About the Authors

Nita Rutkosky began teaching business education courses at Pierce College in Puyallup, Washington, in 1978. Since then she has taught a variety of software applications to students in postsecondary Information Technology certificate and degree programs. In addition to *Marquee Office 2007*, she has authored *Using Computers in the Medical Office: Microsoft Word, Excel, and PowerPoint 2003* as well as textbooks on keyboarding, WordPerfect, desktop publishing, and voice recognition for Paradigm Publishing, Inc.

Denise Seguin has been teaching at Fanshawe College in London, Ontario, since 1986. She has taught a variety of software applications to learners in postsecondary Information Technology diploma programs and in Continuing Education courses. In addition to *Marquee Office 2007*, she has authored *Macromedia Flash MX: Design and Application*; *Microsoft Outlook 2007, 2003, 2002*, and *2000*; and has co-authored *Office 2003*, *Office XP*, and *Using Computers in the Medical Office* for Paradigm Publishing, Inc.

Audrey Rutkosky Roggenkamp has been teaching courses in the Business Information Technology department at Pierce College in Puyallup including keyboarding, skill building, and Microsoft Office programs. In addition to this title, she has co-authored *Using Computers in the Medical Office* for Paradigm Publishing, Inc.

System Requirements

This interactive text is designed for the student to complete section work on a computer running a standard installation of Microsoft Office 2007, Professional Edition, and the Microsoft Windows XP operating system with Service Pack 2 or later. To effectively run this suite and operating system, your computer should be outfitted with the following:

- 500 megahertz (MHz) processor or higher; 256 megabyte (MB) of RAM
- DVD or CD-ROM drive
- 2 gigabyte (GB) of available hard-disk space
- 1024 by 768 monitor resolution ***Note: Screen captures in this book were created using 1024 by 768 resolution; screens with higher resolution may look different.***
- Computer mouse or compatible pointing device

Marquee Series

Paradigm PUBLISHING

Microsoft® Office 2007

with Windows XP and Internet Explorer 7.0

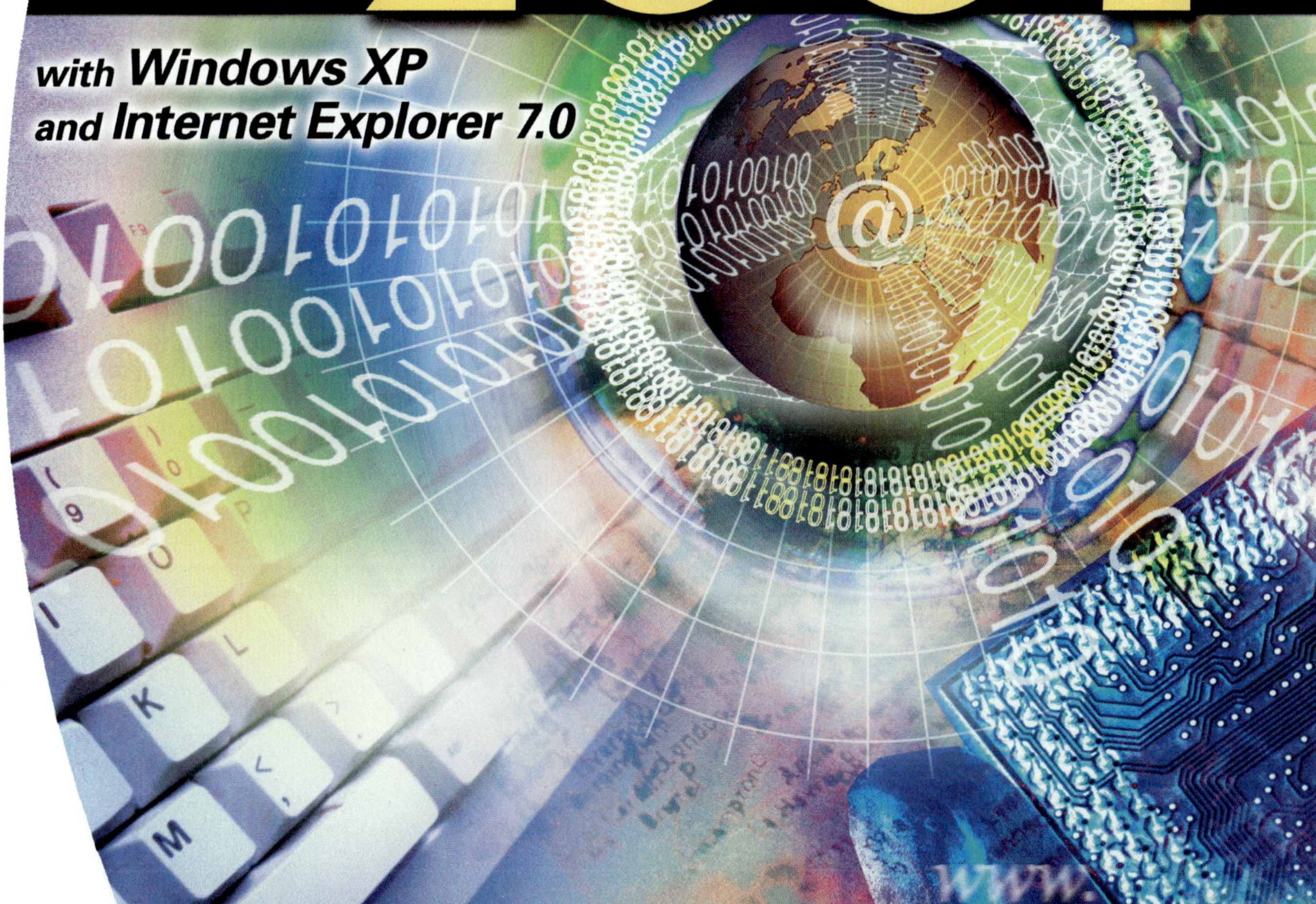

Nita Rutkosky
Pierce College at Puyallup, Puyallup, Washington

Denise Seguin
Fanshawe College, London, Ontario

Audrey Rutkosky Roggenkamp
Pierce College at Puyallup, Puyallup, Washington

Managing Editor Sonja Brown
Senior Developmental Editor Christine Hurney
Production Editor Donna Mears
Cover and Text Designer Leslie Anderson
Copy Editor Susan Capecchi
Desktop Production John Valo, Desktop Solutions
Proofreaders Laura Nelson, Amanda Tristano
Testers Desiree Faulkner, Brady Silver
Indexer Ina Gravitz

Photo Credits: Page 2: (top) © Paradigm Publishing, Inc.; Page 3: (top) Ramin Talaie/Corbis, (middle) courtesy Hewlett-Packard Company, (bottom left) istockphoto.com/Sharon Dominick, (bottom right) © Microsoft Corporation; Page 4: (top) © Lian-Li Industrial Company, Ltd., (middle left) © Eastman Kodak Company, (middle right) © Sintec Corp., (bottom) courtesy McKesson Provider Technologies; Page 5: (top) James Leynse/Corbis, (middle) © Intel Corporation; Page 6: (top) Monica Davey/epa/Corbis, (middle left and right) © Hewlett-Packard Company, (bottom) Corbis; Page 7: (middle) © Memorex Products Inc., (bottom left) © Paradigm Publishing, Inc., (bottom right) © ePerformance; Page 8: (top) © Paradigm Publishing, Inc.; Page 9: (middle) David; Page 11: (bottom) Corbis; Page 13: (bottom left) Corbis, (bottom right) istockphoto.com/Jill Fromer; Page 14: (top) © Hewlett-Packard Company, (middle) Lars Langemeier/A.B./Zefa/Corbis, (bottom) Robert Galbraith/Reuters/Corbis; Page:18: (top) Lawrence Manning/Corbis, (middle) © Cisco Systems Inc.; Page 19: a division of Calendar Club © 2002-2005 Calendars.com LLC. All rights reserved.; Page 22: (top) James Leynse/Corbis, (middle) Screenshots © Google Inc., and are used with permission; Page 23: (top) © 2006, UCAR, (bottom) Premium Stock/Corbis; Page 26: (top left) © 2003-2007 McAfee Inc. All rights reserved., (top right) © 1995-2007 Symantec Corporation, (bottom) Shutter & Mouse/Corbis; Page 28: © 2006 The New York Times.

Text: ISBN 978-0-76383-348-0
Text + CD: ISBN 978-0-76383-350-3

875 Montreal Way
St. Paul, MN 55102
E-mail: educate@emcp.com
Web site: www.emcp.com

Printed in the United States of America

16 15 14 13 12 11 10 09 2 3 4 5 6 7 8 9 10

Contents

Preface

Marquee Series, Microsoft Office 2007 prepares students to work with Microsoft Office 2007 in a business office or for personal use. Incorporating an accelerated, step-by-step, project-based approach, this text builds student competency in Word, Excel, Access, and PowerPoint 2007 and the essential features of Windows XP and Internet Explorer 7.0.

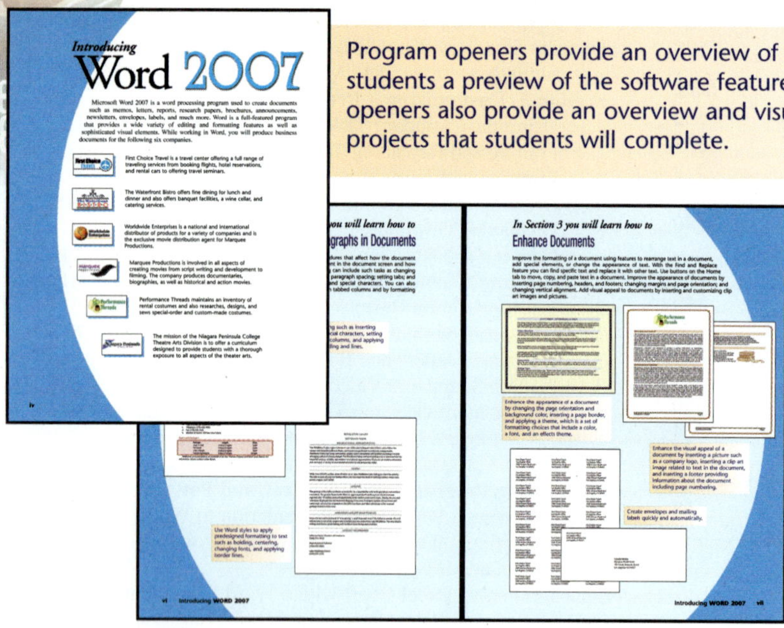

Program openers provide an overview of the software's best uses and give students a preview of the software features and workplace applications. The openers also provide an overview and visual representation of some of the projects that students will complete.

Each program section begins with a list of the skills to be taught and an overview of the projects completed in that section.

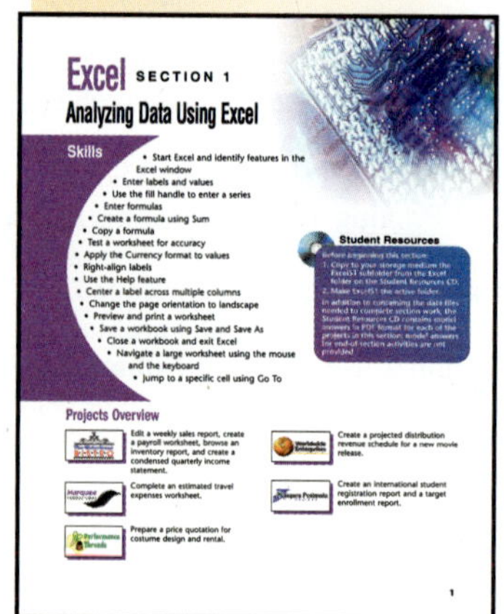

Activities begin with a short explanation of the program features followed by streamlined, point-and-click instruction that pares reading to a minimum.

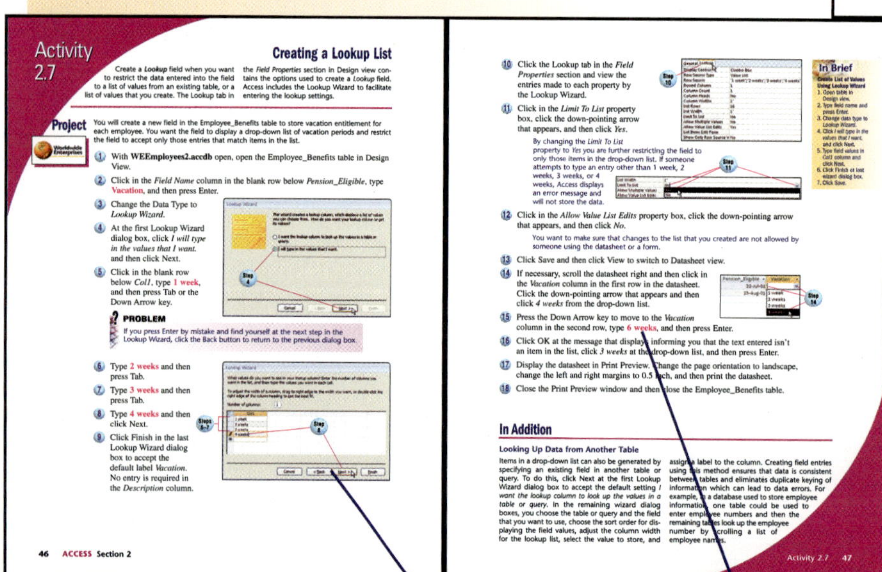

In Brief—Bare-bones summaries of major commands and features provide instant review and a quick reference of the steps required to accomplish a task.

In Addition—Sidebars offer extra information on key features and subfeatures.

Problem boxes—Troubleshooting hints anticipate common obstacles or missteps and redirect students toward success.

Screen captures correlated with exercise steps provide instant reinforcement.

Magenta color highlights text to be typed.

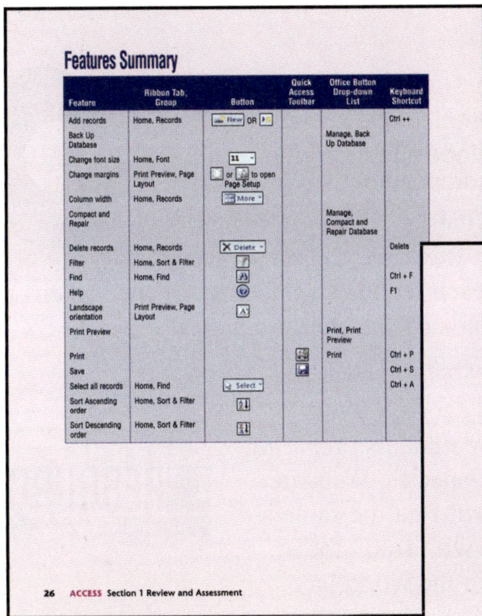

Features Summary—Commands taught in the section are listed with button, ribbon tab, Quick Access toolbar, and keyboard actions.

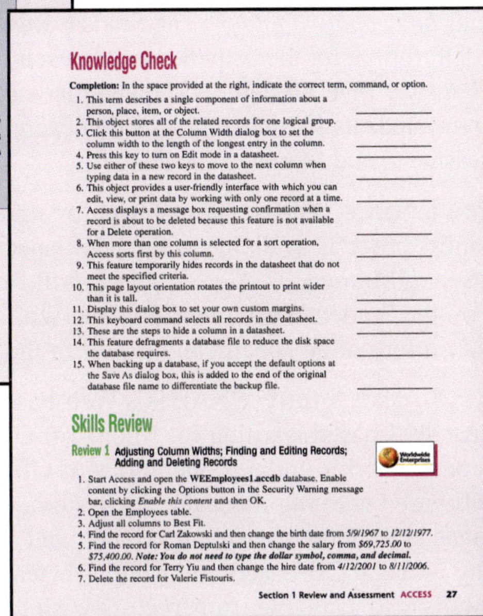

Knowledge Check—Objective completion exercises allows students to assess their comprehension and recall of program features, terminology, and functions.

Skills Review—Activities provide additional hands-on computer exercises to reinforce learning. These activities include some guidance, but less than the intrasection projects.

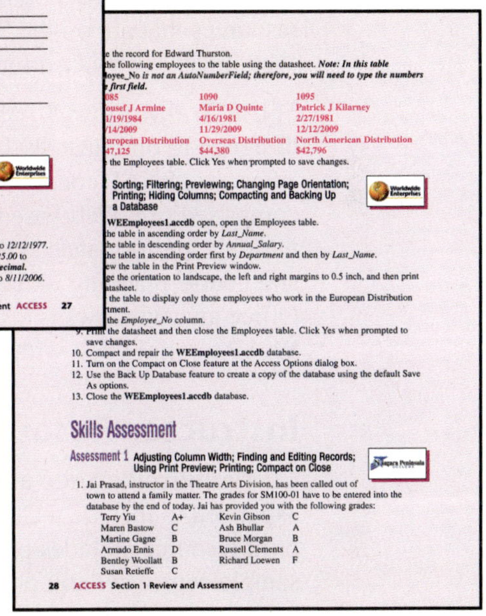

Skills Assessment—Framed in a workplace project perspective, these less-guided assessments evaluate students' abilities to apply section skills and concepts in solving realistic problems. They require demonstrating program skills as well as decision-making skills and include Help and Internet-based activities.

Marquee Challenge—Culminating assessments test students' mastery of program features and their problem-solving abilities.

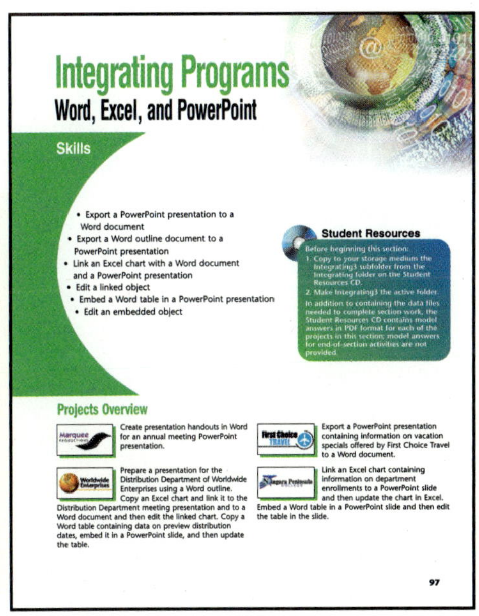

Integrating Programs—Activities devoted to integrating information among Microsoft Office 2007 programs highlight the benefits of using the Office suite. Projects include copying, exporting, linking, and embedding data. Students learn how to manage data efficiently in the business office or for personal use.

Student Courseware

Student Resource CD Each textbook comes with a Student Resources CD that contains typed documents and files required for completing activities and exercises. A CD icon and folder name displayed on the opening page of a section indicates that the student needs to copy a folder of files from the CD to a storage medium before beginning the section projects and activities. *(See the inside back cover for instructions on copying a folder.)* The Student Resource CD also contains model answers in PDF format for the activities within each section so students can check their work. These model answer PDF files are locked and marked with a watermark. Model answers are not provided to the students for the end-of-section exercises—Knowledge Check, Skills Review, Skills Assessment, and Marquee Challenge.

Internet Resource Center Additional material for students preparing to work in the business office is available at the book-specific Web site at www.emcp.net/SchoolMarquee07. Here students will find the same resources that are on the Student Resource CD along with study tools, Web links, and other information specifically useful in the workplace.

SNAP Training and Assessment SNAP is a Web-based program designed to optimize skill-based learning for Microsoft Office 2007 and Windows. SNAP course work simulates operations of Office 2007 and is comprised of a Web-based learning management system, multimedia tutorials, performance skill items, concept test bank, and online grade book and course planning tools. A CD-based set of tutorials teaching the basics of Office and Windows is also available if instructors wish to assign additional SNAP tutorial work without utilizing the Web-based SNAP program.

Instructor Resources

Curriculum Planner and Resources Instructor-support for the Marquee series has been expanded to include a Curriculum Planner and Resources binder with CD. This all-in-one print resource includes planning resources such as Lesson Blueprints, teaching hints, and sample course syllabi; presentation resources such as PowerPoint presentations and handouts; and assessment resources including an overview of available assessment venues, live and PDF model answers for section activities, and live and annotated PDF model answers for end-of-section exercises. Contents of the Curriculum Planner and Resources binder are also available on the password-protected section of the Internet Resource Center for this title at www.emcp.net/SchoolMarquee07.

Computerized Test Generator Instructors can use ExamView test generating software and the provided bank of multiple choice items to create customized Web-based or print tests.

Information Technology Essentials

The Information Processing Cycle

Computers process information in the same way that humans make decisions. We use our eyes and ears to read or "input" facts and data into our brains. We use our brains to "process" that data and organize it into information. The resulting "output" is a thought or decision that we can display or present by drawing it, writing it, or making a voice recording of it. If we decide to keep the results for future use, we "store" the paper or recording in a file cabinet.

As shown in Figure 1, the information processing cycle can be divided into four segments: input, processing, output, and storage. It relies on computer hardware to mimic the human procedure. Hardware refers to the devices you can physically see and touch in and on the computer.

Input

Input involves getting data into the computer so that it can be processed. Some commonly used input devices are described in the following sections.

Keyboard Based on the layout of keys on a typewriter, the keyboard is primarily used for typing text. Although numbers are found in a row above the letters, most PC keyboards also include a calculator-style number pad for the convenience of bookkeepers, accountants, and others who work with numbers a lot.

Twelve keys labeled F1 through F12, as well as several other named keys, can be programmed to perform special functions in software applications. For example, the F1 key usually displays a help window where you might type a request for instructions on how to print what has just been typed. The Home key might move the cursor to the left side of a line in one program, but to the upper left corner of the page in another. (The cursor is the flashing bar, dash, or other symbol that indicates where the next character you type will appear on the screen.)

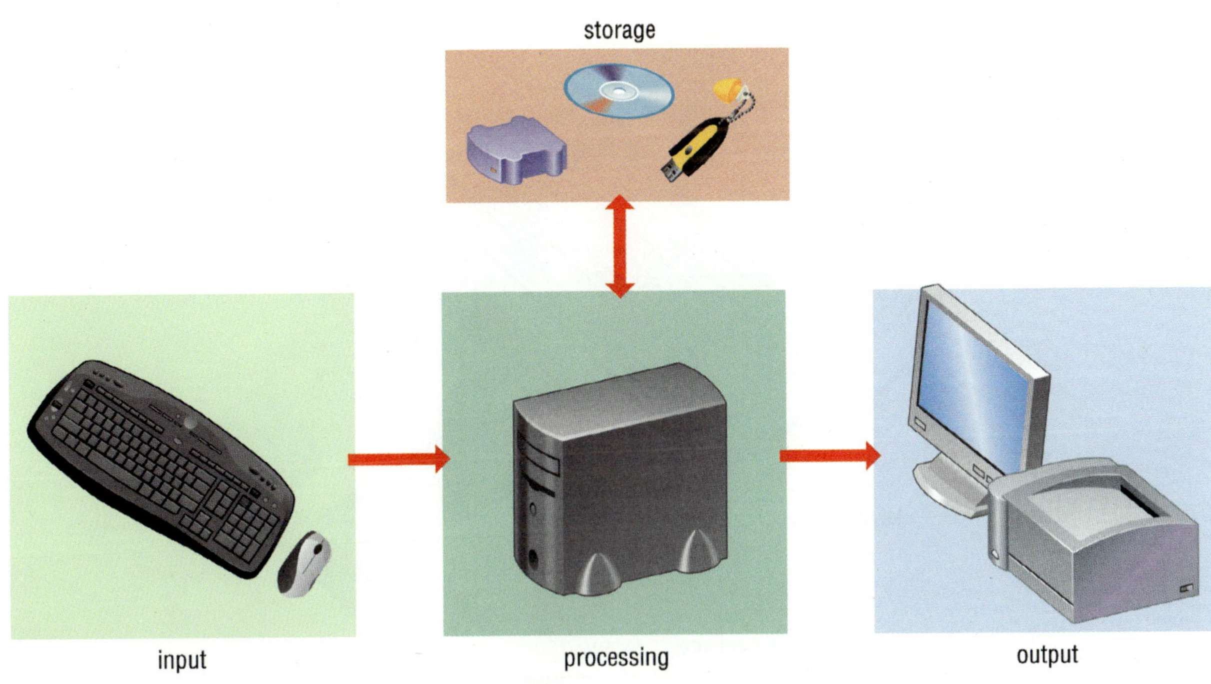

FIGURE 1 The Information Processing Cycle

Mouse A mouse is a pointing device used for issuing commands and selecting text or files for processing. Moving the mouse on the desktop causes a pointer to move on the screen. If you point to the Office button at the top left corner of the Microsoft Word screen, for example, then click the left mouse button, a drop-down menu will appear, allowing you to click *Open* (shown with an open manila file folder icon) if you want to access a file you have previously saved.

If you want to delete several words or lines, you can point to the beginning of the first word, then hold down the left mouse button, "drag" the mouse to highlight the text, and then click the Delete key to remove the text from the document.

Touch Pad Some laptop computers provide a touch pad instead of a mouse as a pointing device. You move your forefinger across the pad to position the cursor, then use your thumb to press the equivalent of the mouse "button."

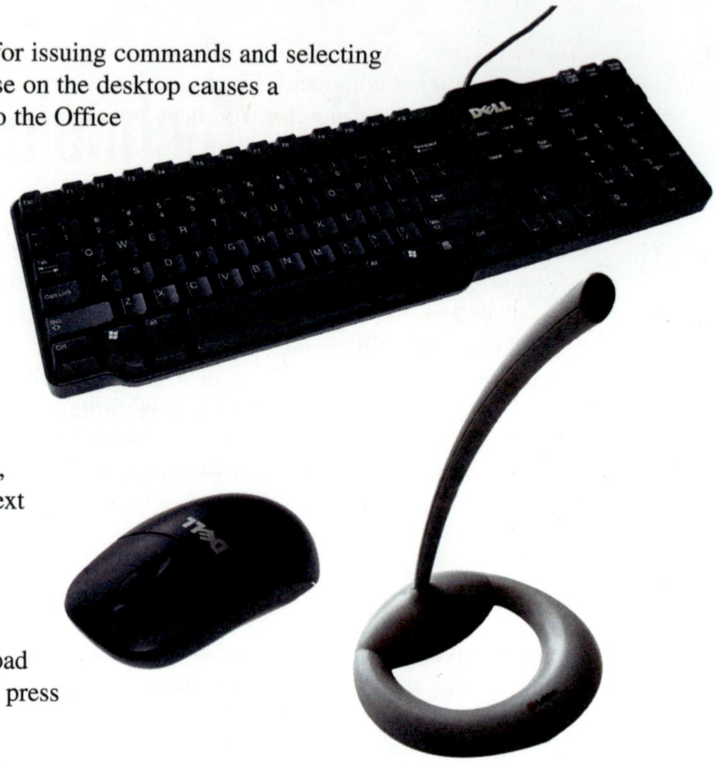

A keyboard, mouse, and microphone are all examples of common input devices.

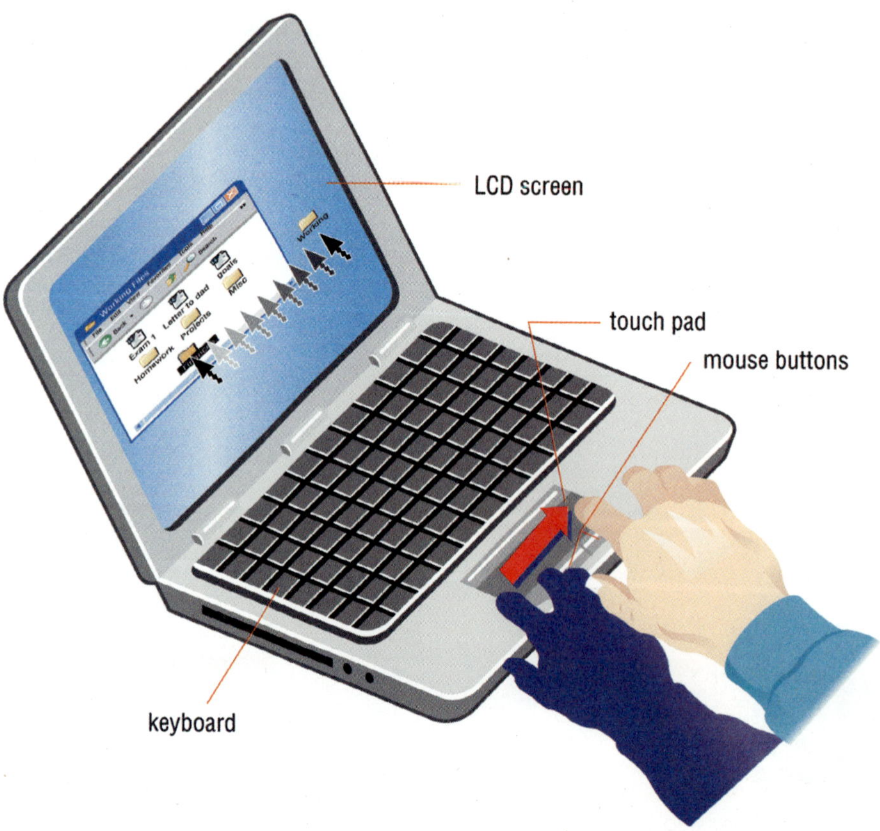

FIGURE 2 Touch Pad Interface
Some laptops use a touch pad instead of a mouse to control the pointer or click commands.

Touch Screen A touch screen allows you to select an item and input commands by physically touching a specific area of the monitor. You have probably used one if you use ATM machines for banking. They are also used at information kiosks to provide an easy-to-use way to select items of interest, without the necessity of a keyboard. Servers at restaurants use them to place orders. (Touch screens are much easier to clean than keyboards, and they can be used with only one hand.)

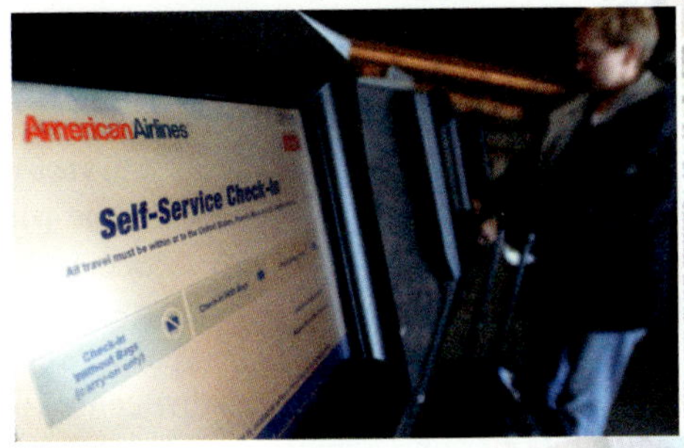

Commonly used at airport check-in counters, touch screens allow travelers to obtain boarding passes and check luggage by touching options on the monitor.

Scanner A scanner works like a photocopier to transfer pictures or text into the computer. If you don't have a digital camera, you can scan your photos into a PC, then organize or enhance them with photo editing software.

A scanner is a tool to input either pictures or text.

Digitizing Pen and Drawing Tablet Although a mouse can be used for drawing designs and pictures, it is very clumsy. Better detail can be achieved with a digitizing pen and drawing tablet. Some handheld and laptop computers now accept "handwritten" input with a digitizing pen called a stylus.

Engineers, architects, and designers often use a very sophisticated type of graphics tablet to make precise drawings such as those used in building construction and the manufacture of circuit boards for computers. Such graphics tablets are made up of hundreds of tiny intersecting wires forming an electronic matrix embedded in the tablet surface. A stylus or crosshair cursor activates these intersection points, which collectively represent the image.

A digitizing pen (stylus) can be used to input information or commands into a handheld computer.

Graphics tablets use a digitizing pen for input.

Joystick A joystick is an input device (named after the control lever used to fly fighter planes) consisting of a small box that contains a vertical lever that, when pushed in a certain direction, moves the graphics cursor correspondingly on the screen. Most often used to control fast-moving images in computer games, joysticks can also be used by people who have difficulty using a mouse.

A joystick is an input device used for moving objects on a computer screen and is a common input device for computer gaming.

Digital Camera Digital cameras can be used to transfer still and moving pictures into the computer. Webcams are a popular example of a video camera that can be used in combination with headphones and a microphone to communicate by "video phone" with people in all corners of the world.

A digital camera captures images in a digital format and often contains an output device for viewing those images.

This SmileCam is a webcam that can be controlled remotely over the Internet.

Microphone With a microphone you can add a "sound bite" to a computerized slide presentation or speak to a friend over the Internet. Microphones can stand on the desk or be worn as part of a headset.

Bar Code Reader Bar code readers are used for entering the Universal Product Code (UPC) found on items in grocery and retail stores. They also are used to track medication administration in hospitals.

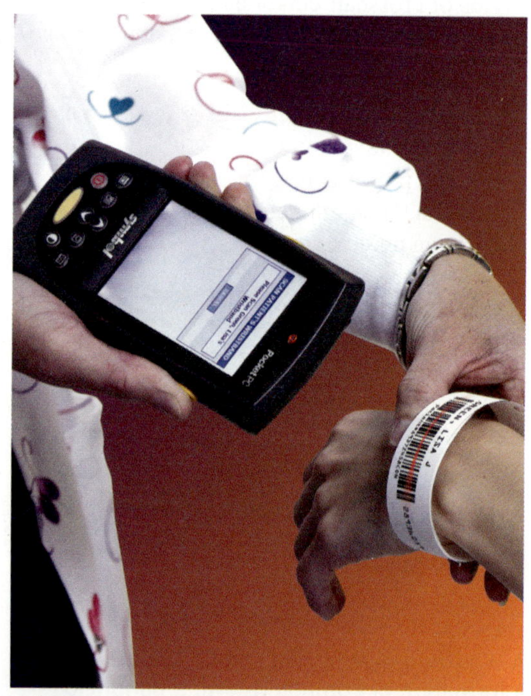

A bar code reader scans a UPC and resulting input can be used to check a patient's identity and medication requirements.

Dual Purpose Devices Although usually thought of as storage devices, floppies, compact discs (CDs), digital video discs (DVDs), flash drives, and hard drives all allow you to reenter data into the computer quickly and easily, without having to retype it. Floppy diskettes were once widely used in PCs, but are quickly becoming obsolete because they can only hold 1.44 megabytes (MB)—that is, 1,440,000 characters—of data. The other devices mentioned will be discussed in the "Storage" section.

Processing

Processing involves using a computer to make calculations (when you want to manage your money) or to move text from one paragraph to another (when you write a report). A spelling and grammar checker can analyze what you write and highlight errors. The central processing unit (CPU) is the brain of the computer that handles those tasks. The rate at which the CPU can process data is known as the "clock speed."

Processors Most IBM-compatible PCs use a central processing unit made by Intel or AMD. They process data at clock speeds from 2.0 to 4.0 gigahertz (GHz). (One gigahertz equals one billion cycles per second.) The first Apple Macintosh computers ran on Motorola 68000 processors, but now use Intel processors and can run IBM-compatible PC operating systems.

For intensive gaming programs and video editing, a dual-core processor is an alternative that can increase computing speed. Such devices are essentially two processors in one. Single-core processors use a technique called "multi-tasking" in which one processor switches back and forth between programs so quickly that the user doesn't perceive any interruption, but both programs are actually running more slowly than they would with two separate processors, or with one dual-core processor.

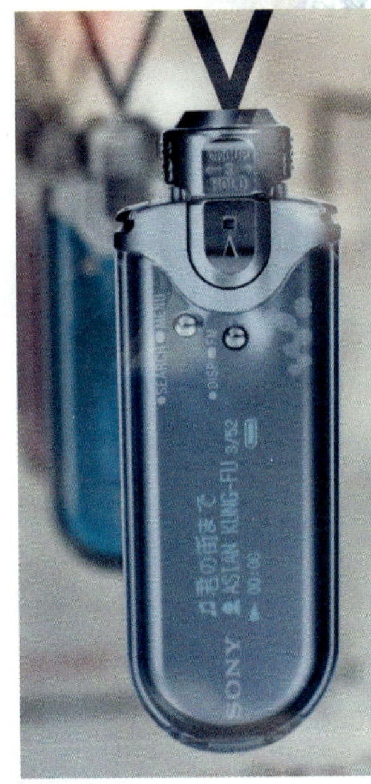

Flash drives are portable and often worn on a lanyard around a person's neck. They can be used to input information from one computer to another computer.

Memory Chips Memory chips are the hardware that provides the workspace for the data and instructions the computer is processing. The user workspace is called random access memory (RAM) because the user has quick access to it and does not have to search through it "page by page." Having a large amount of RAM is like having a large work table where you can spread out books, papers, pencils, a calculator, and other tools you need to do your work. RAM is considered volatile or temporary "storage" because it disappears completely when the power to the computer is shut off.

This Intel® Itanium® dual-core processor provides the brains for a computer.

Today's personal computers usually have at least 512 megabytes of RAM. That's the minimum amount needed by Windows XP. However, Windows Vista requires at least one gigabyte of random access memory. A gigabyte (GB) equals about one billion characters.

Read only memory (ROM) is sometimes confused with RAM due to the similarity of their names. ROM is non-volatile and contains the getting-started instructions that the PC needs when the power is first turned on. As its name implies, ROM can only be used as programmed by the PC manufacturer. You can't make any changes to it; you can only cause its contents to be "read" into the computer.

Figure 3 shows the location of RAM and ROM on a computer's motherboard.

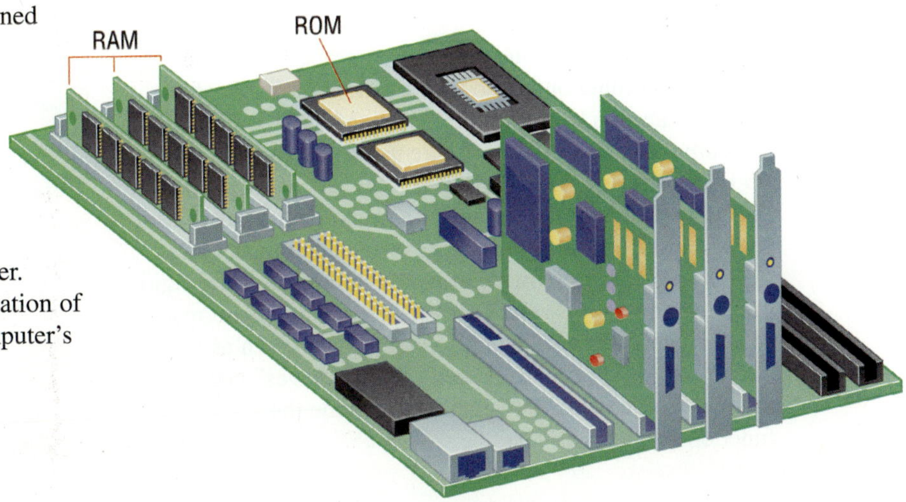

FIGURE 3 **Location of RAM and ROM on the motherboard**

A flat screen, LCD monitor is a commonly used output device.

Output

Output is processed data that can be used immediately or stored in computer-usable form for later use. Output may be produced in either hard copy or soft copy, or in both forms. Hard copy is a permanent version of output, such as a letter printed on paper using a printer. Soft copy is a temporary version and includes any output that cannot be physically handled. Soft copy output devices include monitors and speakers.

Monitor A monitor is the screen used for displaying graphics and text. Although older picture-tube type cathode ray tube (CRT) monitors are still available, most new PCs are sold with flat screen, liquid crystal display (LCD) monitors. In an LCD, liquid crystals are sandwiched between two sheets of material. Electric current passing through the crystals causes them to twist. This twisting effect blocks some light waves and allows other light waves to pass through, creating images on the screen.

Ink-jet printers provide good-quality, inexpensive output.

Printer Printers provide hard copy printouts on paper and other similar media. Ink-jet printers brought low-cost color printing to home computers. Laser printers offer faster, black-and-white printing, and since the late 1990s, laser printers have been affordable for personal use. The prices for color laser printers have also decreased dramatically.

Laser printers produce output of exceptional quality and are among the most popular printers.

Speakers and Headphones Speakers and headphones provide audio output in stereo for movies, radio programs, streaming video, online learning courses, and telephone calls.

Storage

The storage portion of the information processing cycle refers to recording output so that it will be available after the computer has been shut off and RAM has been erased.

Output can be stored for future use on hard drives, CDs, DVDs, and flash drives. A drive is a PC device that can read and write data onto the surface of a round platter (disk) as it spins. Hard disk platters are made of metal; compact and digital video discs are made of plastic. All of them are rigid, in contrast to the first disks (or "diskettes") that were made of a bendable Mylar film and soon became known as "floppy disks." Flash drives aren't really "drives" because they have no moving parts, but they provide the same function as a hard drive.

Computer speakers provide sound output.

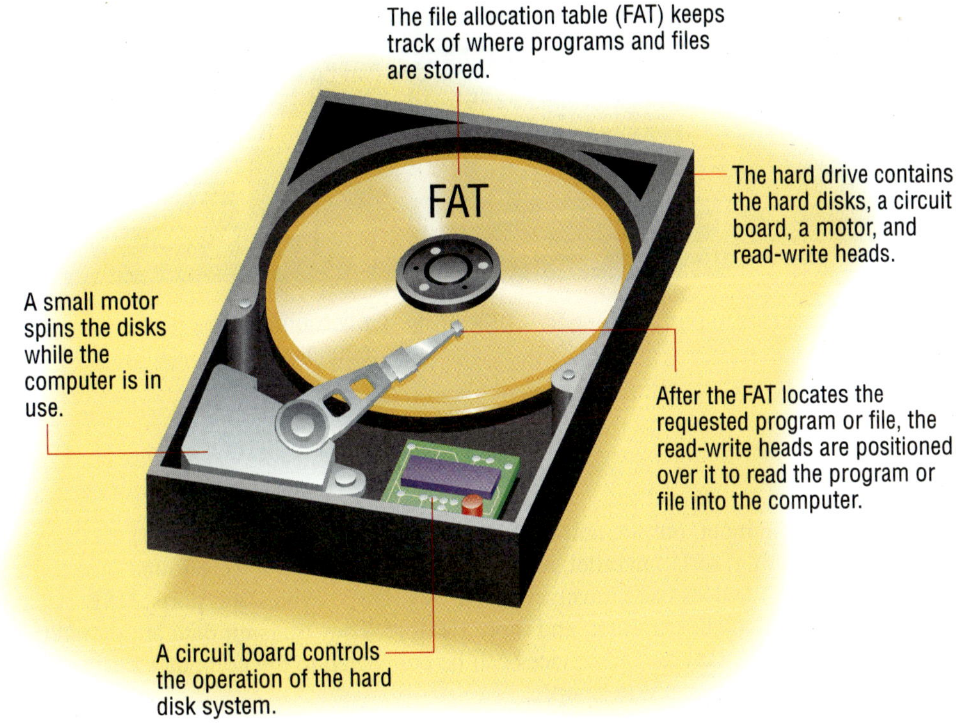

FIGURE 4 Inner Workings of a Hard Drive
A hard drive contains one or more hard disks on which data are stored. When activated, read/write heads move in and out between the disks to record and/or read data.

Hard drives contain a stack of metal platters (disks), a drive motor, and read/write heads that are positioned to access the top and bottom of each platter. Figure 4 shows the inner workings of a hard drive. Capacities of over 200 GB are common in inexpensive desktop PCs.

Data CDs are made of the same material that is used for music CDs. In fact, you can play your favorite music CDs in the CD drive of your PC. They can hold about 700 MB of data. DVDs can hold from 4 GB to 8 GB, depending on whether they can record on both sides and on one or two layers per side.

The flash drives on the market today can hold from 128 megabytes to 4 gigabytes of data on a printed circuit board inside a protective plastic case. They are the size and shape of a person's thumb or a package of chewing gum. Some drives even provide fingerprint authorization. Flash drives connect directly to a USB port and thus do not require the installation of any device driver programs to support them.

CD-R discs offer an inexpensive way for individuals and businesses to create their own CDs.

A DVD disc looks like its relative, the compact disc, but can store five times more data.

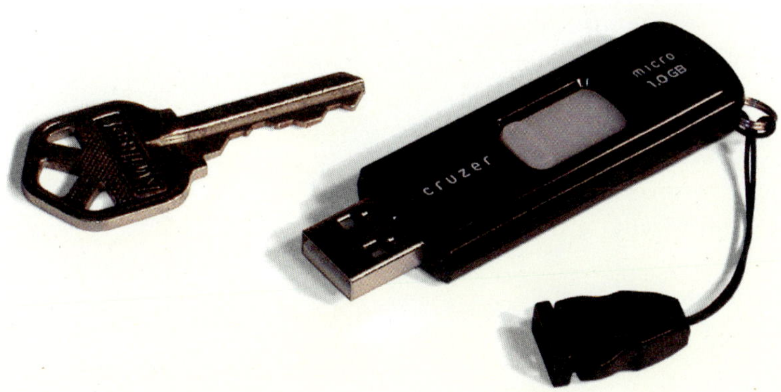

This flash drive storage device has a USB connector that fits into a standard USB port.

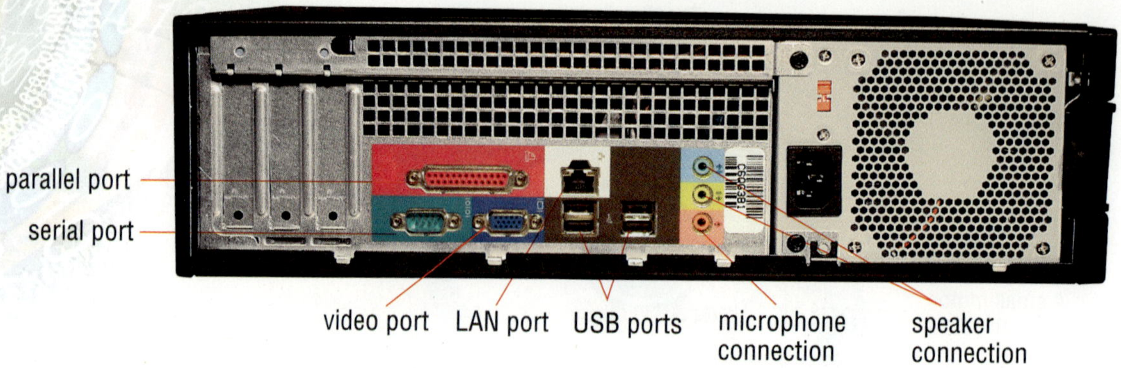

FIGURE 5 System Unit Ports

System Unit Ports

Ports are the "sockets" that the input, output, and storage devices plug into (see Figure 5). In the early days of personal computing, serial, parallel, and printer cables and ports were found on all PCs. Today, most "peripheral" devices use Universal Serial Bus (USB) cables and ports. USB cables and connector plugs are smaller, thinner, and more flexible. They transmit data at up to 480 megabits per second (Mbps). As many as 127 devices can be connected to the computer host at once through a daisy-chain–style connection setup.

USB hubs provide extra connection options for computers with only one or two USB ports. You might even discover that you can make backup copies of your data to an external hard drive that is connected to your computer via the USB port on your keyboard!

EXPLORING TECHNOLOGY 1

Identify the processor, clock speed, and amount of random access memory (RAM) in a computer you often use. *Hint: With Windows XP, follow* **Start > Control Panel > Performance and Maintenance > System**. *With Windows Vista, follow* **Start > Control Panel System and Maintenance > System**. ***In either operating system, if the control panel is displayed using Classic view, double-click the System icon.***

EXPLORING TECHNOLOGY 2

Identify the hardware you have on your computer and categorize each piece as input, output, or both.

Computer Software

Software refers to the operating instructions and applications that allow computers to process the numbers, pictures, sounds, and text we enter into them. We can touch the disk that contains the software, but not the lines of programming code that make up the software.

The Windows Vista operating system requires a CPU that runs at 800 MHz.

Personal Computer Operating Systems

IBM-compatible PC operating systems primarily include those made by Microsoft, such as DOS (Disk Operating System) versions 1 through 6, Windows 95, 98, ME, XP, and Vista. UNIX and Linux are two other PC operating systems.

If a PC has an older CPU with a clock speed that is too slow, it will either run very, very slowly, or it won't be able to run at all. Windows Vista requires, at a minimum, a CPU that runs at 800 MHz. Windows XP, on the other hand, can run at 233 MHz. Both will profit from a higher clock speed.

The operating system for the Apple Macintosh is Mac OS, the first graphical user interface (GUI) brought to market. The Mac was introduced in 1984 in a dramatic and revolutionary Super Bowl commercial. The tenth version of the Mac operating system is called "Mac OS X." Since its release in the spring of 2005, Mac OS X version 10.4 (codenamed "Tiger") can now run on IBM-compatible PCs.

The Mac OS X operating system can run on IBM-compatible PCs.

Applications

People with no technical knowledge of how a PC works can use it to balance their checkbooks or to insert a photograph into a personalized greeting card, print it out, and send it to a friend. The thousands of software applications available provide the instructions that empower users to perform these and other tasks from the mundane to the outright amazing.

In this section we will present the most common types of computer programs on the market today.

Word Processing Word processing software was originally designed as a replacement for the typewriter. Now a word processing program such as Microsoft Word 2007 can support photos and drawings, mathematical calculations, text in table format, text in varying sizes, shapes, and colors—and even sound bites.

Orcas Island

One of the San Juan Islands in Washington State, Orcas Island has long been a favorite destination for generations of vacationers. Located approximately 60 miles north of Seattle, it lies in the Strait of Georgia between Anacortes and Vancouver Island. To the north, on the mainland, is Vancouver, B.C. With its fjord-like bays and sounds, deep harbors, lakes, streams, and waterfalls, Orcas is considered the most spectacular of the islands. The island is over 56 square miles in size and has more than 125 miles of saltwater shoreline. Winding roads fan out from the business and social center of Eastsound village to the nearby communities of Deer Harbor, Orcas, and Olga. One of the greatest assets of the island is Mt. Constitution in Moran State Park, which offers panoramic views of the entire archipelago and is surrounded by miles of trails and sparkling lakes.

Activities on Orcas

Orcas Island offers an unhurried setting to enjoy the spectacular scenery and ... with a wide variety of recreation. ... the year, Orcas Theatre and Community Center offers concerts, plays, art exhibits, dances, workshops, movies, and many special events.

Bicycling Safety

Orcas Island is the most challenging of the islands for bicycles. This is due to the narrow windy roads and hilly terrain. When bicycling on the island, ride single file and keep to the right of the road. Make stops on the straight-of-way rather than at the top of a hill or on a curve. Motorists cannot negotiate blind approaches safely with a bicyclist on the road. When stopping to reset or regroup, enjoy the scenery, but please move completely off the road. As you enjoy the scenery, be alert for potential traffic and the condition of the roadway. When leaving the ferry, pull over to the side of the road and let the automobiles pass.

Marine Parks

These marine parks are accessible only by boat:

- Sucia Island: Cluster of 11 islands; trails, bays, and bluffs; 2.5 miles from Orcas Island

Microsoft Word 2007 is a word processing program that includes several formatting features that can be applied to words, lines, paragraphs, pages, or entire documents.

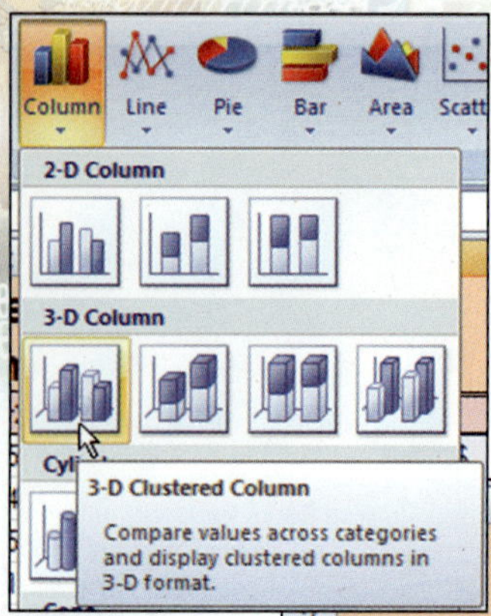

An Excel 2007 spreadsheet can calculate elements of a business proposal, such as operating expenses, and display them in a chart.

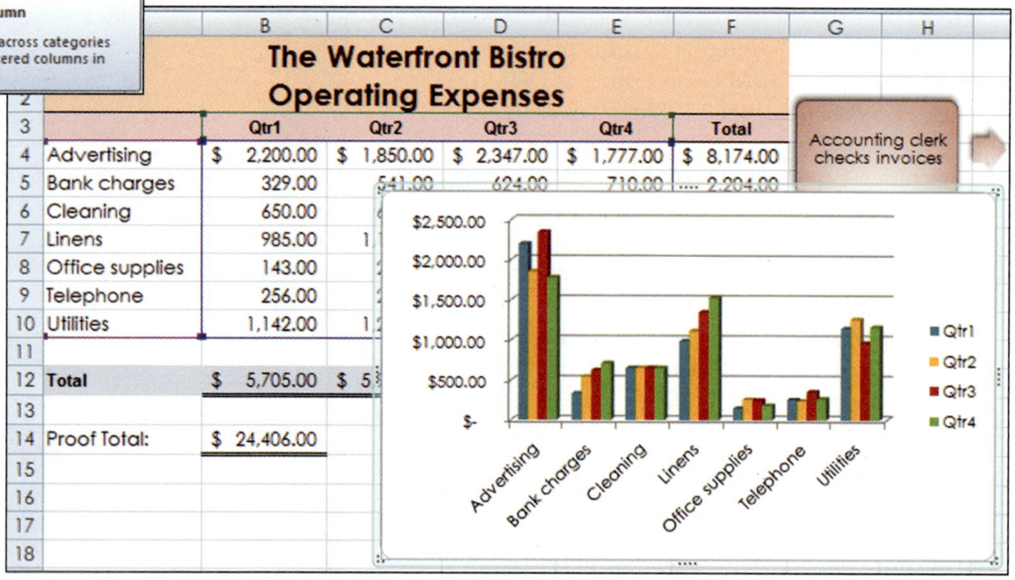

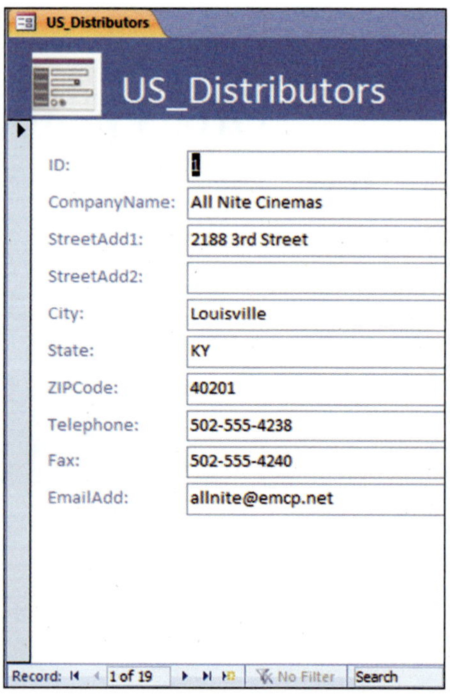

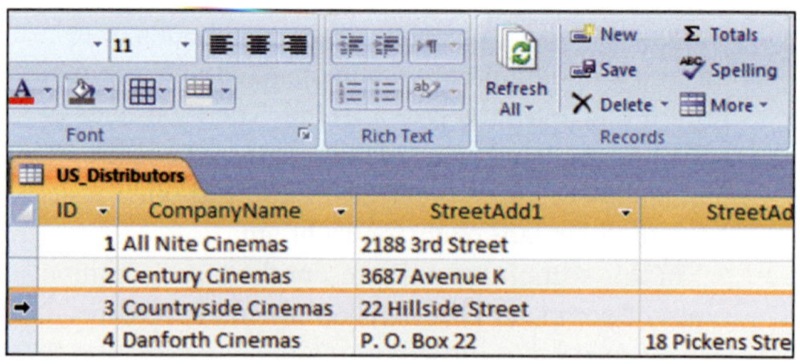

Information can be entered into an Access 2007 database by using a form designed for that purpose.

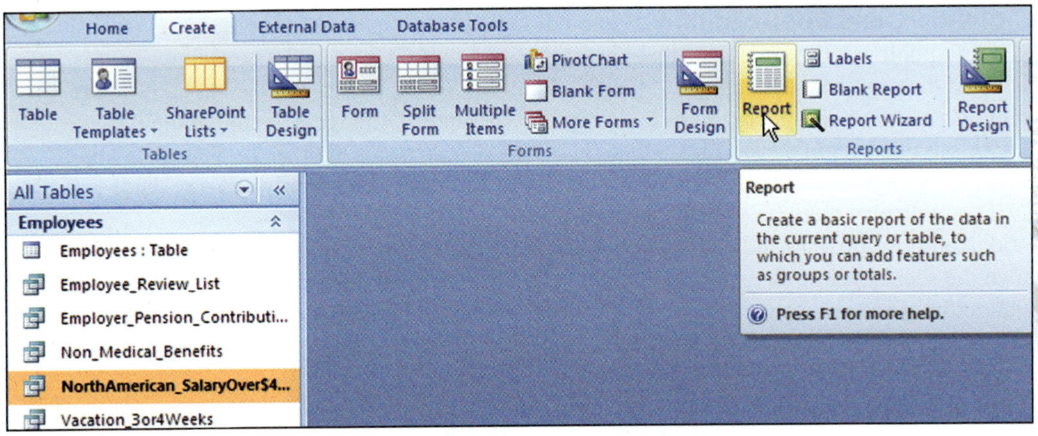

An Access 2007 database report is a selection of data in a database. The user chooses which types of information should be included in the report, and the database automatically finds and organizes the corresponding data.

Spreadsheet Spreadsheet software such as Microsoft Excel 2007 can be used for both simple and very complex calculations. Current versions can also support graphics and perform some database tasks, such as sorting. A series of keystrokes which perform several steps of a repetitive task can be saved as a "macro" and programmed to run at the click of an icon.

Because formulas are used to create calculations, you can ask, "If I spend only $2 per day on coffee instead of $5, how much money will I save at the end of the month?" When you replace one value with another, the program will recalculate your budget automatically.

Database Database software such as Microsoft Access 2007 are designed to keep track of information. They allow you to rearrange it alphabetically, numerically, or chronologically. Or you can filter the data to display only those items that match your criteria, such as the names of customers who spent more than $500 at your online music store last year. Database software can easily do simple calculations, such as showing monthly subtotals and an annual total for each of your customers, but complex math is usually best left to the spreadsheets.

Presentation Presentation software such as Microsoft PowerPoint 2007 allow users to create slide shows that can be viewed on the computer or projected onto a large screen. The shows can include clip art, graphs and charts, photos, drawings, video clips, sound, and text. Features such as arrows and boxes that "fly" into the screen and slide transition effects provide the attention-getting movement that appeals to sales people and teachers.

PowerPoint 2007 can combine text, graphics, sounds, and videos.

Audio, Video, and Photo Editing Photo editing software is used for organizing, retouching, and editing photographs and videos that have been saved on CDs and DVDs, scanned in, or transferred directly from the camera to the PC. Paint Shop Pro, Photo Explosion, and Picture Project allow you to edit photographs and crop out unwanted "strangers," remove the red-eye effect, or put one person's head on another person's body. You can also create your own slide shows with background audio, then e-mail the results to friends and family or copy them to a CD or DVD and display them on your TV set.

Video editing software such as ArcSoft Video Impression can be used to edit video clips to remove the scenes you took of your feet when you forgot to stop recording, or to add music, or to rearrange the scenes to create a more logical flow—or a more creative one. You can also edit the audio tracks. With some relatively inexpensive products, you can fine-tune the sound and achieve a professional level of quality.

Nero StartSmart is an audio editing program that lets you transfer music from cassette tapes and vinyl records to CDs, iPods, and MP3 players. With it you can remove noise, clicks, and crackle; add reverb and other effects; remove the vocals by using a Karaoke filter; and tweak various other sound qualities.

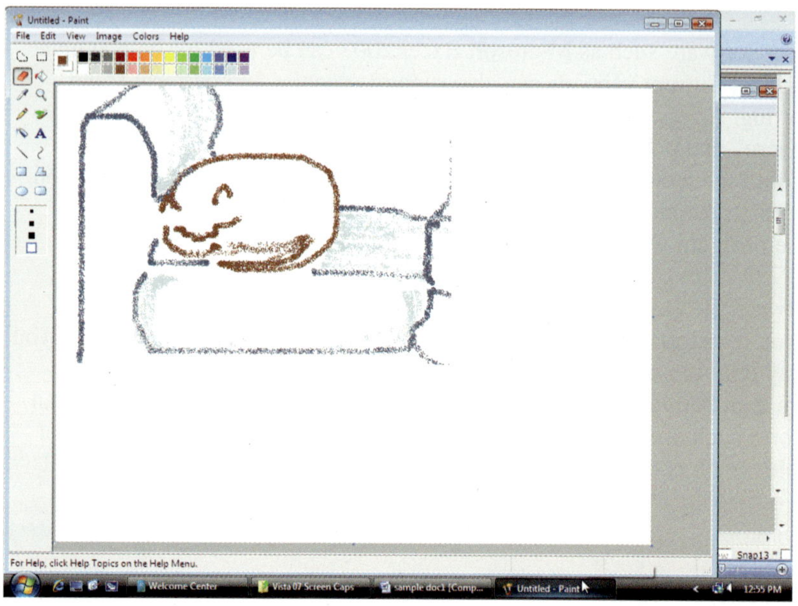

Microsoft Paint is a basic drawing program that is included in the Microsoft Office suite.

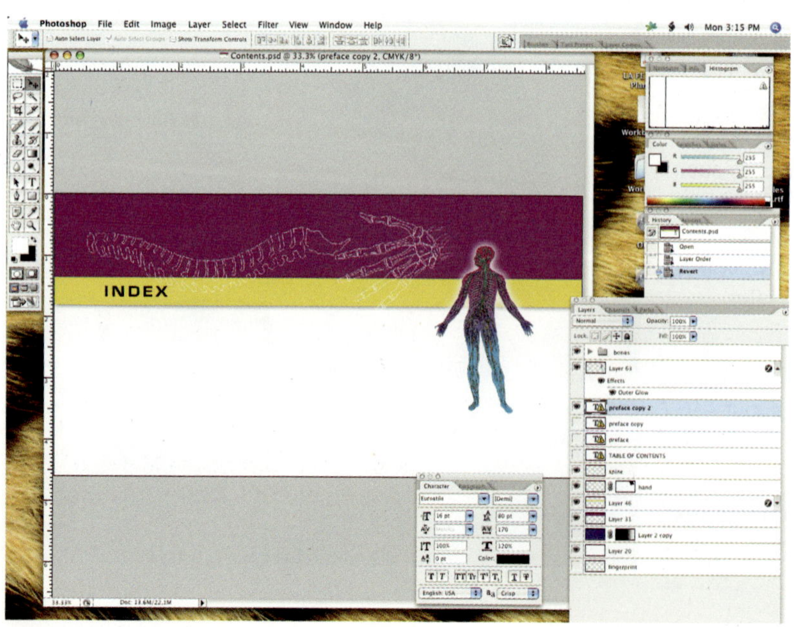

Adobe Photoshop is a popular image-editing program that provides numerous tools for editing an image.

Graphics and Drawing Applications such as CorelDraw, Adobe Illustrator, SmartDraw, Microsoft Paint, and Paint Show Pro are popular software packages that provide the tools to design graphical images that can be used for Web pages, posters, marketing brochures, and greeting cards. Visio is a graphics application that focuses more on technical and business drawings, flow charts, and organizational charts to illustrate complex processes. Visio is vector graphics-based, meaning that it uses points, lines, curves, and geometric shapes to create images. Another method is "raster-based," which uses groups of pixels (picture elements) to make an image. If you can see tiny squares when you magnify an image, you are viewing its individual elements.

A digitized pen and tablet may seem to be a requirement for using drawing applications, but you can do amazing things with a mouse by picking a circle from a group of shapes and making it larger or smaller or turning it into an oval. Free graphics and drawing software includes Inkscape, Skencil, and Open Office DRAW.

Suites Software applications are often bundled into packages called "suites." Widely used versions of the Microsoft Office suite contain the word processor, Word; the spreadsheet, Excel; the database manager, Access; and the presentation manager, PowerPoint.

Money Management Quicken and Microsoft Money are two software applications with an interface that resembles a checkbook. Users can not only write and print checks, but also track their spending habits, create a budget, generate cash flow reports, download their credit card charges, and keep track of their savings and investments.

TurboTax and TaxCut are income tax preparation programs that prompt you to enter your tax information, then print a duplicate of the state and federal forms with your data on the appropriate lines. They also let you file your tax returns electronically and direct your refund to your bank account.

Money management software enables users to manage their money by helping them pay bills, balance checkbooks, keep track of income and expenses, maintain investment records, and other financial activities.

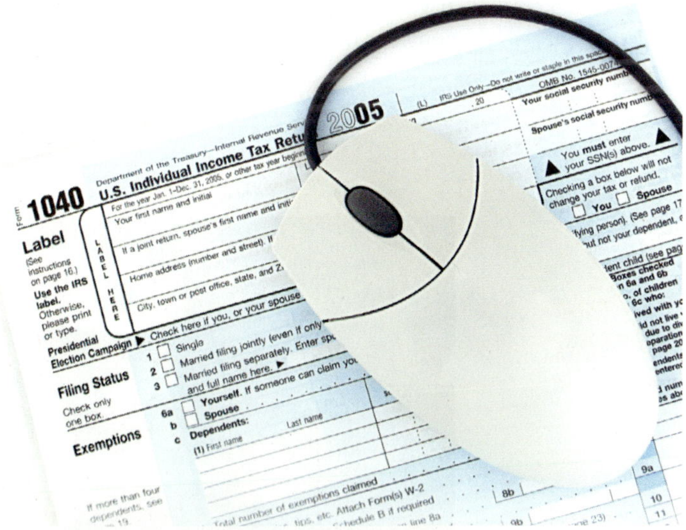

Tax preparation software allows users to efficiently fill out state and federal tax forms and submit them electronically.

Personal Information Management Microsoft Outlook and Lotus Organizer are examples of personal information management (PIM) programs that keep track of your to-do list, address book, and personal calendar. Many PIMs also contain a scheduler with an alarm to alert you of a meeting, whether it occurs daily, weekly, or only once. Handheld devices, such as the Palm, Treo, and Blackberry, also contain this type of software.

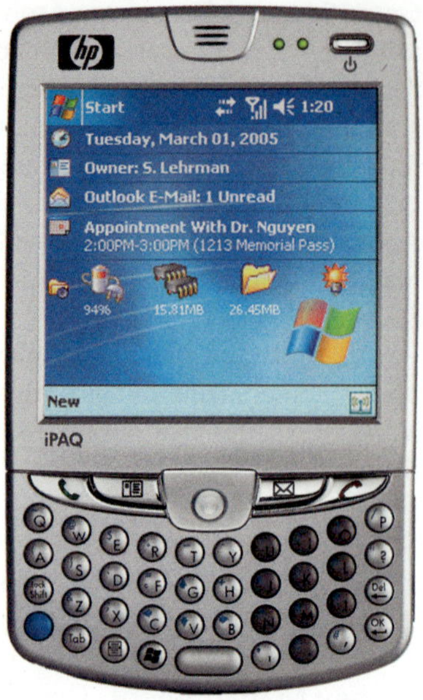

A personal digital assistant (PDA) tracks appointments with a built-in calendar using a PIM program.

Collaboration Businesses often find the need to have several people collaborate on a project. Collaborative software or groupware, such as Lotus Notes and Microsoft Office SharePoint, provides a way to keep track of who has made or suggested changes to documents or plans and to distribute everything electronically. A calendar feature allows users to schedule meetings at times when others are free. Both e-mail and instant messaging (IM) functions are used, providing real-time communication among team members wherever they are in the world. SharePoint allows direct editing of documents through Word, Excel, or PowerPoint and also provides controlled access to shared documents via the Web. A Microsoft application called Office Groove provides similar functionality for the peer-to-peer network environment.

Gaming Computer games have come a long way since the Solitaire program included in the first versions of Windows. Today's games contain high-quality 3D animations, sound, and action that is very realistic. Baseball and football games, auto racing, and fantasy worlds are just a small part of a fast growing industry. You can even play games over the Internet with players in other cities and countries.

Gaming software requires a lot of computer power. If you plan to run gaming software, you will want to consider installing a dual-core processor.

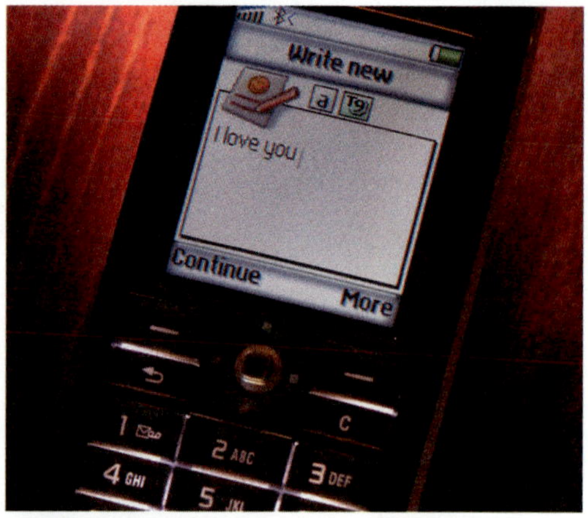

Text messaging allows people to send quick, short messages via cell phones.

Entertainment and gaming software can be so lifelike it can look like an actual TV broadcast of a baseball game.

Open-Source Open-source software is the general term for applications that are provided completely free of charge, with no license fees or restrictions, and no copyrights to worry about. You can download the software, copy it, and give it to your friends. The programming source code is also provided without charge and anyone is allowed to modify and improve it. For further details, go to www.opensource.org.

OpenOffice is a suite of applications that are considered open source and includes a word processor, a spreadsheet, a presentation application, a drawing application, and a database manager.

EXPLORING TECHNOLOGY 3

Identify the operating system version running on your computer. Has it been updated with a Service Pack? ***Hint: Use the same method you used in the first exercise.***

EXPLORING TECHNOLOGY 4

List and categorize the major applications installed on your computer using the terms mentioned in this section. ***Hint: If you don't see icons for them on the Desktop, click the Start button.***

Networks

Computer networks are created when people want to share something such as a printer, an Internet connection, the specific information within the confines of their business, or the wide and abundant variety of information found on the Web. The network allows computers to communicate and to share these resources.

Local Area Networks

A local area network (LAN), illustrated in Figure 6, consists of computers that are connected by physical cables, or wirelessly in an environment that does not *use* public carriers such as Internet service providers (ISPs), telephone, or cable companies. The organization that "owns" the computer systems and data also "owns" the connections between them.

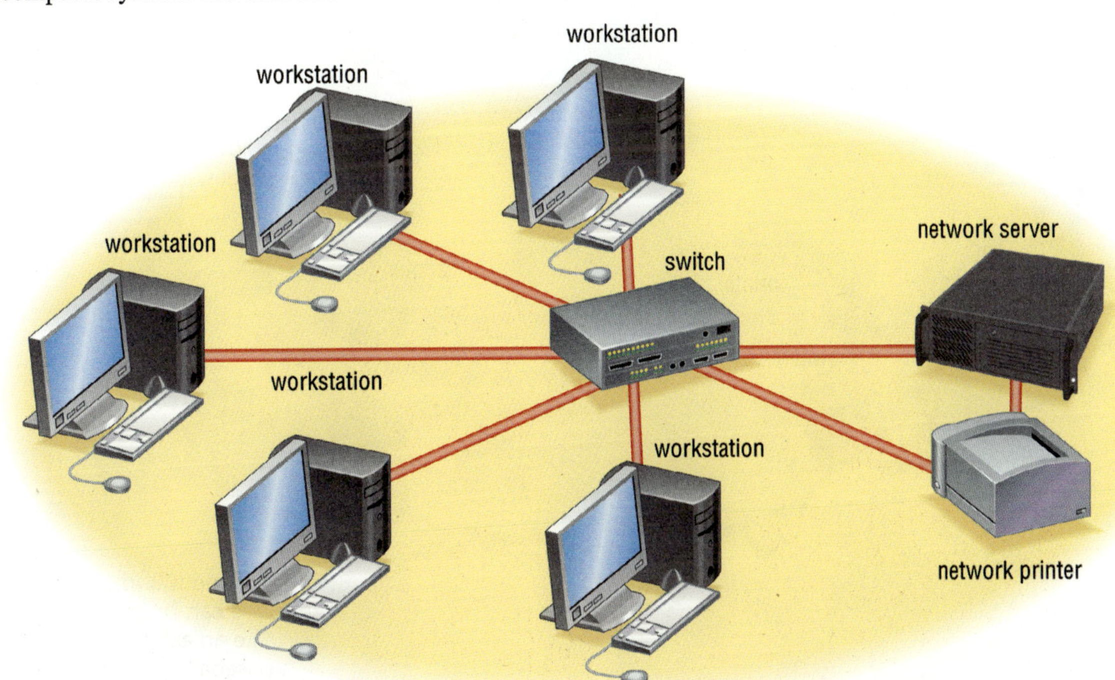

FIGURE 6 **A Local Area Network**

Problems with viruses and access to inappropriate information can be avoided or minimized by using the closed environment that a LAN can provide; access to private, confidential, or proprietary information can be limited to a specific set of known users. Today, however, even very small companies connect their LANs to the Internet to access data on the LANs of their vendors, suppliers, and customers. In doing so, they have transformed their local area network into a wide area network.

Wide Area Networks

A wide area network (WAN) can be thought of as a collection of LANs (see Figure 7). WANs existed long before the Internet became so popular and so public. Since it was neither practical nor, in many cases, possible for large companies to "own" the cable between their branches, they leased exclusive high speed access lines from the public telephone companies. These "T1" lines connected their LANs located in different cities, regions, or countries.

Network Components

Computer networks require specialized hardware and software designed for the sharing of information and other collaborative functions. The various components are explained in this section.

Clients Clients are the computer workstations where end users run the various applications necessary for them to do their jobs. In a client-server network, clients request information from the servers. Figure 8 shows an example of a client-server architecture. In this type of network architecture structure, the networking paths allow a network client computer to send information to a server, which then can relay the information back to the client computer or to another client on the same network. In this network, two fax machines and the laser printer are shared resources, available through their respective servers. In addition, the file server provides access to a shared hard disk.

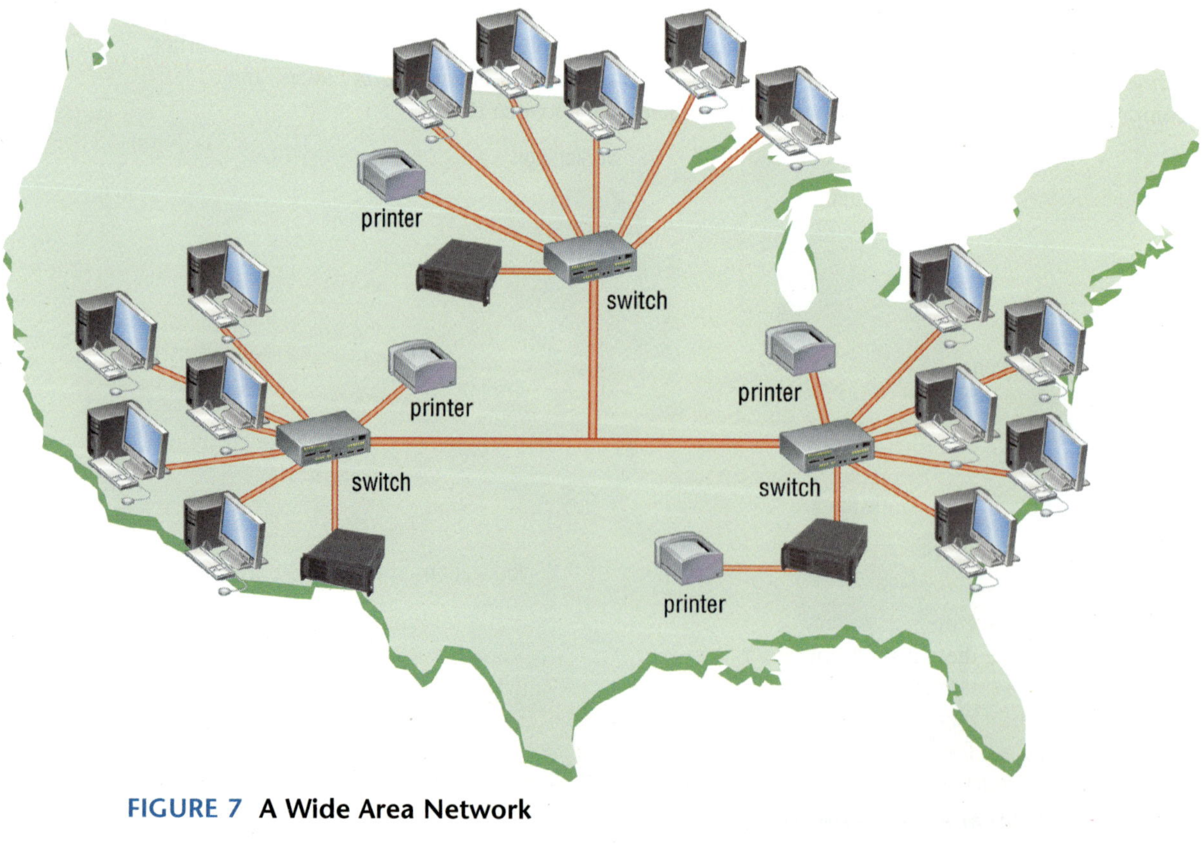

FIGURE 7 A Wide Area Network

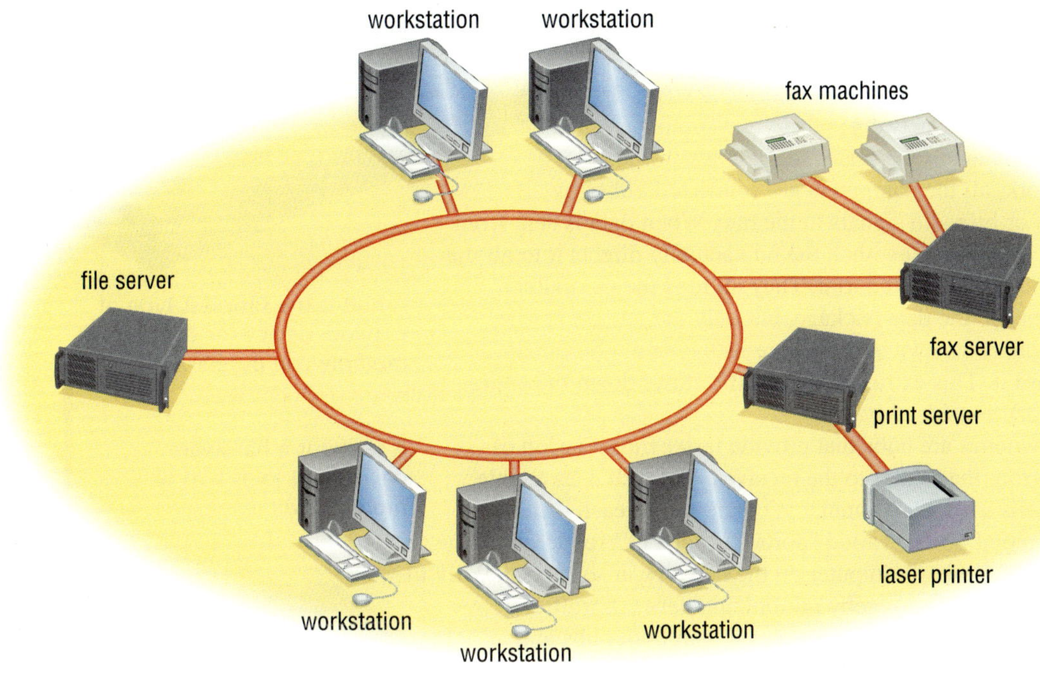

FIGURE 8 **Client-Server Architecture**

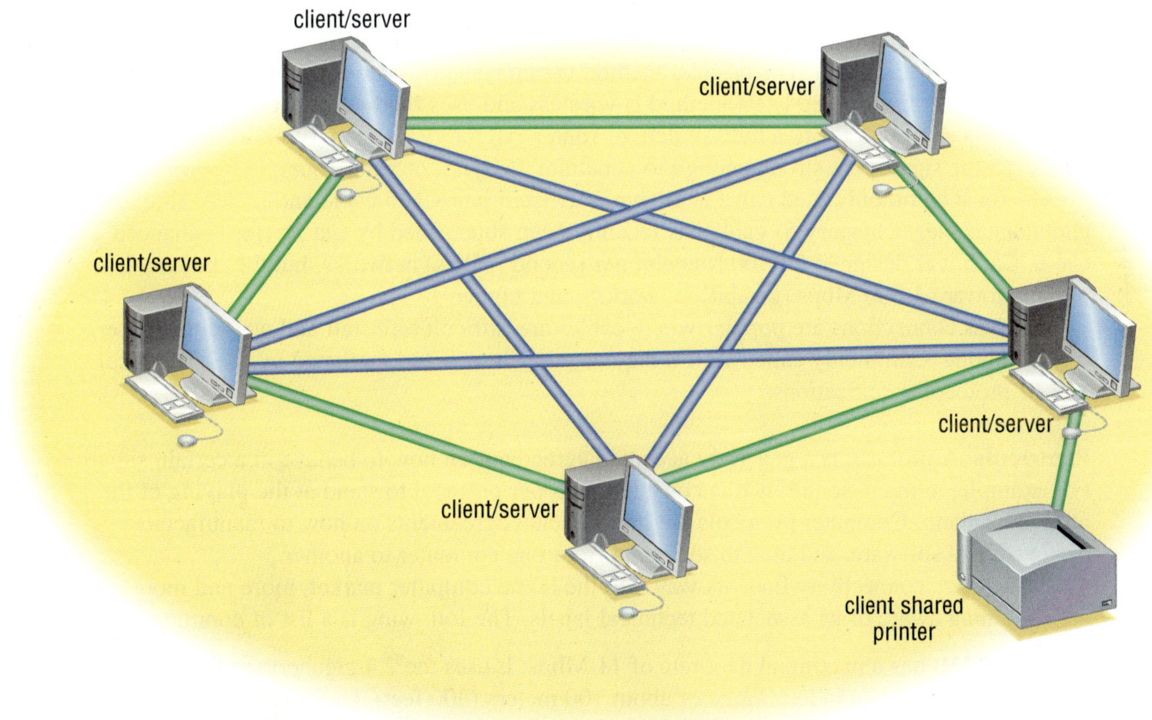

FIGURE 9 **Peer-to-Peer Architecture**

Servers Servers are data providers that are often larger and more powerful computers than clients. They house the network operating system software that organizes the sharing of data among the end users' PCs. They can hold large databases of information that users access to compile the reports that keep their organizations running smoothly. Servers might also be used as the storage location for everything every user creates, so that everyone else has easy access to it.

For small networks, the same computer can function as both client and server in a peer-to-peer network where all computers are equal and each one is both data requester and data provider (see Figure 9).

Hubs, Switches, and Routers Hubs are the devices that physically connect the computers in a LAN or in the local portion of a WAN. In a client-server network, where one computer is designated as the server, or in a peer-to-peer network, all the computers are connected either by cable or by radio signals to the hub. When data is sent from one computer to another, the hub actually directs it to all the computers connected to it. They all read the computer address on the data package, but only the computer that recognizes its own address accepts the data. The others discard it. This extra network traffic slows down the entire network considerably.

A hub is the simplest type of network device for connecting multiple computers.

Switches are hubs that provide faster transmission of data from the sender to the receiver. A switch uses a table that tells it which computer is connected to each of its connection points, called "ports." Instead of broadcasting the data to every computer on the network, it sends it directly to the specific port, thereby minimizing network traffic.

Routers are more sophisticated than both hubs and switches. They know how to pass data from one network to another in a large LAN or WAN, and throughout the Internet.

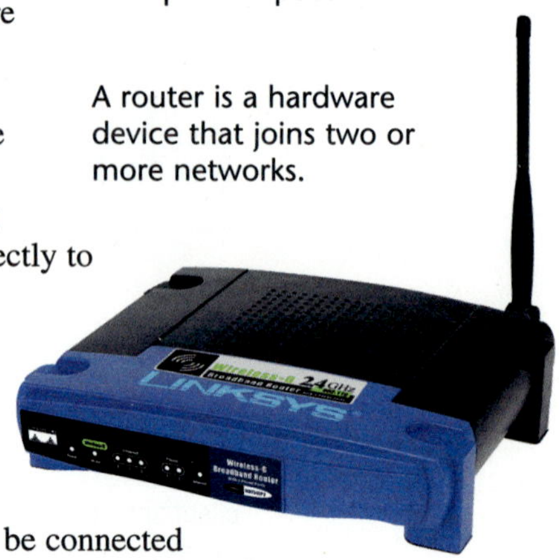

A router is a hardware device that joins two or more networks.

Connectivity The PCs that make up a network have to be connected to each other in some way. The original method uses physical cables containing several strands of wire. The latest method is wireless and uses radio frequencies to carry data over short distances from a PC to a hub, switch, or router. All the devices are often located in the same room, but the signals are strong enough to penetrate the types of walls found in homes and offices.

The most commonly used cable is known as twisted-pair Cat 5 cable and is very similar to telephone cable. "Category 5" cable has recently been superseded by Cat 5e (for "enhanced") and Cat 6. Cat 5 was designed for 100 Megabit per second (Mbps) networks, but the industry is now moving toward 1,000 Mbps (gigabit) networks—and higher.

Wireless connections are popular where cables are difficult to install and where users are highly mobile. Commonly called Wi-Fi, they are also known and marketed by their technical 802.11 protocol specifications.

Protocols A protocol is a generally accepted agreement on how to behave in a certain situation. For example, in many countries it is considered proper protocol to stand at the playing of the national anthem. Computer protocols are international agreements on how to manufacture hardware and software, and how to send data from one computer to another.

As wireless connectivity finds its way into the home computer market, more and more people are becoming aware of its associated technical labels. The following is a list of common protocols.

- **802.11b** has a maximum data rate of 11 Mbps. It uses the 2.4 gigahertz radio frequency band and has an indoor range of about 100 meters (300 feet). Unfortunately, the 2.4 GHz band is also used by cordless telephones, microwave ovens, and Bluetooth short range connectivity devices.

- **802.11a** has a maximum data rate of 54 Mbps. It solves the interference problems associated with its predecessor, 802.11b, by using the 5 GHz radio frequency band. The interference found in the 2.4 GHz band is avoided, but its indoor range is limited to about 30 to 50 meters, or 98 to 164 feet.

- **802.11g** has a maximum data rate of 54 Mbps and uses the 2.4 GHz band.

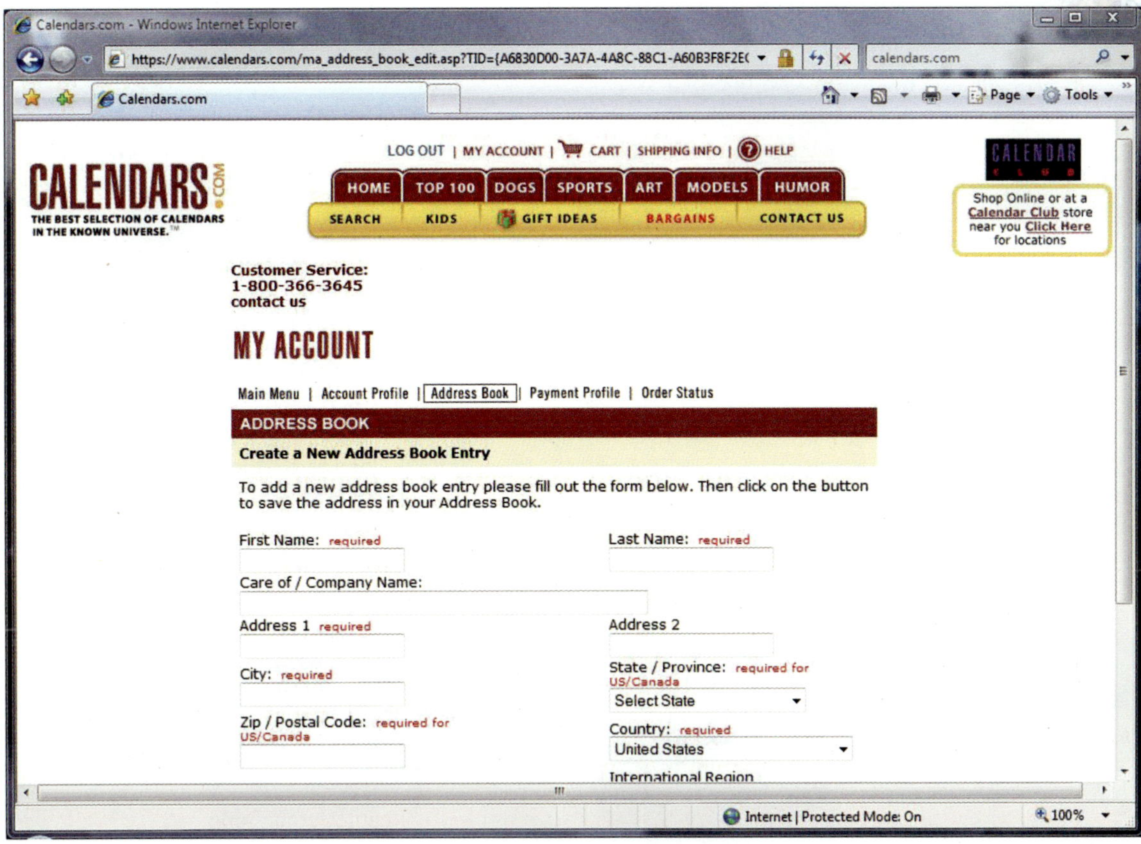

HTTPS is a protocol that protects your personal data. Note the padlock at the right of the address bar at the top of the screen.

- **TCP/IP** (Transmission Control Protocol/Internet Protocol) defines the rules for sending and receiving data from one network with the Internet protocol address 192.200.40.0, for example, to another network with the IP address 192.200.50.0.
- **HTTP** (HyperText Transfer Protocol) defines the rules for sending and receiving Web pages (hypertext) on the Internet. For example, you might see http://emcp/myschool.edu on the uniform resource locator (URL) line of your Internet browser.
- **HTTPS** (HyperText Transfer Protocol Secure Sockets) encrypts data before sending it over the Web. You can see the letters *https* on the URL line when you reach a Web page asking for your credit card number or when you are paying your bills online, such as https://emcp/mybank.com/myaccount.
- **SMTP** (Simple Mail Transfer Protocol) is an e-mail protocol that allows you to send your message to a mail server on the Internet. One day it may be replaced by the "mailto" protocol often seen in Outlook e-mail headers, but backward compatibility remains a big problem. SMTP is an old protocol that was not made for large video file attachments.
- **POP3** is the current version of the Post Office Protocol that holds an e-mail message until the recipient asks for it. The announcement "You've got mail" on the Internet service provider AOL prompts users to open the e-mail folder and access their messages. Figure 10 illustrates the process used for sending electronic mail with SMTP and a POP server.
- **FTP** (File Transfer Protocol) provides a way to send files between computers with incompatible operating systems. It is also used for downloading files that are too large for e-mail attachments, such as PowerPoint presentations, videos, or large graphic files.

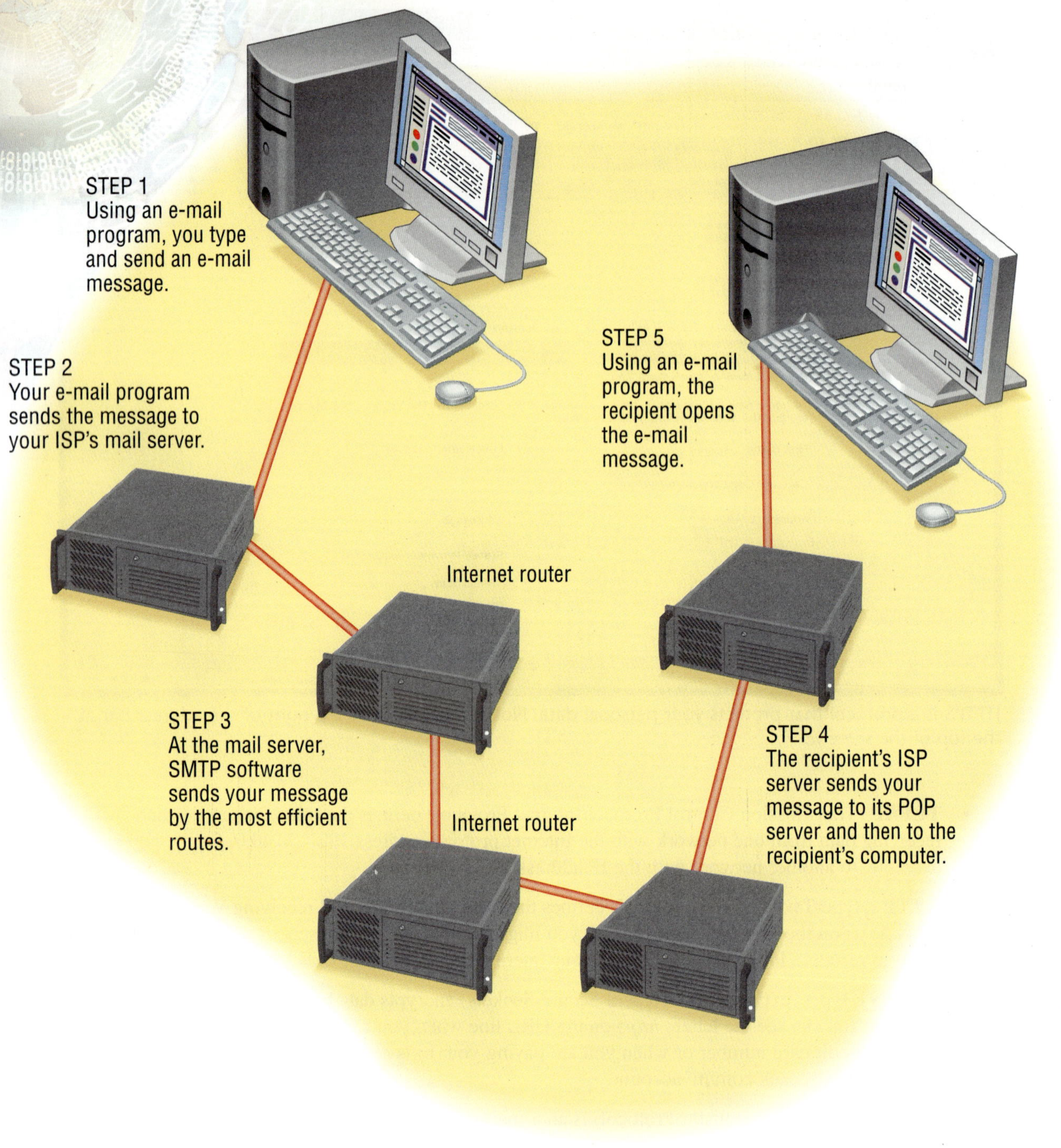

FIGURE 10 The Process for Sending Electronic Mail with SMTP and a POP Server

Connectors and Ports The most popular connectors found these days on the ends of network cables are commonly called RJ45 connectors since they resemble the "Registered Jack" connectors used by the telephone industry. Technically, the computer industry term is 8P8C (8 Positions, 8 Conductors). They plug into an opening called a "port" on the back or side of a computer or other device.

EXPLORING TECHNOLOGY 5

Open the *Control Panel* and click *Network Connections* with XP or *Network and Internet* with Vista. If you find reference to a *Local Area Connection*, open it and look for your system's properties. Explore the other icons and links to learn more about your network. What protocols are installed? What is your connection speed? ***Hint: If you have a dial-up modem connection to the Internet, you may not see any references to a "network," but if you have a DSL or cable modem connection, you probably will—even if you have only one computer in your environment.***

EXPLORING TECHNOLOGY 6

See how far you can trace the connection from your computer through hubs, switches, routers, and modems until it leaves your "local area." Ask your instructor or computer lab assistant for help, if necessary. Does your network include wireless connectivity?

The Internet

The Internet is a global network of computers that allows data of all types and formats to be passed freely from one computer to another (see Figure 11). The Web, e-mail, and FTP are different parts of the Internet.

World Wide Web

The World Wide Web is a collection of hypertext files, containing graphics, audio, and video that can be accessed on the Internet. The Web is only a part of the Internet, albeit a very large one.

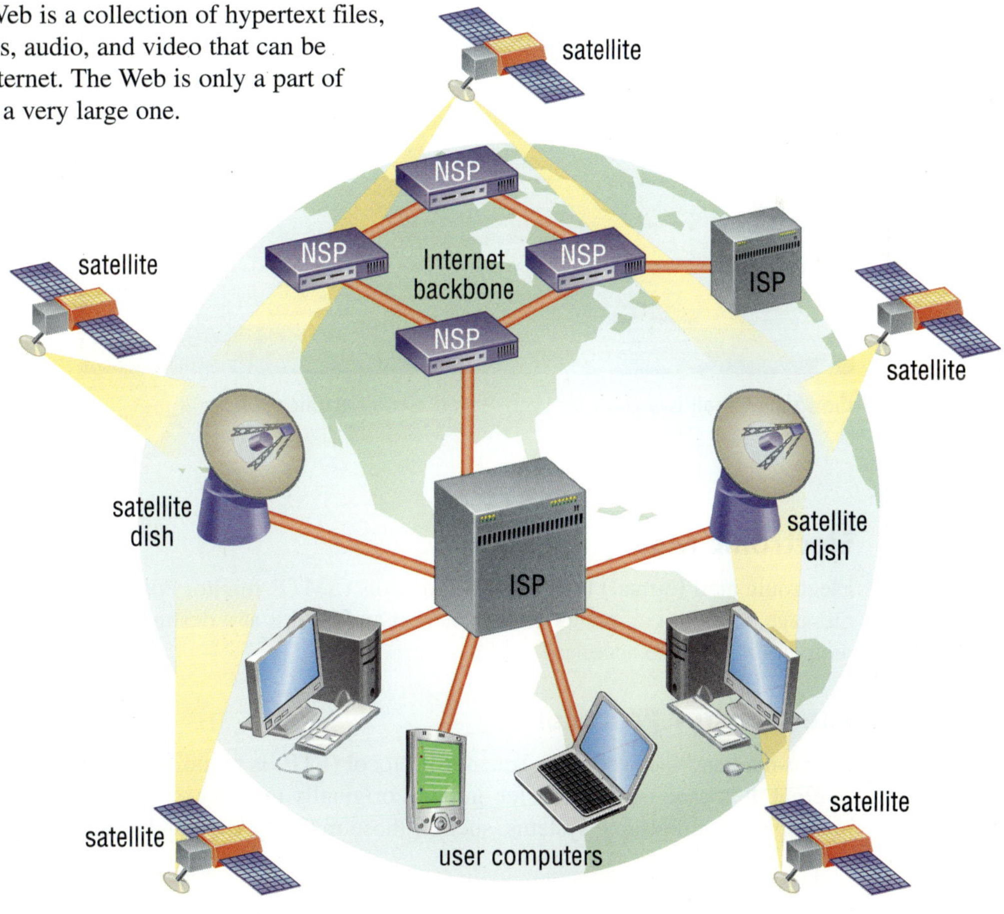

FIGURE 11 The Internet
The Internet is a worldwide network of service providers, individual computers, and networks of all sizes.

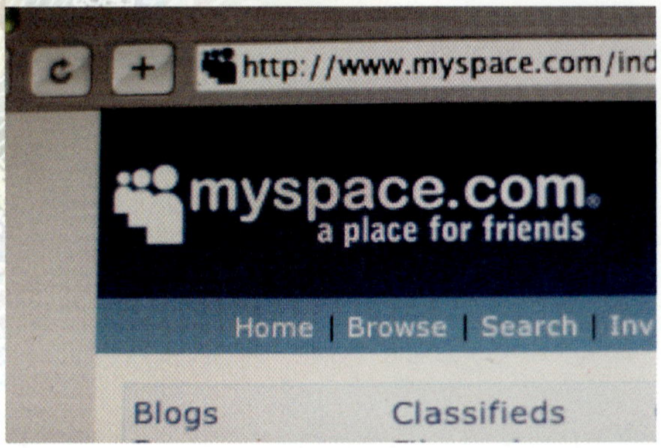

Many, but not all sites on the World Wide Web start with the three letters "www."

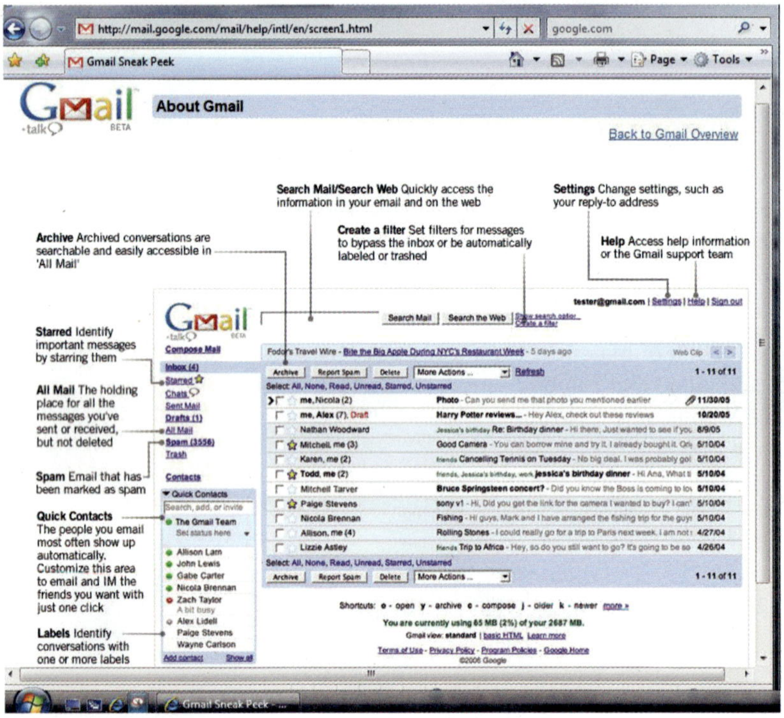

Google's Gmail is a popular Web-based e-mail application.

Electronic Mail

Electronic mail (e-mail) uses its own protocols (SMTP, mailto, Post Office Protocol 3) to route a message between computers on the Internet and hold it at a destination mail server until the recipient is ready to access it.

File Transfer Protocol

Like e-mail and the Web, File Transfer Protocol (FTP) is an information workspace on the Internet. It is used for file transfer and was originally used for exchanging data between incompatible mainframe systems, such as those made by IBM and those made by UNIVAC.

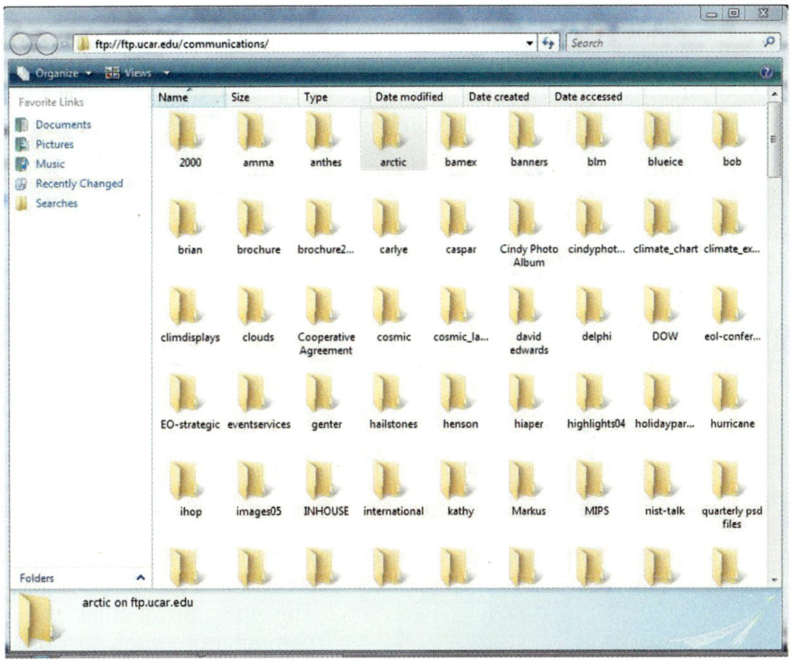

This FTP site shows files available for viewing or downloading.

EXPLORING TECHNOLOGY 7

Open your Internet Browser and navigate to the URL **ftp://ftp.ftpplanet.com**. For Windows XP, select a text file, click *Copy this item* in the Folder Tasks pane, browse to the location of your storage medium in the Copy Items dialog box, and click the Copy button. For Windows Vista, click the Page button, click *Open FTP Site in Windows Explorer*, click Allow (if an Internet Explorer Security message box displays), right-click a text file, click *Copy*, navigate to your storage medium in the Folders list, right-click in the Content pane, and click *Paste*. You have just "ftp-ed" a file to your computer. Close all windows. ***Note: A firewall or other security policy on your network may prevent you from using FTP.***

Security Issues

Malware is a relatively new term describing computer programs that have a malicious intent. Viruses, worms, spyware, and adware programs, discussed in this section, all fall into this category.

Viruses

Viruses are computer programs written by people who want to hurt others by damaging or destroying their computer files or in some way making their computer experience difficult, frustrating, and painful. Viruses are spread through the transfer of files from one computer to another. Before networks were common, they were introduced into computers from floppy diskettes. Macintosh computers seem to be immune to them. Figure 12 illustrates the virus infection process.

Worms

Worms are programs that can spread themselves to any other computer connected to the Internet or any other network. They are easily spread when you open an e-mail attachment or click a hyperlink embedded in the text. The file and link names are often made up of foreign words or seemingly random strings of characters.

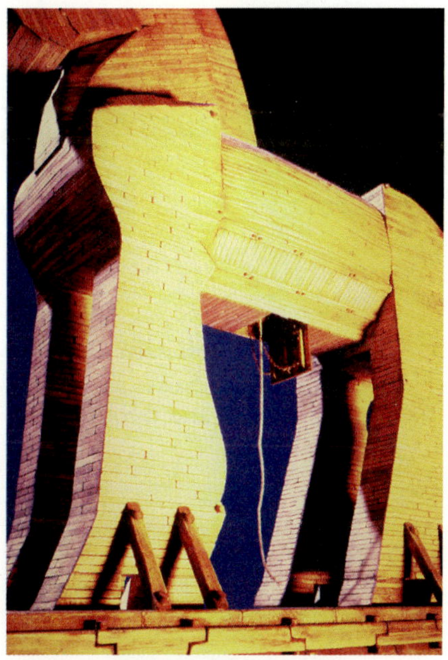

A Trojan Horse virus file hides inside a common file on your PC and then attacks when you open it.

Spyware

Spyware tracks your activity as you surf the Internet and reports it to companies that want to sell you their products—or steal your identity. Spyware takes advantage of cookies, the small files that Web sites put on your computer to remember who you are on your next visit.

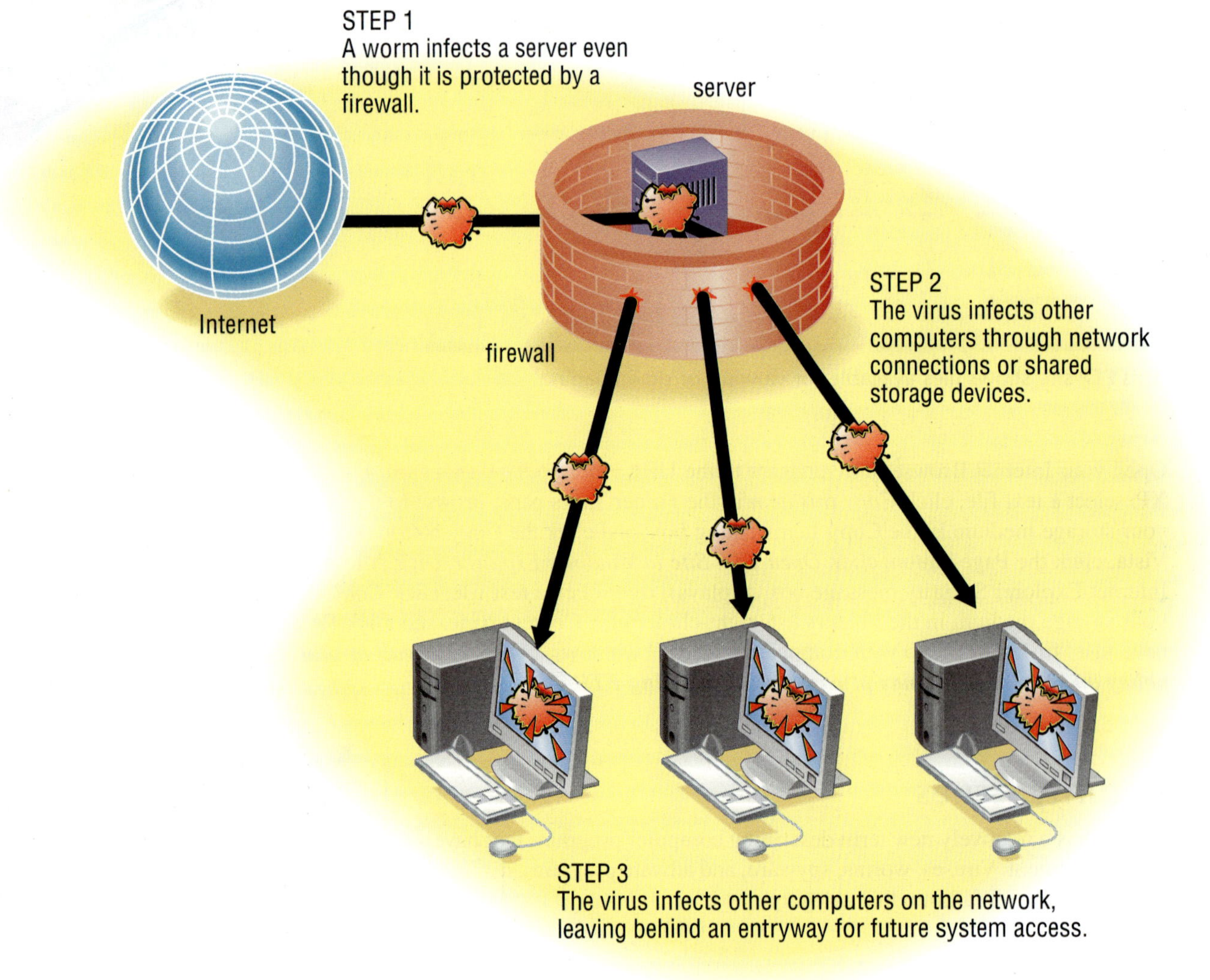

FIGURE 12 The Virus Infection Process
Viruses are often transmitted over the Internet and through shared devices such as flash drives.

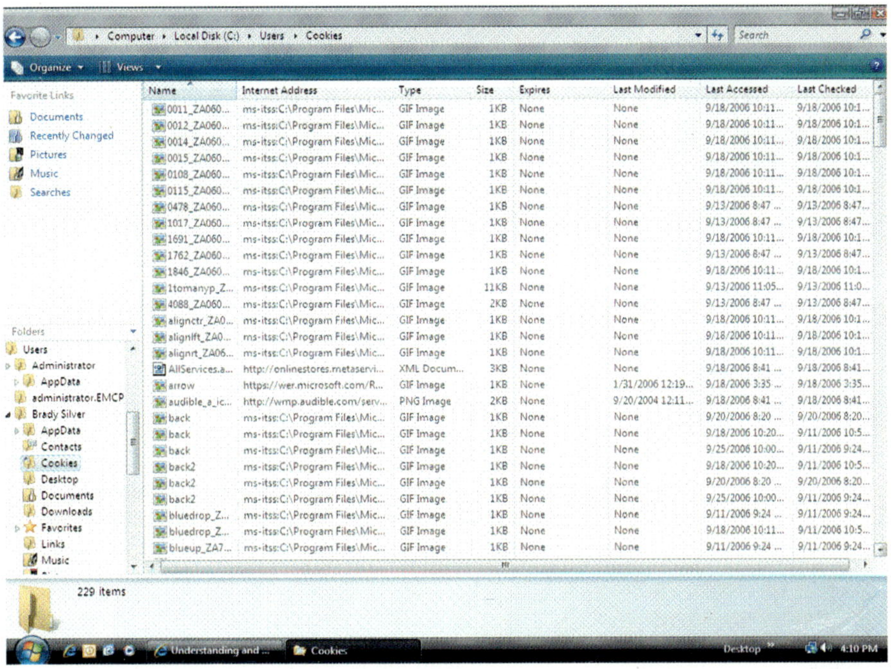

Microsoft Windows includes a Cookies subfolder in the folder structure created for each user. With Internet Explorer, you can manage how cookies are stored in the subfolder.

Adware

Adware looks at files on your computer and then sends pop-up advertisements that try to sell you products and services. Although annoying, adware is not usually destructive, but it can slow down your processor and your Internet access significantly.

Confidentiality and Privacy

Spyware programs can steal your personal information and tell it or sell it to other people who might be able to impersonate you and take money from your bank account or charge large purchases to your credit card.

Phishing is a method of convincing people to reveal their passwords, credit card numbers, social security numbers, and other private or confidential information. Phishers pretend to be representatives of the victim's bank or a government agency by sending official-looking e-mails with obscure links back to Web sites that look exactly like the real Web site. The information they gather is then used in schemes involving identity theft that allow them to gain access to the victim's bank account, which they empty of its funds.

Protection Software

Several computer programs are available to provide protection from virus attacks and from the installation of spyware or adware on your computer. Some examples are McAfee VirusScan and Symantec AntiVirus for viruses; and Spybot Search & Destroy, SpySweeper, AdAware, and Spyware Detector for spyware and adware. Windows Vista includes an anti-adware and anti-spyware program called Windows Defender.

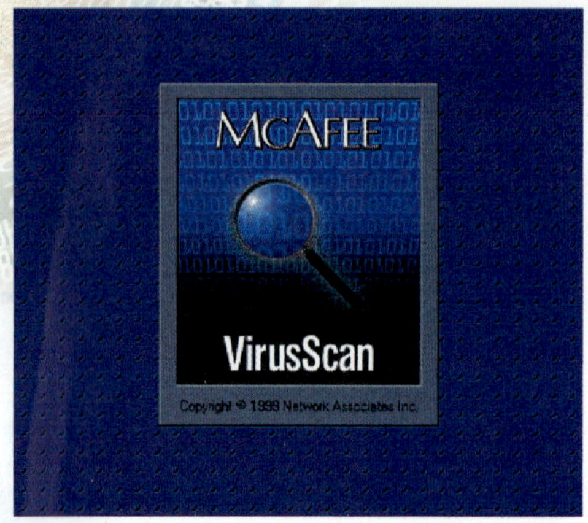

McAfee VirusScan is a popular virus-checking utility.

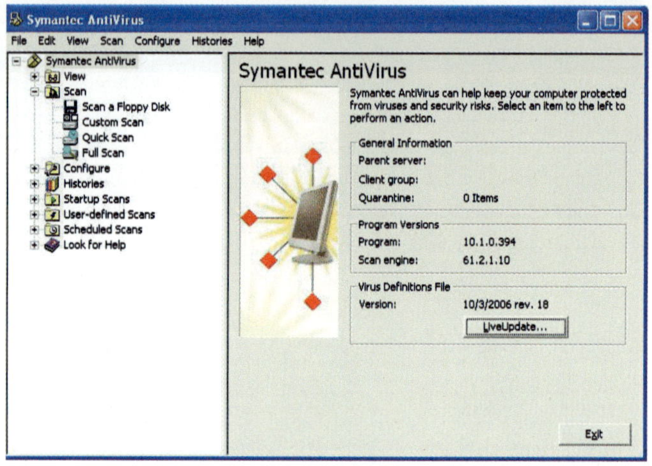

The installation of an antivirus software program such as Symantec AntiVirus is essential for computers connected to the Internet. Keeping these virus definitions up to date will significantly help in the fight against viruses.

To minimize infection, always update your computer with the latest security patches as they become available. Keep your protection software up to date by downloading the latest "signature" files of known viruses.

EXPLORING TECHNOLOGY 8

Explore the programs on your computer and identify what protection software is installed. Verify that it is up to date.

E-mail Etiquette and Computer Ethics

Two types of rules govern and guide behavior: etiquette and ethics. Etiquette refers to the rules that govern courteous behavior, such as holding the door open for someone, or saying "please" and "thank you." We often think of etiquette in terms of knowing which fork to use in a fancy restaurant, but etiquette also involves the rules for language appropriate in a businesslike environment. "Fighting words" are embarrassing to some people, and they can also lead to anger and violence. Showing proper etiquette is a way of showing a person respect. If you show disrespect to someone, that is not proper etiquette. When applied to computer communication, improper etiquette can result in serious misunderstandings or ill will among coworkers. It can even lead to the loss of a lucrative business contract or the loss of a job.

Ethics are the rules we use to determine what is right and wrong, and these rules help guide our choices and actions, both in our personal lives and in our business lives.

Ethics are the moral principles that govern behavior. In the news, we often see reports about corporate executives who have been charged or convicted of funneling company money into their own personal bank accounts. Politicians are accused of taking bribes from lobbyists in return for a favorable vote on a piece of legislation that will be profitable for the lobbyist's organization. Taxpayers claim tax deductions they are not entitled to. Students submit reports that were written by someone else. People offer to copy the latest music CD or software program they just purchased and give it to their friends. Where do you stand on these ethical issues?

Both etiquette and ethics have direct application to computers, especially in relation to e-mail and copyright issues.

E-mail Etiquette

Everyone—friends, relatives, schoolmates, coworkers, employers, teachers, businesses, government officials, and sales and marketing departments—is sending e-mail these days. Speedy communication with other people all over the world can be fun, exciting, and productive. However, it can also cause problems. What you write in an e-mail message can hurt someone's feelings, be misinterpreted, or might accidentally be sent to the wrong person. You can cause yourself embarrassment or even get yourself fired.

Here are ten rules of e-mail etiquette. You might want to add a few of your own.

1. Be brief and to the point. E-mails are supposed to be a fast way to communicate. Don't slow down the process.
2. Don't use ALL CAPITAL letters. It looks and sounds like you're shouting or angry.
3. Remember to attach the attachment. Mentioning what you are "enclosing" in any type of letter is a good idea. Get in the habit of stopping as soon as you type the phrase "I am attaching…" and immediately clicking the Attach button.
4. Use the Spelling Checker (even if you're a great speller). Using the Spelling Checker feature only takes a few seconds and it shows that you care about quality. But watch out! It is very easy to click "Change" instead of "Ignore" and change a person's name to a common word and that, whether humorous or not, is an embarrassing mistake.
5. Reread what you wrote from the perspective of the receiver. Ask yourself how the recipient is likely to interpret your words. Did you leave out or misspell a word that completely changes the meaning?
6. Double-check the address in the *To* box. Confirm that you clicked the correct name in your address list. Once you click the Send button, there is *no* way to stop the message or undo an address mistake.
7. Watch your language. Profanity can come back and haunt you.
8. Assume your e-mail will be read by *lots* of other people. E-mails are often forwarded so others can take action or to inform a supervisor. Avoid cute or friendly asides and comments that you only want a close friend to see.
9. Always put something in the *Subject* line. A well-written subject will help the receiver decide where to file your message and whether to read it now or wait until later.
10. Privacy does not exist in e-mails, especially those in a corporate environment. The e-mail administrator can potentially see the contents of any e-mail. Company policy may allow checking e-mails to ensure that no company secrets are exposed, or to stop harassing or abusive e-mail.

Software manufacturers usually obtain a copyright that prohibits the illegal copying and distribution of software. Warnings such as this one are designed to remind users of the copyright law.

Software Piracy and Copyright Infringement

When you install a software application, you must agree to accept the license agreement that describes the legal contract between the user (you) and the software developer. If you click the "No, I don't accept this agreement" box, the installation process will stop. By accepting the agreement, you agree with everything it says. The contract often covers the number of people who may use the program at the same time. That would usually be one person, but organizations can purchase agreements that cover a specific number of users.

Most software is copyrighted. The exception is open source software mentioned earlier. Copyright laws in the United States and most (but not all) other countries state that authors, music composers, TV show and movie creators, artists, and publishers own the works they create and distribute; no one is allowed to use or copy their work without specific permission. Software license agreements might specify that you can make one backup copy, but you cannot give that copy to a friend. The same rules apply to all copyrighted material including music CDs, DVDs, and songs available on the Web. Infringing on a copyright is illegal, and this law is enforced.

Formerly known as the Software Publishers Association, the Software & Information Industry Association (SIIA, www.siia.net) encourages people who witness software piracy to inform them so that they can investigate the situation. Once they gather enough evidence, they will contact the organization's executives, ask them to prove they have enough licenses, and encourage them to purchase the software legally. In most cases the pressure works, but if necessary, the SIIA may take legal action.

Software piracy is a felony, but even if it was not, other compelling reasons exist for why you should not copy programs, music, or DVDs. It hurts the people who spend a lot of time and money creating products for your enjoyment. They do research. They buy computers, musical instruments, or video cameras. They pay money for studio time to record their songs, and then more money to advertise them and ship them to music stores. They may sell their creations to publishing companies who agree to pay them royalties based on sales. Will you send money to your favorite band every time you give a friend a copy of their latest CD? If graphic artists and musicians can't pay their expenses and cover the cost of making the songs, movies, computer games, and other software you enjoy, how can an individual artist, or even a large company, continue to create more?

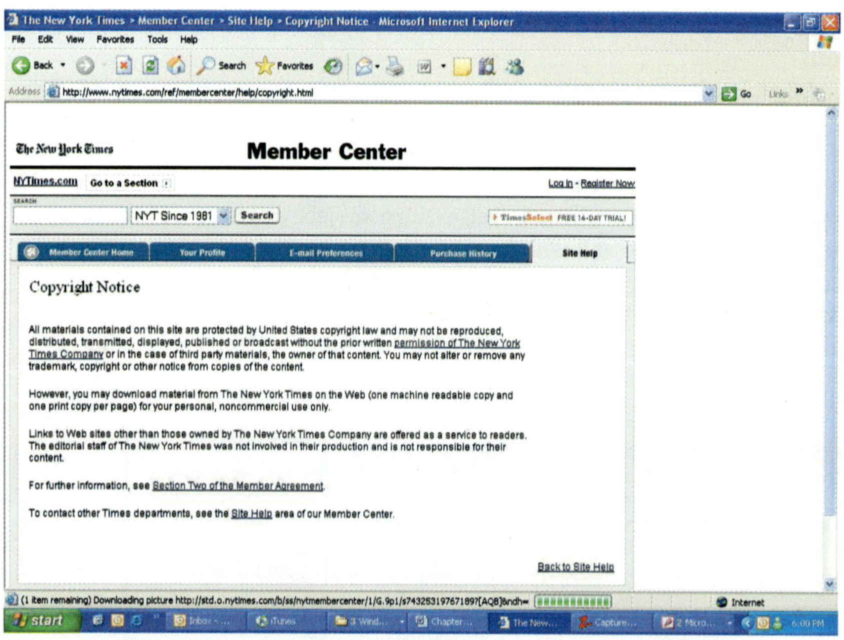

The copyright notice on *The New York Times* home page reminds visitors that the content of the site is copyrighted.

Check to see who is the registered user of each of the applications on your computer by running it and watching for the name on the startup screen. If it isn't registered to your organization, your department, or yourself, ask a supervisor why not. Your action could actually help save your organization from costly litigation and potential fines.

EXPLORING TECHNOLOGY 9

Navigate to www.siia.net and click the *Report Piracy* icon. Read about what you can do to help stop software piracy.

EXPLORING TECHNOLOGY 10

Use your word processor to write the explanation you will use when you decline to give or receive a copy of a music CD, software program, DVD, or any other copyrighted material.

EXPLORING TECHNOLOGY 11

Knowledge Check

Completion: In the space provided at the right, indicate the correct term.

1. What are the four segments of the information processing cycle? __________
2. Besides the keyboard, mouse, and storage devices, list five devices that can be used to enter information into a computer. __________
3. What part of the computer handles the tasks of calculating formulas and editing documents? __________
4. What types of computer applications would be enhanced by a dual-core processor? __________
5. What is the technical name for the volatile computer workspace that is erased whenever the power is turned off? __________
6. Which storage device has no motor or other moving parts? __________
7. What type of port allows up to 127 hardware devices to be connected to the computer host at 480 Mbps? __________
8. What type of software can be copied freely and have no license agreements? __________
9. What it the basic purpose for a computer network? __________
10. What two terms describe the "data requester" and "data provider" in a LAN? __________
11. What is the basic protocol that allows all computers on the Internet to interact? __________
12. Which protocol and application can you use if you need to transfer a file that is too large to e-mail? __________
13. What more common term is used to describe an 8P8C network cable connector? __________
14. List at least three types of malware.
15. What term describes the act of illegally sharing a software application with someone else? __________

Microsoft® Windows XP

Windows XP SECTION 1

Exploring Windows XP

Skills

- Display the Windows XP desktop
- Perform the following actions using the mouse: point, click, double-click, and drag
- Start and close a program
- Open and close a window
- Shut down Windows XP
- Move a window
- Minimize, maximize, and restore a window
- Cascade and tile windows
- Display the Date and Time Properties dialog box
- Use components of a dialog box
- Display the Volume slider
- Display the Taskbar and Start Menu Properties dialog box

Projects Overview

Your department at Worldwide Enterprises has received new computers with the Windows XP operating system. You will explore the Windows XP desktop; open, close, and manipulate windows; open a program using the Start button; use options in the notification area of the Taskbar; and customize the Taskbar.

Activity 1.1

Exploring the Windows XP Desktop

The main portion of the screen that displays when Windows XP is loaded is called the ***desktop***. This desktop can be compared to the top of a desk in an office. A business person places necessary tools—such as pencils, pens, paper, files, calculator—on his or her desktop to perform functions. Like those tools, the Windows XP desktop contains tools for operating the computer. These tools are logically grouped and placed in dialog boxes or windows that can be accessed using the icons located on the Windows XP desktop.

Project

Worldwide Enterprises

You work for Worldwide Enterprises and your department has just received new computers with the Windows XP operating system. You want to explore the Windows XP desktop to familiarize yourself with this new operating system.

1. Complete the steps needed to display the Windows XP desktop.

   Check with your instructor to determine the specific steps required to display Windows XP on your computer. This may be as simple as turning on the computer or may involve additional steps for logging on the computer system. When Windows XP is loaded, you will see a desktop similar to the one shown in Figure 1.1. Your desktop may contain additional icons or have a different background than the desktop shown in Figure 1.1.

2. Move the mouse on the desk and notice how the corresponding pointer moves in the Windows desktop.

   The ***mouse*** is a device that controls the pointer that identifies your location on the screen. Move the mouse on the desk (preferably on a mouse pad) and the pointer moves on the screen. For information on mouse terms, refer to Table 1.1 and for information on mouse icons, refer to Table 1.2.

FIGURE 1.1 Windows XP Desktop

TABLE 1.1 Mouse Terms

Term	Action
point	Position the mouse pointer on the desired item.
click	Quickly tap a button on the mouse once.
double-click	Tap the left mouse button twice in quick succession.
drag	Press and hold down the left mouse button, move the mouse pointer to a specific location, and then release the mouse button.

TABLE 1.2 Mouse Icons

Icon	Description
	The mouse appears as an I-beam pointer in a program screen where you enter text (such as Microsoft Word) and also in text boxes. You can use the I-beam pointer to move the insertion point or select text.
	The mouse pointer appears as an arrow pointing up and to the left (called the *arrow pointer*) on the Windows desktop and also in other program Title bars, Menu bars, and toolbars.
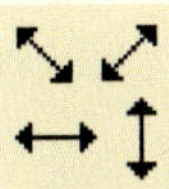	The mouse pointer becomes a double-headed arrow (either pointing left and right, up and down, or diagonally) when performing certain functions such as changing the size of a window.
	Select an object in a program such as a picture or image and the mouse pointer becomes a four-headed arrow. Use this four-headed arrow pointer to move the object left, right, up, or down.
	When a request is being processed or a program is being loaded, the mouse pointer may display with an hourglass beside it. The hourglass means "please wait." When the process is completed, the hourglass image is removed.
	When you position the mouse pointer on certain icons or hyperlinks, it turns into a hand with a pointing index finger. This image indicates that clicking the icon or hyperlink will display additional information.

3 Move the mouse pointer to the current time that displays at the far right side of the Taskbar and after approximately one second, the current day and date will display in a yellow pop-up box.

To identify the location of the Taskbar, refer to Figure 1.1.

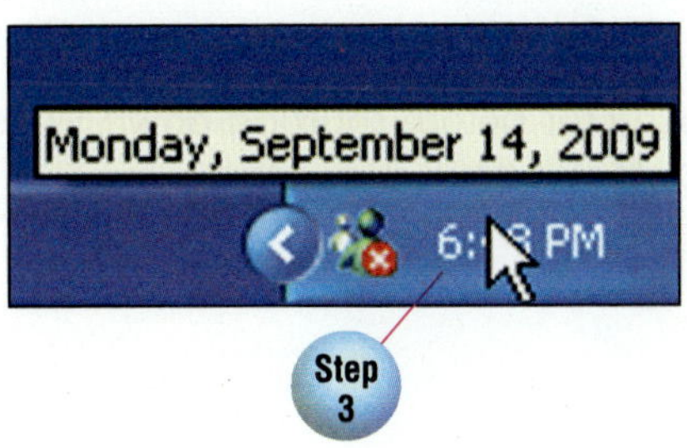

continues

4. Position the mouse pointer on the Start button start on the Taskbar and then click the left mouse button.

   Clicking the Start button causes the Start menu to display. The Start menu contains a list of software programs, documents, and other options available on your computer. The menu is divided into two columns. Links to the most recently used programs display in the left column and links to folders, the Control Panel, online help, and the search feature display in the right column. The bottom of the Start menu contains options for logging off or turning off the computer.

5. At the Start menu, point to *All Programs* and then point to *Microsoft Office*.

   To point to a menu option, simply position the mouse pointer on the option. Do not click a mouse button. Pointing to *All Programs* causes a side menu to display with a list of programs. A right-pointing triangle displays to the right of some options on the Start menu. This triangle indicates that a side menu will display when you point to the option.

6. Move the mouse pointer to *Microsoft Office Word 2007* in the side menu and then click the left mouse button.

   Clicking *Microsoft Office Word 2007* causes the Word program to open and display on the screen.

7. Close Microsoft Word by clicking the Close button x that displays in the upper right corner of the program.

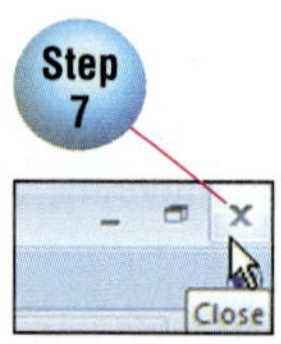

8. At the Windows XP desktop, position the mouse pointer on the *Recycle Bin* icon and then double-click the left mouse button.

   Icons provide an easy method for opening programs or documents. Double-clicking the *Recycle Bin* icon displays the Recycle Bin window. When you open a program, a defined work area, referred to as a ***window***, appears on the screen.

9. Close the Recycle Bin window by clicking the Close button (contains a white X on a red background) that displays in the upper right corner of the window.

10. Shut down Windows XP by clicking the Start button and then clicking *Turn Off Computer* at the Start menu.

    Check with your instructor before shutting down Windows XP. The steps you need to follow to shut down Windows may vary.

11 At the Turn off computer window, click the Turn Off option.

With options at the Turn off computer window, you can shut down Windows, shut down and then immediately restart Windows, tell the computer to go to stand by, or tell the computer to hibernate. Wait for the message that it is okay to turn off the power, or until the computer powers off automatically. Important data is stored in memory while Windows XP is running and this data needs to be written to the hard disk before turning off the computer.

In Brief

Start Program
1. Click Start button.
2. Point to *All Programs*.
3. Click desired program.

Shut Down Windows
1. Click Start button.
2. Click *Turn Off Computer*.
3. At Turn off computer window, click Turn Off.

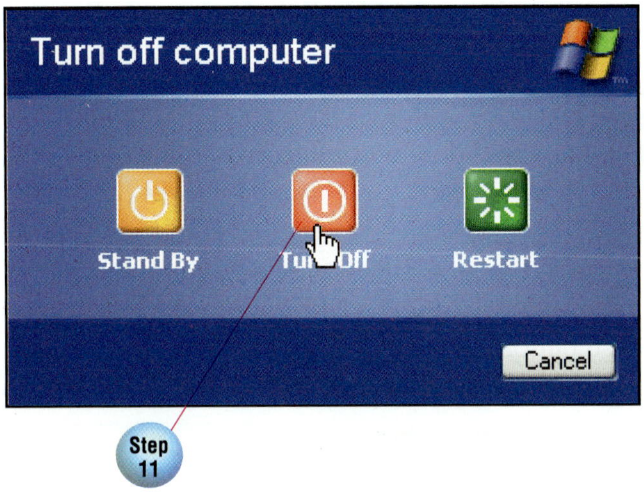

In Addition

Putting the Computer on Stand By or Hibernate

When you shut down Windows, you can choose to shut down the computer completely, shut down and then restart, put the computer on stand by, or tell the computer to hibernate. Click the Stand By option at the Turn off computer window and the computer switches to a low power state causing some devices such as the monitor and hard disks to turn off. With these devices off, the computer uses less power. Stand by is particularly useful for saving battery power for portable computers. Tell the computer to "hibernate" by holding down the Shift key while clicking the Stand By option at the Turn off computer window. In hibernate mode, the computer saves everything in memory on disk, turns off the monitor and hard disk, and then turns off the computer. When you restart the computer, the desktop is restored exactly as you left it. You can generally restore your desktop from either stand by or hibernate by pressing once on the computer's power button. Bringing a computer out of hibernation takes a little longer than bringing a computer out of stand by.

Activity 1.2

Opening and Manipulating Windows

When you open a program, a defined work area, referred to as a ***window***, appears on the screen. You can move a window on the desktop and change the size of a window. The top of a window is called the Title bar and generally contains buttons at the right side for closing the window and minimizing, maximizing, or restoring the size of the window. More than one window can be open at a time and open windows can be cascaded or tiled.

Project

You will continue your exploration of the Windows XP desktop by opening and manipulating windows.

Worldwide Enterprises

1. At the Windows XP desktop, double-click the *Recycle Bin* icon.

   This opens the Recycle Bin window on the desktop. If the Recycle Bin window fills the entire desktop, click the Restore Down button, which is the second button from the right (immediately left of the Close button) located in the upper right corner of the window.

2. Move the window on the desktop. To do this, position the mouse pointer on the window Title bar (the bar along the top of the window), hold down the left mouse button, drag the window to a different location on the desktop, and then release the mouse button.

3. Click the Start button on the Taskbar and then click *My Computer* at the Start menu.

   The *My Computer* option is located in the right column of the Start menu. If the My Computer window fills the entire desktop, click the Restore Down button, which is the second button from the right (immediately left of the Close button) located in the upper right corner of the window. You now have two windows open on the desktop—My Computer and Recycle Bin.

4. Make sure the Title bar of the Recycle Bin window is visible (if not, move the My Computer window) and then click the Recycle Bin Title bar.

   Clicking the Recycle Bin Title bar makes the Recycle Bin window active, moving it in front of the My Computer window.

5. Minimize the Recycle Bin window to a task button on the Taskbar by clicking the Minimize button (contains an underscore symbol) located toward the right side of the Recycle Bin Title bar.

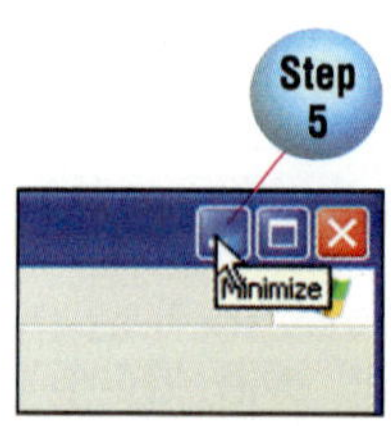

6. Minimize the My Computer window to a task button on the Taskbar by clicking the Minimize button located at the right side of the Title bar.

7. Redisplay the Recycle Bin window by clicking the Recycle Bin task button on the Taskbar.

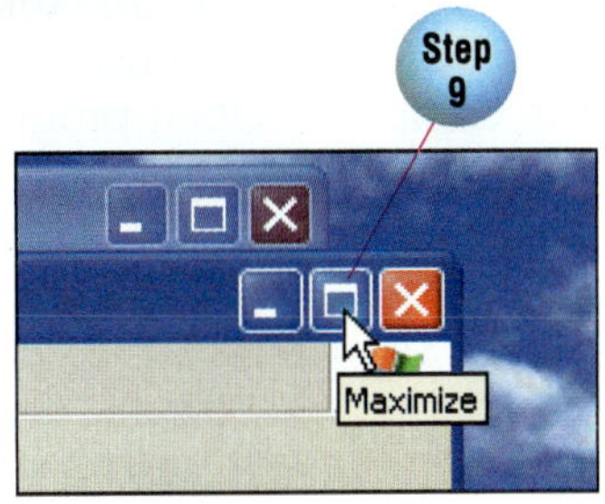

8. Redisplay the My Computer window by clicking the My Computer task button on the Taskbar.
9. Click the Maximize button located at the right side of the My Computer window.

   Clicking the Maximize button causes the window to expand to fill the entire desktop.

10. Click the Restore Down button located at the right side of the My Computer window.

    Clicking the Restore Down button restores the window to the size it was before it was maximized.

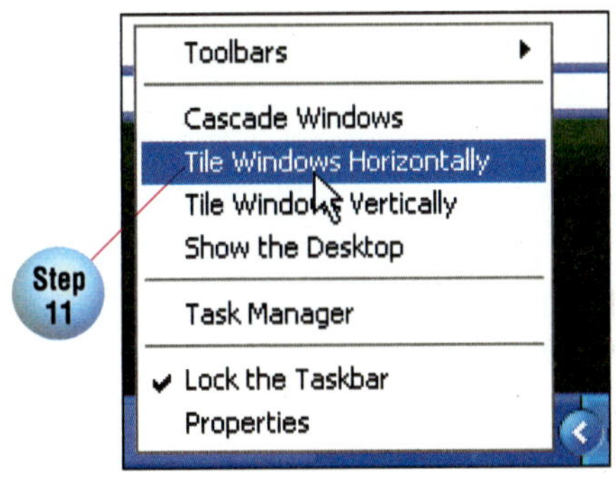

11. Right-click on an empty section of the Taskbar and then click *Tile Windows Horizontally*.

    Tiled windows fill the desktop with the Title bar and a portion of each window visible.

12. Right-click on an empty section of the Taskbar and then click *Cascade Windows* at the shortcut menu.

    Cascaded windows display in the upper left corner of the desktop with the Title bar of each open window visible.

13. Close the My Computer window by clicking the Close button (contains a white X on a red background) located at the right side of the Title bar.
14. Close the Recycle Bin window by clicking the Close button.

In Brief

Move Window

1. Position mouse pointer on window Title bar.
2. Hold down left mouse button.
3. Drag window to desired position.
4. Release mouse button.

Tile Windows Horizontally

1. Right-click an empty section of Taskbar.
2. Click *Tile Windows Horizontally* at shortcut menu.

Cascade Windows

1. Right-click an empty section of Taskbar.
2. Click Cascade Windows at shortcut menu.

In Addition

Sizing a Window

Using the mouse, you can increase or decrease the size of a window. To increase the size horizontally, position the mouse pointer on the border at the right or left side of the window until it turns into a left- and right-pointing arrow. Hold down the left mouse button, drag the border to the right or left, and then release the mouse button. Complete similar steps to increase or decrease the size of the window vertically using the bottom border of the window. To change the size of the window both horizontally and vertically at the same time, position the mouse pointer at the left or right corner of the window until the pointer turns into a diagonally pointing double-headed arrow and then drag to change the size.

Activity 1.3

Exploring the Taskbar

The bar that displays at the bottom of the desktop is called the ***Taskbar*** and it is divided into three sections: the Start button, the task buttons area, and the notification area. Click the Start button to start a program, use the Help and Support feature, change settings, open files, or shut down the computer. Open programs display as task buttons in the task button area of the Taskbar. You can right-click an empty portion of the Taskbar to display a shortcut menu with options for customizing the Taskbar. The notification area displays at the right side of the Taskbar and contains a digital clock and specialized programs that run in the background.

Project

As you continue exploring Windows XP, you want to learn more about the features available on the Taskbar.

Worldwide Enterprises

1. At the Windows XP desktop, double-click the current time that displays at the far right side of the Taskbar.

   Figure 1.2 identifies the components of the Taskbar. Double-clicking the time causes the Date and Time Properties dialog box to display. Please refer to Table 1.3 for information on dialog box components.

2. Check to make sure the correct date and time display in the Date and Time Properties dialog box.

   If the date is incorrect, click the down-pointing arrow at the right side of the month list box in the *Date* section and then click the correct month at the drop-down list. Click the up-or down-pointing arrows in the year text box to increase or decrease the year. Click the correct day in the updated calendar. To change the time, double-click either the hour, minute, or seconds and use the up-and-down-pointing arrows to adjust the time.

3. Click the Time Zone tab located toward the top of the Date and Time Properties dialog box.

   Check to make sure the correct time zone displays. If it is not correct, click the down-pointing arrow at the right side of the list box and then click the desired time zone at the drop-down list.

4. Click OK to close the Date and Time Properties dialog box.

FIGURE 1.2 Taskbar

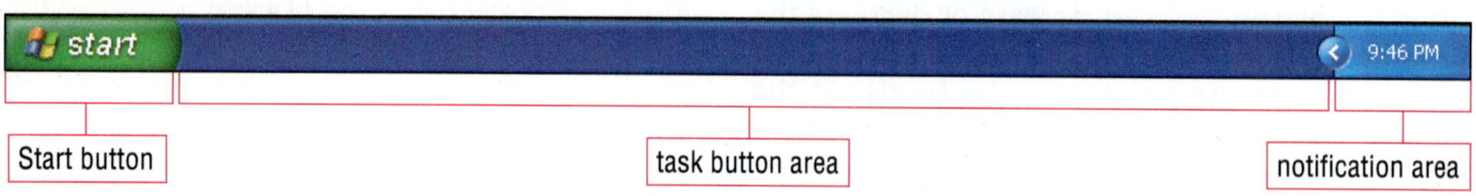

TABLE 1.3 Dialog Box Components

Name	Image	Function
tabs	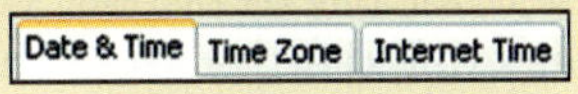	Click a dialog box tab and the dialog box options change.
text box	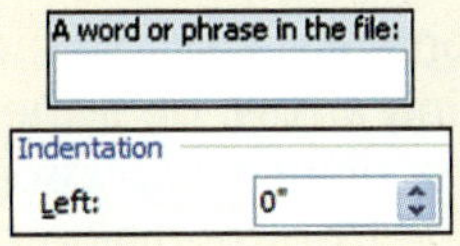	Type or edit text in a text box. A text box may contain up-or-down-pointing arrows to allow you to choose a number or an option instead of typing it in.
drop-down list box	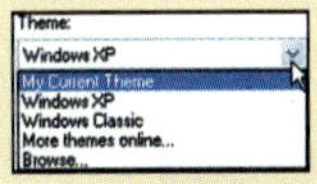	Click the down-pointing arrow at the right side of a drop-down list box and a list of choices displays.
list box		A list box displays a list of options.
check boxes	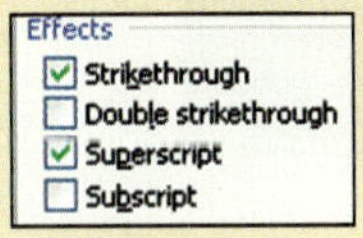	If a check box contains a check mark, the option is active; if the check box is empty, the option is inactive. Any number of check boxes can be active.
option buttons	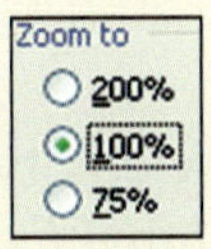	Only one option button in a dialog box section can be selected at any time. An active option button contains a dark or colored circle.
command buttons	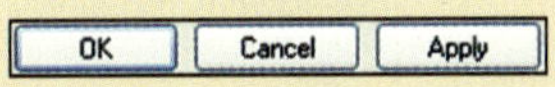	Click a command button to execute or cancel a command. If a command button name is followed by an ellipsis (. . .), clicking the button will open another dialog box.
slider	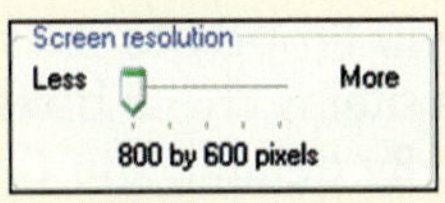	Using the mouse, drag a slider to increase or decrease the number, speed, or percentage of the option.
scroll bar	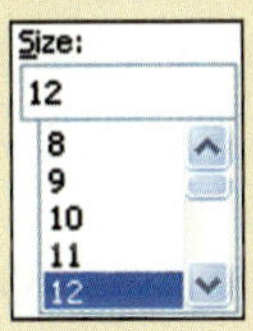	A scroll bar displays when the amount of information in a window is larger than can fit comfortably in a single window.

5. Position the mouse pointer on the Volume button located toward the right side of the Taskbar and then click the left mouse button.

   Clicking the Volume button causes a slider bar to display. Use this slider to increase or decrease the volume. Insert a check mark in the *Mute* check box if you want to turn off the sound. If the Volume button is not visible, click the left-pointing arrow located at the left side of the notification area. This expands the area to show all buttons. If you do not see a left-pointing arrow, or, if the volume button is still not visible, click Start, point to *All Programs*, point to *Accessories*, point to *Entertainment*, and then click *Volume Control*. A Volume Control dialog box opens in which you can increase or decrease the volume.

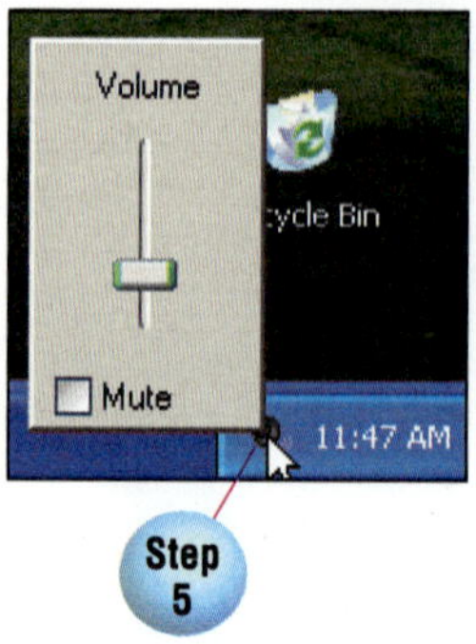

6. After viewing the Volume slider, click on any empty location on the desktop to remove the slider. If you had to open the Volume Control dialog box, click the Close button.
7. Right-click on any empty location on the Taskbar and then click *Properties* at the shortcut menu that displays.

   This displays the Taskbar and Start Menu Properties dialog box with the Taskbar tab selected. Notice that the dialog box contains check boxes. A check mark in a check box indicates that the option is active. By default, the *Group similar taskbar buttons* option is active. With this option active, if the Taskbar becomes crowded with task buttons, task buttons for the same program are collapsed into a single button. Click a button representing collapsed files for the same program and a list of the files displays above the button.
8. Click the *Auto-hide the taskbar* option to insert a check mark in the check box.
9. Click the Apply command button located toward the bottom of the dialog box.

10 Click the OK button to close the Taskbar and Start Menu Properties dialog box.

Notice that the Taskbar is no longer visible.

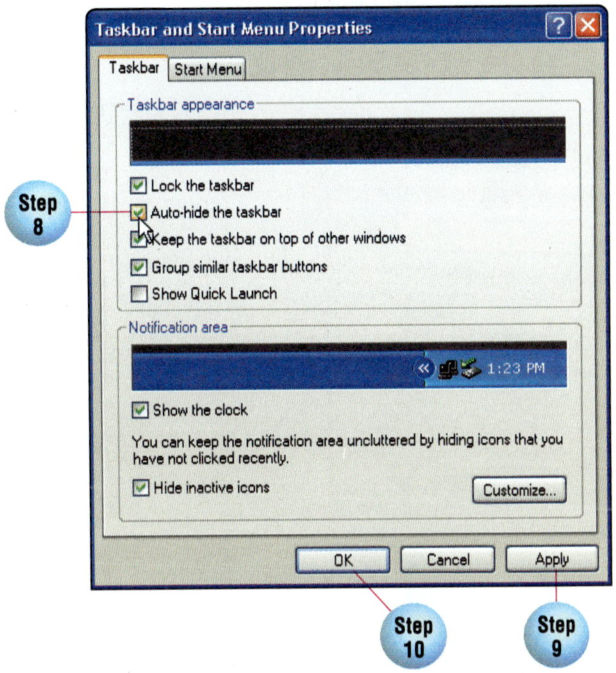

11 Display the Taskbar by moving the mouse pointer to the bottom of the desktop.

12 Right-click on any empty location on the Taskbar and then click *Properties* at the shortcut menu.

13 Click the *Auto-hide the taskbar* option to remove the check mark.

14 Click the Apply command button.

15 Click the OK button to close the Taskbar and Start Menu Properties dialog box.

In Brief

Display Date and Time Properties Dialog Box
Double-click current time at right side of Taskbar.

Display Volume Slider
Click Volume button on Taskbar.

Display Taskbar and Start Menu Properties Dialog Box
1. Right-click an empty location on Taskbar.
2. Click *Properties* at shortcut menu.

In Addition

Using Natural Keyboard Shortcuts

If you are using a Microsoft Natural Keyboard or a compatible keyboard, you can use the Windows logo key and the Application key to access the following features.

Press	To do this
	display the Start menu
+ M	minimize all windows
+ E	open My Computer
+ F	search for a file or folder
+ F1	display Help and Support Center window
+ R	open the Run dialog box
	display the shortcut menu for selected item

Features Summary

Feature	Button	Action
close window		Click Close button on Title bar.
Date and Time Properties dialog box		Double-click time on Taskbar.
maximize window		Click Maximize button on Title bar.
minimize window		Click Minimize button on Title bar.
move window on desktop		Drag window Title bar.
My Computer window		Click Start button, click My Computer.
restore window		Click Restore Down button on Title bar.
shut down computer		Click Start button, click Turn Off Computer, click Turn Off at Turn off computer window.
Start menu	start	Click Start button on Taskbar.
Taskbar and Start Menu Properties dialog box		Right-click empty location on Taskbar, click Properties at shortcut menu.
Taskbar shortcut menu		Right-click empty location on Taskbar.
volume slider		Click Volume button on Taskbar.

Knowledge Check

Completion: In the space provided at the right, indicate the correct term, symbol, button, or command.

1. This mouse term refers to positioning the mouse pointer on the desired item. ______
2. This mouse term refers to tapping the left mouse button twice in quick succession. ______
3. This symbol is attached to the mouse pointer when a request is being processed and means "please wait." ______
4. Click this button on a window Title bar to reduce the window to a task button on the Taskbar. ______
5. Click this button on a window Title bar to expand the window so it fills the entire screen. ______
6. Double-click the time located at the right side of the Taskbar and this dialog box displays. ______
7. This component of a dialog box generally displays when the amount of information is larger than can fit comfortably in the dialog box. ______
8. Drag this component in a dialog box to increase or decrease the number, speed, or percentage of an option. ______

Skills Review

Review 1 Opening and Manipulating Windows

1. At the Windows XP desktop, click the Start button on the Taskbar and then click *My Documents*. (If the My Documents window fills the desktop, click the Restore Down button located in the upper right corner of the window.)
2. Click the Start button on the Taskbar and then click *My Computer*. (If the My Computer window fills the desktop, click the Restore Down button.)
3. Position the mouse pointer on the My Computer Title bar, hold down the left mouse button, and then drag the My Computer window so the My Documents Title bar is visible.
4. Click the My Documents Title bar to make it the active window.
5. Right-click on an empty location on the Taskbar and then click Cascade Windows at the shortcut menu.
6. Click the Minimize button (located toward the right side of the Title bar) on the My Documents window Title bar to reduce the window to a task button on the Taskbar.
7. Click the Minimize button on the My Computer window to reduce the window to a task button on the Taskbar.
8. Click the My Computer task button to restore the My Computer window on the desktop.
9. Click the My Documents task button to restore the My Documents window on the desktop.
10. Click the Maximize button on the My Documents Title bar to expand the window to fill the screen.
11. Click the Restore Down button on the My Documents Title bar to reduce the size of the My Documents window.
12. Close the My Documents window.
13. Close the My Computer window.

Review 2 Exploring the Taskbar

1. At the Windows XP desktop, double-click the time that displays in the notification area at the right side of the Taskbar.
2. At the Date and Time Properties dialog box, click the down-pointing arrow at the right side of the month list box and then click the next month (from the current month) at the drop-down list.
3. Click the OK button.
4. Display the Date and Time Properties dialog box again, change the month back to the current month, and then click OK to close the dialog box.
5. Click the Start button, point to *All Programs*, point to *Microsoft Office*, and then click *Microsoft Office Excel 2007*.
6. Close Excel by clicking the Close button located at the right side of the Microsoft Office Excel Title bar.

Skills Assessment

Assessment 1 Manipulating Windows

1. Click the Start button and then click *My Pictures*. (If the My Pictures window fills the entire desktop, click the Restore Down button.)
2. Click the Start button and then click *My Music*. (If the My Music window fills the entire desktop, click the Restore Down button.)
3. Cascade the two windows.
4. Make the My Pictures window the active window and then reduce it to a task button on the Taskbar.
5. Reduce the My Music window to a task button on the Taskbar.
6. Restore the My Pictures window.
7. Restore the My Music window.
8. Close the My Music window and then close the My Pictures window.

Assessment 2 Exploring the Taskbar

1. At the Windows XP desktop, display the Date and Time Properties dialog box.
2. Change the current hour one hour ahead and then close the dialog box.
3. Open the Date and Time Properties dialog box, change the hour back to the current hour, and then close the dialog box.
4. Display the Volume slider bar, drag the slider to increase the volume, and then click the desktop outside the slider to close it.
5. Display the Volume slider bar and then drag the slider to the original position.
6. Display the Taskbar and Start Menu Properties dialog box, remove the check mark from the *Show the clock* option, and then close the dialog box. (Notice that the time no longer displays on the Taskbar.)
7. Display the Taskbar and Start Menu Properties dialog box, insert a check mark in the *Show the clock* option, and then close the dialog box.

Windows XP SECTION 2

Maintaining Files and Customizing Windows

Skills

- Use the Help and Support feature
- Turn on the display of file extensions
- Create a folder
- Select, move, copy, and paste files
- Delete files/folders to and restore files/folders from the Recycle Bin
- Create and delete a shortcut
- Rename a file
- Explore the Control Panel
- Search for files and/or folders
- Use WordPad and Paint
- Customize the desktop
- Change screen resolution

Student Resources

Before beginning this section:

1. Copy to your storage medium the WindowsS2 folder on the Student Resources CD.
2. Make WindowsS2 the active folder.

Projects Overview

Worldwide Enterprises

You will use the Help feature to learn about new Windows XP features and then organize files for your department at Worldwide Enterprises. This organization includes creating a folder and moving, copying, and deleting files. You will also create a shortcut to a specific file you use when creating reports for your department, search for specific files for your supervisor, prepare a note to the manager of the IS department, and customize your desktop to the corporate computer standard.

Performance Threads

Organize files for Performance Threads including creating folders, copying, moving, renaming, and deleting files; create a shortcut to a document; create a document with file instructions and a text box with a department title.

First Choice TRAVEL

Search for information on setting up a computer for multiple users.

Activity 2.1

Getting Help in Windows XP; Displaying File Extensions

Windows XP includes an on-screen reference guide, called Help and Support, that provides information, explanations, and interactive help on learning Windows features. The Help and Support feature contains complex files with hypertext used to access additional information by clicking a word or phrase. Display the Help and Support Center window by clicking the Start button on the Taskbar and then clicking Help and Support at the Start menu. At the *Help and Support* Center window, you can perform such actions as choosing a specific help topic, searching for a keyword or topic, and displaying an index of help topics.

Project

Worldwide Enterprises

You decide to use the Windows XP Help and Support feature to learn more about new Windows XP features. Your supervisor at Worldwide Enterprises has also asked you to learn how to copy files and create a folder and shortcut in Windows XP. You will also turn on the display of file extensions to prepare for your file management projects.

1. Display the Help and Support Center window by clicking the Start button on the Taskbar and then clicking *Help and Support*.

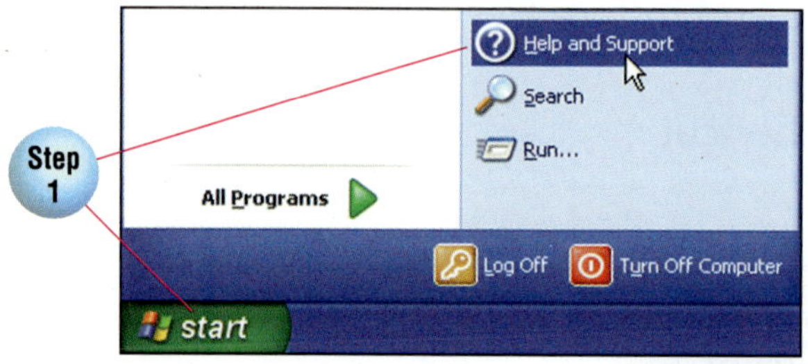

2. At the Help and Support Center window, click the What's new in Windows XP hyperlink located in the *Pick a Help topic* section of the window.

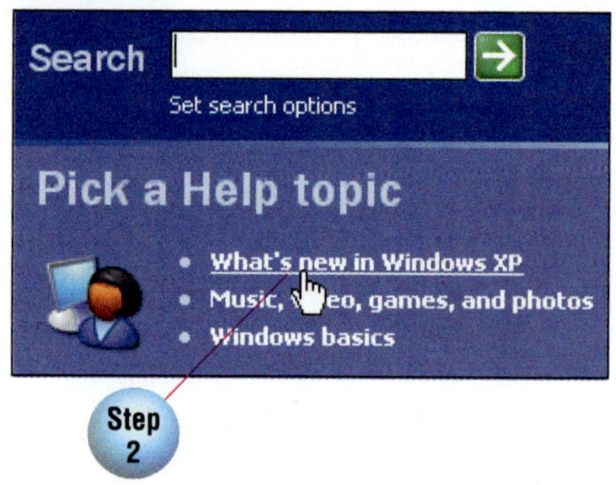

3. Click the What's new hyperlink located in the *What's new in Windows XP* section of the window.

   This displays a list of Help options at the right side of the window.

4. Click the What's new in Windows XP hyperlink located at the right side of the window below the subheading *Overviews, Articles, and Tutorials.*

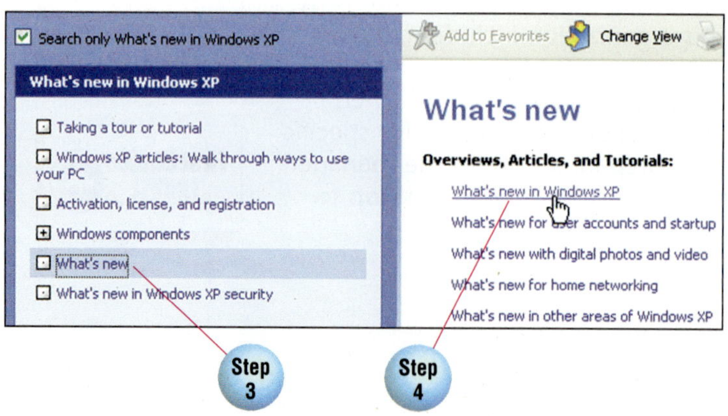

5 Read the information about Windows XP that displays at the right side of the window.

6 Print the information by clicking the Print button located on the toolbar above the information. At the Print dialog box that displays, click the Print button.

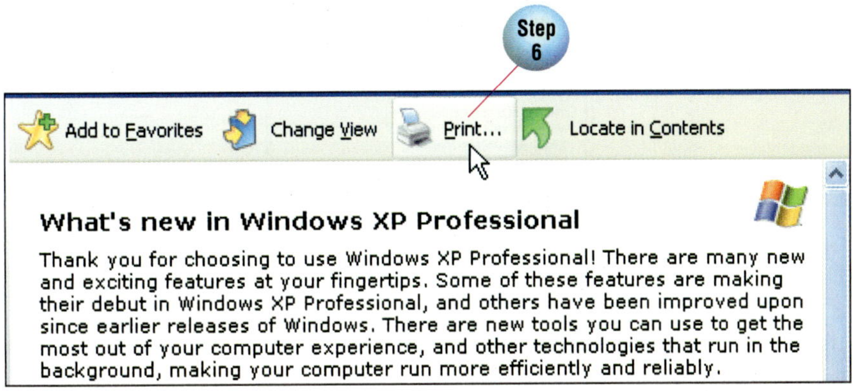

7 Return to the opening Help and Support Center window by clicking the Home button located on the Help and Support Center toolbar.

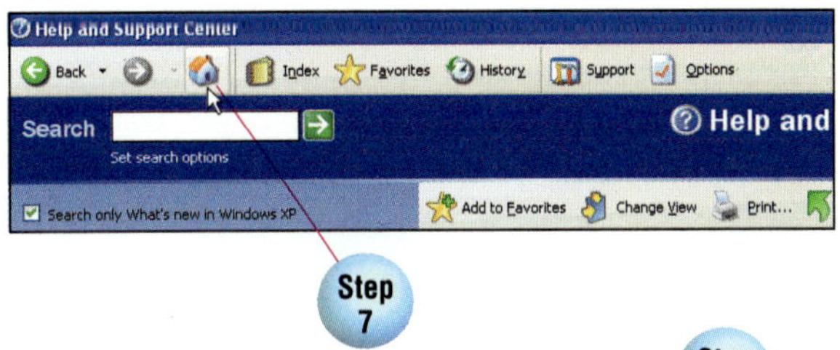

8 Click in the *Search* text box located toward the top of the Help and Support Center window, type **copying files**, and then press Enter.

After typing a search topic you can press Enter or click the Start searching button (white arrow on a green background) that displays at the right of the *Search* text box.

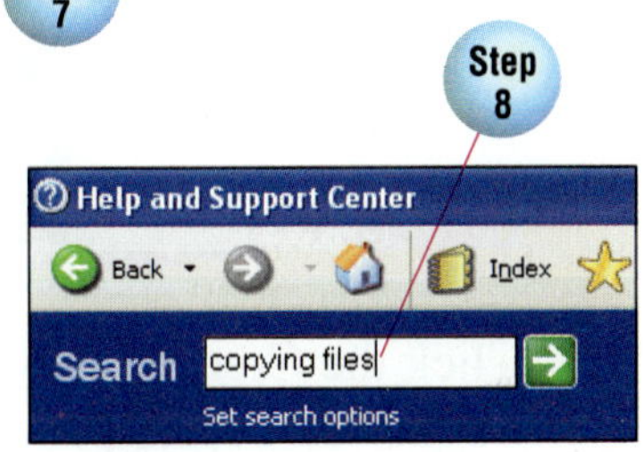

9 Click the Copy a file or folder hyperlink that displays in the *Search Results* section of the window (below the *Pick a task* subheading).

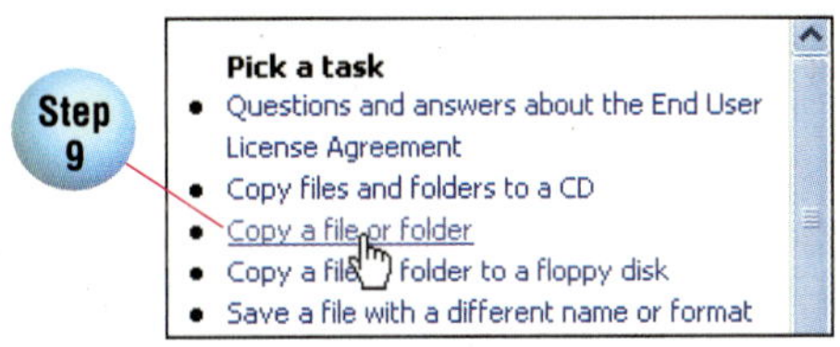

10 Read the information about copying a file or folder that displays at the right side of the window and then print the information by clicking the Print button on the toolbar and then clicking the Print button at the Print dialog box.

11 Click the Index button located on the Help and Support Center toolbar.

12 With the insertion point positioned in the *Type in the keyword to find* text box, type **shortcuts**.

The list of topics in the list box below the *Type in the keyword to find* text box will automatically scroll to related topics.

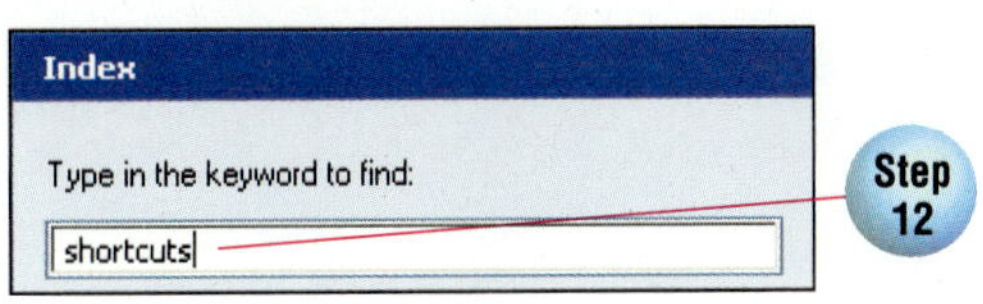

continues

13 Double-click the subheading *for specific programs* that displays below the *shortcuts* heading.

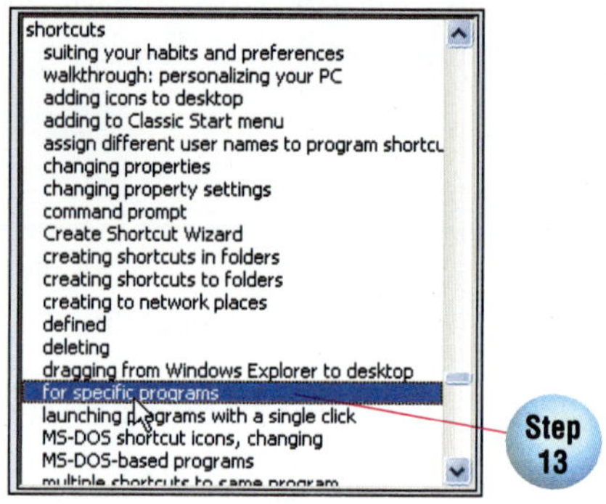

14 Read the information that displays at the right side of the window and then print the information.

15 Click the Home button located on the Help and Support Center toolbar.

16 Click in the *Search* text box located toward the top of the Help and Support Center window, delete existing text, type **create a folder**, and then press Enter.

17 Click the Create a new folder hyperlink located in the *Pick a task* section of the Suggested Topics pane.

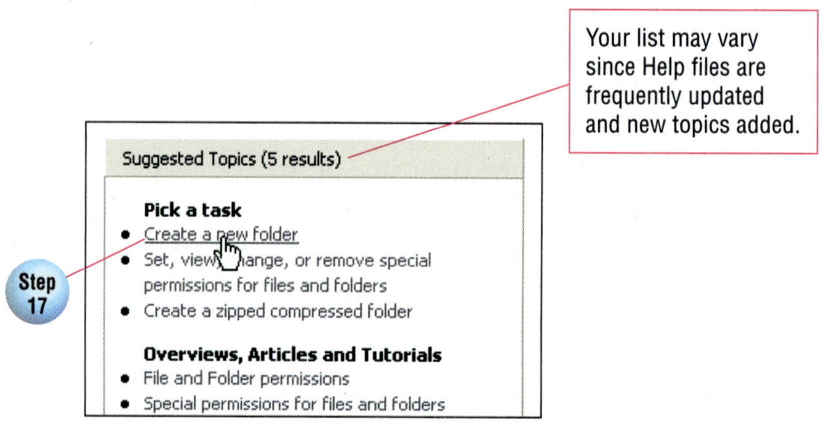

18 Read the information about creating a folder that displays at the right side of the window and then print the information.

19 Click the Locate in Contents button on the toolbar located above the information.

Clicking this button locates the topic in the Help table of contents and displays the information in the Windows basics pane.

20 Click the Home button located on the Help and Support Center toolbar.

21 Close the Help and Support Center window by clicking the Close button located in the upper right corner of the window.

Worldwide Enterprises requires that employees work with the display of file extensions turned on. This practice helps employees identify source applications associated with a file and often prevents an employee from accidentally opening a file attachment in an e-mail that is likely to contain harmful data.

22 Click the Start button on the Taskbar and then click *My Computer* at the Start menu.

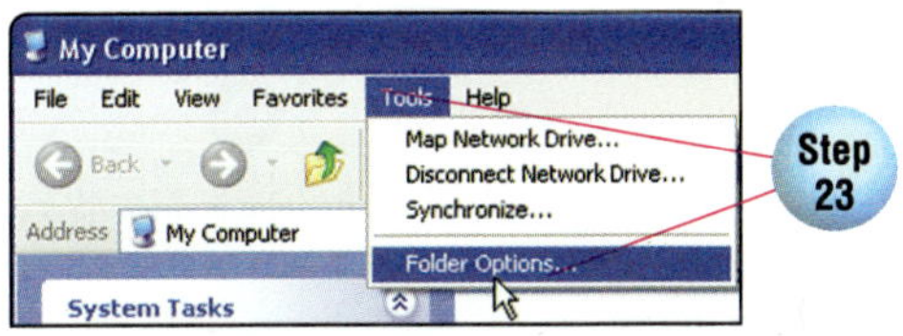

23 Click Tools on the My Computer Menu bar and then click *Folder Options* at the drop-down menu.

24 Click the View tab at the Folder Options dialog box.

25 Click the *Hide extensions for known file types* check box in the *Advanced settings* list box to clear the check mark and then click OK. ***Note: If the check box appears with no check mark in it, then file extensions are already turned on—proceed to Step 26.***

26 Close the My Computer window by clicking the Close button located at the right side of the Title bar.

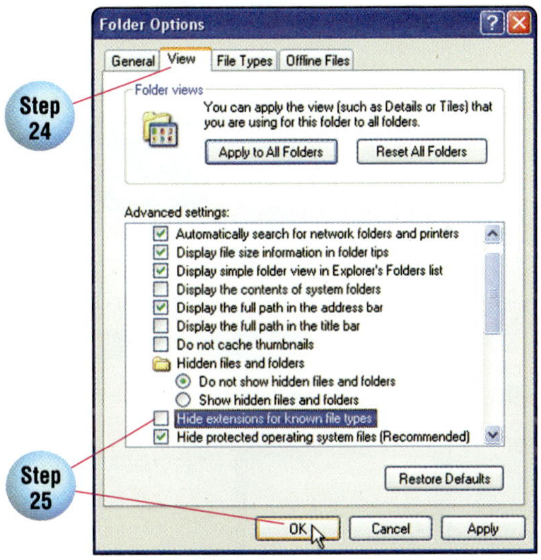

In Brief

Display Help and Support Center Window

1. Click Start button on Taskbar.
2. Click *Help and Support* at Start menu.

In Addition

Adding a Topic to the Favorites List in Help and Support

If you repeatedly use a help topic, you can add it to the Favorites list and then view the Favorites list by clicking the Favorites button on the Help and Support Center window toolbar. To add a help topic to the Favorites list, display the Help and Support Center window and then display the desired topic. Click the Add to Favorites button on the toolbar that displays above the topic information and then click OK at the message that displays. To view the Favorites list, click the Favorites button on the Help and Support Center window toolbar. To remove a topic from the Favorites list, display the Favorites list, click the topic, and then click the Remove button that displays toward the bottom of the list.

Activity 2.2

Creating a Folder

As you begin working with programs in Windows XP, you will create files in which data (information) is saved. A file might contain a Word document, an Excel workbook, or a PowerPoint presentation. As you begin creating files, consider creating folders into which those files will be stored. File management tasks such as creating a folder and copying and moving files and folders can be completed at a variety of locations including the My Computer and My Documents windows.

Project

You have decided you need to organize files for your department at Worldwide Enterprises. The first step is to create a folder at the My Computer window.

Worldwide Enterprises

1. At the Windows XP desktop, click the Start button on the Taskbar and then click *My Computer* at the Start menu.

   The My Computer window displays similar to the one shown in Figure 2.1.

FIGURE 2.1 My Computer Window

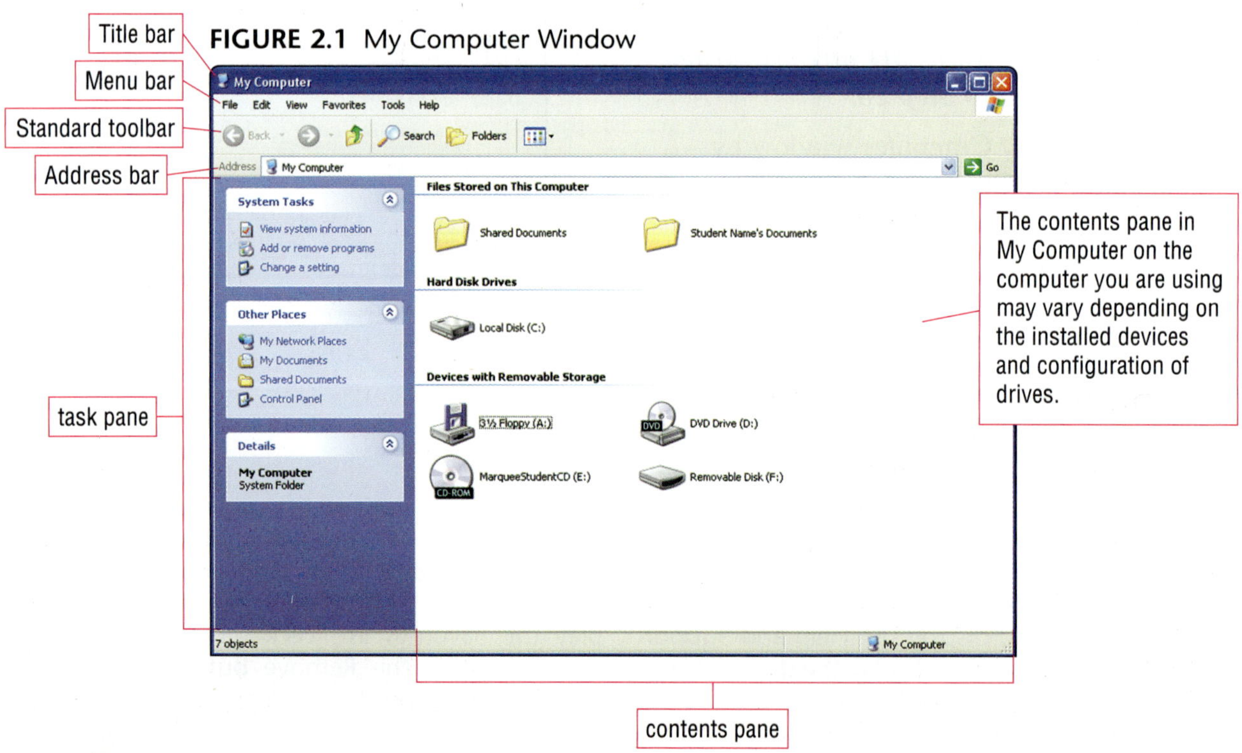

2. Double-click the storage medium label on which you copied the WindowsS2 folder.

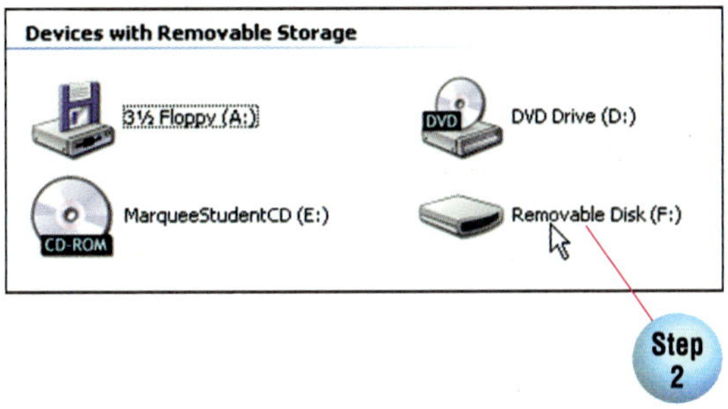

3. Click File on the Menu bar, point to *New*, and then click *Folder*.

4. Type **Revenue** and then press Enter.

   This changes the name from *New Folder* to *Revenue*.

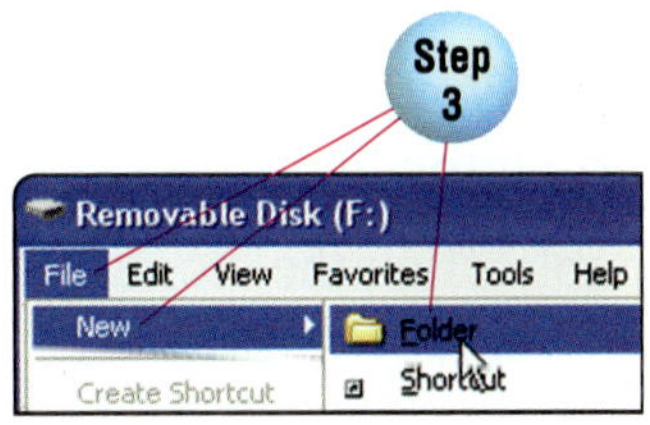

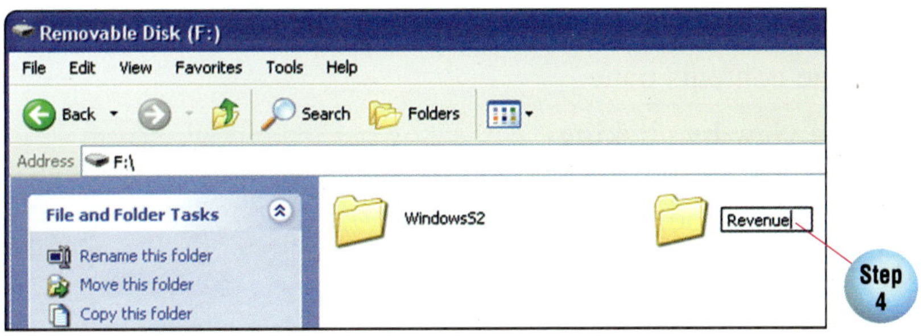

5. Close the window by clicking the Close button located in the upper right corner of the window.

In Brief

Display My Computer Window
1. Click Start button.
2. Click *My Computer*.

Create New Folder
1. Display My Computer window.
2. Double-click device on which to create folder.
3. Click File, point to *New*, click *Folder*.
4. Type folder name and then press Enter.

In Addition

Displaying the Folders Pane

You can display a hierarchical list of folders and drives by displaying the My Computer window and then clicking the Folders button on the Standard Buttons toolbar. This displays the Folders pane at the left side of the window as shown in the image at the right. A plus symbol preceding a folder name indicates that the folder contains additional folders (or drives). Click the folder name in the Folders pane and the contents of the folder display in the Folders pane as well as the contents pane. Turn off the display of the Folders pane by clicking the Folders button.

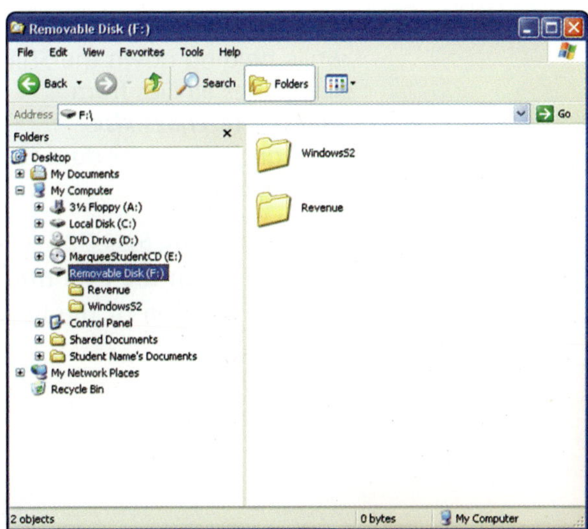

Activity 2.3

Selecting and Copying Files

File and folder management activities might include selecting, moving, copying, or deleting files or folders. The My Computer window offers a variety of methods for completing file management activities. You can use options in the task pane, drop-down menu options, or shortcut menu options. More than one file or folder can be moved, copied, or deleted at one time. Select adjacent files/folders using the Shift key and select nonadjacent files/folders using the Ctrl key. When selecting multiple files or folders, you may want to change the view in the My Computer window. View choices include Thumbnails, Tiles, Icons, List, and Details. List and Details are good choices for selecting multiple files.

Project

Continuing to organize files for your department, you will copy files to the *Revenue* folder you created.

Worldwide Enterprises

1. At the Windows XP desktop, open the My Computer window by clicking the Start button and then clicking *My Computer* at the Start menu.
2. Double-click the storage medium label for the drive containing your student data files in the contents pane.

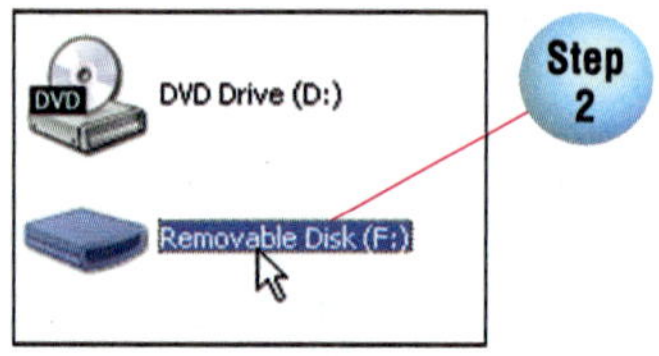

3. Double-click the *WindowsS2* folder in the contents pane.
4. Change the view by clicking the View button on the Standard Buttons toolbar and then clicking *List* at the drop-down list.

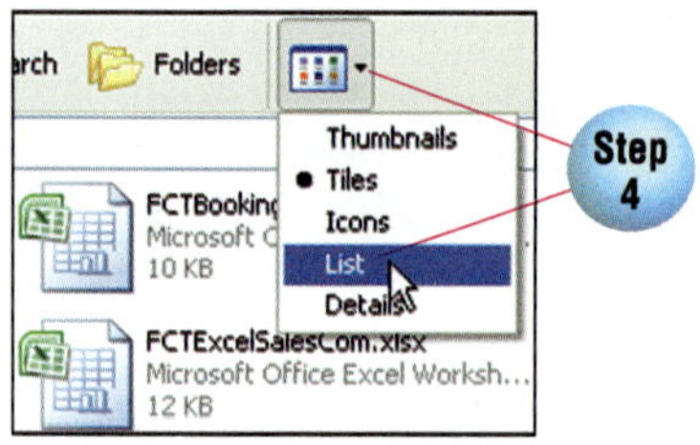

5. Click the file named ***WEExcelRevenues.xlsx*** that displays in the contents pane.
6. Hold down the Shift key, click the file named ***WETable02.docx***, and then release the Shift key.

   Clicking ***WETable02.docx*** while holding down the Shift key causes all files from ***WEExcelRevenues.xlsx*** through ***WETable02.docx*** to be selected.

7. Click the Copy the selected items hyperlink in the *File and Folder Tasks* section of the task pane.

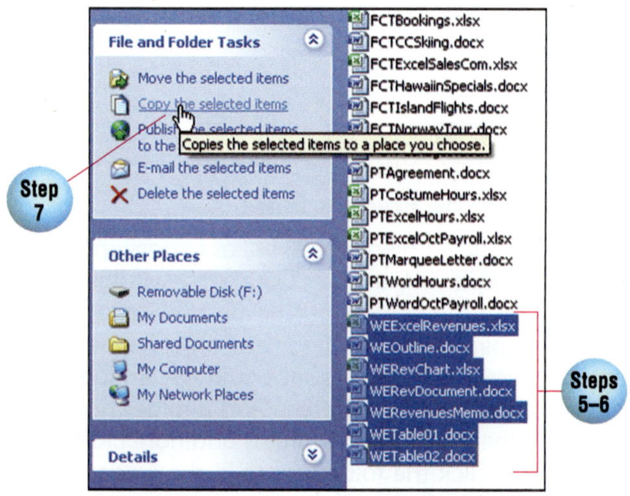

8. At the Copy Items dialog box, click the drive label containing your student data files in the list box.
9. Click *Revenue* in the list box (below your drive label).
10. Click the Copy button that displays toward the bottom of the dialog box.

    A message box with a progress bar appears as the files are copied. Copying the files may take a few seconds.

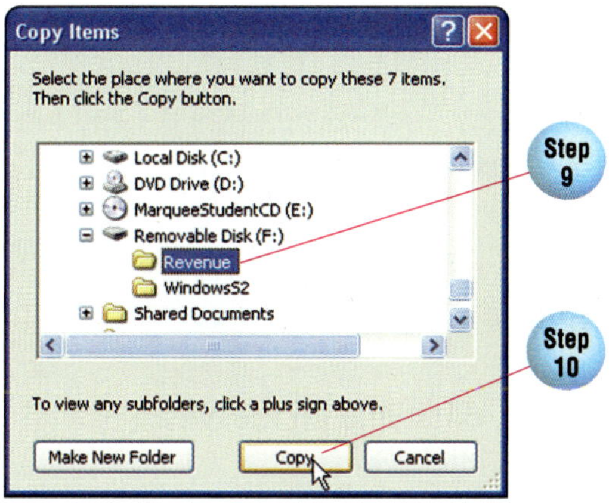

11. Click the drive label containing your student data files that displays in the *Other Places* section of the task pane.
12. Display the files you just copied by double-clicking the *Revenue* folder in the contents pane.
13. Close the window by clicking the Close button located in the upper right corner of the window.

In Brief

Copy Adjacent Files to New Folder

1. Display My Computer window.
2. Click View button on toolbar and then click *List*.
3. Click first file name.
4. Hold down Shift key and then click last file name.
5. Click Copy the selected items hyperlink in task pane.
6. At Copy Items dialog box, specify destination folder, and then click Copy button.

In Addition

Copying by Dragging

You can copy a file/folder to another location by dragging the file/folder. To copy by dragging, display the My Computer window and then click the Folders button on the Standard Buttons toolbar. (This displays the Folders pane at the left side of the window.) Display the desired file or folder in the contents pane of the My Computer window. Position the mouse pointer on the file or folder, hold down the *right* mouse button, drag to the desired drive or folder in the Folders pane, and then release the mouse button. At the shortcut menu that displays, click the *Copy Here* option.

Activity 2.4

Moving Files

Move files in the My Computer window in a manner similar to copying files. You can move a file or folder to a different folder or drive or you can select and then move multiple files or folders. Select the file/folder or files/folders you want to move and then click the appropriate move option in the *File and Folder Tasks* section of the task pane. This displays the Move Items dialog box. At this dialog box, specify where you want to move the file/folder and then click the Move button.

Project

After looking at the files you copied into the Revenue folder, you decide to organize the files by creating another folder and moving some of the files from the Revenue folder into the new folder.

Worldwide Enterprises

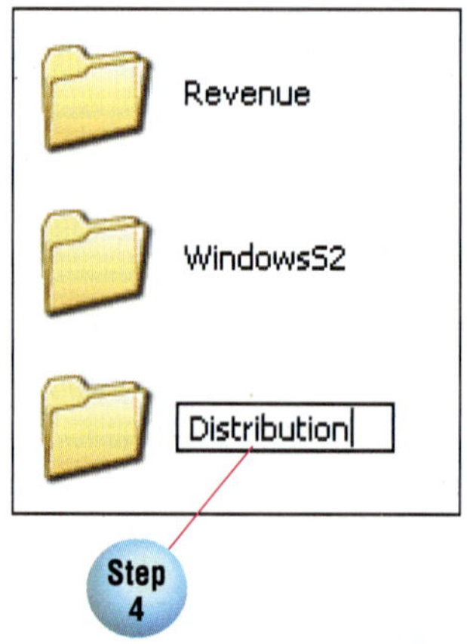

1. At the Windows XP desktop, display the My Computer window.
2. Double-click the storage medium label for the drive containing your student data files in the contents pane.
3. To create a new folder, click File on the Menu bar, point to *New*, and then click *Folder*.
4. Type **Distribution** and then press Enter.

   This changes the name from *New Folder* to *Distribution*.

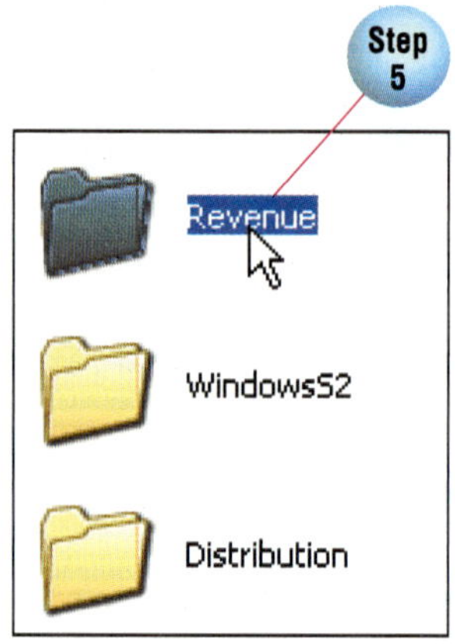

5. Double-click the *Revenue* folder name in the contents pane.
6. Click the View button on the Standard Buttons toolbar and then click *List* at the drop-down list.
7. Click once on ***WEOutline.docx***.

   Clicking once on the file selects the file name to identify the item that you want to move; double-clicking the file would instruct Windows to open Word and then open the document.

8. Hold down the Ctrl key, click once on ***WETable01.docx***, click once on ***WETable02.docx***, and then release the Ctrl key.

   Using the Ctrl key, you can select nonadjacent files.

9. Click the Move the selected items hyperlink in the *File and Folder Tasks* section of the task pane.

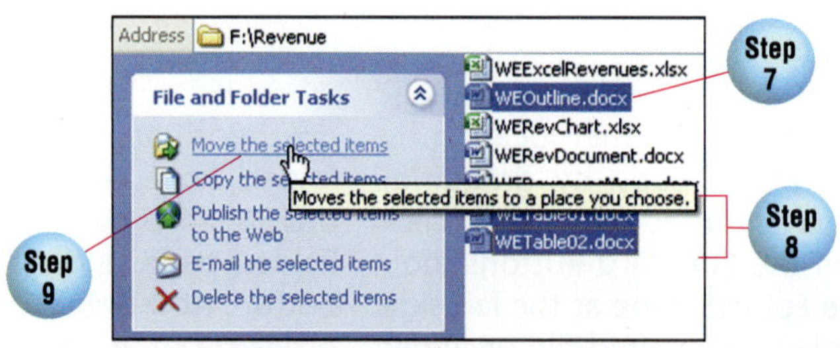

10 At the Move Items dialog box, click the folder named *Distribution* in the list box and then click the Move button.

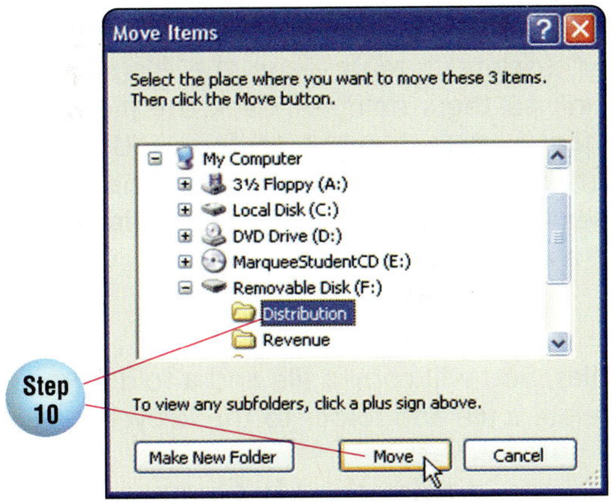

11 Click the Up button on the Standard Buttons toolbar.

This displays the contents of the folder that is up one level from the current folder.

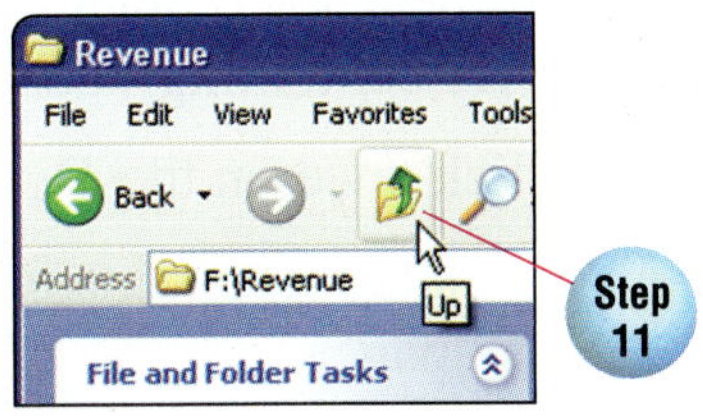

12 Double-click *Distribution* in the contents pane.

The contents pane now displays the files you moved into the Distribution folder.

13 Close the window by clicking the Close button.

In Brief

Move Nonadjacent Files to New Folder

1. Display My Computer window.
2. Click View button on toolbar and then click *List*.
3. Click first file name.
4. Hold down Ctrl key, click each additional file name, and then release Ctrl key.
5. Click Move the selected items hyperlink in task pane.
6. At Move Items dialog box, specify destination folder and then click Move button.

In Addition

Searching for Files/Folders at the My Computer Window

Click the Search button on the My Computer window Standard Buttons toolbar and a Search Companion pane displays at the left side of the window as shown in the image at the right. Specify the type of file for which you are searching and the options in the Search Companion pane. For example, if you are searching for a specific Word document, you would click the *Documents (word processing, spreadsheet, etc.)* option in the Search Companion pane. At the next step, you would specify the document name or a portion of the name and then click the Search button.

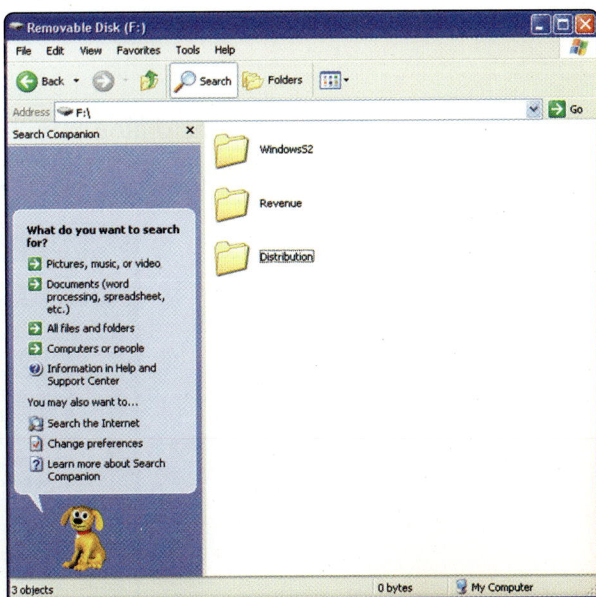

Activity 2.5

Deleting Files/Folders to the Recycle Bin

Deleting the wrong file can be a disaster, but Windows XP helps protect your work with the Recycle Bin. The Recycle Bin acts just like an office wastepaper basket; you can "throw away" (delete) unwanted files, but you can "reach in" to the Recycle Bin and take out (restore) a file if you threw it away by accident. Files or folders deleted from the hard drive are automatically sent to the Recycle Bin. Files or folders deleted from a disk are deleted permanently. (Recovery programs are available, however, that can help you recover deleted data.) To delete a file or folder, display the My Computer window and then display in the contents pane the file(s) and/or folder(s) you want deleted. Click the file or folder or select multiple files or folders and then click the appropriate delete option in the task pane. At the message asking you to confirm the deletion, click the Yes button.

Project

Continuing to organize your files, you will copy a file and a folder from your disk to the My Documents folder and then delete a file and folder to the Recycle Bin.

Worldwide Enterprises

1. At the Windows XP desktop, display the My Computer window.
2. At the My Computer window, double-click the storage medium label for the drive containing your student data files in the contents pane.
3. Click once on the *Distribution* folder in the contents pane to select it.
4. Click the Copy this folder hyperlink in the *File and Folder Tasks* section of the task pane.

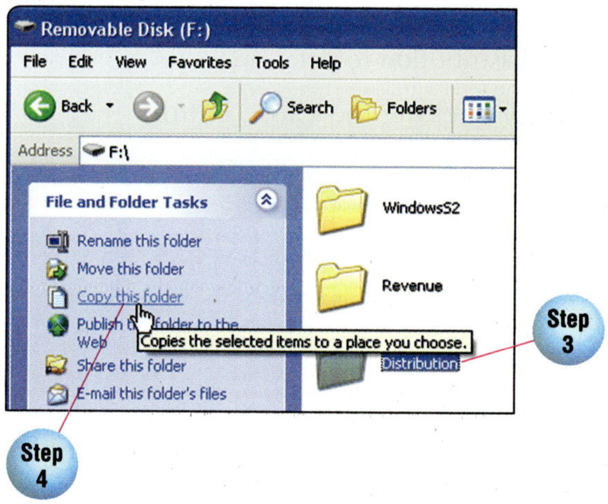

5. At the Copy Items dialog box, click *My Documents* in the list box and then click the Copy button.

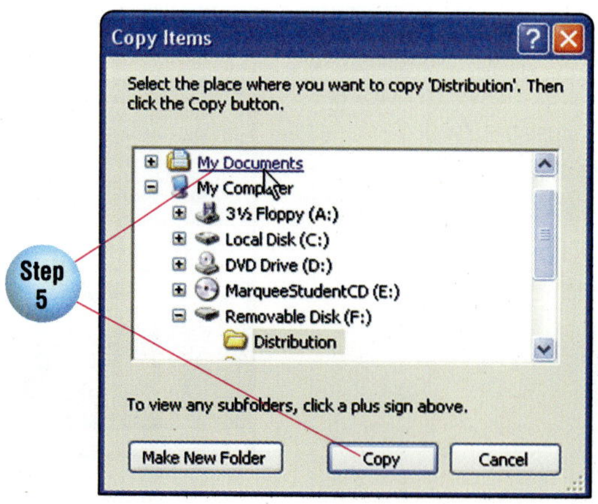

6. Double-click the *Revenue* folder in the contents pane.
7. Click once on ***WERevDocument.docx*** in the contents pane to select it.
8. Click the Copy this file hyperlink in the *File and Folder Tasks* section of the task pane.
9. At the Copy Items dialog box, click *My Documents* in the list box and then click the Copy button.
10. Click My Documents in the *Other Places* section of the task pane.
11. Click once on the *Distribution* folder in the contents pane to select it.
12. Click the Delete this folder hyperlink in the *File and Folder Tasks* section of the task pane.

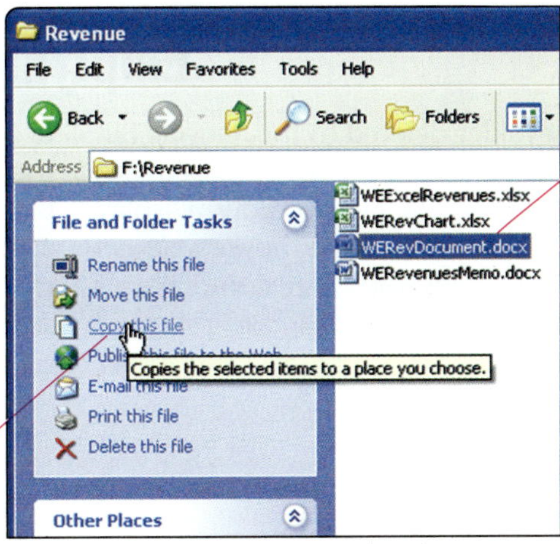

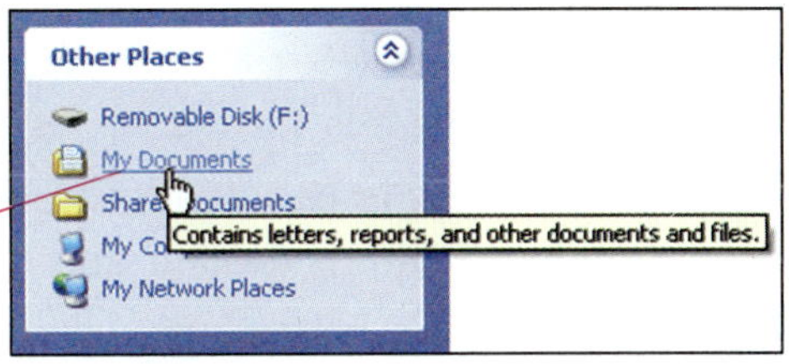

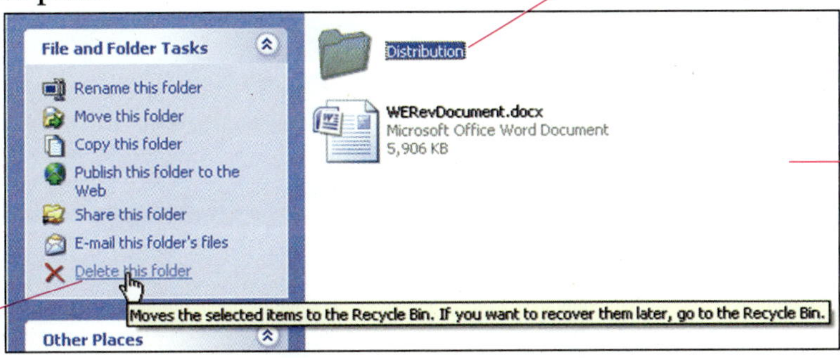

Your My Documents contents pane may show additional files.

13. At the message asking you to confirm the deletion, click the Yes button.
14. Click once on ***WERevDocument.docx*** in the contents pane to select it.
15. Click the Delete this file hyperlink in the *File and Folder Tasks* section of the task pane.
16. At the message asking you to confirm the deletion, click the Yes button.
17. Close the window.

In Brief

Delete File/Folder

1. Display My Computer window.
2. Click file/folder to select it.
3. Click Delete this file hyperlink (or Delete this folder hyperlink) in task pane.
4. At confirmation message, click Yes.

In Addition

Dragging and Dropping Files/Folders

Another method for deleting a file or folder is to drag the file or folder to the *Recycle Bin* icon on the desktop. Drag a file icon to the *Recycle Bin* icon until the icon name *Recycle Bin* displays with a blue background and then release the mouse button. This drops the file you are dragging into the Recycle Bin. You can also select multiple files or folders and then drag and drop the selected items in the Recycle Bin.

Activity 2.6

Restoring Files/Folders and Emptying Files from the Recycle Bin

A file or folder deleted to the Recycle Bin can be restored. Restore a file or folder with options at the Recycle Bin window. Display this window by double-clicking the *Recycle Bin* icon on the Windows desktop. A restored file or folder is removed from the Recycle Bin and returned to its original location. Just like a wastepaper basket, the Recycle Bin can get full. Emptying the Recycle Bin deletes all files and folders. You can also delete a single file or folder from the Recycle Bin (rather than all files and folders).

Project

You decide to experiment with the Recycle Bin and learn how to restore a file and then empty the Recycle Bin.

Worldwide Enterprises

1. At the Windows XP desktop, display the contents of the Recycle Bin by double-clicking the *Recycle Bin* icon.

   The Recycle Bin window displays similar to the one shown in Figure 2.2.

2. At the Recycle Bin window, click the View button on the Standard Buttons toolbar and then click *List* at the drop-down list.

3. Click once on ***WERevDocument.docx*** in the contents pane to select it.

   Depending on the contents of the Recycle Bin, you may need to scroll down the Recycle Bin list to display this document.

4. Click the Restore this item hyperlink in the *Recycle Bin Tasks* section of the task pane.

5. Click once on the *Distribution* folder in the contents pane to select it.

FIGURE 2.2 Recycle Bin Window

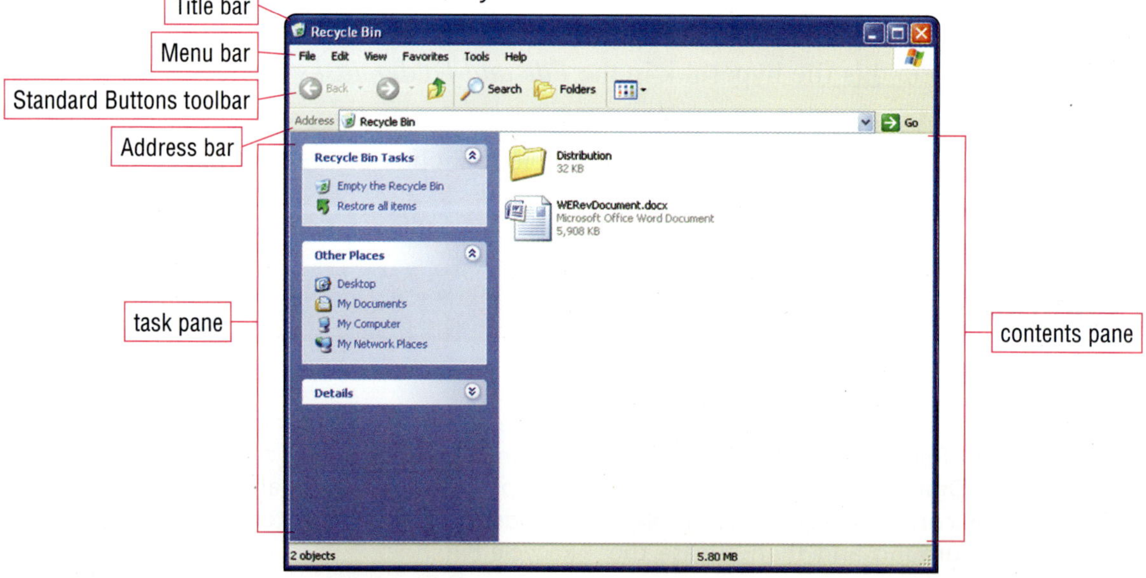

6. Click the Restore this item hyperlink in the *Recycle Bin Tasks* section of the task pane.
7. Close the Recycle Bin window by clicking the Close button that displays in the upper right corner of the window.
8. At the Windows XP desktop, display the My Computer window.
9. Click My Documents in the *Other Places* section of the task pane.
10. Delete the files you restored. To do this, click once on the *Distribution* folder, hold down the Ctrl key, click once on the ***WERevDocument.docx*** file name, and then release the Ctrl key.
11. Click the Delete the selected items hyperlink in the *File and Folder Tasks* section of the task pane.
12. At the message asking you to confirm that you want the items deleted to the Recycle Bin, click the Yes button.
13. Close the window.
14. At the Windows XP desktop, double-click the *Recycle Bin* icon.
15. Click once on the *Distribution* folder, hold down the Ctrl key, click once on the ***WERevDocument.docx*** file name, and then release the Ctrl key.
16. Click File on the Menu bar and then click *Delete* at the drop-down list.

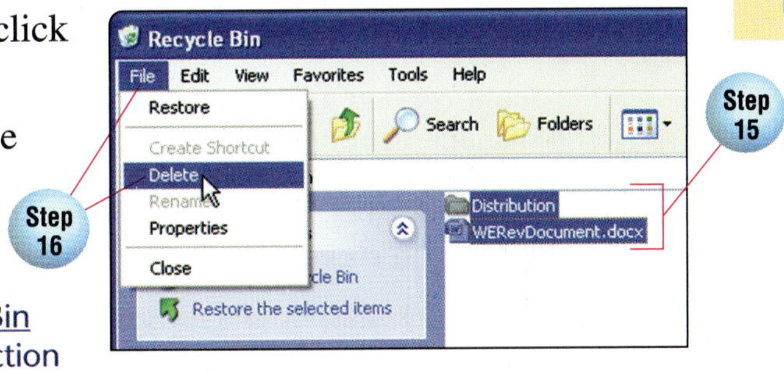

17. At the confirmation message, click the Yes button.

   If you want to empty the entire contents of the Recycle Bin, you would click the Empty the Recycle Bin hyperlink in the *Recycle Bin Tasks* section of the task pane. At the message asking you to confirm the deletion, you would click the Yes button.

18. Close the Recycle Bin window.

In Addition

Arranging Icons in Recycle Bin Window

You can control the arrangement of file and folder icons in the Recycle Bin window with options from the View, *Arrange Icons by* side menu shown at the right. Display this side menu by clicking View on the Recycle Bin Menu bar and then pointing to *Arrange Icons by*. Choose the option that best fits your needs. For example, choose *Name* if you want to see an alphabetic listing of your files and folders or click *Date Deleted* if you want to see files and folders listed by the date they were deleted.

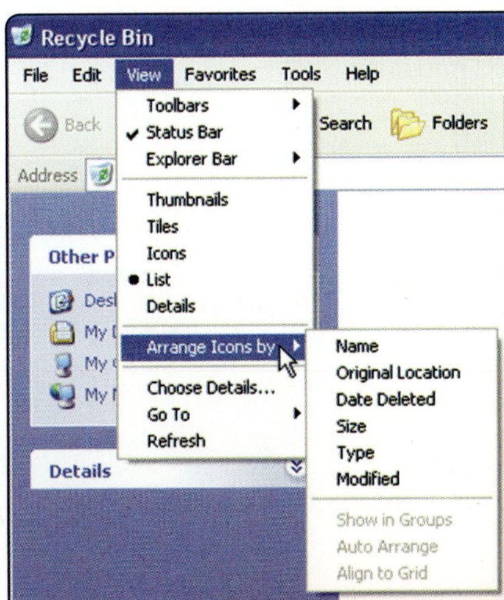

In Brief

Restore File/Folder from Recycle Bin
1. At Windows desktop, double-click *Recycle Bin* icon.
2. At Recycle Bin window, click file/folder to select it (or select multiple files/folders).
3. Click Restore this item hyperlink in task pane.

Delete File/Folder from Recycle Bin
1. At Windows desktop, double-click *Recycle Bin* icon.
2. At Recycle Bin window, click file/folder to select it (or select multiple files/folders).
3. Click File on Menu bar and then click *Delete*.
4. At confirmation message, click Yes.

Activity 2.7

Creating and Deleting a Shortcut and Renaming a File

If you use a file or program on a consistent basis, consider creating a shortcut to the file or program. ***Shortcuts*** are specialized icons and are very small files that point the operating system to the actual item, whether it is a file, a folder, or a program. Double-click a shortcut icon and the file opens in the program in which it was created. Shortcuts provide quick and easy access to files or programs used every day without having to remember where the file is stored. Along with the file management tasks you have learned such as copying, moving, and deleting files/folders, you can also rename a file/folder. Rename a file/folder using an option from a drop-down menu or an option from a shortcut menu.

Project

You use the ***WERevChart.xlsx*** file when creating reports for your department so you decide to rename it and then create a shortcut to the file.

Worldwide Enterprises

1. At the Windows XP desktop, display the My Computer window.
2. At the My Computer window, double-click the storage medium label for the drive containing your student data files in the contents pane.
3. Double-click the *Revenue* folder.
4. If necessary, change the display of files to a list by clicking the View button on the Standard Buttons toolbar and then click *List* at the drop-down list.
5. Right-click on ***WERevChart.xlsx***.

   Right-clicking a file or folder causes a shortcut menu to display containing file management options.
6. At the shortcut menu that displays, click the *Rename* option.

   When you click *Rename*, the name of the file is selected.

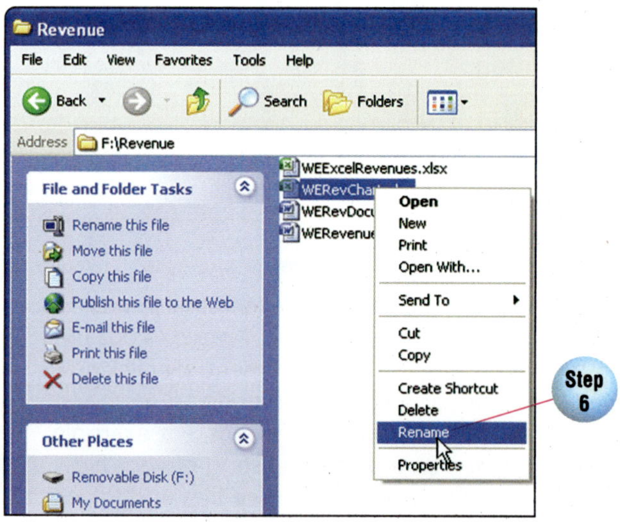

7 Type **RevenueChart.xlsx** and then press Enter.

You can also rename a file by selecting the file, clicking File on the Menu bar, and then clicking *Rename* at the drop-down menu. Type the new name for the file and then press Enter.

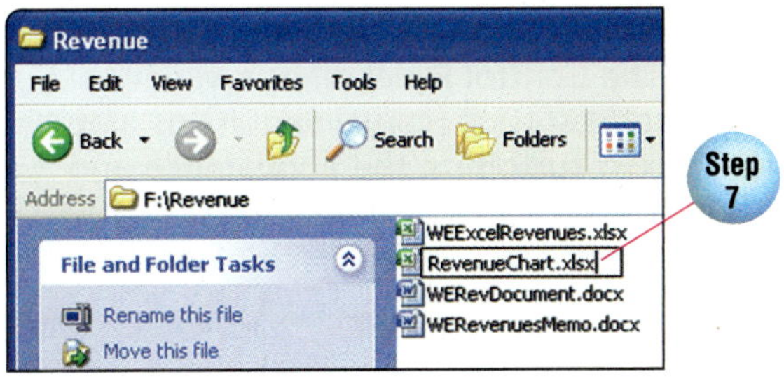

8 Create a shortcut to the file named ***RevenueChart.xlsx***. To do this, position the arrow pointer on ***RevenueChart.xlsx***. Hold down the *right* mouse button, drag the outline of the file to the desktop, and then release the mouse button.

Click the Restore Down button on the Revenue window title bar if the window is currently maximized and you cannot see the desktop in which to drag the file.

9 At the pop-up menu that displays, click *Create Shortcuts Here*.

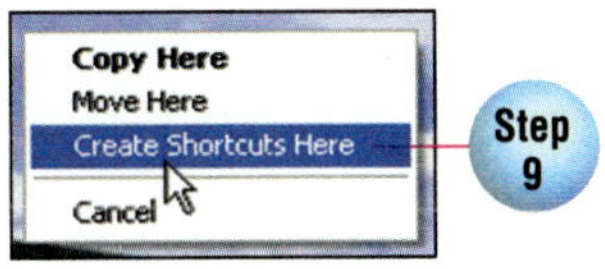

10 Close the Revenue window.

11 Double-click the *Shortcut to RevenueChart.xlsx* shortcut icon on the desktop.

Double-clicking this icon opens Excel and the file named **RevenueChart.xlsx**.

12 After viewing the file in Excel, exit Excel by clicking the Close button that displays in the upper right corner of the window. Click No if prompted to save changes.

13 Delete the *Shortcut to RevenueChart.xlsx* shortcut icon. To do this, position the arrow pointer on the *Shortcut to RevenueChart.xlsx* shortcut icon, hold down the left mouse button, drag the icon on top of the *Recycle Bin* icon, and then release the mouse button.

In Brief

Rename File

1. Display My Computer window.
2. Right-click file to be renamed.
3. At shortcut menu, click *Rename*.
4. Type new file name, press Enter.

Create Shortcut

1. Display My Computer window.
2. Position mouse pointer on desired file.
3. Hold down *right* button, drag outline of file to desktop, then release mouse button.
4. At pop-up menu, click *Create Shortcuts Here*.

In Addition

Displaying Disk or Drive Properties

Information such as the amount of used space and free space on a disk or drive and the disk or drive hardware is available at the Properties dialog box. To display the Local Disk (C:) Properties dialog box, similar to the one shown at the right, display the My Computer window. At the My Computer window, right-click *Local Disk (C:)* in the contents pane and then click *Properties* at the shortcut menu. With the General tab selected, information displays about used and free space on the drive. Click the Tools tab to display error-checking, backup, and defragmentation options. The dialog box with the Hardware tab selected displays the name and type of all disk drives as well as the device properties. Click the Sharing tab to display options for sharing folders and click the Quota tab to display disk quota management options.

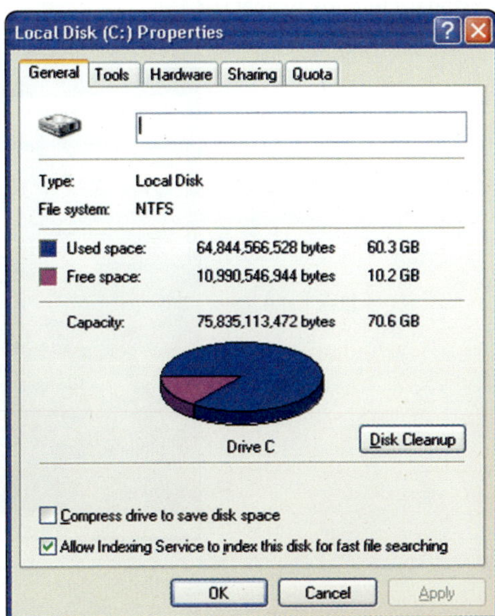

Activity 2.8

Exploring the Control Panel

The Control Panel offers a variety of categories each containing icons you can use to customize the appearance and functionality of your computer. Display the Control Panel window by clicking the Start button and then clicking *Control Panel* at the Start menu. At the Control Panel window, available categories display in the contents pane. Click a category and a list of tasks, a list of icons, or a separate window displays.

Project

You want to know how to customize your computer so you decide to explore the Control Panel window.

Worldwide Enterprises

1. At the Windows XP desktop, click the Start button and then click *Control Panel* at the Start menu.

   The Control Panel window displays similar to the one shown in Figure 2.3.

   PROBLEM

   If your Control Panel is displaying icons, click Switch to Category View in the task pane.

2. At the Control Panel window, click the Appearance and Themes hyperlink in the *Pick a category* section.

3. After viewing the tasks and icons available in the Appearance and Themes category, click the Back button on the Standard Buttons toolbar.

   This displays the opening Control Panel window, which was the previous window.

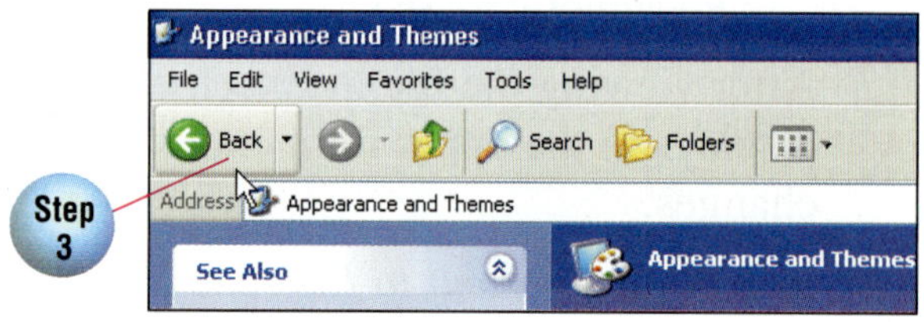

FIGURE 2.3 Control Panel Window

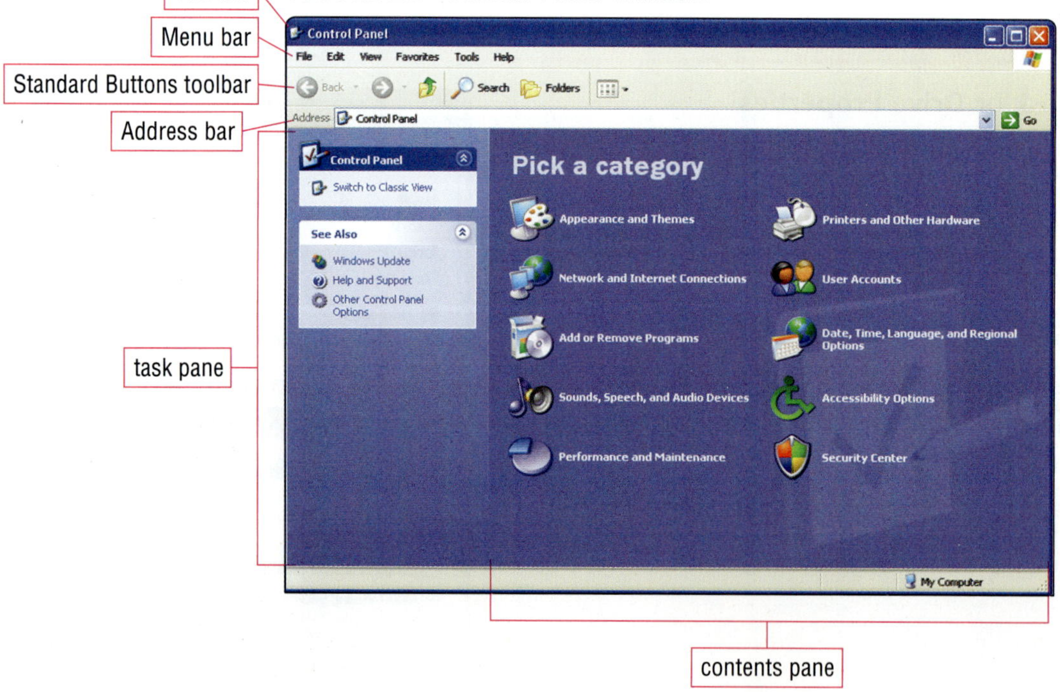

4 Click the Printers and Other Hardware hyperlink in the *Pick a category* section.

5 Click the Mouse hyperlink in the *or pick a Control Panel icon* section.

This displays the Mouse Properties dialog box.

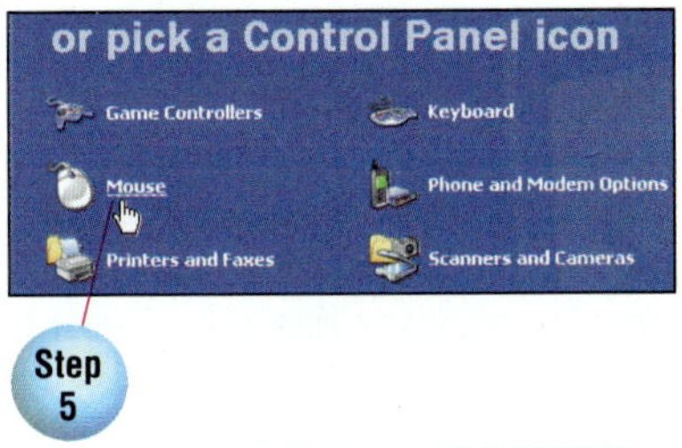

6 At the Mouse Properties dialog box, click each tab and review the available options.

7 Click the Cancel button to close the Mouse Properties dialog box.

8 Click the Back button on the Standard Buttons toolbar.

9 Click the Add or Remove Programs hyperlink in the *Pick a category* section.

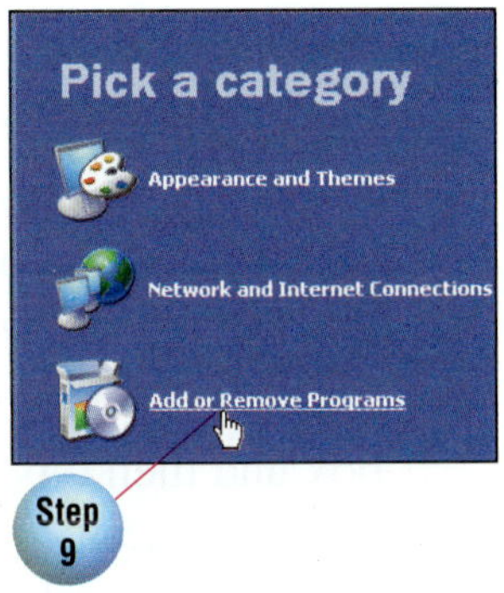

10 At the Add or Remove Programs window, scroll through the list of installed programs and then click the Close button.

11 Click the Performance and Maintenance hyperlink in the *Pick a category* section.

12 Click the System hyperlink in the *or pick a Control Panel icon* section.

This displays the System Properties dialog box.

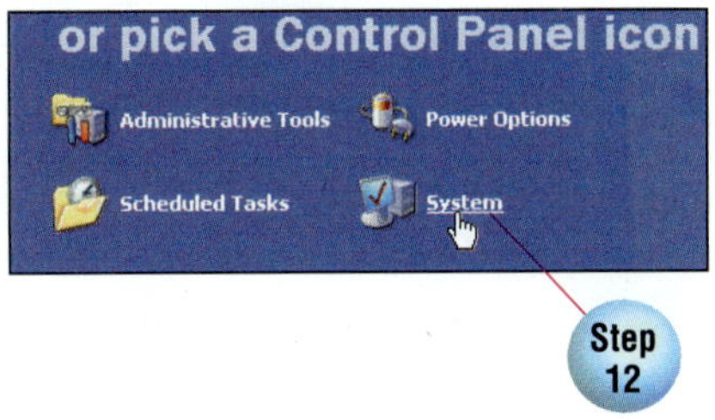

13 At the System Properties dialog box, click each tab and review the available options.

14 Click the Cancel button to close the System Properties dialog box.

15 Close the Control Panel window by clicking the Close button located in the upper right corner of the window.

In Brief

Display Control Panel
1. Click Start button.
2. Click *Control Panel*.

In Addition

Changing the Control Panel View

By default, the Control Panel window displays categories of tasks in what is called the Category View. This view can be changed to the Classic View, which displays icons in a manner similar to that in previous Windows versions (Windows 95, 98, 2000, and Me). Change to the Classic View by clicking the Switch to Classic View hyperlink in the *Control Panel* section of the task pane. This displays the Control Panel window as shown at the right. You can view a description of each icon by changing the view to Details. Changes made to options at the Control Panel window remain in effect each time Windows XP is opened.

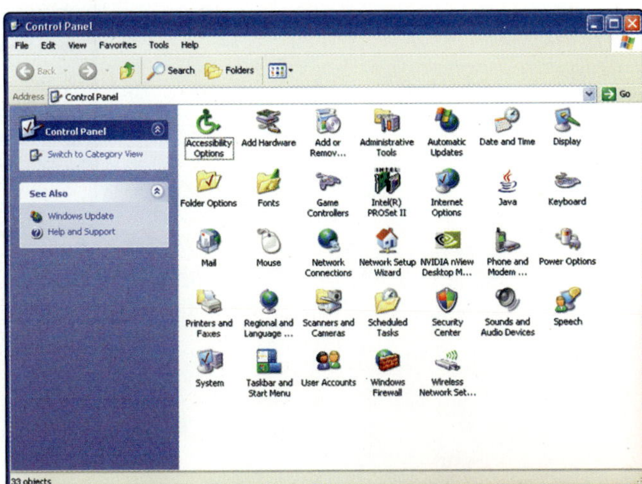

Activity 2.9

Searching for a File or Folder

Windows XP includes a search feature you can use to search for files and/or folders that match specific criteria. To use the Search feature, click the Start button and then click *Search* at the Start menu. At the Search Results window, the Search Companion Wizard is activated automatically and walks you through the steps for completing a search.

Project

Your supervisor has asked you to locate any files on your disk containing the Cinema House company name and any files containing the word *Revenues* in the file name.

Worldwide Enterprises

1. At the Windows XP desktop, click the Start button and then click *Search* at the Start menu.
2. At the Search Results window, click the All files and folders hyperlink in the *What do you want to search for?* section.
3. Click in the *A word or phrase in the file* text box and then type **Cinema House**.

   This specifies that you want to find files containing the words *Cinema House*.
4. Click the down-pointing arrow at the right side of the *Look in* list box and then click the storage medium containing your student data files at the drop-down list.
5. Click the Search button.

   You can stop the search at any time by clicking the Stop button.

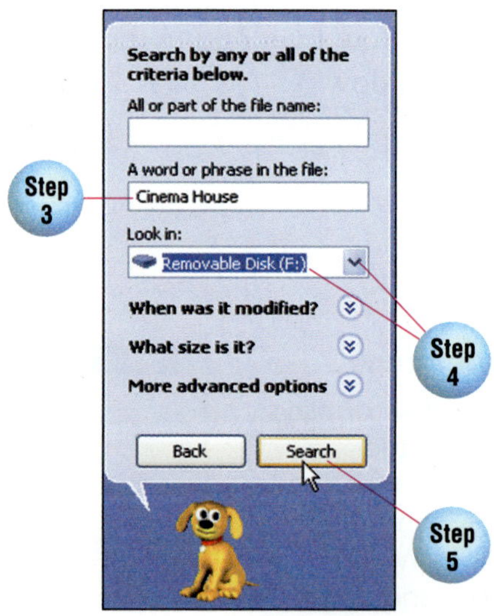

6 Review the list of files found in the Search Results window.

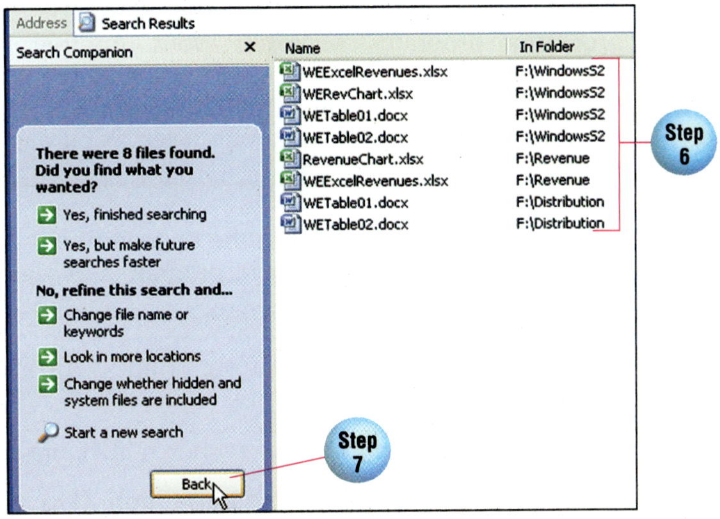

7 Click the Back button (located in the Search Companion Wizard section of the window).

8 With the insertion point positioned in the *All or part of the file name* text box, type **Revenues**.

9 Select and then delete the text *Cinema House* that displays in the *A word or phrase in the file* text box.

10 Make sure the appropriate storage medium still displays in the *Look in* list box.

11 Click the Search button.

12 When the results display in the contents window, click the Yes, finished searching hyperlink in the Search Companion pane.

Clicking this option turns off the Search Companion Wizard.

13 Close the Search Results window.

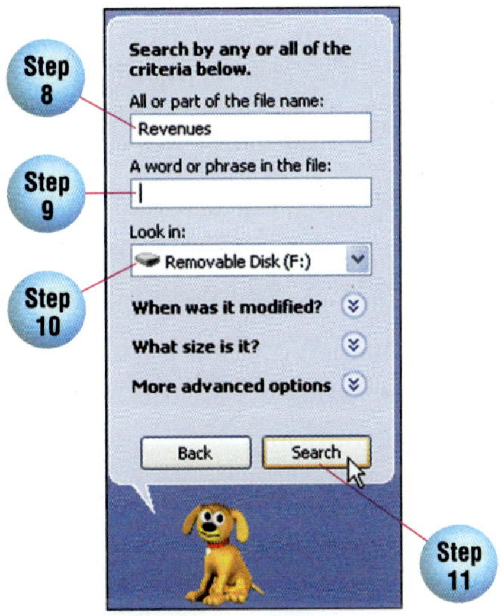

In Brief

Search for File Containing Specific Text

1. Click Start button.
2. Click *Search*.
3. Click All files and folders hyperlink.
4. Click in *A word or phrase in the file* text box.
5. Type specific text.
6. Specify location in *Look in* list box.
7. Click Search button.

Search for File/Folder

1. Click Start button.
2. Click *Search*.
3. Click All files and folders hyperlink.
4. Click in *All or part of the file name* text box.
5. Type specific file or folder name.
6. Specify location in *Look in* list box.
7. Click Search button.

In Addition

Turning Off the Search Companion Wizard

The Windows XP Search feature provides the Search Companion Wizard to help you complete a search. You can turn off this wizard and complete a manual search. To turn off the Search Companion Wizard, display the Search Results window and then click the Change preferences hyperlink that displays at the end of the *What do you want to search for?* section. Click the Without an animated screen character hyperlink below the *How do you want to use Search Companion?* section. To turn on the Search Companion Wizard, display the Search Results window with the Search button active. Click the *Change preferences* option in the *What do you want to search for?* section and then click the With an animated screen character hyperlink.

Activity 2.10

Using WordPad and Paint

Windows XP offers accessory programs such as WordPad and Paint. WordPad is a word processing program with features for preparing, editing, and formatting text documents and documents with graphics. WordPad is a basic word processing program. If you need the features of a full-fledged word processing program consider using Microsoft Word. Another program offered by Windows XP is a drawing program named Paint. Use Paint to draw black-and-white or color images that can be saved as bitmap files.

Project

Worldwide Enterprises

You need to prepare a short note to the manager of the IS department and decide to use the WordPad program. You also want to explore the Paint program and see if you can create a simple shape with an announcement inside.

1. At the Windows desktop, click the Start button, point to *All Programs*, point to *Accessories*, and then click *WordPad*.

   The WordPad window opens and displays as shown in Figure 2.4.

2. At the WordPad window, type the following paragraph. (Do not press the Enter key until you reach the end of the entire paragraph. WordPad contains a word wrap feature that will automatically wrap text to the next line.)

   The Windows XP training is scheduled for Friday from 8:30 to 10:30 a.m. I would like to meet with you this afternoon to go over the details for this training.

3. Press the Enter key twice and then type your first and last names.

4. Print the document by clicking the Print button on the Standard toolbar.

   To save the document, you would click File and then *Save*. At the Save As dialog box, you would type a name for the document and then press Enter.

5. Close WordPad by clicking the Close button located in the upper right corner of the window. At the message asking if you want to save the document, click the No button.

FIGURE 2.4 WordPad Window

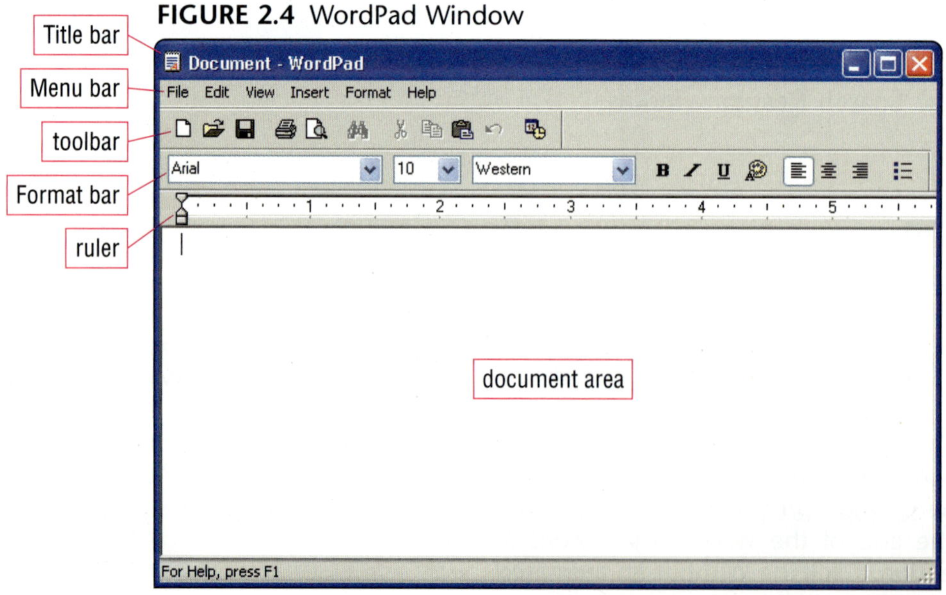

6. At the Windows desktop, click the Start button, point to *All Programs*, point to *Accessories*, and then click *Paint*.

   The Paint window opens and displays as shown in Figure 2.5. Create an image in Paint by clicking the desired tool in the Toolbox and then using the mouse pointer to draw the image.

FIGURE 2.5 Paint Window

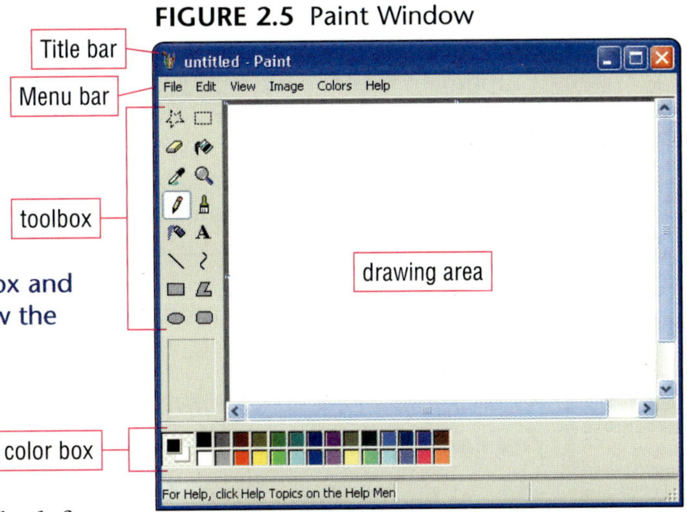

7. Click the Rounded Rectangle tool in the toolbox.
8. Position the pointer in the upper left corner of the drawing area, hold down the left mouse button, drag to the lower right corner of the drawing area, and then release the mouse button.
9. Click the Text tool in the toolbox.
10. Drag to create a text box similar to the one shown at the right.

    When you release the mouse button after drawing the text box, the insertion point is positioned inside the text box.

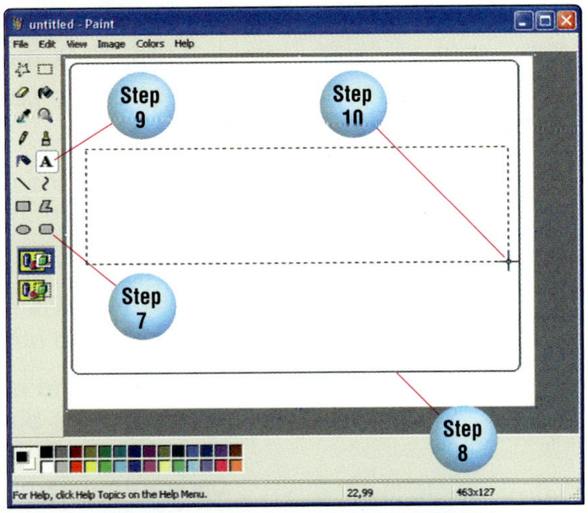

11. Type **Windows XP Training**.
12. Click the down-pointing arrow at the right side of the size list box and then click *26* at the drop-down list.

    If the Text toolbar (displays with Fonts at the left side of the toolbar) is not visible, click View and then Text Toolbar.

13. Click the Fill With Color tool in the toolbox.
14. Click a light turquoise color in the color palette and then click inside the rounded rectangle shape.
15. Notice closed letters did not fill with turquoise. Position the tip of the fill bottle icon inside the closed part of each letter that still displays a white background and click to fill with turquoise.

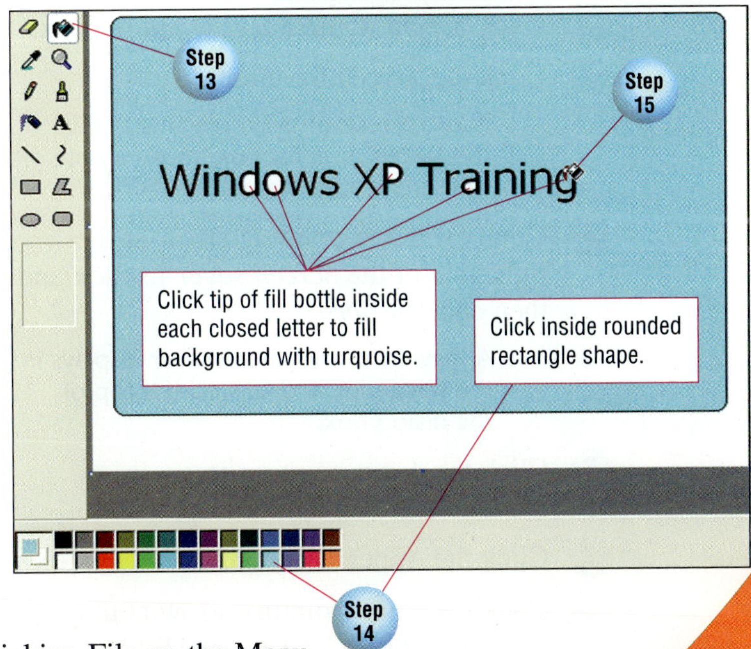

16. Print the image you created by clicking File on the Menu bar and then clicking *Print*. At the Print dialog box, click the Print button.
17. Close Paint by clicking File and then *Exit*. At the message asking if you want to save the changes, click the No button.

Activity 2.11

Customizing the Desktop

The Windows XP operating environment is very customizable. You can change background patterns and colors; specify a screen saver that will display when the screen sits idle for a specific period of time; or change the scheme for windows, menus, title bars, and system fonts. Make these types of changes at the Display Properties dialog box. This dialog box contains five tabs. Clicking each tab displays a different set of options for customizing the desktop. Many companies adopt a corporate computer standard for display properties.

Project

You decide to look at the customization options available for the desktop and set the screen resolution to the corporate standard for computers adopted by Worldwide Enterprises.

Note: Before completing this exercise, check with your instructor to determine if you can customize the desktop.

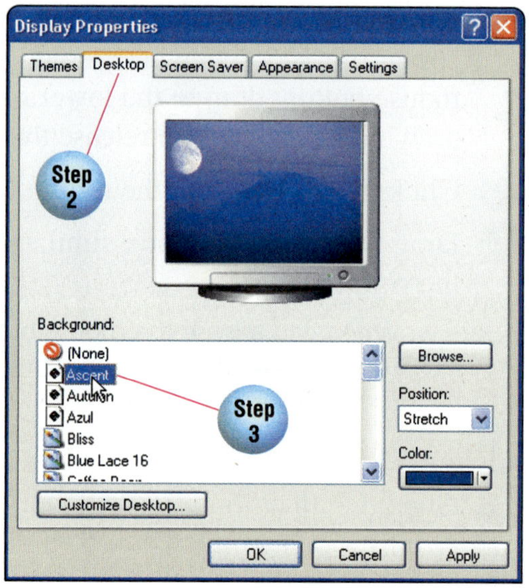

1. At the Windows XP desktop, position the arrow pointer on an empty location on the desktop, click the *right* mouse button, and then click *Properties* at the shortcut menu.

   This displays the Display Properties dialog box with the Themes tab selected.

2. At the Display Properties dialog box, click the Desktop tab.

   If a background is selected in the *Background* list box (other than the *(None)* option), make a note of this background name.

3. Click *Ascent* in the *Background* list box.

4. Click the Screen Saver tab.

   If a screen saver is already selected in the *Screen saver* list box, make a note of this screen saver name.

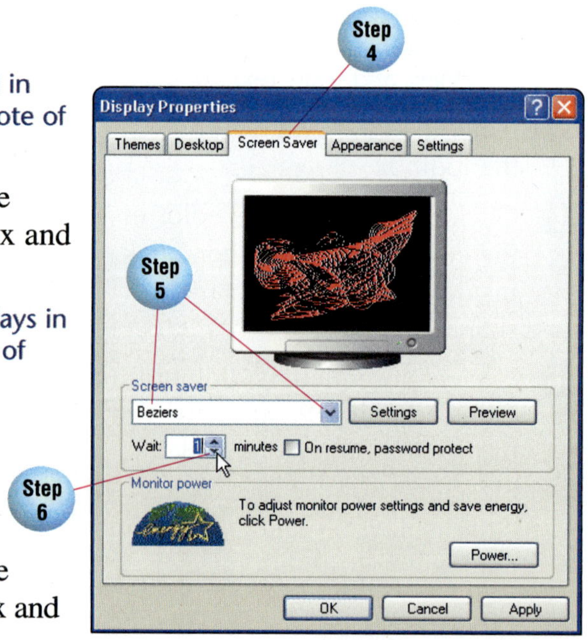

5. Click the down-pointing arrow at the right side of the *Screen saver* list box and then click *Beziers*.

   A preview of the screen saver displays in the screen located toward the top of the dialog box.

6. Click the down-pointing arrow in the *Wait* text box until *1* displays.

7. Click the Appearance tab.

8. Click the down-pointing arrow at the right side of the *Color scheme* list box and then click *Silver* at the drop-down list.

   If a color scheme is selected in the *Color scheme* (other than the *Default (blue)* option), make a note of this color scheme.

9. Click OK to close the Display Properties dialog box.

10. At the Windows XP desktop, notice the Ascent background and the silver Taskbar. Let the screen remain idle for one minute and then notice the screen saver that displays.

11. Move the mouse to deactivate the screen saver and then double-click the *Recycle Bin* icon.

    Notice the silver color scheme applied to the window elements.

12. Close the Recycle Bin window.

13. Reinstate the original desktop settings. To do this, right-click an empty location on the desktop, click *Properties* at the shortcut menu, and then return the Background, Screen Saver, and Color Scheme to the original settings.

Step 7

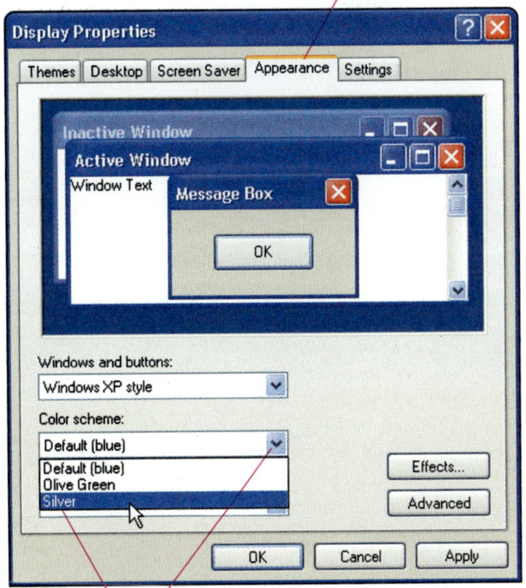

Step 8

In Brief

Open Display Properties Dialog Box

1. Click *right* mouse button on empty location on desktop.
2. Click *Properties* at shortcut menu.

In the next steps, you will set the screen resolution to *1024 by 768 pixels* which is the corporate standard for all desktops at Worldwide Enterprises. Standardizing display properties is considered a best practice in large companies that support many computer users.

14. At the Display Properties dialog box, click the Settings tab.

15. Look in the *Screen resolution* section below the slider bar and check the current screen resolution setting. For example, your screen may be set at *1280 by 1024 pixels*. If your screen is already set to *1024 by 768 pixels*, proceed to Step 17.

    Pixel is the abbreviation of *picture element* and refers to a single dot or point on the display monitor. A monitor displays text and images using thousands of pixels arranged in rows and columns. Changing the screen resolution to a higher number of pixels means that more information can be seen on the screen as items are scaled to a smaller size.

16. Drag the slider bar in the *Screen resolution* section right or left as necessary until the screen resolution is set to *1024 by 768 pixels*.

17. Click OK to close the Display Properties dialog box.

    The screens within the remainder of this textbook assume these options are retained as you work through the applications within the Microsoft Office suite. If you change these settings, differences will occur between what you will see on your screen and the textbook illustrations.

Step 14

Step 16

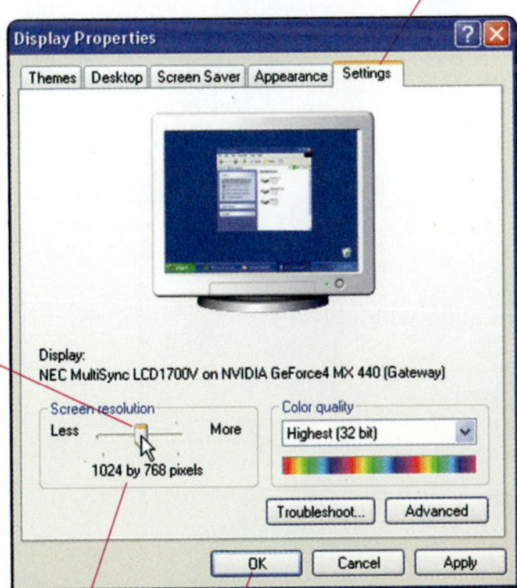

current screen resolution setting

Step 17

Features Summary

Feature	Button/Icon	Action
Control Panel window		Click Start button, click *Control Panel*.
copy selected files/folders		At My Computer window, select files to be copied, click the Copy the selected items hyperlink in the *File and Folder Tasks* section of the task pane, choose destination location in the Copy Items dialog box, click Copy.
create new folder		At My Computer window, click File, point to *New*, click *Folder*.
create shortcut		At My Computer window, position mouse pointer on file, hold down *right* mouse button, drag to desktop, release button, click *Create Shortcuts Here*.
delete files/folders		At My Computer window, select desired files/folders, click the Delete this file hyperlink or Delete this folder hyperlink in the *File and Folder Tasks* section of the task pane, click Yes.
delete shortcut icon		Drag shortcut icon to *Recycle Bin* icon.
display Properties dialog box		Right-click empty location on desktop, click *Properties*.
Help and Support Center window		Click Start button, click *Help and Support*.
move selected files/folders		At My Computer window, select files to be moved, click the Move selected items hyperlink in the *File and Folder Tasks* task pane, choose destination location in the Move Items dialog box, click Move.
My Computer window		Click Start button, click *My Computer*.
Paint		Click Start button, point to *All Programs*, point to *Accessories*, click *Paint*.
Recycle Bin window		Double-click *Recycle Bin* icon.
rename file/folder		At My Computer window, right-click file, click *Rename,* type new name, press Enter.
restore files/folders from Recycle Bin		At Recycle Bin window, select desired files/folders, click the Restore this item hyperlink in the Recycle Bin Tasks task pane.
Search Results window		Click Start button, click *Search*.
select adjacent files/folders		Click first file/folder, hold down Shift key, click last file/folder.
select nonadjacent files/folders		Click first file/folder, hold down Ctrl key, click any other files/folders.
WordPad		Click Start button, point to *All Programs*, point to *Accessories*, click *WordPad*.

Knowledge Check

Completion: In the space provided at the right, indicate the correct term, symbol, button, or command.

1. Click this button on the Help and Support Center toolbar to find information on a topic by typing a keyword, browsing a list of related topics, and then double-clicking the desired topic in the left pane. ________________
2. Click this button on the Help and Support Center toolbar to return to the opening Help and Support Center window. ________________
3. Click this menu sequence to create a new folder in the My Computer window. ________________
4. Change the display of files and folders in the My Computer window to Thumbnails, Tiles, Icons, List, or Details using this button on the Standard Buttons toolbar. ________________
5. To select adjacent files, click the first file, hold down this key, and then click the last file. ________________
6. To select nonadjacent files, click the first file, hold down this key, and then click any other desired files. ________________
7. At the My Computer window, select a file, click the <u>Copy this file</u> hyperlink in the task pane, and this dialog box displays. ________________
8. At the Move Items dialog box, choose the destination location in which to place the selected files or folders and then click this button to complete the action. ________________
9. Files deleted from the hard drive are sent here. ________________
10. Delete a shortcut icon by dragging the icon on top of this icon. ________________
11. Open this window to display a list of categories in which you can customize the appearance and functionality of your computer. ________________
12. This wizard is automatically activated in the Search window to walk you through the steps to complete a search. ________________
13. This Windows accessory program contains features for preparing, editing, and formatting documents. ________________
14. This Windows accessory program contains features for drawing black-and-white or color images that can be saved as bitmap files. ________________
15. Customize the Windows XP desktop such as changing the theme, background, screen saver, color scheme, and so on, with options at this dialog box. ________________

Skills Review

Review 1 Using Help

1. At the Windows XP desktop, learn about keyboard shortcuts. To do this click the Start button on the Taskbar and then click *Help and Support*.
2. At the Help and Support Center window, make sure the insertion point is positioned in the *Search* text box, type **keyboard shortcuts**, and then press Enter.
3. Click Windows keyboard shortcuts overview in the *Overviews, Articles, and Tutorials* section of the *Suggested Topics* list box.
4. Click General keyboard shortcuts in the contents pane below the heading *Windows keyboard shortcuts overview*.
5. Scroll through the list of keyboard shortcuts that displays in the contents pane below the heading *General keyboard shortcuts*.
6. Click the Index button on the Help and Support Center toolbar.
7. Type **keyboard shortcuts** in the *Type in the keyword to find* text box.
8. Double-click *for dialog boxes* in the left pane.
9. Click Dialog box keyboard shortcuts in the contents pane below the heading *Windows keyboard shortcuts overview*.
10. Read the list of keyboard shortcuts that displays in the contents pane.
11. Close the Help and Support Center window.

Review 2 Creating a Folder

1. At the Windows XP desktop, click the Start button and then click *My Computer*.
2. Double-click the storage medium label for the drive containing your student data files in the contents pane.
3. Click File, point to *New*, and then click *Folder*.
4. Type **Worksheets** and then press Enter.
5. Close the window.

Review 3 Selecting, Copying, Moving, and Deleting Files

1. At the Windows XP desktop, open the My Computer window.
2. Double-click the storage medium label for the drive containing your student data files in the contents pane.
3. Double-click the *WindowsS2* folder name in the contents pane.
4. Click the View button on the Standard Buttons toolbar and then click *List*.
5. Click once on ***FCTBookings.xlsx*** to select it, hold down the Shift key, and then click ***FCTPackages.docx***.
6. Click the Copy the selected items hyperlink in the *File and Folder Tasks* section of the task pane.
7. At the Copy Items dialog box, click the drive label containing your student data files in the list box.
8. Click the folder name *Worksheets* in the list box.
9. Click the Copy button.
10. After the files are copied, deselect the files by clicking in any area in the contents pane outside of the selected files.

11. Click ***WEExcelRevenues.xlsx*** in the contents pane, hold down the Ctrl key, and then click ***WERevChart.xlsx***.
12. Click the Move the selected items hyperlink in the *File and Folder Tasks* section of the task pane.
13. At the Move Items dialog box, click *Worksheets* in the list box and then click the Move button.
14. Click ***FCTCCSkiing.docx*** in the contents pane, hold down the Ctrl key, and then click ***FCTNorwayTour.docx***.
15. Click the Delete the selected items hyperlink in the *File and Folder Tasks* section of the task pane.
16. At the confirmation message, click the Yes button.
17. Close the window.

Review 4 Renaming a File; Creating and Deleting a Shortcut

1. At the Windows XP Desktop, open the My Computer window.
2. Double-click the storage medium label for the drive containing your student data files and then double-click the *Worksheets* folder.
3. Right-click ***FCTExcelSalesCom.xlsx*** and then click *Rename*.
4. Type **FCTCommissions.xlsx** and then press Enter.
5. Position the mouse pointer on ***FCTCommissions.xlsx***, hold down *right* mouse button, drag to the desktop, and then release the mouse button.
6. Click *Create Shortcuts Here* at the pop-up menu.
7. Close the window.
8. Double-click the *Shortcut to FCTCommissions.xlsx* icon on the desktop.
9. After viewing the Excel worksheet, close the Excel window. Click No if prompted to save changes.
10. At the Windows XP desktop, drag the *Shortcut to FCTCommissions.xlsx* shortcut icon on top of the *Recycle Bin* icon. (This deletes the shortcut.)

Review 5 Searching for Files

1. At the Windows XP desktop, click the Start button and then click *Search*.
2. Click All files and folders in the *What do you want to search for?* section.
3. Click in the *A word or phrase in the file* text box and then type **Sanderson**.
4. Click the down-pointing arrow at the right side of the *Look in* list box and then click the drive containing your student data files.
5. Click the Search button. (Notice the file names that display in the Search Results pane.)
6. Click the Back button in the Search Companion pane.
7. Type **FCT** in the *All or part of the file name* text box.
8. Select and then delete *Sanderson* in the *A word or phrase in the file* text box.
9. Click the Search button. (Notice the file names that display in the contents pane.)
10. Click the Yes, finished searching hyperlink.
11. Close the Search window.

Review 6 Using WordPad

1. At the Windows XP desktop, click the Start button, point to *All Programs*, point to *Accessories*, and then click *WordPad*.
2. At the WordPad window, type the following:

   Please reserve the conference room for next Thursday from 7 to 9 p.m. We anticipate approximately 25 participants for the "Vacationing on a Budget" workshop.
3. Click the Print button on the toolbar.
4. Click File on the Menu bar and then click *Exit*.
5. At the message asking if you want to save the changes, click the No button.

Review 7 Using Paint

1. At the Windows XP desktop, click the Start button, point to *All Programs*, point to *Accessories*, and then click *Paint*.
2. Click the Ellipse tool in the toolbox.
3. Using the mouse, drag to create an oval shape in the Paint window that fills most of the window.
4. Click the Text tool and then, using the mouse, drag to draw a text box inside the oval.
5. Type **Vacationing on a Budget**.
6. Click the down-pointing arrow at the right side of the size list box and then click *24* at the drop-down list. (You may need to increase or decrease this number to ensure that the text fits on one line in the text box.)
7. Click the Fill With Color tool, click a color of your choice in the color palette, and then click inside the oval shape you drew. Click the tip of the fill color icon inside each closed letter shape that still displays the white background to fill with the same color as the shape.
8. Click File on the Menu bar and then click *Print*. At the Print dialog box, click the Print button.
9. Click File and then *Exit*. At the message asking if you want to save the changes, click the No button.

Skills Assessment

Assessment 1 Managing Folders and Files

1. Create a new folder on your storage medium named *PerformanceThreads.*
2. Display the contents of the WindowsS2 folder.
3. If necessary, change the view to List.
4. Copy all files beginning with *PT* to the PerformanceThreads folder.
5. Display the contents of the PerformanceThreads folder.
6. Change the view to List.
7. Create a new folder within PerformanceThreads named *Payroll.* (A folder created within a folder is referred to as a subfolder.)
8. Move **PTExcelOctPayroll.xlsx** and **PTWordOctPayroll.docx** from the PerformanceThreads folder into the Payroll subfolder.
9. Delete **PTMarqueeLetter.docx** from the PerformanceThreads folder.
10. Rename the file named **PTAgreement.docx** located in the PerformanceThreads folder to **CostumeAgreement.docx**.

Assessment 2 Creating and Then Deleting a Shortcut

1. With the My Computer window open, create a shortcut icon to the file named **CostumeAgreement.docx** located in the PerformanceThreads folder on your storage medium.
2. Close the My Computer window.
3. Double-click the shortcut icon. (This displays the **CostumeAgreement.docx** file in Microsoft Word.)
4. Exit Microsoft Word.
5. Delete the *Shortcut to CostumeAgreement.docx* shortcut icon.

Assessment 3 Using WordPad and Paint

1. Open WordPad and then type the following text:
   I have created a shortcut to the CostumeAgreement.docx file. Print three copies of the agreement and then give one to the customer, one to the Accounting department, and file the third in the Customer filing cabinet.
2. Print the text and then exit WordPad without saving the changes.
3. Open Paint.
4. Create a shape of your choosing with a text box inside. Type the following text in the text box: **Costume Research and Design**.
5. Increase or decrease the size of the text so it spans the text box and fits on one line.
6. Insert a fill color of your choosing in the shape.
7. Print the image.
8. Exit Paint without saving the changes.

Assessment 4 Searching for Information on Multiple User Accounts

1. You have been asked by your supervisor at First Choice Travel to learn about sharing your computer with other users. Your supervisor is considering adding an evening shift and wants to find out how existing computer equipment can be set up for other users who would be working evenings and weekends. Using the Windows XP Help and Support feature, learn how to share computers by creating user accounts. ***Hint: Display the Help and Support Center window, type*** user accounts ***in the*** **Search** ***text box, and then press Enter. Click <u>What's new for user accounts and startup</u> in the <u>Overview, Articles, and Tutorials</u> section and then follow the links to read about sharing your computer.***
2. When the *Sharing your computer* option displays in the right pane, print the help topic.
3. Search for information on creating user accounts and then print the help topic.
4. Search for information on creating user passwords and then print the help topic.
5. Search for information on switching users and then print the help topic.
6. Close the Help and Support Center window.

Microsoft® Internet Explorer 7.0

INTERNET EXPLORER

Browsing the Internet Using Internet Explorer 7.0

Skills

- Visit specific sites by using the site URL
- Click hyperlinks to navigate to specific sites and/or Web pages
- Search for sites containing specific information
- Narrow a search using advanced search options
- Use the Research pane to look up specific information and translate text
- Download a Web page to a separate file
- Download an image to a separate file

Projects Overview

Visit Web sites for two national parks and print the home pages. Search for Web sites pertaining to historical costume design. Use advanced search options to locate information on skydiving companies in the state of Oregon. Search for information on the Royal Ontario Museum and translate English words into French. Locate a Web site for Banff National Park, save the Web page as a file, and save an image as a file.

Print the home pages for the *New York Times* and *USA Today* online newspapers.

Search for and locate the Web page for the Theatre Department at York University and the Web page for the Department of Drama at New York University.

Locate a Web site for a snow skiing resort in Utah and then save the home page as a file and save an image as a file.

Activity 1.1

Browsing the Internet Using Internet Explorer 7.0

Using the Internet, people can access a phenomenal amount of information for private or public use. To use the Internet, three things are generally required—an Internet Service Provider (ISP), a program to browse the Web (called a ***Web browser***), and a ***search engine***. In this section, you will use the Microsoft Internet Explorer Web browser to locate information on the Internet. ***Uniform Resource Locators***, referred to as URLs, are the method used to identify locations on the Internet. The steps for browsing the Internet vary but generally include: opening Internet Explorer, typing the URL for the desired site, navigating the various pages of the site, printing Web pages, and then closing Internet Explorer.

Project

Dennis Chun, the location director for Marquee Productions is gathering information for a new movie project. He has asked you to visit the Web sites for Yosemite National Park and Glacier National Park and print the Web site home pages.

1. Make sure you are connected to the Internet through an Internet Service Provider and that the Windows desktop displays.

   Check with your instructor to determine if you need to complete steps for accessing the Internet.

2. Launch Microsoft Internet Explorer by double-clicking the *Internet Explorer* icon located on the Windows desktop.

   Depending on your system configuration, the steps you complete to open Internet Explorer may vary. Figure 1.1 identifies the elements of the Internet Explorer, version 7, window. The Web page that displays in your Internet Explorer window may vary from what you see in Figure 1.1.

FIGURE 1.1 Internet Explorer Window

3. At the Internet Explorer window, click in the Address bar (refer to Figure 1.1), type **www.nps.gov/yose**, and then press Enter.

   For information on URL names, please refer to the *In Addition* section at the bottom of the page.

4. Scroll down the home page for Yosemite National Park by clicking the down-pointing arrow on the vertical scroll bar located at the right side of the Internet Explorer window.

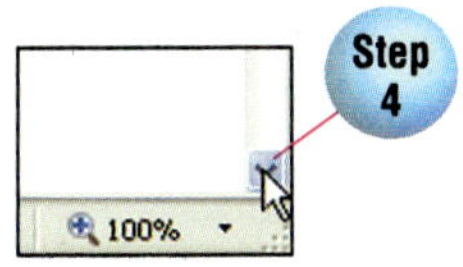

5. Print the home page by clicking the Print button located on the Internet Explorer toolbar.

   Refer to Figure 1.2 for the names of the buttons located on the Internet Explorer toolbar.

6. Display the home page for Glacier National Park by clicking in the Address bar, typing **www.nps.gov/glac**, and then pressing Enter.

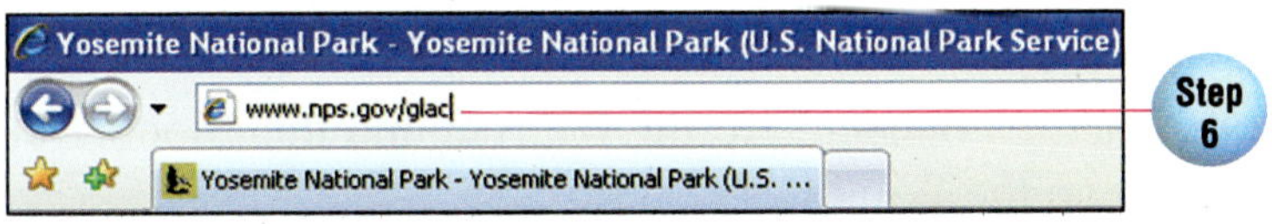

7. Print the home page by clicking the Print button located on the Internet Explorer toolbar.

8. Close Internet Explorer by clicking the Close button (contains an X) located in the upper right corner of the Internet Explorer window.

In Brief

Display Specific Web Site

1. At Windows desktop, double-click *Internet Explorer* icon.
2. Click in Address bar, type Web site URL, press Enter.

FIGURE 1.2 Internet Explorer Toolbar Buttons

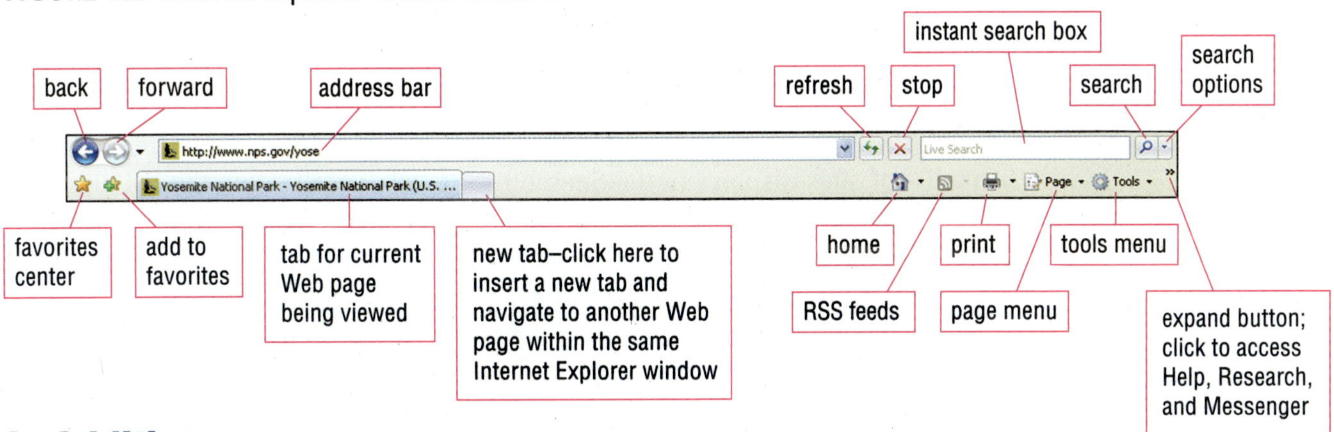

In Addition

Understanding URLs

URLs (Uniform Resource Locators) are the method used to identify locations on the Internet. The format of a URL is *http://server-name.path*. The first part of the URL, *http* stands for HyperText Transfer Protocol, which is the protocol or language used to transfer data within the World Wide Web. The colon and slashes separate the protocol from the server name. The server name is the second component of the URL. For example, in the URL http://www.microsoft.com, the server name is *microsoft*. The last part of the URL specifies the domain to which the server belongs. For example, *.com* refers to "commercial" and establishes that the URL is a commercial company. Other examples of domains include *.edu* for "educational," *.gov* for "government," and *.mil* for "military."

Activity 1.2

Navigating Using Hyperlinks; Searching for Specific Sites

Most Web pages contain ***hyperlinks*** that you click to connect to another page within the Web site or to another site on the Internet. Hyperlinks may display in a Web page as underlined text in a specific color or as images or icons. To use a hyperlink, position the mouse pointer on the desired hyperlink until the mouse pointer turns into a hand and then click the left mouse button. If you do not know the URL for a specific site or you want to find information on the Internet but do not know what site to visit, complete a search with a search engine. A variety of search engines are available on the Internet, each offering the opportunity to search for specific information. One method for searching for information is to click in the Instant Search box, type a keyword or phrase related to your search, and then click the Search button or press Enter. Another method for completing a search is to visit the home page for a search engine and use options at the site.

Project

The research coordinator for Marquee Productions has asked you to locate sites on the Internet on Elizabethan and Renaissance costumes. Historical costumes are needed for the new movie project.

1. Make sure you are connected to the Internet and then double-click the *Internet Explorer* icon on the Windows desktop.
2. At the Internet Explorer window, click in the Instant Search box (currently displays *Live Search*) located at the right end of the Internet Explorer navigation bar.
3. Type **Renaissance costumes** and then click the Search button (or press Enter).

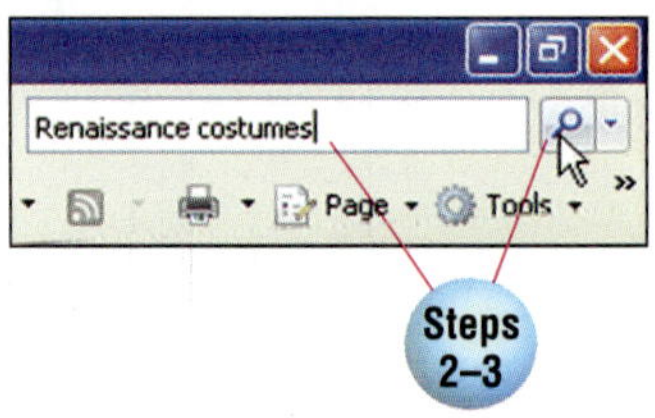

4. When a list of sites displays in the Search results tab, scroll down the list and then click a hyperlink that interests you by positioning the mouse pointer on the hyperlink until the pointer turns into a hand and then clicking the left mouse button.

   By default, Internet Explorer uses Live Search. You can change the search provider default or add search providers using the Search Options button.

5. When the Web site displays, click the Print button.
6. Use the Yahoo! Web site to find sites on Renaissance costumes by clicking in the Address bar, typing **www.yahoo.com**, and then pressing Enter.

   You can also click the Search Options button and click *Yahoo! Search* at the drop-down list if Yahoo! has been added to the search providers list. Internet Explorer automatically repeats the search request using the text in the Instant Search box at Yahoo!'s Web page. Click *Find More Providers* at the search options drop-down list to add your favorite search engines to the search providers list.

7. At the Yahoo! Web site, type **Renaissance costumes** in the search text box and then press Enter.

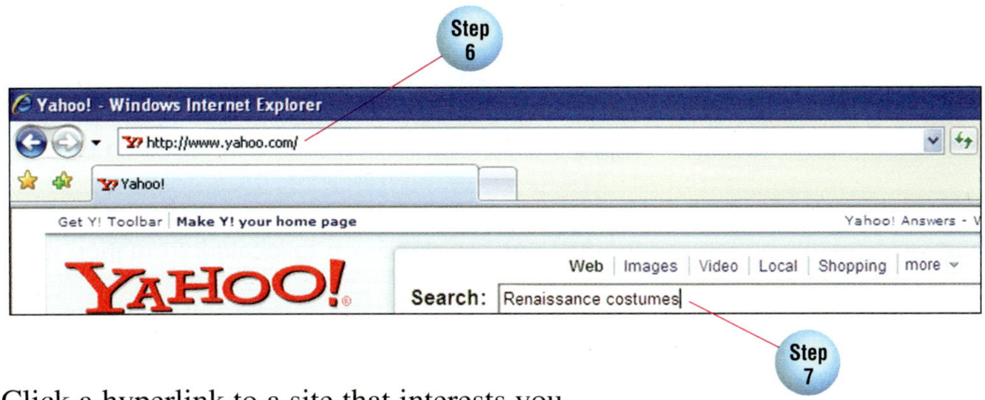

8. Click a hyperlink to a site that interests you.
9. When the site displays, click the Print button on the Internet Explorer toolbar.
10. Use the Google search engine to find sites on Elizabethan costumes by clicking in the Address bar, typing **www.google.com**, and then pressing Enter.
11. When the Google home page displays, type **Elizabethan costumes** in the search text box and then press Enter.

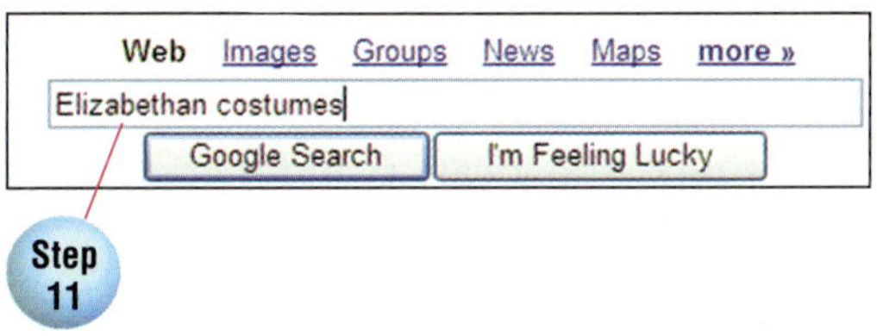

12. Click a hyperlink to a site that interests you.
13. When the Web site displays, click the Print button on the Internet Explorer toolbar.
14. Close Internet Explorer.

In Brief

Search for Web Site
At Internet Explorer window, type text in Instant Search box related to desired Web sites, then click Search button.

In Addition

Adding Favorites to the Favorites Center

If you find a site you want to visit on a regular basis, add the site to the Favorites Center. To do this, click the Add to Favorites button located at the left of the browser tabs and then click *Add to Favorites* at the drop-down list. At the Add a Favorite dialog box that displays, make sure the information in the *Name* text box is the title by which you want to refer to the Web site (if not, select the text and then type your own title for the page) and then click the Add button. The new Web site is added to the Favorites Center drop-down list. Jump quickly to the site by clicking the Favorites Center button and then clicking the site name at the drop-down list.

Activity 1.3

Completing Advanced Searches for Specific Sites

The Internet contains an extraordinary amount of information. Depending on what you are searching for on the Internet and the search engine you use, some searches can result in several thousand "hits" (sites). Wading through a large number of sites can be very time-consuming and counterproductive. Narrowing a search to very specific criteria can greatly reduce the number of hits for a search. To narrow a search, use the advanced search options offered by the search engine.

Project

The stunt coordinator at Marquee Productions has asked you to locate information on skydiving companies in the state of Oregon.

1. Make sure you are connected to the Internet and then double-click the *Internet Explorer* icon on the Windows desktop.
2. Click in the Address bar, type **www.yahoo.com**, and then press Enter.
3. At the Yahoo! home page, click the Web Search button Web Search next to the Search text box and then click the Advanced Search hyperlink.

Step 3

The advanced search hyperlink will probably display at the right side of the search text box. The location and name may vary.

4. At the Advanced Web Search page, click in the *the exact phrase* text box
(the name of this option may vary) and then type **skydiving in Oregon**.

This limits the search to Web sites with the exact phrase "skydiving in Oregon."

5. Click the *Only* ***.com*** *domains* option. (The name of this option may vary.)

Clicking this option tells Yahoo! to only display Web sites with a .com extension and to ignore any other extension.

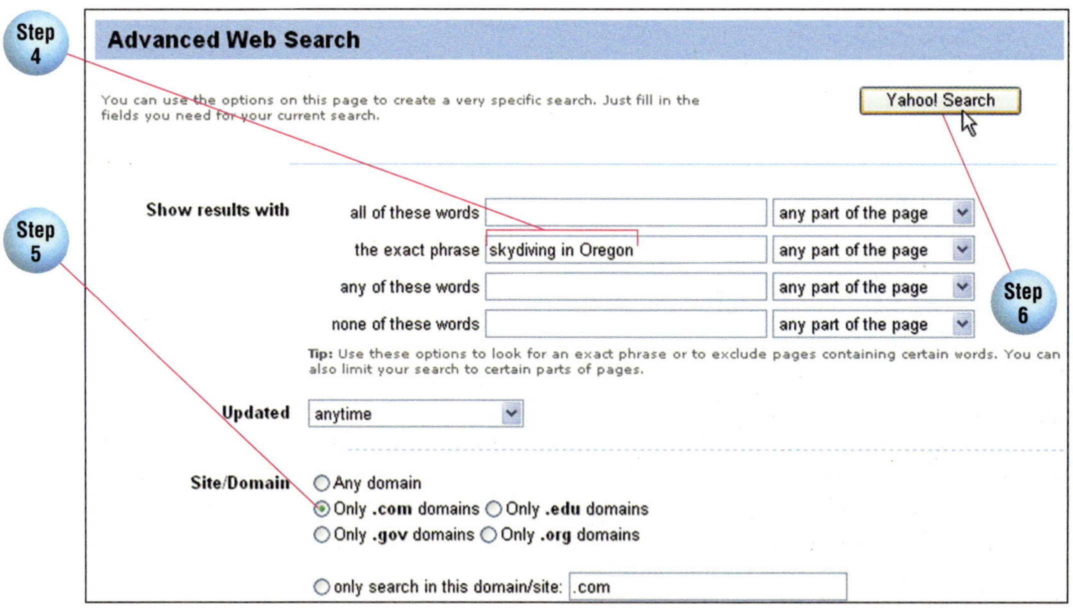

6. Click the Yahoo! Search button.
7. When the list of Web sites displays, click a hyperlink that interests you.
8. Click the Print button on the Internet Explorer toolbar to print the Web page.
9. Click the Back button on the Internet Explorer toolbar until the Yahoo! Advanced Web Search page displays.
10. Select and then delete the text *skydiving in Oregon* located in the *the exact phrase* text box.
11. Click in the *all of these words* text box and then type **skydiving Oregon tandem static line**.

    You want to focus on Web sites that offer tandem and static line skydiving in Oregon.
12. Click the *Any domain* option.

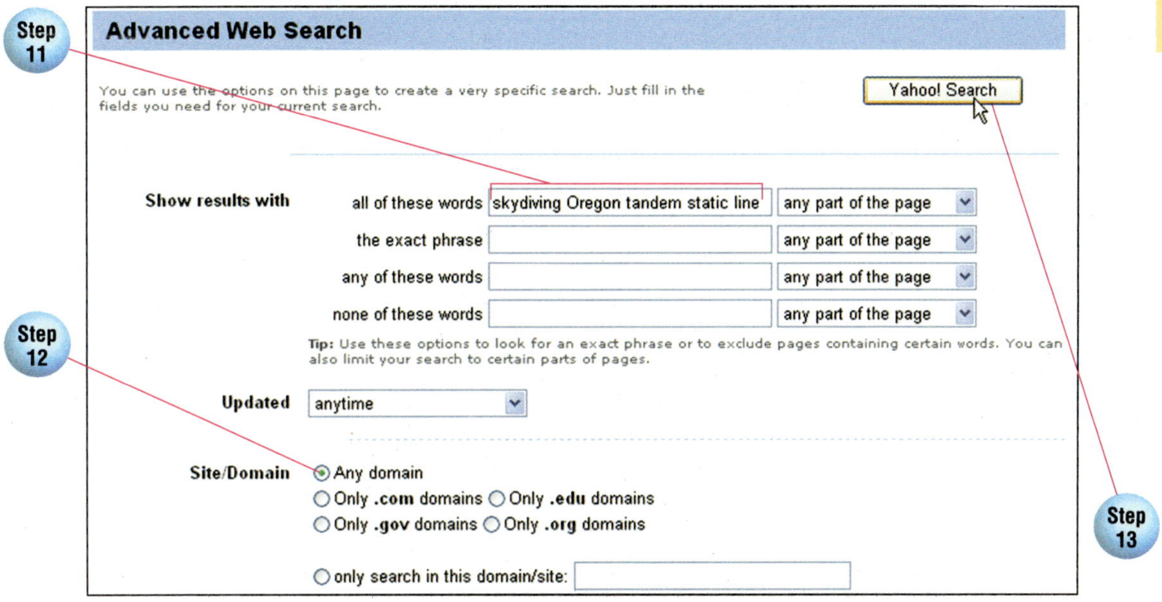

13. Click the Yahoo! Search button.
14. When the list of Web sites displays, click a hyperlink that interests you and then print the Web page.
15. Close Internet Explorer.

In Brief

Complete Advanced Search Using Yahoo!

1. At Internet Explorer window, click in Address bar, type **www.yahoo.com**, then press Enter.
2. Click Web Search button, then click Advanced Search hyperlink.
3. Click in search text box, type specific text related to desired Web sites.
4. Select search method and search area.
5. Click Yahoo! Search button.

In Addition

Displaying a List of Sites Visited

As you view various Web pages, Internet Explorer keeps track of the Web sites visited. Display the History pane by clicking the Tools button on the Internet Explorer toolbar, pointing to *Toolbars* and then clicking *History* at the drop-down list. Click the timeframe for which the Web page would have been viewed to expand the list and display the sites visited. For example, click *Last Week* to expand the list and view the pages that you visited within the past week. Click the desired hyperlink to revisit the page. At the top of the History pane, click the View History down-pointing arrow to change the order in which the history list is displayed. You can display Web sites in the History pane *By Date*, *By Site*, *By Most Visited*, or *By Order Visited Today*. Click *Search History* at the View History drop-down list to search the Web sites in the history pane by keyword or phrase.

Activity 1.4

Researching and Requesting Information

Click the expand button located at the right end of the Internet Explorer toolbar (next to Tools) and then click *Research* at the drop-down list to open the Research pane at the left side of the window. Use options in this pane to search for and request specific information from online sources and to translate words to and from a variety of languages. The online resources available to you depend on the locale to which your system is set, authorization information indicating that you are allowed to download the information, and your Internet service provider. Determine the resources available by clicking the down-pointing arrow at the right of the resources list box. The drop-down list contains lists of reference books, research sites, business and financial sites, and other services. If you want to use a specific reference in your search, click the desired reference at the drop-down list, type the desired word or topic in the *Search for* text box, and then press Enter. Items matching your word or topic display in the pane list box. Depending on the item, the list box may contain hyperlinks you can click to access additional information on the Internet.

Project

Chris Greenbaum, production manager for the Toronto film project, has asked for your assistance. She wants you to use the Research feature of Internet Explorer to search for information on the Royal Ontario Museum and to also use the translation tool to translate two English words into French.

1. Open Internet Explorer.
2. Click the expand button located at the right end of the Internet Explorer toolbar and then click *Research* at the drop-down list.

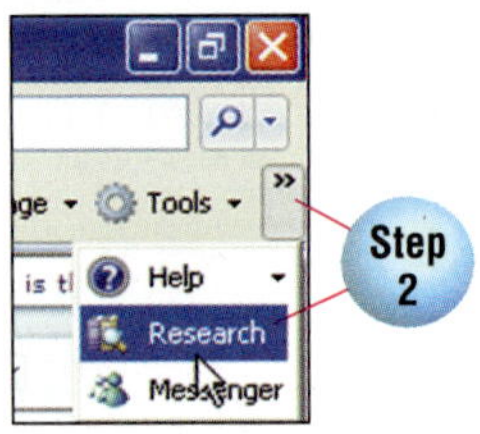

3. Type **Royal Ontario Museum** in the *Search for* text box in the Research pane.
4. Click the down-pointing arrow to the right of the resources list box (the down-pointing arrow immediately below the Start searching button) and then click *Encarta Encyclopedia: English (North America)* at the drop-down list.

   If this reference is not available, click any encyclopedia that is available.

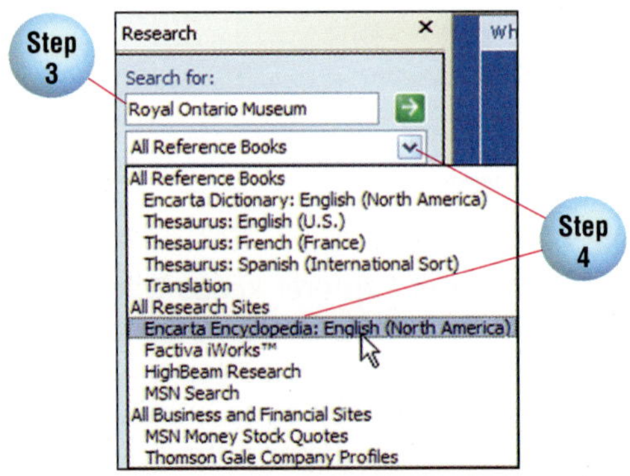

5. Look at the information that displays in the Research pane and then click a hyperlink about the Royal Ontario Museum that interests you.

6 Use the translation feature to translate *script* from English to French. To begin, select the text in the *Search for* text box and then type **script**.

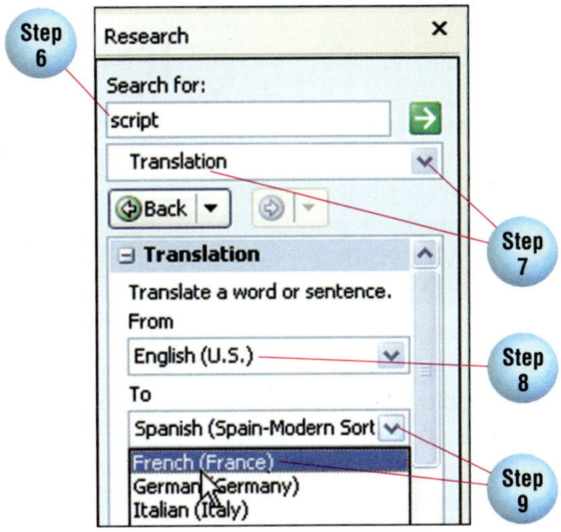

7 Click the down-pointing arrow at the right of the resources list box and then click *Translation* at the drop-down list.

8 Make sure that *English (U.S.)* displays in the *From* option box.

If it does not, click the down-pointing arrow at the right of the *From* option and then click *English (U.S.)* at the drop-down list.

9 Click the down-pointing arrow to the right of the *To* option and then click *French (France)* at the drop-down list.

10 Make a note of the translation of *script* into French.

11 Select *script* in the *Search for* text box, type **documentary**, and then press Enter.

12 When the translation of *documentary* displays in the Research pane, make a note of the translation.

13 Click the Close button located at the top right of the Research pane, or click the expand button located at the right end of the Internet Explorer toolbar and then click *Research* at the drop-down list to close the pane.

14 Close Internet Explorer.

In Brief

Use Research Pane

1. At Internet Explorer window, click expand button.
2. Click *Research*.
3. Click in *Search for* text box, then type specific text.
4. Click down-pointing arrow at right of resources list box, then click desired resource.

In Addition

Choosing Research Options

Determine the resources available by clicking the down-pointing arrow at the right of the resources list box (the list box located below the *Search for* text box). The drop-down list contains lists of reference books, research sites, business and financial sites, and other services. You can control the available research options by clicking the Research options hyperlink located at the bottom of the Research pane. This displays the Research Options dialog box shown at the right. At this dialog box, insert a check mark before those items you want available and remove the check mark from those items you do not want available.

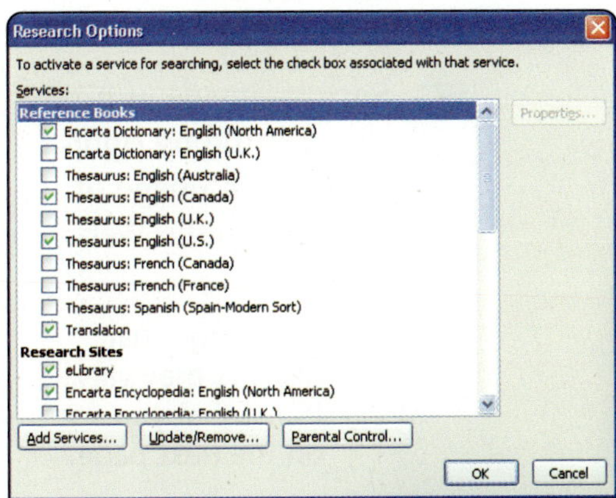

Activity 1.5

Downloading Images, Text, and Web Pages from the Internet

You can save as a separate file the image(s) and/or text that displays when you open a Web page. This separate file can be viewed, printed, or inserted in another file. The information you want to save in a separate file is downloaded from the Internet by Internet Explorer and saved in a folder of your choosing with the name you specify. Copyright laws protect much of the information on the Internet. Before using information downloaded from the Internet, check the site for restrictions. If you do use information, make sure you properly cite the source.

Project

The production manager of the new movie project at Marquee Productions has asked you to locate a site on the Internet for Banff National Park. She wants you to save the Web page as a file and a picture of the park in another file. She needs these files for a presentation she is preparing for the next production meeting.

Note: Saving Web pages and images to a floppy disk is not recommended due to space limitations.

1. Make sure you are connected to the Internet and then double-click the *Internet Explorer* icon on the Windows desktop.
2. Search for sites on the Internet for Banff National Park.
3. From the list of sites that displays, choose a site that contains information about Banff National Park and at least one image of the park.
4. Save the Web page as a separate file by clicking the Page button on the Internet Explorer toolbar and then clicking *Save As* at the drop-down list.

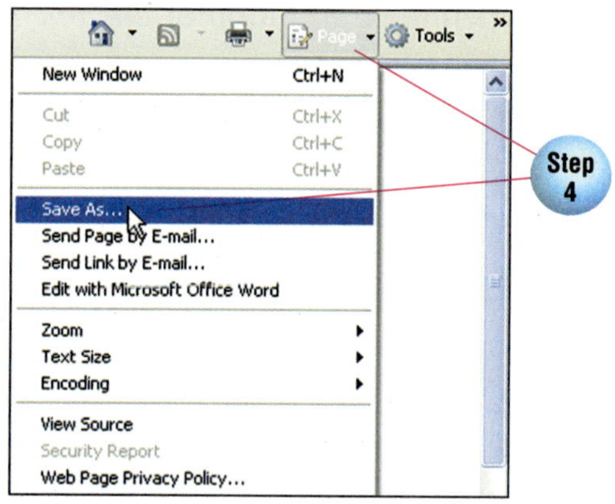

5. At the Save Webpage dialog box, click the down-pointing arrow at the right side of the *Save in* option and then click the drive you are using as your storage medium at the drop-down list.
6. Select the text in the *File name* text box, type **BanffWebPage**, and then click Save or press Enter.
7. Save an image as a separate file by right-clicking an image of the park on the Web page.

   The image that displays may vary from what you see on the next page.

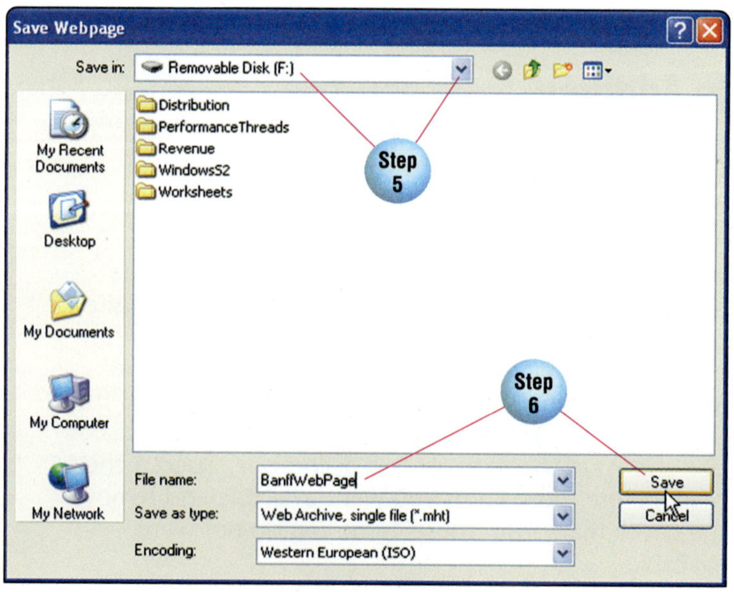

8 At the shortcut menu that displays, click *Save Picture As*.

9 At the Save Picture dialog box, change the location to your storage medium.

10 Select the text in the *File name* text box, type **BanffImage**, and then click Save or press Enter.

11 Close Internet Explorer.

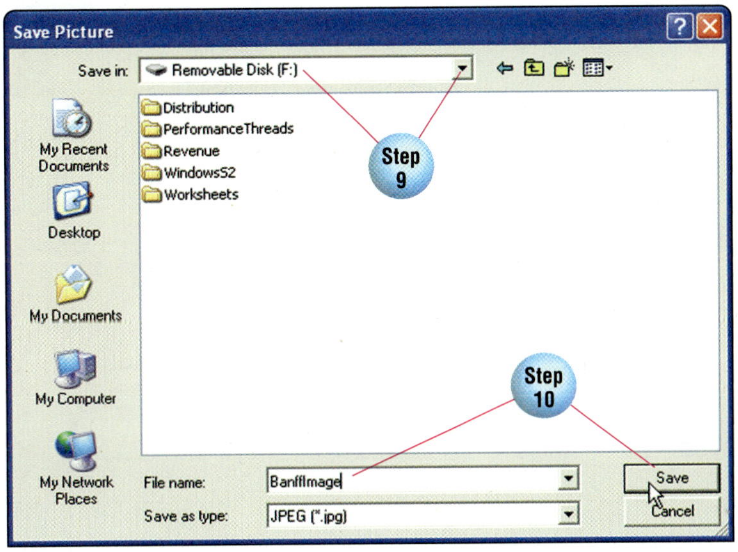

Optional Steps

12 Open Microsoft Word by clicking the Start button on the Taskbar, pointing to *All Programs*, pointing to *Microsoft Office*, and then clicking *Microsoft Office Word 2007*.

13 With Microsoft Word open, click the Insert tab in the ribbon. Click the Picture button in the Illustrations group.

14 At the Insert Picture dialog box, change the *Look in* option to the location where you saved the Banff image and then double-click ***BanffImage.jpg***.

15 When the image displays in the Word document, print the document by clicking the Print button on the Quick Access toolbar.

16 Close the document by clicking the Office button and then clicking *Close* at the drop-down list. At the message asking if you want to save the changes, click No.

17 Open the **BanffWebPage.mht** file by clicking the Office button and then clicking *Open* at the drop-down list.

18 At the Open dialog box, change the *Look in* option to the location where you saved the Banff Web page and then double-click ***BanffWebPage.mht***. Click No if a message appears asking if you want to make Word your default Web page editor.

19 Print the Web page by clicking the Print button on the Quick Access toolbar.

20 Close the **BanffWebPage** file by clicking the Office button and then *Close*.

21 Close Word by clicking the Close button that displays in the upper right corner of the screen.

Features Summary

Feature	Button	Keyboard Shortcut
close Internet Explorer		Alt + F4
go back to previous Web page		Alt + Left Arrow
go forward to next Web page		Alt + Right Arrow
History pane	Tools	Ctrl + Shift + H
launch Internet Explorer		
print current Web page		Ctrl + P
Research pane	»	
save a Web page as separate file	Page	
save image as separate file	Page	
select Address bar	http://www.yahoo.com/	Alt + D
select Instant Search box	Live Search	Ctrl + E

Knowledge Check

Completion: In the space provided at the right, indicate the correct term, symbol, button, or command.

1. Type a URL in this bar at the Internet Explorer window. __________
2. The letters *URL* stand for this. __________
3. Click this button on the Internet Explorer toolbar to display the previous Web page. __________
4. Click in this box located at the right end of the Internet Explorer navigation bar to locate Web pages using a keyword or phrase. __________
5. Use options in this pane to request specific information from online sources and to translate words to and from a variety of languages. __________
6. Save a Web page as a separate file by clicking the Page button on the Internet Explorer toolbar and then clicking this option at the drop-down list. __________
7. Save an image as a separate file by right-clicking the image and then clicking this option at the shortcut menu. __________

Skills Review

Review 1 Browsing the Internet and Navigating with Hyperlinks

1. Launch Internet Explorer.
2. Click in the Address bar, type **www.si.edu**, and then press Enter. (This is the home page for the Smithsonian Institution.)
3. Using hyperlinks navigate to a page in the Smithsonian that interests you and then print the Web page.
4. Click the Back button until the Smithsonian Institution home page displays.

Review 2 Searching for Specific Sites

1. At the Internet Explorer window, use the Instant Search box to look for Web sites on mountain climbing.
2. Visit a site that interests you and then print the Web site.
3. Display the Yahoo! Web site and then use advanced options to search for Web sites on mountain climbing in British Columbia, Canada.
4. Visit a site that interests you and then print the Web site.

Review 3 Requesting Information and Translating Words

1. At the Internet Explorer window, click the Research button to display the Research pane.
2. Use options in the Research pane to find information in an encyclopedia on the decade in the 1900s referred to as the "Roaring Twenties."
3. Click a hyperlink that interests you and then print the Web site.
4. Use options in the Research pane to translate the English word *history* into French.
5. Make a note of the French word and then close the Research pane.

Review 4 Downloading a Web Page

1. Using a search engine of your choosing, search for Web sites on parasailing in Hawaii. Find a site that contains a parasailing image.
2. When the Web page displays, save it as a separate file by clicking the Page button and then *Save As*.
3. At the Save Webpage dialog box, change the location to your storage medium, type **ParasailWebPage** in the *File name* text box, and then press Enter.
4. Save an image by right-clicking an image on the Web page and then clicking *Save Picture As* at the shortcut menu.
5. At the Save Picture dialog box, change the location to your storage medium, type **ParasailImage** in the *File name* text box, and then press Enter.
6. Close Internet Explorer.

Skills Assessment

Assessment 1 Visiting and Printing Web Pages

1. Sam Vestering, a manager at Worldwide Enterprises, likes to keep up-to-date with current events by reading the daily headlines for various newspapers. He has asked you to print the home pages for two online newspapers—the *New York Times* and *USA Today*. To begin, launch Internet Explorer.
2. Visit the Web site of the *New York Times* at www.nytimes.com and then print the home page.
3. Visit the Web site of *USA Today* at www.usatoday.com and then print the home page.

Assessment 2 Navigating Web Sites

1. Cal Rubine, the chair of the Theatre Arts Division at Niagara Peninsula College, has asked you to print the Web pages for the theater and/or drama departments at two universities. Visit the home page for York University, Toronto, Canada, at www.yorku.ca.
2. Using hyperlinks navigate to the Web page for the Theatre department and then print the Web page.
3. Visit the home page for New York University at www.nyu.edu.
4. Using hyperlinks navigate to the Web page for the Department of Drama (undergraduate) and then print the Web page.

Assessment 3 Researching Information

1. You work for First Choice Travel and are preparing a brochure on snow skiing vacations. You need some information and images for the brochure. Using Internet Explorer, search for information on snow skiing resorts in Utah.
2. Visit a Web site that interests you and contains an image of the resort or mountains.
3. Save the Web page as a separate file and name it **UtahSkiResortWebPage**.
4. Save an image as a separate file and name it **UtahResortImage**.
5. Close Internet Explorer.

Optional Steps

6. Open Microsoft Word.
7. Insert the image into a Word document and then print the document.
8. Close the document without saving it.
9. Open the file containing the Web page and then print it.
10. Close the document and then close Word.

Microsoft®

Word 2007

Introducing

Word 2007

Microsoft Word 2007 is a word processing program used to create documents such as letters, reports, research papers, brochures, announcements, newsletters, envelopes, labels, and much more. Word is a full-featured program that provides a wide variety of editing and formatting features as well as sophisticated visual elements. While working in Word, you will produce business documents for the following six companies.

First Choice Travel is a travel center offering a full range of traveling services from booking flights, hotel reservations, and rental cars to offering travel seminars.

The Waterfront Bistro offers fine dining for lunch and dinner and also offers banquet facilities, a wine cellar, and catering services.

Worldwide Enterprises is a national and international distributor of products for a variety of companies and is the exclusive movie distribution agent for Marquee Productions.

Marquee Productions is involved in all aspects of creating movies from script writing and development to filming. The company produces documentaries, biographies, as well as historical and action movies.

Performance Threads maintains an inventory of rental costumes and also researches, designs, and sews special-order and custom-made costumes.

The mission of the Niagara Peninsula College Theatre Arts Division is to offer a curriculum designed to provide students with a thorough exposure to all aspects of the theater arts.

In Section 1 you will learn how to

Create and Edit Documents

Using Microsoft Word, you can create, edit, and format a variety of business documents and use Word's powerful editing and formatting features to produce well-written and visually appealing documents. Some powerful editing features include checking the spelling and grammar in a document and using the Thesaurus to find appropriate synonyms for words; using AutoCorrect to improve the efficiency of entering information in a document; creating a document using a predesigned template; and designing a document using building block organizers.

Prepare multiple-page documents and edit documents by completing a spelling and grammar check and using a thesaurus to find appropriate synonyms for words.

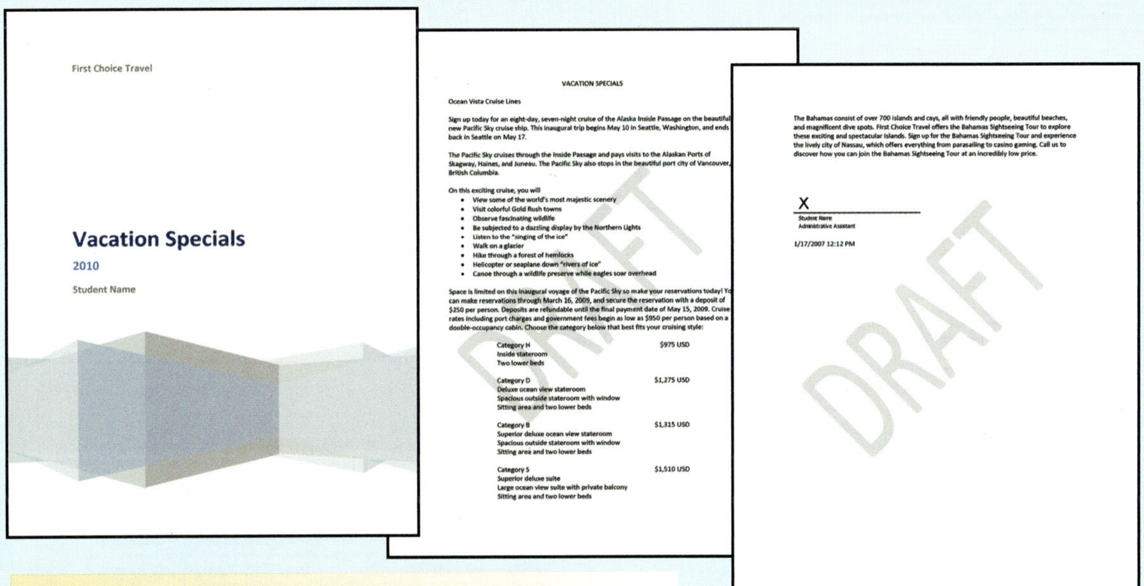

First Choice Travel

Vacation Specials

2010

Student Name

VACATION SPECIALS

Ocean Vista Cruise Lines

Sign up today for an eight-day, seven-night cruise of the Alaska Inside Passage on the beautiful new Pacific Sky cruise ship. This inaugural trip begins May 10 in Seattle, Washington, and ends back in Seattle on May 17.

The Pacific Sky cruises through the Inside Passage and pays visits to the Alaskan Ports of Skagway, Haines, and Juneau. The Pacific Sky also stops in the beautiful port city of Vancouver, British Columbia.

On this exciting cruise, you will

- View some of the world's most majestic scenery
- Visit colorful Gold Rush towns
- Observe fascinating wildlife
- Be subjected to a dazzling display by the Northern Lights
- Listen to the "singing of the ice"
- Walk on a glacier
- Hike through a forest of hemlocks
- Helicopter or seaplane down "rivers of ice"
- Canoe through a wildlife preserve while eagles soar overhead

Space is limited on this inaugural voyage of the Pacific Sky so make your reservations today! Yo can make reservations through March 16, 2009, and secure the reservation with a deposit of $250 per person. Deposits are refundable until the final payment date of May 15, 2009. Cruise rates including port charges and government fees begin as low as $950 per person based on a double-occupancy cabin. Choose the category below that best fits your cruising style:

Category H — $975 USD
Inside stateroom
Two lower beds

Category D — $1,275 USD
Deluxe ocean view stateroom
Spacious outside stateroom with window
Sitting area and two lower beds

Category B — $1,315 USD
Superior deluxe ocean view stateroom
Spacious outside stateroom with window
Sitting area and two lower beds

Category S — $1,510 USD
Superior deluxe suite
Large ocean view suite with private balcony
Sitting area and two lower beds

DRAFT

The Bahamas consist of over 700 islands and cays, all with friendly people, beautiful beaches, and magnificent dive spots. First Choice Travel offers the Bahamas Sightseeing Tour to explore these exciting and spectacular islands. Sign up for the Bahamas Sightseeing Tour and experience the lively city of Nassau, which offers everything from parasailing to casino gaming. Call us to discover how you can join the Bahamas Sightseeing Tour at an incredibly low price.

X
Student Name
Administrative Assistant

1/17/2007 12:12 PM

DRAFT

Use building blocks to create a cover page for a document and insert a text watermark on the page.

Automate the process of inserting a signature line with the Signature Line feature.

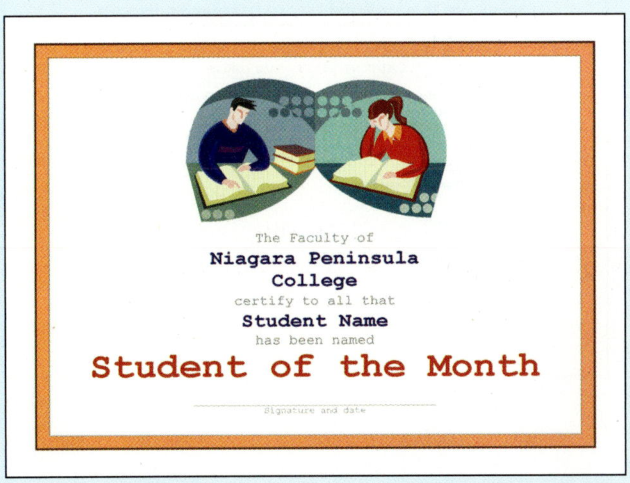

The Faculty of
Niagara Peninsula College
certify to all that
Student Name
has been named
Student of the Month
Signature and date

Download templates from Microsoft Office Online and create a variety of documents including a certificate or award.

In Section 2 you will learn how to

Format Characters and Paragraphs in Documents

Word contains a number of commands and procedures that affect how the document appears when printed. The appearance of a document in the document screen and how it looks when printed is called the ***format***. Formatting can include such tasks as changing the font; aligning and indenting text; changing line and paragraph spacing; setting tabs; and inserting elements such as bullets, numbers, symbols, and special characters. You can also improve the readability of the document by setting text in tabbed columns and by formatting using styles.

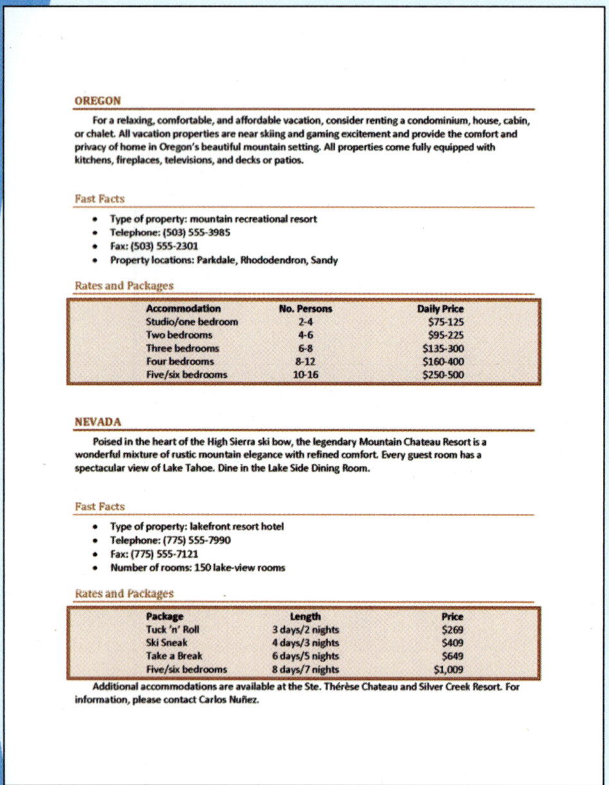

OREGON

For a relaxing, comfortable, and affordable vacation, consider renting a condominium, house, cabin, or chalet. All vacation properties are near skiing and gaming excitement and provide the comfort and privacy of home in Oregon's beautiful mountain setting. All properties come fully equipped with kitchens, fireplaces, televisions, and decks or patios.

Fast Facts

- Type of property: mountain recreational resort
- Telephone: (503) 555-3985
- Fax: (503) 555-2301
- Property locations: Parkdale, Rhododendron, Sandy

Rates and Packages

Accommodation	No. Persons	Daily Price
Studio/one bedroom	2-4	$75-125
Two bedrooms	4-6	$95-225
Three bedrooms	6-8	$135-300
Four bedrooms	8-12	$160-400
Five/six bedrooms	10-16	$250-500

NEVADA

Poised in the heart of the High Sierra ski bow, the legendary Mountain Chateau Resort is a wonderful mixture of rustic mountain elegance with refined comfort. Every guest room has a spectacular view of Lake Tahoe. Dine in the Lake Side Dining Room.

Fast Facts

- Type of property: lakefront resort hotel
- Telephone: (775) 555-7990
- Fax: (775) 555-7121
- Number of rooms: 150 lake-view rooms

Rates and Packages

Package	Length	Price
Tuck 'n' Roll	3 days/2 nights	$269
Ski Sneak	4 days/3 nights	$409
Take a Break	6 days/5 nights	$649
Five/six bedrooms	8 days/7 nights	$1,009

Additional accommodations are available at the Ste. Thérèse Chateau and Silver Creek Resort. For information, please contact Carlos Nuñez.

Apply formatting such as inserting bullets and special characters, setting text in tabbed columns, and applying paragraph shading and lines.

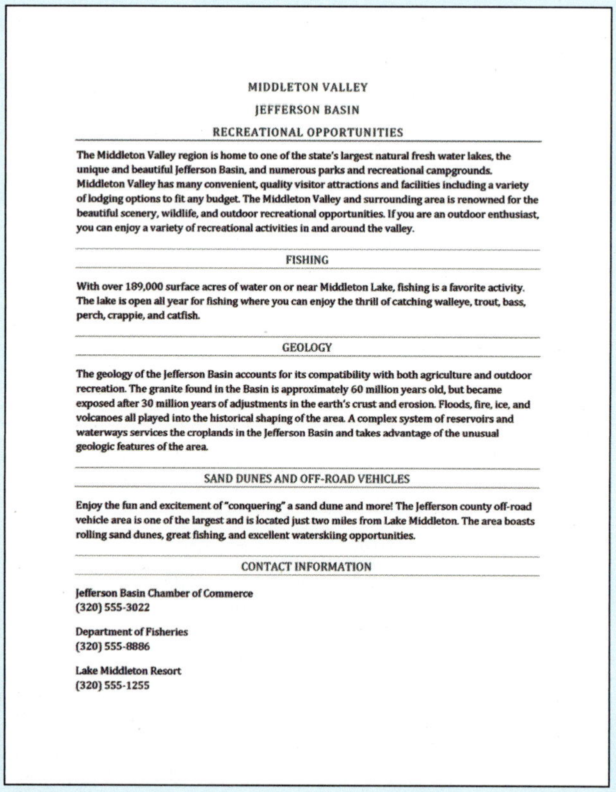

MIDDLETON VALLEY

JEFFERSON BASIN

RECREATIONAL OPPORTUNITIES

The Middleton Valley region is home to one of the state's largest natural fresh water lakes, the unique and beautiful Jefferson Basin, and numerous parks and recreational campgrounds. Middleton Valley has many convenient, quality visitor attractions and facilities including a variety of lodging options to fit any budget. The Middleton Valley and surrounding area is renowned for the beautiful scenery, wildlife, and outdoor recreational opportunities. If you are an outdoor enthusiast, you can enjoy a variety of recreational activities in and around the valley.

FISHING

With over 189,000 surface acres of water on or near Middleton Lake, fishing is a favorite activity. The lake is open all year for fishing where you can enjoy the thrill of catching walleye, trout, bass, perch, crappie, and catfish.

GEOLOGY

The geology of the Jefferson Basin accounts for its compatibility with both agriculture and outdoor recreation. The granite found in the Basin is approximately 60 million years old, but became exposed after 30 million years of adjustments in the earth's crust and erosion. Floods, fire, ice, and volcanoes all played into the historical shaping of the area. A complex system of reservoirs and waterways services the croplands in the Jefferson Basin and takes advantage of the unusual geologic features of the area.

SAND DUNES AND OFF-ROAD VEHICLES

Enjoy the fun and excitement of "conquering" a sand dune and more! The Jefferson county off-road vehicle area is one of the largest and is located just two miles from Lake Middleton. The area boasts rolling sand dunes, great fishing, and excellent waterskiing opportunities.

CONTACT INFORMATION

Jefferson Basin Chamber of Commerce
(320) 555-3022

Department of Fisheries
(320) 555-8886

Lake Middleton Resort
(320) 555-1255

Use Word styles to apply predesigned formatting to text such as bolding, centering, changing fonts, and applying border lines.

In Section 3 you will learn how to

Enhance Documents

Improve the formatting of a document using features to rearrange text in a document, add special elements, or change the appearance of text. With the Find and Replace feature you can find specific text and replace it with other text. Use buttons on the Home tab to move, copy, and paste text in a document. Improve the appearance of documents by inserting page numbering, headers, and footers; changing margins and page orientation; and changing vertical alignment. Add visual appeal to documents by inserting and customizing clip art images and pictures.

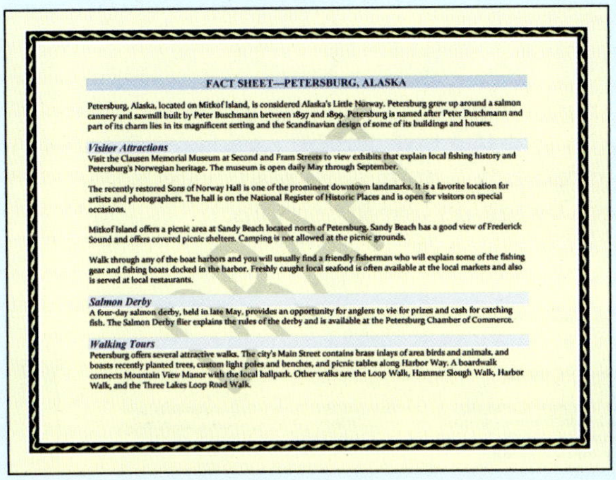

FACT SHEET—PETERSBURG, ALASKA

Petersburg, Alaska, located on Mitkof Island, is considered Alaska's Little Norway. Petersburg grew up around a salmon cannery and sawmill built by Peter Buschmann between 1897 and 1899. Petersburg is named after Peter Buschmann and part of its charm lies in its magnificent setting and the Scandinavian design of some of its buildings and houses.

Visitor Attractions

Visit the Clausen Memorial Museum at Second and Fram Streets to view exhibits that explain local fishing history and Petersburg's Norwegian heritage. The museum is open daily May through September.

The recently restored Sons of Norway Hall is one of the prominent downtown landmarks. It is a favorite location for artists and photographers. The hall is on the National Register of Historic Places and is open for visitors on special occasions.

Mitkof Island offers a picnic area at Sandy Beach located north of Petersburg. Sandy Beach has a good view of Frederick Sound and offers covered picnic shelters. Camping is not allowed at the picnic grounds.

Walk through any of the boat harbors and you will usually find a friendly fisherman who will explain some of the fishing gear and fishing boats docked in the harbor. Freshly caught local seafood is often available at the local markets and also is served at local restaurants.

Salmon Derby

A four-day salmon derby, held in late May, provides an opportunity for anglers to vie for prizes and cash for catching fish. The Salmon Derby flier explains the rules of the derby and is available at the Petersburg Chamber of Commerce.

Walking Tours

Petersburg offers several attractive walks. The city's Main Street contains brass inlays of area birds and animals, and boasts recently planted trees, custom light poles and benches, and picnic tables along Harbor Way. A boardwalk connects Mountain View Manor with the local ballpark. Other walks are the Loop Walk, Hammer Slough Walk, Harbor Walk, and the Three Lakes Loop Road Walk.

DRAFT

Enhance the appearance of a document by changing the page orientation and background color, inserting a page border, and applying a theme, which is a set of formatting choices that include a color, a font, and an effects theme.

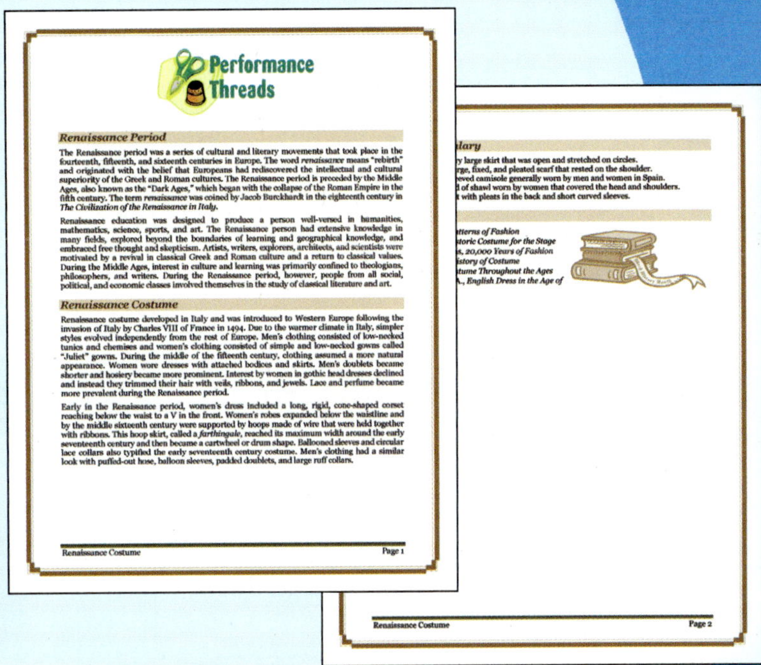

Performance Threads

Renaissance Period

The Renaissance period was a series of cultural and literary movements that took place in the fourteenth, fifteenth, and sixteenth centuries in Europe. The word *renaissance* means "rebirth" and originated with the belief that Europeans had rediscovered the intellectual and cultural superiority of the Greek and Roman cultures. The Renaissance period is preceded by the Middle Ages, also known as the "Dark Ages," which began with the collapse of the Roman Empire in the fifth century. The term *renaissance* was coined by Jacob Burckhardt in the eighteenth century in *The Civilization of the Renaissance in Italy*.

Renaissance education was designed to produce a person well-versed in humanities, mathematics, science, sports, and art. The Renaissance person had extensive knowledge in many fields, explored beyond the boundaries of learning and geographical knowledge, and embraced free thought and skepticism. Artists, writers, explorers, architects, and scientists were motivated by a revival in classical Greek and Roman culture and a return to classical values. During the Middle Ages, interest in culture and learning was primarily confined to theologians, philosophers, and writers. During the Renaissance period, however, people from all social, political, and economic classes involved themselves in the study of classical literature and art.

Renaissance Costume

Renaissance costume developed in Italy and was introduced to Western Europe following the invasion of Italy by Charles VIII of France in 1494. Due to the warmer climate in Italy, simpler styles evolved independently from the rest of Europe. Men's clothing consisted of low-necked tunics and chemises and women's clothing consisted of simple and low-necked gowns called "Juliet" gowns. During the middle of the fifteenth century, clothing assumed a more natural appearance. Women wore dresses with attached bodices and skirts. Men's doublets became shorter and hosiery became more prominent. Interest by women in gothic head dresses declined and instead they trimmed their hair with veils, ribbons, and jewels. Lace and perfume became more prevalent during the Renaissance period.

Early in the Renaissance period, women's dress included a long, rigid, cone-shaped corset reaching below the waist to a V in the front. Women's robes expanded below the waistline and by the middle sixteenth century were supported by hoops made of wire that were held together with ribbons. This hoop skirt, called a *farthingale*, reached its maximum width around the early seventeenth century and then became a cartwheel or drum shape. Ballooned sleeves and circular lace collars also typified the early seventeenth century costume. Men's clothing had a similar look with puffed-out hose, balloon sleeves, padded doublets, and large ruff collars.

Renaissance Costume Page 1

Renaissance Costume Page 2

Enhance the visual appeal of a document by inserting a picture such as a company logo, inserting a clip art image related to text in the document, and inserting a footer providing information about the document including page numbering.

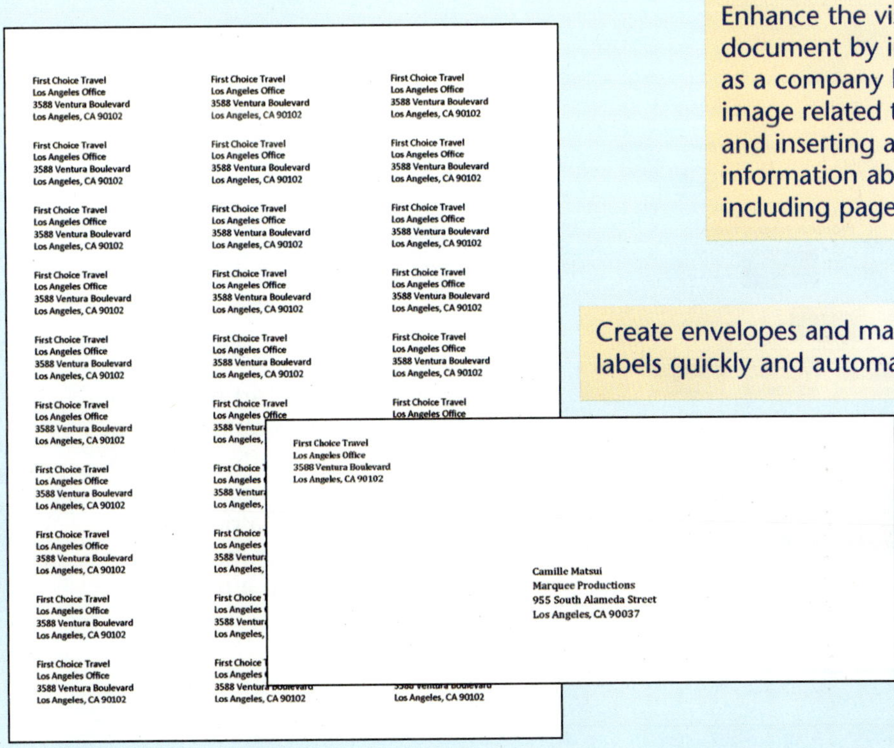

Create envelopes and mailing labels quickly and automatically.

In Section 4 you will learn how to
Apply Special Features

Word contains special formatting features you can apply in a document to enhance the visual display of text. For example, add visual appeal to a document with the WordArt and drop cap features and by inserting shapes and text boxes. Use the SmartArt feature to create visual representations of data such as organizational charts and diagrams, and use the Tables feature to create, modify, and format data in columns and rows. Improve the ease with which a person can read and understand groups of words by setting text in columns. You can save a Word document as a Web page and insert hyperlinks that will link to another document or a location on the Internet.

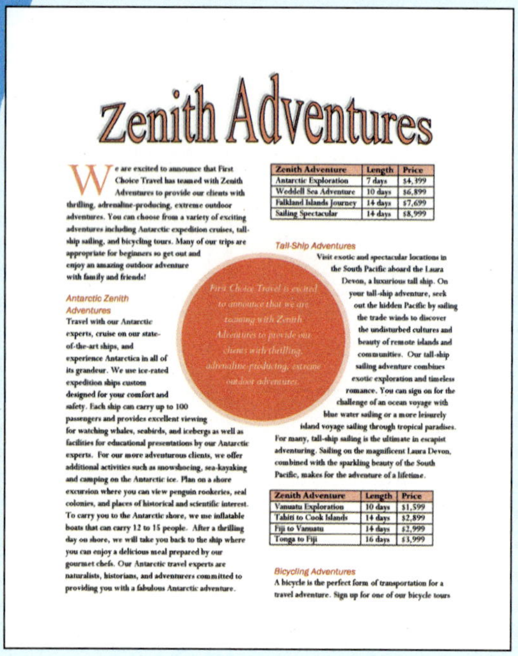

Zenith Adventures

We are excited to announce that First Choice Travel has teamed with Zenith Adventures to provide our clients with thrilling, adrenaline-producing, extreme outdoor adventures. You can choose from a variety of exciting adventures including Antarctic expedition cruises, tall-ship sailing, and bicycling tours. Many of our trips are appropriate for beginners so get out and enjoy an amazing outdoor adventure with family and friends!

Antarctic Zenith Adventures

Travel with our Antarctic experts, cruise on our state-of-the-art ships, and experience Antarctica in all of its grandeur. We use ice-rated expedition ships custom designed for your comfort and safety. Each ship can carry up to 100 passengers and provides excellent viewing for watching whales, seabirds, and icebergs as well as facilities for educational presentations by our Antarctic experts. For our more adventurous clients, we offer additional activities such as snowshoeing, sea-kayaking and camping on the Antarctic ice. Plan on a shore excursion where you can view penguin rookeries, seal colonies, and places of historical and scientific interest. To carry you to the Antarctic shore, we use inflatable boats that can carry 12 to 15 people. After a thrilling day on shore, we will take you back to the ship where you can enjoy a delicious meal prepared by our gourmet chefs. Our Antarctic travel experts are naturalists, historians, and adventurers committed to providing you with a fabulous Antarctic adventure.

Zenith Adventure	Length	Price
Antarctic Exploration	7 days	$4,399
Weddell Sea Adventure	10 days	$6,899
Falkland Islands Journey	14 days	$7,699
Sailing Spectacular	14 days	$8,999

Tall-Ship Adventures

Visit exotic and spectacular locations in the South Pacific aboard the Laura Devon, a luxurious tall ship. On your tall-ship adventure, seek out the hidden Pacific by sailing the trade winds to discover the undisturbed cultures and beauty of remote islands and communities. Our tall-ship sailing adventure combines exotic exploration and timeless romance. You can sign on for the challenge of an ocean voyage with blue water sailing or a more leisurely island voyage sailing through tropical paradises. For many, tall-ship sailing is the ultimate in escapist adventuring. Sailing on the magnificent Laura Devon, combined with the sparkling beauty of the South Pacific, makes for the adventure of a lifetime.

Zenith Adventure	Length	Price
Vanuatu Exploration	10 days	$1,599
Tahiti to Cook Islands	14 days	$2,899
Fiji to Vanuatu	14 days	$2,999
Tonga to Fiji	16 days	$3,999

Bicycling Adventures

A bicycle is the perfect form of transportation for a travel adventure. Sign up for one of our bicycle tours

Use Word's special features to enhance a document with WordArt text, a drop cap, and a built-in text box. Improve the readability of a document by setting text in columns.

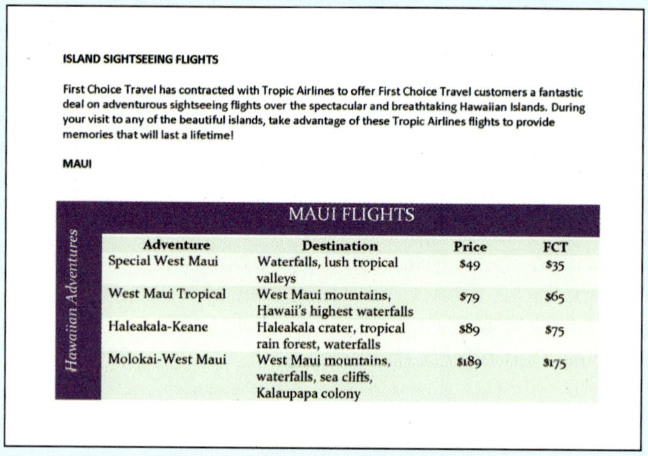

ISLAND SIGHTSEEING FLIGHTS

First Choice Travel has contracted with Tropic Airlines to offer First Choice Travel customers a fantastic deal on adventurous sightseeing flights over the spectacular and breathtaking Hawaiian Islands. During your visit to any of the beautiful islands, take advantage of these Tropic Airlines flights to provide memories that will last a lifetime!

MAUI

Hawaiian Adventures	MAUI FLIGHTS			
	Adventure	Destination	Price	FCT
	Special West Maui	Waterfalls, lush tropical valleys	$49	$35
	West Maui Tropical	West Maui mountains, Hawaii's highest waterfalls	$79	$65
	Haleakala-Keane	Haleakala crater, tropical rain forest, waterfalls	$89	$75
	Molokai-West Maui	West Maui mountains, waterfalls, sea cliffs, Kalaupapa colony	$189	$175

Insert columnar data in a table.

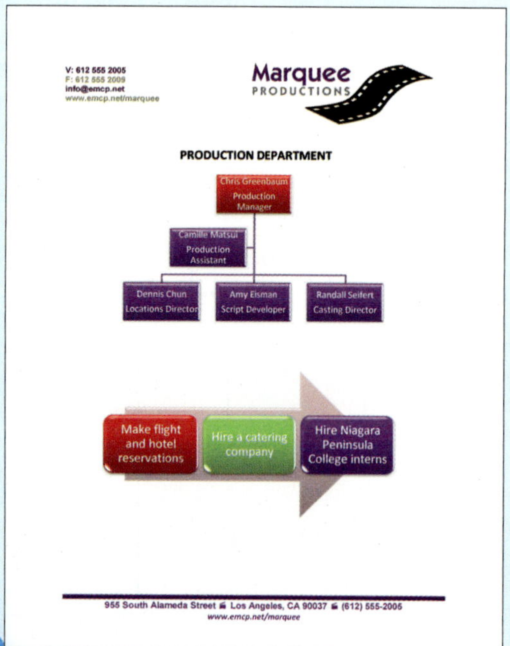

V: 612 555 2005
F: 612 555 2009
info@emcp.net
www.emcp.net/marquee

Marquee PRODUCTIONS

PRODUCTION DEPARTMENT

955 South Alameda Street ■ Los Angeles, CA 90037 ■ (612) 555-2005
www.emcp.net/marquee

Use Word's SmartArt feature to illustrate hierarchical data in an organizational chart or create a diagram for presenting a list of data; showing data processes, cycles, and relationships; and presenting data in a matrix or pyramid.

Word SECTION 1

Creating and Editing a Document

Skills

- Complete the word processing cycle
- Move the insertion point
- Insert, replace, and delete text
- Scroll and navigate in a document
- Select and delete text
- Use Undo and Redo
- Check the spelling and grammar in a document
- Use AutoCorrect
- Use Thesaurus
- Change document views
- Use the Help feature
- Preview a document
- Print a document
- Insert the date and time
- Insert a signature line
- Insert Quick Parts
- Close a document
- Create a document using a template
- Create and rename a folder
- Save a document in a different format

Student Resources

Before beginning this section:

1. Copy to your storage medium the WordS1 subfolder from the Word folder on the Student Resources CD.
2. Make WordS1 the active folder.

In addition to containing the data files needed to complete section work, the Student Resources CD contains model answers in PDF format for each of the projects in this section; model answers for end-of-section activities are not provided.

Projects Overview

First Choice TRAVEL: Prepare a document describing a special vacation package and edit and format three documents describing various vacation specials offered by First Choice Travel.

Marquee PRODUCTIONS: Prepare a letter to First Choice Travel regarding a movie site using a letter template, and prepare a letter to the manager of The Waterfront Bistro requesting catering information.

Worldwide Enterprises: Customize a sample employee incentive agreement and prepare a cover page for the agreement and a fax sheet.

Performance Threads: Edit a letter to Marquee Productions regarding costuming for a film.

The Waterfront B·I·S·T·R·O: Write a letter to Josh Hart at Marquee Productions explaining the catering services offered by The Waterfront Bistro and then prepare a fax sheet for the letter.

Niagara Peninsula COLLEGE: Prepare a student-of-the-month award certificate.

Activity 1.1

Completing the Word Processing Cycle

The process of creating a document in Microsoft Word generally follows a word processing cycle. The steps in the cycle vary but typically include: opening Word; creating and editing the document; saving, printing, and closing the document; and then exiting Word.

Project

As an employee of First Choice Travel, you have been asked to create a short document containing information on a travel package offered by First Choice Travel.

1. At the Windows desktop, click the Start button **start** on the Taskbar, point to *All Programs* at the pop-up menu, point to *Microsoft Office*, and then click *Microsoft Office Word 2007*.

   Depending on your system configuration, these steps may vary.

2. At the Word document screen, identify the various features by comparing your screen with the one shown in Figure 1.1.

   Refer to Table 1.1 for a description of the screen features.

3. Type **First Choice Travel** as shown in Figure 1.2 and then hold down the Shift key, press the Enter key, and then release the Shift key.

   Shift + Enter is the New Line command. Use this command to keep lines of text within the same paragraph, which creates less space between one line and the next.

4. Type **Los Angeles Office** and then press Shift + Enter.
5. Type **Travel Package** and then press Enter.

   Pressing the Enter key begins a new paragraph in the document.

6. Type the remainder of the text shown in Figure 1.2.

   Type the text as shown. When you type *adn* and then press the spacebar, the AutoCorrect feature will automatically correct it to *and*. When you type *teh* and then press the spacebar, AutoCorrect corrects it to *the*. Do not press the Enter key to end a line of text. Word will automatically wrap text to the next line.

FIGURE 1.1 Word Document Screen

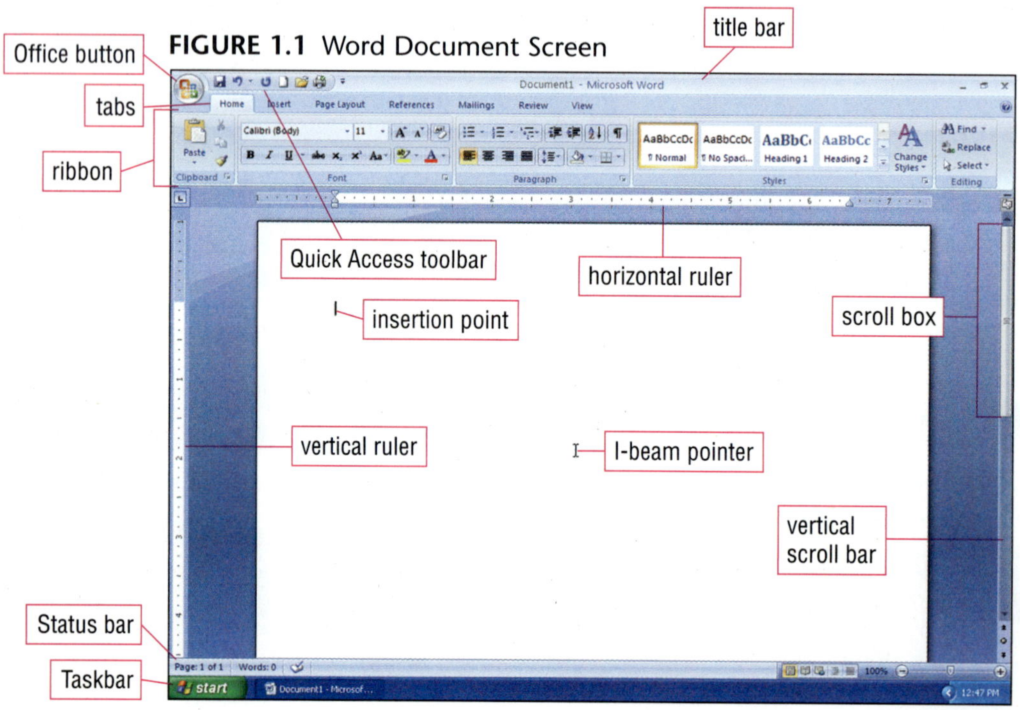

FIGURE 1.2 Steps 3–6

> First Choice Travel
> Los Angeles Office
> Travel Package
>
> Are you spontaneous adn enjoy doing something on a moment's notice? If this describes you, then you will be interested in First Choice Travel Moment's Notice Travel Package. For teh low price of $599 you can fly from New York to London for a four-day stay. The catch to this incredible deal is that you must make your reservations within the next week and complete your London stay within thirty days.

7. Save the document by clicking the Save button on the Quick Access toolbar.

8. At the Save As dialog box, make sure the WordS1 folder on your storage medium is the active folder, type **WordS1-01** in the *File name* text box, and then press Enter (or click the Save button).

   Word automatically adds the file extension *.docx* to the end of a document name. The *Save in* option at the Save As dialog box displays the active folder. If you need to make the WordS1 folder on your storage medium the active folder, click the down-pointing arrow at the right side of the *Save in* option and then click the location of your storage medium. Double-click *WordS1* in the list box.

Step 8

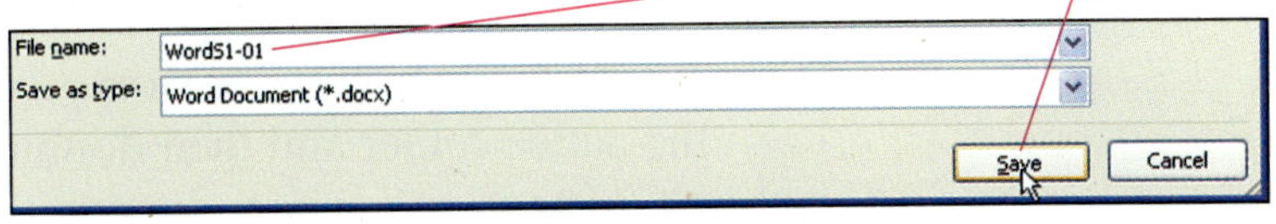

9. Print the document by clicking the Quick Print button on the Quick Access toolbar.

   If the Quick Print button does not display on the Quick Access toolbar, click the Customize Quick Access Toolbar button that displays at the right side of the toolbar and then click *Quick Print* at the drop-down list.

10. Close the document by clicking the Office button and then clicking *Close* at the drop-down list.

    The Office button displays as the Microsoft Office logo and is located in the upper left corner of the screen.

TABLE 1.1 Screen Features and Descriptions

Feature	Description
Office button	displays as a Microsoft Office logo and, when clicked, displays a list of options and most recently opened documents
Quick Access toolbar	contains buttons for commonly used commands
Title bar	displays document name followed by program name
tabs	contains commands and features organized into groups
ribbon	area containing the tabs and commands divided into groups
horizontal ruler	used to set margins, indents, and tabs
vertical ruler	used to set top and bottom margins
I-beam pointer	used to move the insertion point or to select text
insertion point	indicates location of next character entered at the keyboard
vertical scroll bar	used to view various parts of the document
Status bar	displays number of pages and words, View buttons, and Zoom slider bar

In Addition

Default Document Formatting

A Word document is based on a template that applies default formatting. Some of the default formats include 11-point Calibri as the font, line spacing of 1.15, and 10 points of spacing after each paragraph (a press of the Enter key). You will learn more about fonts and paragraph spacing in Section 2.

Correcting Errors

Word contains a spelling feature that inserts a wavy red line below words that are not contained in the Spelling dictionary. You can edit the word or leave it as written. The wavy red line does not print.

Activity 1.2

Moving the Insertion Point; Inserting, Replacing, and Deleting Text

Many documents you create will need to have changes made to them. These changes may include adding text, called ***inserting***, or removing text, called ***deleting***. To insert or delete text, move the insertion point to certain locations without erasing the text through which it passes. To insert text, position the insertion point in the desired location and then type the text. Delete text in a document by pressing the Backspace key or Delete key.

Project

First Choice TRAVEL

First Choice Travel marketing staff members have reviewed your document on vacation specials and have recommended a few changes. You need to create a revised version.

1. At the Word document screen, click the Open button on the Quick Access toolbar.

   If the Open button does not display on the Quick Access toolbar, click the Customize Quick Access Toolbar button that displays at the right side of the toolbar and then click *Open* at the drop-down list.

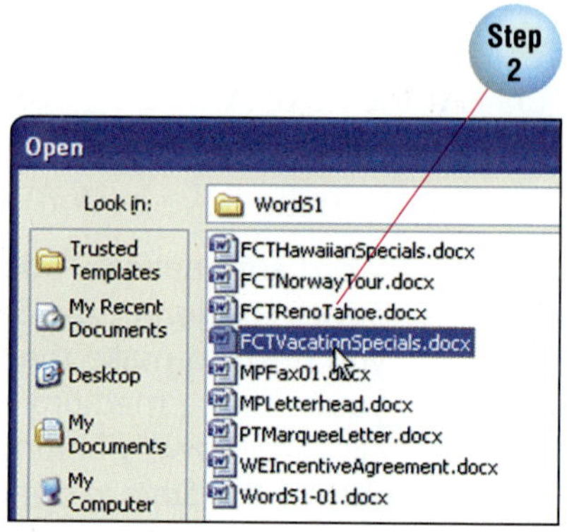

2. At the Open dialog box, make sure the WordS1 folder on your storage medium is the active folder and then double-click ***FCTVacationSpecials.docx*** in the list box.

   PROBLEM

   If the **FCTVacationSpecials.docx** document does not display in the Open dialog box, check with your instructor.

3. Click the Office button and then click *Save As*.

4. At the Save As dialog box, type **WordS1-02** in the *File name* text box and then press Enter.

   If you open an existing document, make changes to it, and then want to save it with the same name, click the Save button on the Quick Access toolbar. If you want to keep the original document and save the document with the changes with a new name, click the Office button and then click *Save As*.

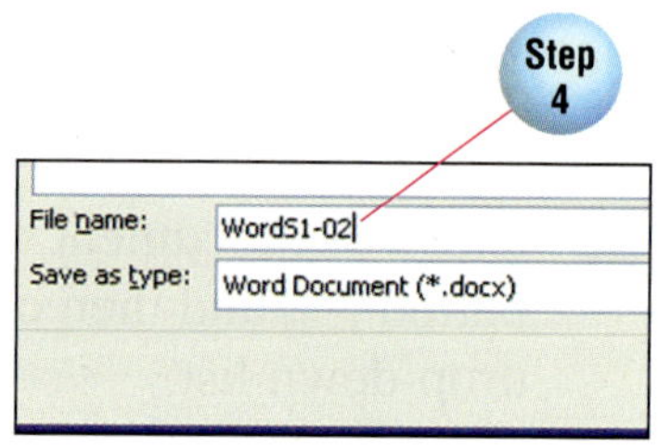

5. Position the mouse pointer at the beginning of the second paragraph and then click the left mouse button.

   This moves the insertion point to the location of the mouse pointer.

6. Press the Up, Down, Left, and Right arrow keys located to the right of the regular keys on the keyboard.

   Use the information shown in Table 1.2 to practice moving the insertion point in the document.

7 Press Ctrl + Home, click at the beginning of the paragraph that begins *Sign up today for . . .* , and then type **Ocean Vista Cruise Lines announces the inaugural voyage of the Pacific Sky ocean liner.** Press the spacebar once after typing the period.

By default, text you type in a document is inserted in the document and existing text is moved to the right.

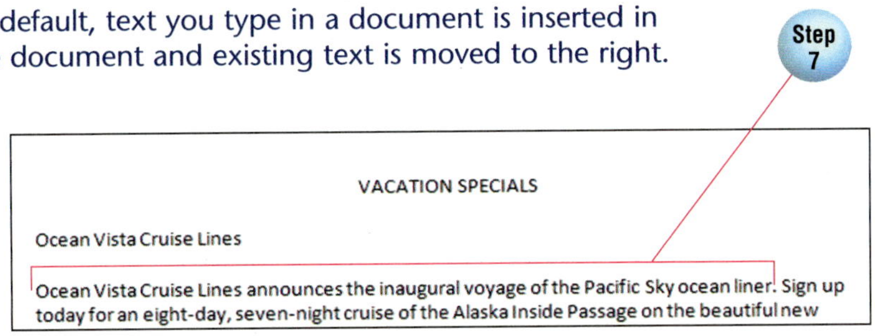
Step 7

VACATION SPECIALS

Ocean Vista Cruise Lines

Ocean Vista Cruise Lines announces the inaugural voyage of the Pacific Sky ocean liner. Sign up today for an eight-day, seven-night cruise of the Alaska Inside Passage on the beautiful new

8 Press Ctrl + End to move the insertion point to the end of the document and then click on any character in the last sentence in the document (the sentence that begins *Let First Choice Travel take . . .*).

9 Press the Backspace key until the insertion point is positioned at the left margin and then press the Delete key until you have deleted the remainder of the sentence.

Pressing the Backspace key deletes any characters left of the insertion point. Press the Delete key to delete any characters to the right of the insertion point.

10 Click the Save button on the Quick Access toolbar.

Clicking the Save button saves the document with the same name (**WordS1-02.docx**).

In Brief

Open Document
1. Click Open button on Quick Access toolbar.
2. Double-click document name.

Save Document
1. Click Save button.
2. Type document name.
3. Click Save or press Enter.

TABLE 1.2 Insertion Point Keyboard Control

Press	To move insertion point
End key	to end of line
Home key	to beginning of line
Pg Up key	up one screen
Pg Down key	down one screen
Ctrl + Home	to beginning of document
Ctrl + End	to end of document

In Addition

Using Overtype Mode

By default, text you type in a document is inserted in the document and existing text is moved to the right. If you want to type over something, you need to turn on the Overtype mode. With the Overtype mode on, anything you type will replace existing text. To turn on the Overtype mode, click the Office button and then click the Word Options button located toward the bottom of the drop-down list. At the Word Options dialog box, click *Advanced* in the left pane. In the *Editing options* section, insert a check mark in the *Use overtype mode* check box if you want the Overtype mode always on in the document. Or, insert a check mark in the *Use the Insert key to control overtype mode* check box if you want to use the Insert key to turn Overtype mode on and off. After making your selection, click the OK button located in the lower right corner of the dialog box.

Activity 1.3

Scrolling and Navigating in a Document

In addition to moving the insertion point to a specific location, you can use the mouse to move the display of text in the document screen. Use the mouse with the vertical scroll bar to scroll through text in a document. The vertical scroll bar displays toward the right side of the screen. Scrolling in a document changes the text displayed but does not move the insertion point. The Select Browse Object button located at the bottom of the vertical scroll bar contains options for browsing through a document. Scrolling in a document changes the text displayed, while browsing in a document moves the insertion point.

Project

To minimize the need for additional editing, you have decided to review carefully the First Choice Travel Vacation Specials document on the screen.

1. With **WordS1-02.docx** open, press Ctrl + Home to move the insertion point to the beginning of the document.

2. Position the mouse pointer on the down scroll arrow on the vertical scroll bar and then click the left mouse button several times.

   This scrolls down the lines of text in the document. Scrolling changes the display of text but does not move the insertion point.

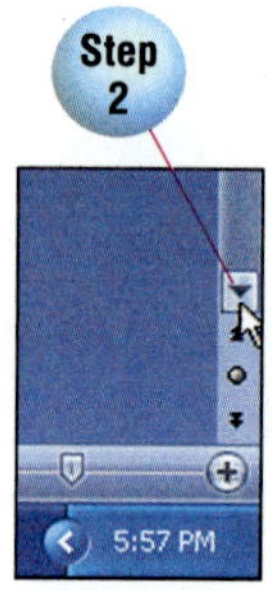

3. Position the mouse pointer on the vertical scroll bar below the scroll box and then click the left mouse button a couple of times.

   The scroll box on the vertical scroll bar indicates the location of the text in the document screen in relation to the remainder of the document. Clicking on the vertical scroll bar below the scroll box scrolls down one screen of text at a time.

4. Position the mouse pointer on the scroll box on the vertical scroll bar, hold down the left mouse button, drag the scroll box to the top of the vertical scroll bar, and then release the mouse button.

   Dragging the scroll box to the top of the vertical scroll bar displays text at the beginning of the document.

5. Click the Select Browse Object button located in the lower right corner of the screen and then click the *Go To* option.

   The location of the *Go To* option may vary. It may be the first option from the left in the top row. Position the arrow pointer on the option and the name of the option displays at the top of the palette. Use other options at the palette to browse to document features such as a field, endnote, footnote, comment, section, heading, and graphic.

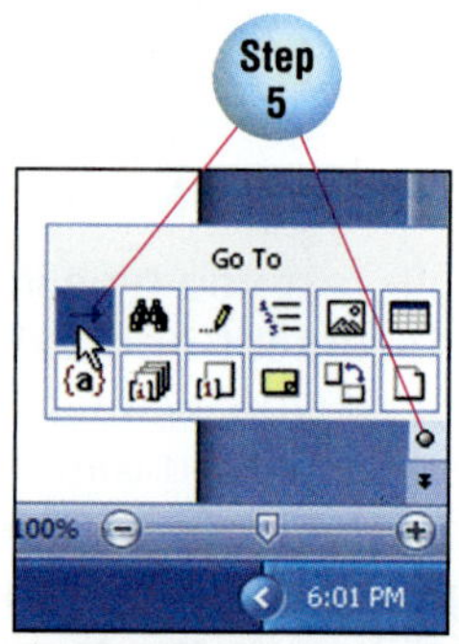

6 At the Find and Replace dialog box with the Go To tab selected, type 2 in the *Enter page number* text box, press the Enter key, and then click Close.

With options at the Find and Replace dialog box with the Go To tab selected, you can move the insertion point to various locations in a document such as a specific page, section, line, bookmark, and so on.

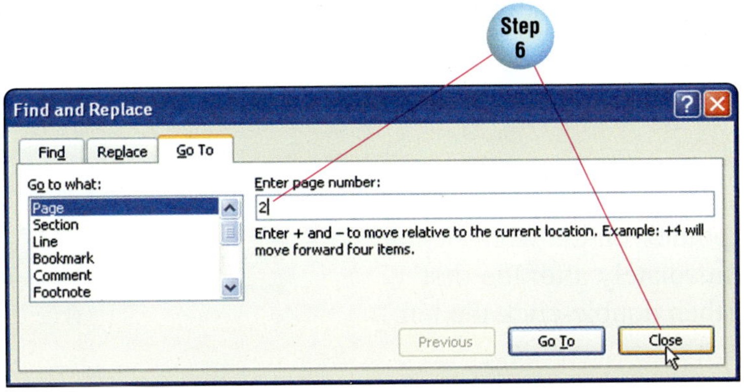

7 Click the Previous Page button located above the Select Browse Object button.

Clicking the Previous Page button moves the insertion point to the beginning of the previous page. The full names of and the tasks completed by the Previous and Next buttons vary depending on the last navigation completed.

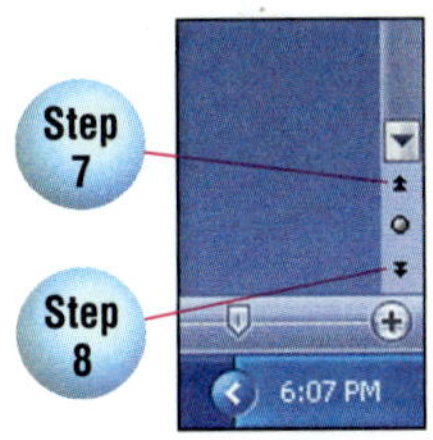

8 Click the Next Page button located below the Select Browse Object button.

9 Press Ctrl + Home to move the insertion point to the beginning of the document.

10 Save the document by clicking the Save button on the Quick Access toolbar.

In Brief

Display Find and Replace Dialog Box

1. Click Select Browse Object button.
2. Click *Go To* option.

In Addition

Option Buttons

As you insert and edit text in a document, you may notice an option button popping up in your text. The name and appearance of this option button varies depending on the action. If a word you type is corrected by AutoCorrect, if you create an automatic list, or if autoformatting is applied to text, the AutoCorrect Options button appears. Click this button to undo the specific automatic action. If you paste text in a document, the Paste Options button appears near the text. Click this button to display options for controlling the formatting of pasted text.

Activity 1.4

Selecting and Deleting Text; Using Undo and Redo

Previously, you learned to delete text by pressing the Backspace key or Delete key. You can also select text and then delete it, replace it with other text, or apply formatting to selected text. If you make a change to text, such as deleting selected text, and then change your mind, use the Undo and/or Redo buttons on the Quick Access toolbar.

Project

Assistant manager, Jordan Keyes, has reviewed the document and has asked you to make a few changes.

1. With **WordS1-02.docx** open, position the mouse pointer on the word *Behold* (located immediately after the first bullet) and then double-click the left mouse button.

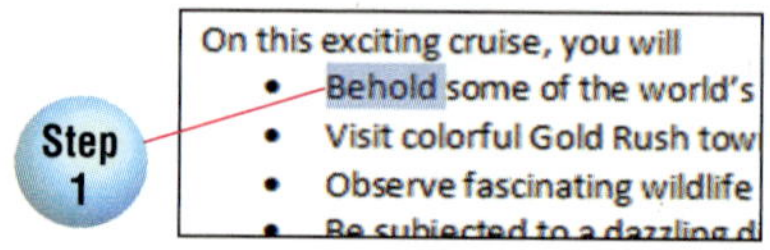

   Selected text displays with a blue background. You can also drag through text with the mouse to select the text. When you select text, a dimmed Mini toolbar displays. You will learn more about the Mini toolbar in Activity 2.1.

   PROBLEM

   If you select the wrong text and want to deselect it, click in the document outside the selected text.

2. Type **View**.

   When you type *View*, it takes the place of *Behold*.

3. Move the insertion point to the beginning of the word *Glacier* (located in the second paragraph) and then press the F8 function key on the keyboard. Press the Right Arrow key until the words *Glacier Bay and* are selected.

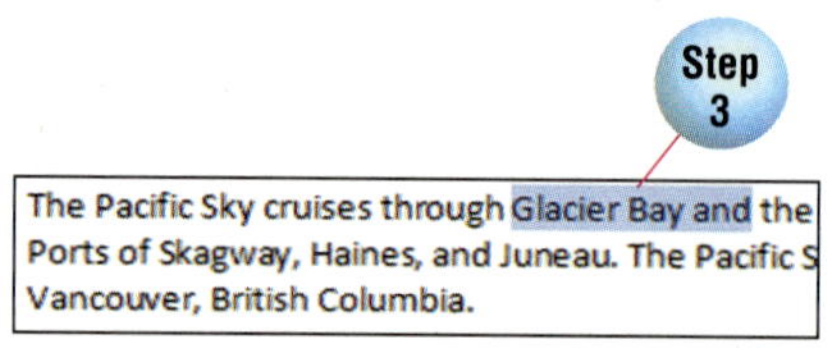

   Pressing the F8 function key turns on the Extend mode. Use the insertion point movement keys to select text in Extend mode.

4. Press the Delete key.

   Pressing the Delete key deletes the selected text. If you want to cancel a selection, press the Esc key and then press any arrow key.

5. Position the mouse pointer on any character in the first sentence that begins *Ocean Vista Cruise Lines announces . . .* , hold down the Ctrl key, click the mouse button, and then release the Ctrl key.

   Holding down the Ctrl key while clicking the mouse button selects the entire sentence.

6. Press the Delete key to delete the selected sentence.

7 Click the Undo button on the Quick Access toolbar.

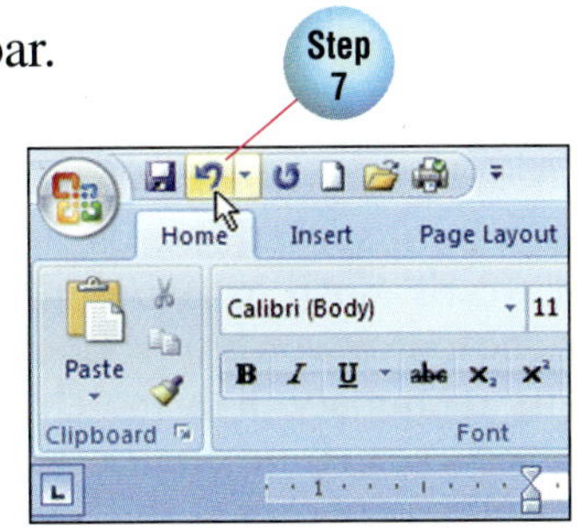

When you click the Undo button, the deleted sentence reappears. Clicking the Undo button reverses the last command or deletes the last entry you typed. Click the down-pointing arrow at the right side of the Undo button and a drop-down list displays containing changes made to the document since it was opened. Click an action and the action, along with any actions listed above it in the drop-down list, is undone.

8 Click the Redo button on the Quick Access toolbar.

Clicking the Redo button deletes the selected sentence. If you click the Undo button and then decide you do not want to reverse the original action, click the Redo button.

9 Position the mouse pointer between the left edge of the page and the first line of text in the second paragraph until the pointer turns into an arrow pointing up and to the right (instead of the left) and then click the left mouse button.

The space between the left edge of the page and the text is referred to as the selection bar. Use the selection bar to select specific amounts of text. Refer to Table 1.3 for more information on selecting text.

10 Deselect the text by clicking in the document outside the selected area.

11 Save the document by clicking the Save button on the Quick Access toolbar.

TABLE 1.3 Selecting with the Mouse

To select	Complete these steps using the mouse
a word	Double-click the word.
a line of text	Click in the selection bar to the left of the line.
multiple lines of text	Drag in the selection bar to the left of the lines.
a sentence	Hold down the Ctrl key and then click anywhere in the sentence.
a paragraph	Double-click in the selection bar next to the paragraph or triple-click anywhere in the paragraph.
multiple paragraphs	Drag in the selection bar.
an entire document	Triple-click in the selection bar.

In Addition

Undoing Multiple Actions

Word maintains actions in temporary memory. If you want to undo an action performed earlier, click the Undo button arrow. This causes a drop-down list to display. To make a selection from this drop-down list, click the desired action. Any actions listed above the selection in the drop-down list are also undone. Multiple actions must be undone in sequence.

Activity 1.5

Checking the Spelling and Grammar in a Document

Use Word's spelling checker to find and correct misspelled words and find duplicated words (such as *and and*). The spelling checker compares words in your document with words in its dictionary. If a match is found, the word is passed over. If no match is found for the word, the spelling checker stops, selects the word, and offers replacements. The grammar checker will search a document for errors in grammar, punctuation, and word usage. The spelling checker and the grammar checker can help you create a well-written document but do not replace the need for proofreading.

Project

Continuing with the editing process, you are ready to check the spelling and grammar in the First Choice Travel Vacation Specials document.

First Choice TRAVEL

1. With **WordS1-02.docx** open, press Ctrl + Home to move the insertion point to the beginning of the document.
2. Click the Review tab and then click the Spelling & Grammar button in the Proofing group.
3. When the word *inagural* is selected in the document and *inaugural* is selected in the *Suggestions* list box, click the Change button in the Spelling and Grammar dialog box.

   Refer to Table 1.4 for an explanation of the buttons in the Spelling and Grammar dialog box.

4. When the sentence that begins *Space are limited . . .* is selected, click the Explain button, read the information on subject-verb agreement that displays in the Word Help window, and then click the Close button.
5. Make sure *Space is* is selected in the *Suggestions* list box and then click the Change button.

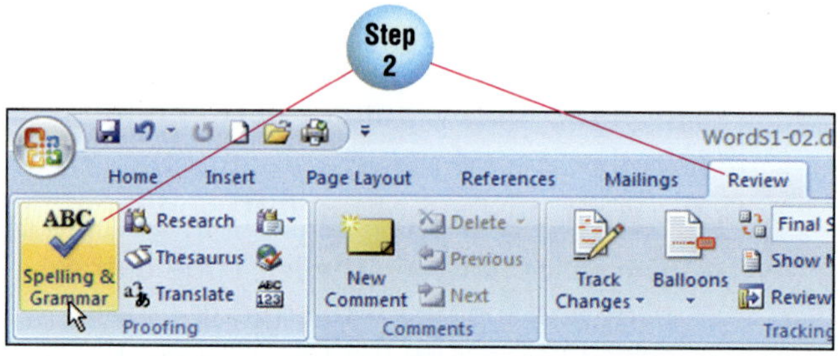

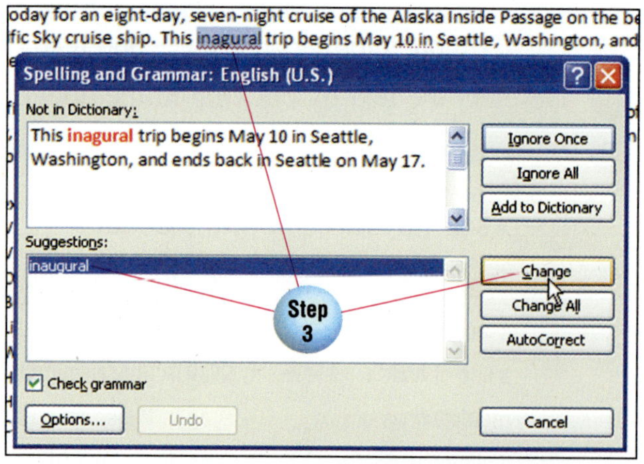

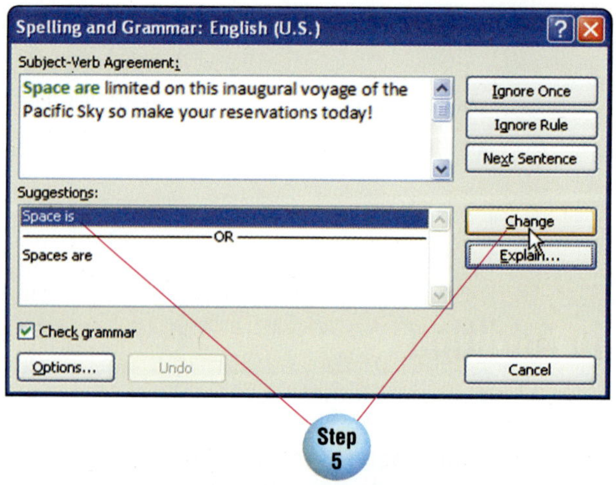

PROBLEM

If you accidentally click outside the Spelling and Grammar dialog box, click the Resume button to continue checking.

TABLE 1.4 Spelling and Grammar Dialog Box Buttons

Button	Function
Ignore Once	during spell checking, skips that occurrence of the word; in grammar checking, leaves currently selected text as written
Ignore All	during spell checking, skips that occurrence and all other occurrences of the word in the document
Ignore Rule	during grammar checking, leaves currently selected text as written and ignores the current rule for remainder of the grammar check
Add to Dictionary	adds selected word to the main spelling check dictionary
Delete	deletes the currently selected word(s)
Change	replaces selected word in sentence with selected word in *Suggestions* list box
Change All	replaces selected word in sentence with selected word in *Suggestions* list box and all other occurrences of the word
Explain	during grammar checking, displays information about the grammar rule
AutoCorrect	inserts selected word and correct spelling of word in AutoCorrect dialog box
Undo	reverses most recent spelling and grammar action
Next Sentence	accepts manual changes made to sentence and then continues grammar checking
Options	displays a dialog box with options for customizing a spelling and grammar check

In Brief

Check Spelling and Grammar

1. Click Review tab.
2. Click Spelling & Grammar button in Proofing group.
3. Ignore or change as needed.
4. Click OK.

6. When the word *the* is selected (this word is repeated twice), click the Delete button in the Spelling and Grammar dialog box.

Step 6

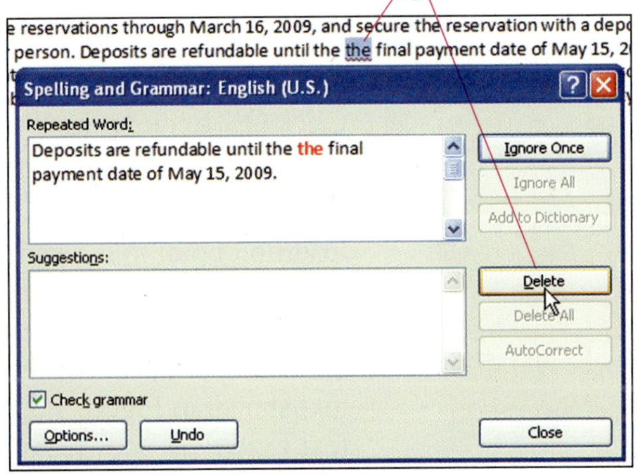

7. When the sentence that begins *You could spent the weekend* . . . is selected, click the Explain button, read the information on Verb Form, and then close the Word Help window.
8. Make sure *spend* is selected in the *Suggestions* list box and then click the Change button.
9. When the word *utah* is selected, click the Change button.
10. Click OK at the message box telling you the spelling and grammar check is complete.
11. Click the Save button on the Quick Access toolbar to save the changes made to the document.

In Addition

Changing Spelling Options

Control spelling and grammar checking options at the Word Options dialog box with the Proofing option selected. Display this dialog box by clicking the Office button and then clicking Word Options at the drop-down list. At the Word Options dialog box, click *Proofing* at the left side of the dialog box. With options in the dialog box, you can tell the spelling checker to ignore certain types of text, create custom dictionaries, show readability statistics, and hide spelling and/or grammar errors in the document.

Editing While Checking Spelling and Grammar

When checking a document, you can temporarily leave the Spelling and Grammar dialog box by clicking in the document. To resume the spelling and grammar check, click the Resume button, which was formerly the Ignore button.

Activity 1.6

Using AutoCorrect and the Thesaurus

The AutoCorrect feature automatically detects and corrects some typographical errors, misspelled words, and incorrect capitalizations. In addition to correcting errors, you can use the AutoCorrect feature to insert frequently used text. Use the Thesaurus program to find synonyms, antonyms, and related words for a particular word.

Project

First Choice TRAVEL

You need to insert additional text in the First Choice Travel vacation specials document. To speed up the process, you will add an entry to AutoCorrect. You will also use the Thesaurus program to find synonyms for specific words in the document.

1. With **WordS1-02.docx** open, click the Office button and then click the Word Options button located at the bottom of the drop-down list.
2. At the Word Options dialog box, click the *Proofing* option located at the left side of the dialog box and then click the AutoCorrect Options button in the *AutoCorrect options* section.
3. At the AutoCorrect dialog box, type **bst** in the *Replace* text box and then press the Tab key.
4. Type **Bahamas Sightseeing Tour** in the *With* text box and then click the Add button.
5. Click OK to close the AutoCorrect dialog box.
6. Click OK to close the Word Options dialog box.
7. Press Ctrl + End to move the insertion point to the end of the document, position the insertion point a double space below the last bulleted item, and then type the text shown in Figure 1.3. (Type the text exactly as shown. AutoCorrect will correct *bst* to *Bahamas Sightseeing Tour*.)

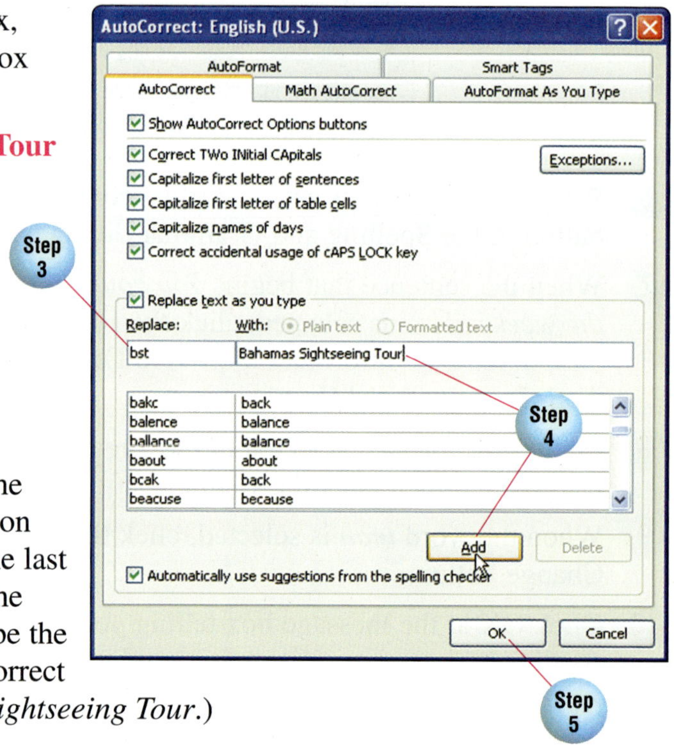

FIGURE 1.3 Step 7

bst

The Bahamas consist of over 700 islands and cays, all with friendly people, beautiful beaches, and magnificent dive spots. First Choice Travel offers the bst to explore these exciting and breathtaking islands. Sign up for the bst and experience the bustling city of Nassau, which offers everything from parasailing to casino gaming. Call us to discover how you can join the bst at an incredibly low price.

8. Click anywhere in the word *breathtaking* located in the second sentence in the paragraph you just typed, click the Review tab, and then click the Thesaurus button in the Proofing group.
9. At the Research task pane, position the mouse pointer on the word *spectacular* in the task pane list box, click the down-pointing arrow, and then click *Insert* at the drop-down list.
10. Close the Research task pane by clicking the Close button located in the upper right corner of the task pane.

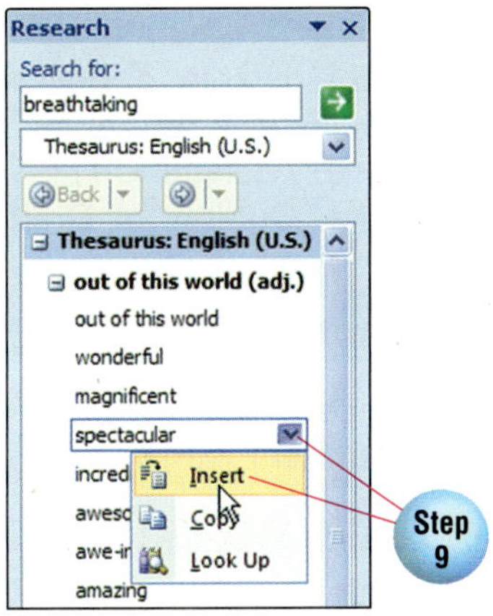

In Brief

Add AutoCorrect Entry
1. Click Office button, Word Options button.
2. Click *Proofing*.
3. Click AutoCorrect Options.
4. Type text in *Replace* text box.
5. Type text in *With* text box.
6. Click Add button.
7. Click OK.
8. Click OK.

Use Thesaurus
1. Click in desired word.
2. Click Review tab.
3. Click Thesaurus button.
4. Click down-pointing arrow at right of desired word.
5. Click *Insert*.

11. Position the mouse pointer on the word *bustling* located in the third sentence in the paragraph you just typed and then click the *right* mouse button. At the shortcut menu that displays, point to *Synonyms* and then click *lively* at the side menu.

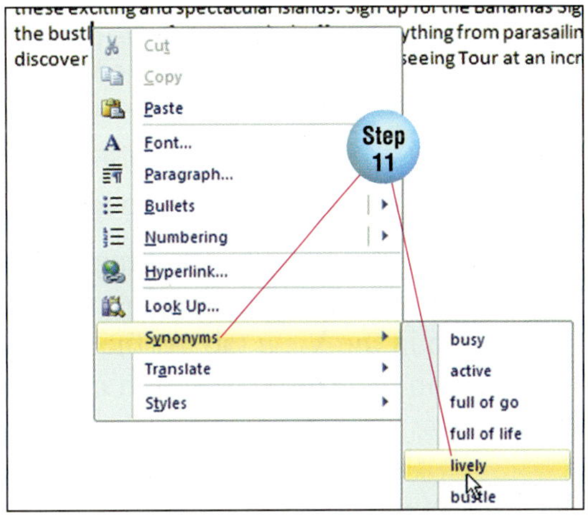

PROBLEM

If the shortcut menu does not display, check to make sure you clicked the *right* mouse button.

12. Click the Save button to save the document with the same name.
13. Click the Office button and then click the Word Options button. Make sure *Proofing* is selected at the left side of the dialog box and then click the AutoCorrect Options button.
14. At the AutoCorrect dialog box, type **bst** in the *Replace* text box.

    This selects *bst* and *Bahamas Sightseeing Tour* in the list box.
15. Click the Delete button and then click OK to close the dialog box.
16. Click OK to close the Word Options dialog box.

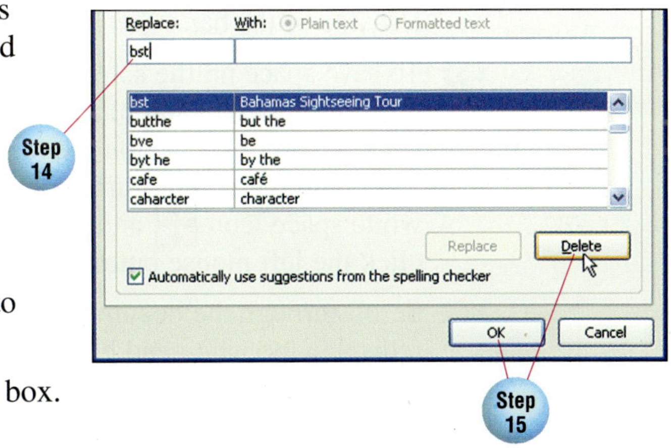

In Addition

Using the Research Task Pane

Depending on the word you are looking up, the words in the Research task pane list box may display followed by *(n.)* for *noun* or *(adj.)* for *adjective*, or *(adv.)* for *adverb*. As you look up synonyms for various words, click the Previous search button or click the Next search button to display the next search in the sequence. You can also click the down-pointing arrow at the right side of the Next search button to display a list of words for which you have looked up synonyms.

Activity 1.7

Changing Document Views

By default, a document generally displays in Print Layout view. You can change this default to Full Screen Reading, Web Layout, Outline, or Draft. You can also change the zoom percentage for viewing a document. In Print Layout view, you can show and/or hide white space at the top and bottom of each page. With the Zoom button in the View tab and the Zoom slider bar on the Status bar, you can change the percentage of display.

Project

Several people will be reviewing the First Choice Travel document on the screen so you decide to experiment with various views to determine the best view for reviewing on the screen.

First Choice TRAVEL

1. With **WordS1-02.docx** open, press Ctrl + Home to move the insertion point to the beginning of the document and then change to Draft view by clicking the View tab and then clicking the Draft button in the Document Views group.

   You can also change to the Draft view by clicking the Draft button located in the View area near the right side of the Status bar.

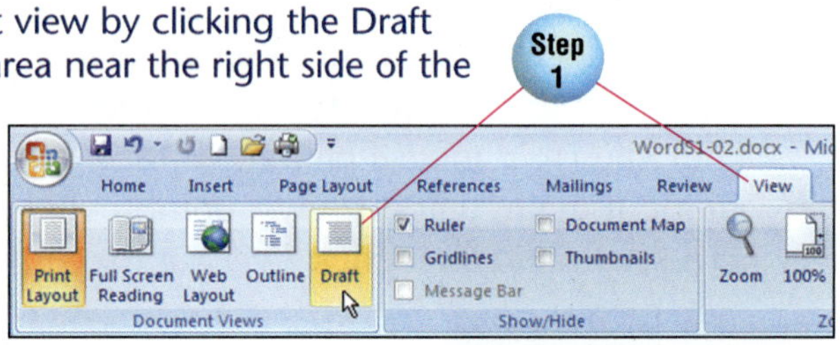

2. Click the Print Layout button in the Document Views group.
3. Change the zoom by clicking the Zoom button in the Zoom group in the View tab. At the Zoom dialog box, click *75%* in the *Zoom to* section and then click OK.

   You can also display the Zoom dialog box by clicking the percentage that displays at the left side of the Zoom slider bar.

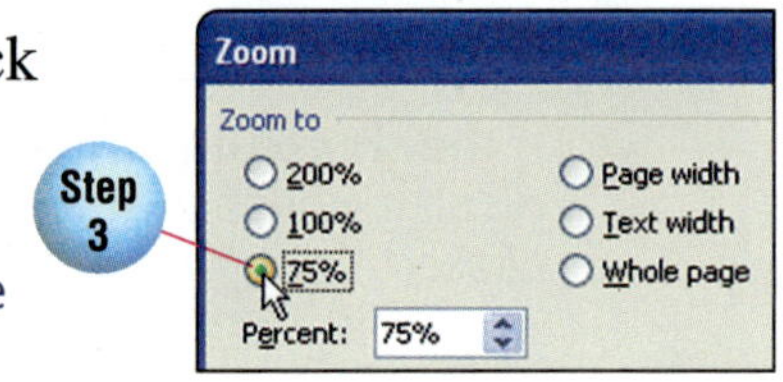

4. Return the view percentage to 100% by positioning the mouse pointer on the button on the Zoom slider bar and then dragging the button to the right until *100%* displays at the left side of the bar.

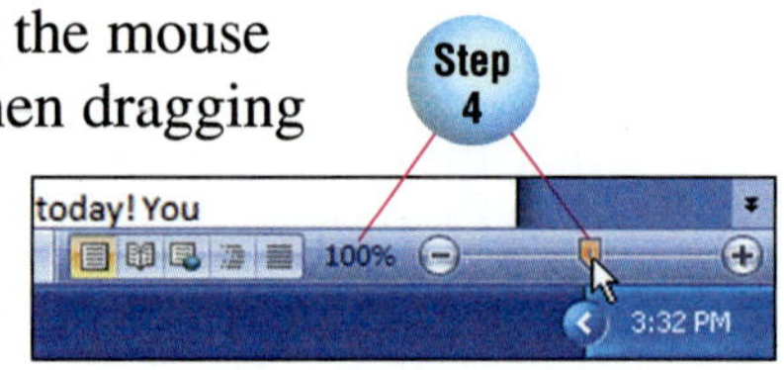

5. To save space on the screen, you decide to remove the white and blue space that displays at the top and bottom of each page. To do this, position the mouse pointer on the blue space at the top of the page until the pointer turns into the hide white space icon and then double-click the left mouse button.

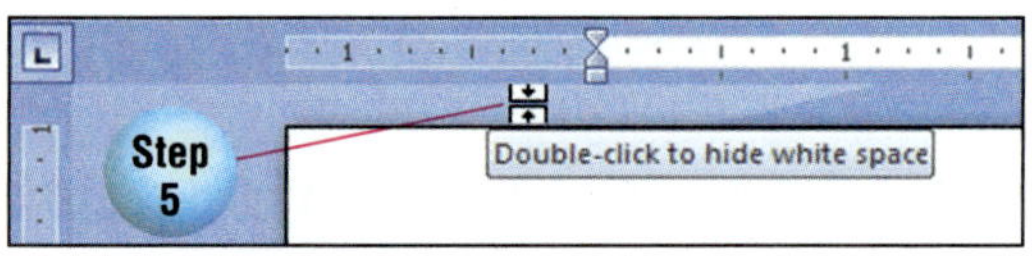

6. Scroll through the document and then redisplay the white and blue space at the top and bottom of each page. To do this, position the mouse pointer on the black line at the top of the page until the pointer turns into a show white space icon and then double-click the left mouse button.

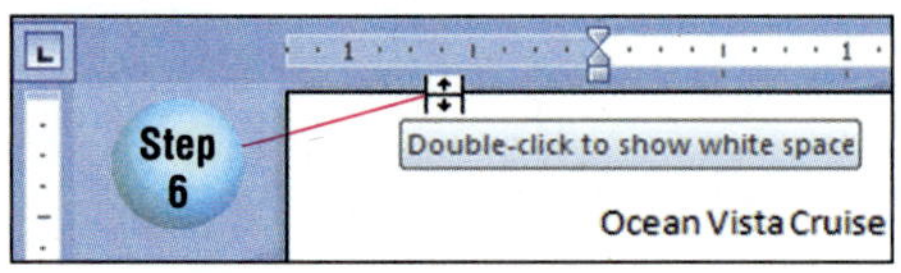

7. Click the Full Screen Reading button in the Document Views group and then navigate in the document using the commands shown in Table 1.5.

   Full Screen Reading view displays a document for easy viewing and reading. You can also display the document in Full Screen Reading view by clicking the Full Screen Reading button located in the View area on the Status bar.

8. Return to Print Layout view by clicking the Close button located in the upper right corner of the screen.
9. Click the *Document Map* check box in the Show/Hide group in the View tab.

   The navigation pane displays at the left side of the screen and displays the main headings in the document.
10. Click the *First Choice Planner* heading to display the page containing the heading.
11. Click the *Document Map* check box to remove the check mark and turn off the display of the navigation pane.
12. Press Ctrl + Home, click the *Thumbnails* check box in the Show/Hide group to display miniatures of each page in the document in the navigation pane, and then click the page 2 thumbnail.
13. Click the *Thumbnail* check box to turn off the display of the navigation pane.
14. Click the Two Pages button in the Zoom group to display two pages on the screen and then click the One Page button in the Zoom group.
15. Click the Page Width button in the Zoom group to display the document so the width of the page matches the width of the window.
16. Drag the button on the Zoom slider bar or click the Zoom Out button or Zoom In button until *100%* displays at the left side of the bar.

TABLE 1.5 Navigating in Full Screen Reading View

Press this key	To complete this action
Page Down or spacebar	Move to next page or section.
Page Up or Backspace key	Move to previous page or section.
Right Arrow	Move to next page.
Left Arrow	Move to previous page.
Home	Move to first page in document.
End	Move to last page in document.
Esc	Return to previous view.

Step 9

Step 10

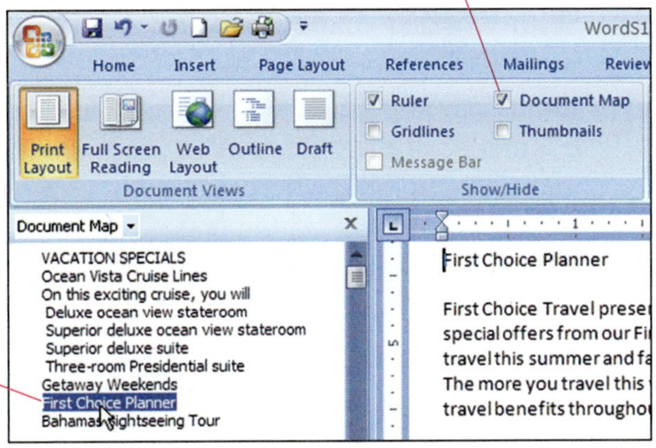

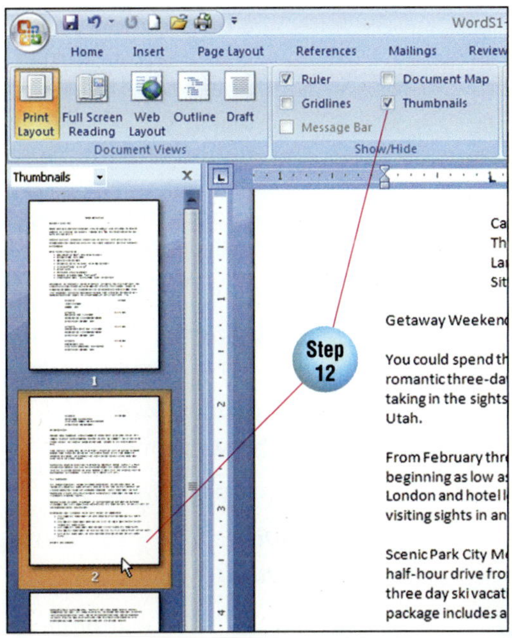

Step 12

In Brief

Display Draft View
1. Click View tab.
2. Click Draft button in Document Views group.

OR

Click Draft button in View area.

Display Full Screen Reading View
1. Click View tab.
2. Click Full Screen Reading button in Document Views group.

OR

Click Full Screen Reading button in View area.

In Addition

Hiding the Ribbon

If you want to view more of your document on the screen, you can hide the ribbon by double-clicking the active tab. The tabs remain on the screen but the groups and commands are removed. Redisplay the ribbon by clicking any tab.

Activity 1.8

Using the Help Feature; Previewing and Printing a Document

Microsoft Word includes a Help feature that contains information on Word features and commands. Click the Microsoft Office Word Help button located in the upper right corner of the screen to display the Word Help window. Before printing a document, previewing a document may be useful. Word's Print Preview feature displays the document on the screen as it will appear when printed. With this feature, you can view a partial page, single page, multiple pages, or zoom in on a particular area of a page. With options at the Print dialog box, you can specify the number of copies to print and also specific pages for printing.

Project

First Choice TRAVEL

You are ready to print certain sections of the First Choice Travel Vacation Specials document. But first you will preview the document on the screen. You decide to use the Help feature to learn about previewing and printing a document.

1. With **WordS1-02.docx** open, press Ctrl + Home to move the insertion point to the beginning of the document and then click the Microsoft Office Word Help button located in the upper right corner of the screen.

   You can also press the F1 function key to display the Word Help window. Many of the dialog boxes contain a Help button that displays with a question mark in the upper right corner of the dialog box. Click this button and the Word Help window opens with information pertinent to the dialog box.

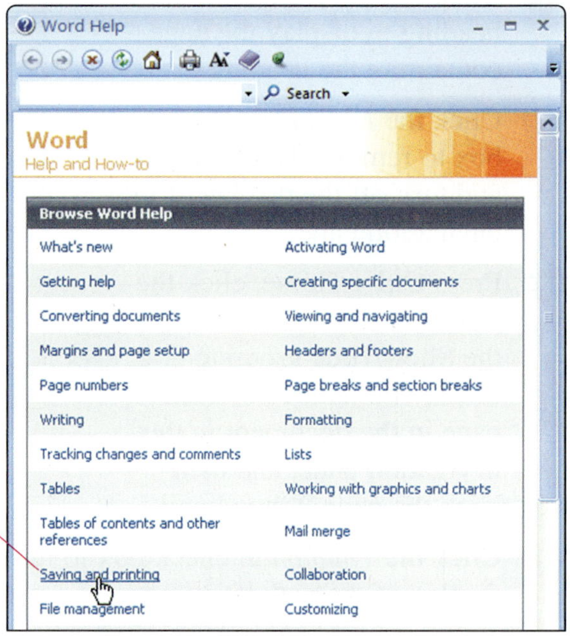

Step 2

2. At the Word Help window, click *Saving and printing* located in the first column in the *Browse Word Help* section of the window.
3. Click *Printing* in the *Subcategories of "Saving and printing"* section.

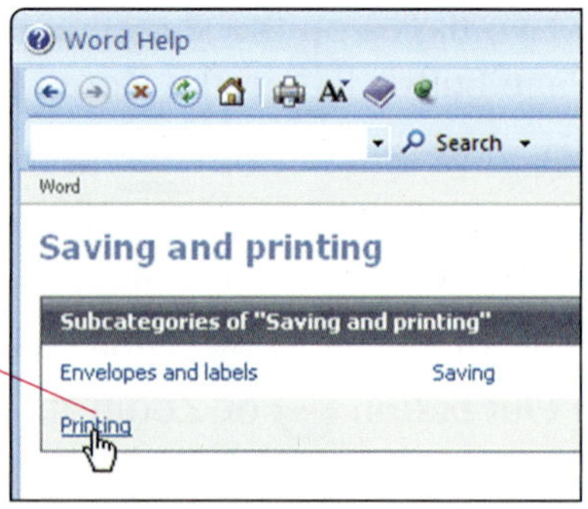

Step 3

4. Click *Preview a page before printing* in the *Printing* section.
5. Read the information that displays in the window and then click the Back button on the Word Help window toolbar.
6. Click *Print a file* located in the *Printing* list box.

7 Read the information that displays in the window and then click the Close button to close the Word Help window.

8 Click the Office button, point to *Print*, and then click *Print Preview*.

Use buttons in the Print Preview tab to customize the document and document display.

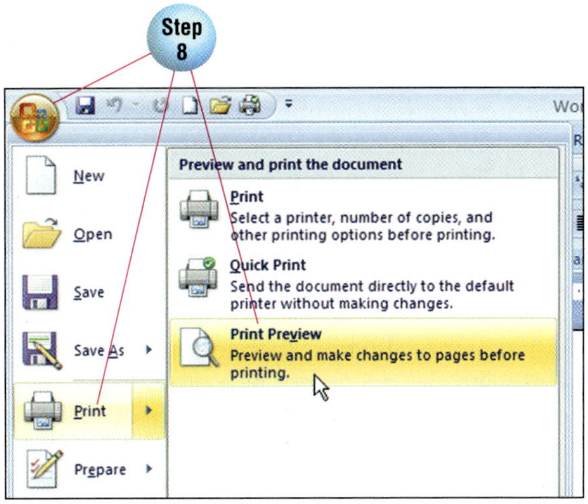

9 Click the Next Page button in the Preview group to display the next page in the document.

10 Click the Two Pages button in the Zoom group to display both pages of the document and then click the One Page button.

11 Click the Close Print Preview button.

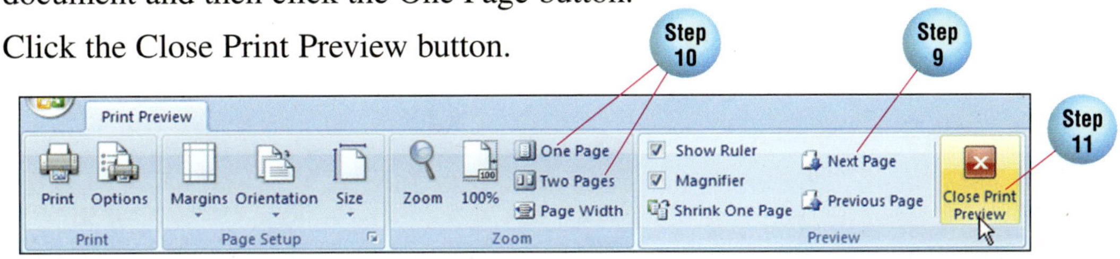

12 Print only page 2 of the document by clicking the Office button and then clicking *Print* at the drop-down list.

13 At the Print dialog box, click in the *Pages* text box in the *Page range* section and then type **2**.

14 Click OK to close the Print dialog box and send page 2 to the printer.

15 Move the insertion point to any character in page 3 and then print page 3 by clicking the Office button and then clicking *Print*.

16 At the Print dialog box, click the *Current page* option in the *Page range* section.

17 Click OK to close the Print dialog box and send page 3 to the printer.

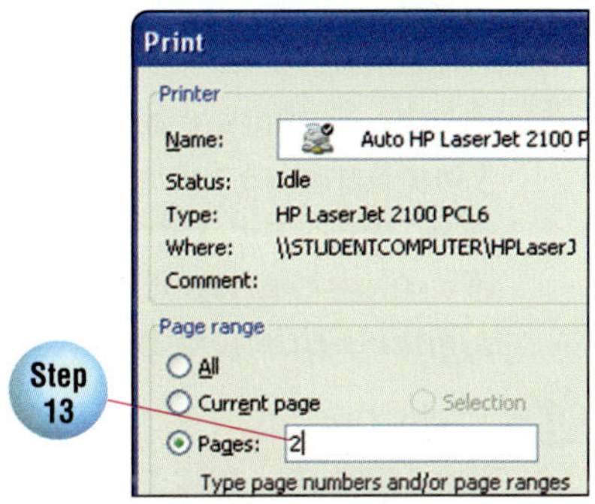

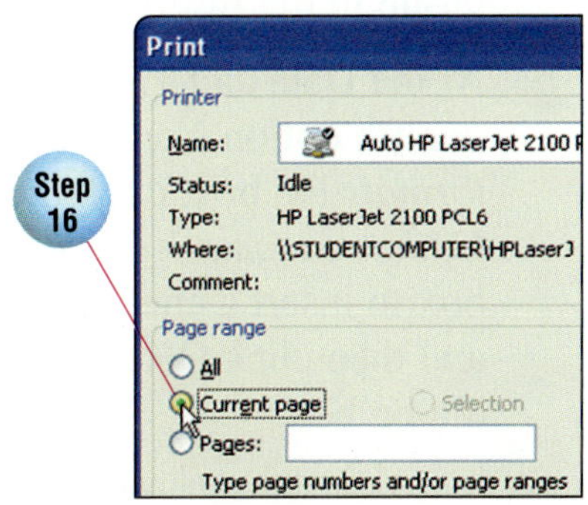

In Brief

Use Help
1. Click Microsoft Office Word Help button.
2. Click desired option in Word Help window.

Preview Document
1. Click Office button.
2. Point to right-pointing arrow at right of *Print* option.
3. Click *Print Preview*.

Print a Specific Page
1. Click Office button, *Print*.
2. Click in *Pages* text box.
3. Type page number.
4. Click OK.

Print Current Page
1. Click Office button, *Print*.
2. Click *Current page* option.
3. Click OK.

In Addition

Printing a Range of Pages

With the *Pages* option in the *Page range* section of the Print dialog box, you can identify a specific page, multiple pages, and/or a range of pages for printing. If you want specific multiple pages printed, use a comma to indicate *and* and use a hyphen to indicate *through*. For example, to print pages 2 and 5, you would type **2,5** in the *Pages* text box. To print pages 6 through 10, you would type **6-10**.

Activity 1.9

Inserting Date, Time, Signature Line, and Quick Parts

Word contains a number of features for inserting information in a document. Use the Date & Time button in the Text group in the Insert tab to insert the current date and time in a document and use the Signature Line button to insert a signature line specifying who should sign. Word also contains a Quick Parts button with options for inserting predesigned building blocks to help you build a document.

Project

To prepare for the next management team meeting, you need to complete the document by identifying the document as a draft, inserting the date and time, inserting a signature line for your name, and creating a cover sheet for the document.

1. With **WordS1-02.docx** open, press Ctrl + End to move the insertion point to the end of the document and then press the Enter key.
2. Insert a signature line by clicking the Insert tab and then clicking the Signature Line button in the Text group. (If a message displays with information about the digital signature, click the OK button.)

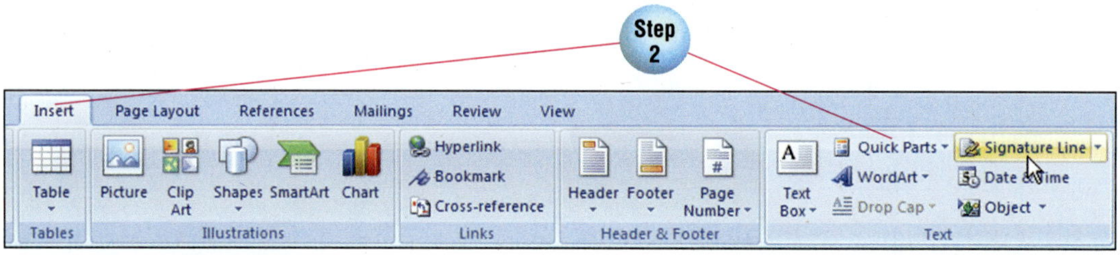

3. At the Signature Setup dialog box, type your name in the *Suggested signer* text box, press the Tab key, type **Administrative Assistant** in the *Suggested signer's title* text box, and then click OK.

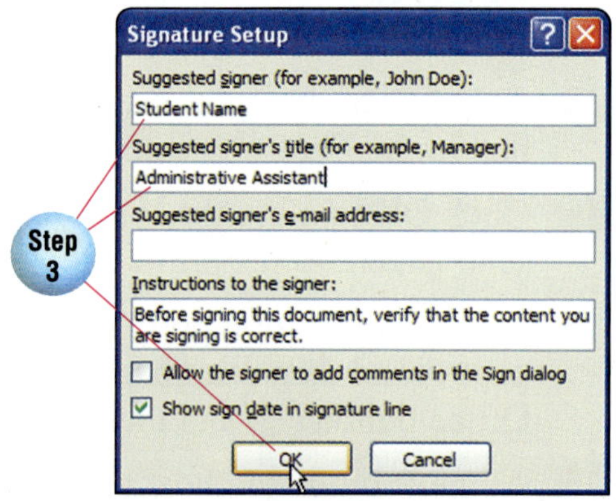

4. Press the Enter key twice and then click the Date & Time button in the Text group in the Insert tab.
5. At the Date and Time dialog box, click the twelfth option from the top in the *Available formats* list box, click the *Update automatically* check box to insert a check mark, and then click OK to close the dialog box.

   Your date will vary from what you see in the Date and Time dialog box at the right. You can use keyboard shortcuts to insert the date and time. Press Alt + Shift + T to insert the current time and press Alt + Shift + D to insert the current date.

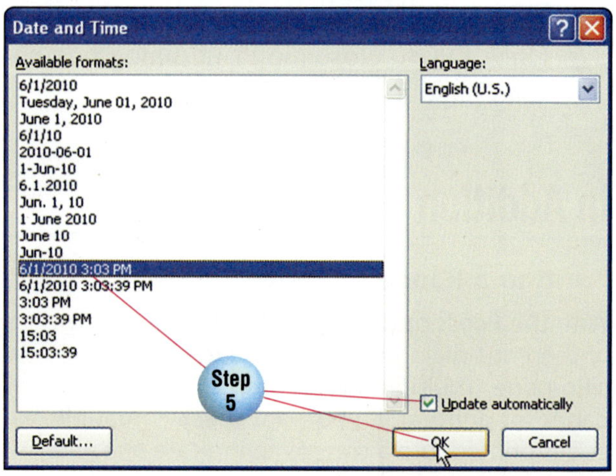

6. You want to identify the document as a draft and decide to insert a building block that displays the word *DRAFT* as a watermark (a lightened image that displays behind text). To begin, click the Quick Parts button [Quick Parts] in the Text group and then click *Building Blocks Organizer* at the drop-down list.

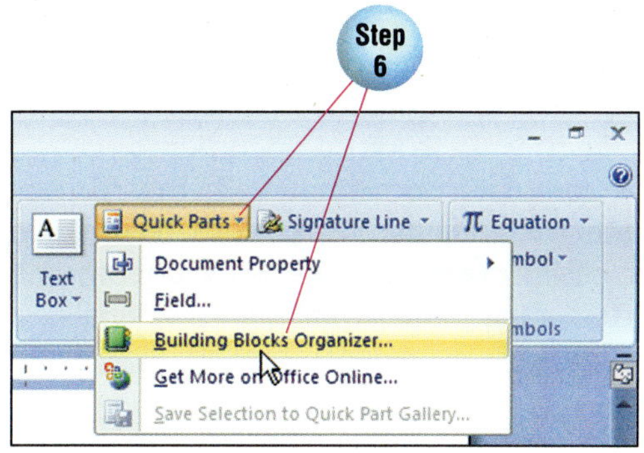

7. At the Building Blocks Organizer dialog box, scroll to the end of the list box, click *DRAFT 1* in the list box, and then click the Insert button.

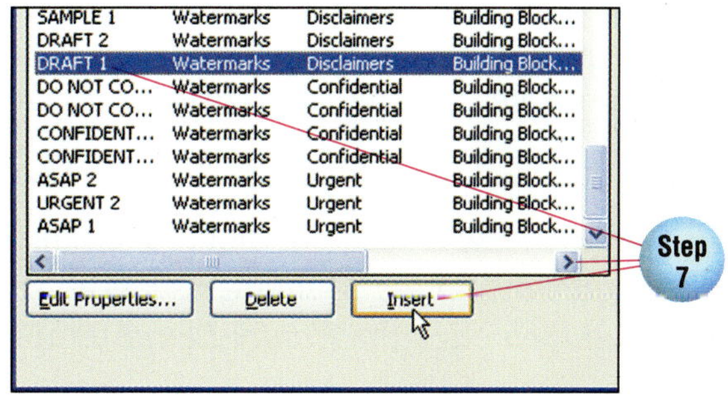

8. You need to insert a cover page for the document and decide to use a predesigned cover page. To begin, press Ctrl + Home to move the insertion point to the beginning of the document, click the Quick Parts button in the Text group, and then click *Building Blocks Organizer* at the drop-down list.

9. At the Building Blocks Organizer dialog box, click *Cubicles* in the list box and then click the Insert button.

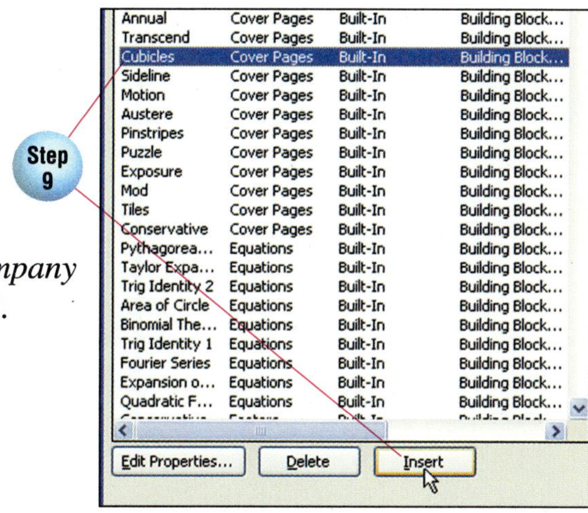

10. Click anywhere in the placeholder text *[Type the company name]* to select it and then type **First Choice Travel**.

11. Click anywhere in the placeholder text *[Type the document title]* and then type **Vacation Specials**.

12. Click anywhere in the placeholder text *[Type the document subtitle]* and then type the current year.

13. Click anywhere in the placeholder text *[Type the author name]* and then type your first and last names.

    Click a placeholder tab to select the placeholder text.

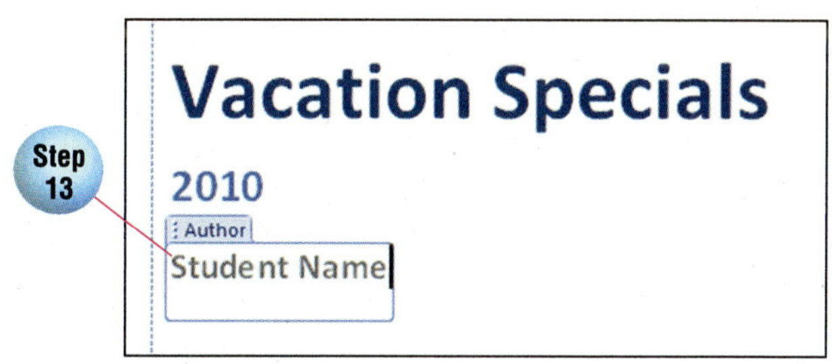

14. Click the placeholder text *[Year]* that displays toward the bottom right side of the page, click the Year tab, and then press the Delete key.

15. Press Ctrl + End to move the insertion point to the end of the document, click anywhere in the date and time text, and then press F9 to update the current time.

    You can also click the Update tab that displays above the selected date and time.

16. Click the Save button on the Quick Access toolbar and then click the Quick Print button.

17. Close the document by clicking the Office button and then clicking *Close* at the drop-down list.

In Brief

Display Signature Setup Dialog Box
1. Click Insert tab.
2. Click Signature Line button in Text group.

Display Date and Time Dialog Box
1. Click Insert tab.
2. Click Insert Date and Time button in Text group.

Display Building Blocks Organizer
1. Click Insert tab.
2. Click Quick Parts button in Text group.
3. Click *Building Blocks Organizer* option.

Activity 1.10

Creating a Document Using a Template

Word includes a number of template documents formatted for specific uses. Each Word document is based on a template document with the *Normal* template the default. With Word templates, you can easily create a variety of documents such as letters, faxes, and awards, with specialized formatting. Templates are available in the *Templates Categories* section of the New Document dialog box. You can choose an installed template or choose from a variety of templates available online. You must be connected to the Internet to download the online templates.

Project

You are the projects coordinator for Marquee Productions, a movie production company involved in all aspects of creating movies. You are a client of First Choice Travel and need to make flight and hotel reservations for personnel involved in filming a movie in and around the Toronto area. You decide to use a letter template to help you format the letter.

1. Click the Office button and then click *New* at the drop-down list.
2. At the New Document dialog box, display available templates by clicking *Installed Templates* in the *Templates* section, scroll through the list of installed templates, and then click the *Equity Letter* template.

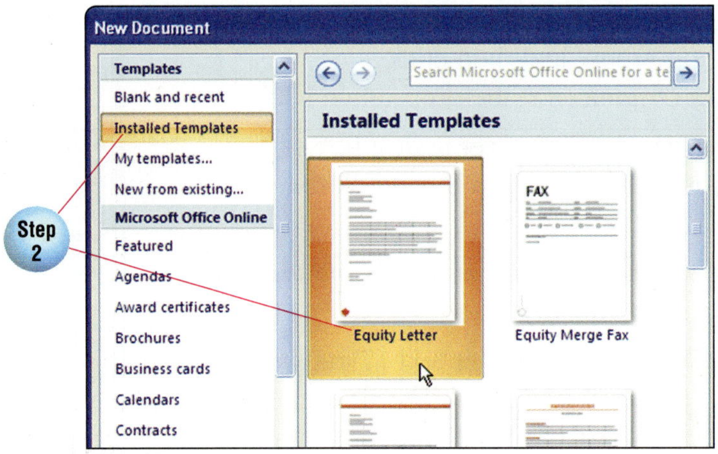

3. Click the Create button.
4. Click the placeholder text *[Pick the date]* and then type the current date. (Your date will automatically change to numbers.)
5. Select the name that displays below the date and then type your first and last names.
6. Click the placeholder text *[Type the sender company name]* and then type **Marquee Productions**.
7. Click the placeholder text *[Type the sender company address]*, type **955 South Alameda Street**, press the Enter key, and then type **Los Angeles, CA 90037**.
8. Click the placeholder text *[Type the recipient name]* and then type **Ms. Melissa Gehring**.
9. Press the Enter key and then type **First Choice Travel**.
10. Click the placeholder text *[Type the recipient address]*, type **3588 Ventura Boulevard**, press the Enter key, and then type **Los Angeles, CA 90102**.
11. Click the placeholder text *[Type the salutation]* and then type **Dear Ms. Gehring:**.

12 Click on any character in the three paragraphs of text in the body of the letter and then type the text shown in Figure 1.4.

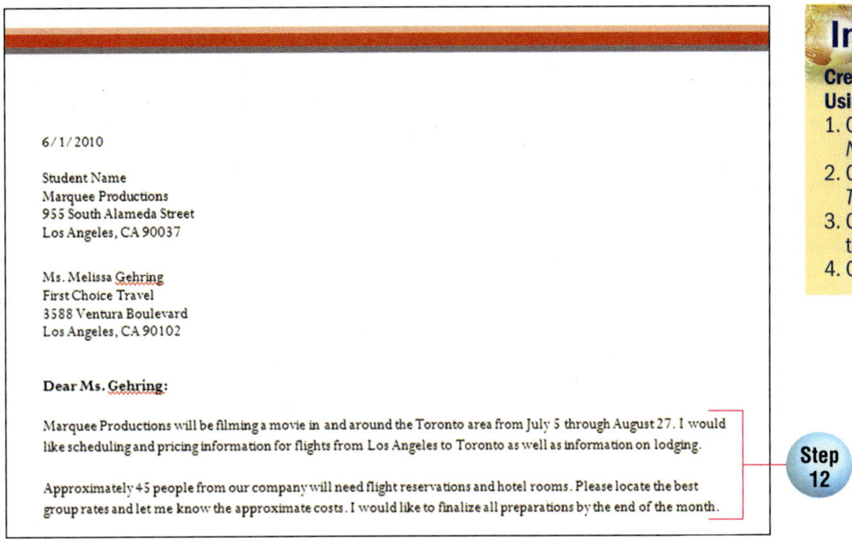
6/1/2010

Student Name
Marquee Productions
955 South Alameda Street
Los Angeles, CA 90037

Ms. Melissa Gehring
First Choice Travel
3588 Ventura Boulevard
Los Angeles, CA 90102

Dear Ms. Gehring:

Marquee Productions will be filming a movie in and around the Toronto area from July 5 through August 27. I would like scheduling and pricing information for flights from Los Angeles to Toronto as well as information on lodging.

Approximately 45 people from our company will need flight reservations and hotel rooms. Please locate the best group rates and let me know the approximate costs. I would like to finalize all preparations by the end of the month.

13 Click the placeholder text *[Type the closing]* and then type **Sincerely,**.

14 Select the current name below Sincerely and then type your first and last names.

15 Click the placeholder text *[Type the sender]* and then type **Projects Coordinator**.

16 Click the Save button on the Quick Access toolbar.

17 At the Save As dialog box, type **WordS1-03** and then press Enter.

18 Click the Quick Print button on the Quick Access toolbar.

19 Close the document by clicking the Office button and then clicking *Close* at the drop-down list.

In Brief

Create Document Using Template

1. Click Office button, *New*.
2. Click *Installed Templates*.
3. Click desired template.
4. Click Create button.

FIGURE 1.4 Step 13

Marquee Productions will be filming a movie in and around the Toronto area from July 5 through August 27. I would like scheduling and pricing information for flights from Los Angeles to Toronto as well as information on lodging.

Approximately 45 people from our company will need flight reservations and hotel rooms. Please locate the best group rates and let me know the approximate costs. I would like to finalize all preparations by the end of the month.

In Addition

Using Online Templates

If you are connected to the Internet, Microsoft offers a number of predesigned templates you can download. Templates are grouped into categories and the category names display in the *Microsoft Office Online* section of the New Document dialog box. Click the desired template category in the list box and available templates display at the right. Click the desired template and then click the Download button.

Activity 1.11

Managing Documents

As you continue working with documents, consider document management tasks such as creating a folder and copying, moving, and deleting documents. You can complete many document management tasks at the Open dialog box on one document or selected documents. By default, Word saves a file as a Word document and adds the extension *.docx* to the name. With the *Save as type* option at the Save As dialog box, you can save a document in a different format such as a Web page, a plain text file, a rich text format, or an earlier version of Word.

Project

First Choice TRAVEL

Since First Choice Travel will be communicating with Marquee Productions, you decide to create a folder into which you will insert Marquee Productions documents. You will also save a document in an older version of Word and as a plain text document.

1. Click the Open button on the Quick Access toolbar.
2. At the Open dialog box with WordS1 the active folder, click the Create New Folder button on the dialog box toolbar.

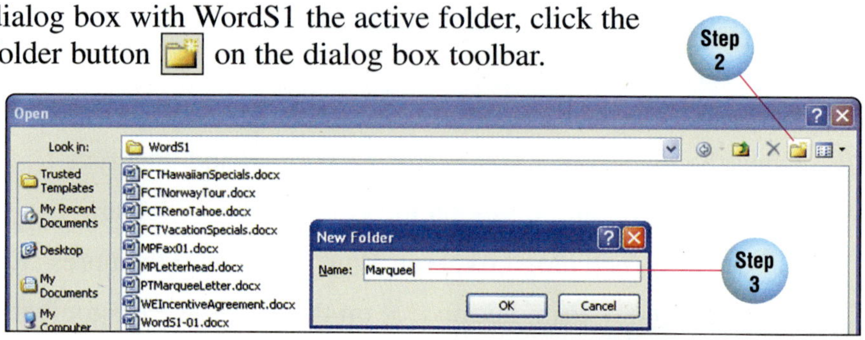

3. At the New Folder dialog box, type **Marquee** and then press Enter.

   The new folder becomes the active folder.

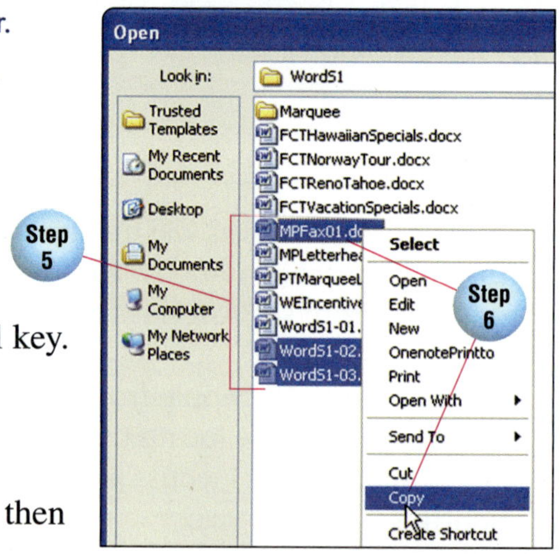

4. Click the Up One Level button on the Open dialog box toolbar to return to the previous folder.
5. Click the document ***MPFax01.docx*** in the Open dialog box list box, hold down the Ctrl key, click ***WordS1-02.docx***, click ***WordS1-03.docx***, and then release the Ctrl key.

   Use the Ctrl key to select nonadjacent documents. Use the Shift key to select adjacent documents.

6. Right-click on any selected document and then click *Copy* at the shortcut menu.
7. Double-click the *Marquee* file folder.

   File folders display in the Open dialog box list box before documents. File folders display preceded by a file folder icon and documents display preceded by a document icon.

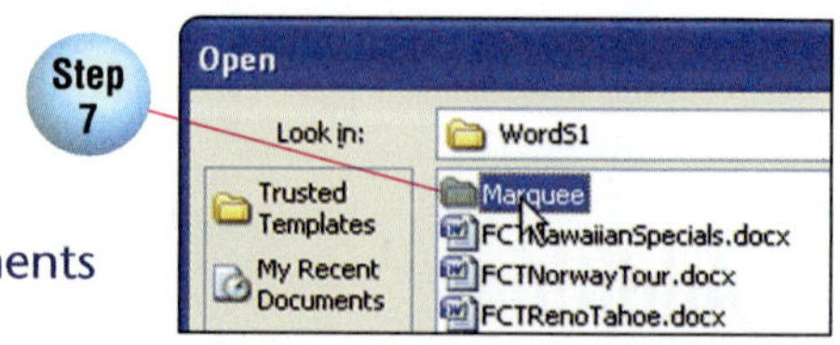

8. Position the mouse pointer in a white portion of the Open dialog box list box, click the *right* mouse button, and then click *Paste* at the shortcut menu.

   The copied documents are inserted in the Marquee folder.

9 You need to send the **WordS1-02.docx** document to a colleague that uses Word 2003, so you need to save the document in that format. At the Open dialog box with the Marquee folder active, double-click ***WordS1-02.docx***.

10 Click the Office button and then *Save As*. At the Save As dialog box, type **WordS1-02Wd2003** in the *File name* text box.

11 Click the down-pointing arrow at the right side of the *Save as type* list box and then click *Word 97-2003 Document (*.doc)*.

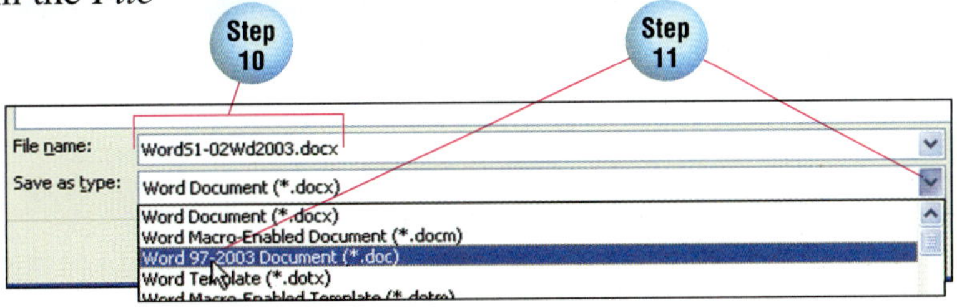

You can also save a document in Word 2003 format by clicking the Office button, pointing to the Save As option, and then clicking *Word 97-2003 Document*.

12 Click the Save button located in the lower right corner of the dialog box and then close the document.

If a compatibility checker message displays, click the Continue button.

13 Display the Open dialog box and then click the Up One Level button on the dialog box toolbar.

14 Rename the Marquee folder. To do this, right-click on the folder name and then click *Rename* at the shortcut menu. Type **MarqueeProductions** and then press Enter.

The new folder name replaces the original folder name. You can also rename a folder by clicking the Tools button, clicking *Rename*, and then typing the new folder name.

15 Delete the MarqueeProductions folder by clicking once on the folder to select it and then clicking the Delete button on the dialog box toolbar. At the message asking if you are sure you want to delete the folder and all its contents, click the Yes button.

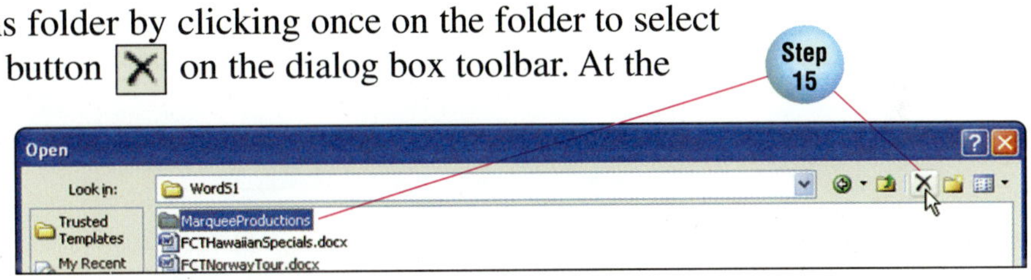

16 Close the Open dialog box.

17 Exit Word by clicking the Close button located in the upper right corner of the screen.

You can also exit Word by clicking the Office button and then clicking the Exit Word button.

In Brief

Create Folder

1. Click Open button on Quick Access toolbar.
2. Click Create New Folder button.
3. Type folder name.
4. Press Enter.

Save Document in Different Format

1. Open document.
2. Click Office button, *Save As*.
3. Type document name.
4. Change *Save as type* option to desired format.
5. Click Save button.

In Addition

Saving a Document for Viewing but Not Editing

If you want to send a document to someone so they can view it but not edit it, consider saving the document in the PDF or XPS file format or as a Web page. Documents saved in the PDF and XPS file formats can be viewed in a variety of software and these formats preserve the page layout of the document. Save a document as a Web page and the document can be viewed in a Web browser. This format, however, does not preserve the page layout of the document.

Features Summary

Feature	Ribbon Tab, Group	Button	Quick Access Toolbar	Office Button Drop-down List	Keyboard Shortcut
AutoCorrect dialog box				Word Options, Proofing, AutoCorrect Options	
close				Close	Ctrl + F4
date	Insert, Text				Shift + Alt + D
Document Map	View, Show/Hide	Document Map			
Draft view	View, Document Views				
exit Word				Exit Word	
Full Screen Reading view	View, Document Views				
Help					F1
new document				New, Blank document	Ctrl + N
New Document dialog box				New	
open				Open	Ctrl + O
Print dialog box				Print	Ctrl + P
print document					
Print Layout view	View, Document Views				
Print Preview				Print, Print Preview	
Quick Parts	Insert, Text	Quick Parts			
redo an action					
Save As dialog box				Save As	F12
save document					Ctrl + S
signature line	Insert, Text				
Spelling & Grammar	Review, Proofing				F7
Thesaurus	Review, Proofing	Thesaurus			Shift + F7
thumbnails	View, Show/Hide	Thumbnails			
time	Insert, Text				Shift + Alt + T

continues

Feature	Ribbon Tab, Group	Button	Quick Access Toolbar	Office Button Drop-down List	Keyboard Shortcut
undo an action					
Word Options dialog box				Word Options	

Knowledge Check

Completion: In the space provided at the right, indicate the correct term, command, or option.

1. This button displays as a Microsoft Office logo. ______________
2. This toolbar contains buttons for commonly used commands. ______________
3. This area on the screen contains tabs and commands divided into groups. ______________
4. Use this keyboard command to move the insertion point to the beginning of the document. ______________
5. To select a sentence, hold down this key and then click anywhere in the sentence. ______________
6. To begin checking the spelling and grammar in a document, click this tab and then click the Spelling & Grammar button in the Proofing group. ______________
7. This feature automatically detects and corrects some typographical errors. ______________
8. Use this feature to find synonyms for a word. ______________
9. Display a document in this view for easy viewing and reading. ______________
10. The Print Layout button is located in this group in the View tab. ______________
11. Display the Signature Setup dialog box by clicking this tab and then clicking the Signature Line button in the Text group. ______________
12. Predesigned cover pages and watermarks are located in this dialog box. ______________
13. Available templates display in this dialog box. ______________
14. Click this button on the Open dialog box toolbar to display the New Folder dialog box. ______________
15. Select nonadjacent documents at the Open dialog box by holding down this key while clicking each document. ______________

Skills Review

Review 1 Formatting a Hawaiian Specials Document

1. Open **FCTHawaiianSpecials.docx** and then save the document with the name **WordS1-R1**.
2. Insert the word *spectacular* between the words *the* and *Pacific* in the first sentence below the White Sands Charters heading.
3. Move the insertion point to the beginning of the paragraph below the *Air Adventures* heading and then type the sentence **Experience beautiful coastlines, magnificent waterfalls, and fly inside an active volcano.**
4. Select and then delete the words *Depending on weather, marine conditions, and access, your* located in the third sentence in the paragraph below the *White Sands Charters* heading.
5. Capitalize the *g* in *guides*. (This word now begins the sentence.)
6. Select and then delete the last sentence in the *Air Adventures* section (the sentence that begins *Chart untouched areas from . . .*).
7. Undo the deletion and then redo the deletion.
8. Select and then delete the fourth bulleted item in the *Bicycle Safari* section (the text that reads *Vista dining*).
9. Undo the deletion and then deselect the text.
10. Move the insertion point to the beginning of the document and then complete a spelling and grammar check on the document. (*Molokini* is spelled correctly.)
11. Display the AutoCorrect dialog box, insert *HA* in the *Replace* text box, insert *Hawaiian* in the *With* text box, click the Add button, and then close the dialog box. Close the Word Options dialog box.
12. Move the insertion point to the end of the document and then type the text shown in Figure 1.5.
13. After typing the text, use Thesaurus to change *lavish* to *sumptuous* and change *exceptional* to *extraordinary*.
14. Move the insertion point to the end of the document, press the Enter key twice, and then insert the current date. (You choose the format.)
15. Press the Enter key and then insert the current time. (You choose the format.)
16. Save, print, and then close **WordS1-R1.docx**.

FIGURE 1.5 Review 1

> Luau Legends
>
> Enjoy a spectacular HA dinner show featuring lavish prime rib and authentic HA buffet. This uniquely HA experience includes a traditional lei greeting, exceptional food and beverages, magic music of the islands, and Hawaii's finest performers. Join us each evening beginning at 7:30 p.m. for an evening of delicious HA food and spectacular performances.

Review 2 Customizing a Sample Agreement and Preparing a Cover Page

1. Open **WEIncentiveAgreement.docx** and then save the document with the name **WordS1-R2**.
2. Complete a spelling and grammar check on the document.
3. Move the insertion point to the end of the document and then insert a signature line using options at the Signature Setup dialog box. Insert the word *Employee* in the signer's text box and leave the signer's title text box empty.
4. Move the insertion point a double space below the signature line and then insert another signature line using options at the Signature Setup dialog box. Insert the word *Company* in the signer's text box and leave the signer's title text box empty.
5. Move the insertion point to the beginning of the document and then insert the word *SAMPLE* in the document as a watermark using an option at the Building Blocks Organizer dialog box.
6. Display the Building Blocks Organizer dialog box, click the *Stacks* cover page in the list box, and then click the Insert button.
7. At the cover page, type the following text in the identified placeholder:
   - [Type the document title] = Retention Incentive Agreement
   - [Type the document subtitle] = Worldwide Enterprises
   - [Type the author name] = (your first and last names)
8. Save, print, and then close **WordS1-R2.docx**.

Review 3 Preparing a Fax Sheet

1. At a blank screen, display the New Document dialog box, click *Installed Templates* in the *Templates* section, click *Equity Fax* in the *Installed Templates* list box, and then click the Create button.
2. Insert the following information in the specified location:
   - To: Scott Drysdale
   - From: (Type your first and last names)
   - Fax: (213) 555-3349
   - Pages: 3
   - Phone: (213) 555-3400
   - Date: (Insert current date)
   - Re: Incentive Agreement
   - cc: (Delete this placeholder)
   - Insert a capital X in the *Please Reply* check box.
   - Type the following comment: **Please review the sample Employee Incentive Agreement and then call me so we can schedule an appointment.**
3. Save the document and name it **WordS1-R3**.
4. Print and then close **WordS1-R3.docx**.

Skills Assessment

Assessment 1 Editing a Letter

1. Open **PTMarqueeLetter.docx** and then save the document with the name **WordS1-A1**.
2. Move the insertion point a double space below the paragraph of text in the letter and then add the following information. (Write the information in paragraph form—do not use bullets.)
   - Costume research takes approximately two to three weeks.
   - If appropriate costumes cannot be found, costumes are sewn.
   - Anticipate five working days to sew a costume.
   - Include the number of costumes and approximate sizes.
   - A price estimate will be provided before costumes are purchased or sewn.
3. Use Thesaurus to replace *regarding* in the first sentence in the letter with an appropriate synonym.
4. Save, print, and then close **WordS1-A1.docx**.

Assessment 2 Writing a Letter

1. Open the Median Letter template from the New Document dialog box and then use the following information to create the letter. (You determine the salutation and closing.)

   Sender's information:

   The Waterfront Bistro
3104 Rivermist Drive
Buffalo, NY 14280

   Recipient's information:

   Mr. Josh Hart, Locations Director
Marquee Productions
955 South Alameda Street
Los Angeles, CA 90037

   Write a letter as Dana Hirsch that covers these points:

   Explain that The Waterfront Bistro is a full-service catering company with a number of menus for breakfast, lunch, and dinner as well as morning and afternoon snacks. Include the price ranges for breakfast, lunch, dinner, and snack menus. (You determine the ranges.) You will offer a discount of 5% on all meals if you cater for the duration of the filming. Tell Mr. Hart that you would like to fax a variety of menu options to him. Close the letter by telling him you are very interested in the business and say something positive about your catering service.
2. Save the completed letter document and name it **WordS1-A2**. Print and then close the document.

Assessment 3 Preparing a Fax

1. Open the Equity Fax template from the New Document dialog box and then insert the necessary information in the specified fields. You are Dana Hirsch and you are sending the fax to Josh Hart (see information in Assessment 2). His fax number is (612) 555-2009 and his telephone number is (612) 555-2005. Insert an x in the *Please Comment* check box and indicate that the fax contains 11 pages.
2. Save the fax document and name it **WordS1-A3**. Print and then close the document.

Assessment 4 Finding Information on Changing Grammar Checking Options

1. Display Help information on spelling and grammar by displaying the Word Options dialog box (click Office button, Word Options), clicking *Proofing*, and then clicking the Help button (contains a question mark) located in the upper right corner of the dialog box. Read the information on spelling and grammar checking. Learn how to change the writing style from *Grammar Only* to *Grammar & Style*.
2. After reading the information, open **FCTNorwayTour.docx** and then save the document with the name **WordS1-A4**.
3. Change the writing style to *Grammar & Style*.
4. Complete a spelling and grammar check on the document. (*Myrdal* is spelled correctly.)
5. Change the *Writing style* option back to *Grammar Only*.
6. Save, print, and then close **WordS1-A4.docx**.

Assessment 5 Using an Online Template

1. Make sure you are connected to the Internet and then display the New Document dialog box, click the *Award certificates* option in the *Microsoft Office Online* list, and then download an award certificate for student of the month. (If the *Award certificates* option is not available, choose a similar certificate.)
2. Identify yourself as the student of the month and Niagara Peninsula College as the school. (Depending on the award certificate template you download, the college name may wrap within the text box. If this occurs, use the Help feature to learn how to resize a text box. Using the information you learn from the Help feature, resize the text box containing the college name so the name remains on one line.)
3. Save the certificate document and name it **WordS1-A5**. Print and then close the document.

Marquee Challenge

Challenge 1 Preparing a Business Letter

1. Open **MPLetterhead.docx** and then save the document with the name **WordS1-C1**.
2. Create the letter shown in Figure 1.6.
3. Save, print, and then close **WordS1-C1.docx**.

Challenge 2 Editing and Formatting a Travel Document

1. Open **FCTRenoTahoe.docx** and then save the document with the name **WordS1-C2**.
2. Edit and format the document so it displays as shown in Figure 1.7. Use the quick parts building block named *Conservative Quote* to create the quote that displays in the middle of the page and use *Accent Bar 2* to create the page number that displays at the bottom of the page.
3. Save, print, and then close **WordS1-C2.docx**.

FIGURE 1.6 Challenge 1

V: 612 555 2005
F: 612 555 2009
info@emcp.net
www.emcp.net/marquee

Marquee
PRODUCTIONS

(Current date)

Ms. Dana Hirsch
The Waterfront Bistro
3104 Rivermist Drive
Buffalo, NY 14280

Dear Ms. Hirsch:

We will be filming a movie in and around Toronto and Buffalo from July 5 to August 27, 2010. During that time, we will require catering services for cast and crew members. The services we request include breakfast, mid-morning snack, lunch, and afternoon snack for each day of filming, including weekends.

Please send information on your breakfast and lunch catering menus and snack choices. We are interested in pricing for meals and snacks for approximately 45 people for the duration of the filming. If you have any questions about our catering needs, please contact me by telephone at (612) 555-2005 or e-mail at JoshH@emcp.net.

Sincerely,

Josh Hart
Locations Director

SN

955 South Alameda Street Los Angeles, CA 90037

FIGURE 1.7 Challenge 2

VACATIONING IN RENO AND LAKE TAHOE

Reno and Lake Tahoe are home to more snow, more ski resorts, and more nightlife than any other ski destination in North America. Come visit our area and experience a vast diversity of ski terrain, scenic beauty, and entertainment options. Getting to Reno and Lake Tahoe is as easy as taking one of over 250 flights that arrive daily at the Reno/Tahoe International Airport. Getting to your accommodations can be as quick as a ten-minute shuttle ride to a hotel casino in Reno or less than a scenic hour through the Sierra foothills to a variety of Lake Tahoe properties. All of the ski slopes are between 45 to 90 minutes from the Reno Airport. Getting around is easy with a variety of transportation options.

Destinations

Convenience and great locations make Incline Village and Crystal Bay desirable destinations at Lake Tahoe. Situated between Squaw Valley and Heavenly Ski Resorts, the two villages, along with other great resorts such as Mt. Rose and Diamond Peak, are just minutes away. Just 30 miles from Reno/Tahoe International Airport, the villages are central to all of the Lake Tahoe ski resorts. Diamond Peak offers 2,000 acres of classic Nordic terrain, over 35 kilometers of groomed track, and skating lanes with incredible views of Lake Tahoe. The resort also boasts a 6.2 million dollar complex including an eight-lane indoor swimming pool, cardiovascular and strength-training center, aerobic studio, and gym. Additional recreational offerings include sledding, sleigh rides, snowshoeing, bowling, and a movie theater.

"Come visit our area and experience a vast diversity of ski terrain, scenic beauty, and entertainment options."

North Lake Tahoe is a favored destination for discriminating vacationers. Visit this beautiful area for the epic powder, seven resorts, downhill and cross-country skiing, and unlimited dining choices all for affordable prices. Consider trying ice-skating at the world's highest ice rink, snowmobiling and snowshoeing in the backcountry, or touring Lake Tahoe on an authentic paddle wheeler. Visit one of 80 restaurants boasting award-winning cuisine in lakeshore and alpine settings. Visit the historic town of Truckee, an old railroad and logging community with quaint shops and sights.

Lake Tahoe South Shore is the ideal destination for variety with an amazing selection of skiing for all skill levels. Almost endless lodging possibilities await you with over 95 luxurious hotels and casinos, all-suite resorts, motels, condominiums, cabins, and homes. Tour the Sierra backcountry on a snowmobile, take a paddle-wheeler cruise to Emerald Bay, try a peaceful sleigh ride, or see the sights from a dog sled.

Page | **1**

Word SECTION 2

Formatting Characters and Paragraphs

Skills

- Apply fonts and font effects
- Use Format Painter
- Repeat a command
- Align text in paragraphs
- Indent text
- Change line and paragraph spacing
- Insert bullets and numbering
- Insert symbols and special characters
- Set tabs and tabs with leaders
- Add borders and shading to text
- Insert a page border
- Apply styles
- Change the document default formatting

Student Resources

Before beginning this section:

1. Copy to your storage medium the WordS2 subfolder from the Word folder on the Student Resources CD.
2. Make WordS2 the active folder.

In addition to containing the data files needed to complete section work, the Student Resources CD contains model answers in PDF format for each of the projects in this section; model answers for end-of-section activities are not provided.

Projects Overview

First Choice TRAVEL

Edit and format fact sheets on Oslo, Norway, and Petersburg, Alaska; format a document on traveling by train in Europe; format documents on vacation packages in Oregon and Nevada and cross-country skiing vacation packages; and use the Internet to find information on museums and galleries in Toronto and then use that information to prepare a letter to Marquee Productions.

Marquee PRODUCTIONS

Prepare a letter to the chair of the Theatre Arts Division at Niagara Peninsula College requesting 20 theater interns.

Worldwide Enterprises

Prepare a movie distribution schedule.

Activity 2.1

Applying Formatting with the Font Group and the Mini Toolbar

Use buttons in the Font group in the Home tab to apply character formatting to text. The top row contains buttons for changing the font and font size and increasing and decreasing the size of the font. The bottom row contains buttons for applying formatting such as bold, italics, underlining, superscript, and subscript. The default font used by Word is Calibri. Change this default with the Font button in the Font group. Click the Clear Formatting button to remove all formatting from selected text. Microsoft Word has taken some commonly used commands and placed them on the Mini toolbar. The Mini toolbar displays in a faded manner when you select text and then becomes solid when you point to it.

Project

You have been asked to improve the appearance of a fact sheet on Oslo, Norway, by applying different font and font effects to the text.

First Choice TRAVEL

1. Open **FCTOslo.docx** and then save the document and name it **WordS2-01**.
2. Select *Oslo Fact Sheet* and then click the Bold button **B** in the Font group in the Home tab.
3. With *Oslo Fact Sheet* still selected, click the Change Case button **Aa** in the Font group and then click *UPPERCASE* at the drop-down list.

   Use options at the Change Case drop-down list to specify the case of selected text.

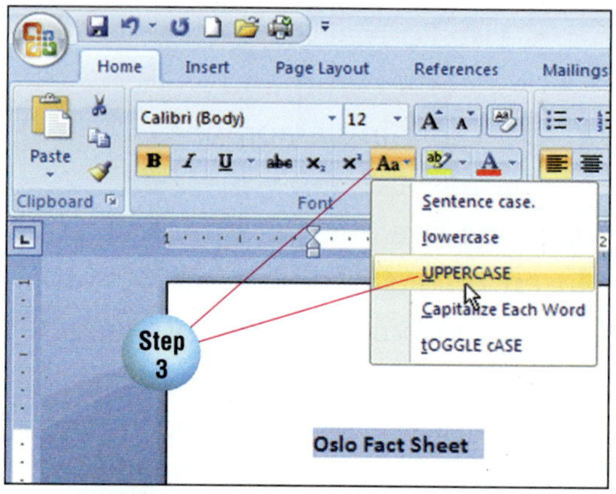

4. Select *History* and then click the Underline button **U** in the Font group.
5. Select and then underline the remaining headings: *Population*; *Commerce and Industry*; *Climate*; *Holiday, Sport, and Leisure*; and *Sightseeing Tours*.

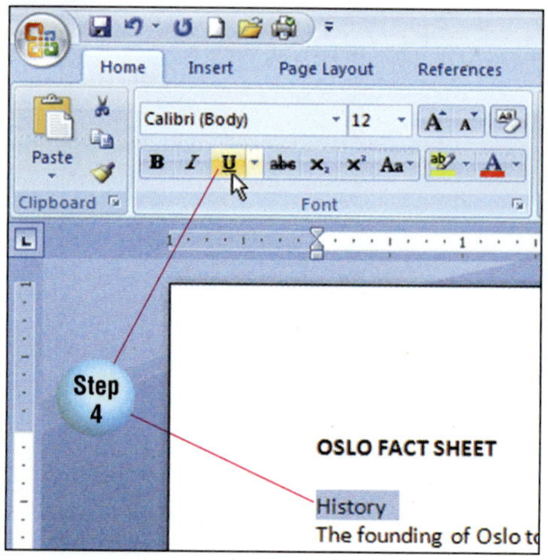

6. Select the words *Viking Age* located in the first paragraph below the *History* heading, point to the Mini toolbar that displays above the selected text, and then click the Italic button *I* on the Mini toolbar.

   The Mini toolbar displays in a faded manner until you point to it and then it becomes solid. The toolbar disappears when you move the mouse pointer away from it and when you click a button on the toolbar.

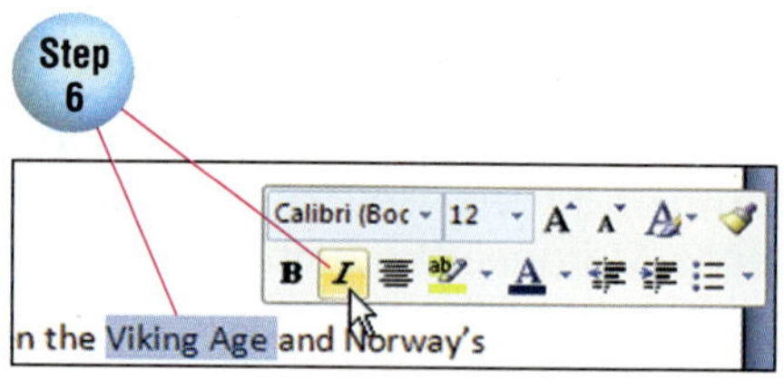

7. Select the words *Catholic Middle Ages* that display in the first paragraph and then click the Italic button *I* on the Mini toolbar.
8. Select the entire document by clicking the Select button in the Editing group in the Home tab and then clicking *Select All* at the drop-down list.

9. Click the Font button arrow in the Font group. Hover the mouse pointer over various typefaces in the drop-down gallery and notice how the text in the document reflects the selected font.

   This feature is referred to as ***live preview*** and provides you with an opportunity to see how the document will appear with font formatting before making a final choice.

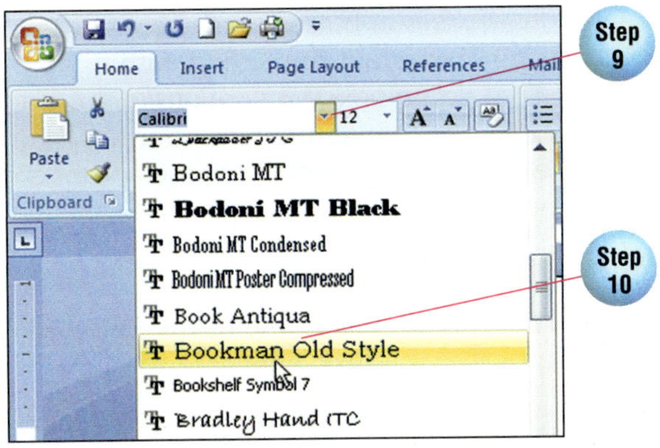

10. Scroll down the gallery and then click *Bookman Old Style*. (If this font is not available, choose another font.)
11. Click the Font Size button arrow and then click *11* at the drop-down gallery.

12. Click the Font Color button arrow and then click *Dark Blue* at the color gallery (second color from the *right* in the *Standard Colors* row).
13. Deselect the text.
14. You want to identify specific text for review by colleagues so you decide to highlight the text. To do this, click the Highlight button in the Font group and then select the first sentence in the second paragraph (the sentence that begins *Oslo's population was substantially . . .*).

    When you click the Highlight button, the mouse pointer displays with a highlighter pen attached. Highlighting stays on until you click the Highlight button again.

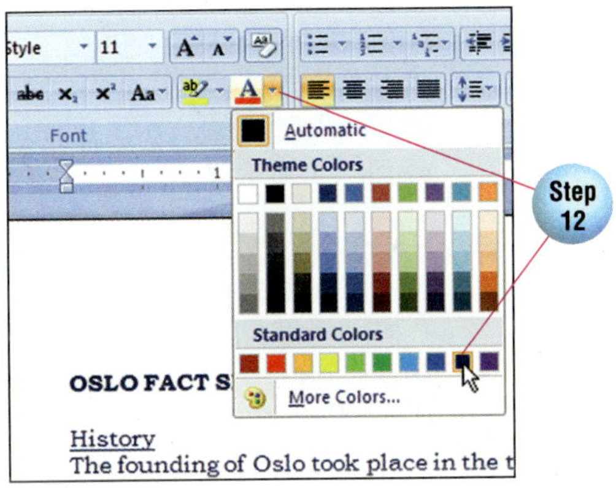

15. Select the first sentence in the *Population* paragraph to highlight it and then click the Highlight button to turn it off.
16. Save and then print **WordS2-01.docx**.

In Addition

Using Typefaces

A typeface is a set of characters with a common design and shape and can be decorative or plain and either monospaced or proportional. Word refers to typeface as ***font***. A monospaced typeface allots the same amount of horizontal space for each character while a proportional typeface allots a varying amount of space for each character. Proportional typefaces are divided into two main categories: ***serif*** and ***sans serif***. A serif is a small line at the end of a character stroke. Consider using a serif typeface for text-intensive documents because the serifs help move the reader's eyes across the page. Use a sans serif typeface for headings, headlines, and advertisements. Microsoft Word 2007 includes six new typefaces designed for extended on-screen reading. These typefaces include the default, Calibri, as well as Cambria, Candara, Consolas, Constantia, and Corbel. Calibri, Candara, and Corbel are sans serif typefaces; Cambria and Constantia are serif typefaces; and Consolas is monospaced.

Activity 2.2

Using the Font Dialog Box and Format Painter; Repeating a Command

In addition to buttons in the Font group, you can apply font formatting with options at the Font dialog box. With options at this dialog box, you can change the font, font size, and font style; change the font color; choose an underlining style; and apply formatting effects. Once you apply font formatting to text, you can copy that formatting to different locations in the document using the Format Painter. If you apply formatting to text in a document and then want to apply the same formatting to other text, use the Repeat command. Repeat a command by pressing the F4 function key.

Project

First Choice TRAVEL

The changes you made to the Oslo fact sheet have enhanced the readability and visual appeal of the text. Now you will turn your attention to the headings.

1. With **WordS2-01.docx** open, press Ctrl + Home to move the insertion point to the beginning of the page and then select the entire document by pressing Ctrl + A.

   Ctrl + A is the keyboard shortcut to select the entire document.

2. Click the Font group dialog box launcher.

   The dialog box launcher displays as a small button containing a diagonal arrow.

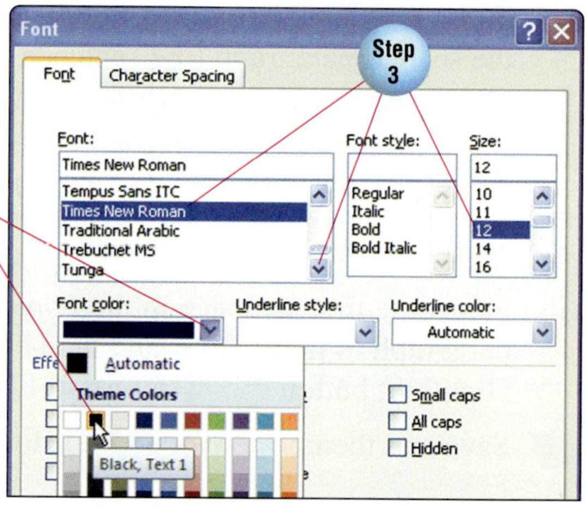

3. At the Font dialog box, click *Times New Roman* in the *Font* list box (you will need to scroll down the list box to display this option) and then click *12* in the *Size* list box.
4. Click the down-pointing arrow at the right side of the *Font color* option and then click *Black, Text 1* (second choice from the left in the top row).
5. Click OK to close the dialog box.
6. Select the heading *History* and then click the Font group dialog box launcher.

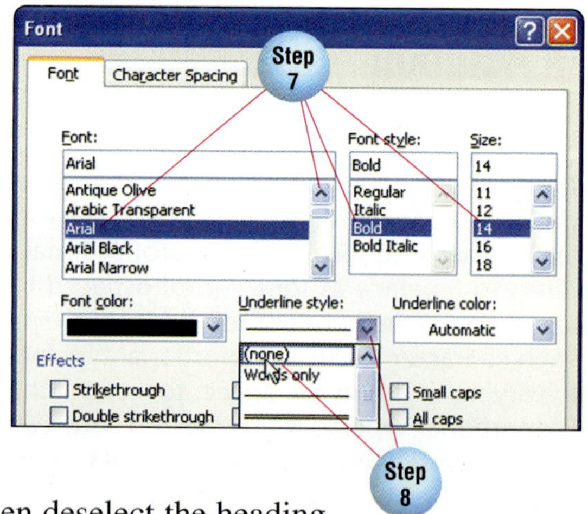

7. Click *Arial* in the *Font* list box (you will need to scroll up the list box to display this option), click *Bold* in the *Font style* list box, and then click *14* in the *Size* list box (you will need to scroll down this list box to display *14*).
8. Click the down-pointing arrow at the right side of the *Underline style* option and then click *(none)* at the drop-down list.
9. Click OK to close the dialog box and then deselect the heading.

10 Click once on any character in the heading *History* and then double-click the Format Painter button in the Clipboard group in the Home tab.

When Format Painter is active, the mouse pointer displays with a paintbrush attached.

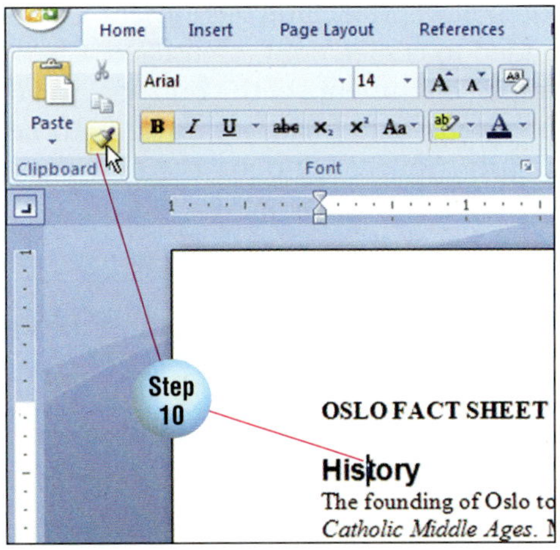

11 Scroll down the document and then select the heading *Population*.

With Format Painter active, selecting text applies formatting.

12 Select individually the remaining headings (*Commerce and Industry*; *Climate*; *Holiday, Sport, and Leisure*; and *Sightseeing Tours*).

13 Click once on the Format Painter button in the Clipboard group to turn off Format Painter.

14 Select the last sentence in the document (the sentence that begins *All tours by boat . . .*) and then click the Font group dialog box launcher.

15 At the Font dialog box, click *Small caps* in the *Effects* section.

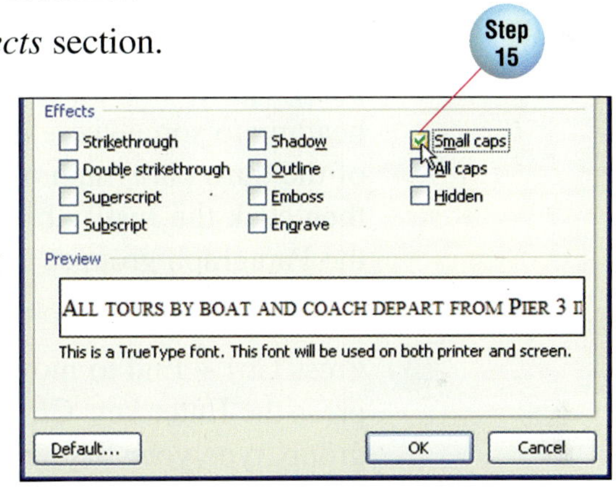

16 Click OK to close the dialog box.

17 Select the text *Tour 1: Mini Cruise* and then click the Font group dialog box launcher.

18 At the Font dialog box, click *Shadow* in the *Effects* section and then click OK to close the dialog box.

19 Select the text *Tour 2: Fjord Cruise* and then press F4. Select the text *Tour 3: Fjord Cruise with Dinner* and then press F4. Select the text *Tour 4: Selected Oslo Sightseeing* and then press F4.

Pressing F4 repeats the previous command and applies the shadow effect to selected text.

20 Select the heading *OSLO FACT SHEET* and then change the font to Arial and the font size to 16.

21 Save **WordS2-01.docx**.

In Brief

Change Font at Font Dialog Box

1. Click Font group dialog box launcher.
2. Choose desired font.
3. Click OK.

Apply Formatting with Format Painter

1. Apply formatting.
2. Double-click Format Painter button.
3. Select text.
4. Click Format Painter button.

Apply Font Effects

1. Select text.
2. Click Font group dialog box launcher.
3. Click desired effect check box.
4. Click OK.

In Addition

Font Keyboard Shortcuts

Along with buttons in the Font group and the Font dialog box, you can apply character formatting with the following keyboard shortcuts.

Font Group Button	Keyboard Shortcut
Font	Ctrl + Shift + F
Font Size	Ctrl + Shift + P
Grow Font	Ctrl + >
Shrink Font	Ctrl + <
Bold	Ctrl + B

Font Group Button	Keyboard Shortcut
Italic	Ctrl + I
Underline	Ctrl + U
Subscript	Ctrl + =
Superscript	Ctrl + Shift + +
Change Case	Shift + F3

Activity 2.3

Aligning and Indenting Text

Paragraphs of text in a document are aligned at the left margin by default. This default alignment can be changed to center, right, or justified. Change paragraph alignment with buttons in the Paragraph group in the Home tab or with keyboard shortcuts. You can indent the first line of text in a paragraph, indent all lines of text in a paragraph, and indent the second and subsequent lines of a paragraph (called a hanging indent). Several methods are available for indenting text, including buttons in the Paragraph group in the Home tab and the Page Layout tab, markers on the Ruler, options at the Paragraph dialog box with the Indents and Spacing tab selected, and keyboard shortcuts.

Project

You will improve the appearance of the Oslo fact sheet by changing text alignment and changing the alignment of specific paragraphs in the document.

First Choice TRAVEL

1. With **WordS2-01.docx** open, position the insertion point on any character in the title *OSLO FACT SHEET* and then click the Center button in the Paragraph group in the Home tab.

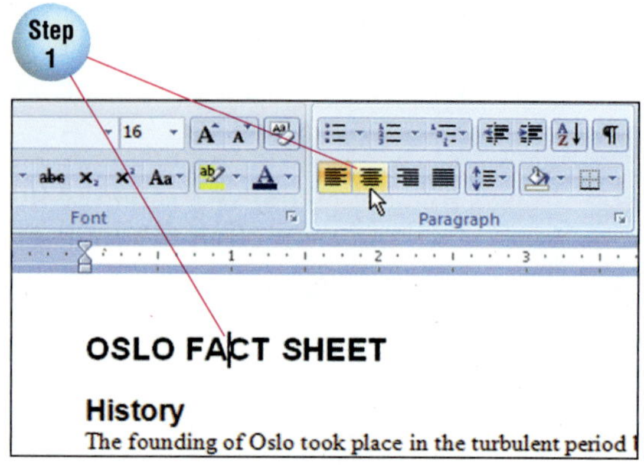

2. Select from the middle of the first paragraph of text below the *History* heading to somewhere in the middle of the third paragraph of text and then click the Justify button in the Paragraph group.

   The entire paragraphs do not have to be selected, only a portion of each paragraph.

3. Press Ctrl + End to move the insertion point to the end of the document and then press the Enter key. Click the Align Text Right button in the Paragraph group, type your first and last names, and then press the Enter key.

4. Type **Date:**, press the spacebar once, and then press Alt + Shift + D. Press the Enter key and then click the Align Text Left button in the Paragraph group.

   Alt + Shift + D is the keyboard shortcut to insert the current date.

5. You decide to return the alignment to left for the paragraphs below the *History* heading and indent the text instead. To begin, select the three paragraphs below the *History* heading and then click the Align Text Left button in the Paragraph group.

6. With the text still selected, position the mouse pointer on the Left Indent marker on the Ruler, hold down the left mouse button, drag the marker to the 0.5-inch mark on the Ruler, and then release the mouse button.

   The ruler indent markers are shown in Figure 2.1. To precisely position a marker on the Ruler, hold down the Alt key while dragging the marker.

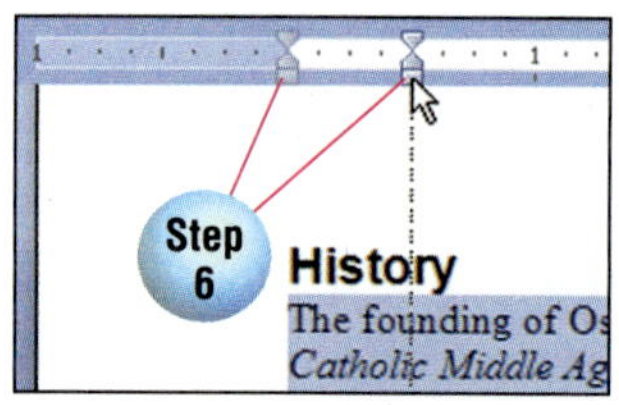

FIGURE 2.1 Ruler Indent Markers

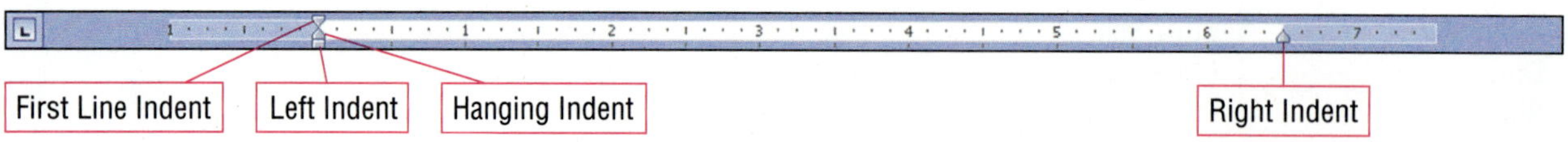

7 Position the mouse pointer on the First Line Indent marker on the Ruler, hold down the left mouse button, and then drag the marker to the 1-inch mark on the Ruler.

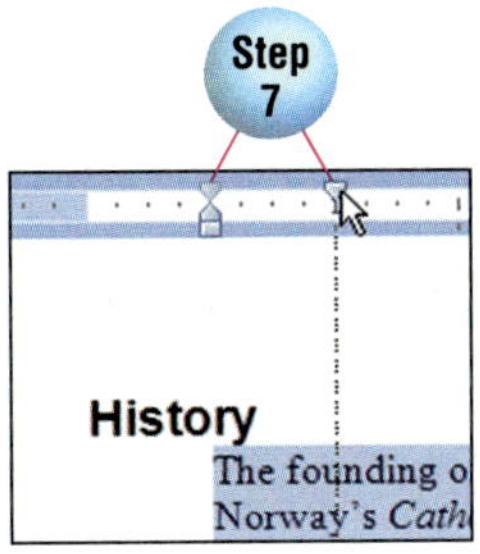

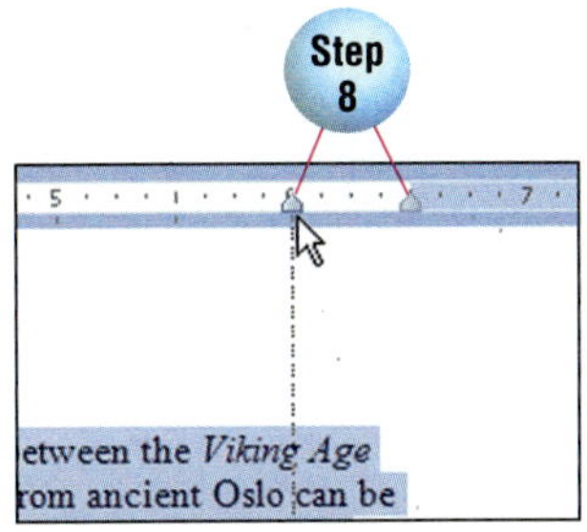

8 Position the mouse pointer on the Right Indent marker on the Ruler, hold down the left mouse button, and then drag the marker to the 6-inch mark on the Ruler.

9 Click anywhere in the paragraph below the *Population* heading and then click the Page Layout tab. In the *Indent* section in the Paragraph group, click in the *Left* text box and then type **0.5**. Click the up-pointing arrow at the right side of the *Right* text box until *0.5″* displays.

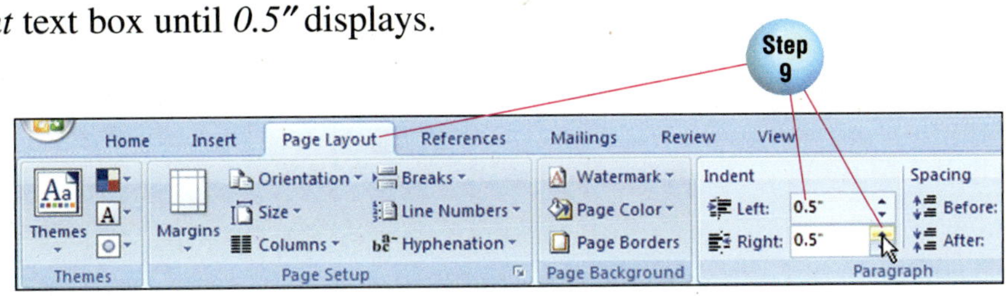

10 Follow the steps in Step 9 to indent the paragraphs below the headings *Commerce and Industry*; *Climate*; *Holiday, Sport, and Leisure*; and *Sightseeing Tours*.

11 Select the three paragraphs below the *History* heading and then click the Paragraph group dialog box launcher.

12 At the Paragraph dialog box, click the down-pointing arrow at the right side of the *Special* list box and then click *Hanging* at the drop-down list.

13 Click OK to close the Paragraph dialog box.

14 Save **WordS2-01.docx**.

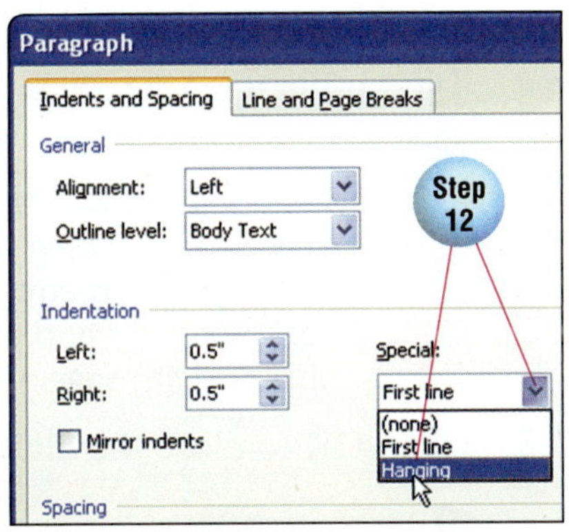

In Addition

Aligning Text

Change text alignment with the following keyboard shortcuts:

Alignment	Keyboard Shortcut
Left	Ctrl + L
Center	Ctrl + E
Right	Ctrl + R
Justified	Ctrl + J

Indenting Text

Indent text with the following keyboard shortcuts:

Indentation	Keyboard Shortcut
Indent text from left margin	Ctrl + M
Decrease indent from left margin	Ctrl + Shift + M
Create a hanging indent	Ctrl + T
Remove hanging indent	Ctrl + Shift + T

Activity 2.4

Changing Line and Paragraph Spacing

By default, line spacing is set at 1.15. This default line spacing can be changed with the Line spacing button in the Paragraph group in the Home tab, keyboard shortcuts, or with the *Line spacing* and *At* options at the Paragraph dialog box. Control spacing above and below paragraphs with options at the Line Spacing button drop-down list, the Spacing Before and Spacing After buttons in the Paragraph group in the Page Layout tab, or with the *Before* and/or *After* options at the Paragraph dialog box with the Indents and Spacing tab selected.

Project

First Choice TRAVEL

The Oslo fact sheet project deadline is at hand. However, you have time to make a few spacing changes in the document before printing the final version.

1. With **WordS2-01.docx** open, select the entire document by pressing Ctrl + A and then click the Home tab.

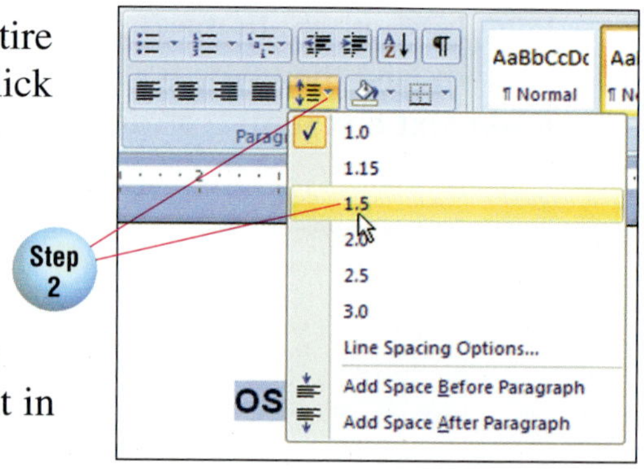

2. Click the Line Spacing button in the Paragraph group in the Home tab and then click *1.5* at the drop-down list.
3. Deselect the text and then scroll through the document. After viewing the document in 1.5 line spacing, you decide to decrease the line spacing to 1.2. To begin, press Ctrl + A to select the entire document, click the Line Spacing button, and then click *Line Spacing Options* at the drop-down list.

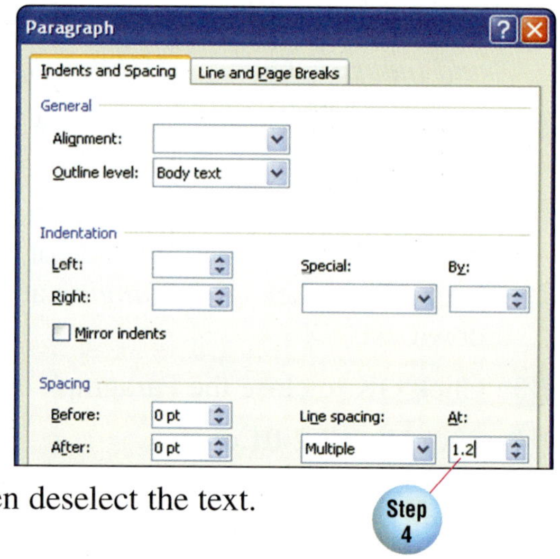

4. Type **1.2** in the *At* text box in the *Spacing* section of the Paragraph dialog box.

   The Paragraph dialog box also contains a *Line spacing* option. Click the down-pointing arrow at the right side of the option and a drop-down list displays with spacing choices.

5. Click OK to close the dialog box and then deselect the text.

PROBLEM

If line spacing seems too spread out, make sure you typed the period in *1.2* in the *At* text box at the Paragraph dialog box.

6. Select from the line of text beginning *Tour 1: Mini Cruise* through the three lines of text pertaining to *Tour 4: Selected Oslo Sightseeing*.
7. Click the Line Spacing button and then click *1.0* at the drop-down list.

   Choosing this option changes the line spacing to single for the selected paragraphs of text. You can also change line spacing with keyboard shortcuts. Press Ctrl + 1 to change to single spacing, Ctrl + 2 to change to double spacing, and Ctrl + 5 to change to 1.5 line spacing.

8. Press Ctrl + End to move the insertion point to the end of the document and then click anywhere in the last sentence (the sentence that begins *All tours by boat . . .*).

9. Click the Line Spacing button and then click *Add Space Before Paragraph*.

   This inserts 12 points of space above the heading.

10. Press Ctrl + Home to move the insertion point to the beginning of the document, click anywhere in the *History* heading, and then click the Paragraph group dialog box launcher.

11. At the Paragraph dialog box, click once on the up-pointing arrow at the right side of the *After* text box and then click OK to close the dialog box.

    Clicking the up-pointing arrow at the right side of the *After* text box inserts *6 pt* in the text box.

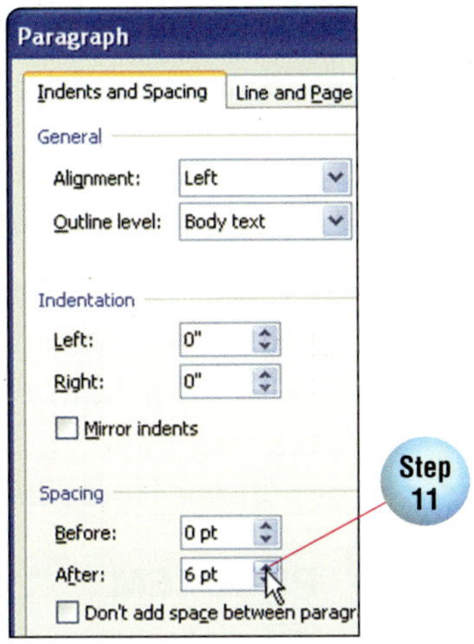

12. Click anywhere in the *Population* heading, click the Page Layout tab, and then click once on the up-pointing arrow at the right side of the Spacing After button in the Paragraph group.

    Clicking once on the up arrow changes the point measurement to *6 pt*.

13. Click anywhere in the *Commerce and Industry* heading and then press F4.

    Pressing F4 repeats the paragraph spacing command.

14. Click individually anywhere in each of the remaining headings (*Climate*; *Holiday, Sport, and Leisure*; and *Sightseeing Tours*) and then press F4.

15. You also decide that you want to remove the hanging indent on the paragraphs in the History section. To do this, select the three paragraphs of text below the *History* heading and then press Ctrl + Shift + T.

16. Save, print, and then close **WordS2-01.docx**.

In Brief

Change Line Spacing

1. Click Line Spacing button.
2. Click desired line spacing option.

OR

1. Click Line Spacing button.
2. Click *Line Spacing Options*.
3. Type desired line spacing in *At* text box.
4. Click OK.

In Addition

Spacing Above or Below Paragraphs

Spacing above or below paragraphs is added in points. A vertical inch contains approximately 72 points and a half inch contains approximately 36 points. For example, to add 9 points of spacing below selected paragraphs, click the Page Layout tab or display the Paragraph dialog box with the Indents and Spacing tab selected. Select the current measurement in the *After* text box and then type 9. You can also click the up-pointing or down-pointing arrows to increase or decrease the amount of spacing before or after paragraphs.

Activity 2.5

Inserting Bullets and Numbering

If you want to draw the reader's attention to a list of items, consider inserting a bullet before each item. Click the Bullets button in the Paragraph group in the Home tab to insert a bullet before items in a list. If a list of items is in a sequence, consider inserting numbers before each item with the Numbering button in the Paragraph group. Create multiple-level bulleted or numbered paragraphs with options from the Multilevel List button in the Paragraph group.

Project

First Choice Travel has a new document on traveling in Europe by train. After reviewing the document, you decide to insert numbers and bullets before selected paragraphs to make the information easier to read.

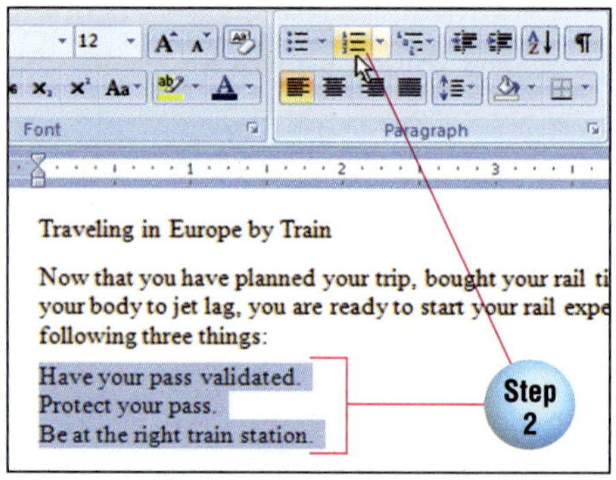

1. Open **FCTRailTravel.docx** and then save the document and name it **WordS2-02**.
2. Select text from the paragraph *Have your pass validated.* through the paragraph *Be at the right train station.* and then click the Numbering button in the Paragraph group in the Home tab.

PROBLEM

If you click the wrong button, immediately click the Undo button.

3. Position the insertion point at the end of the second numbered paragraph (the paragraph that displays as *2. Protect your pass.*) and then press the Enter key once.

   Pressing the Enter key automatically inserts the number *3.* and renumbers the third paragraph to *4.*

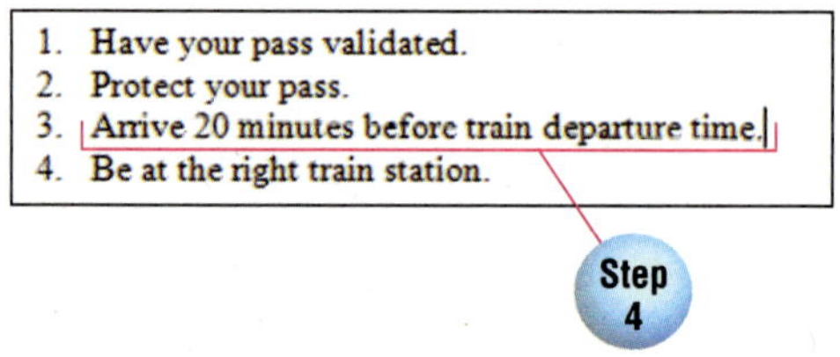

4. Type **Arrive 20 minutes before train departure.**

   Numbering before paragraphs is changed automatically when paragraphs of text are inserted and/or deleted.

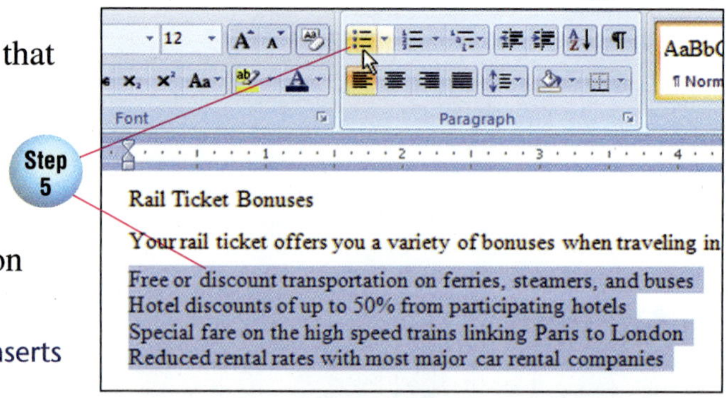

5. Select text from the paragraph that begins *Free or discount transportation* . . . through the paragraph that begins *Reduced rental rates with* . . . and then click the Bullets button in the Paragraph group.

   Clicking the Bullets button inserts a round bullet before each paragraph. Other bullet options are available by clicking the Bullets button arrow.

6. With the text still selected, you decide to replace the round bullet with a custom bullet. To begin, click the Bullets button arrow and then click *Define New Bullet* at the drop-down list.
7. At the Define New Bullet dialog box, click the Symbol button in the *Bullet character* section.

8. At the Symbol dialog box, click the down-pointing arrow at the right side of the *Font* list box, scroll down the drop-down list, and then click *Webdings*.
9. Scroll to the end of the symbol list, click the earth symbol that is the fourth symbol from the *right* in the bottom row, and then click OK to close the Symbol dialog box.
10. Click OK to close the Define New Bullet dialog box.

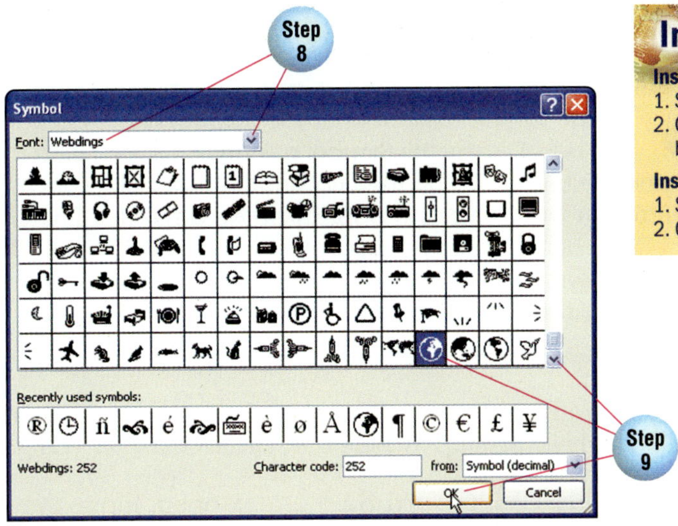

In Brief

Insert Numbers
1. Select text.
2. Click Numbering button.

Insert Bullets
1. Select text.
2. Click Bullets button.

11. Select the text from *Rail Passes* through *Greece-Italy*, click the Multilevel List button in the Paragraph group, and then click the middle option in the top row in the *List Library* section.

    This applies multiple-level numbering to the selected text.

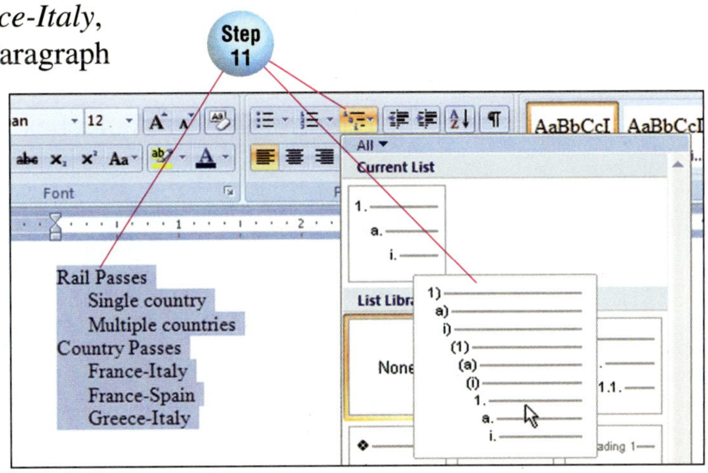

12. With the text still selected, you decide to change to bullets instead of numbers. To do this, click the Multilevel List button and then click the first option from the left in the middle row in the *List Library* section.
13. Deselect the text.
14. Save and then print **WordS2-02.docx**.

In Addition

Creating Numbered and/or Bulleted Text

If you type 1., press the spacebar, type a paragraph of text, and then press the Enter key, Word indents the number approximately 0.25 inch and then hang indents the text in the paragraph approximately 0.5 inch from the left margin. Additionally, *2.* is inserted 0.25 inch from the left margin at the beginning of the next paragraph. Continue typing items and Word inserts the next number in the list. Press Enter to turn off numbering or click the Numbering button in the Paragraph group. Bulleted lists with hanging indents are automatically created when you begin a paragraph with the symbol *, > , or -. Type one of the symbols, press the spacebar, type text, and then press Enter. The type of bullet inserted depends on the type of character entered. For example, if you use the asterisk (*) symbol, a round bullet is inserted, and an arrow bullet is inserted if you type the greater than symbol (>).

Turning Off Automatic Numbering and/or Bulleting

If you do not want automatic numbering or bulleting in a document, turn off the features at the AutoCorrect dialog box with the AutoFormat As You Type tab selected. To display this dialog box, click the Office button and then click the Word Options button. At the Word Options dialog box, click the *Proofing* option and then click the AutoCorrect Options button. At the AutoCorrect dialog box, click the AutoFormat As You Type tab. Click the *Automatic numbered lists* check box and/or *Automatic bulleted lists* check box to remove the check mark.

Activity 2.6

Inserting Symbols and Special Characters

You can insert special symbols such as é, ö, and Ā with options at the Symbol palette or at the Symbol dialog box. Display the Symbol palette by clicking the Insert tab and then clicking the Symbol button in the Symbols group. Click the desired symbol to insert it in the document. To display additional symbols, display the Symbol dialog box by clicking the Symbol button and then clicking the *More Symbols* option. Click the desired symbol at the dialog box, click the Insert button, and then click the Close button. At the Symbol dialog box with the Symbols tab selected, you can change the font and display different symbols. Click the Special Characters tab at the dialog box and a list displays containing special characters and the keyboard shortcuts to insert the characters.

Project

You have identified a few city names in the train travel document that need special letters in their spellings as well as a special character you need to insert in the document.

First Choice TRAVEL

1. With **Word S2-02.docx** open, move the insertion point to the end of the document and then select and delete the multiple-level bulleted text.
2. With the insertion point positioned at the end of the document a double space below the bulleted text, type the text shown in Figure 2.2 up to the Å in Århus. To insert the Å symbol, click the Insert tab, click the Symbol button Ω in the Symbols group, and then click *More Symbols* at the bottom of the palette.
3. At the Symbol dialog box with the Symbols tab selected, click the down-pointing arrow at the right side of the *Font* list box and then click *(normal text)* at the drop-down list. (You may need to scroll up to see this option. Skip this step if *(normal text)* is already selected.)
4. Scroll down the list box until the ninth row is visible and then click the Å symbol (approximately the fifth symbol from the left in the ninth row).

PROBLEM

If you do not see the Å symbol, make sure *(normal text)* is selected at the *Font* list box.

5. Click the Insert button and then click the Close button.
6. Type text up to the ø symbol. To insert the ø symbol, click the Symbol button Ω and then click *More Symbols*.

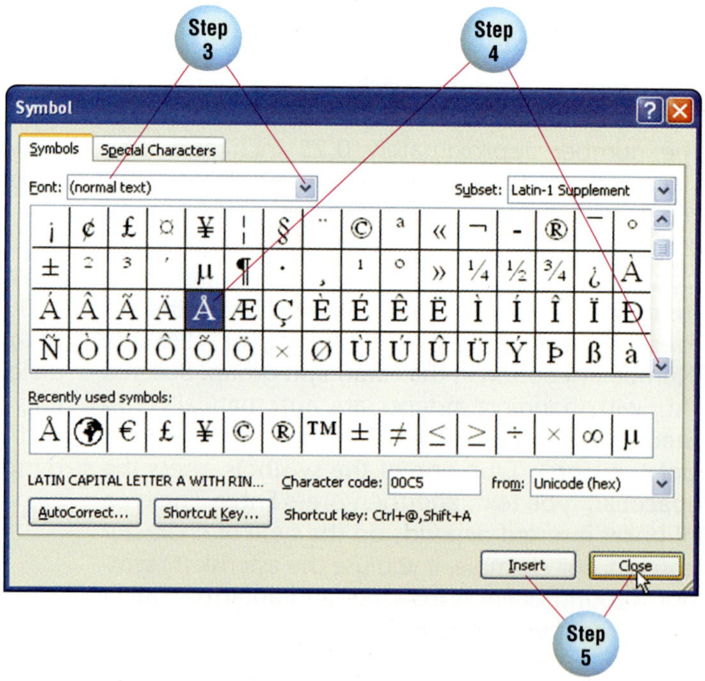

FIGURE 2.2 Steps 2–13

> Some companies offer outstanding reductions on transportation. For example, you can travel on the ferry in Denmark between Århus and Kalundborg and between Nyborg and Korsør at a 75% discount! ScanTravel, a travel company located in Stockholm, offers the StarPass® ticket that provides you with incredible discounts on travel by train, ferry, and bus in Sweden, Norway, and Denmark.

7. At the Symbol dialog box, click the ø symbol (approximately the eighth symbol from the left in the twelfth row).

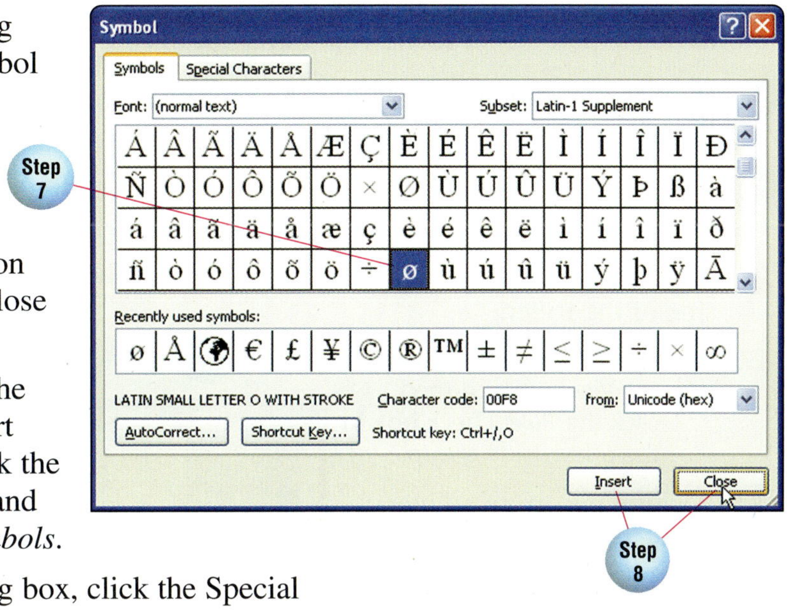

8. Click the Insert button and then click the Close button.
9. Type the text up to the ® character. To insert the ® character, click the Symbol button and then click *More Symbols*.
10. At the Symbol dialog box, click the Special Characters tab.
11. Click the ® character in the dialog box list box.
12. Click the Insert button and then click the Close button.
13. Type the remaining text in Figure 2.2.
14. Save **WordS2-02.docx**.

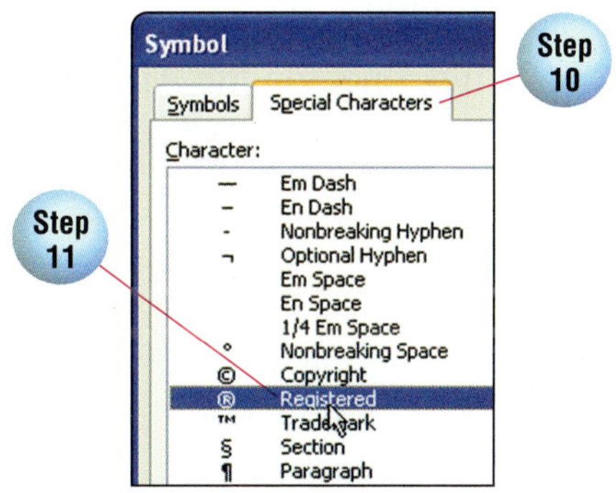

In Brief

Insert Symbol

1. Click Insert tab.
2. Click Symbol button.
3. Click *More Symbols*.
4. Click desired symbol.
5. Click Insert button.
6. Click Close button.

Insert Special Character

1. Click Insert tab.
2. Click Symbol button.
3. Click *More Symbols*.
4. Click Special Characters tab.
5. Click desired character.
6. Click Insert button.
7. Click Close button.

In Addition

Inserting Symbols with Keyboard Shortcuts

Another method for inserting symbols in a document is to use a keyboard shortcut. Click a symbol at the Symbol dialog box and the keyboard shortcut displays toward the bottom of the dialog box. For example, click the ø symbol and the keyboard shortcut *Ctrl+/,O* displays toward the bottom of the dialog box. To insert the ø symbol in a document using the keyboard shortcut, hold down the Ctrl key and then press the / key. Release the Ctrl key and then press the o key. Not all symbols contain a keyboard shortcut.

Inserting Symbols Using the Palette

When you click the Symbol button in the Symbols group, a drop-down palette displays with symbol choices. The palette displays the most recently used symbols. If the palette contains the desired symbol, click the symbol and it is inserted in the document.

Activity 2.7

Setting Tabs

Word offers a variety of default settings including left tabs set every 0.5 inch. You can set your own tabs using the Ruler or at the Tabs dialog box. Use the Ruler to set, move, and delete tabs. The default tabs display as tiny vertical lines along the bottom of the Ruler. With a left tab, text aligns at the left edge of the tab. The other types of tabs that can be set on the Ruler are center, right, decimal, and bar. The small button at the left side of the Ruler is called the Alignment button. Each time you click the Alignment button, a different tab or paragraph alignment symbol displays. To set a tab, display the desired alignment button on the Ruler and then click on the Ruler at the desired position.

Project

You have completed some additional research on train travel in Europe with train connections. You will add airport names to the train travel document.

First Choice TRAVEL

1. With **WordS2-02.docx** open, move the insertion point a double space below the last paragraph of text in the document.
2. Type **International Airports with Train Connections** and then press the Enter key twice.
3. Make sure the left tab symbol displays in the Alignment button at the left side of the Ruler.

   If the Ruler is not visible, click the View tab and then click the *Ruler* check box in the Show/Hide group.

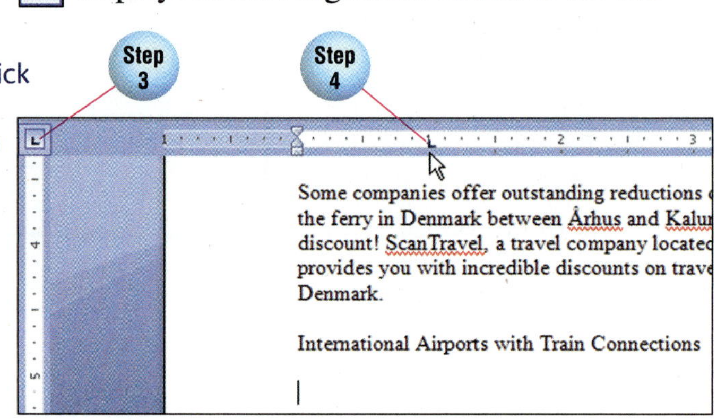

4. Position the arrow pointer below the 1-inch mark on the Ruler and then click the left mouse button.
5. Click once on the Alignment button located at the left side of the Ruler to display the center tab symbol.

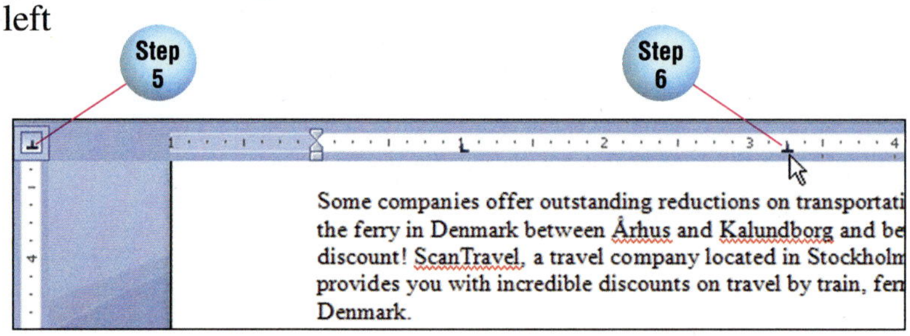

6. Position the arrow pointer below the 3.25-inch mark on the Ruler and then click the left mouse button.
7. Click once on the Alignment button located at the left side of the Ruler to display the right tab symbol.
8. Position the arrow pointer below the 5.5-inch mark on the Ruler and then click the left mouse button.

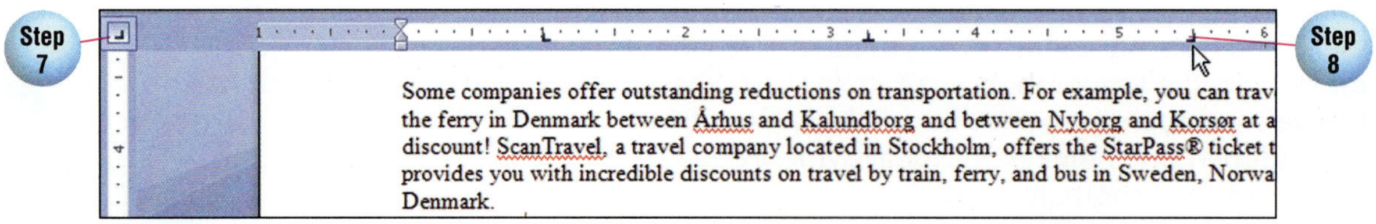

9 Type the text shown in Figure 2.3, pressing the Tab key before typing each tabbed entry. Make sure you press the Tab key before typing the entry in the first column and that you bold the text in the first row.

PROBLEM

If your columns of text do not look similar to those in Figure 2.3, check to make sure you inserted the tab symbols at the correct locations on the Ruler and that you pressed the Tab key before typing each entry in the first column.

In Brief

Set Tab on Ruler

1. Display desired alignment symbol on Alignment button.
2. Click on Ruler at desired position.

10 After typing the last entry in the third column (*Fiumicino*), press the Enter key twice and then click the Clear Formatting button in the Font group in the Home tab.

Clicking the Clear Formatting button removes paragraph and character formatting. You can also remove paragraph formatting by pressing the keyboard shortcut Ctrl + Q and remove character formatting by pressing the keyboard shortcut Ctrl + spacebar.

11 Save **WordS2-02.docx**.

FIGURE 2.3 Step 9

Country	**City**	**Airport**
Austria	Vienna (Wein)	Schwechat
Belgium	Brussels	Nationaal
France	Paris	Orly
Germany	Berlin	Schoenefeld
Great Britain	London	Heathrow
Italy	Rome	Fiumicino

In Addition

Moving a Tab

Move a tab on the Ruler by positioning the mouse pointer on the tab symbol on the Ruler. Hold down the left mouse button, drag the symbol to the new location on the Ruler, and then release the mouse button.

Deleting a Tab

Delete a tab from the Ruler by positioning the arrow pointer on the tab symbol, holding down the left mouse button, dragging the symbol down into the document screen, and then releasing the mouse button.

Setting a Decimal Tab

Set a decimal tab for column entries you want aligned at the decimal point. To set a decimal tab, click the Alignment button located at the left side of the Ruler until the decimal tab symbol displays and then click on the desired position on the Ruler.

Activity 2.8

Setting Tabs with Leaders

The four types of tabs can be set with leaders. Leaders are useful for material where you want to direct the reader's eyes across the page. Leaders can be periods, hyphens, or underlines. Tabs with leaders are set with options at the Tabs dialog box. To display this dialog box, click the Paragraph group dialog box launcher and then click the Tabs button at the Paragraph dialog box. At the Tabs dialog box, choose the type of tab, the type of leader, and then enter a tab position measurement.

Project

The information you found listing airports with train connections also includes schedule times. You will add this data to the train travel document.

First Choice TRAVEL

1. With **WordS2-02.docx** open, move the insertion point to the end of the document.
2. Click the Alignment button at the left side of the Ruler until the left tab symbol displays.
3. Position the arrow pointer below the 1-inch mark on the Ruler and then click the left mouse button.
4. Click the Alignment button at the left side of the Ruler until the right tab symbol displays.
5. Position the arrow pointer below the 5.5-inch mark on the Ruler and then click the left mouse button.
6. Type the headings shown in Figure 2.4 by pressing the Tab key, clicking the Bold button in the Font group, and then typing **Airport**.
7. Press the Tab key and then type **Service**.
8. Press the Enter key once and then click the Clear Formatting button to remove the bold formatting and the paragraph tab formatting.
9. Set a left tab and a right tab with leaders at the Tabs dialog box. To begin, click the Paragraph group dialog box launcher and then click the Tabs button located in the lower left corner of the Paragraph dialog box.
10. At the Tabs dialog box, make sure *Left* is selected in the *Alignment* section of the dialog box. (If it is not, click *Left*.) With the insertion point positioned in the *Tab stop position* text box, type **1** and then click the Set button.

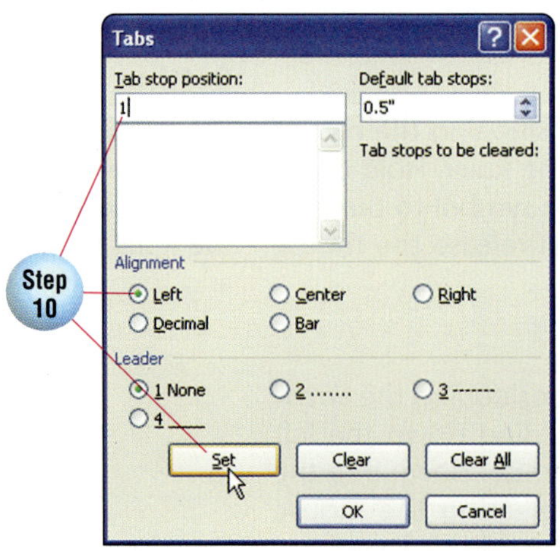

FIGURE 2.4 Steps 6 and 13

Airport	**Service**
Schwechat	Train every 30 minutes
Nationaal	Train every 20 minutes
Orly	RER train every 20 minutes
Schoenefeld	S-Bahn train every 20 minutes
Heathrow....................................	LT train every 10 minutes
Fiumicino................................	Train every 10 to 20 minutes

In Brief

Set Tab with Leaders

1. Click Paragraph group dialog box launcher.
2. Click Tabs button.
3. Type tab measurement.
4. Click desired alignment.
5. Click desired leader.
6. Click Set.
7. Click OK.

11. Type 5.5 in the *Tab stop position* text box, click *Right* in the *Alignment* section of the dialog box, and click *2 . . . . .* in the *Leader* section of the dialog box.
12. Click the Set button and then click OK to close the dialog box.

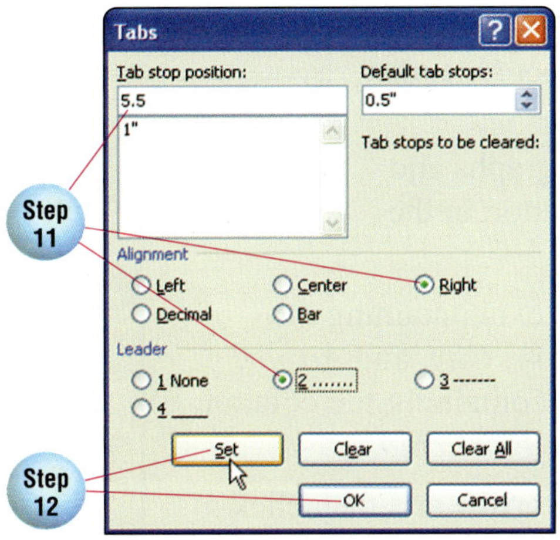

13. Type the remaining text shown in Figure 2.4, making sure you press the Tab key before typing the first text entry.

PROBLEM

If your columns of text do not look similar to those in Figure 2.4, check to make sure you inserted the tab symbols at the correct measurements and that you pressed Tab before typing each entry in the first column.

14. Save **WordS2-02.docx**.

In Addition

Clearing Tabs at the Tabs Dialog Box

At the Tabs dialog box, you can clear an individual tab or all tabs. To clear all tabs, click the Clear All button. To clear an individual tab, specify the tab position and then click the Clear button.

Activity 2.9

Adding Borders and Shading

Insert a border around text and/or apply shading to text in a paragraph or selected text with the Border button and Shading button in the Paragraph group in the Home tab or at the Borders and Shading dialog box. At the Borders and Shading dialog box with the Borders tab selected, you can specify the border type, style, color, and width. Click the Shading tab and the dialog box contains options for choosing a fill color and pattern style. Click the Page Border tab and the dialog box contains options for applying a page border.

Project

To highlight certain information in First Choice Travel's train travel document, you will apply a border to selected text and apply border and shading formatting to the column text. You will also apply a page border to add visual appeal.

1. With **WordS2-02.docx** open, select the numbered paragraphs, click the Border button arrow in the Paragraph group in the Home tab, and then click *Outside Borders* at the drop-down list.

   The name of the button changes when you choose a border option at the drop-down list.

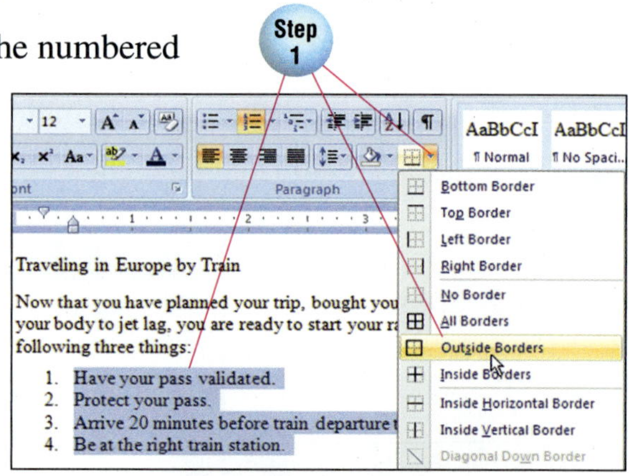

2. Select the bulleted paragraphs and then click the Border button in the Paragraph group.
3. Select from the line of text containing the column headings *Country*, *City*, and *Airport* through the line of text containing the column entries *Italy*, *Rome*, and *Fiumicino*.
4. Click the Border button arrow and then click *Borders and Shading* at the drop-down list.
5. At the Borders and Shading dialog box with the Borders tab selected, click the down-pointing arrow at the right side of the *Style* list box until the first double-line option displays and then click the double-line option.

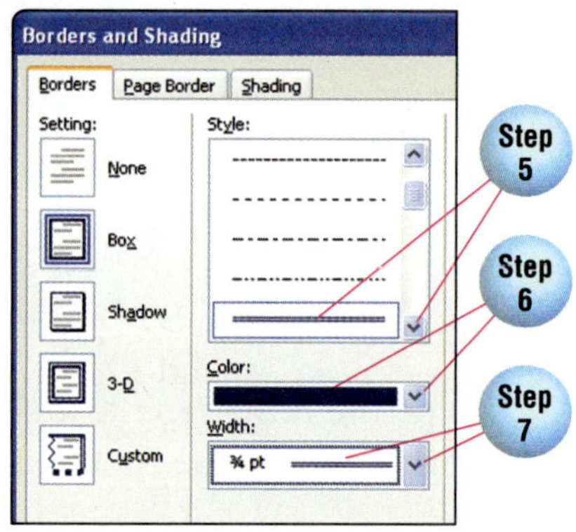

6. Click the down-pointing arrow at the right side of the *Color* list box and then click the *Dark Blue* option (second option from the *right* in the *Standard Colors* row).
7. Click the down-pointing arrow at the right side of the *Width* list box and then click *¾ pt* at the drop-down list.
8. Click the Shading tab, click the down-pointing arrow at the right side of the *Fill* option, and then click the *Aqua, Accent 5, Lighter 80%* color (the second color in the second column from the right).

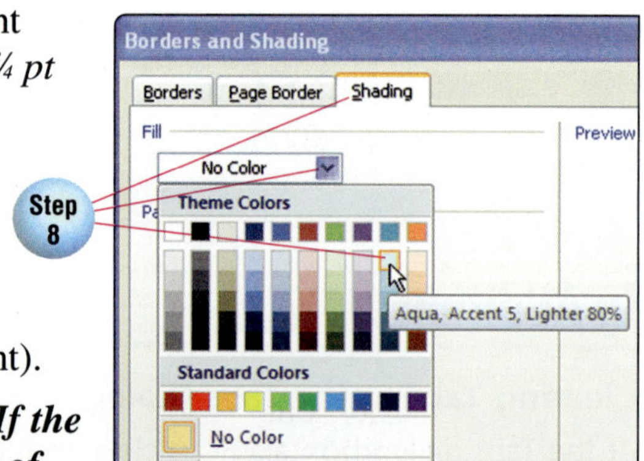

9. Click OK to close the dialog box. ***Hint: If the border does not appear around all sides of the column text, display the Borders and Shading dialog box with the Borders tab selected and then click the* Box *option in the* Setting *section.***

10 Add the same border and shading to the other columns of text by selecting from the line of text containing the column headings *Airport* and *Service* through the line of text containing the column entries *Fiumicino* and *Train every 10 to 20 minutes* and then pressing F4.

11 Apply shading to the title by positioning the insertion point on the title *Traveling in Europe by Train*, clicking the Shading button arrow, and then clicking the *Aqua, Accent 5, Lighter 80%* color.

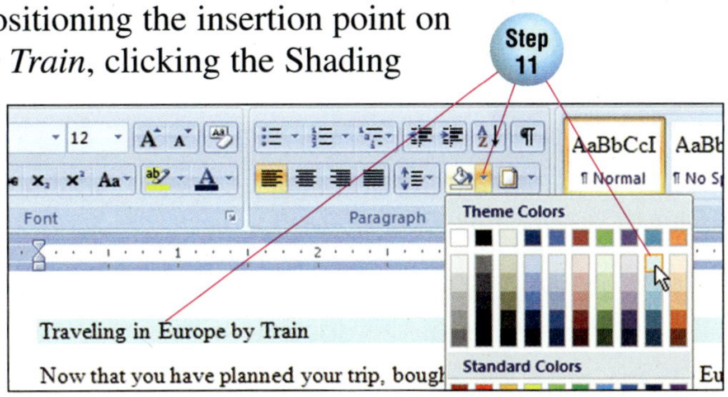

12 Apply a page border to the document. To begin, click the Border button arrow and then click *Borders and Shading* at the drop-down list.

13 At the Borders and Shading dialog box, click the Page Border tab, click the *Shadow* option in the *Setting* section, click the down-pointing arrow at the right side of the *Width* option, and then click *2 ¼ pt* at the drop-down list.

You can also display the Borders and Shading dialog box with the Page Border tab selected by clicking the Page Layout tab and then clicking the Page Borders button in the Page Background group.

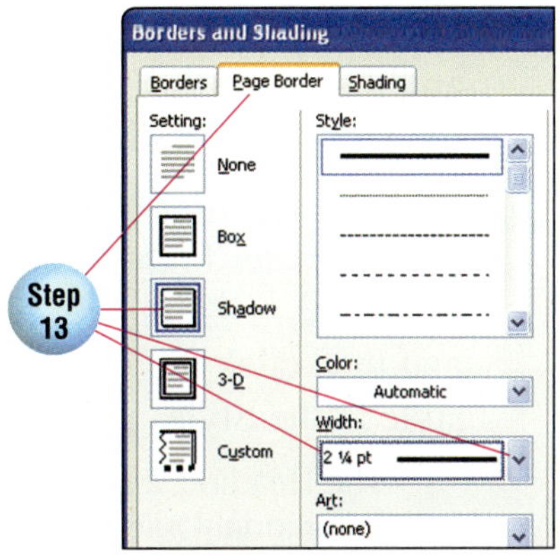

14 Click OK to close the dialog box.

15 Change the page border to an art image. To begin, click the Border button arrow and then click Borders and Shading. At the Borders and Shading dialog box, click the Page Border tab.

16 Click the *Box* option in the *Setting* section, click the down-pointing arrow at the right side of the *Art* option box, scroll down the list until the globe art images display, and then click the first set of globe images.

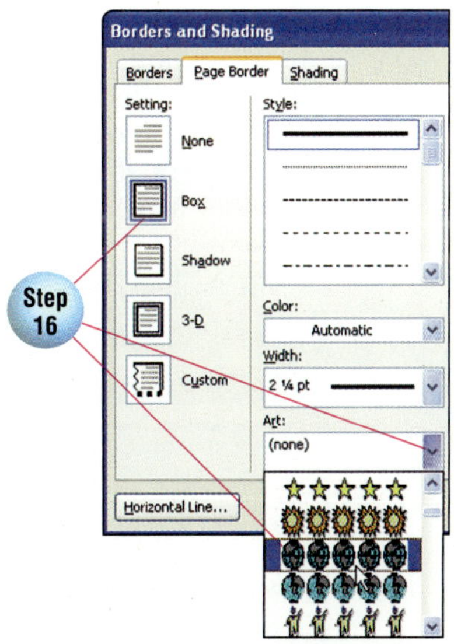

17 Select the measurement in the *Width* text box, type **10**, and then click OK to close the dialog box.

18 Save **WordS2-02.docx**.

In Addition

Inserting Horizontal Lines

Word includes a horizontal line feature that inserts a graphic horizontal line in a document. To display the Horizontal Line dialog box, display the Borders and Shading dialog box with any tab selected and then click the Horizontal Line button [Horizontal Line...] located toward the bottom of the dialog box. Click the desired horizontal line in the list box and then click OK and the line is inserted in the document.

In Brief

Insert Borders and Shading

1. Select text.
2. Click Border button arrow.
3. Click *Borders and Shading*.
4. Choose desired border(s).
5. Click Shading tab.
6. Choose desired shading and/or pattern.
7. Click OK.

Insert Page Border

1. Click Border button arrow.
2. Click *Borders and Shading*.
3. Click Page Border tab.
4. Choose desired options.
5. Click OK.

Activity 2.10

Applying Styles

A Word document contains a number of predesigned formats grouped into style sets called Quick Styles. Display the available Quick Styles sets by clicking the Change Styles button in the Styles group in the Home tab and then pointing to Style Set. Choose a Quick Styles set and two of the four styles visible in the Styles group change to reflect the set. To display additional available styles, click the More button (contains a horizontal line and a down-pointing triangle) that displays at the right side of the styles. Styles are also available in the Styles window. Display this window by clicking the Styles group dialog box launcher.

Project

To further enhance the train travel document, you decide to apply paragraph and character styles to specific text.

First Choice TRAVEL

1. With **WordS2-02.docx** open, press Ctrl + Home to move the insertion point to the beginning of the document.
2. Click the Change Styles button in the Styles group in the Home tab, point to *Style Set*, and then click *Traditional* at the drop-down gallery.
3. Position the insertion point on any character in the heading *Traveling in Europe by Train* and then click the Heading 2 style in the Styles group.

   The Heading 2 style in the Traditional Quick Styles set changes the font color, adds spacing before and after the heading, and inserts a bottom border. The heading style also removes the shading you inserted in the previous activity.

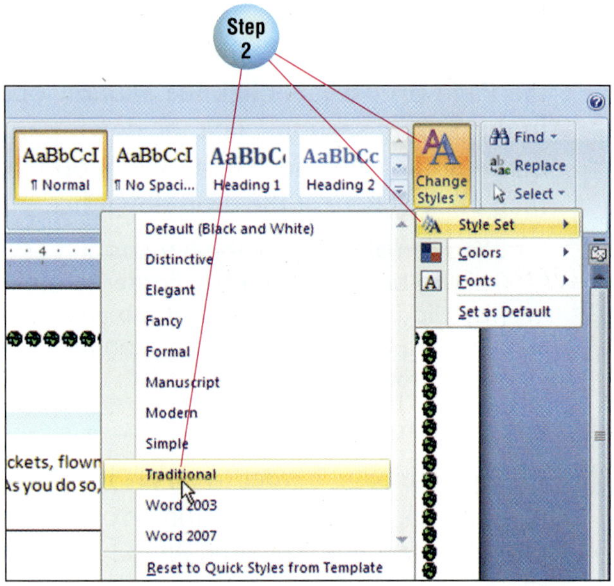

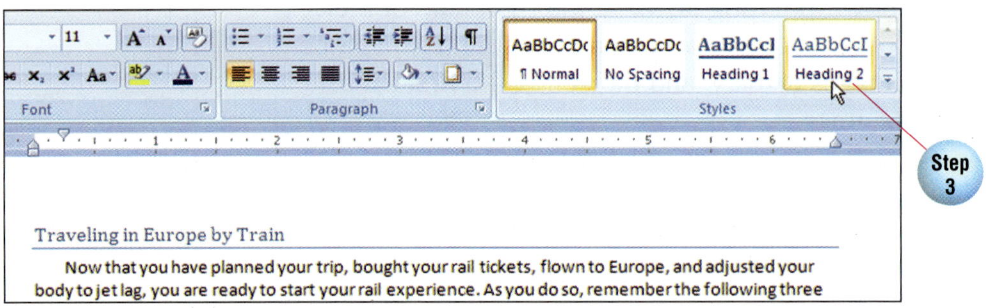

4. Click anywhere in the heading *Rail Ticket Bonuses* and then click the Heading 2 style in the Styles group.
5. Click anywhere in the heading *International Airports with Train Connections* and then click the Heading 2 style button.

6 Click the Styles group dialog box launcher.

This displays the Styles window containing available styles. Styles that apply only paragraph formatting display followed by a paragraph symbol (¶), styles that apply paragraph and character formatting display followed by a paragraph symbol and the **a** character (¶a), and styles that apply only character formatting display followed by the **a** character.

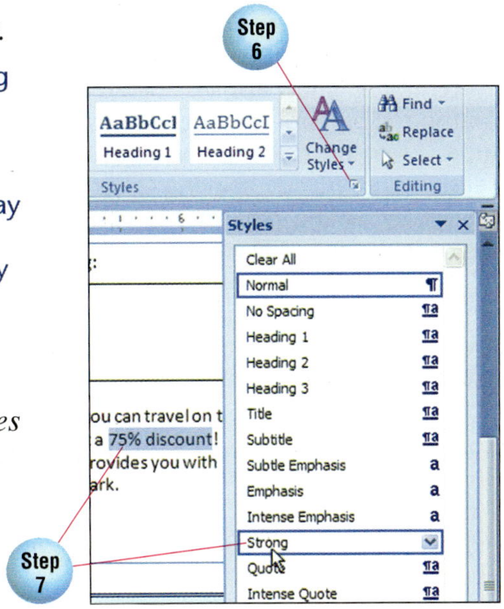

7 Select the words *75% discount* located in the last paragraph in the *Rail Ticket Bonuses* section and then click the *Strong* style in the Styles window.

8 Select the four numbered items that begin with *Have your pass validated.* and then click the *Intense Emphasis* style in the Styles window.

In Brief

Change Quick Styles Set

1. Click Change Styles button.
2. Point to Style Set.
3. Click desired set.

Apply Quick Style

1. Position insertion point at desired location.
2. Click style in Styles group or click More button and then click desired style.

Apply Style from Styles Window

1. Position insertion point at desired location.
2. Click Styles group dialog box launcher.
3. Click desired style in Styles window.

9 Close the Styles window by clicking the Close button (contains an X) located in the upper right corner of the window.

10 With the numbered text selected, remove the border around the paragraphs by clicking the Border button arrow and then clicking the *No Border* option at the drop-down list.

11 Remove the border around the bulleted paragraphs by selecting the paragraphs and then pressing the F4 function key. Deselect the text.

Pressing F4 repeats the most recent command.

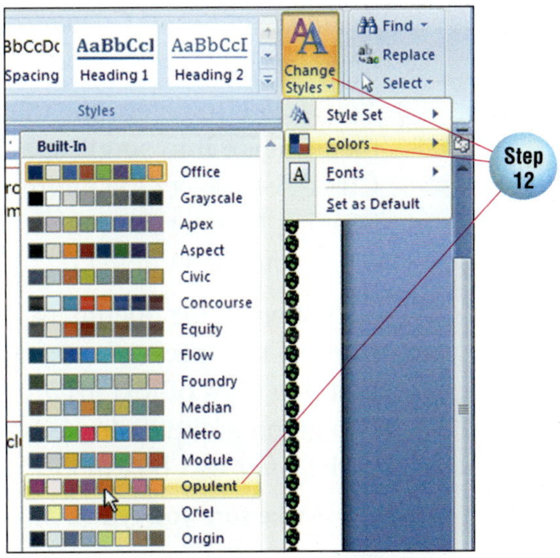

12 Click the Change Styles button in the Styles group, point to *Colors*, and then click *Opulent* at the drop-down gallery.

13 Click the Change Styles button in the Styles group, point to *Fonts*, and then click *Apex* at the drop-down gallery.

14 Save, print, and then close **WordS2-02.docx**.

In Addition

Displaying All Styles

The Styles window displays some of the most commonly used styles but not all of the predesigned styles. To display all styles, click the Styles group dialog box launcher and then click *Options* (located in the lower right corner) at the Styles window. At the Styles Gallery Options dialog box, click the down-pointing arrow at the right side of the *Select styles to show* option box and then click *All styles* at the drop-down list. Click OK to close the dialog box. All styles are now available in the Styles window.

Activity 2.11

Changing Default Document Formatting

A Word document is based on a template that applies default formatting. Some of the default formats include 11-point Calibri, line spacing of 1.15, and 10 points of spacing after each paragraph. Many of the documents you have opened from your student CD have had changes made to them including changes to the font, line spacing, and paragraph spacing. If you create a document with the default formatting, you may need to use the New Line command, Shift + Enter, to keep lines of text within the same paragraph, creating less space between one line and the next. If you turn on the display of nonprinting characters, by clicking the Show/Hide ¶ button in the Paragraph group in the Home tab, a line that ends with Shift + Enter displays as a curved arrow pointing left. This symbol can help you identify whether or not a line begins a new paragraph. You can modify the default formatting by manually changing individual features, change formatting by applying styles, or change formatting by applying a Quick Styles set.

Project

Your supervisor at First Choice Travel has asked you to complete a fact sheet on Middleton Valley. You need to type additional information and then apply formatting to improve the visual appeal of the document.

1. Open **FCTMiddleton.docx** and then save the document and name it **WordS2-03A**.

   This document has been prepared with default formatting.

2. Press Ctrl + End to move the insertion point to the end of the document and then type the text shown in Figure 2.5. Press the Enter key once after *Contact Information* and each of the telephone numbers. Press the New Line command, Shift + Enter, after *Jefferson Basin Chamber of Commerce*, *Department of Fisheries*, and *Lake Middleton Resort*.

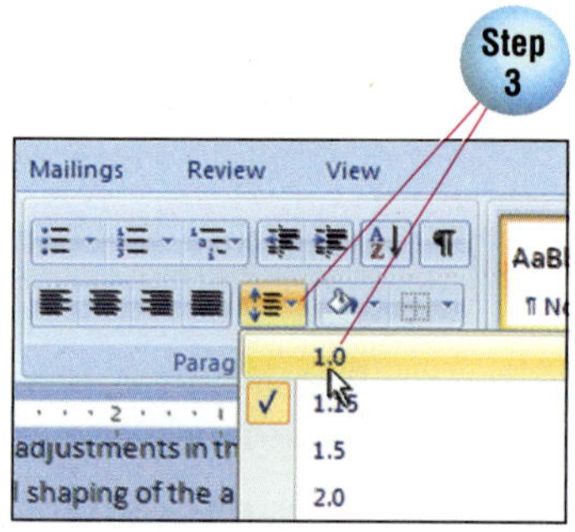

3. You decide to determine the current line spacing and then change it to single spacing. To do this, press Ctrl + A to select the entire document, click the Line Spacing button (notice the current setting is *1.15*), and then click *1.0*.

4. As you view the document, you decide to remove some of the spacing between the first three lines of text. To do this, select the first two lines of text *Middleton Valley* and *Jefferson Basin* and then click the Paragraph group dialog box launcher. At the Paragraph dialog box, select *10 pt* in the *After* text box in the *Spacing* section, type 0, and then click OK.

   Make sure you type a zero and not a capital O.

5. To improve the visual appeal of the document you decide to apply a Quick Styles set. To do this, click the Change Styles button, point to *Style Set*, and then click *Fancy* at the drop-down gallery.

6. Select the first three lines of text and then click the Heading 2 style in the Styles group.

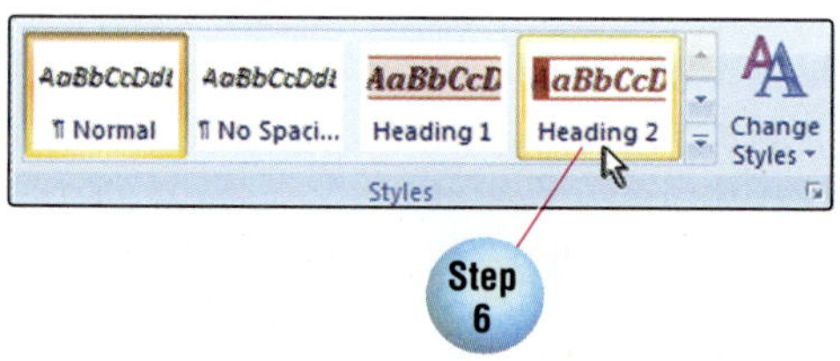

FIGURE 2.5 Step 2

Contact Information

Jefferson Basin Chamber of Commerce
(320) 555-3022

Department of Fisheries
(320) 555-8886

Lake Middleton Resort
(320) 555-1255

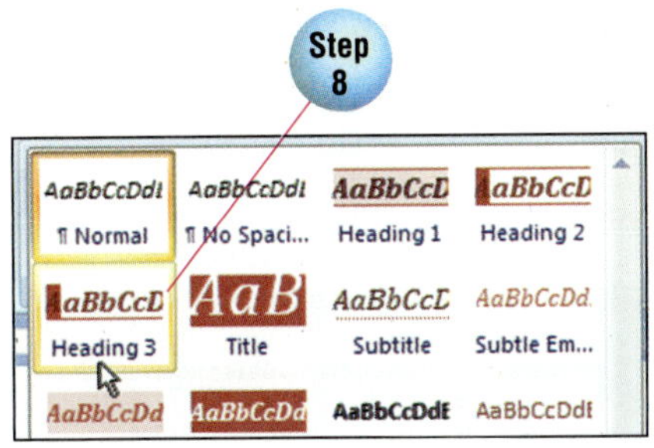

7. Position the insertion point on any character in the heading *Fishing* and then click the More button at the right side of the Styles group.
8. Click *Heading 3* at the drop-down gallery.
9. Apply the Heading 3 style to the remaining headings: *Geology*, *Sand Dunes and Off-Road Vehicles*, and *Contact Information*.

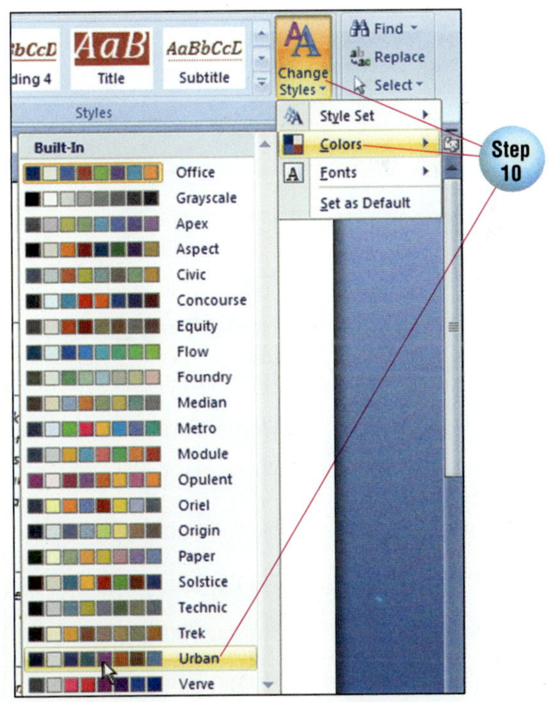

10. Change the style set color by clicking the Change Styles button, pointing to *Colors*, and then clicking *Urban* at the drop-down gallery.
11. Save and then print **WordS2-03A.docx**.
12. You decide to experiment with another Quick Styles set. To do this, click the Change Styles button, point to *Style Set*, and then click *Formal*.
13. Notice how the Formal style set increased the spacing above and below the first three lines of text. Remove some of the spacing by selecting the first three lines of text and then clicking the Paragraph group dialog box launcher.
14. At the Paragraph dialog box, change the *Before* measurement to *0 pt*, the *After* measurement to *6 pt*, and then click OK to close the dialog box.
15. Deselect the text.
16. Save the document with Save As and name it **WordS2-03B**.
17. Print and then close **WordS2-03B.docx**.

Features Summary

Feature	Ribbon Tab, Group	Button	Keyboard Shortcut
1.5 line spacing	Home, Paragraph		Ctrl + 5
align text left	Home, Paragraph		Ctrl + L
align text right	Home, Paragraph		Ctrl + R
bold	Home, Font		Ctrl + B
border	Home, Paragraph		
bullets	Home, Paragraph		
center	Home, Paragraph		Ctrl + E
change case	Home, Font		Shift + F3
change styles	Home, Styles		
clear formatting	Home, Font		
decrease indent	Home, Paragraph		Ctrl + Shift + M
double line spacing	Home, Paragraph		Ctrl + 2
font	Home, Font	Calibri (Body)	
font color	Home, Font		
Font dialog box	Home, Font		Ctrl + Shift + F
font size	Home, Font	11	Ctrl + Shift + P
Format Painter	Home, Clipboard		
hanging indent			Ctrl + T
highlight	Home, Font		
increase indent	Home, Paragraph		Ctrl + M
insert symbol	Insert, Symbols		
italics	Home, Font		Ctrl + I
justify	Home, Paragraph		Ctrl + J
line spacing	Home, Paragraph		
multilevel list	Home, Paragraph		
numbering	Home, Paragraph		
Paragraph dialog box	Home, Paragraph		
Quick Parts	Insert, Text	Quick Parts	
remove hanging indent			Ctrl + Shift + T
shading	Home, Paragraph		
single line spacing	Home, Paragraph		Ctrl + 1

continues

Feature	Ribbon Tab, Group	Button	Keyboard Shortcut
spacing after	Page Layout, Paragraph	0 pt	
spacing before	Page Layout, Paragraph	0 pt	
styles	Home, Styles		
Styles window	Home, Styles		
Tabs dialog box	Home, Paragraph OR Page Layout, Paragraph	, Tabs...	
underline	Home, Font	U	Ctrl + U

Knowledge Check

Completion: In the space provided at the right, indicate the correct term, command, or option.

1. The Bold button is located in this group in the Home tab ________
2. Click this button in the Font group and then click the *UPPERCASE* option to change selected text to uppercase letters. ________
3. Press these keys on the keyboard to italicize selected text. ________
4. The *Small caps* option is located in this section of the Font dialog box. ________
5. Click this button in the Paragraph group in the Home tab to align text at the right margin. ________
6. Indent text from the left margin by dragging the Left Indent marker on this. ________
7. The Line Spacing button displays in this group in the Home tab. ________
8. Click this button in the Paragraph group in the Home tab to number selected paragraphs. ________
9. Create multiple-level bulleted or numbered paragraphs with options from this button. ________
10. Display the Symbol palette by clicking this tab and then clicking the Symbol button in the Symbols group. ________
11. This is the name of the button that displays at the left side of the Ruler. ________
12. Set tabs at the Tabs dialog box or using this. ________
13. Click this button in the Font group in the Home tab to remove paragraph formatting from selected text. ________
14. These can be added to a tab to help guide the reader's eyes across the page. ________
15. Insert a page border with options at this dialog box with the Page Border tab selected. ________
16. A document contains a number of predesigned formats grouped into sets called this. ________
17. Click the Styles group dialog box launcher and this displays. ________
18. At a new document screen, this is the default line spacing. ________

Skills Review

Review 1 Formatting a Fact Sheet

First Choice TRAVEL

1. Open **FCTFactSheet01.docx** and then save it and name it **WordS2-R1**.
2. Change the font to Bookman Old Style and the font size to 11 points for the entire document. (If the Bookman Old Style font is not available, choose a similar font such as Garamond or Century Schoolbook.)
3. Set the title *FACT SHEET—PETERSBURG, ALASKA* in 16-point Arial bold.
4. Set the heading *Services* in 14-point Arial bold and then use Format Painter to apply the same formatting to the remaining headings (*Visitor Attractions*, *Walking Tours*, *Accommodations*, and *Transportation*).
5. Apply small caps to the last sentence in the document (the sentence that begins *If you would like more . . .*).
6. Apply a shadow effect to the title *FACT SHEET—PETERSBURG, ALASKA*.
7. Change the paragraph alignment to Justify for the paragraph below the title *FACT SHEET—PETERSBURG, ALASKA*.
8. Change the paragraph alignment to Center for the last sentence in the document (the sentence that begins *If you would like more . . .*).
9. Change the paragraph alignment to Justify and indent text 0.5 inch from the left margin for the two paragraphs below the *Services* heading. Apply the same formatting to the four paragraphs below the *Visitor Attractions* heading, the one paragraph below the *Walking Tours* heading, the two paragraphs below the *Accommodations* heading, and the two paragraphs below the *Transportation* heading.
10. Move the insertion point to the end of the document, press the Enter key twice, and then insert the current date and time.
11. Select the entire document, change the line spacing to 1.15, and then deselect the document.
12. Click anywhere in the *Services* heading and then change the paragraph spacing after to 6 points.
13. Use the Repeat command to insert 6 points of spacing after the remaining headings (*Visitor Attractions*, *Walking Tours*, *Accommodations*, and *Transportation*).
14. Save, print, and then close **WordS2-R1.docx**.

Review 2 Formatting a Vacation Package Document

First Choice TRAVEL

1. Open **FCTPackages.docx** and then save the document and name it **WordS2-R2**.
2. Select the entire document and then change the line spacing to 1 and remove the 10 points of spacing after paragraphs.
3. Select the four paragraphs of text below *Fast Facts* in the *OREGON* section, click the Decrease Indent button to remove the indent, and then insert bullets.
4. Select the four paragraphs of text below *Fast Facts* in the *NEVADA* section, click the Decrease Indent button to remove the indent, and then insert bullets.
5. Move the insertion point to the end of the document and then type the text shown in Figure 2.6.

6. Move the insertion point to the line below the heading *Rates and Packages* in the *OREGON* section and then create the tabbed text shown in Figure 2.7. Set a left tab at the 1-inch mark on the Ruler, a center tab at the 3.25-inch mark, and a right tab at the 5.5-inch mark on the Ruler.
7. Move the insertion point to the line below the heading *Rates and Packages* in the *NEVADA* section and then create the tabbed text shown in Figure 2.8 using the measurements from Step 6.
8. Select the tabbed text below the *Rates and Packages* heading in the *OREGON* section, insert a border and shading of your choosing, and then deselect the text.
9. Select the tabbed text below the *Rates and Packages* heading in the *NEVADA* section, insert the same border and shading you chose in Step 8, and then deselect the text.
10. Change the Quick Styles set to *Traditional*.
11. Apply the Heading 1 style to *OREGON* and *NEVADA*.
12. Apply the Heading 2 style to the headings *Fast Facts* and *Rates and Packages* in the *OREGON* section and the *NEVADA* section.
13. Change the Quick Styles set color to *Civic*.
14. Make sure the text fits on one page.
15. Save, print, and then close **WordS2-R2.docx**.

FIGURE 2.6 Review 2, Step 5

Additional accommodations are available at the Ste. Thérèse Chateau and Silver Creek Resort. For information, please contact Carlos Nuñez.

FIGURE 2.7 Review 2, Step 6

Accommodation	**No. Persons**	**Daily Price**
Studio/one bedroom	2–4	$75–125
Two bedrooms	4–6	$95–225
Three bedrooms	6–8	$135–300
Four bedrooms	8–12	$160–400
Five/six bedrooms	10–16	$250–500

FIGURE 2.8 Review 2, Step 7

Package	**Length**	**Price**
Tuck 'n' Roll	3 days/2 nights	$269
Ski Sneak	4 days/3 nights	$409
Take a Break	6 days/5 nights	$649
Ultimate	8 days/7 nights	$1,009

Skills Assessment

Assessment 1 Formatting a Cross Country Skiing Document

First Choice TRAVEL

1. Open **FCTCCSkiing.docx** and then save the document and name it **WordS2-A1**.
2. Make the following changes to the document:
   a. Set the entire document in Century Schoolbook. (If this typeface is not available, choose a similar typeface such as Bookman Old Style or Garamond.)
   b. Set the title in 14-point Tahoma bold. (If Tahoma is not available, choose Arial.)
   c. Set the names of the cross-country skiing resorts in 12-point Tahoma bold and add a shadow effect.
   d. Change the line spacing for the entire document to 1.3.
   e. Insert 6 points of space after each of the names of the cross-country skiing resorts.
   f. Center-align the title.
   g. Indent one-half inch from the left margin and change the alignment to Justify for the paragraph of text below each cross-country skiing resort name.
3. Save, print, and then close **WordS2-A1.docx**.

Assessment 2 Preparing and Formatting a Letter

Marquee PRODUCTIONS

1. Open **MPLetterhead.docx** and then save the document and name it **WordS2-A2**.
2. You are Neva Smith-Wilder, Educational Liaison for Marquee Productions. Write a letter using the date April 19, 2010, to Cal Rubine, Chair, Theatre Arts Division, Niagara Peninsula College, 2199 Victoria Street, Niagara-on-the-Lake, ON L0S 1J0 and include the following information:
   - Marquee Productions will be filming in and around the city of Toronto during the summer of 2010.
   - Marquee Productions would like to use approximately 20 theater interns to assist in the shoot.
   - Interns will perform a variety of tasks including acting as extras, assisting the camera crew, working with set designers on set construction, and providing support to the production team.
   - Interns can work approximately 15 to 30 hours per week and will be compensated at minimum wage.
   - Close your letter by asking Mr. Rubine to screen interested students and then send approximately 20 names to you.
   - If Mr. Rubine has any questions, he may contact you at (612) 555-2005 or send the names to you by e-mail at NevaSW@emcp.net
3. After typing the letter, apply the following formatting:
   a. Select the letter text (do not select the letterhead image or text) and then change to a font other than Calibri.
   b. Change the paragraph alignment to Justify for the paragraph(s) in the body of the letter.
4. Save, print, and then close **WordS2-A2.docx**.

Assessment 3 Setting Leader Tabs

1. At a blank document screen, type the text shown in Figure 2.9 with the following specifications:
   a. Center, bold, and italicize the text as shown.
   b. Set the tabbed text as shown using a left tab for the first column and a right tab with leaders for the second column.
   c. After typing the text, select the entire document, change to a typeface of your choosing (other than Calibri), and then change the spacing after paragraphs to 0 points.
2. Save the document and name it **WordS2-A3**.
3. Print and then close **WordS2-A3.docx**.

FIGURE 2.9 Assessment 3

WORLDWIDE ENTERPRISES

Distribution Schedule

Two by Two

United States...May 10

Canada...June 7

Japan...July 26

Australia/New Zealand............................August 2

Mexico...September 20

Assessment 4 Finding Information on the Widow/Orphan Feature and Keeping Text Together

HELP

1. Use Word's Help feature to learn how to prevent page breaks between paragraphs and how to place at least two lines of a paragraph at the top or bottom of a page to prevent a widow (last line of a paragraph by itself at the top of a page) or orphan (first line of a paragraph by itself at the bottom of a page).
2. Create a document containing the following information:
   a. Create a title for the document.
   b. Write a paragraph discussing how to prevent page breaks between paragraphs and list the steps required to complete the task.
   c. Write a paragraph discussing how to prevent a widow or orphan on a page in a document and list the steps required to complete the task.
3. Save the completed document and name it **WordS2-A4A**.
4. Print and then close **WordS2-A4A.docx**.

5. Open **FCTVacationSpecials.docx**.
6. Save the document with Save As and name it **WordS2-A4B**.
7. Select the entire document and then change the font to 12-point Times New Roman.
8. Complete a spelling and grammar check on the document.
9. Select the heading *Category S* (located toward the bottom of the first page) and the three lines of text below it.
10. Insert a command to keep all lines of text together with the next line.
11. Save the document and then print only page 2 of **WordS2-A4B.docx**.
12. Close **WordS2-A4B.docx**.

Assessment 5 Locating Information and Writing a Letter

1. You are a travel consultant for First Choice Travel and Camille Matsui, production assistant for Marquee Productions, has asked you to find information on art galleries and museums in Toronto, Ontario, Canada. Connect to the Internet and search for information on at least three art galleries and/or museums in the Toronto area.
2. Using the information you find on the Internet, open the **FCTLetterhead.docx** document and then write a letter to Camille Matsui, Production Assistant, Marquee Productions, 955 South Alameda Street, Los Angeles, CA 90037. Tell her about three galleries and/or museums, providing a brief description of each.
3. Use your name in the complimentary close and include the title, Travel Consultant.
4. Save the completed letter and name it **WordS2-A5**.
5. Print and then close **WordS2-A5.docx**.

Marquee Challenge

Challenge 1 Editing and Formatting a Fact Sheet

1. Open **FCTFactSheet02.docx** and then save the document with the name **WordS2-C1**.
2. Edit and format the document so it displays as shown in Figure 2.10. Change line and paragraph spacing to match the document and apply border and shading formatting as shown.
3. Save, print, and then close **WordS2-C1.docx**.

Challenge 2 Creating and Formatting a Flyer about a Skiing Vacation Package

1. Create the document shown in Figure 2.11. Set the text in the Cambria font and apply the page, border, shading, and bullet formatting as shown in the figure.
2. Save the completed document and name it **WordS2-C2**.
3. Print and then close **WordS2-C2.docx**.

FIGURE 2.10 Challenge 1

FACT SHEET—PETERSBURG, ALASKA

Petersburg, Alaska, located on Mitkof Island, is considered Alaska's Little Norway. Petersburg grew up around a salmon cannery and sawmill built by Peter Buschmann between 1897 and 1899. Petersburg is named after Peter Buschmann and part of its charm lies in its magnificent setting and the Scandinavian design of some of its buildings and houses.

Services

Downtown merchants sell a variety of products including gifts and souvenirs, hunting and fishing gear and licenses, camping supplies, groceries, hardware, marine supplies, automotive parts, and clothing. Unique and colorful gifts and clothes imported from Norway are available at some specialty shops. Artwork by local artists is sold at downtown shops and at an art gallery located near the ferry terminal.

The business district contains two banks, several restaurants, a laundry, a movie theater, and a bookstore. The U.S. Post Office and the U.S. Forest Service ranger district office are both located in the federal office building. Other merchants offer nearly all visitor services, including gas stations and car repair, air taxi services and charters, car rentals, RV parking, propane, and boat repairs and rentals.

Visitor Attractions

Visit the Clausen Memorial Museum at Second and Fram Streets to view exhibits that explain local fishing history and Petersburg's Norwegian heritage. The museum is open daily May through September.

The recently restored Sons of Norway Hall is one of the prominent downtown landmarks. It is a favorite location for artists and photographers. The hall is on the National Register of Historic Places and is open for visitors on special occasions.

Mitkof Island offers a picnic area at Sandy Beach located north of Petersburg. Sandy Beach has a good view of Frederick Sound and offers covered picnic shelters. Camping is not allowed at the picnic grounds.

Walk through any of the boat harbors and you will usually find a friendly fisherman who will explain some of the fishing gear and fishing boats docked in the harbor. Freshly caught local seafood is often available at the local markets and also is served at local restaurants.

Walking Tours

Petersburg offers several attractive walks. The city's Main Street contains brass inlays of area birds and animals, and boasts recently planted trees, custom light poles and benches, and picnic tables along Harbor Way. A boardwalk connects Mountain View Manor with the local ballpark. Other walks are the Loop Walk, Hammer Slough Walk, Harbor Walk, and the Three Lakes Loop Road Walk.

FIGURE 2.11 Challenge 2

Ski Lake Tahoe

Super Value Ski Package®

Our exciting new Super Value Ski Package features special rates on a full line of top-quality resort and hotel rentals for three days or more. Ask for the Super Value Ski Package and receive a blizzard of valuable savings for one low, inclusive price. Whatever resort or hotel you choose, you will receive the following items for free or at a considerable discount.

- Receive one free adult day lift ticket and ski all day.
- If you would like to travel throughout the Lake Tahoe area, rent any vehicle and receive a 25% discount coupon.
- For your comfort and convenience, we will include a coupon for a free ski rack rental.
- Book a Super Value Ski Package by October 31 and receive four $25 gift certificates you can use at any of the fine dining restaurants in the area.

Accommodations

Resort	*3 to 5 Nights*	*7+ Nights*
Ambassador Inn	$699	$959
Hanover's at Lake Tahoe	$679	$929
Moore Creek Lodge	$629	$879
Evergreen Suites	$619	$859
St. Rémi Resort	$607	$837
Cedar Ridge Lodge	$547	$757
Mountain Lodge	$539	$729
River Creek Resort	$525	$715
Alpine Lodge	$477	$677

Word SECTION 3

Formatting and Enhancing a Document

Skills

- Find and replace text
- Reveal formatting
- Cut, copy, and paste text
- Use the Clipboard task pane to copy and paste items
- Change page margins, orientation, and size
- Apply a theme
- Insert a watermark, page color, and page border
- Insert page numbering
- Insert a header and footer
- Use the Click and Type feature
- Vertically align text
- Insert, size, and move images
- Prepare an envelope
- Prepare labels

Student Resources

Before beginning this section:

1. Copy to your storage medium the WordS3 subfolder from the Word folder on the Student Resources CD.
2. Make WordS3 the active folder.

In addition to containing the data files needed to complete section work, the Student Resources CD contains model answers in PDF format for each of the projects in this section; model answers for end-of-section activities are not provided.

Projects Overview

First Choice TRAVEL: Edit and format fact sheets on Petersburg and Juneau, Alaska; prepare an announcement about a workshop on traveling on a budget; prepare a document on special vacation activities in Hawaii; prepare envelopes and labels for mailing fact sheets and announcements.

Niagara Peninsula College: Prepare an announcement about internship positions available at Marquee Productions; prepare an envelope and labels for the Theatre Arts Division.

Performance Threads: Format a costume rental agreement.

Worldwide Enterprises: Create an announcement for a stockholders' meeting; prepare an envelope.

Marquee Productions: Prepare an announcement about a workshop on employment opportunities in the movie industry; prepare a banner with information on the Royal Ontario Museum.

Activity 3.1

Finding and Replacing Text

Use the Find and Replace feature to find specific text and replace with other text. For example, you can use abbreviations for common phrases when entering text and then replace the abbreviations with the actual text later, or you can set up standard documents with generic names and replace the names with other names to make a personalized document. You can also find and replace some formatting. These options are available at the Find and Replace dialog box with the Replace tab selected.

Project

First Choice TRAVEL

You are working on a First Choice Travel document containing information on Petersburg, Alaska. Your quick review identifies some spelling and capitalization errors that you will correct using the Find and Replace feature.

1. Open **FCTPetersburg.docx** and then save the document and name it **WordS3-01**.
2. Press Ctrl + A to select the entire document, click the No Spacing style that displays in the Styles group in the Home tab, and then press Ctrl + Home to move the insertion point to the beginning of the document.

   Clicking the No Spacing style removes the default 10 points of spacing after the paragraph and changes the line spacing to 1.

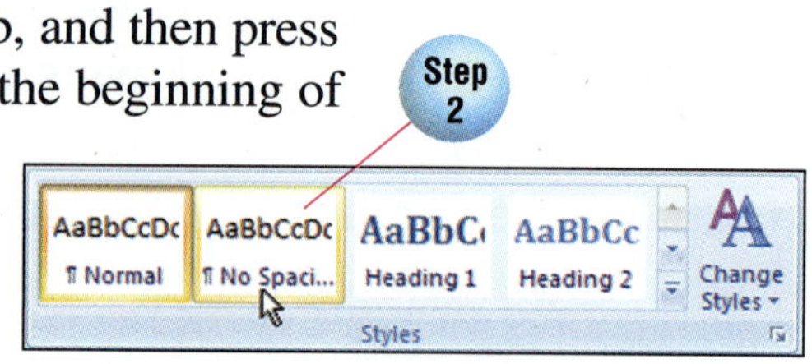

3. After looking over the document, you realize that Mitkof is spelled incorrectly as *Mitkoff*. Display the Find and Replace dialog box by clicking the Replace button [Replace] in the Editing group in the Home tab.
4. At the Find and Replace dialog box with the Replace tab selected, type **Mitkoff** in the *Find what* text box and then press the Tab key.

   Pressing the Tab key moves the insertion point to the *Replace with* text box.

5. Type **Mitkof** in the *Replace with* text box and then click the Replace All button located toward the bottom of the dialog box.

   Clicking the Replace All button replaces all occurrences of the text in the document. If you want control over what is replaced in a document, click the Replace button to replace text or click the Find Next button to move to the next occurrence of the text.

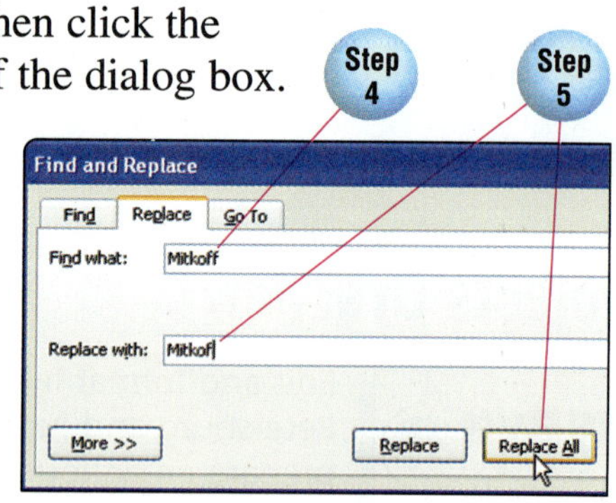

6. At the message telling you that two replacements were made, click the OK button.
7. Click the Close button to close the Find and Replace dialog box.
8. Looking at the document, you determine that Alaska Marine Highway is a proper name and should display in the document with the first letter of each word capitalized. To begin, click the Replace button [Replace] in the Editing group in the Home tab.
9. At the Find and Replace dialog box with the Replace tab selected, type **Alaska marine highway**.

   When you open the Replace dialog box, *Mitkoff* is automatically selected in the *Find what* text box. When you begin typing *Alaska marine highway*, the selected text is automatically deleted.

10 Press Tab, type **Alaska Marine Highway** in the *Replace with* text box, and then click the Replace All button.

11 At the message telling you that two replacements were made, click the OK button.

12 Click the Close button to close the Find and Replace dialog box.

13 Select the title *FACT SHEET—PETERSBURG, ALASKA* and then change the font to 16-point Arial bold and change the alignment to center.

14 Select the heading *Services* and then change the font to 14-point Arial bold. Use Format Painter to format the remaining headings (*Visitor Attractions*, *Walking Tours*, *Accommodations*, and *Transportation)* with 14-point Arial bold.

15 Save **WordS3-01.docx**.

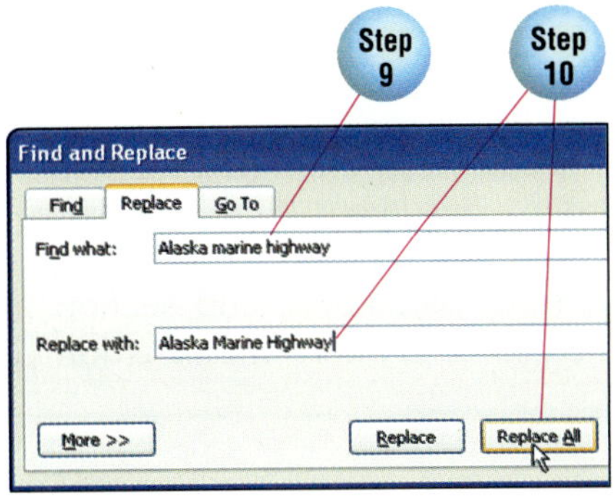

In Brief

Find and Replace Text

1. Click Replace button in Editing group.
2. Type find text.
3. Press Tab key.
4. Type replace text.
5. Click Replace All button.

In Addition

Options at the Expanded Find and Replace Dialog Box

The Find and Replace dialog box contains a variety of check boxes with options you can choose for completing a find and replace. To display these options, click the More button located at the bottom of the dialog box. This causes the Find and Replace dialog box to expand as shown at the right. The options are described below.

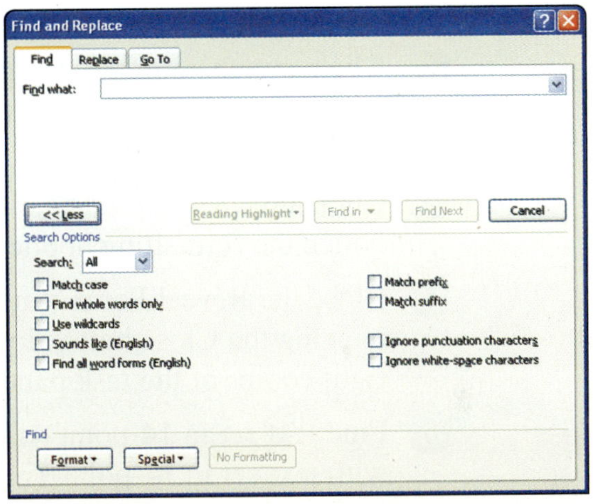

Option	Action
Match case	Exactly match the case of the search text. For example, if you search for *Book*, Word will stop at *Book* but not *book* or *BOOK*.
Find whole words only	Find a whole word, not a part of a word. For example, if you search for *her* and did *not* select *Find whole words only*, Word would stop at t*here*, *here*, *her*s, and so on.
Use wildcards	Search for wildcards, special characters, or special search operators.
Sounds like	Match words that sound alike but are spelled differently such as *know* and *no*.
Find all word forms	Find all forms of the word entered in the *Find what* text box. For example, if you enter *hold*, Word will stop at *held* and *holding*.
Match prefix	Find only those words that begin with the letters in the *Find what* text box. For example, if you enter *per*, Word will stop at words such as *perform* and *perfect* but skip over words such as *super* and *hyperlink*.
Match suffix	Find only those words that end with the letters in the *Find what* text box. For example, if you enter *ly*, Word will stop at words such as *accurately* and *quietly* but skip over words such as *catalyst* and *lyre*.
Ignore punctuation characters	Ignore punctuation within characters. For example, if you enter *US* in the *Find what* text box, Word will stop at *U.S.*
Ignore white space characters	Ignore spaces between letters. For example, if you enter *F B I* in the *Find what* text box, Word will stop at *FBI*.

Activity 3.2

Revealing Formatting; Finding and Replacing Formatting

Display formatting applied to specific text in a document at the Reveal Formatting task pane. The Reveal Formatting task pane displays font, paragraph, and section formatting applied to text where the insertion point is positioned or to selected text. With options at the Find and Replace dialog box with the Replace tab selected, you can search for specific formatting or characters containing specific formatting and replace it with other characters or formatting.

Project

After reviewing the Petersburg document, you decide that the headings would look better set in a different font and font color. To display the formatting applied to specific text, you will use the Reveal Formatting task pane and then find and replace font formatting.

1. With **WordS3-01.docx** open, press Ctrl + Home to move the insertion point to the beginning of the document and then press Shift + F1.

   Pressing Shift + F1 displays the Reveal Formatting task pane with information on the formatting applied to the title. Generally, a minus symbol precedes *Font* and *Paragraph* and a plus symbol precedes *Section* in the *Formatting of selected text* section. Click the minus symbol to hide any items below a heading and click the plus symbol to reveal items. Some items in the Reveal Formatting task pane are hyperlinks. For example, click the Font hyperlink and the Font dialog box displays. Use these hyperlinks to make changes to the document formatting.

2. Click anywhere in the paragraph below the title and look at the Reveal Formatting task pane to determine the formatting.
3. Click anywhere in the heading *Services* and then notice the formatting applied to the text.
4. Close the Reveal Formatting task pane by clicking the Close button located in the upper right corner of the task pane.
5. Find text set in 14-point Arial bold and replace it with text set in 14-point Times New Roman bold italic and in dark blue color. To begin, position the insertion point at the beginning of the document and then click the Replace button in the Editing group in the Home tab.
6. At the Find and Replace dialog box, press the Delete key. (This deletes any text that displays in the *Find what* text box.)
7. Click the More button. (If a check mark displays in the *Find all word forms* check box, click the option to remove the mark.)
8. Click the Format button located at the bottom of the dialog box and then click *Font* at the pop-up list.

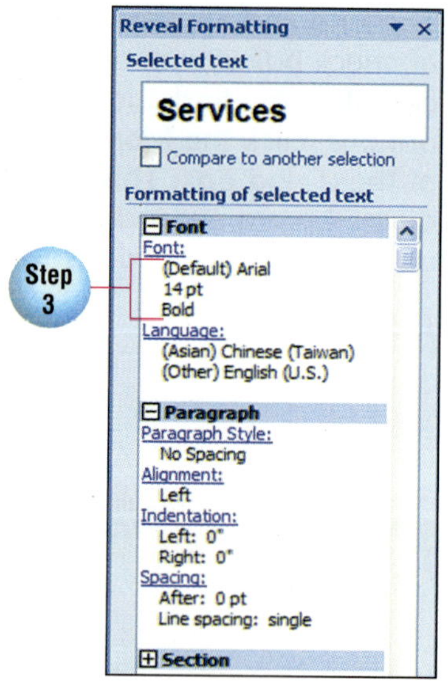

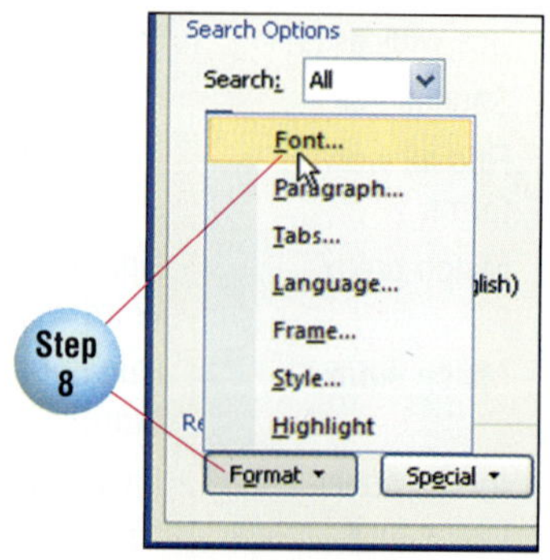

9 At the Find Font dialog box, change the font to Arial, the font style to bold, and the size to 14, and then click OK to close the dialog box.

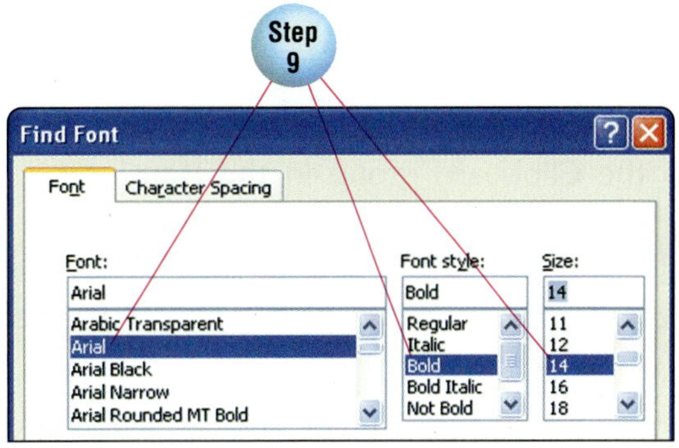

10 At the Find and Replace dialog box, select and then delete any text that displays in the *Replace with* text box.

11 With the insertion point positioned in the *Replace with* text box, click the Format button located at the bottom of the dialog box and then click *Font* at the pop-up list.

12 At the Replace Font dialog box, change the font to Times New Roman, the font style to bold italic, the size to 14, and the font color to Dark Blue.

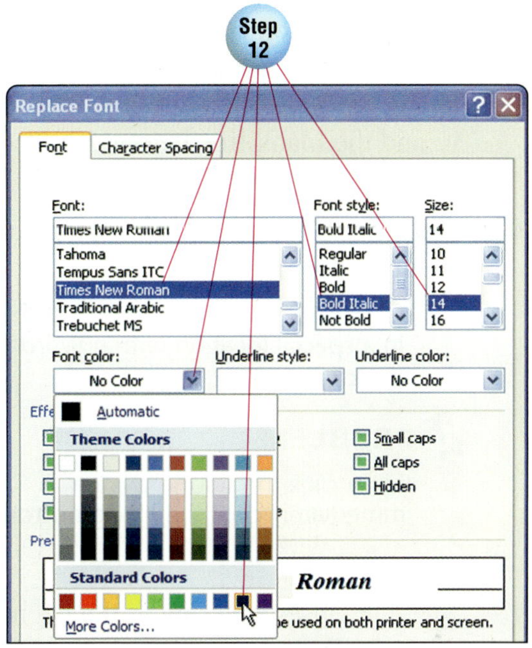

13 Click OK to close the dialog box.

14 At the Find and Replace dialog box, click the Replace All button. At the message telling you that the search of the document is complete and five replacements were made, click OK.

15 With the Find and Replace dialog box open and the insertion point positioned in the *Find what* text box, click the No Formatting button that displays at the bottom of the dialog box. Click in the *Replace with* text box and then click the No Formatting button.

16 Click the Less button to reduce the size of the Find and Replace dialog box and then close the dialog box.

17 Select the title *FACT SHEET—PETERSBURG, ALASKA* and then change the font to 14-point Times New Roman bold and the font color to Dark Blue.

18 Save **WordS3-01.docx**.

In Brief

Reveal Formatting
1. Click in desired text.
2. Press Shift + F1.

In Addition

Comparing Formatting

Along with displaying formatting applied to text, you can use the Reveal Formatting task pane to compare formatting of two text selections to determine what formatting is different. To compare formatting, display the Reveal Formatting task pane and then select the first instance of formatting to be compared. Click the *Compare to another selection* check box to insert a check mark and then select the second instance of formatting to compare. Any differences between the two selections will display in the *Formatting differences* list box.

Activity 3.3

Cutting, Copying, and Pasting Text; Using Paste Special

With the Cut, Copy, and Paste buttons in the Clipboard group in the Home tab, you can move and/or copy words, sentences, or entire sections of text to other locations in a document. You can cut and paste text or copy and paste text within the same document or between documents. Specify the formatting of pasted text with options at the Paste Special dialog box.

Project

You decide that some of the text in the fact sheet about Petersburg, Alaska, should be reorganized and you also decide to add additional information to the document.

First Choice TRAVEL

1. With **WordS3-01.docx** open, move the *Services* section below the *Walking Tours* section. Begin by selecting the *Services* heading, the two paragraphs of text below it, and the blank line below the second paragraph.

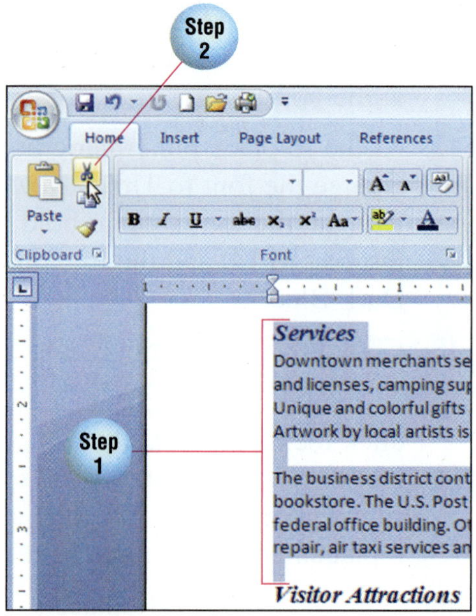

2. Click the Cut button in the Clipboard group in the Home tab.

   Clicking the Cut button places the text in a special location within Word called the ***clipboard***.

   PROBLEM

   If you click the wrong button, immediately click the Undo button.

3. Move the insertion point to the beginning of the *Accommodations* heading and then click the Paste button in the Clipboard group in the Home tab.

   A Paste Options button displays below the pasted text. Click this button and options display for specifying the formatting of the pasted text. The default setting keeps source formatting for the pasted text. You can also choose to match the destination formatting or keep only the text and not the formatting.

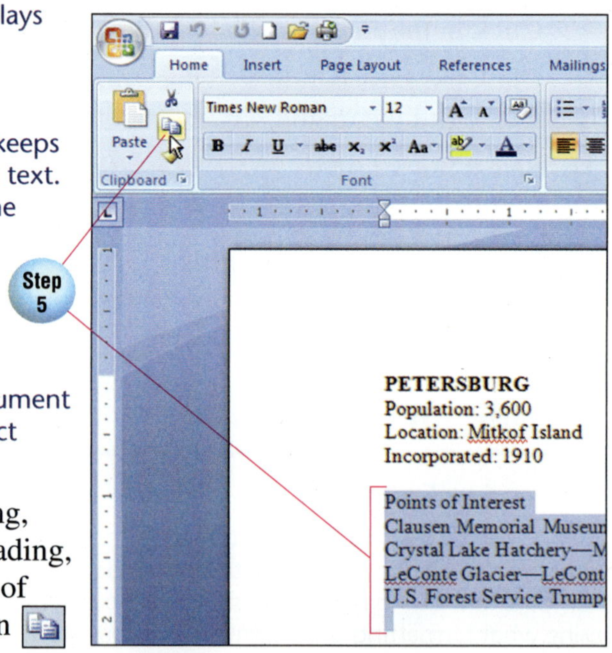

4. Open **FCTPA01.docx**.

   You will copy text from this document and paste it in the Petersburg fact sheet.

5. Select the *Points of Interest* heading, the four lines of text below the heading, and the blank line below the lines of text and then click the Copy button in the Clipboard group.

6 Click the button on the Taskbar representing **WordS3-01.docx**.

7 Position the insertion point at the beginning of the sentence *If you would like more information . . .* located toward the end of the document and then click the Paste button in the Clipboard group.

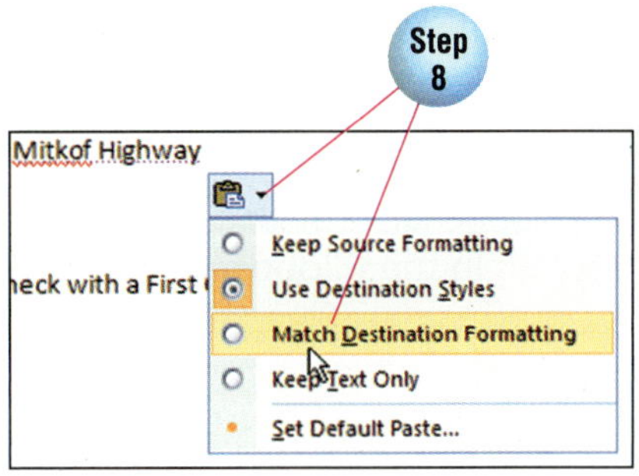

8 Click the Paste Options button and then click *Match Destination Formatting* at the drop-down list.

9 Click the button on the Taskbar representing **FCTPA01.docx**.

10 Select the text *Resources:* and the three lines below it and then click the Copy button .

11 Click the button on the Taskbar representing **WordS3-01.docx**.

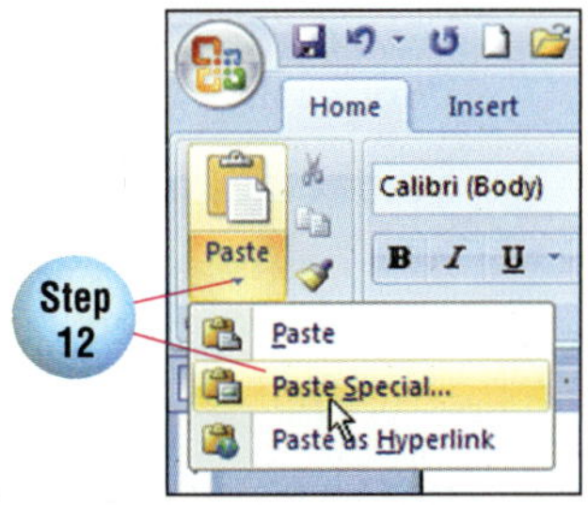

12 Move the insertion point to the end of the document and then press the Enter key once. Paste the copied text into the document without the formatting by clicking the Paste button arrow and then clicking *Paste Special* at the drop-down list.

13 At the Paste Special dialog box, click *Unformatted Text* in the *As* list box and then click OK.

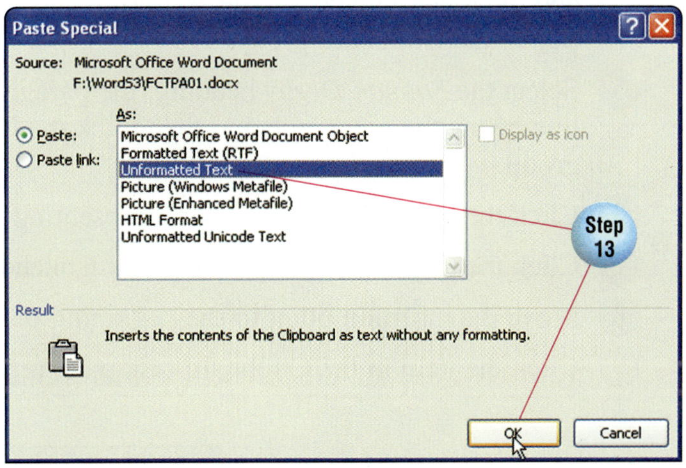

14 Save **WordS3-01.docx**.

15 Click the button on the Taskbar representing the **FCTPA01.docx** document and then close the document.

Closing the **FCTPA01.docx** document displays the **WordS3-01.docx** document.

In Brief

Cut and Paste Text

1. Select text.
2. Click Cut button in Clipboard group.
3. Move insertion point to desired position.
4. Click Paste button in Clipboard group.

Copy and Paste Text

1. Select text.
2. Click Copy button in Clipboard group.
3. Move insertion point to desired position.
4. Click Paste button in Clipboard group.

Display Paste Special Dialog Box

1. Cut or copy text.
2. Click Paste button arrow.
3. Click *Paste Special*.
4. Click desired format in *As* list box.
5. Click OK.

In Addition

Moving and Copying Text with the Mouse

You can move selected text using the mouse. To do this, select the text with the mouse and then move the I-beam pointer inside the selected text until the I-beam pointer turns into an arrow pointer. Hold down the left mouse button, drag the arrow pointer (displays with a gray box attached) to the location where you want the selected text inserted, and then release the button. You can copy and move selected text by following similar steps. The difference is that you need to hold down the Ctrl key while dragging with the mouse. With the Ctrl key down, a box containing a plus symbol displays near the gray box by the arrow pointer.

Activity 3.4

Using the Clipboard Task Pane

Using the Clipboard task pane, you can collect up to 24 different items and then paste them in various locations in a document. Display the Clipboard task pane by clicking the Clipboard dialog box launcher. Cut or copy an item and the item displays in the Clipboard task pane. If the item is text, the first 50 characters display. Paste an item by positioning the insertion point at the desired location and then clicking the item in the Clipboard task pane. When all desired items are inserted, click the Clear All button located in the upper right corner of the task pane.

Project

You will open another fact sheet document, copy items in the document, and then paste the items into the Petersburg fact sheet document.

First Choice TRAVEL

1. Make sure **WordS3-01.docx** is open and then open the **FCTPA02.docx** document.
2. In the **FCTPA02.docx** document, display the Clipboard task pane by clicking the Clipboard group dialog box launcher. If any items display in the Clipboard task pane, click the Clear All button located in the upper right corner of the task pane.
3. Select the *Sightseeing* heading, the two paragraphs of text below it, and the blank line below the second paragraph and then click the Copy button in the Clipboard group.

   Notice how the copied item is represented in the Clipboard task pane.
4. Select the *Little Norway Festival* heading, the two paragraphs of text below it, and the blank line below the second paragraph and then click the Copy button in the Clipboard group.
5. Select the *Salmon Derby* heading, the paragraph of text below it, and the blank line below the paragraph and then click the Copy button in the Clipboard group.
6. Click the button on the Taskbar representing **WordS3-01.docx**.
7. Click the Clipboard group dialog box launcher to display the Clipboard task pane.
8. Move the insertion point to the beginning of the *Walking Tours* heading.
9. Click the item in the Clipboard task pane representing *Salmon Derby*.

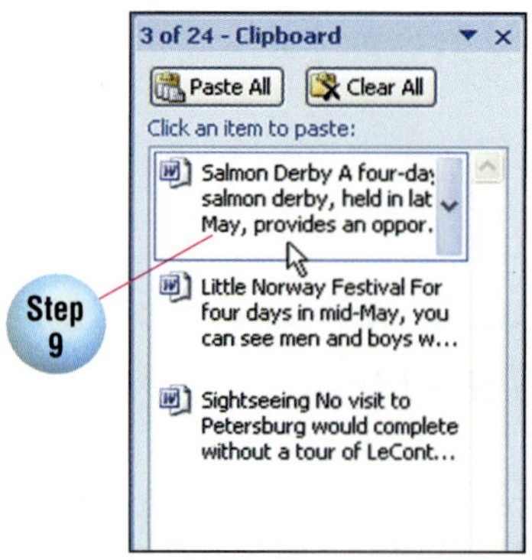

10 Move the insertion point to the beginning of the *Points of Interest* heading.

11 Click the item in the Clipboard task pane representing *Sightseeing*.

12 Click the Clear All button located toward the upper right corner of the Clipboard task pane.

13 Close the Clipboard task pane by clicking the Close button located in the upper right corner of the task pane.

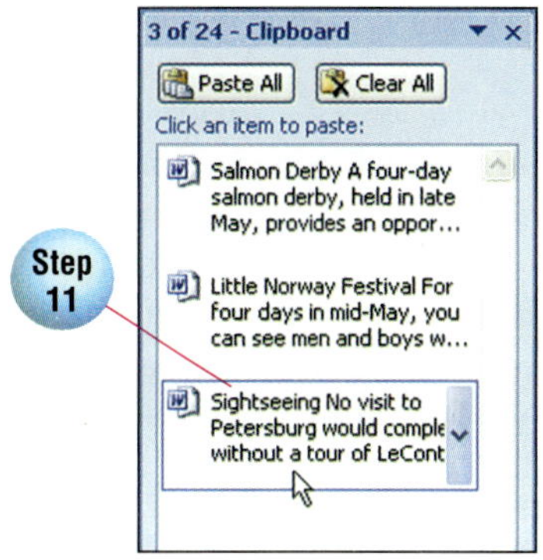

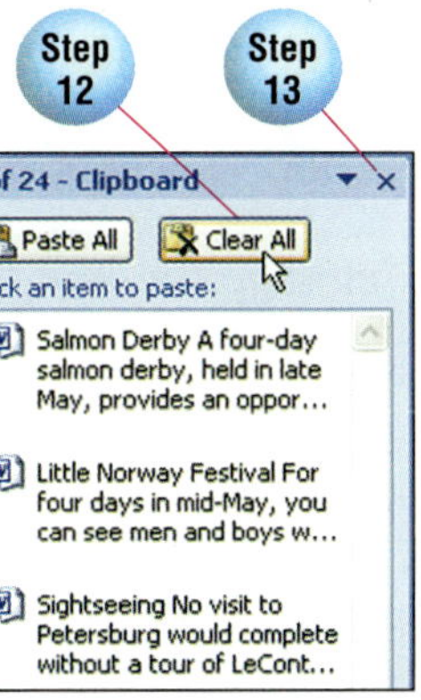

14 Click the button on the Taskbar representing **FCTPA02.docx** and then close the document.

The **WordS3-01.docx** document displays when you close **FCTPA02.docx**.

15 Click anywhere in the heading *Visitor Attractions* and then double-click the Format Painter button in the Clipboard group in the Home tab.

16 Select the headings *Salmon Derby*, *Sightseeing*, and *Points of Interest*.

17 Click the Format Painter button to turn off the feature.

18 Save **WordS3-01.docx**.

In Brief

Use Clipboard Task Pane

1. Click Clipboard group dialog box launcher.
2. Select text.
3. Click Copy button.
4. Select and copy any additional items.
5. Move insertion point to desired position.
6. Click item in Clipboard task pane representing desired item.
7. Paste any other desired items from Clipboard task pane.
8. Click Clear All button.

In Addition

Clipboard Task Pane Options

Click the Options button located toward the bottom of the Clipboard task pane and a pop-up menu displays with five options as shown at the right. Insert a check mark before those options that you want active. For example, you can choose to display the Clipboard task pane automatically when you cut or copy text, press Ctrl + C twice to display the Clipboard task pane, cut and copy text without displaying the Clipboard task pane, display the Office Clipboard icon near the Taskbar when the clipboard is active, and display the item message when copying items to the Clipboard.

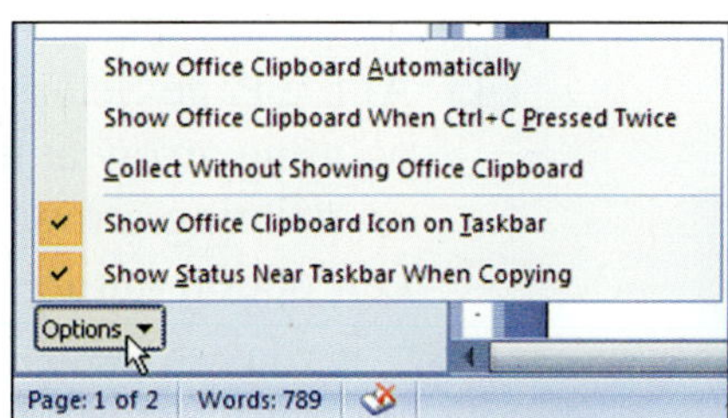

Activity 3.5

Changing Page Margins, Orientation, and Size; Applying a Theme

In Word, a page contains a number of defaults such as a page size of 8.5 inches by 11 inches; top, bottom, left, and right margins of one inch; a portrait page orientation; and a page break after approximately nine inches of vertical text on a page. Change these default settings with buttons in the Page Setup group in the Page Layout tab. You can apply formatting to a document using a theme. A theme applies formatting in much the same way as the Quick Style sets discussed in Activities 2.10 and 2.11. A document theme is a set of formatting choices that include a color theme (a set of colors), a font theme (a set of heading and body text fonts), and an effects theme (a set of lines and fill effects). Apply a theme with buttons in the Themes group in the Page Layout tab.

Project

To customize the Petersburg fact sheet you will change the document margins, orientation, and page size and then customize and add visual appeal by applying a theme.

1. With **WordS3-01.docx** open, change the margins by clicking the Page Layout tab, clicking the Margins button in the Page Setup group, and then clicking the *Office 2003 Default* option at the drop-down list.

   The *Office 2003 Default* option changes the left and right margins to 1.25, which is the default for Word 2003.

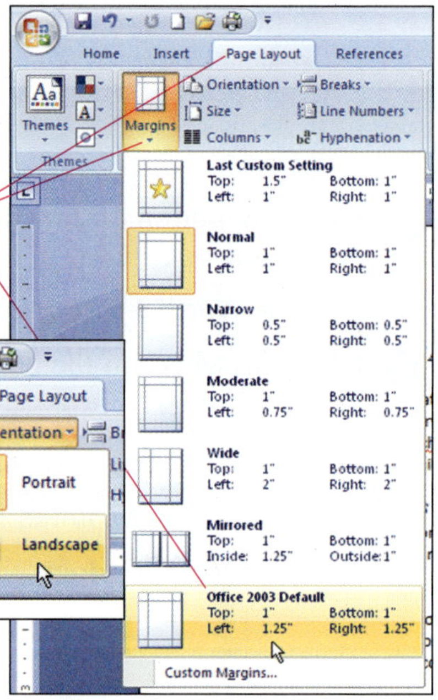

2. Change the page orientation by clicking the Orientation button in the Page Setup group in the Page Layout tab and then clicking *Landscape* at the drop-down list.

   By default, a page is set in portrait orientation. At this orientation, Word considers a page 8.5 inches wide and 11 inches tall. Change to landscape orientation and Word considers a page 11 inches wide and 8.5 inches tall. You can also change page orientation at the Page Setup dialog box with the Margins tab selected.

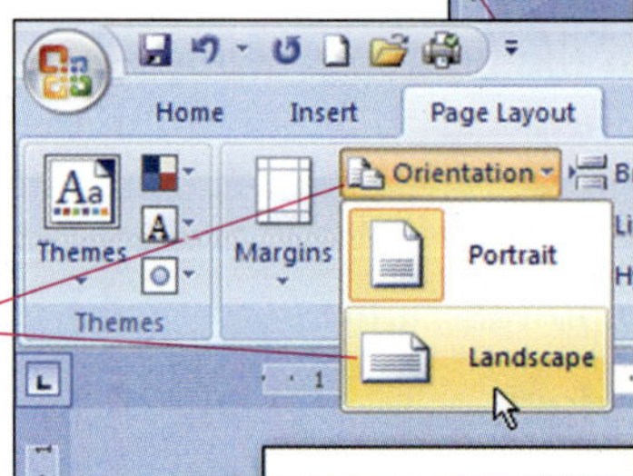

3. With the document in landscape orientation, you decide to make changes to the margins. To begin, click the Margins button in the Page Setup group in the Page Layout tab and then click the *Custom Margins* option that displays at the bottom of the drop-down list.

4. At the Page Setup dialog box with the Margins tab selected, click the down-pointing arrow at the right side of the *Bottom* option until *1"* displays. Click the up-pointing arrow at the right side of the *Left* option until *1.5"* displays.

   You can also change a margin measurement by selecting the measurement and then typing the new measurement.

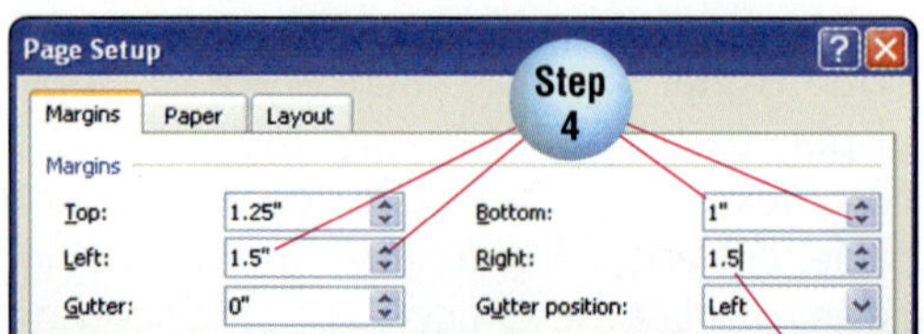

5. Select the current measurement in the *Right* text box and then type **1.5**.

6. Click OK to close the Page Setup dialog box.

7. Apply a theme to the document by clicking the Themes button in the Themes group and then clicking *Oriel* at the drop-down gallery.

   Apply formatting to an entire document using a theme. A document theme is formatting that includes a font theme, a color theme, and an effects theme.

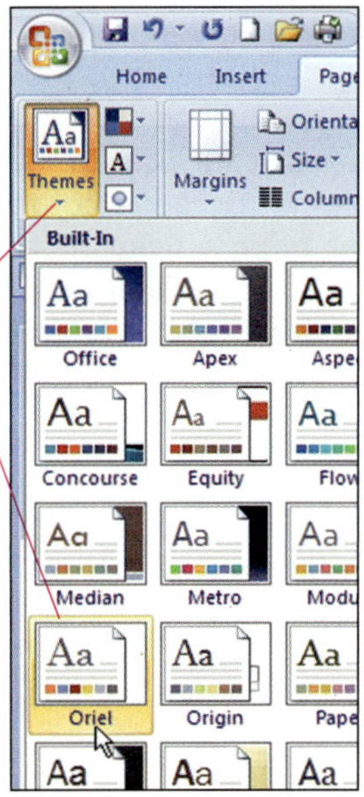

8. You like the color of the theme but you decide to change the font. To do this, click the Theme Fonts button in the Themes group, scroll down the drop-down gallery, and then click *Paper*.

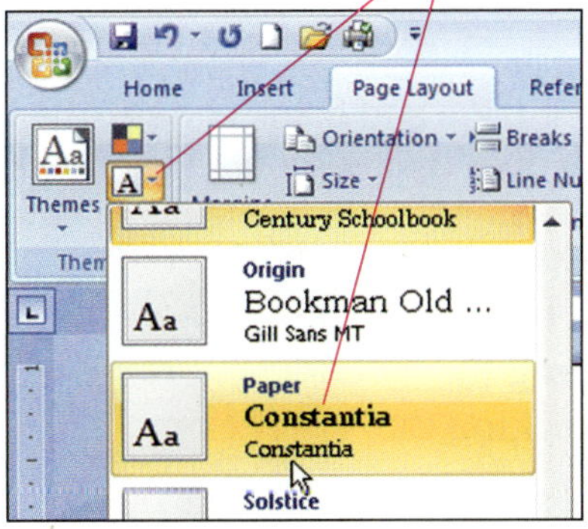

9. You decide to experiment with paper size by clicking the Size button in the Page Setup group, and then clicking the *Legal* option at the drop-down list.

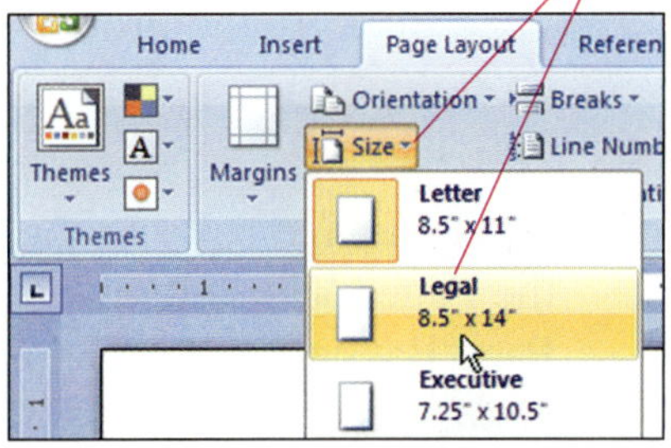

10. Scroll through the document and notice how the document is affected by the Legal page size. After looking at the document you decide to return to the default page size. To do this, click the Size button in the Page Setup group and then click *Letter* at the drop-down list.

11. Move the insertion point to the title *FACT SHEET—PETERSBURG, ALASKA*, click the Home tab, click the Shading button arrow, and then click the *Blue, Accent 2, Lighter 60%* color.

12. Move the insertion point to the heading *Visitor Attractions*, click the Shading button arrow, and then click the *Blue, Accent 2, Lighter 80%* color.

13. Apply the same shading (Blue, Accent 2, Lighter 80%) to the remaining headings in the document (*Salmon Derby*, *Walking Tours*, *Services*, *Accommodations*, *Transportation*, *Sightseeing*, and *Points of Interest*).

14. Save **WordS3-01.docx**.

In Brief

Changing Margins
1. Click Page Layout tab.
2. Click Margins button.
3. Click desired option.

Changing Orientation
1. Click Page Layout tab.
2. Click Orientation button.
3. Click desired orientation option.

Changing Page Size
1. Click Page Layout tab.
2. Click Size button.
3. Click desired size option.

Apply a Theme
1. Click Page Layout tab.
2. Click Themes button.
3. Click desired theme.

Activity 3.6

Customizing the Page and Page Background

The Page Background group in the Page Layout tab contains buttons you can use to insert a watermark, change the page color, and insert a page border. In an activity in Section 1, you applied a watermark to a document using options at the Building Blocks Organizer dialog box. You can also apply a watermark with the Watermark button. In a project in Section 2, you applied a page border to a document. You can also apply a page border using the Page Borders button in the Page Background group. The Pages group in the Insert tab contains buttons for adding a cover page, a blank page, and a page break.

Project

To add visual appeal to the Petersburg fact sheet, you will apply page color and a page border. You will add a cover page and blank page at the beginning of the document and identify the document as a draft by inserting a watermark.

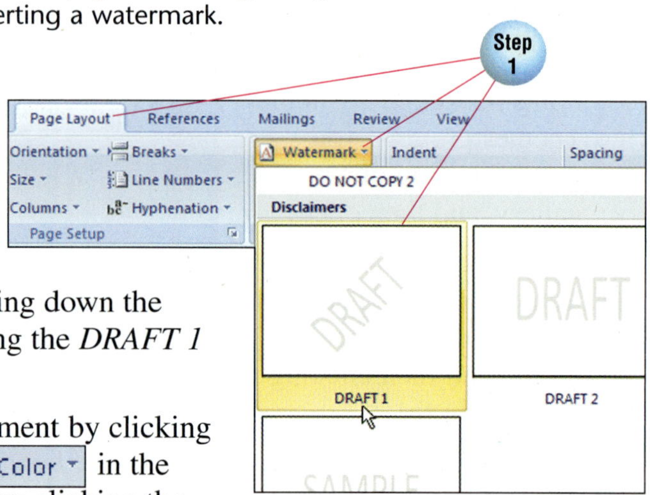

1. With **WordS3-01.docx** open, press Ctrl + Home. Insert a watermark by clicking the Page Layout tab, clicking the Watermark button Watermark in the Page Background group, scrolling down the drop-down list, and then clicking the *DRAFT 1* option.

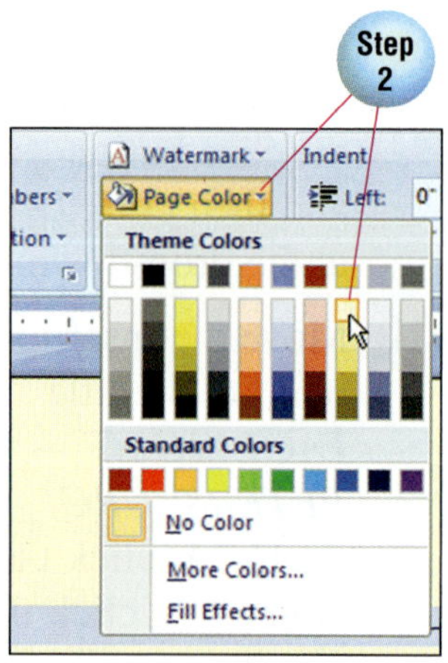

2. Apply a page color to the document by clicking the Page Color button Page Color in the Page Background group and then clicking the *Gold, Accent 4, Lighter 80%* color.

   Page color is designed for viewing a document on screen and does not print.

3. Click the Page Borders button Page Borders in the Page Background group.

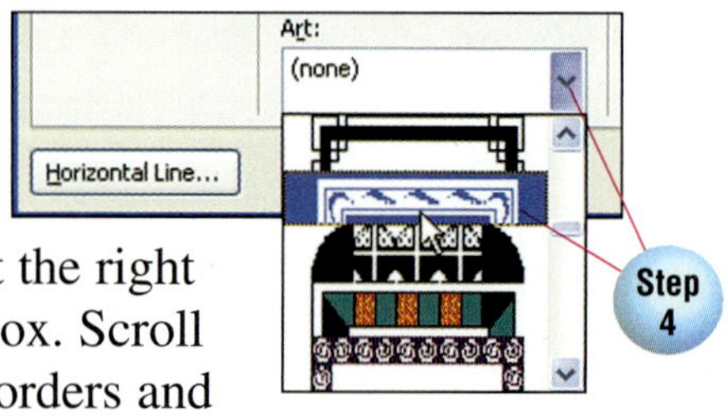

4. At the Borders and Shading dialog box with the Page Border tab selected, click the down-pointing arrow at the right side of the *Art* option box. Scroll down the list of page borders and then click the art border option shown above. Click OK to close the dialog box.

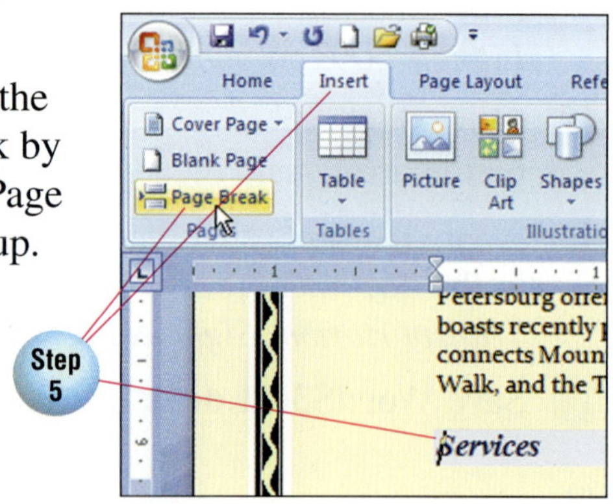

5. Move the insertion point to the beginning of the heading *Services* and then insert a page break by clicking the Insert tab and then clicking the Page Break button Page Break in the Pages group.

   You can also insert a page break by clicking the Page Layout tab, clicking the Breaks button Breaks in the Page Setup group, and then clicking *Page* at the drop-down list.

6. Move the insertion point to the beginning of the *Sightseeing* heading and then insert a hard page break by pressing Ctrl + Enter.
7. Save and then print **WordS3-01.docx**. (The page background color does not print.)
8. After looking at the printed document, you decide to make some changes. Remove the page color by clicking the Page Layout tab, clicking the Page Color button [Page Color] in the Page Background group, and then clicking the *No Color* option.

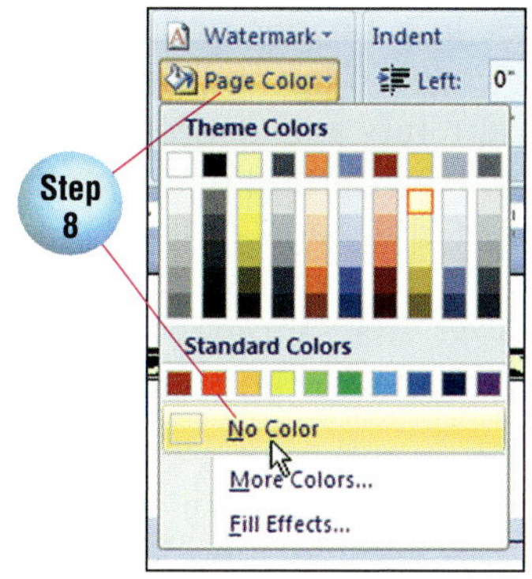

9. Change the orientation by clicking the Orientation button in the Page Setup group and then clicking *Portrait*.
10. Remove the page border by clicking the Page Borders button [Page Borders], clicking *None* in the *Setting* section of the Borders and Shading dialog box, and then clicking OK.
11. Click the Home tab and then click the Show/Hide ¶ button.

    Clicking the Show/Hide ¶ button turns on the display of nonprinting characters.

12. Delete the page break before *Services* by positioning the insertion point at the beginning of the page break that displays toward the bottom of the first page and then pressing the Delete key twice.
13. Delete the page break that displays toward the bottom of the second page and then insert a page break at the beginning of the heading *Points of Interest*.
14. Click the Show/Hide ¶ button to turn off the display of nonprinting characters.
15. You need a blank page at the end of the document for information that will be added later. Press Ctrl + End, click the Insert tab, and then click the Blank Page button in the Pages group.
16. Press Ctrl + Home and then insert a cover page by clicking the Cover Page button [Cover Page], scrolling down the drop-down list, and then clicking *Motion*.

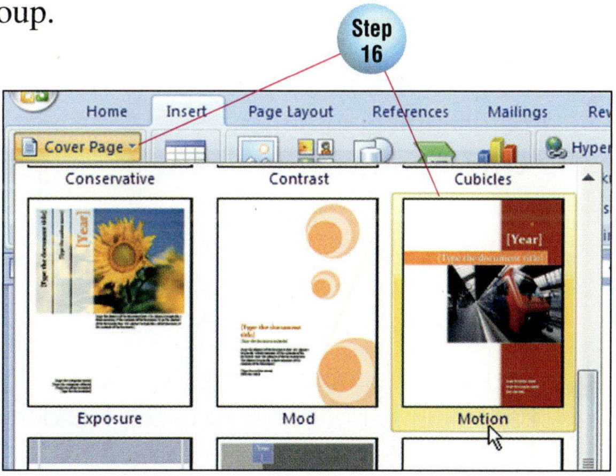

17. Insert the current year in the *[Year]* placeholder and type **Alaska Fact Sheets** in the *[Type the document title]* placeholder.
18. Type your first and last names in the *[Type the author name]* placeholder, type **First Choice Travel** in the *[Type the company name]* placeholder, and then change the date below the company name to the current date.
19. Save **WordS3-01.docx**.

In Brief

Apply Watermark
1. Click Page Layout tab.
2. Click Watermark button.
3. Click desired watermark option.

Apply Page Color
1. Click Page Layout tab.
2. Click Page Color button.
3. Click desired color.

Insert Page Border
1. Click Page Layout tab.
2. Click Page Borders button.
3. Click desired options at Borders and Shading dialog box.
4. Click OK.

Insert Page Break
1. Click Insert tab.
2. Click Page Break button.

Insert Blank Page
1. Click Insert tab.
2. Click Blank Page button.

Insert Cover Page
1. Click Insert tab.
2. Click Cover Page button.
3. Click desired option.
4. Type text in appropriate fields.

Activity 3.7

Inserting Page Numbering, Headers, and Footers

Insert page numbering in a document with options from the Page Number button or in a header or footer. Click the Page Number button in the Header & Footer group in the Insert tab and a drop-down list displays with options for inserting page numbers at the top or bottom of the page or in the page margins, removing page numbers, and formatting page numbers. Text that appears at the top of every page is called a ***header*** and text that appears at the bottom of every page is referred to as a ***footer***. Headers and footers are common in manuscripts, textbooks, reports, and other publications. Insert a predesigned header in a document with the Header button in the Header & Footer group in the Insert tab. Insert a predesigned footer in the same manner as a header. Headers and footers are visible in Print Layout view but not Draft view. Predesigned headers and footers contain formatting which you can customize.

Project

Insert identifying information in the document using a header and footer and insert page numbering in the Petersburg fact sheet.

First Choice TRAVEL

1. With **WordS3-01.docx** open, remove the blank page by clicking the Home tab and then clicking the Show/Hide ¶ button. Position the insertion point at the beginning of the page break that displays below the text on the fourth page and then press the Delete key. Click the Show/Hide ¶ button to turn off the display of nonprinting characters.
2. Move the insertion point to the beginning of the title *FACT SHEET—PETERSBURG, ALASKA* and then number pages at the bottom of each page by clicking the Insert tab, clicking the Page Number button in the Header & Footer group, and then pointing to *Bottom of Page*.

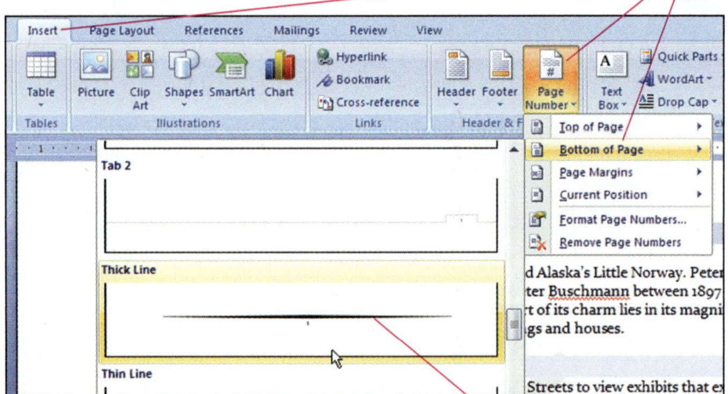

3. At the gallery of predesigned page numbers, scroll down the list and then click the *Thick Line* option.
4. Double-click in the body of the document and then scroll through the document and notice how the page numbers display toward the bottom of each page except the cover page.
5. Remove page numbering by clicking the Insert tab, clicking the Page Number button in the Header & Footer group, and then clicking *Remove Page Numbers* at the drop-down list.
6. Insert a header in the document by clicking the Header button in the Header & Footer group, scrolling down the header list, and then clicking the *Mod (Even Page)* header.

   Notice how the document title you entered in the cover page is inserted in the header along with the current date.

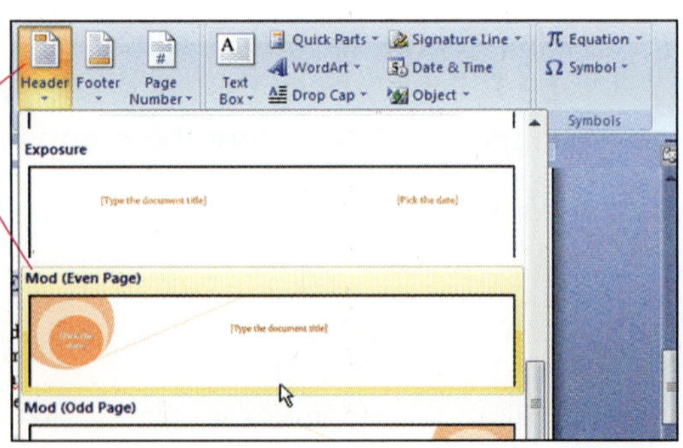

7 Double-click in the body of the document.

This makes the document active and dims the header.

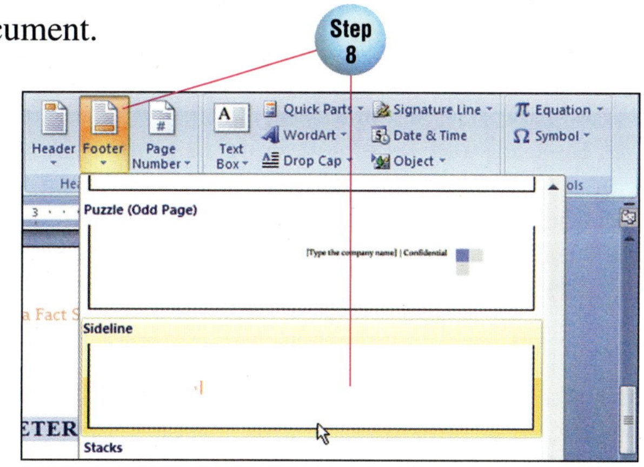

8 Insert a footer in the document by clicking the Insert tab, clicking the Footer button in the Header & Footer group, scrolling down the footer list, and then clicking the *Sideline* footer.

9 Double-click in the body of the document.

10 Scroll through the document and notice how the header and footer appear on each page except the cover page.

11 Remove the footer by clicking the Insert tab, clicking the Footer button in the Header & Footer group, and then clicking the *Remove Footer* option at the drop-down menu.

12 Insert a new footer by clicking the Insert tab, clicking the Footer button in the Header & Footer group, scrolling through the footer list, and then clicking the *Mod (Odd Page)* footer.

13 Double-click in the body of the document.

14 Edit the header by clicking the Insert tab, clicking the Header button in the Header & Footer group, and then clicking *Edit Header* at the drop-down list.

15 Click on any character in the title *Alaska Fact Sheets* and then click the Title tab.

Clicking the Title tab selects the title text.

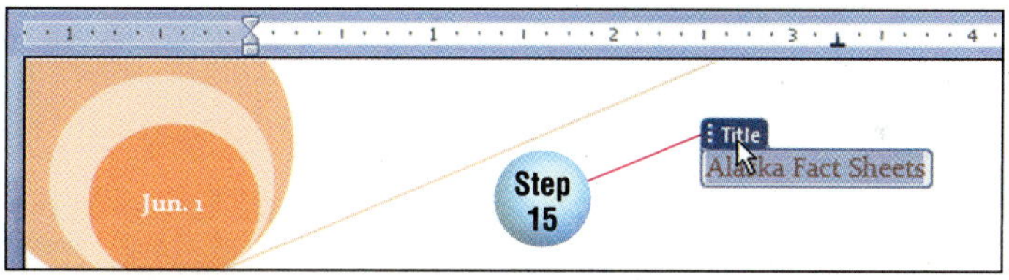

16 Change the font size by clicking the Home tab, clicking the Font Size button arrow, and then clicking *16* at the drop-down list.

17 Double-click in the document.

18 Save, print, and then close **WordS3-01.docx**.

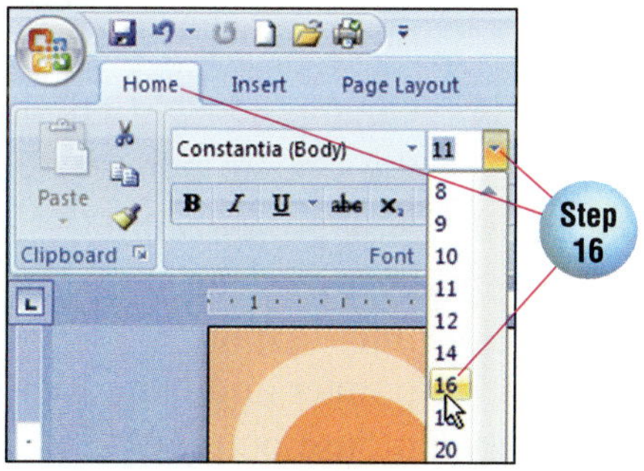

In Brief

Insert Page Numbers
1. Click Insert tab.
2. Click Page Number button.
3. Point to desired location.
4. Click desired option at drop-down gallery.

Insert Header
1. Click Insert tab.
2. Click Header button.
3. Click desired option at drop-down gallery.

Insert Footer
1. Click Insert tab.
2. Click Footer button.
3. Click desired option at drop-down gallery.

In Addition

Creating Your Own Header or Footer

You can create your own header or footer using the Edit Header or Edit Footer options from the drop-down list. For example, to create a header, click the Insert tab, click the Header button, and then click *Edit Header* at the drop-down list. This displays a Header pane in the document and also displays the Header & Footer Tools Design tab with buttons and options for editing the header. Make the desired edits to the header with options in the tab and then close the header window by clicking the Close Header and Footer button located in the Close group in the Header & Footer Tools Design tab.

Activity 3.8

Using Click and Type; Vertically Aligning Text; Inserting, Sizing, and Moving an Image

You can change paragraph alignment with the Click and Type feature. To use the Click and Type feature, position the mouse pointer at the left margin, in the center of the page, or at the right margin until the pointer displays with the desired alignment symbol and then double-click the mouse button. By default, text is aligned at the top of the page. You can change this alignment to Center, Justified, or Bottom with the *Vertical alignment* option at the Page Setup dialog box with the Layout tab selected. Microsoft Office includes a gallery of media images you can insert in a document such as clip art, photographs, and movie images, as well as sound clips. Use buttons in the Insert tab to insert a clip art image or insert a picture or image from a specific file location.

Project

First Choice TRAVEL

First Choice Travel is planning a workshop for people interested in traveling on a budget. You will create an announcement that contains center- and right-aligned text, vertically center the text on the page, and then add visual appeal by inserting a clip art image and the company logo.

1. Press Ctrl + N to display a blank document.
2. Position the I-beam pointer between the left and right margins at about the 3.25-inch mark on the horizontal ruler and the top of the vertical ruler. When the center alignment lines display below the I-beam pointer, double-click the left mouse button.

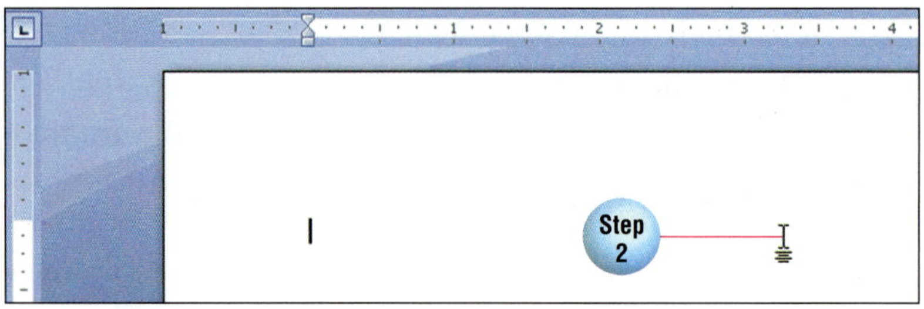

3. Type the centered text shown in Figure 3.1, pressing the Enter key once between each line of text.
4. Change to right alignment by positioning the I-beam pointer near the right margin at approximately the 2-inch mark on the vertical ruler until the right alignment lines display at the left side of the I-beam pointer and then double-clicking the left mouse button.

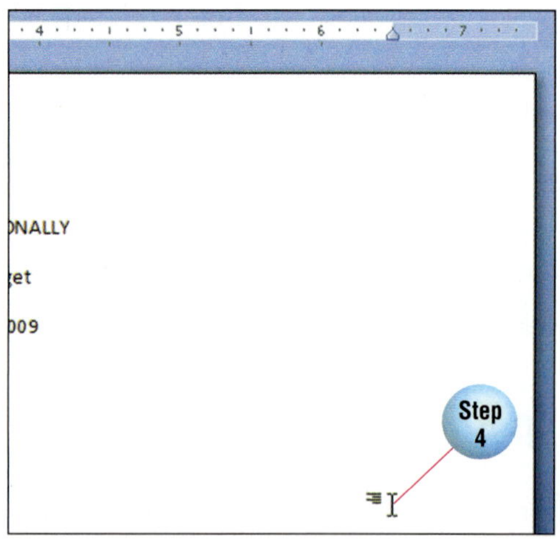

5. Type the right-aligned text shown in Figure 3.1. After typing the first line of right-aligned text, press Shift + Enter to move the insertion point to the next line.
6. Select the centered text and then change the font to 14-point Arial bold. Select the right-aligned text, change the font to 8-point Arial bold, and then deselect the text.

FIGURE 3.1 Steps 3 and 5

TRAVELING INTERNATIONALLY

Traveling on a Budget

Thursday, April 23, 2009

7:00 to 8:30 p.m.

Sponsored by
First Choice Travel

7 Vertically center the text on the page. To do this, click the Page Layout tab and then click the Page Setup group dialog box launcher.

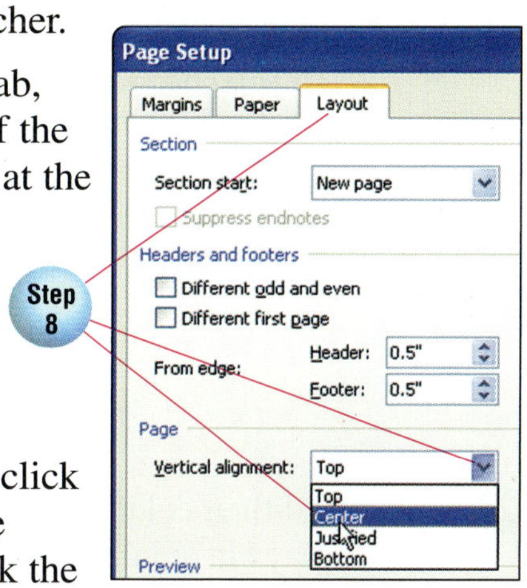

8 At the Page Setup dialog box, click the Layout tab, click the down-pointing arrow at the right side of the *Vertical alignment* option, and then click *Center* at the drop-down list.

9 Click OK to close the Page Setup dialog box.

10 Save the document and name it **WordS3-02**.

11 Print **WordS3-02.docx**.

12 Return the vertical alignment to Top. To do this, click the Page Setup group dialog box launcher. At the Page Setup dialog box, click the Layout tab, click the down-pointing arrow at the right side of the *Vertical alignment* option, and then click *Top* at the drop-down list. Click OK to close the dialog box.

13 Click the Insert tab and then click the Clip Art button in the Illustrations group.

This displays the Clip Art task pane at the right side of the screen.

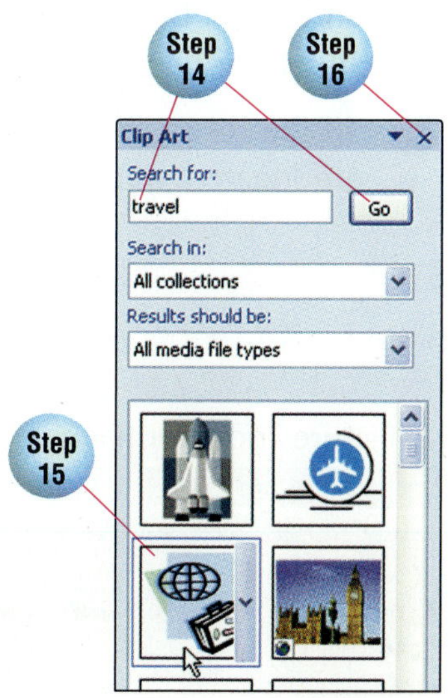

14 Type **travel** in the *Search for* text box and then click the Go button.

If you are connected to the Internet, a message may display asking if you want to include thousands of clip art images and photos from Microsoft Office Online. Check with your instructor to determine if you should click the Yes button or the No button.

15 Click the image shown at the right. If this image is not available, choose another image related to travel.

The image is inserted in the document, it is selected (sizing handles display around the image), and the Picture Tools Format tab displays as shown in Figure 3.2.

continues

16 Close the Clip Art task pane by clicking the Close button located in the upper right corner of the task pane.

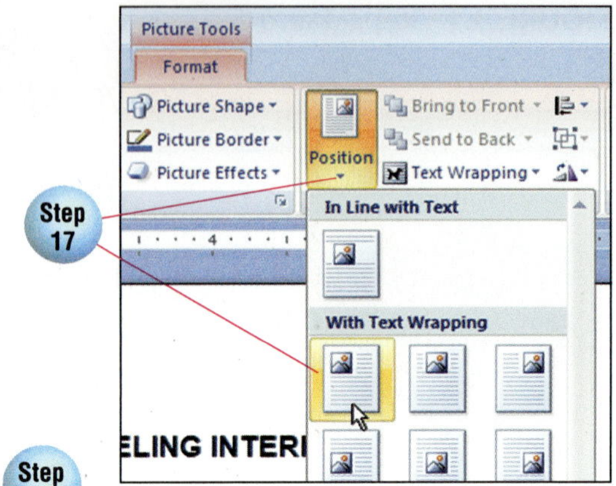

17 With the image selected, click the Position button in the Arrange group and then click the first option from the left in the top row of the *With Text Wrapping* section (the option named *Position in Top Left with Square Text Wrapping*).

18 Add a shadow effect to the clip art image by clicking the fourth option from the left in the Picture Styles group (*Drop Shadow Rectangle*).

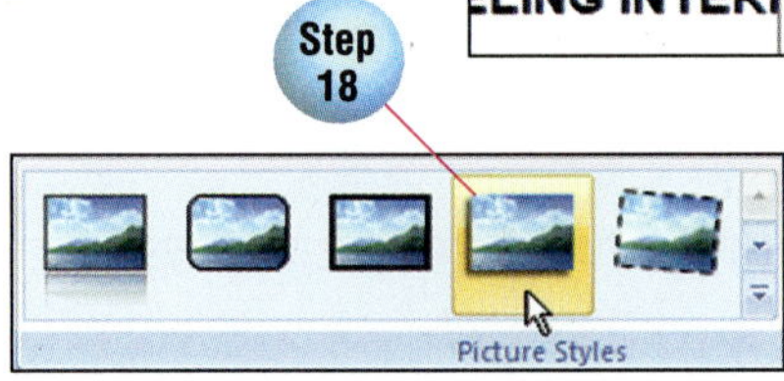

19 Click in the Shape Height box in the Size group and then type **1.7**.

When you change the height measurement, the width measurement is automatically changed to maintain the proportions of the image.

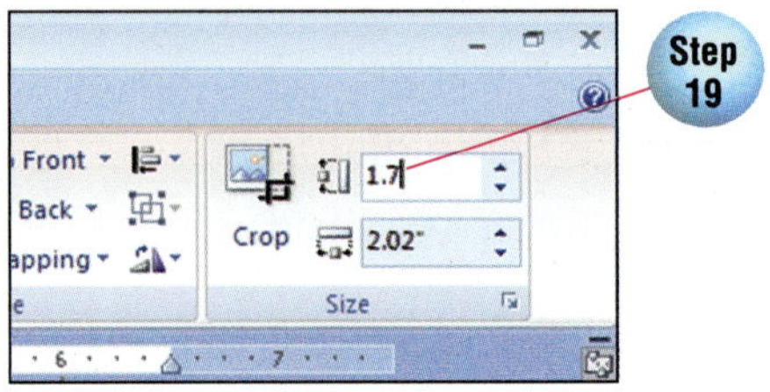

20 Select and then delete the text *First Choice Travel* that displays in small font size at the right side of the document.

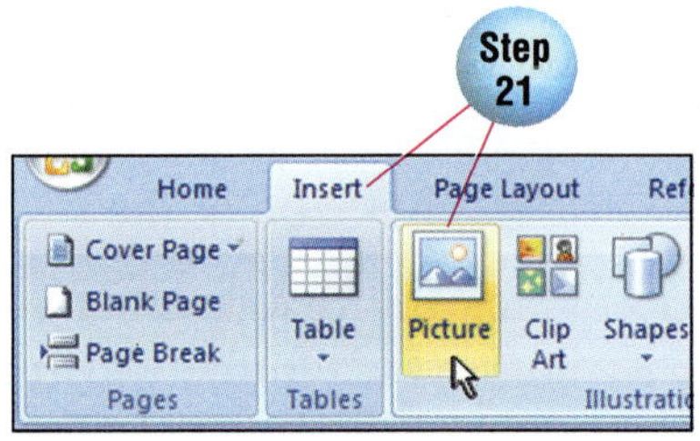

21 Insert the First Choice Travel logo below *Sponsored by*. To begin, click the Insert tab and then click the Picture button in the Illustrations group.

22 At the Insert Picture dialog box, display the folder where your data documents are located and then double-click ***FCTLogo.jpg***.

FIGURE 3.2 Picture Tools Format Tab

23 With the image selected in the document, hold down the Shift key and then drag one of the corner sizing handles (circles) to reduce the size of the logo so it displays as shown in Figure 3.3.

Holding down the Shift key while increasing or decreasing the size of an image maintains the proportions of the image.

24 With the image still selected, click the Text Wrapping button [Text Wrapping] and then click *Tight* at the drop-down list.

With a wrapping style applied, you can move the image.

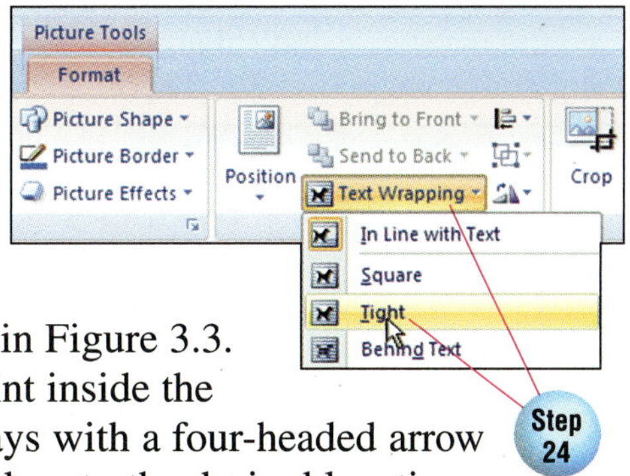

25 Drag the image so it is positioned as shown in Figure 3.3. To drag the image, position the insertion point inside the selected image until the arrow pointer displays with a four-headed arrow attached. Hold down the left mouse button, drag to the desired location, and then release the mouse button.

26 Click outside the logo to deselect it.

27 Save, print, and then close **WordS3-02.docx**.

FIGURE 3.3 Step 26

In Brief

Vertically Center Text
1. Click Page Layout tab.
2. Click Page Setup group dialog box launcher.
3. Click Layout tab.
4. Click *Vertical alignment* option.
5. Click *Center* at drop-down list.
6. Click OK.

Insert Clip Art Image
1. Click Insert tab.
2. Click Clip Art button.
3. Type category information in *Search for* text box.
4. Click Go button.
5. Click desired clip art image.

Insert Picture
1. Click Insert tab.
2. Click Picture button.
3. Navigate to desired folder.
4. Double-click desired picture file.

In Addition

Formatting an Image with Buttons in the Picture Tools Format Tab

Images inserted in a document can be formatted in a variety of ways, which might include adding fill color and border lines, increasing or decreasing the brightness or contrast, choosing a wrapping style, and cropping the image. Format an image with buttons in the Picture Tools Format tab as shown in Figure 3.2. With buttons in the Picture Tools group you can control the brightness and contrast of the image; recolor the image; change to a different image; reset the image to its original size, position, and color; and compress the picture. Compress a picture to reduce resolution or discard extra information to save room on the hard drive or to reduce download time. Use buttons in the Picture Styles group to apply a predesigned style, insert a picture border, or apply a picture effect. The Arrange group contains buttons for positioning the image, wrapping text around the image, and aligning and rotating the image. Use options in the Size group to crop the image and specify the height and width of the image.

Activity 3.9

Preparing an Envelope

Word automates the creation of envelopes with options at the Envelopes and Labels dialog box with the Envelopes tab selected. At this dialog box, type a delivery address and a return address. If you open the Envelopes and Labels dialog box in a document containing a name and address, the name and address are inserted automatically as the delivery address. If you enter a return address, Word will ask you before printing if you want to save the new return address as the default return address. Answer yes if you want to use the return address for future envelopes or answer no if you will use a different return address for future envelopes.

Project

You need to create an envelope for sending the fact sheet about Petersburg, Alaska, to Camille Matsui at Marquee Productions.

First Choice TRAVEL

1. Click the New button on the Quick Access toolbar to display a blank document.

   If the New button does not display on the Quick Access toolbar, click the Customize Quick Access Toolbar button that displays at the right side of the toolbar and then click *New* at the drop-down list.

2. Click the Mailings tab and then click the Envelopes button in the Create group.

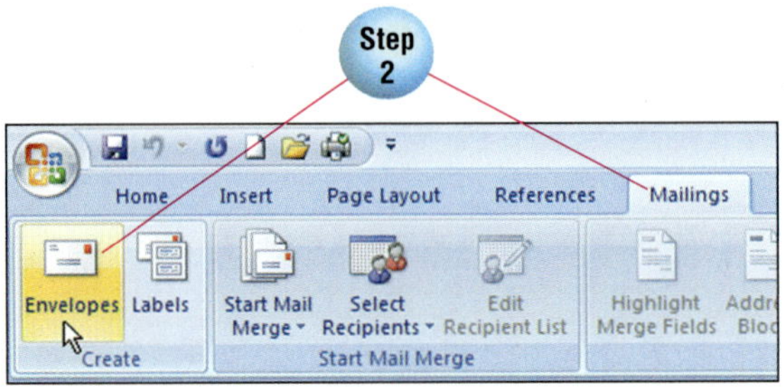

3. At the Envelopes and Labels dialog box with the Envelopes tab selected, type the following name and address in the *Delivery address* text box. (Press Enter at the end of each line, except the last line containing the city name, state, and ZIP code.)

   Camille Matsui
   Marquee Productions
   955 South Alameda Street
   Los Angeles, CA 90037

4. If any text displays in the *Return address* text box, delete it and then type the following name and address:

   First Choice Travel
   Los Angeles Office
   3588 Ventura Boulevard
   Los Angeles, CA 90102

5. Click the Add to Document button.

   Clicking the Add to Document button inserts the envelope in the document. You can also send the envelope directly to the printer by clicking the Print button.

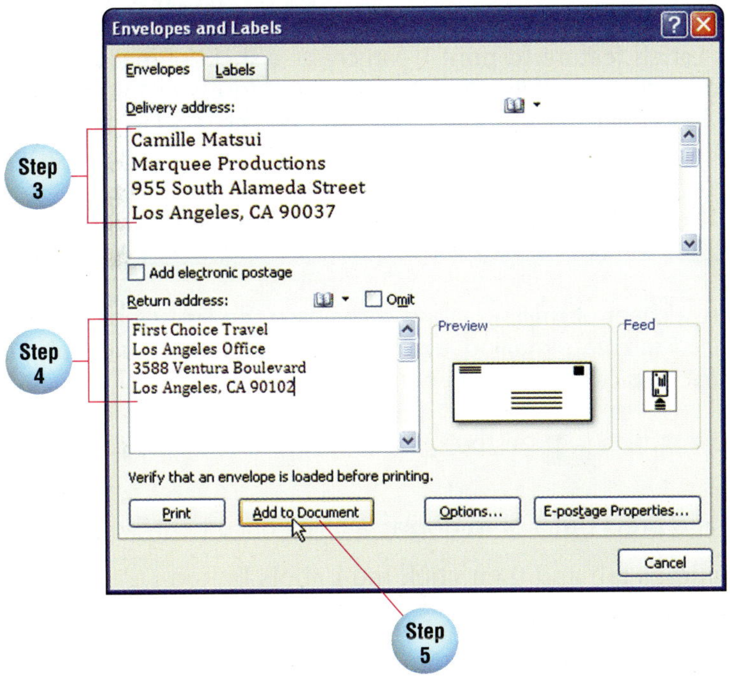

In Brief

Prepare Envelope
1. Click Mailings tab.
2. Click Envelopes button.
3. Type delivery address.
4. Type return address.
5. Click either Add to Document button or Print button.

6. At the message asking if you want to save the new return address as the default address, click the No button.
7. Save the document and name it **WordS3-03**.
8. Print and then close **WordS3-03.docx**. ***Note: Manual feed of the envelope may be required. Please check with your instructor.***

In Addition

Customizing Envelopes

With options at the Envelope Options dialog box shown at the right, you can customize an envelope. Display this dialog box by clicking the Options button at the Envelopes and Labels dialog box. At the Envelope Options dialog box, you can change the envelope size, change the font for the delivery and return addresses, and specify the positioning of the addresses in relation to the left and top edges of the envelope.

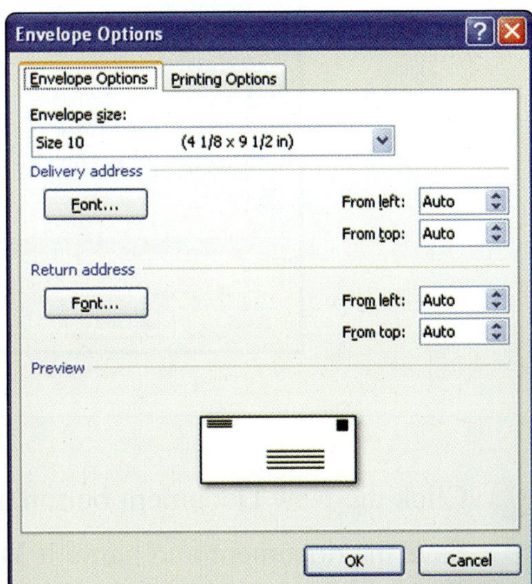

Activity 3.10

Preparing Mailing Labels

Use Word's Labels feature to print text on mailing labels, file labels, disk labels, or other types of labels. You can create labels for printing on a variety of predefined labels, which you can purchase at an office supply store. With the Labels feature, you can create a sheet of mailing labels with the same name and address or enter a different name and address on each label. Create a label with options at the Envelopes and Labels dialog box with the Labels tab selected.

Project

You decide to create a sheet of mailing labels containing the First Choice Travel name and address. You also need to create mailing labels for sending the fact sheet about Petersburg, Alaska, to several First Choice Travel customers.

1. Click the New button on the Quick Access toolbar to display a blank document.

   You can also press Ctrl + N to display a blank document.

2. Click the Mailings tab and then click the Labels button in the Create group.
3. Type the following information in the *Address* text box. (Press Enter at the end of each line, except the last line containing the city name, state, and ZIP code.)

   First Choice Travel
   Los Angeles Office
   3588 Ventura Boulevard
   Los Angeles, CA 90102

4. Click the Options button.
5. At the Label Options dialog box, click the down-pointing arrow at the right side of the *Label vendors* list box and then click Avery US Letter.
6. Click the down-pointing arrow at the right side of the *Product number* list box, click *5630* in the list box, and then click OK to close the dialog box.

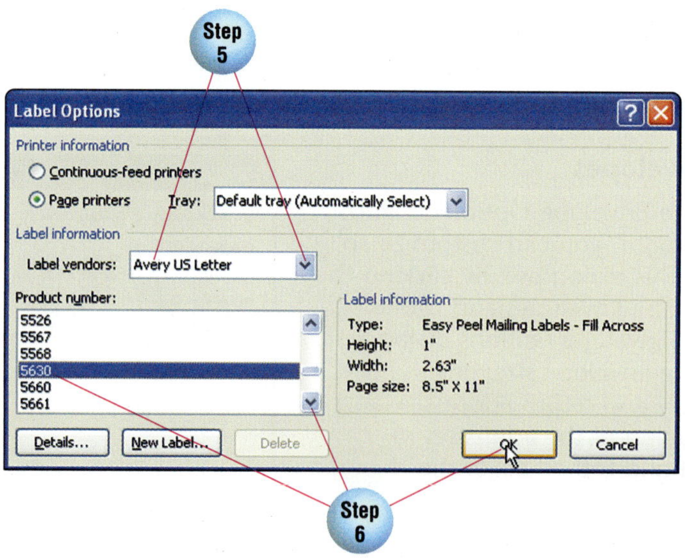

7. Click the New Document button at the Envelopes and Labels dialog box.
8. Save the document and name it **WordS3-04**.

9. Print and then close **WordS3-04.docx**.

   The number of labels printed on the page varies depending on the label selected at the Envelopes and Labels dialog box.

10. Click the Mailings tab and then click the Labels button in the Create group.
11. At the Envelopes and Labels dialog box, click the New Document button.
12. At the document, type the first name and address shown in Figure 3.4 in the first label. Press the Tab key twice to move the insertion point to the next label and then type the second name and address shown in Figure 3.4. Continue in this manner until you have typed all of the names and addresses in Figure 3.4.
13. Save the document and name it **WordS3-05**.
14. Print and then close **WordS3-05.docx**.
15. Close the blank document.

In Brief

Prepare Mailing Labels with Same Name and Address

1. Click Mailings tab.
2. Click Labels button.
3. Type name and address in *Address* text box.
4. Click either New Document button or Print button.

Prepare Mailing Labels with Different Names and Addresses

1. Click Mailings tab.
2. Click Labels button.
3. Click New Document button.
4. At document screen, type names and addresses.

FIGURE 3.4 Step 12

Moreno Products 350 Mission Boulevard Pomona, CA 91767	Mr. Miguel Santos 12120 Barranca Parkway Irvine, CA 92612
Dr. Esther Riggins 9077 Walnut Street Los Angeles, CA 90097	Automated Services, Inc. 4394 Seventh Street Long Beach, CA 92602

In Addition

Customizing Labels

Click the Options button at the Envelopes and Labels dialog box with the Labels tab selected and the Label Options dialog box displays as shown at the right. At this dialog box, choose the type of printer, the desired label vendor, and the product number. This dialog box also displays information about the selected label such as type, height, width, and paper size. When you select a label, Word automatically determines label margins. If, however, you want to customize these default settings, click the Details button at the Label Options dialog box.

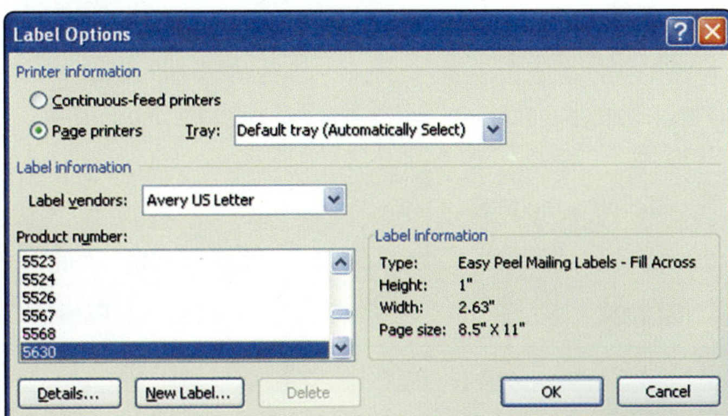

Features Summary

Feature	Ribbon Tab, Group	Button	Keyboard Shortcut
Clip Art task pane	Insert, Illustrations		
Clipboard task pane	Home, Clipboard		
copy selected text	Home, Clipboard		Ctrl + C
cut selected text	Home, Clipboard		Ctrl + X
Find and Replace dialog box with Find tab selected	Home, Editing		Ctrl + F
Find and Replace dialog box with Replace tab selected	Home, Editing	Replace	Ctrl + H
Envelopes and Labels dialog box with Envelopes tab selected	Mailings, Create		
Envelopes and Labels dialog box with Labels tab selected	Mailings, Create		
footer	Insert, Header & Footer		
header	Insert, Header & Footer		
Insert Picture dialog box	Insert, Illustrations		
page border	Page Layout, Page Background	Page Borders	
page break	Insert, Pages	Page Break	Ctrl + Enter
page color	Page Layout, Page Background	Page Color	
page margins	Page Layout, Page Setup		
page number	Insert, Header & Footer		
page orientation	Page Layout, Page Setup		
Page Setup dialog box	Page Layout, Page Setup		
page size	Page Layout, Page Setup		
paste selected text	Home, Clipboard		Ctrl + V
Paste Special dialog box	Home, Clipboard	Paste, Paste Special	
Reveal Formatting task pane			Shift + F1
theme	Page Layout, Themes		
watermark	Page Layout, Page Background	Watermark	

Knowledge Check

Completion: In the space provided at the right, indicate the correct term, command, or option.

1. Click this button at the Find and Replace dialog box to replace all occurrences of text. ______________
2. Click this button at the Find and Replace dialog box to display additional options. ______________
3. This is the keyboard shortcut to display the Reveal Formatting task pane. ______________
4. The Cut button is located in this group in the Home tab. ______________
5. Click this button to insert selected text in the document. ______________
6. Click this to display the Clipboard task pane. ______________
7. Click this tab to display the Margins button. ______________
8. This is the default measurement for the top, bottom, left, and right margins. ______________
9. This is the default page orientation. ______________
10. This is the default page size. ______________
11. A document theme is a set of formatting choices that includes a font theme, an effects theme, and this. ______________
12. This is the keyboard shortcut to insert a page break. ______________
13. Insert a footer by clicking the Footer button in this group in the Insert tab. ______________
14. Use this feature to position the mouse pointer at the left margin, center of the page, or right margin. ______________
15. This is the default page alignment. ______________
16. Change page alignment with the *Vertical alignment* option at this dialog box. ______________
17. The Clip Art button displays in this group in the Insert tab. ______________
18. Click this button in the Picture Tools Format tab to choose a wrapping style. ______________
19. Click this button in the Insert tab to display the Insert Picture dialog box. ______________
20. When changing the size of an image, maintain the image proportions by holding down this key while dragging a corner sizing handle. ______________
21. To display the Envelopes and Labels dialog box, click this tab and then click the Envelopes button or the Labels button. ______________

Skills Review

Review 1 Formatting a Fact Sheet on Juneau, Alaska

First Choice TRAVEL

1. Open **FCTJuneau.docx** and then save the document and name it **WordS3-R1**.
2. Select the entire document, click the No Spacing style in the Styles group, and then deselect the text.

3. Apply the *Module* theme. (To display the Themes button, click the Page Layout tab.)
4. Find every occurrence of *Mendanhall* and replace it with *Mendenhall.*
5. Find every occurrence of *Treadwill* and replace it with *Treadwell.*
6. Select the heading *Visitor Centers*, the three paragraphs of text below it, and the blank line below the three paragraphs and then move the selected text before the heading *Visitor Attractions.*
7. Select the heading *Museums*, the three paragraphs of text below it, and the blank line below the three paragraphs and then move the selected text before the heading *Visitor Attractions.*
8. With **WordS3-R1.docx** open, open the document named **FCTJA01.docx**.
9. Display the Clipboard task pane and then make sure the task pane is empty.
10. In the **FCTJA01.docx** document, select and then copy from the heading *Visitor Services* through the two paragraphs of text below the heading and the blank line below the two paragraphs.
11. Select and then copy from the heading *Transportation* through the paragraph of text below the heading and the blank line below the paragraph.
12. Select and then copy from the heading *Points of Interest* through the columns of text below the heading and the blank line below the columns of text.
13. Make **WordS3-R1.docx** the active document.
14. Display the Clipboard task pane.
15. Move the insertion point to the end of the document and then paste the text that begins with the heading *Points of Interest.*
16. Move the insertion point to the beginning of the heading *Museums* and then paste the text that begins with the heading *Transportation.*
17. Move the insertion point to the beginning of the heading *Points of Interest* and then paste the text that begins with the heading *Visitor Services.*
18. Clear the contents of the Clipboard task pane and then close the task pane.
19. Make **FCTJA01.docx** the active document and then close it.
20. Change the left and right margins to 1 inch and the top and bottom margins to 1.5 inches.
21. Apply the Heading 1 style to the title *FACT SHEET—JUNEAU, ALASKA.*
22. Apply the Heading 2 style to the headings in the document including *History*, *Visitor Centers*, *Transportation*, *Museums*, *Visitor Attractions*, *Visitor Services,* and *Points of Interest.*
23. Change the page orientation to landscape.
24. Insert page numbering at the bottom of the page. (You determine the page number style.)
25. Insert a watermark that prints the word *Sample* across the page.
26. Save and then print **WordS3-R1.docx**.
27. Change the page orientation to portrait and remove page numbering and the watermark.
28. Change the top and bottom margins to 1 inch and the left and right margins to 1.5 inches.
29. Insert a footer of your choosing that includes the text *Juneau, Alaska* and the page number.
30. Save, print, and then close **WordS3-R1.docx**.

Review 2 Preparing and Formatting an Announcement

1. At a blank document, use the Click and Type feature to type the text shown in Figure 3.5.
2. Select the centered text you just typed and then change the font to 14-point Arial bold.
3. Select the right-aligned text you just typed and then change the font to 10-point Arial bold.

4. Change the vertical alignment of the text on the page to Center.
5. Save the document and name it **WordS3-R2A**.
6. Print **WordS3-R2A.docx**.
7. Save the document with Save As and name it **WordS3-R2B**.
8. Change the vertical alignment of the text on the page back to Top.
9. Insert a clip art image of your choosing related to the announcement. (You determine the clip art image as well as the size and position of the image.) If you have access to Office Online (through the Clip Art task pane), consider downloading an appropriate image. If you are limited to the clip art images provided with Office 2007, consider using the key word *business* to look for a clip art image.
10. Delete the text *Marquee Productions* from the document and then insert the Marquee Productions logo image named **MPLogo.jpg** below the text *Sponsored by*. ***Hint: Do this at the Insert Picture dialog box.*** Adjust the size and position of the image so it displays below *Sponsored by* and is approximately one inch wide.
11. Save, print, and then close **WordS3-R2B.docx**.

FIGURE 3.5 Review 2

EMPLOYMENT OPPORTUNITIES

Working in the Movie Industry

Wednesday, March 17, 2010

7:00 to 8:30 p.m.

Sponsored by
Marquee Productions

Review 3 Preparing an Envelope

First Choice TRAVEL

1. At a blank document, prepare an envelope with the return address and delivery address shown below and add the envelope to the document.
   Delivery address:
   Chris Greenbaum
   Marquee Productions
   955 South Alameda Street
   Los Angeles, CA 90037
   Return address:
   First Choice Travel
   Los Angeles Office
   3588 Ventura Boulevard
   Los Angeles, CA 90102
2. Save the document and name it **WordS3-R3**. Print and then close **WordS3-R3.docx**. (Manual feed may be required.)

Review 4 Preparing Mailing Labels

First Choice TRAVEL

1. At a blank document, prepare a sheet of mailing labels for the following name and address using the Avery US Letter 5160 labels option.

   First Choice Travel
   Toronto Office
   4277 Yonge Street
   Toronto, ON M4P 2E6

2. Save the mailing label document and name it **WordS3-R4**. Print and then close **WordS3-R4.docx**.

Skills Assessment

Assessment 1 Formatting a Costume Rental Agreement

Performance Threads

1. Open **PTAgreement.docx** and then save the document and name it **WordS3-A1**.
2. Search for all occurrences of *Customer* and replace with *Marquee Productions*.
3. Move the *4. Alterations* section above the *3. Marquee Productions Agrees* section. Renumber the two sections.
4. Select the entire document, change the font to 12-point Constantia, and then deselect the document.
5. Change the top margin to 1.5 inches.
6. Insert a footer of your choosing that prints at the bottom of each page.
7. Save, print, and then close **WordS3-A1.docx**.

Assessment 2 Creating an Announcement

Niagara Peninsula COLLEGE

1. At a blank document, create an announcement for Niagara Peninsula College by typing the text shown in Figure 3.6.
2. Change the font for the entire document to a decorative font, size, and color of your choosing.
3. Change the line spacing to double for the entire document.
4. Insert, size, and move a clip art image of your choosing in the document. Choose a clip art image related to the subject of the announcement. If you have access to Office Online (through the Clip Art task pane), consider downloading an appropriate image.
5. Save the document and name it **WordS3-A2**.
6. Print and then close **WordS3-A2.docx**.

FIGURE 3.6 Assessment 2

NIAGARA PENINSULA COLLEGE
Internship Opportunities
Marquee Productions, Toronto Office
June 16 through August 29, 2010
Contact Cal Rubine, Theatre Arts Division

Assessment 3 Preparing Mailing Labels

1. Prepare return mailing labels with the following information:
   Niagara Peninsula College
   Theatre Arts Division
   2199 Victoria Street
   Niagara-on-the-Lake, ON L0S 1J0
2. Save the labels document and name it **WordS3-A3**. Print and then close **WordS3-A3.docx**.

Assessment 4 Finding Information on Creating a Picture Watermark

1. Open **WordS3-R2A.docx** and then save the document and name it **WordS3-A4**.
2. Use Word's Help feature to learn how to insert a picture watermark.
3. Insert the **MPLogo.jpg** file located in the WordS3 folder as a watermark.
4. Save, print, and then close **WordS3-A4.docx**.

HELP

Assessment 5 Locating Information and Creating a Banner

1. You are Camille Matsui, production assistant for Marquee Productions. You have been asked by Chris Greenbaum, the production manager, to find information on the Royal Ontario Museum. Marquee Productions will need to do some interior shots and would like to contact the museum as a possible site. Ms. Greenbaum wants to include the information on the museum in a packet of information that will be made available to all employees at the Toronto filming site. Connect to the Internet and search for information on the Royal Ontario Museum. Find the following information: the museum address, telephone number, and hours of operation.
2. Using the information you find on the museum, create a flyer containing the museum information. Apply formatting to the document to enhance the visual appeal and include a page border and a clip art image.
3. Save the document and name it **WordS3-A5**.
4. Print and then close **WordS3-A5.docx**.

Marquee Challenge

Challenge 1 Formatting a Costume Document

1. Open **PTRenaissanceCostume.docx** and then save the document with the name **WordS3-C1**.
2. Apply the Civic theme to the document, change the font, and apply shading to the headings as shown in Figure 3.7. Apply a page border and any other formatting required so your document displays similar to the document in Figure 3.7. If you have access to clip art on Office Online (available at the Clip Art task pane), apply a different book image than the one shown on the second page of the document.
3. Save, print, and then close **WordS3-C1.docx**.

FIGURE 3.7 Challenge 1

Performance Threads

Renaissance Period

The Renaissance period was a series of cultural and literary movements that took place in the fourteenth, fifteenth, and sixteenth centuries in Europe. The word *renaissance* means "rebirth" and originated with the belief that Europeans had rediscovered the intellectual and cultural superiority of the Greek and Roman cultures. The Renaissance period is preceded by the Middle Ages, also known as the "Dark Ages," which began with the collapse of the Roman Empire in the fifth century. The term *renaissance* was coined by Jacob Burckhardt in the eighteenth century in *The Civilization of the Renaissance in Italy*.

Renaissance education was designed to produce a person well-versed in humanities, mathematics, science, sports, and art. The Renaissance person had extensive knowledge in many fields, explored beyond the boundaries of learning and geographical knowledge, and embraced free thought and skepticism. Artists, writers, explorers, architects, and scientists were motivated by a revival in classical Greek and Roman culture and a return to classical values. During the Middle Ages, interest in culture and learning was primarily confined to theologians, philosophers, and writers. During the Renaissance period, however, people from all social, political, and economic classes involved themselves in the study of classical literature and art.

Renaissance Costume

Renaissance costume developed in Italy and was introduced to Western Europe following the invasion of Italy by Charles VIII of France in 1494. Due to the warmer climate in Italy, simpler styles evolved independently from the rest of Europe. Men's clothing consisted of low-necked tunics and chemises and women's clothing consisted of simple and low-necked gowns called "Juliet" gowns. During the middle of the fifteenth century, clothing assumed a more natural appearance. Women wore dresses with attached bodices and skirts. Men's doublets became shorter and hosiery became more prominent. Interest by women in gothic head dresses declined and instead they trimmed their hair with veils, ribbons, and jewels. Lace and perfume became more prevalent during the Renaissance period.

Early in the Renaissance period, women's dress included a long, rigid, cone-shaped corset reaching below the waist to a V in the front. Women's robes expanded below the waistline and by the middle sixteenth century were supported by hoops made of wire that were held together with ribbons. This hoop skirt, called a *farthingale*, reached its maximum width around the early seventeenth century and then became a cartwheel or drum shape. Ballooned sleeves and circular lace collars also typified the early seventeenth century costume. Men's clothing had a similar look with puffed-out hose, balloon sleeves, padded doublets, and large ruff collars.

Renaissance Costume Page 1

continues

Costume Vocabulary

1. **Basquine:** A very large skirt that was open and stretched on circles.
2. **Berne:** A very large, fixed, and pleated scarf that rested on the shoulder.
3. **Jupon:** Long-sleeved camisole generally worn by men and women in Spain.
4. **Mantilla:** A kind of shawl worn by women that covered the head and shoulders.
5. **Marlotte:** A coat with pleats in the back and short curved sleeves.

Costume Books

- Arnold, Janet, *Patterns of Fashion*
- Barton, Lucy, *Historic Costume for the Stage*
- Boucher, Francois, *20,000 Years of Fashion*
- Brooke, Iris, *A History of Costume*
- Evans, Mary, *Costume Throughout the Ages*
- LaMar, Virginia A., *English Dress in the Age of Shakespeare*

Renaissance Costume Page 2

Challenge 2 Preparing an Announcement

1. At a blank document, create the document shown in Figure 3.8.
2. Save the completed document and name it **WordS3-C2**.
3. Print and then close **WordS3-C2.docx**.

FIGURE 3.8 Challenge 2

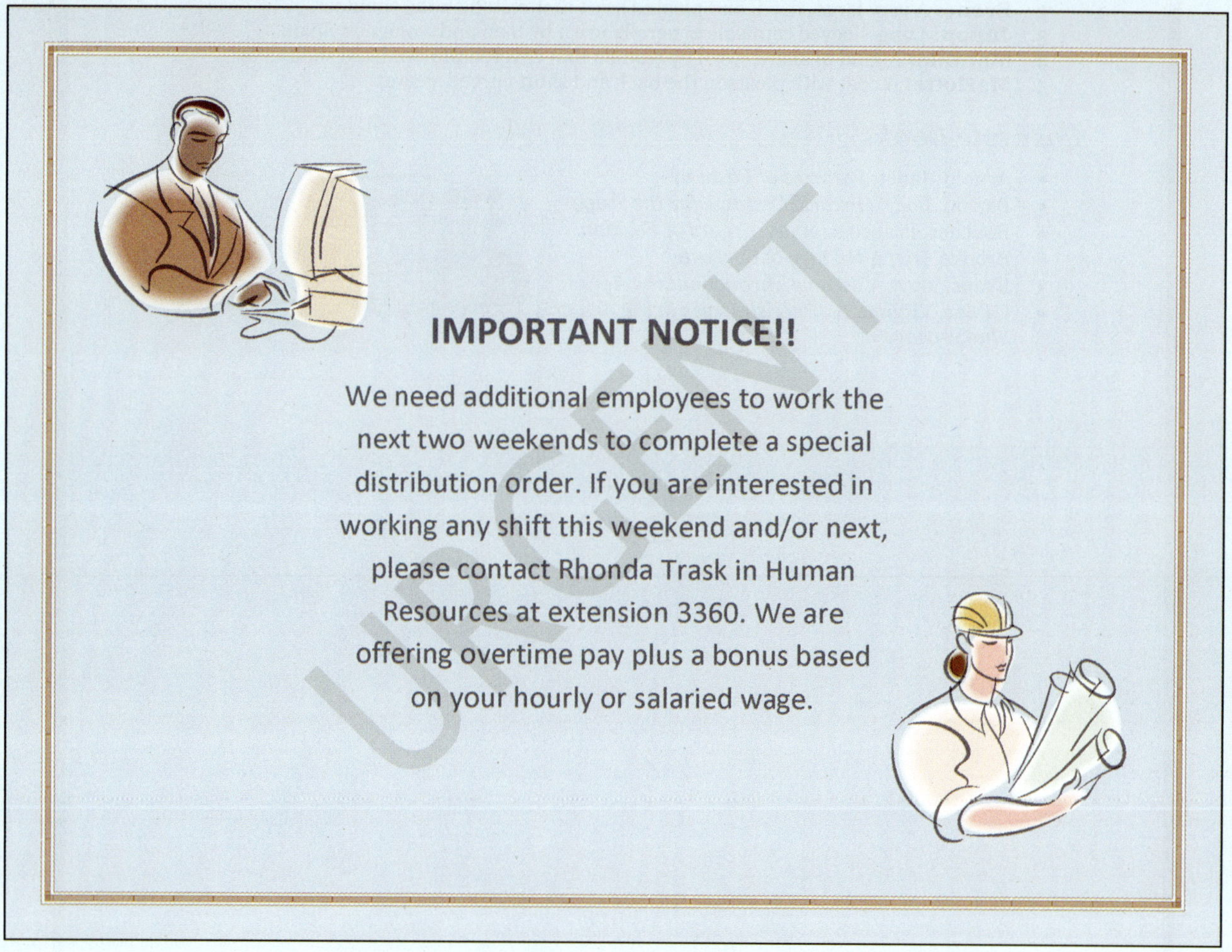

URGENT

IMPORTANT NOTICE!!

We need additional employees to work the next two weekends to complete a special distribution order. If you are interested in working any shift this weekend and/or next, please contact Rhonda Trask in Human Resources at extension 3360. We are offering overtime pay plus a bonus based on your hourly or salaried wage.

Word SECTION 4

Formatting with Special Features

Skills

- Create and modify WordArt text
- Create a drop cap
- Insert a text box and draw a text box
- Insert and modify shapes
- Use SmartArt to create organizational charts and diagrams
- Create, format, and modify tables
- Insert one file into another
- Insert a continuous section break
- Create and modify columns
- Save a document as a single file Web page
- Insert a hyperlink
- Merge letters and envelopes

Student Resources

Before beginning this section:

1. Copy to your storage medium the WordS4 subfolder from the Word folder on the Student Resources CD.
2. Make WordS4 the active folder.

In addition to containing the data files needed to complete section work, the Student Resources CD contains model answers in PDF format for each of the projects in this section; model answers for end-of-section activities are not provided.

Projects Overview

First Choice TRAVEL: Format a document on special vacation activities in Hawaii; prepare an organizational chart and diagram of services; create and modify a table containing information on scenic flights on Maui; format and modify a fact sheet containing information on Petersburg, Alaska; save the fact sheet as a single file Web page and insert hyperlinks to an additional document and a Web site; create a data source and then merge a letter on cruise specials and an envelope document with the data source; format a newsletter containing information on Zenith Adventures; create a table with information on rental cars.

Marquee PRODUCTIONS: Create an organizational chart and diagram for the production department.

Niagara Peninsula COLLEGE: Create and format a table with information on classes offered by the Theatre Arts Division; format and modify a newsletter.

Performance Threads: Create an organizational chart and diagram for the design department; create a data source and then merge it with a letter asking for fabric pricing.

Worldwide Enterprises: Create and format an announcement about an upcoming stockholders' meeting; insert a formula in a table that calculates total sales.

The Waterfront B·I·S·T·R·O: Create and format a table containing information on catered lunch options.

Activity 4.1

Creating and Modifying WordArt Text

Use the WordArt feature to distort or modify text to conform to a variety of shapes. Consider using WordArt to create a company logo, letterhead, flier title, or heading. With WordArt, you can change the font, style, and alignment of text; use different fill patterns and colors; customize border lines; and add shadow and three-dimensional effects. Selected WordArt text can be sized and moved in the document.

Project

To increase the visual appeal of a document on Hawaiian specials, you decide to insert and format WordArt.

First Choice TRAVEL

1. Open **FCTHASpecials.docx** and then save the document and name it **WordS4-01**.
2. Complete a spelling and grammar check on the document. You determine what to correct and what to ignore. (The name *Molokini* is spelled correctly in the document.)
3. Apply a theme by clicking the Page Layout tab, clicking the Themes button in the Themes group, and then clicking *Flow* at the drop-down gallery.
4. Select and then delete the title *HAWAIIAN SPECIALS*.
5. With the insertion point positioned at the beginning of the document, click the Insert tab.
6. Insert WordArt by clicking the WordArt button in the Text group and then clicking the fourth option from the left in the third row (*WordArt style 16*).
7. At the Edit WordArt Text dialog box, type **Hawaiian Specials** and then click OK to close the dialog box.
8. Increase the height of the WordArt text by positioning the mouse pointer on the bottom middle sizing handle until the pointer turns into an arrow pointing up and down. Hold down the left mouse button, drag down approximately one-half inch, and then release the mouse button.

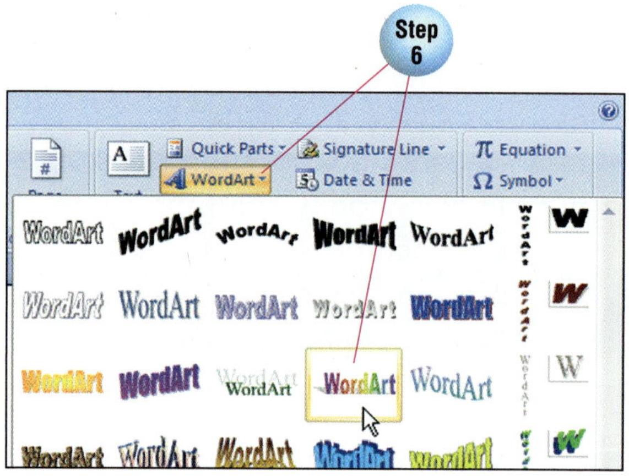

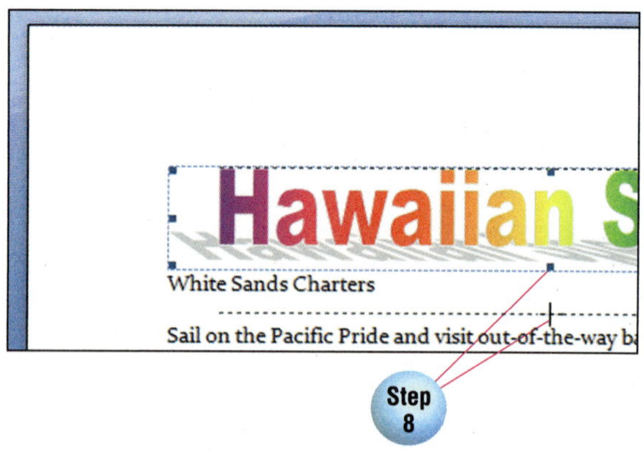

PROBLEM

If you are not satisfied with the size of the WordArt, click the Undo button and then size it again.

9 In the WordArt Tools Format tab, click in the Shape Width measurement box in the Size group, type 5.5, and then press Enter.

10 Click the Position button in the Arrange group and then click the *Position in Top Center with Square Text Wrapping* option in the *With Text Wrapping* section.

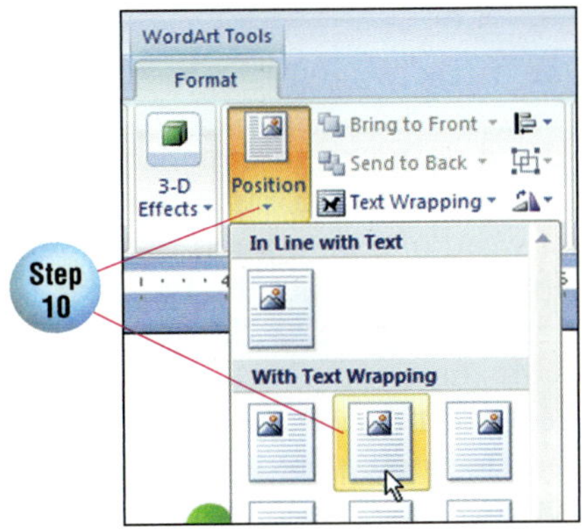

Customize WordArt with buttons in the WordArt Tools Format tab.

11 Click the Text Wrapping button [Text Wrapping] and then click *Top and Bottom* at the drop-down list.

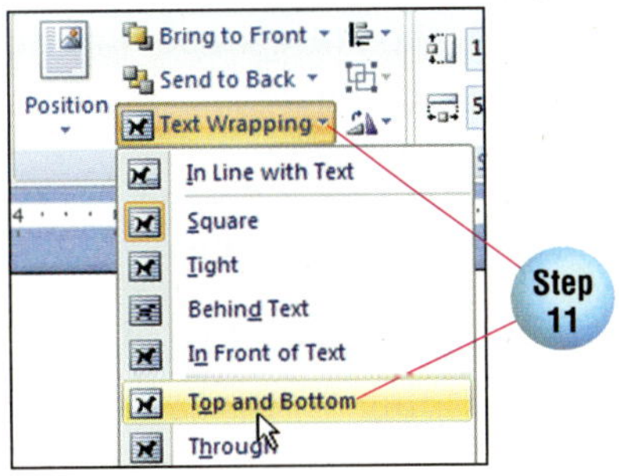

12 In the WordArt Tools Format tab, click the Shape Outline button arrow in the WordArt Styles group and then click the yellow color (fourth option from the left in the *Standard Colors* section).

13 Click the Shadow Effects button in the Shadow Effects group and then click the *Shadow Style 20* option (last option in the *Additional Shadow Styles* group).

14 Click outside the WordArt area to deselect it.

15 Apply the Heading 2 style to the following headings: *White Sands Charters*, *Air Adventures*, *Deep Sea Submarines*, *Snorkeling Fantasies*, and *Bicycle Safari*.

16 Press Ctrl + A to select the entire document and then change the font color to blue. To do this, click the Home tab, click the Font Color button arrow, and then click the blue color (third color from the *right* in the *Standard Colors* section).

17 Save **WordS4-01.docx**.

In Brief

Insert WordArt

1. Click Insert tab.
2. Click WordArt button.
3. Click desired option at drop-down gallery.
4. At Edit WordArt Text dialog box, type desired text.
5. Click OK.

In Addition

Changing WordArt Shape

Customize the shape of WordArt with options at the Change Shape drop-down gallery shown at the right. Display this gallery by clicking the Change Shape button in the WordArt Styles group in the WordArt Tools Format tab.

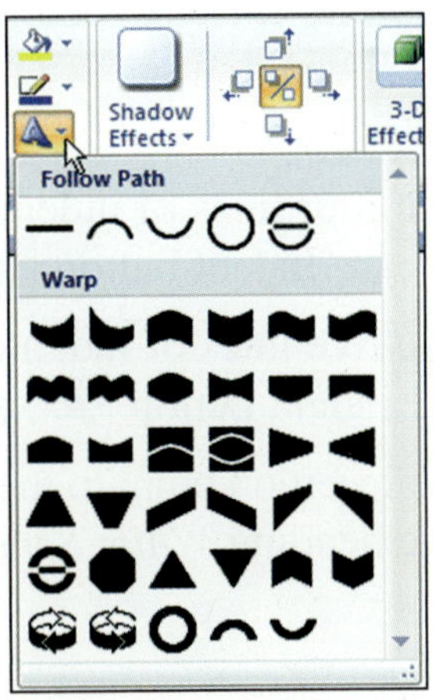

Activity 4.2

Creating Drop Caps and Text Boxes; Drawing Shapes

Use a drop cap to enhance the appearance of text. A drop cap is the first letter of the first word of a paragraph that is set into a paragraph. Drop caps identify the beginning of major sections or parts of a document. Create a drop cap with the Drop Cap button in the Text group in the Insert tab. Use the Text Box button in the Text group to insert a predesigned text box in a document or create your own text box. The Shapes button in the Insert tab contains a number of shape options you can use to draw shapes in a document including lines, basic shapes, block arrows, flow chart shapes, callouts, stars, and banners. Click a shape and the mouse pointer displays as crosshairs (plus sign). Position the crosshairs where you want the image to begin, hold down the left mouse button, drag to create the shape, and then release the mouse button. This inserts the shape in the document and also displays the Drawing Tools Format tab. Use buttons in this tab to change the shape, apply a style to the shape, arrange the shape, and change the size of the shape.

Project

You continue to add visual appeal to the Hawaiian Specials document by creating a drop cap, text boxes, and a shape.

First Choice TRAVEL

1. With **WordS4-01.docx** open, position the insertion point on any character in the heading *White Sands Charters*, click the Border button arrow in the Paragraph group in the Home tab, and then click the *Borders and Shading* option at the drop-down list.
2. At the Borders and Shading dialog box, make sure the single line is selected in the *Style* section, click the down-pointing arrow at the right side of the *Color* option box, and then click the blue color (third color from the *right* in the *Standard Colors* section).
3. Click the bottom of the diagram in the *Preview* section of the dialog box.

   This inserts a single blue line in the diagram.

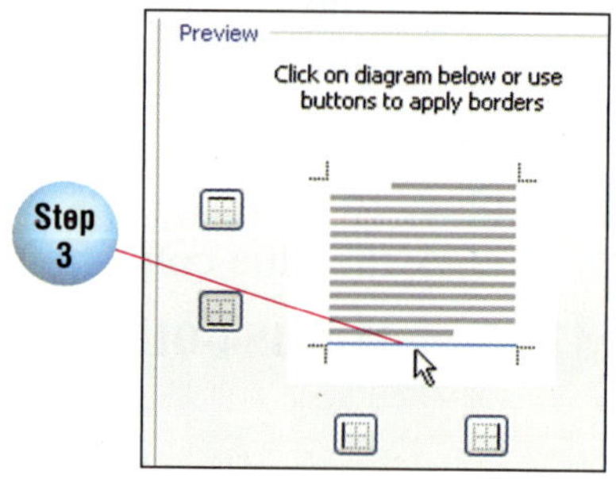

4. Click OK to close the Borders and Shading dialog box.
5. Use the Repeat command, F4, to apply the same bottom blue border to the remaining headings in the document (*Air Adventures*, *Deep Sea Submarines*, *Snorkeling Fantasies*, and *Bicycle Safari*).
6. Select the four lines of indented text in the *Air Adventures* section, click the Decrease Indent button in the Paragraph group, and then click the Bullets button.
7. Select the four lines of indented text in the *Deep Sea Submarines* section, click the Decrease Indent button, and then click the Bullets button.
8. Select the five lines of indented text in the *Bicycle Safari* section, click the Decrease Indent button, and then click the Bullets button.
9. Move the insertion point to the beginning of the word *Sail* that displays immediately below the heading *White Sands Charters* and then click the Insert tab.

10 Click the Drop Cap button Drop Cap in the Text group and then click *Dropped* at the drop-down gallery.

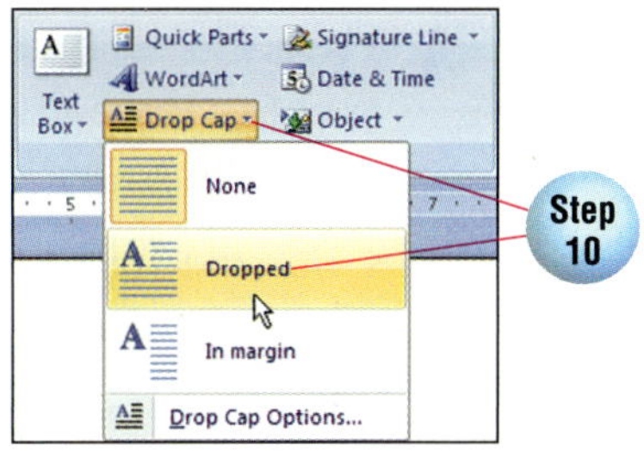

If you click *Drop Cap Options*, the Drop Cap dialog box displays with options for positioning the drop cap, changing the font, identifying the number of lines for the drop cap, and the distance from the drop cap to the text.

11 Click anywhere in the text on the first page to deselect the *S*.

12 Insert a text box on the first page by clicking the Text Box button in the Text group in the Insert tab, scrolling down the drop-down list, and then clicking the *Cubicles Quote* option.

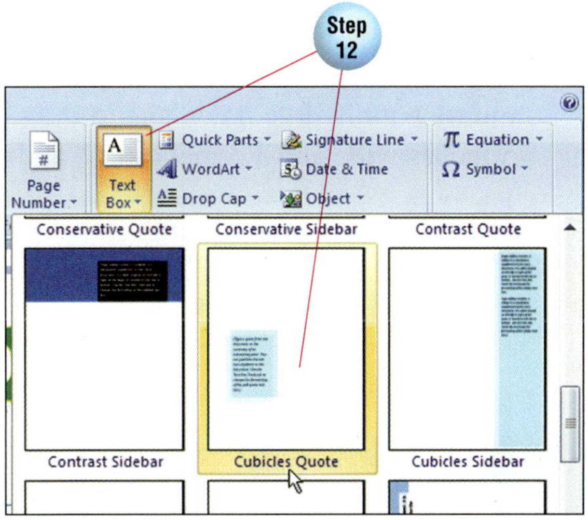

13 Type the following text in the text box: **Sign up today for your Hawaiian adventure and enjoy spectacular beaches, fly over untouched areas, journey through Hawaii's natural undersea world, and snorkel in beautiful, out-of-the-way bays.**

14 Select the text in the text box, click the Home tab, and then change the font size to 10 and the font color to purple.

PROBLEM

If all of the text is not visible in the text box, increase the size of the box.

15 With the text box selected, position and size the text box as shown below.

When sizing the text box, hold down the Shift key while dragging the box border. This maintains the proportion of the box.

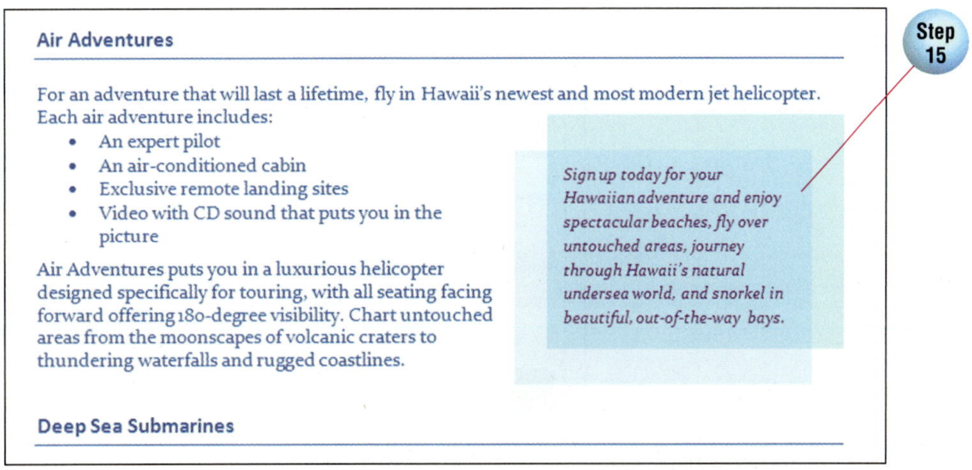

continues

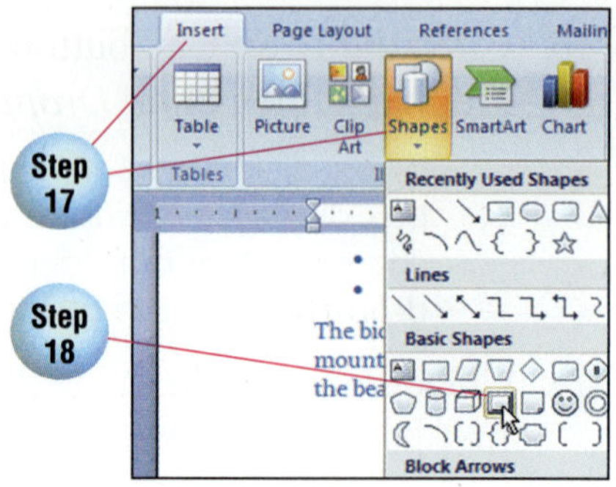

16 Press Ctrl + End to move the insertion point to the end of the document and then press the Enter key twice.

17 Click the Insert tab and then click the Shapes button in the Illustrations group.

18 Click the *Bevel* shape in the *Basic Shapes* section (fourth shape from the left in the middle row).

19 Position the mouse pointer (displays as crosshairs) below the text at approximately the 0.5-inch mark on the horizontal ruler, hold down the left mouse button, drag down and to the right until the banner is approximately 5 inches wide and 1.5 inches tall, and then release the mouse button.

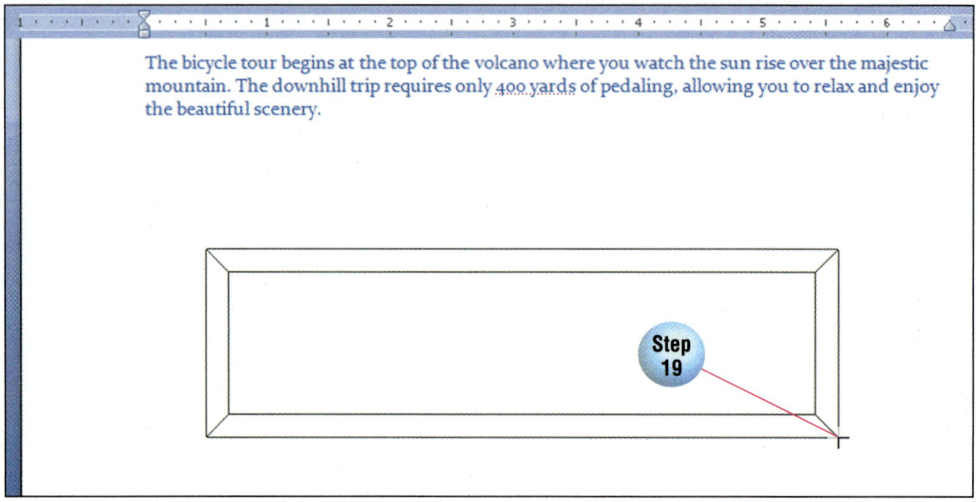

20 Apply a shape style by clicking the More button that displays at the right side of the Shape Styles group in the Drawing Tools Format tab and then clicking *Diagonal Gradient - Accent 1* from the gallery (second option from the left in the sixth row).

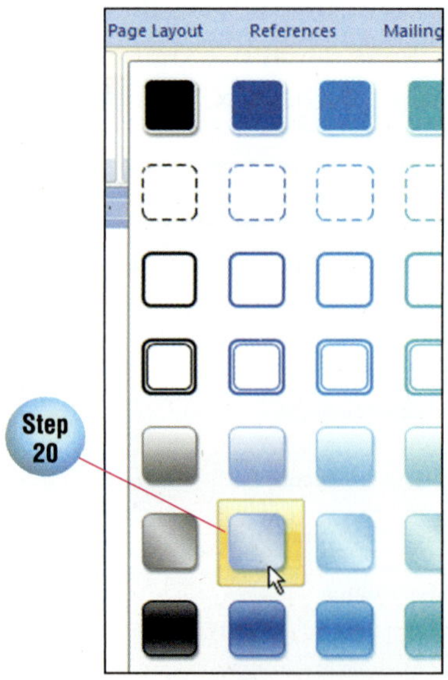

21 Click in the Shape Height measurement box, type **1.5**, and then press Enter.

22. Click in the Shape Width measurement box, type **5**, and then press Enter.
23. Draw a text box inside the shape by clicking the Insert tab, clicking the Text Box button [A] in the Text group, and then clicking *Draw Text Box* at the drop-down list.
24. Position the crosshairs inside the banner and then drag to create a text box similar to the one shown below.

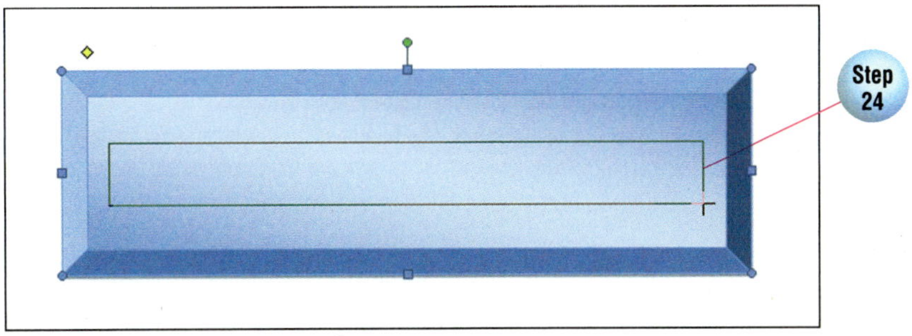

25. Click the Shape Fill button arrow in the Text Box Styles group in the Text Box Tools tab and then click *No Fill* at the drop-down gallery.
26. Click the Shape Outline button arrow in the Text Box Styles group and then click *No Outline* at the drop-down gallery.
27. Click the Home tab and then change the font size to 14 and the font color to purple. Click the Bold button, click the Italic button, click the Center button, and then type **Sign up today for your Hawaiian adventure!**

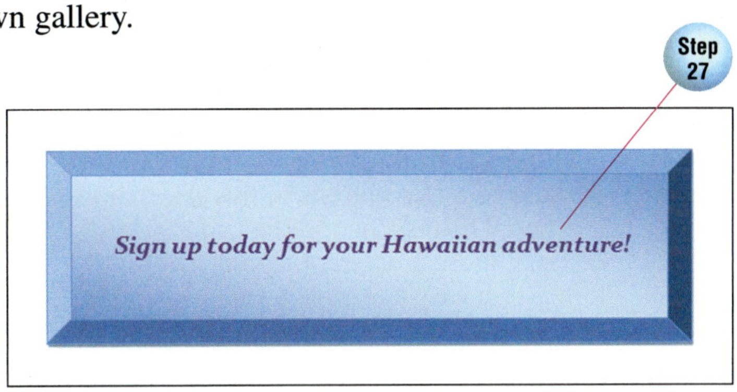

Your text box should appear as shown above.

28. Press Ctrl + Home to move the insertion point to the beginning of the document.
29. Save, print, and then close **WordS4-01.docx**.

In Brief

Create Drop Cap
1. Click Insert tab.
2. Click Drop Cap button.
3. Click desired location.

Insert Text Box
1. Click Insert tab.
2. Click Text Box button.
3. Click desired preformatted text box option.

Create Text Box
1. Click Insert tab.
2. Click Text Box button.
3. Click *Draw Text Box* option.
4. Drag with mouse to draw text box.

In Addition

Drawing Lines

The Shapes drop-down list contains a number of options you can use to draw lines in a document. With the *Curve* option in the *Lines* section, you can draw curved lines by clicking at the beginning position, dragging to the location where you want the curve to appear, and then clicking the mouse button again. Continue in this manner until you have drawn all the desired curved lines. Use the *Freeform* option in the *Lines* section to draw free-form in a document. Click the *Freeform* option and then drag in the document screen. When you want to stop drawing, double-click the left mouse button. You can also use the *Scribble* option to draw free-form in a document. The difference between the *Freeform* option and the *Scribble* option is that you have to double-click to stop drawing with *Freeform* but you only need to release the mouse button to stop drawing with the *Scribble* option.

Activity 4.3

Using SmartArt to Create an Organizational Chart

If you need to visually illustrate hierarchical data, consider creating an organizational chart with a SmartArt option. To display a menu of SmartArt choices, click the Insert tab and then click the SmartArt button in the Illustrations group. This displays the Choose a SmartArt Graphic dialog box. At this dialog box, click *Hierarchy* in the left panel and then double-click the desired organizational chart in the middle panel. This inserts the organizational chart in the document. Some diagrams are designed to include text. You can type text in a diagram by selecting the shape and then typing text in the shape or you can type text in the *Type your text here* window that displays at the left side of the diagram.

Project

Terry Blessing, president of First Choice Travel, has asked you to prepare a document containing information on the organizational structure of the company.

First Choice TRAVEL

1. Open **FCTStructure.docx** and then save the document and name it **WordS4-02**.
2. Move the insertion point a double space below the heading *ORGANIZATIONAL CHART* and then create the organizational chart shown in Figure 4.1. To begin, click the Insert tab and then click the SmartArt button in the Illustrations group.
3. At the Choose a SmartArt Graphic dialog box, click *Hierarchy* in the left panel of the dialog box and then double-click the first option in the middle panel, *Organization Chart*.

   This displays the organizational chart in the document with the SmartArt Tools Design tab selected. Use buttons in this tab to add additional boxes, change the order of the boxes, choose a different layout, apply formatting with a SmartArt Style, and reset the formatting of the organizational chart.

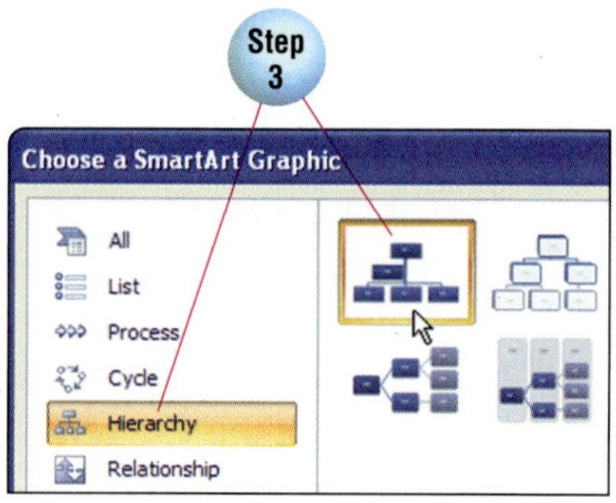

4. If a *Type your text here* window displays at the left side of the organizational chart, close it by clicking the Text Pane button Text Pane in the Create Graphic group.

   You can also close the window by clicking the Close button that displays in the upper right corner of the window.

5. Delete one of the boxes in the organizational chart by clicking the border of the box in the lower right corner to select it and then pressing the Delete key.

   Make sure that the selection border that surrounds the box is a solid line and not a dashed line. If a dashed line displays, click the box border again. This should change it to a solid line.

FIGURE 4.1 Organizational Chart

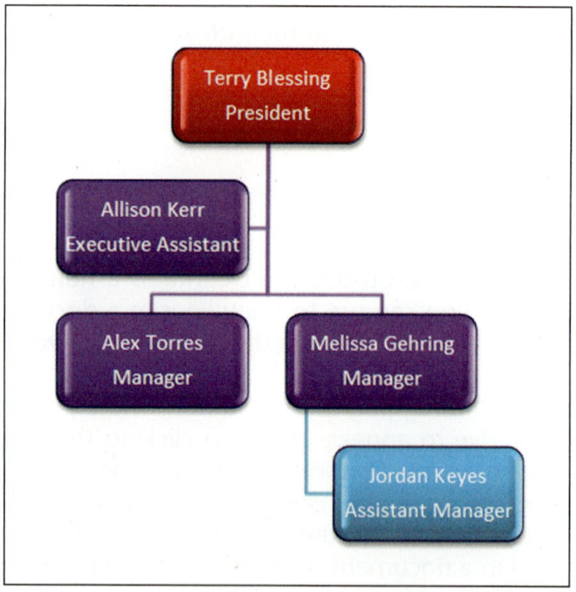

6. With the bottom right box selected, click the Add Shape button arrow in the Create Graphic group and then click the *Add Shape Below* option.

   Your organizational chart should contain the same boxes as shown in Figure 4.1.

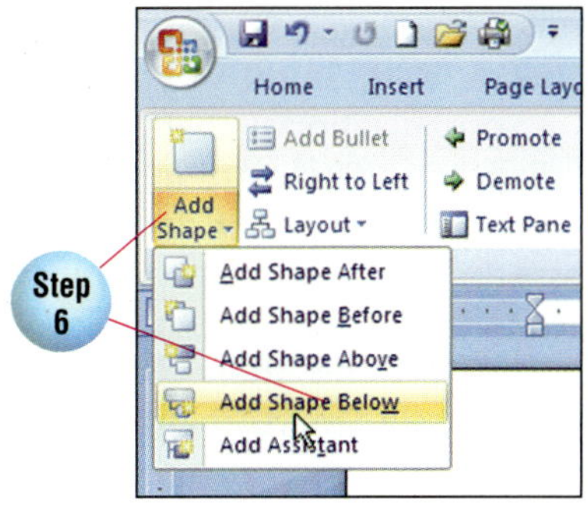

In Brief

Create Organizational Chart
1. Click Insert tab.
2. Click SmartArt button.
3. Click *Hierarchy* at Choose a SmartArt Graphic dialog box.
4. Double-click desired organizational chart.

7. Click *[Text]* in the top box, type **Terry Blessing**, press the Enter key, and then type **President**. Click in each of the remaining boxes and type the text as shown in Figure 4.1.

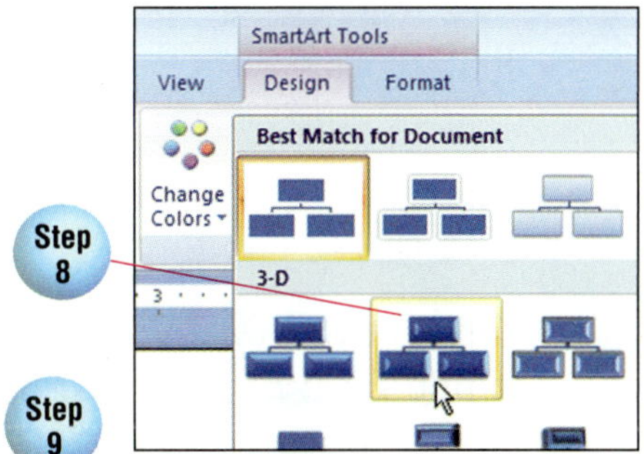

8. Click the More button located at the right side of the SmartArt Styles group and then click the *Inset* option located in the *3-D* section.
9. Click the Change Colors button in the Quick Styles group and then click the *Colorful Range - Accent Colors 3 to 4* option in the *Colorful* section.

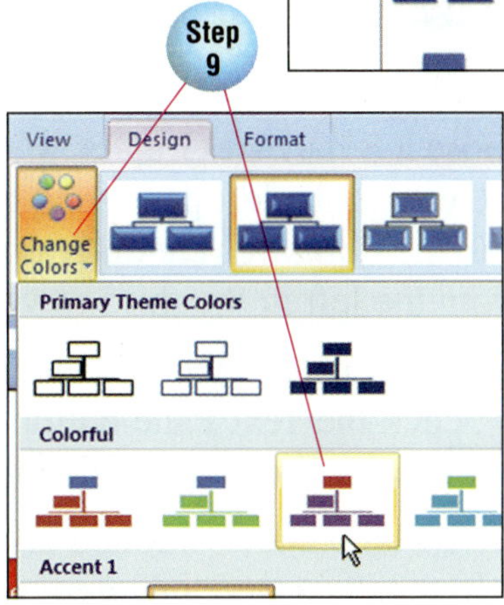

10. Click the SmartArt Tools Format tab.

    The SmartArt Tools Format tab contains buttons for changing the box shape; applying shape styles; applying WordArt styles to text; applying text fill, outline, and effects; and arranging and sizing the organizational chart.

11. Click the tab (displays with a right- and left-pointing triangle) that displays at the left side of the diagram border and then, using the mouse, select the text that displays in the *Type your text here* window.
12. Click the Change Shape button Change Shape in the Shapes group and then click the rounded rectangle shape (second shape from the left in the top row) in the *Rectangles* section.

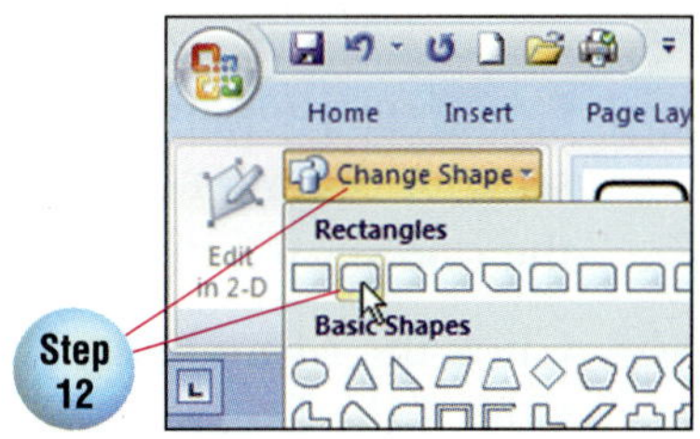

13. Click the Shape Outline button arrow in the Shape Styles group and then click the dark blue color (second color from the right in the *Standard Colors* section).
14. Click the Size button located at the right side of the tab and then click the up arrow to change the *Height* to *4″* and the *Width* to *6.5″*.
15. Click outside the chart to deselect it.
16. Save **WordS4-02.docx**.

Activity 4.4

Using SmartArt to Create a Diagram

With SmartArt you can create an organizational chart as well as other diagrams. SmartArt includes diagrams for presenting a list of data; showing data processes, cycles, and relationships; and presenting data in a matrix or pyramid. When you click the Insert tab and then click the SmartArt button, the Choose a SmartArt Graphic dialog box displays. At this dialog box, *All* is selected in the left panel of the dialog box and all available predesigned diagrams display in the middle panel. Click the desired diagram type in the left panel and then use the scroll bar at the right side of the middle panel to scroll down the list of diagram choices. Click a diagram in the middle panel and the name of the diagram displays in the right panel along with a description of the diagram type. Double-click a diagram in the middle panel of the dialog box and the diagram is inserted in the document. Use buttons in the SmartArt Tools Design tab and the SmartArt Tools Format tab to customize a diagram.

Project

Terry Blessing has asked you to include a diagram in the document that illustrates the services provided by First Choice Travel.

First Choice TRAVEL

1. With **WordS4-02.docx** open, press Ctrl + End to move the insertion point below the title *TRAVEL SERVICES* located on the second page.
2. Click the Insert tab and then click the SmartArt button in the Illustrations group.
3. At the Choose a SmartArt Graphic dialog box, click *Cycle* in the left panel and then double-click the *Radial Cycle* diagram (first diagram from the left in the third row).

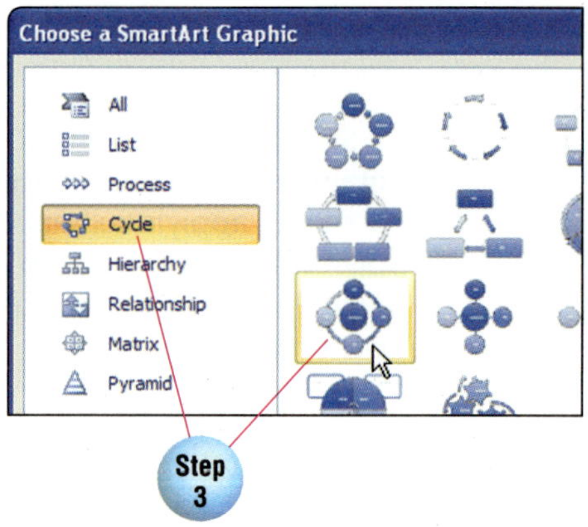

4. If the *Type your text here* window does not display, click the Text Pane button Text Pane in the Create Graphic group.
5. With the insertion point positioned after the first bullet in the *Type your text here* window, type **Travel and Reservation Services**.
6. Click *[Text]* that displays after the first indented bullet and then type **Cruise Packages**.

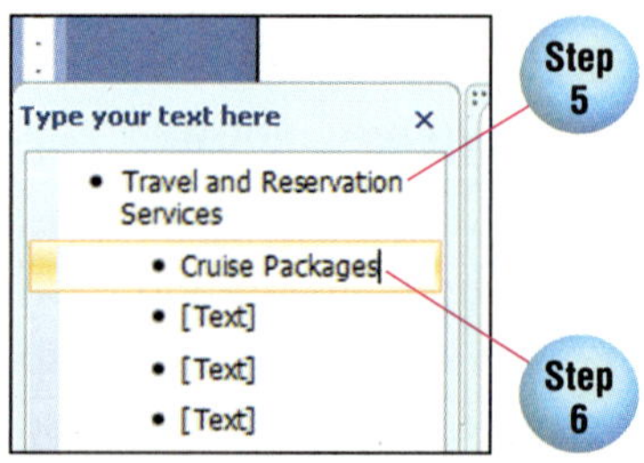

7. Continue clicking *[Text]* and typing text so your diagram contains the same text as the one shown in Figure 4.2.
8. Click the More button located at the right side of the SmartArt Styles group and then click the *Inset* option in the *3-D* section.

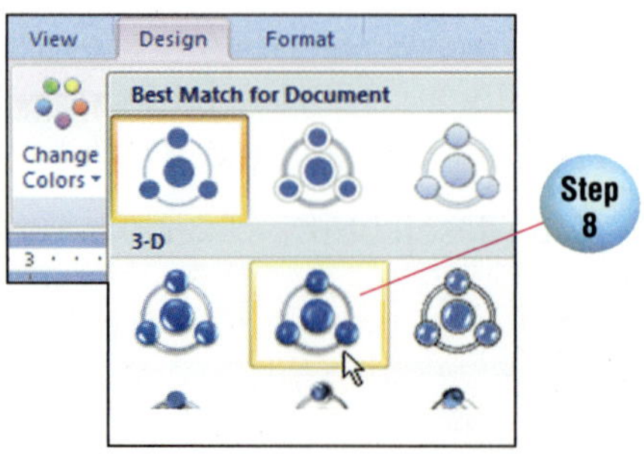

9. Click the Change Colors button in the SmartArt Styles group and then click the *Colorful Range - Accent Colors 4 to 5* option in the *Colorful* section.
10. Click the SmartArt Tools Format tab.
11. Using the mouse, select the text that displays in the *Type your text here* window.
12. Click once on the Larger button in the Shapes group to slightly increase the size of the diagram circles.

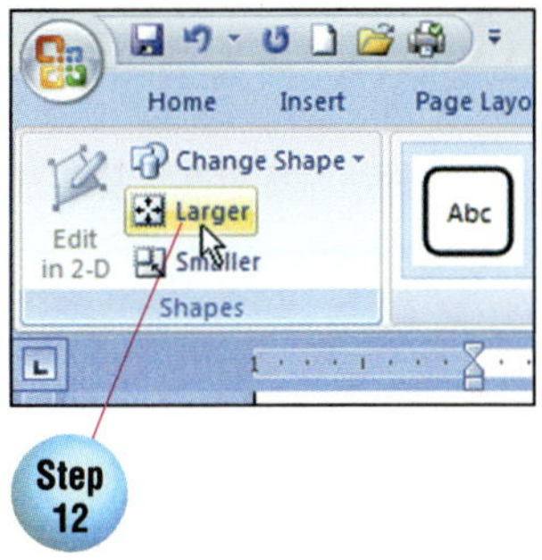

13. Click the Shape Outline button arrow in the Shape Styles group and then click the dark blue color (second color from the right in the *Standard Colors* section).
14. Click the Size button located at the right side of the tab and then click the up arrow to change the *Height* to *4″* and the *Width* to *6.5″*.
15. Click outside the chart to deselect it.
16. Save, print, and then close **WordS4-02.docx**.

In Brief

Create Diagram
1. Click Insert tab.
2. Click SmartArt button.
3. Click desired category in left panel of Choose a SmartArt graphic dialog box.
4. Double-click desired chart.

FIGURE 4.2 Services Diagram

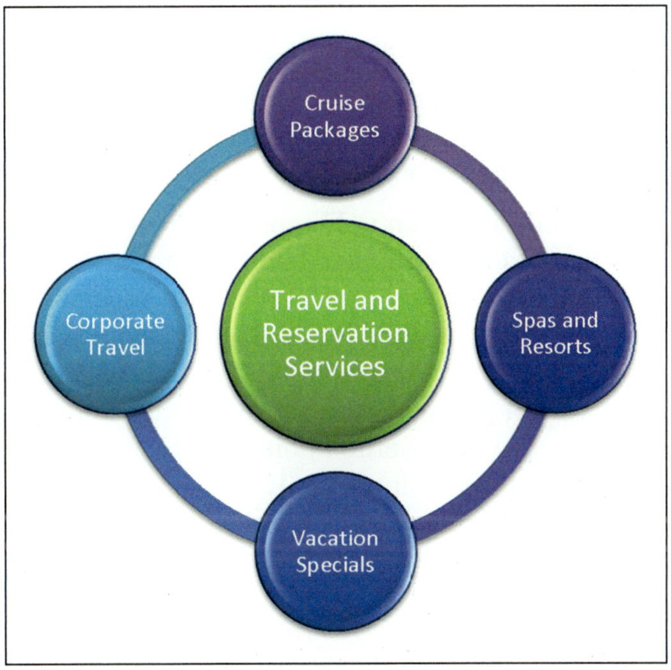

In Addition

Moving a SmartArt Organizational Chart or Diagram

Before moving a SmartArt diagram, you must select a text wrapping style. To do this, select the diagram, click the SmartArt Tools Format tab, and then click the Arrange button. At the list of options that displays, click *Text Wrapping* and then click the desired wrapping style at the drop-down list. Move the diagram by positioning the arrow pointer on the diagram border until the pointer displays with a four-headed arrow attached, holding down the left mouse button, and then dragging the diagram to the desired location. You can increase the size of the diagram with the *Height* and *Width* options or by dragging a corner of the diagram border. If you want to maintain the proportions of the diagram, hold down the Shift key while dragging the border to increase or decrease the size.

Activity 4.5

Creating and Modifying a Table

Word's Table feature is useful for displaying data in columns and rows. This data may be text, values, and/or formulas. You can create a table using the Table button in the Insert tab or with options at the Insert Table dialog box. Once you specify the desired number of rows and columns, Word displays the table and you are ready to enter information into the cells. A ***cell*** is the "box" created by the intersection of a row and a column. Cells are designated with a letter-number label representing the column and row intersection. Columns are lettered from left to right, beginning with A. Rows are numbered from top to bottom, beginning with 1. You can modify the structure of the table by inserting or deleting columns and/or rows and merging cells.

Project

First Choice TRAVEL

You are developing a new First Choice Travel information document about sightseeing flights around the island of Maui. You decide to create a table to display the data and then modify the table.

1. Open **FCTIslandFlights.docx** and then save the document and name it **WordS4-03**.
2. Press Ctrl + End to move the insertion point to the end of the document.
3. Click the Insert tab and then click the Table button in the Tables group.
4. Drag the mouse pointer down and to the right until the number above the grid displays as *3 × 6* and then click the mouse button.
5. Type the text in the cells as shown in Figure 4.3. Press the Tab key to move the insertion point to the next cell or press Shift + Tab to move the insertion point to the previous cell. When typing text in the cells in the second column, do not press the Enter key to end a line. Type the text and let the word wrap feature wrap the text within the cell. After typing text in the last cell, do not press the Tab key. This will insert another row. If you press the Tab key accidentally, immediately click the Undo button. To move the insertion point to different cells within the table using the mouse, click in the desired cell. If you type the incorrect text in a cell, press Shift + Tab until the incorrect text is selected and then type the correct text.

FIGURE 4.3 Step 5

Adventure	Destination	Price
Special West Maui	Waterfalls, lush tropical valleys	$49
West Maui Tropical	West Maui mountains, Hawaii's highest waterfalls	$79
Haleakala-Keane	Haleakala crater, tropical rain forest, waterfalls	$89
Special Circle Island	Hana, Haleakala, West Maui mountains, tropical rain forest, waterfalls	$169
Molokai-West Maui	West Maui mountains, waterfalls, sea cliffs, Kalaupapa colony	$189

6. You decide to add First Choice Travel discount prices to the table. To do this, position the insertion point in the *Price* cell, click the Table Tools Layout tab, and then click the Insert Right button in the Rows & Columns group.

   Figure 4.4 displays the Table Tools Layout tab.

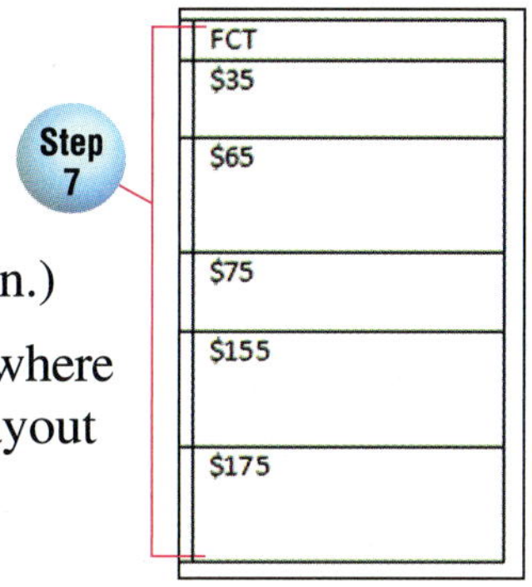

7. Click in the top cell of the new column, type **FCT**, and then press the Down Arrow key. Type the money amounts in the remaining cells as shown at the right. (Press the Down Arrow key to move to the next cell down.)

8. Delete the *Special Circle Island* row. To do this, click anywhere in the text *Special Circle Island*, click the Table Tools Layout tab, click the Delete button in the Rows & Columns group, and then click *Delete Rows* at the drop-down list.

9. Insert a row above *Adventure*. To do this, click anywhere in the text *Adventure* and then click the Insert Above button in the Rows & Columns group.

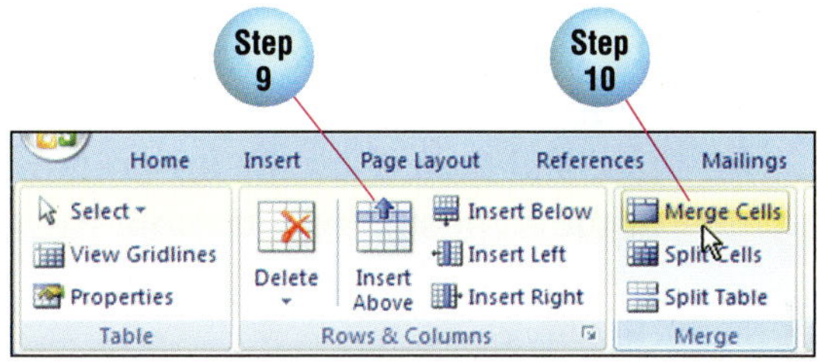

10. With the new top row selected, merge the cells by clicking the Merge Cells button in the Merge group.

11. Type **MAUI FLIGHTS** in the top row.

12. Select all cells in the table by clicking the table move handle that displays in the upper left corner of the table (square with a four-headed arrow inside).

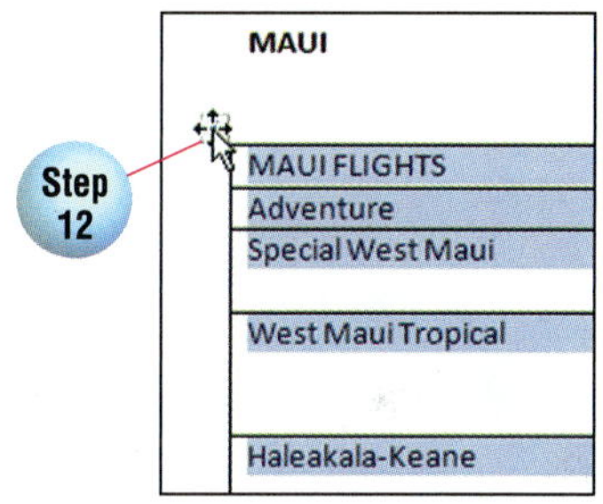

13. Click the Home tab, change the font to Constantia, the font size to 12, and then click outside the table to deselect it.

14. Save **WordS4-03.docx**.

In Brief

Create Table

1. Click Insert tab.
2. Click Table button.
3. Drag in grid to select desired number of columns and rows.

FIGURE 4.4 Table Tools Layout Tab

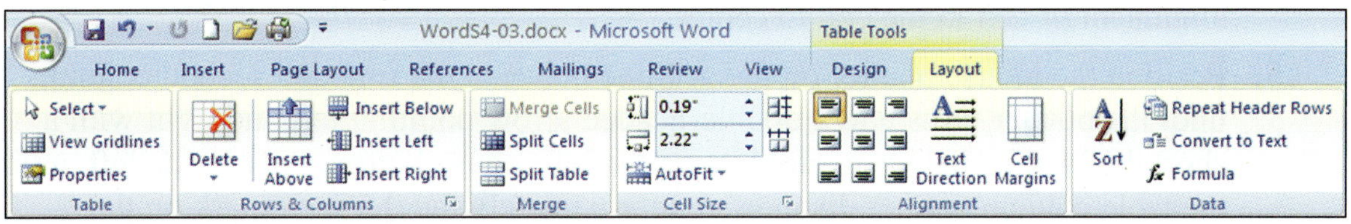

In Addition

Other Methods for Creating a Table

Other methods for creating a table include using options from the Insert Table dialog box or drawing a table. Display the Insert Table dialog box by clicking the Insert tab, clicking the Table button, and then clicking *Insert Table* at the drop-down list. Specify the desired number of columns and rows and then click OK to close the dialog box.

Another method for creating a table is to draw a table by clicking the Table button and then clicking *Draw Table* at the drop-down list. The mouse pointer changes to a pencil. Drag in the document screen to create the desired columns and rows.

Activity 4.6

Changing the Table Layout

In the previous activity, you added a column and a row and deleted a row using buttons in the Table Tools Layout tab. This tab contains additional buttons for customizing the table layout such as changing cell size, alignment, direction, and margins; sorting data; and converting a table to text. When you create a table, columns are the same width and rows are the same height. The width of columns depends on the number of columns as well as the document margins. You can change column widths and row height using a variety of methods including dragging the gridlines. You can apply formatting to text in cells by selecting text or selecting multiple cells and then applying formatting.

Project

First Choice TRAVEL

The Maui Flights table needs adjustments to improve its appearance. You will increase and decrease column widths, increase the height of a row, and apply formatting to the entire table and to specific cells in the table.

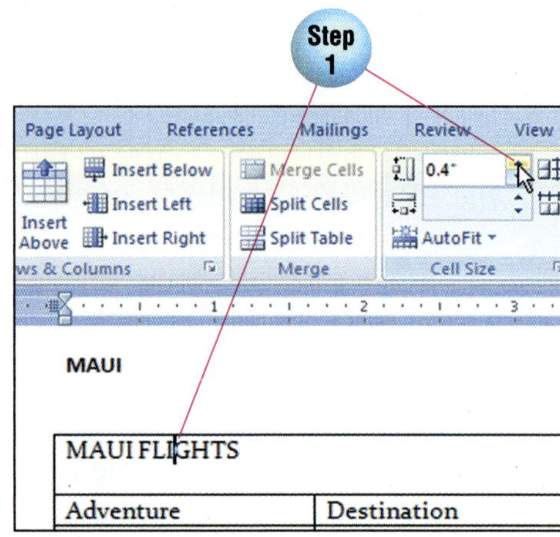

1. With **WordS4-03.docx** open, click in the top cell containing the text *MAUI FLIGHTS*, click the Table Tools Layout tab, and then click the up-pointing arrow at the right side of the Table Row Height text box in the Cell Size group until *0.4"* displays.
2. Click the Insert Left button [Insert Left] in the Rows & Columns group in the Table Tools Layout tab.
3. With the cells in the new column selected, click the Merge Cells button [Merge Cells] in the Merge group.
4. Type **Hawaiian Adventures** in the new cell and then click twice on the Text Direction button in the Alignment group.
5. Click the Align Center button in the Alignment group to change the horizontal and vertical alignment of text in the cell to center.

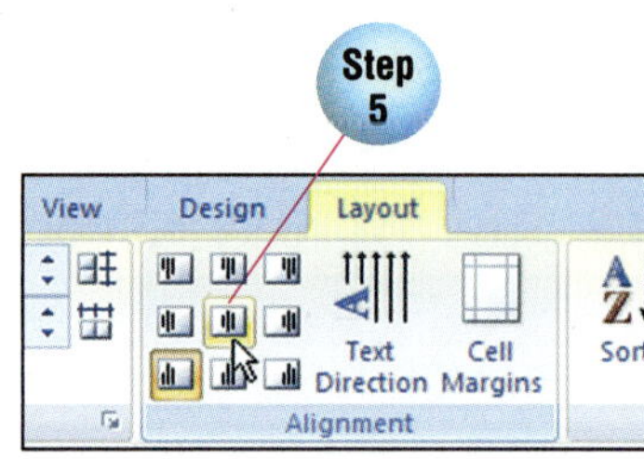

6. Position the mouse pointer on the gridline between the first and second columns until the pointer turns into a double-headed arrow pointing left and right with a short double line between. Hold down the left mouse button, drag to the left until the table column marker displays at approximately the 0.5-inch mark on the horizontal ruler, and then release the mouse button.

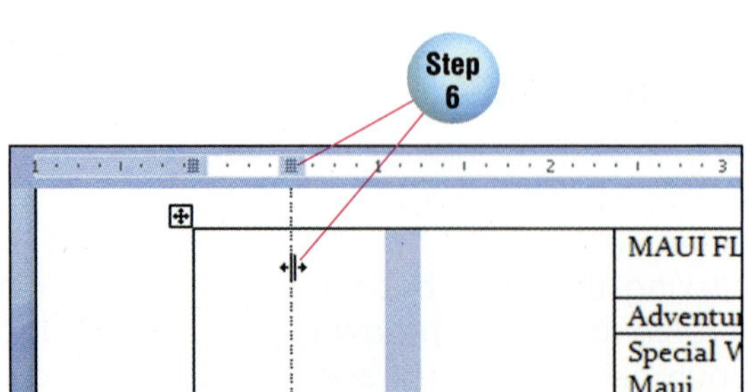

7 Position the mouse pointer on the gridline between the fourth and fifth columns until the pointer turns into a double-headed arrow pointing left and right, and then drag to the left until the table column marker displays at the 5.5-inch mark on the horizontal ruler.

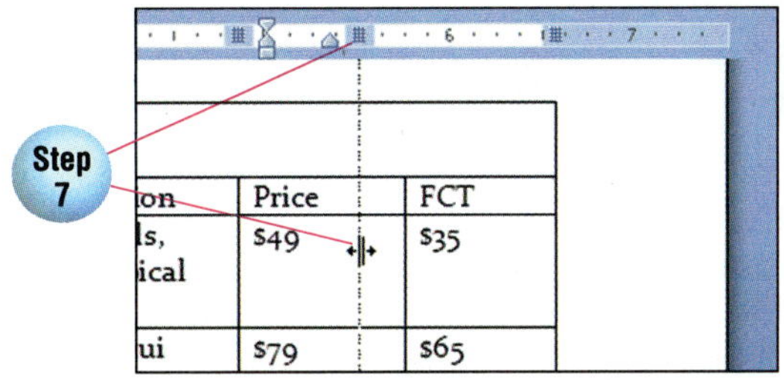

8 Following the same procedure, drag the gridline between the third and fourth columns to the left until the table column marker displays at the 4.5-inch mark on the horizontal ruler.

9 Drag the gridline between the second and third columns to the right until the table column marker displays at the 2.25-inch mark on the horizontal ruler.

10 Click anywhere in the *MAUI FLIGHTS* text, click the Align Center button in the Alignment group in the Table Tools Layout tab.

This changes the horizontal and vertical alignment to center for text in the cell.

11 Select the four cells containing the headings *Adventure*, *Destination*, *Price*, and *FCT*; click the Align Center button in the Alignment group; and then press Ctrl + B to apply bold formatting.

12 Select all of the cells containing prices and then click the Align Top Center button in the Alignment group.

13 Click anywhere outside the table to deselect the cells.

14 Save **WordS4-03.docx**.

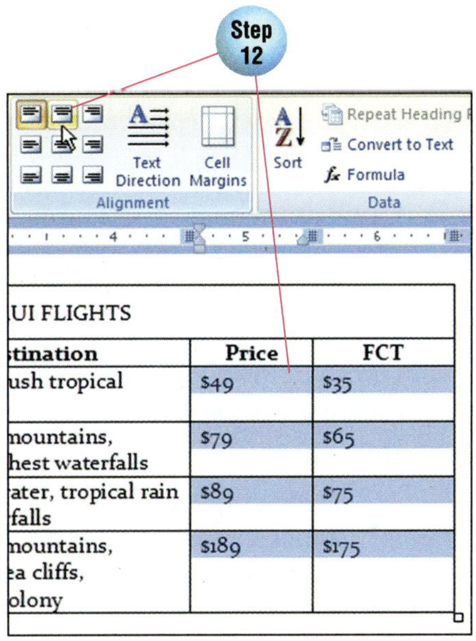

In Brief

Increase/Decrease Column/Row

1. Position mouse pointer on gridline until it turns into double-headed arrow.
2. Hold down left mouse button, drag to desired position, then release mouse button.

In Addition

Selecting Cells with the Keyboard

Besides using the mouse, you can also select cells using keyboard shortcuts by completing the following steps:

To select	Press
the next cell's contents	Tab
the preceding cell's contents	Shift + Tab
the entire table	Alt + 5 (on the numeric keypad with Num Lock off)
adjacent cells	Hold Shift key and then press an arrow key repeatedly.
a column	Position insertion point in top cell of column, hold down the Shift key, and then press Down Arrow key until column is selected.

Activity 4.7

Changing the Table Design

The Table Tools Design tab contains a number of options for enhancing the appearance of the table. With options in the Table Styles group, apply a predesigned style that applies color and border lines to a table. Maintain further control over the predesigned style formatting applied to columns and rows with options in the Table Style Options group. For example, if your table contains a row for totals, you would insert a check mark in the *Total Row* option. Apply additional design formatting to cells in a table with the Shading and Borders buttons in the Table Styles group. Draw a table or draw additional rows and/or columns in a table by clicking the Draw Table button in the Draw Borders group. Click this button and the mouse pointer turns into a pencil. Drag in the table to create the desired columns and rows. Click the Eraser button and the mouse pointer turns into an eraser. Drag through the column and/or row lines you want to erase in the table.

Project

You will add final design formatting to the Maui Flights table by applying a table style and then customizing the formatting with additional options.

1. With **WordS4-03.docx** open, select *MAUI FLIGHTS*, click the Home tab, and then change the font size to 16 and turn on bold.
2. Select the text *Hawaiian Adventures*, change the font size to 14, and then turn on bold and italics.
3. Click anywhere in the table and then click the Table Tools Design tab.
4. Click the More button that displays at the right side of the Table Styles group.

   This displays a drop-down gallery of style choices.
5. Click the *Medium Shading 1 - Accent 5* option (second option from the right in the fourth row in the *Built-In* section).

   Notice the color and border style formatting applied and also notice how the style changed the cell alignment for *MAUI FLIGHTS* and *Hawaiian Adventures* from Align Center to Align Top Center.

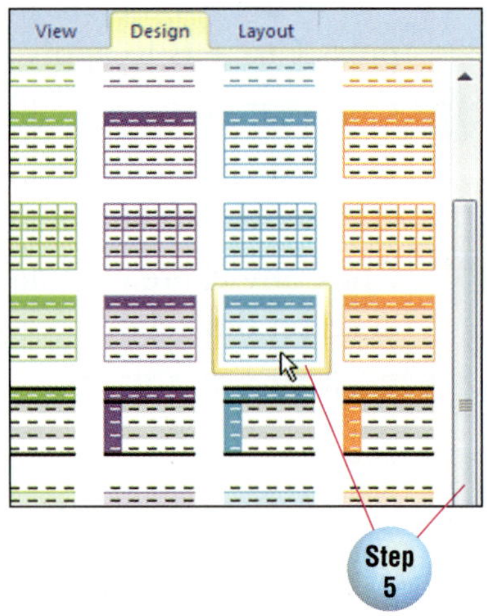

6. Experiment with an additional style by clicking the More button at the right side of the Table Styles group and then clicking the *Medium Shading 1 - Accent 1* option (second option from the left in the fourth row in the *Built-In* section).

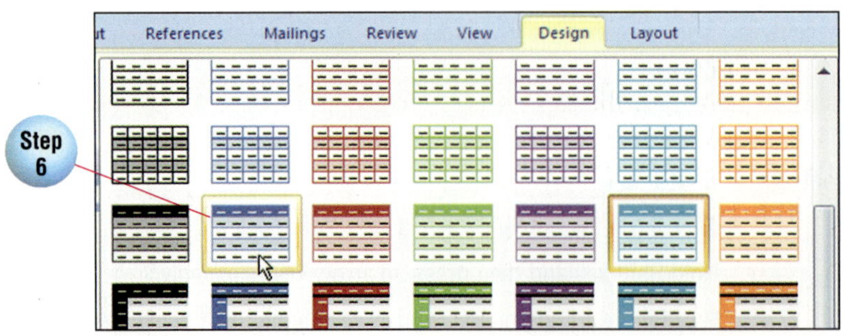

7. Change the formatting by clicking the *Banded Rows* option in the Table Style Options group to remove the check mark. Click the *Banded Columns* option to insert a check mark. Click the *Header Row* option to remove the check mark and click the *First Column* option to remove the check mark.
8. Save and then print **WordS4-03.docx**.
9. With the insertion point positioned in a cell in the table and the Table Tools Design tab selected, click the *Header Row* option in the Table Style Options group to insert a check mark and click the *First Column* option to insert a check mark. Click the *Banded Columns* option to remove the check mark and click the *Banded Rows* option to insert a check mark.
10. Click the More button that displays at the right side of the Table Styles group, scroll down to the bottom of the drop-down gallery, and then click the *Colorful List - Accent 3* option (fourth option from the left in the thirteenth row).
11. Save, print, and then close **WordS4-03.docx**.

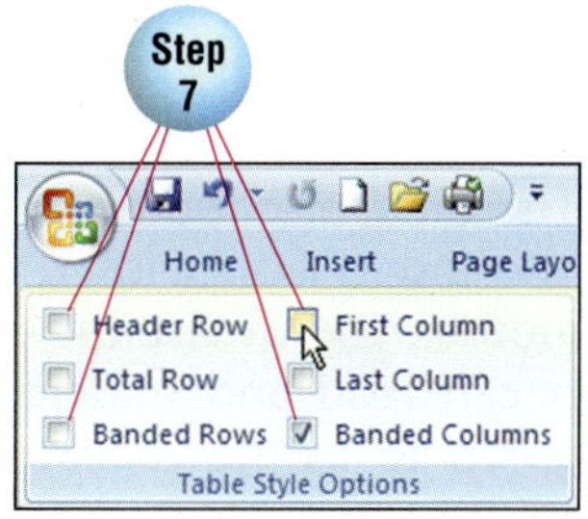

In Addition

Sorting in a Table

Sort text in a table alphabetically, numerically, or by date with options at the Sort dialog box shown at the right. Display this dialog box by positioning the insertion point in a cell in the table and then clicking the Sort button in the Data group in the Table Tools Layout tab. Make sure the column you want to sort is selected in the *Sort by* option and then click OK. If the first row in the table contains data such as headings that you do not want to include in the sort, click the *Header row* option in the *My list has* section of the Sort dialog box. If you want to sort specific cells in a table, select the cells first and then click the Sort button.

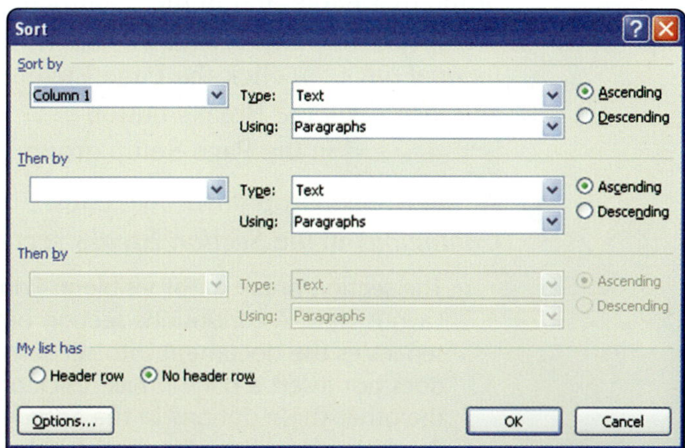

Activity 4.8

Inserting a File and Section Break; Creating and Modifying Newspaper Columns

Use the Object button in the Text group in the Insert tab to insert one document into another. To increase the ease with which a person can read and understand groups of words (referred to as the ***readability*** of a document), consider setting text in the document in newspaper columns. Newspaper columns contain text that flows up and down on the page. Create newspaper columns with the Columns button in the Page Layout tab or with options at the Columns dialog box. If you want to apply column formatting to only a portion of a document, insert a section break in the document. Insert a section break in a document with options at the Breaks button drop-down list.

Project

First Choice TRAVEL

You are working on a fact sheet for Petersburg, Alaska, and realize that you need to insert additional information from another file. You also decide to improve the readability of the Petersburg fact sheet document by setting the text in newspaper columns.

1. Open **FCTPA03.docx** and then save the document and name it **WordS4-04**.
2. Press Ctrl + End to move the insertion point to the end of the document and then click the Insert tab.
3. Insert a document into **WordS4-04.docx** by clicking the Object button arrow in the Text group and then clicking the *Text from File* option at the drop-down list.
4. At the Insert File dialog box, navigate to the WordS4 folder on your storage medium and then double-click ***FCTPAActivities.docx***.

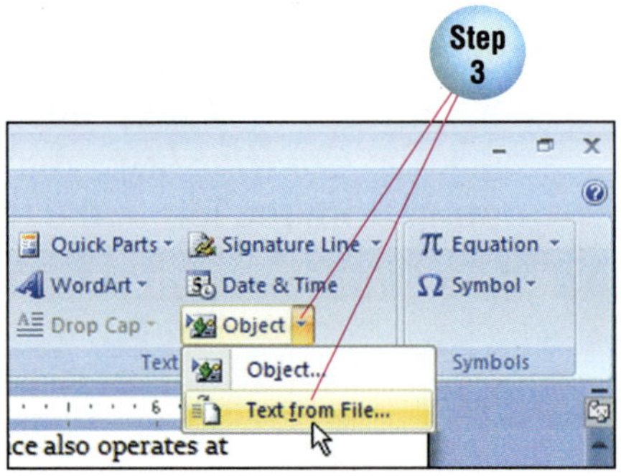

5. Select the text you just inserted and then change the font to Constantia.
6. Apply the Heading 1 style to the title *FACT SHEET—PETERSBURG, ALASKA* and apply the Heading 2 style to the headings in the document including *Services*, *Visitor Attractions*, *Walking Tours*, *Accommodations*, *Transportation*, and *Guided Activities*.
7. Position the insertion point at the beginning of the first paragraph in the document (the paragraph that begins *Petersburg, Alaska, located on . . .*), click the Page Layout tab, and then click the Breaks button [Breaks] in the Page Setup group.
8. At the Breaks drop-down list, click *Continuous* in the *Section Breaks* section.

   The section break is not visible in Print Layout view. A continuous section break separates the document into sections but does not insert a page break. Click one of the other three options in the *Section Breaks* section of the Breaks drop-down list if you want to insert a section break that begins a new page.

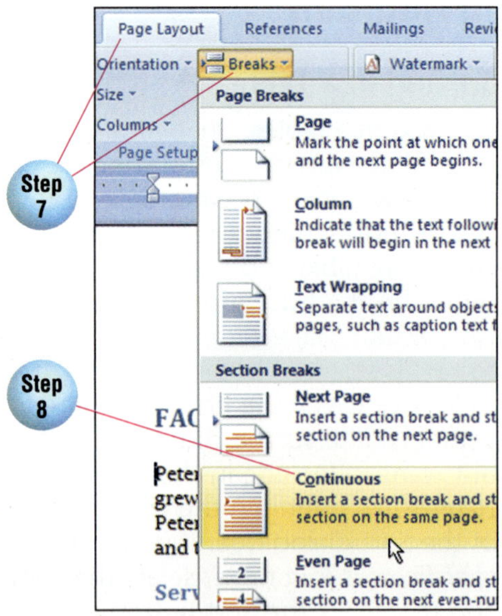

9. Click the Draft button in the View section of the Status bar.

   In Draft view, the section break displays in the document as a double row of dots with the words *Section Break (Continuous)* in the middle.

10. With the insertion point positioned below the section break, format the text below the section break into three newspaper columns by clicking the Columns button in the Page Setup group in the Page Layout tab and then clicking *Three* at the drop-down list.

   Formatting text into columns automatically changes the view to Print Layout.

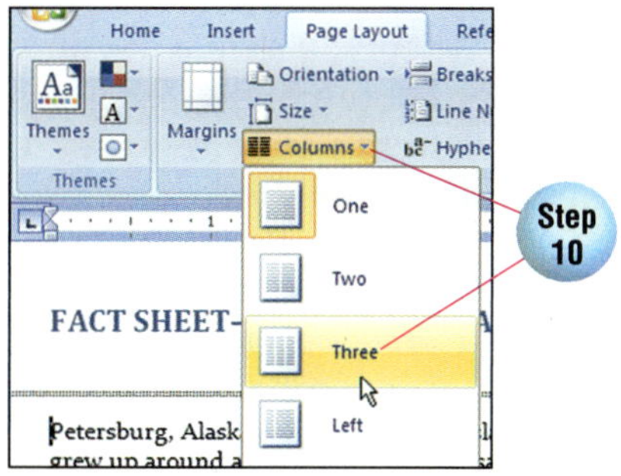

11. As you view the document, you decide that the three columns are too narrow. To change and customize columns, click the Columns button in the Page Setup group in the Page Layout tab and then click *More Columns* at the drop-down list.
12. At the Columns dialog box, click *Two* in the *Presets* section.
13. Increase the spacing between the two columns by clicking the up-pointing arrow at the right side of the *Spacing* option in the *Width and spacing* section until *0.7″* displays in the text box and make sure a check mark displays in the *Equal column width* check box. (If not, click the option to insert the check mark.)
14. Click the *Line between* option to insert a check mark and then click OK to close the dialog box.

   Choosing the *Line between* option inserts a line between the two columns. The *Preview* section of the dialog box provides a visual representation of the columns.

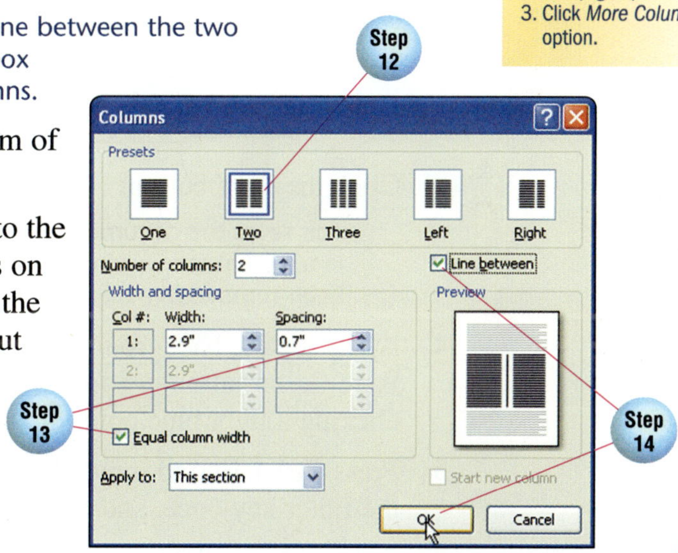

15. Insert page numbering that prints at the bottom of each page.
16. Press Ctrl + End to move the insertion point to the end of the document. Looking at the columns on the last (second) page, you decide to balance the two columns. To do this, click the Page Layout tab, click the Breaks button in the Page Setup group, and then click *Continuous* in the *Section Breaks* section.
17. Save and then print **WordS4-04.docx**.

In Brief

Insert File into Another

1. Click Insert tab.
2. Click Object button arrow in Text group and then click *Text from File*.
3. At Insert File dialog box, double-click desired document.

Insert Continuous Section Break

1. Click Page Layout tab.
2. Click Breaks button in Page Setup group.
3. Click *Continuous*.

Format Text into Columns

1. Click Page Layout tab.
2. Click Columns button in Page Setup group.
3. Click desired number of columns.

Display Columns Dialog Box

1. Click Page Layout tab.
2. Click Columns button in Page Setup group.
3. Click *More Columns* option.

In Addition

Changing Column Width

One method for changing column width in a document is to drag the column marker on the horizontal ruler. To change the width (and also the spacing) of columns of text, position the arrow pointer on the left or right edge of a column marker on the horizontal ruler until it turns into a double-headed arrow pointing left and right. Hold down the left mouse button, drag the column marker to the left or right to make the column of text wider or narrower, and then release the mouse button. Hold down the Alt key while dragging the column marker and measurements display on the horizontal ruler.

Activity 4.9

Saving a Document as a Web Page; Creating a Hyperlink

You can save a Word document as a Web page and apply formatting to the Web page. When you save a document as a Web page, Word automatically changes to the Web Layout view. In this view, the page displays as it will appear when published to the Web or an intranet. In an organization, a Word document can be saved as a Web page and posted on the company intranet as a timely method of distributing the document to the company employees. You can save a Word document as a single Web page or as a conventional Web page. If you choose the *Single File Web Page* option, all data in the document such as graphics and other supplemental data is saved in a single Web file. If you choose the *Web Page* option, Word creates additional files for supplemental data and saves the files in a subfolder. A third option *Web Page, Filtered*, is similar to the *Web Page* option except only the essential data is saved. You can create a hyperlink in a document or Web page that connects to a site on the Internet or to another document.

Project

First Choice TRAVEL

Since many of First Choice Travel's clients have Internet access, you decide to save the Petersburg document as a Web page, and then insert hyperlinks to another document containing information on Petersburg as well as an Alaska travel Web site.

1. With **WordS4-04.docx** open, save the document as a single Web page by clicking the Office button and then clicking *Save As*.
2. At the Save As dialog box, click the down-pointing arrow at the right side of the *Save as type* list box, scroll down the drop-down list, and then click the *Single File Web Page (*.mht; *.mhtml)* option.

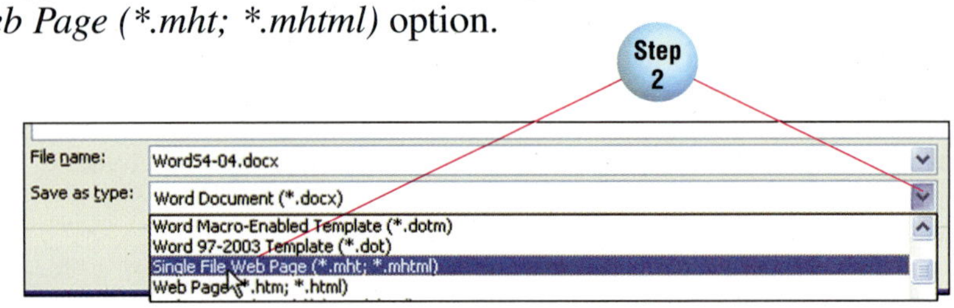

3. Click the Save button.

   This saves the document with the name **WordS4-04.mht** and displays the document in a format for viewing on the Internet. Notice how some of the formatting has been removed.

4. Apply a page background color by clicking the Page Layout tab, clicking the Page Color button Page Color in the Page Background group, and then clicking a light blue color of your choosing.
5. Press Ctrl + End to move the insertion point to the end of the document, press the Enter key once, and then type **Additional Information**.
6. Select the text *Additional Information*.
7. Insert a hyperlink by clicking the Insert tab and then clicking the Hyperlink button Hyperlink in the Links group.

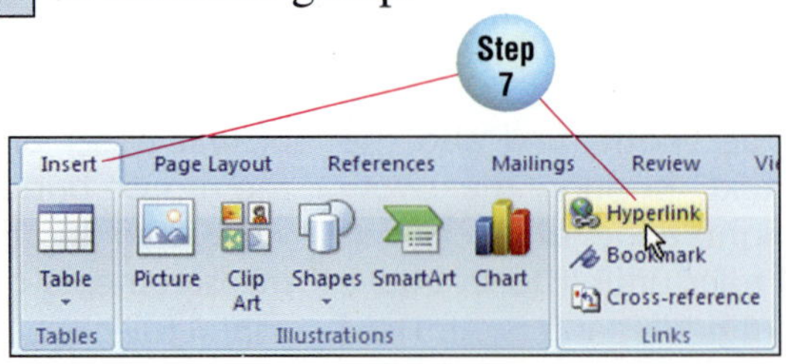

8 At the Insert Hyperlink dialog box, click the down-pointing arrow at the right side of the *Look in* option, navigate to the WordS4 folder on your storage medium, and then double-click ***FCTPA01.docx***.

The Insert Hyperlink dialog box closes and *Additional Information* displays as hyperlink text.

9 Press Ctrl + End, press the Enter key once, and then type **Alaska Tourism**.

10 Create a hyperlink to the tourism site by selecting *Alaska Tourism* and then clicking the Hyperlink button Hyperlink in the Links group.

11 At the Insert Hyperlink dialog box, type **www.travelalaska.com** in the *Address* text box and then click OK.

Word automatically adds *http://* to the beginning of the Web address. If this Web site is not available, try www.state.ak.us.

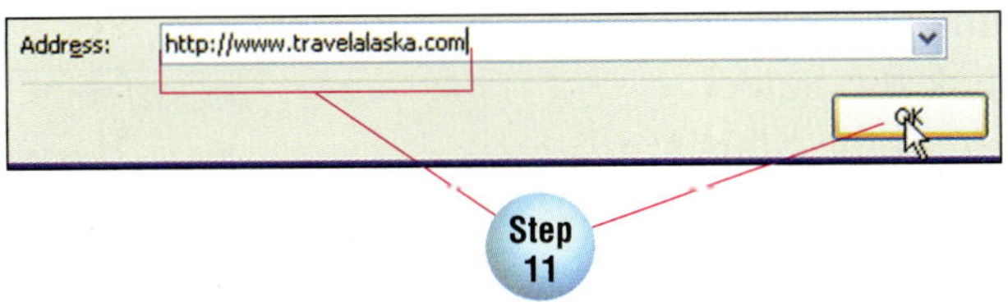

12 Display the document containing additional information on Petersburg by holding down the Ctrl key and then clicking the Additional Information hyperlink.

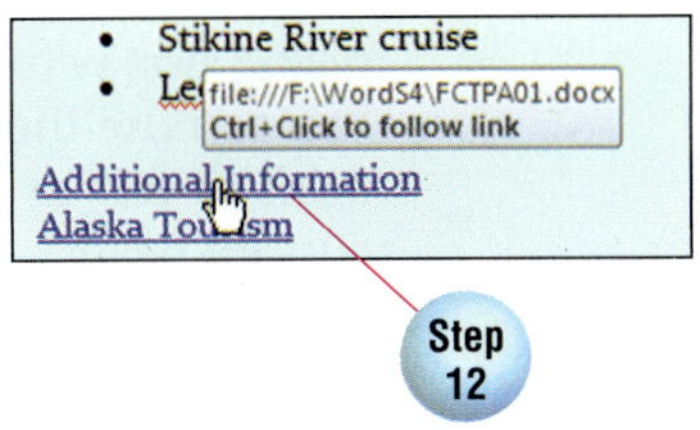

13 After reading the information in the document, close the document.

14 Make sure you are connected to the Internet and then connect to the Alaska tourism site by holding down the Ctrl key and then clicking the Alaska Tourism hyperlink.

15 At the Alaska Tourism Web page, click on any hyperlinks that interest you. When you are finished, click the Close button in the upper right corner of the browser window.

16 Save, print, and then close **WordS4-04.mht**.

The document prints with the original formatting applied.

In Brief

Save Document as Single File Web Page
1. Click Office button and then Save As.
2. Click down-pointing arrow at right side of *Save as type* list box.
3. Click *Single File Web Page (*.mht; *.mhtml)*.
4. Click Save.

Insert Hyperlink
1. Select text.
2. Click Insert tab.
3. Click Hyperlink button in Links group.
4. Type file name or Web address.
5. Click OK.

In Addition

Downloading and Saving Web Pages and Images

You can save the image(s) and/or text that displays when you open a Web page as well as the Web page itself. Copyright laws protect much of the information on the Internet so check the site for restrictions before copying or downloading. If you do use information, make sure you properly cite the source. To save a Web page as a file, display the desired page, click File on the Internet Explorer Menu bar, and then click *Save As*. At the Save Web Page dialog box, specify the folder where you want to save the Web page. Select the text in the *File name* text box, type a name for the page, and then click the Save button. Save a specific Web image by right-clicking the image and then clicking *Save Picture As*. At the Save Picture dialog box, type a name for the image in the *File name* text box and then press Enter.

Activity 4.10

Merging Documents and Envelopes

If you need to mail the same basic letter to a number of clients or customers, consider using the mail merge feature to make the job easier and to make the letter more personalized. With mail merge you can use a data source containing information on your clients to merge with a main document containing the letter. You can also create an envelope document you can merge with a data source. Click the Mailings tab to display a number of buttons for preparing a mail merge document. Generally, a merge takes two documents —the ***data source*** and the ***main document***. The data source document contains the variable information that will be inserted in the main document. Use buttons in the Mailings tab to create main documents and data source documents for merging.

Project

First Choice Travel is offering a special cruise package and Melissa Gehring has asked you to prepare a data source document with client information and merge it with a letter describing the cruise special and then print envelopes for the letters.

1. At a blank document, click the Mailings tab, click the Select Recipients button in the Start Mail Merge group, and then click *Type New List* at the drop-down list.

   This displays the New Address List dialog box with predesigned fields. You can use these predesigned fields as well as create your own custom fields.

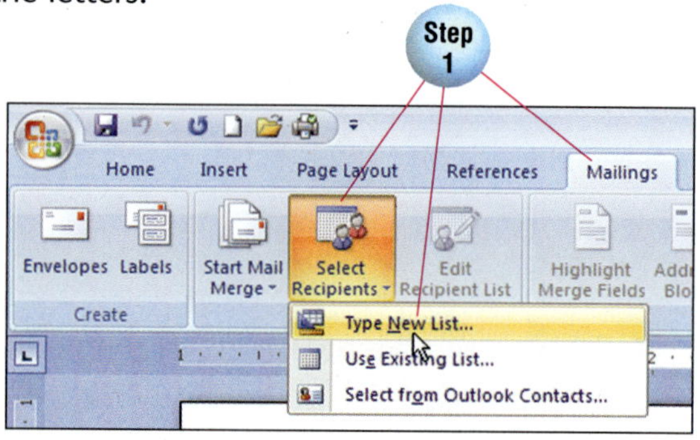

2. Click the Customize Columns button located toward the bottom of the dialog box.

   The predesigned fields offer most of the fields you need for your data source document but you decide to delete six of the predesigned fields and insert two of your own field.

3. At the Customize Address List dialog box, click *Company Name* to select it and then click the Delete button.

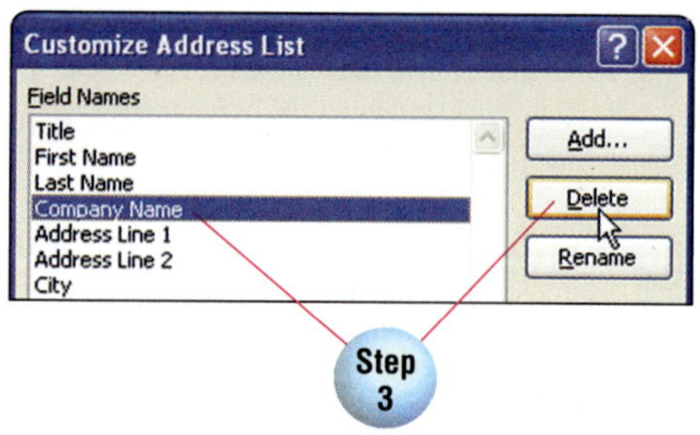

4. At the message asking if you are sure you want to delete the field, click Yes.
5. Complete steps similar to those in Steps 3 and 4 to delete the following fields: *Address Line 2*, *Country or Region*, *Home Phone*, *Work Phone*, and *E-mail Address*.
6. Click the Add button.

   If the New Address List dialog box does not provide for all variable information, create your own custom field.

7. At the Add Field dialog box, type **Membership** and then click OK.

8. Click the Add button, type **Discount**, and then click OK.
9. Click OK to close the Customize Address List dialog box.

10 At the New Address List dialog box with the insertion point positioned in the *Title* field, type **Mrs.** and then press the Tab key.

This moves the insertion point to the *First Name* field. You can also press the Enter key to move to the next field and press Shift + Tab to move to the previous field.

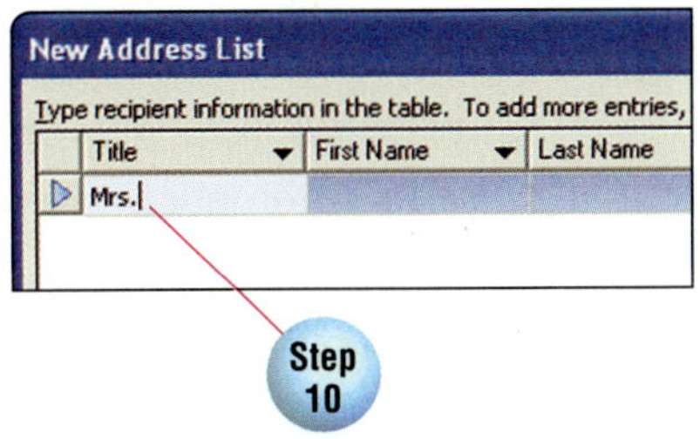

11 Continue typing text in the specified fields as indicated in Figure 4.5. After entering all of the information for the last client in Figure 4.5, click the OK button.

After typing **3 percent** for Jerome Ellington, do not press the Tab key. If you do, a new blank client record will be created.

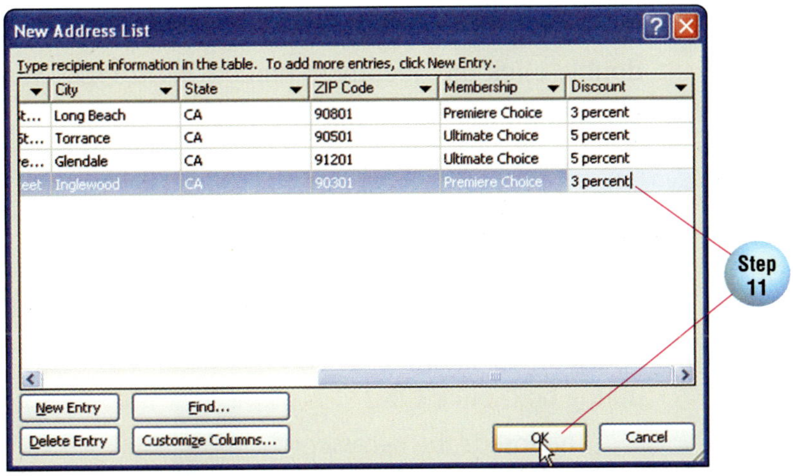

FIGURE 4.5 Step 11

Title	**Mrs.**	*Title*	**Mr. and Mrs.**
First Name	**Kristina**	*First Name*	**Walter**
Last Name	**Herron**	*Last Name*	**Noretto**
Address Line 1	**4320 Jackson Street**	*Address Line 1*	**3420 114th Avenue**
City	**Long Beach**	*City*	**Glendale**
State	**CA**	*State*	**CA**
ZIP Code	**90801**	*ZIP Code*	**91201**
Membership	**Premiere Choice**	*Membership*	**Ultimate Choice**
Discount	**3 percent**	*Discount*	**5 percent**
Title	**Ms.**	*Title*	**Mr.**
First Name	**Cathy**	*First Name*	**Jerome**
Last Name	**Washington**	*Last Name*	**Ellington**
Address Line 1	**321 Wildwood Street**	*Address Line 1*	**12883 22nd Street**
City	**Torrance**	*City*	**Inglewood**
State	**CA**	*State*	**CA**
ZIP Code	**90501**	*ZIP Code*	**90301**
Membership	**Ultimate Choice**	*Membership*	**Premiere Choice**
Discount	**5 percent**	*Discount*	**3 percent**

continues

12 At the Save Address List dialog box, navigate to your WordS4 folder. Click in the *File name* text box, type **WordS4DS**, and then press Enter.

Word automatically saves the data source as an Access database.

13 Open **FCTCruiseLetter.docx** and then save the document and name it **WordS4MD**.

14 Click the Mailings tab, click the Select Recipients button in the Start Mail Merge group, and then click *Use Existing List* at the drop-down list.

15 At the Select Data Source dialog box, navigate to your WordS4 folder and then double-click the document named ***WordS4DS.mdb***.

16 Move the insertion point a double space above the first paragraph of text in the letter and then click the Address Block button in the Write & Insert Fields group.

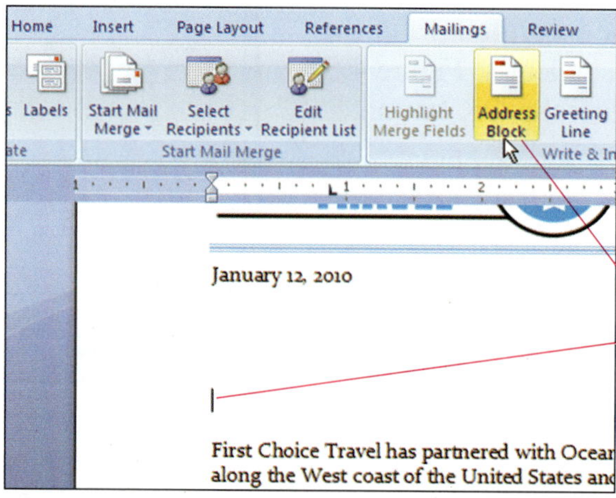

17 At the Insert Address Block dialog box, click OK.

This inserts the necessary fields to insert the client name and address in the letter.

18 Press the Enter key twice and then click the Greeting Line button in the Write & Insert Fields group.

19 At the Insert Greeting Line dialog box, click the down-pointing arrow at the right side of the option box containing the comma (the box to the right of *Mr. Randall*) and then click the colon at the drop-down list.

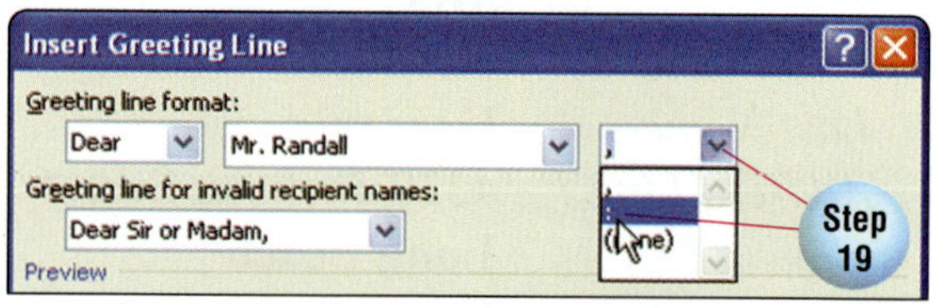

20 Click OK to close the dialog box.

21 Move the insertion point to the end of the first paragraph, type **With your**, press the spacebar, and then insert the *Membership* field by clicking the Insert Merge Field button arrow and then clicking *Membership* at the drop-down list.

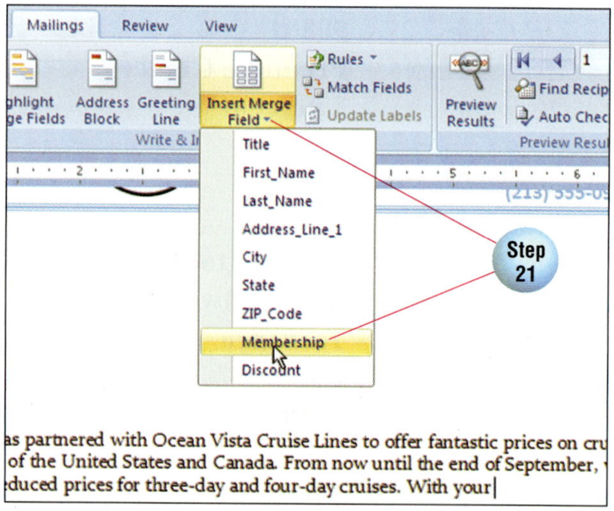

22 Press the spacebar and then type **membership, you will receive an additional**.

23 Press the spacebar and then insert the *Discount* field by clicking the Insert Merge Field button arrow and then clicking *Discount* at the drop-down list.

24. Press the spacebar, type **discount**, and then type a period.

    The sentence you just typed should look like this: *With your «Membership» membership, you will receive an additional «Discount» discount.*

25. Click the Save button on the Quick Access toolbar.

Step 26

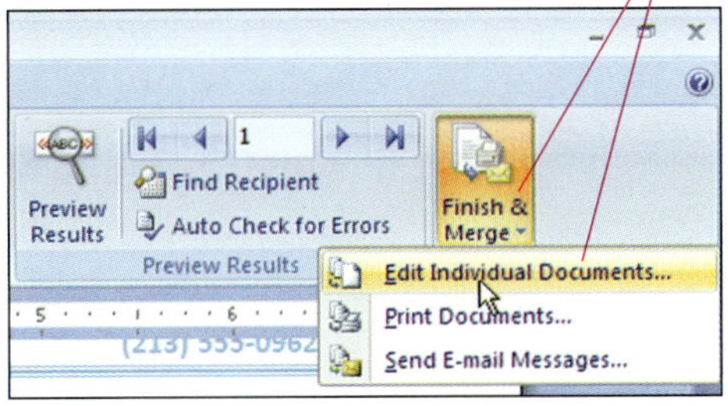

26. Merge the letter with the records in the data source. Begin by clicking the Finish & Merge button in the Finish group in the Mailings tab and then clicking *Edit Individual Documents* at the drop-down list.

27. At the Merge to New Document dialog box, click the OK button.

    The letters are merged with the records and displayed in a new document.

28. Save the merged letters in the normal manner and name the document **WordS4MergedDocs**.

Step 31

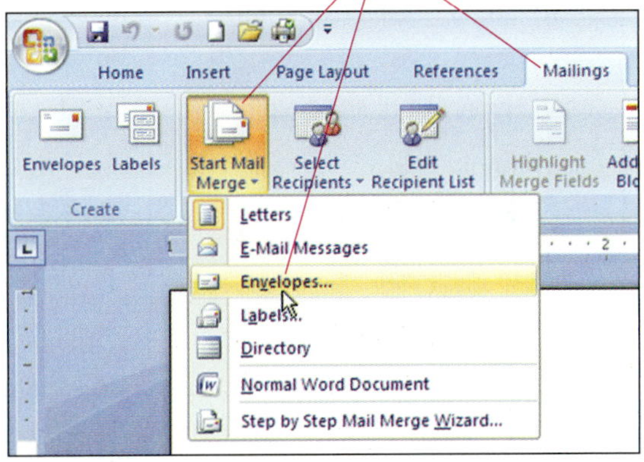

29. Print and then close **WordS4MergedDocs.docx**.

    Four letters will print.

30. Save and then close **WordS4MD.docx**.

31. Click the New button on the Quick Access toolbar and then prepare envelopes for the four letters. Begin by clicking the Mailings tab, clicking the Start Mail Merge button, and then clicking *Envelopes* at the drop-down list.

32. At the Envelope Options dialog box, click OK.

33. Click the Select Recipients button in the Start Mail Merge group and then click *Use Existing List* at the drop-down list.

34. At the Select Data Source dialog box, navigate to the WordS4 folder and then double-click ***WordS4DS.mdb***.

35. Click in the approximate location in the envelope in the document window where the client's name and address will appear.

    This causes a box with a dashed blue border to display. If you do not see this box, try clicking in a different location on the envelope.

36. Click the Address Block button in the Write & Insert Fields group.

37. At the Insert Address Block dialog box, click OK.

38. Click the Finish & Merge button in the Finish group and then click *Edit Individual Documents* at the drop-down list.

39. At the Merge to New Document dialog box, click OK.

40. Save the merged envelopes document and name it **WordS4MergedEnvs**.

41. Print **WordS4MergedEnvs.docx**.

    This document will print four envelopes. Check with your instructor about specific steps for printing envelopes. You may need to hand feed envelopes into your printer.

42. Close **WordS4MergedEnvs.docx**.

43. Close the envelope main document without saving it.

Features Summary

Feature	Ribbon Tab, Group	Button	Option
columns	Page Layout, Page Setup	Columns	
Columns dialog box	Page Layout, Page Setup	Columns	More Columns
draw text box	Insert, Text		Draw Text Box
drop cap	Insert, Text	Drop Cap	
Drop Cap dialog box	Insert, Text	Drop Cap	Drop Cap Options
Insert Address Block dialog box	Mailings, Write & Insert Fields		
insert file	Insert, Text		Text from File
Insert Greeting Line dialog box	Mailings, Write & Insert Fields		
Insert Hyperlink dialog box	Insert, Links	Hyperlink	
insert merge field	Mailings, Write & Insert Fields		
Insert Table dialog box	Insert, Tables		Insert Table
merge documents	Mailings, Finish		
section break (continuous)	Page Layout, Page Setup	Breaks	Continuous
select recipients	Mailings, Start Mail Merge		
shapes	Insert, Illustrations		
SmartArt	Insert, Illustrations		
start mail merge	Mailings, Start Mail Merge		
table	Insert, Tables		
text box	Insert, Text		
WordArt	Insert, Text	WordArt	

Knowledge Check

Completion: In the space provided at the right, indicate the correct term, command, or option.

1. Use this feature to distort or modify text to conform to a variety of shapes. ________________
2. This is the first letter of the first word of a paragraph that is set into a paragraph. ________________
3. Insert a text box by clicking the Text Box button in this group in the Insert tab. ________________
4. When you draw a shape in a document, this tab becomes active. ________________
5. To display a menu of SmartArt choices, click the Insert tab and then click the SmartArt button in this group. ________________
6. In a SmartArt diagram, click this button in the Create Graphic group to close the *Type your text here* window. ________________
7. You can create a table using the Table button in the Insert tab or with options at this dialog box. ________________
8. Press this key to move the insertion point to the next cell in a table. ________________
9. Press these keys to move the insertion point to the previous cell in a table. ________________
10. To insert a row in a table above the current row, click this button in the Rows & Columns group of the Table Tools Layout tab. ________________
11. Merge selected cells in a table by clicking the Merge Cells button in this group. ________________
12. Rotate text in a cell by clicking this button in the Alignment group in the Table Tools Layout tab. ________________
13. Use this button in the Text group in the Insert tab to insert one file into another. ________________
14. Insert a section break in a document with options at this button drop-down list. ________________
15. To display the Columns dialog box, click the Page Layout tab, click the Columns button, and then click this option at the drop-down list. ________________
16. If you want to save a Word document as a single file Web page, choose this option at the *Save as type* option at the Save As dialog box. ________________
17. To navigate to a hyperlinked document or Web site, hold down this key while clicking the hyperlink. ________________
18. A merge generally takes two documents—the main document and this. ________________
19. Use buttons in this tab to merge documents. ________________

Skills Review

Review 1 Formatting a First Choice Travel Document

First Choice TRAVEL

1. Open **FCTZenithAdventures.docx** and then save the document and name it **WordS4-R1**.
2. Apply the Equity theme to the document.
3. Move the insertion point to the beginning of the heading *Upcoming Adventures* and then insert the file named **FCTBicycling.docx**. ***Hint: Do this with the Object button in the Insert tab.***
4. Position the insertion point in the top cell in the first column in the table in the *Bicycling Adventures* section and then change the width to 1.5″. ***Hint: Do this with the Table Column Width text box in the Cell Size group in the Table Tools Layout tab.*** Position the insertion point in the top cell in the middle column and then change the width to 0.6″. Position the insertion point in the top cell in the last column and then change the width to 0.6″.
5. Select the first row of the table in the *Bicycling Adventures* section, turn on bold, and then apply the Orange, Accent 1, Lighter 60% shading. ***Hint: Apply shading with options from the Shading button drop-down gallery.***
6. Select the top row in the table in the *Antarctic Zenith Adventures* section, turn on bold, and then apply Orange, Accent 1, Lighter 60% shading.
7. Select the top row in the table in the *Tall-Ship Adventures* section, turn on bold, and then apply Orange, Accent 1, Lighter 60% shading.
8. Apply the Heading 4 style to the four headings in the document.
9. Move the insertion point to the beginning of the document and then insert WordArt with the following specifications:
   a. Use the WordArt style named WordArt style 20 (second option from the left in the fourth row).
   b. Type **Zenith Adventures** in the Edit WordArt Text dialog box.
   c. Change the shadow effect to Shadow Style 16.
   d. Change the shape fill color to Orange, Accent 1, Lighter 40%.
   e. Change the height to 1.2″ and the width to 5.5″.
   f. Change the position to Position in Top Center with Square Text Wrapping.
   g. Change the text wrapping to Top and Bottom.
10. Move the insertion point to the beginning of the first paragraph in the document and then insert a continuous section break.
11. Create two newspaper columns with 0.4″ of spacing between columns.
12. Insert the Mod Quote text box in the document and then type the following in the text box: **First Choice Travel is excited to announce that we are teaming with Zenith Adventures to provide our clients with thrilling, adrenaline-producing, extreme outdoor adventures.**
13. Change the height of the quote text box to 2.8″.
14. Create a drop cap with the first letter of the first paragraph in the document (the letter *W* in *We*) and then change the font color for the letter to Orange, Accent 1, Lighter 40%.
15. Move the insertion point to the end of the document and then insert a continuous section break (this balances the columns on the second page). If the *Upcoming Adventures* heading at the beginning of the second column on the second page displays with a blank line above, delete the blank line.

16. Press Ctrl + End to move the insertion point to the end of the document after the continuous section break.
17. Click the Page Layout tab, click the Columns button, and then click *One* at the drop-down list.
18. Draw and format the shape and draw and format the text box as shown in Figure 4.6 using the following specifications:
    a. Draw the shape with the Up Ribbon shape in the *Stars and Banners* section.
    b. Change the height of the drawn shape to 1.5″ and the width to 4.5″.
    c. Center the shape between the left and right margins below the text in the document.
    d. Change the shape style to Diagonal Gradient - Accent 1.
    e. Draw the text box and then remove the shape fill and shape outline.
    f. Type the text in the text box as shown in Figure 4.6 and then turn on bold, change the font size to 26, center the text, and then change the font color to Orange, Accent 1, Darker 25%.
19. Save, print, and then close **WordS4-R1.docx**.

FIGURE 4.6 Review 1

Review 2 Preparing and Formatting an Organizational Chart and Diagram

1. Open **MPProdDept.docx** and then save the document and name it **WordS4-R2**.
2. Press Ctrl + End and then create the organizational chart shown in Figure 4.7 with the following specifications:
    a. Display the Choose a SmartArt Graphic dialog box, click *Hierarchy* in the left panel, and then double-click *Organization Chart*.
    b. Change the SmartArt style to Polished.
    c. Change the color to Colorful Range - Accent Colors 3 to 4.
    d. Click the SmartArt Tools Format tab, click the Size button, and then change the height to 2.5″ and the width to 5″.
    e. Click the Arrange button and then change the text wrapping to Top and Bottom.
    f. Drag the organizational chart so it is centered between the left and right margins.
    g. Type the text in the boxes as shown in Figure 4.7.
3. Create the diagram shown in Figure 4.8 with the following specifications:
    a. Press Ctrl + End to move the insertion point to the end of the document and then press the Enter key twice.
    b. Display the Choose a SmartArt Graphic dialog box, click *Process* in the left panel, and then double-click *Continuous Block Process*.
    c. Change the SmartArt style to Polished.
    d. Change the color to Colorful - Accent Colors.
    e. Click the SmartArt Tools Format tab, click the Size button, and then change the height to 2.5″ and the width to 5″.

f. Click the Arrange button and then change the text wrapping to Top and Bottom.
g. Drag the diagram so it is centered between the left and right margins.
h. Type the text in the boxes as shown in Figure 4.8.

4. Make sure the organizational chart and diagram fit on the page.
5. Save, print, and then close **WordS4-R2.docx**.

FIGURE 4.7 Review 2 Organizational Chart

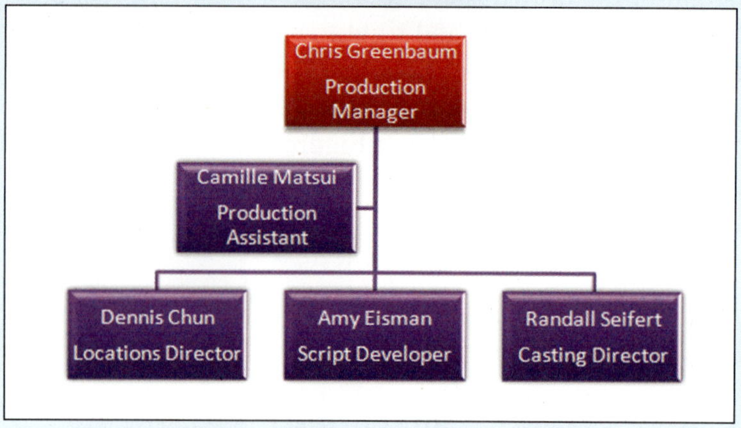

FIGURE 4.8 Review 2 Diagram

Review 3 Preparing, Modifying, and Formatting a Table

Niagara Peninsula College

1. At a blank document, create a table with four columns and six rows.
2. Type the text in the cells as shown in Figure 4.9.
3. Insert a new column at the right side of the table and then type the following text in the new cells:

   Instructor
   Crowe
   Crowe
   Rubine
   McAllister
   Auve

4. Insert a new row above the first row and then with the new row selected, merge the cells.
5. Type **THEATRE ARTS DIVISION FALL SCHEDULE** in the cell and then bold and center the text.

6. Select the second row (contains the text *Course*, *Name*, *Days*, and so on) and then bold and center the text.
7. Decrease the width of the cells so the table appears as shown in Figure 4.10.
8. Display the Table Tools Design tab, remove all check marks from the options in the Table Style Options group *except* the *Header Row* and *Banded Rows* options.
9. Apply the Medium Shading 1 - Accent 1 table style.
10. Save the document and name it **WordS4-R3**.
11. Print and then close **WordS4-R3.docx**.

FIGURE 4.9 Review 3

Course	Name	Days	Time
TR 101	Intro to Theater	MTWRF	8:00-8:50 a.m.
TR 101	Intro to Theater	MW	1:00-2:40 p.m.
TR 125	Beginning Acting	MTWR	9:00-9:50 a.m.
TR 211	Set Design	MTW	10:00-10:50 a.m.
TR 251	Costume Design	MW	3:00-4:20 p.m.

FIGURE 4.10 Review 3

THEATRE ARTS DIVISION FALL SCHEDULE				
Course	**Name**	**Days**	**Time**	**Instructor**
TR 101	Intro to Theater	MTWRF	8:00-8:50 a.m.	Crowe
TR 101	Intro to Theater	MW	1:00-2:40 p.m.	Crowe
TR 125	Beginning Acting	MTWR	9:00-9:50 a.m.	Rubine
TR 211	Set Design	MTW	10:00-10:50 a.m.	McAllister
TR 251	Costume Design	MW	3:00-4:20 p.m.	Auve

Review 4 Saving a Document as a Web Page; Inserting a Hyperlink

First Choice TRAVEL

1. Open **FCTON01.docx** and then save the document and name it **WordS4-R4**.
2. Apply the Solstice theme to the document.
3. Apply the Title style to the text *Oslo, Norway* and apply the Heading 2 style to the headings in the document (*History*; *Population*; *Commerce and Industry*; *Climate*; *Holiday, Sport, and Leisure*; and *Sightseeing Tours*).
4. Move the insertion point to the beginning of the heading *History*, insert a continuous section break, and then create two newspaper columns with a line between.
5. Save and then print **WordS4-R4.docx**.
6. Save the document as a single file Web page with the name **WordS4-R4.mht**.
7. Move the insertion point to the end of the document, press the Enter key twice, and then type **Additional Information on Norway**.
8. Select the text *Additional Information on Norway* and then insert a hyperlink to the official site of Norway for the United States at www.norway.org.
9. Make sure you are connected to the Internet, hold down the Ctrl key, and then click the Additional Information on Norway hyperlink.
10. At the Norway site, click on any hyperlink that interests you. When you are finished, click File and then *Close*.
11. Save and then close **WordS4-R4.mht**.

Review 5 Merging Letters and Envelopes

Performance Threads

1. Create a data source document with the following names and addresses. (You determine the fields to delete; use the *State* field for the ON [Ontario] province.)

Mr. Frank Tolentino Royal Fabrics and Supplies 3220 Wilson Avenue Toronto, ON M2F 4T7	Mrs. Andrea Jones-Leigh JL Fabrics and Crafts 1230 Sheppard Avenue Toronto, ON L2H 5T8
Mrs. Anna Strassburg Millwood Fabrics 550 Jane Street Toronto, ON P2H 9T7	Mr. Donald Enslow Premiere Fabrics and Design 8744 Huron Street London, ON 3J4 T3H

2. Save the data source document with the name **WordS4R5DS**.
3. Open **PTFabricLetter.docx**, save the document, and then name it **WordS4R5MD**.
4. Specify **WordS4R5DS.mdb** as the data source.
5. Insert the *Address Block* field and the *Greeting Line* field in the appropriate locations in the letter.
6. Move the insertion point immediately right of the word *company* located in the last sentence of the third paragraph, type a comma, and then press the spacebar. Insert the *Title* field, press the spacebar, insert the *Last Name* field, and then type a comma.
7. Merge all of the records to a new document.
8. Save the merged letters document and name it **WordS4R5MergedLtrs**. Print and then close the document. Save and then close **WordS4R5MD.docx**.
9. Create an envelope document, specify **WordS4R5DS.mdb** as the data source, and then merge the envelopes.
10. Save the merged envelopes document and name it **WordS4R5MergedEnvs**. Print and then close the document.
11. Close the envelope main document without saving it.

Skills Assessment

Assessment 1 Formatting a Theatre Arts Division Newsletter

Niagara Peninsula College

1. Open **NPCTheatreNewsletter.docx** and then save the document and name it **WordS4-A1**.
2. Move the insertion point to the end of the document and then insert the document named **NPCProductions.docx**.
3. Apply the Flow theme to the document and change the theme colors to Solstice.
4. Insert a continuous section break at the beginning of the *Division Description* heading and then format the text into two columns.
5. Apply the Heading 2 style to the headings in the document.
6. Move the insertion point to the beginning of the document and then insert the text *Theatre Arts Division* as WordArt. You determine the layout and format of the WordArt. Position the WordArt text at the top of the page centered between the left and right margins.

7. Move the insertion point to any character in the heading *Division Description* and then insert a built-in text box of your choosing that contains the text "The Niagara Peninsula College theater experience can be the beginning of a lifelong interest in the art of theater."
8. Move the insertion point to the end of the document and then insert a continuous section break.
9. Save, print, and then close **WordS4-A1.docx**.

Assessment 2 Creating an Organization Chart

1. Open **PTDesignDept.docx** and then save the document and name it **WordS4-A2**.
2. Move the insertion point to the end of the document and then create an organizational chart with the following information:

Camilla Yong
Design Manager

Scott Bercini
Designer

Terri Cantrell
Designer/Sewer

Paul Gottlieb
Designer/Sewer

3. Apply formatting and/or design to enhance the visual display of the organizational chart.
4. Move the insertion point below the organizational chart and then create a diagram with the following text (use the Converging Radial diagram in the *Relationship* group in the Choose a SmartArt Graphic dialog box):

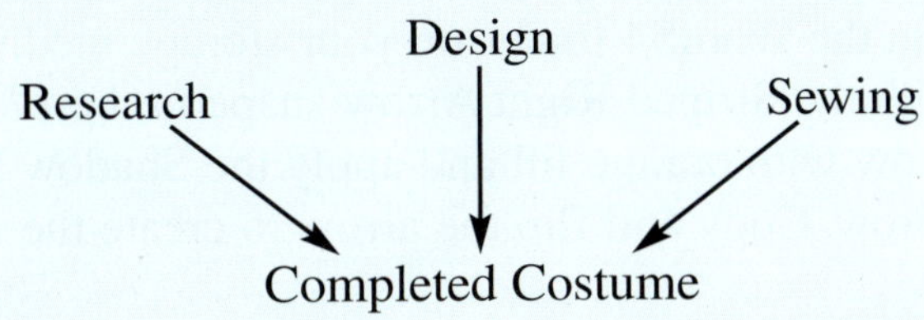

5. Apply formatting and/or design to enhance the visual display of the diagram. Make any necessary adjustments to spacing and/or size to ensure that the organizational chart and diagram fit on one page.
6. Save, print, and then close **WordS4-A2.docx**.

Assessment 3 Creating a Table for The Waterfront Bistro

1. At a blank document, create a table with the text shown in Figure 4.11.
2. Apply design and layout features to enhance the visual appeal of the table.
3. Save the document and name it **WordS4-A3**.
4. Print and then close **WordS4-A3.docx**.

FIGURE 4.11 Assessment 3

CATERED LUNCH OPTIONS			
Option	Contents	Cost per Person	Discount Price
Option A: Hot	Vegetarian quiche, Caesar salad, vegetables, dressing, dessert, and beverages	$11.75	$10.95
Option B: Deli	Turkey or ham sandwiches, chips, vegetables, dressing, brownies, and beverages	$9.75	$9.30
Option C: Continental	Bagels, rolls, cream cheese, vegetables, dressing, cookies, and beverages	$8.95	$8.50

Assessment 4 Finding Information on Flipping and Copying Objects

1. Use Word's Help feature to learn how to flip objects and copy objects.
2. At a blank document, create the document shown in Figure 4.12. Use the Picture button in the Illustrations group in the Insert tab to insert the logo **WELogo.jpg** located in the WordS4 folder on your storage medium. Create the arrow at the left with the Striped Right Arrow shape in the *Block Arrows* section. Format the arrow with orange fill and apply the Shadow Style 3 shadow effect to the arrow. Copy and flip the arrow to create the arrow at the right side.
3. Save the completed document and name it **WordS4-A4**.
4. Print and then close **WordS4-A4.docx**.

HELP

FIGURE 4.12 Assessment 4

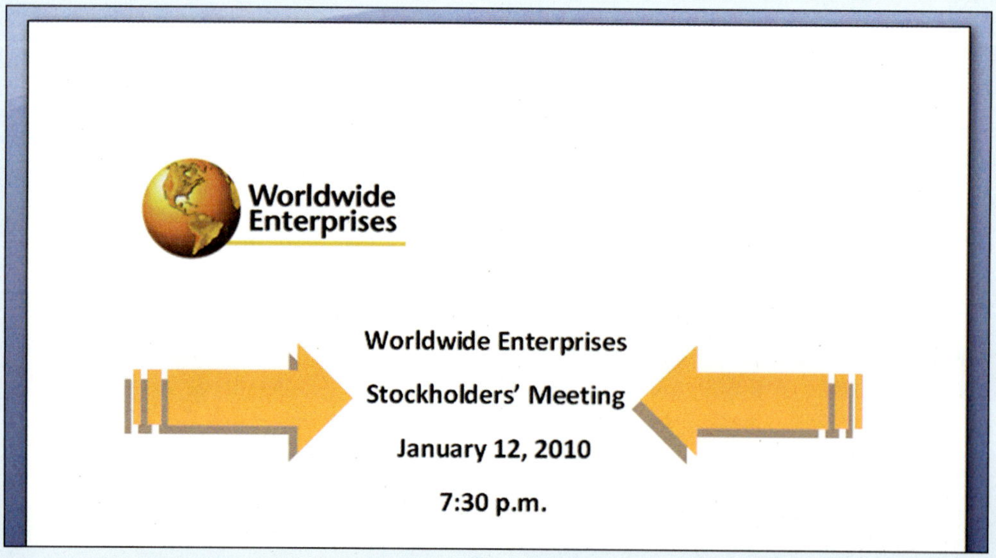
Worldwide Enterprises

Worldwide Enterprises

Stockholders' Meeting

January 12, 2010

7:30 p.m.

Assessment 5 Inserting Formulas in a Table

1. Use Word's Help feature to learn how to perform calculations in a table and specifically how to total numbers in a row or column.
2. Open **WESales.docx** and then save the document and name it **WordS4-A5**.
3. Using the information you learned about totaling numbers in a row or column, insert a formula in the cell immediately below *Total* that sums the amount in the cell immediately below *First Half* and the amount in the cell immediately below *Second Half*.
4. Insert a formula in each of the remaining cells in the *Total* column that sums the amount in the *First Half* column with the amount in the *Second Half* column.
5. Save, print, and then close **WordS4-A5.docx**.

Assessment 6 Locating Information and Writing a Letter

1. You are Jordan Keyes, assistant manager at First Choice Travel. Chris Greenbaum, the production manager at Marquee Productions, has asked you to find information on renting a car in Toronto. Connect to the Internet and search for a car rental company in the Toronto area. Locate pricing information on economy and midsize cars and also minivans. Find out the daily rental fees for each as well as the weekly rental fee.
2. Open **FCTLetterhead.docx** and then save the document and name it **WordS4-A6**.
3. Using the information you find on the Internet, write a letter to Chris Greenbaum at Marquee Productions, 955 South Alameda Street, Los Angeles, CA 90037, that includes a table containing the information you found on car rentals. Modify and format the table so the information in the table is attractive and easy to read.
4. Save, print, and then close **WordS4-A6.docx**.

Marquee Challenge

Challenge 1 Formatting a Fact Sheet on Orcas Island

1. Open **FCTOIFactSheet.docx** and then save the document with the name **WordS4-C1**.
2. Format the document so it displays as shown in Figure 4.13. Apply the Flow theme and the Foundry color theme and apply the Heading 2 style to the headings in the document.
3. Save, print, and then close **WordS4-C1.docx**.

Challenge 2 Preparing a Flier for The Waterfront Bistro

1. At a blank document, create the document shown in Figure 4.14.
2. Save the completed document and name it **WordS4-C2**.
3. Print and then close **WordS4-C2.docx**.

FIGURE 4.13 Challenge 1

Orcas Island

One of the San Juan Islands in Washington State, Orcas Island has long been a favorite destination for generations of vacationers. Located approximately 60 miles north of Seattle, it lies in the Strait of Georgia between Anacortes and Vancouver Island. To the north, on the mainland, is Vancouver, B.C. With its fjord-like bays and sounds, deep harbors, lakes, streams, and waterfalls, Orcas is considered the most spectacular of the islands. The island is over 56 square miles in size and has more than 125 miles of saltwater shoreline. Winding roads fan out from the business and social center of Eastsound village to the nearby communities of Deer Harbor, Orcas, and Olga. One of the greatest assets of the island is Mt. Constitution in Moran State Park, which offers panoramic views of the entire archipelago and is surrounded by miles of trails and sparkling lakes.

Activities on Orcas

Orcas Island offers an unhurried setting to enjoy the spectacular scenery and wildlife, with a wide variety of recreation. Activities include hiking, biking, golfing, sailing, kayaking, shopping, flying, and fishing. During the summer and on weekends and holidays, several resorts and lounges offer live music. Throughout the year, Orcas Theatre and Community Center offers concerts, plays, art exhibits, dances, workshops, movies, and many special events.

Bicycling Safety

Orcas Island is the most challenging of the islands for bicycles. This is due to the narrow windy roads and hilly terrain. When bicycling on the island, ride single file and keep to the right of the road. Make stops on the straight-of-way rather than at the top of a hill or on a curve. Motorists cannot negotiate blind approaches safely with a bicyclist on the road. When stopping to reset or regroup, enjoy the scenery, but please move completely off the road. As you enjoy the scenery, be alert for potential traffic and the condition of the roadway. When leaving the ferry, pull over to the side of the road and let the automobiles pass.

Marine Parks

These marine parks are accessible only by boat:

- Sucia Island: Cluster of 11 islands; trails, bays, and bluffs; 2.5 miles from Orcas Island
- Patos: Two buoys, four campsites, trails (no water)
- Matis: One hundred and fifty acres, two buoys, and ten campsites

1

continues

FIGURE 4.13 Challenge 1—*Continued*

Directions to Orcas Island

You can reach Orcas Island either by ferry or by airplane. The primary departure point for the Washington State Ferry is Anacortes. To reach Anacortes, take Interstate 5 to State Highway 20 (exit 230) and travel west about 20 miles to the ferry terminal. The ferry ride lasts approximately one hour and fifteen minutes. Consider arriving at least one hour ahead of your desired departure time. Kenmore Air and West Isle Air each offer scheduled flights from Anacortes and Bellingham to Orcas Island. Flights arrive either at Eastsound Airport or Rosario or West Sound. Landings in Rosario and West Sound require float planes.

Contact:

First Choice TRAVEL

2

FIGURE 4.14 Challenge 2

The Waterfront
B·I·S·T·R·O

3104 Rivermist Drive
Buffalo, NY 14280
(716) 555-3166

Breakfast, Lunch, and Dinner–Sunday through Saturday

Fine dining in casual elegance

Full-service catering at reasonable prices

Specialty and vintage wines

Fine dining

Specialty wines

Catering

Microsoft®

Excel 2007

Introducing Excel 2007

Microsoft Excel 2007 is a popular choice among individuals and companies to organize, analyze, and present data in columns and rows in a document called a ***worksheet***. More than one worksheet can be created and saved in a file called a ***workbook***. Entries are placed in a worksheet in a ***cell***, which is the intersection of a column with a row. A cell is labeled with the column letter and row number, such as A1. Worksheets can be created to track, analyze, and chart any type of data that can be set up in a column and row format. Expenses, sales, assets, liabilities, grades, statistics, research study data, machine production records, weather records, and gas usage are just a few examples of the type of information that can be stored in an Excel workbook. While working in Excel, you will create and edit worksheets for the following six companies.

First Choice Travel is a travel center offering a full range of traveling services from booking flights, hotel reservations, and rental cars to offering travel seminars.

The Waterfront Bistro offers fine dining for lunch and dinner and also offers banquet facilities, a wine cellar, and catering services.

Worldwide Enterprises is a national and international distributor of products for a variety of companies and is the exclusive movie distribution agent for Marquee Productions.

Marquee Productions is involved in all aspects of creating movies from script writing and development to filming. The company produces documentaries, biographies, as well as historical and action movies.

Performance Threads maintains an inventory of rental costumes and also researches, designs, and sews special-order and custom-made costumes.

The mission of the Niagara Peninsula College Theatre Arts Division is to offer a curriculum designed to provide students with a thorough exposure to all aspects of the theater arts.

In Section 1 you will learn how to

Create Worksheets to Analyze Data

Begin your work in Excel by entering labels in columns or rows to create the worksheet layout. Next, add the values that correspond to the labels. Finally, create formulas to add, subtract, multiply, or divide to calculate the desired results. Once a worksheet has been created, the power and versatility of Excel is put to use by performing *what-if* analyses. What happens to net profit if sales increase by 4 percent? What happens to monthly cash flow if the wages of all employees are raised 3 percent? To answer these types of questions, you edit a value and then watch Excel's recalculation feature automatically update all other values dependent on the number you changed.

Enter labels to organize worksheet layout, values to record quantities and prices, and formulas to calculate total costs.

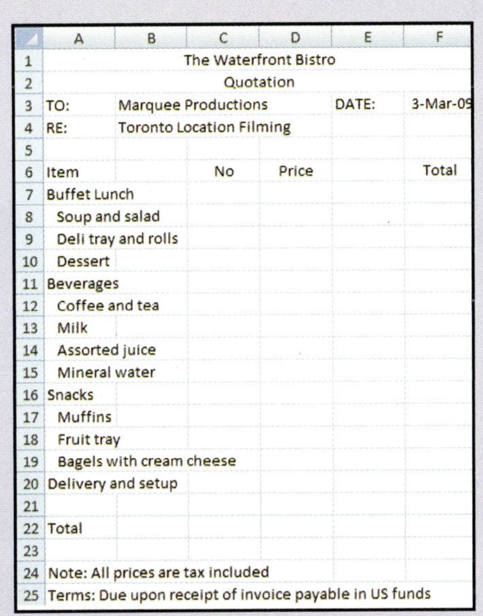

	A	B	C	D	E	F
1			The Waterfront Bistro			
2			Quotation			
3	TO:	Marquee Productions			DATE:	3-Mar-09
4	RE:	Toronto Location Filming				
5						
6	Item		No	Price		Total
7	Buffet Lunch					
8	Soup and salad					
9	Deli tray and rolls					
10	Dessert					
11	Beverages					
12	Coffee and tea					
13	Milk					
14	Assorted juice					
15	Mineral water					
16	Snacks					
17	Muffins					
18	Fruit tray					
19	Bagels with cream cheese					
20	Delivery and setup					
21						
22	Total					
23						
24	Note: All prices are tax included					
25	Terms: Due upon receipt of invoice payable in US funds					

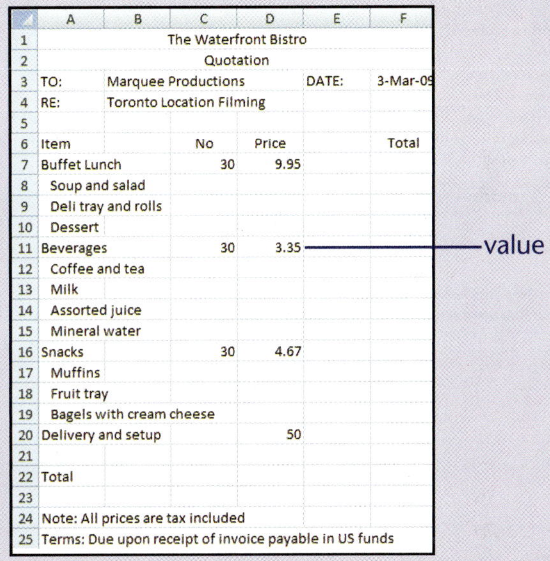

	A	B	C	D	E	F
1			The Waterfront Bistro			
2			Quotation			
3	TO:	Marquee Productions			DATE:	3-Mar-09
4	RE:	Toronto Location Filming				
5						
6	Item		No	Price		Total
7	Buffet Lunch		30	9.95		
8	Soup and salad					
9	Deli tray and rolls					
10	Dessert					
11	Beverages		30	3.35		
12	Coffee and tea					
13	Milk					
14	Assorted juice					
15	Mineral water					
16	Snacks		30	4.67		
17	Muffins					
18	Fruit tray					
19	Bagels with cream cheese					
20	Delivery and setup			50		
21						
22	Total					
23						
24	Note: All prices are tax included					
25	Terms: Due upon receipt of invoice payable in US funds					

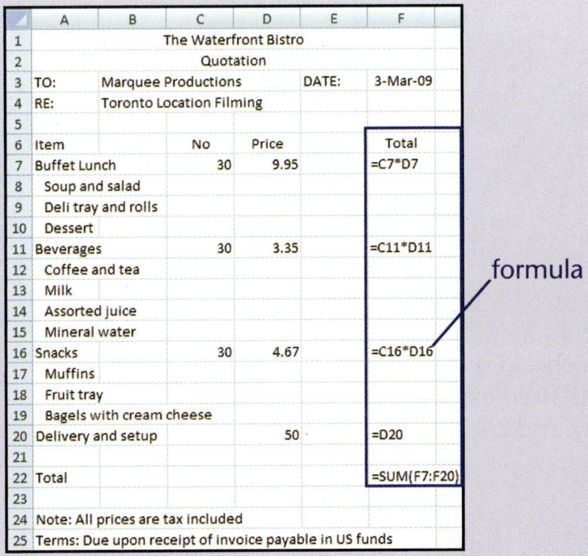

	A	B	C	D	E	F
1			The Waterfront Bistro			
2			Quotation			
3	TO:	Marquee Productions			DATE:	3-Mar-09
4	RE:	Toronto Location Filming				
5						
6	Item		No	Price		Total
7	Buffet Lunch		30	9.95		=C7*D7
8	Soup and salad					
9	Deli tray and rolls					
10	Dessert					
11	Beverages		30	3.35		=C11*D11
12	Coffee and tea					
13	Milk					
14	Assorted juice					
15	Mineral water					
16	Snacks		30	4.67		=C16*D16
17	Muffins					
18	Fruit tray					
19	Bagels with cream cheese					
20	Delivery and setup			50		=D20
21						
22	Total					=SUM(F7:F20)
23						
24	Note: All prices are tax included					
25	Terms: Due upon receipt of invoice payable in US funds					

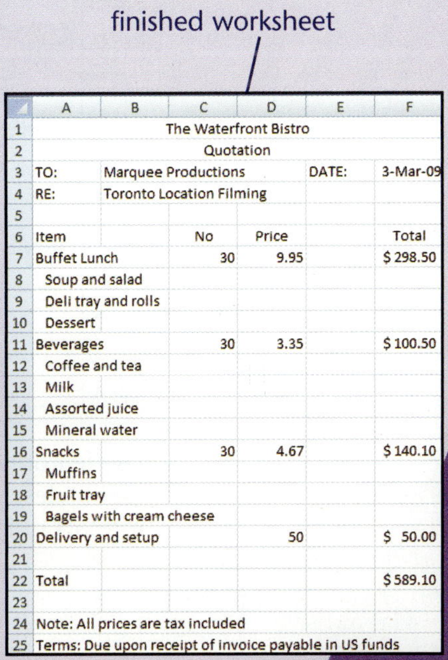

	A	B	C	D	E	F
1			The Waterfront Bistro			
2			Quotation			
3	TO:	Marquee Productions			DATE:	3-Mar-09
4	RE:	Toronto Location Filming				
5						
6	Item		No	Price		Total
7	Buffet Lunch		30	9.95		$ 298.50
8	Soup and salad					
9	Deli tray and rolls					
10	Dessert					
11	Beverages		30	3.35		$ 100.50
12	Coffee and tea					
13	Milk					
14	Assorted juice					
15	Mineral water					
16	Snacks		30	4.67		$ 140.10
17	Muffins					
18	Fruit tray					
19	Bagels with cream cheese					
20	Delivery and setup			50		$ 50.00
21						
22	Total					$ 589.10
23						
24	Note: All prices are tax included					
25	Terms: Due upon receipt of invoice payable in US funds					

In Section 2 you will learn how to

Edit and Format Worksheets

Excel allows you to apply formatting attributes and add color to enhance the appearance of the worksheet and draw a reader's attention to important titles, totals, or other results. A new feature in Excel 2007 is the ability to apply a theme which coordinates colors, fonts, and effects to provide a worksheet with a professional appearance in just a few mouse clicks. A variety of formats, grouped into categories, are available for numbers, dates, and times.

The Waterfront Bistro			
Quotation			
TO: Marquee Productions		DATE	3-Mar-09
RE: Toronto Location Filming			
Item	No	Price	Total
Buffet Lunch	30	9.95	$ 298.50
Soup and salad			
Deli tray and rolls			
Dessert			
Beverages	30	3.35	$ 100.50
Coffee and tea			
Milk			
Assorted juice			
Mineral water			
Snacks	30	4.67	$ 140.10
Muffins			
Fruit tray			
Bagels with cream cheese			
Delivery and setup		50.00	$ 50.00
Total			**$ 589.10**

Note: All prices include tax.
Terms: Due upon receipt of invoice payable in U.S. funds

Apply formatting enhancements including:

- adding borders
- adding fill color
- adjusting row height
- adjusting column width
- applying a cell style
- applying a theme
- changing text alignment within cells
- changing font, font size, font color
- changing font attributes to bold and/or italic
- indenting text within a cell
- formatting numbers

The Waterfront Bistro

Westview Room Schedule — Week: September 6–12

Time	Sunday	Monday	Tuesday	Wednesday	Thursday	Friday	Saturday
11:00 AM							
12:00 PM					Tyler Santini	Tyler Santini	Jason Hill
1:00 PM	Pat Cardenas		Paula Soulliere	Carl Doxtator	Pat Cardenas	Pat Cardenas	Pat Cardenas
2:00 PM	Carl Doxtator		Moira Su-Lin	Dayna McGuire			
3:00 PM							
4:00 PM					Jason Hill	Jason Hill	
5:00 PM		CLOSED			Tammy Williams	Tammy Williams	Carl Doxtator
6:00 PM				Jason Hill			Dayna McGuire
7:00 PM	Heather Kiley		Tammy Williams	Paula Soulliere	Heather Kiley	Heather Kiley	
8:00 PM	Tyler Santini						
9:00 PM			Pat Cardenas		Paula Soulliere	Paula Soulliere	Paula Soulliere
10:00 PM				Heather Kiley Tyler Santini	Moira Su-Lin	Moira Su-Lin	Moira Su-Lin
11:00 PM							

Use features such as Format Painter, Cell Styles, and Themes to apply formats quickly and consistently.

In Section 3 you will learn how to

Use Function Formulas and Add Visual Elements

Excel's functions make the task of writing formulas easier. Functions are grouped by category such as statistical, financial, date, and logical. Excel provides over 300 prebuilt formulas to perform calculations. The Insert Function dialog box is available to assist with locating and creating a function. Create charts from data to emphasize trends or compare data sets. Add emphasis to worksheets or charts by drawing arrows and adding text boxes. Insert images such as clip art or a logo to enhance a worksheet or add a corporate identity.

The Waterfront B·I·S·T·R·O

Item	Unit	January	February	March
Cloves	case	1	0	0
Allspice	case	1	0	0
Seasoned Salt	case	1	0	0
Salt	case	1	1	1
Pepper	case	1	0	0
Total		**101**	**65**	**81**
Proof Total	1033			
Average Units Purchased		2	1	2
Maximum Units Purchased		6	5	6
Minimum Units Purchased		0	0	0
Count of Inventory Items		50		

Enter formulas using Excel's built-in functions.

The Waterfront B·I·S·T·R·O

Patio Expansion Loan Analysis

	Funds Unlimited	Capital Venture Inc.	
Interest Rate	8.65%	9.25%	annual rate
Amortization	15	12	years for repayment
Loan Amount	$ 385,000	$ 385,000	principal amount borrowed
Monthly Payment	($3,825.17)	($4,435.80)	includes principal and interest
Monthly Principal Payment (1st payment)	($1,049.97)	($1,468.09)	payment on principal for the first month of the loan
Total Loan Payments	($688,531.46)	($638,755.48)	

...ased on a constant interest rate and a constant payment

Add a logo to add a corporate identity and clip art to add visual interest.

The Waterfront B·I·S·T·R·O

The Waterfront Bistro
Operating Expenses

	Qtr1	Qtr2	Qtr3	Qtr4	Total
Advertising	$ 2,200.00	$ 1,850.00	$ 2,347.00	$ 1,777.00	$ 8,174.00
Bank charges	329.00	541.00	624.00	710.00	2,204.00
Cleaning	650.00	650.00	650.00	650.00	2,600.00
Linens	985.00	1,110.00	1,344.00	1,526.00	4,965.00
Office supplies	143.00	255.00	249.00	182.00	829.00
Telephone	256.00	241.00	355.00	268.00	1,120.00
Utilities	1,142.00	1,254.00	961.00	1,157.00	4,514.00
Total	$ 5,705.00	$ 5,901.00	$ 6,530.00	$ 6,270.00	$ 24,406.00

Proof Total: $ 24,406.00

Abnormally cold spring

Use arrows and text boxes to draw a reader's attention to an item.

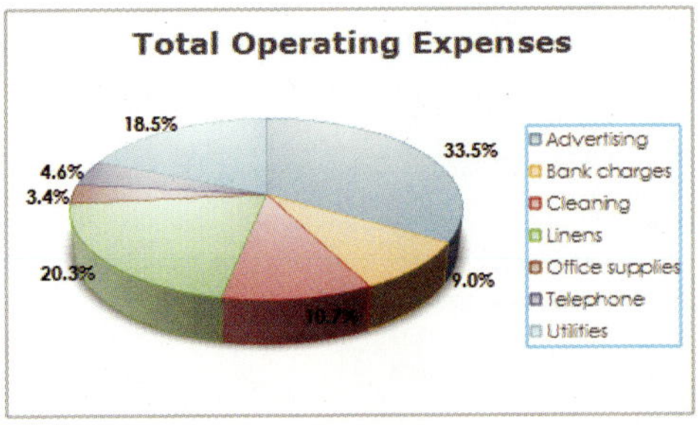

Illustrate trends or comparisons of data sets using charts.

In Section 4 you will learn how to

Work with Multiple Worksheets and Tables

Large amounts of data are managed easily if they are separated into individual worksheets. Worksheets can be copied or moved to rearrange the order and logically organized by renaming and applying a tab color to the sheet tabs. Formulas can be created that reference cells in other worksheets or a cell can be linked to another worksheet to ensure the data flows from one worksheet to another. A new feature in Excel 2007 is the ability to format a list as a table. A table can be sorted, filtered, and formatted as a separate entity within a worksheet.

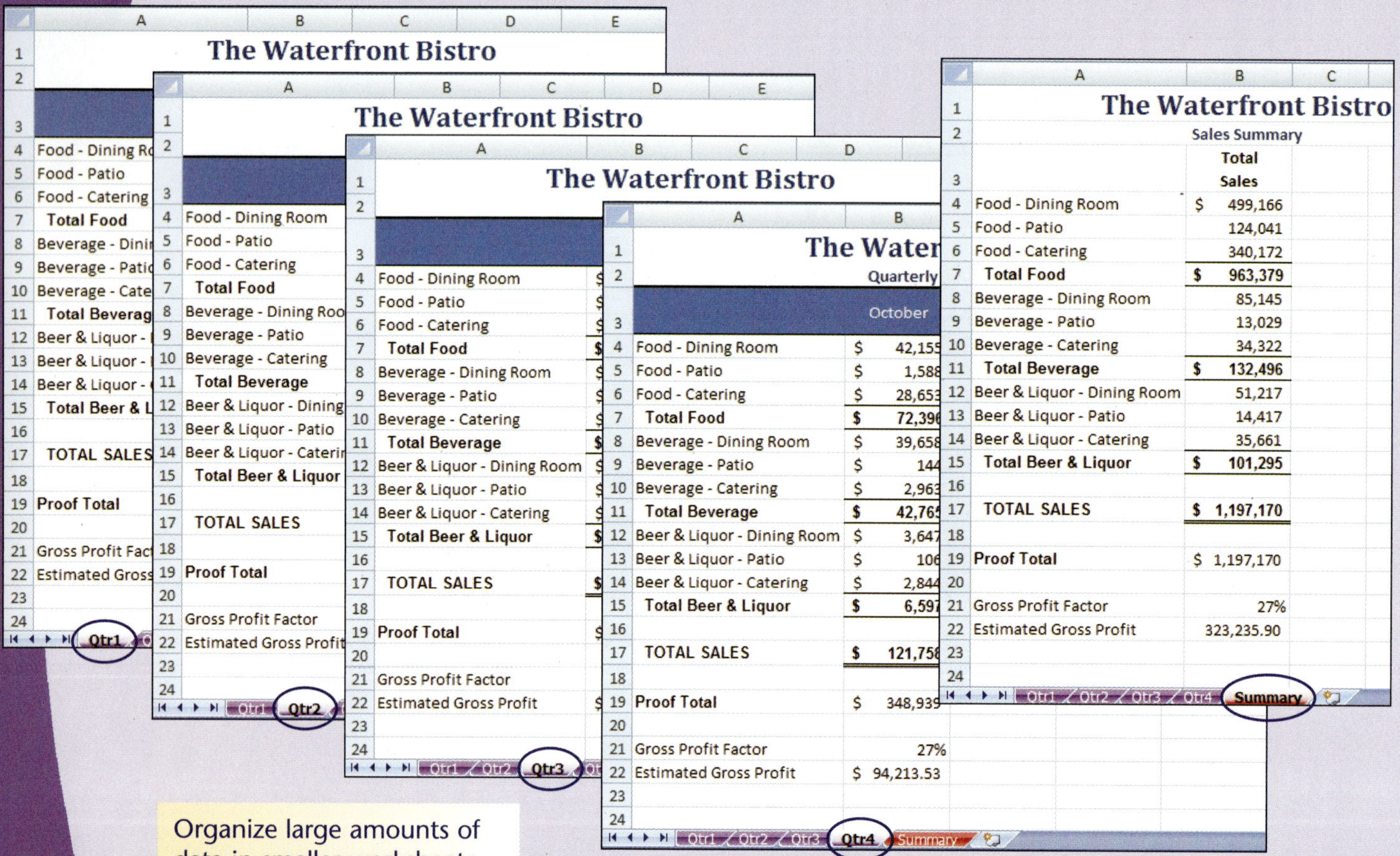

Organize large amounts of data in smaller worksheets.

Create formulas and link cells to summarize worksheets.

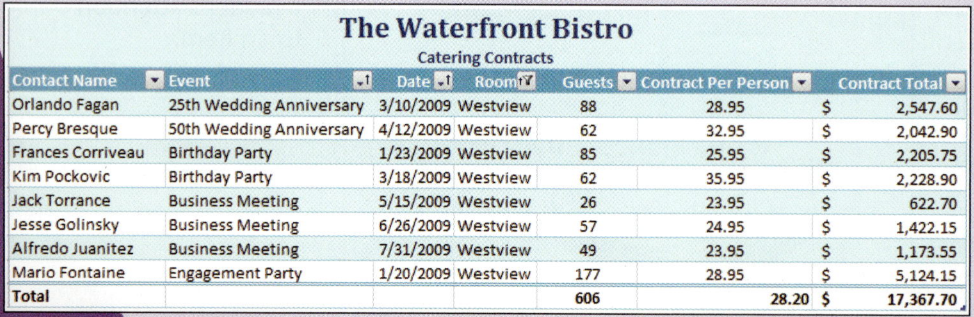

The Waterfront Bistro

Catering Contracts

Contact Name	Event	Date	Room	Guests	Contract Per Person		Contract Total
Orlando Fagan	25th Wedding Anniversary	3/10/2009	Westview	88	28.95	$	2,547.60
Percy Bresque	50th Wedding Anniversary	4/12/2009	Westview	62	32.95	$	2,042.90
Frances Corriveau	Birthday Party	1/23/2009	Westview	85	25.95	$	2,205.75
Kim Pockovic	Birthday Party	3/18/2009	Westview	62	35.95	$	2,228.90
Jack Torrance	Business Meeting	5/15/2009	Westview	26	23.95	$	622.70
Jesse Golinsky	Business Meeting	6/26/2009	Westview	57	24.95	$	1,422.15
Alfredo Juanitez	Business Meeting	7/31/2009	Westview	49	23.95	$	1,173.55
Mario Fontaine	Engagement Party	1/20/2009	Westview	177	28.95	$	5,124.15
Total				606	28.20	$	17,367.70

Format a list as a table to filter and format the list as a separate entity.

Excel SECTION 1

Analyzing Data Using Excel

Skills

- Start Excel and identify features in the Excel window
- Enter labels and values
- Use the fill handle to enter a series
- Enter formulas
- Create a formula using Sum
- Copy a formula
- Test a worksheet for accuracy
- Apply the Currency format to values
- Right-align labels
- Use the Help feature
- Center a label across multiple columns
- Change the page orientation to landscape
- Preview and print a worksheet
- Save a workbook using Save and Save As
- Close a workbook and exit Excel
- Navigate a large worksheet using the mouse and the keyboard
- Jump to a specific cell using Go To

Student Resources

Before beginning this section:

1. Copy to your storage medium the ExcelS1 subfolder from the Excel folder on the Student Resources CD.
2. Make ExcelS1 the active folder.

In addition to containing the data files needed to complete section work, the Student Resources CD contains model answers in PDF format for each of the projects in this section; model answers for end-of-section activities are not provided.

Projects Overview

The Waterfront B·I·S·T·R·O: Edit a weekly sales report, create a payroll worksheet, browse an inventory report, and create a condensed quarterly income statement.

Marquee Productions: Complete an estimated travel expenses worksheet.

Performance Threads: Prepare a price quotation for costume design and rental.

Worldwide Enterprises: Create a projected distribution revenue schedule for a new movie release.

Niagara Peninsula College: Create an international student registration report and a target enrollment report.

Activity 1.1

Completing the Excel Worksheet Cycle

Information is created in Excel in a ***worksheet*** and is saved in a file called a ***workbook***. A workbook can contain several worksheets. Imagine a worksheet as a page with horizontal and vertical lines drawn in a grid representing columns and rows. Data is entered into a ***cell***, which is the intersection of a column with a row. Columns are lettered A to Z, AA to AZ, BA to BZ, and so on. The last column in the worksheet is labeled *XFD*. Rows are numbered 1, 2, 3, and so on. A column letter and a row number identify each cell. For example, A1 is the cell address for the intersection of column A with row 1. Each worksheet in Excel contains 16,384 columns and 1,048,576 rows. An Excel workbook initially contains three worksheets labeled *Sheet1*, *Sheet2*, and *Sheet3*. Additional sheets can be inserted as needed.

Project

You have been asked to update a weekly sales report for The Waterfront Bistro by adding data and viewing the impact of changing a cell used to calculate gross margin.

The Waterfront B·I·S·T·R·O

1. At the Windows XP desktop, click the Start button **start** on the Taskbar.
2. Point to *All Programs*.
3. Point to *Microsoft Office*.
4. Click *Microsoft Office Excel 2007*.

   Depending on your operating system and/or system configuration, the steps you complete to open Excel may vary.

5. At the Excel screen, identify the various features by comparing your screen with the one shown in Figure 1.1. If necessary, maximize the Excel window. Depending on your screen resolution, your screen may vary slightly. Refer to Table 1.1 for a description of the screen features.

FIGURE 1.1 The Excel Screen

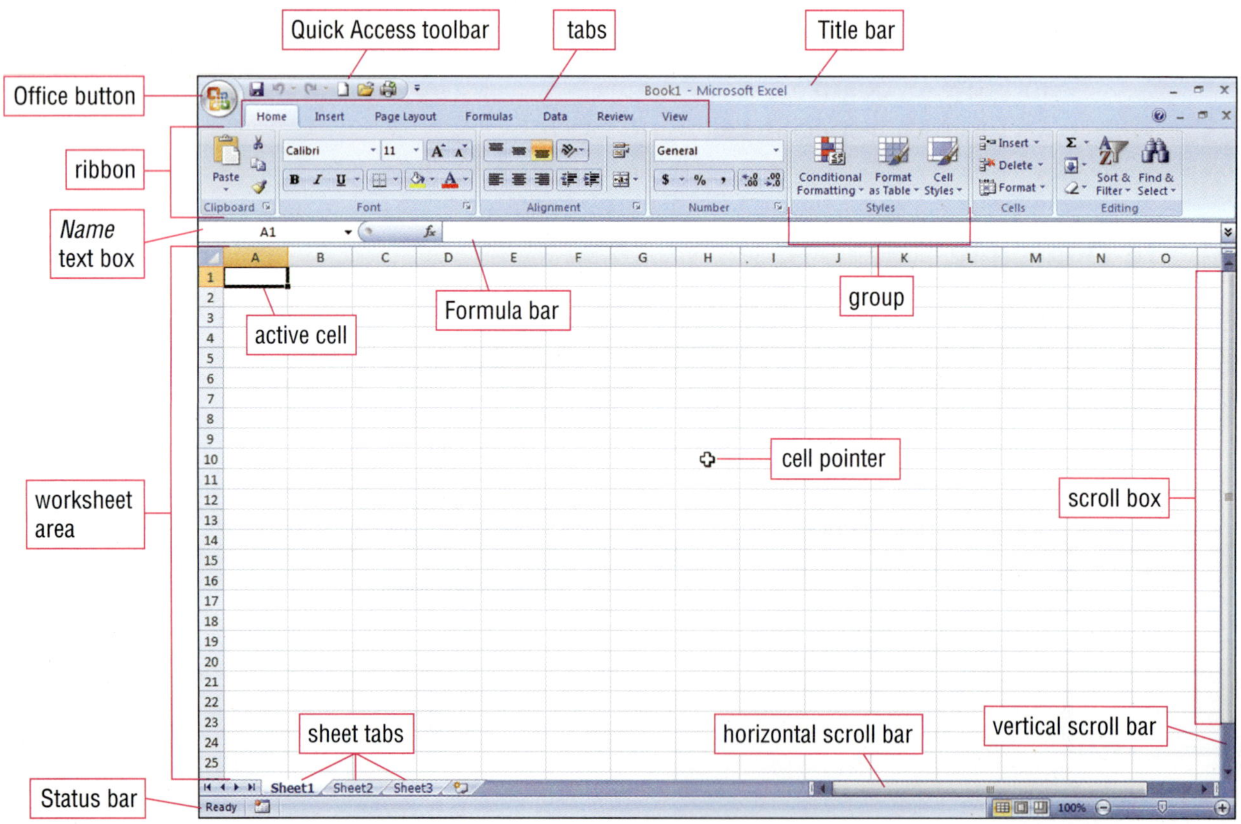

TABLE 1.1 Excel Screen Features

Feature	Description
Office button	Displays as a Microsoft Office logo and, when clicked, displays a list of document management actions, such as save or print, and a list of recently opened workbooks.
Quick Access toolbar	Contains buttons for commonly used commands which can be executed with a single mouse click.
tabs	Commands and features in the ribbon are organized into related groups which are accessed by clicking a tab name.
Title bar	Displays workbook name followed by Microsoft Excel.
ribbon	Area from which commands and features for performing actions on a cell or worksheet are accessed. Begin by selecting a tab and then choosing the command or feature.
Name text box	Displays the active cell address or name assigned to active cell.
Formula bar	Displays the contents stored in the active cell.
active cell	Location in the worksheet that will display typed data or that will be affected by a command.
worksheet area	Contains cells used to create the worksheet.
cell pointer	Select cells when you see this icon by clicking or dragging the mouse.
vertical and horizontal scroll bars	Used to view various parts of the worksheet beyond the current screen.
sheet tabs	Identifies the worksheets in the workbook. Use these tabs to change the active worksheet.
Status bar	Displays current mode, action messages, View buttons, and Zoom slider.

6 Click the Open button on the Quick Access toolbar.

If the Open button does not display on the Quick Access toolbar, click the Customize Quick Access Toolbar button that displays at the right side of the toolbar and then click *Open* at the drop-down list.

7 If necessary, navigate to the ExcelS1 folder on your storage medium.

To change to a different drive, click the down-pointing arrow at the right of the *Look in* list box and then select the correct drive or folder from the drop-down list. Double-clicking a folder name in the file list box changes the active folder.

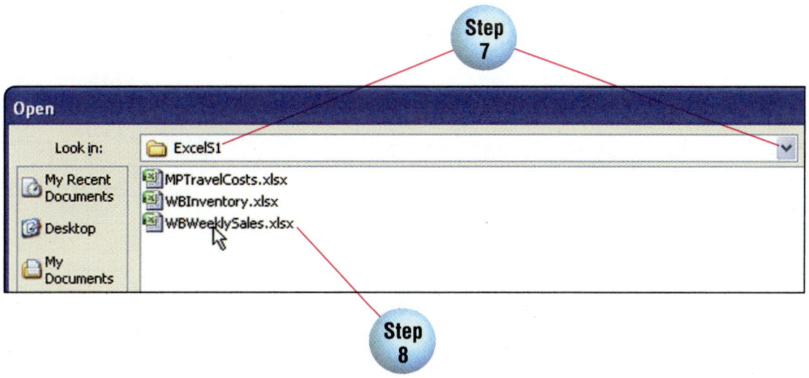

8 Double-click ***WBWeeklySales.xlsx***.

This workbook contains one worksheet with sales for The Waterfront Bistro for the week ended September 26, 2009. The formulas to sum the sales have already been created. Notice some of the cells in the column labeled *Saturday* are empty. You will enter these values in Steps 11 through 14.

continues

9 Click the Office button and then click Save As.

Use the Save option to save a file using the same name. If you want to keep the original workbook and save the workbook with the changes under a new name, use Save As.

10 At the Save As dialog box, make sure the ExcelS1 folder on your storage medium is the active folder, type **ExcelS1-01** in the *File name* text box, and then press Enter or click Save.

Excel automatically adds the file extension *.xlsx* to the end of a workbook name. The *Save in* option at the Save As dialog box displays the active folder. If you need to make ExcelS1 the active folder, click the down-pointing arrow at the right of the *Save in* list box, navigate to the correct file storage location, and then double-click *ExcelS1* in the file list box.

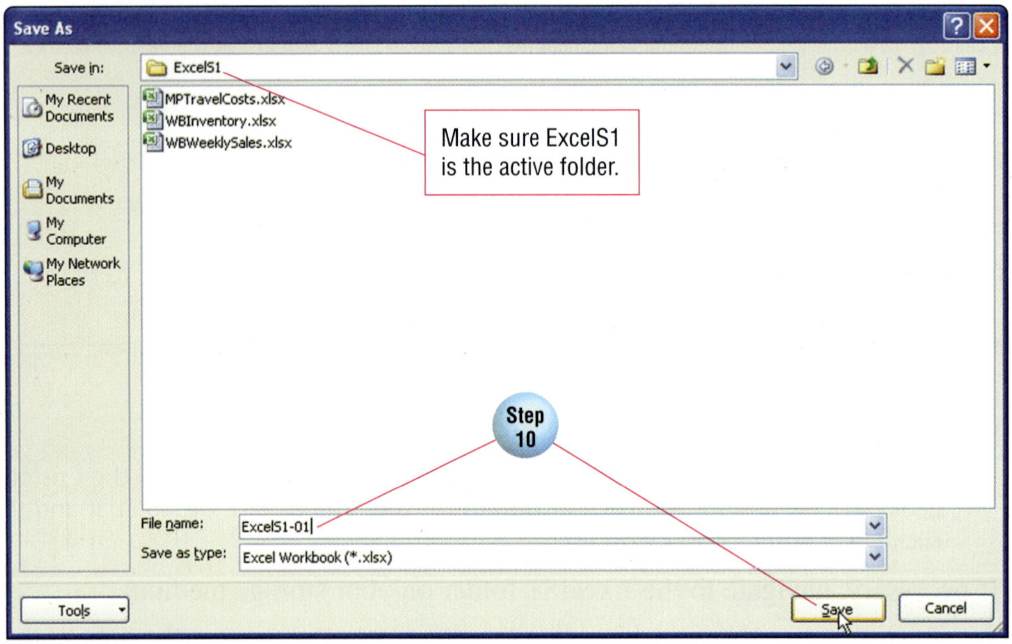

11 Move the cell pointer over the intersection of column H with row 6 (H6) and then click to make H6 the active cell.

12 Type **2976** and then press Enter.

Notice that the entry in H7 has changed. This is because the formula created in H7 was dependent on H6. As soon as you enter a value in H6, any other dependent cells are automatically updated. Can you identify other cells that changed as a result of the new value in H6?

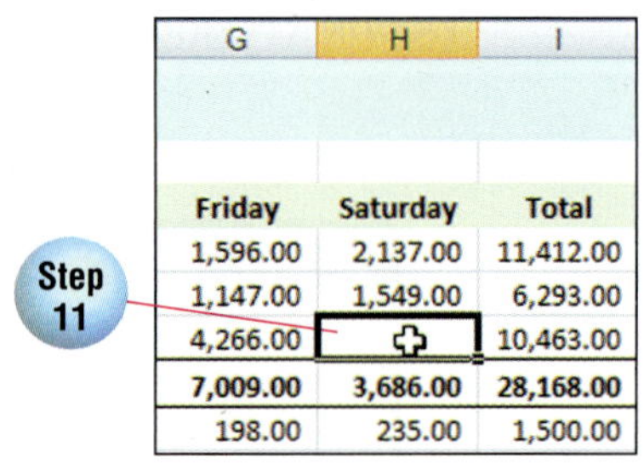

PROBLEM

Typing mistake? Press Backspace to delete the characters to the left of the insertion point and then type the correct text

13 Make H10 the active cell and then type **156**.

14 Make H14 the active cell, type **542**, and then press Enter.

15 Look at the entry in B19. This percentage is used to calculate the Estimated Gross Profit in row 20 (Total Sales times the Gross Profit Factor). Next, you will change the entry in B19 to see the effect on the estimated gross profit values.

16 Make B19 the active cell, type **29%**, and then press Enter.

Notice the new estimated gross profit values in cells B20 through I20.

G	H	I
Friday	Saturday	Total
1,596.00	2,137.00	11,412.00
1,147.00	1,549.00	6,293.00
4,266.00	2,976.00	13,439.00
7,009.00	6,662.00	31,144.00
198.00	235.00	1,500.00
84.00	128.00	786.00
394.00	156.00	1,763.00
676.00	519.00	4,049.00
224.00	485.00	3,545.00
168.00	227.00	1,461.00
884.00	542.00	3,165.00
1,276.00	1,254.00	8,171.00
8,961.00	8,435.00	43,364.00

Step 12

Step 13

Step 14

Step 16

17	TOTAL SALES	10,666.00	1,686.00	2,391.00	5,342.00	5,883.00	8,961.00	8,435.00	43,364.00
18									
19	Gross Profit Factor	29%							
20	Estimated Gross Profit	3,093.14	488.94	693.39	1,549.18	1,706.07	2,598.69	2,446.15	12,575.56

New Estimated Gross Profit values as a result of changing the percent value in B19.

17 Click the Save button on the Quick Access toolbar.

18 Click the Quick Print button on the Quick Access toolbar.

If the Quick Print button does not display on the Quick Access toolbar, click the Customize Quick Access Toolbar button that displays at the right side of the toolbar and then click *Quick Print* at the drop-down list. The worksheet prints on two pages. In a later activity you will learn how to change to landscape page orientation to fit a wide worksheet on one page.

19 Click the Office button and then click Close at the drop-down list.

Excel displays a blank blue screen in the worksheet area when no workbooks are currently open.

In Brief

Start Excel
1. Click Start.
2. Point to All Programs.
3. Point to Microsoft Office.
4. Click Microsoft Office Excel 2007.

Open Workbook
1. Click Open button on Quick Access toolbar.
2. Navigate to storage medium and folder.
3. Double-click workbook name.

Save Workbook with New Name
1. Click Office button.
2. Click Save As.
3. Type new workbook name.
4. Click Save or press Enter.

In Addition

AutoComplete

The AutoComplete feature in Excel will complete text entries for you as you start to type a new entry in a cell. If the first few letters that you type match another entry in the column, Excel automatically fills in the remaining text. Press Tab or Enter to accept the text Excel suggests, or continue typing the correct text. You can turn off AutoComplete by clicking the Office button and then clicking the Excel Options button near the bottom right of the drop-down list. Click Advanced in the left pane of the Excel Options dialog box, click the *Enable AutoComplete for cell values* check box to clear the box, and then click OK.

Activity 1.2

Entering Labels and Values; Using Fill Options

A *label* is an entry in a cell that helps the reader relate to the values in the corresponding column or row. Labels are generally entered first when creating a new worksheet since they define the layout of the data in the columns and rows. By default, Excel aligns labels at the left edge of the column. A *value* is a number, formula, or function that can be used to perform calculations in the worksheet. By default, Excel aligns values at the right edge of the column. Take a few moments to plan or sketch out the layout of a new worksheet before entering labels and values. Decide the calculations you will need to execute and how to display the data so that it will be easily understood and interpreted.

Project

You need to create a new payroll worksheet for the hourly paid staff at The Waterfront Bistro. Begin by entering labels and values.

The Waterfront B·I·S·T·R·O

1. At the blank Excel screen, click the New button on the Quick Access toolbar to start a new blank workbook.

   If the New button does not display on the Quick Access toolbar, click the Customize Quick Access Toolbar button that displays at the right side of the toolbar and then click *New* at the drop-down list. Ctrl + N is the keyboard shortcut to begin a new blank workbook. In a later section, you will learn how to start a new workbook using a template.

2. Type **Payroll** as the title for the new worksheet in A1.

   When you type a new entry in a cell, the entry appears in the Formula bar as well as within the active cell in the worksheet area. To end a cell entry, press Enter, move to another cell in the worksheet, or click the Enter button on the Formula bar.

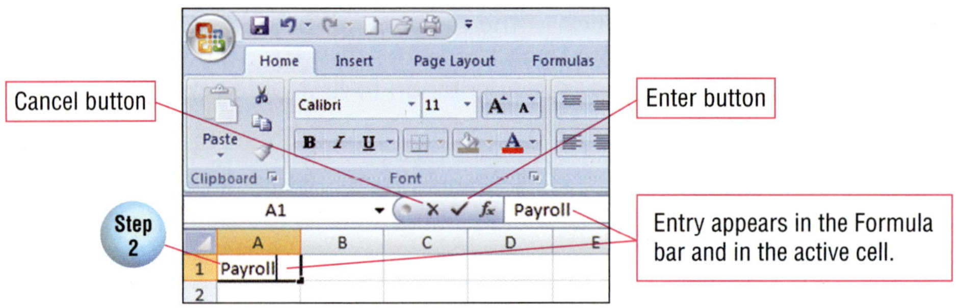

3. Press Enter.

PROBLEM

If you catch a typing error after a cell has been completed, activate the cell, retype the entry, and press Enter, or double-click the cell to open the cell for editing.

4. With A2 the active cell, type **Week Ended: September 26, 2009** and then press Enter.

   Notice the entry in A2 is overflowing into columns B, C, and D. You can allow a label to spill over into adjacent columns as long as you do not plan to enter other data in the overflow cells. In a later section, you will learn how to adjust column widths.

5 Enter the remaining labels as shown below by making the appropriate cell active, typing the label, and then pressing Enter or clicking another cell. (Do not complete the labels for the days of the week beyond *Sun*, as this will be done in Steps 6–8.)

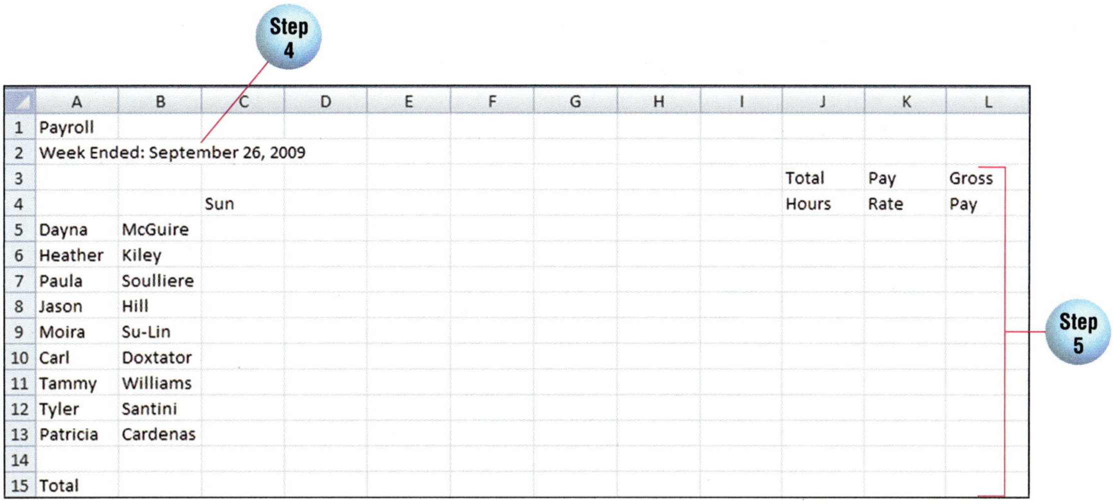

6 Click C4 to make the cell active.

A thick black border surrounds the active cell. A small black square displays at the bottom right corner of the active cell. This black square is called the ***fill handle***. The fill handle is used to fill adjacent cells with the same data or consecutive data. The entries that are automatically inserted in the adjacent cells are dependent on the contents of the active cell. You will use the fill handle in C4 to automatically enter the remaining days of the week in D4 through I4.

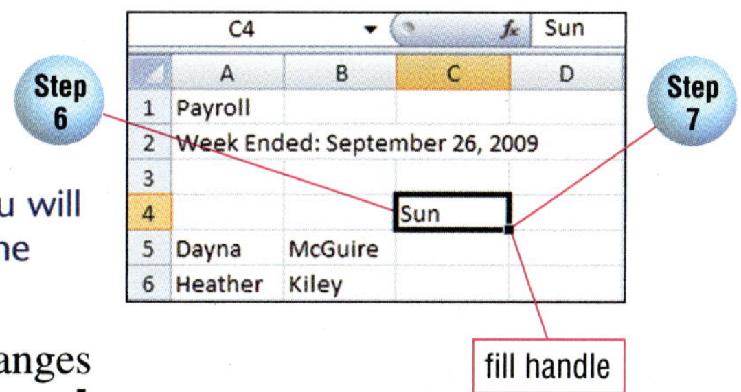

7 Point at the fill handle in C4. The cell pointer changes from the large white cross to a thin black cross.

8 Hold down the left mouse button, drag the pointer to I4, and then release the mouse.

The entries *Mon* through *Sat* appear in D4 to I4. As you drag the pointer to the right, a gray border surrounds the selected cells and a ScreenTip appears below the pointer indicating the label or value that will be inserted. When you release the left mouse button, the cells remain selected and the Auto Fill Options button appears. Clicking the Auto Fill Options button causes a drop-down list to appear with various alternative actions for filling text or data into the cells.

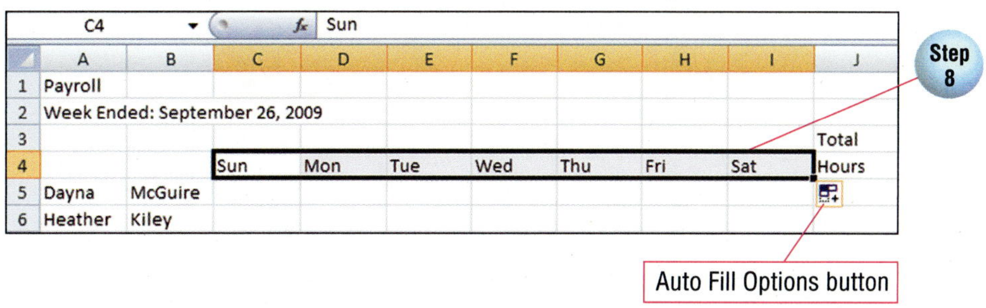

PROBLEM

Mon through *Sat* does not appear? You probably dragged the mouse using the cell pointer instead of the fill handle. This action selects cells instead of filling them. Go back to Step 6 and try again.

continues

9 Click C5 to make the cell active.

10 Type **8** and then press the Right Arrow key.

11 Type **5** in D5 and then press the Right Arrow key.

12 Type the following values in the cells indicated:

E5	**6**
F5	**8**
G5	**7**
H5	**0**
I5	**4**

13 Make F5 the active cell.

14 Point at the fill handle in F5 and then drag the pointer down to F13.

This time the active cell contained a value. The value *8* is copied to the adjacent cells.

B	C	D	E	F	G
ed: September 26, 2009					
	Sun	Mon	Tue	Wed	Thu
McGuire	8	5	6	8	
Kiley				8	
Soulliere				8	
Hill				8	
Su-Lin				8	
Doxtator				8	
Williams				8	
Santini				8	
Cardenas				8	

Step 14

15 Enter the remaining values for employee hours as shown below. Use the fill handle where there are duplicate values in adjacent cells to enter the data as efficiently as possible.

	A	B	C	D	E	F	G	H	I	J
1	Payroll									
2	Week Ended: September 26, 2009									
3										Total
4			Sun	Mon	Tue	Wed	Thu	Fri	Sat	Hours
5	Dayna	McGuire	8	5	6	8	7	0	4	
6	Heather	Kiley	0	8	6	8	5	5	8	
7	Paula	Soulliere	8	8	0	8	7	7	0	
8	Jason	Hill	8	0	8	8	0	8	6	
9	Moira	Su-Lin	0	8	0	8	7	7	8	
10	Carl	Doxtator	0	0	8	8	7	7	8	
11	Tammy	Williams	8	0	0	8	8	7	4	
12	Tyler	Santini	8	0	8	8	6	7	0	
13	Patricia	Cardenas	8	0	4	8	0	7	8	

Step 15

16 Click K5 to make the cell active, type **8.15**, and then press Enter.

17 Position the cell pointer over cell K5, hold down the left mouse button, drag down to K13, and then release the mouse.

A group of adjacent cells is referred to as a ***range***. Select a range of cells when you want to perform an action on a group of cells.

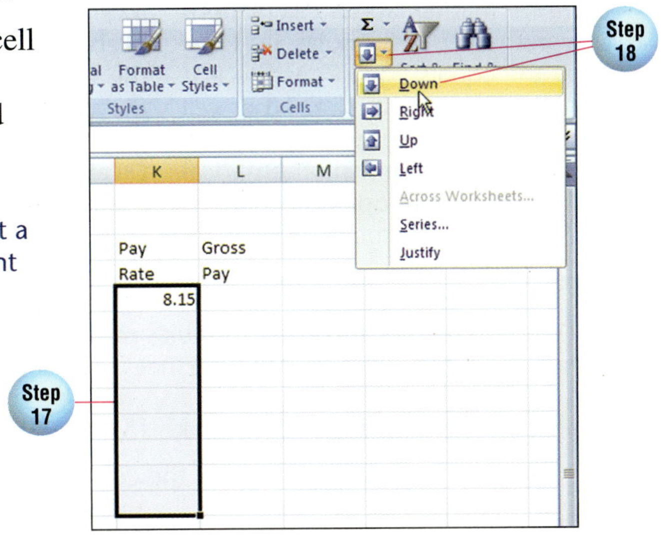

18 With Home the active tab in the ribbon, click the Fill button arrow in the Editing group and then click *Down* at the drop-down list.

19 Click in any cell in the worksheet to deselect the range of cells in column K.

20 Click the Save button on the Quick Access toolbar.

21 At the Save As dialog box with ExcelS1 the active folder, type **ExcelS1-02** in the *File name* text box and then press Enter.

In Addition

More about the Fill Command

In this activity you used the fill handle to continue the days of the week and copy a static value to adjacent cells. The fill handle is versatile and can be used to enter a series of values, dates, times, or other labels as a pattern. The pattern is established based on the cells you select before dragging the fill handle. In the worksheet shown below, the cells in columns C through J were all populated using the fill handle. In each row, the first two cells in columns A and B were selected and then the fill handle dragged right to column J. Notice the variety of patterns used to extend a series.

Use the Auto Fill Options button drop-down list to control how the series is entered. After dragging the fill handle, the Auto Fill Options button is displayed at the end of the series. Pointing at the button causes the button to expand and display a down-pointing arrow. Click the down-pointing arrow and then select the desired fill action from the options in the drop-down list. By default, *Fill Series* is active.

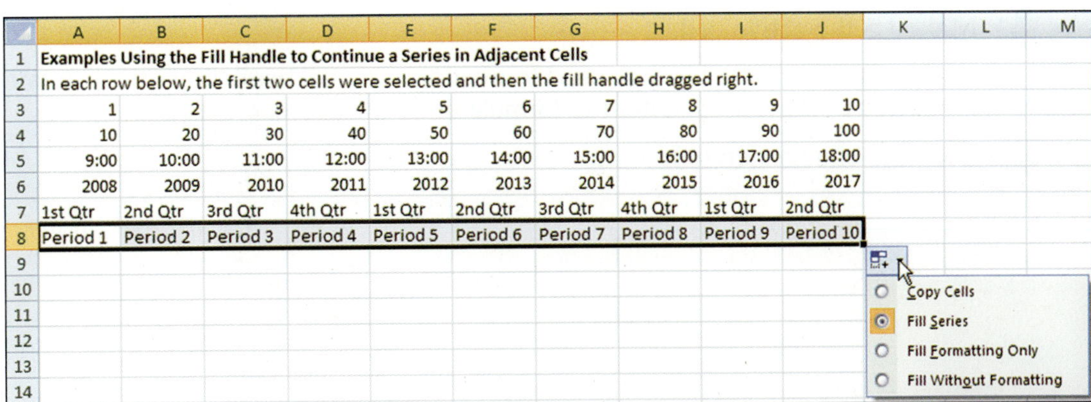

	A	B	C	D	E	F	G	H	I	J
1	Examples Using the Fill Handle to Continue a Series in Adjacent Cells									
2	In each row below, the first two cells were selected and then the fill handle dragged right.									
3	1	2	3	4	5	6	7	8	9	10
4	10	20	30	40	50	60	70	80	90	100
5	9:00	10:00	11:00	12:00	13:00	14:00	15:00	16:00	17:00	18:00
6	2008	2009	2010	2011	2012	2013	2014	2015	2016	2017
7	1st Qtr	2nd Qtr	3rd Qtr	4th Qtr	1st Qtr	2nd Qtr	3rd Qtr	4th Qtr	1st Qtr	2nd Qtr
8	Period 1	Period 2	Period 3	Period 4	Period 5	Period 6	Period 7	Period 8	Period 9	Period 10

Activity 1.3

Performing Calculations Using Formulas

A ***formula*** is entered into a cell to perform mathematical calculations in a worksheet. All formulas in Excel begin with the equals sign (=) as the first character. After the equals sign, the cell addresses that contain the values you want to calculate are entered between mathematical operators. The mathematical operators are + (addition), – (subtraction), * (multiplication), / (division), and ^ (exponentiation). An example of a valid formula is *=A3*B3*. The value in A3 is multiplied by the value in B3 and the result is placed in the formula cell. By including the cell address in the formula rather than typing the actual value, you can utilize the powerful recalculation feature in Excel. If you change a cell's content, the worksheet is automatically recalculated so that all values are current.

Project

You will use two methods to enter formulas to calculate total hours and gross pay for the first two employees listed in the Payroll worksheet for The Waterfront Bistro.

1. With **ExcelS1-02.xlsx** open, make J5 the active cell.

   Begin a formula by activating the cell in which you want the result placed.

2. Type **=c5+d5+e5+f5+g5+h5+i5** and then press Enter.

   The values in C5 through I5 are added and the result, *38*, is displayed in J5.

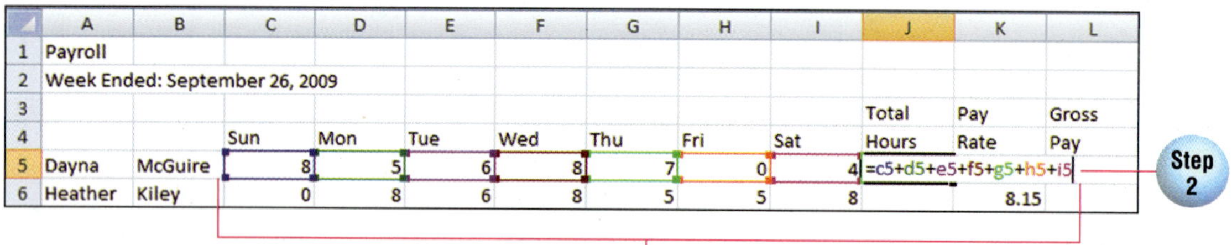

Cell references in the formula bar are color-coded to the originating cell for quick reference and error checking.

3. Press the Up Arrow key to move the active cell back to J5.

   Notice that the result of the formula is displayed in the worksheet area and the formula used to calculate the result is shown in the Formula bar. Notice also that the column letters in cell addresses are automatically converted to uppercase.

4. Make J6 the active cell, type the formula **=c6+d6+e6+f6+g6+h6+i6**, and then press Enter.

   Seem like too much typing? A more efficient way to add a series of cells is available. This method will be introduced in the next activity after you learn the pointing method for entering formulas.

5. Make L5 the active cell.

   To calculate gross pay you need to multiply the total hours times the pay rate. In Steps 6–10, you will enter this formula using the pointing method.

6. Type the equals sign (**=**).

7 Click J5.

A moving dashed border (called a ***marquee***) displays around J5, indicating it is the cell included in the formula, and the cell address is added to the formula cell (J5) with a blinking insertion point after the reference. Notice also that the Status bar displays the action *Point*.

PROBLEM

Click the wrong cell by mistake? Simply click the correct cell, or press Esc to start the formula over again.

8 Type an asterisk (*).

The marquee surrounding cell J5 disappears and J5 is color-coded with the cell reference J5 within the formula cell.

9 Click K5.

10 Click the Enter button on the Formula bar.

The result 309.7 is displayed in L5. In Activity 1.6 you will learn how to display two decimal places for cells containing dollar values.

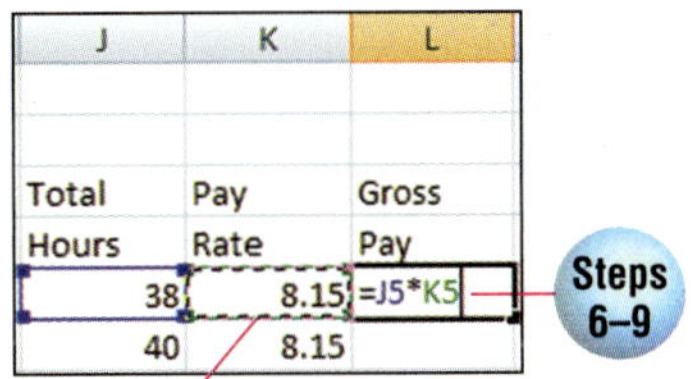

Marquee displays around cell K5 in Step 9.

11 Use the pointing method or type the formula **=j6*k6** to calculate the gross pay for Heather Kiley in L6.

12 Click the Save button on the Quick Access toolbar.

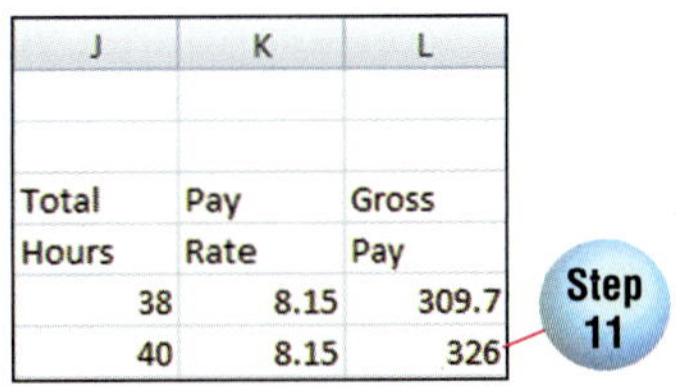

In Brief

Enter Formula

1. Activate formula cell.
2. Type =.
3. Type first cell address.
4. Type operator symbol.
5. Type second cell address.
6. Continue Steps 3-5 until finished.
7. Press Enter or click Enter button.

Enter Formula Using Pointing Method

1. Activate formula cell.
2. Type =.
3. Click first cell.
4. Type operator symbol.
5. Click second cell.
6. Repeat Steps 3-5 until finished.
7. Press Enter or click Enter button.

In Addition

Order of Operations

If you include several operators in a formula, Excel calculates the result using the order of operations as follows: negations (e.g., –1) first, then percents (%), then exponentiations (^), then multiplication and division (* and /), and finally addition and subtraction (+ and –). If a formula contains more than one operator at the same level of precedence—for example, both an addition and a subtraction operation—Excel calculates the equation from left to right. To change the order of operations, use parentheses around the part of the formula you want calculated first.

Formula	Calculation
=B5*C5/D5	Both operators are at the same level of precedence—Excel would multiply the value in B5 times the value in C5 and then divide the result by the value in D5.
=(B5+B6+B7)*A10	Excel would add the values in B5 through B7 before multiplying times the value in A10.

Activity 1.4

Using the SUM Function

The formulas to calculate the hours worked by the first two employees were lengthy. A more efficient way to calculate the total hours for Dayna McGuire in J5 would be to enter the formula *=SUM(C5:I5)*. This formula includes one of Excel's built-in functions called SUM. A ***function*** is a preprogrammed formula. The structure of a formula utilizing a function begins with the equals sign (=), followed by the name of the function, and then the ***argument***. Argument is the term given to the values identified within parentheses. In the example provided, the argument C5:I5 contains the starting cell and the ending cell separated by a colon (:). This is called a ***range*** and is used when the values to be added are located in a rectangular-shaped block of cells. Since the SUM function is used frequently, a Sum button is available in the Home tab.

Project

The office manager of The Waterfront Bistro wants you to use a more efficient method of payroll calculation, so you will use the SUM function to complete the hours worked for the Payroll worksheet.

The Waterfront B·I·S·T·R·O

1. With **ExcelS1-02.xlsx** open, make J5 the active cell and then press the Delete key.

   This deletes the formula in the cell. There was nothing wrong with the formula already entered in J5. You are deleting it so that the formulas in the completed worksheet will be consistent.

2. Click the Sum button Σ in the Editing group in the Home tab. (Do not click the down-pointing arrow to the right of the Sum button.)

   A moving marquee surrounds cells C5 through I5 and a ScreenTip appears below the formula cell indicating the correct format for the SUM function. Excel enters the formula *=SUM(C5:I5)* in J5. The suggested range C5:I5 is selected within the formula so that you can highlight a different range with the mouse if the suggested range is not correct.

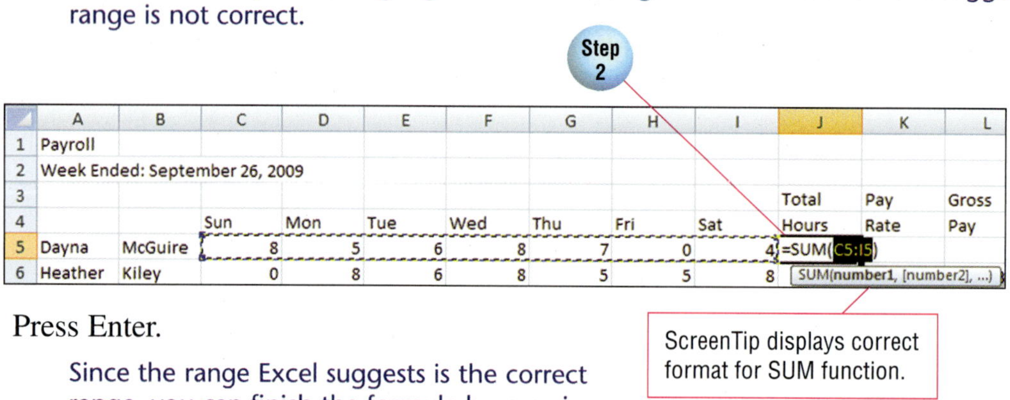

3. Press Enter.

   Since the range Excel suggests is the correct range, you can finish the formula by pressing Enter or by clicking the Enter button on the Formula bar.

4. With J6 the active cell, press the Delete key to delete the existing formula in the cell.

5. Click the Sum button. When Excel displays the formula *=SUM(C6:I6)*, click the Enter button in the Formula bar.

6. Make J7 the active cell and then click the Sum button.

   Notice this time the range of cells Excel is suggesting to add (J5:J6) is the wrong range. When you click the Sum button, Excel looks for multiple values in the cells immediately above the active cell. If no more than one value exists above the active cell, Excel looks in the cells to the left. In this case, there were multiple values above J7. You need to correct the range of cells that you want to add.

7. Position the cell pointer over C7, hold down the left mouse button, drag the pointer to the right to I7, and then release the mouse button.

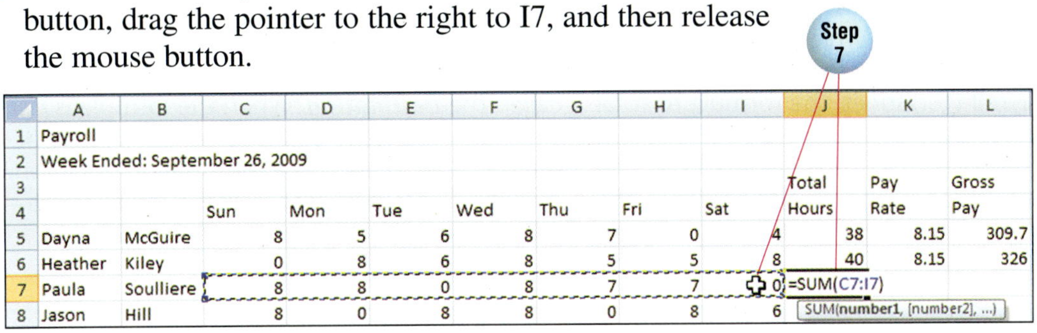

	A	B	C	D	E	F	G	H	I	J	K	L
1	Payroll											
2	Week Ended: September 26, 2009											
3										Total	Pay	Gross
4			Sun	Mon	Tue	Wed	Thu	Fri	Sat	Hours	Rate	Pay
5	Dayna	McGuire	8	5	6	8	7	0	4	38	8.15	309.7
6	Heather	Kiley	0	8	6	8	5	5	8	40	8.15	326
7	Paula	Soulliere	8	8	0	8	7	7	0	=SUM(C7:I7)		
8	Jason	Hill	8	0	8	8	0	8	6	SUM(number1, [number2], ...)		

8. Press Enter.

   Now that you have seen how the Sum button operates, you already know that the suggested range for the next employee's total hours will be incorrect. In Step 9, you will select the range of cells *first* to avoid the incorrect suggestion.

9. Position the cell pointer in C8, hold down the left mouse button, drag the pointer to the right to J8, and then release the mouse button.

   Notice you are including J8, the cell that will display the result, in the range of cells.

10. Click the Sum button.

    The result, *38,* appears in cell J8.

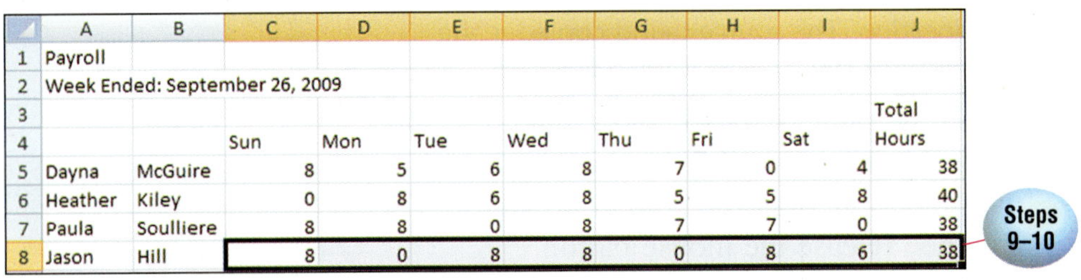

	A	B	C	D	E	F	G	H	I	J
1	Payroll									
2	Week Ended: September 26, 2009									
3										Total
4			Sun	Mon	Tue	Wed	Thu	Fri	Sat	Hours
5	Dayna	McGuire	8	5	6	8	7	0	4	38
6	Heather	Kiley	0	8	6	8	5	5	8	40
7	Paula	Soulliere	8	8	0	8	7	7	0	38
8	Jason	Hill	8	0	8	8	0	8	6	38

11. Click J8 and look in the Formula bar at the formula the SUM function created: *=SUM(C8:I8).*

    Since Excel created the correct SUM formula from a range of selected cells, you decide to try calculating total hours for more than one employee in one step using the method employed in Steps 9 and 10 but with an expanded range.

12. Position the cell pointer in C9, hold down the left mouse button, drag the pointer down and right to J13, and then release the mouse button.

13. Click the Sum button.

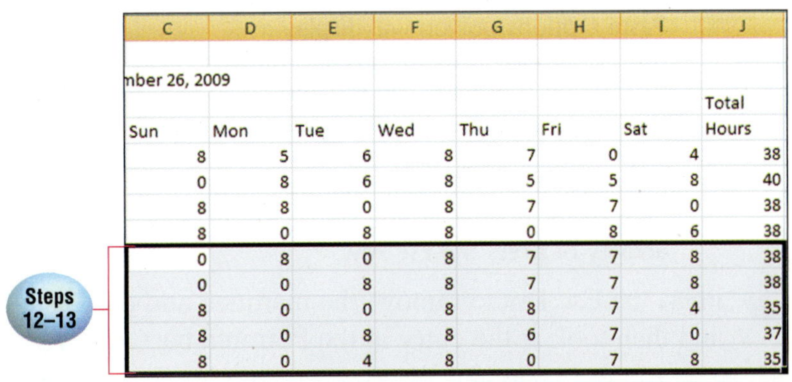

C	D	E	F	G	H	I	J
mber 26, 2009							
							Total
Sun	Mon	Tue	Wed	Thu	Fri	Sat	Hours
8	5	6	8	7	0	4	38
0	8	6	8	5	5	8	40
8	8	0	8	7	7	0	38
8	0	8	8	0	8	6	38
0	8	0	8	7	7	8	38
0	0	8	8	7	7	8	38
8	0	0	8	8	7	4	35
8	0	8	8	6	7	0	37
8	0	4	8	0	7	8	35

14. Click cells J9, J10, J11, J12, and J13 to confirm that the correct formulas appear in the Formula bar.

15. Click the Save button on the Quick Access toolbar.

Activity 1.5

Copying Formulas

Many times you may create a worksheet in which several formulas are basically the same. For example, in the payroll worksheet, the formula to total the hours for Dayna McGuire is *=SUM(C5:I5)*, for Heather Kiley *=SUM(C6:I6)*, and so on. The only difference between the two formulas is the row number. Whenever formulas are this similar, you can use the Copy and Paste feature to copy the formula from one cell to another. The cell containing the original formula is called the ***source***, and the cell(s) to which the formula is copied is called the ***destination***. When the formula is pasted, Excel automatically changes column letters or row numbers to reflect the destination location. By default, Excel assumes ***relative addressing***—cell addresses update relative to the destination.

Project

To simplify your completion of the Payroll worksheet for The Waterfront Bistro, you will copy formulas using two methods: Copy and Paste and the fill handle.

1. With **ExcelS1-02.xlsx** open, make L6 the active cell.

   This cell contains the formula *=J6*K6* to calculate the gross pay for Heather Kiley. You will copy this formula to the remaining cells in column L to finish the *Gross Pay* column.

2. Click the Copy button in the Clipboard group in the Home tab.

   A moving marquee surrounds the active cell indicating the source contents are copied to the Clipboard, which is a temporary storage location. The source being copied is the formula *=J6*K6*—not the value *326*.

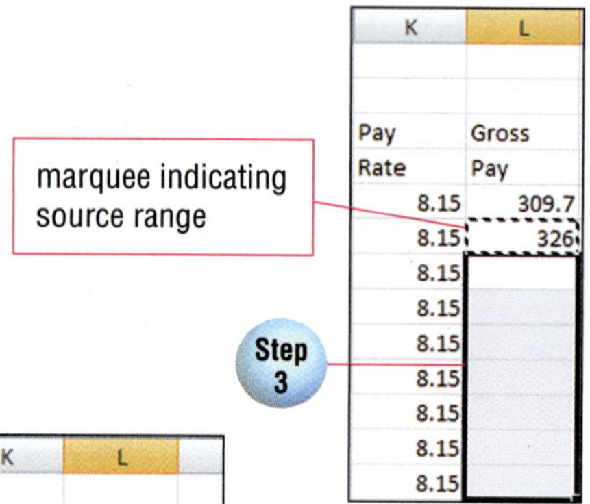

3. Select the range L7:L13. To do this, position the cell pointer over L7, hold down the left mouse button, drag the pointer down to L13, and then release the mouse button.

4. Click the Paste button in the Clipboard group in the Home tab. (Do not click the down-pointing arrow on the button.)

   Excel copies the formula to the selected cells, displays the results, and the Paste Options button appears. Clicking the Paste Options button will display a drop-down list with various alternatives for pasting the data. The moving marquee remains around the source cell and the destination cells remain highlighted. The moving marquee disappears as soon as you start another activity or press the Esc key.

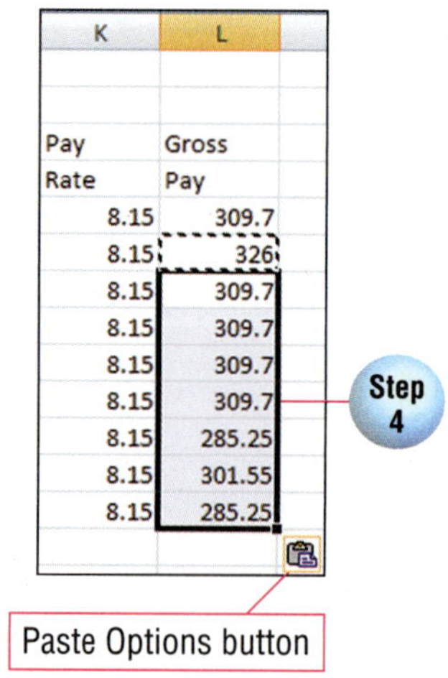

5. Press the Esc key to remove the marquee and the Paste Options button, click L7, and then look at the entry in the Formula bar: *=J7*K7*.

   The row number in the source formula was increased by one to reflect the destination.

6. Use the Down Arrow key to check the remaining formulas in column L.

7. Make C15 the active cell.

8. Click the Sum button and then click the Enter button in the Formula bar.

   The SUM function inserts the formula *=SUM(C5:C14)*. Next, you will copy the formula using the fill handle.

9. Drag the fill handle in C15 right to L15.

   When the active cell contains a formula, dragging the fill handle causes Excel to copy the formula and change cell references relative to each destination location.

	A	B	C	D	E	F	G	H	I	J	K	L
1	Payroll											
2	Week Ended: September 26, 2009											
3										Total	Pay	Gross
4			Sun	Mon	Tue	Wed	Thu	Fri	Sat	Hours	Rate	Pay
5	Dayna	McGuire	8	5	6	8	7	0	4	38	8.15	309.7
6	Heather	Kiley	0	8	6	8	5	5	8	40	8.15	326
7	Paula	Soulliere	8	8	0	8	7	7	0	38	8.15	309.7
8	Jason	Hill	8	0	8	8	0	8	6	38	8.15	309.7
9	Moira	Su-Lin	0	8	0	8	7	7	8	38	8.15	309.7
10	Carl	Doxtator	0	0	8	8	7	7	8	38	8.15	309.7
11	Tammy	Williams	8	0	0	8	8	7	4	35	8.15	285.25
12	Tyler	Santini	8	0	8	8	6	7	0	37	8.15	301.55
13	Patricia	Cardenas	8	0	4	8	0	7	8	35	8.15	285.25
14												
15	Total		48	29	40	72	47	55	46	337	73.35	2746.55

Step 9

PROBLEM

If the results do not appear in D15 through L15, you probably dragged the cell pointer instead of the fill handle. Click C15 and try again.

10. Make K15 the active cell and then press the Delete key.

    The sum of the *Pay Rate* column is not useful information.

11. Make D15 the active cell and look at the entry in the Formula bar: *=SUM(D5:D14)*.

    The column letter in the source formula was changed to reflect the destination.

12. Use the Right Arrow key to check the formulas in the remaining columns.

13. Click the Save button on the Quick Access toolbar.

In Brief

Copy Formula

1. Activate source cell.
2. Click Copy button.
3. Select destination cell(s).
4. Click Paste button.

In Addition

Copy and Paste versus Fill

What is the difference between Copy and Paste and the fill handle? When you use Copy, the contents of the source cell(s) are placed in the Clipboard. The data will remain in the Clipboard and can be pasted several times in the current worksheet, into any other worksheet that is open, or into an open document in another program. Use Copy and Paste when the formula is to be inserted more than once or into non-adjacent cells. Use the fill handle when the formula is only being copied to adjacent cells.

Activity 1.6

Testing the Worksheet; Improving the Worksheet Appearance; Sorting

When you have finished building the worksheet, verifying that the formulas you entered are accurate is a good idea. The worksheet could contain formulas that are correct in structure but not mathematically correct for the situation. For example, the wrong range may be included in a SUM formula, or parentheses missing from a multioperator formula may cause an incorrect result. Various methods can be employed to verify a worksheet's accuracy. One method is to create a proof formula in a cell beside or below the worksheet that will verify the totals. For example, in the payroll worksheet the *Total Hours* column can be verified by creating a formula that adds all of the hours for all of the employees.

Data in Excel can be rearranged by sorting rows in either ascending order or descending order. You can select a single column or define a custom sort to specify multiple columns that determine the sort order.

Project

To confirm the accuracy of your calculations in the Payroll worksheet for The Waterfront Bistro, you will enter proof formulas to test the worksheet and then use two formatting options to improve the worksheet's appearance.

1. With **ExcelS1-02.xlsx** open, make A17 the active cell.
2. Type **Hours**, press Alt + Enter, type **Proof**, and then press Enter.

   Alt + Enter is the command to insert a line break in a cell. This command is used when you want multiple lines within the same cell. The height of the row is automatically expanded to accommodate the multiple lines.

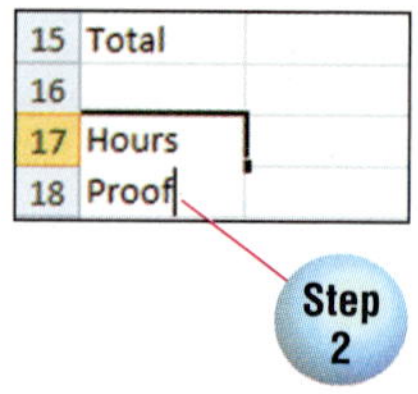

3. Make B17 the active cell.
4. Click in the Formula bar, type **=sum(c5:i13)**, and then click the Enter button or press Enter. (Alternatively, you could click the Sum button and then drag the pointer across the range C5 through I13.)

   Excel displays the result, *337,* which verifies that your total hours in J15 is correct. Can you think of another formula that would have accomplished the same objective? ***Hint: Think of the direction you added to arrive at the total hours in J15.***

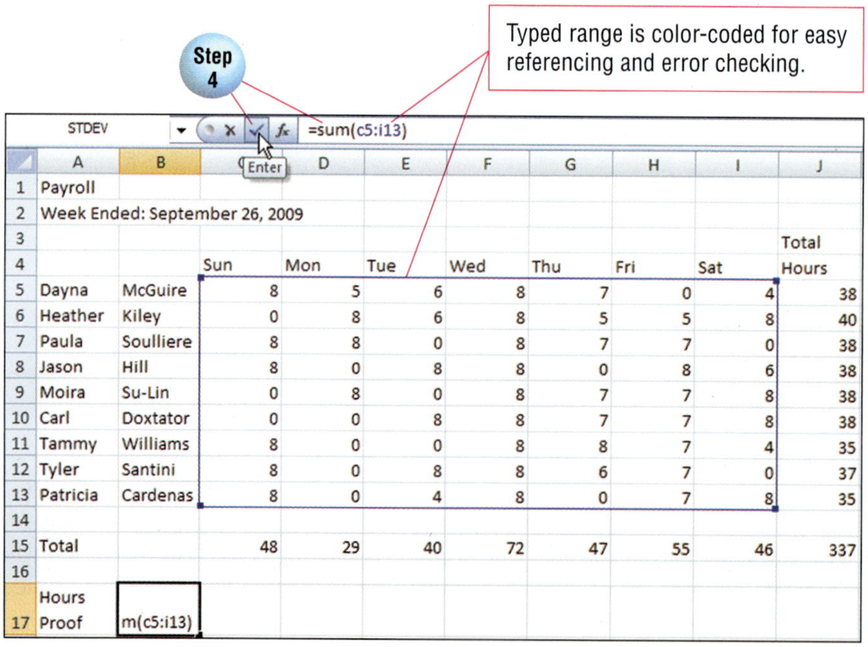

	A	B	C	D	E	F	G	H	I	J
1	Payroll									
2	Week Ended: September 26, 2009									
3										Total
4			Sun	Mon	Tue	Wed	Thu	Fri	Sat	Hours
5	Dayna	McGuire	8	5	6	8	7	0	4	38
6	Heather	Kiley	0	8	6	8	5	5	8	40
7	Paula	Soulliere	8	8	0	8	7	7	0	38
8	Jason	Hill	8	0	8	8	0	8	6	38
9	Moira	Su-Lin	0	8	0	8	7	7	8	38
10	Carl	Doxtator	0	0	8	8	7	7	8	38
11	Tammy	Williams	8	0	0	8	8	7	4	35
12	Tyler	Santini	8	0	8	8	6	7	0	37
13	Patricia	Cardenas	8	0	4	8	0	7	8	35
14										
15	Total		48	29	40	72	47	55	46	337
16										
17	Hours Proof	m(c5:i13)								

? PROBLEM

Didn't get 337? Then one of the cell entries is incorrect. Look through previous pages to see if the difference between 337 and your result equals a cell entry that you missed.

5. Make A18 the active cell.
6. Type **Gross**, press Alt + Enter, type **Pay Proof**, and then press Enter.
7. Make B18 the active cell.

   Since all of the employees are paid the same rate of pay, you can verify the *Gross Pay* column by multiplying the total hours times the pay rate.

8. Type **=j15*k5** and then press the Right Arrow key.

   The result, *2746.55*, confirms that the value in L15 is correct. The importance of testing a worksheet cannot be emphasized enough. Worksheets often contain important financial or statistical data that can form the basis for strategic business decisions.

Step 8

15	Total		48
16			
17	Hours Proof	337	
18	Gross Pay Proof	=j15*k5	

9. Look at the completed worksheet shown below. Notice that some of the values in column L show no decimals while others show 1 or 2 decimal places. Also notice the labels do not align directly over the values below them.

Labels do not align directly over values.

	A	B	C	D	E	F	G	H	I	J	K	L
1	Payroll											
2	Week Ended: September 26, 2009											
3										Total	Pay	Gross
4			Sun	Mon	Tue	Wed	Thu	Fri	Sat	Hours	Rate	Pay
5	Dayna	McGuire	8	5	6	8	7	0	4	38	8.15	309.7
6	Heather	Kiley	0	8	6	8	5	5	8	40	8.15	326
7	Paula	Soulliere	8	8	0	8	7	7	0	38	8.15	309.7
8	Jason	Hill	8	0	8	8	0	8	6	38	8.15	309.7
9	Moira	Su-Lin	0	8	0	8	7	7	8	38	8.15	309.7
10	Carl	Doxtator	0	0	8	8	7	7	8	38	8.15	309.7
11	Tammy	Williams	8	0	0	8	8	7	4	35	8.15	285.25
12	Tyler	Santini	8	0	8	8	6	7	0	37	8.15	301.55
13	Patricia	Cardenas	8	0	4	8	0	7	8	35	8.15	285.25
14												
15	Total		48	29	40	72	47	55	46	337		2746.55
16												
17	Hours Proof	337										
18	Gross Pay Proof	2746.55										

Decimal places are not consistent.

continues

10 Select the range L5:L15.

These final steps in building a worksheet are meant to improve the appearance of cells. In column L, Excel uses up to 15 decimal places for precision when calculating values. Since the *Gross Pay* column represents a sum of money, you will format these cells to the Currency format.

ScreenTip describes purpose for down-pointing arrow on the button, which displays a drop-down list of alternative currency formats.

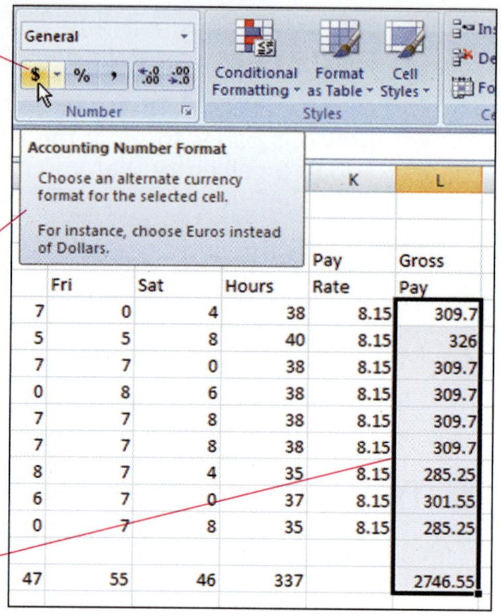

11 Click the Accounting Number Format button [$] in the Number group in the Home tab.

The Accounting Number format adds a dollar sign, a comma in the thousands place, and two decimal places to each value in the selection.

12 Make B18 the active cell and then click the Accounting Number Format button.

13 Select the range C3:L4.

As previously mentioned, labels are aligned at the left edge of a column while values are aligned at the right edge. In the next step, you will align the labels at the right edge of the column so they appear directly over the values they represent.

14 Click the Align Text Right button in the Alignment group in the Home tab.

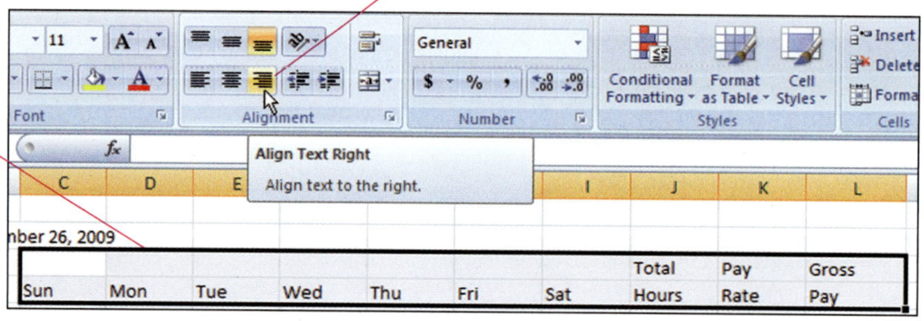

15 Click in any cell to deselect the range.

In the next steps, you will rearrange the names in the payroll worksheet so that they are in alphabetical order by last name. Since the last name is not the first column in the worksheet, you will need to define a custom sort.

16 Select the range A5:L13.

You are selecting the range before executing the sort command since you do not want to include the cells above and below the list of names in the sort action.

17 Click the Sort & Filter button in the Editing group in the Home tab.

18 Click *Custom Sort* at the drop-down list.

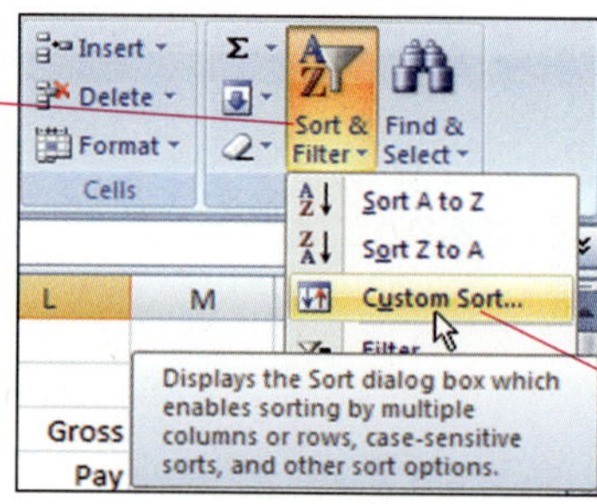

19 At the Sort dialog box, click the down-pointing arrow at the right of *Sort by* in the *Column* section and then click *Column B* at the drop-down list.

The default entries of *Values* for *Sort On* and *A to Z* for *Order* are correct since you want the cells sorted by the text entries in column B in ascending order.

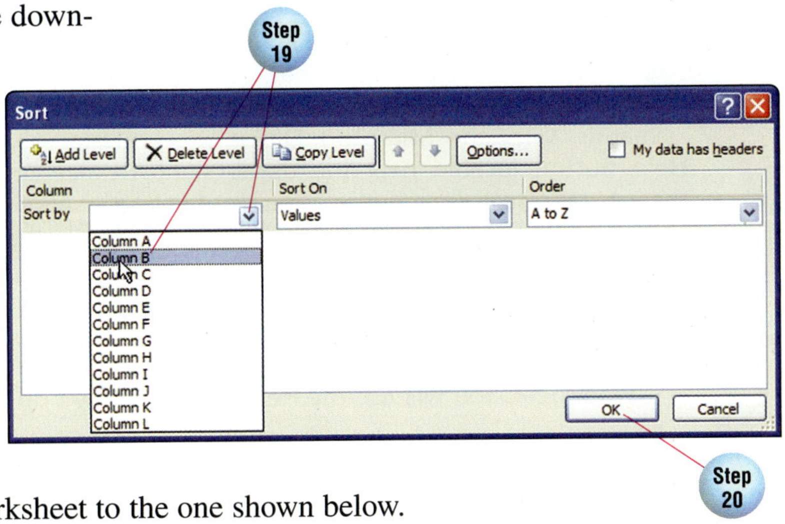

20 Click OK.

21 Click in any cell to deselect the range. Compare your sorted worksheet to the one shown below.

employees rearranged by last name in column B

	A	B	C	D	E	F	G	H	I	J	K	L
1	Payroll											
2	Week Ended: September 26, 2009											
3										Total	Pay	Gross
4			Sun	Mon	Tue	Wed	Thu	Fri	Sat	Hours	Rate	Pay
5	Patricia	Cardenas	8	0	4	8	0	7	8	35	8.15	$ 285.25
6	Carl	Doxtator	0	0	8	8	7	7	8	38	8.15	$ 309.70
7	Jason	Hill	8	0	8	8	0	8	6	38	8.15	$ 309.70
8	Heather	Kiley	0	8	6	8	5	5	8	40	8.15	$ 326.00
9	Dayna	McGuire	8	5	6	8	7	0	4	38	8.15	$ 309.70
10	Tyler	Santini	8	0	8	8	6	7	0	37	8.15	$ 301.55
11	Paula	Soulliere	8	8	0	8	7	7	0	38	8.15	$ 309.70
12	Moira	Su-Lin	0	8	0	8	7	7	8	38	8.15	$ 309.70
13	Tammy	Williams	8	0	0	8	8	7	4	35	8.15	$ 285.25
14												
15	Total		48	29	40	72	47	55	46	337		$2,746.55
16												
17	Hours Proof	337										
18	Gross Pay Proof	$2,746.55										

22 Click the Save button on the Quick Access toolbar.

In Addition

Rotating Text in Cells

The Alignment group in the Home tab contains an Orientation button, which can be used to rotate text within cells. Text can be rotated counterclockwise, clockwise, changed to a vertical alignment, rotated up vertically, or rotated down vertically. Often, text set in narrow columns is angled to improve the label appearance. In the screen shown at the right, the cells containing the days of the week in the payroll worksheet are angled counterclockwise.

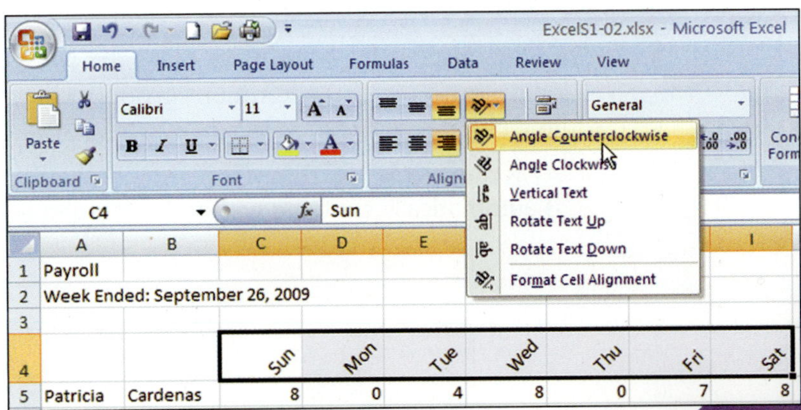

Activity 1.7

Using Help

An extensive online Help resource is available that contains information on Excel features and commands. Click the Microsoft Office Excel Help button located near the upper right corner of the screen (below the Minimize button on the Title bar) to open the Excel Help window. By default, the Help feature searches for an Internet connection. A message at the bottom right corner of the window will indicate whether Help will display information in Excel resources at Office Online or in the Offline Help file.

Another method to use Help resources is to point to a button in the tab and then press function key F1.

Project

After reviewing the Payroll worksheet, the office manager of The Waterfront Bistro thinks the first two title rows would look better if the text was centered over the columns in the worksheet. You will use the Help feature to look up the steps to do this.

1. With **ExcelS1-02.xlsx** open, make A1 the active cell.

   To center the title rows above the columns in the worksheet, you decide to browse the buttons in the Alignment group in the Home tab. The Merge & Center button in the group seems appropriate but you are not sure of the steps to work with this feature.

2. Point to the Merge & Center button in the Alignment group in the Home tab and read the information that displays in the ScreenTip.

3. With the pointer still resting on the Merge & Center button, press function key F1 and then read the paragraph below the title *Merge cells or split merged cells* in the Excel Help window.

4. Click *Merge adjacent cells* below the subtitle *What do you want to do?* and then read the information describing the steps to merge cells.

5. Close the Excel Help window.

6. Select the range A1:L1 and then click the Merge & Center button in the Alignment group in the Home tab.

   A1 is merged across columns A through L and the text *Payroll* is automatically centered within the merged cell.

Step 2

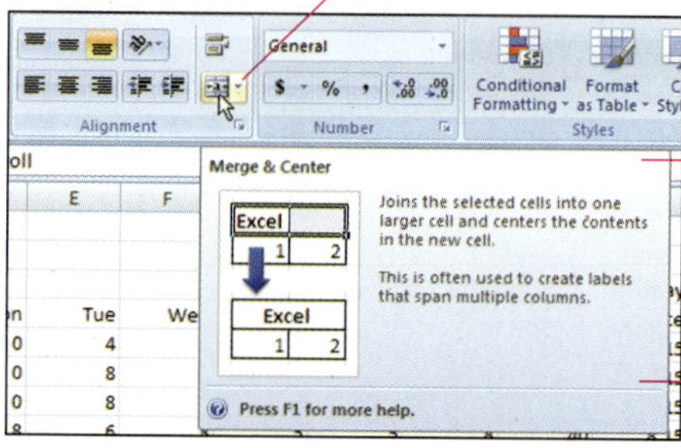

ScreenTip describes what the feature will do and when it might be useful.

Step 3

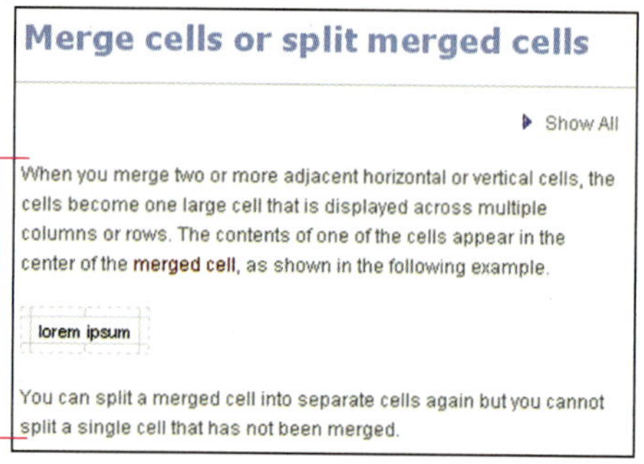

Step 4

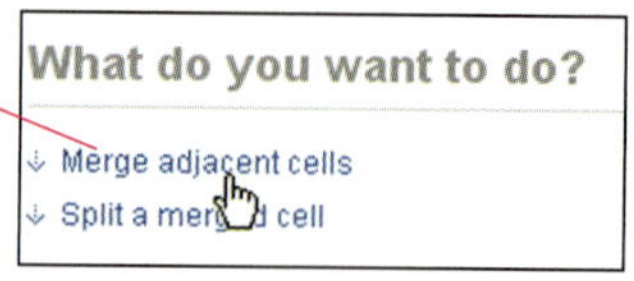

Step 6

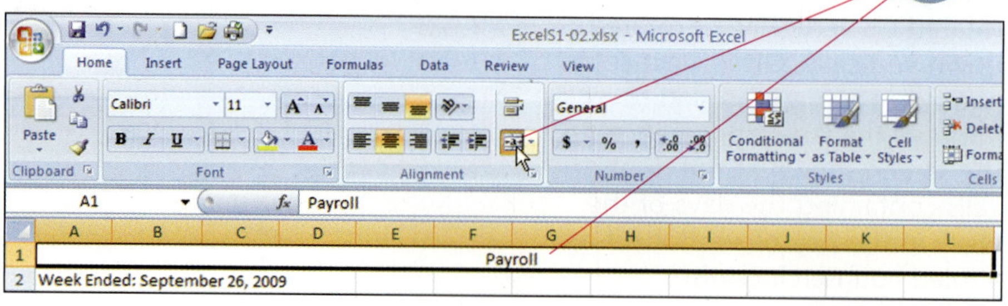

7 Select the range A2:L2 and then click the Merge & Center button.

The two titles in the payroll worksheet are now centered over the cells below them.

8 Click the Microsoft Office Excel Help button located near the upper right corner of the screen (below the Minimize button on the Title bar).

You can also access Help resources by typing a search phrase and browsing related topics in the Help window.

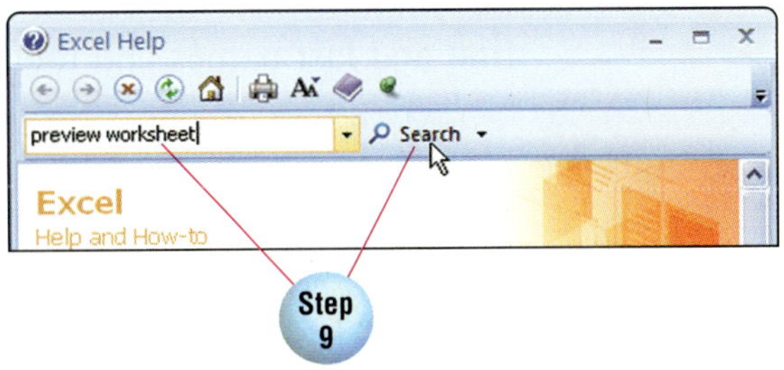

9 With the insertion point positioned in the search text box, type **preview worksheet** and then click the Search button or press Enter.

10 Click the Preview worksheet pages before printing hyperlink and then read the information that displays in the window.

11 Close the Excel Help window.

12 Click the Save button on the Quick Access toolbar.

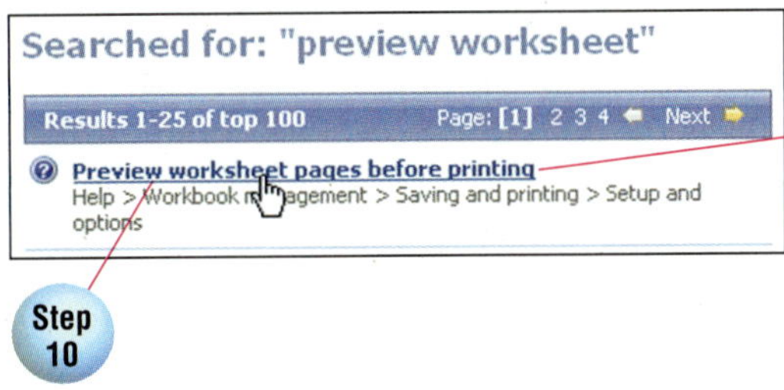

Since Microsoft Office Online is updated frequently, your search results list may vary, including the title or position in the list of this hyperlink.

In Addition

Using Offline Help

By default Excel checks for a live Internet connection when the Help feature is activated. If no connection is found, Excel displays the Help window shown at the right. Office Online provides additional resources such as online training and templates along with the most up-to-date information. You can disable online Help searches if you want to turn off the online access for reasons similar to the following:

- You are currently experiencing a slow Internet connection.
- You are working away from your normal site where you have to pay for Internet access.
- You are working away from your normal site and are concerned about privacy.

Click the down-pointing arrow to the right of the Search button and then click *Excel Help* in the *Content from this computer* section at the drop-down list to temporarily suspend online searches.

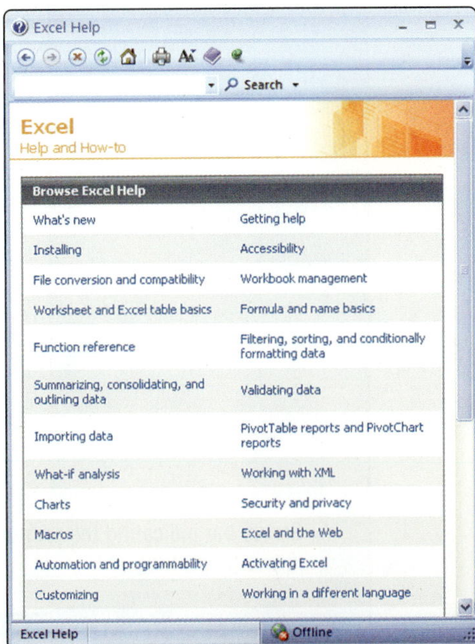

Activity 1.8

Previewing, Printing, and Closing a Workbook

Many times a worksheet is printed to have a paper copy, or ***hard copy***, to file or to attach to a report. Large, complex worksheets are often easier to proofread and check from a paper copy. The Quick Print button on the Quick Access toolbar will print the active worksheet using default print options. Display the Print dialog box to modify print options. For example, if more than one worksheet exists in a workbook, open the Print dialog box by clicking the Office button and then Print. At the Print dialog box, change the *Print what* option to *Entire workbook*. Use Print Preview before printing to avoid wasted paper by checking in advance whether the entire worksheet will fit on one page, or to preview other page layout options.

Project

The Payroll worksheet for The Waterfront Bistro is finished. You want to preview the worksheet and then print a copy for the office manager.

1. With **ExcelS1-02.xlsx** open, make A20 the active cell and then type the student information your instructor has directed for printouts. For example, type your first and last names and then press Enter.

   Make sure you have checked if other identifying information such as your program or class number should be included.

2. Click the Office button, point to Print, and then click Print Preview to display the worksheet in the Print Preview window shown in Figure 1.2.

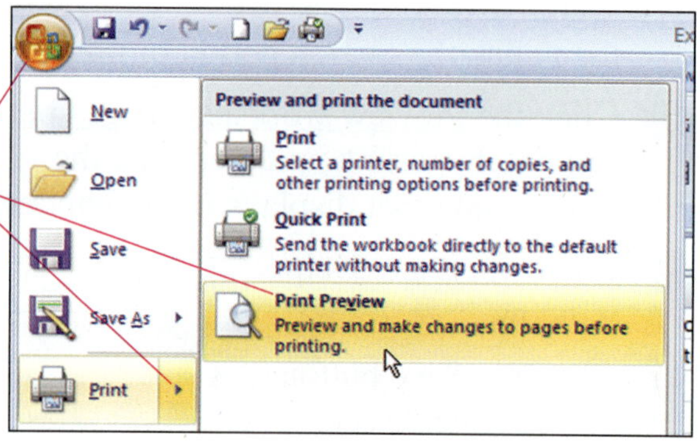

FIGURE 1.2 Print Preview Window

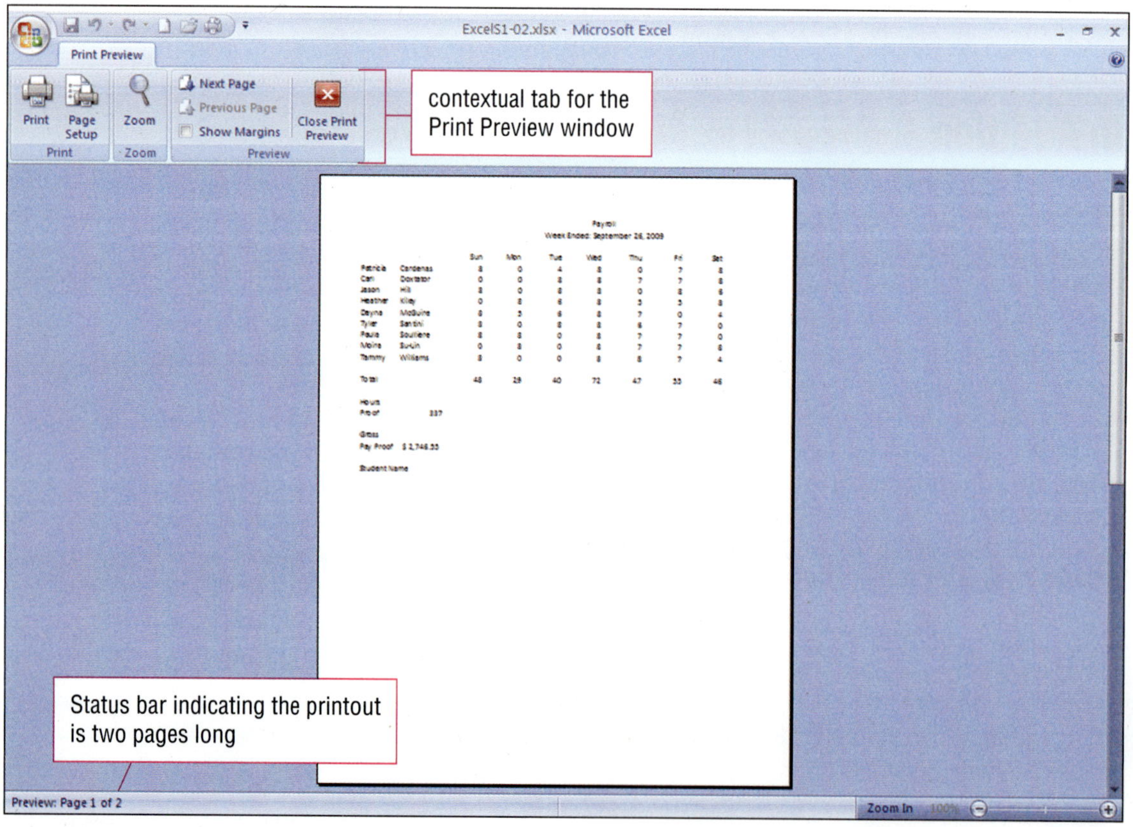

3 The Print Preview window displays a picture of what the printed page will look like. Notice the Status bar is indicating *Page 1 of 2*. Click the Next Page button in the Preview group in the Print Preview tab.

4 The second page of the printout appears showing the columns that could not fit on page 1. The mouse pointer displays as a magnifying glass in the preview screen. Move the mouse pointer over the columns at the top left of page 2 and then click the left mouse button.

This causes the display to enlarge so that you can read the data in the columns.

5 Click the mouse anywhere on the page to return to the full-page view and then click the Previous Page button in the Preview group.

6 Click the Page Setup button in the Print group.

One method to reduce the printout to one page is to change the orientation of the paper from portrait to landscape. In ***portrait*** orientation, the page is printed on paper taller than it is wide. In ***landscape*** orientation, the data is rotated to print on paper that is wider than it is tall.

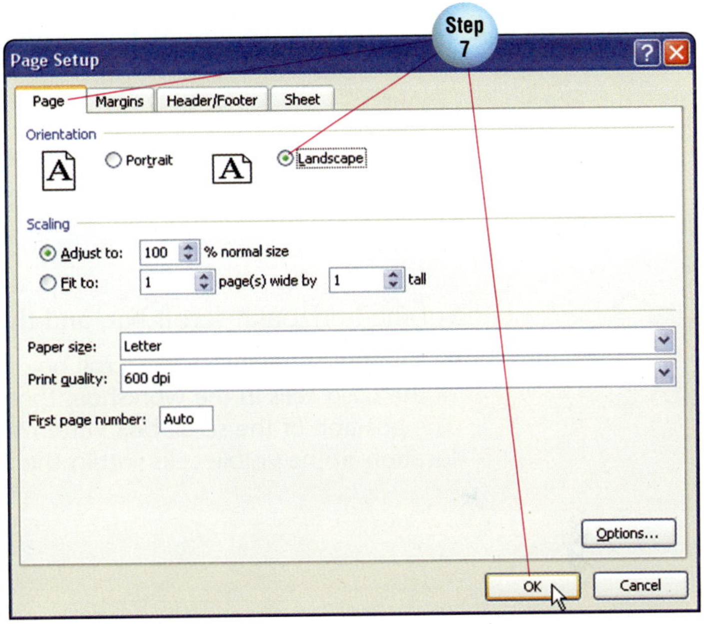

7 If necessary, click the Page tab in the Page Setup dialog box, click *Landscape* in the *Orientation* section, and then click OK.

Print Preview updates to show the worksheet in landscape orientation. Notice that all of the columns now fit on one page.

8 Click the Print button in the Print group.

Print Preview closes and the Print dialog box appears.

9 The default settings in the Print dialog box are to print one copy of all pages in the active sheet. Click OK.

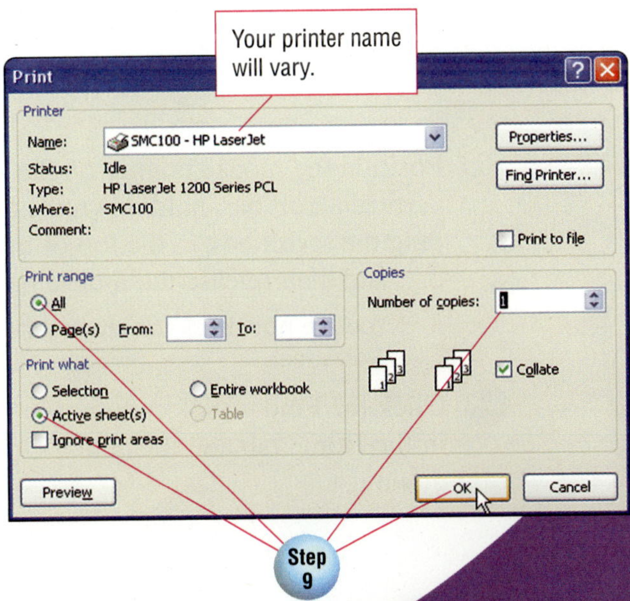

10 If necessary, scroll right until you see the vertical dashed line between columns located to the right of the *Gross Pay* column.

The dashed vertical line is a page break. Page breaks appear after you have used Print Preview or Print and indicate how much information from the worksheet can fit on a page.

11 Click the Save button on the Quick Access toolbar.

12 Click the Office button and then click Close at the drop-down list.

Activity 1.9

Navigating a Worksheet

Until now, you have been working with small worksheets that generally fit within the viewing area. Once worksheets become larger, you will need to scroll to the right or scroll down to locate cells with which you need to work. The horizontal and vertical scroll bars are used to scroll with the mouse. Scrolling using the scroll bars does not move the position of the active cell. You can also scroll using the arrow keys or with keyboard commands. Scrolling using the keyboard moves the active cell.

Project

To prepare for the creation of another report, you will open a workbook and practice various scrolling techniques using the mouse and the keyboard

1. Click the Open button on the Quick Access toolbar.
2. At the Open dialog box with ExcelS1 the active folder, double-click the workbook ***WBInventory.xlsx***.
3. Position the mouse pointer on the down scroll arrow at the bottom of the vertical scroll bar and then click the left mouse button a few times to scroll down the worksheet.
4. Position the mouse pointer on the right scroll arrow at the right edge of the horizontal scroll bar and then click the left mouse button a few times to scroll to the right edge of the worksheet.
5. Position the mouse pointer on the scroll box in the horizontal scroll bar, hold down the left mouse button, drag the scroll box to the left edge of the horizontal scroll bar, and then release the mouse button.

   The width or height of the scroll box indicates the proportional amount of the used cells in the worksheet that is visible in the current window. The position of the scroll box within the scroll bar indicates the relative location of the visible cells within the remainder of the worksheet.

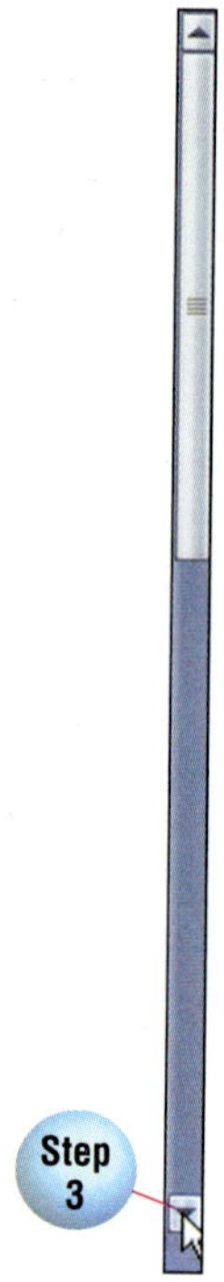

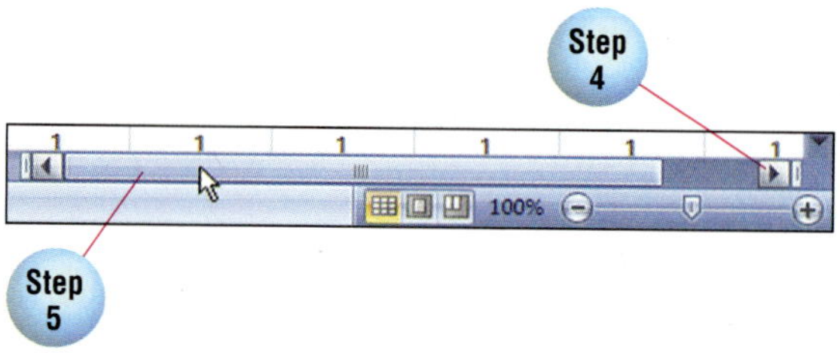

6. Position the mouse pointer on the scroll box in the vertical scroll bar, hold down the left mouse button, drag the scroll box to the top of the vertical scroll bar, and then release the mouse button.

   You are now back to viewing the beginning of the worksheet.

7. Click the Find & Select button in the Editing group in the Home tab and then click *Go To* at the drop-down list.

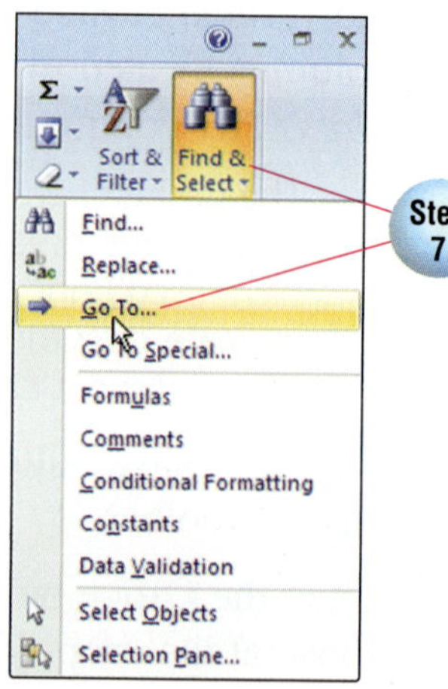

8 At the Go To dialog box, type **o54** in the *Reference* text box and then click OK or press Enter.

The active cell is positioned in O54, the bottom right edge of the worksheet, which is the total of all of the inventory units for all 12 months. Notice using Go To moved the position of the active cell.

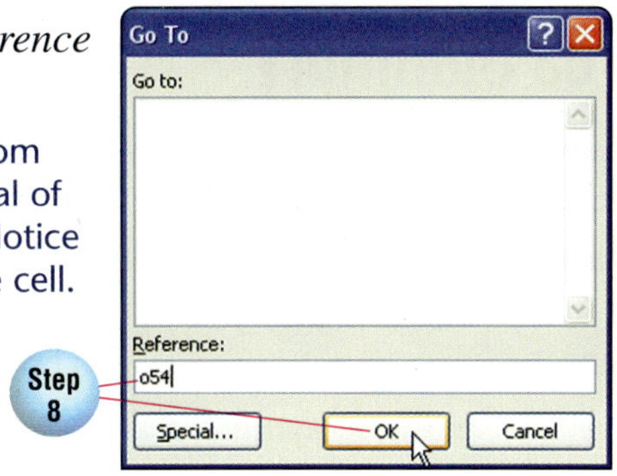

In Brief

Go to Specific Cell

1. Click Find & Select button.
2. Click *Go To*.
3. Type cell address.
4. Click OK.

9 Press Ctrl + Home.

Ctrl + Home makes A1 the active cell.

10 Press the Page Down button twice.

Each time you press the Page Down key you move down one screen.

11 Press the Right Arrow key four times.

Each time you press the Right Arrow key, you move the active cell one cell to the right.

12 Use the Up, Down, Left, and Right Arrow keys to practice moving around the worksheet.

Holding down a directional arrow key causes the screen to scroll very quickly. Table 1.2 illustrates more keyboard scrolling techniques.

13 Click the Office button and then click Close to close **WBInventory.xlsx**.

14 Click the Office button and then click the Exit Excel button [Exit Excel] located at the bottom right of the drop-down menu.

TABLE 1.2 Keyboard Movement Commands

Press	To move to
Arrow keys	one cell up, down, left, or right
Ctrl + Home	A1
Ctrl + End	last cell in worksheet
Home	beginning of row
Page Down	down one screen
Page Up	up one screen
Alt + Page Down	one screen to the right
Alt + Page Up	one screen to the left

In Addition

Viewing a Large Worksheet by Splitting the Window

You can split a worksheet into more than one window to facilitate viewing different sections of the worksheet at the same time. The split window allows you to view different sections of a large worksheet at the same time by scrolling in each window to different locations. For example, to view January's and December's inventory purchases in the same window, you could split the window vertically as shown below. Each window contains a set of scroll bars to allow you to scroll to different areas within each window. To split a worksheet into two vertical windows, drag the split box located immediately right of the right scroll arrow in the horizontal scroll bar to the position you want the split to occur. Drag the split bar back to the right edge of the screen to remove the split. Drag the split box at the top of the vertical scroll bar down to create a horizontal split.

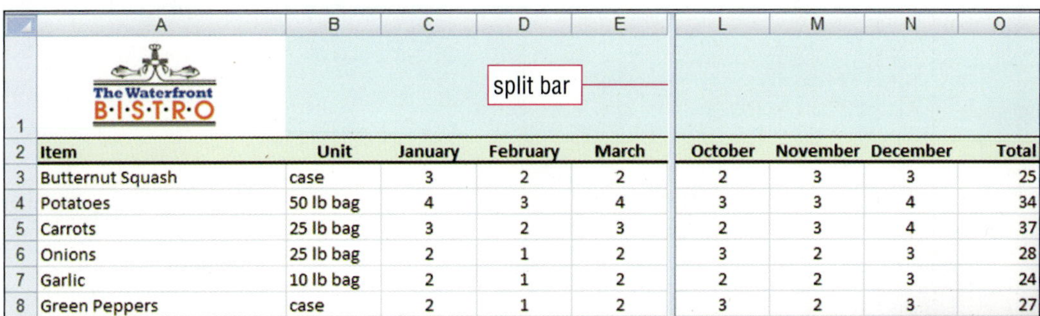

	A	B	C	D	E	L	M	N	O
2	Item	Unit	January	February	March	October	November	December	Total
3	Butternut Squash	case	3	2	2	2	3	3	25
4	Potatoes	50 lb bag	4	3	4	3	3	4	34
5	Carrots	25 lb bag	3	2	3	2	3	4	37
6	Onions	25 lb bag	2	1	2	3	2	3	28
7	Garlic	10 lb bag	2	1	2	2	2	3	24
8	Green Peppers	case	2	1	2	3	2	3	27

Features Summary

Feature	Ribbon Tab, Group	Button	Quick Access Toolbar	Office Button Drop-down List	Keyboard Shortcut
Accounting Number format	Home, Number	$			
align text left	Home, Alignment				
align text right	Home, Alignment				
close a workbook				Close	Ctrl + F4
copy	Home, Clipboard				Ctrl + C
exit Excel		Exit Excel		Exit Excel	Alt + F4
fill down	Home, Editing				Ctrl + D
fill left	Home, Editing				
fill right	Home, Editing				Ctrl + R
fill up	Home, Editing				
Go To	Home, Editing				Ctrl + G
Help					F1
merge and center	Home, Alignment				
new workbook				New	Ctrl + N
open				Open	Ctrl + O
paste	Home, Clipboard				Ctrl + V
Print Preview				Print, Print Preview	Ctrl + F2
print using Print dialog box				Print	Ctrl + P
print using Quick Print					
save				Save	Ctrl + S
save with a new name				Save As	F12
SUM function	Home, Editing	Σ			Alt + =

Knowledge Check

Completion: In the space provided at the right, indicate the correct term, command, or option.

1. This area contains commands and features for performing actions divided into tabs and groups. ______________
2. This area displays the formula stored within the cell (not the result). ______________
3. The cell pointer changes to this when pointing at the small black square at the bottom right corner of the active cell. ______________
4. This would be the formula entry to divide the contents of cell C6 by the contents in cell C12. ______________
5. This is the term for the method used to create a formula by typing the equals sign and operator symbols while clicking reference cells between the typed symbols. ______________
6. This term is used to refer to the values identified within parentheses in the SUM function. ______________
7. The SUM function button is located in this group in the Home tab. ______________
8. Do this action if Excel suggests the wrong range after clicking the Sum button. ______________
9. This button appears after copied cells are pasted into the destination range. ______________
10. This is the term for the formulas entered beside or below a worksheet that are designed to verify the worksheet's accuracy. ______________
11. This format adds a dollar sign, a comma in the thousands place, and two decimal places to each value in the selected range. ______________
12. Click the Sort & Filter button in the Editing group in the Home tab and then click this option at the drop-down list to display the Sort dialog box. ______________
13. This keyboard shortcut will open the Excel Help window when pointing to a button. ______________
14. Display the active worksheet in Print Preview by clicking the Office button, pointing to this option, and then clicking Print Preview. ______________
15. Open this dialog box to type a cell reference to which you want to move the active cell. ______________

Skills Review

Review 1 Creating Labels, Values, and Formulas

The Waterfront B·I·S·T·R·O

1. Start Excel.
2. Create the worksheet shown in Figure 1.3. Use the fill handle whenever possible to facilitate data entry. In rows 8, 13, and 17, press the spacebar twice before typing the cell entry to indent the text.
3. Format E6:H17 to the Accounting Number format.

FIGURE 1.3 Review 1 Worksheet

	A	B	C	D	E	F	G	H
1	The Waterfront Bistro							
2	Condensed Quarterly Statement of Income							
3	For the Quarter Ended September 30, 2009							
4	In Thousands							
5					Jul	Aug	Sep	Total
6	Sales				49.5	51.4	53.7	
7	Cost of Goods Sold				33.1	42.6	43.9	
8	Gross Margin							
9								
10	Advertising Expense				1.8	1.8	1.8	
11	Wages and Benefits Expense				8.1	7.8	8.4	
12	Miscellaneous and Overhead Expense				0.8	0.8	0.8	
13	Total Expenses							
14								
15	Net Income Before Taxes							
16	Taxes							
17	Net Income After Taxes							

4. Create the following formulas by typing the entry, using the pointing method, or by using the Sum button:
   a. In cell E8, subtract *Cost of Goods Sold* from *Sales* by entering **=e6-e7**.
   b. In cell E13, add the three expenses by entering **=SUM(e10:e12)**.
   c. In cell E15, subtract *Total Expenses* from *Gross Margin* by entering **=e8-e13**.
   d. In cell E16, multiply *Net Income Before Taxes* by 22% by entering **=e15*22%**.
   e. In cell E17, subtract *Taxes* from *Net Income Before Taxes* by entering **=e15-e16**.
5. Copy and paste formulas in column E to columns F and G as follows:
   a. Copy the formula in E8 and then paste the formula to the range F8:G8.
   b. Copy the formula in E13 and then paste the formula to the range F13:G13.
   c. Select and copy the range E15:E17 and then paste the formulas to the range F15:G17.
6. Click in cell H6 and then use the Sum button to enter the formula to add E6:G6.
7. Copy the formula in H6 to the remaining cells in column H.
8. Save the workbook and name it **ExcelS1-R1.xlsx**.

Review 2 Improving the Appearance of the Worksheet; Previewing and Printing

1. With **ExcelS1-R1.xlsx** open, merge and center the title in row 1 across columns A through H.
2. Merge and center A2, A3, and A4 across columns A through H.
3. Change the alignment of the range E5:H5 to Align Text Right.
4. Use the Help feature to find out how to display fewer decimal places.
5. Select the range E6:H17 and then decrease the number of decimal places to one decimal place.
6. Deselect the range E6:H17 and then display the worksheet in Print Preview.
7. Save, print, and then close **ExcelS1-R1.xlsx**.

Skills Assessment

Assessment 1 Adding Values and Formulas to a Worksheet

1. Open **MPTravelCosts.xlsx**.
2. Save the workbook with Save As and name it **ExcelS1-A1**.
3. You have received a message from Melissa Gehring of First Choice Travel with quotations for return airfare, hotel, and airport transfers for the film crew to travel to Toronto, Ontario, for a film shoot July 5 to August 27, 2010. This information is summarized below.
   - Return airfare from Los Angeles to Toronto is $676.20 per person.
   - Melissa has negotiated with a local hotel for a flat room rate of $5,850.00 per room for the entire duration of the film shoot with two persons per room.
   - Airport Transfer Limousine Service has quoted a flat rate of $1,125.00 in Toronto and $895.00 in Los Angeles.
   - All of the above prices include taxes and are quoted in U.S. dollars.
4. Enter the appropriate values and formulas to complete the worksheet.
5. Apply alignment and formatting options you learned in this section to any cells that you consider would improve the appearance of the worksheet.
6. Save, print, and then close **ExcelS1-A1.xlsx**.

Assessment 2 Creating a New Workbook

1. You work with Bobbie Sinclair, business manager at Performance Threads. You are preparing a price estimate for costumes needed by Marquee Productions for its Toronto film shoot July 5 to August 27, 2010. Create a new workbook that will calculate the costume price quotation using the following information.
   - Five costumes must be researched, designed, and custom-made at $2,755.00 per costume. Marquee Productions will own all five of these costumes after the film shoot.
   - Seven costumes are in stock and can be rented at $118.50 per day. Marquee Productions will need all seven of these costumes for 17 days.
   - Eighteen costumes require size and length adjustments. These 18 costumes are subject to the same rental fee, but are only required for 11 days. A flat fee for alterations is $210.00 per costume.
2. Apply alignment and formatting options you learned in this section to any cells that you consider would improve the appearance of the worksheet.
3. Save the workbook and name it **ExcelS1-A2**.
4. Print and then close **ExcelS1-A2.xlsx**.

Assessment 3 Creating a New Workbook

1. You work with Sam Vestering, manager of North American Distribution for Worldwide Enterprises. You are preparing a projected distribution revenue schedule for Marquee Productions' latest film *Two by Two*, to be released February 12, 2010. Create a new workbook that will estimate Worldwide's projected revenue using the following information (see Table 1.3):
   - Preview cities receive the film on the Friday before the general release date and pay Worldwide Enterprises 1.27% of projected box office revenues.

TABLE 1.3 Assessment 3

City	Release Category	Projected Box Office Sales in Millions
New York	Preview	42.7
Tuscon	General	12.5
Los Angeles	Preview	46.8
Denver	Preview	22.3
Orlando	General	32.1
Des Moines	General	11.2
Wichita	Preview	10.6
Boston	General	24.5
Philadelphia	General	19.6
Dallas	General	21.4
Milwaukee	General	17.8
Atlanta	Preview	34.9
Vancouver	General	26.4
Calgary	General	19.2
Toronto	Preview	31.7
Montreal	Preview	21.6

- General release cities pay Worldwide Enterprises 1% of projected box office revenues.
- All distribution fees and projected revenues are in U.S. dollars.
- Include a total of the projected revenue for Worldwide Enterprises. ***Hint: Consider creating this worksheet by grouping the preview cities and the general release cities separately.***

2. Apply alignment and formatting options you learned in this section to any cells that you consider would improve the appearance of the worksheet.
3. Use the Sort feature to rearrange the order of the cities in ascending order.
4. Save the workbook and name it **ExcelS1-A3**.
5. Print and then close **ExcelS1-A3.xlsx**.

Assessment 4 Finding Information on Displaying Formulas in Cells

1. Use Excel Help to find out how to hide or display cell formulas in a worksheet.
2. Open **ExcelS1-A1.xlsx**.
3. Display the cell formulas in the worksheet.
4. Print the worksheet.
5. Hide the cell formulas in the worksheet.
6. Close **ExcelS1-A1.xlsx**. Click No if prompted to save changes.

HELP

Assessment 5 Locating and Completing Excel Training in Office Online

1. Display a new blank worksheet.
2. Open the Excel Help window.
3. Click the down-pointing arrow at the right of the Search button and then click *Excel Training* at the drop-down list.
4. Type **formulas** in the search text box and then click the Search button.
5. Click the hyperlink to one of the training courses that interests you.
6. Complete the online training course. ***Note: You can skip through sections of the course that are teaching skills you have already mastered by clicking the next topic in the navigation pane.***
7. Close Internet Explorer when you have completed the course.
8. Close the Excel Help window and then close the worksheet.

Marquee Challenge

Challenge 1 Preparing an International Student Registration Report

1. You work at Niagara Peninsula College in the Registrar's Office. The Registrar has asked you to create the annual report for international student registrations. Create the worksheet shown in Figure 1.4.
2. Calculate the tuition fees in column K by multiplying the credit hours times the fee per hour.
3. Use the SUM function to calculate the total international student fees.
4. Apply format options as shown and format the values in column K to an appropriate number format.
5. Add the current date and your name in rows 4 and 19 respectively.
6. Save the workbook and name it **ExcelS1-C1**.
7. Print and then close **ExcelS1-C1.xlsx**.

FIGURE 1.4 Challenge 1

	A	B	C	D	E	F	G	H	I	J	K
1	Niagara Peninsula College										
2	International Student Registrations										
3	for the 2009/2010 Academic Year										
4	Report Date: (Current Date)										
5			Last	First	Home				Credit	Fee per	Tuition
6	Student Number		Name	Name	Country		Program	Semester	Hours	Hour	Fee
7	124-444-854		Cano	Sergio	Spain		BIS11	1	15	566	
8	111-785-156		Bastow	Maren	Ireland		BIS11	1	22	566	
9	138-456-749		Yiu	Terry	Hong Kong		BMK12	1	18	566	
10	165-874-316		Chan	Joseph	Hong Kong		BIN32	2	16	566	
11	137-854-632		Alivero	Maria	Mexico		CMP12	2	17	566	
12	138-598-648		Torres	Phillip	Ecuador		CTN14	2	21	566	
13	124-875-458		Davis	Caitlyn	Australia		OAM24	3	23	566	
14	328-745-856		Muir	Christa	Australia		GRD13	4	25	566	
15	348-758-986		Figueria	Marlo	Bahamas		HTC24	2	24	566	
16	348-854-861		Cervinka	Mary	Greece		TTM14	4	20	566	
17											
18							TOTAL INTERNATIONAL STUDENT FEES:				
19	Prepared by: (Student Name)										

Challenge 2 Preparing a Theatre Arts Target Enrollment Report

1. You work with Cal Rubine, chair of the Theatre Arts division at Niagara Peninsula College. Cal needs the target student enrollment report shown in Figure 1.5 to assist with the revenue projections for the upcoming budget preparation. Create the worksheet shown in Figure 1.5.
2. Cal has provided percentages to use for calculating the 2010/2011 target enrollment. Cal uses the actual enrollments from the prior year (2009/2010) to calculate the target for the next year. In some programs, Cal expects that enrollment will be higher than the previous year due to new registrants, transfers from other programs, and students returning to pick up missed credits. In other programs, Cal expects that enrollment will decline from the previous year due to students dropping the program, transfers to other colleges, and students failing to meet the minimum GPA for progression. Use the percentages in Table 1.4 to create the target formulas.
3. Use the SUM function to calculate the total target enrollment for the division.
4. Apply alignment options as shown.
5. Add the current date and your name in rows 8 and 9 respectively.
6. Format the values in the Target column to zero decimal places.
7. Save the workbook and name it **ExcelS1-C2**.
8. Print and then close **ExcelS1-C2.xlsx**.

FIGURE 1.5 Challenge 2

	A	B	C	D	E	F	G	H	I	J
1	Niagara Peninsula College									
2	Target Student Enrollments									
3	For the 2010/2011 Academic Year									
4	Theatre Arts Division									
5										
6	Academic chair: Cal Rubine									
7										
8	Report date: (current date)									
9	Prepared by: (student name)							Actual		
10					Program	Semester		Enrollment		
11	Program Name				Code	Offering		2009/2010		Target
12	Theatre Arts: Acting				TAA12	1 2 3 4		188		
13	Theatre Arts: Stage Management				TAM23	1 2		49		
14	Theatre Arts: Lighting & Effects				TAL42	1 2 3		65		
15	Theatre Arts: Production				TAP32	1 2 3 4		168		
16	Theatre Arts: Sound				TAS14	1 2		45		
17	Theatre Arts: Business Management				TAB25	1 2 3 4		74		
18										
19					ESTIMATED ENROLLMENTS FOR 2010/2011:					

TABLE 1.4 Challenge 2

Program Name	Target Percent
Theatre Arts: Acting	93%
Theatre Arts: Stage Management	104%
Theatre Arts: Lighting & Effects	110%
Theatre Arts: Production	87%
Theatre Arts: Sound	108%
Theatre Arts: Business Management	78%

Excel SECTION 2

Editing and Formatting Worksheets

Skills

- Edit the content of cells
- Clear cells and cell formats
- Use proofing tools
- Insert and delete columns and rows
- Move and copy cells
- Use Paste Options to link cells
- Create formulas using absolute references
- Adjust column width and row height
- Change the font, size, style, and color of cells
- Apply numeric formats and adjust the number of decimal places
- Use Undo, Redo, and Repeat
- Change cell alignment and indentation
- Add borders and shading
- Copy formats using Format Painter
- Apply cell styles
- Find and replace cell entries and formats
- Freeze and unfreeze panes
- Change the zoom percentage

Student Resources

Before beginning this section:

1. Copy to your storage medium the ExcelS2 subfolder from the Excel folder on the Student Resources CD.
2. Make ExcelS2 the active folder.

In addition to containing the data files needed to complete section work, the Student Resources CD contains model answers in PDF format for each of the projects in this section; model answers for end-of-section activities are not provided.

Projects Overview

The Waterfront B·I·S·T·R·O — Edit and format a quotation and invoice for catering services.

Performance Threads — Complete and format a costume cost report and an invoice for costume production.

Worldwide Enterprises — Edit and format a revenue summary report for movie distribution.

Marquee Productions — Create a direct wages budget for a remote film shoot.

Niagara Peninsula College — Create a room timetable.

Activity 2.1

Editing and Clearing Cells; Using Proofing Tools

The contents of a cell can be edited directly within the cell or in the Formula bar. Clearing a cell can involve removing the cell contents, format, or both. The Spelling feature is a useful tool to assist with correcting typing errors within a worksheet. After completing a spelling check, you will still need to proofread the worksheet since the spelling checker will not highlight all errors and cannot check the accuracy of values. Other Proofing tools available include a Research feature to search for external information, a Thesaurus to find a word with similar meaning, and a Translate tool to translate a selected word into a different language.

Project

Dana Hirsch, manager of The Waterfront Bistro, has begun a catering services quotation for Marquee Productions. Dana has asked you to finish the quotation by correcting spelling, following up on costs, and improving the appearance. You will be working on this quotation through most of this section.

1. Open **WBQuote-MarqueeProd.xlsx**. ***Note: This worksheet contains intentional spelling errors that will be corrected in this activity.***
2. Save the workbook with Save As in the ExcelS2 folder and name it **ExcelS2-01**.
3. Double-click I21.

   Double-clicking a cell inserts a blinking insertion point in the cell; *Edit* appears in the Status bar. The insertion point position varies depending on the location of the cell pointer when *Edit* mode is activated.
4. Press the Right or Left Arrow key as needed to move the insertion point between the decimal point and *4* and then press the Delete key.
5. Type **3** and then press Enter.
6. Make I27 the active cell.
7. Move the pointer after *1* in the Formula bar and then click the left mouse button.

   The cell pointer changes to an I-beam pointer when positioned in the Formula bar.
8. Press Backspace to delete *1*, type **4**, and then click the Enter button on the Formula bar.
9. Make A9 the active cell and then press Delete.

   Delete or Backspace clears only the contents of the cell; formats or comments applied to the cell remain in effect.
10. Select the range I17:I18. Click the Clear button in the Editing group in the Home tab and then click *Clear All* at the drop-down list.

    Clear All removes everything from a cell including formats or comments.
11. Press Ctrl + Home to make A1 the active cell.
12. Click the Review tab in the ribbon and then click the Spelling button.

    Spell check begins at the active cell. Words within the worksheet that are not found in the dictionary are highlighted as potential errors. Use buttons in the Spelling dialog box to skip the word (Ignore Once or Ignore All), replace the word with the highlighted word in the *Suggestions* list box (Change), or add the word to the dictionary (Add to Dictionary) if spelled correctly.

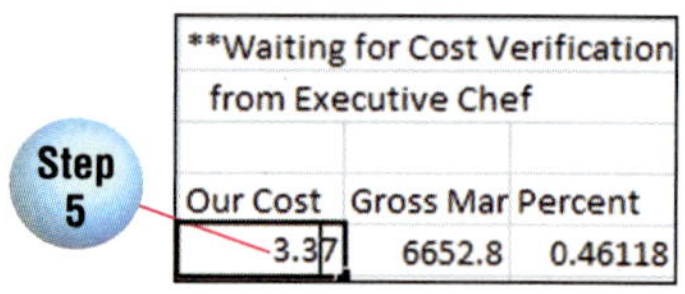

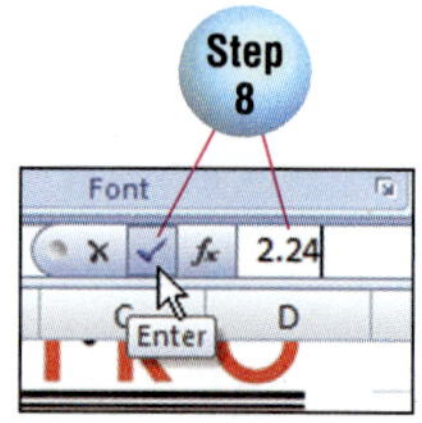

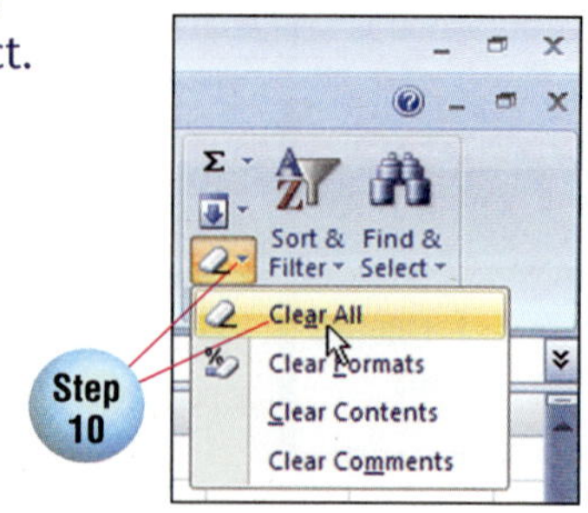

13 Click the Ignore All button in the Spelling dialog box to skip all occurrences of *Rivermist* in the worksheet since the street name is spelled correctly.

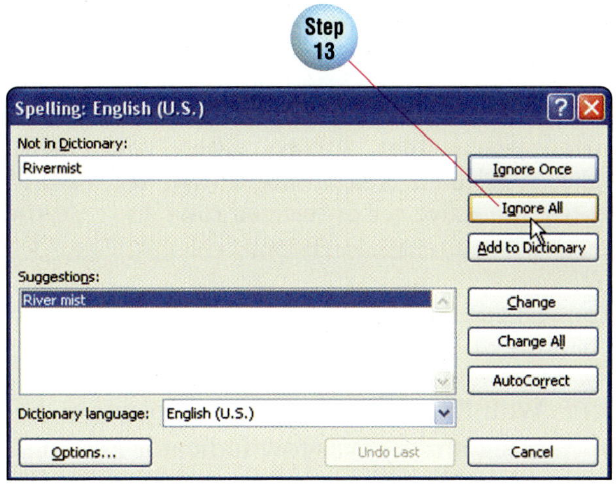

14 Click the Change button in the Spelling dialog box to replace *Torontow* with *Toronto*.

15 Click the Change button in the Spelling dialog box to replace *Persns* with *Persons*.

16 Complete the spell check, changing words as required. Click OK at the message that the spelling check is complete.

Double-click the correct spelling in the *Suggestions* list box if the correct word is not initially selected. Click in the *Not in Dictionary* text box if the correct spelling is not in the list, edit as required, and then click Change. You can drag the Spelling dialog box out of the way if you need to see the selected word within the worksheet.

17 Make A39 the active cell.

18 Click the Thesaurus button in the Proofing group in the Review tab.

Use the Thesaurus to replace a word in the worksheet with another word of similar meaning. Thesaurus is a feature within the Research task pane.

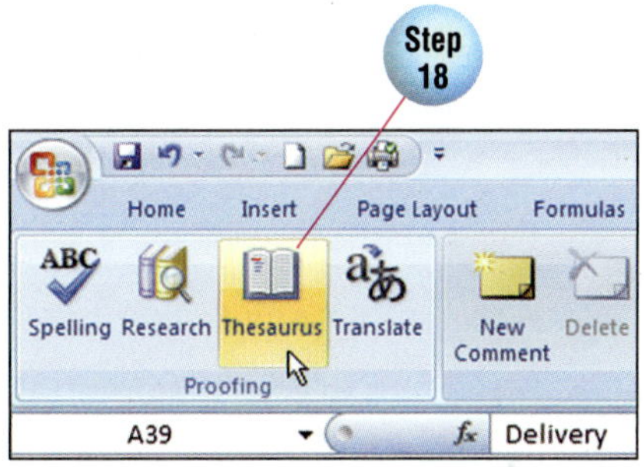

19 Point to the word *transport* in the task pane word list, click the down-pointing arrow that appears, and then click *Insert* at the drop-down list.

The word *Delivery* is replaced with *Transport* in A39.

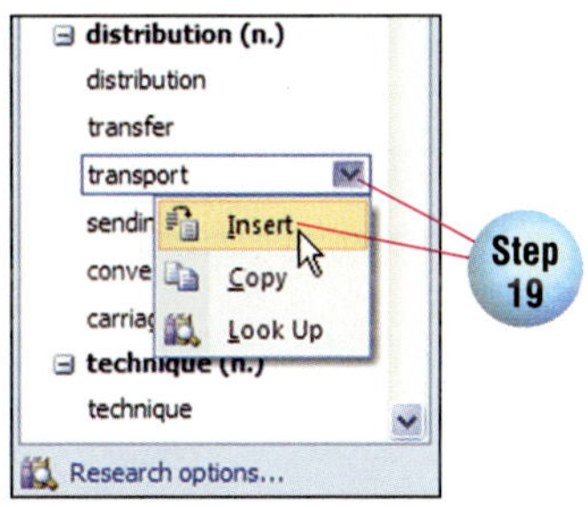

20 Click the Research button in the Proofing group to turn off the Research task pane.

21 Save **ExcelS2-01.xlsx**.

In Brief

Edit Cell
1. Double-click cell.
2. Insert and/or delete text.
3. Press Enter or click another cell.

Clear Cell
1. Click Clear button arrow in Home tab.
2. Click *Clear All*, *Clear Formats*, *Clear Contents*, or *Clear Comments*.

Spell Check
1. Click Review tab.
2. Click Spelling button.
3. Click Ignore Once, Ignore All, Change, or Add to Dictionary as required.

In Addition

Research Task Pane

You can use the Research task pane to search for information online without leaving the worksheet. For example, you can conduct an Internet search, look up information in online encyclopedias or business reference sites, or find a current stock quote using MSN Money Stock Quote. Choose the online source by clicking the down-pointing arrow at the right of the resources list box (located below the *Search for* text box).

Activity 2.2

Inserting and Deleting Columns and Rows

Insert rows or columns using options from the Insert button in the Home tab or from the context-sensitive shortcut menu that displays when you right-click a selected area. Inserted rows are placed above the active cell or selected rows and existing rows are shifted down. Columns are inserted left of the active cell or selected columns and existing columns are shifted right. When rows or columns are deleted, data automatically is shifted up or left to fill space and references in formulas are updated.

Project

You will add to and delete items from the quotation by inserting and deleting rows and columns.

1. With **Excel S2-01.xlsx** open, position the cell pointer (displays as a right-pointing black arrow) over row indicator *24*, hold down the left mouse button, and then drag the mouse down over *25*.

   This selects rows 24 and 25. Inserted rows are placed *above* the selected rows and columns are inserted to the *left*.

2. Click the Home tab, click the Insert button arrow (Insert) in the Cells group, and then click *Insert Sheet Rows* at the drop-down list.

   Two blank rows are inserted. All rows below the inserted rows are shifted down.

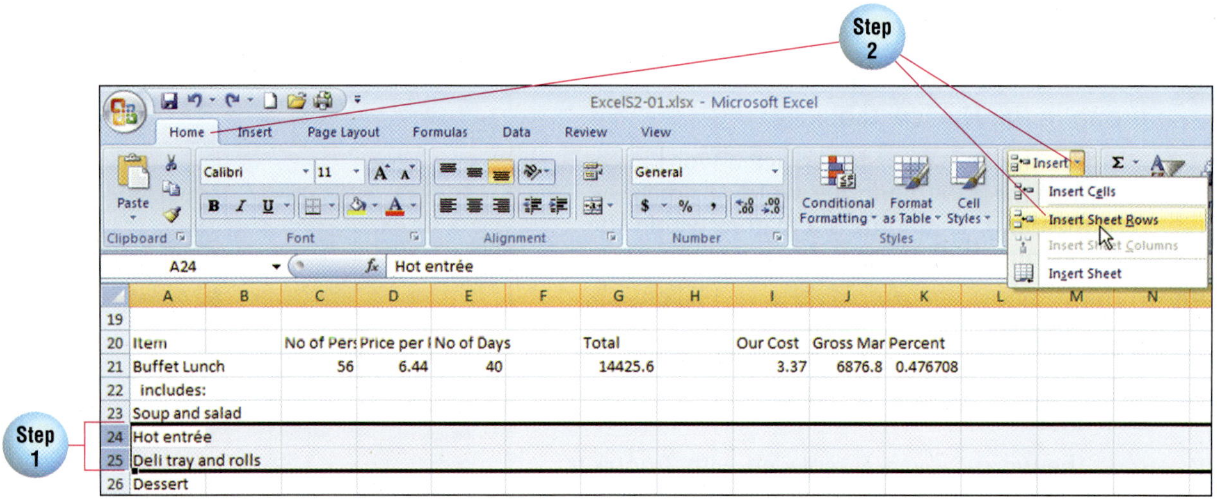

3. Click A24, type **Vegetable tray with dip**, and then press Enter.
4. Type **Seafood hors d'oeuvres** and then press Enter.
5. Select row 32.
6. Click the Delete button arrow in the Cells group and then click *Delete Sheet Rows* at the drop-down list.

   The data in row 32 is removed from the worksheet. All rows below the deleted row shift up to fill in the space.

7. Select row 22. Hold down the Ctrl key and then select rows 30 and 35.

   Hold down the Ctrl key to select multiple rows or columns that are not adjacent.

8. Position the pointer within any of the three selected rows, right-click to display the shortcut menu and Mini toolbar, and then click *Delete*.

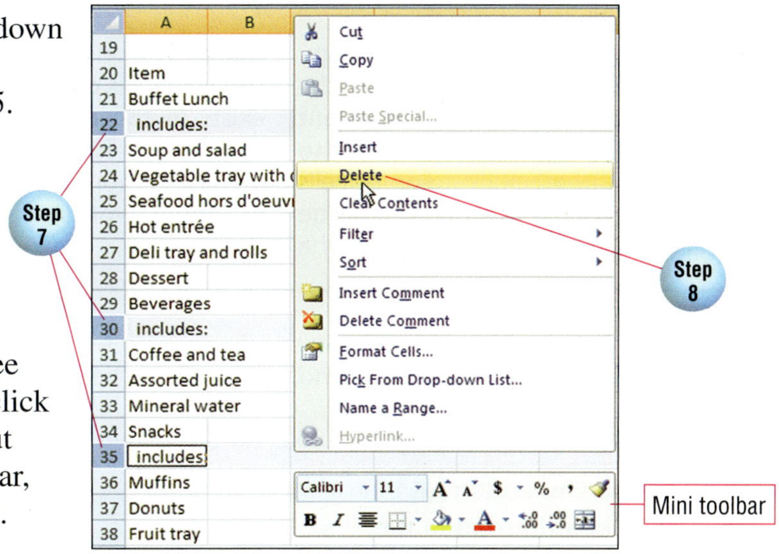

9. Select column F and display the shortcut menu and Mini toolbar by positioning the cell pointer over column indicator letter *F* (displays as a down-pointing black arrow) and right-clicking the mouse.

10. At the shortcut menu, click *Delete*.

    Data in columns to the right of the deleted column are shifted left to fill in the space.

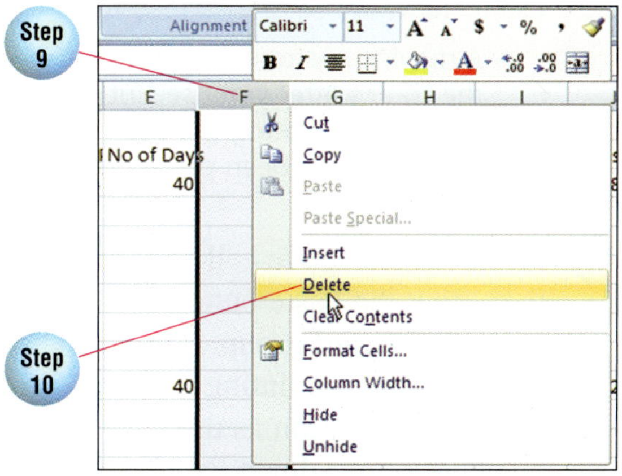

11. Click in any cell to deselect the column.

12. Make F11 the active cell, type **November 5, 2009**, and then press Enter.

    By default, Excel displays dates in the format *dd-mmm-yy* (5-Nov-09).

13. Save **Excel S2-01.xlsx**.

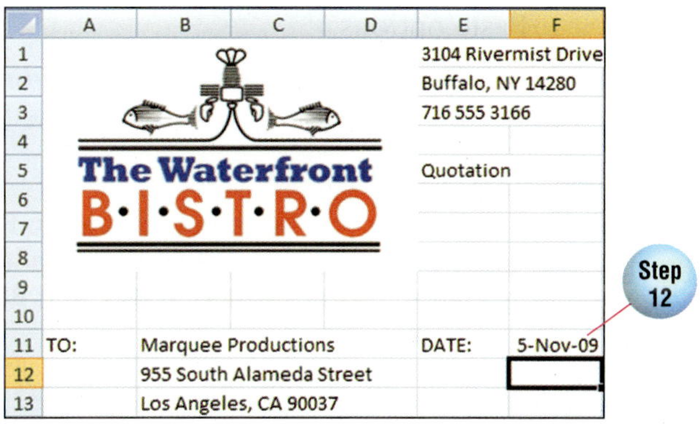

In Brief

Insert Rows or Columns

1. Select required number of rows or columns.
2. Click Insert button arrow.
3. Click *Insert Sheet Rows* or *Insert Sheet Columns*.

Delete Rows or Columns

1. Select rows or columns to be deleted.
2. Click Delete button arrow.
3. Click *Delete Sheet Rows* or *Delete Sheet Columns*.

In Addition

Inserting and Deleting Cells

In this activity, you selected entire rows and columns before inserting or deleting. This practice is the more common method when you need to add or delete data to a worksheet. Another method used less frequently is to insert new blank cells or delete a range of cells within the worksheet area. To insert new blank cells, select the range of cells you need to add and then click the Insert button in the Cells group, or click the Insert button arrow and then click *Insert Cells* at the drop-down list to display the dialog box shown at the right. Using the dialog box you can choose to shift existing cells right or down. Click the Delete button in the Cells group to delete a selected range of cells and shift up the cells below the deleted range. Click the Delete button arrow and then click *Delete Cells* to open the Delete dialog box with similar options as Insert.

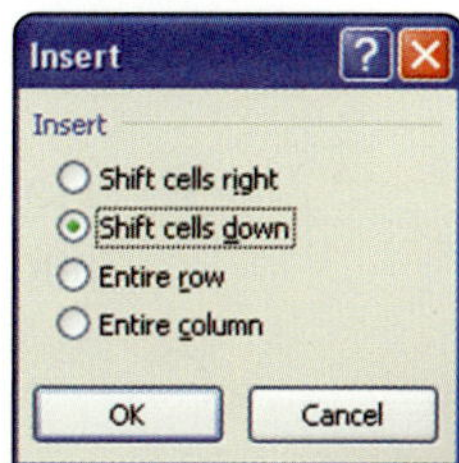

Activity 2.3

Moving and Copying Cells

You learned how to use copy and paste to copy formulas in the payroll worksheet for The Waterfront Bistro. You can also use cut and paste to move the contents of a cell or range of cells to another location in the worksheet. The selected cells being cut or copied are called the ***source***. The cell or range of cells that is receiving the source data is called the ***destination***. If data already exists in the destination cells, Excel replaces the contents. Cells cut or copied to the Clipboard can be pasted more than once in the active workbook, in another workbook, or in another Office application.

Project

Continue to work on the catering quotation by moving text in the quotation, duplicating a price, linking cells containing prices, and by copying a food item description.

1. With **ExcelS2-01.xlsx** open, make E5 the active cell.

2. Click the Cut button in the Clipboard group in the Home tab.

   A moving marquee surrounds the source after you use Cut or Copy, indicating the cell contents have been placed in the Clipboard.

3. Make A9 the active cell and then click the Paste button in the Clipboard group. (Do not click the down-pointing arrow on the Paste button as this displays a drop-down list of Paste options.)

   The text *Quotation* is removed from E5 and placed in A9. In the next step, you will move a range of cells using a method called ***drag and drop***.

4. Select the range A17:B18.

   You are only selecting to column B since the entries *Toronto Location Filming* and *July 5 to August 27* are stored in B17 and B18, respectively.

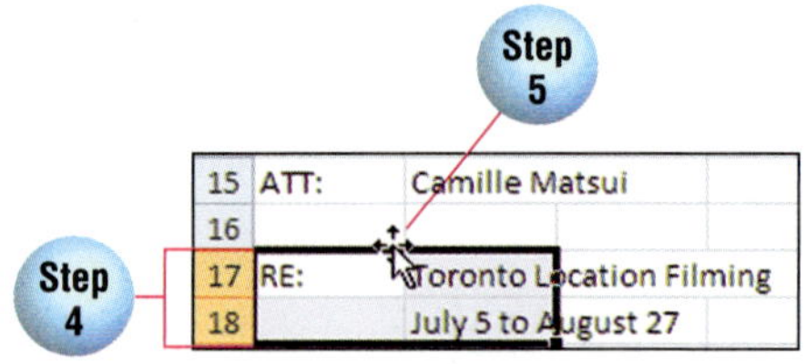

5. Point at any one of the four borders surrounding the selected range.

   When you point at a border, the pointer changes from the thick white cross to a white arrow with the move icon attached to it (four-headed arrow).

6. Hold down the left mouse button, drag the top left corner of the range to E15, and then release the mouse.

   A gray border will appear as you drag, indicating the placement of the range when you release the mouse. The destination range displays in a ScreenTip below the gray border.

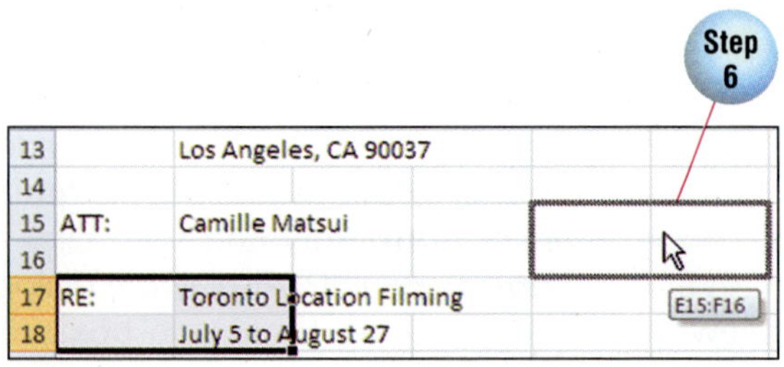

7. Make D28 the active cell.
8. Click the Copy button in the Clipboard group.
9. Make D32 the active cell, click the Paste button arrow in the Clipboard group, and then click *Paste Link* at the drop-down list.

   The existing data in D32 is replaced with the value copied from D28 and the source and destination cells are now linked. Linking the source and destination cells means that any change made to one cell will automatically be applied to the other cell.

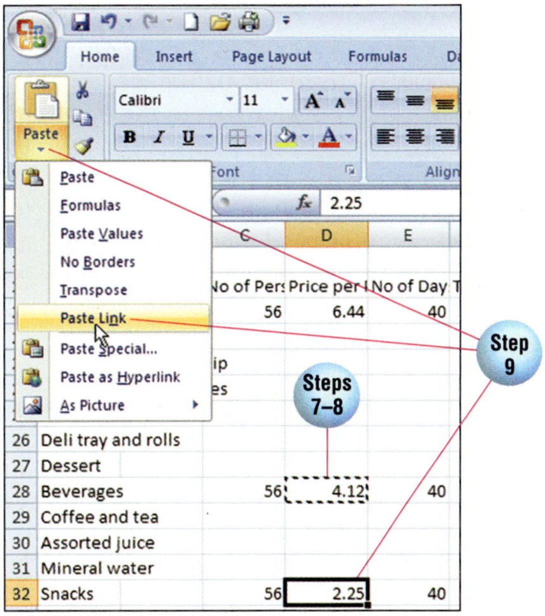

10. Press Esc to remove the moving marquee from D28.
11. Make D28 the active cell and edit the value to *4.09*.

   Notice the value in D32 is also changed to 4.09 automatically.

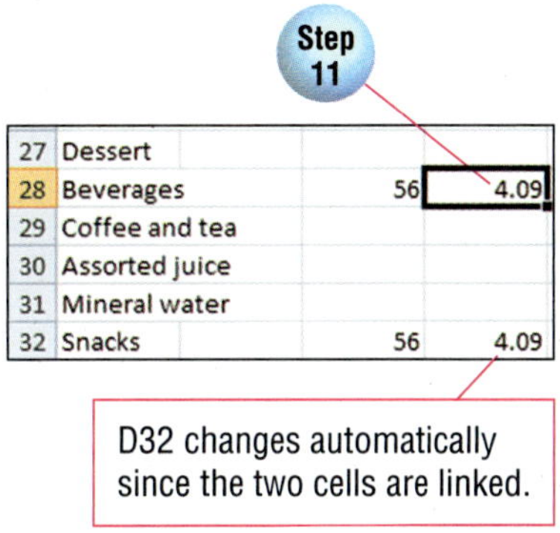

12. Make A23 the active cell. Point at any one of the four borders surrounding A23 until the pointer displays as a white arrow with the move icon attached to it, hold down the Ctrl key, and then drag the mouse to A36.

13. Release the mouse button first and then release the Ctrl key.

   A plus sign attached to the pointer indicates the source contents are being *copied* when you drag and drop using the Ctrl key.

14. Save **Excel S2-01.xlsx**.

In Brief

Move or Copy Cells
1. Select source cells.
2. Click Cut or Copy button.
3. Select starting destination cell.
4. Click Paste button.

Copy and Link Cells
1. Select source cells.
2. Click Copy button.
3. Select destination cell.
4. Click Paste button arrow.
5. Click *Paste Link*.

In Addition

Paste Options

The Paste button arrow contains several options for controlling how cut or copied text is pasted into the destination. The list shown at the right includes options to paste *Formulas*, *Paste Values* (instead of source formulas), *No Borders* (borders in source cell are not duplicated), and *Transpose* (rows are converted to columns and vice versa). Click *Paste Special* to open the Paste Special dialog box with more paste options. The bottom of the Paste drop-down list contains hyperlink and picture options.

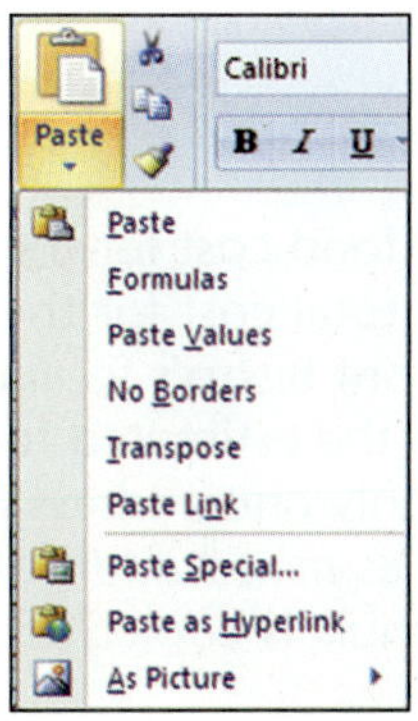

Activity 2.4

Creating Formulas with Absolute Addressing

In Section 1, when you copied and pasted formulas in the payroll worksheet, the cell addresses in the destination cells changed automatically *relative* to the destination row or column. The formulas in the payroll worksheet used ***relative addressing***. Sometimes you need a cell address to remain fixed when it is copied to another location in the worksheet. To do this, the formulas must include ***absolute addressing*** for those cell addresses that you do not want changed. Make a cell address absolute by typing a dollar symbol ($) in front of the column letter or row number that cannot be changed. You can also use the function key F4 to toggle through variations of the address as relative, absolute, or mixed in which either the row is absolute and the column is relative or vice versa.

Project

Dana has provided you with estimated cost percentages for food, food preparation, and servers for the Marquee quotation. You will use these values to create formulas to calculate the extended cost at the right side of the quotation. These values are estimates and are likely to change as you move closer to the actual catering date.

The Waterfront B·I·S·T·R·O

1. With **ExcelS2-01.xlsx** open, make K20 the active cell and then type **Food**.
2. Make L20 the active cell and then type **Prep**.
3. Make M20 the active cell and then type **Server**.
4. Type the decimal values in K19, L19, and M19 as shown below.

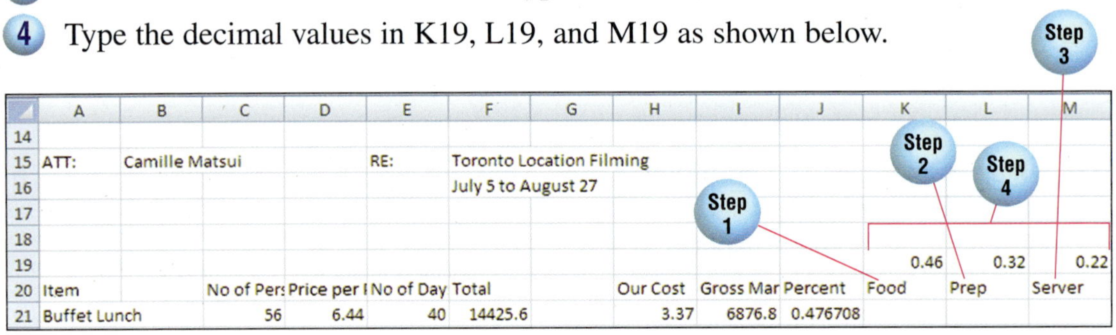

5. Make K21 the active cell, type **=(c21*e21*h21)*k19**, and then press function key F4.

   Pressing F4 causes Excel to insert dollar symbols in front of the row and column number immediately left of the insertion point—*k19* becomes $K$19, an absolute address.

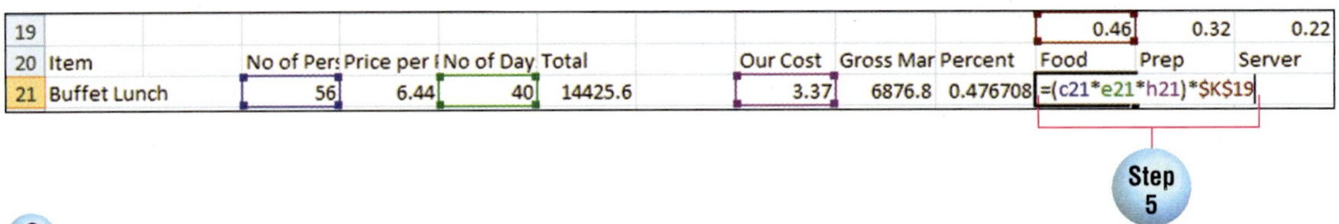

6. Press Enter.

   The extended food cost for the buffet lunch is *3472.448*. The formula first calculates the total cost for the buffet lunch (56 people × 40 days × 3.37, which is The Waterfront Bistro's total cost). Next, the formula multiplies the result times 0.46, which is the estimated food cost portion of the total cost. Notice in the formula that only one address has been made absolute. This is an example of a formula that has ***mixed addressing*** with some addresses relative and some absolute. When the formula is copied later in this activity, only K19 will remain the same.

7 Make L21 the active cell, type the formula **=(c21*e21*h21)*l19**, and then press Enter.

You can also type the dollar symbols into the formula rather than use F4.

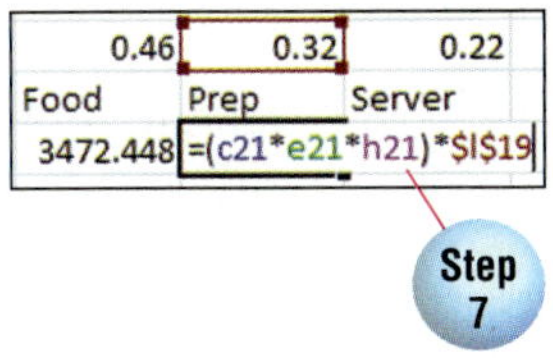

8 Make M21 the active cell and then enter the formula **=(c21*e21*h21)*m19** by either typing the dollar symbols or by pressing F4.

In the next steps, you will copy and paste the three cost formulas to rows 28 and 32.

9 Select the range K21:M21 and then click the Copy button in the Clipboard group in the Home tab.

10 Select the range K28:M28, hold down the Ctrl key, and then select the range K32:M32.

11 Click the Paste button in the Clipboard group. (Do not click the down-pointing arrow on the Paste button.)

12 Press the Esc key to remove the moving marquee from the selected range.

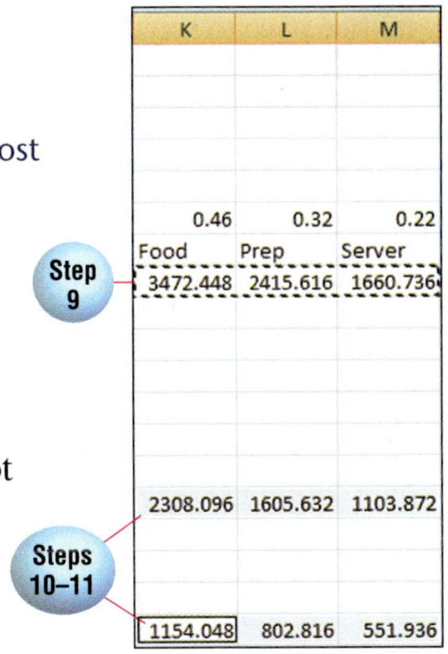

13 Click K28 and then look at the Formula bar to see the formula that was pasted into the cell: *=(C28*E28*H28)*$K$19*.

Notice in the formula that the address of the cells in parentheses changed relative to the destination (row 28), while the address for the food cost percent, K19, remained the same.

14 Click L32 and then look at the Formula bar to see the formula that was pasted into the cell. Notice in this column, the address for the Prep cost, L19, remained absolute as $L$19.

15 Enter a Sum function to calculate the totals in K39, L39, and M39.

16 Save **ExcelS2-01.xlsx**.

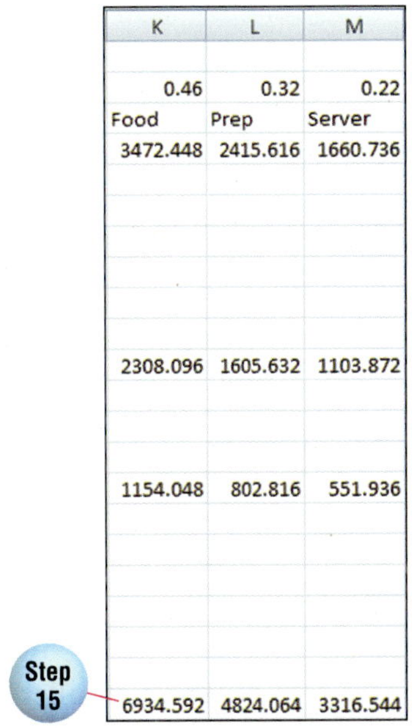

In Brief

Make Cell Address Absolute

With insertion point positioned just after cell address or with cell address selected in Formula bar, press F4.

OR

Type dollar symbols immediately preceding column letter and/or row number.

In Addition

More about Mixed Addressing

Excel can be instructed to fix only the row number or the column letter of a cell that is copied and pasted to another location. Following are more ways that a cell address can use absolute referencing. Pressing F4 repeatedly causes Excel to scroll through each of these variations for the selected cell address.

Example	Action
=$A$12*.01	Neither the column nor the row will change.
=$A12*.01	The column will remain fixed at column A, but the row will change.
=A$12*.01	The column will change, but the row remains fixed at row 12.
=A12*.01	Both the column and row will change.

Activity 2.5

Adjusting Column Width and Row Height

By default, columns are all the same width and rows are all the same height with columns set by default to a width of 8.43 characters (64 pixels) and rows to a height of 15 points (110 pixels). In some cases you do not have to increase the width when the text is too wide for the column, since labels "spill over" into the next cell if it is empty. Some column headings in the quotation are truncated because an entry exists in the column immediately to the right. Excel automatically adjusts the height of rows to accommodate the size of the text within the cells. Manually increasing the row height adds more space between rows, which can be used to improve readability or as a design technique to draw attention to a series of cells.

Project

You will adjust the column widths for columns in which labels are truncated to make sure each entry is entirely visible to readers and increase the height of the row containing the column headings to make them stand out from the text below.

The Waterfront B·I·S·T·R·O

1. With **ExcelS2-01.xlsx** open, make any cell in column C the active cell.
2. Click the Format button in the Cells group in the Home tab and then click *Column Width* at the drop-down list.

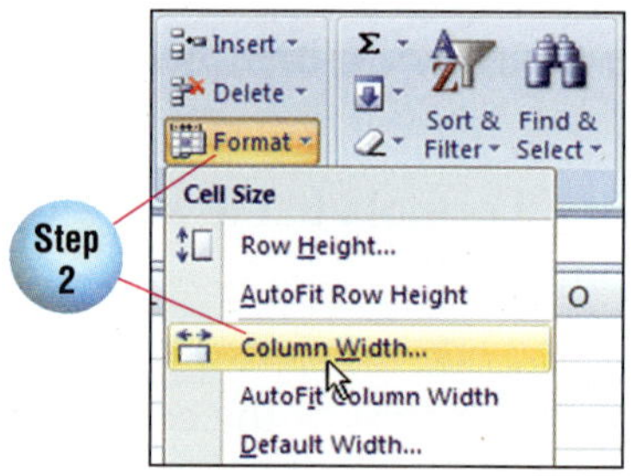

3. At the Column Width dialog box, type **14** and then click OK or press Enter.

   In the next step, you will adjust the width of column D using the mouse.

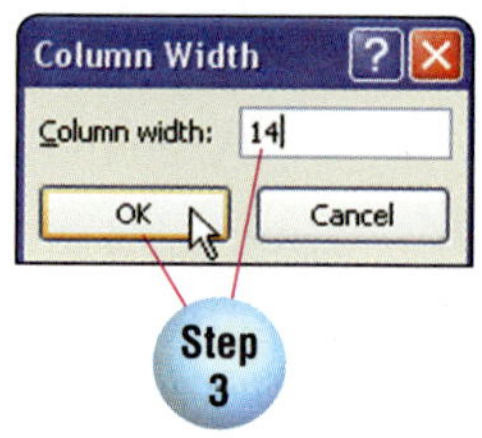

4. Position the mouse pointer on the boundary line in the column indicator row between columns D and E until the pointer changes to a vertical line with a left- and right-pointing arrow ↔.
5. Hold down the left mouse button, drag the boundary line to the right until *Width: 15.00 (110 pixels)* displays in the ScreenTip, and then release the mouse button.

   As you drag the boundary line to the right or left, a dotted line appears in the column in the worksheet area indicating the new width.

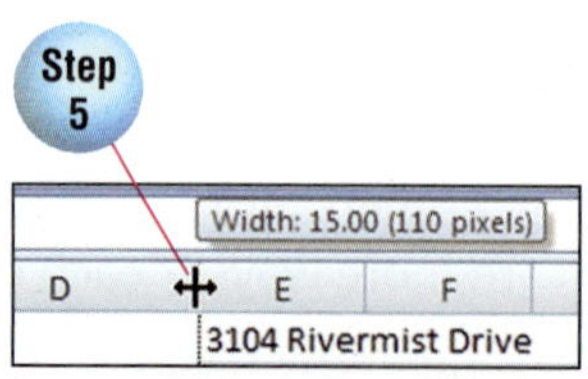

6. Position the mouse pointer on the boundary line in the column indicator row between columns E and F until the pointer changes to a vertical line with a left- and right-pointing arrow and then double-click the left mouse button.

   Double-clicking the boundary line sets the width to fit the length of the longest entry within the column, referred to as ***AutoFit***.

7. Increase the width of column B to *12 (89 pixels)* using either the Column Width dialog box or by dragging the column boundary.

   After reviewing the worksheet, you decide all of the columns with numeric values should be the same width. In the next steps, you will learn how to set the width of multiple columns in one operation.

8. Position the mouse pointer on column indicator letter *C*, hold down the left mouse button, and then drag the mouse right to column M.

   This selects columns C through M.

9. Position the mouse pointer on *any* of the right boundary lines to the right of column E within the selected range of columns until the pointer changes to a vertical line with a left- and right-pointing arrow.

   Any changes made to the width of one column boundary will affect all of the selected columns.

10. Drag the boundary line right until *Width: 15.00 (110 pixels)* displays in the ScreenTip and then release the mouse button.

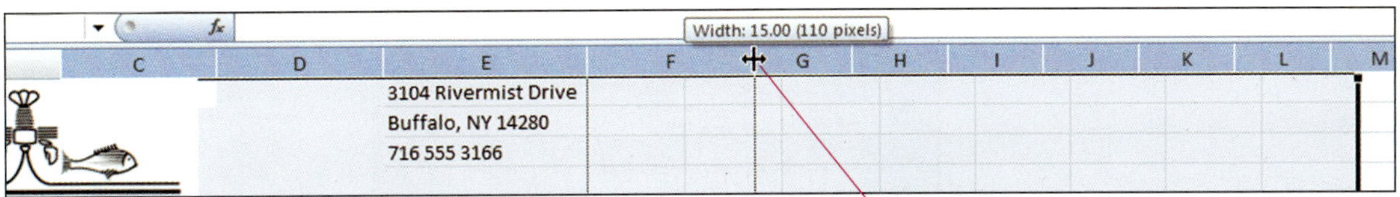

Step 10

11. Click in any cell to deselect the columns.

    Do not be concerned that the columns are now too wide after this step—you have many formatting tasks to complete that will improve the layout as you work through the next four activities.

12. Move E15:F16 to A17:B18 and then click in any cell to deselect the range. Refer to Activity 2.3 if you need assistance with this step.

    In the next steps, you will adjust row height using the mouse.

13. Position the mouse pointer on the boundary line below row 20 until the pointer changes to a horizontal line with an up- and down-pointing arrow.

14. Drag the boundary line down until *Height: 19.50 (26 pixels)* displays in the ScreenTip and then release the mouse button.

Step 14

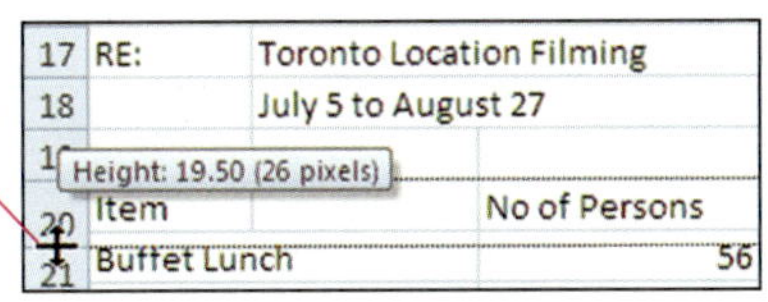

15. Save **ExcelS2-01.xlsx**.

In Brief

Increase or Decrease Column Width
1. Select column(s).
2. Click Format button in Cells group.
3. Click *Width*.
4. Type desired width.
5. Click OK.

Increase or Decrease Row Height
1. Select row(s).
2. Click Format button in Cells group.
3. Click *Height*.
4. Type desired height.
5. Click OK.

Adjust Width or Height Using Mouse
Drag boundary to right of column or below row, or double-click boundary to AutoFit.

In Addition

Row Height Dialog Box

A sequence of steps similar to the one used for adjusting column width using the Column Width dialog box can be used to increase or decrease the height of a row with the Row Height dialog box, shown at the right. Click any cell within the row, click the Format button in the Cells group in the Home tab, and then click *Row Height* at the drop-down list. Type the desired height and press Enter or click OK.

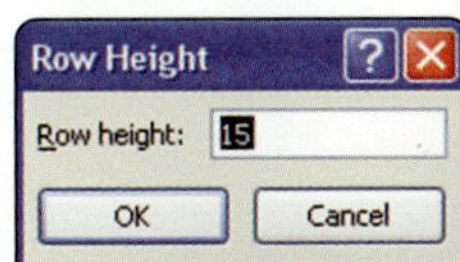

Activity 2.6

Changing the Font, Size, Style, and Color of Cells

The *font* is the typeface used to display and print data. The default font in Excel is Calibri, but several other fonts are available. The size of the font is measured in units called ***points***. A point is approximately 1/72 of an inch measured vertically. The default font size used by Excel is 11-point. The larger the point size, the larger the type. Each font's style can be enhanced to **bold**, *italic*, or ***bold italic***. Cell entries display in black with a white background. Changing the color of the font and/or the color of the background (called ***fill***) adds interest or emphasis to the text.

Project

To add to the visual appeal of the quotation, you will change the font and font size and apply attributes such as font and fill color to the title *Quotation*.

1. With **Excel S2-01.xlsx** open, make A9 the active cell.
2. Click the Font button arrow in the Font group in the Home tab, scroll down the list of fonts, and then point to *Impact* at the drop-down gallery. Notice that Excel applies the font you are pointing at to the active cell so that you can preview the result. This feature is called ***Live Preview***. Click *Impact* at the drop-down gallery.

Live Preview shows you how the cell will look before you choose the font so you can try different font options before making your selection.

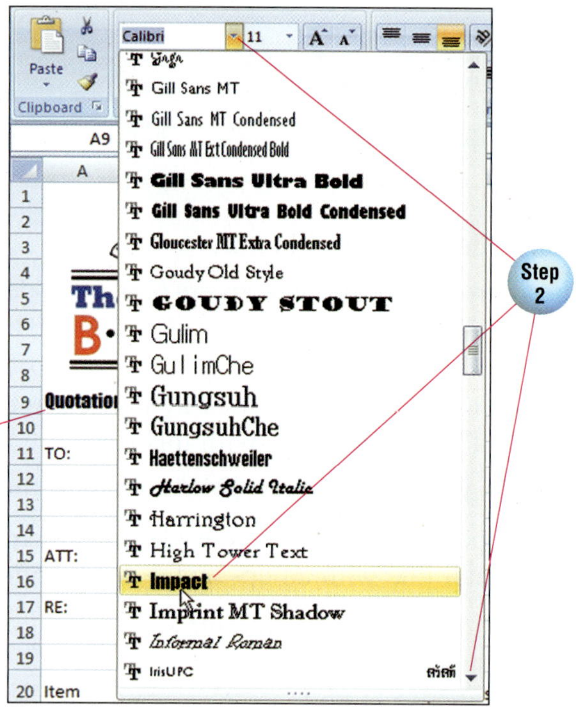

3. Click the Font Size button arrow in the Font group and then click *18* at the drop-down list.

   The row height is automatically increased to accommodate the larger type size.

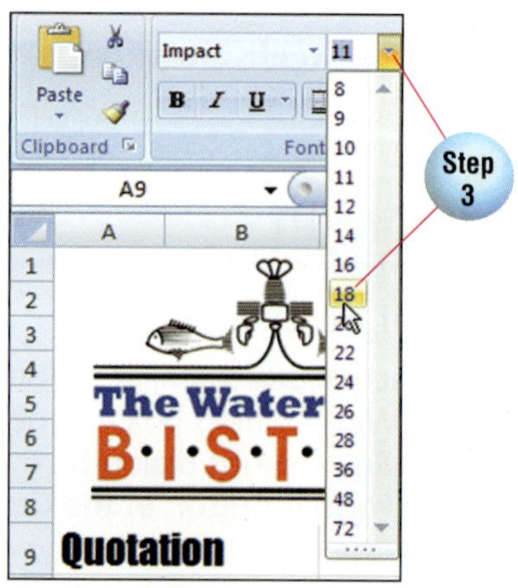

4. With A9 still the active cell, click the Font Color button arrow in the Font group and then click the Blue color box (third from right) in the *Standard Colors* section of the color gallery.

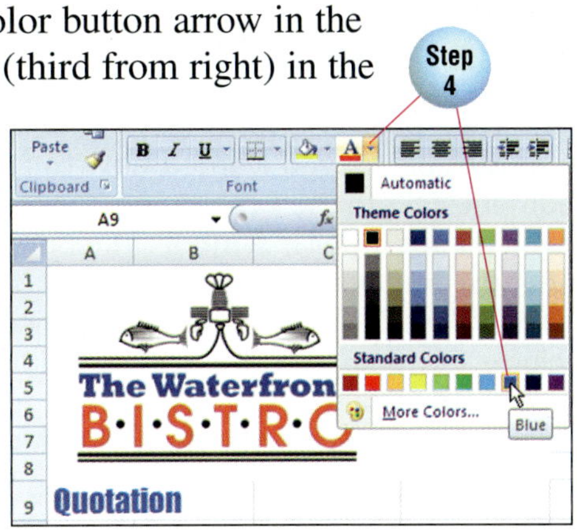

5. Select A9:F9 and then click the Merge & Center button in the Alignment group.

   The cells in the range A9:F9 have now been merged into one large cell that spans across the six columns. The text within A9, *Quotation*, is now centered within this large cell. As you learned in Section 1, Merge & Center centers titles over multiple columns.

6. With merged cell A9 still selected, click the Fill Color button arrow in the Font group and then click the *Aqua, Accent 5, Lighter 80%* color box (second from right in second row) in the *Theme Colors* section of the color gallery.

   Fill is the color of the background in the cell. Changing the fill color is sometimes referred to as ***shading*** a cell.

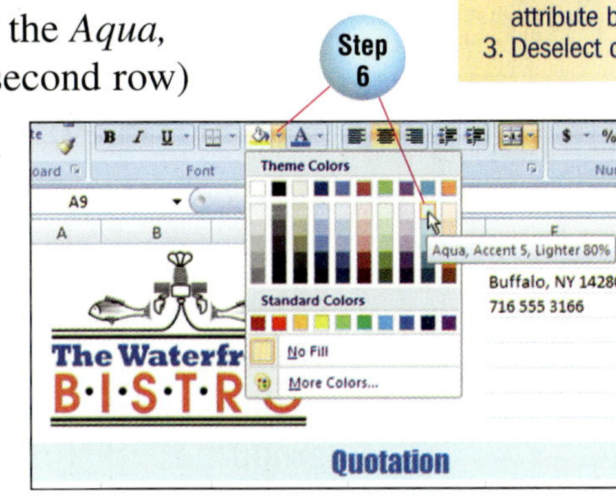

7. Make A39 the active cell.
8. Hold down the Ctrl key and then click F39.

   You can select multiple cells and/or ranges and apply font changes or attributes to the group in one step.

9. Click the Bold button **B** and the Italic button *I* in the Font group.

   You can also apply multiple format operations since the cells stay selected after you apply a format command.

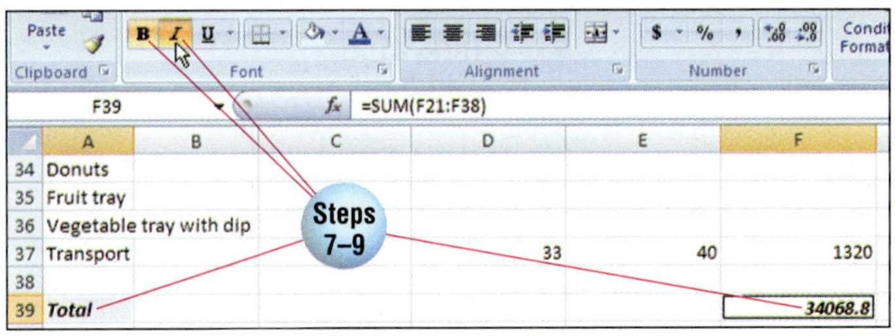

10. Click in any cell to deselect A39 and F39.
11. Save **ExcelS2-01.xlsx**.

In Brief

Change Font
1. Select cells.
2. Click Font button arrow.
3. Click desired font.
4. Deselect cells.

Change Font Size
1. Select cells.
2. Click Font Size button arrow.
3. Click desired size.
4. Deselect cells.

Change Font Attributes
1. Select cells.
2. Click desired attribute button.
3. Deselect cells.

In Addition

Format Cells Dialog Box

You can use the Format Cells dialog box with the Font tab selected (shown at the right) to change the font, font size, font style, and color of text. Additional Underline style options such as *Single, Double, Single Accounting*, and *Double Accounting* are available, as well as special effects options *Strikethrough, Superscript*, and *Subscript*. Select the cells you want to change and then click the Font group dialog box launcher button to open the Format Cells dialog box with the Font tab active.

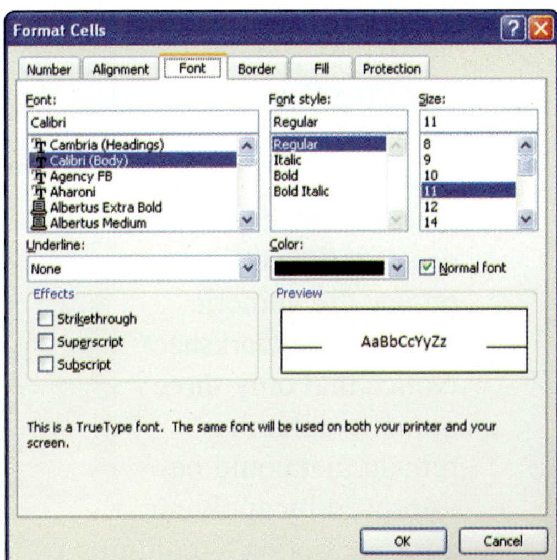

Activity 2.7

Formatting Numeric Cells; Adjusting Decimal Places; Using Undo and Redo

In the payroll worksheet for The Waterfront Bistro, you learned how to format numeric cells to the Accounting Number Format which adds a dollar symbol ($), comma in the thousands, and two decimal places and displays negative values in brackets. Other numeric formats include Comma, Percent, and Currency. By default, cells are initially set to the General format which has no specific numeric style. The number of decimal places in a selected range of cells can be increased or decreased using the Increase Decimal and Decrease Decimal buttons in the Number group of the Home tab.

Use the Undo button on the Quick Access toolbar to reverse the last action. Excel stores up to 100 actions that can be undone or redone and you can repeat actions as many times as you need. Some actions (such as Save) cannot be reversed with Undo.

Project

To display a consistent number of characters for the numeric values, you will apply the Accounting Number, Comma, and Percent formats to selected ranges within the quotation.

The Waterfront BISTRO

1. With **ExcelS2-01.xlsx** open, make F21 the active cell.
2. Hold down the Ctrl key and click I21, K21:M21, F39, I39, and K39:M39.

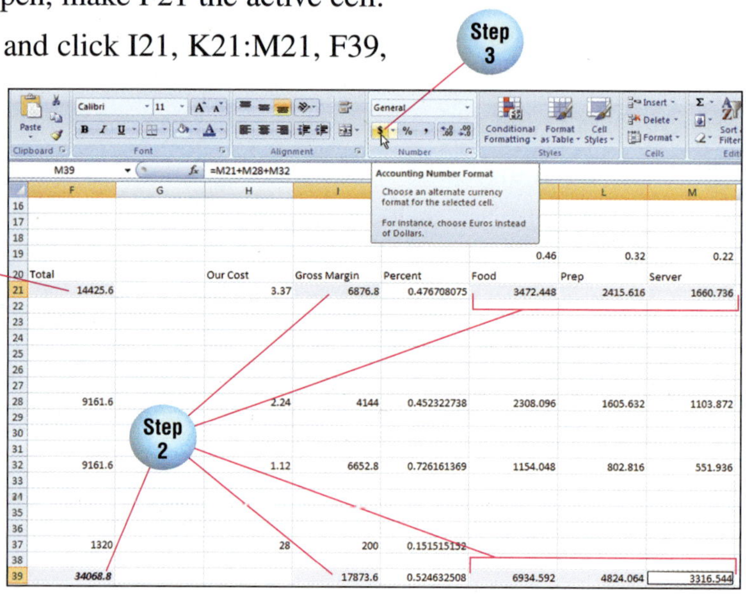

3. Click the Accounting Number Format button in the Number group in the Home tab.
4. Click in any cell to deselect the cells.
5. Select F28:F37, I28:I37, and K28:M32.
6. Click the Comma Style button in the Number group.

Comma Style formats cells the same as the Accounting Number format with the exception of the dollar or alternative currency symbol.

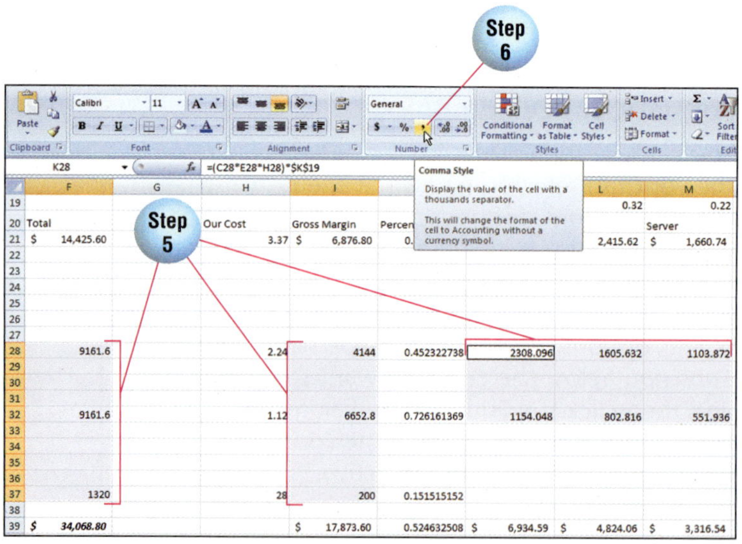

7. Click in any cell to deselect the cells and review the numeric values in the worksheet. Notice that only three numeric columns remain that could be improved by applying a format option—columns D, H, and J.

8 Select J21:J39.

9 Click the Percent Style button in the Number group.

Percent Style causes Excel to multiply cell values by 100 and add a percent symbol (%) to the end of each result in the selected range.

10 With the range J21:J39 still selected, click the Increase Decimal button twice in the Number group.

One decimal place is added to or removed from the cells in the selected range each time you click Increase Decimal or Decrease Decimal.

11 With the range J21:J39 still selected, click the Decrease Decimal button once in the Number group.

12 Click in any cell to deselect the range.

13 Select D37 and H37 and then click the Increase Decimal button in the Number group twice to display two decimal places.

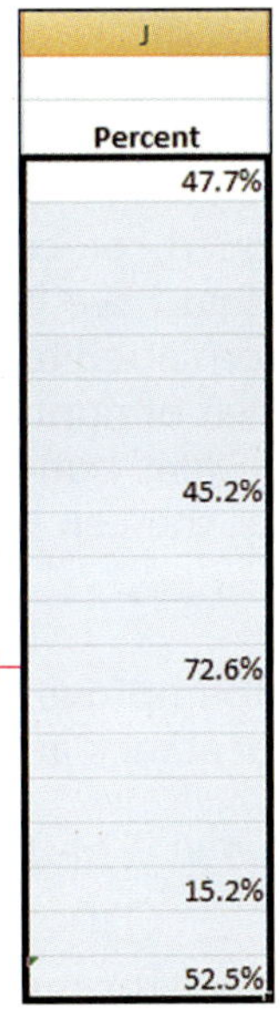

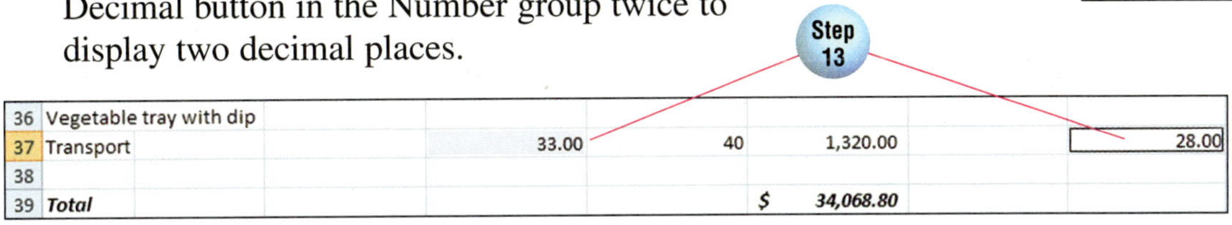

In Brief

Change Numeric Format
1. Select cells.
2. Click desired format style button in Number group.
3. Deselect cells.

Undo Action
Click Undo button on Quick Access toolbar or press Ctrl + Z.

Redo Action
Click Redo button on Quick Access toolbar or press Ctrl + Y.

14 Deselect the cells.

15 Click the Undo button on the Quick Access toolbar.

Excel removes one decimal place.

16 Click the Undo button a second time.

Both decimal places are removed. With the Undo button arrow, you can display a drop-down list of actions from which you can undo multiple actions in one step.

17 Click the Redo button on the Quick Access toolbar two times.

18 Save **ExcelS2-01.xlsx**.

In Addition

Additional Number Format Options

Click the Number Format button arrow in the Number group to display a drop-down list (shown at the right) with additional numeric format options including date, time, fraction, and scientific options. Click *More Number Formats* at the bottom of the list to open the Format Cells dialog box with the Number tab selected. Using this dialog box, you can access further customization options for a format, such as display negative values in red, or create your own custom format code.

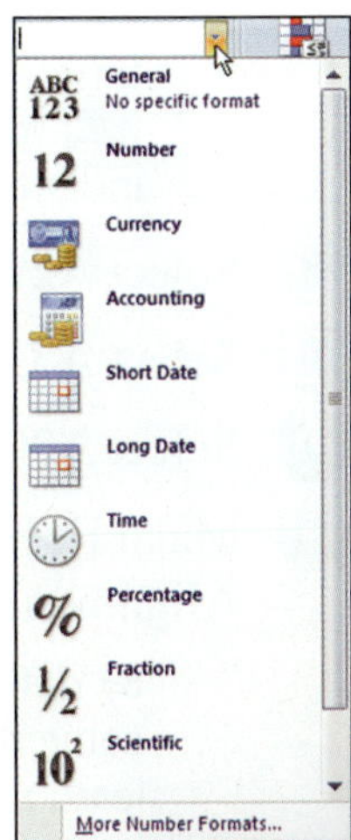

Activity 2.8

Changing the Alignment and Indentation of Cells; Using Repeat

Data in a cell can be left-aligned, right-aligned, or centered within the column. Cells that have had Merge & Center applied can be formatted to align the text in the merged cell at the left or right. Use the Increase Indent and Decrease Indent buttons to indent text from the left edge of the cell approximately one character width each time the button is clicked. Using buttons along the top row in the Alignment group in the Home tab you can change vertical alignment, rotate text, or wrap text. Use the Repeat keyboard shortcut Ctrl + Y to replicate the last action on another cell. This is useful if you need to perform the same action several times in a row.

Project

To improve the appearance of the quotation, you will change the alignment of column headings and values and indent labels from the left edge of column A.

1. With **ExcelS2-01.xlsx** open, edit the column headings in C20 and E20 to include a period (.) after the abbreviation for number. For example, the edited column heading in C20 will be *No. of Persons*.

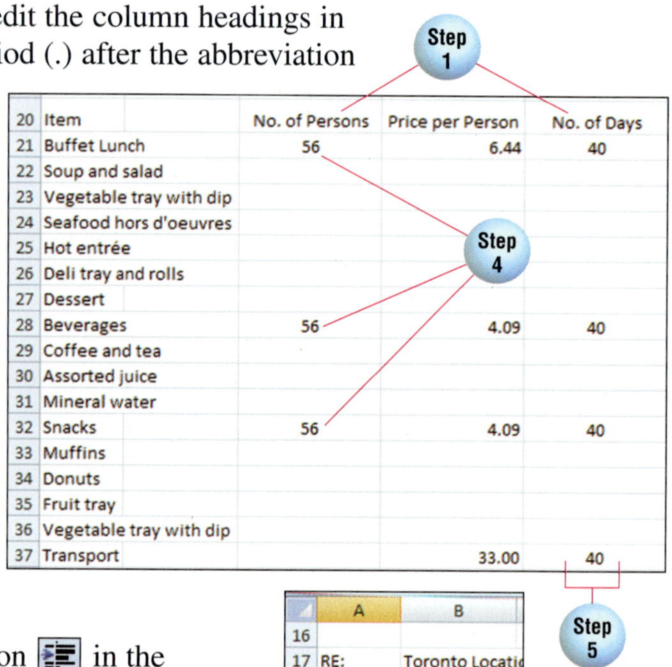

2. Select C20:M20.
3. Click the Center button in the Alignment group in the Home tab.
4. Select C21, C28, and C32 and then change the alignment to center.
5. Center the entries in column E.
6. Select A22:A27.
7. Click the Increase Indent button in the Alignment group.

   Each time you click Increase Indent, the contents of the selected cells are indented by approximately one character width. If you click Increase Indent one too many times, click the Decrease Indent button to return the text to the previous indent position.

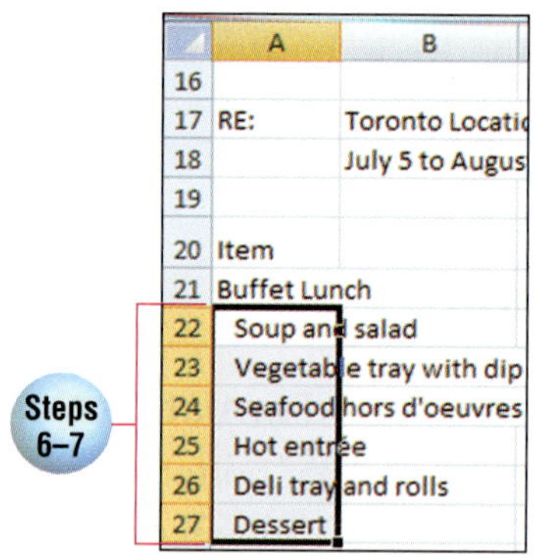

8. Select A29:A31 and then click the Increase Indent button.
9. Select A33:A36 and then click the Increase Indent button.
10. Select A20:M20 and then bold the cells.
11. Make F11 the active cell and then click the Align Text Left button in the Alignment group.

    By default, Excel aligns date entries at the right edge of a column since dates are converted to a serial number and treated in a similar manner to values. You will learn more about using dates in Excel in Section 3.

In Brief

Change Horizontal or Vertical Alignment
1. Select cells.
2. Click desired alignment button.
3. Deselect cells.

Indent Text within Cells
1. Select cells.
2. Click Increase Indent button.
3. Deselect cells.

Repeat Command
Press Ctrl + Y.

12 Select A20:M20.

In Activity 2.5, you increased the height of row 20 to 19.50. The Alignment group contains buttons that also allow you to control the alignment of the text between the top and bottom of the cell boundaries. In the next step, you will center the text vertically within the cells.

13 Click the Middle Align button in the Alignment group.

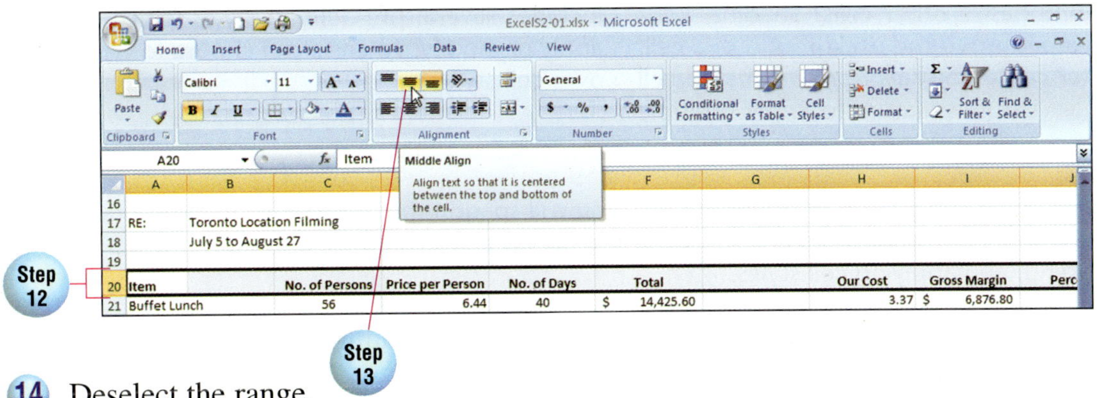

14 Deselect the range.

15 Select E1:F1 and then click Merge & Center in the Alignment group.

16 Select E2:F2 and then press Ctrl + Y (the Repeat command).

You can add a Repeat button to the Quick Access toolbar. To do this, click the Customize Quick Access Toolbar button that displays at the right side of the toolbar and then click *More Commands* at the drop-down list. At the Excel Options dialog box, click Repeat in the list box, click the Add button, and then click OK.

17 Select E3:F3 and then press Ctrl + Y.

You can merge and center in only one row at a time in this situation because data already exists in all three rows.

18 Select E1:E3 and then click the Align Text Right button in the Alignment group.

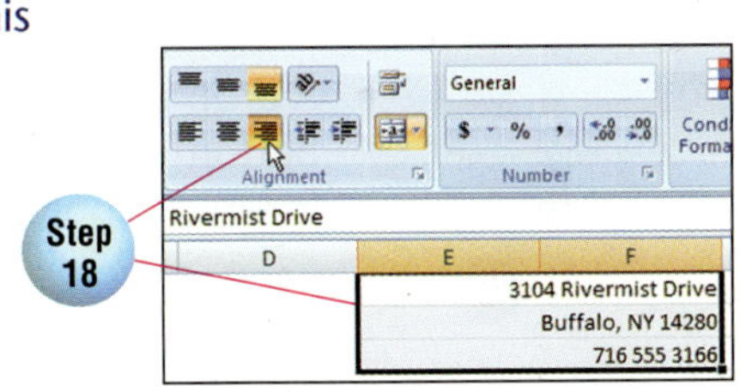

19 Deselect the range.

20 Save **ExcelS2-01.xlsx**.

In Addition

Wrapping Text within a Cell

A Wrap Text button is available in the Alignment group which you can use to wrap text within a cell if you do not want to widen the column width. Text too wide for the column is displayed on multiple lines and the height of the row is automatically increased. In the example shown below, the original cells are shown on the left and the wrapped cells displayed on the right.

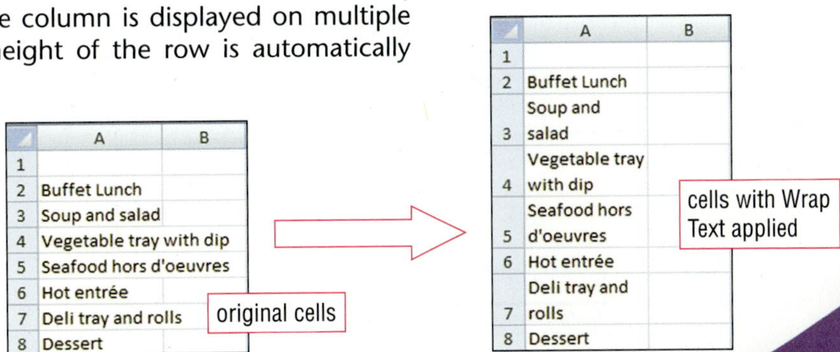

Activity 2.9

Adding Borders and Shading; Copying Formats with Format Painter; Using Cell Styles

Borders in various styles and colors can be applied to display and print in selected cells within the worksheet. Borders can be added to the top, left, bottom, or right edge of a cell. Use borders to underscore headings or totals or to emphasize other cells. Shading adds color and/or a pattern to the background of a cell. Format Painter copies formats from a selected cell to another cell. Use this feature to apply multiple format options from one cell to another cell. Cell Styles contain a group of predefined formatting options stored in a name. Styles are an efficient method to consistently apply formats, creating a professional, consistent worksheet appearance. Excel includes several pre-defined styles which you can apply or modify; you also can choose to create your own cell style.

Project

As you near completion of the quotation, you will spend time improving the presentation of the worksheet by adjusting column widths, deleting extra columns, adding borders and shading, and applying cell styles.

1. With **ExcelS2-01.xlsx** open, change the width of column A to *11.00 (82 pixels)*. Refer to Activity 2.5 if you need help with this step.

   Before applying borders, shading, and styles, you will take a few moments to finalize column settings in the worksheet.

2. AutoFit columns C–F and H–M.
3. Change the width of column G to *4.00 (33 pixels)*.
4. Select A20:M20.

   In the next steps, you will add a border to the top and bottom of the column headings using the Bottom Border button in the Font group of the Home tab.

5. Click the Bottom Border button arrow in the Font group in the Home tab.

   A drop-down list of border style options displays. The *More Borders* option at the bottom of the list opens the Format Cells dialog box with the Border tab selected in which you can create a custom border.

6. Click *Top and Bottom Border* at the drop-down list.

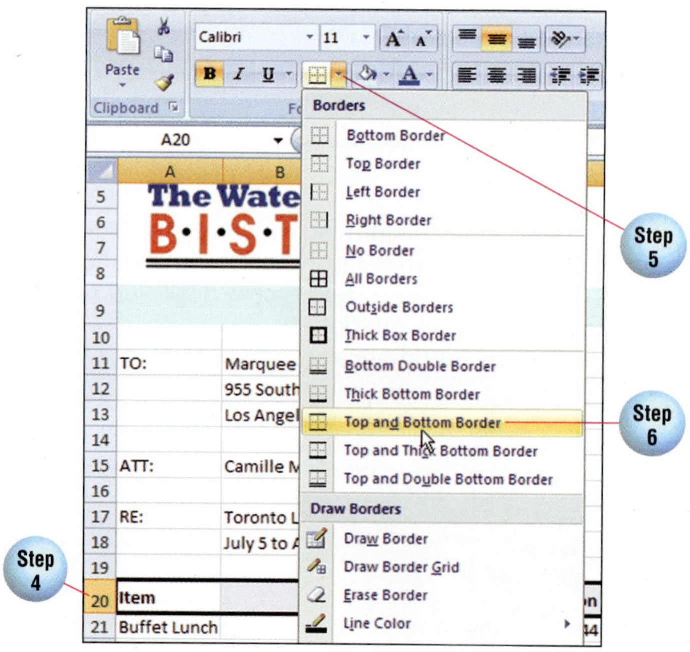

7 Click in any cell to deselect the range and view the border.

8 Select A21:B21, click the Top and Bottom Border button arrow, and then click *Outside Borders* at the drop-down list.

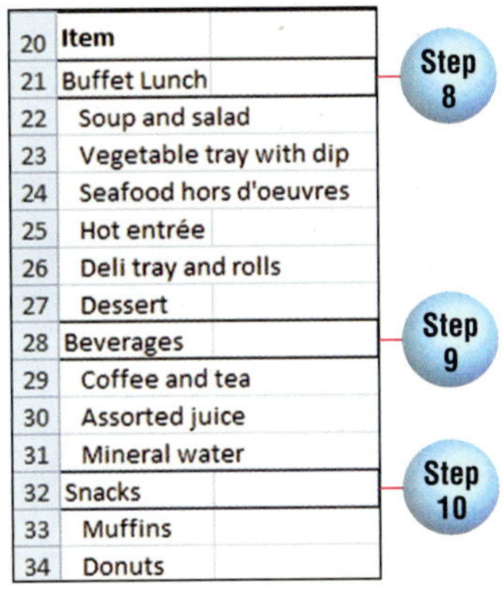

9 Select A28:B28 and then click the Outside Borders button. (Do not click the arrow.)

Since the Borders button updates to the most recently selected border style, you can apply the Outside Borders option to the active cell without displaying the drop-down list.

10 Select A32:B32 and then click the Outside Borders button.

11 Deselect the range.

12 Make F39 the active cell, click the Outside Borders button arrow, and then click *Top and Double Bottom Border* at the drop-down list.

In the next steps, you will copy the formats from F39 to the other values in row 39 using Format Painter.

13 With F39 still the active cell, double-click the Format Painter button in the Clipboard group.

A moving marquee surrounds the source cell and a paintbrush displays attached to the cell pointer. This icon means that the formats are copied from the source cell and can be pasted to multiple cells or ranges. Single-clicking Format Painter allows you to copy formats to the next cell or range that you click. Double-click the Format Painter button to toggle the feature on until you turn it off by clicking Format Painter again.

14 Click I39 and then drag the cell pointer to select K39:M39. Click the Format Painter button to turn off the feature.

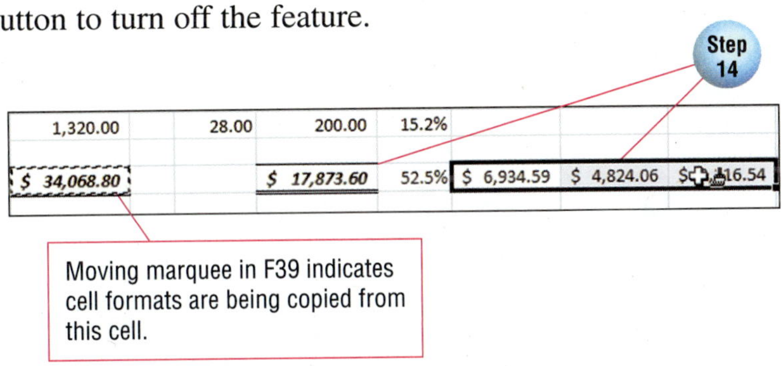

15 Select E1:F8.

In the original quotation, Dana applied a white fill color to the background of the cells behind the bistro's logo. You decide to carry the white fill to remaining cells in the top portion of the quotation to improve the display of the worksheet. Cell gridlines do not print, so this action has no effect on a printout of the quotation.

continues

16 Click the Fill Color button arrow [Fill Color button] in the Font group and then click the white color box *(White, Background 1)* that displays in the color gallery.

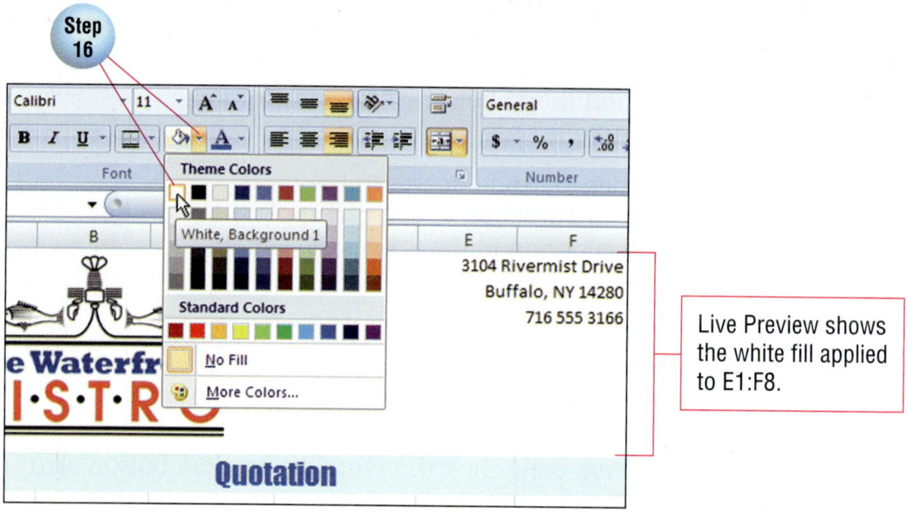

17 Deselect the range.

In the next steps, you will use Cell Styles to apply shading and other format options to selected cells.

18 Select A9.

You decide to change the formatting of the *Quotation* title to one of the predefined cell styles that Excel provides.

19 Click the Cell Styles button in the Styles group in the Home tab.

20 Move the mouse over several of the cell style designs in the drop-down gallery and watch Live Preview show you the style applied to the title in A9.

21 Click the *Title* style in the *Titles and Headings* section of the gallery.

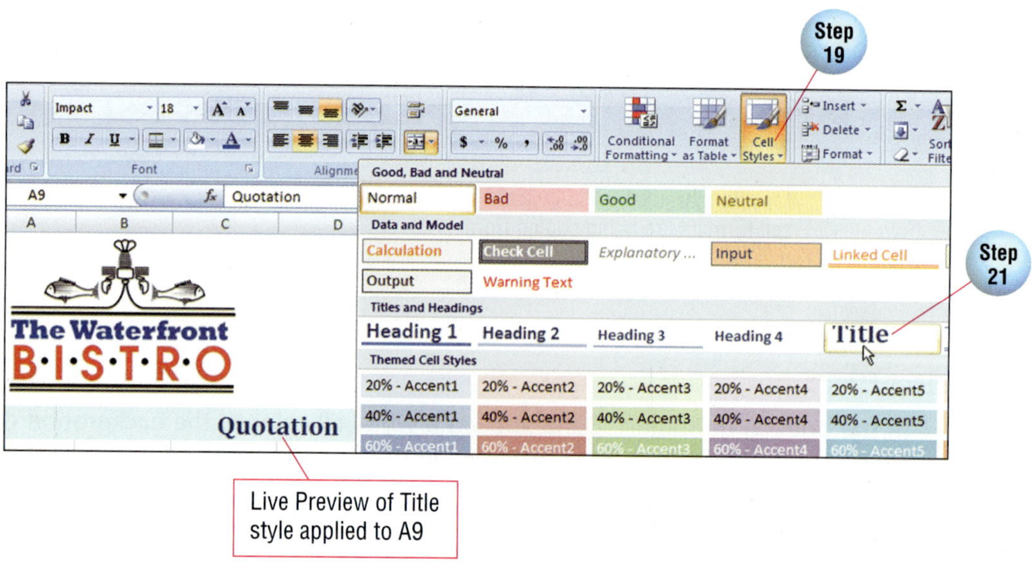

22 Select A20:M20, click the Cell Styles button in the Styles group, and then click the *Accent2* style in the *Themed Cell Styles* section.

23 Select A21:B21, A28:B28, and A32:B32 and apply the *Accent1* style in the *Themed Cell Styles* section in the Cell Styles drop-down gallery.

24 Select K19:M19 and apply the *Note* style in the *Data and Model* section in the *Cell Styles* drop-down gallery.

In the next steps, you will print two copies of the completed quotation. One copy will not include the confidential cost information and the second copy will include all cells.

25 Select A1:F42.

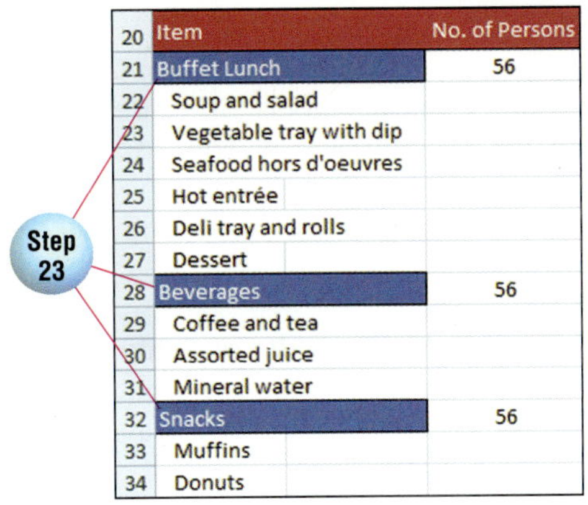

In Brief

Add Borders
1. Select cells.
2. Click Borders button arrow in Font group.
3. Click desired border style.
4. Deselect cells.

Copy Formats
1. Make active cell containing source formats.
2. Click Format Painter button in Clipboard group.
3. Click destination cells.

Apply Cell Styles
1. Select cells.
2. Click Cell Styles button.
3. Click desired style in drop-down gallery.

PROBLEM

Point to the top left corner of A1 to select the cell rather than the logo. If you click the logo by mistake, point at the space left of the logo and when you see the cell pointer icon, click and drag to F42.

26 Click the Office button and then click *Print*.

27 At the Print dialog box, click *Selection* in the *Print what* section and then click OK.

28 Deselect the range.

29 Click the Page Layout tab.

30 Click the Orientation button in the Page Setup group in the Page Layout tab and then click *Landscape* at the drop-down list.

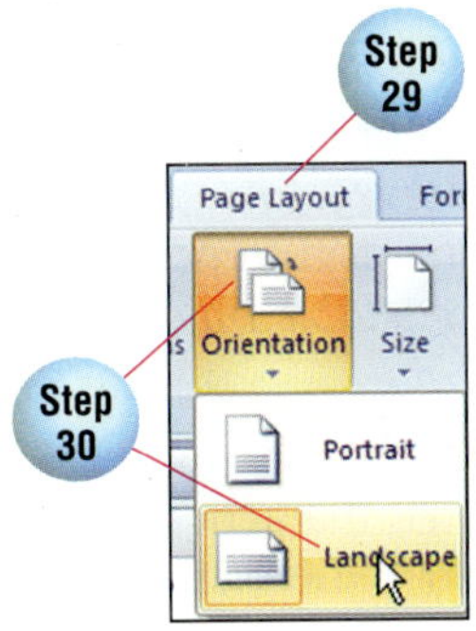

31 Click the Width button arrow (currently displays *Automatic*) in the Scale to Fit group and then click *1 page* at the drop-down list.

32 Click the Height button arrow (currently displays *Automatic*) in the Scale to Fit group and then click *1 page* at the drop-down list.

33 Click the Quick Print button on the Quick Access toolbar.

34 Save **ExcelS2-01.xlsx**.

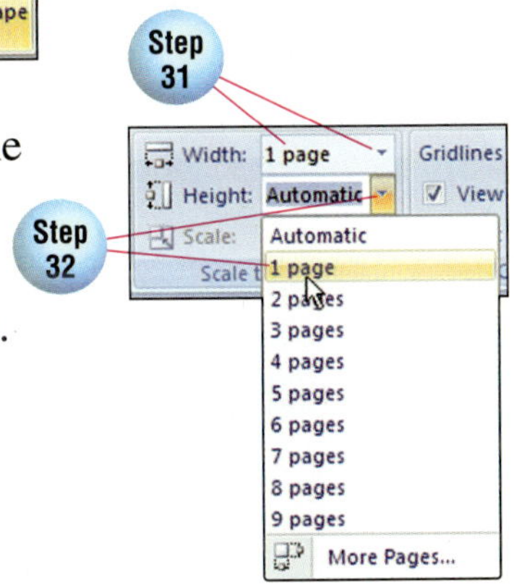

In Addition

Hiding Columns

Another method you could consider to print the worksheet without the confidential cost information is to temporarily hide the columns containing cost data—columns H–M. The data is removed from view but is not deleted. Do this with a worksheet that contains confidential information that you do not want someone to see on your screen or to prevent the data from printing. Select the rows or columns you want hidden, right-click in the selected area, and then click Hide at the shortcut menu. Unhide the rows or columns by selecting the columns or rows immediately before and after the hidden data, right-clicking, and then clicking Unhide at the shortcut menu.

Activity 2.10

Using Find and Replace

Use the Find command to search for specific labels or values that you want to verify or edit. The Find command will move to each cell containing the text you specify. The Replace command will search for a label, value, or format and automatically will replace it with another label, value, or format. The Find and Replace feature ensures that all occurrences of the specified text are included.

Project

The Waterfront B·I·S·T·R·O

Use Find to review the quantity and type of trays that are to be supplied for the film crew. Camille Matsui of Marquee Productions sent an e-mail today advising that they will need catering services for three additional days. You will use the Replace command to adjust the quotation.

1. With **ExcelS2-01.xlsx** open, press Ctrl + Home to make A1 the active cell.
2. Click the Home tab.
3. Click the Find & Select button in the Editing group in the Home tab and then click *Find* at the drop-down list.

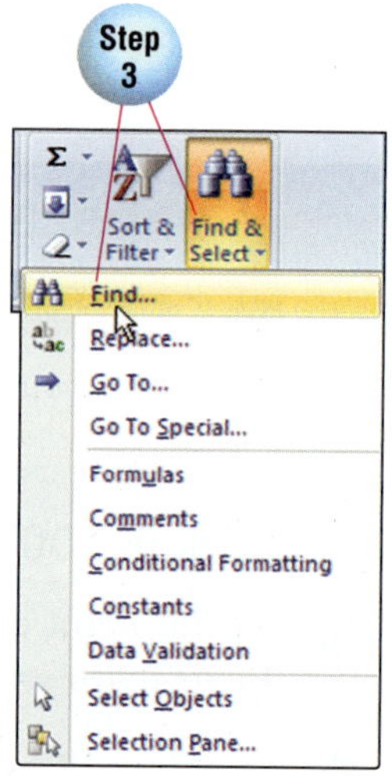

4. Type ***tray*** in the *Find what* text box and then click the Find Next button.

   The asterisk character is called a ***wildcard character***. You can type * within a search string in place of characters that you do not want to specify so that you see all variations of a string. For example, in this search Excel can return cells that contain *vegetable tray* or *vegetable tray with dip* or *fruit tray*. The first occurrence in A23 becomes active and contains the text *Vegetable tray with dip*.

PROBLEM

Can't see the active cell? Drag the Find and Replace dialog box out of the way if the box is obscuring your view of the worksheet.

5. Click Find Next.

   The cell containing *Deli tray with rolls* (A26) becomes active.

6. Click Find Next.

   The cell containing *Fruit tray* (A35) becomes active.

7. Click Find Next.

   The cell containing *Vegetable tray with dip* (A36) becomes active.

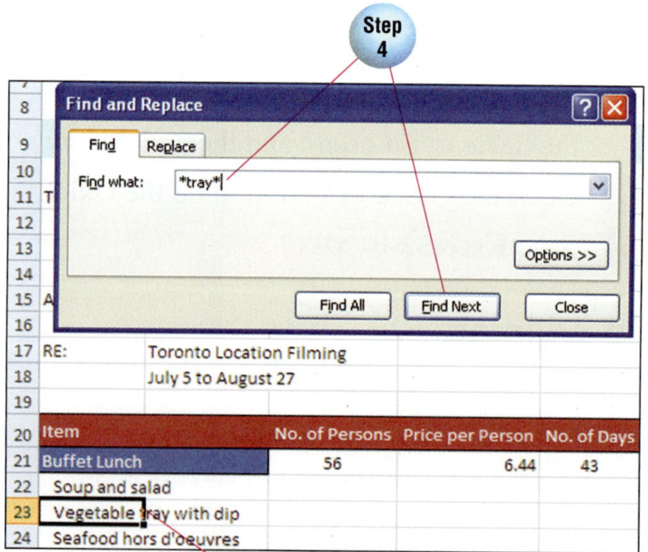

Active cell moves to the next occurrence each time you click Find Next.

8. Click Find Next.

   Excel returns to the first occurrence in A23. You now know that the quotation contains four trays. Although in this small worksheet you could easily have found this information by scanning column A, in a large worksheet with many rows and columns, the Find command is an efficient method of moving to a specific cell. Typing a specific value into the *Find what* text box could move you to a section title or label very quickly.

9. Click the Close button to close the Find and Replace dialog box.
10. Click the Find & Select button in the Editing group and then click *Replace* at the drop-down list.
11. Drag to select **tray** in the *Find what* text box and then type **40**.
12. Press Tab to move the insertion point to the *Replace with* text box and then type **43**.
13. Click the Replace All button.

    Excel searches through the entire worksheet and automatically changes all occurrences of *40* to *43*.

14. Click OK at the message that Excel has completed the search and has made four replacements.
15. Click the Close button to close the Find and Replace dialog box.
16. Review the *No. of Days* column in the worksheet (column E) and note that four replacements were made in E21, E28, E32, and E37.
17. Save **ExcelS2-01.xlsx**.

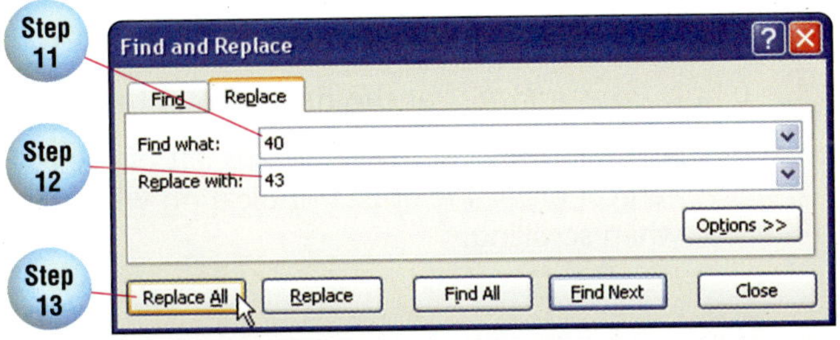

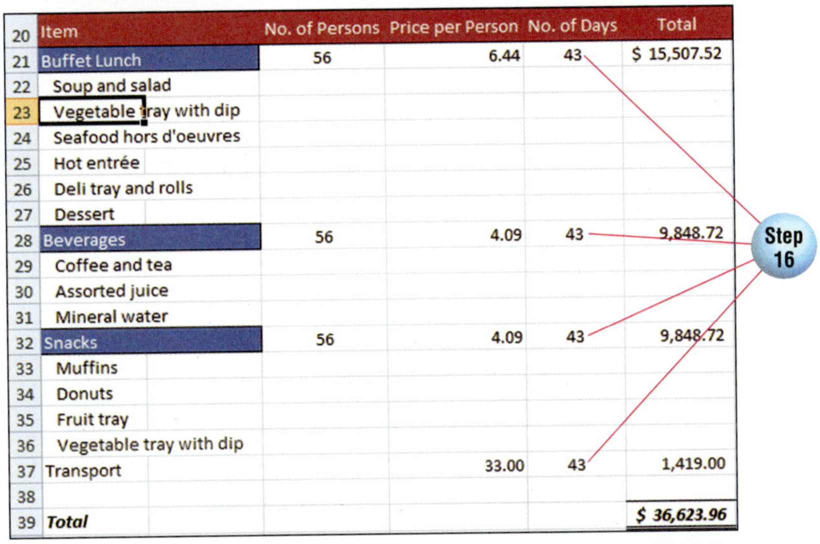

	Item	No. of Persons	Price per Person	No. of Days	Total
21	Buffet Lunch	56	6.44	43	$ 15,507.52
22	Soup and salad				
23	Vegetable tray with dip				
24	Seafood hors d'oeuvres				
25	Hot entrée				
26	Deli tray and rolls				
27	Dessert				
28	Beverages	56	4.09	43	9,848.72
29	Coffee and tea				
30	Assorted juice				
31	Mineral water				
32	Snacks	56	4.09	43	9,848.72
33	Muffins				
34	Donuts				
35	Fruit tray				
36	Vegetable tray with dip				
37	Transport		33.00	43	1,419.00
38					
39	*Total*				*$ 36,623.96*

In Brief

Find Label or Value

1. Click Find & Select button.
2. Click *Find*.
3. Type label or value in *Find what* text box.
4. Click Find Next.

Replace Label or Value

1. Click Find & Select button.
2. Click *Replace*.
3. Type label or value in *Find what* text box.
4. Type replacement label or value in *Replace with* text box.
5. Click Find Next or Replace All.

In Addition

Replacing Formats

You can use the Replace feature to find formats and replace them with other formats or no formatting. For example, you could use Excel to find all occurrences of bold and blue font color applied to a cell and replace with bold and green font color. At the Find and Replace dialog box with the Replace tab selected, click the Options button to display Format buttons to the right of the *Find what* and *Replace with* text boxes (shown at the right). Use these buttons to specify the required format options. The Preview box to the left (initially displays *No Format Set*) displays the formats Excel will find and replace.

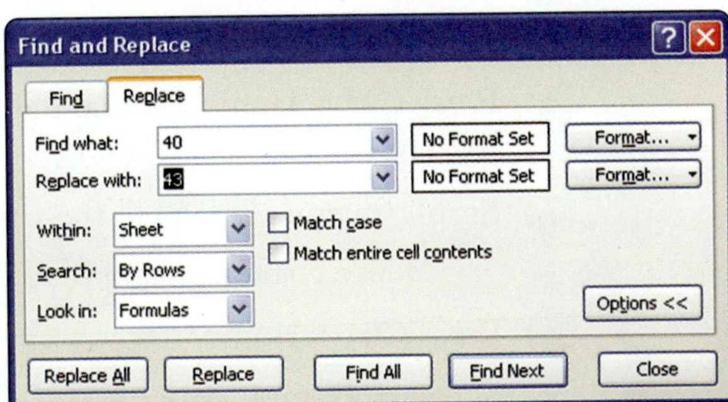

Activity 2.11

Freezing Panes; Changing the Zoom

When you scroll to the right or down to view parts of a worksheet that do not fit in the current window, some column or row headings may scroll off the screen making it difficult to relate text or values. The Freeze Panes option causes rows and columns to remain fixed when scrolling. Magnify or reduce the worksheet display by dragging the Zoom slider bar button, clicking the Zoom In or Zoom Out buttons, or by specifying a percentage to zoom to at the Zoom dialog box. Changing the magnification does not affect printing since worksheets print at 100% unless scaling options are changed.

Project

You will freeze column and row headings in the quotation to facilitate scrolling and practice with various Zoom settings to view more cells within the current window.

1. With **ExcelS2-01.xlsx** open, make C10 the active cell.
2. Click the View tab.
3. Click the Freeze Panes button in the Window group.
4. Click *Freeze Panes* at the drop-down list.

   All rows above and all columns left of the active cell are frozen. A horizontal and a vertical black line appear indicating which rows and which columns remain fixed when scrolling.

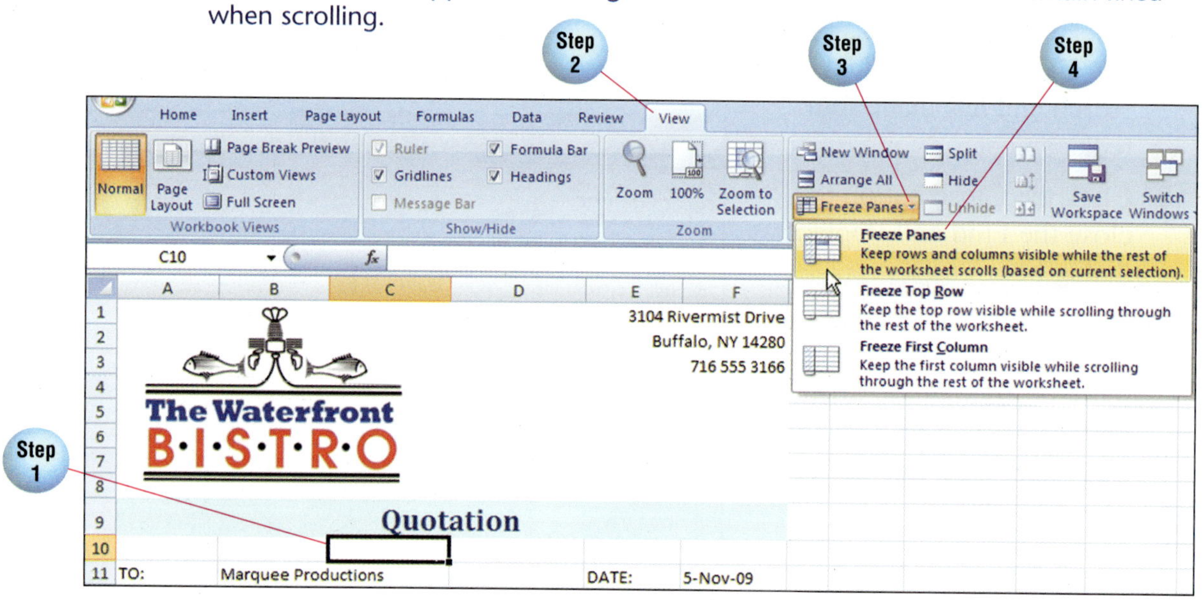

5. Press the Page Down key several times to scroll down the worksheet.

   Notice rows 1 through 9 do not scroll off the screen.

6. Press Ctrl + Home. Notice that Excel returns to C10 instead of A1 since A1 is frozen.
7. Scroll several screens to the right.

   Notice columns A and B do not scroll off the screen.

8. Press Ctrl + Home.
9. Scroll right until column H is immediately right of column B and then scroll down until row 20 is immediately below row 9.

   You can now view the cost information directly beside the labels as shown on the next page.

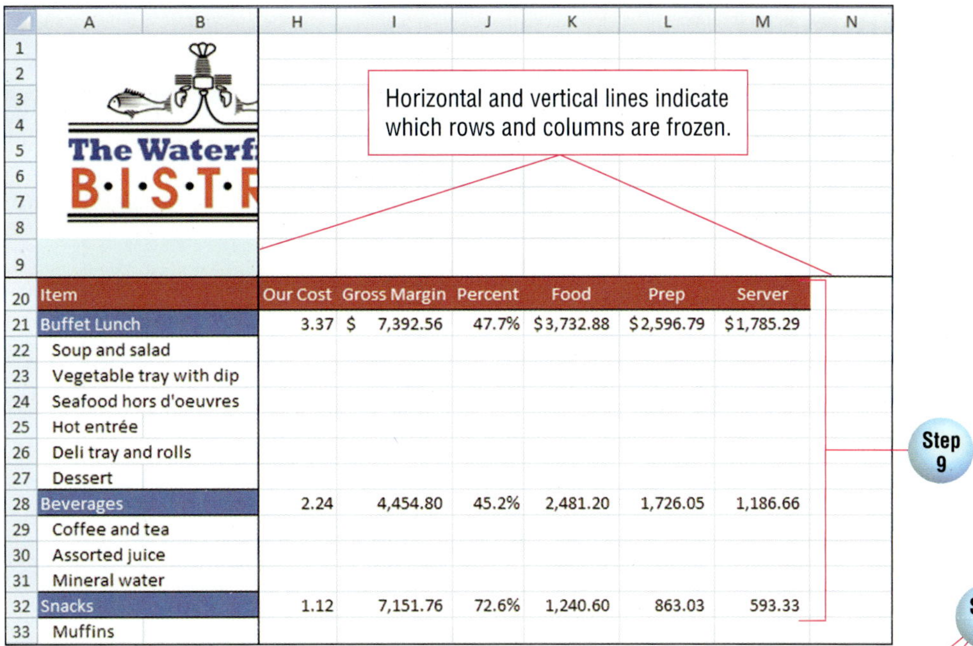

In Brief

Freeze Panes

1. Make cell active below and right of row or column headings you want to freeze.
2. Click View tab.
3. Click Freeze Panes button.
4. Click *Freeze Panes*.

Change Zoom Setting

Drag Zoom slider bar button.

OR

Click Zoom In or Zoom Out buttons.

OR

Click zoom percentage value and choose magnification option at Zoom dialog box.

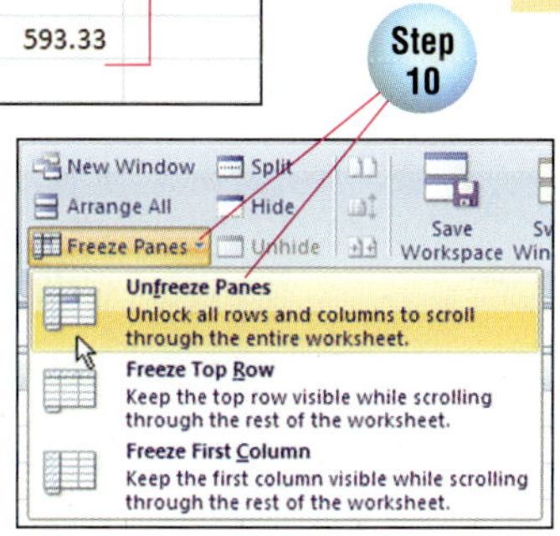

10. Click the Freeze Panes button in the Window group and then click *Unfreeze Panes*.

    The Freeze Panes option changes to Unfreeze Panes when rows or columns have been frozen.

11. Practice dragging the button on the Zoom slider bar (located at the right end of the Status bar above the system time) and watch the cells magnify and shrink as you drag right and left.

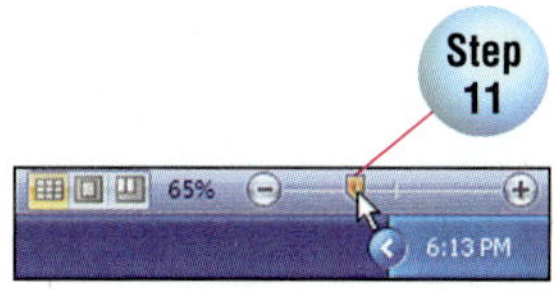

12. Drag the slider bar button to the halfway mark on the slider bar to redisplay the worksheet at 100%.
13. Click over *100%* at the left edge of the slider bar to open the Zoom dialog box.
14. Click *75%* and then click OK.

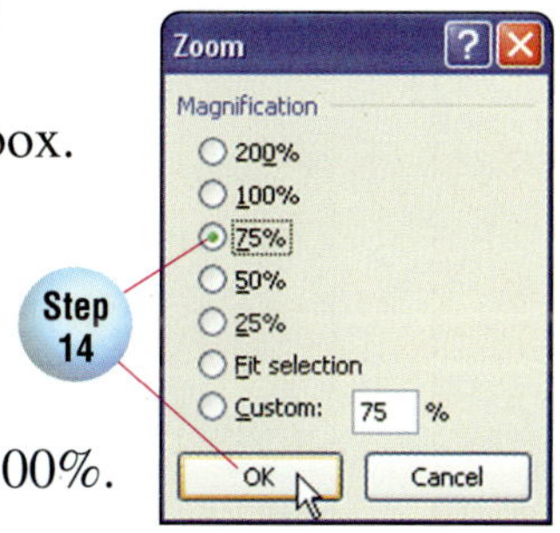

15. Click the Zoom In button at the right side of the Zoom slider bar (displays as a plus symbol inside a circle).
16. Continue to click the Zoom In button until the zoom percentage returns to 100%.

    When the worksheet is set to 100% magnification, clicking the Zoom In or Zoom Out buttons at either side of the slider bar magnifies or shrinks the display of the worksheet by 10% each time the button is clicked.

17. Save and then close **ExcelS2-01.xlsx**.

In Addition

Zoom to Selection

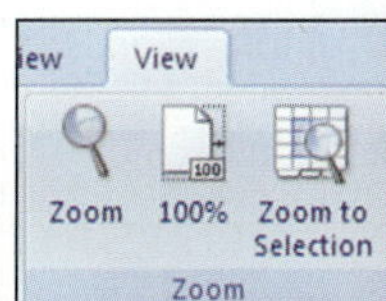

The View tab contains a Zoom group with three buttons to change zoom settings. Click the Zoom button in the Zoom group to open the Zoom dialog box. This is the same dialog box that you displayed in Step 13. Click the 100% button to return the view to 100%. Select a range of cells and then click the Zoom to Selection button to cause Excel to scale the zoom setting so that the selected range fills the worksheet area.

Features Summary

Feature	Ribbon Tab, Group	Button	Quick Access Toolbar	Keyboard Shortcut
Accounting Number format	Home, Number	$		
align text left	Home, Alignment			
align text right	Home, Alignment			
bold	Home, Font	B		Ctrl + B
borders	Home, Font			
cell styles	Home, Styles			
center	Home, Alignment			
clear cell	Home, Editing			
column width	Home, Cells	Format		
Comma style	Home, Number	,		
copy	Home, Clipboard			Ctrl + C
cut	Home, Clipboard			Ctrl + X
decrease decimal	Home, Number			
decrease indent	Home, Alignment			
delete cell, column, or row	Home, Cells	Delete		
fill color	Home, Font			
find	Home, Editing			Ctrl + F
font	Home, Font	Calibri		Ctrl + 1
font color	Home, Font	A		Ctrl + 1
font size	Home, Font	11		Ctrl + 1
Format Painter	Home, Clipboard			
freeze panes	View, Window	Freeze Panes		
increase decimal	Home, Number			
increase indent	Home, Alignment			
insert cell, column, or row	Home, Cells	Insert		
italic	Home, Font	I		Ctrl + I
merge and center	Home, Alignment			
middle-align	Home, Alignment			
paste	Home, Clipboard			Ctrl + V

continues

Feature	Ribbon Tab, Group	Button	Quick Access Toolbar	Keyboard Shortcut
Percent style	Home, Number	%		Ctrl + Shift + %
redo an action				Ctrl + Y
repeat				Ctrl + Y
replace	Home, Editing			Ctrl + H
row height	Home, Cells	Format		
Spelling	Review, Proofing			F7
Thesaurus	Review, Proofing			Shift + F7
undo an action				Ctrl + Z
zoom	View, Zoom			

Knowledge Check

Completion: In the space provided at the right, indicate the correct term, command, or option.

1. Use this feature to remove everything from a cell including text and formats. ____________
2. Make a cell active anywhere in this row to insert a new row between 11 and 12. ____________
3. Make a cell active anywhere in this column to insert a new column between E and F. ____________
4. Use this function key to add dollar symbols in front of row or column numbers to make the addresses absolute references. ____________
5. Perform this action with the mouse on a column boundary to adjust the width to the length of the longest entry. ____________
6. This term refers to the feature where Excel shows the results of a format option while pointing to the option in a drop-down list or gallery. ____________
7. By default, cells are initially set to this format. ____________
8. Click this button in the Alignment group of the Home tab to center cells vertically between the top and bottom cell boundaries. ____________
9. Click this button in the Clipboard group of the Home tab to copy the formats of the active cell. ____________
10. This feature stores predefined format options. ____________
11. This is the term used to describe the asterisk (*) when typed in a search string. ____________
12. Make this cell active to freeze rows 1 through 9 and columns A and B. ____________
13. List three methods for changing the zoom magnification to view more cells in the current window. ____________

Skills Review

Review 1 Editing, Moving, Copying, and Clearing Cells; Performing a Spell Check; Inserting and Deleting Rows

1. Open **WBInvoice-NPCollege.xlsx**.
2. Save the workbook with Save As and name it **ExcelS2-R1**.
3. Change the cost in I20 from *6.17* to *6.85* and then clear the contents of I16:I17.
4. Change the label in A21 from *Soup* to *French Onion Soup*.
5. Type new data in the cells indicated.
   E14 **PO No.** F14 **TA-09-643**
6. Delete rows 7, 8, and 9.
7. Complete a spelling check of the worksheet. (All names are spelled correctly.)
8. Move D5 to A15 and move E7:F7 to E10:F10 and then copy A24 to A30.
9. Delete those rows that contain the labels *Milk*, *Assorted Juice*, and *Donuts*.
10. Insert a new row between *Prime Rib* and *Mixed Vegetables* and then type **Seafood Pasta** in column A of the new row.
11. Save **ExcelS2-R1.xlsx**.

Review 2 Adjusting Column Widths; Replacing Data; Moving Cells; Applying Formatting Features

1. With **ExcelS2-R1.xlsx** open, adjust the width of column A to *10.00 (75 pixels)*.
2. Change the width of column C to AutoFit (length of the longest entry).
3. Change the width of column D to *15.00 (110 pixels)* and column E to *7.00 (54 pixels)*.
4. Adjust the width of columns I–K to AutoFit.
5. Use the Replace feature to replace the value *30* with *36*.
6. Create a SUM formula in F32 to total the cells in the column.
7. Apply numeric formats as follows:
   a. Format F17 and F32 to Accounting Number Format.
   b. Format F27 and F30 to Comma Style.
   c. Format K17 and K27 to Percent Style with one decimal place.
8. Indent once A18:A26 and A28:A29.
9. Select D1:D3 and change the font to 10-point Bookman Old Style bold. (Substitute another font of your choosing if Bookman Old Style is not available.)
10. Move D1:D3 to F1:F3 and then align the text at the right edge of the cells.
11. Apply the Input cell style (*Data and Model* section) to the ranges A17:B17 and A27:B27.
12. Merge and center A15 across columns A–F.
13. Apply the Title cell style to A15.
14. Center the values in columns C and D and in F16.
15. Add a top and bottom border to A16:K16 and turn on bold.
16. Add a top and double bottom border to F32 and turn on bold.
17. Add the fill color Olive Green, Accent 3, Lighter 80% from the Fill Color palette to A15.
18. Add the fill color Olive Green, Accent 3, Lighter 60% from the Fill Color palette to A16:K16.
19. Delete column H.
20. Print the entire worksheet scaled to fit 1 page in height and 1 page in width in landscape.
21. Save and then close **ExcelS2-R1.xlsx**.

Skills Assessment

Assessment 1 Editing Cells; Inserting Columns; Absolute References; Copying Formulas; Applying Formatting Features

Performance Threads

1. Bobbie Sinclair of Performance Threads has started preparing a workbook that tracks the costs of costume research, design, and production for the Marquee Productions project. You have been asked to complete the workbook.
2. Open **PT-MarqueeCostumes.xlsx**.
3. Save the workbook with Save As and name it **ExcelS2-A1**.
4. Complete the worksheet using the following information:
   a. Design costs for all costumes should be *157.50* instead of *27.50*.
   b. Insert a new column between *Fabric* and *Total Cost* and type the column heading **Notions** in J9. Type the values in J10:J14 as follows:

Val Wingfield	**110.00**	Celia Gopf	**77.56**
Eunice Billings	**79.73**	Jade Norwich	**112.42**
Tony Salvatore	**98.41**		

   c. The formula to calculate total cost for each costume is incorrect. Enter the correct formula for the first costume (K10) and then copy the formula to K11:K14. ***Hint: The current formula does not include the fabric and notions costs.***
   d. Add the label and value in the cells indicated:
      A18 **Costume Fee Markup** A19 **155%**
   e. Create a formula in L10 to calculate the costume fee that will multiply the total cost in K10 by the costume fee markup percent in A19 and then copy the formula to L11:L14. ***Hint: You will need to use an absolute reference in the formula so that it copies correctly.***
   f. Create a formula in M10 to calculate the profit as costume fee minus total cost and then copy the formula to M11:M14.
   g. Format the numeric cells in an appropriate style.
   h. Change the alignment of any headings that could be improved in appearance.
   i. Merge and center the titles in A6 and A7 over the columns.
   j. Apply font, border, and color changes to enhance the appearance of the worksheet.
5. Print the worksheet in landscape orientation with the width scaled to fit 1 page.
6. Save and then close **ExcelS2-A1.xlsx**.

Assessment 2 Completing and Formatting a Worksheet

Performance Threads

1. Camille Matsui, production assistant for Marquee Productions, has requested the invoice in advance for the five custom-made costumes so that she can make sure the budget funds are allocated. Bobbie Sinclair has started the invoice and has asked you to finish it. ***Note: Completion of Assessment 1 is required to finish the invoice for this assessment.***
2. Open **PT-MarqueeInvoice.xlsx**.
3. Save the workbook with Save As and name it **ExcelS2-A2**.
4. Complete the invoice using the following information:
   a. Type the current date in G6.
   b. Refer to your printout of the costumes in Assessment 1, Step 5. Type the values from the *Costume Fee* column into the appropriate cells in F15:F19.

c. Total the costume fees in F20. ***Hint: Make sure the total agrees with the total costume fee on your printout from Assessment 1.***
d. A transportation and storage container for each of the five costumes is *$125.00*. Enter the appropriate formula in F22 that will calculate the fee for five containers.
e. Enter in F23 the delivery for all five costumes as *$150.00*.
f. Enter the formula in F24 that will add the total for the costume fees with the additional charges.
g. Enter the formula in F25 that will calculate 6% GST (Goods and Services Tax) on the total including additional charges.
h. Enter the formula to total the invoice in F26 as the sum of F24 and F25.

5. Improve the appearance of the worksheet by applying formatting features that you learned in this section.
6. Save **ExcelS2-A2.xlsx**.
7. Print and then close **ExcelS2-A2.xlsx**.

Assessment 3 Performing a Spelling Check; Adjusting Column Width; Editing Cells; Using Find and Replace; Applying Formatting Features

Worldwide Enterprises

1. Sam Vestering, manager of North American Distribution for Worldwide Enterprises, has created a workbook to summarize revenues from distribution of Marquee Productions' film *Two by Two*. You have been asked to review the worksheet and make corrections and enhancements to the appearance.
2. Open **WE-2by2Revenue.xlsx**.
3. Save the workbook with Save As and name it **ExcelS2-A3**.
4. Make the following corrections:
   a. Perform a spelling check.
   b. Adjust column widths so all data is completely visible.
   c. Check the Projected Box Office Sales in column H with the data in **ExcelS1-A3.xlsx** and change any values that do not match. ***Note: You can check these values in Figure 1.3 for Assessment 3 in Section 1.***
   d. In I8, enter the formula to calculate the box office variance as box office sales minus projected box office sales. Copy the formula to the remaining rows in the column and then increase the column width so that all values are visible.
   e. Change all of the theaters named *Cinema House* to *Cinema Magic*.
   f. In A3, type **Date:** and then enter today's date in B3.
   g. Improve the appearance of the worksheet by applying formatting features that you learned in this section.
5. Print the worksheet in portrait orientation with the width scaled to fit 1 page.
6. Save and then close **ExcelS2-A3.xlsx**.

Assessment 4 Finding the Select All Button

The Waterfront B·I·S·T·R·O

1. Use the Help feature to find out where the Select All button is located in the Excel window.
2. Open **WBInventory.xlsx**.
3. Save the workbook with Save As and name it **ExcelS2-A4**.
4. Adjust all column widths to AutoFit.
5. Click the Select All button.

HELP

6. Apply italic formatting and change the alignment to Align Text Right.
7. Scroll the worksheet to view the new formats.
8. Change the page orientation to landscape, scale the width to fit 1 page, and then print the worksheet.
9. Save and then close **ExcelS2-A4.xlsx**.

Assessment 5 Locating Information on Theater Arts Programs

1. You are considering enrolling in a drama/theater arts program at a college or university. Search the Internet for available programs in postsecondary schools in the United States and Canada. Choose five schools that interest you the most and find out as much as you can about the costs of attending these schools. Try to find information on costs beyond tuition and books, such as transportation and room and board.
2. Create a workbook that summarizes the information on the schools you selected.
3. Apply formatting features that you learned in this section to the worksheet.
4. Save the workbook and name it **ExcelS2-A5**.
5. Print and then close **ExcelS2-A5.xlsx**.

Marquee Challenge

Challenge 1 Creating a Direct Wages Budget Report for a Film Shoot

1. You work with Chris Greenbaum, production manager at Marquee Productions. Chris has asked you to create the direct wages budget for the company's location film shoot in Toronto. Create the worksheet shown in Figure 2.1.
2. Link the values in the *Estimated per Diem Rates* table (columns I and J) to the *Per Diem Rate* column (column F) in the budget section.
3. Calculate the extended cost by summing the number of days for site prep, shoot, and cleanup and then multiplying by the per diem rate.
4. Calculate the total in G16.
5. Apply formatting options as shown and format the values in column G to an appropriate number format. Use your best judgment to determine the font, font size, column widths, borders, and fill colors.
6. Although not visible in the figure, a border should also be applied along the top (columns A–G) and left edges (rows 1–14) of the budget cells so that when printed, the entire budget has a perimeter border.
7. Save the workbook and name it **ExcelS2-C1**.
8. Print and then close **ExcelS2-C1.xlsx**.

Challenge 2 Creating a Room Timetable

1. You are an assistant to the person who schedules classroom space in the Theatre Arts Division at Niagara Peninsula College. You have been given the room schedule for the large theater classroom for next semester. The division posts a printed copy of the timetable outside the classroom door so that students know when the room is available to work on theater projects and practice for upcoming plays. You want

to use Excel to create and format the timetable so that the printed copy is easy to read and has a more professional appearance.

2. Refer to the data in Figure 2.2 and then create the timetable in a new workbook. Apply formatting features learned in this section to create a colorful, easy-to-read room timetable.
3. Save the workbook and name it **ExcelS2-C2**.
4. Print and then close **ExcelS2-C2.xlsx**.

FIGURE 2.1 Challenge 1

Marquee Productions

Location Film Shoot

Toronto, Ontario, Canada

July 5 to August 27, 2010

Personnel	Site Prep Days	Shoot Days	Cleanup Days	Per Diem Rate	Extended Cost
	Direct Wages Budget				
Crew	9	32	2		
Cast	0	32	0		
Actor Assistants	0	32	0		
Extras	0	19	0		
Cleaners	9	0	5		
Security	7	32	0		
Administration	9	32	0		
		Total Direct Wages Budget			

Estimated per Diem Rates *Subject to Change*	
Crew	1,575
Cast	10,500
Actor Assistants	2,400
Extras	2,000
Cleaners	750
Security	4,000
Administration	3,700

FIGURE 2.2 Challenge 2

Niagara Peninsula College					
Room:	T1101		Period Covered: January 1 toApril 30		
Time	Monday	Tuesday	Wednesday	Thursday	Friday
8:00 AM	SM100-01	AC215-03		MG210-01	SM240-03
9:00 AM	Prasad	McLean	LE100-03	Spelberger	Prasad
10:00 AM	LE253-03	(lab)	Das	SM355-02	SD350-04
11:00 AM	Das			Prasad	Attea
12:00 PM	SD451-01	PD250-02	Common	PD320-03	
1:00 PM	Attea	Kemper	Period	Kemper	LE310-02
2:00 PM	PD340-02	MG410-03	AC478-01	AC480-01	Das
3:00 PM	Kemper	Spelberger	Simmons	Simmons	MG210-01
4:00 PM	MG150-02	SM165-01	AC140-01	(lab)	Spelberger
5:00 PM	Spelberger	Prasad	Chou		
Use of this facility is restricted to staff and registered students only of Niagara Peninsula College. Failure to abide by this policy is considered a serious violation of the college's code of conduct.					
Note 1:	Monday through Thursday evenings, room is booked for Continuing Education department.				
Note 2:	Room is booked 8:00 AM to 5:00 PM the second Saturday of each month for the local community theater group.				

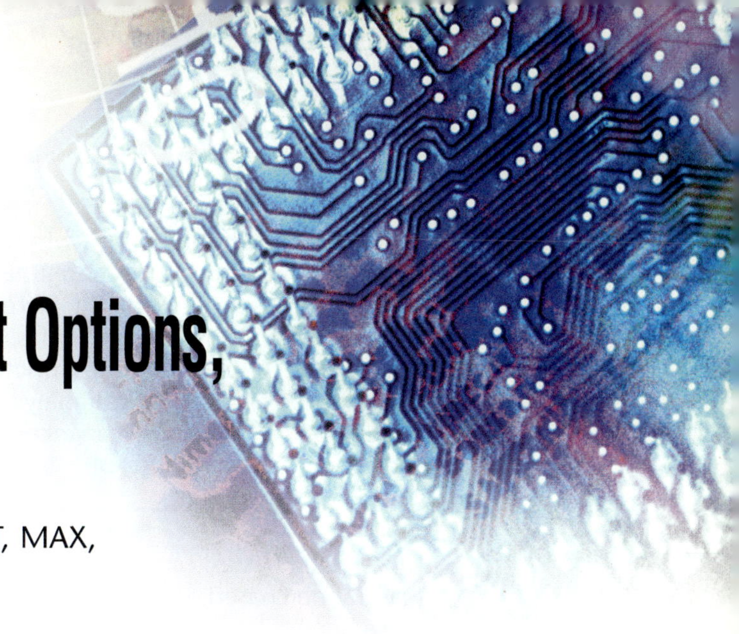

Excel SECTION 3

Using Functions, Setting Print Options, and Adding Visual Elements

Skills

- Create AVERAGE, COUNT, MAX, and MIN formulas to perform statistical analysis
- Create TODAY, NOW, and DATE formulas
- Create PMT and PPMT formulas to calculate loan payments
- Create an IF formula to return a result based on a logical test
- Change margins
- Center a worksheet horizontally and vertically
- Scale a worksheet to fit within a set number of pages
- Work with a worksheet in Page Layout view
- Insert headers and footers
- Format a worksheet using a theme
- Create a SmartArt diagram
- Create, edit, and format a column chart
- Create, edit, and format a pie chart
- Insert, size, and move a picture and clip art
- Draw shapes and text boxes

Student Resources

Before beginning this section:

1. Copy to your storage medium the ExcelS3 subfolder from the Excel folder on the Student Resources CD.
2. Make ExcelS3 the active folder.

In addition to containing the data files needed to complete section work, the Student Resources CD contains model answers in PDF format for each of the projects in this section; model answers for end-of-section activities are not provided.

Projects Overview

The Waterfront B·I·S·T·R·O: Add functions and set print options for inventory purchases and quarterly expenses report; finish an invoice by entering dates; calculate loan payment amounts for a patio expansion loan; calculate year-end bonuses; create charts, insert images and shapes, and customize printing for a quarterly expense and cost of sales report.

Niagara Peninsula College: Create and format charts for a grades analysis report; format a worksheet including inserting images and create a chart for an international student registration report.

First Choice Travel: Calculate and analyze sales commissions data; insert a picture and apply formatting enhancements to a European Destinations report.

Worldwide Enterprises: Calculate payments for an office renovation loan for two finance companies.

Marquee Productions: Create two charts that depict movie attendance statistics for a staff development workshop.

Activity 3.1

Using Statistical Functions AVERAGE, COUNT, MAX, and MIN

You learned about functions when you used the Sum button in Section 1. Excel includes numerous other built-in formulas that are grouped into function categories. The Statistical category contains several functions that can be used to perform statistical analysis on data, such as calculating medians, variances, frequencies, and so on. The structure of a function formula begins with the equals sign (=), followed by the name of the function, and then the argument within parentheses. ***Argument*** is the term given to the values to be included in the calculation. The structure of the argument is dependent on the function being used and can include a single range of cells, multiple ranges, single cell references, or a combination thereof.

Project

The Waterfront B·I·S·T·R·O

Dana Hirsch has asked you to add statistics in an inventory worksheet such as the average quantity purchased, the maximum units purchased, minimum units purchased, and a count of the items.

1. Open **WBInventory.xlsx**.
2. Save the workbook with Save As and name it **ExcelS3-01**.
3. Make C3 the active cell and then freeze the panes.
4. Type the following labels in the cells indicated:

   A58 **Average Units Purchased**
   A59 **Maximum Units Purchased**
   A60 **Minimum Units Purchased**
   A61 **Count of Inventory Items**

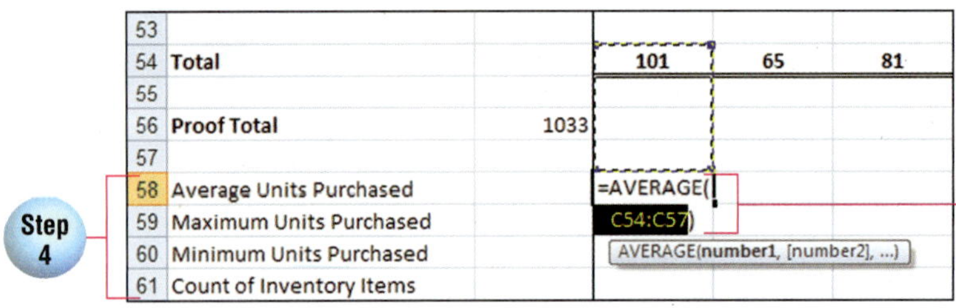

AVERAGE function inserted in C58 with suggested range highlighted (Step 7)

5. Make C58 the active cell.

   In the next steps, you will insert the AVERAGE function to determine the arithmetic mean of the cells in column C. If an empty cell or a cell containing text is included in the argument, Excel ignores the cell when determining the result. If, however, the cell contains a zero value, it is included in the average calculation.

6. Click the Sum button arrow in the Editing group in the Home tab.
7. Click *Average* at the drop-down list.

   Excel inserts the formula *=AVERAGE(C54:C57)* in the active cell with the suggested range highlighted. In the next step, you will drag to select the correct range and then complete the formula.

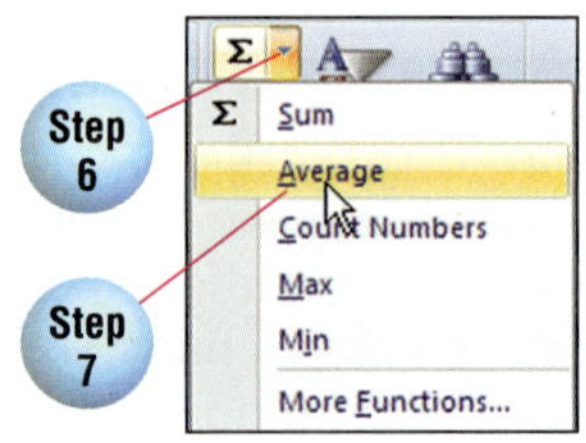

8. Scroll up the worksheet until you can see C3. Position the cell pointer over C3, hold down the left mouse button, drag down to C52, and then release the left mouse button.

Excel inserts the range *C3:C52* in the formula and the moving marquee expands to display the selected cells.

9. Press Enter or click the Enter button on the Formula bar.

   Excel returns the result *2.02* in C58.

10. Make C59 the active cell.

11. Click the Sum button arrow and then click *Max* at the drop-down list.

    The MAX function returns the largest value in the argument.

12. Type **c3:c52** and then press Enter.

    Excel returns the result *6* in C59. Typing the range into the formula is sometimes faster if you are sure of the starting and ending cell references.

13. With C60 the active cell, type the function **=min(c3:c52)** and then press Enter.

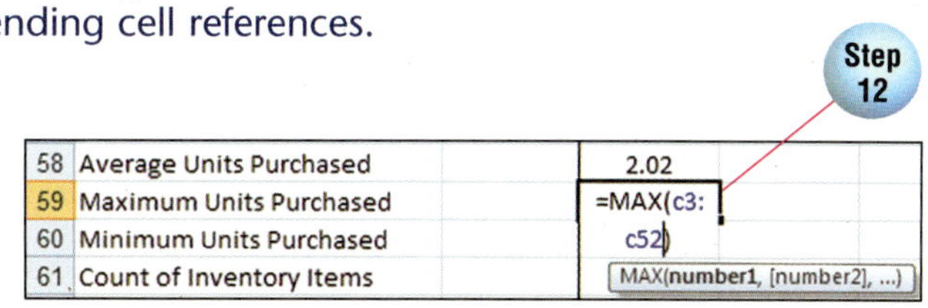

    MIN returns the smallest value in the argument. As soon as you type the letter *m* after the equals sign, the Formula AutoComplete feature displays a drop-down list of functions that begin with the letter typed. Formula AutoComplete helps you to write formulas by displaying function names, descriptions, and argument syntax. You can scroll the list and point to a function name to display in a ScreenTip the function's purpose. Double-click a function name in the list to enter the function into the cell.

14. With C61 the active cell, type the function **=count(c3:c52)** and then press Enter.

    COUNT returns the number of cells that contain numbers or numbers that have been formatted as text and dates. Empty cells, text labels, or error values in the range are ignored.

15. Format C58:C61 to the Number format with zero decimal places.

    To change the Number format, click the Number Format button arrow and then click Number at the drop-down list. Use the Decrease Decimals button to remove decimal values.

16. Select C58:C60 and then drag the fill handle right to column O. (You are not including the Count formula in C61 since the count value (50) does not change from February through December.)

    This copies the AVERAGE, MAX, and MIN formulas to columns D through O.

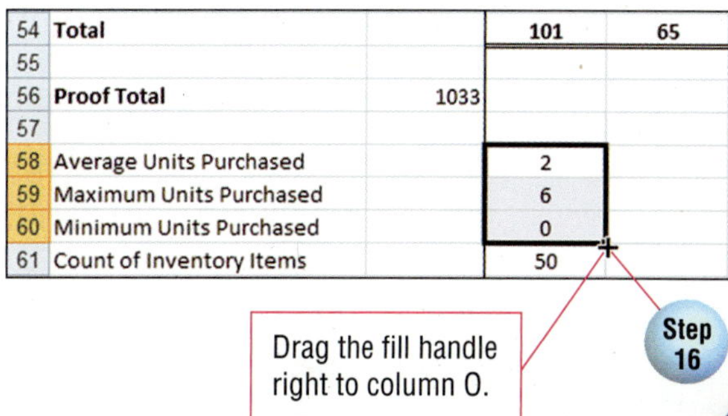

17. Click in any cell to deselect C58:O60.

18. Save and then close **ExcelS3-01.xlsx**.

? PROBLEM

Scrolling too fast as you drag right? Don't let go of the mouse—drag slowly in the opposite direction if the screen moves too quickly.

In Brief

AVERAGE, MAX, MIN, COUNT Functions

1. Make desired cell active.
2. Click Sum button arrow.
3. Click desired function.
4. Type or select argument range.
5. Press Enter or click Enter button.

Activity 3.2

Using Date Functions TODAY, NOW, and DATE

Dates are stored as a serial number starting from January 1, 1900, as serial number 1 and increased sequentially. Times are stored as decimal fractions representing portions of a day. Storing these entries as numbers enables calculations to be performed on cells containing a date or a time. The Date & Time category in the Insert Function dialog box contains functions that can be used to write formulas for cells containing dates. Cells containing dates and times can be formatted using the Number Format drop-down list in the Number group in the Home tab or using the Format Cells dialog box. Various combinations of year, month, day, hour, minutes, and seconds are available for displaying dates and times.

Project

An invoice to Performance Threads needs to be completed by entering the invoice date and the due date. You will open the invoice and experiment with the TODAY and NOW functions to enter the invoice date and then create a formula to calculate the due date. Finally, you will use a DATE function to enter the date The Waterfront Bistro opened in the invoice header.

1. Open **WBInvoice-PerfThreads.xlsx**.
2. Save the workbook with Save As and name it **ExcelS3-02**.
3. Make E7 the active cell, type **=now()**, and then press Enter.

   The current date and time is inserted in E7 and the column width automatically expands to accommodate the length of the entry. In the next step, you will try the TODAY function to see the difference between the two.

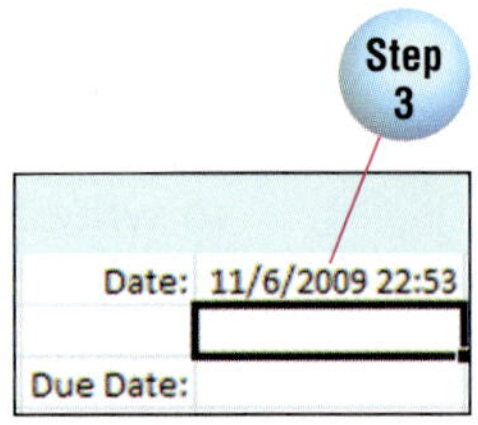

4. Make E7 the active cell, press Delete to clear the cell, type **=today()**, and then press Enter.

   The current date is inserted in the cell with the time displayed as *0:00*. Normally, the time does not display when TODAY is used; however, since we first entered the NOW function, Excel retained the time format for the cell. In a later step, you will format the cell to display the month, day, and year only.

5. Make E9 the active cell, type **=e7+30**, and then press Enter to calculate the due date as 30 days from the invoice date.

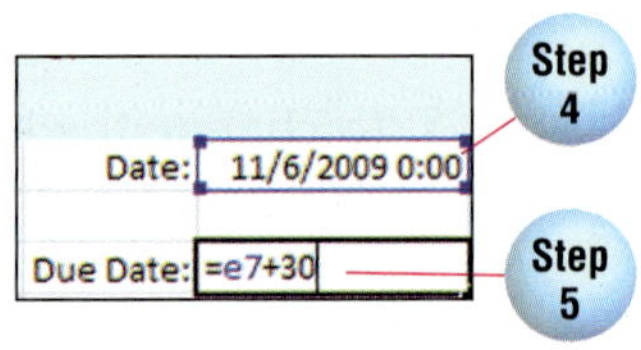

6. Make E5 the active cell, click the Sum button arrow, and then click *More Functions* at the drop-down list.

   The Insert Function dialog box opens. Search for a function by typing a phrase describing the type of formula you want in the *Search for a function* text box and then clicking the Go button or by selecting a category name and then browsing a list of functions.

7. At the Insert Function dialog box, click the down-pointing arrow to the right of the *Or select a category* list box and then click *Date & Time* at the drop-down list.

   The *Select a function* list box displays an alphabetical list of date and time functions. Clicking a function name causes the formula with its argument structure and a description to appear below the list box.

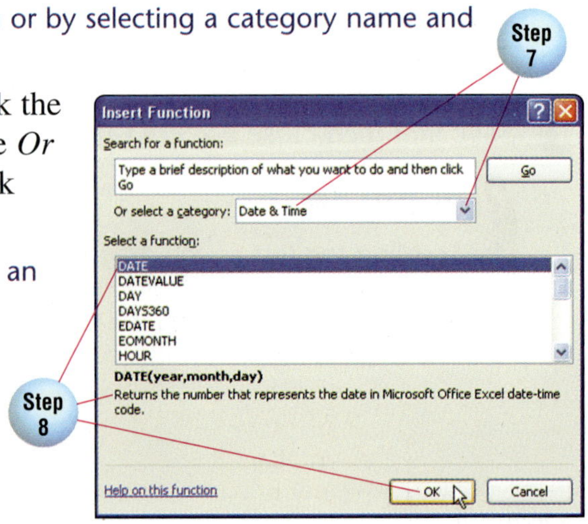

8. With *DATE* already selected in the *Select a function* list box, read the description of the formula and then click OK.

   The Function Arguments dialog box opens with a text box for each section of the function argument.

9. Type **1977** in the *Year* text box.

10. Press Tab to move the insertion point to the *Month* text box and then type **06**.

11. Press Tab to move the insertion point to the *Day* text box, type **15**, and then click OK.

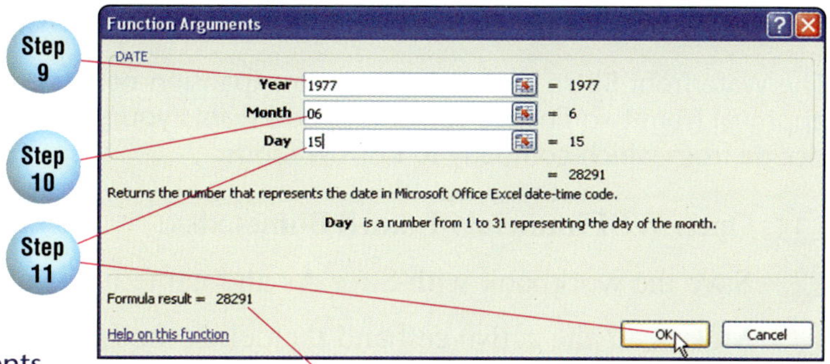

   The Function Arguments dialog box displays the serial number for June 15, 1977, as *28291* which is the value Excel stores in the cell. Notice the formula in the Formula bar is *=DATE(1977,6,15).*

12. Right-click E5 and then click *Format Cells* at the shortcut menu.

13. If necessary, click the Number tab in the Format Cells dialog box.

    Since the active cell contains a date function, the *Date* category will be automatically selected in the *Category* list box.

14. Scroll down the list of formats in the *Type* list box; click *Mar-01*, the format that will display the date as mmm-yy; and then click OK.

15. Format E5 to 9-point Candara italic and left-align the text.

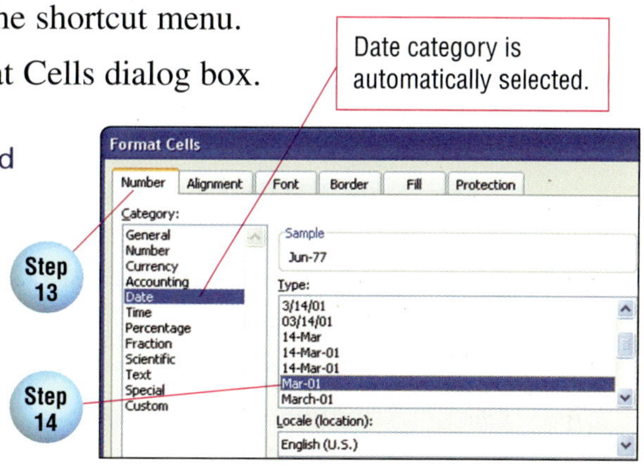

16. Select E7:E9 and then display the Format Cells dialog box with the Number tab selected.

17. Click *Date* in the *Category* list box. Scroll down the *Type* list box; click *14-Mar-2001*, the format that displays the date as dd-mmm-yyyy; and then click OK.

18. Click in any cell to deselect E7:E9.

19. Save and then close **ExcelS3-02.xlsx**.

In Brief

Date Functions

1. Make desired cell active.
2. Click Sum button arrow.
3. Click *More Functions*.
4. Change category to *Date & Time*.
5. Click desired function name.
6. Click OK.
7. Enter references in Function Arguments dialog box.
8. Click OK.

In Addition

TIME Function

Time values are stored as decimal numbers that represent the portion of a day starting at 0 (12:00:00 AM) and continuing up to 0.999988426, representing (23:59:59 PM). The format of the TIME function using the 24-hour clock is *=TIME(hour,minute,second)*. In the worksheet shown at the right, the formula *=(C2-B2)*24* is used to calculate how many hours the employee worked.

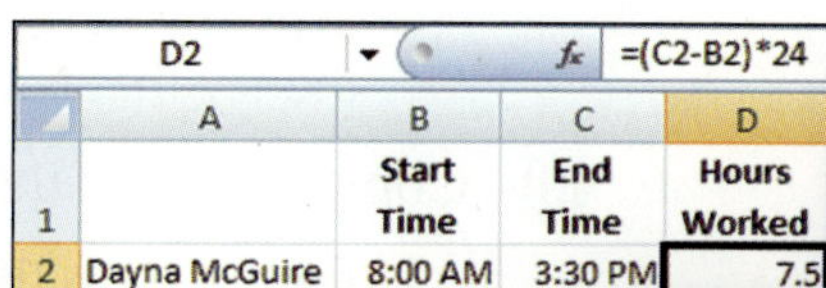

Activity 3.3

Using Financial Functions PMT and PPMT

You can use Excel's financial functions to calculate depreciation, interest rates, payments, terms, present values, future values, and so on. The PMT function is used to calculate a payment for a loan based on constant payments, a constant interest rate, and a set period of time. Using PPMT, you can calculate the principal portion of a specific payment for a loan. For example, you can ask Excel for the amount of principal on the first payment or the last payment of a mortgage to see the amount that you are actually paying down on the loan.

Project

The Waterfront Bistro is planning a patio expansion next year. Dana Hirsch has received preapproval from two finance companies and wants you to calculate payments for each to help decide from which company to borrow funds.

1. Open **WBFinancials-Loan&Bonus.xlsx**.
2. Save the workbook with Save As and name it **ExcelS3-03**.
3. Make C12 the active cell and then click the Insert Function button on the Formula bar.
4. At the Insert Function dialog box, with *Type a brief description of what you want to do and then click Go* already selected in the *Search for a function* text box, type **loan payments** and then click the Go button.

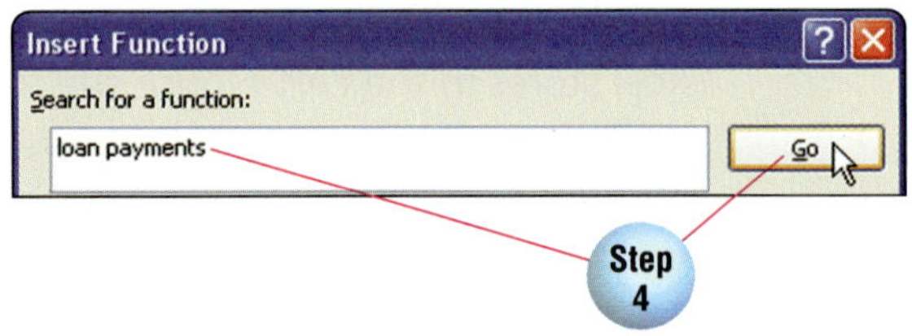

5. With *PMT* already selected in the *Select a function* list box, read the description below the list box and then click OK.

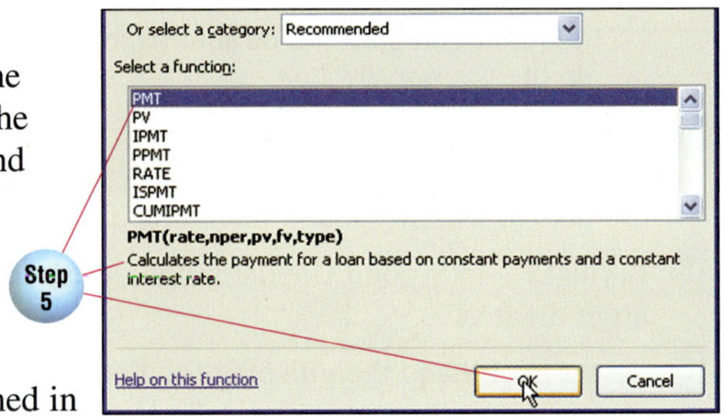

6. If necessary, drag the Function Arguments Title bar to the right of column C.
7. With the insertion point positioned in the *Rate* text box, click the mouse in C8 and then type **/12**.

   Typing */12* divides the annual interest rate by 12 to obtain a monthly interest rate.

8. Click in the *Nper* text box, click C9, and then type ***12**.

   Typing **12* calculates the number of payments that will be made on the loan.

9. Click in the *Pv* text box, click C10, and then click OK.

   Pv stands for *present value* and represents the principal amount that is being borrowed. Excel returns the payment amount *–$3,825.17* for the Funds Unlimited loan in C12. Payments are displayed as negative values. Consider loan payments as money that is subtracted from your cash balance.

10. Copy and paste the formula from C12 to E12.

    Excel returns the payment *–$4,435.80* for Capital Venture Inc.

11. If necessary, press the Esc key to remove the moving marquee around the copied cell in C12.

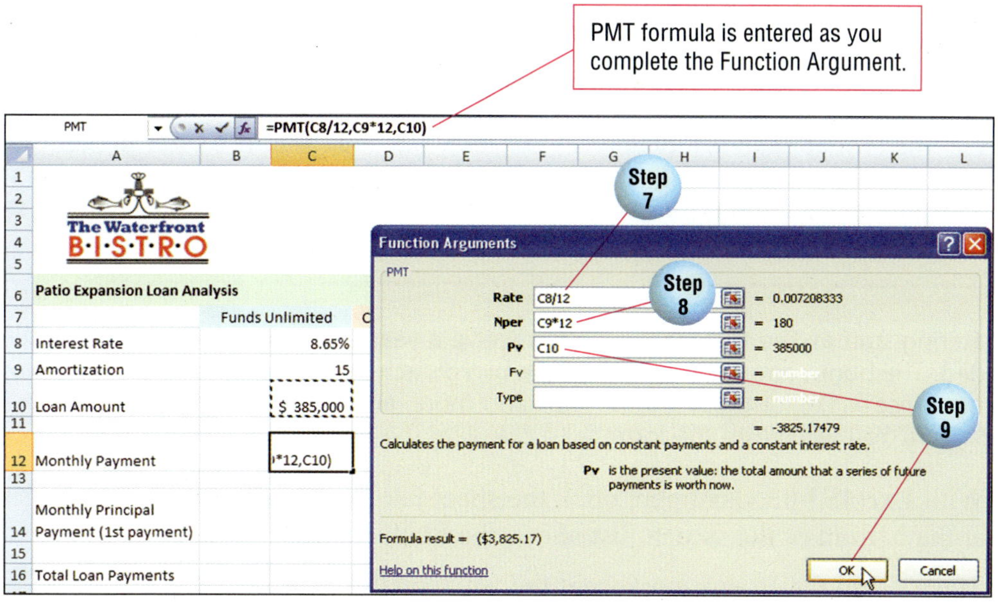

In Brief

Financial Functions

1. Make desired cell active.
2. Click Insert Function button.
3. Change category to *Financial* or search for function by description.
4. Click desired function name.
5. Click OK.
6. Enter references in Function Arguments dialog box.
7. Click OK.

12 Make C14 the active cell and then click the Insert Function button on the Formula bar.

13 At the Insert Function dialog box, type **principal payments** in the *Search for a function* text box and then click Go.

14 Click *PPMT* in the *Select a function* list box and then click OK.

15 At the Function Arguments dialog box, enter the parameters as indicated and then click OK.

Rate **c8/12** Nper **c9*12**
Per **1** Pv **c10**

Per refers to the period for which you want to find the principal portion of the payment. Typing *1* indicates the first payment's principal. To find the principal for the last payment, you would type 180 (15 years × 12 payments).

16 Copy and paste the formula from C14 to E14 and then press the Esc key to remove the moving marquee from C14.

17 Make C16 the active cell, type **=c9*12*c12**, and then press Enter.

18 AutoFit column C.

19 Copy and paste the formula from C16 to E16, remove the moving marquee, and then AutoFit column E.

7		Funds Unlimited	Capital Venture Inc.	
8	Interest Rate	8.65%	9.25%	annual rate
9	Amortization	15	12	years for repayment
10	Loan Amount	$ 385,000	$ 385,000	principal amount borrowed
11				
12	Monthly Payment	($3,825.17)	($4,435.80)	includes principal and interest
13				
14	Monthly Principal Payment (1st payment)	($1,049.97)	($1,468.09)	payment on principal for the first month of the loan
15				
16	Total Loan Payments	($688,531.46)	($638,755.48)	

Steps 12–16

Steps 17–19

Notice that the loan from Capital Venture Inc. is a better choice for The Waterfront Bistro provided the bistro can afford the higher monthly payments. Although the interest rate is higher than Funds Unlimited's loan, the shorter term means the loan is repaid faster.

20 Save **ExcelS3-03.xlsx**.

Activity 3.4

Using the Logical IF Function

The IF function returns one of two values in a cell based on a true or false answer to a question called a *logical test*. The format of an IF function is =*IF(logical_test,value_if_true,value_if_false)*. For example, assume a salesperson earns a 3 percent commission if sales are greater than or equal to $100,000, or a 2 percent commission for sales less than $100,000. Assume the sales value resides in B4. The statement B4>=100000 (*logical_test*) can only return a true or false answer. Depending on the answer, the salesperson's commission will be calculated at either B4*3% (*value_if_true*) or B4*2% (*value_if_false*).

Project

The catering staff at The Waterfront Bistro receive a year-end bonus if the profit target is exceeded. The bonus amount is based on the bistro's actual profit earned and the employee's years of service—1% for those with 5 years and more, and 0.50% for those with service less than 5 years. You will create the formula to calculate the bonuses due each employee.

1. With **ExcelS3-03.xlsx** open, click the sheet tab labeled *Bonus* located at the bottom of the screen just above the Status bar.

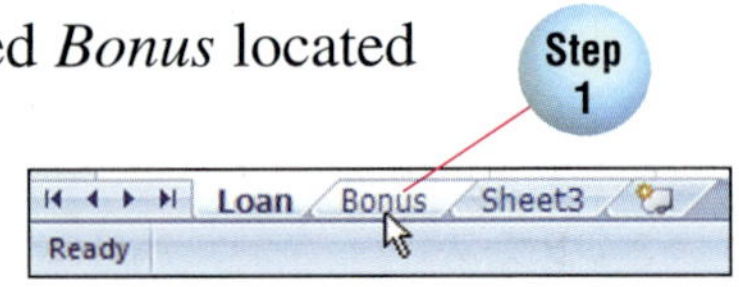

2. Make C7 in the Bonus worksheet the active cell.
3. Type **=i** and then read the ScreenTip that appears next to *IF* in the Formula AutoComplete list box below the cell.

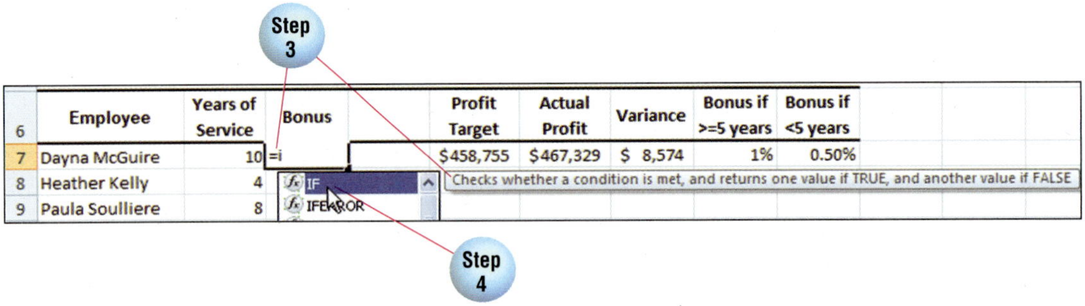

4. Double-click *IF* in the Formula AutoComplete list box.

   Excel completes the entry in the cell to the first bracket =*IF(* and displays in a ScreenTip the required syntax for the argument. The ScreenTip displays the next required entry in the formula in bold (*logical_test*). At any point, you can click the Insert Function button to display the dialog box to assist you.

5. Click the Insert Function button on the Formula bar.
6. Position the cell pointer on the Function Arguments dialog box Title bar and then drag the dialog box down and right until you can see all of the cells in row 7.
7. With the insertion point positioned in the *Logical_test* text box, type **b7<5** and then press Tab.

   To begin the IF statement you want Excel to test whether the value in B7 is less than 5. This test determines whether Excel calculates the bonus using the lower percent paid to employees with fewer than five years of service or the higher percent paid to employees with five or more years of service.

8. With the insertion point positioned in the *Value_if_true* text box, type **f7*i7** and then press Tab.

   If the value in B7 is less than 5, the formula calculates the actual profit (F7) times .50% (I7). Since the formula will be copied to rows 8–15, absolute references are required for those cells that reference the actual profit and the percent.

9. With the insertion point positioned in the *Value_if_false* text box, type **f7*h7** and then click OK.

   If the value in B7 is greater than or equal to 5, the formula calculates the actual profit (F7) times 1% (H7). Notice Excel displays *= FALSE* next to the *Logical_test* text box, *2336.645* next to *Value_if_true*, and *4673.29* next to *Value_if_false*. Below the text boxes, Excel shows the result that will be placed in the active cell *Formula result = 4673.29*.

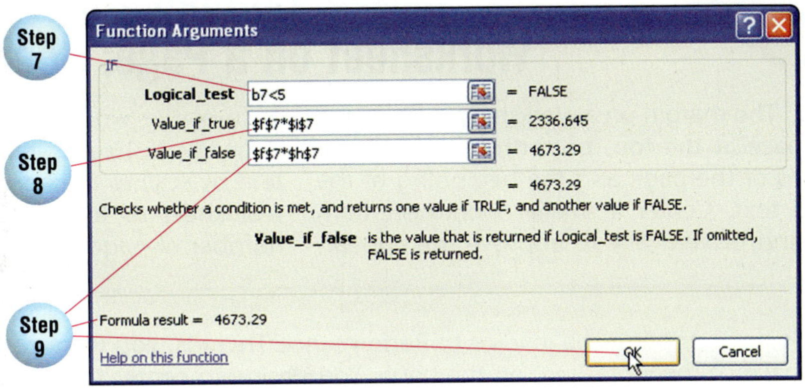

10. Drag the fill handle in C7 down to row 15 and then click in any cell to deselect the range.

    The cell address containing the years of service changed relative to each row (B7 is changed to B8, B9, and so on); however, the cell addresses containing the actual profit and percents (F7, H7, and I7) did not change. Recall from Section 2 that the term for a formula with some addresses relative and some absolute is mixed addressing.

11. Make C17 the active cell and then create a SUM function to calculate the total bonuses to be paid.

12. Format the values in column C to Comma Style.

13. Click each cell individually within the range C8 to C15 and review the formula in the Formula bar.

14. Save and then close **ExcelS3-03.xlsx**.

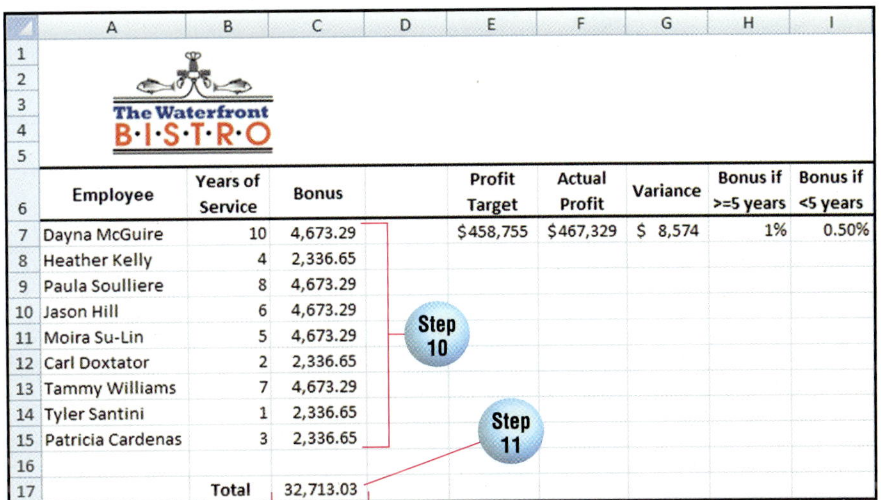

	A	B	C	D	E	F	G	H	I
6	Employee	Years of Service	Bonus		Profit Target	Actual Profit	Variance	Bonus if >=5 years	Bonus if <5 years
7	Dayna McGuire	10	4,673.29		$458,755	$467,329	$ 8,574	1%	0.50%
8	Heather Kelly	4	2,336.65						
9	Paula Soulliere	8	4,673.29						
10	Jason Hill	6	4,673.29						
11	Moira Su-Lin	5	4,673.29						
12	Carl Doxtator	2	2,336.65						
13	Tammy Williams	7	4,673.29						
14	Tyler Santini	1	2,336.65						
15	Patricia Cardenas	3	2,336.65						
16									
17		Total	32,713.03						

values in column C formatted to Comma Style in Step 12

In Brief

IF Function

1. Make desired cell active.
2. Click Insert Function button.
3. Change category to *Logical*.
4. Click *IF*.
5. Click OK.
6. Enter conditional formula in *Logical_test* text box.
7. Enter formula or value in *Value_if_true* text box.
8. Enter formula or value in *Value_if_false* text box.
9. Click OK.

In Addition

Nested IF Function

If more than two actions are required when a logical test is performed, a nested IF function is used. For example, if three bonus rates were dependent on years of service the IF function entered in C7 would not have been able to calculate the correct bonus amount. Assume the dining room staff receive 1% if they have 5 years of service or more, 0.50% for 2–5 years, and 0.25% for less than 2 years. An example of the IF function that would calculate the bonus is:

=IF(B7>=5,$F$7*1%,IF(B7>=2,
$F$7*0.50%,$F$7*0.25%))

The two parentheses at the end of the argument are required to close both IF statements. Excel allows you to nest up to 64 IF statements.

Activity 3.5

Changing Margins; Centering a Worksheet on a Page; Scaling a Worksheet

The margin on a worksheet is the blank space at the top, bottom, left, and right edges of the page and the beginning of the printed text. Center a smaller worksheet horizontally and/or vertically to improve the appearance of the worksheet for printing purposes. For larger worksheets, you can choose to shrink the text by scaling the height and/or the width of the worksheet to force the printout to a maximum number of pages.

Project

The Waterfront B·I·S·T·R·O

Prior to printing the invoice to Performance Threads, you want to adjust the left margin to balance the worksheet on the page. You decide to center the *Bonus* worksheet horizontally and vertically and print the worksheet in landscape orientation. Finally, you will scale the inventory units purchased report to fit on two landscape pages.

1. Open **ExcelS3-02.xlsx**.
2. Click the Office button, point to *Print*, and then click *Print Preview*.

   Notice the invoice is unbalanced at the left edge of the page with a larger amount of white space on the right side. One method of correcting this is to change the left margin.

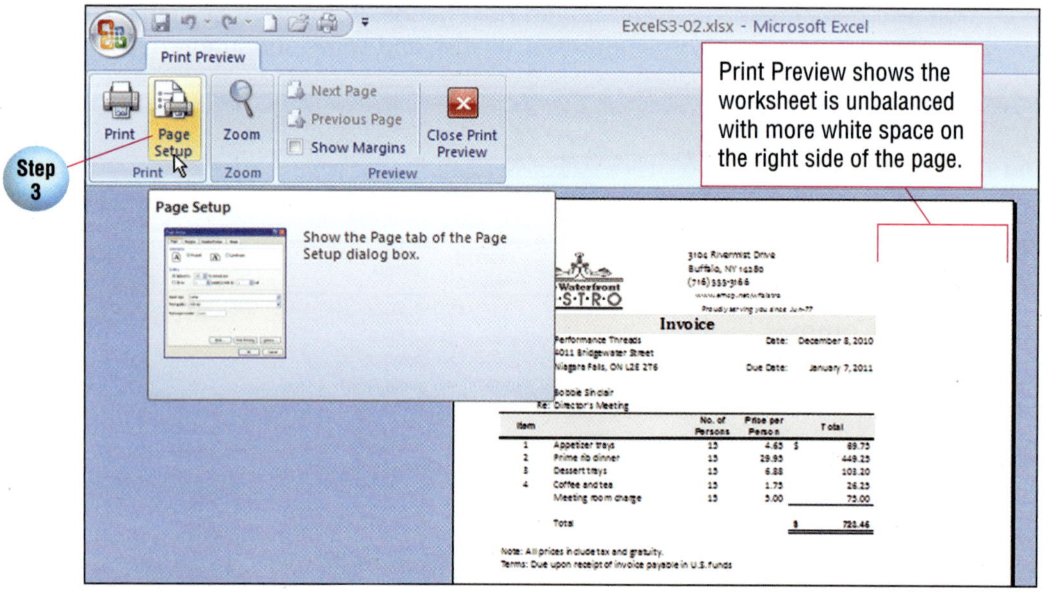

3. Click the Page Setup button in the Print group in the Print Preview tab.
4. If necessary, click the Margins tab at the Page Setup dialog box.
5. Select the current entry in the *Left* text box, type **1.25**, and then click OK.

   The worksheet now appears balanced between the left and right edges of the page.
6. Click the Print button in the Print group.

   The Print Preview window closes and the Print dialog box appears.

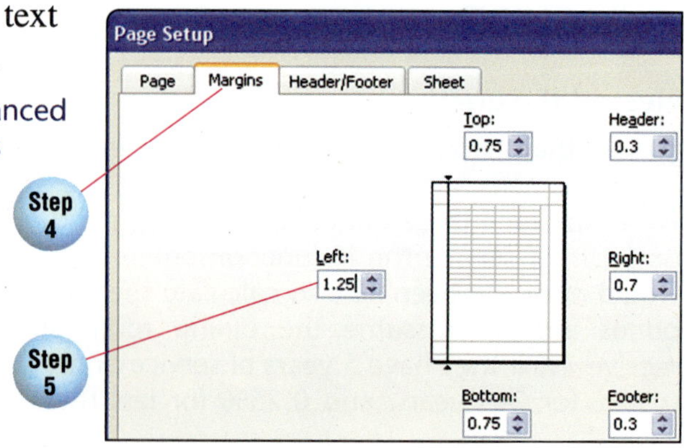

7. At the Print dialog box, click OK.
8. Save and then close **ExcelS3-02.xlsx**.
9. Open **ExcelS3-03.xlsx** and make sure the Bonus worksheet is the active worksheet. (Click the Bonus worksheet tab at the bottom of the worksheet area if the worksheet is not currently displayed.)
10. Click the Page Layout tab, click the Orientation button in the Page Setup group, and then click *Landscape*.
11. Click the Margins button in the Page Setup group and then click *Custom Margins* at the drop-down list.

    The Page Setup dialog box opens with the Margins tab active.

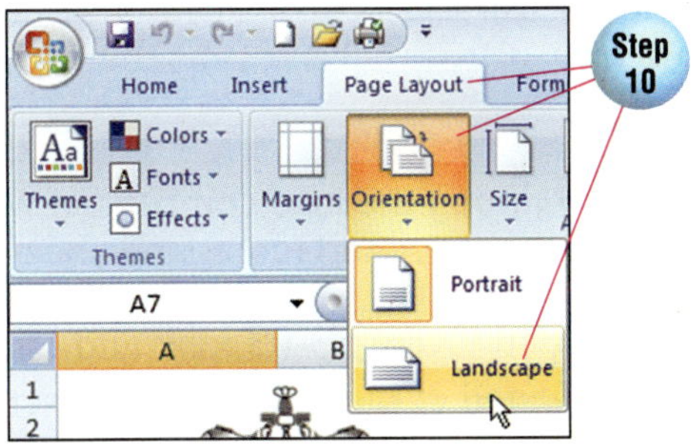

12. Click the *Horizontally* check box in the *Center on page* section and then click OK.

    Centering the worksheet horizontally is another method that can be used to ensure the worksheet prints balanced between the left and right edges of the page. You can choose both the *Horizontally* and *Vertically* check boxes to print a worksheet that is centered between both the left and right edges (horizontally), and the top and bottom edges (vertically) of the page.

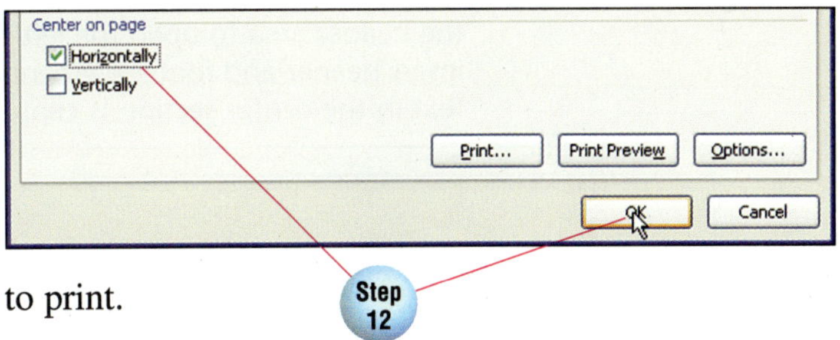

13. Click the Quick Print button on the Quick Access toolbar.
14. Save and then close **ExcelS3-03.xlsx**.
15. Open **ExcelS3-01.xlsx**.
16. Display the worksheet in Print Preview. Notice the worksheet requires four pages to print.
17. Click the Close Print Preview button in the Preview group.
18. With the Page Layout tab active, click the Orientation button in the Page Setup group and then click *Landscape*.
19. Click the Width button arrow (currently displays *Automatic*) in the Scale to Fit group and then click *1 page* at the drop-down list.
20. Click the Height button arrow (currently displays *Automatic*) in the Scale to Fit group and then click *2 pages* at the drop-down list.
21. Print the worksheet.
22. Save and then close **ExcelS3-01.xlsx**.

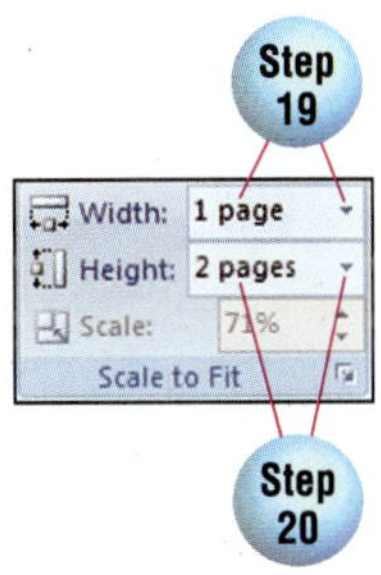

In Brief

Change Margins and/or Center Worksheet

1. Display worksheet in Print Preview.
2. Click Page Setup button.
3. Change required margin setting and/or click *Horizontally* and/or *Vertically* check box.
4. Click OK.

Scale Worksheet

1. Click Page Layout tab.
2. Click Width button arrow.
3. Click desired number of pages to scale width.
4. Click Height button arrow.
5. Click desired number of pages to scale height.

In Addition

Printing Column or Row Headings on Multiple Pages

Use the Print Titles button in the Page Setup group in the Page Layout tab to define column or row headings that you want repeated at the top or left edge of each page to make the data in rows and columns in a multi-page printout easier to identify.

Activity 3.6

Using Page Layout View; Inserting Headers and Footers

Page Layout view allows you to view the worksheet along with the print settings. Page Layout view also displays a horizontal and vertical ruler to assist with measurements. A header is text that prints at the top of each worksheet and a footer is text that prints at the bottom of each worksheet. Excel includes predefined headers and footers that can be selected from a drop-down list or you can create your own custom header or footer text.

Project

Before printing the loan comparison worksheet, you want to add identifying information in a custom header and footer and check other print options using Page Layout view.

1. Open **Excel S3-03.xlsx** and click the sheet tab labeled *Loan* located at the bottom of the screen just above the Status bar.

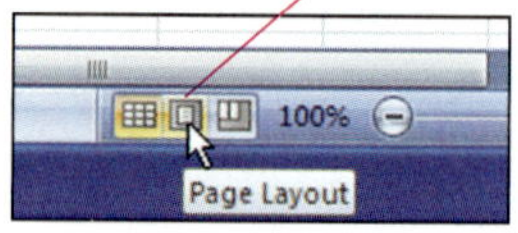

2. Click the Page Layout button located at the right side of the Status bar near the Zoom slider bar.
3. If necessary, use the horizontal and vertical scroll bars to adjust the window so that the Loan worksheet including the white space for the top, left, and right margins is entirely visible.
4. Click over the text *Click to add header* near the top center of the page.

   A header and footer are divided into three sections. Click at the left or right side of the header area to open the left or right section text box in which you can type or insert header and footer elements. By default, text in the left section is left-aligned, text in the center section is centered, and text in the right section is right-aligned.

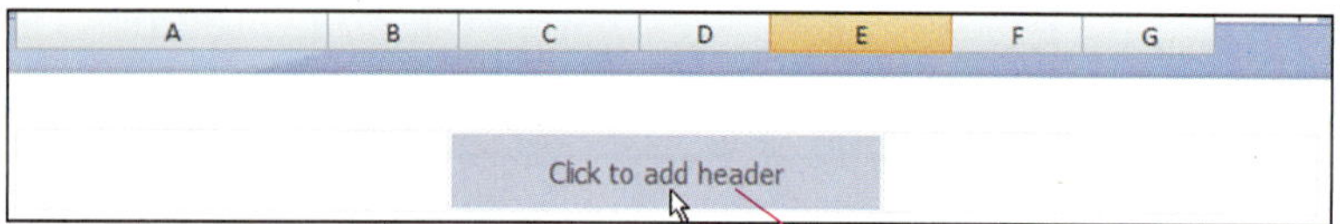

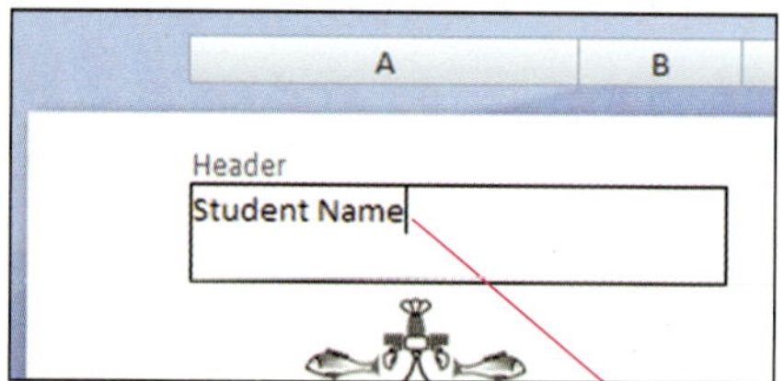

5. Click at the left edge of the Header area to open the left section text box and then type your first and last names.
6. Click at the right edge of the Header area to open the right section text box, type **Date Printed:**, and then press the spacebar once.
7. Click the Current Date button in the Header & Footer Elements group in the Header & Footer Tools Design tab.

   Excel inserts the code *&[Date]*, which causes the current date to be inserted at the location of the code when the worksheet is printed.

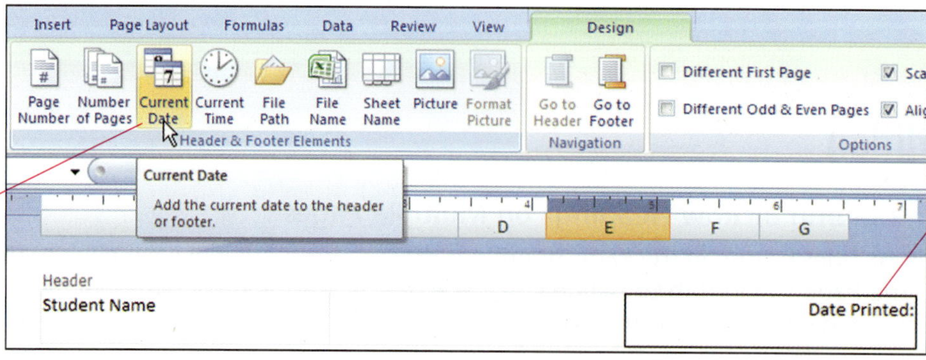

In Brief

Insert Header or Footer

1. Switch to Page Layout view.
2. Click over *Click to add header* or *Click to add footer.*
3. Insert desired header and footer elements and/or type text in left, center, or right section.
4. Click in worksheet area to end header or footer editing.

8 Click the Go to Footer button in the Navigation group in the Header & Footer Tools Design tab.

The right footer section at the bottom of the page opens for editing.

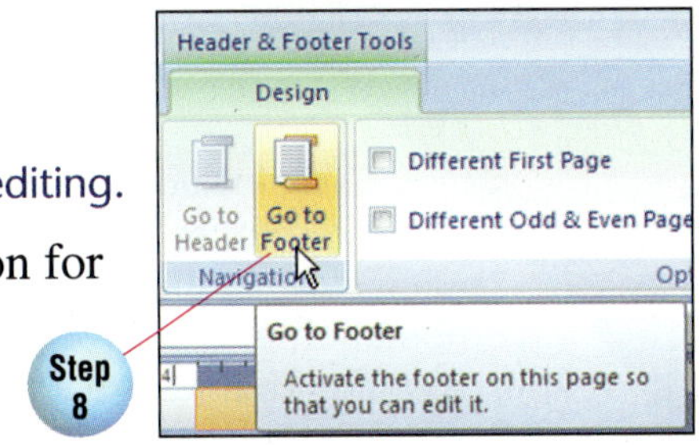

9 Click in the center of the Footer area to open the center section for editing.

10 Click the File Name button in the Header & Footer Elements group, press the spacebar once, and then click the Sheet Name button in the same group.

Excel inserts the codes *&[File]* and *&[Tab]*, which causes the workbook file name followed by the worksheet name to be inserted at the location of the codes when printed.

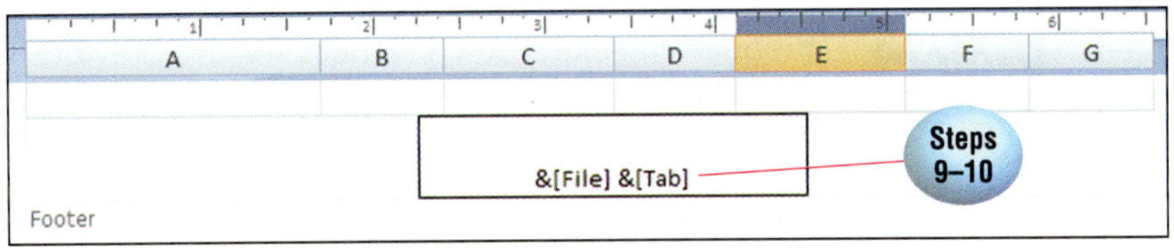

11 Click anywhere in the worksheet area outside the footer to close the footer section.

12 Scroll to the top of the worksheet to view the header. Notice that Excel now displays the current date in place of the *&[Date]* code.

13 Scroll to the bottom of the worksheet and notice that the *&[File]* and *&[Tab]* codes now display the workbook file name followed by the sheet name.

14 Click the Page Layout tab.

15 Click the Margins button in the Page Setup group, click *Custom Margins* at the drop-down list, and then change the margin settings as indicated below at the Page Setup dialog box with the Margins tab active:

Left	**1**	Bottom	**1**
Top	**1**	Footer	**0.5**
Header	**0.5**		

16 Click OK to close the Page Setup dialog box.

17 Review the new margin settings in Page Layout view.

Review new margin settings in Page Layout view in Step 17.

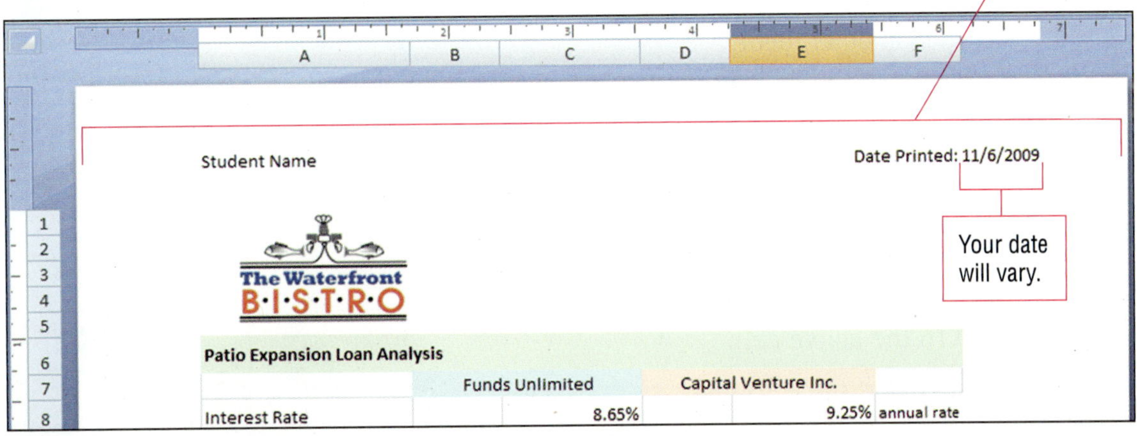

18 Print the worksheet.

19 Click the Normal button located at the right side of the Status bar near the Zoom slider bar (immediately left of the Page Layout View button).

20 Save and then close **ExcelS3-03.xlsx**.

Activity 3.7

Formatting a Worksheet Using a Theme; Inserting a SmartArt Diagram

Excel includes several predefined workbook themes which you can apply to quickly format the workbook in a coordinated combination of color, fonts, and effects such as lines and fills. Themes are shared in Word, Excel, and PowerPoint so that you can create a consistent look for all business publications. Enter values or text into a SmartArt diagram to visually present a process or a relationship between data. SmartArt includes over 80 layouts grouped according to the categories: list, process, cycle, hierarchy, relationship, matrix, and pyramid.

Project

The quarterly expense worksheet for the previous year is finished. You want to experiment with themes to find a professional look for the report and add a diagram to emphasize the expense approval process.

1. Open **WBQtrExpenses.xlsx**.
2. Save the workbook with Save As and name it **ExcelS3-04**.
3. Click the Page Layout tab.
4. Click the Themes button in the Themes group.
5. Move the mouse over each of the themes in the drop-down gallery and watch live preview apply the theme's colors and fonts to the worksheet.
6. Click *Verve*.

   In the next step, assume that you prefer the font in the Verve theme but want to change the color scheme to one used in another theme.

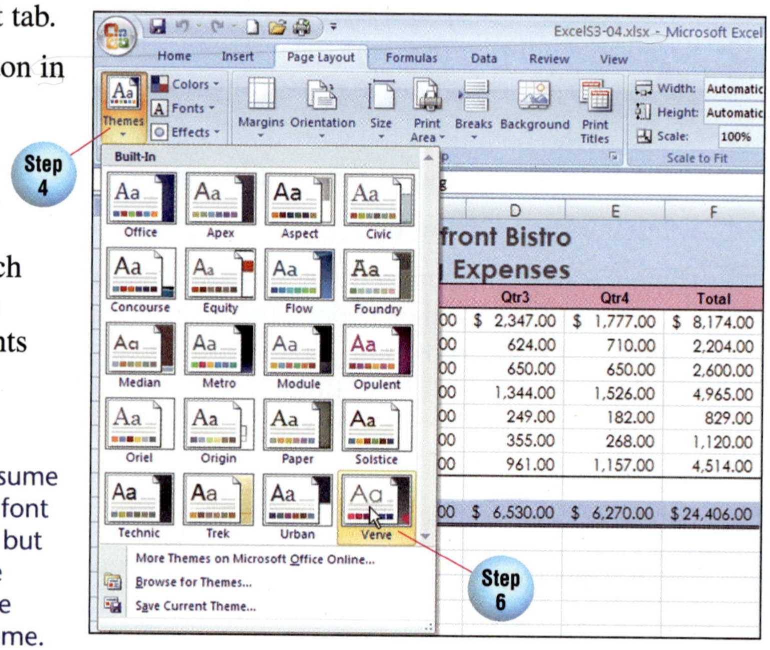

7. Click the Colors button Colors in the Themes group.
8. Click *Solstice* at the drop-down gallery.

   Notice that in Steps 4–8 you did not have to select cells before applying theme formatting; themes automatically apply to all cells in the worksheet.

9. Make A16 the active cell.
10. Click the Insert tab.
11. Click the SmartArt button in the Illustrations group.

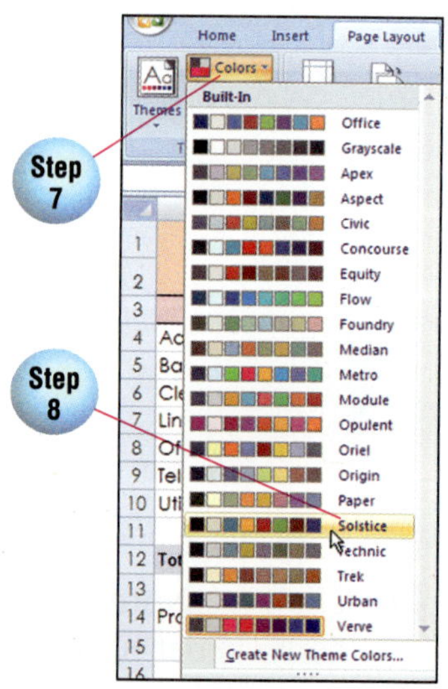

In Brief

Apply Worksheet Theme

1. Click Page Layout tab.
2. Click Themes button.
3. Click desired theme.

Create SmartArt Object

1. Click Insert tab.
2. Click SmartArt button.
3. Click category in left pane.
4. Click desired layout in center pane.
5. Click OK.
6. Type text inside text pane or inside boxes.
7. Move and/or resize as required.
8. Apply design options.
9. Click outside SmartArt object.

12 At the Choose a SmartArt Graphic dialog box, click *Process* in the left pane and then click *Basic Bending Process* in the center pane (first option in fifth row). Examine the preview of the graphic in the right pane and read the description below. Click OK.

A SmartArt object is dropped over the worksheet. Text to be contained within the objects can either be typed in the left pane or directly within the box. The object can be moved and resized; do not be concerned that the graphic is overlapping the worksheet cells.

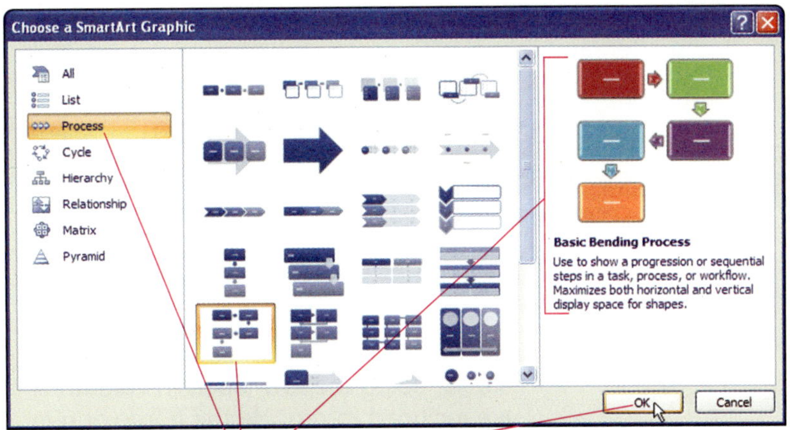

Step 12

13 If a *Type your text here* window displays at the left side of the diagram, click the Text Pane button in the Create Graphic group.

Step 14

14 Click over *[Text]* in the top left box within the SmartArt object and then type **Accounting clerk checks invoices**.

The font size is automatically scaled to fit the text within the box.

15 Enter text in the remaining boxes as indicated by clicking the box and then typing the text. After entering text into the last box, click outside the box within the perimeter of the SmartArt object.

Top Middle Box	**Executive chef approves food purchases**
Top Right Box	**Dining Room manager approves other purchases**
Bottom Left Box	**Final approval by bistro manager**
Bottom Right Box	**Accounting clerk inputs invoices into computer**

16 Point to the border of the SmartArt object until the pointer displays with the four-headed arrow move icon, hold down the left mouse button, and then drag the SmartArt object to the top right of the worksheet (top left corner begins in G1).

Step 19

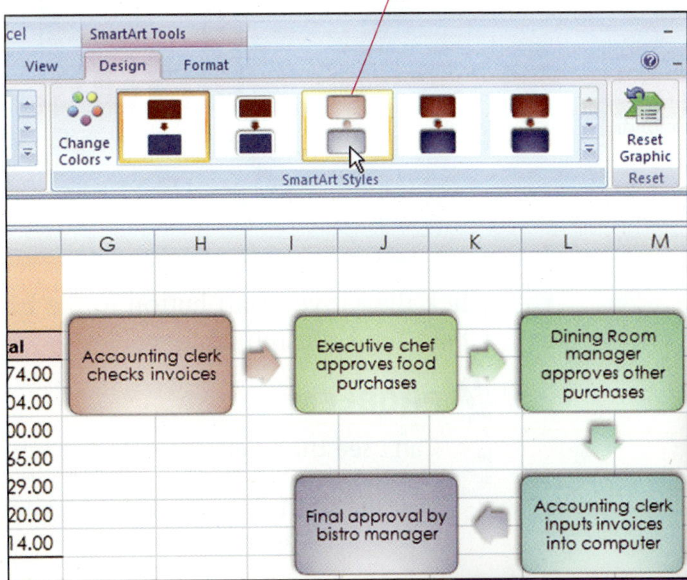

17 If necessary, click the SmartArt Tools Design tab.

18 Click the Change Colors button in the SmartArt Styles group and then click *Colorful Range - Accent Colors 5 to 6* at the drop-down gallery (last option in the *Colorful* section).

19 Click the *Subtle Effect* option in the SmartArt Styles group (third option from left).

20 Click outside the SmartArt graphic to deselect the object.

21 Save **ExcelS3-04.xlsx**.

Activity 3.8

Creating a Column Chart

Numerical values are often more easily understood when presented visually in a chart. Excel includes several chart types such as column, line, pie, bar, area, scatter, and others with which you can graphically portray data. The chart can be placed in the same worksheet as the data or it can be inserted into its own sheet. To create a chart, first select the cells containing the data you want to graph and then choose the chart type. Excel graphs the data in a separate object which can be moved, resized, and formatted.

Project

Continuing with the quarterly operating expenses worksheet, Dana Hirsch has asked you to create a chart to compare the expenses in each quarter.

1. With **ExcelS3-04.xlsx** open, select A3:E10.

   The first step in creating a chart is to select the range of cells containing the data you want to chart. Notice in the range that you are including the row labels in column A. Labels are included to provide the frame of reference for each bar, column, or other chart series.

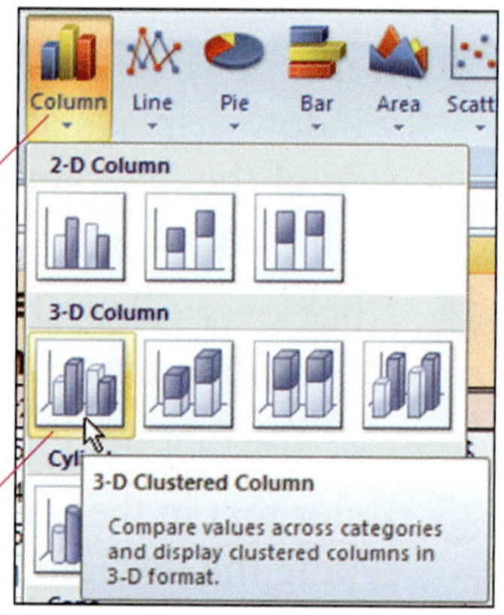

Step 3

Step 4

2. Click the Insert tab.
3. Click the Column button in the Charts group.
4. Click *3-D Clustered Column* at the drop-down list (first from left in *3-D Column* section).

   Excel graphs the data in a 3-D column chart and places the chart inside an object box in the center of the worksheet.

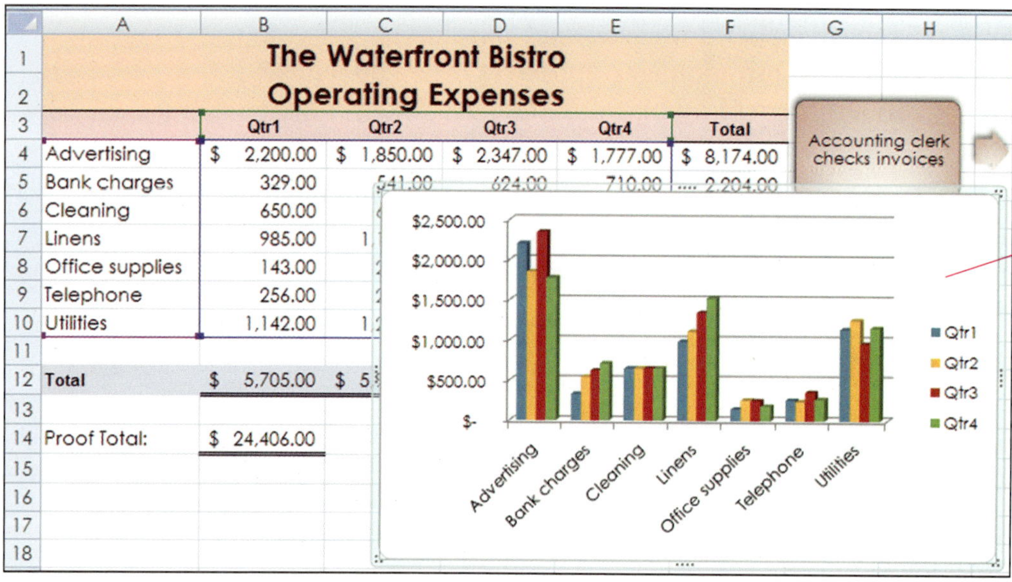

3-D column chart created in Step 4 is placed in an object box which can be moved, resized, and formatted as needed.

Step 5

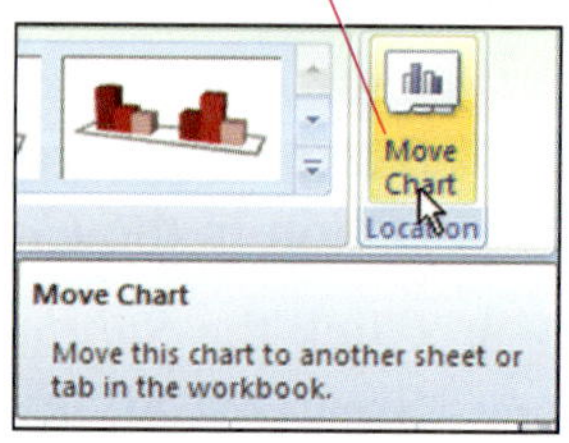

5. Click the Move Chart button in the Location group in the Chart Tools Design tab.

PROBLEM

Can't see the Chart Tools Design tab? You probably clicked outside the chart to deselect the object and the contextual tab disappeared. Click over the chart to select the object and the contextual Chart Tools Design tab reappears.

6. At the Move Chart dialog box, click *New sheet*.
7. With *Chart1* selected in the *New sheet* text box, type **ColumnChart** and then click OK.

   The chart object is moved to a new sheet in the workbook with a tab labeled *ColumnChart*. The chart is automatically scaled to fill the entire page in landscape orientation

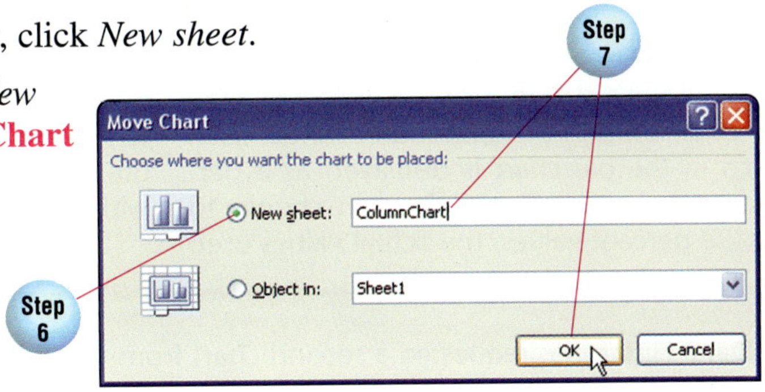

8. Click *Layout 3* in the Chart Layouts group.

   This layout adds a title to the top center of the chart and moves the legend to the bottom center.

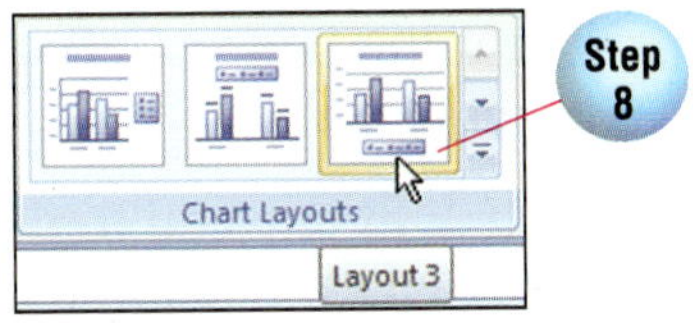

9. Click once over *Chart Title* to select the title object, click a second time at the beginning of the text to place an insertion point inside the chart title box, delete *Chart Title*, and then type **Operating Expenses by Quarter**.

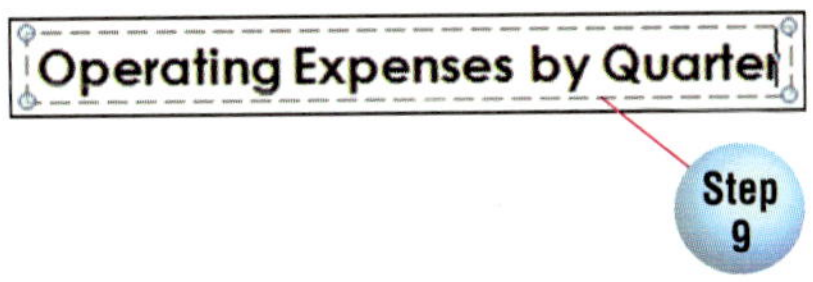

10. Click inside the chart area to deselect the title text.
11. Click the More arrow button in the Chart Styles group in the Chart Tools Design tab.

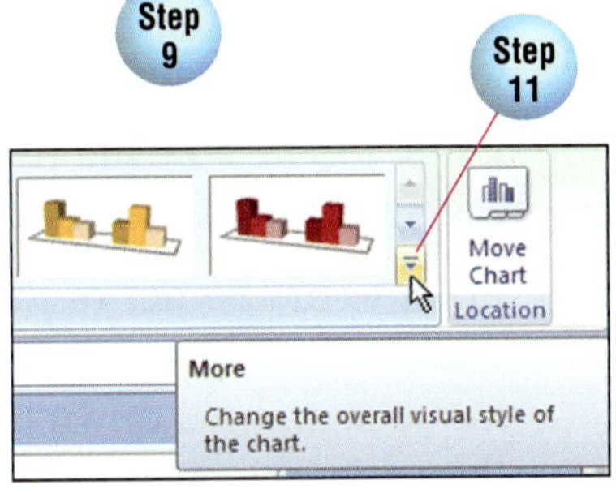

12. Click *Style 8* in the drop-down list (last option in the first row).
13. Save **ExcelS3-04.xlsx**.

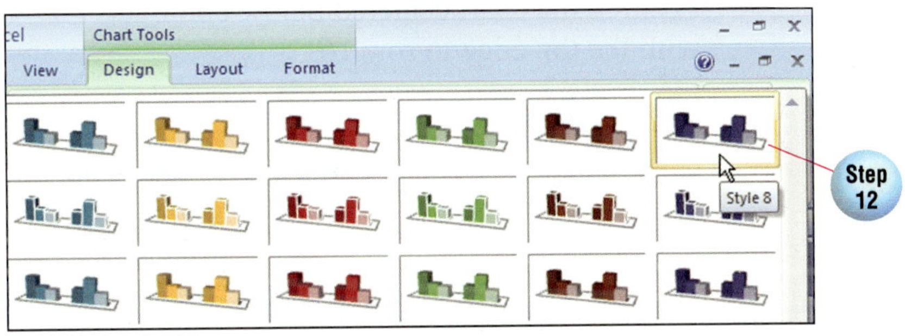

In Brief

Create Column Chart

1. Select cells.
2. Click Insert tab.
3. Click Column button.
4. Click desired chart type.
5. Move and/or resize as required.
6. Apply design options.

In Addition

Changing the Data in a Chart

Click the Select Data button in the Data group in the Chart Tools Design tab to add cells to, or delete cells from, the source range that was selected to generate the chart. At the Select Data Source dialog box shown at the right, you can add, edit, or delete a data series or edit the category axis labels.

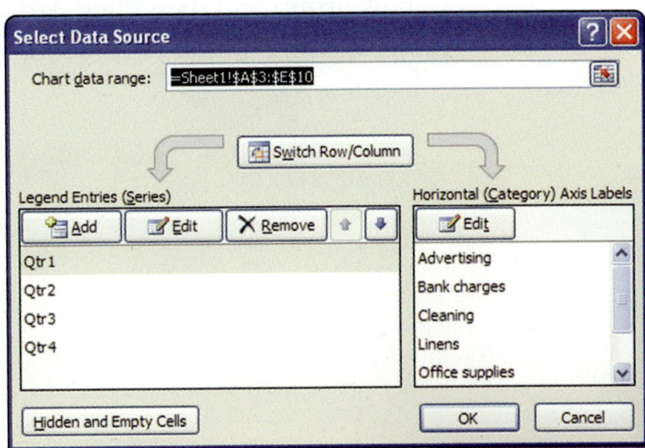

Activity 3.9

Creating a Pie Chart

Pie charts illustrate each data point's size in proportion to the total of all items in the data source range. Each slice in the pie chart is displayed as a percentage of the whole pie. You can choose to display the percent values, the actual values used to generate the chart, or both values as data labels inside or outside the pie slices. Use a pie chart when you have only one data series you want to graph and there are no negative or zero values within the data range.

Project

Dana Hirsch has requested a second chart from the quarterly operating expenses worksheet that depicts each expense as a proportion of the total expenses.

The Waterfront B·I·S·T·R·O

1. With **ExcelS3-04.xlsx** open, click the tab labeled *Sheet1* near the bottom left corner of the window above the Status bar.

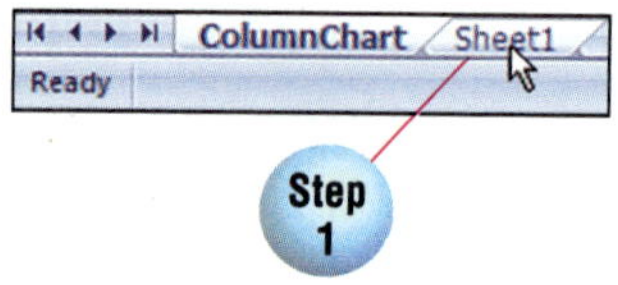

2. Click in any cell to deselect the range that was used to generate the column chart in the previous activity.
3. Select the range A3:A10, hold down the Ctrl key, and then select the range F3:F10.
4. Click the Insert tab.
5. Click the Pie button in the Charts group.
6. Click *Pie in 3-D*, the first pie chart in the *3-D Pie* section in the drop-down list.
7. Point to the border of the chart object until the pointer displays with the four-headed arrow move icon, hold down the left mouse button, and then drag the chart below the worksheet. Position the chart centered below columns A–F with the top edge in row 16.

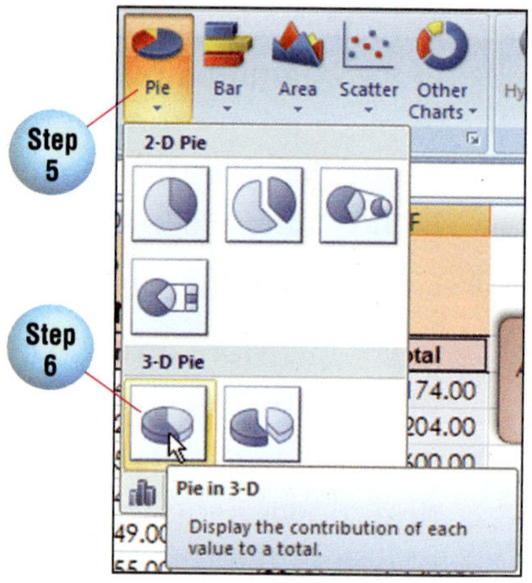

? PROBLEM

You may find it helpful to scroll the worksheet until you see several blank rows below row 16 before moving the chart.

8. Click the Chart Tools Layout tab.
9. Click the Data Labels button in the Labels group and then click *More Data Label Options* at the drop-down list.

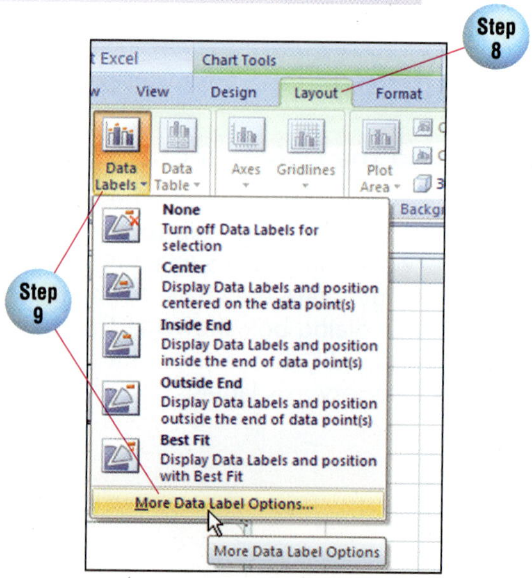

10. At the Format Data Labels dialog box with *Label Options* selected in the left pane, click the *Value* check box in the *Label Contains* section to clear the box and then click the *Percentage* check box to add a check mark.

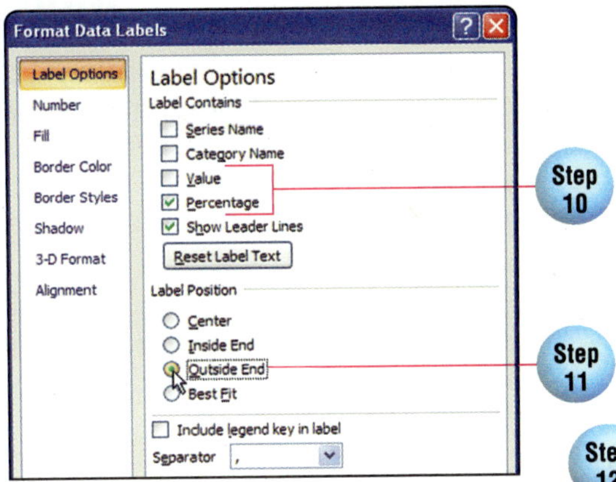

11. Click *Outside End* in the *Label Position* section.
12. Click *Number* in the left pane, click *Percentage* in the *Category* list box, select the number in the *Decimal places* text box, and then type **1**.

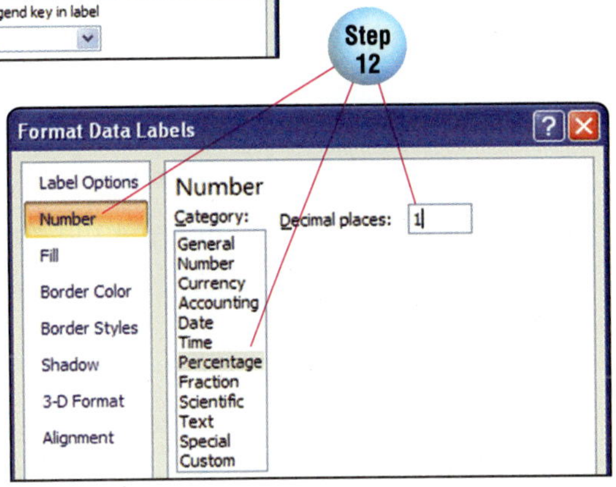

13. Close the Format Data Labels dialog box.
14. Click the Chart Tools Design tab.
15. Click the More arrow button in the Chart Styles group and then click *Style 10* at the drop-down list (second from left in second row).
16. Change the chart title to **Total Operating Expenses**. Refer to Activity 3.8, Steps 9–10 if you need assistance with this step.
17. Click in the worksheet area outside the chart to deselect the chart.
18. Save **ExcelS3-04.xlsx**.

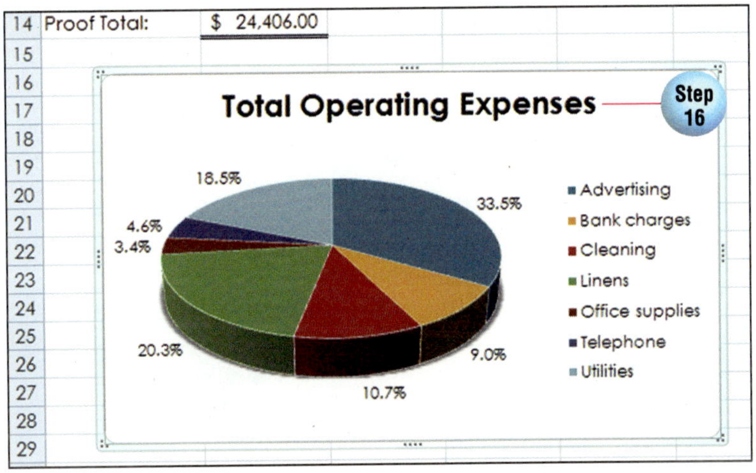

In Brief

Create Pie Chart

1. Select cells.
2. Click Insert tab.
3. Click Pie button.
4. Click desired pie type.
5. Move and/or resize as required.
6. Apply design options.

In Addition

Other Chart Types

Deciding the most appropriate chart type for graphing data can be difficult. Following are descriptions of a few chart types and the type of data for which each is designed.

Area	Emphasizes magnitude by summing the plotted values and then graphing the relationship of each range to the whole.
Bar	Displays individual figures at a specific time or shows variations between data ranges. Bars are displayed horizontally.
Doughnut	Shows the relationship of parts to a whole in a similar manner as a pie chart.
Line	Depicts trends and change over time intervals.
Scatter	Also called an *XY chart*; shows relationships among numeric values or plots interception points between *x* and *y* values.

Activity 3.10

Modifying and Formatting Charts

To make changes to an existing chart, click inside a chart or chart element to display the translucent border around the perimeter of the chart object. Point to the border to move the chart or point to one of the eight sizing handles to resize the chart. When the chart is selected, the Chart Tools Design, Layout, and Format tabs become available. Use these tabs to add, delete, or modify the chart or chart elements.

Project You will modify the charts created for the Operating Expenses worksheet by formatting the legend, changing the font in the chart title, and changing the chart type.

1. With **ExcelS3-04.xlsx** open, click anywhere inside the pie chart to select the chart object.

   Once a chart is selected, the three contextual Chart Tools tabs become available—Design, Layout, and Format.

2. Click inside the pie chart legend.

   Eight sizing handles appear around the legend indicating the object is selected. You can drag the legend to another location or resize the legend using one of the handles.

3. Click the Chart Tools Format tab.

4. Click the Shape Outline button in the Shape Styles group and then click the *Light Blue* color box in the color palette (fourth from right in *Standard Colors* section).

   This adds a thin, light blue border around the legend.

Step 3

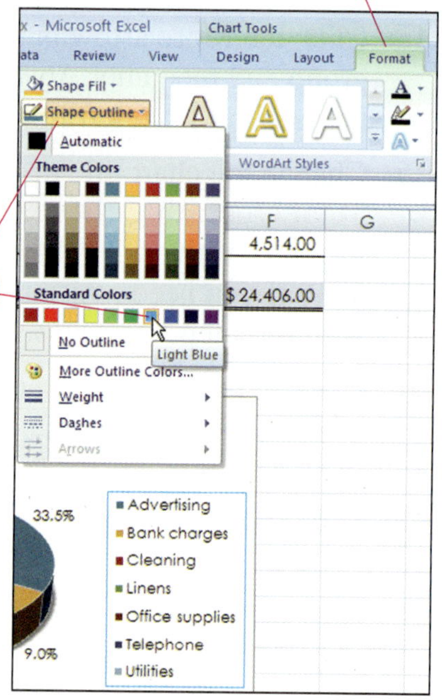

Step 4

5. Right-click the chart title and then use the Font and Font Size buttons in the Mini toolbar to change the title to 16-point Verdana.

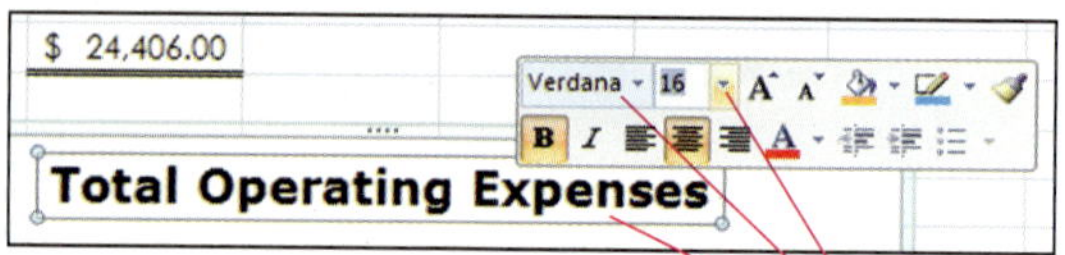

Step 5

6. Click inside the chart area to deselect the chart title.

7. Click inside any one of the percent values around the edge of the pie.

   This selects all seven data labels.

8. Click *10.7%* to select only the one data point. The handles surrounding the other six data points disappear.

9. Point to the border of the data label and then drag the label until it is approximately centered below the pie slice.

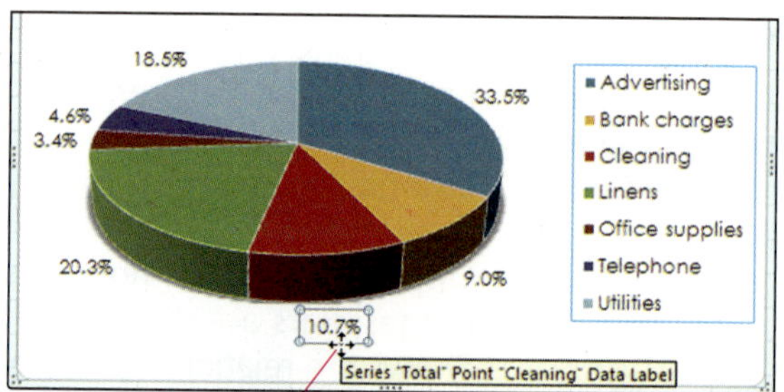

Step 9

10 Click in the worksheet area outside the pie chart.

11 Click the ColumnChart tab and then click inside the column chart to select the chart.

12 Click the Chart Tools Design tab and then click the Change Chart Type button in the Type group.

13 At the Change Chart Type dialog box, click *Bar* in the left pane and then click *Clustered Bar in 3-D* in the *Bar* section in the right pane (fourth from left in first row).

Step 13

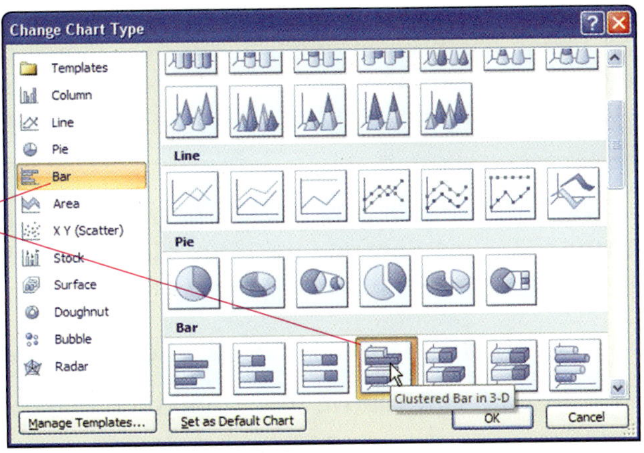

14 Click OK.

15 Click *Layout 1* in the Chart Layouts group.

This layout moves the legend to the right side of the chart where there is more room.

16 Click the More arrow button in the Chart Styles group and then click *Style 2* in the drop-down list.

17 Save **ExcelS3-04.xlsx**.

Layout 1 and Style 2 applied to bar chart in Steps 15–16

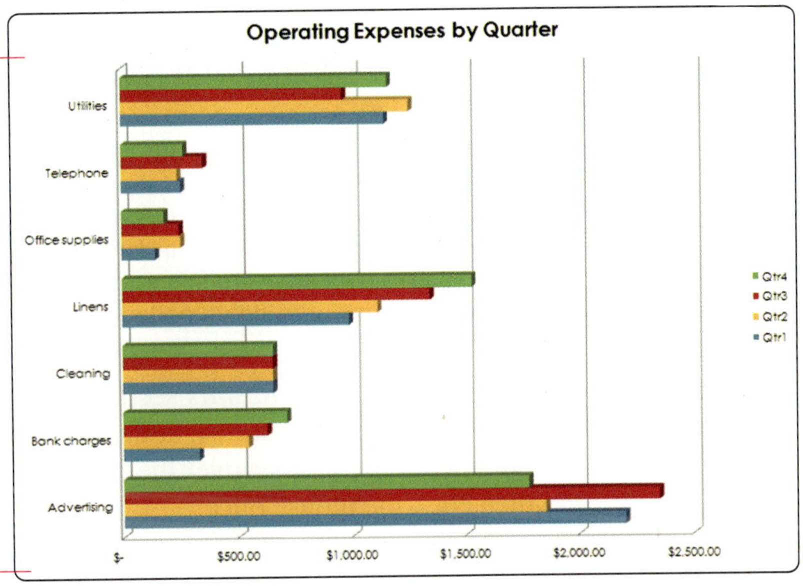

In Brief

Modify Chart

1. Click to select chart or chart element.
2. Use Design, Layout, or Format Chart Tools tabs to add or change options.

In Addition

Chart Elements

Another method to edit a chart is to right-click a chart element to display a context-sensitive shortcut menu. For example, right-clicking the axis labels in the bar chart displays the shortcut menu shown at the right. The bottom section of the shortcut menu changes dependent on the element you clicked.

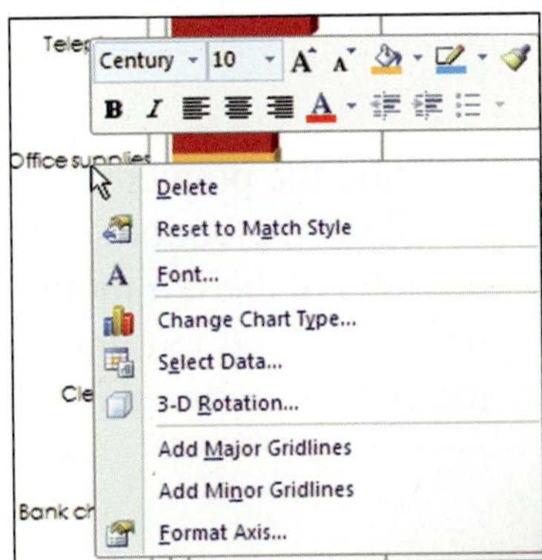

Activity 3.11

Inserting, Moving, and Resizing Pictures and Clip Art

When connected to Office Online, the Microsoft Office suite includes a clip art gallery containing thousands of images. Once a clip art image has been inserted, it can be moved, resized, or deleted. The Clip Art task pane allows you to view images in the gallery and insert them into the worksheet with a single click. By default, Excel searches Office Online if you are connected to the Internet. A company logo or other digital picture can also be inserted into a worksheet using the Picture button in the Illustrations group of the Insert tab.

Project

The Waterfront B·I·S·T·R·O

As you near completion of the quarterly operating expenses worksheet, you will add a clip art image to the top right and the bistro's logo to the top left of the worksheet. After inserting the images, you will resize and move them.

1. With **ExcelS3-04.xlsx** open, click the Sheet1 tab.
2. Insert 5 rows above row 1 and then make A1 the active cell.
3. Click the Insert tab and then click the Clip Art button in the Illustrations group.

   The Clip Art task pane opens at the right side of the worksheet area.

4. Click in the *Search for* text box at the top of the Clip Art task pane. Delete existing text if necessary, type **seafood**, and then click Go.

   Available images associated with the keyword *seafood* display in the *Results* section of the Clip Art task pane. By default, Excel searches all media collections (clip art, photographs, movies, and sounds) in all categories of the Office gallery, in Office Online, and in all favorites, unclassified clips, and downloaded clips that have been added to the computer you are using.

Step 4

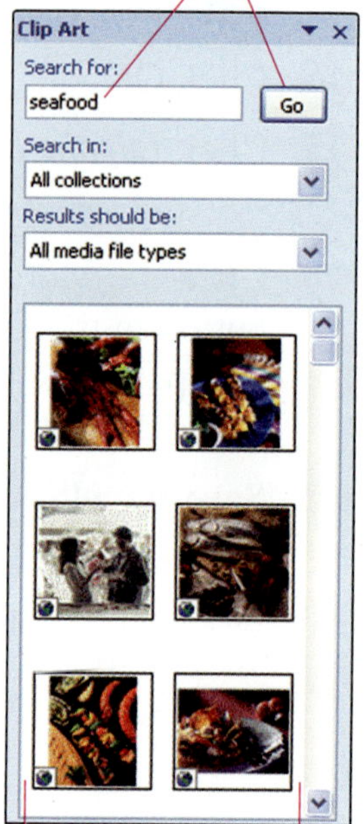

Images shown may vary.

5. Scroll the images in the *Results* section until you see the clip art shown at the right. Position the mouse pointer over the picture and then click the mouse once.

Step 5

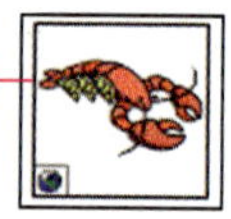

   The picture is inserted in the worksheet starting at A1.

? PROBLEM

Select an alternative image if the clip art shown is not available.

6. Position the pointer on the round white sizing handle at the bottom right corner of the image, hold down the left mouse button, and drag the pointer up and left until the image fits within the first five rows above the worksheet title.

Step 6

7. Move the pointer over the image until the four-headed arrow move icon appears attached to the pointer, hold down the left mouse button, and then drag the image until the right edge of the picture is aligned at the right edge of the worksheet.

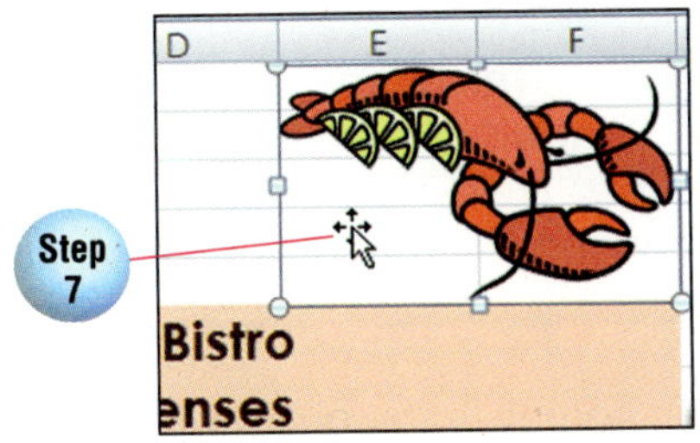

8. Click the Close button in the upper right corner of the Clip Art task pane.
9. Click A1 and then click the Picture button in the Illustrations group of the Insert tab.
10. At the Insert Picture dialog box, navigate to the ExcelS3 folder on your storage medium and then double-click the file named ***TWBLogo.jpg***.

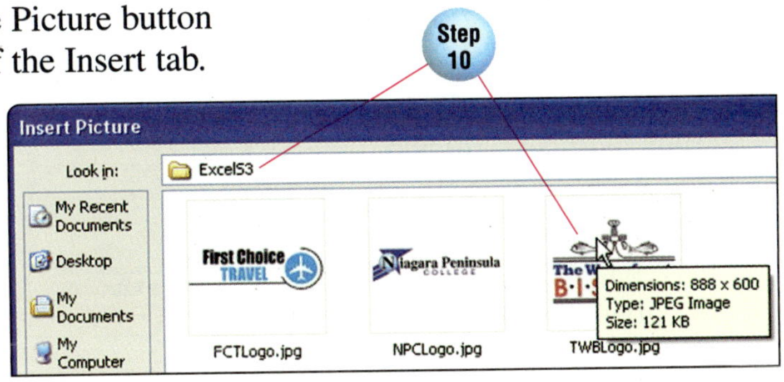

11. Use the sizing handles to resize the picture until the logo image fits above the top left edge of the worksheet.

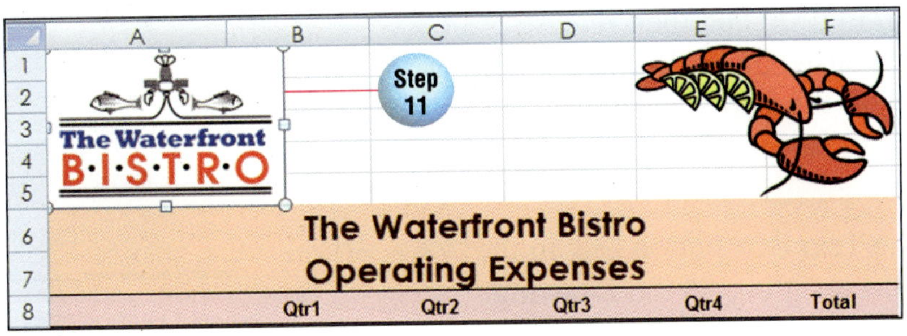

12. Click in any cell to deselect the logo image.
13. Save **ExcelS3-04.xlsx**.

In Brief

Insert Clip Art

1. Click Insert tab.
2. Click Clip Art button.
3. Search for image by keyword.
4. Click desired image in *Results* section.
5. Move and/or resize as required.
6. Close Clip Art task pane.

Insert Picture from File

1. Click Insert tab.
2. Click Picture button.
3. Navigate to drive and/or folder.
4. Double-click file containing picture.
5. Move and/or size as required.

In Addition

Picture Tools

When a clip art image or picture inserted from a file is selected, the contextual Picture Tools Format tab becomes available. Customize the image using picture tools or picture styles. Use the crop button to cut an unwanted area or set a specific height or width measurement for the image. Buttons in the Arrange group allow you to control the alignment, rotation, or order of the image within the worksheet.

Activity 3.12

Inserting Shapes and Text Boxes

The Shapes button in the Insert tab includes buttons with which you can draw lines, rectangles, basic shapes, block arrows, equation shapes, flowchart symbols, stars and banners, and callouts. Enclosed shapes can also contain text. Draw shapes, arrows, or add text boxes to add emphasis or insert explanatory notes in a worksheet.

Project

To complete the quarterly operating expenses worksheet, you will draw an arrow and text box to insert an explanatory note regarding the second quarter utilities expense.

1. With **ExcelS3-04.xlsx** open, click the Insert tab.

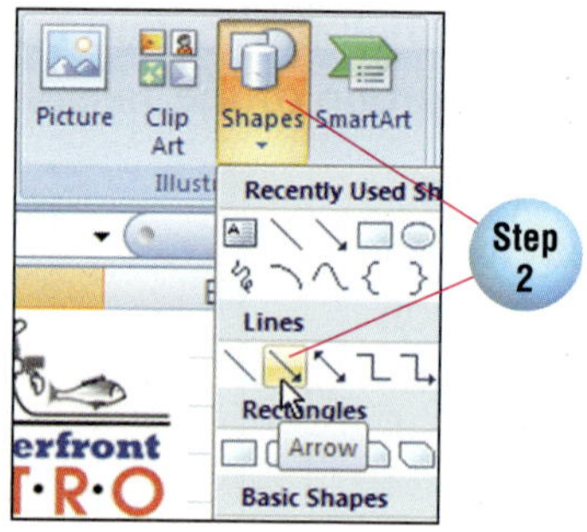

2. Click the Shapes button in the Illustrations group and then click the Arrow button in the Lines group.

   When a shape object tool has been selected, the pointer changes to a crosshairs +.

3. Position the crosshairs near the bottom left boundary of D18, drag the crosshairs up toward the value *1,254.00* in C15, and then release the left mouse button. If you are not happy with the arrow, press Delete to delete the arrow and then try again.

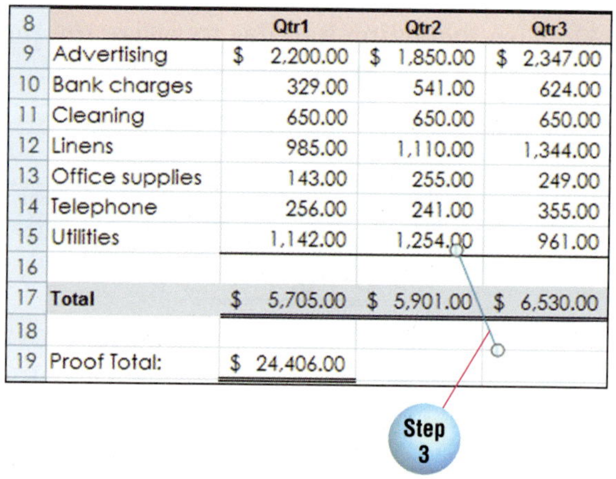

4. Click the Text Box button in the Insert Shapes group in the Drawing Tools Format tab.

   When the Text Box tool has been selected, the pointer changes to a downward-pointing arrow ↓.

5. Position the pointer at the top left boundary of D19 and then drag the pointer down and right to draw the text box the approximate size shown in the illustration.

   An insertion point appears inside the box when you release the left mouse button, indicating you can begin typing the text.

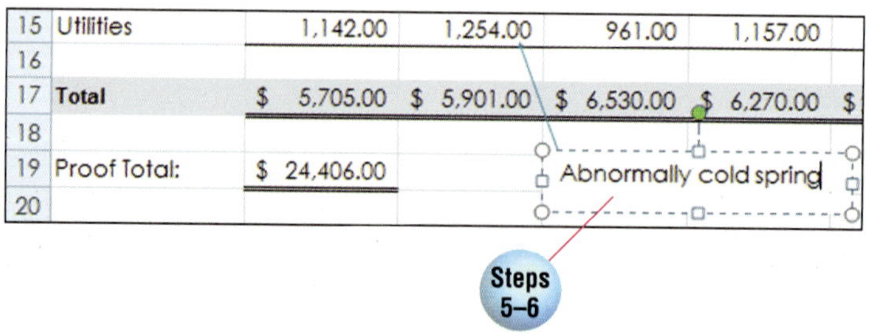

6. Type **Abnormally cold spring** inside the text box.

7. Click outside the text box to deselect the object.
8. Click the arrow to select the drawn object, hold down the Ctrl key, and then click the text box object. Both drawn shapes are now selected.
9. Click the Drawing Tools Format tab.
10. Click the Shape Outline button in the Shape Styles group and then click the *Light Blue* color box in the color palette (fourth from right in *Standard Colors* section).
11. Click the Shape Outline button a second time, point to *Weight*, and then click *1½ pt* at the weight gallery.
12. Click in any cell to deselect the drawn shapes.

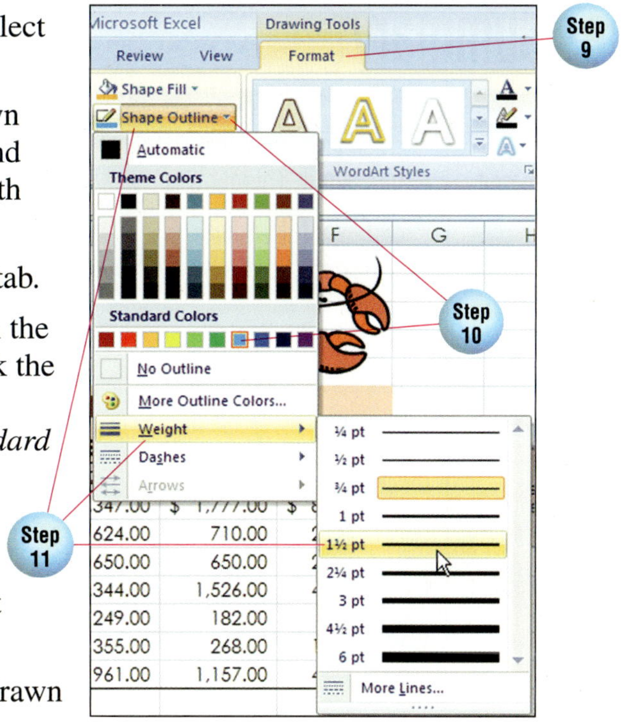

In Brief

Draw Shape
1. Click Insert tab.
2. Click Shapes button.
3. Click desired shape.
4. Drag to create shape.
5. Move, resize, or format as required.

Draw Text Box
1. Click Insert tab.
2. Click Text Box button.
3. Drag to create box size.
4. Type text.
5. Click outside text box object.

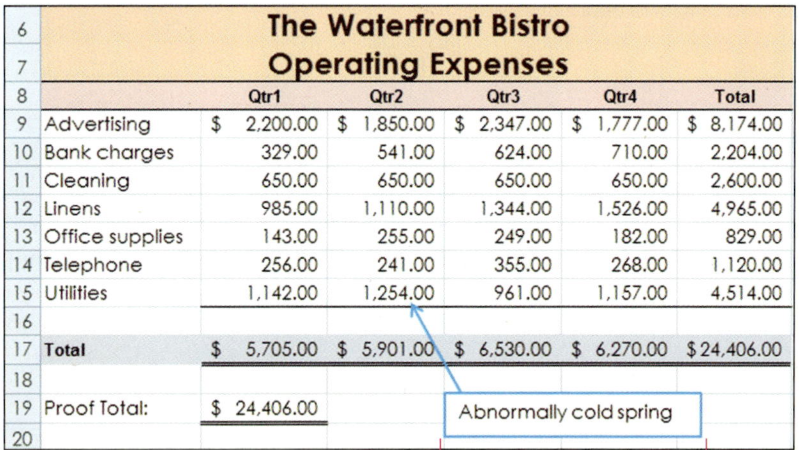

6	The Waterfront Bistro					
7	Operating Expenses					
8		Qtr1	Qtr2	Qtr3	Qtr4	Total
9	Advertising	$ 2,200.00	$ 1,850.00	$ 2,347.00	$ 1,777.00	$ 8,174.00
10	Bank charges	329.00	541.00	624.00	710.00	2,204.00
11	Cleaning	650.00	650.00	650.00	650.00	2,600.00
12	Linens	985.00	1,110.00	1,344.00	1,526.00	4,965.00
13	Office supplies	143.00	255.00	249.00	182.00	829.00
14	Telephone	256.00	241.00	355.00	268.00	1,120.00
15	Utilities	1,142.00	1,254.00	961.00	1,157.00	4,514.00
16						
17	Total	$ 5,705.00	$ 5,901.00	$ 6,530.00	$ 6,270.00	$ 24,406.00
18						
19	Proof Total:	$ 24,406.00		Abnormally cold spring		
20						

text box and arrow after formatting options applied

13. Switch to Page Layout view and then click the Page Layout tab.
14. Change the orientation to landscape and then scale the width to 1 page.
15. Change the zoom settings until you can view as much of the worksheet, images, pie chart, and SmartArt diagram as possible.
16. Print the worksheet.
17. Click the ColumnChart tab located near the bottom left corner of the window above the Status bar and then print the bar chart.
18. Save and then close **ExcelS3-04.xlsx**.

Features Summary

Feature	Ribbon Tab, Group	Button
apply worksheet theme	Page Layout, Themes	
change margins	Page Layout, Margins	
create a column chart	Insert, Charts	
create a pie chart	Insert, Charts	
draw a shape	Insert, Illustrations	
draw a text box	Insert, Text	
insert clip art	Insert, Illustrations	
insert function	Formulas, Function Library	
insert header or footer	Insert, Text	
insert picture	Insert, Illustrations	
insert SmartArt diagram	Insert, Illustrations	
Page Layout view	View, Workbook Views	OR
scale page width and/or height	Page Layout, Scale to Fit	

Knowledge Check

Completion: In the space provided at the right, indicate the correct term, command, or option.

1. AVERAGE and COUNT are two of the functions grouped in this function category. __________
2. This Date and Time function inserts the current date (without the time) in the active cell. __________
3. This financial function returns the principal portion of a specified payment on a loan. __________
4. The IF function returns one of two values based on this criterion. __________
5. This feature formats a worksheet using predefined coordinated colors, fonts, and effects. __________
6. This type of graphic is used to illustrate a cycle, hierarchy, process, or other type of relationship. __________
7. This type of chart is used to illustrate each data point as a proportion of the total. __________
8. When a chart is selected, these three contextual Chart Tools tabs appear. __________
9. Click this tab and button to insert an image stored in a file. __________
10. Click this tab and button to search for art on Office Online. __________
11. The mouse pointer changes to this as you are drawing a shape. __________

Skills Review

Review 1 Inserting Statistical, Date, and IF Functions; Setting Print Options

1. Open **WBQtrExpenses.xlsx**.
2. Save the workbook and name it **ExcelS3-R1**.
3. Type labels in the cells as indicated and then increase the width of column A to 18.00 (131 pixels).
   A16 **Average Expense** A17 **Maximum Expense** A18 **Minimum Expense**
4. In B16, B17, and B18, enter the function formulas that will calculate the average, maximum, and minimum expense values within the range B4:B10.
5. Copy the formulas in B16:B18 to C16:F18.
6. Make A20 the active cell and then type **Date Created**.
7. Enter in B20 a DATE function that will insert the current date. ***Note: You do not want to use TODAY or NOW functions, because the date will update each time you open the file.***
8. Format B20 to display the date in the format *14-Mar-2001*.
9. Type the label **Next Revision Date** in A21 and then enter a formula in B21 that will add 350 days to the date in B20.
10. Make A23 the active cell, type **Expense Target**, press Alt + Enter, type **Variance**, and then press Enter.
11. Dana Hirsch set a target of $6,000 for the total expenses in each quarter. Calculate in B23 the amount over target the quarter's total expenses are if the total expenses exceeded $6,000 by entering the following IF formula: **=if(b12>6000,b12-6000,0)**
12. Drag the fill handle from B23 to C23:E23.
13. Print the worksheet.
14. Assume that Dana Hirsch has changed the expense target to a different amount for each quarter. The revised targets are: *Qtr1–$5,850*; *Qtr2–$5,900*; *Qtr3–$6,150*; *Qtr4–$6,300*. Revise the IF functions in B23:E23 to reflect these new targets.
15. Change the top margin to 2 inches, the left margin to 1.25 inches, and the header and footer margins to 0.5 inch.
16. Create a custom header that will print your first and last names at the left margin and the current date and time at the right margin separated by one space.
17. Create a custom footer that will print the word *Page* followed by the page number separated by one space at the left margin and the file name at the right margin.
18. Save, print, and then close **ExcelS3-R1.xlsx**.

Review 2 Creating a Chart; Drawing Shapes; Inserting Images; Applying a Theme

1. Open **WBQtrCostofSales.xlsx**.
2. Save the workbook with Save As and name it **ExcelS3-R2**.
3. Select the range A3:E6 and then create a column chart with the following options:
   a. Choose the *Clustered Column* in the *2-D Column* section (first chart option).
   b. Move the chart to a new sheet with the sheet label ColumnChart.
   c. Apply the Layout 2 chart layout.
   d. Apply the Style 1 chart style.
   e. Change the chart title to *Quarterly Cost of Sales*.

4. With Sheet1 the active sheet, draw an arrow that starts below the total row and points to the value in E6. Draw a text box anchored to the end of the arrow and then type the following text inside the box. (You determine the best location for the two shapes.)

   Catering staff wage increase of 5% this quarter
5. Format the Shape Outline for the arrow and text box to Dark Red (Standard Color) with a 1-pt weight.
6. Insert 5 blank rows above the worksheet and then insert the file named **TWBLogo.jpg** at the top left of the worksheet. Resize the logo as needed.
7. Search for a clip art image using the keyword *budgets*. Insert an appropriate image from the *Results* section of the Clip Art task pane at the top right of the worksheet. Move and resize the image as needed.
8. Apply the Foundry theme to the worksheet. Make adjustments to the arrow and text box if necessary after the theme is applied.
9. Print both the worksheet and the column chart.
10. Save and then close **ExcelS3-R2.xlsx**.

Skills Assessment

Assessment 1 Using Statistical and IF Functions

First Choice TRAVEL

1. Alex Torres, manager of the Toronto office for First Choice Travel, has started a workbook to calculate sales commission for the Toronto sales agents. First Choice Travel has implemented a new bonus commission based upon the number of cruises booked. Alex has asked for your help in writing the correct formulas to calculate the commission owed to the agents and analyze the results.
2. Open **FCTSalesComm.xlsx**.
3. Save the workbook and name it **ExcelS3-A1**.
4. Create a formula to calculate the commission for D. Lopez in D4 using the information in the Commission Parameters table in B20:C23. When writing your IF statement, use references to the percent values in C22 and C23. Alex is considering revising the percents so the worksheet should be flexible in the event of a change. ***Hint: The formula will be copied in the next step, so you must make the references in C22 and C23 absolute.***
5. Copy the formula to the remaining rows in column D.
6. Calculate the total commissions owed in D18.
7. Format the values to an appropriate number style.
8. Starting in F16, enter appropriate labels for average, maximum, and minimum commissions and then create the required formulas below the labels in row 18. For example, enter **Average** in F16, **Commission** in F17, and the average function in F18. AutoFit columns F, G, and H.
9. Change the top and left margins to 1.5 inches and the page orientation to landscape.
10. Save, print, and then close **ExcelS3-A1.xlsx**.

Assessment 2 Applying the PMT and PPMT Functions

1. You are the assistant to Sam Vestering, manager of North American Distribution for Worldwide Enterprises. Sam has entered in a workbook details on financing from two companies for a proposed office renovation loan. Sam would like you to enter the formulas to calculate the monthly loan payments, the principal portion for the first and last payments, and the total cost of each loan.
2. Open **WEOfficeRenoLoan.xlsx**.
3. Save the workbook and name it **ExcelS3-A2**.
4. Calculate the monthly payments on the loan in B7 and D7.
5. Calculate the principal portion of the loan payments for the first payment in B11 and D11, and for the last payment in B12 and D12.
6. Calculate the total payments required for each loan in B14 and D14.
7. Save, print, and then close **ExcelS3-A2.xlsx**.

Assessment 3 Creating Charts; Drawing Shapes

1. Cal Rubine, chair of the Theatre Arts Division at Niagara Peninsula College, has asked you to create charts from the grades analysis report to present at a divisional meeting. After reviewing the grades, you decide to create a line chart depicting the grades for all of the courses and a pie chart summarizing the total grades.
2. Open **NPCGrades.xlsx**.
3. Save the workbook and name it **ExcelS3-A3**.
4. Create a line chart in a new sheet labeled *LineChart* that displays the A+ through F grades for all five courses. Include an appropriate chart title. You determine the line chart style, layout, and any other chart elements and formats that will make the chart easy to interpret.
5. Create a 3-D pie chart that displays the total of each grade as a percentage of 100. ***Hint: Select the ranges B4:G4 and B11:G11 to create the chart.*** Include an appropriate chart title and display percents around the outside of the pie slices as well as the Category names. Position the pie chart below the grades worksheet starting in row 14.
6. Draw an arrow pointing to the value in G11. Create a text box at the end of the arrow containing the text *Lowest attrition since 2005!* Change the Shape Outline of the arrow and text box to an appropriate color and weight.
7. Print the worksheet centered horizontally in landscape orientation and print the line chart.
8. Save and then close **ExcelS3-A3.xlsx**.

Assessment 4 Inserting, Moving, and Resizing Images; Applying Themes

1. Melissa Gehring, manager of the Los Angeles office for First Choice Travel, has prepared a worksheet listing European destinations and the current package pricing options. Melissa wants you to improve the worksheet by adding images and formatting before she presents it at the next staff meeting.
2. Open **FCTEurope.xlsx**.
3. Save the workbook and name it **ExcelS3-A4**.
4. Insert six rows above the worksheet.

5. Insert the file named **FCTLogo.jpg** at the top left of the worksheet. Resize the logo as needed. Search for an appropriate clip art image using the keyword *Europe* and insert your selection at the top right of the worksheet. Resize the image as needed.
6. Increase the height of row 7 to *19.50 (26 pixels)* and row 8 to *27.00 (36 pixels)*.
7. Apply the *Origin* theme to the worksheet.
8. Apply the *Accent1* cell style to the range A7:G8.
9. Format the values in B9:G17 to Accounting Number format with zero decimals.
10. Horizontally and vertically center the labels within rows 7 and 8.
11. Apply other formatting attributes that you think would enhance the appearance of the remainder of the worksheet.
12. Save, print, and then close **ExcelS3-A4.xlsx**.

Assessment 5 Finding Information on WordArt

1. Use the Help feature to find information on how to create a WordArt object in a worksheet.
2. Open **FCTEurope.xlsx**.
3. Save the workbook and name it **ExcelS3-A5**.
4. Insert six rows above the worksheet.
5. Create a WordArt object with the text *Europe this summer!*
6. Move and resize the object to fit centered over the worksheet within the first six rows and format the WordArt object as desired.
7. Save, print, and then close **ExcelS3-A5.xlsx**.

Assessment 6 Searching for Vacation Destinations

1. You are trying to choose among vacation alternatives. Use the Internet to locate information on three cities that you would like to visit. Look for detailed travel information such as round-trip airfare, hotel, car rental, and currency exchange. Look for tourist destinations such as museums, theme parks, zoos, or other tours within the cities of your choice and find entrance fees or other charges for visiting these locations.
2. Create an Excel workbook that compares the travel costs for the three cities you researched.
3. Apply formatting enhancements to the worksheet.
4. Create a chart that graphs the total cost of each vacation destination. Position the chart centered below the worksheet.
5. Apply layouts, styles, and chart elements to make the chart easy to interpret.
6. Save the workbook and name it **ExcelS3-A6**.
7. Print and then close **ExcelS3-A6.xlsx**.

Marquee Challenge

Challenge 1 Creating Charts on Movie Attendance Statistics for a Staff Development Workshop

1. You are working with Shannon Grey, president of Marquee Productions, on presentation materials for an upcoming staff development workshop on producing and marketing movies. As part of Shannon's research for the workshop, she compiled a workbook with statistics related to movie attendance by age group and by household income. Shannon has asked you to create two charts for the workshop based on this source data.
2. Open **MPMovieAttendanceStats.xlsx**.
3. Using the data in the workbook, create the two charts shown in Figure 3.1.
4. Use your best judgment to determine chart style, layout, font, and other formatting options. Explore the various formatting options for elements such as the chart area, walls, axes, and gridlines. The question text is inserted in each chart in a text box.
5. Position the bar chart in a new sheet with the label *AgeChart.*
6. Position the doughnut chart in a new sheet with the label *IncomeChart.*
7. Save the revised workbook and name it **ExcelS3-C1**.
8. Print each chart and then close **ExcelS3-C1.xlsx**.

FIGURE 3.1 Challenge 1

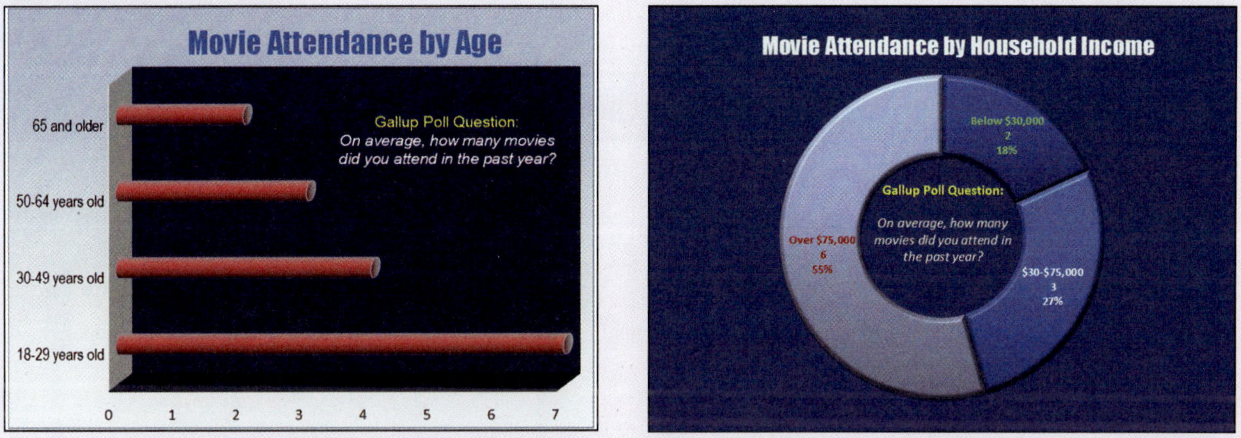

Challenge 2 Preparing an International Student Registration Report

1. You work in the Registrar's Office at Niagara Peninsula College. Terri VanDaele, the registrar, has sent you a workbook with the top ten countries of origin for international students registered for the 2010 academic year. Terri would like you to format the workbook to improve the appearance and create a chart next to the data for inclusion with the annual report to the board.
2. Open **NPCTop10International.xlsx**.
3. Using the data in the workbook, create the chart shown in Figure 3.2.
4. Insert the Niagara Peninsula College logo as shown in Figure 3.2 using the file named **NPCLogo.jpg**.
5. Format the worksheet as shown including adding the clip art. If the clip art images are not available on the computer you are using, select an appropriate alternative image. Use your best judgment to determine theme, colors, and other formatting elements.
6. Change the page orientation to landscape and make sure the workbook fits on one page.
7. Save the revised workbook and name it **ExcelS3-C2**.
8. Print and then close **ExcelS3-C2.xlsx**.

FIGURE 3.2 Challenge 2

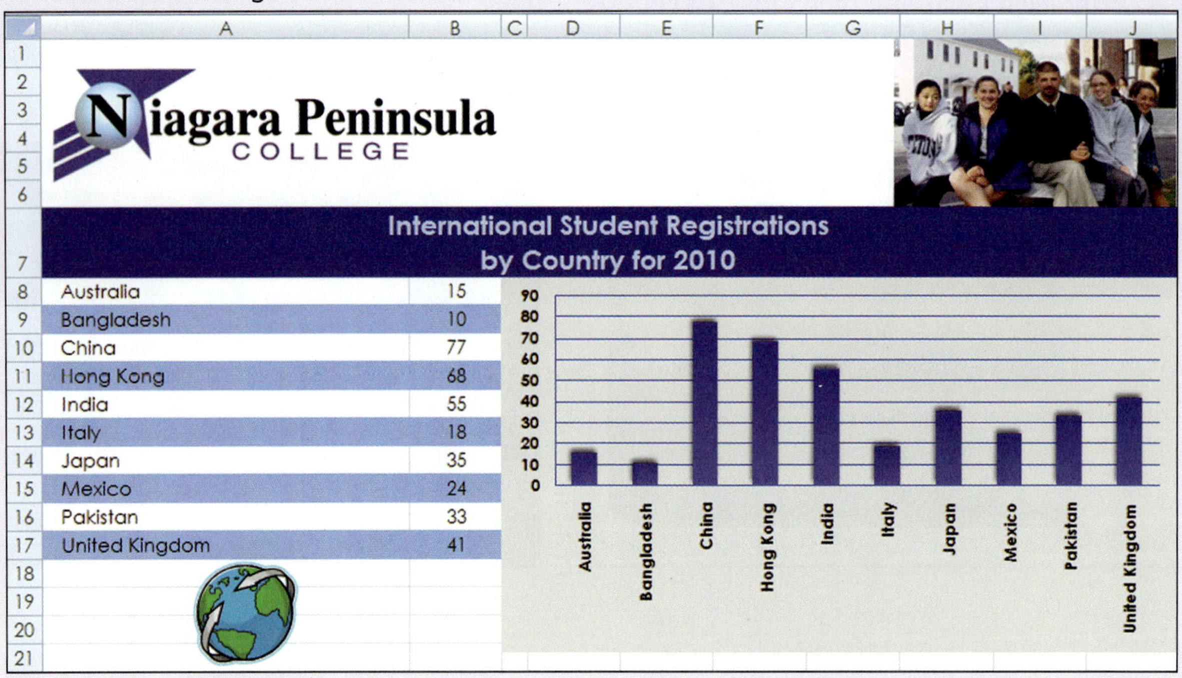

Excel SECTION 4

Working with Multiple Worksheets, Tables, and Other File Formats

Skills

- Insert, delete, and rename a worksheet
- Format sheet tabs
- Move and copy a worksheet
- Group and ungroup worksheets
- Link cells between worksheets
- Create 3-D references in formulas
- Add a graphic as a background
- Print multiple worksheets
- Set and clear a print area
- View a worksheet in Page Break Preview
- Format data as a table
- Insert rows and columns into a table
- Add a total row to a table
- Sort by single and multiple criteria
- Filter a table by single and multiple criteria
- Insert, edit, delete, and print comments
- Create a new workbook using a template
- Open and save a workbook in a previous Excel version
- Save a workbook as a text file

Student Resources

Before beginning this section:

1. Copy to your storage medium the ExcelS4 subfolder from the Excel folder on the Student Resources CD.
2. Make ExcelS4 the active folder.

In addition to containing the data files needed to complete section work, the Student Resources CD contains model answers in PDF format for each of the projects in this section; model answers for end-of-section activities are not provided.

Projects Overview

The Waterfront B·I·S·T·R·O

Complete the quarterly sales report and the payroll report; format, sort, filter, and insert comments in the catering event and inventory workbooks; create invoices and a billing statement for catering services; open an employee schedule saved in an earlier Excel version; save an investment summary in Excel 2003 format; convert the inventory file to comma delimited file format.

Niagara Peninsula College

Create a grade summary worksheet for the Theatre Arts Co-op Internships report.

Performance Threads

Produce a list of costumes with a final delivery date of July 8; insert comments in the production schedule in preparation for the design team meeting; format the rental costume inventory, calculate the rental fees due, and then save the 2003 workbook in 2007 file format.

Worldwide Enterprises

Import U.S. and Canadian distributor information from two text files, combine the information into one workbook, and then format and sort the report.

Activity 4.1

Inserting, Deleting, and Renaming a Worksheet; Formatting Sheet Tabs

A new workbook initially contains three sheets named Sheet1, Sheet2, and Sheet3. Additional sheets can be added or deleted as needed. Organizing large amounts of data by grouping related topics in individual worksheets makes the task of creating, editing, and analyzing data more manageable. For example, you could keep track of your test grades in one worksheet and assignment grades in another. A summary sheet at the beginning or end of the workbook would be used to consolidate the test and assignment grades and calculate a final mark. By breaking down the data into smaller units, you are able to view, enter, and edit cells quickly. Format sheet tabs using different colors to visually group related sheets.

Project

Dana Hirsch, the manager of The Waterfront Bistro, has asked you to complete the quarterly sales report. To begin this project, you will insert, rename, and delete a worksheet and then organize the sheets by applying color to the sheet tabs.

1. Open **WBQuarterlySales.xlsx**.
2. Save the workbook and name it **ExcelS4-01**.
3. Click the Qtr2 tab and then view the worksheet.

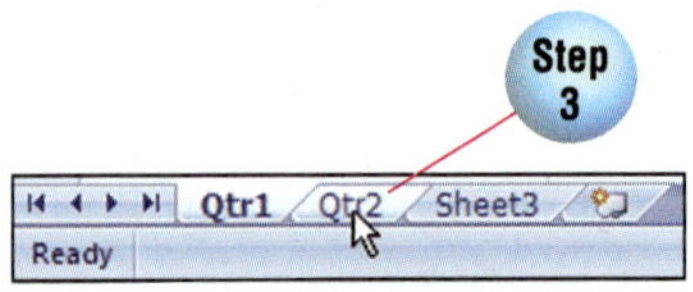

4. Click the Sheet3 tab and then view the worksheet.

   The quarterly sales report has been organized with each quarter's sales in a separate worksheet. In the next step, you will insert a worksheet for the fourth quarter.

5. Click the Insert Worksheet button located at the end of the Sheet tabs (immediately right of Sheet3).

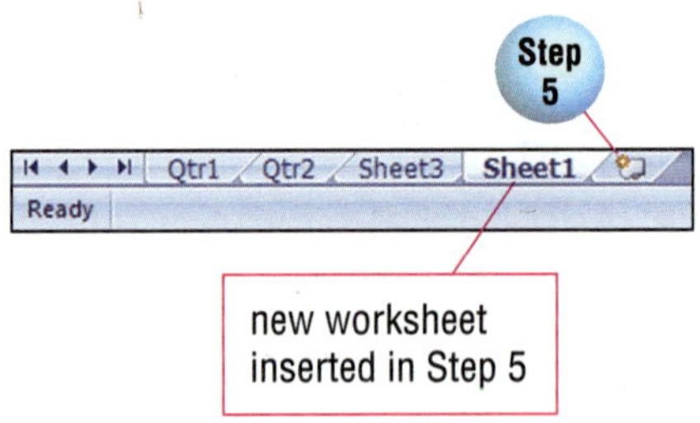

   Clicking the Insert Worksheet button inserts a new worksheet at the end of the existing sheets. In the next step, you will insert at the beginning of the workbook a new worksheet that will be used to summarize the sales data from the four quarters.

6. Right-click the Qtr1 tab.

   Right-clicking a worksheet tab activates the worksheet and displays the worksheet shortcut menu.

7. Click *Insert* at the shortcut menu.
8. With *Worksheet* already selected in the General tab in the Insert dialog box, click OK.

   Five worksheets now exist in **ExcelS4-01.xlsx**: Sheet2, Qtr1, Qtr2, Sheet3, and Sheet1.

9. Right-click the Sheet2 tab and then click *Rename* at the shortcut menu.

   This selects the current worksheet name in the sheet tab.

10. Type **Summary** and then press Enter.

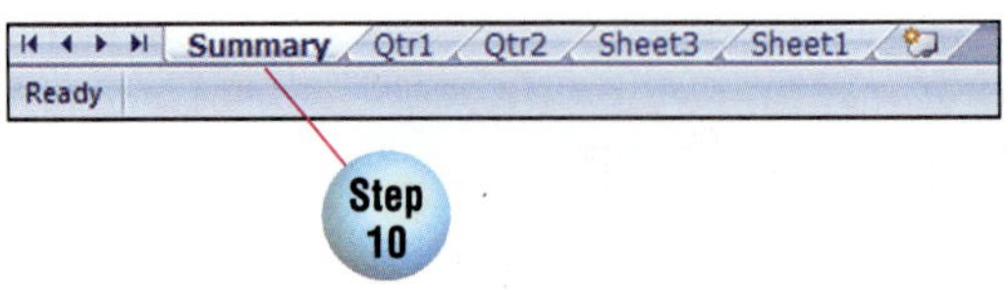

11. Double-click the Sheet3 tab.

    You can also rename a worksheet by double-clicking the sheet tab.

12. Type **Qtr3** and then press Enter.

13. Right-click the Sheet1 tab and then click *Delete* at the shortcut menu.

    You can also click the Delete button arrow in the Cells group of the Home tab and then click *Delete Sheet* at the drop-down list to delete the active worksheet from the workbook. If the worksheet selected for deletion contains data, a message box appears warning you that data may exist in the sheet. Click the Delete button at the Microsoft Office Excel message box to confirm the deletion. Be careful when deleting worksheets since Undo does not restore a deleted sheet.

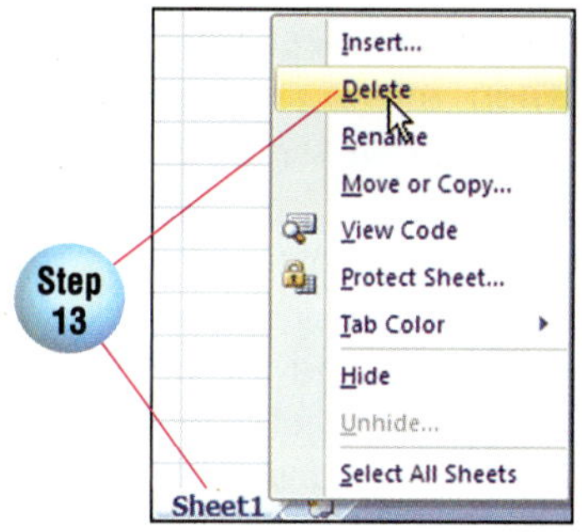

14. Right-click the Summary tab to activate the Summary worksheet and display the shortcut menu.

15. Point to Tab Color and then click the *Dark Red* color in the *Standard Colors* section of the color palette (first option).

    Changing the color of sheet tabs can help to visually identify related worksheets or the organizational structure of the workbook.

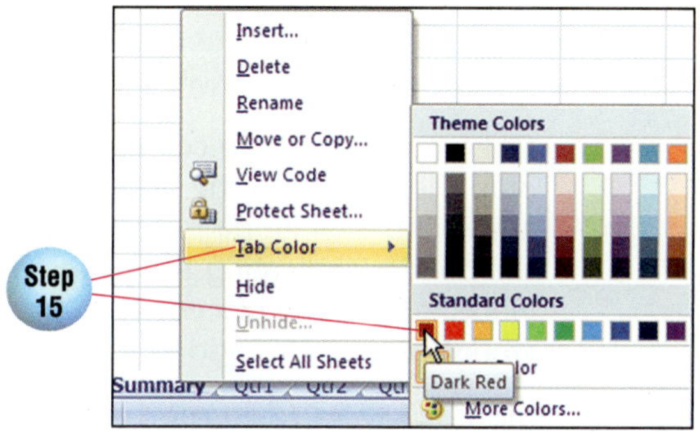

16. Right-click the Qtr1 tab, point to *Tab Color*, and then click the *Purple* color in the *Standard Colors* section of the color palette (last option).

17. Repeat Step 16 for the Qtr2 and Qtr3 sheet tabs.

    The three worksheets containing the quarterly sales data are now organized with the same tab color (purple). The worksheet that will later contain the summary data for the entire year is differentiated by the dark red tab color.

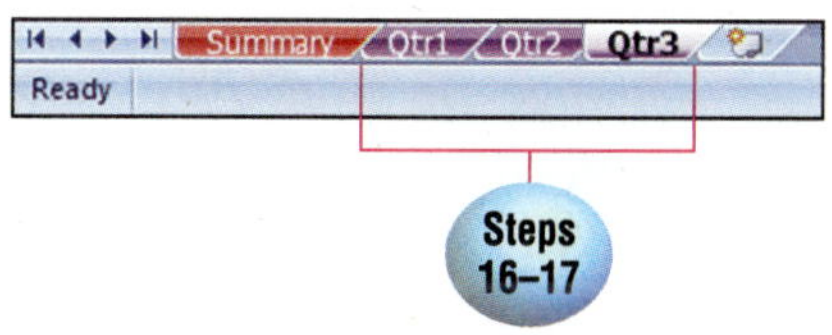

18. Save **ExcelS4-01.xlsx**.

In Brief

Insert Worksheet
1. Right-click sheet tab.
2. Click *Insert*.
3. Click OK.

OR

Click Insert Worksheet button.

Rename Worksheet
1. Right-click sheet tab.
2. Click *Rename*.
3. Type new name.
4. Press Enter.

OR

Double-click sheet tab, type new name, and then press Enter.

Delete Worksheet
1. Right-click sheet tab.
2. Click *Delete*.

In Addition

Tab Scrolling Buttons

The tab scrolling buttons are located at the left edge of the horizontal scroll bar as shown below. Use these buttons to scroll the worksheet tabs if there are more tabs than currently displayed. Drag the tab split box to the right or left to increase or decrease the number of worksheet tabs displayed or to change the size of the horizontal scroll bar.

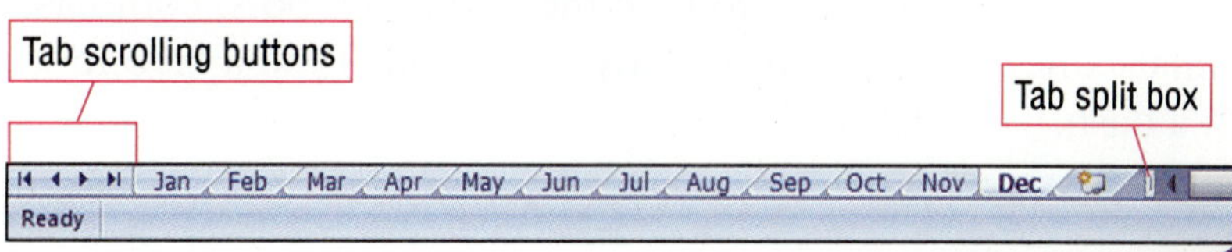

Activity 4.2

Moving and Copying Worksheets; Grouping and Ungrouping Worksheets

Drag a sheet tab to move a worksheet to a different position within the open workbook. Hold down the Ctrl key while dragging a worksheet tab to copy it. Exercise caution when moving or copying a worksheet since calculations may become inaccurate after the worksheet has been repositioned or copied. A workbook with multiple worksheets that all have similar column and row structure can have formatting options applied to all sheets in one step by first grouping the worksheets.

Project

The Waterfront B·I·S·T·R·O

Continue your work on the quarterly sales report by copying the Qtr3 worksheet, renaming the sheet, and then entering data for the fourth quarter's sales. Next, you will move the Summary sheet after the Qtr4 sheet. Finally, you will apply formatting options to all four quarters by grouping the sheets.

1. With **ExcelS4-01.xlsx** open and Qtr3 the active sheet, position the mouse pointer over the Qtr3 tab, hold down the Ctrl key, drag the pointer to the right (on top of the Insert Worksheet button), release the mouse button, and then release the Ctrl key.

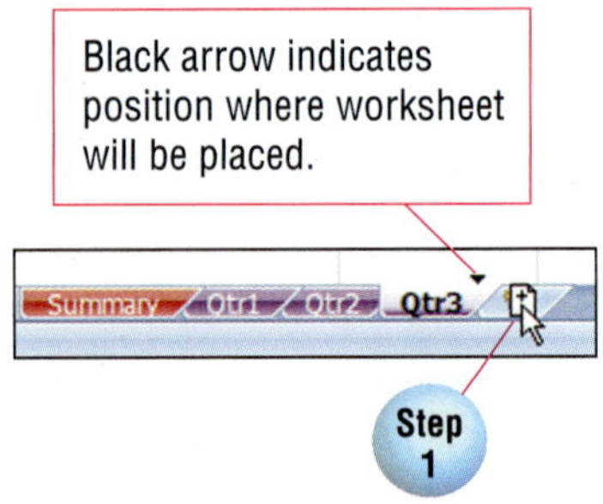

   Ctrl + dragging a tab copies a worksheet. As you drag the pointer to the right, a black down-pointing arrow and a white page with a plus sign display with the pointer, indicating the position where the copied worksheet will be placed. The copied worksheet is labeled the same as the source worksheet with *(2)* added to the end of the name.

2. Double-click *Qtr3 (2)*, type **Qtr4**, and then press Enter.
3. With Qtr4 the active worksheet, select the following ranges and then press Delete:
   B4:D6
   B8:D10
   B12:D14
4. Change B3 from *July* to *October;* C3 from *August* to *November;* and D3 from *September* to *December*.

   The worksheet is now cleared of the third quarter's data. As new data is typed, the totals will automatically update. First, you will move the Summary worksheet after the four quarterly sales worksheets.

5. Position the pointer over the Summary tab, hold down the left mouse button and drag the pointer right after Qtr4 (on top of the Insert Worksheet button), and then release the mouse button.

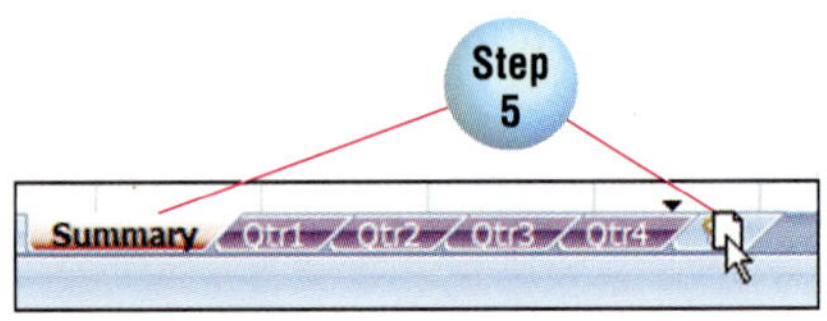

   Dragging a tab moves the worksheet. As you drag the pointer to the right, a black down-pointing arrow and a white page display with the pointer, indicating the position where the worksheet will be repositioned.

6. Click Qtr4 and enter the data for the fourth quarter as shown in Figure 4.1 on page 341. You do not need to type the dollar symbols, commas, or zeros after decimals since the cells are already formatted. Type a zero in the cells displayed with a dash.

7. Click Qtr1, hold down the Shift key, and then click Qtr4.

   The four worksheets are now grouped. Any formatting options that you change apply to all four worksheets. Use the Shift key to select a group of sheets starting with the first tab selected through to the last tab selected. Use the Ctrl key to group nonadjacent sheets.

8. Select A1:A2 and then change the Fill Color to White (click *White, Background 1* in the *Theme Colors* section).

9. Select A3:E3 and then apply the *Accent1* cell style (first option in the bottom row in the *Themed Cell Styles* section of the Cell Styles drop-down gallery).

10. Right-click any of the Qtr sheet tabs and then click *Ungroup Sheets* at the shortcut menu.

   The worksheets are no longer grouped and can be individually formatted.

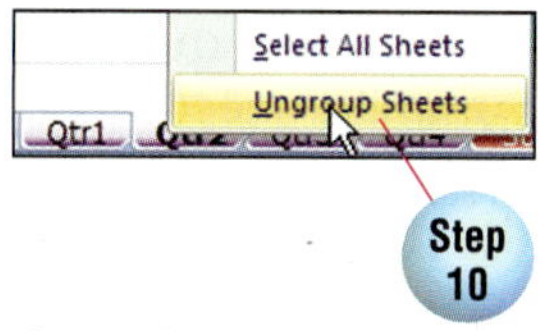

11. Click Qtr1 and view the formatting applied in Steps 8–9. Click each of the other quarterly sales worksheets to view the same formats.

12. Save **ExcelS4-01.xlsx**.

In Brief

Copy Worksheet
Ctrl + drag sheet tab to desired location.

Move Worksheet
Drag sheet tab to desired location.

Group Worksheets
1. Click first sheet tab.
2. Shift + click last sheet tab OR Ctrl + click other sheets.

FIGURE 4.1 Data for Fourth Quarter

	A	B	C	D	E
1	The Waterfront Bistro				
2	Quarterly Sales Report				
3		October	November	December	Quarter Total
4	Food - Dining Room	$ 42,155	$ 45,876	$ 52,144	$ 140,175
5	Food - Patio	$ 1,588	$ -	$ -	$ 1,588
6	Food - Catering	$ 28,653	$ 31,455	$ 60,488	$ 120,596
7	**Total Food**	**$ 72,396**	**$ 77,331**	**$ 112,632**	**$ 262,359**
8	Beverage - Dining Room	$ 39,658	$ 4,477	$ 5,103	$ 49,238
9	Beverage - Patio	$ 144	$ -	$ -	$ 144
10	Beverage - Catering	$ 2,963	$ 2,966	$ 5,843	$ 11,772
11	**Total Beverage**	**$ 42,765**	**$ 7,443**	**$ 10,946**	**$ 61,154**
12	Beer & Liquor - Dining Room	$ 3,647	$ 4,655	$ 4,761	$ 13,063
13	Beer & Liquor - Patio	$ 106	$ -	$ -	$ 106
14	Beer & Liquor - Catering	$ 2,844	$ 3,264	$ 6,149	$ 12,257
15	**Total Beer & Liquor**	**$ 6,597**	**$ 7,919**	**$ 10,910**	**$ 25,426**
16					
17	TOTAL SALES	**$ 121,758**	**$ 92,693**	**$ 134,488**	**$ 348,939**

In Addition

Move or Copy Dialog Box

In Steps 1 and 5 you copied and moved a worksheet by dragging the sheet tab with the pointer. You can also use the Move or Copy dialog box (shown at the right) to move or copy worksheets within the active workbook or to another open workbook. Right-click the sheet to be moved or copied and then click *Move* or *Copy* at the shortcut menu. Click the worksheet in front of which you want to place the moved or copied worksheet in the *Before sheet* list box and click OK to move, or click *Create a copy* and then click OK to copy. To move or copy to another open workbook, select the destination file name in the *To book* drop-down list.

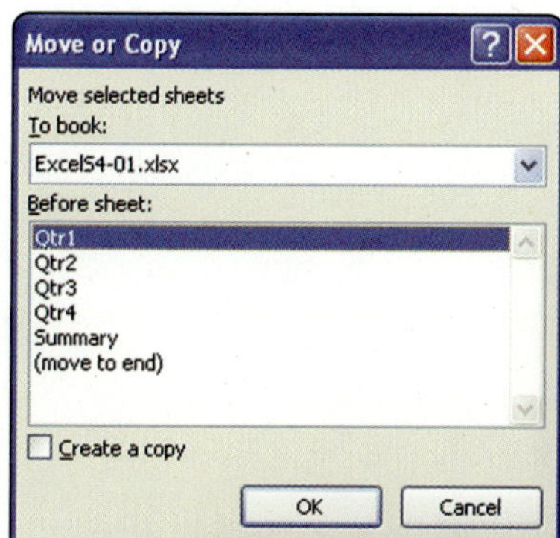

Activity 4.3

Using 3-D References; Linking Cells; Adding a Background

A formula with ***3-D references*** is used to consolidate data from several worksheets into one worksheet. Linking worksheets within the same workbook or between different workbooks involves entering a formula that references a cell containing the source data. If the source data changes, the cell that is linked to the source will automatically update to reflect the change. A file containing a picture or other graphics image can be added as the background to a worksheet similar to the backgrounds you might see on Web pages. The background image affects the display of the worksheet only; backgrounds do not print.

Project

To finish the quarterly sales report, you will copy labels from the Qtr1 worksheet to the Summary sheet and enter 3-D formulas that reference the total sales cells in the four quarterly sales worksheets. You will also copy formats and link to a cell in another worksheet to enter the percent of gross profit. Finally, you will add a background to the sales worksheets.

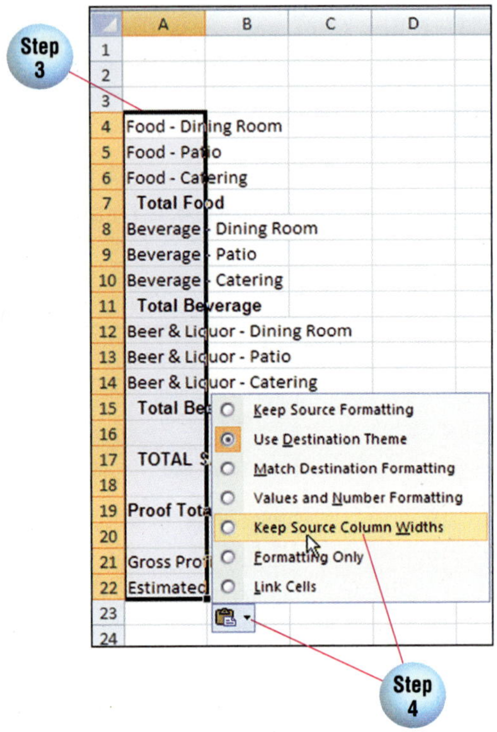

1. With **ExcelS4-01.xlsx** open, click the Qtr1 tab.
2. Select A4:A22 and then click the Copy button in the Clipboard group in the Home tab.
3. Make Summary the active worksheet, click A4, and then click the Paste button in the Clipboard group. (Do not click the Paste button arrow.)
4. Click the Paste Options button and then click *Keep Source Column Widths* at the pop-up menu.
5. Make B3 the active cell, type **Total**, press Alt + Enter, type **Sales**, and then press Enter.
6. Bold and center B3.
7. Make Qtr1 the active worksheet, copy A1, and then paste to A1 in the Summary worksheet.
8. Create the subtitle **Sales Summary** merged and centered in A2:E2. Apply bold and the *Dark Blue, Text 2* font color to the subtitle.
9. Change the width of column B to 12.00 (89 pixels).

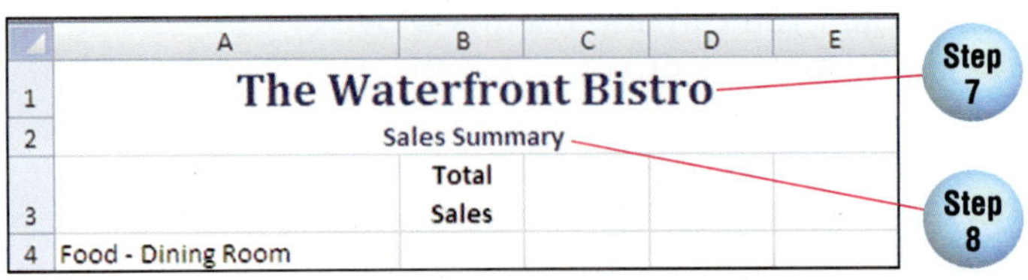

10 Save **ExcelS4-01.xlsx**.

Saving the workbook before consolidating data using 3-D references is a good idea in case you encounter difficulties when performing the consolidation. In Steps 11–14, you will enter a 3-D formula using the point-and-click method.

11 With Summary still the active worksheet, make B4 the active cell.

12 Type **=sum(**.

13 Click the Qtr1 tab, hold down the Shift key, and then click the Qtr4 tab.

This groups the four quarterly sales worksheets and Qtr1 is the worksheet now displayed. Watch the formula bar each time you click the mouse to view the formula that is being built.

14 Click E4 and then press Enter.

15 Press the Up Arrow key to return the active cell back to B4 and then read the formula in the Formula bar, *=SUM('Qtr1:Qtr4'!E4).*

Notice Excel inserted the closing bracket automatically. The result, *499166,* appears in B4, which is the total of the values in E4 in all four quarterly sales worksheets. The formula is called a ***3-D reference*** since it references a cell spanning two or more worksheets. The argument in the SUM function begins with the range of worksheets *Qtr1:Qtr4* (in single quotes) followed by the exclamation point to separate the worksheet range from the cell reference. The argument ends with the cell to be summed in the worksheet range.

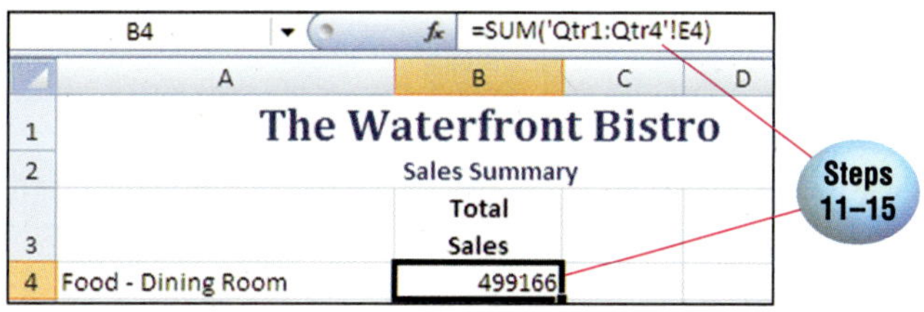

16 Drag the fill handle from B4 down through B15 to copy the 3-D formula to the remaining rows.

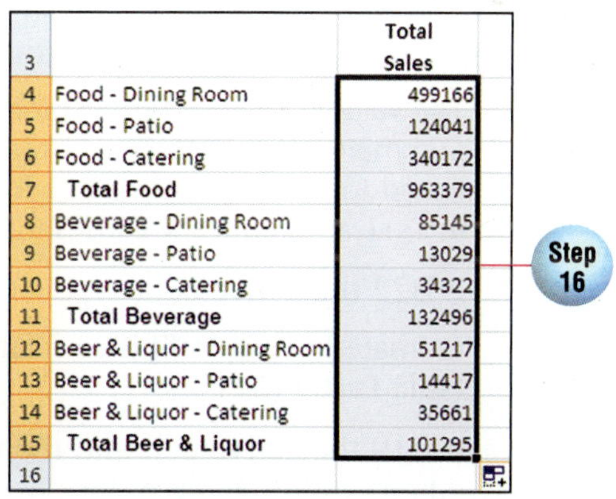

17 Make B17 the active cell, type the formula **=b7+b11+b15**, and then press Enter.

18 Apply the Comma Style format to B4:B15.

19 With B4:B15 still selected, decrease the decimals so that zero decimals display.

20 Deselect the range.

21 Make E7 in the Qtr4 worksheet the active cell and then double-click the Format Painter button in the Clipboard group.

Double-clicking Format Painter toggles the copy format feature on so that you can paste formats multiple times.

continues

22 Click the Summary tab, click B7, click B11, and click B15.

23 Click the Format Painter button.

Turn off the feature by clicking the button to toggle off copy formats.

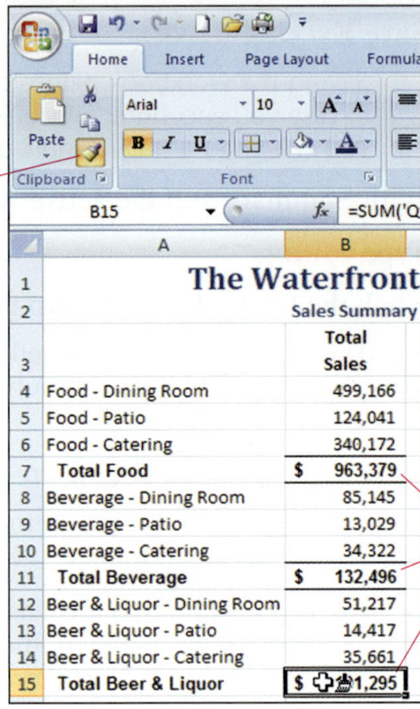

24 Make E4 in the Qtr4 worksheet the active cell and then click the Format Painter button.

25 Click the Summary tab and then click B4.

26 Use Format Painter to copy the formats from E17 in the Qtr4 worksheet to B17 in the Summary worksheet.

4	Food - Dining Room	$ 499,166
5	Food - Patio	124,041
6	Food - Catering	340,172
7	Total Food	$ 963,379
8	Beverage - Dining Room	85,145
9	Beverage - Patio	13,029
10	Beverage - Catering	34,322
11	Total Beverage	$ 132,496
12	Beer & Liquor - Dining Room	51,217
13	Beer & Liquor - Patio	14,417
14	Beer & Liquor - Catering	35,661
15	Total Beer & Liquor	$ 101,295
16		
17	TOTAL SALES	$ 1,197,170

Step 25

Step 26

27 Make B21 in the Summary sheet the active cell.

28 Type **=**.

29 Click the Qtr1 tab, click B21, and then press Enter.

30 Press the Up Arrow key to return the active cell back to B21.

The value *27%* displays and the formula *='Qtr1'!B21* is stored in B21 of the Summary worksheet. The contents of B21 in the Summary worksheet are now linked to the contents of B21 in the Qtr1 worksheet. Any change made to B21 in Qtr1 automatically causes B21 in Summary to update as well.

31 Make B22 the active cell, type **=b17*b21**, and then press Enter.

Estimated Gross Profit is calculated by multiplying Total Sales (B17) times the Gross Profit Factor (B21).

32 Make B19 the active cell and then type a formula that will check the accuracy of the total sales in cell B17. ***Hint: Look at the proof total formulas in the Qtr1–Qtr4 worksheets as an example.***

17	TOTAL SALES	$ 1,197,170
18		
19	Proof Total	$ 1,197,170
20		
21	Gross Profit Factor	27%
22	Estimated Gross Profit	323,235.90

Steps 28–29

Step 31

Steps 32–33

33 Use Format Painter to apply the formatting in B4 to B19.

34. Click the Page Layout tab.

35. Click the Background button in the Page Setup group.

    A graphics file can be inserted as a pattern that is tiled to fill the background of a worksheet. Add a background to apply an image to the worksheet area similar to the backgrounds you see on Web pages. The background image does not print. Background colors and/or patterns should not be too dark or overwhelming as to obscure the data that you need to see.

36. At the Sheet Background dialog box, navigate to the storage medium in which the student data files are stored and then double-click ***WBBackground.jpg***.

    The Background button changes to Delete Background after an image has been applied to the background of the cells. Clicking Delete Background removes the image from the worksheet.

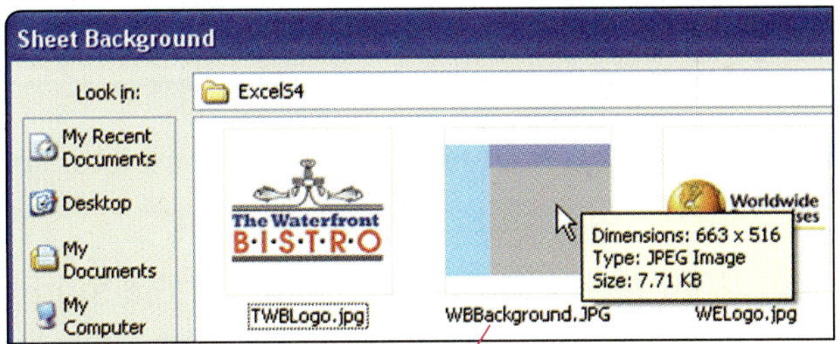

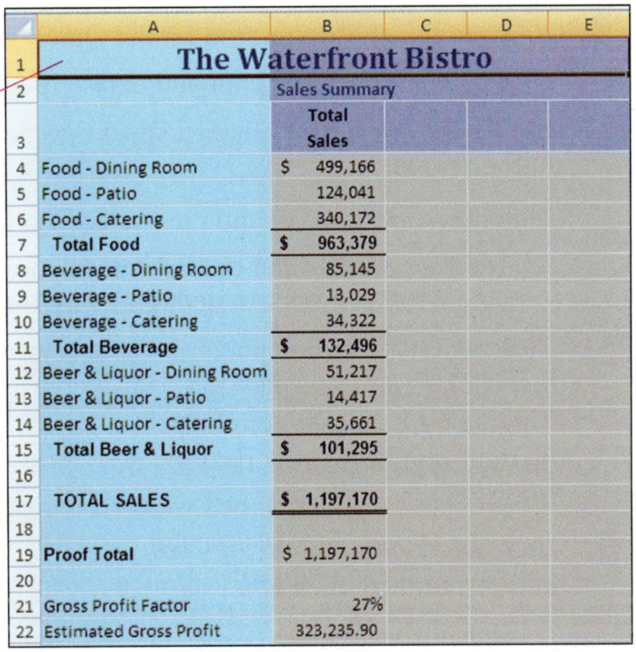

	A	B	C	D	E
1	The Waterfront Bistro				
2		Sales Summary			
3		Total Sales			
4	Food - Dining Room	$ 499,166			
5	Food - Patio	124,041			
6	Food - Catering	340,172			
7	Total Food	$ 963,379			
8	Beverage - Dining Room	85,145			
9	Beverage - Patio	13,029			
10	Beverage - Catering	34,322			
11	Total Beverage	$ 132,496			
12	Beer & Liquor - Dining Room	51,217			
13	Beer & Liquor - Patio	14,417			
14	Beer & Liquor - Catering	35,661			
15	Total Beer & Liquor	$ 101,295			
16					
17	TOTAL SALES	$ 1,197,170			
18					
19	Proof Total	$ 1,197,170			
20					
21	Gross Profit Factor	27%			
22	Estimated Gross Profit	323,235.90			

37. Click A1 and then click the Home tab.

38. Click the Fill Color button arrow and then click *No Fill* at the drop-down gallery.

39. Save **ExcelS4-01.xlsx**.

In Brief

Create Formula with 3-D Reference
1. Make desired cell active.
2. Type **=sum(**.
3. Click first sheet tab.
4. Shift + click last sheet tab.
5. Click cell containing data to be summed in all sheets.
6. Press Enter.

Link Worksheet
1. Make destination cell active.
2. Type **=**.
3. Click sheet tab for source cell.
4. Click source cell.
5. Press Enter.

Apply Background
1. Click Page Layout tab.
2. Click Background button.
3. Navigate to drive and/or folder.
4. Double-click file name.

In Addition

3-D References and Moving, Inserting, and Deleting Sheets

The following actions apply to a formula when worksheets are moved, added, or deleted within a 3-D range.

- **Move:** Values are removed from the calculation if a worksheet is moved to a location outside the 3-D range.
- **Insert new sheet:** 3-D formula is adjusted to include all values in the same range of cells in the new worksheet(s).
- **Delete:** Values are removed from the 3-D formula. If the worksheet that is deleted is the beginning or ending sheet in the 3-D range, the formula is automatically adjusted to the new range of worksheets.

Activity 4.4

Printing Multiple Worksheets; Using Page Break Preview; Setting the Print Area

To print more than one worksheet at once, select multiple worksheets prior to printing, or display the Print dialog box and change the *Print what* option to *Entire workbook*. To print a portion of a worksheet, select the cells and then change the *Print what* option to *Selection* in the Print dialog box. Setting a print area allows you to save one or more ranges of cells to print so that you do not need to define the selection range again the next time you print. Page Break Preview displays the worksheet with page break information to provide a reference to the amount of cells that will print on each page. In this view, you can adjust the page break locations.

Project

Now that the quarterly sales report is complete, you will experiment with various printing methods.

1. With **ExcelS4-01.xlsx** open and the Summary sheet active, click the Qtr1 tab, hold down the Shift key, and then click the Qtr4 tab.

   As you learned in Activity 4.2, this action selects and groups all of the worksheets from the first tab through the last tab (Qtr1–Qtr4). To select multiple nonadjacent worksheets, hold down the Ctrl key while clicking each tab.

2. Click the Quick Print button on the Quick Access toolbar.

   The four worksheets print and remain grouped.

3. Right-click any of the selected sheet tabs and then click *Ungroup Sheets* at the shortcut menu.

4. Click the Summary tab and then select the range A3:B17.

   The *Print what* section of the Print dialog box contains the option *Selection* that is used when you want to print only a portion of the active worksheet.

5. Click the Office button and then click *Print* to display the Print dialog box. (Do not click the right-pointing arrow next to Print.)

6. Click *Selection* in the *Print what* section and then click OK.

   Only the cells within A3:B17 print.

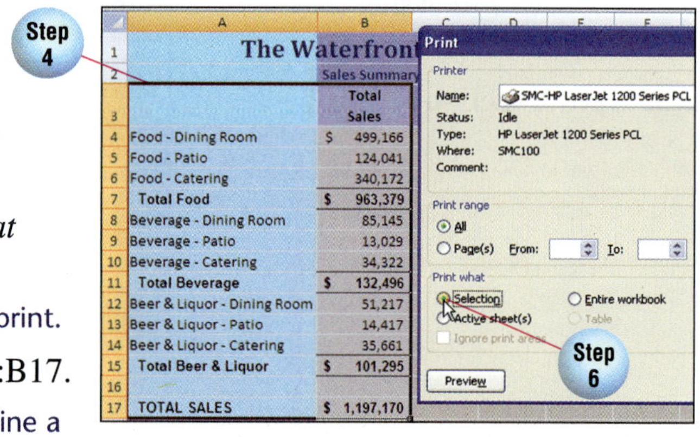

7. Click in any cell to deselect A3:B17.

   In the next steps, you will define a print area that will be saved with the workbook.

8. Click the Qtr1 tab and then click the Page Break Preview button located next to the Zoom slider bar near the right side of the Status bar. ***Hint: Click OK if the Welcome to Page Break Preview message box displays.***

9. Change the Zoom setting to 90%.

   In Page Break Preview, page breaks are shown as dashed or solid blue lines. You can adjust a page break by dragging the blue line to the desired position. In Steps 10–11, you will store a range of cells with the workbook as the print area to use by default whenever the worksheet is printed.

10. Select A1:E17.

11 Position the mouse pointer within the selected range, right-click, and then click *Set Print Area* at the shortcut menu.

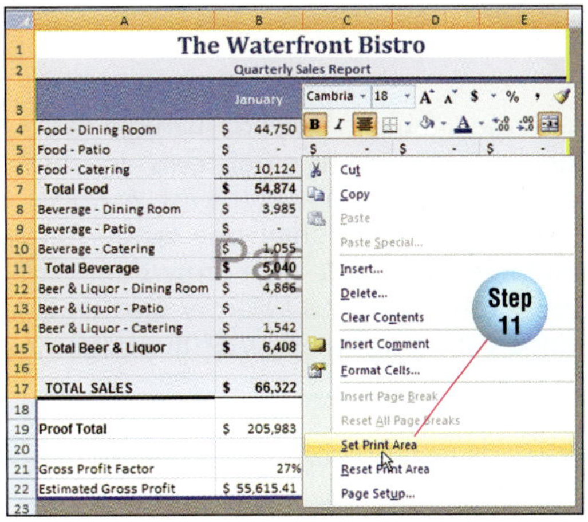

12 Click in any cell to deselect the range.

The cells not included in the print area are shown outside the solid blue border in a shaded background.

13 Click the Print button on the Quick Access toolbar.

Only the cells within the print area are printed. In the next steps, you will use the blue border to adjust the location of the page break.

14 Click the Qtr4 tab.

15 Switch to Page Break Preview and then change the Zoom setting to 90%.

16 Drag the blue solid line up until the border is on the boundary line between rows 17 and 18 as shown at the right.

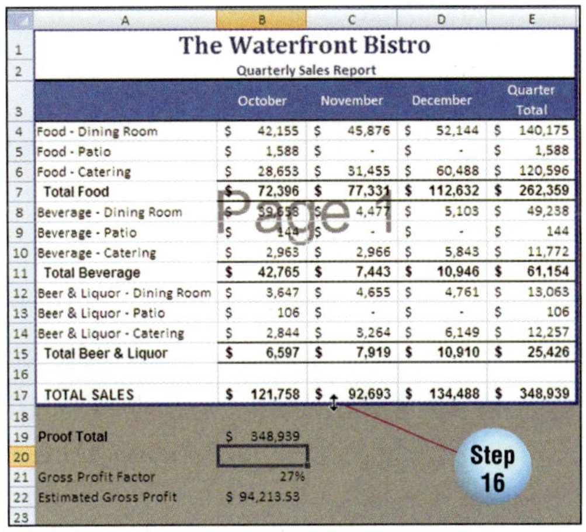

17 Click the Qtr1 tab, hold down the Ctrl key, and then click the Qtr4 tab.

18 Click the Office button, point to *Print*, and then click *Print Preview*.

The Qtr1 worksheet displays in Print Preview and the Status bar at the bottom of the Preview window displays *Page 1 of 2*.

19 Click the Next Page button in the Preview group of the Print Preview tab to view the Qtr4 worksheet.

20 Click the Close Print Preview button.

You decide after viewing the worksheets in Print Preview to remove the print area from the Qtr1 worksheet.

21 Click the Qtr3 tab to deselect the two grouped worksheets.

22 Click the Qtr1 tab, click the Page Layout tab, click the Print Area button in the Page Setup group, and then click *Clear Print Area* in the drop-down list.

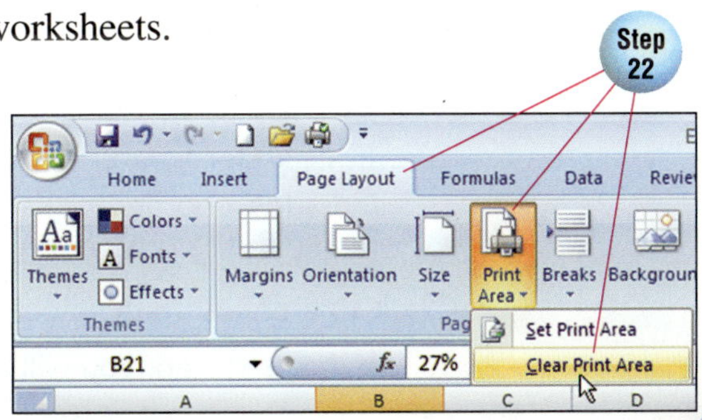

23 Click the Qtr4 tab and then drag the solid blue line down until the border is on the boundary line between rows 22 and 23.

24 Click the Summary tab, switch to Page Break Preview, and then change the zoom to 90%.

25 With *Page 1* displayed in the worksheet background as printing the range A1:E22, click the Print button on the Quick Access toolbar.

26 Save and then close **Excel S4-01.xlsx**.

In Brief

Print Multiple Worksheets
1. Group worksheets to be printed.
2. Click Quick Print button on Quick Access toolbar.

Print Selection
1. Select range to be printed.
2. Click Office button.
3. Click Print.
4. Click *Selection*.
5. Click OK.

Set Print Area
1. Display Page Break Preview.
2. Select range to be printed.
3. Right-click within range.
4. Click *Set Print Area*.

Clear Print Area
1. Click Page Layout tab.
2. Click Print Area button.
3. Click *Clear Print Area*.

Activity 4.5

Formatting Data as a Table; Applying Table Design Options

Create a table in Excel to manage data independently from other cells in the worksheet, or to filter and sort a list. A worksheet can contain more than one range formatted as a table. By default, filter arrows appear in the first row of the table and a border surrounds the table range with a sizing arrow at the bottom right corner. In previous versions of Excel, this feature was called a List. Excel includes a variety of predefined table styles to apply attractive formatting features to the range within a table. The contextual Table Tools Design tab becomes available when a range of cells is defined as a table.

Project

Dana Hirsch has given you information for a new catering contract in August. You will open the catering workbook and format the list as a table, add a record to the list, and create a new calculated column to extend the catering contract amounts. Finally, you will add a totals row to the bottom of the table to sum the catering contracts.

The Waterfront B·I·S·T·R·O

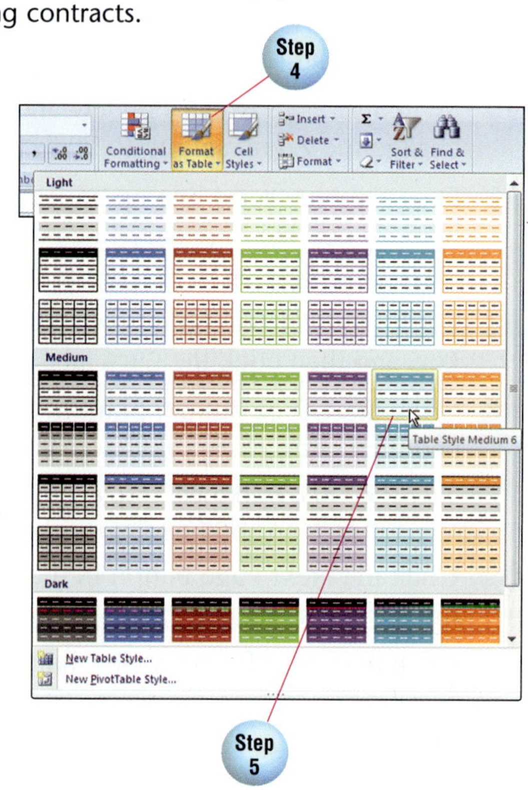

1. Open **WBCatering.xlsx**.
2. Save the workbook and name it **ExcelS4-02**.
3. Select A3:H23.
4. Click the Format as Table button in the Styles group in the Home tab.
5. Click *Table Style Medium 6* (sixth from left in first row in *Medium* section) at the drop-down gallery.

   Excel includes 60 predefined table styles grouped into *Light*, *Medium*, and *Dark* categories with which you can add color, borders, and shading formats to cells within the table. In addition, you can create your own custom table style saved with the current workbook.

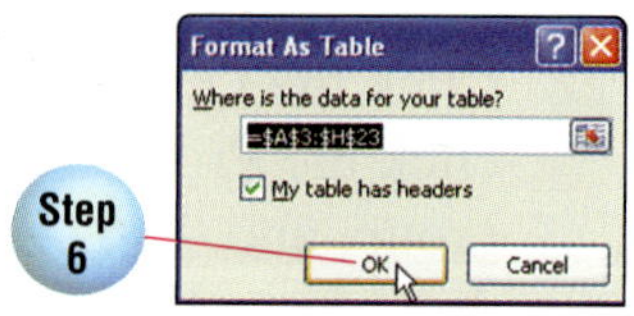

6. At the Format As Table dialog box, with *=$A$3:$H$23* selected in the *Where is the data for your table?* text box, click OK.

   Excel applies the table style formats to the range, displays filter arrows in the first row of the table, and adds a border to the table, including a sizing handle to the bottom right cell.

7. Click in any cell to deselect the range.

   In the next step, you will add a new record to the table.

8. Make A24 the active cell and then type the new record in the columns indicated. Press Enter after typing the contract per person price.

Contact Name	**Sing Ping Yee**
Contact Phone	**716 555 2668**
Event	**Graduation Party**
Date	**8/6/2009**

Room	**Starlake**
Guests	**73**
Special Menu	**Yes**
Contract per Person	**31.95**

Since you typed data in the row immediately below the table, Excel automatically expands the table to include the new row and applies the table style formats. You can also insert a new row by pressing Tab at the last cell in the table to insert a new blank row below and then type the data.

9. Make I3 the active cell, type **Contract Total**, and then press Enter.

   Typing new data in a column immediately right of the table also automatically expands the table list range.

10. With I4 the active cell, type the formula **=f4*h4** and then press Enter.

    Typing a formula in a table column causes Excel to automatically categorize the column as a calculated column and duplicate the formula in the remainder of the table.

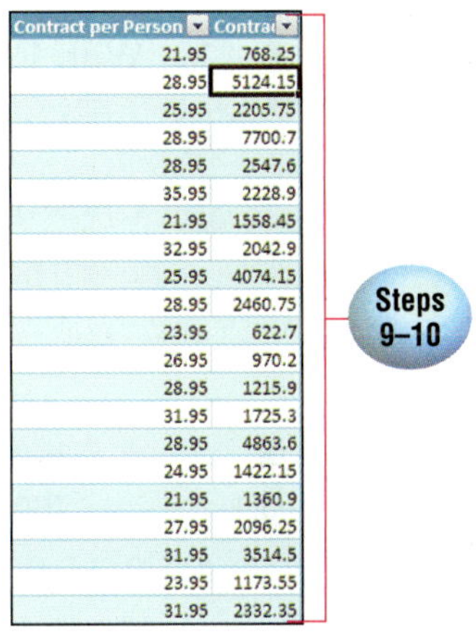

11. AutoFit the width of column I.
12. Click the Table Tools Design tab.
13. Click the *Total Row* check box in the Table Style Options group.

    Excel adds the word *Total* in the leftmost cell in the row below the table and sums the cells in column I.

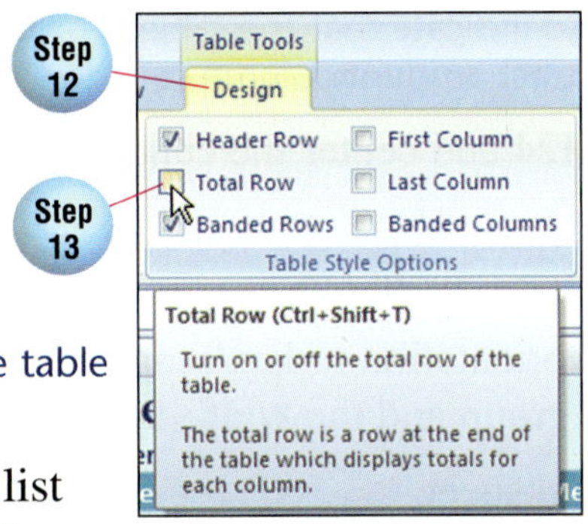

14. Make F25 the active cell, click the list arrow that appears, and then click *Sum* at the pop-up list.
15. Make H25 the active cell, click the list arrow that appears, and then click *Average* at the pop-up list.
16. Decrease the decimals in H25 to two decimal places.
17. Apply the Accounting Number Format to I4:I25.
18. Select A1:I1 and then click the Merge & Center button in the Alignment group in the Home tab to remove the merging of columns A through H.
19. With A1:I1 still selected, click the Merge & Center button a second time to merge columns A through I.
20. Correct the centering of the title in row 2 by completing steps similar to those in Steps 18–19.
21. Save **ExcelS4-02.xlsx**.

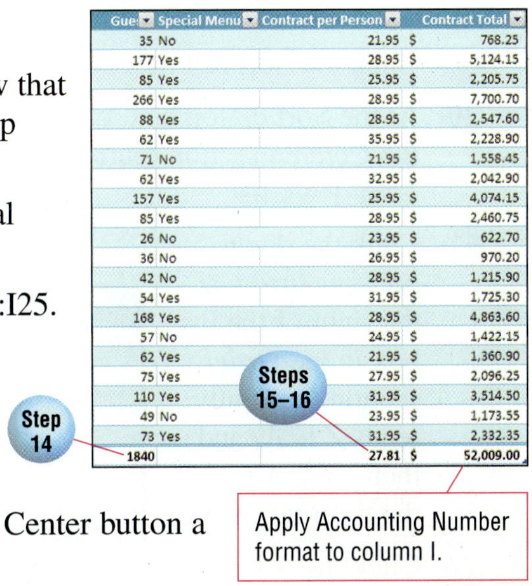

In Brief

Format Table
1. Select range.
2. Click Format as Table button.
3. Click desired table style.

Add Total Row
1. Click Table Tools Design tab.
2. Click *Total Row* check box.
3. If necessary, choose desired function in numeric columns.

Activity 4.6

Sorting a Table by Single and Multiple Criteria

In Activity 1.6 you learned to sort the payroll worksheet alphabetically by last names. To sort rows in a table by single or multiple criteria involves the same process as the one used in Section 1. To sort by a single column, click in any cell in the column by which you wish to sort and then use the *Sort Ascending* or *Sort Descending* options at the Sort & Filter drop-down list. To group the rows first by one column and then sort the rows within each group by another column, open the Sort dialog box. You can continue to group and sort by multiple criteria as needed.

Project

You decide to print the catering data sorted in descending order by the extended contract amount. Next, you want a printout of the catering list grouped first by the event, then by room, and then by date.

1. With **ExcelS4-02.xlsx** open, click any cell in column I within the table range.
2. Click the Sort & Filter button in the Editing group in the Home tab.
3. Click *Sort Largest to Smallest* at the drop-down list.

   The table is rearranged in descending order by contract amount with the highest contract amount at the top of the list. Excel displays a down-pointing black arrow in the filter arrow button to indicate that the table is ordered by the contract amount column.

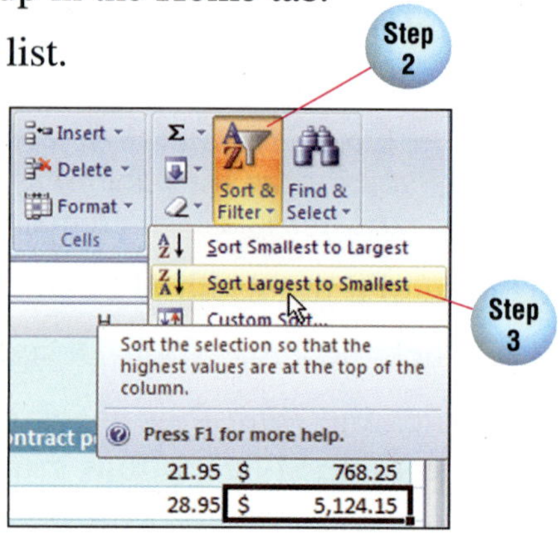

4. Select G4:H24 and center the cells within the range.
5. Click the Page Layout tab.
6. Change the orientation to landscape in the Page Setup group and the width to 1 page in the Scale to Fit group.
7. Print the worksheet.
8. Click the Home tab.
9. Click the Sort & Filter button and then click *Custom Sort* at the drop-down list.
10. At the Sort dialog box, click the down-pointing arrow at the right of *Sort by* in the *Column* section (currently reads *Contract Total*) and then click *Event* at the drop-down list.
11. Click the down-pointing arrow at the right of the list box in the *Order* section (currently reads *Z to A*) and then click *A to Z* at the drop-down list.
12. Click the Add Level button in the Sort dialog box.

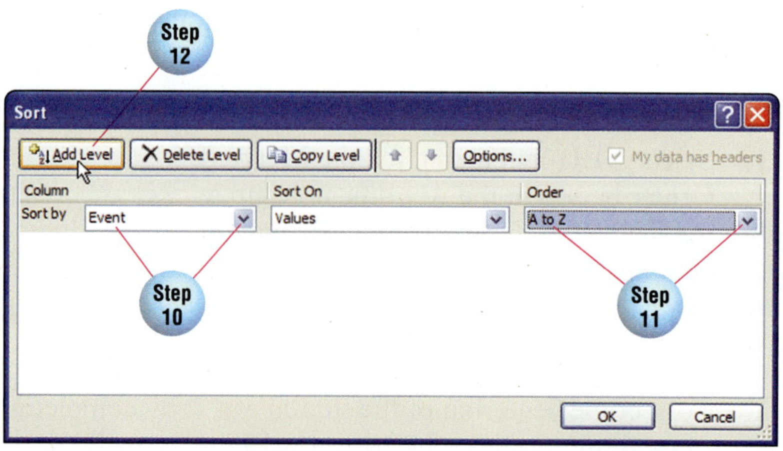

In Brief

Sort Table by Single Column

1. Click in any row within column by which to sort.
2. Click Sort & Filter button.
3. Click *Sort Smallest to Largest* or *Sort Largest to Smallest.*

Sort Table by Multiple Columns

1. Click Sort & Filter button.
2. Click *Custom Sort.*
3. Select first column to sort by.
4. Select sort order.
5. Click Add Level.
6. Repeat Steps 3-5 for each sort column.
7. Click OK.

13 Click the down-pointing arrow at the right of *Then by* in the *Column* section and then click *Room* at the drop-down list.

The default entries of *Values* for *Sort On* and *A to Z* for *Order* are correct since you want the cells sorted by the room names in ascending order.

14 Click the Add Level button.

15 Click the down-pointing arrow at the right of the second *Then by* list box in the *Column* section and then click *Date* at the drop-down list.

The default entries of *Values* for *Sort On* and *Oldest to Newest* for *Order* are correct since you want to sort the dates in ascending order.

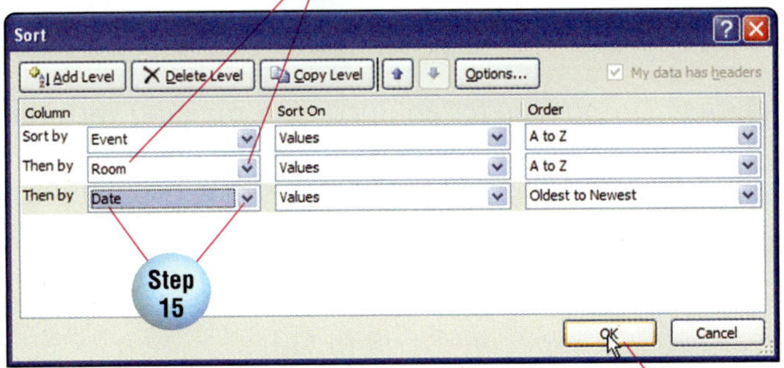

16 Click OK to begin the sort.

17 Examine the sorted worksheet and compare your results with the worksheet shown below. Notice the rows are grouped and sorted first by event starting with *25th Wedding Anniversary*. Within each event group, the rows are next arranged by room and then within each room group the rows are arranged by date.

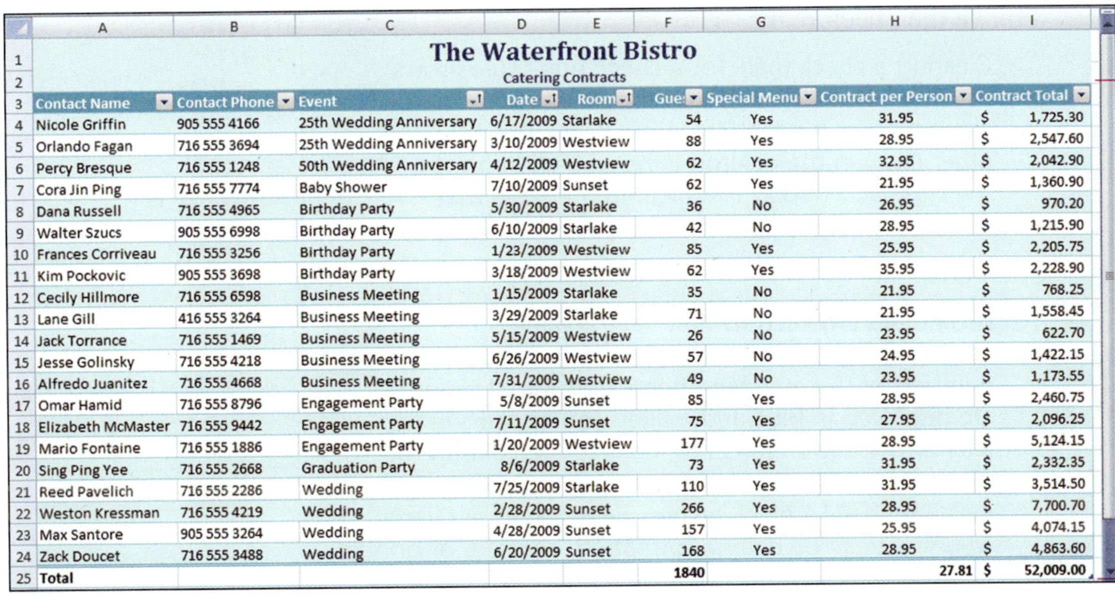

	A	B	C	D	E	F	G	H	I
1	The Waterfront Bistro								
2	Catering Contracts								
3	Contact Name	Contact Phone	Event	Date	Room	Gue	Special Menu	Contract per Person	Contract Total
4	Nicole Griffin	905 555 4166	25th Wedding Anniversary	6/17/2009	Starlake	54	Yes	31.95	$ 1,725.30
5	Orlando Fagan	716 555 3694	25th Wedding Anniversary	3/10/2009	Westview	88	Yes	28.95	$ 2,547.60
6	Percy Bresque	716 555 1248	50th Wedding Anniversary	4/12/2009	Westview	62	Yes	32.95	$ 2,042.90
7	Cora Jin Ping	716 555 7774	Baby Shower	7/10/2009	Sunset	62	Yes	21.95	$ 1,360.90
8	Dana Russell	716 555 4965	Birthday Party	5/30/2009	Starlake	36	No	26.95	$ 970.20
9	Walter Szucs	905 555 6998	Birthday Party	6/10/2009	Starlake	42	No	28.95	$ 1,215.90
10	Frances Corriveau	716 555 3256	Birthday Party	1/23/2009	Westview	85	Yes	25.95	$ 2,205.75
11	Kim Pockovic	905 555 3698	Birthday Party	3/18/2009	Westview	62	Yes	35.95	$ 2,228.90
12	Cecily Hillmore	716 555 6598	Business Meeting	1/15/2009	Starlake	35	No	21.95	$ 768.25
13	Lane Gill	416 555 3264	Business Meeting	3/29/2009	Starlake	71	No	21.95	$ 1,558.45
14	Jack Torrance	716 555 1469	Business Meeting	5/15/2009	Westview	26	No	23.95	$ 622.70
15	Jesse Golinsky	716 555 4218	Business Meeting	6/26/2009	Westview	57	No	24.95	$ 1,422.15
16	Alfredo Juanitez	716 555 4668	Business Meeting	7/31/2009	Westview	49	No	23.95	$ 1,173.55
17	Omar Hamid	716 555 8796	Engagement Party	5/8/2009	Sunset	85	Yes	28.95	$ 2,460.75
18	Elizabeth McMaster	716 555 9442	Engagement Party	7/11/2009	Sunset	75	Yes	27.95	$ 2,096.25
19	Mario Fontaine	716 555 1886	Engagement Party	1/20/2009	Westview	177	Yes	28.95	$ 5,124.15
20	Sing Ping Yee	716 555 2668	Graduation Party	8/6/2009	Starlake	73	Yes	31.95	$ 2,332.35
21	Reed Pavelich	716 555 2286	Wedding	7/25/2009	Starlake	110	Yes	31.95	$ 3,514.50
22	Weston Kressman	716 555 4219	Wedding	2/28/2009	Sunset	266	Yes	28.95	$ 7,700.70
23	Max Santore	905 555 3264	Wedding	4/28/2009	Sunset	157	Yes	25.95	$ 4,074.15
24	Zack Doucet	716 555 3488	Wedding	6/20/2009	Sunset	168	Yes	28.95	$ 4,863.60
25	Total					1840		27.81	$ 52,009.00

18 Print the worksheet.

19 Save **ExcelS4-02.xlsx**.

In Addition

More about Sorting

By default, Excel sorts the data in a column alphanumerically. Alphanumeric sorting arranges rows with entries that begin with symbols first, then numbers, then letters. Notice in the catering events workbook that the events beginning with numbers such as *25th Wedding Anniversary* and *50th Wedding Anniversary* are the first rows in the sorted worksheet.

Activity 4.7

Filtering a Table

A *filter* is used to display only certain records within the table that meet specified criteria. The records that do not meet the filter criteria are temporarily hidden from view. Using a filter, you can view and/or print a subset of rows within a table. For example, you might want to print a list of catering events that have been booked into a certain room. Once you have printed the list, removing the filter redisplays all of the rows. Excel displays filter arrows in the first row of the table with which you specify the filter criteria.

Project

The Waterfront B·I·S·T·R·O

To prepare for an upcoming meeting with the executive chef, Dana Hirsch has asked for a printout of the catering events that require a special menu. Another printout of the events booked into the Starlake room is needed for planning staff requirements. Finally, Dana Hirsch wants a printed list of the weddings booked into the Sunset room.

1. With **ExcelS4-02.xlsx** open, click the filter arrow button next to the label *Special Menu* in G3.

   Filter a table by selecting the criterion from a drop-down list. For each column in the table, a filter arrow button appears. Excel looks in the active column and includes in the filter drop-down list each unique field value that exists within the column. In addition, the entries *Sort A to Z, Sort Z to A,* and *Sort by Color* appear at the top of the list.

2. Click the check box next to *No* in the drop-down list to remove the check mark.

   Clearing a check mark for a check box causes rows with the value that matches the entry in the filtered column to be hidden from view. Since the only other entry in the column is *Yes*, the criterion for the filter is to display rows within the table that have the text entry *Yes* in column G.

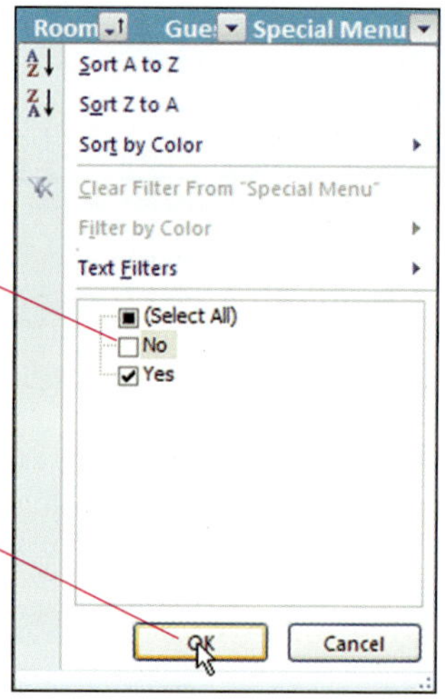

Step 2

Step 3

3. Click OK.

   Excel hides any records that have a value other than *Yes* in the column as shown below. The row numbers of the matching items that were found are displayed in blue and a filter icon appears in the filter arrow button in G3 to indicate the column that was used to filter by. The Status bar also shows the message that 14 of 21 records were found. A filtered worksheet can be edited, formatted, charted, or printed.

4. Print the filtered worksheet.

Filter icon indicates the column used to filter the table.

3	Contact Name	Contact Phone	Event	Date	Room	Gue	Special Menu
4	Nicole Griffin	905 555 4166	25th Wedding Anniversary	6/17/2009	Starlake	54	Yes
5	Orlando Fagan	716 555 3694	25th Wedding Anniversary	3/10/2009	Westview	88	Yes
6	Percy Bresque	716 555 1248	50th Wedding Anniversary	4/12/2009	Westview	62	Yes
7	Cora Jin Ping	716 555 7774	Baby Shower	7/10/2009	Sunset	62	Yes
10	Frances Corriveau	716 555 3256	Birthday Party	1/23/2009	Westview	85	Yes
11	Kim Pockovic	905 555 3698	Birthday Party	3/18/2009	Westview	62	Yes
17	Omar Hamid	716 555 8796	Engagement Party	5/8/2009	Sunset	85	Yes
18	Elizabeth McMaster	716 555 9442	Engagement Party	7/11/2009	Sunset	75	Yes
19	Mario Fontaine	716 555 1886	Engagement Party	1/20/2009	Westview	177	Yes
20	Sing Ping Yee	716 555 2668	Graduation Party	8/6/2009	Starlake	73	Yes
21	Reed Pavelich	716 555 2286	Wedding	7/25/2009	Starlake	110	Yes
22	Weston Kressman	716 555 4219	Wedding	2/28/2009	Sunset	266	Yes
23	Max Santore	905 555 3264	Wedding	4/28/2009	Sunset	157	Yes
24	Zack Doucet	716 555 3488	Wedding	6/20/2009	Sunset	168	Yes
25	Total					1524	

Excel hides rows that do not meet the criterion. Matching row numbers are displayed in blue.

5. Point to the filter icon in the filter arrow button in G3. Notice the filter criterion displays in the ScreenTip.

Step 5

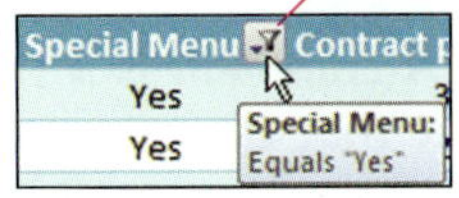

6. Click the filter arrow button in G3.
7. Click *Clear Filter from "Special Menu"* at the filter drop-down list.

   All rows within the table are restored to view.

Step 7

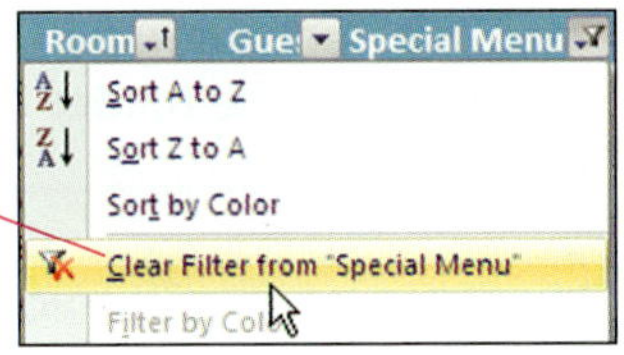

8. Click the filter arrow button in E3.
9. Clear the check marks in the *Westview* and *Sunset* check boxes at the drop-down list and then click OK.

   Only the catering events where Starlake is the specified room are displayed.

3	Contact Name	Contact Phone	Event	Date	Room
4	Nicole Griffin	905 555 4166	25th Wedding Anniversary	6/17/2009	Starlake
8	Dana Russell	716 555 4965	Birthday Party	5/30/2009	Starlake
9	Walter Szucs	905 555 6998	Birthday Party	6/10/2009	Starlake
12	Cecily Hillmore	716 555 6598	Business Meeting	1/15/2009	Starlake
13	Lane Gill	416 555 3264	Business Meeting	3/29/2009	Starlake
20	Sing Ping Yee	716 555 2668	Graduation Party	8/6/2009	Starlake
21	Reed Pavelich	716 555 2286	Wedding	7/25/2009	Starlake
25	Total				

table filtered by *Starlake* in Step 9

10. Print the filtered worksheet.
11. Click the filter arrow button in E3.
12. Click the *(Select All)* check box to insert a check mark and then click OK.

    Choosing the *(Select All)* check box is another method to redisplay the entire table. In the next steps, you will filter by the event and then filter the subset of rows again to further refine a report.

13. Click the filter arrow button in C3.
14. Click the *(Select All)* check box to clear the check marks from all check boxes in the drop-down list, click the *Wedding* check box to insert a check mark, and then click OK.
15. Click the filter arrow button in E3.

    Notice the drop-down list of text filters displays only the two rooms that are shown in the filtered table.

16. Clear the check mark from the *Starlake* check box and then click OK.

Step 14

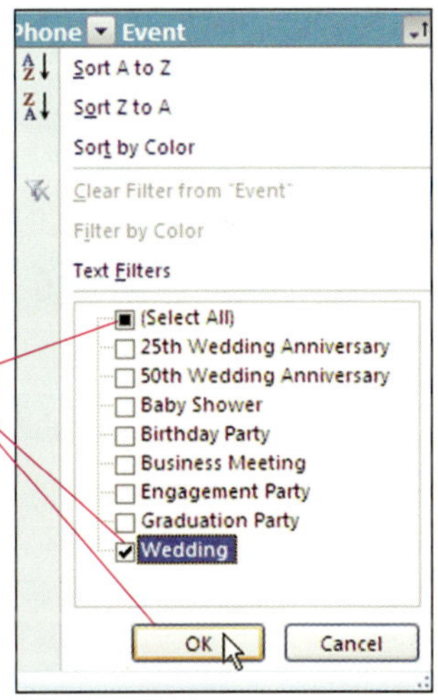

table filtered first by Wedding *Event* and then by Sunset *Room* in Steps 13–16

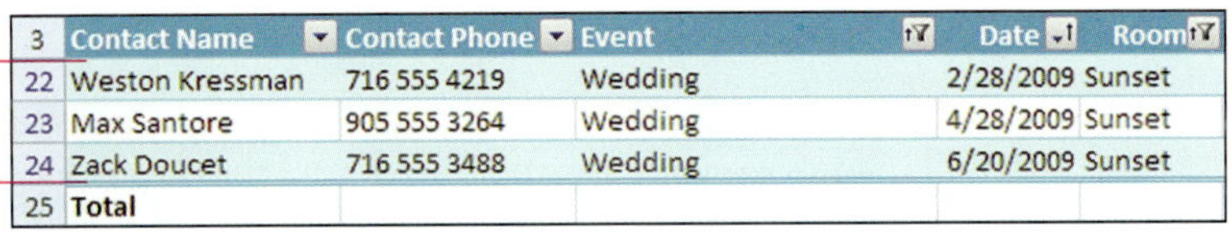

3	Contact Name	Contact Phone	Event	Date	Room
22	Weston Kressman	716 555 4219	Wedding	2/28/2009	Sunset
23	Max Santore	905 555 3264	Wedding	4/28/2009	Sunset
24	Zack Doucet	716 555 3488	Wedding	6/20/2009	Sunset
25	Total				

17. Print the filtered worksheet.
18. Redisplay all records for both filtered columns.
19. Save **ExcelS4-02.xlsx**.

In Brief

Filter Table
1. Click desired filter arrow button.
2. Clear check boxes for items you do not want to view.
3. Click OK.

Remove Filter
1. Click desired filter arrow button.
2. Click *Clear Filter from (column title)*.

In Addition

Filtering Data Not Formatted as a Table

Data in a worksheet that has not been formatted as a table can also be filtered using similar techniques as you learned in this activity. Select the range of cells that you wish to filter, click the Sort & Filter button in the Editing group in the Home tab, and then click *Filter* at the drop-down list. Excel adds filter arrows in each column of the first row of the selected range.

Activity 4.8

Inserting, Editing, Deleting, and Printing Comments

A *comment* is a pop-up box containing text that displays when the cell pointer is positioned over a cell with an attached comment. A diagonal red triangle in the upper right corner of the cell alerts the reader that a comment exists. The Review tab contains buttons to insert and delete comments, show or hide all comment boxes, and scroll through comments within a worksheet. Use comments to provide instructions, ask questions, or add other explanatory text to a cell.

Project

Dana Hirsch has given you two notes and a reminder that should be inserted into the appropriate event information in the catering contracts workbook.

1. With **ExcelS4-02.xlsx** open, make F10 the active cell.
2. Click the Review tab.
3. Click the New Comment button in the Comments group.

    A comment box displays anchored to the active cell with the user's name inserted in bold text at the top of the box. In worksheets accessed by multiple people, the name helps the reader identify the person who made the comment.

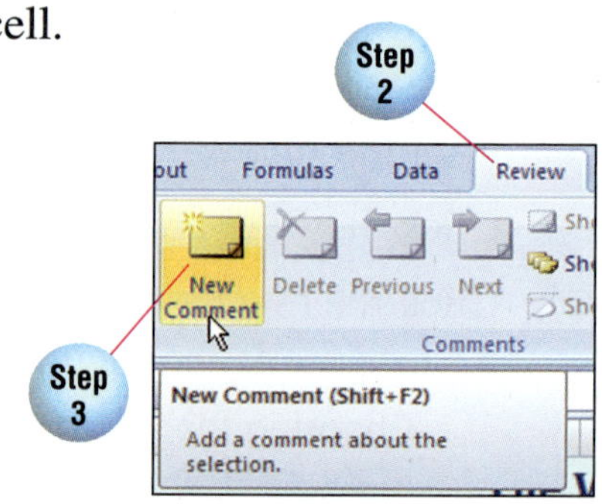

4. Type **Waiting for Frances to confirm the final number of guests.**
5. Click in the worksheet outside the comment box.

    A diagonal red triangle appears in the upper right corner of F10 indicating a comment exists for the cell.

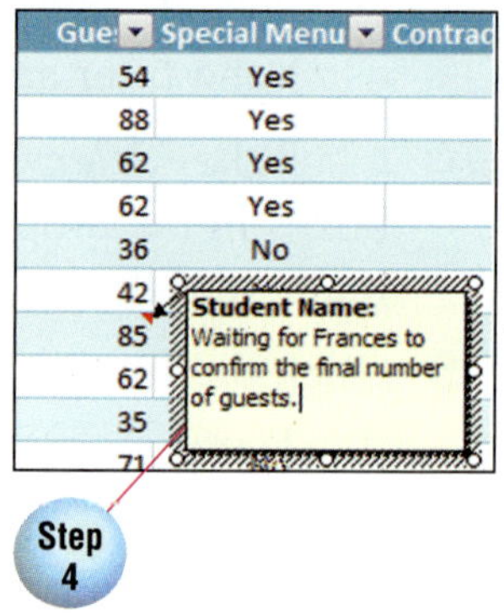

6. Right-click G19 and then click *Insert Comment* at the shortcut menu.
7. Type **Remind Pierre that five guests require a diabetic menu.**

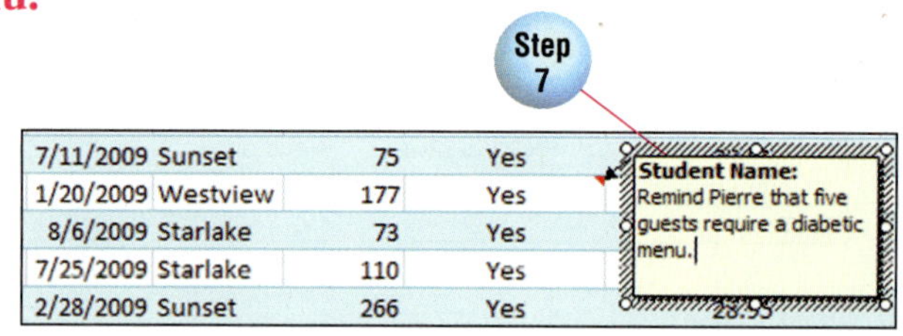

8. Click in the worksheet outside the comment box.
9. Hover the cell pointer over F10.

    Hovering the cell pointer over a cell that contains a comment causes the comment box to pop up.

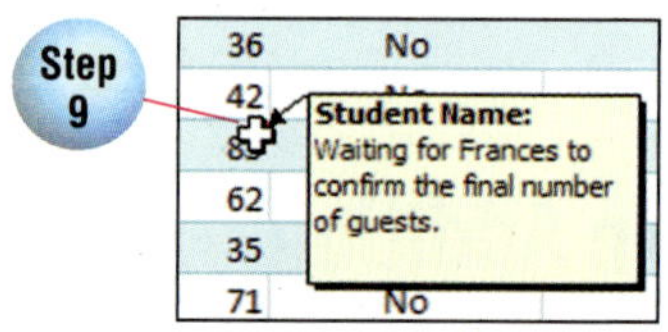

10. Click H24, click the New Comment button in the Comments group, type **Signed contract not yet received. Follow-up in two weeks.**, and then click in the worksheet outside the comment box.

11. Right-click G19 and then click *Edit Comment* at the shortcut menu.
12. Move the cursor and insert and delete text as necessary to change the comment text from *five* to *six* guests require a diabetic menu.

Steps 11–12

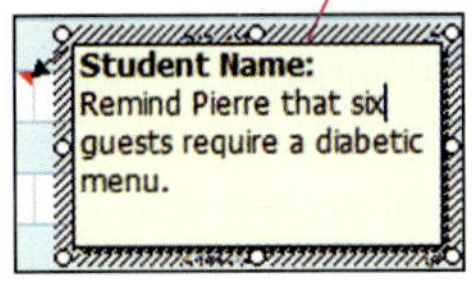

13. Click in the worksheet outside the comment box and then press Ctrl + Home to move the active cell to A1.
14. Click the Next button in the Comments group.

    Excel opens the comment box in F10.

Step 14

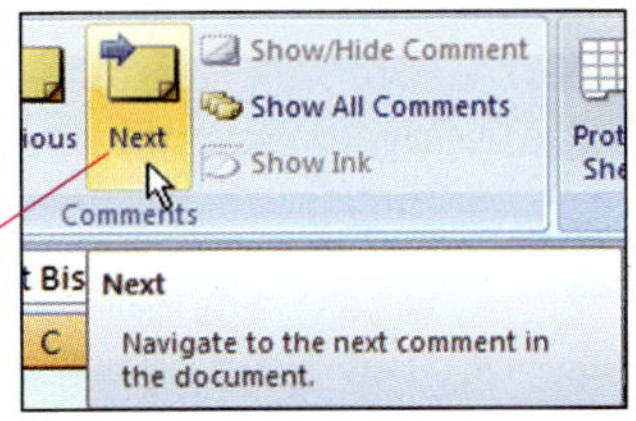

15. Click the Next button to scroll to the next comment box in G19.
16. Click the Next button to scroll to the third comment box and then click the Delete button in the Comments group.

    By default, comments do not print with the worksheet. In the next steps, you will print the worksheet with the comment text displayed next to the cells.

Step 16

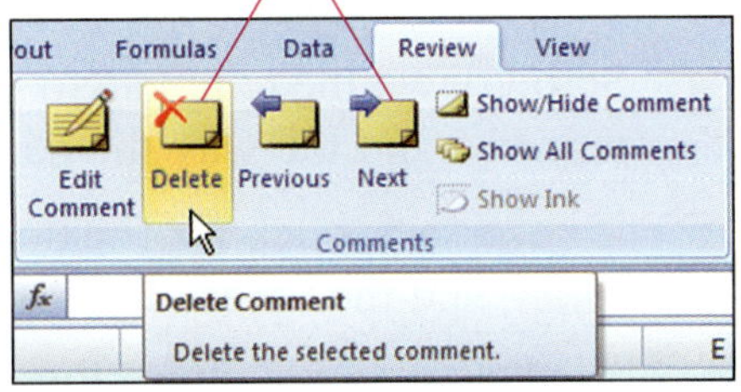

17. Click the Show All Comments button in the Comments group.
18. Click the Page Layout tab.
19. Click the Page Setup group dialog box launcher located at the bottom right corner of the Page Setup group.

Step 18

Step 19

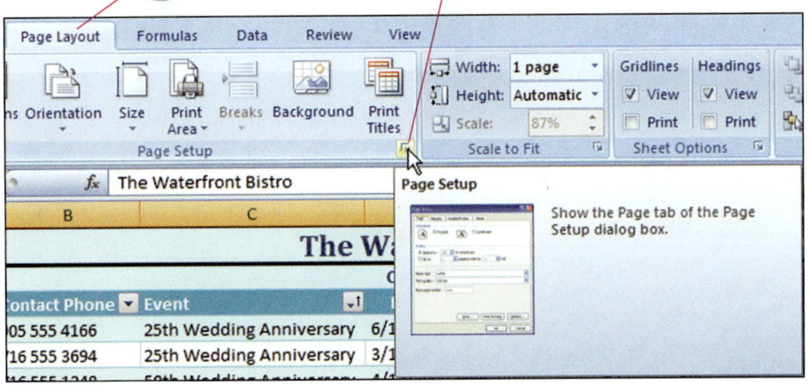

20. Click the Sheet tab at the Page Setup dialog box, click the down-pointing arrow next to *Comments* in the *Print* section, click *As displayed on sheet*, and then click OK.
21. Print the worksheet.
22. Click the Review tab and then click the Show All Comments button to remove the display of the comment boxes.
23. Save and then close **ExcelS4-02.xlsx**.

In Brief

Insert Comment

1. Make active cell in which to insert comment.
2. Click Review tab.
3. Click New Comment button.
4. Type comment text.
5. Click in worksheet outside comment box.

Print Comments with Worksheet

1. Click Page Layout tab.
2. Click Page Setup group dialog box launcher.
3. Click Sheet tab in Page Setup dialog box.
4. Click down-pointing arrow to right of *Comments*.
5. Click *As displayed on sheet* or *At end of sheet*.
6. Click OK.
7. Print worksheet.

Activity 4.9

Creating a Workbook from a Template

Excel includes worksheets that are formatted and have text and formulas created for specific uses such as creating sales invoices, expenses, timecards, and financial statements. These preformatted worksheets are called ***templates***. Templates can be customized and saved with a new name to reflect individual company data. Additional templates can be downloaded from Office Online.

Project

Aparna Patel, the administrative assistant to Dana Hirsch, has provided her hours worked for submission to payroll. You will use the Time Card template to fill out the paperwork.

1. Click the Office button and then click *New* at the drop-down list.
2. At the New Workbook dialog box, click *Installed Templates* in the *Templates* list in the left pane.

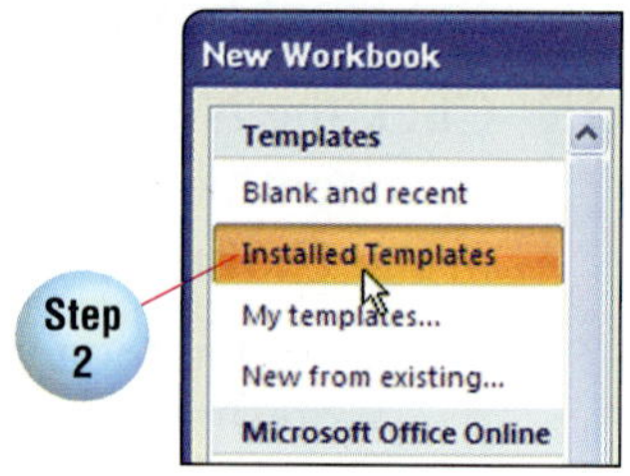

3. Scroll down the list of installed templates in the center pane and then double-click *Time Card*.
4. Scroll down the template to view the type of information required and the way the data is arranged on the page.
5. If necessary, click *C7* (next to *Employee*), type **Aparna Patel**, and then press Enter twice.

   Pressing Enter moves the active cell next to *[Street Address]* (C9) in the template.
6. Type **15 Pearl Street** and then press Enter four times.
7. With the active cell next to *[City, ST ZIP Code]*, type **Buffalo, NY 14202** and then press Enter three times.

   The active cell moves next to *Week ending:* (C16).
8. Type **11/8/2009** and then click *G7* (next to *Manager:*).

   Notice the dates in the table below *Week ending* update once you change the date in C16.

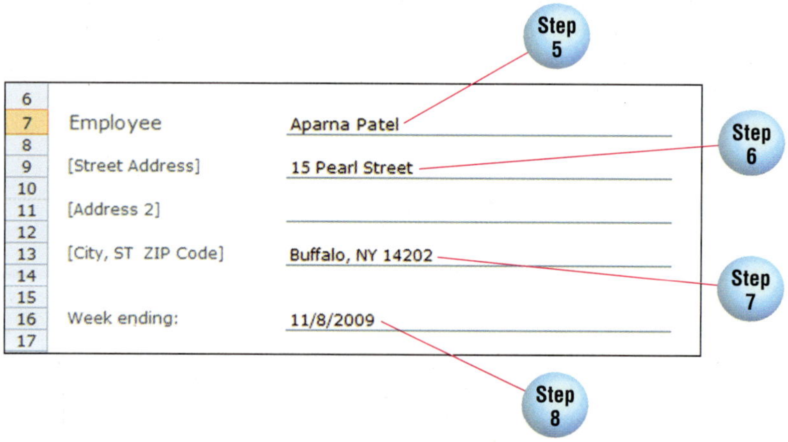

9. Type **Dana Hirsch** and then press Enter twice.

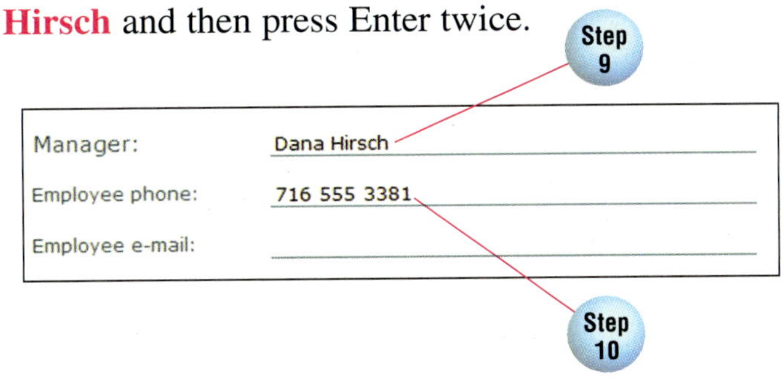

10. With the active cell next to *Employee phone:*, type **716 555 3381** and then click D21.

11. Type the remaining entries in the time card as shown below by typing the value and then pressing Enter or clicking the next cell as needed. The cells in the shaded *Total* column, and *Total hours* and *Total pay* rows calculate automatically.

Day	Date	Regular Hours	Overtime	Sick	Vacation	Total
Monday	11/2/2009	8.00	2.00			10.00
Tuesday	11/3/2009	7.00				7.00
Wednesday	11/4/2009	8.00				8.00
Thursday	11/5/2009	8.00				8.00
Friday	11/6/2009	7.00				7.00
Saturday	11/7/2009					
Sunday	11/8/2009					
Total hours		38.00	2.00			40.00
Rate per hour		$ 14.73	$ 22.10			
Total pay		$ 559.74	$ 44.20	$ -	$ -	$ 603.94

Step 11

12. Click the Save button.

13. At the Save As dialog box, type **ExcelS4-03** in the *File name* text box and then press Enter.

14. Print and then close **ExcelS4-03.xlsx**.

In Brief

Create Workbook from Template

1. Click Office button, then *New*.
2. Click *Installed Templates* or Office Online category.
3. Double-click desired template in center pane.
4. Fill in data or other information as needed.
5. Save, print, close.

In Addition

Templates from Microsoft Office Online

Microsoft maintains a Templates page on Office Online from which you can browse hundreds of predesigned templates for all products in the Office 2007 suite. Browse for an Excel template in the *Microsoft Office Online* categories list in the left pane of the New Workbook dialog box, or click *Featured* in the Microsoft Office Online category, scroll to the bottom of the center pane, and then click the hyperlink to Templates below *More on Office Online*. At the Microsoft Office Online Templates Web page you can browse template categories or type a description of the template you need and search the site for available templates. Once you have located an appropriate template you can download the template to your computer.

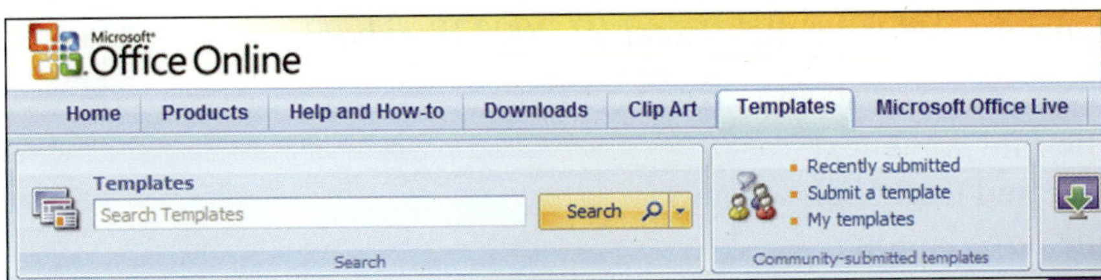

Activity 4.10

Opening and Saving a Workbook in a Different File Format

The default file format for an Excel workbook is Extensible Markup (XML), which is different than the format used for previous versions of Excel. Opening a file created in a version of Excel earlier than 2007 causes Excel to switch to compatibility mode. In this mode, you can edit and save the workbook retaining the original file format or use *Save As* to convert to Excel 2007. If you plan to exchange a workbook created in Excel 2007 with someone who does not have the same version, you have to save the file using Excel 97-2003 file format since the file is not backward compatible. A variety of other file formats are available to save workbooks for use in other applications.

Project

The Waterfront B·I·S·T·R·O

You will open an employee schedule created in Excel 2003 by Aparna Patel and work in compatibility mode. Another file on your system needs to be given to Aparna so you will save the workbook in the earlier Excel version. Finally, the inventory workbook needs to be converted to another file format for the executive chef.

1. Open **WBSchedule-Feb16.xls**.

   Notice the title bar displays *[Compatibility Mode]* next to the file name since the file you opened was created in a version of Excel prior to Excel 2007.

2. Insert a new row between rows 1 and 2 and then type the label **Pier Dining Room** merged and centered in columns A–H.
3. Change the font size of A2 to 16-point.
4. Make B9 the active cell, type **All schedule changes must be approved in advance by Dana Hirsch.**, and then press Enter.
5. Click the Office button and then click *Save As*.

   Notice the *Save as type* option is set to *Excel 97-2003 Workbook (*.xls)*.

6. Type **ExcelS4-04** in the *File name* text box.
7. Click the down-pointing arrow next to *Save as type* and then click *Excel Workbook (*.xlsx)*.

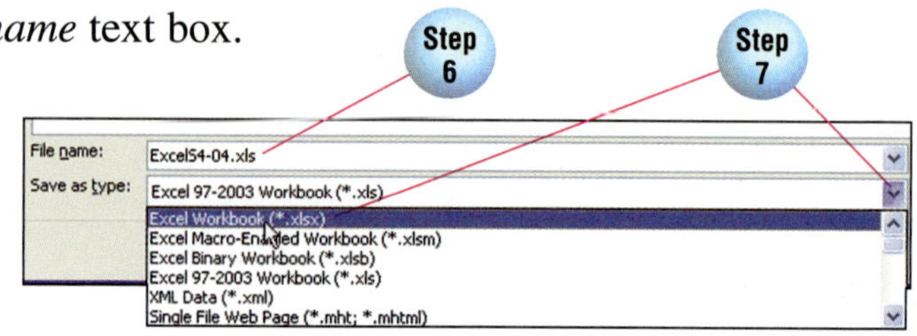

8. Click the *Save* button.
9. Close **ExcelS4-04.xlsx**.

   In the next steps, you will open an Excel 2007 workbook related to a cash investment and save it in Excel 2003 format so that Aparna can update the file when the investment details are completed.

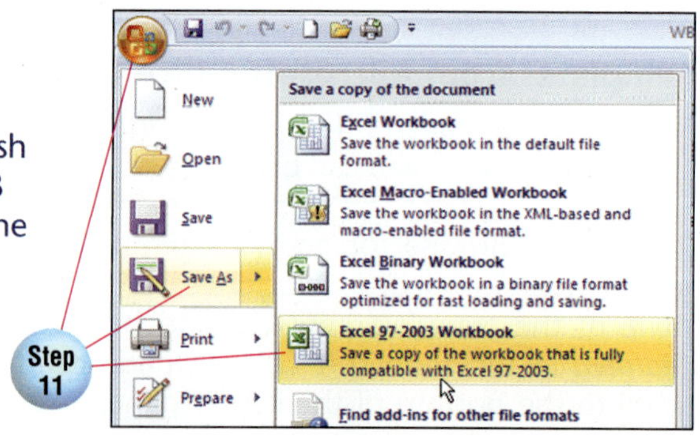

10. Open **WBInvestment.xlsx**.
11. Click the Office button, point to *Save As*, and then click *Excel 97-2003 Workbook*.
12. Type **ExcelS4-05** in the *File name* text box and then click the *Save* button.

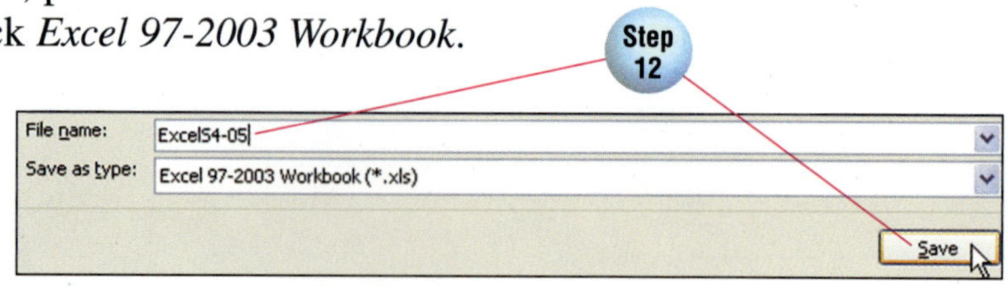

13 At the Microsoft Office Excel - Compatibility Checker dialog box advising you that one formatting occurrence is not supported in the selected file format, click the *Continue* button.

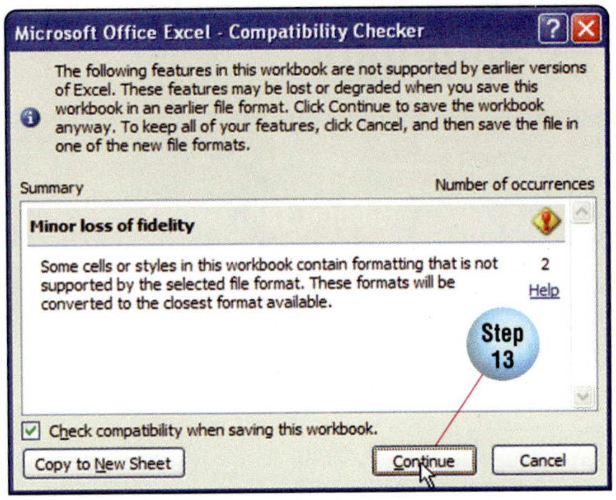

Earlier versions of Excel did not include the cell styles, themes, and table format galleries. Excel will match the formatting as closely as possible but some minor loss of fidelity will occur when the file is opened in Excel 2003. When you know you have to exchange files with others that do not have Excel 2007, avoid using these features if possible or apply colors from the standard color palette.

14 Close **ExcelS4-05.xls**.

The executive chef uses an inventory program that does not recognize Excel workbooks; however, the program can import data stored in ***comma delimited (csv)*** file format. The csv format saves the data as it is displayed in cells, with a comma separating the data between columns and a paragraph mark at the end of each row. Formulas are converted to text and all formatting within the worksheet is stripped from the file.

15 Open **WBInventory.xlsx**.

16 Click the Office button and then click *Save As*.

17 Type **ExcelS4-06** in the *File name* text box.

18 Click the down-pointing arrow to the right of *Save as type*, scroll down the list box, and then click *CSV (Comma delimited) (*.csv)*.

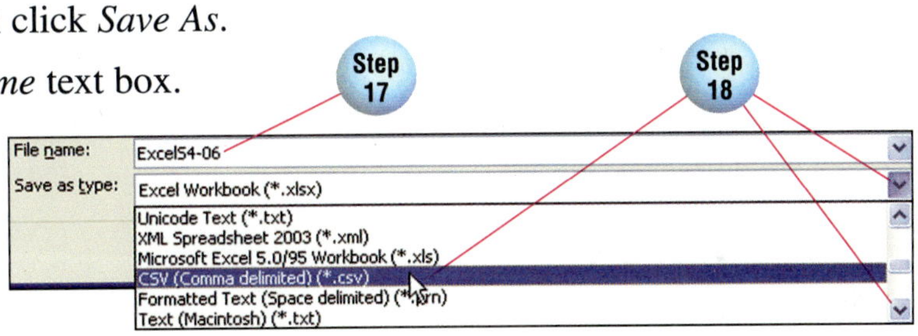

19 Click the *Save* button.

20 Click OK at the Microsoft Office Excel message box that says the selected file type does not support workbooks that contain multiple sheets and that clicking OK will save only the active worksheet.

21 Click Yes to save the workbook at the Microsoft Office Excel message box that says *ExcelS4-06.csv* may contain features that are not compatible with csv (comma delimited).

22 Close **ExcelS4-06.csv**. Click No when prompted to save changes since the file has already been converted.

In Brief

Save Workbook in Earlier Excel File Format

1. Click Office button.
2. Point at right-pointing arrow next to *Save As*.
3. Click *Excel 97-2003 Format*.
4. Type file name.
5. Click Save.
6. Click Continue at Compatibility Checker dialog box.

Save Workbook in Another File Format

1. Click Office button, *Save As*.
2. Type file name.
3. Change *Save as type* to desired file format.
4. Click Save.
5. Respond to message boxes as they occur.

In Addition

More about File Format Converters in Excel

The list of file formats shown in the *Save as type* list box varies depending on the active worksheet. Excel can convert only the active worksheet in most file formats. If a workbook contains multiple sheets, you may need to convert each sheet separately.

Features Summary

Feature	Ribbon Tab, Group	Button	Office Button Drop-down List	Keyboard Shortcut
background	Page Layout, Page Setup			
clear print area	Page Layout, Page Setup			
delete comment	Review, Comments			
delete worksheet	Home, Cells	Delete		
edit comment	Review, Comments			
filter table	Home, Editing			
format sheet tab	Home, Cells	Format		
format table	Home, Styles			
insert comment	Review, Comments			Shift + F2
insert worksheet	Home, Cells	OR Insert		Shift + F11
move or copy worksheet	Home, Cells	Format		
print comments	Page Layout, Page Setup			
print multiple worksheets			Print	Ctrl + P
rename worksheet	Home, Cells	Format		
save in different file format			Save As	F12
save in earlier Excel version			Save As, Excel 97-2003 Workbook	F12
set print area	Page Layout, Page Setup			
show all comments	Review, Comments	Show All Comments		
sort	Home, Editing			
templates			New	

Knowledge Check

Completion: In the space provided at the right, indicate the correct term, command, or option.

1. A new workbook initially contains this many sheets.
2. Perform this action with multiple sheets to apply the same formatting options to all of them in one operation.
3. Perform this action with the mouse while pointing at a sheet tab to change the worksheet name.
4. Hold down this key while dragging a sheet tab to copy the sheet.
5. The formula *=SUM('Expense1:Expense4'!G4)* includes this type of reference.
6. Link a cell in one worksheet to a cell in another worksheet by creating this type of entry in the destination cell.
7. One or more ranges that you print frequently can be stored using this feature to avoid having to select the cells each time you print.
8. Click this button in the Styles group in the Home tab to define an area of a worksheet as an independent range that can be formatted and managed separately from the rest of the worksheet.
9. Select this option from the Sort & Filter list to open a dialog box in which to define more than one sort column.
10. This term refers to temporarily hiding rows that do not meet a specified criterion.
11. Use this feature to type additional information about a cell that appears in a pop-up box when the cell pointer is positioned over the cell.
12. Predesigned formatted worksheets that have labels and formulas created for specific uses can be accessed at this dialog box.
13. This is the default file format for Excel workbooks.
14. Opening a workbook created in an earlier version of Excel causes Excel to switch to this mode.

Skills Review

Review 1 Managing and Formatting Worksheets; Using 3-D References; Linking Cells; Printing Multiple Worksheets

The Waterfront B·I·S·T·R·O

1. Open **WBPayroll.xlsx**.
2. Save the workbook and name it **ExcelS4-R1**.
3. Copy the Week2 worksheet, positioning the new sheet after Week3.
4. Rename the Week2 *(2)* worksheet as Week4.
5. Delete the Week3 worksheet.
6. Copy the Week2 worksheet, positioning the new sheet between Week2 and Week4.
7. Rename the Week2 *(2)* worksheet as Week3.
8. Insert a new worksheet positioned before Week1 and then rename the worksheet Summary.

9. Make Week3 the active worksheet and then edit the following cells:
   Change E9 from *0* to *5*.
   Change I6 from *6* to *0*.
   Change H14 from *0* to *4*.
10. Make Week4 the active worksheet and then edit the following cells:
    Change C11 from *0* to *8*.
    Change G11 from *9* to *0*.
    Change I14 from *6* to *9*.
11. Apply a dark blue color to the Week1 through Week4 sheet tabs and a dark red to the Summary tab.
12. Copy A1:A2 from any worksheet to A1:A2 in the Summary worksheet keeping the source column widths.
13. Copy A5:B15 from any worksheet to A5:B15 in the Summary worksheet.
14. Copy J5:L5 from any worksheet to C5:E5 in the Summary worksheet keeping the source column widths.
15. With Summary the active worksheet, create a SUM formula with a 3-D reference in C6 that sums the hours for Dayna McGuire for all four weeks.
16. Drag the fill handle in C6 to row 14.
17. In B17 enter a formula that links B17 in the Summary worksheet to B17 in the Week1 worksheet.
18. In C3 in Week1 use the DATE function to enter the date November 8, 2009.
19. Type a formula in C4 that will add three days to the date in C3.
20. Complete steps similar to those in Steps 18–19 to enter the week ended and payment dates in the remaining worksheets as follows:
    C3 in Week2 **November 15, 2009**
    C3 in Week3 **November 22, 2009**
    C3 in Week4 **November 29, 2009**
21. In K6 in *Week1* type the formula **=if(j6>40,j6-40,0)**, drag the fill handle from K6 to K14, and then calculate the total in K15. ***Note: A green error flag may appear if error checking is turned on for the computer you are using. You can ignore this error which Excel has flagged. Excel flags J15 as a potential error because the SUM function in column K is adding the cells above while the SUM function in column J adds the cells left.***
22. In L6 type the formula **=(j6*b17)+(k6*b17*.5)**, drag the fill handle from L6 to L14 and then calculate the total in L15.
23. Complete the overtime hours and gross pay column entries for Week2–Week4 and then adjust any column widths as necessary. ***Hint: Consider copying and pasting the formulas from Week1.***
24. Make Summary the active worksheet and then enter the 3-D reference formulas in D6 and E6 to sum the overtime hours and gross pay for Dayna McGuire from all four worksheets.
25. Copy the 3-D formulas in D6:E6 to D7:E14 and then calculate totals in C15:E15.
26. Format the *Gross Pay* column to Accounting Number format.
27. Adjust the titles in rows 1 and 2 to merge and center across columns A through E. ***Hint: Turn off merge and center first to split the cells and then remerge.***
28. Center the Summary worksheet horizontally on the page.
29. Group the Week1–Week4 sheets and then scale the width to fit 1 page.
30. Open the Print dialog box and print *Entire workbook* in the *Print what* section.
31. Save and then close **ExcelS4-R1.xlsx**.

Review 2 Formatting a Table; Sorting; Filtering; and Inserting and Printing Comments

1. Open **WBInventory.xlsx**.
2. Save the workbook and name it **ExcelS4-R2**.
3. Select A2:O54 and format the range as a table using *Table Style Light 2* (second from left in first row of *Light* section).
4. Filter the table to display only those items that are purchased in units by the flat.
5. Scale the width to fit 1 page in landscape orientation and then print the filtered worksheet.
6. Redisplay all rows in the table.
7. Using the filter arrow button in the *January* column, filter the table to display items that have the value of *1* or *2*.
8. Filter the subset of rows by case units.
9. Sort the filtered table by item from A to Z.
10. Add a comment to B12 with the text **Dana, is this the right unit for this item?**
11. Add a comment to A50 with the text **Vendor reports that this item is difficult to source. Dana, should we consider replacing this item with something else?**
12. Set comments to print at the end of the worksheet.
13. Select cells in the filtered table starting in A2 and ending with the last cell displayed in column C and then print only the selection.
14. Deselect the range, save, and then close **ExcelS4-R2.xlsx**.

Review 3 Creating a Workbook Using a Template

1. Start a new workbook using the installed template named Billing Statement.
2. Enter data into the template as shown in Figure 4.2.
3. Save the workbook and name it **ExcelS4-R3**.
4. Print and then close **ExcelS4-R3.xlsx**.

FIGURE 4.2 Data for Review 3

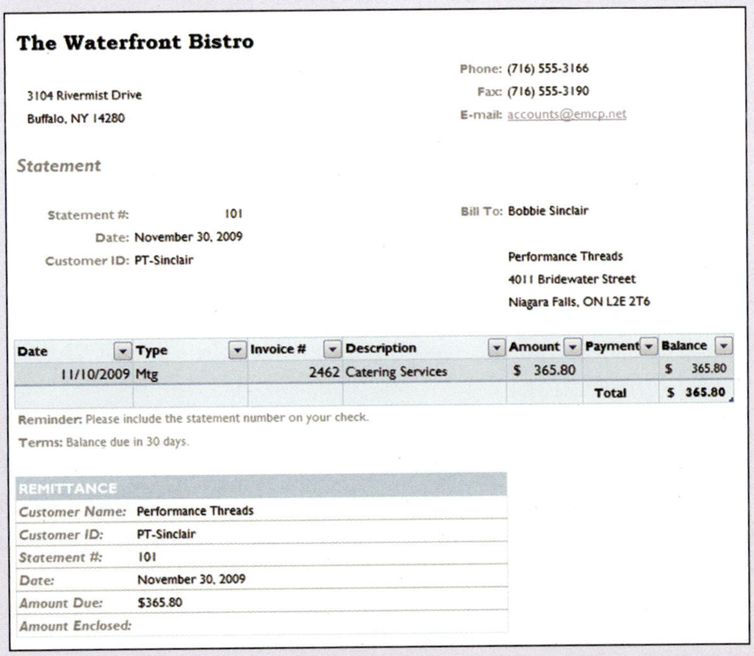
The Waterfront Bistro

3104 Rivermist Drive
Buffalo, NY 14280

Phone: (716) 555-3166
Fax: (716) 555-3190
E-mail: accounts@emcp.net

Statement

Statement #: 101
Date: November 30, 2009
Customer ID: PT-Sinclair

Bill To: Bobbie Sinclair
Performance Threads
4011 Bridewater Street
Niagara Falls, ON L2E 2T6

Date	Type	Invoice #	Description	Amount	Payment	Balance
11/10/2009	Mtg	2462	Catering Services	$ 365.80		$ 365.80
					Total	$ 365.80

Reminder: Please include the statement number on your check.
Terms: Balance due in 30 days.

REMITTANCE	
Customer Name:	Performance Threads
Customer ID:	PT-Sinclair
Statement #:	101
Date:	November 30, 2009
Amount Due:	$365.80
Amount Enclosed:	

Skills Assessment

Assessment 1 Inserting, Deleting, and Renaming Worksheets; Linking Worksheets

1. You are the assistant to Cal Rubine, chair of the Theatre Arts Division at Niagara Peninsula College. The co-op consultant has entered grades for the internships at Marquee Productions and Performance Threads into separate worksheets in the same workbook. You need to create a worksheet to summarize the data.
2. Open **NPCCo-opGrades.xlsx**.
3. Save the workbook and name it **ExcelS4-A1**.
4. Insert a new worksheet, position it before the MarqueeProductions worksheet, and rename the sheet *GradeSummary*.
5. Delete Sheet3.
6. Complete the GradeSummary worksheet by completing the following tasks:
   a. Copy A3:B7 in MarqueeProductions to A3:B7 in GradeSummary keeping the source column widths.
   b. Copy A4:B8 in PerformanceThreads to A8:B12 in GradeSummary.
   c. Copy G3:H3 in MarqueeProductions to C3:D3 in GradeSummary keeping the source column widths.
   d. Link the cells in columns C and D of the GradeSummary worksheet to the corresponding grades and dates in MarqueeProductions and PerformanceThreads.
   e. Copy the title and subtitle in rows 1 and 2 from MarqueeProductions to GradeSummary. Change the font size of rows 1 and 2 in GradeSummary to 12-point and then adjust the merge and center to columns A–D. Change the Fill Color in E1:H2 to No Fill.
   f. Center the grades in column C.
7. Save **Excel S4-A1.xlsx**.
8. Group the three worksheets and then change the page orientation to landscape.
9. Change the left margin for the GradeSummary sheet only to 3 inches.
10. Print all three worksheets and then close **ExcelS4-A1.xlsx**.

Assessment 2 Formatting a Table; Filtering; Sorting

1. Bobbie Sinclair, business manager at Performance Threads, needs a list of costumes for Marquee Productions that have a final delivery date of July 8. You decide to format the list as a table and use sorting and filtering features to do this task.
2. Open **PTMarqueeSchedule.xlsx**.
3. Save the workbook and name it **ExcelS4-A2**.
4. Select A10:H15 and then format the range as a table using *Table Style Light 15* (first from left in third row of *Light* section).
5. AutoFit the width of columns A–H.
6. Filter the table to show only those costumes with a final delivery date of July 8. ***Note: Since* Start Date *and* End Date *are repeated as column headings in the table, Excel adds numbers after the first occurrences to make each column heading unique.***
7. Sort the filtered list by Costume from A to Z.
8. Change the page orientation to landscape, center the worksheet horizontally, and then print the filtered list.

9. Redisplay all rows in the table.
10. Sort the table first by the final delivery date from oldest to newest and then by costume from A to Z.
11. Print the worksheet.
12. Save and then close **ExcelS4-A2.xlsx**.

Assessment 3 Inserting and Printing Comments

Performance Threads

1. The design team for the Marquee Productions costumes is meeting at the end of the week to discuss the production schedule. In preparation for this meeting, Bobbie Sinclair, business manager at Performance Threads, has asked you to review the schedule and send a copy with your comments inserted.
2. Open **PTMarqueeSchedule.xlsx**.
3. Save the workbook and name it **ExcelS4-A3**.
4. Make D11 the active cell and then create the following comment:

   Sue is not yet done with the research for this costume. Design may not be able to start June 10.
5. Make D15 the active cell and then create the following comment:

   This costume is the most complex in this project. These dates may need adjustment.
6. Show all comments.
7. Change the page orientation to landscape and center the worksheet horizontally.
8. Turn on printing of comments *As displayed on sheet*.
9. Print **ExcelS4-A3.xlsx**.
10. Save and then close **ExcelS4-A3.xlsx**.

Assessment 4 Formatting Columns and Formatting a Table; Opening an Excel 2003 Workbook and Saving as an Excel 2007 Workbook

Performance Threads

1. Bobbie Sinclair, business manager at Performance Threads, has a workbook file exported from the accounting system in Excel 2003 format with information on rental costumes the company has in inventory. Bobbie has asked you to open the Excel 2003 workbook, modify the data to create a report, and save it in the 2007 file format.
2. Open **PTRentalCostumes.xls**.
3. AutoFit the width of each column and then right-align column headings in columns C–E.
4. Insert two rows at the top of the worksheet and add the label **Performance Threads** in A1.
5. Add the subtitle **Rental Costume Inventory** in A2.
6. Add the label **DaysRented** right-aligned in F3 and then AutoFit the column width.
7. Add the label **TotalDue** right-aligned in G3 and then AutoFit the column width.
8. Enter the formula **=e4-d4** in F4 and then format the result to Comma Style with no decimals.
9. Copy the formula in F4 to the remaining rows in column F.
10. Create the formula **=f4*c4** in G4 and then format the result to Accounting Number format.
11. Copy the formula in G4 to the remaining rows in column G.
12. Select A3:G53 and then format the range as a table using *Table Style Light 9* (second from left in second row of *Light* section).
13. Insert a total row at the bottom of the table.
14. If necessary, AutoFit column G so that all data is visible.
15. Merge and center the title and subtitle across columns A through G and then apply appropriate font and fill color formats to the cells.

16. Scale the width to fit 1 page and the height to fit 2 pages.
17. Print the worksheet.
18. Use Save As to save the workbook as an Excel 2007 file named **ExcelS4-A4**.
19. Close **ExcelS4-A4.xlsx**.

Assessment 5 Finding Information on File Management in Excel

1. Use the Help feature to find information on creating a folder and moving a file in Excel. The category *Workbook management* in *Browse Excel Help* at the main Excel Help window will link to these topics. Print the Help topics that you find with the steps on creating a folder and moving a file.
2. Display the Open dialog box and create three new folders within the ExcelS4 folder named *SectionProjects, Review*, and *Assessments*.
3. Move the files created by completing Activity 4.1 through Activity 4.10 to the folder named *SectionProjects*. ***Hint: To move the text file, you will have to change the* files of type *option.***
4. Move the files created by completing Review 1 through Review 3 to the folder named *Review*.
5. Move the files created by completing Assessment 1 through Assessment 4 to the folder named *Assessments*.
6. Close the Open dialog box.

Assessment 6 Finding Information on File Formats Supported by Excel

1. You want to create a reference list of file formats that can be opened directly within Excel using the default file format converters. Open Internet Explorer and go to the Excel home page at Microsoft Office Online. Search for information on file format converters and Excel.
2. Create three tables in an Excel workbook with each table organized in a separate sheet. Use Table 1 to list the file formats for Lotus 1-2-3, Table 2 to list the file formats for text files, and Table 3 to list the file formats for other spreadsheet and database files. Name each sheet appropriately and format each tab to a different color. Include the file extension for each product, the version number related to the file extension, and any explanatory information. ***Note: Copying and pasting information from the Microsoft Web site is not acceptable.***
3. Apply a table style to each table.
4. Make sure the information is easy to read and understand.
5. Save the workbook and name it **ExcelS4-A6**.
6. Group the three worksheets and set print options to ensure the entire worksheet will fit on one page.
7. Print the entire workbook and then close **ExcelS4-A6.xlsx**.

Marquee Challenge

Challenge 1 Creating a Sales Invoice by Searching and Downloading a Template

1. Dana Hirsch, manager of The Waterfront Bistro, has asked you to find and download a professionally designed sales invoice template and then use the template to create an invoice to First Choice Travel for catering their business meeting.
2. Open the New Workbook dialog box, click the *Featured* option in the left pane, and then click the hyperlink to Templates in the *More on Office Online* section at the bottom of the center pane. At the Templates Web site, search for the template named *Sales invoice (Blue Gradient design)* in Microsoft Office Online. Be careful to locate the template that is created for Excel and not Word. Download the template to your computer. If you cannot find the template shown in Figure 4.3, download another suitable template for a sales invoice.
3. Complete the customer invoice using today's date. All other information can be found in Figure 4.3.
4. To insert the logo, select the logo container object and then click the Picture Tools Format tab. Click the Change Picture button in the Picture Tools group, navigate to the data file **TWBLogo.jpg**, and then double-click the file name. Move and resize the logo image as shown in Figure 4.3.
5. Delete the unused rows between the billing address and the body of the invoice.
6. Delete the unused rows between the last line item and the subtotal row.
7. Format the *QTY* column as shown in Figure 4.3.
8. Type **The Waterfront Bistro** next to *Make all checks payable to* near the bottom of the invoice.
9. Save the invoice and name it **ExcelS4-C1**.
10. Print and then close **ExcelS4-C1.xlsx**.

FIGURE 4.3 Challenge 1

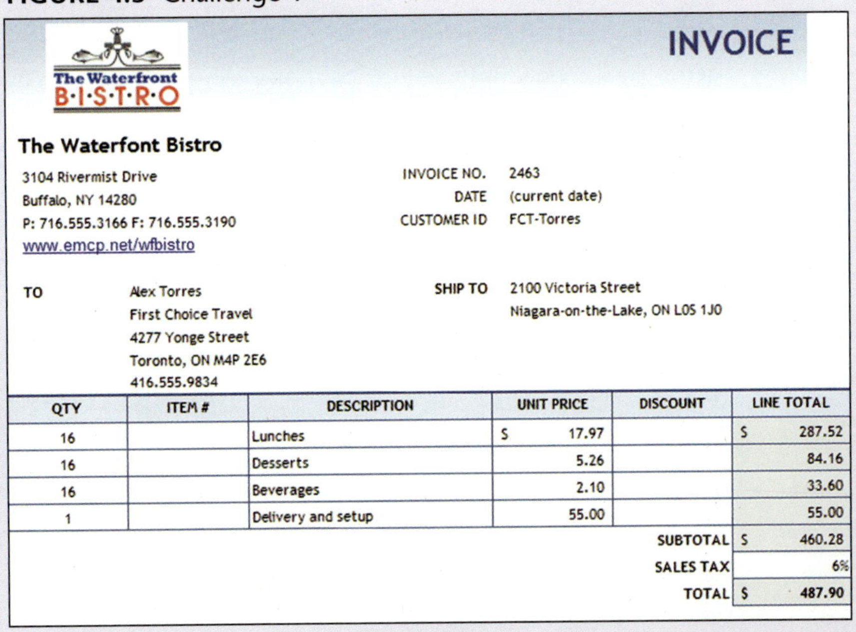

INVOICE

The Waterfront Bistro

3104 Rivermist Drive
Buffalo, NY 14280
P: 716.555.3166 F: 716.555.3190
www.emcp.net/wfbistro

INVOICE NO. 2463
DATE (current date)
CUSTOMER ID FCT-Torres

TO Alex Torres
First Choice Travel
4277 Yonge Street
Toronto, ON M4P 2E6
416.555.9834

SHIP TO 2100 Victoria Street
Niagara-on-the-Lake, ON L0S 1J0

QTY	ITEM #	DESCRIPTION	UNIT PRICE	DISCOUNT	LINE TOTAL
16		Lunches	$ 17.97		$ 287.52
16		Desserts	5.26		84.16
16		Beverages	2.10		33.60
1		Delivery and setup	55.00		55.00
				SUBTOTAL	$ 460.28
				SALES TAX	6%
				TOTAL	$ 487.90

Challenge 2 Importing, Formatting and Sorting a Distributor List

1. Sam Vestering, manager of North American Distribution at Worldwide Enterprises, has provided you with two text files exported from the corporate head office computer. One file contains a list of U.S. distributors and the other contains a list of Canadian distributors. Sam would like you to import each file into Excel and then combine the U.S. and Canadian information into one workbook. Sam would like the workbook attractively presented and sorted.
2. Research in Help how to import a text file by opening the file. The files used in this challenge were exported as delimited files with a comma as the delimiter character to separate data.
3. Open the text file named **WEUSDistibutors.txt** and follow the steps in the Text Import Wizard as you learned in Help.
4. Open the file named **WECdnDistributors.txt** and follow the steps in the Text Import Wizard as you learned in Help.
5. Delete the second address and e-mail address columns in each workbook.
6. Move or copy one of the worksheets to the bottom of the other worksheet.
7. Add a row above the data with the labels shown in Figure 4.4.
8. Insert the logo named **WELogo.jpg**, add the title rows, and format the data as a table as shown in Figure 4.4. Use your best judgment to determine the table style and other formatting options to apply to the table.
9. Look closely at Figure 4.4 to determine the sort order and then custom sort the table. ***Hint: The table is sorted by three levels.***
10. Save the worksheet as an Excel workbook and name it **ExcelS4-C2**.
11. Print the worksheet centered horizontally and vertically on one page.
12. Close **ExcelS4-C2.xlsx**.
13. Close any other Excel workbooks that are open without saving changes.

FIGURE 4.4 Challenge 2

Worldwide Enterprises		North American Distributor List				
Name	**Mailing Address**	**City**	**State**	**ZIP code**	**Telephone**	**Fax**
Olypmic Cinemas	P. O. Box 1439	Calgary	AB	T2C 3P7	403-651-4587	403-651-4589
LaVista Cinemas	111 Vista Road	Phoenix	AZ	86355-6014	602-555-6231	602-555-6233
West Coast Movies	P. O. Box 298	Vancouver	BC	V6Y 1N9	604-555-3548	604-555-3549
Marquee Movies	1011 South Alameda Street	Los Angeles	CA	90045	612-555-2398	612-555-2377
Sunfest Cinemas	341 South Fourth Avenue	Tampa	FL	33562	813-555-3185	813-555-3177
Liberty Cinemas	P. O. Box 998	Atlanta	GA	73125	404-555-8113	404-555-2349
O'Shea Movies	59 Erie	Oak Park	IL	60302	312-555-7719	312-555-7381
Midtown Moviehouse	1033 Commercial Street	Emporia	KS	66801	316-555-7013	316-555-7022
All Nite Cinemas	2188 3rd Street	Louisville	KY	40201	502-555-4238	502-555-4240
Eastown Movie House	P. O. Box 722	Cambridge	MA	02142	413-555-0981	413-555-0226
Riverview Cinemas	1011-848 Sheppard Street	Winnipeg	MB	R2P 0N6	204-555-6538	204-555-6533
New Age Movies	73 Killarney Road	Moncton	NB	E1B 2Z9	506-555-8376	506-555-8377
EastCoast Cinemas	62 Mountbatten Drive	St.John's	NF	A1A 3X9	709-555-8349	709-555-8366
Hillman Cinemas	55 Kemble Avenue	Baking Ridge	NJ	07920	201-555-1147	201-555-1143
Seaboard Movie House Inc.	P. O. Box 1005	Dartmouth	NS	B2V 1Y8	902-555-3948	902-555-3950
Northern Reach Movies	P. O. Box 34	Yellowknife	NW	X1A 2N9	867-555-6314	867-555-6316
Mainstream Movies	P. O. Box 33	Buffalo	NY	14601	212-555-3269	212-555-3270
Victory Cinemas	12119 South 23rd	Buffalo	NY	14288	212-555-8746	212-555-8748
Waterfront Cinemas	P. O. Box 3255	New York	NY	14288	212-555-3845	212-555-3947
Westview Movies	1112 Broadway	New York	NY	10119	212-555-4875	212-555-4877
Mooretown Movies	P. O. Box 11	Dublin	OH	43107	614-555-8134	614-555-8339
Millennium Movies	4126 Yonge Street	Toronto	ON	M2P 2B8	416-555-9335	416-555-9338
Redwood Cinemas	P. O. Box 112F	Portland	OR	97466-3359	503-555-8641	503-555-8633
Wellington 10	1203 Tenth Southwest	Philadelphia	PA	19178	215-555-9045	215-555-9048
Waterdown Cinemas	575 Notre Dame Street	Summerside	PE	C1N 1T8	902-555-8374	902-555-8376
MountainView Movies	5417 RoyalMount Avenue	Montreal	PQ	H4P 1H8	514-555-3584	514-555-3585
Danforth Cinemas	P. O. Box 22	Columbia	SC	29201	803-555-3487	803-555-3421
Plains Cinema House	P. O. Box 209	Regina	SK	S4S 5Y9	306-555-1247	305-555-1248
Century Cinemas	3687 Avenue K	Arlington	TX	76013	817-555-2116	817-555-2119
Countryside Cinemas	22 Hillside Street	Bennington	VT	05201	802-555-1469	802-555-1470
Northern Stars Movies	811 Cook Street	Whitehorse	YK	Y1A 2S4	867-555-6598	867-555-6599

Integrating Programs
Word and Excel

Skills

- Copy and paste Word data into an Excel worksheet
- Link an Excel worksheet with a Word document
- Update linked data
- View linked data as an icon
- Link an Excel chart with a Word document
- Embed an Excel worksheet into a Word document
- Edit an embedded worksheet

Student Resources

Before beginning this section:

1. Copy to your storage medium the Integrating1 subfolder from the Integrating folder on the Student Resources CD.
2. Make Integrating1 the active folder.

In addition to containing the data files needed to complete section work, the Student Resources CD contains model answers in PDF format for each of the projects in this section; model answers for end-of-section activities are not provided.

Projects Overview

Performance Threads

Copy data in a Word document on costume research, design, and sewing hours for employees into an Excel worksheet. Copy data in an Excel worksheet on employee payroll and then link the data to a Word document. Update the payroll hours for the employees for the next week. Copy employee payroll data in an Excel worksheet to a Word document and then update the data in Word.

First Choice TRAVEL

Link a chart containing sales commissions for agents with a Word document and then update the sales commissions to reflect a higher percentage.

Niagara Peninsula College

Copy Word data on student scores into an Excel worksheet. Copy an Excel chart containing data on student areas of emphasis in the Theatre Arts Division into a Word document and then update the chart in Excel.

Worldwide Enterprises

Copy data in an Excel worksheet on theater company revenues into a Word document and then update the data in Word.

Activity 1.1

Copying and Pasting Word Data into an Excel Worksheet

Microsoft Office is a suite that allows integration, which is the combining of data from two or more programs into one document. Integration can occur by copying and pasting data between programs. The program containing the data to be copied is called the *source* program and the program where the data is pasted is called the *destination* program. For example, you can copy data from a Word document into an Excel worksheet. Copy and paste data between programs in the same manner as you would copy and paste data within a program.

Project

You have been handed a Word document containing data on costume research, design, and sewing hours and need to copy the data to an Excel worksheet.

1. Open Word and then open the document named **PTWordHours.docx**.
2. Open Excel and then open **PTExcelHours.xlsx**.
3. Save the worksheet with Save As and name it **IntE1-01**.
4. Click the button on the Taskbar representing the Word document **PTWordHours.docx**.

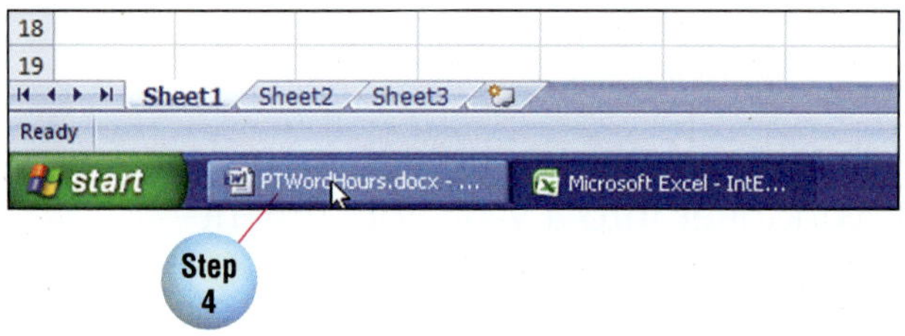

5. Select the five lines of text in columns as shown below.
6. Click the Copy button in the Clipboard group in the Home tab.

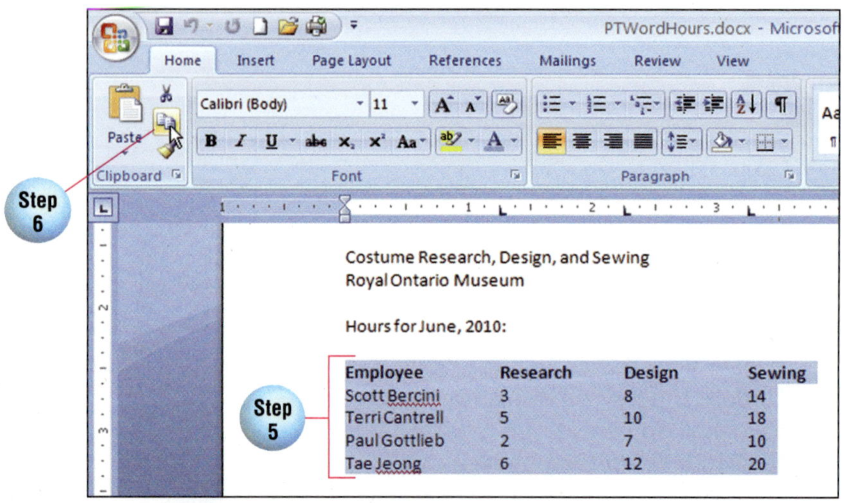

7. Click the button on the Taskbar representing the Excel workbook **IntE1-01.xlsx**.

8. Make sure cell A2 is the active cell and then click the Paste button [Paste icon] in the Clipboard group.
9. Click in cell E2 to deselect the text and then double-click the blue column boundary line between columns A and B.

   This increases the width of column A so the names display.

In Brief

Copy Data from One Program to Another

1. Open desired programs and documents.
2. Select data in source program.
3. Click Copy button.
4. Click button on Taskbar representing destination program.
5. Click Paste button.

10. With cell E2 active, click the Bold button **B** and then type **Total**.
11. Make cell E3 the active cell, click the Sum button Σ in the Editing group, and then press Enter.

    This inserts a formula that calculates the total number of hours for Scott Bercini.

12. Copy the formula down to cells E4 through E6.
13. Make cell A7 active, click the Bold button **B**, and then type **Total**.
14. Make cell B7 active, click the Sum button Σ in the Editing group, and then press Enter.

    This inserts a formula that calculates the total number of research hours.

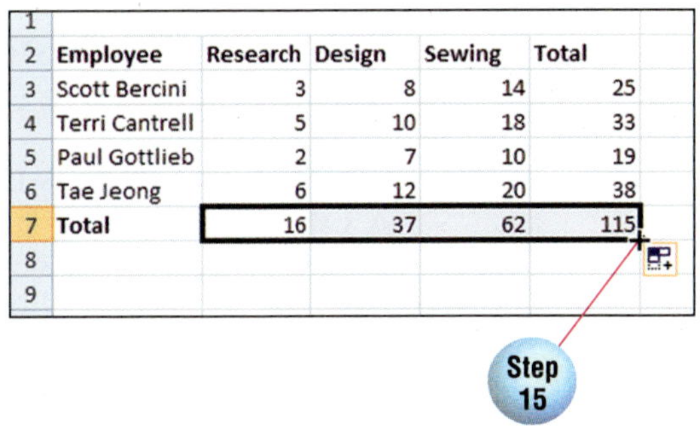

	Employee	Research	Design	Sewing	Total
3	Scott Bercini	3	8	14	25
4	Terri Cantrell	5	10	18	33
5	Paul Gottlieb	2	7	10	19
6	Tae Jeong	6	12	20	38
7	Total	16	37	62	115

15. Copy the formula in cell B7 to cells C7 through E7.
16. Select cells A2 through E7.
17. Click the Format as Table button [Format as Table icon] in the Styles group and then click *Table Style Light 11* (fourth option from the left in the second row in the *Light* section).
18. At the Format As Table dialog box, click OK.
19. Make any other changes needed to improve the visual display of the data in cells A2 through E7.
20. Save, print, and then close **IntE1-01.xlsx**.
21. Click the button on the Taskbar representing the Word document **PTWordHours.docx**.
22. Close **PTWordHours.docx**.

In Addition

Cycling between Open Programs

Cycle through open programs by clicking the button on the Taskbar representing the desired program. You can also cycle through open programs by pressing Alt + Tab. Pressing Alt + Tab causes a menu to display. Continue holding down the Alt key and pressing the Tab key until the desired program icon is selected by a border in the menu and then release the Tab key and the Alt key.

Activity 1.2

Linking an Excel Worksheet with a Word Document

In the previous activity, you copied data from a Word document and pasted it into an Excel worksheet. If you continuously update the data in the Word document, you would need to copy and paste the data each time into the Excel worksheet. If you update data on a regular basis that is copied to other programs, consider copying and linking the data. When data is linked, the data exists in the source program but not as separate data in the destination program. The destination program contains only a code that identifies the name and location of the source program, document, and the location in the document. Since the data is located only in the source program, changes made to the data in the source program are reflected in the destination program. Office updates a link automatically whenever you open the destination program or you edit the linked data in the destination program.

Project

Copy data in an Excel worksheet on employee payroll for Performance Threads and then link the data to a Word document.

1. With Word the active program, open the document named **PTWordOctPayroll.docx**.
2. Save the document with Save As and name it **IntW1-01**.
3. Make Excel the active program and then open the workbook named **PTExcelOctPayroll.xlsx**.
4. Save the workbook with Save As and name it **IntE1-02**.
5. Link the data in cells in the worksheet into the Word document by selecting cells A3 through D8.
6. Click the Copy button in the Clipboard group in the Home tab.

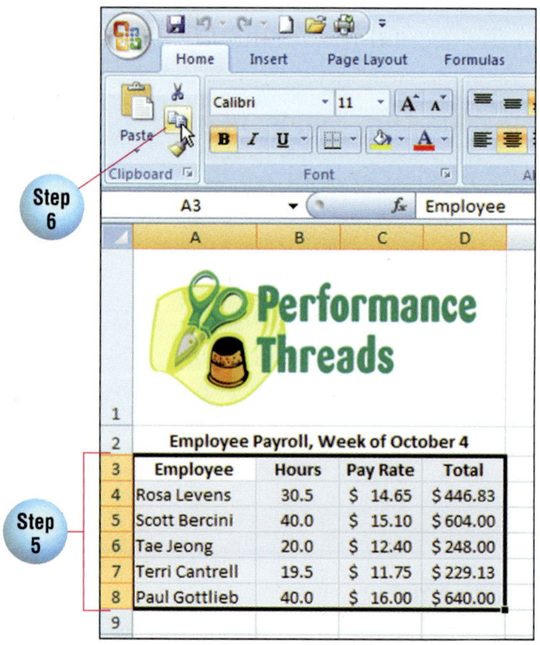

7. Click the button on the Taskbar representing the Word document **IntW1-01.docx**.

8. Press Ctrl + End to move the insertion point to the end of the document (the insertion point is positioned a double space below *Week of October 4, 2010:*).
9. Click the Paste button arrow and then click *Paste Special* at the drop-down list.
10. At the Paste Special dialog box, click *Microsoft Office Excel Worksheet Object* in the *As* list box.
11. Click the *Paste link* option located at the left side of the dialog box.
12. Click OK to close the dialog box.

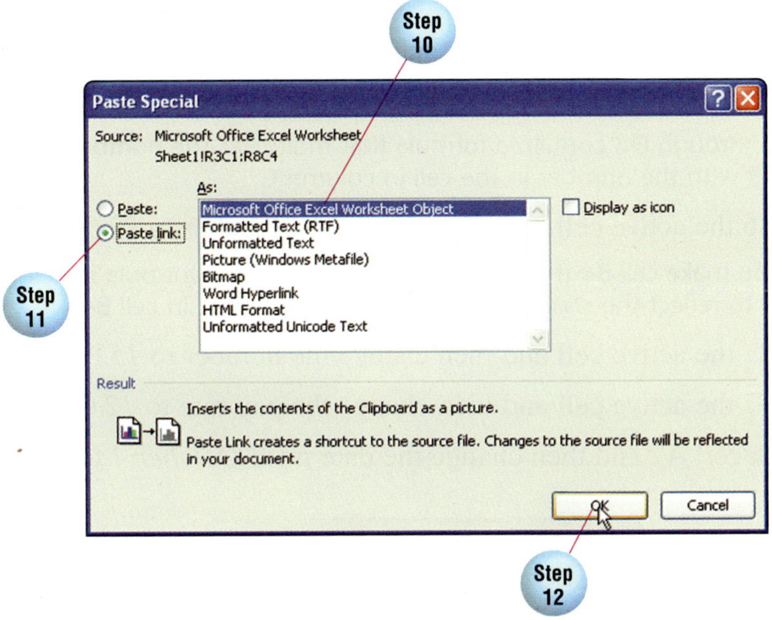

13. Save, print, and then close **IntW1-01.docx**.

    The table gridlines do not print.

14. Click the button on the Taskbar representing the Excel workbook **IntE1-02.xlsx**.
15. Press the Esc key on the keyboard to remove the moving marquee around cells A3 through D8 and then click cell A3 to make it the active cell.
16. Save, print, and then close **IntE1-02.xlsx**.

In Brief

Link Data between Programs

1. Open desired programs and documents.
2. Select data in source program.
3. Click Copy button.
4. Click button on Taskbar representing destination program.
5. Click Paste button arrow, *Paste Special*.
6. Click object in *As* list box.
7. Click *Paste link*.
8. Click OK.

In Addition

Linking Data within a Program

Linking does not have to be between two different programs—you can link data between files in the same program. For example, you can create an object in a Word document such as a table or chart and then link the object with another Word document (or several Word documents). If you make a change to the object in the original document, the linked object in the other document (or documents) is automatically updated.

Activity 1.3

Updating Linked Data; Viewing a Link

The advantage of linking data over copying data is that editing the data in the source program will automatically update the data in the destination program. To edit linked data, open the document in the source program, make the desired edits, and then save the document. The next time you open the document in the destination program, the data is updated. The display of the linked data in the destination program can be changed to an icon. The icon represents the document and program to which the object is linked.

Project

Update the payroll hours for the employees of Performance Threads in the Excel worksheet for the week of October 11.

1. Make Excel the active program and then open **IntE1-02.xlsx**.
2. Make cell B4 the active cell and then change the number to *20.0*.

   Cells D4 through D8 contain a formula that multiplies the number in the cell in column B with the number in the cell in column C.
3. Make cell B6 the active cell and then change the number to *25.5*.

   When you make cell B6 the active cell, the result of the formula in cell D4 is updated to reflect the change you made to the number in cell B4.
4. Make cell B7 the active cell and then change the number to *15.0*.
5. Make cell C7 the active cell and then change the pay rate to *12.00*.
6. Double-click cell A2 and then change the date from *October 4* to *October 11*.

7. Save **IntE1-02.xlsx**.
8. Print and then close **IntE1-02.xlsx**.
9. Make Word the active program and then open **IntW1-01.docx**.
10. At the message asking if you want to update the document, click Yes.

    The document opens and is automatically updated to reflect the changes you made in **IntE1-02.xlsx**.

11. Change the date above the table from *October 4* to *October 11*.

12. Save and then print **IntW1-01.docx**.
13. Display the linked table as an icon. Begin by right-clicking in the table, pointing to *Linked Worksheet Object*, and then clicking *Convert*.
14. At the Convert dialog box, click the *Display as icon* check box to insert a check mark and then click OK.

    Notice how the table changes to an icon representing the linked document.

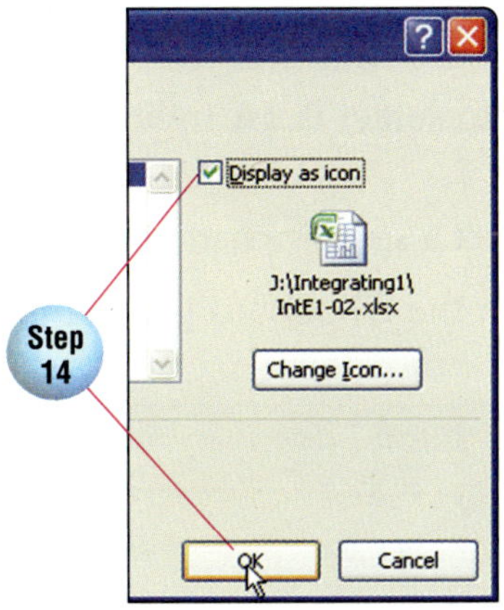

15. Print **IntW1-01.docx**.
16. Make sure the linked object icon is still selected and then redisplay the table. To begin, right-click the icon, point to *Linked Worksheet Object*, and then click *Convert*.
17. At the Convert dialog box, click the *Display as icon* check box to remove the check mark and then click OK.
18. Save and then close **IntW1-01.docx**.

In Brief

Update Linked Data

1. Open document in source program.
2. Make desired edits.
3. Save and close document.
4. Open document in destination program.
5. Save and close document.

Display Linked Object as an Icon

1. Select object.
2. Right-click in table.
3. Click *Linked Worksheet Object*, *Convert*.
4. At Convert dialog box, click *Display as icon* check box.
5. Click OK.

In Addition

Breaking a Link

The link between an object in the destination and source programs can be broken. To break a link, right-click on the object, point to *Linked Worksheet Object*, and then click *Links*. At the Links dialog box, click the Break Link button. At the question asking if you are sure you want to break the link, click the Yes button.

Activity 1.4

Linking an Excel Chart with a Word Document

While a worksheet does an adequate job of representing data, you can present some data more visually by charting the data. A chart is a visual representation of numeric data and, like a worksheet, can be linked to a document in another program. Link a chart in the same manner as you would link a worksheet.

Project

Link a chart containing sales commissions for agents of First Choice Travel with a Word document. Change the sales commission in the worksheet chart from 3% to 4%.

1. Make Word the active program and then open **FCTWordSalesCom.docx**.
2. Save the document with Save As and name it **IntW1-02**.
3. Make Excel the active program and then open **FCTExcelSalesCom.xlsx**.
4. Save the workbook with Save As and name it **IntE1-03**.
5. Click once in the chart area to select it. (A light turquoise border displays around the chart.)

   Make sure you do not select a specific chart element.

6. Click the Copy button in the Clipboard group in the Home tab.

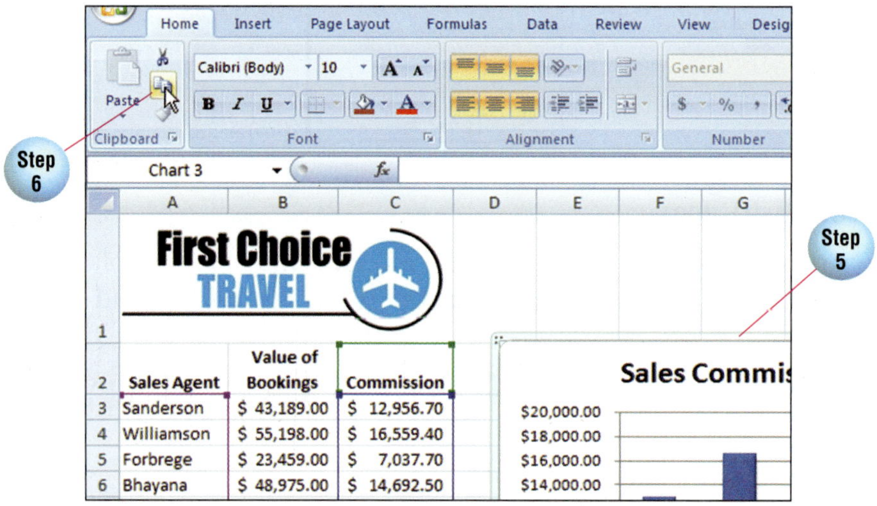

7. Click the button on the Taskbar representing the Word document **IntW1-02.docx**.
8. Press Ctrl + End to move the insertion point to the end of the document.
9. Link the chart by clicking the Paste button arrow and then clicking *Paste Special* at the drop-down list.

10 At the Paste Special dialog box, click the *Microsoft Office Excel Chart Object* option in the *As* list box, click *Paste link*, and then click OK.

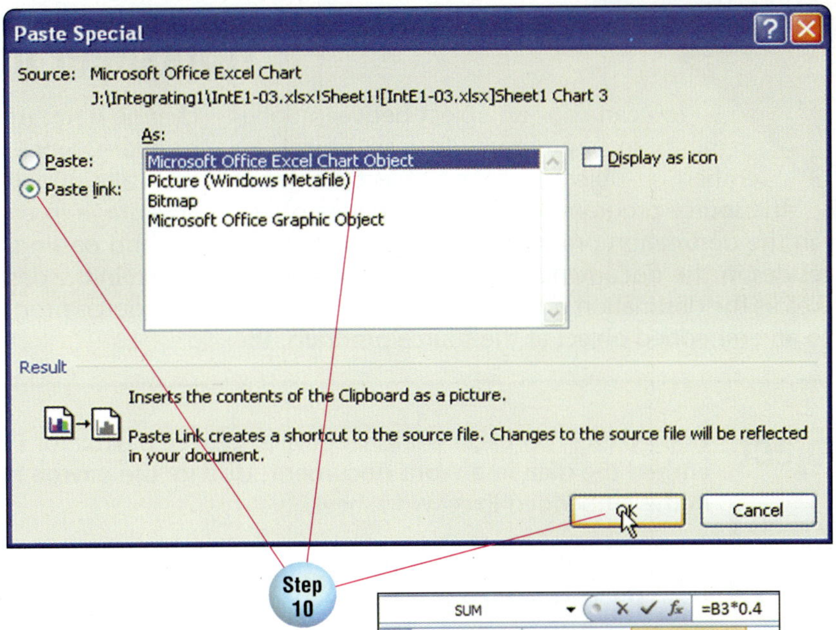

11 Save, print, and then close **IntW1-02.docx**.

12 Click the button on the Taskbar representing the Excel workbook **IntE1-03.xlsx**.

13 The chart is based on a sales commission of 30 percent. Change the formula so it calculates a sales commission of 40 percent by double-clicking in cell C3 and then changing the *0.3* in the formula to a *0.4*.

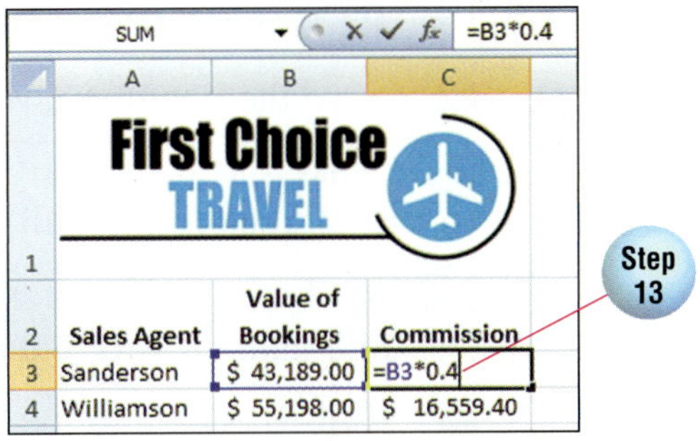

14 Press the Enter key.

Pressing Enter displays the result of the formula calculating commissions at 40 percent.

15 Make cell C3 the active cell and then copy the new formula down to cells C4 through C8.

16 Save and then close **IntE1-03.xlsx**.

17 Click the button on the Taskbar representing Word and then open the **IntW1-02.docx** document.

18 At the message asking if you want to update the document, click Yes.

Notice the change in the amounts in the chart.

19 Save, print, and then close **IntW1-02.docx**.

In Addition

Customizing a Link

By default, a linked object is updated automatically and a linked object can be edited. You can change these defaults with options at the Links dialog box. Display this dialog box by selecting the linked object, clicking the Office button, pointing to *Prepare*, and then clicking the *Edit Links to Files* option. At the Links dialog box, click the *Manual update* option if you want to control when to update linked data. With the *Manual update* option selected, update linked objects by clicking the Update Now button at the right side of the Links dialog box. If you do not want a linked object updated, click the *Locked* check box in the Links dialog box to insert a check mark.

Activity 1.5

Embedding an Excel Worksheet into a Word Document

You can copy an object between documents in a program, link an object, or embed an object. A linked object resides in the source program but not as a separate object in the destination program. An embedded object resides in the document in the source program as well as the destination program. If a change is made to an embedded object at the source program, the change is not made to the object in the destination program. Since an embedded object is not automatically updated as is a linked object, the only advantage to embedding rather than simply copying and pasting is that you can edit an embedded object in the destination program using the tools of the source program.

Project

Copy data in an Excel worksheet on employee payroll for Performance Threads and then embed the data in a Word document. Update the payroll hours for the week of October 18 in the embedded Excel worksheet.

1. With Word open and the active program, open the document named **PTWordOctPayroll.docx**.
2. Save the document with Save As and name it **IntW1-03**.
3. Make Excel the active program and then open the workbook named **PTExcelOctPayroll.xlsx**.
4. Save the workbook with Save As and name it **IntE1-04**.
5. Embed cells into the Word document by selecting cells A3 through D8.
6. Click the Copy button in the Clipboard group in the Home tab.
7. Click the button on the Taskbar representing the Word document **IntW1-03.docx**.
8. Press Ctrl + End to move the insertion point to the end of the document (the insertion point is positioned a double space below *Week of October 4, 2010:*).

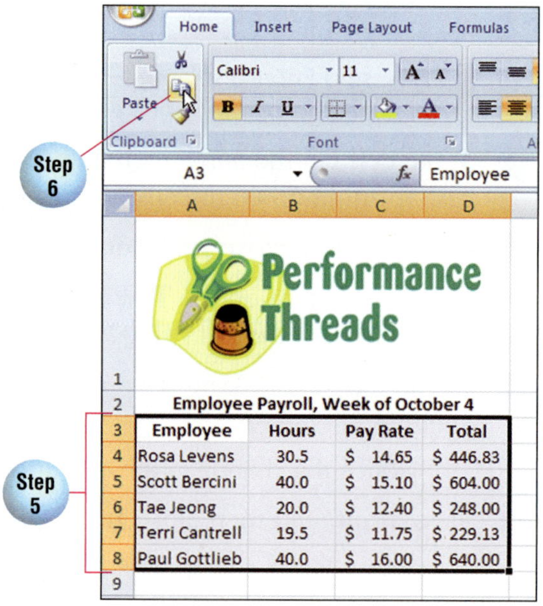

9. Click the Paste button arrow and then click *Paste Special* at the drop-down list.
10. At the Paste Special dialog box, click *Microsoft Office Excel Worksheet Object* in the *As* list box.
11. Click OK.

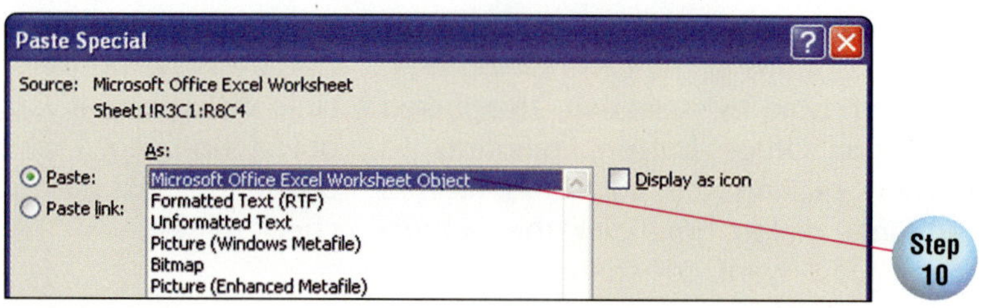

12. Click outside the table to deselect it and then save and print **IntW1-03.docx**.
13. Click the button on the Taskbar representing the Excel workbook **IntE1-04.xlsx**.
14. Press the Esc key to remove the moving marquee around cells A3 through D8.
15. Click in cell A2 to make it the active cell and then save and close **IntE1-04.xlsx**.
16. Click the button on the Taskbar representing the Word document **IntW1-03.docx**.
17. Change the date above the table from *October 4* to *October 18*.
18. Position the arrow pointer anywhere in the worksheet and then double-click the left mouse button.

    In a few moments, the worksheet displays surrounded by column and row designations and the Excel tabs.

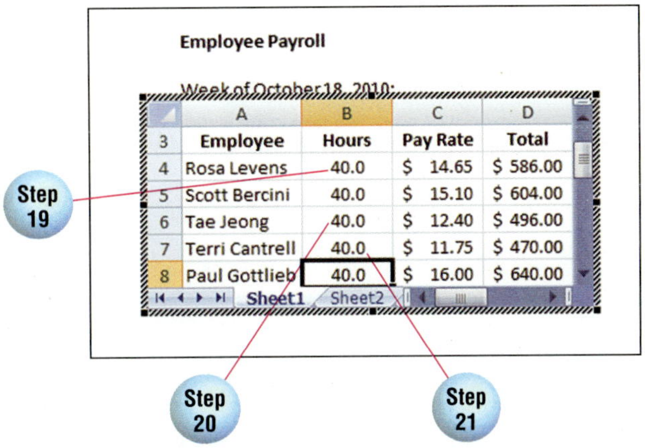

19. To produce the ordered costumes on time, the part-time employees worked a full 40 hours for the week of October 18. Make cell B4 the active cell and then change the number to 40.
20. Make cell B6 the active cell and then change the number to 40.
21. Make cell B7 the active cell and then change the number to 40.
22. Bobbie Sinclair, Business Manager, wants to know the payroll total for the week of October 18 to determine the impact it has on the monthly budget. Add a new row to the table by making cell A8 the active cell and then pressing the Enter key.
23. With cell A9 the active cell, type **Total**.
24. Make cell D9 the active cell and then click the Sum button [Σ] in the Editing group.
25. Make sure *D4:D8* displays in cell D9 and then press the Enter key.
26. Increase the height of the worksheet by one row by positioning the arrow pointer on the bottom middle black sizing square until the pointer turns into a double-headed arrow pointing up and down. Hold down the left mouse button, drag down one row, and then release the mouse button.

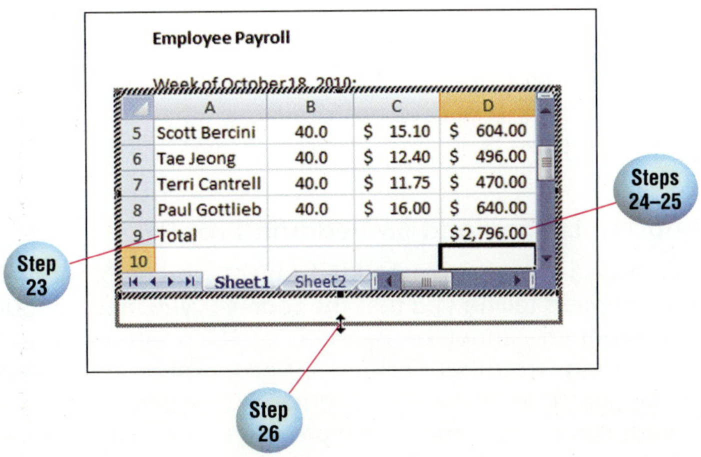

continues

In Brief

Embed Data

1. Open desired programs and documents.
2. Select data in source program.
3. Click Copy button.
4. Click button on Taskbar representing destination program.
5. Click Paste button arrow, *Paste Special*.
6. Click object in *As* list box.
7. Click OK.

Edit Embedded Object

1. In source program, double-click embedded object.
2. Make desired edits.
3. Click outside object.

27 Using the arrow keys on the keyboard, make cell A3 the active cell and position cell A3 in the upper left corner of the worksheet. (This will display all cells in the worksheet containing data.)

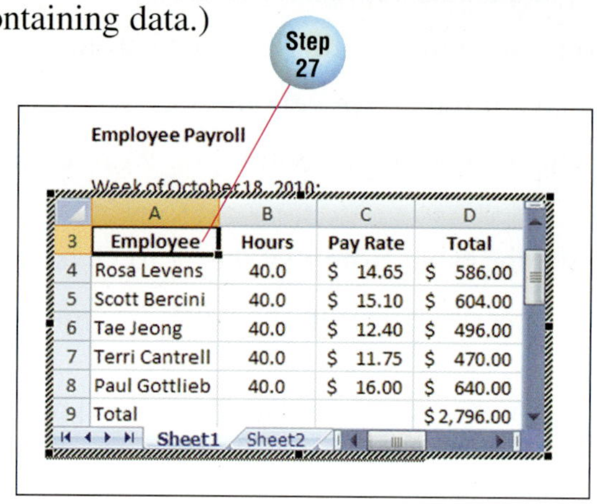

28 Click outside the worksheet to deselect it.

29 Save, print, and then close **IntW1-03.docx**.

The gridlines do not print.

In Addition

Inserting an Embedded Object from an Existing File

You embedded an Excel worksheet in a Word document using the Copy button and options at the Paste Special dialog box. Another method is available for embedding an object from an existing file. In the destination program document, position the insertion point where you want the object embedded and then click the Object button in the Text group. At the Object dialog box, click the Create from File tab. At the Object dialog box with the Create from File tab selected as shown at the right, type the desired file name in the *File name* text box or click the Browse button and then select the desired file from the appropriate folder. At the Object dialog box, make sure the *Link to file* check box does not contain a check mark and then click OK.

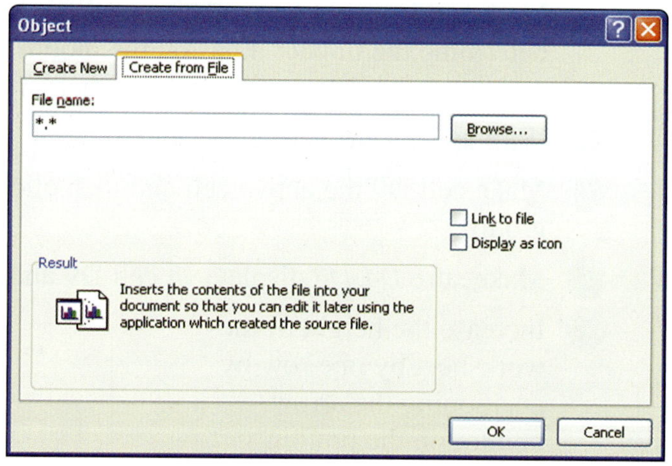

Troubleshooting Linking and Embedding Problems

If you double-click a linked or embedded object and a message appears telling you that the source file or source program cannot be opened, consider the following troubleshooting options. Check to make sure that the source program is installed on your computer. If the source program is not installed, convert the object to the file format of a program that is installed. Try closing other programs to free memory and make sure you have enough memory to run the source program. Check to make sure the source program does not have any dialog boxes open and, if it is a linked object, check to make sure someone else is not working in the source file.

Skills Review

Review 1 Copying and Pasting Data

1. With Word the active program, open the document named **NPCWordScores.docx**.
2. Make Excel the active program and then open **NPCExcelScores.xlsx**.
3. Save the workbook with Save As and name it **IntE1-R1**.
4. Click the button on the Taskbar representing the Word document **NPCWordScores.docx**.
5. Select the nine lines of text in columns (the line beginning *Student* through the line beginning *Yiu, Terry*) and then click the Copy button in the Clipboard group in the Home tab.
6. Click the button on the Taskbar representing the Excel file **IntE1-R1.xlsx**.
7. With cell A5 active, paste the text into the worksheet.
8. Insert the text *Average* in cell E5.
9. Make cell E6 active. Insert a formula that averages the numbers in cells B6 through D6.
10. Copy the formula in cell E6 down to cells E7 through E13.
11. With cells E6 through E13 selected, change the font to 12-point Cambria and then click three times on the Decrease Decimal button in the Number group in the Home tab.
12. Select cells B6 through D13 and then click once on the Increase Decimal button in the Number group in the Home tab. (This displays two numbers after the decimal point.)
13. Select cells B6 through E13, click the Center button in the Alignment group in the Home tab, and then deselect the cells.
14. Save, print, and then close **IntE1-R1.xlsx**.
15. Click the button on the Taskbar representing the Word document **NPCWordScores.docx** and then close the document.

Review 2 Linking an Object and Editing a Linked Object

1. With Word the active program, open the document named **NPCWordEnrollment.docx**.
2. Save the document with Save As and name it **IntW1-R1**.
3. Make Excel the active program and then open the workbook named **NPCExcelChart.xlsx**.
4. Save the workbook with Save As and name it **IntE1-R2**.
5. Link the chart to the Word document **IntW1-R1.docx** a triple space below the *Student Enrollment* subtitle. (Make sure you use the Paste Special dialog box.)
6. Center the chart below the subtitle *Student Enrollment*. To do this, right-click the chart and then click *Format Object* at the shortcut menu. At the Format Object dialog box, click the Layout tab. Click the *Square* option in the *Wrapping style* section, click the *Center* option in the *Horizontal alignment* section, and then click OK.
7. Save, print, and close **IntW1-R1.docx**.
8. Click the button on the Taskbar representing **IntE1-R2.xlsx**.
9. Click outside the chart to deselect it.
10. Save and then print **IntE1-R2.xlsx**.

11. With **IntE1-R2.xlsx** open, make the following changes to the data in the specified cells:
    A2 Change *Fall Term* to *Spring Term*
    B4 Change *75* to *98*
    B5 Change *30* to *25*
    B6 Change *15* to *23*
    B7 Change *38* to *52*
    B8 Change *25* to *10*
12. Make cell A2 active.
13. Save, print, and then close **IntE1-R2.xlsx**.
14. Make Word the active program and then open **IntW1-R1.docx**. (At the message asking if you want to update the document, click Yes.)
15. Save, print, and then close **IntW1-R1.docx**.

Review 3 Embedding an Object

Worldwide Enterprises

1. With Word the active program, open the document named **WERevenuesMemo.docx**.
2. Save the document with Save As and name it **IntW1-R2**.
3. Make Excel the active program and then open the workbook named **WEExcelRevenues.xlsx**.
4. Save the workbook with Save As and name it **IntE1-R3**.
5. Embed the data in cells A2 through D8 to the Word document **IntW1-R2.docx** a double space below the paragraph of text in the body of the memo.
6. Save and then print **IntW1-R2.docx**.
7. Click the button on the Taskbar representing **IntE1-R3.xlsx**.
8. Press the Esc key to remove the moving marquee and then click outside the selected cells.
9. Save, print, and then close **IntE1-R3.xlsx**.
10. With **IntW1-R2.docx** open, double-click the worksheet and then make the following changes to the data in the specified cells:
    A2 Change *July Revenues* to *August Revenues*
    B4 Change *1,356,000* to *1,575,000*
    B5 Change *2,450,000* to *2,375,000*
    B6 Change *1,635,000* to *1,750,000*
    B7 Change *950,000* to *1,100,000*
    B8 Change *1,050,000* to *1,255,000*
11. Click outside the worksheet to deselect it.
12. Make the following changes to the memo:
    Change the date from *August 10, 2010* to *September 7, 2010*.
    Change the subject from *July Revenues* to *August Revenues*.
13. Save, print, and then close **IntW1-R2.docx**.

Microsoft® Access 2007

Introducing Access 2007

Microsoft Access 2007 is a ***database management system (DBMS)*** included with the Microsoft Office suite. Interacting with a DBMS occurs often as one performs daily routines such as withdrawing cash from the ATM, purchasing gas using a credit card, or looking up a telephone number in an online directory. In each of these activities a DBMS is accessed to retrieve information, and data is viewed, updated, and/or printed. Any application that involves storing and maintaining a large amount of data in an organized manner can be set up as an Access database. Examples include customers and invoices, suppliers and purchases, inventory and orders. While working in Access, you will create and maintain databases for the following six companies.

First Choice Travel is a travel center offering a full range of traveling services from booking flights, hotel reservations, and rental cars to offering travel seminars.

The Waterfront Bistro offers fine dining for lunch and dinner and also offers banquet facilities, a wine cellar, and catering services.

Worldwide Enterprises is a national and international distributor of products for a variety of companies and is the exclusive movie distribution agent for Marquee Productions.

Marquee Productions is involved in all aspects of creating movies from script writing and development to filming. The company produces documentaries, biographies, as well as historical and action movies.

Performance Threads maintains an inventory of rental costumes and also researches, designs, and sews special-order and custom-made costumes.

The mission of the Niagara Peninsula College Theatre Arts Division is to offer a curriculum designed to provide students with a thorough exposure to all aspects of the theater arts.

In Section 1 you will learn how to

Work with Tables

Access databases are comprised of a series of objects. A table is the first object that is created in a new Access database. Information in the database is organized by topic and a table stores data for one topic. For example, one table in a customer database might store customer names and addresses while another table stores the customer invoices and another table stores the customer payments. Table datasheets are organized like a spreadsheet with columns and rows. Each column in the table represents one ***field***, which is a single unit of information about a person, place, item, or object. Each row in the table represents one ***record***, which includes all of the related fields for one person, place, item, or object. Working in tables involves adding or deleting records, editing fields, sorting, filtering, or formatting datasheets. Access provides the Navigation pane for managing database objects.

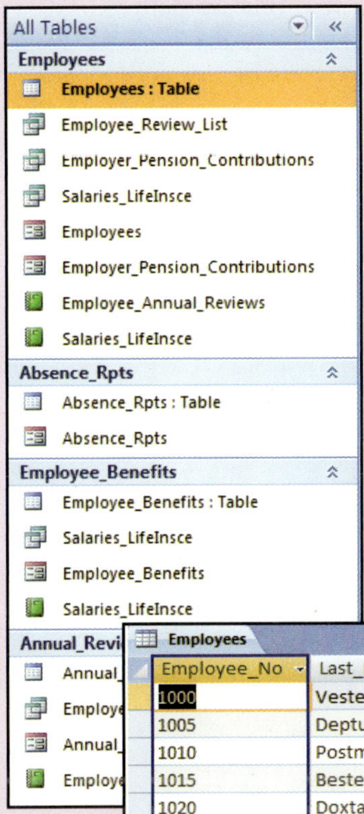

Group objects in the database by various catagories and display them in the Navigation pane.

Data in tables display in a datasheet comprised of columns and rows similar to an Excel worksheet. Each column in a table datasheet represents one field. Each row in a table datasheet represents one record.

Employees

Employee_No	Last_Name	First_Name	Middle_Initial	Birth_Date	Hire_Date	Department	Annual_Salary
1000	Vestering	Sam	L	2/18/1957	7/22/1998	North American Distribution	$69,725.00
1005	Deptulski	Roman	W	3/12/1948	8/15/1998	Overseas Distribution	$69,725.00
1010	Postma	Hanh	A	12/10/1952	1/30/1999	European Distribution	$69,725.00
1015	Besterd	Lyle	C	10/15/1959	5/17/1999	North American Distribution	$45,651.00
1020	Doxtator	Angela	B	5/22/1963	8/3/2000	North American Distribution	$45,558.00
1025	Biliski	Jorge	N	6/18/1970	12/1/1999	North American Distribution	$44,892.00
1030	Hicks	Thom	P	7/27/1977	1/22/1999	Overseas Distribution	$42,824.00
1035	Fitsouris	Valerie	E	2/4/1970	3/15/2001	European Distribution	$44,694.00
1040	Lafreniere	Guy	F	9/14/1972	3/10/2001	Overseas Distribution	$45,395.00
1045	Yiu	Terry	M	6/18/1961	4/12/2001	European Distribution	$42,238.00
1050	Zakowski	Carl	W	5/9/1967	2/9/2002	European Distribution	$44,387.00
1055	Thurston	Edward	S	1/3/1960	6/22/2002	Overseas Distribution	$42,248.00
1060	McKnight	Donald	Z	1/6/1964	6/22/2003	European Distribution	$42,126.00
1065	Liszniewski	Norm	M	11/16/1970	2/6/2003	North American Distribution	$43,695.00
1070	Jhawar	Balfor	R	9/3/1973	11/22/2004	Overseas Distribution	$44,771.00
1075	Fitchett	Mike	L	4/18/1966	3/19/2004	Overseas Distribution	$42,857.00
1080	Couture	Leo	S	1/8/1978	1/17/2004	European Distribution	$43,659.00

record

field

In Section 2 you will learn how to

Create New Tables and Establish Relationships

New tables can be created by adding records to a blank datasheet, creating the table structure by defining fields, or by accessing a table template. Each field in a table has a set of ***field properties***, which are a set of characteristics that control how the field interacts with data in objects such as tables, forms, queries, or reports. The ability to create a relationship between two tables allows one to maintain or extract data in multiple tables as if they were one large table.

Create a new table in Table Design view by assigning each field a field name, a data type, and field properties.

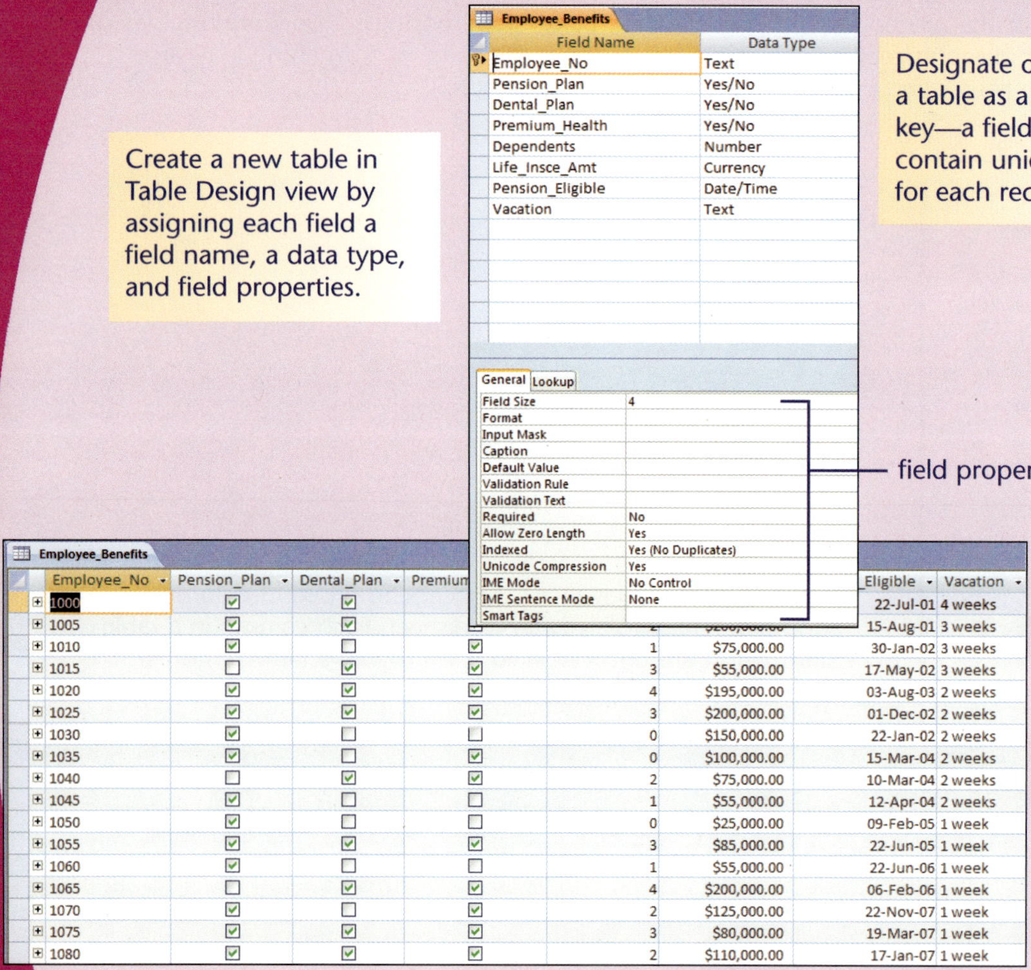

Designate one field in a table as a primary key—a field that will contain unique data for each record.

field properties

Create relationships between tables by joining one table to another on a common field. These relationships are displayed in the Relationships window by black join lines between table field list boxes.

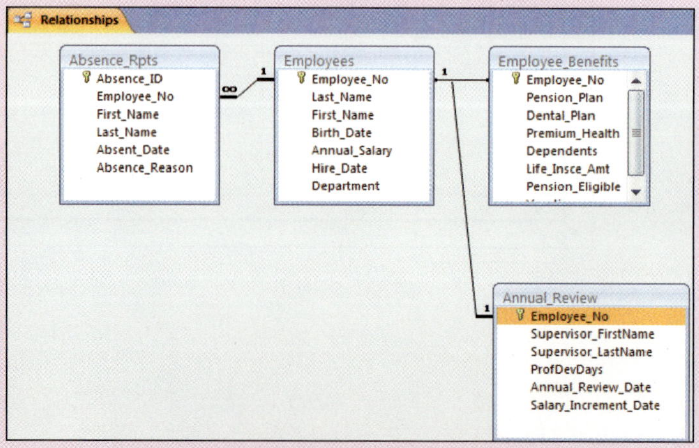

In Section 3 you will learn how to

Create Queries, Forms, and Reports

Queries and forms are objects based on tables and are created to extract, view, and maintain data. Queries can be used to view specific fields from tables that meet a particular criterion. For example, create a query to view customers from a specific state or ZIP code. Forms provide a more user-friendly interface for entering, editing, deleting, and viewing records in tables. Create a report to generate professionally designed printouts of information from tables or queries.

Field:	Employee_No	First_Name	Last_Name	Supervisor_FirstName	Supervisor_LastName	Annual_Review_Date
Table:	Employees	Employees	Employees	Annual_Review	Annual_Review	Annual_Review
Sort:						
Show:	☑	☑	☑	☑	☑	☑
Criteria:				"Sam"	"Vestering"	
or:						

Use queries and criteria statements to extract data from one or more tables.

The query created in Design view (shown above) produces query results datasheet (shown below).

Employee_Review_List

Employee_No	First_Name	Last_Name	Supervisor_FirstName	Supervisor_LastName	Annual_Review_Date
1015	Lyle	Besterd	Sam	Vestering	20-May-09
1020	Angela	Doxtator	Sam	Vestering	03-Aug-09
1025	Jorge	Biliski	Sam	Vestering	01-Dec-09
1065	Norm	Liszniewski	Sam	Vestering	06-Feb-10
1080	Leo	Couture	Sam	Vestering	17-Jan-10

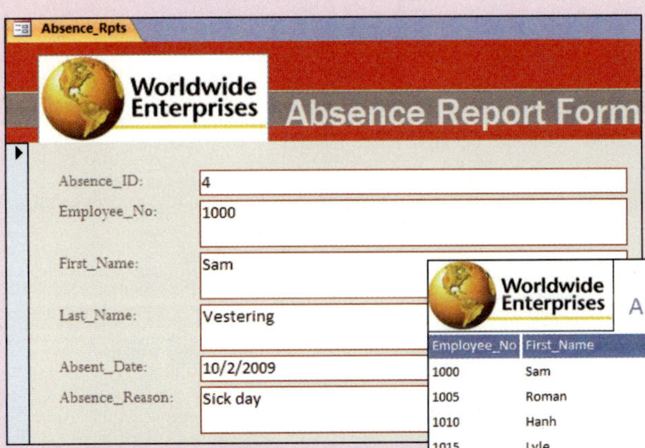

Use forms to provide a user-friendly interface for adding, deleting, and editing records in a table.

Worldwide Enterprises — Annual and Monthly Salary Report

Wednesday, August 26, 2009
12:20:09 PM

Employee_No	First_Name	Last_Name	Hire_Date	Life_Insce_Amt	Annual_Salary	Monthly_Salary
1000	Sam	Vestering	7/22/1998	$190,000.00	$69,725.00	$5,810.42
1005	Roman	Deptulski	8/15/1998	$200,000.00	$69,725.00	$5,810.42
1010	Hanh	Postma	1/30/1999	$75,000.00	$69,725.00	$5,810.42
1015	Lyle	Besterd	5/17/1999	$55,000.00	$45,651.00	$3,804.25
1020	Angela	Doxtator	8/3/2000	$195,000.00	$45,558.00	$3,796.50
1025	Jorge	Biliski	12/1/1999	$200,000.00	$44,892.00	$3,741.00
1030	Thom	Hicks	1/22/1999	$150,000.00	$42,824.00	$3,568.67
1035	Valerie	Fitsouris	3/15/2001	$100,000.00	$44,694.00	$3,724.50
1040	Guy	Lafreniere	3/10/2001	$75,000.00	$45,395.00	$3,782.92
1045	Terry	Yiu	4/12/2001	$55,000.00	$42,238.00	$3,519.83
1050	Carl	Zakowski	2/9/2002	$25,000.00	$44,387.00	$3,698.92
1055	Edward	Thurston	6/22/2002	$85,000.00	$42,248.00	$3,520.67
1060	Donald	McKnight	6/22/2003	$55,000.00	$42,126.00	$3,510.50
1065	Norm	Liszniewski	2/6/2003	$200,000.00	$43,695.00	$3,641.25
1070	Balfor	Jhawar	11/22/2004	$125,000.00	$44,771.00	$3,730.92
1075	Mike	Fitchett	3/19/2004	$80,000.00	$42,857.00	$3,571.42
1080	Leo	Couture	1/17/2004	$110,000.00	$43,659.00	$3,638.25
					$824,170.00	$68,680.83

Page 1 of 1

Create professional-quality printed reports using the Report tool or the Report Wizard. Incorporate report elements such as a logo, the date and time, page numbering, and grand totals in Layout view using buttons available in the ribbon.

In Section 4 you will learn how to

Summarize Data

Large amounts of data in tables can be summarized using various tools available within Access. Aggregate functions calculate statistics such as the sum, average, maximum, and minimum values on a numeric field. Crosstab queries use functions on a numeric field to group data by two fields. PivotTables and PivotCharts are interactive summaries of data grouped by two or more fields that can be filtered to pivot the table or chart by showing a subset of data. Add a calculated field to a form and/or report to calculate a result from a numeric field.

Salary_Statistics_byDept

Total Salaries	Average Salary	Maximum Salary	Minimum Salary	Department
$325,004.00	$46,429.14	$69,725.00	$38,175.00	European Distribution
$327,871.00	$46,838.71	$69,725.00	$38,175.00	North American Distribution
$325,995.00	$46,570.71	$69,725.00	$38,175.00	Overseas Distribution

Summarize data by calculating statistics such as sum, average, maximum, and minimum. Show statistics for the entire table or group them by a field.

Use a crosstab query to group data by two fields. In this example, tuition payments are grouped by employee (rows) and by quarter (columns).

Tuition_byEmp_byQtr

Last_Name	Total Of Tuition	Qtr 1	Qtr 2	Qtr 4
Deptulski	$1,895.00	$1,145.00		$750.00
Doxtator	$995.00		$510.00	$485.00
Hicks	$674.00	$674.00		
Postma	$1,472.00	$887.00	$585.00	
Vestering	$2,118.00	$1,575.00	$543.00	
Yiu	$2,130.00	$985.00	$1,145.00	
Total	$9,284.00	$5,266.00	$2,783.00	$1,235.00

Department: North American Distribution

	Date_Reimbursed: 24-Dec-09	05-Jan-10	01-May-10	Grand Total
Last_Name	Tuition	Tuition	Tuition	Total Tuition
Doxtator	$485.00		$510.00	$995.00
	$485.00		$510.00	
Vestering		$1,575.00	$543.00	$2,118.00
		$1,575.00	$543.00	
Grand Total	$485.00	$1,575.00	$1,053.00	$3,113.00

Transform data from a table or query datasheet to analyze in an interactive PivotTable (shown at left) or PivotChart (shown below).

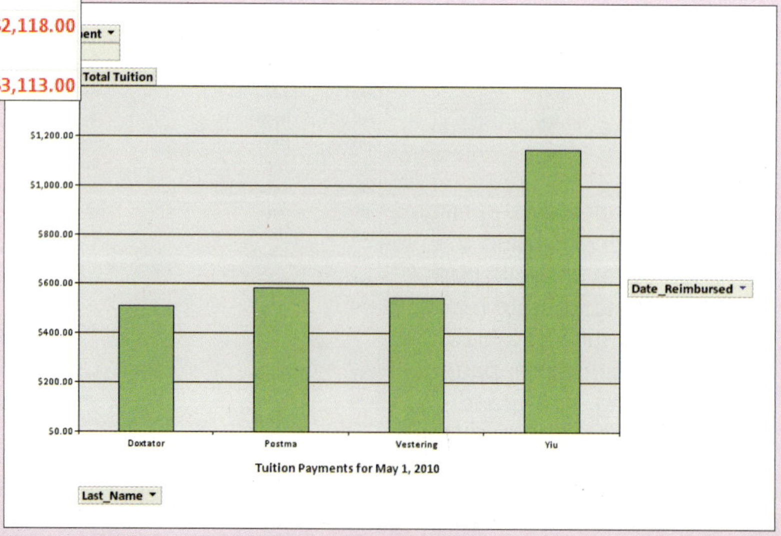

Access SECTION 1

Maintaining Data in Access Tables

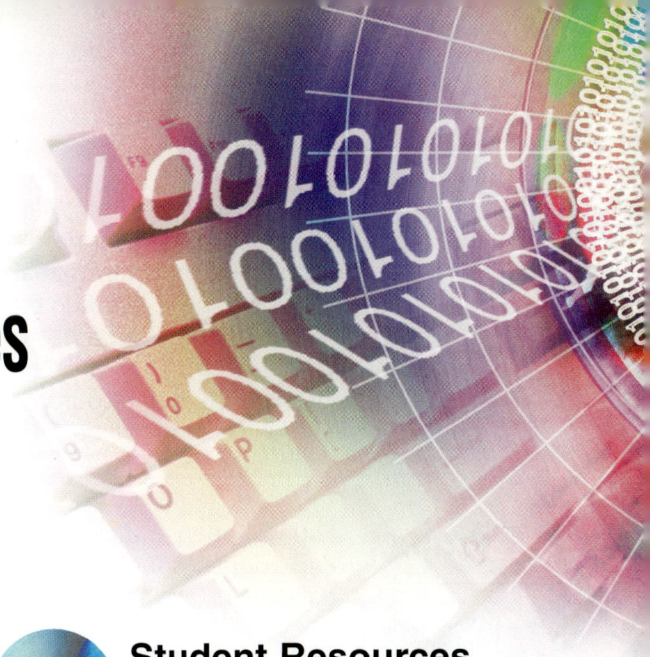

Skills

- Define *field, record, table, datasheet,* and *database*
- Start and exit Access
- Identify features in the Access window
- Open and close a database
- Open and close tables
- Open and close forms
- Adjust column widths
- Navigate in Datasheet view
- Find and edit records
- Add records
- Delete records
- Sort records
- Move columns in a datasheet
- Apply and remove a filter in a datasheet
- Preview and print a table
- Change margins
- Change the page orientation
- Use the Help feature
- Change the font size for selected records
- Hide columns in a datasheet
- Compact and repair a database
- Back up a database

Student Resources

Before beginning this section:

1. Copy to your storage medium the AccessS1 subfolder from the Access folder on the Student Resources CD.
2. Make AccessS1 the active folder.

In addition to containing the data files needed to complete section work, the Student Resources CD contains model answers in PDF format for each of the projects in this section; model answers for end-of-section activities are not provided.

Projects Overview

Worldwide Enterprises

Add, delete, find, sort, and filter records; preview, change page orientation and margins, and print tables; format and hide columns in a datasheet; compact and back up the Distributors database; find, edit, add, delete, sort, and filter records; preview, change page setup, and print; compact and back up the Employees database.

Niagara Peninsula College

Find student records and enter grades into the Grades database; compact and back up the Grades database.

The Waterfront B·I·S·T·R·O

Maintain the Inventory database by adding and deleting records; compact the Inventory database. Add, delete, and modify records; sort, filter, and set print options for a catering event database.

Performance Threads

Delete records, sort and filter records, and print two reports from the Costume Inventory database; compact the Inventory database; create field names and table names for a new custom costume database.

Activity 1.1

Exploring Database Objects and the User Interface

A ***database*** is comprised of a series of objects used to enter, manage, and view data. Data, the basic building block of a database, is organized into ***tables***. A table contains information for related items such as customers, suppliers, inventory, or human resources broken down into individual units of information. The interface in Access is different from the other applications within the Microsoft Office suite. The Navigation pane at the left side of the screen displays the objects in the database organized into categories and is used to open an object. Unlike other Microsoft Office applications, only one database can be open at a time.

Project

Worldwide Enterprises

You will open and close two tables and a form in a database used to store distributor names and addresses for Worldwide Enterprises to define and identify objects, fields, records, tables, datasheets, and forms.

1. At the Windows desktop, click the Start button on the Taskbar.
2. Point to *All Programs*.
3. Point to *Microsoft Office*.
4. Click *Microsoft Office Access 2007*.

   Depending on your operating system and/or system configuration, the steps you complete to open Access may vary.

5. Click the Office button located at the upper left corner of the screen and then click *Open* at the drop-down list, or click the More hyperlink in the Open Recent Database pane.

   The *Getting Started with Microsoft Office Access* screen is divided into three sections. The *Template Categories* section at the left is used to preview and download database templates. The *New Blank Database* section in the center is used to start a new database and the *Open Recent Database* section is used to open an existing database file.

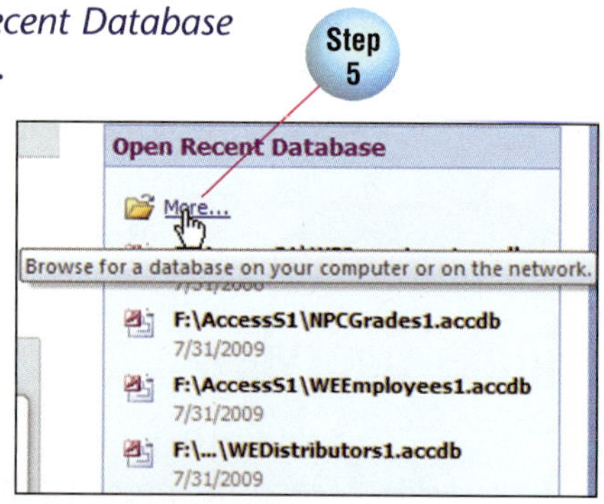

6. If necessary, change the *Look in* location to the storage medium on which you copied the student data files. To change to a different drive, click the down-pointing arrow to the right of the *Look in* option box and then click the correct drive at the drop-down list.
7. Double-click the folder named *AccessS1* and then double-click ***WEDistributors1.accdb***.

   Access 2007 database file names end with the file name extension *accdb*.

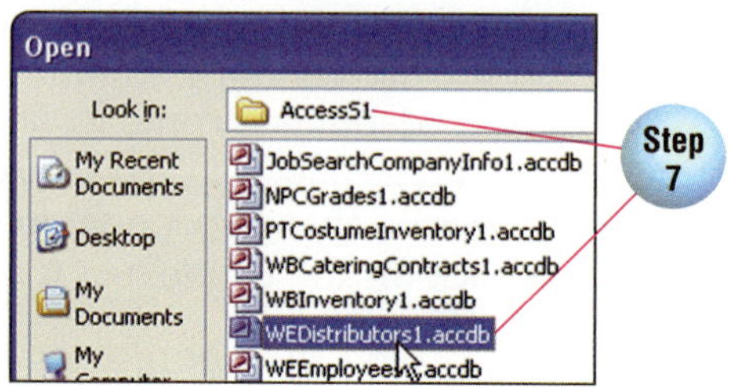

8. At the Access screen, identify the various features by comparing your screen with the one shown in Figure 1.1.

   Descriptions of the types of objects are presented in Table 1.1 on page 5. The Navigation pane displays the names of the objects within the database grouped by tables.

FIGURE 1.1 The Access Screen

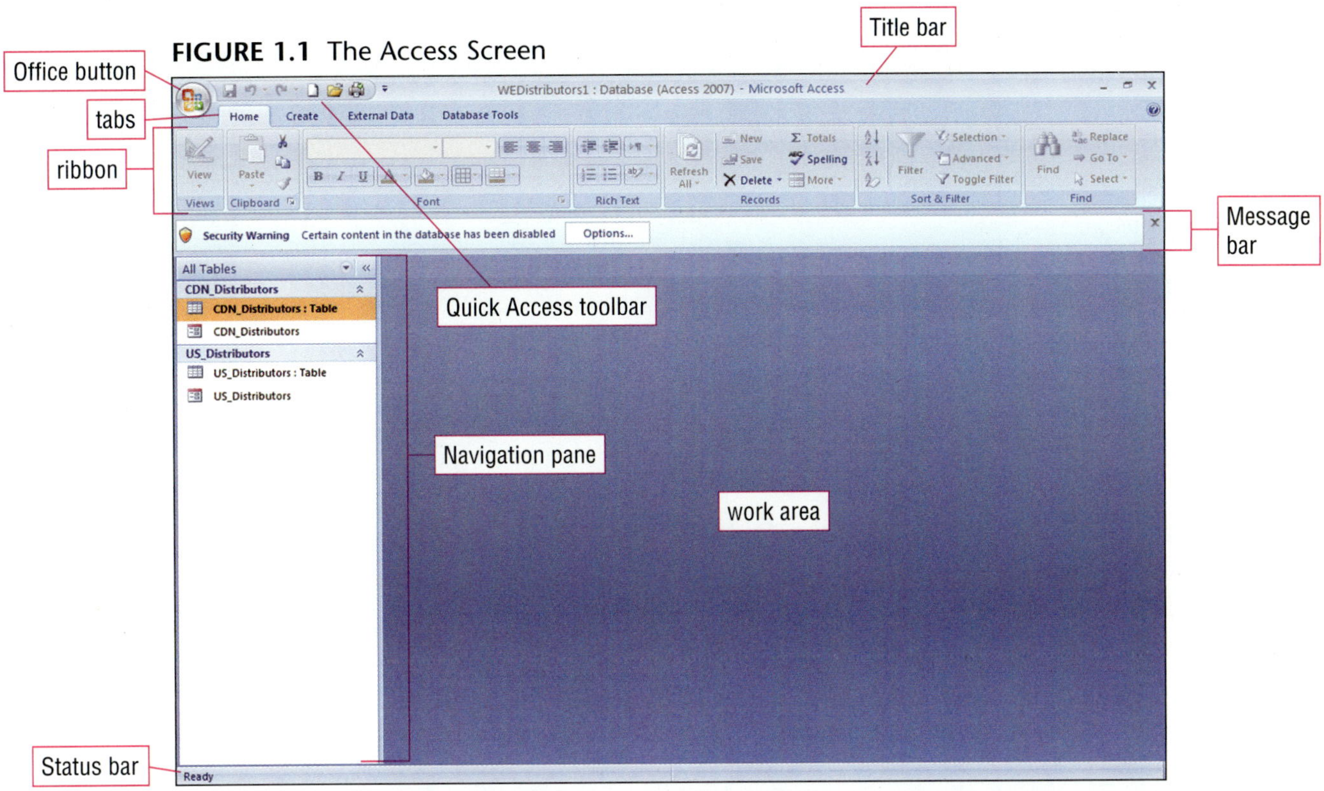

9 With the *All Tables* group displayed in the Navigation pane, double-click *CDN_Distributors : Table.*

Double-clicking the CDN_Distributors : Table object name opens the table in Datasheet view in the work area. Datasheets display the contents of a table in a column and row format.

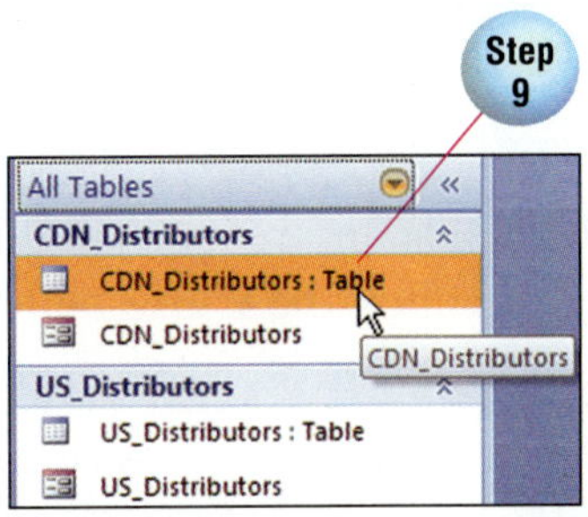

10 Compare your screen with the one shown in Figure 1.2 on page 4 and examine the identified elements.

The identified elements are further described in Table 1.2 on page 5.

11 Identify the fields and the field names in the CDN_Distributors table. Notice each field contains only one unit of information.

The field names *ID, CompanyName, StreetAdd1, StreetAdd2, City,* and so on are displayed in the header row at the top of the datasheet.

12 Identify the records in the CDN_Distributors table. Each record is one row in the table.

13 Press the Down Arrow key four times to move the active record.

Notice the record number in the Record Navigation bar at the bottom of the datasheet changes to indicate you are viewing record 5 of a total of 12 records.

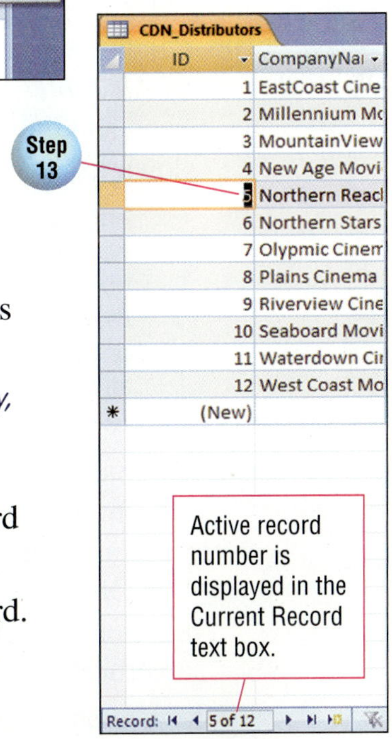

continues

FIGURE 1.2 CDN_Distributors Table in Datasheet View

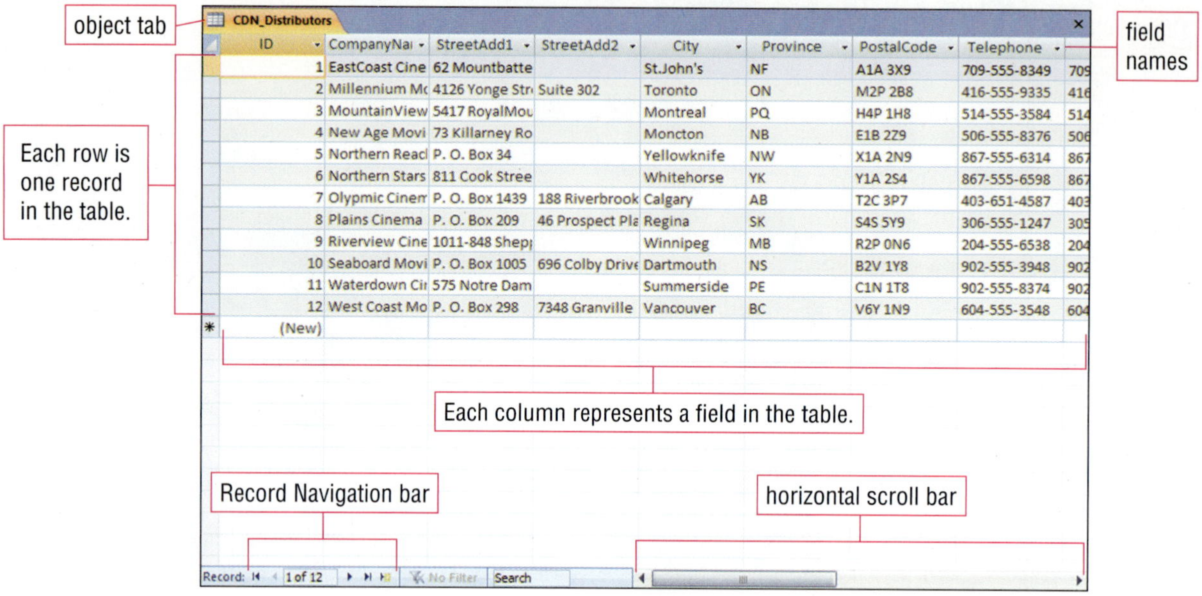

ID	CompanyNa	StreetAdd1	StreetAdd2	City	Province	PostalCode	Telephone	
1	EastCoast Cine	62 Mountbatte		St.John's	NF	A1A 3X9	709-555-8349	709
2	Millennium Mc	4126 Yonge Str	Suite 302	Toronto	ON	M2P 2B8	416-555-9335	416
3	MountainView	5417 RoyalMou		Montreal	PQ	H4P 1H8	514-555-3584	514
4	New Age Movi	73 Killarney Ro		Moncton	NB	E1B 2Z9	506-555-8376	506
5	Northern Reacl	P. O. Box 34		Yellowknife	NW	X1A 2N9	867-555-6314	867
6	Northern Stars	811 Cook Stree		Whitehorse	YK	Y1A 2S4	867-555-6598	867
7	Olympic Cinem	P. O. Box 1439	188 Riverbrook	Calgary	AB	T2C 3P7	403-651-4587	403
8	Plains Cinema	P. O. Box 209	46 Prospect Pl	Regina	SK	S4S 5Y9	306-555-1247	306
9	Riverview Cine	1011-848 Shep		Winnipeg	MB	R2P 0N6	204-555-6538	204
10	Seaboard Movi	P. O. Box 1005	696 Colby Drive	Dartmouth	NS	B2V 1Y8	902-555-3948	902
11	Waterdown Cir	575 Notre Dam		Summerside	PE	C1N 1T8	902-555-8374	902
12	West Coast Mo	P. O. Box 298	7348 Granville	Vancouver	BC	V6Y 1N9	604-555-3548	604
(New)								

14 Click the Close button **X** at the top right corner of the work area.

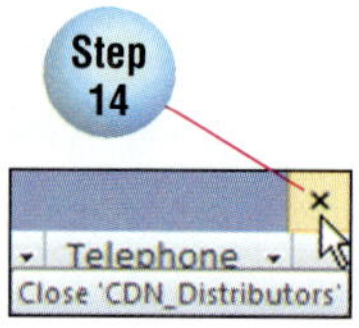

15 Move the mouse pointer over the object named US_Distributors : Table and then right-click.

16 Click *Open* at the shortcut menu.

17 Review the fields and records in the US_Distributors table and then click the Close button at the top right corner of the work area.

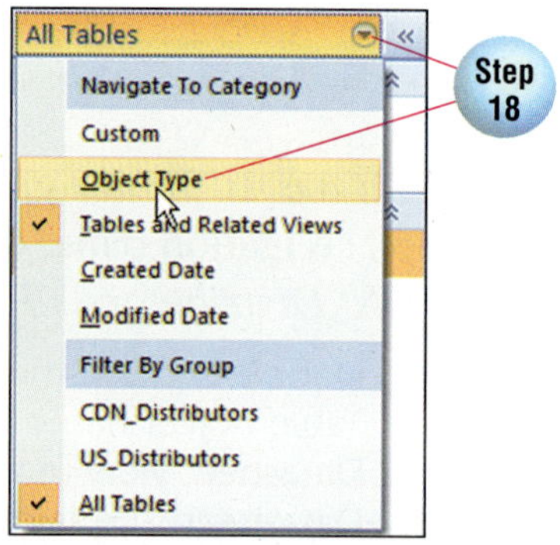

18 Click the down-pointing arrow to the right of *All Tables* at the top of the Navigation pane and then click *Object Type* at the drop-down list.

The current view for the Navigation pane was *Tables and Related Views*. In this view, objects are grouped by the table to which they are associated. The *Object Type* view displays objects grouped by type such as all table objects, all form objects, and so on.

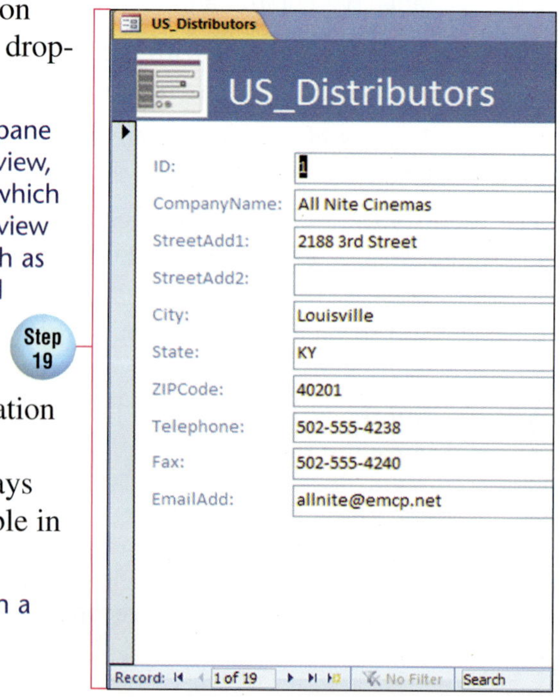

19 Double-click *US_Distributors* below the group heading *Forms* in the Navigation pane and then review the fields in the US_Distributors form. The form displays the fields from the US_Distributors table in a vertical layout.

A form is used to view and edit data in a table one record at a time.

20 Click the Close button at the top right corner of the work area.

21 Click the Office button and then click *Close Database* at the drop-down list.

In Brief

Start Access
1. Click Start.
2. Point to *All Programs.*
3. Point to *Microsoft Office.*
4. Click *Microsoft Office Access 2007.*

Open Objects
1. Open database file.
2. Double-click object name in Navigation pane.

TABLE 1.1 Database Objects

Object	Description
Table	Organizes data in fields (columns) and rows (records). A database must contain at least one table. The table is the base upon which other objects are created.
Query	Used to display data from a table that meets a conditional statement and/or to perform calculations. For example, display only those records in which the city is Toronto.
Form	Allows fields and records to be presented in a different layout than the datasheet. Used to facilitate data entry and maintenance.
Report	Prints data from tables or queries.
Macro	Automates repetitive tasks.
Module	Advanced automation through programming using Visual Basic for Applications.

TABLE 1.2 Basic Elements of a Database

Element	Description
Field	A single component of information about a person, place, item, or object.
Record	All of the fields related to one logical unit in the table such as a customer, supplier, contact, or inventory item.
Table	All of the related records for one logical group.
Database	A file containing related tables and objects.

In Addition

Planning and Designing a Table

One of the first steps in designing a table for a new database is to determine the best way to break down all of the information into individual fields. Discuss with others what the future needs will be for both input and output. Include fields you anticipate will be used in the future. For example, add a field for a Web site address even if you do not currently have URLs for your customers. Refer to Skills Assessment 5 and Marquee Challenge 2 at the end of this section for exercises on designing a new database.

Activity 1.2

Adjusting Column Width; Navigating in Datasheet View

A table opened in Datasheet view displays data in a manner similar to a spreadsheet with a grid of columns and rows. Columns contain the field values, with the field names in the header row at the top of the datasheet, and records are represented as rows. A Record Navigation bar at the bottom contains buttons with which to navigate the datasheet.

Project

You will adjust column widths and practice scrolling and navigating through records in the US_Distributors table.

Worldwide Enterprises

1. At the *Getting Started with Microsoft Office Access* screen, click **WEDistributors1.accdb** in the Open Recent Database pane.

   New security features in Access 2007 cause the message bar with the Security Warning message to appear below the ribbon when you open an Access 2007 database outside of a trusted location (a list of drives and folder names stored in the Trust Center dialog box). If you are sure the database is virus-free you can use the message bar to enable the full content.

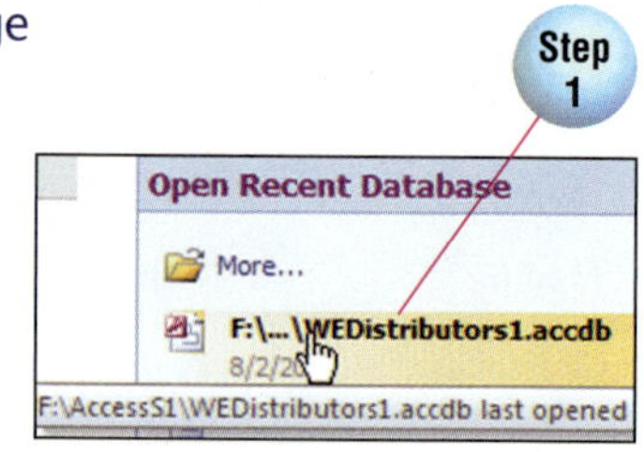

2. Click the Options button in the Message bar.

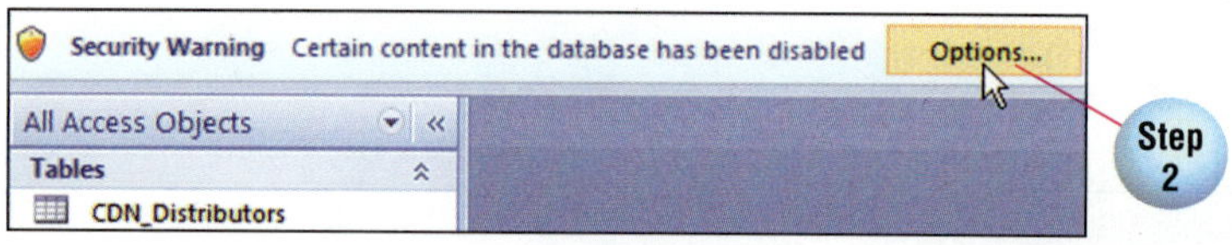

3. At the Microsoft Office Security Options dialog box, click *Enable this content* and then click OK.

   The message bar closes once you indicate the database in use can be trusted.

4. Double-click *US_Distributors* in the Tables group in the Navigation pane.

   Notice that some columns contain data that is not entirely visible. In Steps 5–7, you will learn how to adjust the column widths using two methods.

5. With the insertion point positioned at the left edge of the number *1* in the *ID* field of the first row in the datasheet, click the More button More in the Records group in the Home tab and then click *Column Width* at the drop-down list.

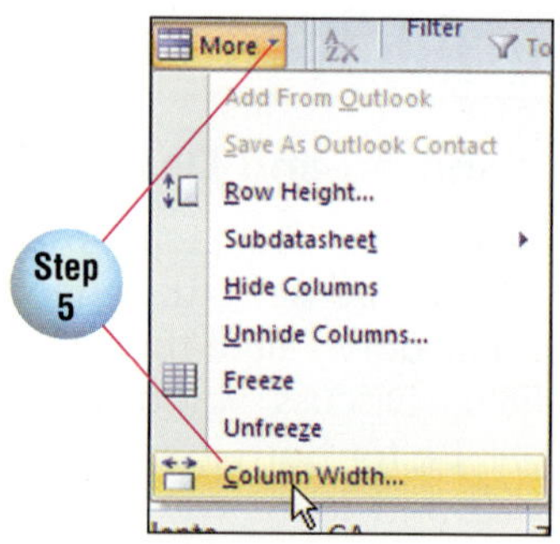

6. At the Column Width dialog box, with the current entry already selected in the *Column Width* text box, type **6** and then press Enter or click OK.

   Type a value to increase or decrease the column width or use the Best Fit button to set the width to accommodate the length of the longest entry. In the next step, you will use the mouse to best fit a column.

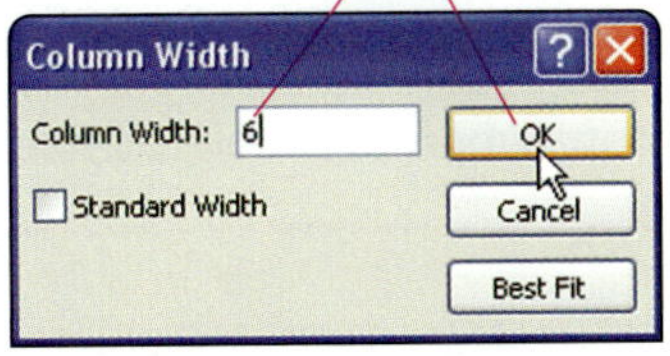

7. Position the mouse pointer on the right column boundary line in the header row between columns two and three *(CompanyName* and *StreetAdd1)* until the pointer changes to a vertical line with a left- and right-pointing arrow and then double-click the left mouse button.

   Double-clicking the column boundary performs the Best Fit command, which automatically sets the width to the length of the longest entry within the field.

8. Best Fit the *StreetAdd1, StreetAdd2, City, State* and *ZIPCode* columns using either method learned in Steps 5–6 or Step 7.
9. Click the right-pointing horizontal scroll arrow as many times as necessary to scroll the datasheet to the right and view the remaining columns. (See Table 1.3 for keyboard scrolling commands.)
10. Best Fit the *EmailAdd* column.
11. Drag the scroll box to the left edge of the horizontal scroll bar.

12. Click the Save button on the Quick Access toolbar.
13. Click the Last record button on the Record Navigation bar to move to the last row in the table.
14. Click the Previous record button on the Record Navigation bar to move up one row in the table and then click the Next record button to move down one row.
15. Click the First record button on the Record Navigation bar to move to the first row in the table.

In Brief

Adjust Column Width

1. Position insertion point in desired column.
2. Click More button.
3. Click *Column Width*.
4. Type *Column Width* value or click Best Fit.
5. Click OK.

OR

Drag or double-click right column boundary line in header row.

TABLE 1.3 Scrolling Techniques Using the Keyboard

Press	To move to
Home	first field in the current record
End	last field in the current record
Tab	next field in the current record
Shift + Tab	previous field in the current record
Ctrl + Home	first field in the first record
Ctrl + End	last field in the last record

In Addition

Saving Data

Access differs from other Office applications in that *data* is *automatically* saved as soon as you move to the next record or close the table. Database management systems store critical data related to business activities and saving is not left to chance. The Save button was used in this topic to save the layout changes that were made when the column widths were enlarged.

Activity 1.3

Finding and Editing Records

The Find command can be used to quickly move the insertion point to a specific record in a table. This is a time-saving feature when the table contains several records that are not all visible in one screen. Once a record has been located, click the insertion point within a field and insert or delete text as required to edit the record.

Project

Worldwide Enterprises

You have received a note from Sam Vestering that Waterfront Cinemas has changed its fax number and Eastown Movie House has a new post office box number. You will use the Find feature to locate the records and make the changes.

1. With the US_Distributors table open, press Tab or click the insertion point in the *CompanyName* column in the first row and then click the Find button in the Find group in the Home tab.

   This displays the Find and Replace dialog box.

2. Type **Waterfront Cinemas** in the *Find What* text box and then click the Find Next button.

   The active record moves to record 17 and the text *Waterfront Cinemas* is selected in the *CompanyName* field. If necessary, move the dialog box up to view the datasheet.

Step 2

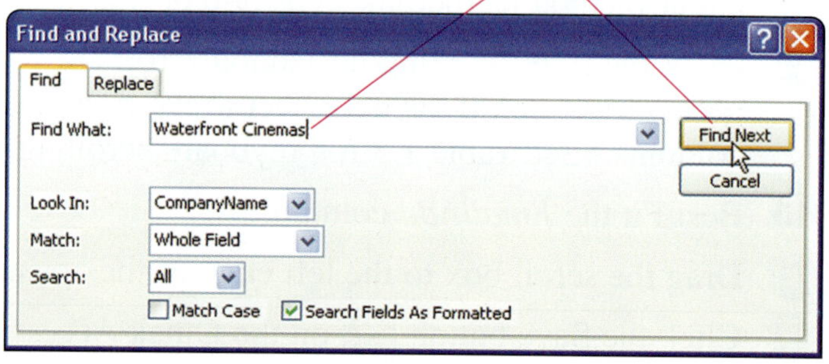

Current record *ID* is 17 and the search text is automatically selected in the field.

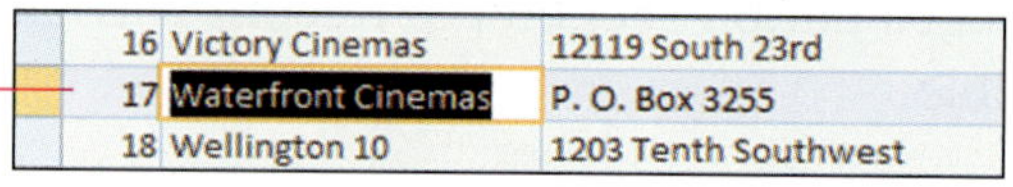

3. Click the Close button on the Find and Replace dialog box Title bar.
4. Press Tab or Enter seven times to move to the *Fax* column.

   The entire field value is selected when you move from column to column using Tab or Enter. If you need to edit only a few characters within the field you will want to use *Edit* mode. As an alternative, you could scroll and click the insertion point within the field to avoid having to turn on *Edit* mode.

5. Press F2 to turn on *Edit* mode.
6. Press Backspace four times to delete *3947* and then type **4860**.

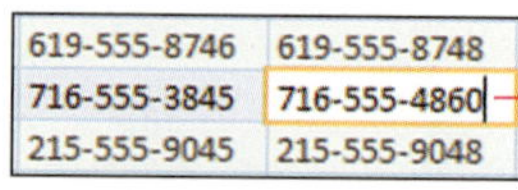

Step 6

7. Look at the record selector bar (blank column at the left edge of the datasheet) at record 17 and notice the pencil icon that is displayed.

   The pencil icon indicates the current record is being edited and the changes have not yet been saved.

Step 7

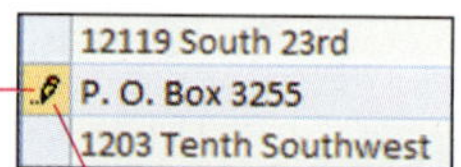

Pencil icon indicates a record is being edited. Changes to data are not saved until you move to another record in the table.

8 Press Enter twice to move to the next record in the table.

The pencil icon disappears, indicating the changes have now been saved.

9 Click in any record in the *StreetAdd1* column and then click the Find button.

10 Type **Box 722** in the *Find What* text box.

11 Click the down-pointing arrow next to the *Match* option box and then click *Any Part of Field* in the drop-down list.

Using the options from the *Match* option box you can find records without specifying the entire field value. Specifically, you can instruct Access to stop at records where the entry typed in the *Find What* text box is the *Whole Field*, is *Any Part of Field*, or is the *Start of Field*.

12 Click Find Next.

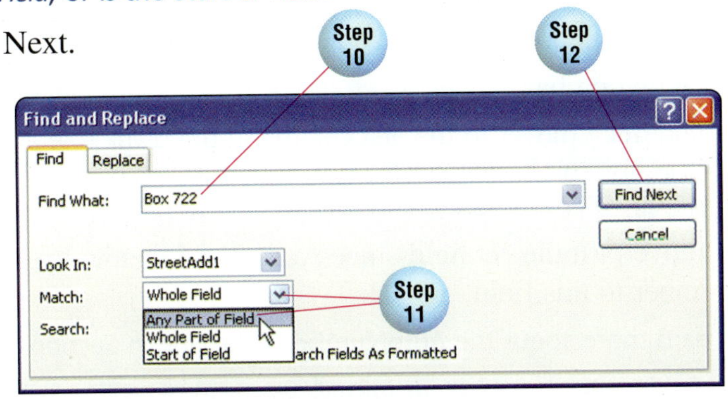

13 Close the Find and Replace dialog box.

The insertion point moved to record 5. You were able to correctly locate the record for Eastown Movie House using only a portion of the field value for *StreetAdd1*. Notice that Access has selected *Box 722* in the field—only the text specified in the *Find What* text box (not P. O. Box 722, which is the entire field value).

14 Press F2 to turn on *Edit* mode, press Backspace three times, type **429**, and then click in any other record to save the changes to record 5.

In Brief

Find a Record

1. Click in any row in field by which you want to search.
2. Click Find button.
3. Type search text.
4. Click Find Next.

In Addition

Using the Replace Command

Use the Replace tab in the Find and Replace dialog box to automatically change a field entry to something else. For example, in Steps 9–12 you searched for *Box 722* and then edited the field to change the box number to *429*. The Replace command could have been used to change the text automatically. To do this, click the Replace button [Replace] in the Find group in the Home tab, type **Box 722** in the *Find What* text box, type **Box 429** in the *Replace With* text box, change the option in the *Match* option box to *Any Part of Field*, and then click the Find Next button. Click the Replace button when the record is found. Use the Replace All button in the dialog box to change multiple occurrences of a field.

Activity 1.4

Adding Records to a Datasheet

New records can be added to a table in either Datasheet view or Form view. To add a record in Datasheet view, open the table and then click the New (blank) record button on the Record Navigation bar, or click the New button in the Records group in the Home tab. When you press Tab or Enter after typing the last field, the record is saved automatically. When a datasheet is opened, the records are sorted alphanumerically by the primary key. A ***primary key*** is a field that provides Access with a unique identifier for each record. In the US_Distributors table, the *ID* field is the primary key. The In Addition section at the end of this activity describes the function of a primary key field.

Project

Worldwide Enterprises has signed two new distributors in the United States. You will add the information in two records in the US_Distributors table using the datasheet.

1. With the US_Distributors table open, click the New (blank) record button in the Record Navigation bar.

   The insertion point moves to the first column in the blank row at the bottom of the datasheet and the *Current Record* box in the Record Navigation bar indicates you are editing record *20 of 20* records.

2. Press Tab to move past the *ID* field since Access automatically assigns the next sequential number to this field.

   You will learn more about the AutoNumber data type in Section 2.

3. Type **Dockside Movies** in the *CompanyName* field and then press Tab.

Step 3

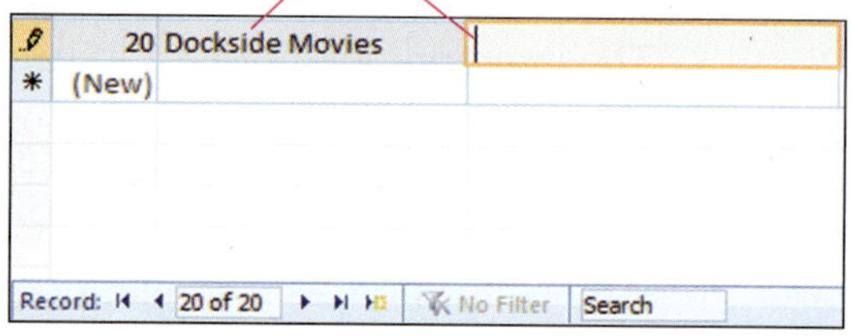

4. Type **P. O. Box 224** and then press Tab.
5. Type **155 S. Central Avenue** and then press Tab.
6. Type **Baltimore** and then press Tab.
7. Type **MD** and then press Tab.
8. Type **21203** and then press Tab.

   If you use the numeric keypad to type numbers, consider using the Enter key to move to the next field since it will be more comfortable.

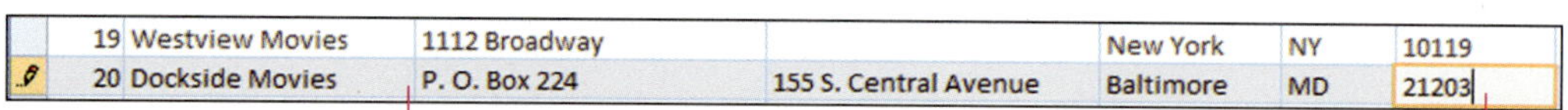

Steps 4–8

9. Type **301-555-7732** and then press Tab.
10. Type **301-555-9836** and then press Tab.
11. Type **dockside@emcp.net** and then press Tab.

    The insertion point moves to a new row when you press Tab or Enter after the last field in a new record to allow you to continue typing the next new record in the table. The record just entered is saved automatically.

12 Type the following information in the next row:

Renaissance Cinemas
3599 Woodward Avenue
Detroit, MI 48211
313-555-1693
313-555-1699
renaissance-cinemas@emcp.net

20	Dockside Movies	P. O. Box 224	155 S. Central Avenue	Baltimore	MD	21203
21	Renaissance Cinemas	3599 Woodward Avenue		Detroit	MI	48211
(New)						

name and address fields of new record added in Step 12

13 Drag the right column boundary line of the *EmailAdd* column until you can view all of the data.

14 Close the US_Distributors table. Click Yes when prompted to save changes to the layout of the table.

US_Distributors

ZIPCode	Telephone	Fax	EmailAdd	Add New Field
40201	502-555-4238	502-555-4240	allnite@emcp.net	
76013	817-555-2116	817-555-2119	centurycinemas@emcp.net	
05201	802-555-1469	802-555-1470	countryside@emcp.net	
29201	803-555-3487	803-555-3421	danforth@emcp.net	
02142	413-555-0981	413-555-0226	eastown@emcp.net	
07920	201-555-1147	201-555-1143	hillman@emcp.net	
86355-6014	602-555-6231	602-555-6233	lavista@emcp.net	
73125	404-555-8113	404-555-2349	libertycinemas@emcp.net	
98220-2791	206-555-3269	206-555-3270	mainstream@emcp.net	
90045	612-555-2398	612-555-2377	marqueemovies@emcp.net	
66801	316-555-7013	316-555-7022	midtown@emcp.net	
43107	614-555-8134	614-555-8339	mooretown@emcp.net	
60302	312-555-7719	312-555-7381	oshea@emcp.net	
97466-3359	503-555-8641	503-555-8633	redwoodcinemas@emcp.net	
33562	813-555-3185	813-555-3177	sunfest@emcp.net	
97432-1567	619-555-8746	619-555-8748	victory@emcp.net	
14288	716-555-3845	716-555-4860	waterfrontcinemas@emcp.net	
19178	215-555-9045	215-555-9048	wellington10@emcp.net	
10119	212-555-4875	212-555-4877	westview@emcp.net	
21203	301-555-7732	301-555-9836	dockside@emcp.net	
48211	313-555-1693	313-555-1699	renaissance-cinemas@emcp.net	
*				

Step 13

In Brief

Add Records to Datasheet

1. Open table.
2. Click New (blank) record button in Navigation bar OR click New button in Records group.
3. Type data in fields.

In Addition

Primary Key Field

Generally, in each table one field is designated as the ***primary key***. A primary key is the field by which the table is sorted whenever the table is opened. The primary key field must contain unique data for each record. When a new record is being added to the table, Access checks to ensure there is no existing record with the same data in the primary key. If there is, Access displays an error message indicating there are duplicate values and will not allow the record to be saved. The primary key field cannot be left blank when a new record is being added, since it is the field that is used to sort and check for duplicates. When you elect to create a new table by adding records, a new feature in Access 2007 is the automatic inclusion of a field named *ID* that is defined as the primary key. The *ID* field uses the AutoNumber data type, which assigns each new record the next sequential number.

Activity 1.5

Adding Records Using a Form

Forms are used to enter, edit, view, and print data. Forms provide a user-friendly interface between the user and the underlying table of data. Adding records in a form is easier than using a datasheet since all of the fields in the table are presented in a different layout which usually allows all fields to be visible in the current screen. Other records in the table do not distract the user since only one record displays at a time. Forms can be customized to present a variety of layouts. You will learn how to create and edit forms in Section 3.

Project

Worldwide Enterprises has just signed two new distributors in New York. You will add the information in two records in the US_Distributors table using a form.

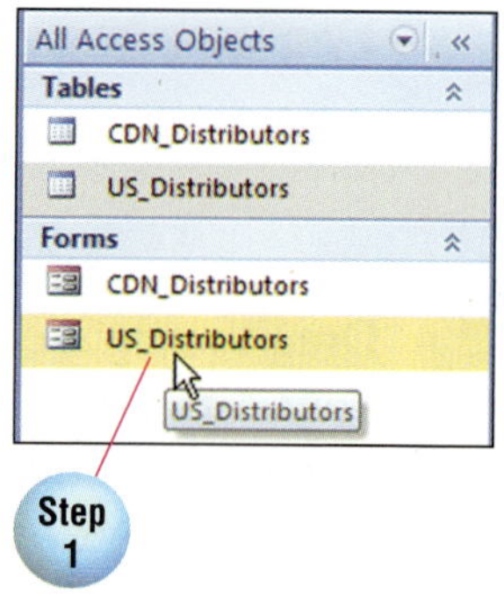

1. With the **WEDistributors1.accdb** database open, double-click *US_Distributors* in the *Forms* group of the Navigation pane.

   The US_Distributors form opens with the first record in the US_Distributors table displayed in the form.

2. Click the New button [New] in the Records group in the Home tab.

   A blank form appears in Form view and the Record Navigation bar indicates you are editing record number 22. Notice the New (blank) record and Next record buttons on the Record Navigation bar are dimmed.

3. Press Tab to move to the *CompanyName* field since Access automatically assigns the next sequential number to the *ID* field.

   The *ID* field does not display a field value until you begin to type data in another field in the record.

4. Type **Movie Emporium** and then press Tab or Enter.

5. Type **203 West Houston Street** and then press Tab or Enter.

   Use the same navigation methods you learned in Activity 1.4 on adding records to a datasheet.

6. Type the remaining fields as shown at the right. Press Tab or Enter after typing the last field.

   When you press Tab or Enter after the *EMailAdd* field, a new form will appear in the work area.

7. Type the following information in the new form for record 23:

   Cinema Festival
   318 East 11th Street
   New York, NY 10003
   212-555-9715
   212-555-9717
   cinemafestival@emcp.net

8 Click the First record button [|◀] in the Record Navigation bar.

This displays the information for All Nite Cinemas in Form view.

9 Click the Last record button [▶|] in the Record Navigation bar.

This displays the information for Cinema Festival in Form view.

10 Use the Previous record button [◀] to scroll the records one at a time back to the first record.

11 Click the insertion point within the *CompanyName* field and then click the Find button in the Find group in the Home tab.

You can use the Find feature to find a record that you need to view or edit in Form view using the same method as you learned in Activity 1.3 for finding and editing records in a datasheet.

12 With existing text already selected in the *Find What* text box, type **Dockside Movies** and then click Find Next.

Access scrolls the form to make the *ID* 20 record active, which is the record in which the search string *Dockside Movies* exists in the *CompanyName* field.

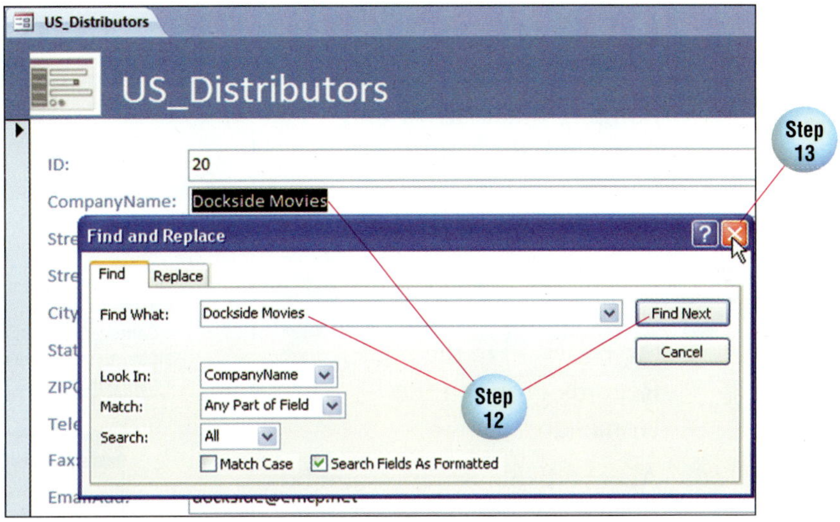

13 Close the Find and Replace dialog box to view the record for Dockside Movies.

PROBLEM

Record not found? Check your spelling in the *Find What* text box. A typing mistake will mean Access could not match the search string with a *CompanyName* field value.

14 Close the US_Distributors form.

15 Open the US_Distributors table and then view the two records added to the table using the form.

16 Close the US_Distributors table.

In Brief

Add Record in Form View

1. Open form.
2. Click New (blank) record button in Navigation bar OR click New button in Records group.
3. Type data in fields.

In Addition

Scrolling in Form View Using the Keyboard

Records can be scrolled in Form view using the following keyboard techniques:

- Page Down displays the next record.
- Page Up displays the previous record.
- Ctrl + End moves to the last field in the last record.
- Ctrl + Home moves to the first field in the first record.

Activity 1.6

Deleting Records in a Datasheet and Form

Records can be deleted in either Datasheet view or Form view. To delete a record, open the datasheet or form, activate any field in the record to be deleted, and then click the Delete button in the Records group in the Home tab. Access displays a message indicating the selected record will be permanently removed from the table. Click Yes to confirm the record deletion.

Project

Worldwide Enterprises

The Countryside Cinemas and Victory Cinemas distributor agreements have lapsed and you have just been informed that they have signed agreements with another movie distributing company. You will delete their records in the US_Distributors table using the datasheet and the form.

1. With the **WEDistributors1.accdb** database open, double-click *US_Distributors* in the *Tables* group of the Navigation pane.
2. Position the mouse pointer in the record selector bar (empty column to the left of *ID*) for record 3 until the pointer changes to a right-pointing black arrow and then click the left mouse button.

    This selects the entire record.

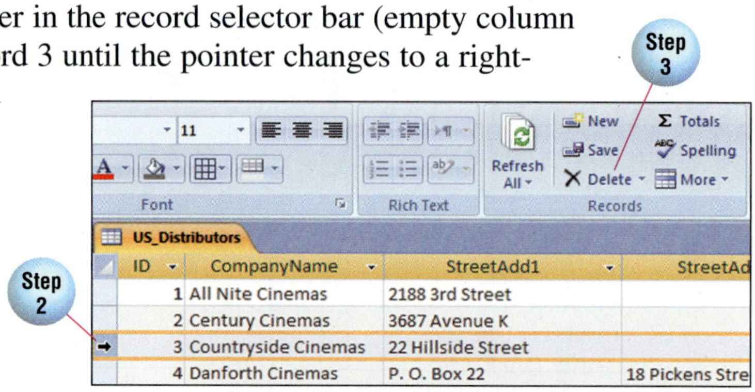

3. Click the Delete button Delete in the Records group in the Home tab.
4. Access displays a message box indicating you are about to delete 1 record and that the undo operation is not available after this action. Click Yes to confirm the deletion.

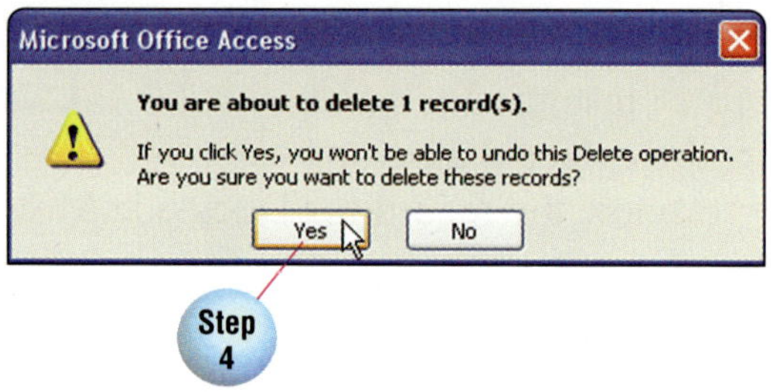

PROBLEM

Check that you are deleting the correct record before clicking Yes. Click No if you selected the wrong record by mistake.

5. Notice that Access does not renumber the remaining records in the *ID* field once record 3 has been deleted from the table.

    Once a number has been used for an *ID*, Access does not make the number available again for another record even after the record is deleted.

6. Close the US_Distributors table.
7. Open the US_Distributors form.
8. Click in the *CompanyName* field and then use the Find feature to locate the record for Victory Cinemas.
9. Close the Find and Replace dialog box when the record has been located.

10 Click the Delete button arrow in the Records group in the Home tab and then click *Delete Record* at the drop-down list.

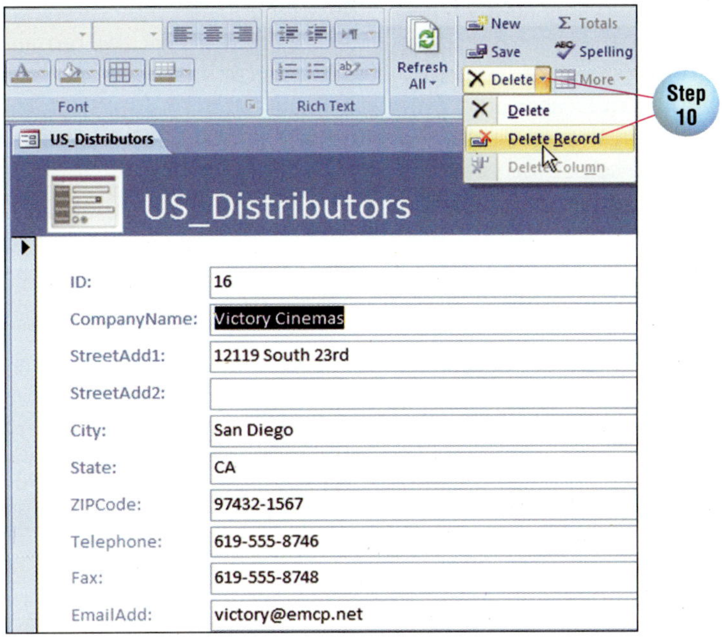

In Brief

Delete Record

1. Open table datasheet or form.
2. Make record to be deleted active.
3. Click Delete button.
4. Click Yes.

11 Click Yes to confirm the deletion.

12 Click the First record button in the Record Navigation bar to move the active record to All Nite Cinemas.

13 Click the Next record button in the Record Navigation bar twice to move the active record to Danforth Cinemas.

14 Notice the *ID* field value for Danforth Cinemas is *4* while the Record Navigation bar displays *3 of 21* in the *Current Record* text box.

Do not get confused between the record numbers in the navigation bar and the *ID* field values. They are separate identifiers. The *ID* field values are assigned as new records are added to the table. Deleting a record does not make the number available for use again. In other words, the field values in *ID* are not dynamic—they do not change once the number has been assigned in the field. The numbers in the navigation bar are dynamic and update to reflect the current number of records that exist in the table.

15 Close the US_Distributors form.

In Addition

More about Deleting Records

In a multiuser environment, deleting records is a procedure that should be performed only by authorized personnel; once the record is deleted, crucial data can be lost. It is a good idea to back up the database file before deleting records. Activity 1.11 on page 412 describes how to back up a database.

Activity 1.7

Sorting Records

Records in a table are displayed alphanumerically and sorted in ascending order by the primary key field values. To rearrange the order of the records, click in any record in the column you want to sort by and then click the Ascending or Descending buttons in the Sort & Filter group in the Home tab. To sort by more than one column, select the columns first and then click the Ascending or Descending button. Access sorts first by the leftmost column in the selection, then by the next column, and continues this pattern for the remainder of the sort keys. Columns can be moved in the datasheet if necessary to facilitate a multiple-column sort. Access saves the sort order when the table is closed.

Project

You will perform one sort routine using a single field and then perform a multiple-column sort. To do the multiple-column sort, you will have to move columns in the datasheet.

Worldwide Enterprises

1. With the **WEDistributors1.accdb** database open, open the US_Distributors table.
2. Click in any record in the *City* column.

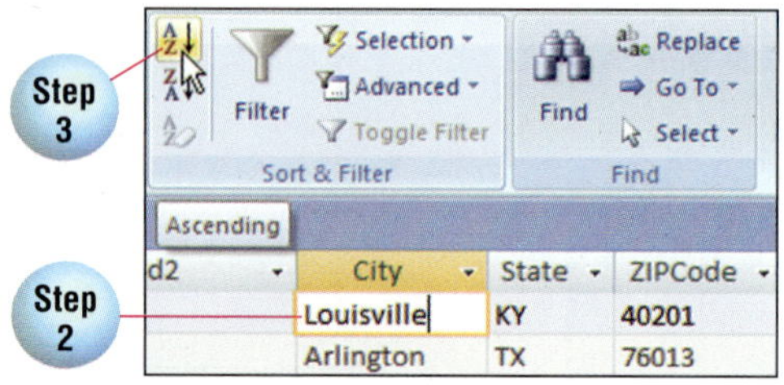

3. Click the Ascending button in the Sort & Filter group in the Home tab.

   The records are rearranged to display in order of the city names starting with *A* through *Z*.

4. Click the Descending button in the Sort & Filter group.

   The records are rearranged to display the cities starting with *Z* through *A*. Notice also that the *City* column heading displays with a downward pointing arrow to indicate the field that is being used to sort the datasheet in descending order. In Steps 5–9 you will move the *State* and *City* columns to the left of the *CompanyName* column to perform a multiple-column sort.

5. Position the mouse pointer in the *State* column heading until the pointer changes to a downward-pointing black arrow and then click the left mouse button.

   The selected *State* column can be moved by dragging the column heading to another position in the datasheet.

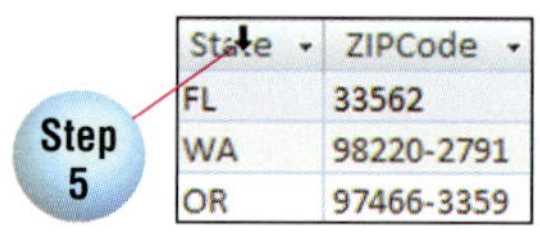

6. With the *State* column selected, move the pointer to the column heading *State* until the white arrow pointer appears.

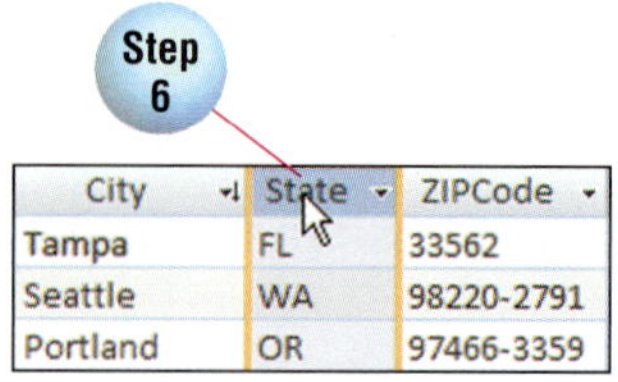

7. Hold down the left mouse button, drag the column between *ID* and *CompanyName*, and then release the mouse. *State* is now positioned before the *CompanyName* field in the datasheet.

   A thick black line appears between columns as you drag, indicating the position to which the column will be moved when you release the mouse. In addition, the pointer displays with the outline of a gray box attached to it, indicating you are performing a move operation.

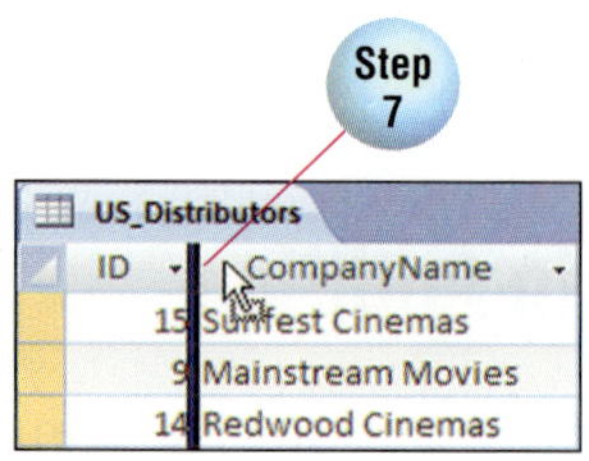

8. Click in any field to deselect the *State* column.
9. Move the *City* column between *State* and *CompanyName* by completing steps similar to those in Steps 5–8.

10 Position the mouse pointer in the *State* column heading until the pointer changes to a downward-pointing black arrow; hold down the left mouse button; drag right until the *State, City,* and *CompanyName* columns are selected; and then release the left mouse button.

Step 10

US_Distributors

ID	State	City	CompanyName
15	FL	Tampa	Sunfest Cinemas
9	WA	Seattle	Mainstream Movies
14	OR	Portland	Redwood Cinemas

11 Click the Ascending button and then click in any cell to deselect the three columns.

The records are sorted first by *State*, then by *City* within each State, and then by *CompanyName* within each City.

12 Look at the four records for the state of New York. Notice the order of the records is Waterfront Cinemas in Buffalo first, then Cinema Festival, Movie Emporium, and Westview Movies in New York City next.

US_Distributors

ID	State	City	CompanyName	StreetAdd1
7	AZ	Phoenix	LaVista Cinemas	111 Vista Road
10	CA	Los Angeles	Marquee Movies	1011 South Alameda Street
15	FL	Tampa	Sunfest Cinemas	
8	GA	Atlanta	Liberty Cinemas	P. O. Box 998
13	IL	Oak Park	O'Shea Movies	59 Erie
11	KS	Emporia	Midtown Moviehouse	1033 Commercial Street
1	KY	Louisville	All Nite Cinemas	2188 3rd Street
5	MA	Cambridge	Eastown Movie House	P. O. Box 429
20	MD	Baltimore	Dockside Movies	P. O. Box 224
21	MI	Detroit	Renaissance Cinemas	3599 Woodward Avenue
6	NJ	Baking Ridge	Hillman Cinemas	55 Kemble Avenue
17	NY	Buffalo	Waterfront Cinemas	P. O. Box 3255
23	NY	New York	Cinema Festival	318 East 11th Street
22	NY	New York	Movie Emporium	203 West Houston Street
19	NY	New York	Westview Movies	1112 Broadway
12	OH	Dublin	Mooretown Movies	P. O. Box 11
14	OR	Portland	Redwood Cinemas	P. O. Box 112F
18	PA	Philadelphia	Wellington 10	1203 Tenth Southwest
4	SC	Columbia	Danforth Cinemas	P. O. Box 22
2	TX	Arlington	Century Cinemas	3687 Avenue K
9	WA	Seattle	Mainstream Movies	P. O. Box 33

Step 12

13 Close the US_Distributors table. Click Yes when prompted to save the design changes.

In Brief

Sort Datasheet by Single Field

1. Open table.
2. Click in column by which to sort.
3. Click Ascending or Descending button.

Sort Datasheet by Multiple Fields

1. Open table.
2. If necessary, move columns to accommodate desired sort order.
3. Select columns from left to right in order of the sort.
4. Click Ascending or Descending button.

In Addition

More about Sorting

When you are ready to sort records, consider the following alphanumeric rules:

- Numbers stored in fields that are not defined as numeric (i.e., social security number or telephone number) are sorted as characters (not numeric values). To sort them as if they were numbers, all field values must be the same length.
- Records in which the selected field is empty are listed first.
- Numbers are sorted before letters.

Activity 1.8

Applying and Removing Filters

A *filter* is used to view only those records that meet specified criteria. The records that do not meet the filter criteria are hidden from view temporarily. Using a filter, you can view, edit, and/or print a subset of rows within the table. For example, you might want to view only those records of distributors in one state.

Project

You want to view a list of distributors in New York state and then further filter the list to display only those in the city of New York. In a second filter operation you will view the distributors located in California and Georgia.

Worldwide Enterprises

1. With **WEDistributors1.accdb** open, open the US_Distributors table.
2. Click the insertion point within any record in the *State* column.
3. Click the Filter button in the Sort & Filter group of the Home tab.

   A field is filtered by selecting criteria from a drop-down list. Access looks in the active column and includes in the filter list box each unique field value that exists within the column. Adjacent to each field value is a check box. Clear the check box for those states that you do not wish to view. When you click OK, only those records with a field value that match the states with a check mark retained in the check box are displayed; all other records are temporarily hidden.

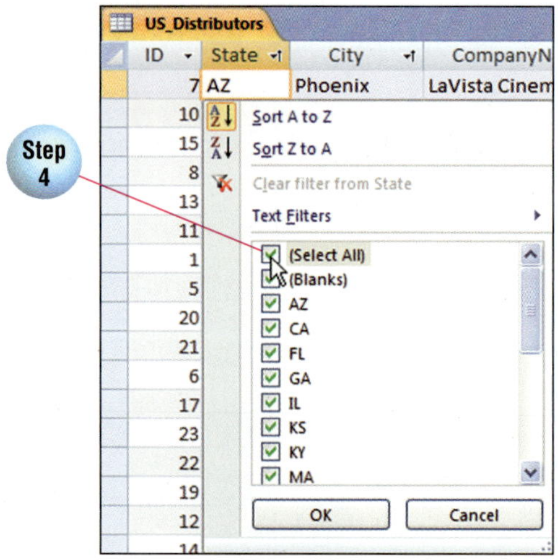

4. Click the *Select All* check box to clear the check marks from all of the check boxes.
5. Scroll down the filter list box, click the check box next to *NY*, and then click OK.

   The filter list box closes and only four records remain, as shown below. Notice the two icons next to *State* indicating the field is both filtered and sorted. Notice also the message *Filtered* displays in the Record Navigation bar. In the next step, you will further filter the records to display only those in New York City.

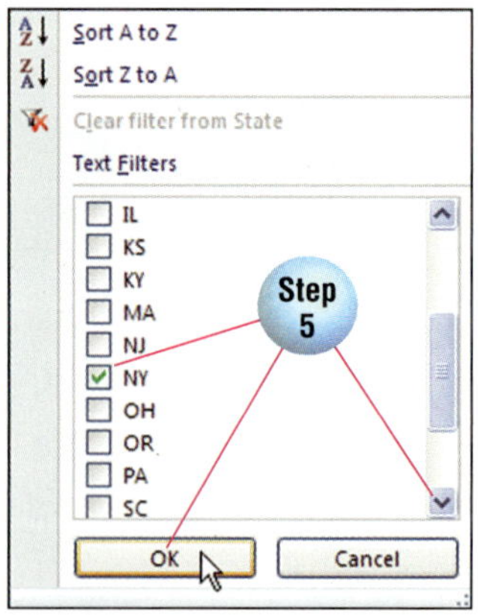

Only those records that meet the filter criterion, *State* is *NY*, are displayed in Step 5.

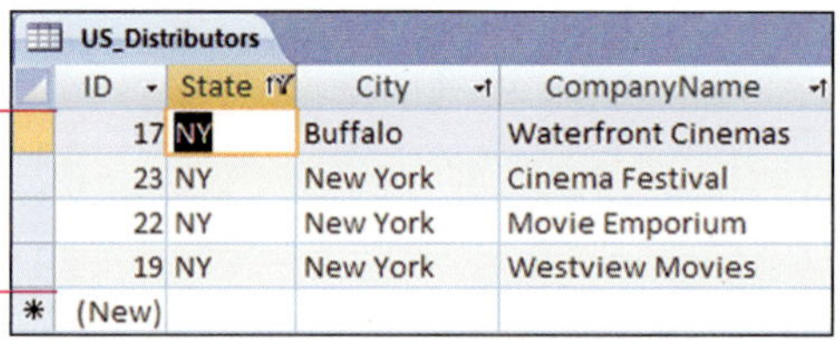

6. Click the filter arrow (displays as a down-pointing arrow) next to *City* to open the filter list box.

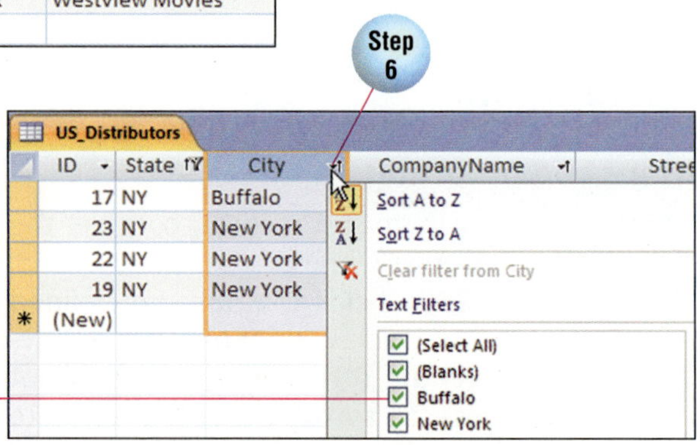

Clear this check box in Step 7.

7. Click the check box next to *Buffalo* to clear the check mark and then click OK.

   This action removes the record from the datasheet for the company located in Buffalo. Now only three records remain, as shown below.

The filtered datasheet is filtered again to show only those distributors in New York City in Step 7.

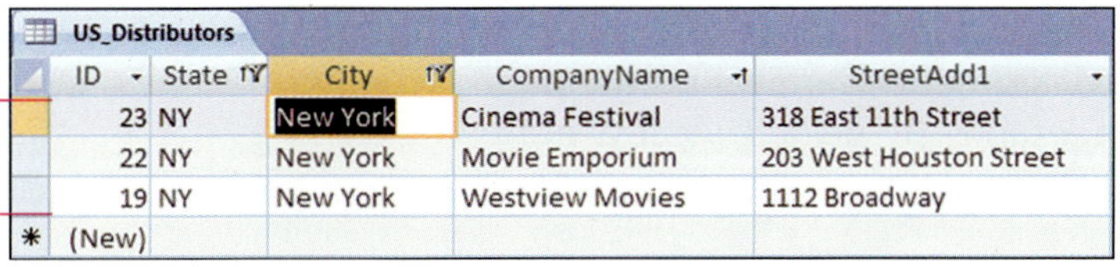

8. Click the Toggle Filter button **Toggle Filter** in the Sort & Filter group.

   When a filter has been applied to a datasheet, clicking Toggle Filter acts as the Remove Filter command. The Toggle Filter button switches between Apply Filter and Remove Filter, depending on the state of the datasheet. Notice all records are redisplayed in the datasheet. Notice also that the message in the Record Navigation bar has changed to *Unfiltered*.

9. Click the Advanced button in the Sort & Filter group of the Home tab.

10. Click *Filter By Form* at the drop-down list.

    All records are temporarily removed from the datasheet. Specify the field value in the field by which you want to filter by using the drop-down lists in the fields in the blank row. Access retains the most recent filter settings. In the next step, you will clear the previous settings so that you can begin a new filter.

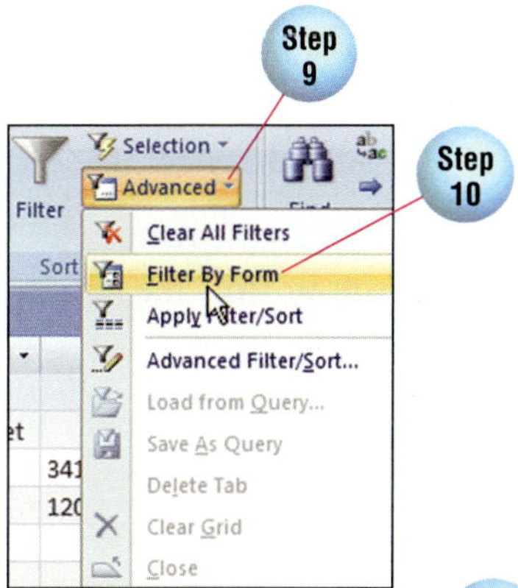

11. Click the Advanced button and then click *Clear Grid* at the drop-down list.

    This clears all previous filter options.

12. Click in the *State* column, click the down-pointing arrow that appears, and then click *CA* at the drop-down list.

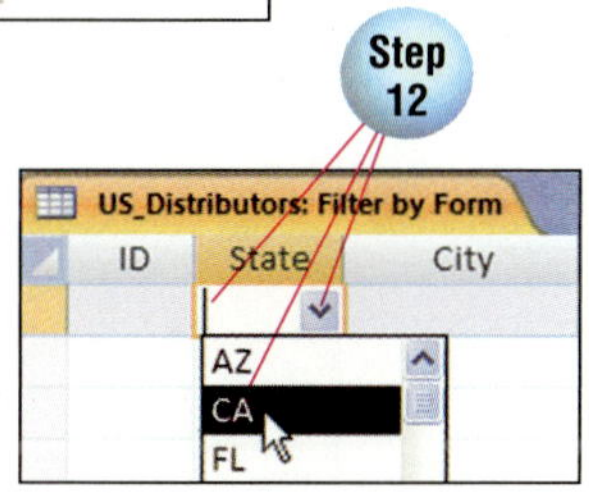

13. Click the Or tab located at the bottom of the datasheet.

    Using the Or tab you can filter by more than one state. A new blank form appears in which you specify a second filter criteria.

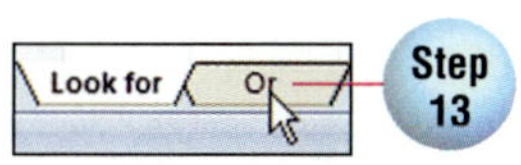

14. With *State* the active column, click the down-pointing arrow that appears and then click *GA*.

15. Click the Toggle Filter button (displays the ScreenTip Apply Filter) to apply the filter settings.

    Two records display in the filtered datasheet: Marquee Movies in Los Angeles, CA and Liberty Cinemas in Atlanta, GA.

16. Click the Toggle Filter button (displays the ScreenTip Remove Filter) to redisplay the entire datasheet.

17. Close the US_Distributors table. Click Yes when prompted to save the design changes.

In Brief

Filter Records

1. Open table.
2. Click in field by which to filter.
3. Click Filter button or click down-pointing arrow next to field name.
4. Clear check boxes for items you do not want to view.
5. Click OK.

Remove Filter

Click Toggle Filter button when datasheet is filtered.

Clear Filter Settings

1. Click Advanced button.
2. Click *Clear Grid*.

Activity 1.9

Previewing and Printing; Changing Margins and Page Orientation

Click the Print button on the Quick Access toolbar to print the table in Datasheet view. To avoid wasting paper, use Print Preview to view how the datasheet will appear on the page before you print a table. By default, Access prints a datasheet on letter size paper in portrait orientation. You can change the paper size, orientation, or margins using buttons in the Page Layout group in the Print Preview tab.

Project

Worldwide Enterprises

Sam Vestering has requested a list of the U.S. distributors. You will open the US_Distributors table, preview the printout, change the page orientation, change the left and right margins, and then print the datasheet.

1. With the **WEDistributors1.accdb** database open, open the US_Distributors table.
2. Click the Office button, point to *Print*, and then click *Print Preview* to display the datasheet in the Print Preview window shown in Figure 1.3.
3. Move the mouse pointer (displays as a magnifying glass) over the top center of the table and click the left mouse button.

   The zoom changes to 100% magnification. Notice that Access prints the table name at the top center and the current date at the top right of the page. At the bottom center, Access prints the word *Page* followed by the current page number.
4. Click the left mouse button again to zoom the datasheet back to fit the current page within the window.
5. Click the Next Page button located on the Navigation bar at the bottom left of the Print Preview window two times.

FIGURE 1.3 Print Preview Window

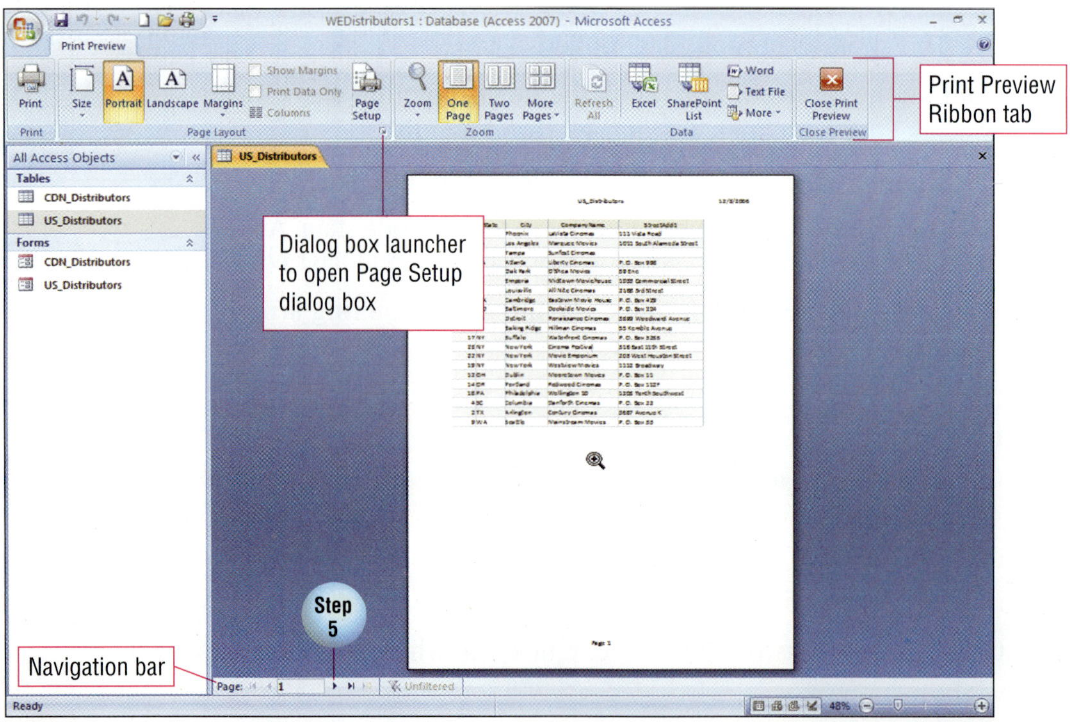

The US_Distributors table requires three pages to print with the default margins and orientation. In the next step, you will change the orientation to landscape to see if all of the columns will fit on one page.

6. Click the Landscape button in the Page Layout group in the Print Preview tab.

   Landscape orientation rotates the printout to print wider than it is tall. Changing to landscape allows more columns to fit on a page.

7. Look at the page number in the Navigation bar at the bottom of the Print Preview window. Notice that the page number is now 2. In landscape orientation, the US_Distributors table still needs two pages to print.

   Another method to fit more text on a page is to reduce the margins. In the next step, you will try reducing the left and right margins to see the effect on the number of pages.

8. Click the Margins button in the Page Layout group and then review the predefined margin options in the drop-down list.

   You decide you want to set your own custom margins since none of the predefined margin settings meet your needs.

9. Click outside the drop-down list to remove it and then click the Page Setup button in the Page Layout group.

10. At the Page Setup dialog box with the Print Options tab active, drag across *1* in the *Left* text box and then type **0.25**.

11. Press Tab, type **0.25** in the *Right* text box, and then click OK.

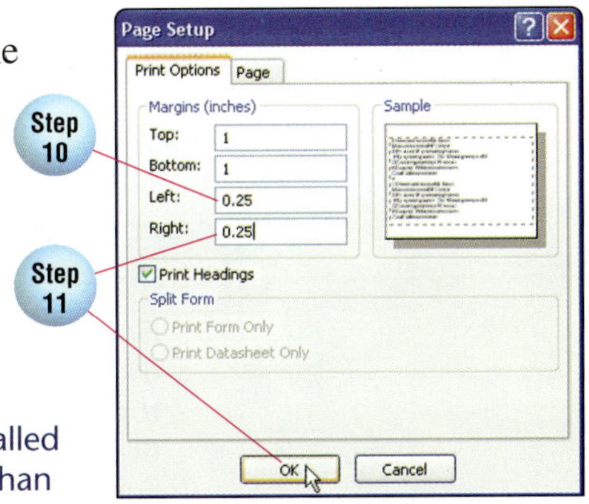

12. Click the Print button in the Print group and then click OK at the Print dialog box.

    In a few seconds the table will print on the default printer installed on your computer. Making the left and right margins smaller than 0.25 inch would still not allow the entire datasheet to fit on one page. In Section 3, titled "Creating Queries, Forms, and Reports," you will learn how to create a report for a table. Using a report you can control the data layout on the page and which columns are printed.

13. Click the Close Print Preview button in the Close Preview group.

14. Close the US_Distributors table.

In Brief

Change to Landscape Orientation

1. Display datasheet in Print Preview window.
2. Click Landscape button.
3. Click Close Print Preview button.

Set Custom Margins

1. Display datasheet in Print Preview window.
2. Click Page Setup button in Page Layout group.
3. Change margins to desired settings.
4. Click OK.

In Addition

Previewing Multiple Pages

Use buttons in the Preview group of the Print Preview tab to view a datasheet that requires multiple pages all in one window. Click the Two Pages button to view the datasheet with two pages side-by-side. Click the More pages button and then choose from *Four Pages*, *Eight Pages*, or *Twelve Pages* at the drop-down list. The US_Distributors datasheet is shown with multiple pages set to *Four Pages* at the right.

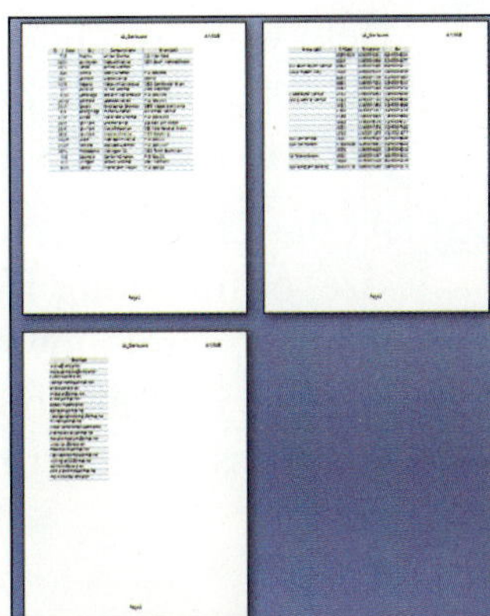

Activity 1.10

Using Help; Hiding Columns in a Datasheet

An extensive online Help resource is available that contains information on Access features and commands. Click the Microsoft Office Access Help button located near the upper right corner of the screen (below the Close button on the Title bar) to open the Access Help window. By default, the Help feature searches for an Internet connection. A message at the bottom right corner of the window reads *Connected to Office Online* when an Internet connection is found. Help information is available without Internet access; however, fewer resources display for help topics when using the Offline Help file.

Project

Worldwide Enterprises

After printing the US_Distributors table, you decide that you do not need to see the *ID* and *EmailAdd* columns on the printout. You will use the Help feature to learn how to format the datasheet and then reprint the table with two of the field columns hidden.

Note: The following steps assume you are connected to the Internet to access Office Online.

1. With the **WEDistributors1.accdb** database open, open the US_Distributors table.
2. Click the Microsoft Office Access Help button located near the upper right corner of the screen (below the Close button on the Title bar).

   Find information in Help resources by clicking links to categories of Help topics in the main Access Help window or by typing a search word or phrase and then clicking the Search button.

3. At the main Access Help window, click *Tables* located in the first column in the *Browse Access Help* list.
4. At the Tables Help window, click *Fonts and formatting* in the *Subcategories of "Tables"* list.
5. At the Fonts and formatting Help window, click *Change the font, font size, or font color* in the Topics list.
6. At the Change the font, font size, or font color Help window, scroll down and read the information related to Access on how to change the font size.

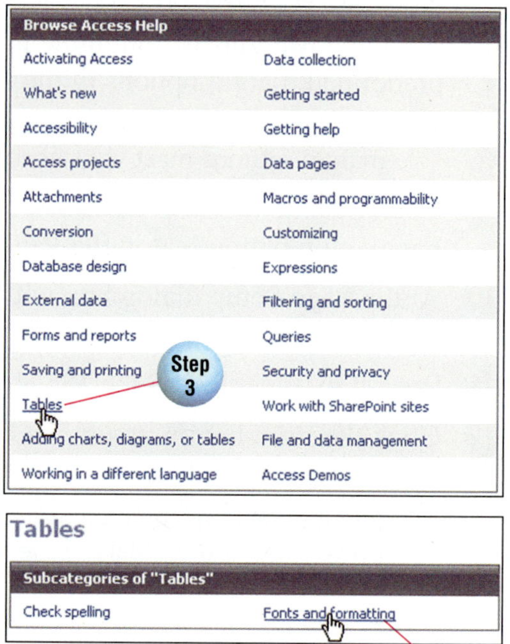

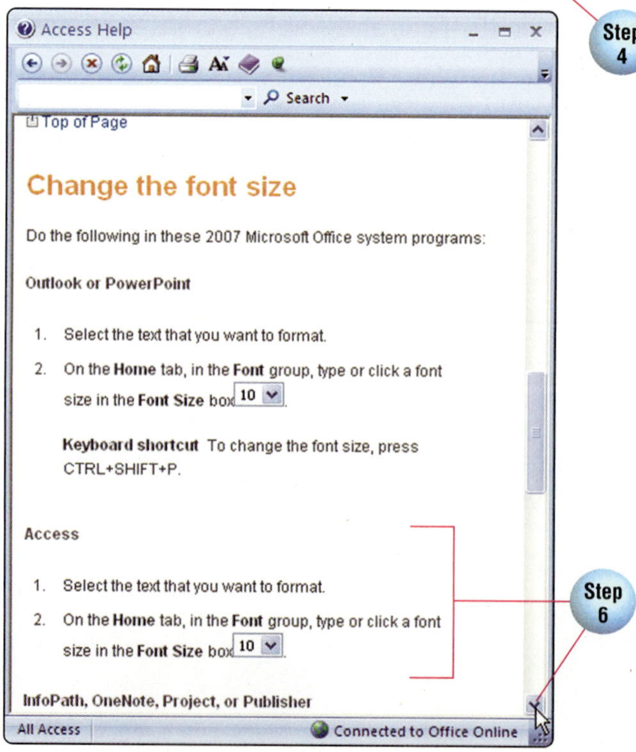

7. Click in the Search text box located at the top of the Access Help window below the toolbar, type **keyboard shortcuts**, and then click the Search button.

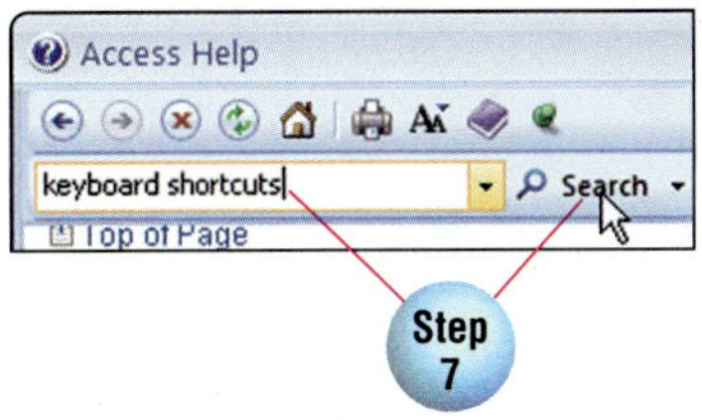

Now that you know how to change the font size for records, you want to find a quick way to select all of the records in the datasheet. Using Help you will find out if there is a keyboard shortcut to select all of the records.

8. Click *Keyboard shortcuts for Access* in the Results list.

9. At the Keyboard shortcuts for Access Help window, scroll down and then click *Select text and data* in the *Keys for working with text and data* section.

10. Click *Selecting a field or record* in the expanded list of topics.

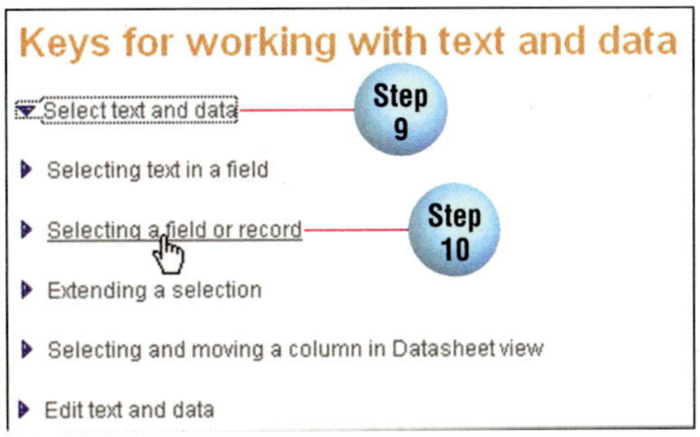

11. Read the descriptions and keyboard shortcuts in the table that is displayed. Notice the keyboard shortcut for the last option, *Select all records*, is *Ctrl + A* or *Ctrl + Shift + Spacebar*.

12. Close the Help window.

13. At the US_Distributors datasheet, press Ctrl + A to select all records.

14. Click the Font Size button arrow in the Home tab and then click *10* at the drop-down list.

15. Click in any field to deselect the records.

16. Right-click the *ID* field name at the top of the column and then click *Hide Columns* at the shortcut menu.

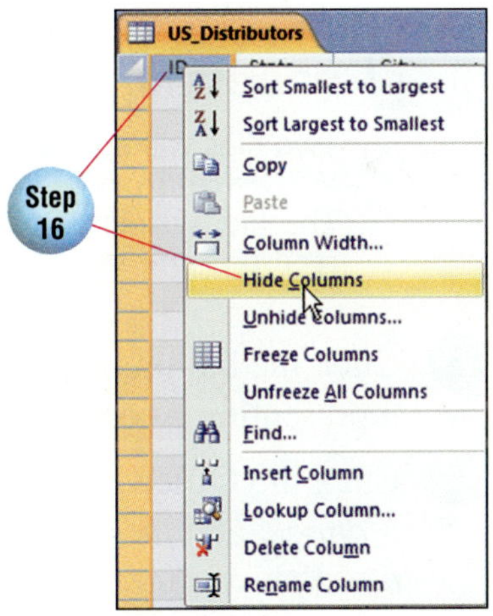

17. Scroll the datasheet right, right-click the *EmailAdd* field name, and then click *Hide Columns* at the shortcut menu.

18. Display the datasheet in Print Preview.

19. Change the orientation to landscape and set the left and right margins to 0.5 inch.

20. Print the datasheet.

21. Close the Print Preview window and then close the US_Distributors table. Click Yes when prompted to save the layout changes.

In Brief

Use Help Resources

1. Click Microsoft Office Access Help button.
2. Type term, phrase, or question.
3. Click Search button.
4. Click topic from Results list.
5. If necessary, continue selecting topics or hyperlinks.
6. Close Access Help window.

Activity 1.11

Compacting and Repairing a Database; Backing Up a Database

Once you have been working with a database file for a period of time, the data can become fragmented because of records and objects that have been deleted. The disk space that the database uses may be larger than is necessary. Compacting the database defragments the file and reduces the required disk space. Compacting and repairing a database also ensures optimal performance while using the file. The database can be set to compact automatically each time the file is closed. Regular backups of a database should be maintained to protect a business from data loss and to provide a historical record of tables before records are added, deleted, or modified. Access includes a backup utility to facilitate this process.

Project

Worldwide Enterprises

You decide to compact the WEDistributors1 database and then turn on the Compact on Close option so that the database is compacted automatically each time the file is closed. You will also create a backup copy of the database.

1. With the **WEDistributors1.accdb** database open, click the Minimize button on the Microsoft Access Title bar to reduce Access to a button on the Taskbar.
2. Open a My Computer window and then navigate to the drive and AccessS1 folder in which the student data files are stored. (This is the location from which you opened the **WEDistributors1** database.)
3. If necessary, change to the Tiles view by clicking View and then *Tiles* at the drop-down menu.
4. Locate the file **WEDistributors1.accdb** and then write down the file size in kilobytes (KB) of the database.

   File size = ________________

PROBLEM

Two files will appear in the file list: **WEDistributors1.accdb** and **WEDistributors1.laccdb**. Notice the *.laccdb* displays with a lock icon. This file is used to lock records so that two users cannot request the same record at the same time.

5. Click the button on the Taskbar representing Access.
6. Click the Office button, point at *Manage*, and then click *Compact and Repair Database*.

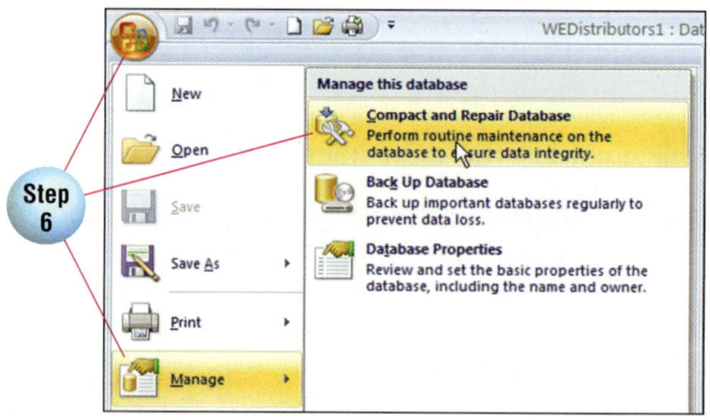

7. Click the button on the Taskbar representing the AccessS1 folder in My Computer.
8. Write down the new file size of **WEDistributors1.accdb**. Notice that the amount of disk space used for the database is lower.

   File size = ________________

9. Close the My Computer window.

   In the next steps, you will set the database to compact automatically each time you close the file.

10 With the **WEDistributors1.accdb** database open, click the Office button and then click the Access Options button [Access Options] located near the bottom right of the drop-down list.

11 Click *Current Database* in the left pane, click the *Compact on Close* check box in the *Application Options* section, and then click OK.

12 Click OK at the message that appears that you must close and reopen the current database for the option to take effect.

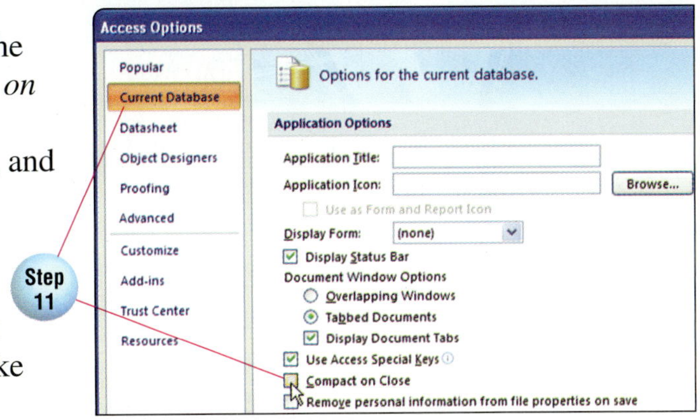

13 Click the Office button, point at *Manage*, and then click *Back Up Database*.

14 At the Save As dialog box, click the Save button to accept the default settings.

By default, Access saves the backup copy of the database using the original file name with the current date appended to the end of the name after an underscore character. The backup copy is stored in the same location as the original database unless you change the drive and/or folder before saving. You can move the file after it has been created to an archive storage medium such as a CD-R.

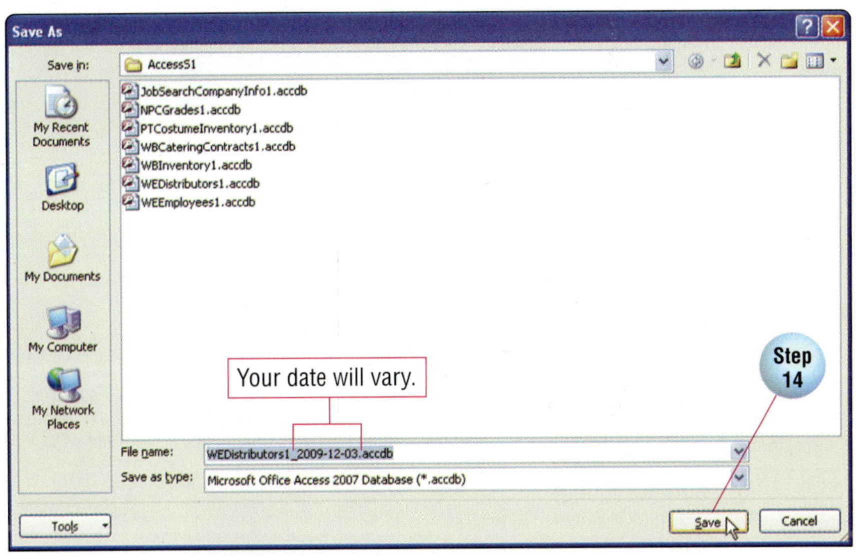

15 Close the **WEDistributors1.accdb** database.

In Brief

Compact and Repair Database

1. Click Office button.
2. Point to *Manage*.
3. Click *Compact and Repair Database*.

Turn on Compact on Close Option

1. Click Office button.
2. Click Access Options button.
3. Click *Current Database*.
4. Click *Compact on Close*.
5. Click OK.

Back Up Database

1. Click Office button.
2. Point to *Manage*.
3. Click *Back Up Database*.
4. Click Save.

In Addition

Database Properties

The Database Properties dialog box (shown at the right) can be used to store additional information about the database. For example, you could add information in the *Comments* text box about the data history in the backup copy of a database. To do this, open the backup copy of the database, click the Office button, point to *Manage*, and then click *Database Properties*.

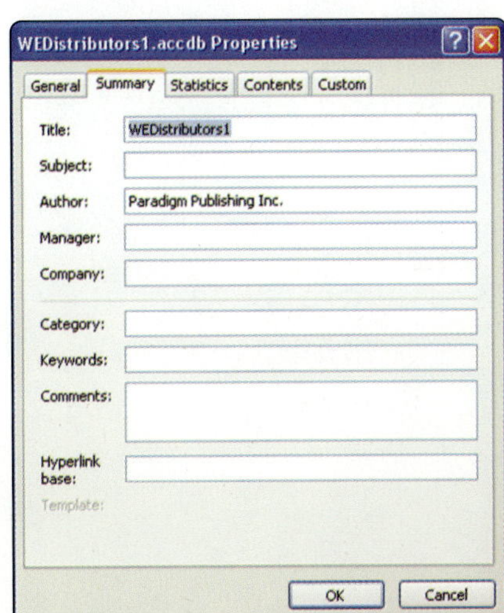

Features Summary

Feature	Ribbon Tab, Group	Button	Quick Access Toolbar	Office Button Drop-down List	Keyboard Shortcut
add records	Home, Records	New OR			Ctrl + +
back up database				Manage, Back Up Database	
change font size	Home, Font	11			
change margins	Print Preview, Page Layout	OR to open Page Setup			
column width	Home, Records	More			
compact and repair database				Manage, Compact and Repair Database	
delete records	Home, Records	Delete			Delete
filter	Home, Sort & Filter				
Find	Home, Find				Ctrl + F
Help					F1
landscape orientation	Print Preview, Page Layout				
print				Print	Ctrl + P
Print Preview				Print, Print Preview	
save					Ctrl + S
select all records	Home, Find	Select			Ctrl + A
sort ascending order	Home, Sort & Filter				
sort descending order	Home, Sort & Filter				

Knowledge Check

Completion: In the space provided at the right, indicate the correct term, command, or option.

1. This term describes a single component of information about a person, place, item, or object. ________________
2. This object stores all of the related records for one logical group. ________________
3. Click this button at the Column Width dialog box to set the column width to the length of the longest entry in the column. ________________
4. Press this key to turn on Edit mode in a datasheet. ________________
5. Use either of these two keys to move to the next column when typing data in a new record in the datasheet. ________________
6. This object provides a user-friendly interface with which you can edit, view, or print data by working with only one record at a time. ________________
7. Access displays a message box requesting confirmation when a record is about to be deleted because this feature is not available for a Delete operation. ________________
8. When more than one column is selected for a sort operation, Access sorts first by this column. ________________
9. This feature temporarily hides records in the datasheet that do not meet the specified criteria. ________________
10. This page layout orientation rotates the printout to print wider than it is tall. ________________
11. Display this dialog box to set your own custom margins. ________________
12. This keyboard command selects all records in the datasheet. ________________
13. These are the steps to hide a column in a datasheet. ________________
14. This feature defragments a database file to reduce the disk space the database requires. ________________
15. When backing up a database, if you accept the default options at the Save As dialog box, this is added to the end of the original database file name to differentiate the backup file. ________________

Skills Review

Review 1 Adjusting Column Widths; Finding and Editing Records; Adding and Deleting Records

Worldwide Enterprises

1. Start Access and open the **WEEmployees1.accdb** database. Enable content by clicking the Options button in the Security Warning message bar, clicking *Enable this content* and then OK.
2. Open the Employees table.
3. Adjust all columns to Best Fit.
4. Find the record for Carl Zakowski and then change the birth date from *5/9/1967* to *12/12/1977*.
5. Find the record for Roman Deptulski and then change the salary from *$69,725.00* to *$75,400.00*. ***Note: You do not need to type the dollar symbol, comma, and decimal.***
6. Find the record for Terry Yiu and then change the hire date from *4/12/2001* to *8/11/2006*.
7. Delete the record for Valerie Fistouris.

8. Delete the record for Edward Thurston.
9. Add the following employees to the table using the datasheet. ***Note: In this table* Employee_No *is not an AutoNumberField; therefore, you will need to type the numbers in the first field.***

1085	**1090**	**1095**
Yousef J Armine	**Maria D Quinte**	**Patrick J Kilarney**
11/19/1984	**4/16/1981**	**2/27/1981**
3/14/2009	**11/29/2009**	**12/12/2009**
European Distribution	**Overseas Distribution**	**North American Distribution**
$47,125	**$44,380**	**$42,796**

10. Close the Employees table. Click Yes when prompted to save changes.

Review 2 Sorting; Filtering; Previewing; Changing Page Orientation; Printing; Hiding Columns; Compacting and Backing Up a Database

1. With **WEEmployees1.accdb** open, open the Employees table.
2. Sort the table in ascending order by *Last_Name*.
3. Sort the table in descending order by *Annual_Salary*.
4. Sort the table in ascending order first by *Department* and then by *Last_Name*.
5. Preview the table in the Print Preview window.
6. Change the orientation to landscape, the left and right margins to 0.5 inch, and then print the datasheet.
7. Filter the table to display only those employees who work in the European Distribution department.
8. Hide the *Employee_No* column.
9. Print the datasheet and then close the Employees table. Click Yes when prompted to save changes.
10. Compact and repair the **WEEmployees1.accdb** database.
11. Turn on the Compact on Close feature at the Access Options dialog box.
12. Use the Back Up Database feature to create a copy of the database using the default Save As options.
13. Close the **WEEmployees1.accdb** database.

Skills Assessment

Assessment 1 Adjusting Column Width; Finding and Editing Records; Using Print Preview; Printing; Compact on Close

1. Jai Prasad, instructor in the Theatre Arts Division, has been called out of town to attend a family matter. The grades for SM100-01 have to be entered into the database by the end of today. Jai has provided you with the following grades:

Terry Yiu	A+	Kevin Gibson	C
Maren Bastow	C	Ash Bhullar	A
Martine Gagne	B	Bruce Morgan	B
Armado Ennis	D	Russell Clements	A
Bentley Woollatt	B	Richard Loewen	F
Susan Retieffe	C		

2. Open the **NPCGrades1.accdb** database and enable content at the Security Warning message bar.
3. Open the SM100-01_Grades table.
4. Adjust column widths to Best Fit.
5. Enter the grades provided in Step 1 in the appropriate records.
6. Preview and then print the table.
7. Close the SM100-01_Grades table. Click Yes when prompted to save changes.
8. Turn on the Compact on Close feature.
9. Close the **NPCGrades1.accdb** database.

Assessment 2 Finding, Adding, and Deleting Records; Formatting Datasheet; Compact on Close

1. Dana Hirsch, manager, has ordered three new inventory items and decided to discontinue three others. Dana has asked you to update the inventory database.
2. Open the **WBInventory1.accdb** database and enable content at the Security Warning message bar.
3. Open the Inventory_List table.
4. Locate and then delete the inventory items *Pita Wraps*, *Tuna*, and *Lake Erie Perch*.
5. Add the following new records to the Inventory_List table.

ItemNo	**ItemDescription**	**Unit**	**SupplierCode**
051	**Atlantic Scallops**	**case**	**9**
052	**Lake Trout**	**case**	**9**
053	**Panini Rolls**	**flat**	**1**

6. Adjust all column widths to Best Fit.
7. Change the font size for all records to 10.
8. Preview the table in Print Preview and adjust the top and/or bottom margin settings until all of the records will print on one page and then print the table and close Print Preview.
9. Close the Inventory_List table. Click Yes when prompted to save changes.
10. Turn on the Compact on Close feature.
11. Close the **WBInventory1.accdb** database.

Assessment 3 Finding, Sorting, Filtering, and Deleting Records; Compact on Close

1. You are the assistant to Bobbie Sinclair, business manager. You have just been informed that several costumes in the rental inventory have been destroyed in a fire at an offsite location. These costumes will have to be written off since the insurance policy does not cover them when they are out on rental. After updating the costume inventory, you will print two datasheets.
2. Open the **PTCostumeInventory1.accdb** database and enable content at the Security Warning message bar.
3. Open the CostumeInventory table and then adjust all column widths to Best Fit.
4. Locate and then delete the records for the following costumes that were destroyed in a fire at a Shakespearean festival:

Macbeth	Othello
Lady Macbeth	King Lear
Hamlet	Richard III

5. Sort the table in ascending order by *CostumeTitle*.
6. Preview the table, adjust margins so that all data fits on one page, and then print the table.
7. Sort the table in ascending order first by *Date Out*, then by *Date In*, and then by *CostumeTitle*.
8. Filter the table so that only those records that were rented out on *10/1/2009* are displayed.
9. Print the filtered list.
10. Redisplay all records.
11. Close the CostumeInventory table. Click Yes when prompted to save changes.
12. Turn on the Compact on Close feature.
13. Close the **PTCostumeInventory1.accdb** database.

Assessment 4 Backing Up a Database; Compact on Close

1. You have been reading articles on disaster recovery planning in a computer-related periodical. Cal Rubine, chair of the Theatre Arts Division, has advised you that the department does not currently have an up-to-date recovery plan for the information systems and has asked you to begin researching best practices. In the meantime, you decide that the grades database needs to be backed up immediately.
2. Open the **NPCGrades1.accdb** database and enable content at the Security Warning message bar.
3. Create a backup copy of the database using the default options at the Save As dialog box.
4. Close the **NPCGrades1.accdb** database.
5. Open the backup copy of the **NPCGrades1.accdb** database and enable all content.
6. Open and view each table to ensure the data was copied correctly.
7. Turn on the Compact on Close feature.
8. Close the backup copy of the **NPCGrades1.accdb** database.

Assessment 5 Finding Information on Designing a Database

HELP

1. Open an Access Help window and then use the following navigation guidelines to find information on the steps involved in designing a database.
   a. Click *Database design* in the *Browse Access Help* list.
   b. Click *Database design basics* in the *Database design* Topics list.
   c. Scroll down and read the information in the sections titled *What is good database design?* and *The design process*.
2. The help information for the design process lists several basic steps that should be followed when designing a database. Read the information presented in the first four bullets.
3. Use Microsoft Word to create a memo to your instructor as follows:
   - Use one of the memo templates.
   - Include an opening paragraph describing the body of the memo.
   - List all of the basic steps to designing a database in a bulleted list.
   - Briefly describe the first four steps. ***Note: Copying and pasting the text from the Help window is not acceptable—describe the four steps using your own words.***
4. Save the memo in Word and name it **AccessS1-A5Memo**.
5. Print and close **AccessS1-A5Memo.docx** and then exit Word.

Assessment 6 Creating a Job Search Company Database

1. You are starting to plan ahead for your job search after graduation. You decide to maintain a database of company information in Access.
2. Search the Internet for at least eight companies in your field of study (four out of state or out of province.) Include company name, address, telephone and fax numbers, and a contact person in their human resources department, if possible.
3. Open the **JobSearchCompanyInfo1.accdb** database.
4. Open the CompanyInformation table.
5. Enter at least eight records for the companies you researched on the Internet.
6. Adjust column widths as necessary.
7. Sort the records in ascending order by the *CompanyName* field.
8. Preview the table. Format all records to a smaller font size, hide the *ID* and *Fax* columns, and then change page layout options as necessary so that the entire table will fit on one page.
9. Print and then close the CompanyInformation table.
10. Turn on the Compact on Close feature.
11. Close the **JobSearchCompanyInfo1.accdb** database.

Marquee Challenge

Challenge 1 Updating and Printing a Catering Event Database

1. Dana Hirsch, manager, has given you information related to five new catering events that were recently booked at the bistro. Dana would like you to update the catering database and produce two reports.
2. Open **WBCateringContracts1.accdb** and enable content.
3. Open the CateringContracts table and then add the following information. Dana advises that deposits have been received for all of these events. The columns in the table that have check boxes displayed are defined as a Yes/No field. In these columns, click to insert a check mark in the box indicating "Yes"; otherwise leave the check box empty to indicate "No".

Name	Phone	Event	Date	Room	Guests	Charge	Special Menu
Cora Spriet	905-555-1623	Wedding	8/8/2009	Westview	150	26.95	Yes
Sean Vezina	716-555-3846	Business Meeting	8/12/2009	Starlake	24	23.75	No
William Graham	716-555-8694	25th Wedding Anniversary	8/15/2009	Sunset	80	24.95	No
Helena Kosjovic	716-555-3441	Engagement Brunch	8/16/2009	Sunset	56	22.95	No
Pieter Borman	716-555-6994	Business Meeting	8/22/2009	Starlake	41	24.95	Yes

4. Jack Torrance has called and cancelled his business meeting on May 15. Delete the record.
5. Dana has updated the charge for the Pavelich wedding to 33.50 per person.

6. Dana would like a report that is sorted by the room booked first and then by the last name. Make sure the data is entirely visible in all columns and that the printout is only 1 page. For this report Dana does not need to see the *ID* or the *ContactPhone* fields.
7. Dana needs a second report that prints only the events booked in the Westview room. You can use the same print settings for this report as for the previous report.
8. Close the CateringContracts table saving design changes.
9. Close the **WBCateringContracts1.accdb** database.

Challenge 2 Determining Fields and Table Names for a New Database

Performance Threads

1. Bobbie Sinclair, business manager, is considering having you create a new database to store the custom costume business at Performance Threads. Bobbie has jotted down rough notes regarding the information to be stored in the new database in Table 1.4.
2. Using Microsoft Word, create a document that provides the proposed field names and table names for each table. Incorporate the information in the additional notes as you develop the tables. As you create this document, consider the following two database design practices:
   - The use of spaces in field names or table names is discouraged.
   - Within each table, one field must contain unique identifying information.
3. At this stage of the design process, you are only considering the breakdown of fields to accommodate the information in Table 1.4. Other elements of the table and database design such as data type, properties, and relationships will be added in a challenge project for Section 2.
4. Save the Word document and name it **AccessS1-C2**.
5. Print and then close the document

TABLE 1.4 Challenge 2

Customer Information	**Order Information**
Customer's name, address, contact telephone numbers	Description of costume Customer for whom costume is being made Contract price Date due Seamstress Estimated hours for each of the main cost centers: Research, Design, Production Deposit amount received in advance
Contract Seamstresses Name, address, and contact telephone numbers for seamstresses on contract with Performance Threads	**Ship To Information** Customer Costume Address for delivery of costume Shipping company Shipping charge
Additional notes: Costumes are quoted a contract price which the customer accepts in advance by signing a contract document. The signed document must be on file before work begins. The hours for the three cost centers are estimated at the time of the quote. Bobbie wants to use the database to also enter actual hours after the costume is complete to generate hours variance reports.	

Access SECTION 2

Creating Tables and Relationships

Skills

- Create a table by adding records
- Change field names
- Insert and modify fields in Design view
- Create a table using Design view
- Set the primary key for a table
- Limit the number of characters allowed in a field
- Enter a default value in a field
- Verify data entry using a validation rule
- Restrict data entered into a field using an input mask
- Set the format for displaying data
- Create a Lookup list in a field
- Move and delete fields
- Format a datasheet
- Create a one-to-many relationship between two tables
- Edit relationship options
- Create a one-to-one relationship between two tables
- Print a relationship report
- Display records from a related table in a subdatasheet

Student Resources

Before beginning this section:

1. Copy to your storage medium the AccessS2 subfolder from the Access folder on the Student Resources CD.
2. Make AccessS2 the active folder.

In addition to containing the data files needed to complete section work, the Student Resources CD contains model answers in PDF format for each of the projects in this section; model answers for end-of-section activities are not provided.

Projects Overview

Worldwide Enterprises: Create and modify tables to store employee absences, employee benefit information, and annual employee review and professional development days; format a datasheet; create relationships between the tables and view and edit records from a related table in a subdatasheet. Review tables in an existing database and improve the table design.

Niagara Peninsula College: Create a table to store student grades for a course in the Theatre Arts Division.

The Waterfront B·I·S·T·R·O: Create a new database to store local event information.

First Choice Travel: Create a new database to store employee expense claims.

Performance Threads: Modify and correct field properties in a costume inventory table to improve the design. Continue design work on a new database for custom costume activities and then create the database tables and relationships.

Activity 2.1

Creating a Table by Adding Records

Creating a new table generally involves the following steps: entering field names, assigning a data type to each field, modifying properties, designating the primary key, and naming the table object. All of the preceding steps are part of a process referred to as "defining the table ***structure***." Fields comprise the structure of a table. To simplify the process, a new table can be created by simply typing new records into a blank datasheet. Access sets a data type for each field based on the type of data entered into each column. For example, a column that contains dates is automatically assigned the Date/Time data type. You will learn more about data types in Activity 2.3.

Project

Worldwide Enterprises

Rhonda Trask, human resources manager for Worldwide Enterprises, has asked you to create a new table in the employees database in which to store the days each employee is absent from work and the reason for each absence. You decide to create the table by adding a few sample records to create the required fields and field names.

1. Open **WEEmployees2.accdb** and enable content.
2. Click the Create tab in the ribbon.
3. Click the Table button in the Tables group.

   A blank datasheet appears. Notice the column with the field name *ID* has been created automatically. Access creates *ID* as an AutoNumber field in which the field value is assigned automatically by Access as you enter each record.

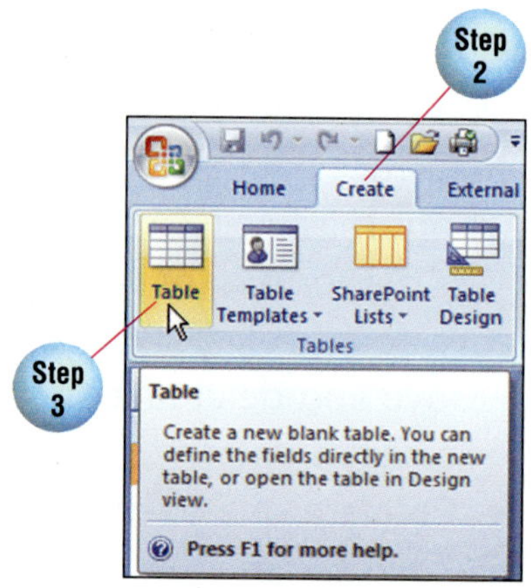

4. Type **Sam** and then press Tab or Enter to move to the next column.
5. Type **Vestering** and then press Tab or Enter.
6. Type **October 2, 2009** and then press Tab or Enter.

   Access converts the date you entered to the format m/d/yyyy. When entering dates, be careful to use the proper punctuation and spacing between the month, day, and year so that Access recognizes the entry as a valid date.

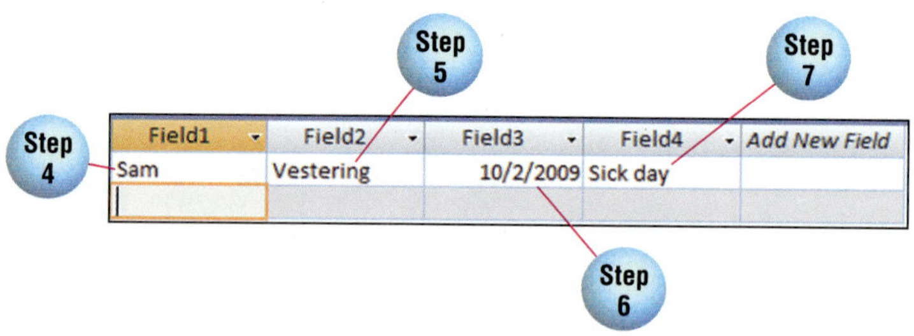

7. Type **Sick day** and then press Tab or Enter.
8. Press Enter to end the record in the *Add New Field* column and then press Enter in the second row to move to *Field1* after *ID*.

9. Type the data in the next two rows as shown at the right.

   A new feature in Access 2007 is the Date button that appears whenever a date field is being edited. As an alternative to typing a date, click the Date button and then select the correct date from the drop-down calendar.

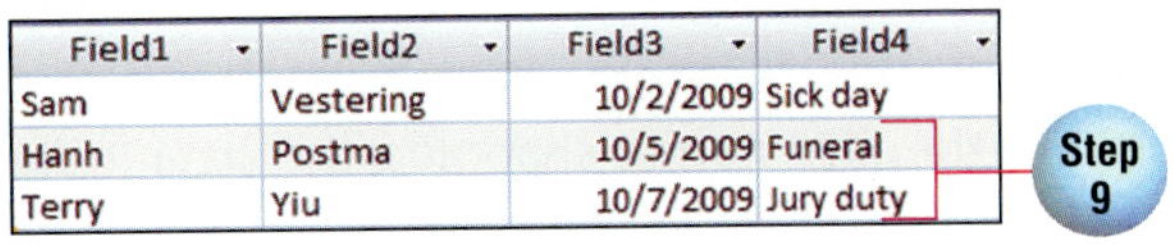

10. Move the mouse pointer over the column heading *Field1* and then double-click to select the column heading.

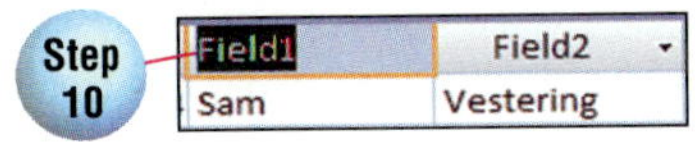

11. Type **First_Name** and then press Enter.

    This changes the field name for the first column from *Field1* to *First_Name*.

12. Double-click *Field2*, type **Last_Name**, and then press Enter.
13. Double-click *Field3*, type **Absent_Date**, and then press Enter.
14. Double-click *Field4*, type **Absence_Reason**, and then click in any field.

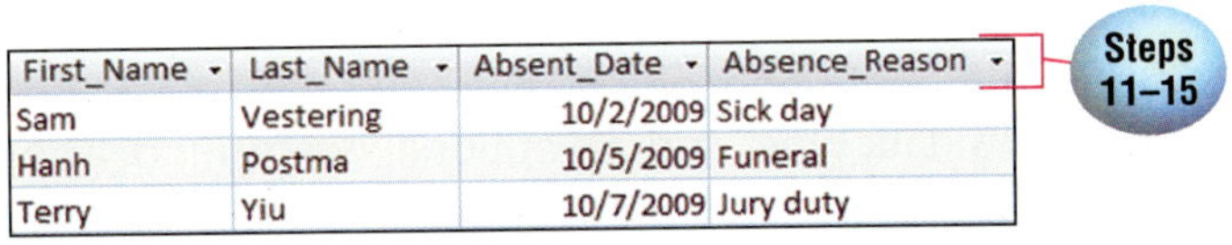

15. Best Fit the *Absent_Date* and *Absence_Reason* columns.
16. Click the Save button on the Quick Access toolbar.
17. At the Save As dialog box with *Table1* selected in the *Table Name* text box, type **Absence_Rpts** and then press Enter or click OK.

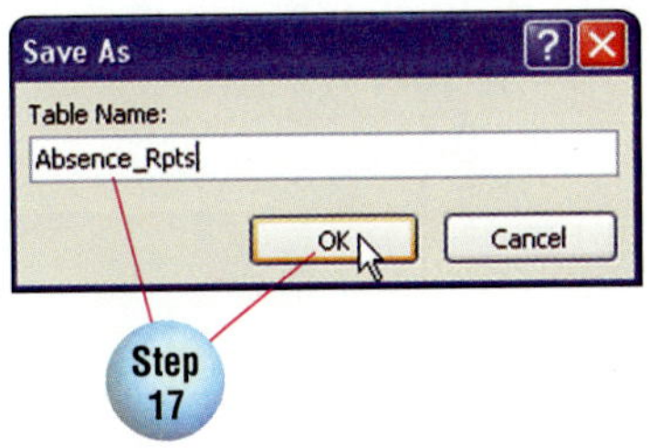

    Note: The ID field may have assigned numbering beginning with 4 instead of 1 for the first record. This is a known issue at time of publication.

18. Close the Absence_Rpts table.

In Brief

Create Table by Adding Records

1. Click Create.
2. Click Table.
3. Type records in blank datasheet.
4. Double-click *Field1*.
5. Type desired field name.
6. Press Enter or click outside field.
7. Repeat Steps 4-6 for remaining columns.
8. Click Save button.
9. Type table name.
10. Press Enter or click OK.

In Addition

Data Type Assumptions

Each field in an Access table has a data type associated which is used by Access to prevent invalid data from being entered into records. When you create a table by adding records, Access assigns the data type based on the type of entries in the column. The following are the assumptions made by Access for four commonly used data types:

Column Entry Examples	Data Types
Sam, 706-555-1275, 55102-4245	Text
October 2, 2009, 10/2/2009, Oct 2, 2009, 10:23 pm	Date/Time
$124, $155.43	Currency
124, 1,500.33, 155.43	Number

Activity 2.2

Inserting and Modifying Fields in Design View

Changes to a field can include editing the field name, changing the data type, adding a field description, or modifying the field's properties. ***Field properties*** are a set of characteristics used to control how the field displays or how the field interacts with the data. New fields can be inserted in the table using the *Add New Field* column in Datasheet view or by inserting the field in Design view.

Project

Worldwide Enterprises

You decide to change the field name and add a description to the *ID* column of the Absence_Rpts table to explain the purpose of the field to another user. You also think that each record should have the employee number entered for verification of each absence report. Using Design View, you will make these changes.

1. With **WEEmployees2.accdb** open, right-click Absence_Rpts: Table in the Navigation pane and then click *Design View* at the shortcut menu.

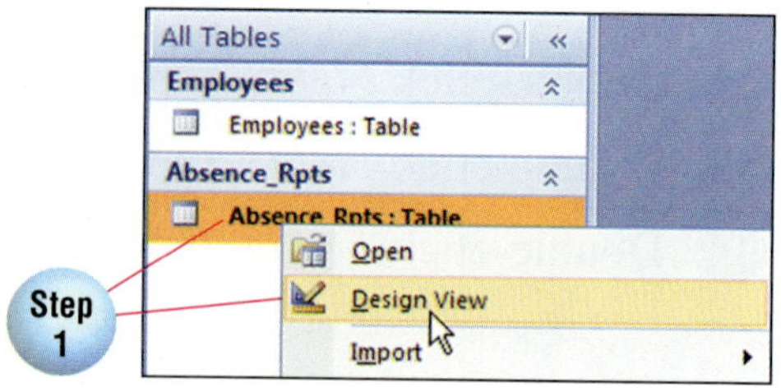

   This opens the table in Design view in the work area. Design view is used to define or modify the structure of the table. Each row in the top section represents one field in the table and is used to define the field name, the field's data type, and an optional description. The *Field Properties* section in the lower half of the work area displays the properties for the active field. The properties will vary depending on the active field.

2. With the insertion point positioned in the first row in the *Field Name* column and the text *ID* already selected, type **Absence_ID** and then press Tab twice to move to the *Description* column.

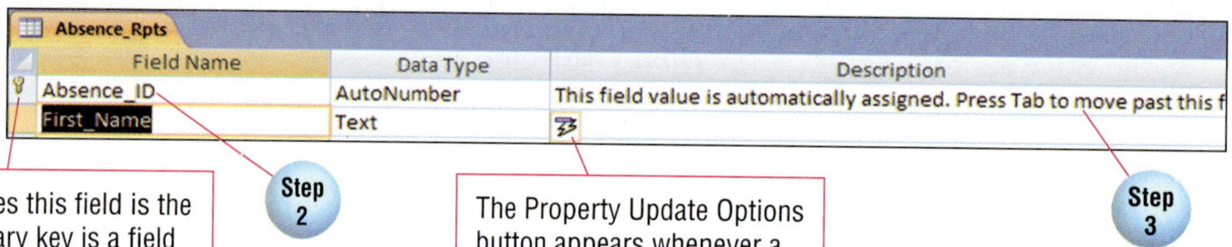

The key icon indicates this field is the *primary key*. A primary key is a field that stores unique information—no two records can have the same field value in this field.

The Property Update Options button appears whenever a field is changed.

3. Type **This field value is automatically assigned. Press Tab to move past this field.** and then press Enter.

   Descriptions are optional. When the field is active in a form, text typed in this area is displayed at the bottom left of the window. You can use descriptive text to explain a field's purpose and/or display messages to the user for data entry. The Property Update Options button displays whenever changes are made to an existing field.

4. Move the mouse pointer in the field selector bar beside *First_Name* (empty column to left of field names) until the pointer changes to a right-pointing black arrow.

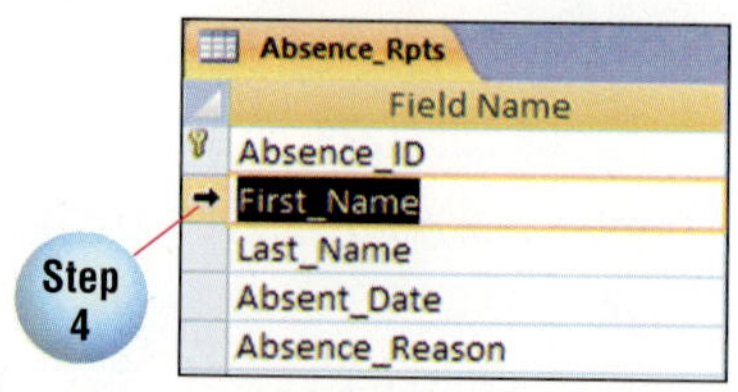

5. Click the left mouse button to select the field.

   In the next step, you will insert a new row between *Absence_ID* and *First_Name* so that you can add a new field to the table. New rows are inserted above the active field.

6. Click the Insert Rows button [Insert Rows] in the Tools group in the Table Tools Design tab.

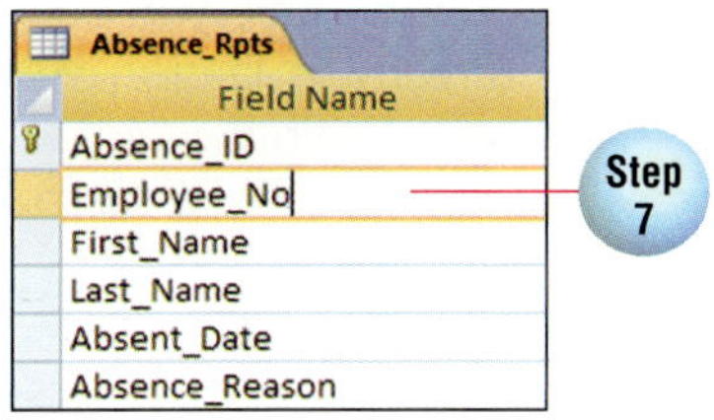

7. Click in the *Field Name* column in the new blank row and then type **Employee_No**.
8. Click the Save button on the Quick Access toolbar to save the changes to the table design.
9. Click the View button in the Views group in the Table Tools Design tab to switch to Datasheet view. (Do *not* click the down-pointing arrow on the button.)

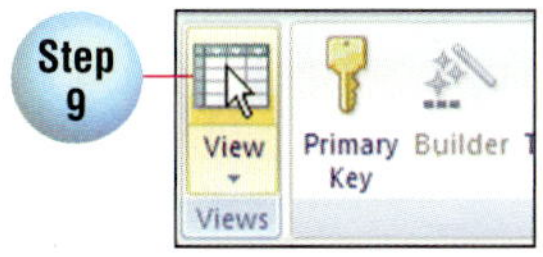

   A new column displays in the datasheet with the title *Employee_No* between *Absence_ID* and *First_Name*.

10. Click in the first row of the *Employee_No* column, type **1000**, and then press the Down Arrow key to move to the second row in the same column.
11. Type **1010** in the second row and then press the Down Arrow key.
12. Type **1045** in the third row and then click in any field in the first two rows to save the changes.

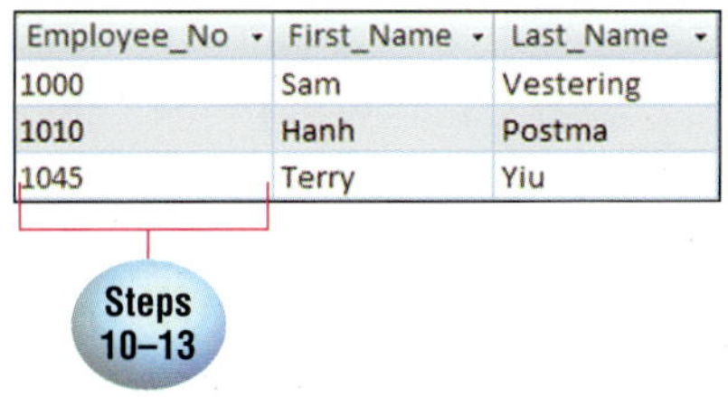

13. Best Fit the *Employee_No* column.
14. Close the Absence_Rpts table. Click Yes to save changes to the table layout.

In Brief

Modify Field in Design View

1. Open table in Design View.
2. Make active field that you want to change.
3. Change field name, data type, description, or field properties as desired.
4. Click Save button.

Insert Field in Design View

1. Open table in Design View.
2. Make desired field active.
3. Click Insert Rows button.
4. Click in *Field Name* area of new row and type field name.
5. Change data type, description, or field properties as desired.
6. Click Save button.

In Addition

Inserting a New Field Using the Datasheet

You can also insert a new field to the table using the *Add New Field* column in the datasheet. Typing data in the first row of the table in the column labeled *Add New Field* causes Access to change the column heading to *Field1* and moves *Add New Field* to another new column in the datasheet. Change the *Field1* column heading to the desired field name by double-clicking the heading and typing a new name. You can also right-click the column heading and choose *Rename column.* An example of this method is shown in the graphic at the right.

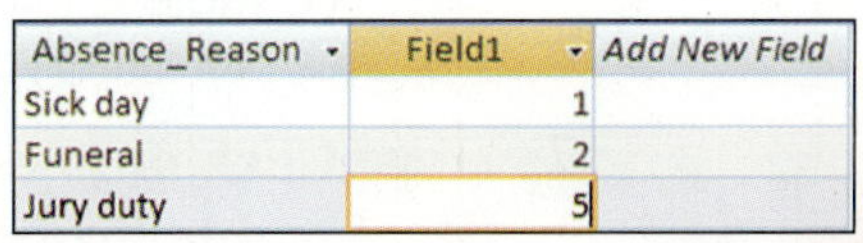

Activity 2.3

Creating a Table in Design View; Setting the Primary Key

As an alternative to creating a new table by adding records and then modifying the structure in Design view, you can create the table structure directly in Design view and add data later. By starting in Design view, you can set the field properties the way you need them right away. When you use Design view, Access does not add the *ID* field to the new table automatically. As you saw in the Absence_Rpts table, *ID* was the designated primary key field. Each table should have a field used to store a unique field value. Examples of fields suitable for a primary key are fields that store an identification value such as an employee number, a part number, a vendor number, or a customer number.

Project

Rhonda Trask, human resources manager, has asked you to create a new table to store the employee benefit plan information. You decide to create this table using Design view.

Worldwide Enterprises

1. With **WEEmployees2.accdb** open, click the Create tab and then click the Table Design button in the Tables group.

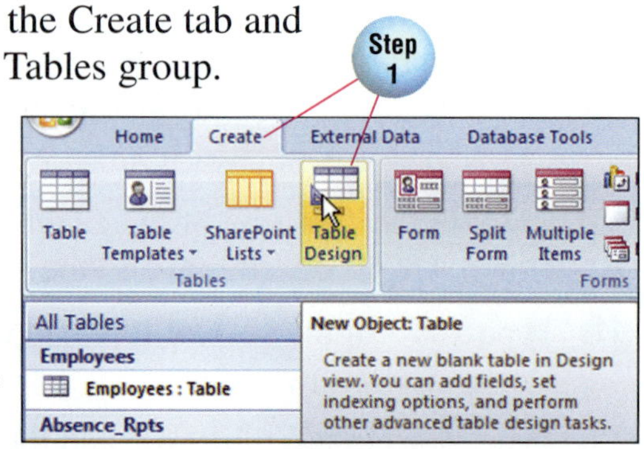

2. With the insertion point positioned in the *Field Name* column in the first row, type **Employee_No** and then press Enter or Tab to move to the next column.
3. With *Text* already entered in the *Data Type* column, press Enter or Tab to move to the next column.

   Table 2.1 provides a list and brief description of the available data types. The *Employee_No* field will contain numbers; however, leave the data type defined as *Text* since no calculations will be performed with employee numbers.

4. Type **Enter the four-digit employee number** in the *Description* column and then press Enter to move to the second row.

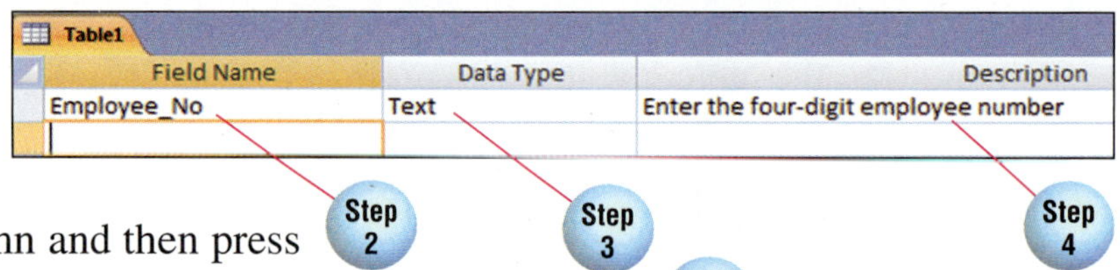

5. Type **Pension_Plan** in the *Field Name* column in the second field row and then press Enter.
6. Click the down-pointing arrow at the right of the *Data Type* column, click *Yes/No* at the drop-down list, and then press Enter.

   See Table 2.1 for a description of the Yes/No data type.

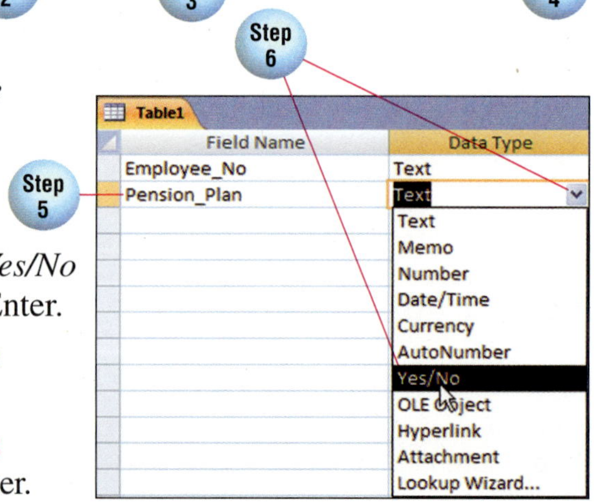

7. Type **Click or press spacebar for Yes; leave empty for No** and then press Enter.
8. Enter the remaining field names, data types, and descriptions as shown in Figure 2.1 by completing steps similar to those in Steps 5–7.

   Although descriptions are optional, the description text displays above the Status bar when the end user is adding records to a datasheet or form and can provide useful information.

9 Click the insertion point in any character in the *Employee_No* field row.

In the next step, you will designate *Employee_No* as the primary key field for the table.

10 Click the Primary Key button in the Tools group in the Table Tools Design tab.

A key icon appears in the field selector bar to the left of *Employee_No* indicating the field is the primary key. A primary key field contains unique data for each record. Access automatically sorts the table data by the primary key field when the table is opened.

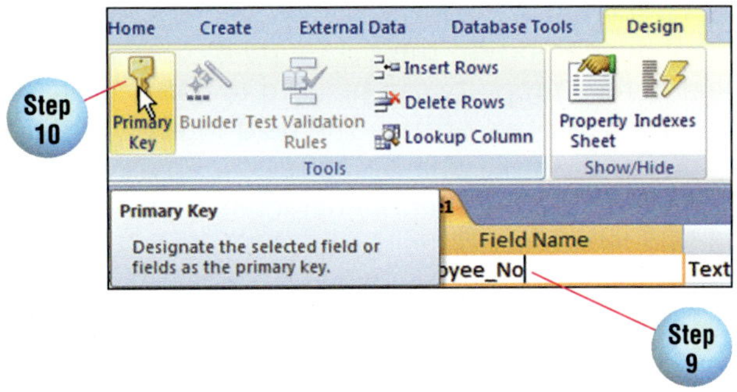

11 Click the Save button on the Quick Access toolbar.

12 At the Save As dialog box, type **Employee_Benefits** in the *Table Name* text box and then press Enter or click OK.

13 Close the Employee_Benefits table.

In Brief

Create Table in Design View

1. Click Create tab.
2. Click Table Design.
3. Type field names, change data types, add descriptions, or modify other field properties as desired.
4. Assign primary key.
5. Click Save button.
6. Type table name.
7. Click OK.

Assign Primary Key

1. Open table in Design view.
2. Make active desired primary key field.
3. Click Primary Key button.
4. Save table.

TABLE 2.1 Data Types

Data Type	Description
Text	Alphanumeric data up to 255 characters in length, such as a name, address, or value such as a telephone number or social security number that is used as an identifier and not for calculating.
Memo	Alphanumeric data up to 64,000 characters in length.
Number	Positive or negative values that can be used in calculations. Do *not* use for values that will calculate monetary amounts (see Currency).
Date/Time	Use this type to ensure dates and times are entered and sorted properly.
Currency	Values that involve money. Access will not round off during calculations.
AutoNumber	Access automatically numbers each record sequentially (incrementing by 1) when you begin typing a new record.
Yes/No	Data in the field will be either Yes or No, True or False, On or Off.
OLE Object	Used to embed or link objects created in other Office applications.
Hyperlink	Field that will store a hyperlink such as a URL.
Attachment	Use this data type to add file attachments to a record such as a Word document or an Excel workbook.
Lookup Wizard	The Lookup Wizard can be used to enter data in the field from another existing table or display a list of values in a drop-down list for the user to choose from.

FIGURE 2.1 Design View Table Entries

Table1

Field Name	Data Type	Description
Employee_No	Text	Enter the four-digit employee number
Pension_Plan	Yes/No	Click or press spacebar for Yes; leave empty for No
Dental_Plan	Yes/No	Click or press spacebar for Yes; leave empty for No
Premium_Health	Yes/No	Click or press spacebar for Yes; leave empty for No
Dependents	Number	Type the number of dependents related to this employee
Life_Insce_Amt	Currency	Type the amount of life insurance subscribed by this employee

Activity 2.4

Modifying Field Size and Default Value Properties

In Design view, the available field properties displayed in the lower half of the work area vary depending on the data type of the active field. A field property can be used to control how the field displays or how the field interacts with data. For example, the *Field Size* property can be used to limit the number of characters that are allowed in a field entry. A field size of 4 for an employee number field would prevent employee numbers longer than four characters from being stored in a record. This practice can help avoid data entry errors. Use the *Default Value* property when most records are likely to contain the same field value since the contents of this property display automatically when a new record is added to the table.

Project

Worldwide Enterprises

Worldwide Enterprises uses a four-digit employee number. You will modify the *Employee_No* Field Size property in the Employee_Benefits table to set the maximum number of characters to 4. Since most employees opt into the Pension Plan, you will set the default value for the *Pension Plan* field to *Yes.*

1. With **WEEmployees2.accdb** open, right-click the Employee_Benefits table name in the Navigation pane and then click *Design View* at the shortcut menu.

2. With *Employee_No* already selected in the *Field Name* column, double-click the value *255* that appears in the *Field Size* property box in the *Field Properties* section and then type **4**.

   Alternatively, click in the *Field Size* property box to activate the insertion point, delete *255*, and then type **4**.

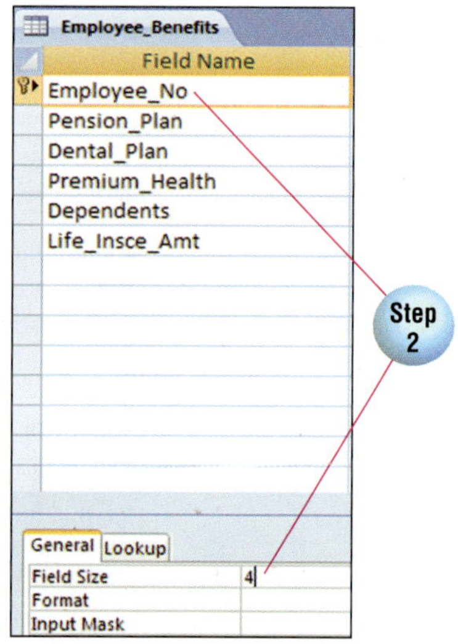

3. Click in the *Pension_Plan* row in the *Field Name* column to display the *Pension_Plan* properties in the *Field Properties* section.

   Notice the list of available properties has changed. The items displayed in the *Field Properties* section change to reflect the options for the active field's data type. Since *Pension_Plan* is a Yes/No field, the list of properties shown is different than those for *Employee_No* which is a Text field.

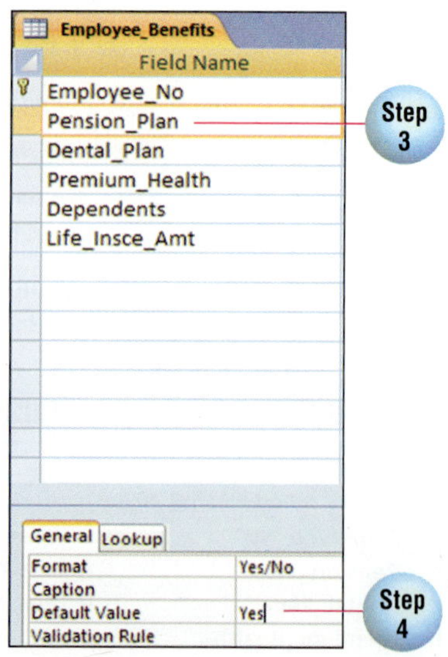

4. Select the current entry in the *Default Value* field property box and then type **Yes**.

5. Click the Save button.

   If a field property is changed after data has been entered into records, Access displays warning messages when you save the table that some data could be lost if, for example, a field size is changed to a shorter size. If a large amount of data was entered into a table before a property such as field size is changed, consider making a backup copy of the database before modifying the table design. Check for errors by comparing the field data in the backup copy with the data in the working copy after Access saves the table.

6. Click the View button in the Views group in the Table Tools Design tab to switch to Datasheet view. (Do *not* click the down-pointing arrow on the button.)

7. Type **1000111** in the *Employee_No* field in the first blank row of the datasheet and then press Enter.

   A beep sounds if the computer's speakers are on and the volume is not muted each time you type a character that extends beyond the field size of 4. Access does not display any characters in the field after the fourth character typed.

8. At the *Pension_Plan* field, notice a check mark already exists in the check box since the default value was set to *Yes*. Press Enter to accept the default value.

   When presented with a default value in a field, you have the option of accepting the default value by pressing Enter or Tab, or of overwriting the default value by typing another entry. In the case of a Yes/No field, you would press the spacebar or click to clear the check box.

9. Enter the following data in the remaining fields in the first row:

Dental_Plan	**Yes**
Premium_Health	**Yes**
Dependents	**0**
Life_Insce_Amount	**100000**

10. Adjust all column widths to Best Fit.

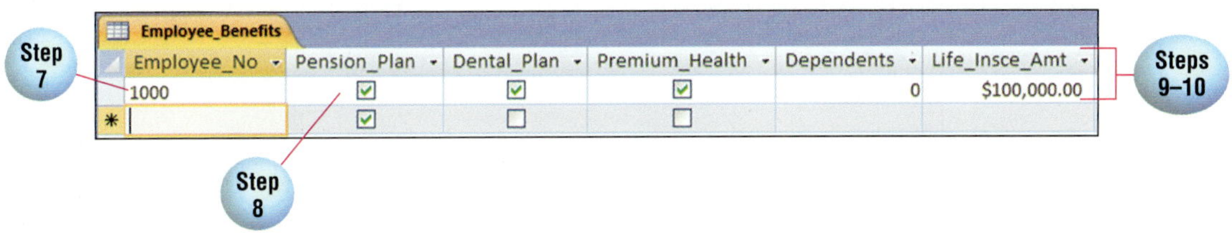

11. Close the Employee_Benefits table. Click Yes when prompted to save the changes to the layout.

In Brief

Set Field Size
1. Open table in Design view.
2. Click in desired field row.
3. Select current value in *Field Size* property box.
4. Type maximum number of characters for field.
5. Click Save.

Set Default Value
1. Open table in Design view.
2. Click in desired field row.
3. Click or select current entry in *Default Value* property box.
4. Type default value.
5. Click Save.

In Addition

More about the Field Size Property

The default field size property varies depending on the data type. The default value for a Text field is 255. In an AutoNumber or Numeric field, the default field size is Long Integer. Long Integer stores whole numbers from –2,147,483,648 to 2,147,483,648 (negative to positive). The field size property is not available for fields with a data type set to Memo, Date/Time, Currency, Yes/No, OLE Object, Hyperlink, or Attachment.

Activity 2.5

Validating Field Entries

The ***Validation Rule*** property can be used to enter a statement containing a conditional test that is checked each time data is entered into a field. When data is entered that fails to satisfy the conditional test, Access does not accept the entry and displays an error message. For example, suppose a customer number must be within a certain range of values. By entering a conditional statement in the Validation Rule property that checks each entry against the acceptable range, you can reduce errors and ensure that only valid numbers are stored in the customer number field. Enter in the ***Validation Text*** property the content of the error message that you want the user to see.

Project

Worldwide Enterprises

Worldwide Enterprises offers life insurance benefits up to a maximum of $200,000. You will add a validation rule and enter an error message in the Validation Text property for the *Life_Insce_Amt* field in the Employee_Benefits table to ensure no benefit exceeds this maximum.

1. With **WEEmployees2.accdb** open, open the Employee_Benefits table in Design view.
2. Click in the *Life_Insce_Amt* field row to display the associated field properties.
3. Click in the *Validation Rule* property box, type **<=200000**, and then press Enter.

   Pressing Enter after typing the validation rule moves the insertion point to the *Validation Text* property box.
4. Type **Enter a value that is less than or equal to $200,000** and then press Enter.

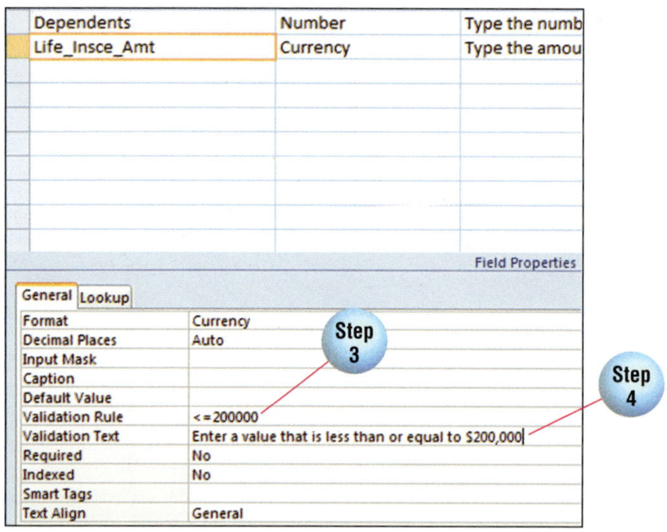

5. Click the Save button.

   Since a validation rule has been created *after* data has been entered into the table, Access displays a warning message warning that some data may not be valid.
6. At the Microsoft Office Access message box, click Yes to instruct Access to test the data with the new rules.

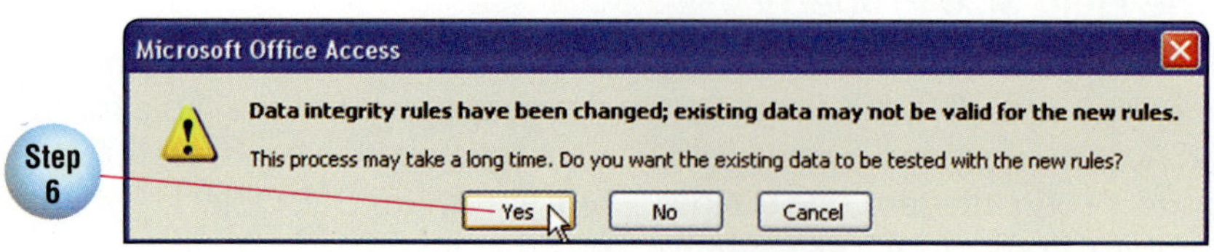

7. Click the View button in the Views group in the Table Tools Design tab to switch to Datasheet view.

8. Add the following record to the table:

Employee_No	**1005**
Pension_Plan	**Yes**
Dental_Plan	**Yes**
Premium_Health	**Yes**
Dependents	**2**
Life_Insce_Amt	**210000**

When you enter *210000* into the *Life_Insce_Amt* field and press Enter or Tab, Access displays an error message. The text in the error message is the text you entered in the *Validation Text* property box.

9. Click OK at the Microsoft Office Access error message.

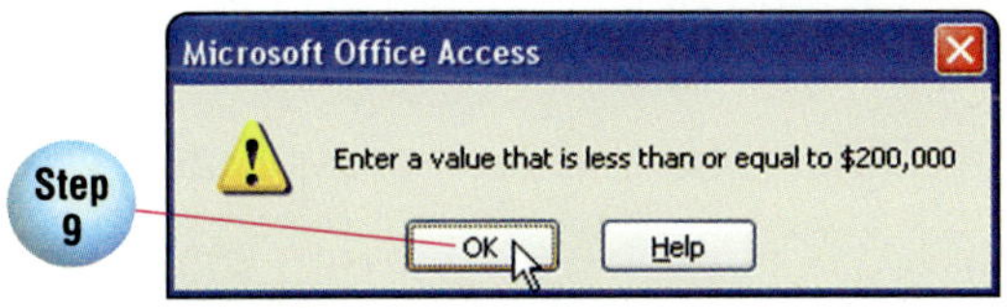

10. Backspace to delete *210000*, type **200000**, and then press Enter.

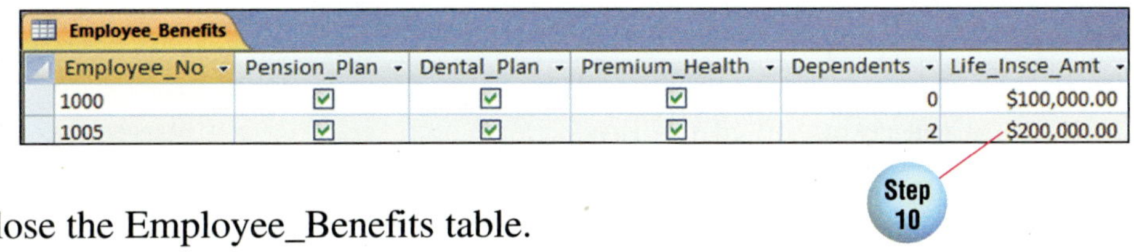

11. Close the Employee_Benefits table.

In Brief

Create Validation Rule

1. Open table in Design view.
2. Click in desired field row.
3. Click in *Validation Rule* property box.
4. Type conditional statement.
5. Click in *Validation Text* property box.
6. Type error message.
7. Click Save.

In Addition

Other Validation Rule Examples

Validation rules should be created whenever possible to avoid data entry errors. The examples below illustrate various ways to use the validation rule to verify data.

Field Name	Validation Rule	Data Check
Customer_No	>1000 And <1100	Limits customer numbers to 1001 through 1099.
Credit_Limit	<=5000	Restricts credit limits to values of 5000 or less.
State	"CA"	Only the state of California is accepted.
Country	"CA" Or "US"	Only the United States or Canada is accepted.
Order_Qty	>=25	Quantity ordered must be a minimum of 25.

Activity 2.6

Creating Input Masks; Formatting a Field

An ***input mask*** displays a pattern in the datasheet or form indicating how data is to be entered into the field. For example, an input mask in a telephone number field that displays (___)___-____ indicates to the user that the three-digit area code is to be entered in front of all telephone numbers. Input masks ensure that data is entered consistently in tables. In addition to specifying the position and amount of characters in a field you can create masks that restrict the data entered to digits, letters, or characters, and whether or not each digit, letter, or character is required or optional. The ***Format*** property controls how the data is *displayed* in the field *after* it has been entered.

Project

You will create a new field in the Employee_Benefits table for Pension Plan eligibility dates and include an input mask and format property in the field.

Worldwide Enterprises

1. With **WEEmployees2.accdb** open, open the Employee_Benefits table in Design view.
2. Click in the *Field Name* column in the blank row below *Life_Insce_Amt*, type **Pension_Eligible**, and then press Enter.
3. Change the data type to *Date/Time* and then press Enter.
4. Type **Type date employee is eligible for pension plan in the format dd-mmm-yy (example: 12-Dec-09)**.
5. Click Save.
6. With *Pension_Eligible* the active field, click in the *Input Mask* property box in the *Field Properties* section and then click the Build button **...** at the right end of the box.
7. Click *Medium Date* at the first Input Mask Wizard dialog box and then click Next.

   The input masks that display in the list in the first dialog box are dependent on the data type for the field for which you are creating an input mask.

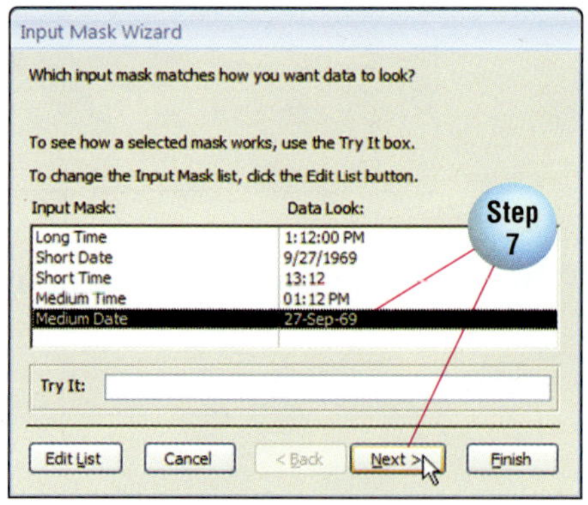

8. Click Next at the second Input Mask Wizard dialog box.

   This dialog box displays the input mask code in the *Input Mask* text box and sets the placeholder character that displays in the field. The default placeholder is the underscore character.

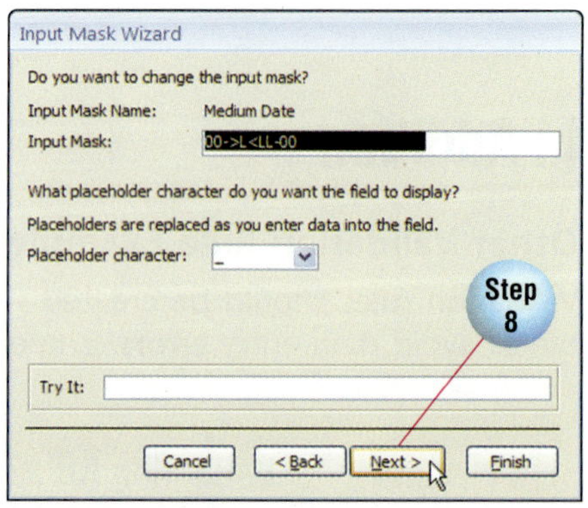

9. Click Finish at the last Input Mask Wizard dialog box to complete the entry in the *Input Mask* property box and then press Enter.

   The mask built by the wizard broken down into parts is: *00*\- two required digits for the day followed by a hyphen displayed in the field; >*L*<LL\- three required letters for the month, first letter uppercase and remaining two lowercase, followed by a hyphen displayed in the field; 00 two required digits for the year. Following the date requirement ;0 instructs Access to store literal characters used in the field (hyphens between dates). The mask ends with ;_ which is the placeholder character.

10 Click in the *Format* property box.

The input mask controls how a date is entered in to the field; however, by default, Access displays dates in the format *m/dd/yyyy*. To avoid confusion, you will format the field to display the date in the same format that the input mask accepts the data.

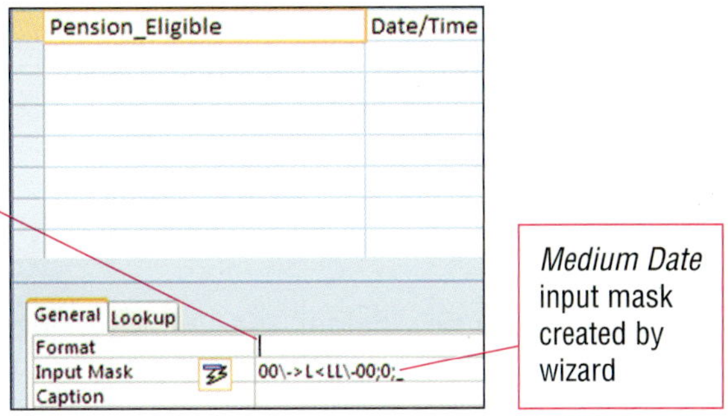

11 Click the down-pointing arrow at the end of the property box and then click *Medium Date* at the drop-down list.

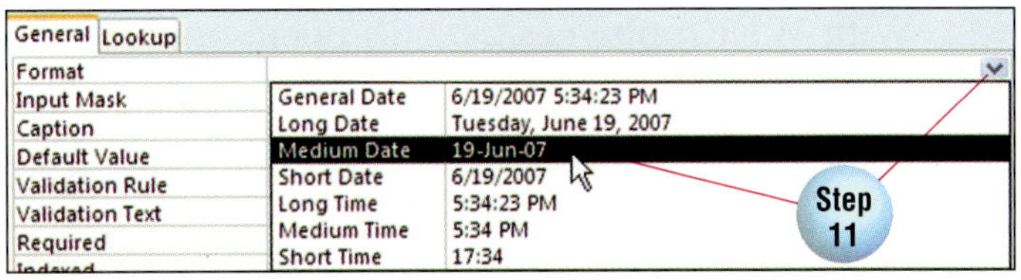

12 Click the Save button and then switch to Datasheet view.

13 Click in *Pension_Eligible* column for the first row in the datasheet.

The input mask __-___-__ appears in the field.

14 Type **22jul01** and then press the Down Arrow key.

Notice the hyphens are not required to enter the date and the first character in the month is converted to uppercase. The greater than symbol (>) preceding *L* in the mask causes Access to convert the first character to uppercase.

15 Type **150801**.

A beep sounds as you type every character after *15*. The only characters allowed after the first hyphen are letters. Notice the insertion point remains in the month section of the field.

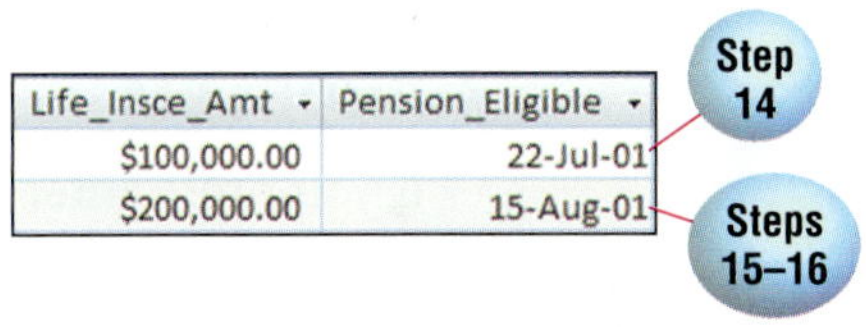

16 Type **aug01** and then press Enter.

17 Adjust the column width of *Pension_Eligible* to Best Fit.

18 Close the Employee_Benefits table. Click Yes when prompted to save changes to the layout.

In Brief

Use Input Mask Wizard

1. Open table in Design view.
2. Click in desired field row.
3. Click in *Input Mask* property box.
4. Click Build button.
5. Click input mask you want to create.
6. Click Next.
7. Select placeholder character.
8. Click Next.
9. Click Finish at last wizard dialog box.
10. Click Save button.

In Addition

Input Mask Codes

The Input Mask Wizard is only available for fields with a data type set to Text or Date/Time. For fields such as Number or Currency or for an input mask for which the wizard does not provide an option, you can create your own by entering the codes directly into the property box. Following is a list of commonly used input mask codes.

Use	To restrict data entry to
0	digit, zero through nine, entry is required
9	digit or space, entry is not required
L	letter, A through Z, entry is required
?	letter, A through Z, entry is not required
>	all characters following are converted to uppercase
<	all characters following are converted to lowercase

Activity 2.7

Creating a Lookup List

Create a ***Lookup*** field when you want to restrict the data entered into the field to a list of values from an existing table, or a list of values that you create. The Lookup tab in the *Field Properties* section in Design view contains the options used to create a *Lookup* field. Access includes the Lookup Wizard to facilitate entering the lookup settings.

Project

Worldwide Enterprises

You will create a new field in the Employee_Benefits table to store vacation entitlement for each employee. You want the field to display a drop-down list of vacation periods and restrict the field to accept only those entries that match items in the list.

1. With **WEEmployees2.accdb** open, open the Employee_Benefits table in Design View.
2. Click in the *Field Name* column in the blank row below *Pension_Eligible*, type **Vacation**, and then press Enter.
3. Change the Data Type to *Lookup Wizard.*
4. At the first Lookup Wizard dialog box, click *I will type in the values that I want.* and then click Next.
5. Click in the blank row below *Col1*, type **1 week**, and then press Tab or the Down Arrow key.

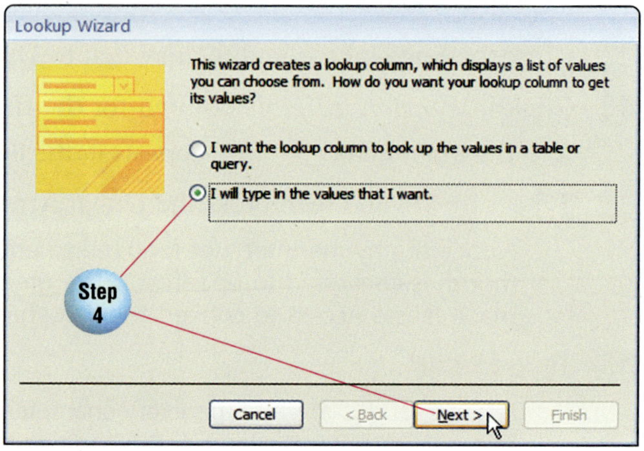

PROBLEM

If you press Enter by mistake and find yourself at the next step in the Lookup Wizard, click the Back button to return to the previous dialog box.

6. Type **2 weeks** and then press Tab.
7. Type **3 weeks** and then press Tab.
8. Type **4 weeks** and then click Next.
9. Click Finish in the last Lookup Wizard dialog box to accept the default label *Vacation*. No entry is required in the *Description* column.

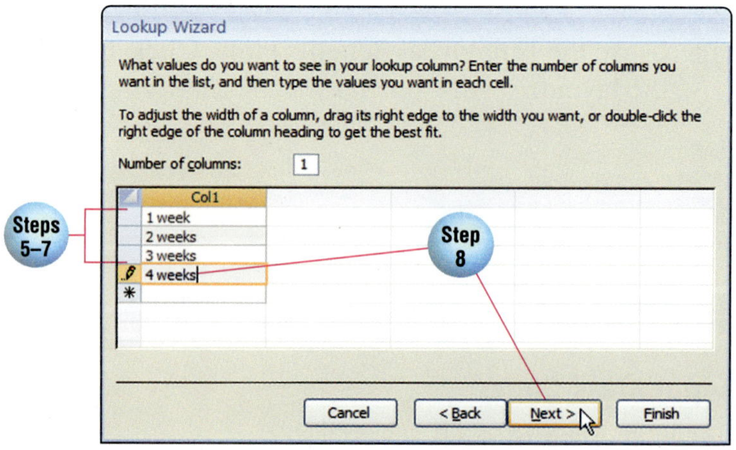

10 Click the Lookup tab in the *Field Properties* section and view the entries made to each property by the Lookup Wizard.

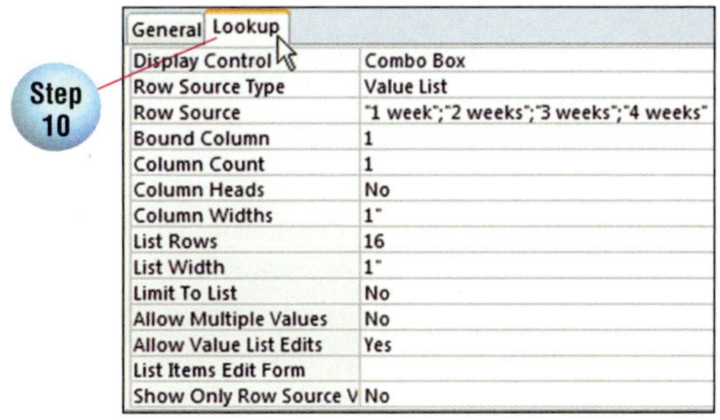

11 Click in the *Limit To List* property box, click the down-pointing arrow that appears, and then click *Yes*.

By changing the *Limit To List* property to *Yes* you are further restricting the field to only those items in the drop-down list. If someone attempts to type an entry other than 1 week, 2 weeks, 3 weeks, or 4 weeks, Access displays an error message and will not store the data.

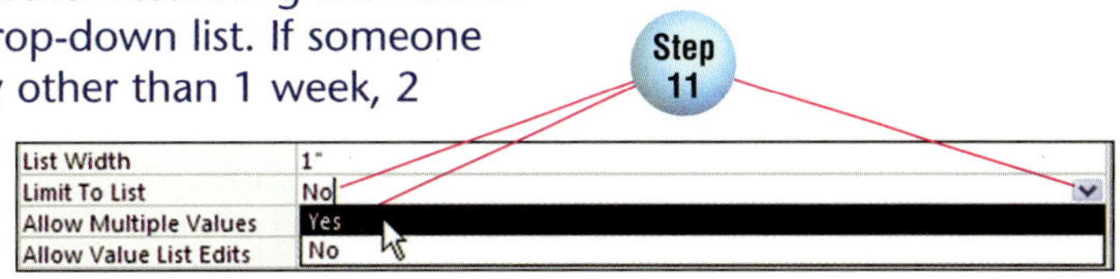

12 Click in the *Allow Value List Edits* property box, click the down-pointing arrow that appears, and then click *No*.

You want to make sure that changes to the list that you created are not allowed by someone using the datasheet or a form.

13 Click Save and then click View to switch to Datasheet view.

14 If necessary, scroll the datasheet right and then click in the *Vacation* column in the first row in the datasheet. Click the down-pointing arrow that appears and then click *4 weeks* from the drop-down list.

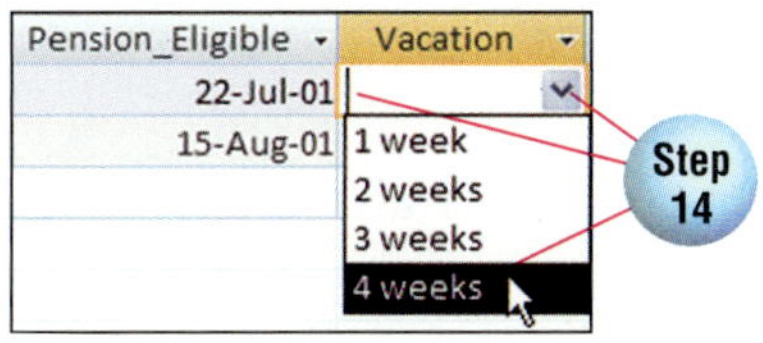

15 Press the Down Arrow key to move to the *Vacation* column in the second row, type **6 weeks**, and then press Enter.

16 Click OK at the message that displays informing you that the text entered isn't an item in the list, click *3 weeks* at the drop-down list, and then press Enter.

17 Display the datasheet in Print Preview. Change the page orientation to landscape, change the left and right margins to 0.5 inch, and then print the datasheet.

18 Close the Print Preview window and then close the Employee_Benefits table.

In Brief

Create List of Values Using Lookup Wizard

1. Open table in Design view.
2. Type field name and press Enter.
3. Change data type to *Lookup Wizard*.
4. Click *I will type in the values that I want.* and click Next.
5. Type field values in *Col1* column and click Next.
6. Click Finish at last wizard dialog box.
7. Click Save.

In Addition

Looking Up Data from Another Table

Items in a drop-down list can also be generated by specifying an existing field in another table or query. To do this, click Next at the first Lookup Wizard dialog box to accept the default setting *I want the lookup column to look up the values in a table or query*. In the remaining wizard dialog boxes, you choose the table or query and the field that you want to use, choose the sort order for displaying the field values, adjust the column width for the lookup list, select the value to store, and assign a label to the column. Creating field entries using this method ensures that data is consistent between tables and eliminates duplicate keying of information which can lead to data errors. For example, in a database used to store employee information, one table could be used to enter employee numbers and then the remaining tables look up the employee number by scrolling a list of employee names.

Activity 2.8

Moving and Deleting Fields; Formatting the Datasheet; Inserting Totals

Fields can be moved or deleted in either Datasheet or Design view. Exercise caution when deleting fields since data will be lost and the operation cannot be reversed with the Undo command. As a precaution, consider making a backup copy of the database before deleting a field. Enhance the appearance of the datasheet by using options in the Font group of the Home tab. A new feature in Access 2007 is the ability to add a total row to a datasheet and then choose from a list of functions to add, find the average, maximum, minimum, count, standard deviation, or variance result in a numeric column.

Project

Worldwide Enterprises

You will make changes to the structure of the Employees table by deleting a field and repositioning a field in the table. In Datasheet view, you decide to enhance the appearance by changing the background color and gridlines and increasing the font size. Finally, you decide to add a total to the *Annual_Salary* column.

1. With **WEEmployees2.accdb** open, open the Employees table in Design view.
2. Click the insertion point in any text in the *Middle_Initial* row.
3. Click the Delete Rows button [Delete Rows] in the Tools group in the Table Tools Design tab.

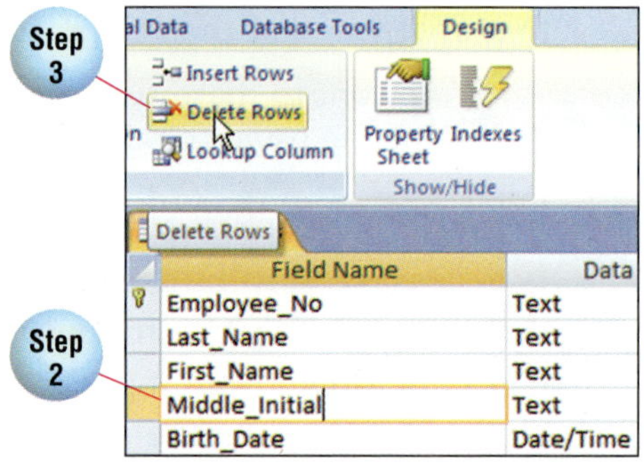

4. At the Microsoft Office Access message box asking you to confirm that you want to permanently delete the selected field(s) and all of the data in the field(s), click Yes.

If you have more than one field to delete and they are adjacent, use the field selector bar to select the multiple fields and delete all of them in one operation.

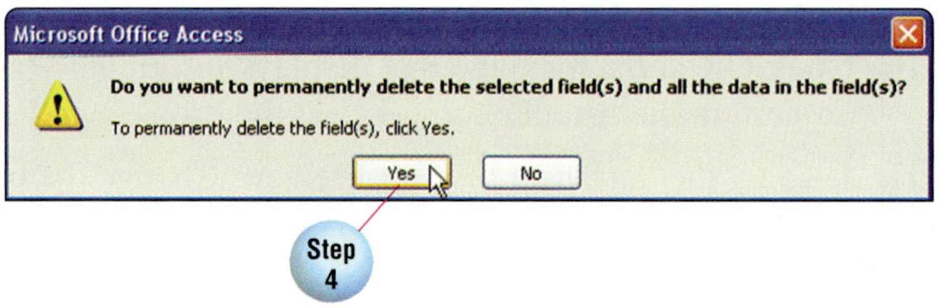

5. Move the mouse pointer in the field selector bar beside *Annual_Salary* until the pointer changes to a right-pointing black arrow and then click the left mouse button to select the field.
6. With the pointer still positioned in the field selector bar beside *Annual_Salary* (pointer now displays as a white arrow), drag the pointer up between the *Birth_Date* and *Hire_Date* fields and then release the left mouse button.

As you drag the mouse, a black line appears between existing field names, indicating where the selected field will be repositioned when the mouse button is released and the white arrow pointer displays with a gray shaded box attached to it.

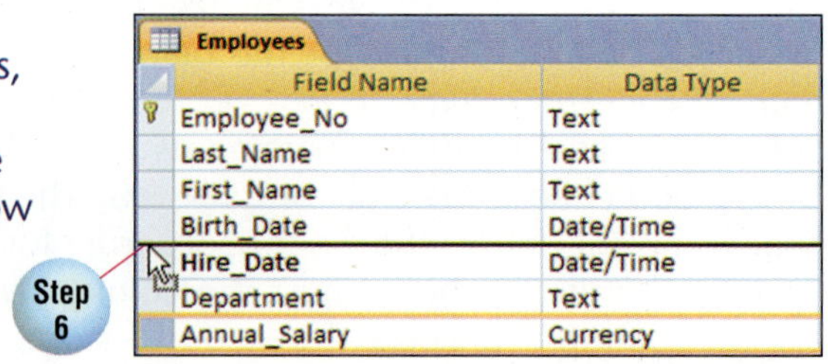

7. Click in any field to deselect the *Annual_Salary* row and then click the Save button.
8. Switch to Datasheet view.

   Review the changes in the datasheet with *Middle_Initial* deleted and *Annual_Salary* repositioned in the table.

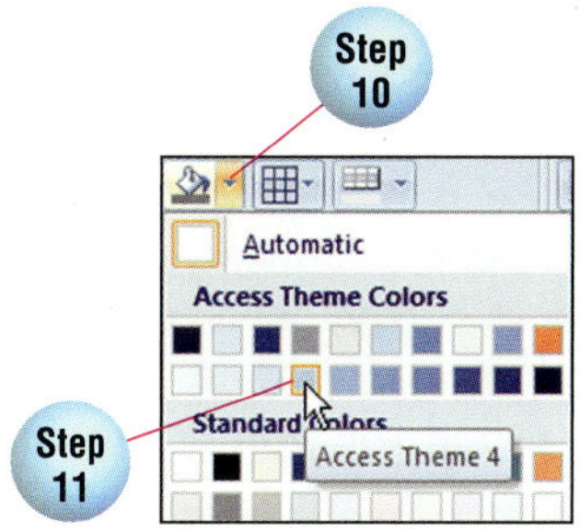

9. Adjust all column widths to Best Fit.
10. Click the down-pointing arrow to the right of the Fill Color button in the Font group in the Home tab.
11. Click *Access Theme 4* (fourth color box from left in second row in the *Access Theme Colors* section) in the drop-down color palette.

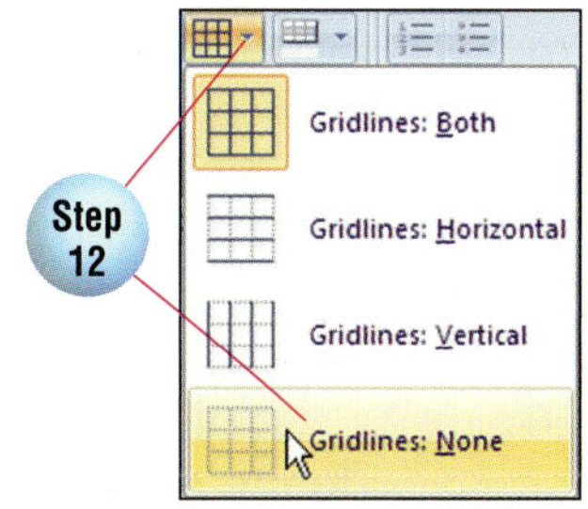

12. Click the Gridlines button in the Font group and then click *Gridlines: None* at the drop-down list.
13. Click the down-pointing arrow next to the Font Size button in the Font group and then click *12* at the drop-down list.
14. Click the Totals button **Σ Totals** in the Records group in the Home tab.

   A new feature in Access 2007 includes the Totals row in datasheets. When you click the Totals button, Access adds a row to the bottom of the datasheet with the label *Total* at the left. In the next step, you will apply the SUM function to the *Annual_Salary* field.

15. Click in the *Total* row at the bottom of the *Annual_Salary* column, click the down-pointing arrow that appears, and then click *Sum* at the pop-up list.

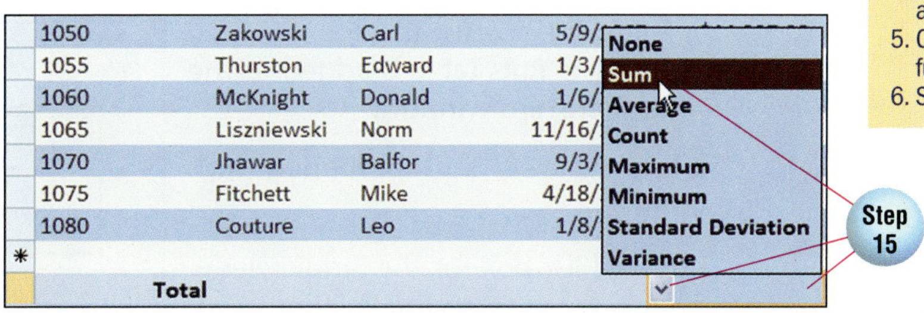

   Access displays the result *$824,170.00*.

16. Display the datasheet in Print Preview, change the page orientation to landscape, and then print the datasheet.
17. Close the Print Preview window and then close the Employees table. Click Yes when prompted to save changes to the layout of the table.

In Brief

Delete Field
1. Open table in Design view.
2. Make desired field active.
3. Click Delete Rows button.
4. Click Yes.
5. Save table.

Move Field
1. Open table in Design view.
2. Select field using field selector bar.
3. With pointer in field selector bar, drag field to desired position.
4. Save table.

Format Datasheet
1. Open table.
2. Click desired formatting button in Font group.
3. Save table.

Insert Total
1. Open table.
2. Click Totals button.
3. Click in *Total* row in desired field.
4. Click down-pointing arrow.
5. Click desired function.
6. Save table.

In Addition

Working with Wide Datasheets

When working in a datasheet with many columns, scrolling right can make it difficult to relate to the record in which you need to make a change since descriptor fields such as *Employee_No* or *Last_Name* have scrolled off the screen. To alleviate this problem, you can freeze columns so they do not disappear when the datasheet is scrolled right. To do this, select the columns that you want to freeze, click the More button in the Records group in the Home tab, and then click Freeze.

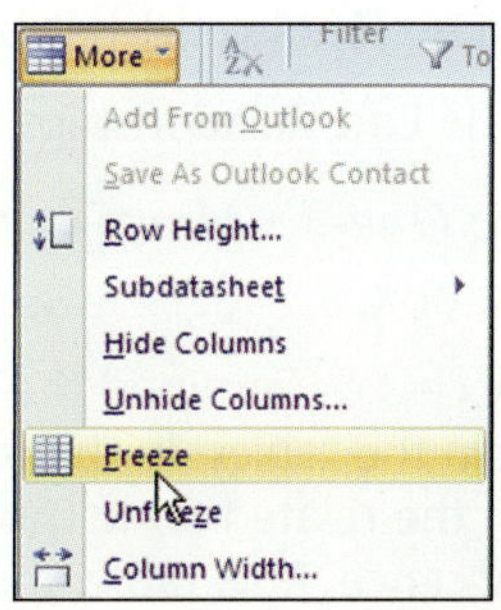

Activity 2.9

Creating a One-to-Many Relationship; Editing a Relationship

Access is referred to as a ***relational database management system***. A relational database is one in which relationships exist between tables, allowing two or more tables to be treated as if they were one when generating reports or looking up data. One table in a relationship is called the ***primary*** table and the other table is called the ***related*** table. A one-to-many relationship means that one table in the relationship contains one unique record in the field used to join the tables while the related table can have several records with a matching field value in the joined field. This is the most common type of relationship created between Access tables.

Project

Worldwide Enterprises

You will create a one-to-many relationship between the Employees table and the Absence_Rpts table using the common field *Employee_No*.

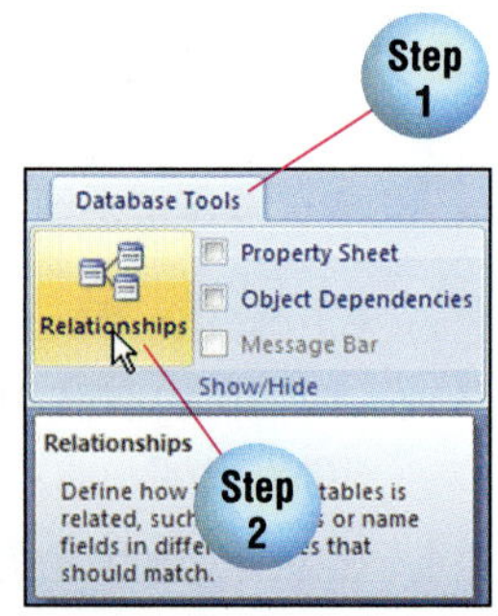

1. With **WEEmployees2.accdb** open, click the Database Tools tab.
2. Click the Relationships button in the Show/Hide group.

   In the relationship, Employees will be the primary table since the table contains only one record per employee and Absence_Rpts will be the related table since an employee can be absent more than once.

3. With *Absence_Rpts* already selected at the Show Table dialog box with the *Tables* tab selected, click the Add button.

   A field list box for the Absence_Rpts table is added to the Relationships window.

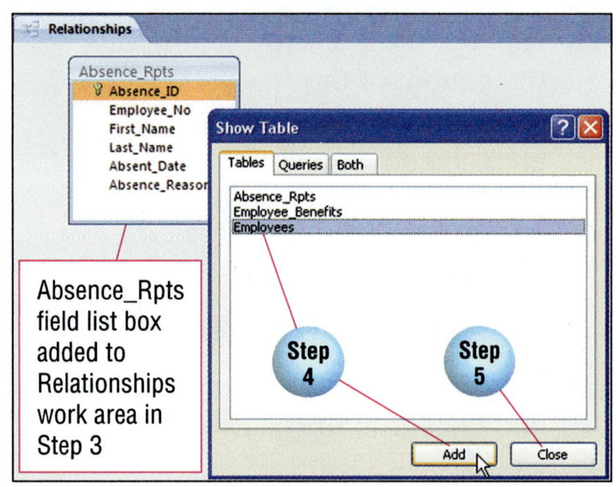

4. Click *Employees* and then click the Add button.

   A field list box for the Employees table is added to the Relationships window.

5. Click the Close button to close the Show Table dialog box.

   A common field in two tables is the basis upon which the tables are joined. In the next step, you will drag the common field *Employee_No* from the primary table (Employees) to the related table (Absence_Rpts).

6. Position the mouse pointer over *Employee_No* in the Employees field list box, hold down the left mouse button, drag the pointer left to *Employee_No* in the Absence_Rpts field list box, and then release the mouse button.

   The Edit Relationships dialog box appears when you release the mouse button.

7. Notice *One-To-Many* is in the *Relationship Type* section of the Edit Relationships dialog box.

   Access determined the relationship type based on the common field that was used to join the tables. In the primary table (Employees), *Employee_No* is the primary key while in the related table (Absence_Rpts) *Employee_No* is not the primary key. In the Absence_Rpts table, the field *Employee_No* is referred to as the ***foreign key***. A foreign key is the field used to relate a table that references the primary key in the other table.

8 Click the *Enforce Referential Integrity* check box at the Edit Relationships dialog box and then click Create.

Referential integrity means that Access will ensure that a record with the same employee number already exists in the primary table when a new record is being added to the related table.

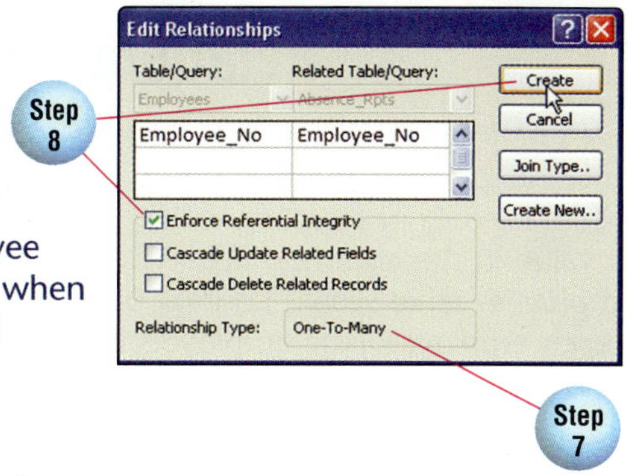

9 Click the Save button.

A black line (referred to as a ***join line***) joins the two tables at the common field. A *1* appears next to the primary table, indicating the *one* side of the relationship and the infinity symbol ∞ appears next to the related table, indicating the *many* side of the relationship.

Join line illustrating the relationship that links the tables at the common field in each table.

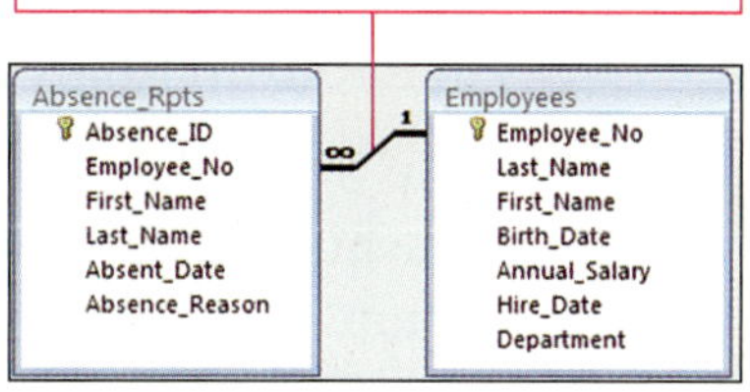

10 Close the Relationships window.

11 Open the Absence_Rpts table.

In Steps 12–14 you will test referential integrity by attempting to add a record for an employee that does not have a record in the primary table.

12 Click the New button [New] in the Records group in the Home tab, press Tab to move past the *Absence_ID* column, type **1099** in the *Employee_No* column, and then press Enter.

13 Type the entries in the next three fields as follows:

First_Name **Fiona**
Last_Name **Campbell**
Absent_Date **October 9, 2009**

14 Type **Sick day** at the *Absence_Reason* column and then press Tab or Enter.

Access displays an error message indicating you cannot add or change a record because a related record is required in the Employees table.

15 Click OK at the Microsoft Office Access message box.

16 Close the Absence_Rpts table. Click OK at the Microsoft Office Access error message that appears for the second time.

17 Click Yes at the second error message box to close the table and confirm that the data changes will be lost.

In Brief

Create One-to-Many Relationship

1. Click Database Tools.
2. Click Relationships button.
3. Add desired tables to Relationships window.
4. Close Show Table dialog box.
5. Drag common field name from primary table field list box to related table field list box.
6. Click *Enforce Referential Integrity* at Edit Relationships dialog box.
7. Click Create.
8. Click Save.

In Addition

Cascade Relationship Options

At the Edit Relationships dialog box, two additional options are dimmed until you turn on referential integrity: *Cascade Update Related Fields* and *Cascade Delete Related Records*. If you change the field value in the field used to join the tables, you can elect to have Access make the same change in the record in the related table. If you delete a record in the primary table you can also instruct Access to delete the records with the same field value in the joined field in the related table.

Activity 2.10

Creating a One-to-One Relationship; Printing a Relationship Report

A one-to-one relationship exists when both the primary table and the related table contain only one record with a matching field value in the common field. For example, the Employees table would contain only one record for each employee. The Employee_Benefits table would also contain only one record for each employee. If these tables are joined on the common *Employee_No* field, a one-to-one relationship would be created. Notice also that *Employee_No* is the primary key field in each table. Once all relationships are created, you can print a relationship report to file away for future reference.

Project

You will create a one-to-one relationship between the Employees and the Employee_Benefits table and then print a relationship report for the WEEmployees2 database.

Worldwide Enterprises

1. With **WEEmployees2.accdb**, click the Database Tools tab.
2. Click the Relationships button in the Show/Hide group.
3. Click the Show Table button in the Relationships group in the Relationship Tools Design tab.

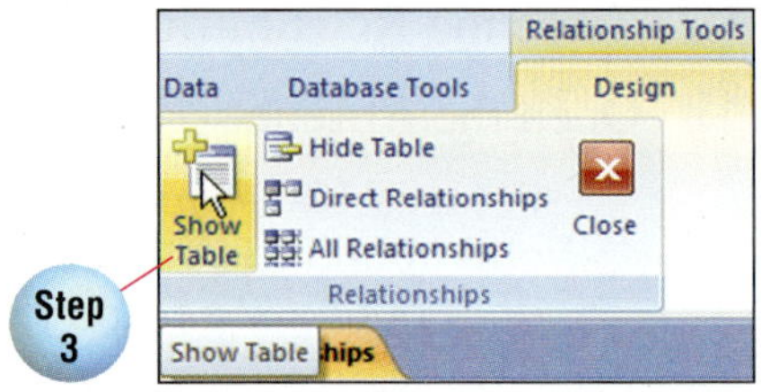

4. At the Show Table dialog box with the Tables tab selected, click *Employee_Benefits*, click the Add button, and then click the Close button.

   A field list box for Employee_Benefits is added to the Relationships window.

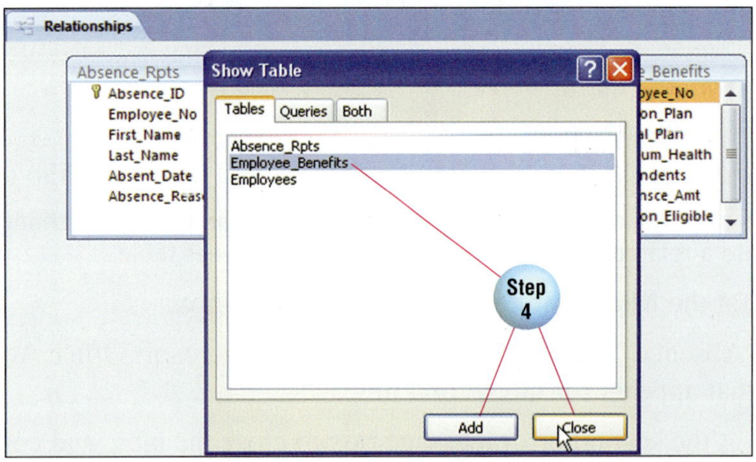

5. Position the mouse pointer over *Employee_No* in the Employees field list box, hold down the left mouse button, drag the pointer to *Employee_No* in the Employee_Benefits field list box, and then release the mouse button.

6 Notice *One-To-One* displays in the *Relationship Type* section of the Edit Relationships dialog box.

Access determined the relationship type as one-to-one since the common field that was used to join the two tables is the primary key field in each table. In both tables, only one record can exist for each unique employee number.

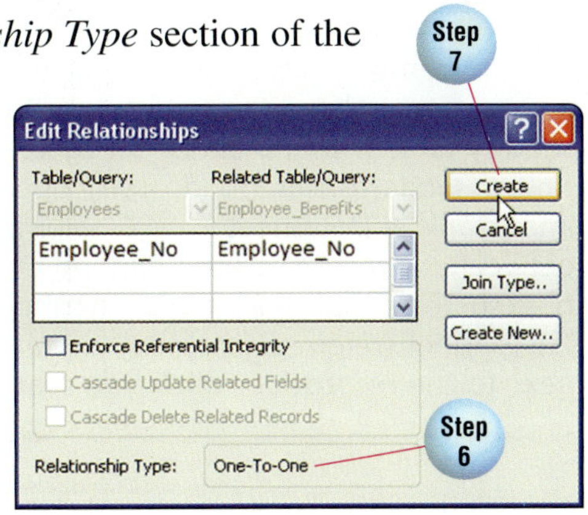

7 Click Create.

A black join line connecting the two *Employee_No* fields appears between the two tables in the Relationships window. The join line does not show a 1 at each end similar to that shown in the previous activity because referential integrity was not turned on.

8 Click the Relationship Report button [Relationship Report] in the Tools group in the Relationship Tools Design tab.

join line illustrating the one-to-one relationship at the two primary key fields

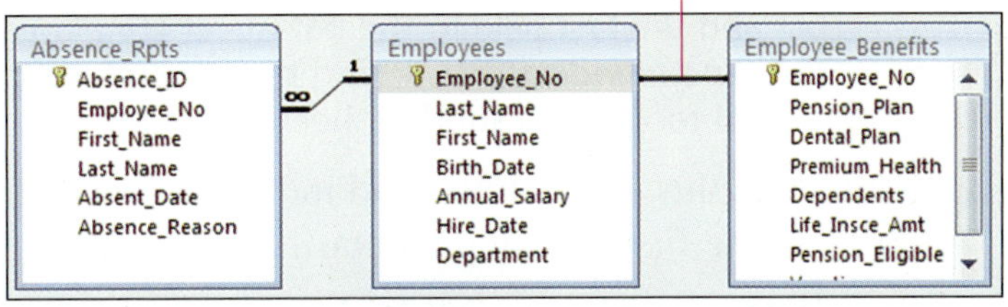

9 With the Relationships for WEEmployees2 report active in the work area, click the Print button on the Quick Access toolbar. ***Note: If the Print button is not displayed on the Quick Access toolbar, click the Customize Quick Access Toolbar button and then click Quick Print at the drop-down list.***

relationship report created in Step 8

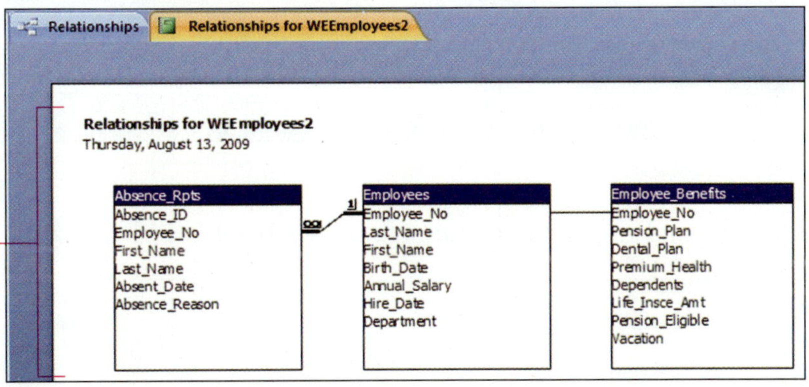

10 Close the Relationships for WEEmployees2 report. Click No when prompted to save the changes to the design of the report.

11 Close the Relationships window.

In Brief

Create One-to-One Relationship

1. Click Database Tools.
2. Click Relationships button.
3. Add desired tables to Relationships window.
4. Close Show Table dialog box.
5. Drag common field from primary table field list box to related table field list box.
6. Turn on desired relationship options.
7. Click Create.
8. Click Save.

In Addition

Deleting a Relationship

To delete a relationship between tables, open the Relationships window, click the black join line representing the relationship you want to remove, and then press the Delete key. At the Microsoft Office Access message asking if you are sure you want to delete the selected relationship permanently from your database, click Yes.

Activity 2.11

Displaying Records in a Subdatasheet

When two tables are joined, you can view related records from the primary table within a datasheet by displaying a ***subdatasheet***. To do this, open the primary table in Datasheet view. A column appears between the record selector bar and the first field in each row displaying a plus symbol. Click the plus symbol (referred to as the ***expand indicator***) next to the record for which you want to view the record(s) in the related table. A subdatasheet opens below the selected record. To remove the subdatasheet, click the minus symbol (referred to as the ***collapse indicator***) to collapse it (the plus symbol changes to a minus symbol after the record has been expanded). If a table has more than one relationship defined, you can choose the subdatasheet you want to see using the More button in the Records group in the Home tab.

Project

You will open the Employees table datasheet and then view related records in subdatasheets from the Absence_Rpts and Employee_Benefit tables.

Worldwide Enterprises

1. With **WEEmployees2.accdb** open, open the Employees table.

   A new column containing a plus symbol (+) appears between the record selector bar and the first field in the datasheet (*Employee_No*). The plus symbol is called the ***expand indicator***. Clicking the expand indicator next to a record displays the related record in a subdatasheet.

2. Click the plus symbol (expand indicator) between the record selector bar and *1000* in the first row in the datasheet.

   The subdatasheet opens to display the record for the same employee (Employee_No 1000) in the related table (Absence_Rpts). Notice the *Employee_No* field is not displayed in the subdatasheet since this is the field by which the two tables are joined.

Plus symbol (expand indicator) changes to minus symbol (collapse indicator) when record has been expanded.

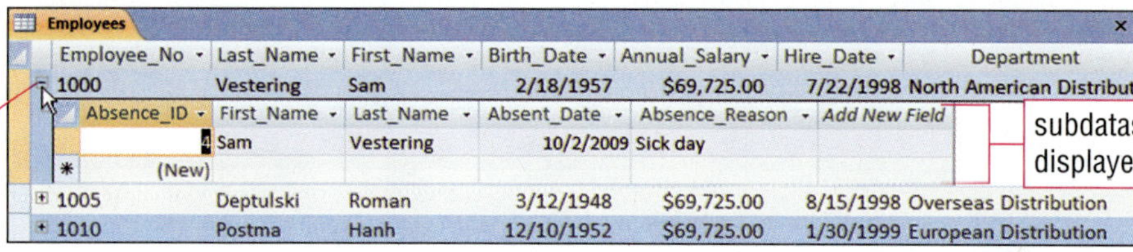

subdatasheet displayed in Step 2

3. Click the expand indicator for *Employee_No* 1010.
4. Click the minus symbol (collapse indicator) for *Employee_No* 1000.
5. Click the collapse indicator for *Employee_No* 1010.
6. Click the More button in the Records group in the Home tab.
7. Point to *Subdatasheet* at the drop-down list and then click *Expand All*.

Step 6

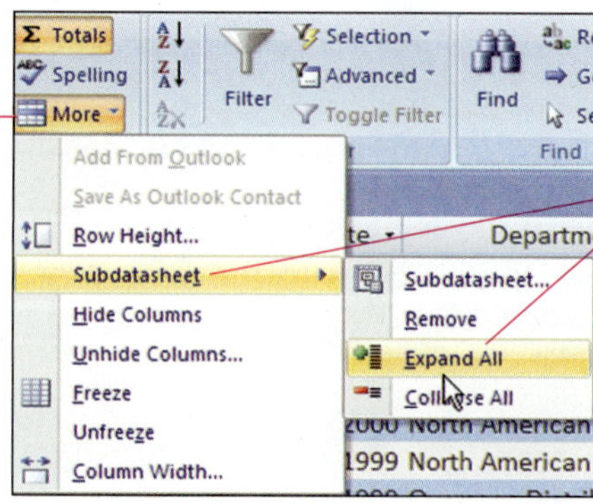

Step 7

8. Click the More button, point to *Subdatasheet*, and then click *Collapse All*.

   In the next steps, you will use the Subdatasheet dialog box to instruct Access to display the related record from the Employee_Benefits table instead of the Absence_Rpts table.

9. Click the More button, point to *Subdatasheet*, and then click *Subdatasheet*.

10. At the Insert Subdatasheet dialog box with the Tables tab selected, click *Employee_Benefits* and then click OK.

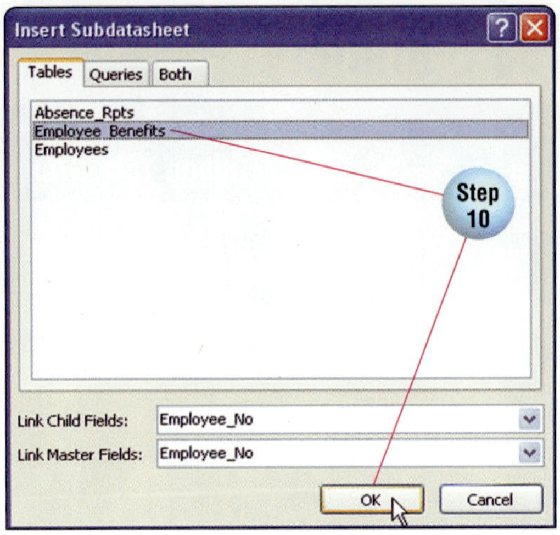

11. Expand the record for *Employee_No* 1000.

    One of the advantages to displaying subdatasheets is the ability to edit in a table while viewing related information from another table. Since the Employee_Benefits table does not include employee names, viewing the benefit record in a subdatasheet from the Employees table which does display employee names ensures you are editing the correct record.

12. Drag across the value $100,000.00 in the *Life_Insce_Amt* field and then type **190000**.

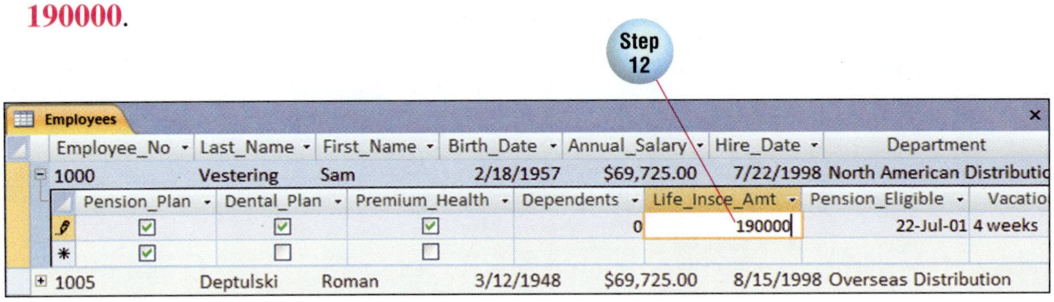

13. Press Enter to complete the entry.

14. Close the Employees table. Click Yes to save the layout changes.

    Saving the layout change means that the next time you open the Employees table and use the expand indicator to display a subdatasheet, the Employee_Benefits table appears instead of Absence_Rpts.

15. Reopen the Employees table and expand all records.

    Notice the related record displayed for each employee is drawn from the Employee_Benefits table.

16. Close the Employees table. Click Yes if prompted to save changes.

17. Close **WEEmployees2.accdb**.

In Brief

Display Records in Subdatasheet

1. Open primary table.
2. Click expand indicator for desired record.
3. View or edit as required.
4. Click collapse indicator.

Choose Subdatasheet to Display

1. Open primary table.
2. Click More button.
3. Point to *Subdatasheet*.
4. Click *Subdatasheet*.
5. Click related table name.
6. Click OK.
7. Click expand indicator for desired record.
8. View or edit as required.
9. Click collapse indicator.

In Addition

Remove a Subdatasheet

If you prefer not to expand records, click the More button in the Records group of the Home tab, point to *Subdatasheet*, and then click *Remove*. This removes the column in the datasheet that displays the expand indicator buttons.

Features Summary

Feature	Ribbon Tab, Group	Button	Keyboard Shortcut
Datasheet view	Home, Views		
delete fields	Table Tools Design, Tools	Delete Rows	Delete
Design view	Home, Views		
fill color	Home, Font		
font size	Home, Font	11	
gridlines	Home, Font		
insert fields	Table Tools Design, Tools	Insert Rows	
insert totals	Home, Records	Σ Totals	
primary key	Table Tools Design, Tools		
relationship report	Relationship Tools Design, Tools	Relationship Report	
relationships	Database Tools, Show/Hide		
subdatasheet	Home, Records	More	

Knowledge Check

Completion: In the space provided at the right, indicate the correct term, command, or option.

1. Display a table in this view to modify a field's properties. ____________
2. Assign a field this data type if the field will contain dollar values that you do not want rounded off in calculations. ____________
3. This is the term for the field in a table that must contain unique information for each record. ____________
4. Enter a value in this field property if you want the value to appear automatically in the field whenever a new record is created. ____________
5. Enter a conditional statement in this field property to prevent data that does not meet the criteria from being entered into the field. ____________
6. This is the field property that controls data as it is being entered by ensuring data typed in the field conforms to the code entered in the property box. ____________
7. This field property controls how data is displayed after it has been accepted for entry in the field. ____________
8. This is the name of the wizard used to create a drop-down list in a field. ____________
9. This button can be used to add a SUM function to the bottom of a numeric field in the datasheet. ____________

10. One table in a relationship is referred to as the primary table. The other table is referred to as this. ____________
11. In this type of relationship one table can have only one record with a matching field value in the common field while the other table can have several records with a matching field value. ____________
12. This is the term for the black line that displays between the common field name in the two field list boxes after a relationship has been created. ____________
13. This type of relationship is created when the field used to join the two tables is the primary key in both tables. ____________
14. Once a relationship has been created between two tables you can open the primary table and click this button to display the subdatasheet for a record. ____________
15. Open this dialog box to specify the table that you want the subdatasheet to be generated from when the primary table has more than one relationship defined. ____________

Skills Review

Review 1 Creating and Modifying a Table in Design View

Worldwide Enterprises

1. Open the **WEEmployees2.accdb** database and enable content.
2. Create a table in Design view using the following field names and data types. You decide whether to add an appropriate description. Do *not* set any field properties since these will be changed later in this activity.

Field Name	**Data Type**
Employee_No	Text
Supervisor_LastName	Text
Supervisor_FirstName	Text
Annual_Review_Date	Date/Time
Salary_Increment_Date	Date/Time
ProfDevDays	Number

3. Define *Employee_No* as the primary key field.
4. Save the table and name it Annual_Review.
5. Switch to Datasheet view and then enter the following two records:

Employee_No	**1015**	*Employee_No*	**1030**
Supervisor_LastName	**Vestering**	*Supervisor_LastName*	**Deptulski**
Supervisor_FirstName	**Sam**	*Supervisor_First_Name*	**Roman**
Annual_Review_Date	**5/20/09**	*Annual_Review_Date*	**1/23/09**
Salary_Increment_Date	**7/01/09**	*Salary_Increment_Date*	**3/02/09**
ProfDevDays	**5**	*ProfDevDays*	**10**

6. Adjust all columns to Best Fit.
7. Save the changes to the datasheet layout.
8. Switch to Design view and then make the following changes to the field properties.
   a. Change the field size for the *Employee_No* field to 4.

b. Create a validation rule for the *ProfDevDays* field to ensure that no number greater than 10 is entered into the field. Enter an appropriate validation text error message.
c. Save the table and click Yes at each message that indicates some data may be lost and to test the data with the new validation rule.
d. Create an input mask for both date fields to set the pattern for entering dates to *Medium Date*. Use the default entry for the placeholder character. Click Yes if prompted to save the table before displaying the Input Mask Wizard.
e. Change the Format property for both date fields to display the date in the Medium Date format.

9. Save the table.
10. Switch to Datasheet view and add the following two records:

Employee_No	**1035**	*Employee_No*	**1040**
Supervisor_LastName	**Postma**	*Supervisor_LastName*	**Deptulski**
Supervisor_FirstName	**Hanh**	*Supervisor_FirstName*	**Roman**
Annual_Review_Date	**14-Mar-09**	*Annual_Review_Date*	**10-Mar-09**
Salary_Increment_Date	**01-May-09**	*Salary_Increment_Date*	**01-May-09**
ProvDevDays	**8**	*ProfDevDays*	**6**

11. Display the datasheet in Print Preview.
12. Change the page orientation to landscape and the left and right margins to 0.5 inch and then print the table.
13. Close Print Preview and then close the Annual_Review table.

Review 2 Moving Fields; Formatting Datasheets; Creating Relationships

Worldwide Enterprises

1. With **WEEmployees2.accdb** open, open the Annual_Review table in Design view.
2. Move the *ProvDevDays* field between *Supervisor_FirstName* and *Annual_Review_Date*.
3. Move *Supervisor_FirstName* before *Supervisor_LastName*.
4. Save the table and then switch to Datasheet view.
5. Format the datasheet as follows:
   a. Change the Fill Color to *Dark Blue 3* (fourth from left in fourth row of *Standard Colors*).
   b. Change gridlines to *Gridlines: Vertical*.
   c. Change the font size to 10.
   d. Adjust all column widths to Best Fit.
6. Close the Annual_Review table saving changes.
7. Create a one-to-one relationship between the Employees table (primary table) and the Annual_Review table (related table) using the *Employee_No* field. Turn on referential integrity. ***Hint: You can drag the title bar of a field list box to another location in the work area so that you are not overlapping join lines with other field list boxes when creating a relationship.***
8. Save the changes to the relationships.
9. Print a relationship report and then close the report without saving.
10. Close the relationships window.
11. Close **WEEmployees2.accdb**.

Skills Assessment

Assessment 1 Creating a Table in Design View; Creating a Lookup Field

1. Gina Simmons, instructor in the Theatre Arts Division, has asked you to create a new table to store the grades for the AC478-01 course she is currently teaching. Gina would prefer to enter grades by selecting from a drop-down list.
2. Open the **NPCGrades2.accdb** database and enable content.
3. Create a new table in Design view using the following field names: *Student_No*; *Last_Name*; *First_Name*; *Grade*. Set the data type to Text for each field except *Grade*. At the *Grade* field, use the Lookup Wizard to create a drop-down list with the following grades: A+, A, B, C, D, F.
4. Restrict the *Grade* lookup properties to items within the list only and do *not* allow the values within the list to be edited from the datasheet.
5. Define *Student_No* field as the primary key.
6. Save the table and name it AC478-01_Grades.
7. Enter the following four records in the datasheet:

Student_No	**111-785-156**	*Student_No*	**118-487-578**
Last_Name	**Bastow**	*Last_Name*	**Andre**
First_Name	**Maren**	*First_Name*	**Ian**
Grade	**A+**	*Grade*	**C**
Student_No	**137-845-746**	*Student_No*	**138-456-749**
Last_Name	**Knowlton**	*Last_Name*	**Yiu**
First_Name	**Sherri**	*First_Name*	**Terry**
Grade	**B**	*Grade*	**D**

8. Adjust all column widths to Best Fit.
9. Print and then close the AC478-01_Grades table saving changes.
10. Close the **NPCGrades2.accdb** database.

Assessment 2 Changing Field Size; Validating Entries; Creating an Input Mask; Formatting Dates; Formatting a Datasheet

1. Bobbie Sinclair, business manager, has asked you to look at the design of the CostumeInventory table and try to improve it with data restrictions and validation rules. While reviewing the table design, you discover an error has been made in assigning the data type for one of the fields.
2. Open the **PTCostumeInventory2.accdb** database and enable content.
3. Open the CostumeInventory table in Design view.
4. Change *DateIn* to a Date/Time field.
5. Change the field size for *CostumeNo* to 5.
6. Performance Threads has a minimum daily rental fee of $85.00. Create a validation rule and validation text that will ensure no one enters a value less than $85.00 in the *DailyRentalFee* field.
7. To ensure no one mixes the order of the month and day when entering the *DateOut* and *DateIn* fields, create an input mask for these two fields to require that the date be entered in the *Medium Date* format.

8. Since Performance Threads is open seven days a week, format the *DateOut* and *DateIn* fields to display the dates in the *Long Date* format. This adds the day of the week to the entry and spells the month in full.
9. Save the table and then switch to Datasheet view.
10. Adjust the column widths of the two date columns to Best Fit. (Access displays pound symbols (#) across a column when the width is not wide enough to display the data.)
11. Change the font size of the datasheet to 10 and then adjust all column widths to Best Fit.
12. Preview the datasheet. Change the margins for the page as necessary so that the entire datasheet fits on one page.
13. Save, print, and then close the CostumeInventory table.
14. Close the **PTCostumeInventory2.accdb** database.

Assessment 3 Creating a New Database

First Choice TRAVEL

1. Alex Torres, manager of the Toronto office, has asked you to help the accounting staff by creating a database to track employee expense claims information. You will create the database from scratch.
2. At the *Getting Started with Microsoft Office Access* screen, complete the following steps:
   a. Click *Blank Database* in the *New Blank Database* section of the center pane.
   b. Select the existing text in the *File Name* text box in the *Blank Database* section of the right pane and then type **FCTExpenses**.
   c. Click the Browse button (displays as a folder icon) at the right of the *File Name* text box. At the File New Database dialog box, if necessary, navigate to the AccessS2 folder on your storage medium and then click OK.
   d. Click the Create button in the *Blank Database* section of the right pane.
3. Look at the sample expense form in Figure 2.2. On your own or with another student in the class, make a list of the fields that would be needed to store the information from this form in a table. Alex has advised that you do *not* need to include fields for the mailing address for the employee. For each field on your list, determine the appropriate data type and field properties that could be used.
4. Create a new table named *Expense_Claims* in Design view. Use the information from Step 3 to enter the field names, data types, and field properties.
5. Create an ID field with the AutoNumber data type and assign the field as the primary key.
6. Switch to Datasheet view and then enter the expense claim information shown in Figure 2.2 in a record.
7. Preview, print, and then close the Expense_Claims table. Use landscape orientation and change margins as necessary to print using only one page if possible.
8. Turn on the Compact on Close feature.
9. Close **FCTExpenses.accdb**.

FIGURE 2.2 Assessment 3

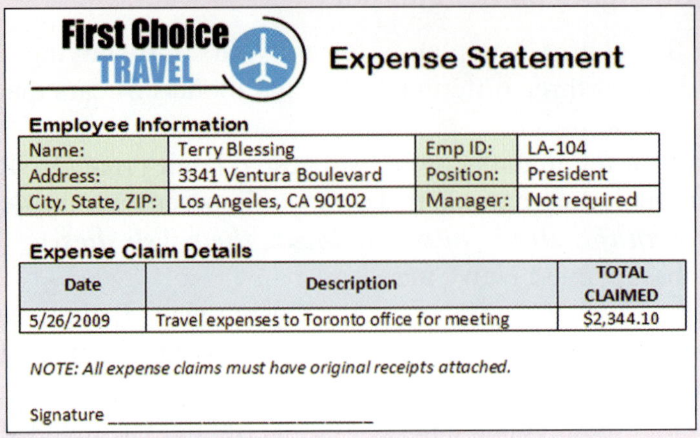

First Choice TRAVEL

Expense Statement

Employee Information

Name:	Terry Blessing	Emp ID:	LA-104
Address:	3341 Ventura Boulevard	Position:	President
City, State, ZIP:	Los Angeles, CA 90102	Manager:	Not required

Expense Claim Details

Date	Description	TOTAL CLAIMED
5/26/2009	Travel expenses to Toronto office for meeting	$2,344.10

NOTE: All expense claims must have original receipts attached.

Signature ______________________

Assessment 4 Finding Information on Table Templates

1. Use the Help feature to find information on creating a new table using a table template.
2. Print the Help topic you find.
3. Create a new blank database named **WBEvents** and then close the empty datasheet that appears.
4. Create a new table in the database using the Events table template.
5. Save the table and name it Local_Events.
6. Display the table in Design view and then delete the field named *Attachments*.
7. Rename the *ID* field to *EventID*.
8. Delete the space between the words in the field names *Start Time* and *End Time*.
9. Add the following event information to the datasheet:

Title	*StartTime*	*EndTime*	*Location*	*Description*
Sailing Regatta	**June 12, 2009**	**June 14, 2009**	**Buffalo Yacht Club**	**Daily races at yacht club**
Sunfest Festival	**July 28, 2009**	**July 31, 2009**	**Broderick Park**	**Celebration of world cultures featuring music, crafts, and cuisine**

10. Adjust all column widths to Best Fit.
11. Preview the datasheet. Change the page orientation to landscape, adjust the margins so the datasheet fits on one page, and then print the datasheet.
12. Close Print Preview and then close the Local_Events table saving changes.
13. Turn on the Compact on Close feature and then close the **WBEvents.accdb** database.

Assessment 5 Car Shopping on the Internet

1. After completing this course, you plan to reward yourself by buying a new car. Identify at least three different makes and models of cars that you like.
2. Search the Internet for the manufacturer's suggested retail price (MSRP) for the cars you would like to own, including options that you would order with the vehicle. ***Hint: Try searching by the manufacturers' names to locate their Web sites.***
3. Create a new database named **NewCars**.
4. Create a table named New_Car_Pricing using Design view. Include the manufacturer's name, brand, model of the car, options, and MSRP. Include other fields that you might want to track such as exterior color choice and interior color choice. Include a field in the table that will contain unique data and then define the field as the primary key.
5. Adjust all column widths to Best Fit.
6. Preview and then print the New_Car_Pricing table.
7. Close the New_Car_Pricing table.
8. Turn on the Compact on Close feature and then close the **NewCars.accdb** database.

Marquee Challenge

Challenge 1 Refining Tables in a Database; Creating Relationships

1. Sam Vestering has sent you a database that was created to keep track of corporate logo wear purchases and vendors. A former intern created the database but was not able to complete it before returning to school. Sam would like you to review the tables and modify field properties wherever possible to refine the table design and then relate the two tables.
2. Open **WEPurchases2.accdb** and enable content.
3. Open each table and look at the sample data entered in the datasheet and then, in Design view, modify field properties to maximize Access features that can control or otherwise validate data entered. Consider the following practices at Worldwide Enterprises as you complete this task:
   a. Worldwide uses a 4-character purchase order numbering system.
   b. All vendors are assigned a 3-character vendor number.
   c. Staff at Worldwide are used to entering dates in the format dd-mmm-yy.
   d. Telephone numbers must all include the area code using a format such as (212) 555-6549.
   e. Worldwide will not issue a purchase order for corporate wear that has a value less than $300.00.
4. Sam asked that you set up a new field in the Purchases table to enter the shipment method. Worldwide will only receive shipments from the following carriers with whom credit accounts have been set up: *UPS, Fedex, Express Freight,* and *Global Transport*. After creating the new field, populate the existing records with one of the carrier companies to test the field.
5. Create a relationship between the Vendors tables and the Purchases table.
6. Print the relationship report.
7. Print each datasheet making sure all data is visible.
8. Create a memo to your instructor that documents the field properties in each table that you modified including the property box entry. Save the memo and name it **AccessS2-C1**. Print and then close the memo.
9. Close **WEPurchases2.accdb**.

Challenge 2 Creating a New Database

Performance Threads

1. Bobbie Sinclair, business manager, has approved the project to create the new database that will store the custom costume business at Performance Threads.
2. Open **AccessS1-C2.docx**. (This document was created in Marquee Challenge 2 in Section 1.)
3. Use Save As and name the document **AccessS2-C2**.
4. Continue your work on the table design for this database by documenting next to each field name the properties that you will set. For each field, consider applying properties learned in this section that will help maintain data integrity. Consider making assumptions about some business rules and then setting field properties that will conform to those rules. You may make any reasonable assumptions that you think would protect the data in a business setting similar to a custom costume manufacturer. For example, you may assume a minimum price for a custom costume. You determine any acceptable limits. Document all of your assumptions.
5. Consider the relationships in the new database. Document in **AccessS2-C2.docx** on a separate page the tables that will be related and the type of relationship created. Include the common field name upon which you will join each table.
6. Create a new blank database named **AccessS2-C2-PTCostumes**.
7. Create the tables as per your design document. Make sure that you change your design document if you change your mind about a field property once you create the table.
8. Populate each table with a few sample records to ensure your properties work as expected.
9. Create relationships between the tables as per your design document.
10. Print the relationships report.
11. Print each datasheet.
12. Turn on the Compact on Close feature and then close **AccessS2-C2-PTCostumes.accdb**.
13. Save the revised Word document and then print **AccessS2-C2.docx**.

Access SECTION 3

Creating Queries, Forms, and Reports

Skills

- Create a select query using the Simple Query Wizard
- Create a select query in Design view
- Add multiple tables to a query
- Sort the query results
- Add criteria statements to a query
- Prevent columns in the query design grid from displaying in the query results datasheet
- Perform calculations in a query
- Create a form using the Simple Form tool
- Create a split form
- Create a form using the Form Wizard
- Add a logo image to a form
- Resize and format an object on a form
- Change the style for a form
- Add a field to a form
- Create a report using the Report tool
- Create a report using the Report Wizard
- Move and resize columns in a report

Student Resources

Before beginning this section:

1. Copy to your storage medium the AccessS3 subfolder from the Access folder on the Student Resources CD.
2. Make AccessS3 the active folder.

In addition to containing the data files needed to complete section work, the Student Resources CD contains model answers in PDF format for each of the projects in this section; model answers for end-of-section activities are not provided.

Projects Overview

Worldwide Enterprises

Create queries to produce custom employee lists, add criteria, and calculate pension contributions and monthly salaries; create and modify forms to facilitate data entry and viewing of records; create and modify reports to produce custom printouts of data.

Niagara Peninsula College

Create and print a query to extract records of students who achieved A+ in all of their courses.

Performance Threads

Create a query, and create and print a report that lists all costumes rented in a particular month; create and modify a form for browsing the costume inventory and entering new records; continue design work on a new database for custom costume activities by creating forms and a report.

The Waterfront B·I·S·T·R·O

Create queries and design a report for the catering events database to extract event information for each banquet room, extract all events booked in a particular month, and calculate the estimated revenue from the catering events.

Activity 3.1

Creating a Query Using the Simple Query Wizard

A ***query*** is an Access object designed to extract data from one or more tables. A query can be created to serve a variety of purposes, from very simple field selection to complex conditional statements or calculations. In its simplest form, a query selects some of the fields from the table(s) to display or print rather than viewing all fields in a table datasheet. Access includes the Simple Query Wizard to facilitate creating a query.

Project

Worldwide Enterprises

You need to print a list of records using fields from two tables. Using the Simple Query Wizard, you will generate a list of each employee's first and last names, number of dependents, life insurance amount, pension plan eligibility date, and vacation entitlement.

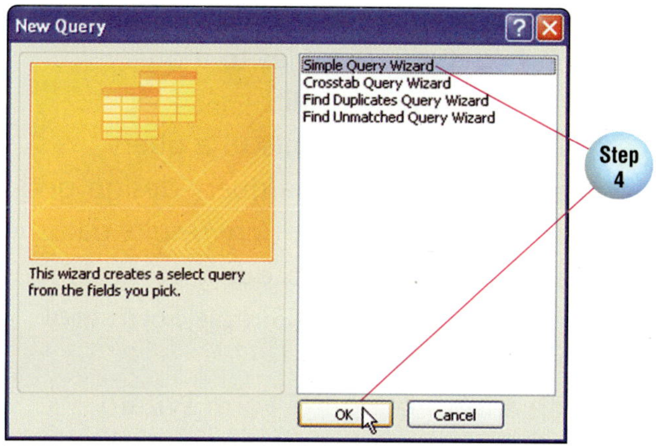

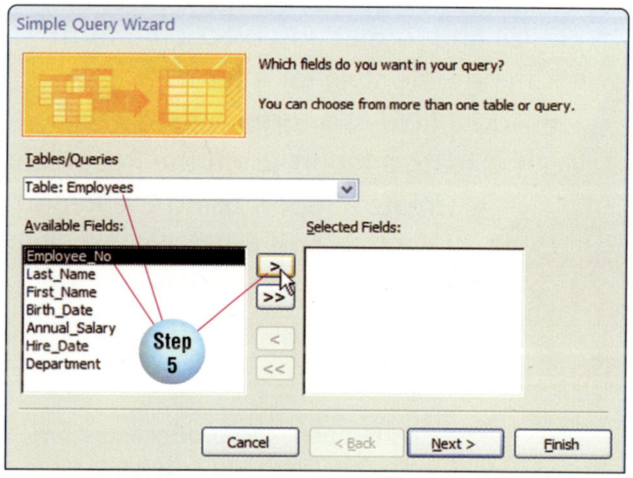

1. Open **WEEmployees3.accdb** and enable content.
2. Click *Employees: Table* in the Navigation pane and then click the Create tab.
3. Click the Query Wizard button in the Other group.
4. At the New Query dialog box, with *Simple Query Wizard* already selected in the list box, click OK.
5. At the first Simple Query Wizard dialog box, with *Table: Employees* already selected in the *Tables/Queries* list box and with *Employee_No* already selected in the *Available Fields* list box, click the Add Field button > to move *Employee_No* to the *Selected Fields* list box.
6. With *Last_Name* now selected in the *Available Fields* list box, click the Add Field button to move *Last_Name* to the *Selected Fields* list box.
7. Click the Add Field button to move *First_Name* to the *Selected Fields* list box.
8. Click the down-pointing arrow at the right of the *Tables/Queries* list box and then click *Table: Employee_Benefits* at the drop-down list.

   The list of fields in the *Available Fields* list box changes to display the field names from the Employee_Benefits table.
9. Double-click *Dependents* in the *Available Fields* list box.

   Double-clicking a field name is another way to move a field to the *Selected Fields* list box.

10 Double-click the following fields in the *Available Fields* list box to move them to the *Selected Fields* list box:

Life_Insce_Amt
Pension_Eligible
Vacation

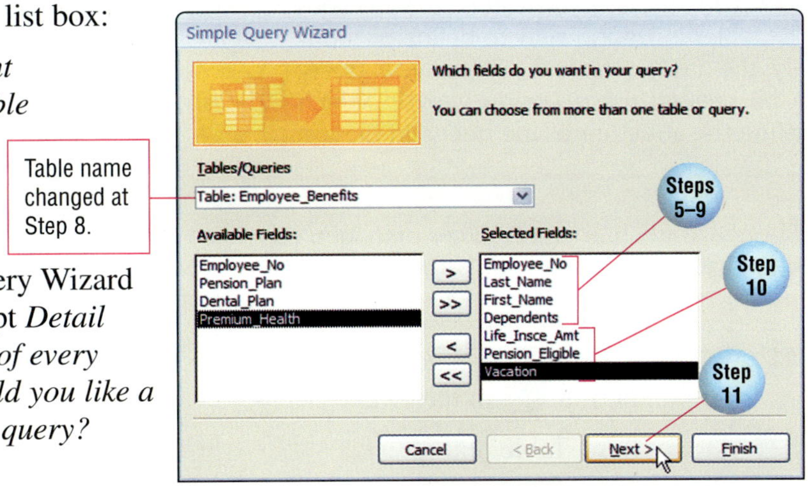

11 Click Next.

12 Click Next at the second Simple Query Wizard dialog box to accept *Detail (shows every field of every record)* in the *Would you like a detail or summary query?* section.

13 At the third Simple Query Wizard dialog box, select the current text in the *What title do you want for your query?* text box, type **Non-Medical_Benefits**, and then click Finish.

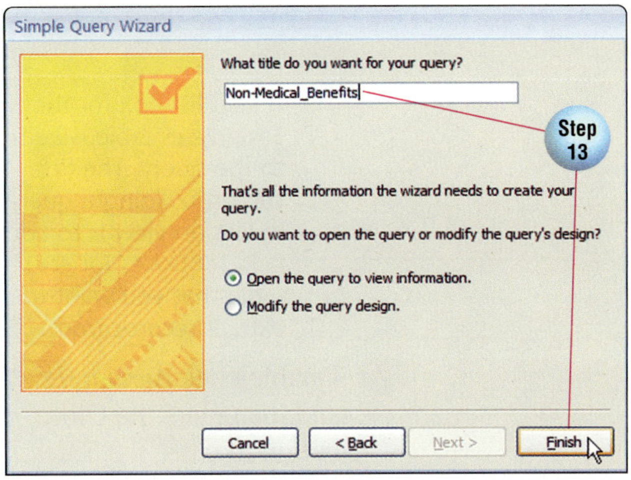

14 View the query results datasheet shown in Figure 3.1.

The query results datasheet shown in Figure 3.1 can be sorted, edited, or formatted in a manner similar to a table datasheet. Data displayed in query results is not stored as a separate entity—the query is simply another interface for viewing and editing data in the associated table(s). When a saved query is opened, the query results are updated dynamically each time by running the query.

15 Display the datasheet in Print Preview, change the orientation to landscape, and then print the datasheet.

16 Close the Print Preview window and then close the Non-Medical_Benefits query.

FIGURE 3.1 Query Results Datasheet

Non-Medical_Benefits

Employee_No	Last_Name	First_Name	Dependents	Life_Insce_Amt	Pension_Eligible	Vacation
1000	Vestering	Sam	0	$190,000.00	22-Jul-01	4 weeks
1005	Deptulski	Roman	2	$200,000.00	15-Aug-01	3 weeks
1010	Postma	Hanh	1	$75,000.00	30-Jan-02	3 weeks
1015	Besterd	Lyle	3	$55,000.00	17-May-02	3 weeks
1020	Doxtator	Angela	4	$195,000.00	03-Aug-03	2 weeks
1025	Biliski	Jorge	3	$200,000.00	01-Dec-02	2 weeks
1030	Hicks	Thom	0	$150,000.00	22-Jan-02	2 weeks
1035	Fitsouris	Valerie	0	$100,000.00	15-Mar-04	2 weeks
1040	Lafreniere	Guy	2	$75,000.00	10-Mar-04	2 weeks
1045	Yiu	Terry	1	$55,000.00	12-Apr-04	2 weeks
1050	Zakowski	Carl	0	$25,000.00	09-Feb-05	1 week
1055	Thurston	Edward	3	$85,000.00	22-Jun-05	1 week
1060	McKnight	Donald	1	$55,000.00	22-Jun-06	1 week
1065	Liszniewski	Norm	4	$200,000.00	06-Feb-06	1 week
1070	Jhawar	Balfor	2	$125,000.00	22-Nov-07	1 week
1075	Fitchett	Mike	3	$80,000.00	19-Mar-07	1 week
1080	Couture	Leo	2	$110,000.00	17-Jan-07	1 week

In Brief

Create Query Using Simple Query Wizard

1. Click Create tab.
2. Click Query Wizard.
3. Click OK.
4. Choose table(s) and field(s) to include in query.
5. Click Next.
6. Choose *Detail* or *Summary* query.
7. Click Next.
8. Type title for query.
9. Click Finish.

Activity 3.2

Creating a Query in Design View

In Section 2 you learned to work with tables in Design view to define or modify the table structure. Similarly, a query can be created using Design view in which you define the structure of the query. In Design view, you choose the table(s) you wish to extract records from and then use field list box(es) to choose the field(s) to display in the query results datasheet.

Project

Worldwide Enterprises

Rhonda Trask, human resources manager, has asked for a list that includes employee number, employee name, supervisor name, and annual review date. This data is stored in two different tables. You will create a query to obtain the required fields from each table to generate the list.

1. With **WEEmployees3.accdb** open and the Create tab active, click the Query Design button in the Other group.

2. At the Show Table dialog box with the Tables tab selected, double-click *Employees*.

   A field list box for the Employees table is added to the query. The first step in building a query in Design view is to add field list boxes for each table that you want to extract records from.

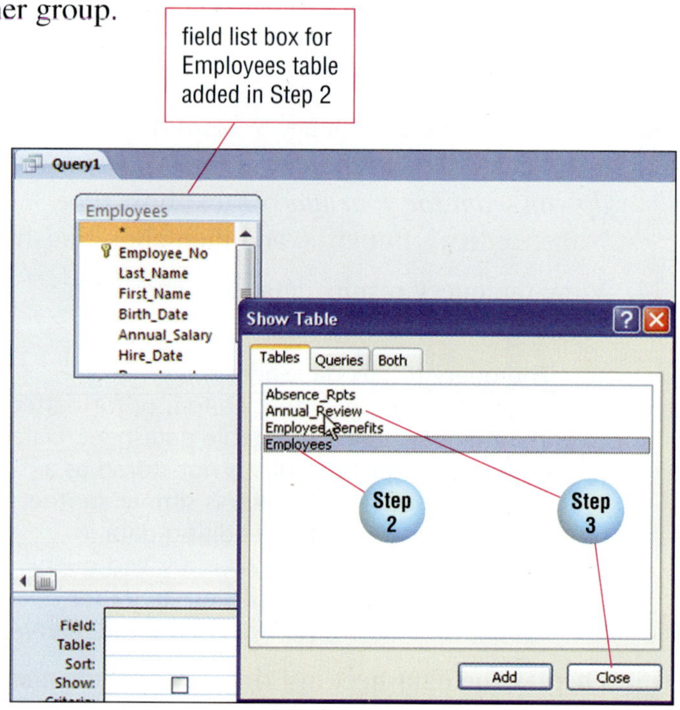

3. Double-click *Annual_Review* and then click the Close button to close the Show Table dialog box.

   A black join line with 1 at each end of the line between the Employees and the Annual_Review tables illustrates the one-to-one relationship that has been defined between the two tables.

4. Double-click *Employee_No* in the Employees table field list box.

   The blank columns at the bottom represent the columns in the query results datasheet and are referred to as the *design grid*. You place the field names in the columns in the order in which you want the fields displayed in the query results datasheet. Double-clicking a field name adds the field to the next available column. In Steps 5 and 6, you will practice two other methods of adding fields to the design grid.

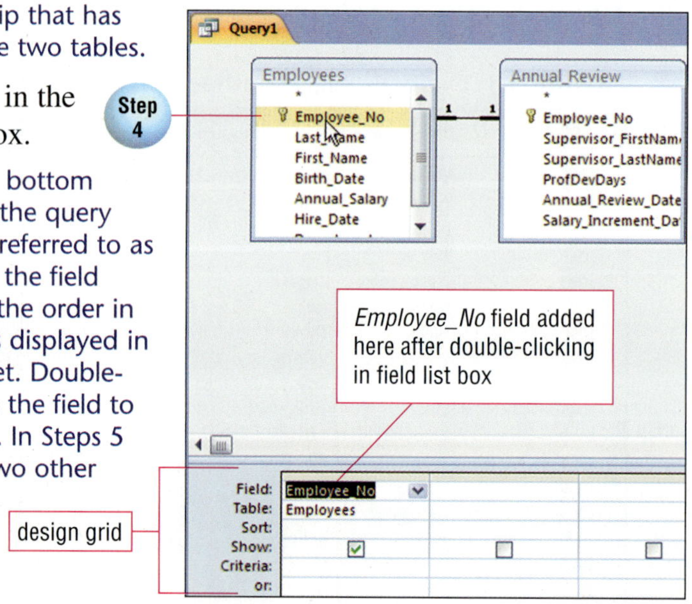

5 Position the mouse pointer on the *First_Name* field in the Employees table field list box, hold down the left mouse button, drag to the *Field* row in the second column of the design grid, and then release the mouse button.

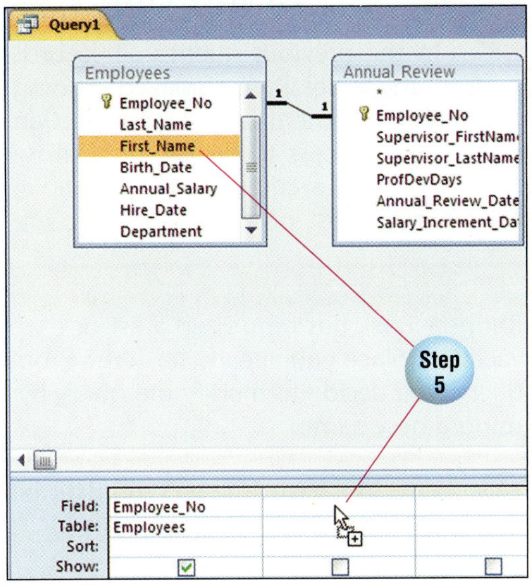

6 Click in the *Field* row in the third column of the design grid, click the down-pointing arrow that appears, and then click *Employees.Last_Name* at the drop-down list.

7 Using any of the three methods learned in Steps 4–6, add the fields *Supervisor_FirstName*, *Supervisor_LastName*, and *Annual_Review_Date* from the Annual_Review table field list box to the design grid.

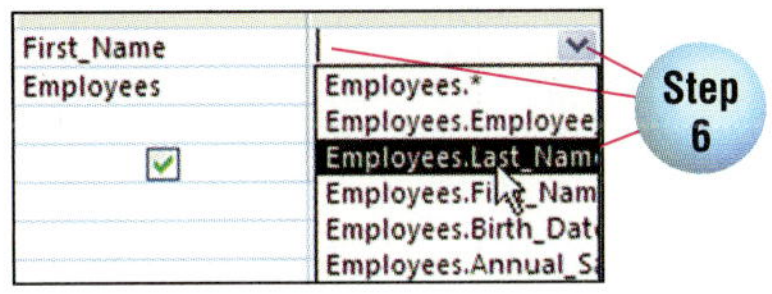

8 Click the Save button on the Quick Access toolbar.

9 At the Save As dialog box, type **Employee_Review_List** in the *Query Name* text box and then press Enter or click OK.

10 Click the Run button [!] in the Results group in the Query Tools Design tab.

A query stores instructions on how to extract data. The Run command instructs Access to carry out the instructions and display the results.

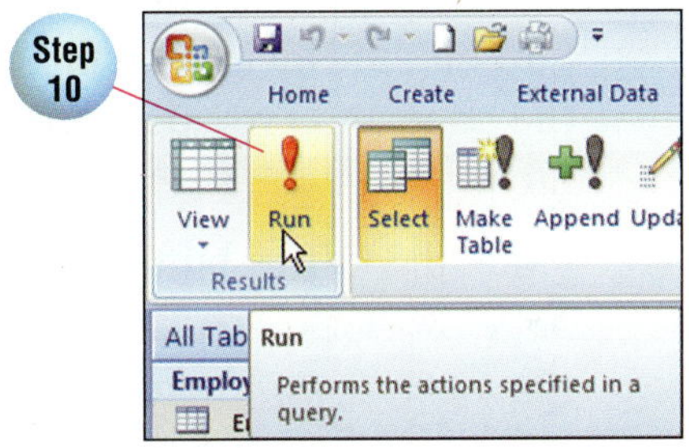

11 Adjust the column widths for the last three columns in the query results datasheet to Best Fit.

12 Display the datasheet in Print Preview, change the orientation to landscape, and then print the datasheet.

13 Close the Print Preview window and then close the Employee_Review_List query, saving changes to the layout of the query.

In Brief

Create Query in Design View

1. Click Create tab.
2. Click Query Design button.
3. Double-click required table(s) in Show Table dialog box.
4. Close Show Table dialog box.
5. Add required field names from field list box(es) to columns in design grid.
6. Click Save button.
7. Type query name and click OK.
8. Click Run button.

In Addition

Action Queries

In the last activity and in this activity, you created ***select queries*** that displayed selected fields from tables. Another type of query, called an ***action query***, makes changes to a group of records. Four types of action queries are available in Access: delete, update, append, and make-table. A delete query deletes records. An update query makes global changes to a field. Append queries add a group of records from one table to the end of another table. A make-table query creates a new table from all or part of data in existing tables.

Activity 3.3

Extracting Records Using Criteria Statements

In the previous queries all records from the tables were displayed. Adding a criterion statement to the query design grid will cause Access to display only those records that meet the criterion. For example, you could generate a list of employees who are entitled to four weeks of vacation. Extracting specific records from the tables is where the true power in creating queries is found since you are able to separate out only those records that serve your purpose.

Project

Rhonda Trask has requested a list of employees who receive either three or four weeks of vacation. Since you already have the employee names and vacation fields set up in an existing query, you decide to modify the query by adding the vacation criteria and then save the query using a new name.

1. With **WEEmployees3.accdb** open, right-click *Non-Medical_Benefits* in the Navigation pane and then click *Design View* at the shortcut menu.

? PROBLEM

Not sure which Non-Medical_Benefits to open? The current view for the Navigation pane is *Table and Related Views*. This means that objects are grouped by tables. Since the Non-Medical_Benefits query was generated using two tables, the object name is displayed in two categories: Employees and Employee_Benefits. You can right-click either name because they both refer to the same object.

2. Click the Shutter Bar Open/Close Button « on the Navigation pane to minimize the pane and provide a larger working area.

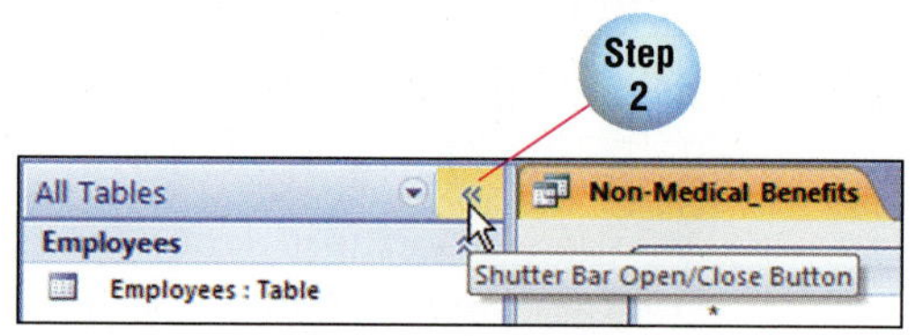

3. Click the Office button and then click *Save As*. Type **Vacation_3or4Weeks** in the *Save 'Non-Medical_Benefits' to* text box at the Save As dialog box and then click OK.

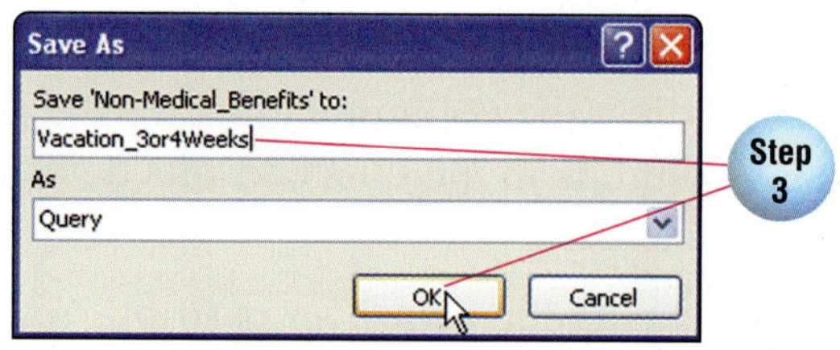

4. Click in the *Criteria* row in the *Vacation* column in the design grid.
5. Type **4 weeks** and then press Enter.

   The insertion point moves to the *Criteria* row in the next column and Access inserts quotation marks around *4 weeks* in the *Vacation* column. Since quotation marks are required in criteria statements for text fields, Access automatically inserts them if they are not typed into the *Criteria* text box.

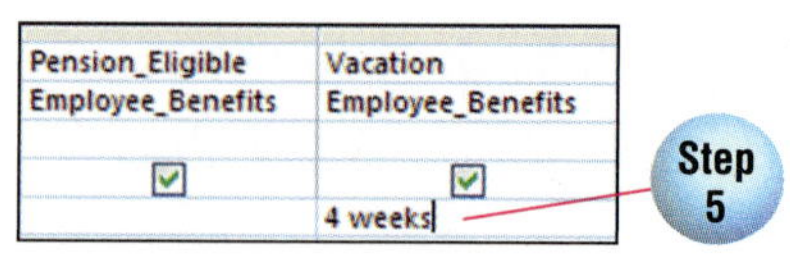

6. Click in the *or* row in the *Vacation* column in the design grid (blank row below *"4 weeks"*), type **3 weeks**, and then press Enter.

   Including a second criteria statement below the first one instructs Access to display records that meet either of the two criteria.

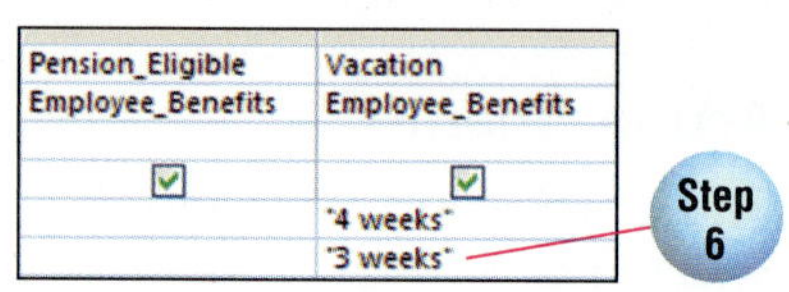

7. Click the Run button in the Results group in the Query Tools Design tab.

8 View the query results in the datasheet and then click the View button in the Views group in the Home tab to switch to Design view. (Do *not* click the down-pointing arrow on the View button.)

Since Rhonda Trask is interested only in the employee names and vacation weeks, you will instruct Access not to display the other fields in the query results datasheet.

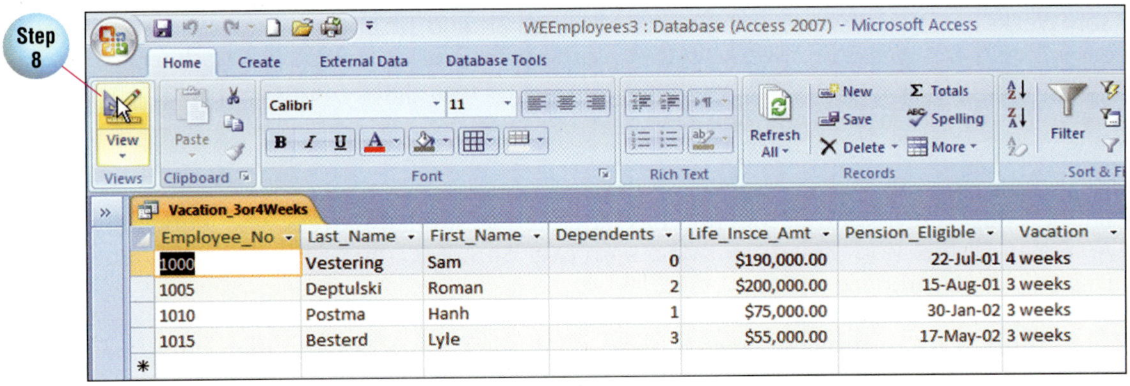

9 Click the check box in the *Show* row in the *Dependents* column to clear the box.

Clearing the check box instructs Access to hide the column in the query results datasheet.

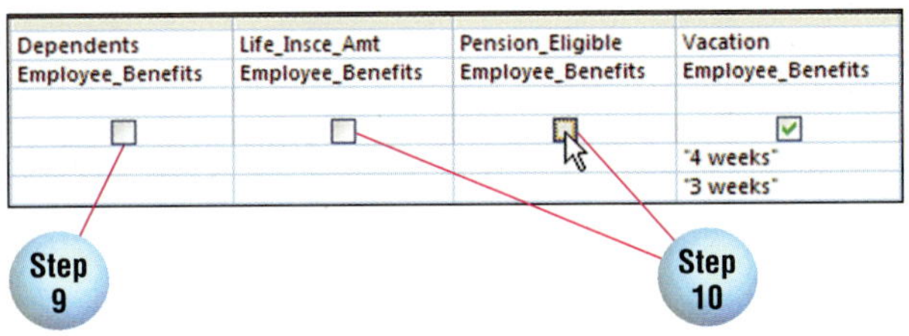

10 Clear the *Show* check boxes in the *Life_Insce_Amt* and *Pension_Eligible* columns in the design grid.

11 Click the View button to switch to Datasheet view.

The columns for which the *Show* check box was cleared do not display in the query results.

12 Print the query results datasheet.

13 Close the Vacation_3or4Weeks query. Click Yes to save changes to the design of the query and then click the Shutter Bar Open/Close Button to redisplay the Navigation pane.

In Brief

Add Criteria Statement to Query

1. Open query in Design view.
2. Click in *Criteria* row in column to attach criterion to.
3. Type criterion statement.
4. Save revised query.
5. Run query.

In Addition

Criteria Statement Examples

The following are examples of criteria statements for text, number, and date fields showing the proper syntax required by Access. For text and date fields, Access inserts the quotation symbols (") and pound symbols automatically (#).

Criterion Statement	Records That Would Be Extracted
"Finance Department"	Those with *Finance Department* in the field
Not "Finance Department"	All *except* those with *Finance Department* in the field
"Fan*"	Those that begin *Fan* and end with any other characters in the field
>15000	Those with a value greater than 15,000 in the field
>=15000 And <=20000	Those with a value from 15,000 to 20,000 in the field
#05/01/09#	Those that contain the date May 1, 2009 in the field
>#05/01/09#	Those that contain dates after May 1, 2009 in the field
Between #05/01/09# And #05/31/09#	Those that contain dates May 1, 2009 through May 31, 2009 in the field

Activity 3.4

Extracting Records Using Multiple Field Criteria; Sorting Data in a Query

In the previous query, entering more than one criterion below another in the *Vacation* field is an example of extracting records using an *Or* statement. In the Vacation_3or4Weeks query, Access selected records of employees with either 4 weeks or 3 weeks in the vacation field. You can also select records by entering criteria statements into more than one field. Multiple criteria all entered in the same row becomes an *And* statement where each criterion must be met for the record to be selected. Use the Sort row in the design grid to specify the field by which records should be sorted. Sort a query using the same principles as sorting a datasheet—columns are sorted from left to right for multiple sort keys.

Project

Worldwide Enterprises

Rhonda Trask is reviewing salaries and has requested a list of employees who work in the North American Distribution department who earn over $45,000. You will create a new query in Design view to produce the list.

1. With **WEEmployees3.accdb** open, click the Create tab and then click the Query Design button in the Other group.
2. At the Show Table dialog box, double-click the table named *Employees* and then click the Close button.
3. Double-click the following fields in order to add the fields to the design grid. ***Note: You may have to scroll down the field list box to see all of the fields.***

   First_Name
   Last_Name
   Department
   Hire_Date
   Annual_Salary

4. Click in the *Criteria* row in the *Department* column in the design grid, type **North American Distribution**, and then press Enter.
5. Position the mouse pointer on the right column boundary line for the *Department* field in the gray header row at the top of the design grid until the pointer changes to a black vertical line with a left- and right-pointing arrow and then double-click to best fit the column width.

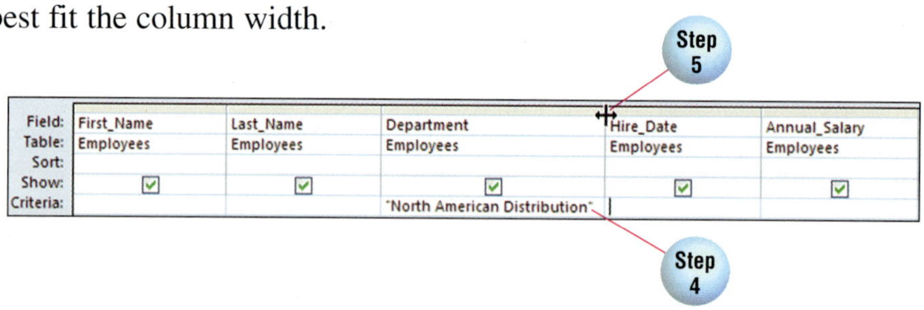

6. Click in the *Criteria* row in the *Annual_Salary* column, type **>45000**, and then press Enter.

   Placing multiple criterion statements on the same row in the design grid means that each criterion must be satisfied in order for Access to select the record.

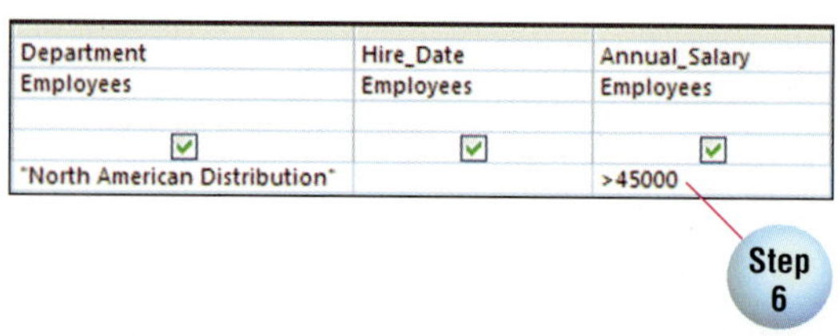

7 Click in the *Sort* row in the *Last_Name* column, click the down-pointing arrow that appears, and then click *Ascending* at the drop-down list.

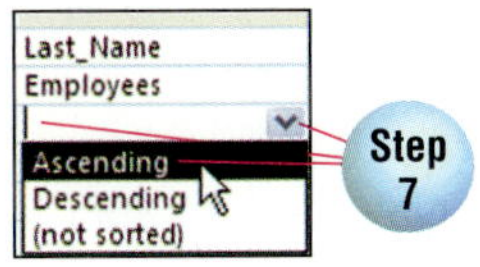

8 Click the Run button.

9 Review the records selected in the query results datasheet. Notice that the *Department* field value for each record is *North American Distribution* **and** the field values in the *Annual_Salary* column are all greater than $45,000. The list is also displayed sorted by the employee's last name.

Query1

First_Name	Last_Name	Department	Hire_Date	Annual_Salary
Lyle	Besterd	North American Distribution	5/17/1999	$45,651.00
Angela	Doxtator	North American Distribution	8/3/2000	$45,558.00
Sam	Vestering	North American Distribution	7/22/1998	$69,725.00

Step 9

10 Click the Save button, type **NorthAmerican_SalaryOver$45K** in the *Query Name* text box, and then press Enter or click OK.

11 Print the query results datasheet.

12 Close the NorthAmerican_SalaryOver$45K query.

In Brief

Extracting Using Multiple Field Criteria

1. Start new query in Design view.
2. Add desired table(s) and field(s) to design grid.
3. Click in *Criteria* row in column in which to attach criterion.
4. Type criterion statement.
5. Repeat Steps 3–4 for remaining criterion fields.
6. Save query.
7. Run query.

Sort Query Results

1. Open query in Design view.
2. Click in *Sort* row in field by which to sort.
3. Click down-pointing arrow.
4. Click *Ascending* or *Descending*.
5. Save query.
6. Run query.

In Addition

Combining And and Or Statements

Assume that Rhonda Trask requested a list of employees who work in the North American Distribution department *and* earn over $45,000 per year *or* the European Distribution department *and* earn over $45,000 per year. To perform this query, you would use two rows in the design grid to enter the criteria as shown below.

Department	Hire_Date	Annual_Salary
Employees	Employees	Employees
☑	☑	☑
"North American Distribution"		>45000
"European Distribution"		>45000

multiple and/or criteria

First_Name	Last_Name	Department	Hire_Date	Annual_Salary
Lyle	Besterd	North American Distribution	5/17/1999	$45,651.00
Angela	Doxtator	North American Distribution	8/3/2000	$45,558.00
Hanh	Postma	European Distribution	1/30/1999	$69,725.00
Sam	Vestering	North American Distribution	7/22/1998	$69,725.00

resulting query results datasheet

Activity 3.5

Performing Calculations in a Query; Formatting Columns

Calculations such as adding or multiplying two fields can be included in a query. In a blank field text box in Query Design view, type the text that you want to appear as the column heading followed by a colon and then the mathematical expression for the calculated values. Field names in the mathematical expression are encased in square brackets. For example, the entry *Total_Salary:[Base_Salary]+[Commission]* would add the value in the field named *Base_Salary* to the value in the field named *Commission*. The result would be placed in a new column in the query datasheet with the column heading *Total_Salary*. Calculated columns do not exist in the associated table; the values are calculated dynamically each time the query is run. Format the appearance of data using buttons in the Font group in the Home tab. Numeric format and decimal places are set using the property sheet in Design view.

Project

Worldwide Enterprises contributes 5% of each employee's annual salary to a registered pension plan. You will create a new query to calculate the employer's annual pension contributions.

1. With **WEEmployees3.accdb** open, click the Create tab and then click the Query Design button.
2. At the Show Table dialog box, double-click the table named *Employees* and then click the Close button.
3. Double-click the following fields in the order shown to add the fields to the design grid. ***Note: You may have to scroll down the field list box to see all of the fields.***
   Employee_No
   First_Name
   Last_Name
   Annual_Salary

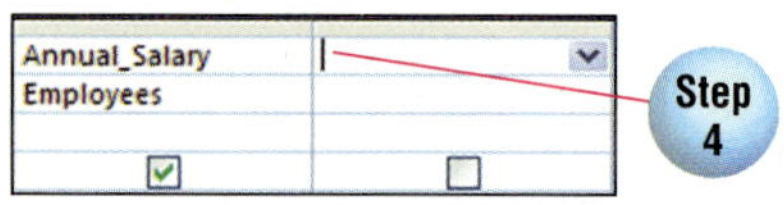

4. Click in the blank *Field* row next to the *Annual_Salary* column in the design grid.
5. Type **Pension_Contribution:[Annual_Salary]*.05** and then press Enter.

PROBLEM

Message appears stating expression contains invalid syntax? Check that you have used the correct type of brackets, typed a colon, and that there are no other typing errors.

6. Position the mouse pointer on the right vertical boundary line for the *Pension_Contribution* column in the gray field selector bar at the top of the design grid until the pointer changes to a black vertical line with a left- and right-pointing arrow and then double-click the left mouse button.

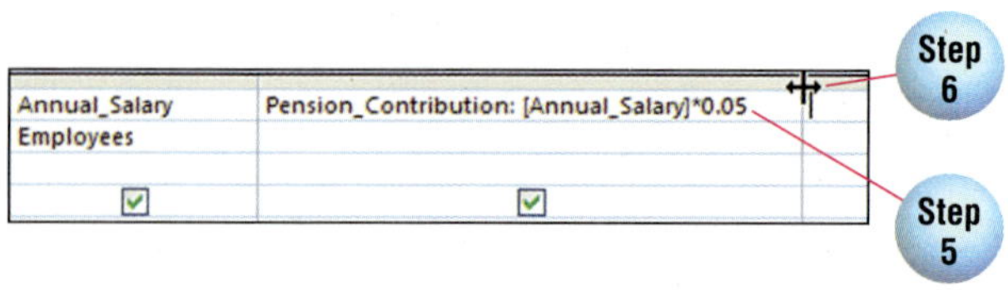

7. Click the Save button. At the Save As dialog box, type **Employer_Pension_Contributions** in the *Query Name* text box and then press Enter or click OK.
8. Click the Run button.

9. In the query results datasheet, adjust the column width for the *Pension_Contribution* column to Best Fit.

   The values in the calculated column need to be formatted to display a consistent number of decimal places. You will correct this in the next steps by changing the format option in the *Pension_Contribution* field's *Field Properties* sheet.

10. Switch to Design view.
11. Click the insertion point anywhere within the *Pension_Contribution* field row in the design grid.
12. Click the Property Sheet button Property Sheet in the Show/Hide group of the Query Tools Design tab.

   Available properties for the active field display in the Property Sheet task pane at the right side of the work area.

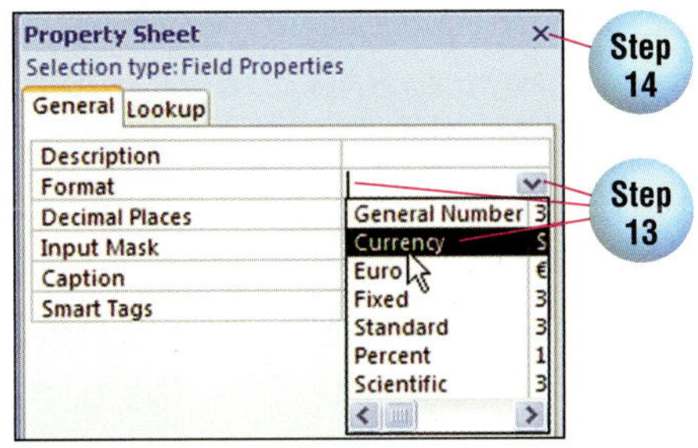

13. Click in the *Format* property box in the Property Sheet task pane, click the down-pointing arrow that appears, and then click *Currency* at the drop-down list.
14. Click the Close button at the top right of the Property Sheet task pane.
15. Click the Save button and then click the Run button.

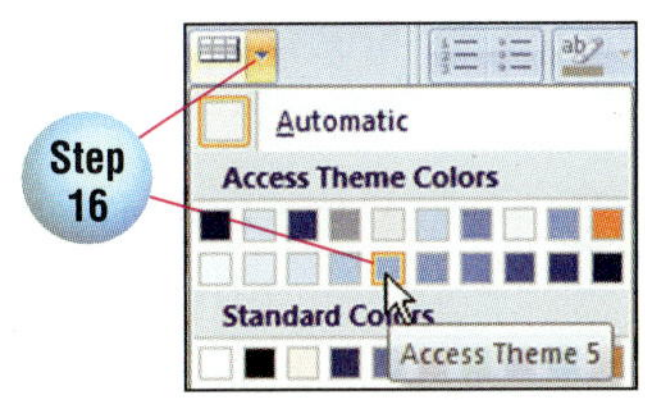

16. At the query results datasheet, click the down-pointing arrow at the right of the Alternate Fill/Back Color button in the Font group in the Home tab and then click *Access Theme 5* (fifth from left in second row of *Access Theme Colors* section) at the drop-down color palette.
17. Print the query results datasheet.
18. Close the Employer_Pension_Contributions query. Click Yes when prompted to save changes to the layout of the query.

Employer_Pension_Contributions

Employee_No	First_Name	Last_Name	Annual_Salary	Pension_Contribution
1000	Sam	Vestering	$69,725.00	$3,486.25
1005	Roman	Deptulski	$69,725.00	$3,486.25
1010	Hanh	Postma	$69,725.00	$3,486.25
1015	Lyle	Besterd	$45,651.00	$2,282.55
1020	Angela	Doxtator	$45,558.00	$2,277.90
1025	Jorge	Biliski	$44,892.00	$2,244.60
1030	Thom	Hicks	$42,824.00	$2,141.20
1035	Valerie	Fitsouris	$44,694.00	$2,234.70
1040	Guy	Lafreniere	$45,395.00	$2,269.75
1045	Terry	Yiu	$42,238.00	$2,111.90
1050	Carl	Zakowski	$44,387.00	$2,219.35
1055	Edward	Thurston	$42,248.00	$2,112.40
1060	Donald	McKnight	$42,126.00	$2,106.30
1065	Norm	Liszniewski	$43,695.00	$2,184.75
1070	Balfor	Jhawar	$44,771.00	$2,238.55
1075	Mike	Fitchett	$42,857.00	$2,142.85
1080	Leo	Couture	$43,659.00	$2,182.95

query results datasheet with Alternate Fill/Back Color applied in Step 16

In Brief

Create Calculated Field in Query

1. Open query in Design view.
2. Click in first available blank field row in design grid.
3. Type column heading for calculated field.
4. Type colon (:).
5. Type mathematical expression.
6. Press Enter or click in another field.
7. Click Save button.
8. Click Run button.

Format Calculated Field

1. Open query in Design view.
2. Click in field containing calculated expression.
3. Click Query Tools Design tab.
4. Click Property Sheet button.
5. Click in *Format* property box.
6. Click down-pointing arrow.
7. Click desired format at drop-down list.
8. Close Property Sheet task pane.
9. Save query.
10. Run query.

Activity 3.6

Creating Forms Using the Form Tool, Split Form Tool, and Form Wizard

Recall from Section 1 that forms provide a user-friendly interface for viewing, adding, editing, and deleting records. The Form tool creates a new form with one click. A split form shows two views for a form, with the top half displaying the form using Form view while the same form displays in the bottom half using Datasheet view. The two views are synchronized so that scrolling one view causes the other view to scroll to the same location. The Form Wizard provides more choices for the form's design than the Form tool. In the Form Wizard, the user is guided through a series of dialog boxes to generate the form, including selecting the fields to be included and the form layout.

Project

Worldwide Enterprises

You decide to create forms for maintaining records in tables to make the task easier for the employees not familiar with using a database. You decide to practice creating forms using three form tools that Access provides: the Form tool, the Split Form tool, and the Form Wizard.

1. With **WEEmployees3.accdb** open, click once on *Absence_Rpts : Table* in the Navigation pane.

   In order to use the Form tool, you must first select the table object upon which to base the new form.

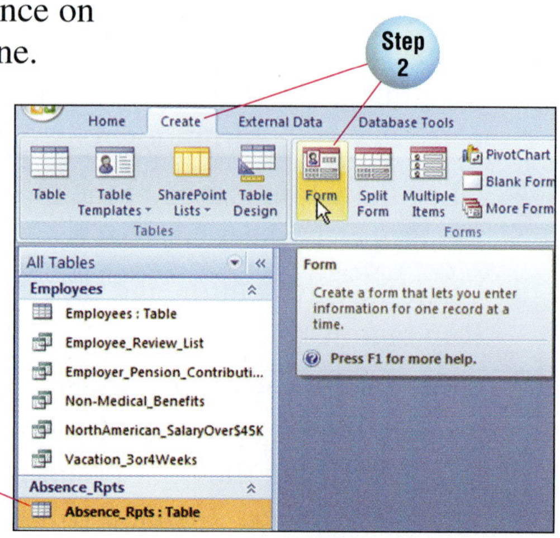

2. Click the Create tab and then click the Form button in the Forms group.

   Access creates the form using all fields in the table in a vertical layout and displays the form in Layout view with the Form Layout Tools Format tab active.

3. Click the Form View button located at the right end of the Status bar in the lower right corner.

4. Click the Next record button on the Record navigation bar a few times to scroll through a few records in Form view.

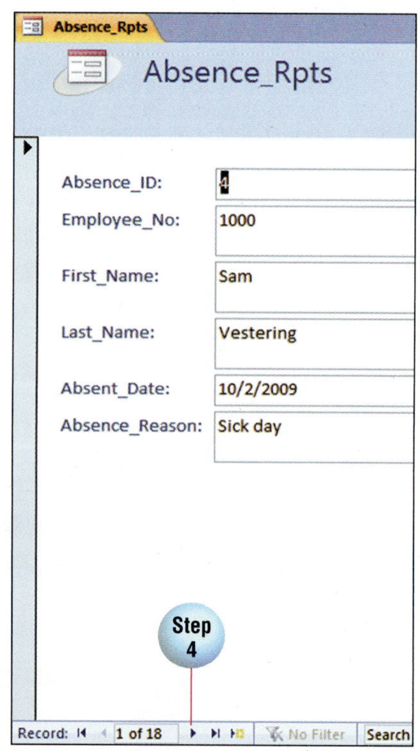

5. Close the Absence_Rpts form. Click Yes to save the changes to the design. At the Save As dialog box, click OK to save the form using the default name *Absence_Rpts*.

6. Click once to select *Employee_Benefits : Table* in the Navigation pane, click the Create tab, and then click the Split Form button in the Forms group.

   Access creates a split screen in the work area with the Employee_Benefits form in Datasheet view in the bottom half and the same form in Layout view in the top half. Separating the two views is a split bar which can be used to resize the height of the two forms.

7. Click the Form View button located at the right end of the Status bar.

8. Click the Next record button on the Record navigation bar two times and watch the two form views scroll synchronously.

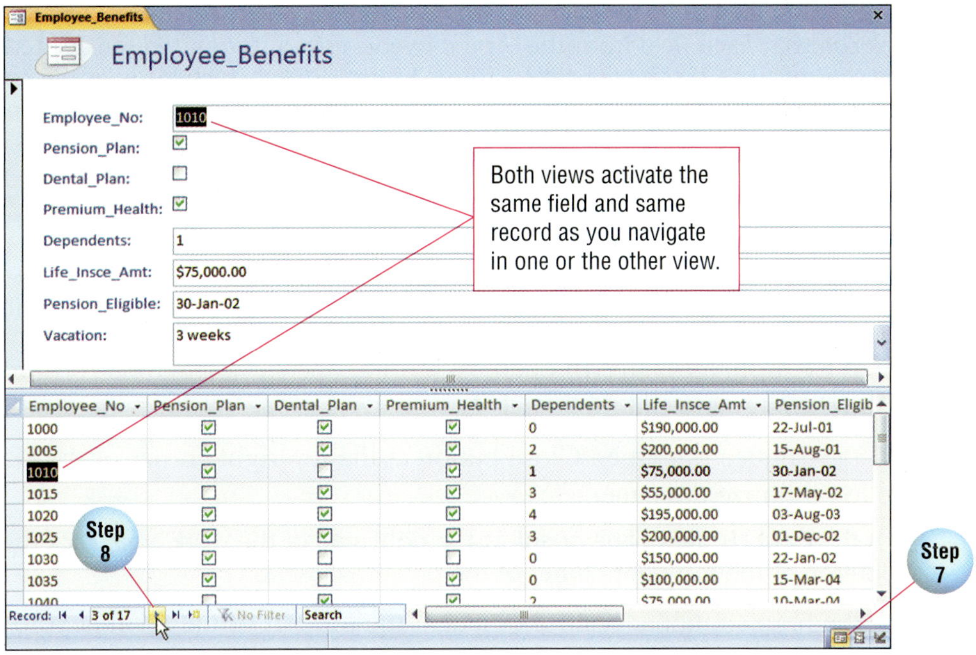

9. Close the Employee_Benefits form. Click Yes to save the changes to the form design and then click OK at the Save As dialog box to accept the default form name *Employee_Benefits*.

10. Click the Create tab, click the More Forms button [More Forms] in the Forms group, and then click *Form Wizard* at the drop-down list.

11. At the first Form Wizard dialog box, click the down-pointing arrow at the right of the *Tables/Queries* list box and then click *Table: Employees* at the drop-down list.

12. Click the Add All Fields button [>>] to move all of the fields in the *Available Fields* list box to the *Selected Fields* list box and then click Next.

13. At the second Form Wizard dialog box with *Columnar* already selected as the form layout, click Next.

14. At the third Form Wizard dialog box, click several style names in the list box to preview each style's colors and backgrounds in the preview window. Click *Flow* and then click Next.

15. Click Finish at the last Form Wizard dialog box to accept the default title of *Employees* and *Open the form to view or enter information.*

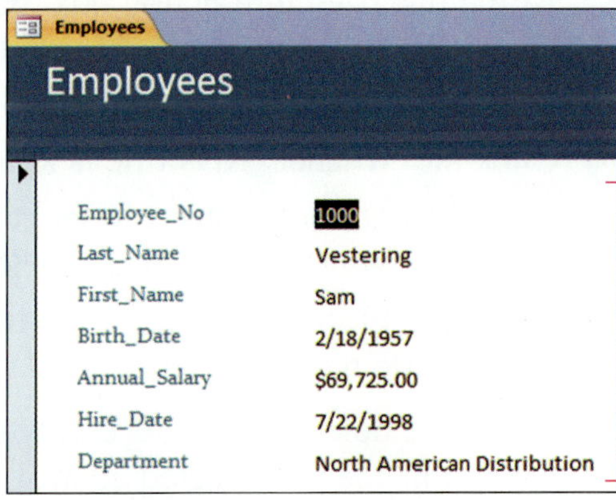

completed form created through Form Wizard in Steps 10–15

The completed form appears in Form view in the work area.

16. Click the Next record button on the Record navigation bar a few times to scroll through a few records in Form view.

17. Close the Employees form.

In Brief

Create Form Using Form Tool
1. Click once to select table name in Navigation pane.
2. Click Create tab.
3. Click Form button.

Create Form Using Split Form Tool
1. Click once to select table name in Navigation pane.
2. Click Create tab.
3. Click Split Form button.

Create Form Using Form Wizard
1. Click Create tab.
2. Click More Forms button.
3. Click *Form Wizard*.
4. Choose table for which to create form.
5. Select fields to include in form.
6. Click Next.
7. Choose form layout.
8. Click Next.
9. Choose form style.
10. Click Next.
11. Type form title.
12. Click Finish.

Activity 3.7

Adding a Logo; Resizing and Formatting Objects

A form is comprised of a series of objects referred to as ***controls***. Each field from the table has a ***label control*** and a ***text box control*** placed side-by-side, with the label control object placed first. The label control contains the field name. The text box control is the field placeholder where data is entered or edited. The controls can be moved, resized, formatted, or deleted from the form. A form's style, which includes the color theme and fonts, can be changed after the form has been created by applying a different style.

Project

You decide to customize the Absence_Rpts form by adding the Worldwide Enterprises logo, editing the title text, resizing the controls in which data is typed, and changing the form style.

1. With **WEEmployees3.accdb** open, right-click the *Absence_Rpts* form name in the Navigation pane and then click *Layout View* at the shortcut menu.
2. Click the Shutter Bar Open/Close button at the top right corner of the Navigation pane to minimize the pane.

   If the Field List task pane opens at the right side of the work area, click the Close button at the top right corner of the pane to close it.

3. Click the logo container control object at the top left of the form next to the Absence_Rpts title.

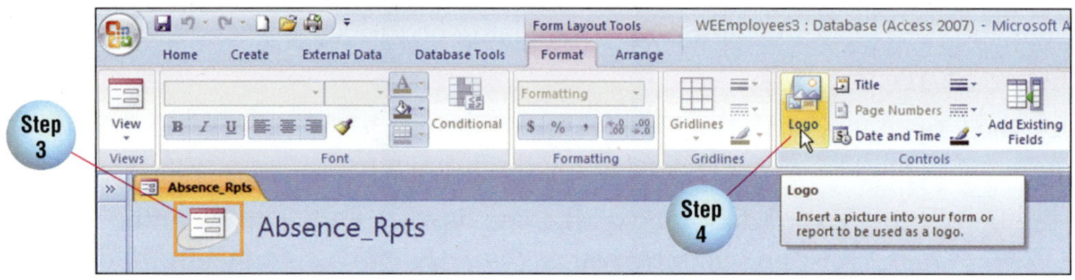

4. Click the Logo button in the Controls group in the Form Layout Tools Format tab.
5. At the Insert Picture dialog box, navigate to the storage medium containing your student data files, double-click the *AccessS3* folder, and then double-click ***WELogo-Small.jpg***.
6. Click the Absence_Rpts title next to the logo image.

   Click once on an object to select the control. Once the control is selected you can apply formatting or layout changes to the object.

7. Click the selected Absence_Rpts title a second time to place an insertion point inside the control object.

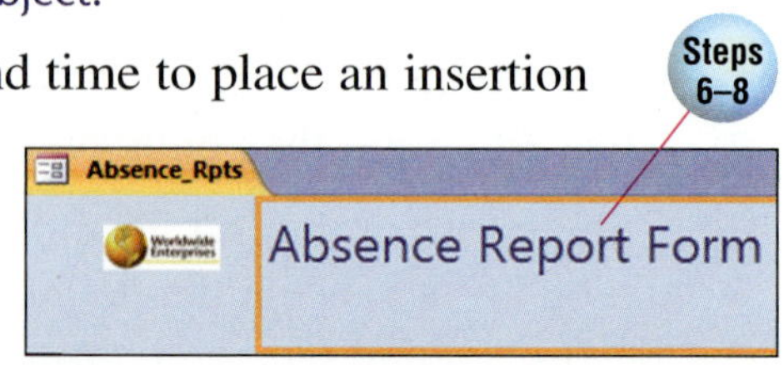

8. Insert and delete text as necessary to change the text inside the selected control to **Absence Report Form**.
9. Click outside the title to deselect the control object.
10. Click the *Absence_ID* text box control. This is the control object that displays the data next to the label *Absence_ID*.

    The width of the controls in which data is typed are much wider than necessary. In the next steps, you will shorten these controls.

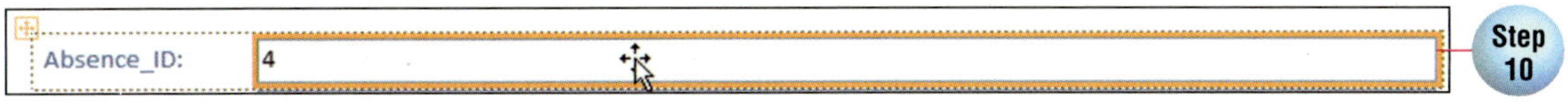

11 Hold down the Shift key and then click each of the text box controls below *Absence_ID* to *Absence_Reason* (contains the text *Sick day*).

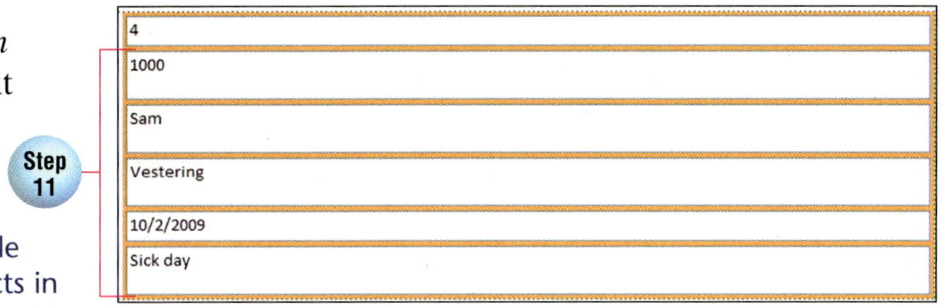

Use the Shift key to select multiple control objects in a form or report.

12 Position the mouse pointer on the right edge of any of the selected control objects until the pointer changes to a left- and right-pointing arrow, drag the right border left to the approximate width shown (align at right edge of form title), and then release the mouse.

13 Click in a blank area of the form to deselect the control objects.

In the next steps, you will change the form's style using the AutoFormat style gallery.

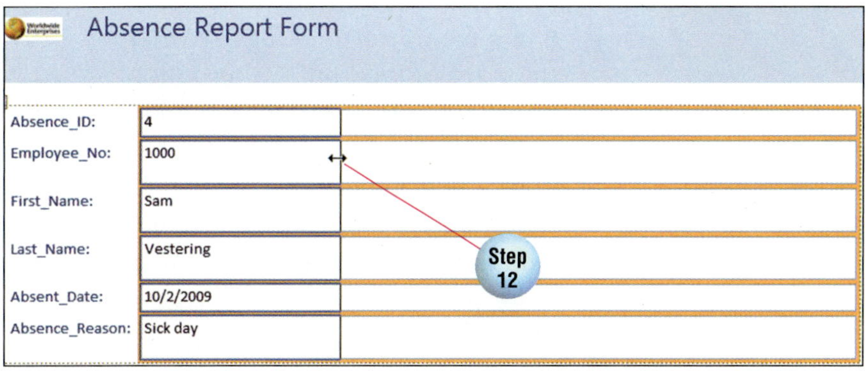

14 Click the More button located at the bottom of the vertical scroll bar in the AutoFormat group in the Form Layout Tools Format tab to display the drop-down style gallery.

15 Click the *Equity* style button (fourth from left in second row) at the drop-down list.

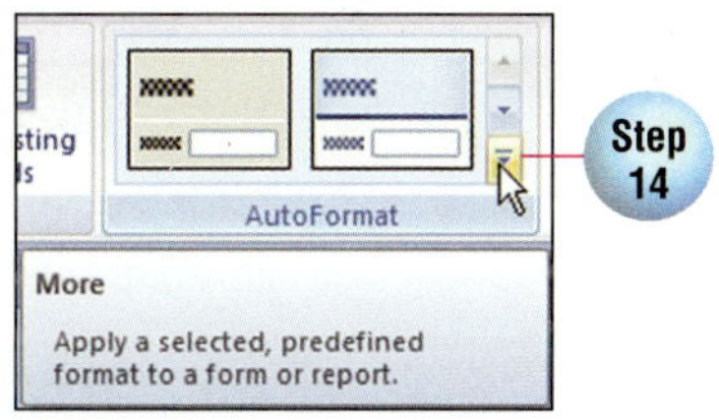

16 Click to select the Absence Report Form title control object. Position the mouse pointer on the left border of the control object until the pointer changes to a left- and right-pointing arrow, and then drag the border right to align the beginning of the title text as shown below.

17 Click to select the logo image. Drag the right and bottom borders of the selected logo control object to resize the image the approximate height and width shown.

18 Click in a blank area of the form to deselect the logo control object.

19 Click the Save button and then close the Absence_Rpts form.

20 Click the Shutter Bar Open/Close button to redisplay the Navigation pane.

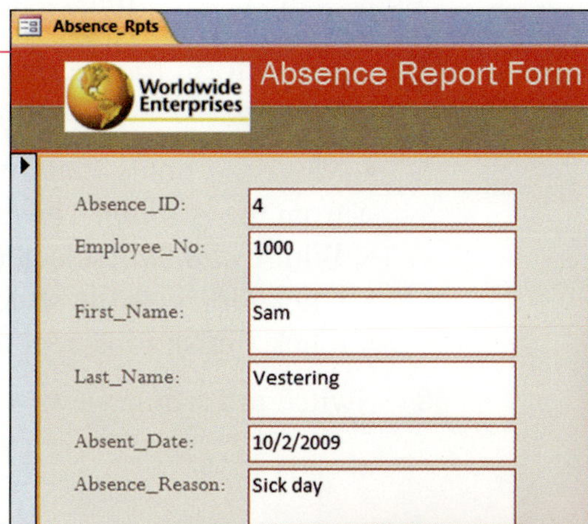

Absence_Rpts form after revisions in this project

In Brief

Add Logo to Form
1. Open form in Layout view.
2. Click logo container object.
3. Click Logo button.
4. Navigate to location of graphic file.
5. Double-click graphic file name.

Resize Control Object
1. Open form in Layout view.
2. Select desired control object.
3. Point to left, right, top, or bottom edge.
4. Drag height or width to desired size.

Change Form Style
1. Open form in Layout view.
2. Click More button in AutoFormat group.
3. Click desired style.

Activity 3.8

Adding Control Objects to a Form Using Layout View

The Controls group in the Form Layout Tools Format tab contains buttons with which you can add control objects to a form such as a title, the date and time, a logo image, page numbers, or additional fields. Open a form in Layout view or Design view to add objects.

Project

You will edit the title in the Employees form and then create and modify another form using the Form Wizard for the Employer_Pension_Contribution query.

Worldwide Enterprises

1. With **WEEmployees3.accdb** open, double-click the *Employees* form in the Navigation pane to open the form and then change the view to Layout view.
2. Double-click the Employees title to place an insertion point in the control object and then press the End key.
3. With the insertion point positioned at the end of *Employees* in the control object, insert and delete text as necessary to change the title to **Employee Record Entry Form** and then press Enter. Drag the right border to resize the object until all text is on one line.

   In the next step, you will format the text by changing the font color.

4. Click the down-pointing arrow at the right of the Font Color button in the Font group in the Form Layout Tools Format tab and then click *Light Label Text* (second button in first row of *Access Theme Colors* section) at the drop-down color palette.

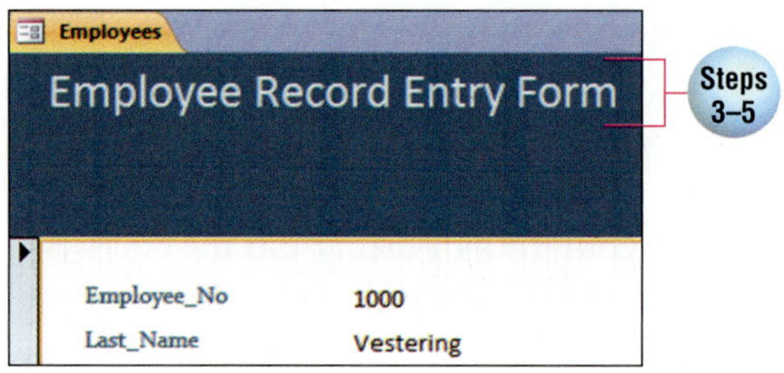

5. Click in a blank area of the form to deselect the title object.
6. Click the Save button and then close the Employees form.

   In the next steps, you will create a new form using the Form Wizard and then add a title and a field to the form.

7. Click the *Employer_Pension_Contributions* query in the Navigation pane to select the query object, click the Create button, click the More Forms button, and then click *Form Wizard* at the drop-down list.
8. Create a form for the Employer_Pension_Contributions query using the wizard as follows:
   - Move the fields *Employee_No, First_Name, Last_Name,* and *Annual_Salary* from the *Available Fields* list box to the *Selected Fields* list box and click Next.
   - With *Columnar* selected as the layout, click Next.
   - Click *Office* as the style and then click Next.
   - Click Finish to accept the default title.
9. Switch to Layout view.

10 Edit the title text to Employer Pension Contributions by double-clicking the title, moving the insertion point, deleting the underscore characters, and inserting space.

In the next steps, you will add the *Pension_Contribution* field from the query to the form.

11 Click outside the title object and then click the Add Existing Fields button in the Controls group in the Form Layout Tools Format tab.

Access opens the Field List task pane at the right side of the work area.

Step 11

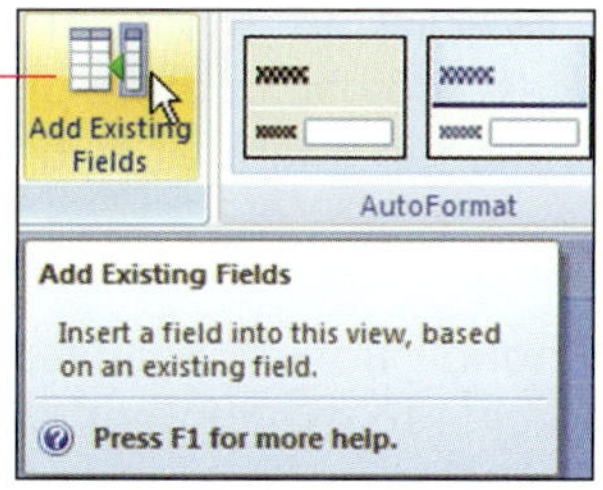

12 Position the mouse pointer on *Pension_Contribution* in the Field List task pane and then drag the field name below *Annual_Salary* in the form.

Access adds the field to the form aligned below the existing objects. A horizontal orange bar displays illustrating the position at which the label control and text box control objects for the new field will be placed on the form.

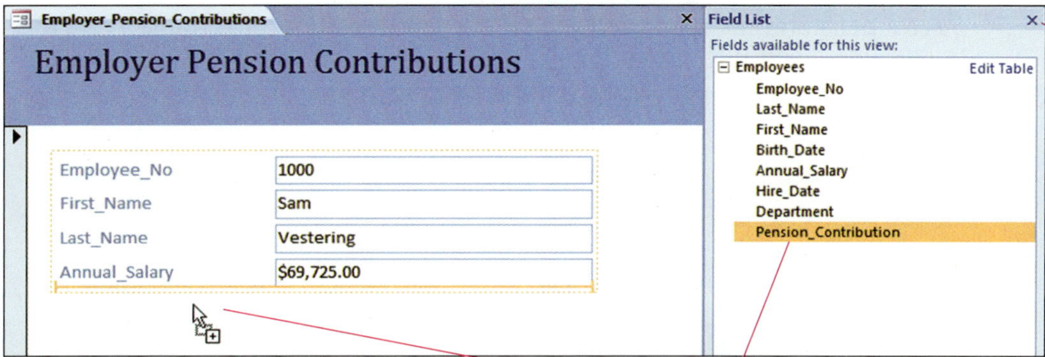

Step 13

Step 12

13 Close the Field List task pane, click the Save button, and then switch to Form view.

14 Close the Employer_Pension_Contributions form.

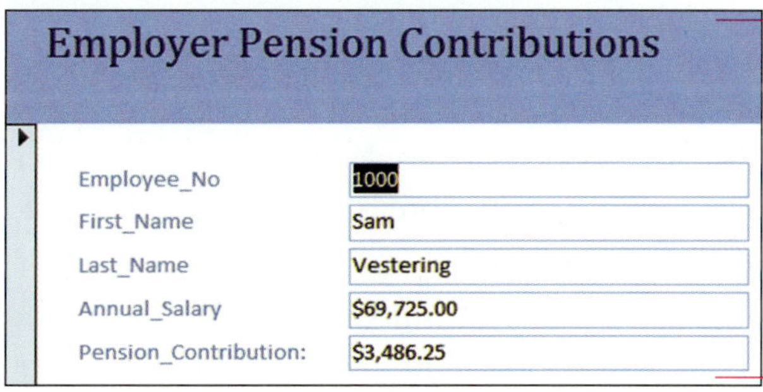

Employer_Pension_Contributions form after revisions in this project

In Brief

Add Existing Fields to Form

1. Open form in Layout view.
2. Click Add Existing Fields button.
3. Drag desired field name from Field List task pane to desired location on form.

In Addition

Moving and Deleting Control Objects

With a form displayed in Layout view, clicking a control object displays an orange border around the control. Press Delete to remove the object from the form. Point inside the selected object to display the pointer with the four-headed arrow move pointer attached and then drag the object to reposition it on the form.

Activity 3.9

Creating, Editing, and Printing a Report

Information from the database can be printed while viewing tables in Datasheet view, while viewing a query results datasheet, or while browsing through forms by clicking the Print button on the Quick Access toolbar. In these printouts all of the fields are printed in a tabular layout for datasheets or in the designed layout for forms. Create a report when you want to specify which fields to print and to have more control over the report layout and format. Access includes a Report tool and the Report Wizard which operate in a similar manner as the Form tool and Form Wizard.

Project

Worldwide Enterprises

Rhonda Trask, human resources manager, has requested updated printouts for two queries. You decide to experiment with the Report tool and the Report Wizard to create the two reports.

1. With **WEEmployees3.accdb** open, click the *NorthAmerican_SalaryOver$45K* query in the Navigation pane and then click the Create tab.

   As with the Form tool, a table or query must be selected first before clicking the Report button.

2. Click the Report button in the Reports group.

   Access generates the report using a tabular layout with records displayed in rows. A title along with the current date and time are placed automatically at the top of the report as well as a container for an image such as a logo placed at the left of the title text.

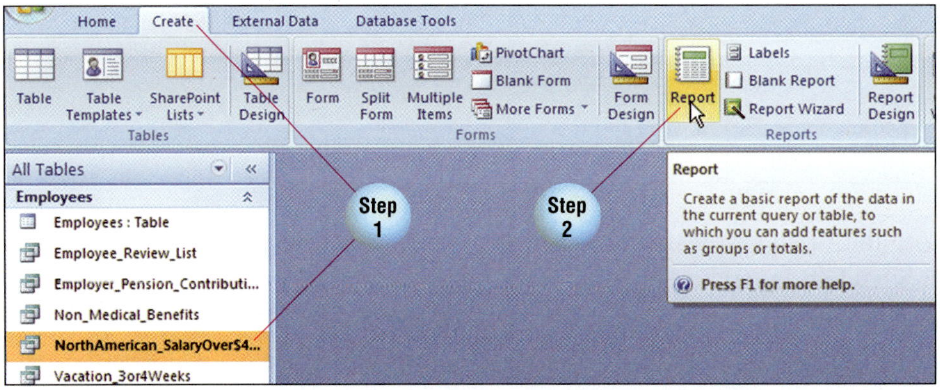

3. Double-click the title text to place an insertion point inside the label control object.
4. Delete the existing text, type **Employees in North American Distribution**, press Shift + Enter to insert a line break, type **Earning over $45,000**, and then press Enter.
5. With the title label control object still selected, click the down-pointing arrow at the right of the Font Size button in the Font group in the Report Layout Tools Format tab and then click *16* at the drop-down list.

6. Click in a blank area of the report to deselect the title label control object.

7. Click the image container control object located next to the report title.
8. Click the Logo button in the Controls group in the Report Layout Tools Format tab.
9. At the Insert Picture dialog box, navigate to the storage medium containing your student data files, double-click the *AccessS3* folder, and then double-click ***WELogo-Small.jpg***. Resize the logo object the approximate height and width shown below.
10. Click the current date located at the top right of the report to select the object and then press Delete.
11. Click the current time located at the top right of the report to select the object and then press Delete.

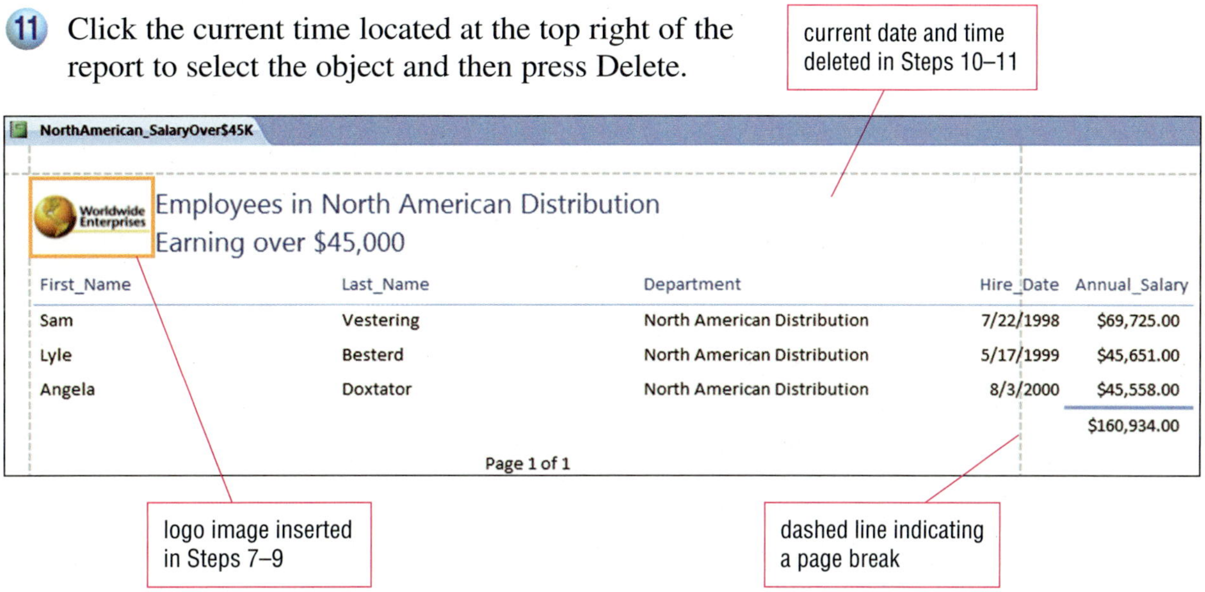

12. Minimize the Navigation pane.
13. Notice the dashed line in the middle of the *Hire_Date* column indicating a page break.
14. Click the Report Layout Tools Page Setup tab.
15. Click the Landscape button in the Page Layout group.

    The page break disappears indicating all columns now fit on one page.

16. Click the Save button. At the Save As dialog box, click OK to accept the default report name *NorthAmerican_SalaryOver$45K*.
17. Print and then close the report.
18. Redisplay the Navigation pane.
19. Click the *Employee_Review_List* query in the Navigation pane, click the Create tab, and then click the Report Wizard button Report Wizard in the Reports group.
20. At the first Report Wizard dialog box with the Employee_Review_List query already selected, move all fields from the *Available Fields* list box to the *Selected Fields* list box and click Next.

continues

21 Click Next at the second Report Wizard dialog box to indicate that there is no grouping in the report.

A grouping level in a report allows you to print records by sections within a table. For example, you could print the review list with the employees grouped by supervisor names. Following this example, you would double-click the *Supervisor_LastName* field to define the grouping level.

22 Click the down-pointing arrow next to the first text box at the third Report Wizard dialog box and then click *Last_Name* at the drop-down list.

You can sort a report by up to four fields in the table or query. By default, Ascending order is used for a sort column. Click the Ascending button to the right of the sort list box to change the sort order from Ascending to Descending.

23 Click Next.

24 Click Next at the fourth Report Wizard dialog box to accept the default *Tabular* layout and *Portrait* orientation.

25 Click *Civic* in the style list box at the fifth Report Wizard dialog box and then click Next.

26 With *Preview the report* selected at the last Report Wizard dialog box, select the existing text in the title text box, type **Employee_Annual_Reviews**, and then click Finish.

In a few seconds the report appears in Print Preview.

27 Minimize the Navigation pane.

28 Move the pointer (displays as a magnifying glass) to the middle of the report and then click the left mouse button.

The zoom changes to *Fit* and the entire page is displayed in the Print Preview window, as shown at the right.

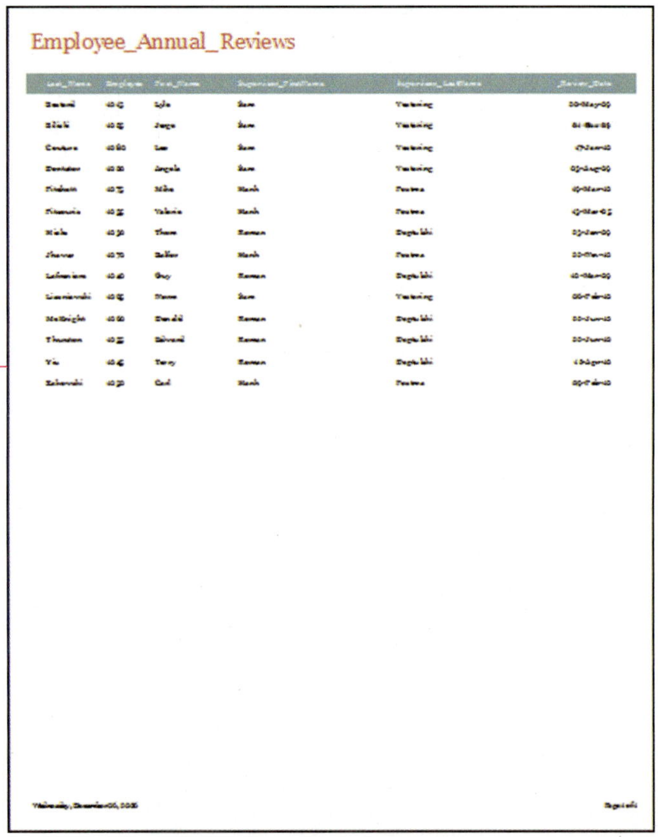

Employee_Annual_Reviews report created using Report Wizard in Steps 19–26 displayed in Print Preview with the zoom set to display the full page

29 Click the Landscape button in the Page Layout group in the Print Preview tab.

30 Click the Margins button in the Page Layout group and then click *Wide* at the drop-down list.

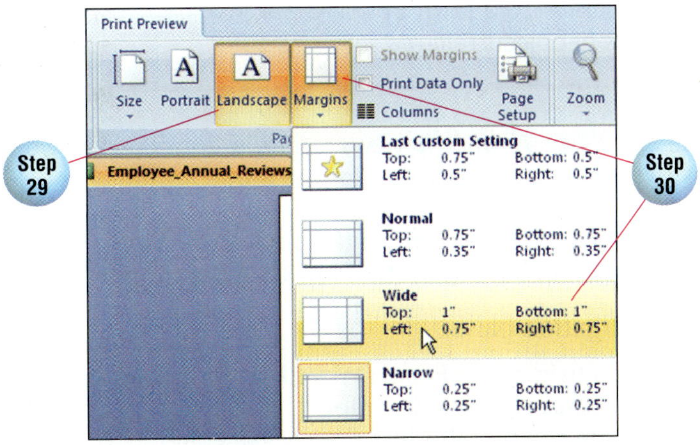

31 Click the Save button and then close Print Preview.

Closing Print Preview displays the report in Design view.

32 Close the Employee_Annual_Reviews report.

33 Redisplay the Navigation pane.

In Brief

Create Report Using Report tool

1. Click object name in Navigation pane.
2. Click Create tab.
3. Click Report button.

Create Report Using Report Wizard

1. Click object name in Navigation pane.
2. Click Create tab.
3. Click Report Wizard.
4. Choose table(s) and field(s) to include in report.
5. Click Next.
6. Choose grouping field.
7. Click Next.
8. Choose sort field.
9. Click Next.
10. Choose layout and orientation.
11. Click Next.
12. Choose style.
13. Click Next.
14. Type report title.
15. Click Finish.

In Addition

The Label Wizard

Access includes a Label Wizard to assist with generating mailing labels for a customer, employee, vendor, contacts list, or other data that you want printed on standard labels. Click the object in the Navigation pane that contains the fields you want printed on the labels and then click the Labels button in the Reports group in the Create tab. This launches the Label Wizard shown at the right.

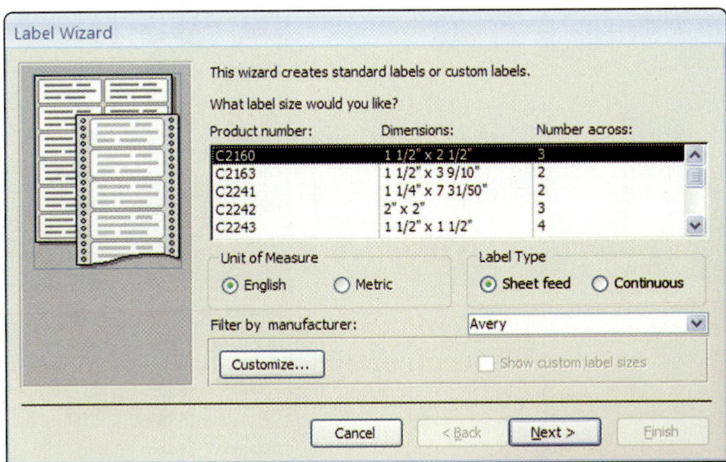

Activity 3.10

Resizing and Moving Columns in a Report

Once a report has been created, the report can be modified by opening it in Layout view or Design view. A report is similar to a form in that it is comprised of a series of objects referred to as controls. A report can be modified using techniques similar to those learned in Activities 3.7 and 3.8.

Project

After previewing the Employee_Annual_Reviews report in Print Preview, you decide to move and resize columns to provide a better layout for the report.

Worldwide Enterprises

1. With **WEEmployees3.accdb** open, right-click the *Employee_Annual_Reviews* report in the Navigation pane and then click Layout View.
2. Minimize the Navigation pane.

   When you sort a field in the Report Wizard, Access places the sort field as the first column in the report. In the next steps, you will move the column after the *First_Name* column.
3. Click the *Last_Name* column heading to select the column.

   A dotted box surrounds the column indicating the data as well as the column heading is selected.
4. Position the pointer inside the dotted box in the first column until the pointer displays with the four-headed move icon attached.
5. Drag the column right between the *First_Name* and *Supervisor_FirstName* columns.

   A vertical orange bar indicates the location at which the column will be placed when you release the mouse.
6. Click the *Employee_No* column heading.

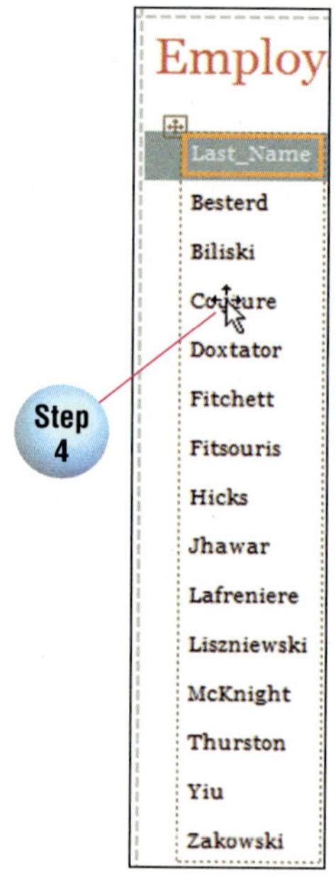

7. Position the mouse pointer on the right border of the selected column heading until the pointer displays as a left- and right-pointing arrow and then drag right to widen the column the approximate width shown so that all of the column heading text is visible.

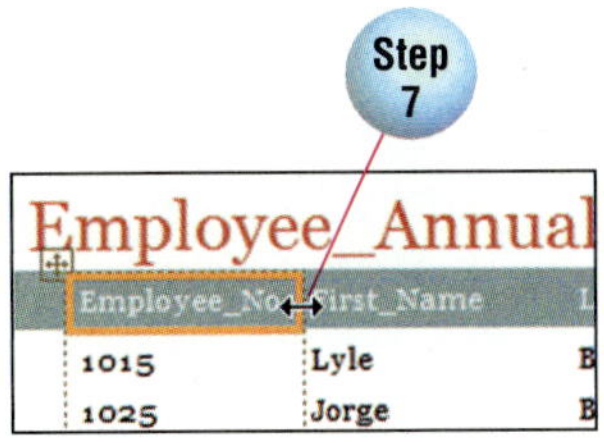

8. Click the *Last_Name* column heading and then widen the column to add the approximate space at the right as shown below.
9. Click the *Annual_Review_Date* column heading and then widen the column so that all of the column heading and data is displayed.
10. Edit the title text to delete the underscore characters between the words and insert a space in place of each of them.

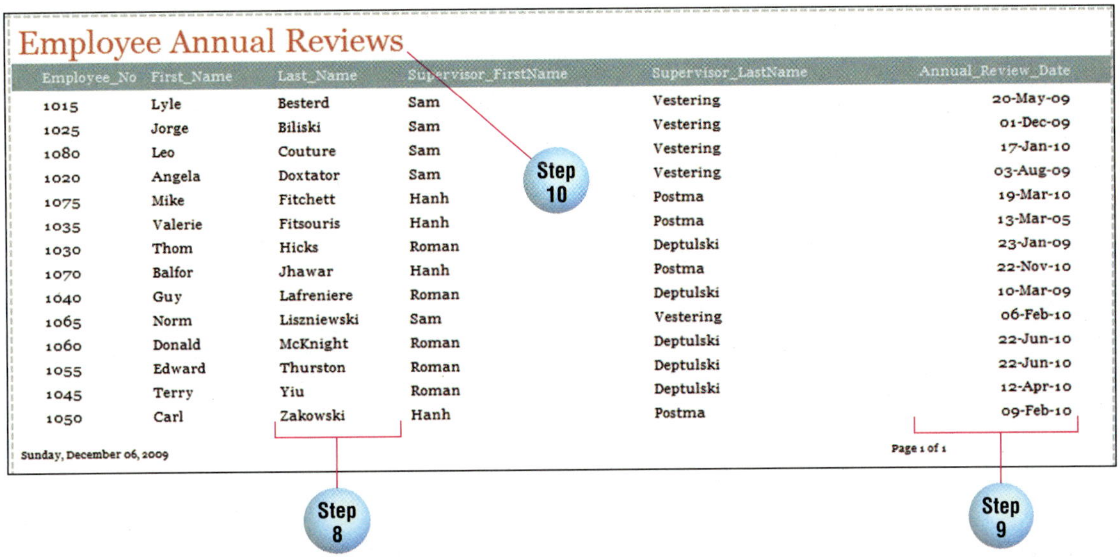

Employee Annual Reviews

Employee_No	First_Name	Last_Name	Supervisor_FirstName	Supervisor_LastName	Annual_Review_Date
1015	Lyle	Besterd	Sam	Vestering	20-May-09
1025	Jorge	Biliski	Sam	Vestering	01-Dec-09
1080	Leo	Couture	Sam	Vestering	17-Jan-10
1020	Angela	Doxtator	Sam	Vestering	03-Aug-09
1075	Mike	Fitchett	Hanh	Postma	19-Mar-10
1035	Valerie	Fitsouris	Hanh	Postma	13-Mar-05
1030	Thom	Hicks	Roman	Deptulski	23-Jan-09
1070	Balfor	Jhawar	Hanh	Postma	22-Nov-10
1040	Guy	Lafreniere	Roman	Deptulski	10-Mar-09
1065	Norm	Liszniewski	Sam	Vestering	06-Feb-10
1060	Donald	McKnight	Roman	Deptulski	22-Jun-10
1055	Edward	Thurston	Roman	Deptulski	22-Jun-10
1045	Terry	Yiu	Roman	Deptulski	12-Apr-10
1050	Carl	Zakowski	Hanh	Postma	09-Feb-10

Sunday, December 06, 2009 Page 1 of 1

11. Save and print the report.
12. Close the Employee_Annual_Reviews report.
13. Redisplay the Navigation pane.
14. Close **WEEmployees3.accdb**.

In Brief

Move Report Columns

1. Open report in Layout view.
2. Click column heading.
3. Position mouse pointer inside selected column border.
4. Drag column to desired location.
5. Save report.

Resize Report Columns

1. Open report in Layout view.
2. Click column heading.
3. Drag right or left border of selected column heading to desired width.
4. Save report.

In Addition

Report Sections

A report is divided into five sections described below.

Report Section	Description
Report Header	Controls in this section are printed once at the beginning of the report, such as the report title.
Page Header	Controls in this section are printed at the top of each page, such as column headings.
Detail	Controls in this section make up the body of the report by printing the data from the associated table or query.
Page Footer	Controls in this section are printed at the bottom of each page, such as the report date and page numbers.
Report Footer	Controls in this section are printed once at the end of the report, such as column totals.

Features Summary

Feature	Ribbon Tab, Group	Button	Keyboard Shortcut
add fields to a form	Form Layout Tools Format, Controls		
change form style	Form Layout Tools, Format, AutoFormat		
create query in Design view	Create, Other		
Design view	Home, Views	OR	
Form tool	Create, Forms		
Form view	Home, Views	OR	
Form Wizard	Create, Forms	More Forms	
insert logo in form or report	Form Layout Tools Format, Controls OR Report Layout Tools Format, Controls		
Layout view	Home, Views	OR	
minimize Navigation pane		«	
property sheet in query	Query Tools Design, Show/Hide	Property Sheet	Alt + Enter
redisplay Navigation pane		»	
Report Print Preview			
Report tool	Create, Reports		
Report view	Home, Views	OR	
Report Wizard	Create, Reports	Report Wizard	
run a query	Query Tools Design, Results	!	
Simple Query Wizard	Create, Other		
Split Form tool	Create, Forms		

Knowledge Check

Completion: In the space provided at the right, indicate the correct term, command, or option.

1. This is the name of the wizard used to facilitate creating a query to select records from a table. ________________
2. Click this button to show the query results datasheet after creating a query using Design view. ________________
3. Type this entry in the *Annual_Salary* criteria row in the query design grid to extract records of employees who earn more than $40,000. ________________
4. Click the check box in this row in the query design grid to prevent a column from being displayed in the query results datasheet. ________________
5. This entry in a blank Field box in the query design grid would add the values in a field named *RegHours* to the values in a field named *OTHours* and title the column in the query results datasheet *TotalHours*. ________________
6. Click this button in the Query Tools Design tab to change a field's format to display in Currency. ________________
7. Create a form using this method if you want the ability to specify the form's layout and style before the form is generated. ________________
8. This type of form displays in two views in the work area: Datasheet view and Form view. ________________
9. Modify a form in this view. ________________
10. A form or report is comprised of a series of objects referred to by this term. ________________
11. A form created using the Form tool adds this object next to the title so you can easily add an image such as a company logo. ________________
12. This button opens the Field List task pane to add fields to a form. ________________
13. List two items that are added to the top of a report automatically when the report is generated using the Report tool. ________________
14. A report's page orientation can be changed from portrait to landscape in this view. ________________
15. A column in a report can be moved or resized by first clicking here. ________________

Skills Review

Review 1 Creating a Query Using the Simple Query Wizard; Sorting a Query; Creating a Calculated Field; Extracting Records

Worldwide Enterprises

1. Open the **WEEmployees3.accdb** database and enable content.
2. Use the Simple Query Wizard to create a query that displays fields from the Employees and Employee_Benefits tables in order as follows:

Employees	**Employee_Benefits**
Employee_No	*Life_Insce_Amt*
First_Name	
Last_Name	
Hire_Date	
Annual_Salary	

3. Accept the default Detail query and type **Salaries_LifeInsce** as the title for the query.
4. View the query results datasheet and then switch to Design view.
5. Sort the query results by the *Last_Name* field in ascending order.
6. Create a calculated field in the column after *Life_Insce_Amt* that divides *Annual_Salary* by 12 and label the new column *Monthly_Salary*.
7. Format *Monthly_Salary* to display the calculated values in the Currency format.
8. Save and run the query and then adjust the column width of *Monthly_Salary* to Best Fit.
9. Print the query results datasheet in landscape orientation.
10. Use Save As to copy the query design and name it **Employees_HiredAfter1999**.
11. Switch to Design view and then type **>December 31, 1999** in the *Criteria* row of the *Hire_Date* column. ***Note: Access will convert the text you type to #12/31/1999# after you press Enter.***
12. Save and then run the query.
13. Print the query results datasheet in landscape orientation and then close the Employees_HiredAfter1999 query.

Review 2 Creating and Modifying a Form

Worldwide Enterprises

1. With **WEEmployees3.accdb** open, create a new form for the Annual_Review table using the Form tool.
2. With the form open in Layout view, make the following changes to the form design.
   a. Add the logo named **WELogo-Small.jpg** to the top of the form and resize the image to fill the space at the top left of the form.
   b. Change the title text to **Annual Review and Salary Increment Dates**.
   c. Change the font size of the title text to 20.
   d. Resize the text box control objects containing the data to align the right edge of the objects below the end of the word *Salary* in the title text.
3. Save the revised form accepting the default name *Annual_Review*.
4. Close the form.

Review 3 Creating and Modifying a Report

1. With **WEEmployees3.accdb** open, use the Report tool to create a report based on the Salaries_LifeInsce query.
2. With the report open in Layout view, make the following changes to the report design.
   a. Add the logo named **WELogo-Small.jpg** to the top of the report and resize the image appropriately.
   b. Change the title text to **Annual and Monthly Salary Report**.
   c. Change the font size of the title text to 20.
   d. Change the page orientation to landscape.
   e. Move the date and time to align at the right edge of the report.
   f. Move the *Life_Insce_Amt* column between *Hire_Date* and *Annual_Salary*.
3. Display the report in Print Preview and ensure all data is visible in all columns.
4. If necessary, switch to Layout view and adjust column widths.
5. Save the report accepting the default name *Salaries_LifeInsce*.
6. Print and then close the report.
7. Close **WEEmployees3.accdb**.

Skills Assessment

Assessment 1 Creating a Query in Design View; Sorting a Query; Extracting Records Using Multiple Criteria

1. The Bursary Selection Committee at Niagara Peninsula College would like you to provide them with the names of students who have achieved an A+ in all three of their courses.
2. Open **NPCGrades3.accdb** and enable content.
3. Create a query in Design view that extracts the records of those students with an A+ grade in all three courses using the following specifications.
   a. Add all three tables to the query design grid and then drag the primary key field name from the first table field list box to the second table field list box. This creates a join line between the first two tables on the *Student_No* field.
   b. Drag the primary key field from the second table field list box to the third table field list box to create a join line between the second and third tables on the *Student_No* field.
   c. Include in the query results the student number, first name, last name, and grade from the first table field list box and sort in ascending order by last name.
   d. Add the grade field from the second and third tables to the design grid.
   e. Enter the required criteria statements to select the records of those students who achieved A+ in all three courses. ***Hint: Type A+ encased in quotation marks in the* Criteria *row to indicate the plus symbol is not part of a mathematical expression.***
4. Save the query and name it *A+_Students*.
5. Run the query.
6. Best Fit the columns in the query results datasheet.
7. Print the query results datasheet in landscape orientation.
8. Close the A+_Students query saving changes and then close **NPCGrades3.accdb**.

Assessment 2 Creating a Query and Report; Modifying a Report

Performance Threads

1. Bobbie Sinclair, business manager, would like a report that lists the costumes that were rented in August 2009.
2. Open **PTCostumeInventory3.accdb** and enable content.
3. Create a new query in Design view using the CostumeInventory table that lists fields in the following order: *CostumeNo, DateOut, DateIn, CostumeTitle, DailyRentalFee.*
4. Type the following criterion statement in the *DateOut* column to extract records for costumes rented in the month of August 2009:

   Between August 1, 2009 and August 31, 2009
5. Expand the column width of the *DateOut* column to view the entire criterion statement. Notice Access converted the long dates to short dates and added pound symbols to the beginning and end of dates in the criterion statement.
6. Sort the query results in ascending order first by *DateOut*, then by *DateIn*, and then by *CostumeTitle*.
7. Save the query and name it *August_2009_Rentals*.
8. Run the query.
9. Close the query after viewing the query results datasheet.
10. Create a report based on the August_2009_Rentals query using the Report tool.
11. Add the logo image **PTLogo-Small.jpg** to the top of the report and resize the image as desired.
12. Change the title text to **Costume Rentals for August 2009**.
13. Adjust column widths in the report until all columns fit on the page in portrait orientation.
14. Save the report accepting the default name *August_2009_Rentals* and then print the report.
15. Close the report and then close **PTCostumeInventory3.accdb**.

Assessment 3 Creating and Modifying a Split Form

Performance Threads

1. Staff at Performance Threads have mentioned that working in the datasheet for CostumeInventory is useful for looking up information but they would prefer a form for entering new records. You decide to create a split form for the staff so they can use Form view to add new records and Datasheet view for looking up a rental record.
2. Open **PTCostumeInventory3.accdb** and enable content.
3. Create a split form for the CostumeInventory table.
4. Adjust all column widths in the datasheet in the lower form to Best Fit.
5. Resize all of the text box control objects for the data in the upper form until the right edge of the objects align with the right edge of the datasheet in the lower half of the work area.
6. Change the AutoFormat to *Oriel*.
7. Drag the split bar between the two views until the split occurs just below the last field in the upper half of the work area.
8. Save the form accepting the default name *CostumeInventory*.
9. Close the form and then close **PTCostumeInventory3.accdb**.

Assessment 4 Finding Information on Creating a Form with a Subform

1. Use the Help feature to find out how to create a form that contains a subform using the Form Wizard.
2. Print the Help topic that you find.
3. Open **WEVendors3.accdb** and enable content.
4. Open the Relationships window and notice there is a one-to-many relationship between the Vendors (primary) and the Purchases (related) tables.
5. Close the Relationships window.
6. Using the Form Wizard, create a form for each vendor that includes a subform that displays the purchases for each vendor in a datasheet below the vendor record. Include the following fields from the Vendors table: *Vendor_No, Vendor_Name, City, Telephone, Fax*. Include all fields except *Vendor_No* from the Purchases table. You determine the layout and style. Accept the default names for the forms.
7. If necessary, modify the form in Layout view to resize columns in the subform to improve the datasheet appearance. ***Hint: You can also resize the subform datasheet object if necessary to widen the datasheet or decrease the height.***
8. Display the first vendor record in Form view. Open the Print dialog box, click *Selected Record(s)* in the *Print Range* section, and then click OK to print the first form.
9. Close the form saving changes to the design.
10. Close **WEVendors3.accdb**.

Assessment 5 Researching Movies on the Internet

1. Choose four to six movies that are currently playing in your vicinity that you have seen or would like to see and then find their Web sites on the Internet. Look for the information listed in Step 3 that you will be entering into a new database.
2. Create a new database named **Movies.accdb**.
3. Create a table named Movie_Facts that will store the following information:

Movie title	Lead Female Actor
Director's name	Supporting Female Actor
Producer's name	Movie category—drama, action, thriller, and so on
Lead Male Actor	Movie rating—R, PG, and so on
Supporting Male Actor	Web site address

4. Create a form to enter the records for the movies you researched. Modify the form by applying the skills learned in this section.
5. Enter records for the movies you researched using the form created in Step 4.
6. Print only the first record displayed in Form view.
7. Create a report for the Movie_Facts table. Modify the report by applying the skills learned in this section.
8. Print the Movie_Facts report.
9. Close **Movies.accdb**.

Marquee Challenge

Challenge 1 Creating Queries and a Report for a Catering Events Database

1. Dana Hirsch, manager, has provided you with a copy of the database file used to track catering events at the bistro. Dana has been filtering records in the datasheet to obtain the lists needed for managing the events but is finding this process too time-consuming. Dana has asked you to figure out how to create queries that can provide the information more efficiently.
2. Open **WBCateringContracts3.accdb** and enable content.
3. Create the following queries.
   a. A query named Westview_Events that displays all events booked in the Westview room. In the query results datasheet, Dana would like the first and last names, event description, date the event is booked, the estimated guests, and the special menu detail. Print the query results datasheet.
   b. A query named Starlake_Events that displays all events booked in the Starlake room. In the query results datasheet, show the same columns as in 3a. Print the query results datasheet.
   c. A query named Sunset_Events that displays all events booked in the Sunset room. In the query results datasheet, show the same columns as in 3a. Print the query results datasheet.
   d. A query named June_Events that displays all of the events booked in June, 2009. In the query results datasheet, show the first and last names, event description, date the event is booked, and the room in which the event will be held. Print the query results datasheet.
   e. A query named Event_Revenue that displays all records. In the query results datasheet, show the last name, event description, date the event is booked, estimated guests, and per person charge. Calculate in the query the estimated revenue by multiplying the estimated guests by the per person charge. You determine an appropriate column label and format for the calculated column. In the query results datasheet, add a total at the bottom of the calculated column.
4. Create a report based on the Event_Revenue query as shown in Figure 3.2. The company logo is stored in the file named **TWBLogo-Small.jpg**. Use your best judgment to determine the style and report formatting elements. Save and print the report.
5. Close **WBCateringContracts3.accdb**.

FIGURE 3.2 Challenge 1

Catering Event Revenue — The Waterfront B·I·S·T·R·O — Monday, December 07, 2009 1:08:24 AM

LastName	DateOfEvent	Event	EstimatedGuests	PerPersonCharge	EstimatedRevenue
Hillmore	15-Jan-09	Business Meeting	35	$21.95	$768.25
Fontaine	20-Jan-09	Engagement Party	177	$28.95	$5,124.15
Corriveau	23-Jan-09	Birthday Party	85	$25.95	$2,205.75
Kressman	28-Feb-09	Wedding	266	$28.95	$7,700.70
Fagan	10-Mar-09	25th Wedding Anniversary	88	$28.95	$2,547.60
Pockovic	18-Mar-09	Birthday Party	62	$35.95	$2,228.90
Gill	29-Mar-09	Business Meeting	71	$21.95	$1,558.45
Bresque	12-Apr-09	50th Wedding Anniversary	62	$32.95	$2,042.90
Santore	28-Apr-09	Wedding	157	$25.95	$4,074.15
Hamid	08-May-09	Engagement Party	85	$28.95	$2,460.75
Torrance	15-May-09	Business Meeting	26	$23.95	$622.70
Russell	30-May-09	Birthday Party	36	$26.95	$970.20
Szucs	10-Jun-09	Birthday Party	42	$28.95	$1,215.90
Griffin	17-Jun-09	25th Wedding Anniversary	54	$31.95	$1,725.30
Doucet	20-Jun-09	Wedding	168	$28.95	$4,863.60
Golinsky	26-Jun-09	Business Meeting	57	$24.95	$1,422.15
Jin Ping	10-Jul-09	Baby Shower	62	$21.95	$1,360.90
McMaster	11-Jul-09	Engagement Party	75	$27.95	$2,096.25
Pavelich	25-Jul-09	Wedding	110	$31.95	$3,514.50
Juanitez	31-Jul-09	Business Meeting	49	$23.95	$1,173.55
					$49,676.65

Challenge 2 Creating Forms and a Report for a Custom Costume Database

Performance Threads

1. Bobbie Sinclair, business manager, is pleased with the way the custom costume database is taking shape. Bobbie would now like forms and a report created to facilitate data entry and printing of the custom orders.
2. Open a My Computer window, navigate to your storage medium, and make a copy of the database **AccessS2-C2-PTCostumes.accdb** in the AccessS3 folder. (This database was created in Marquee Challenge 2 in Section 2.) Rename the copied file **AccessS3-C2-PTCostumes.accdb**.
3. Open **AccessS3-C2-PTCostumes.accdb** and enable content.
4. Create a form for each table in the database. You determine the layout, style, and form design by applying skills learned in this section.
5. For each form, with the first record displayed in Form view, print the selected record.
6. Create a report to print the custom costume orders. You determine the layout, style, and other elements of the report design by applying skills learned in this section. Consider the example shown in Figure 3.3. In this report, the layout is columnar, which allows all fields to print on one page since there are numerous fields in the table. To create your report similar in layout to Figure 3.3, use the Report Wizard to generate the report. At the grouping dialog box, if the preview box shows the report grouped by a field, click the Remove Field button < to move the grouped field out of the grouping order. This action makes the *Columnar* layout option available at the layout dialog box.
7. Save and print the report.
8. Close **AccessS3-C2-PTCostumes.accdb**.

FIGURE 3.3 Challenge 2

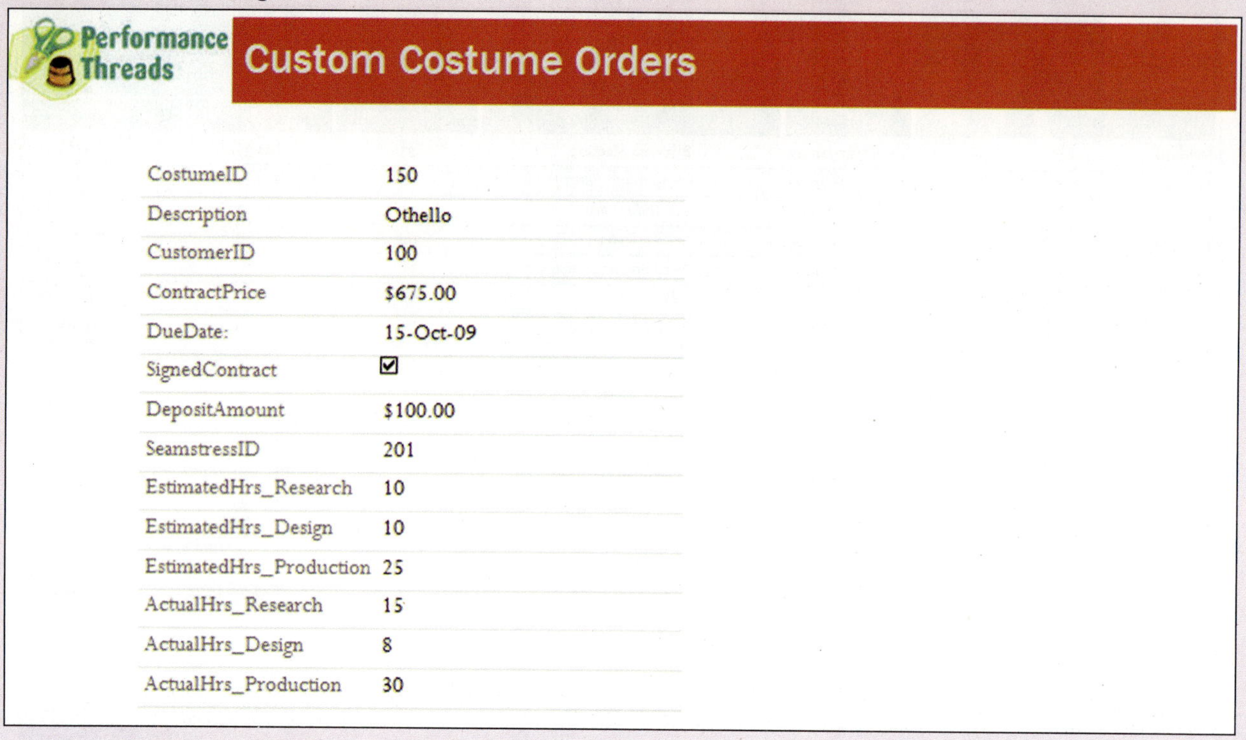

Performance Threads

Custom Costume Orders

CostumeID	150
Description	Othello
CustomerID	100
ContractPrice	$675.00
DueDate:	15-Oct-09
SignedContract	☑
DepositAmount	$100.00
SeamstressID	201
EstimatedHrs_Research	10
EstimatedHrs_Design	10
EstimatedHrs_Production	25
ActualHrs_Research	15
ActualHrs_Design	8
ActualHrs_Production	30

Use this example as a guide for layout purposes only. Your report will vary depending on how you created your table structure in Marquee Challenge 2 in Section 2.

Access SECTION 4

Summarizing Data and Calculating in Forms and Reports

Skills

- Use functions in a query to calculate statistics
- Summarize data in a crosstab query
- Summarize data in a PivotTable
- Summarize data in a PivotChart
- Create a find duplicates query
- Create a find unmatched query
- Create a calculated control object in a form and report
- Create a label control object in a form and report
- Move and resize control objects in a report
- Sort in a form or report
- Create a new database using a template

Student Resources

Before beginning this section:

1. Copy to your storage medium the AccessS4 subfolder from the Access folder on the Student Resources CD.
2. Make AccessS4 the active folder.

In addition to containing the data files needed to complete section work, the Student Resources CD contains model answers in PDF format for each of the projects in this section; model answers for end-of-section activities are not provided.

Projects Overview

Worldwide Enterprises

Create a query to calculate salary statistics; create queries to summarize values grouped by two fields; summarize and filter data in a PivotTable and PivotChart; use a query to find duplicate records; use a query to display records from a table that have no matching record in a related table; modify forms and reports to include descriptive text and calculations; create a new database in which to store contact information; and create and modify a report to print names and addresses of Canadian distributors.

The Waterfront B·I·S·T·R·O

Create a query and PivotChart to summarize inventory purchases; calculate statistics for inventory purchases and create a query to group purchases by item and by supplier code; and create a report and PivotChart to summarize catering event revenue.

Performance Threads

Modify a form to include a calculation that displays the rental fee including tax; create a report that prints costume rental revenue grouped by month including subtotals and a grand total.

Activity 4.1

Calculating Statistics Using Functions

Aggregate functions such as Sum, Avg, Min, Max, or Count can be used in a query to calculate statistics from a datasheet. When an aggregate function is used, Access displays one row in the query results datasheet with the result for each statistic in the query. To display the aggregate function list, click the Totals button in the Show/Hide group in the Query Tools Design tab. Access adds a *Total* row to the design grid with a drop-down list from which you select the desired function. Using the *Group By* option in the *Total* drop-down list, you can add a field to the query upon which Access groups records for statistical calculations.

Project Rhonda Trask has asked for statistics on the salaries currently paid to employees. You will create a new query and use aggregate functions to find the total of all salaries, the average salary, and the maximum and minimum salary. In a second query you will calculate the same statistics by department.

Worldwide Enterprises

1. Open **WEEmployees4.accdb** and enable content.
2. Click the Create tab and then click the Query Design button in the Other group.
3. At the Show Table dialog box with the Tables tab selected, double-click *Employees* and then click the Close button.

   The field upon which the statistics are to be calculated is added to the design grid once for each aggregate function you want to use.

4. Double-click *Annual_Salary* four times in the Employees table field list box.

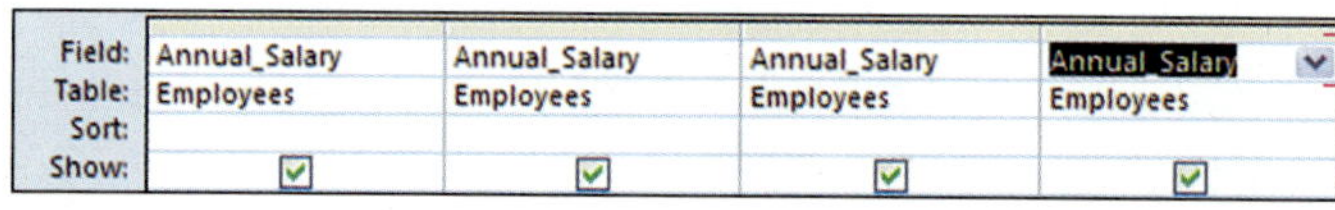

Step 4

5. Click the Totals button [Σ] in the Show/Hide group in the Query Tools Design tab.

   A *Total* row is added to the design grid between *Table* and *Sort* with the default option *Group By*.

6. Click in the *Total* row in the first *Annual_Salary* column in the design grid, click the down-pointing arrow that appears, and then click *Sum* at the drop-down list.

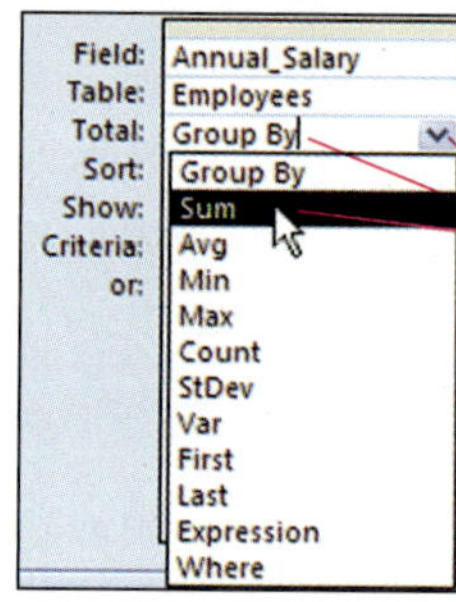

Step 6

7. Click in the *Total* row in the second *Annual_Salary* column, click the down-pointing arrow that appears, and then click *Avg* at the drop-down list.
8. Change the *Total* option to *Max* for the third *Annual_Salary* column.
9. Change the *Total* option to *Min* for the fourth *Annual_Salary* column.
10. Click the Save button, type **Salary_Statistics** in the *Query Name* text box at the Save As dialog, and then press Enter or click OK.
11. Click the Run button.

    Access calculates the Sum, Avg, Max, and Min functions for all salary values and displays one row with the results. Access assigns column headings in the query results datasheet using the function name, the word *Of*, and the field name from which the function has been derived such as *SumOfAnnual Salary*.

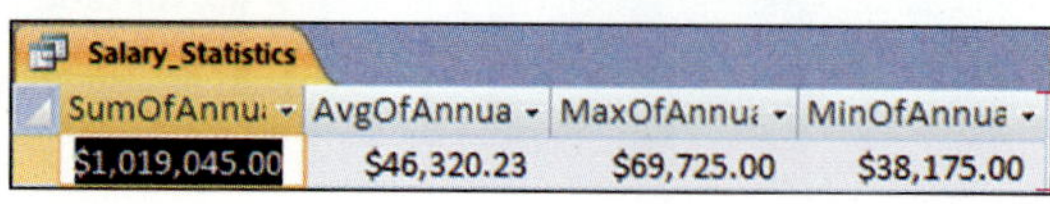

Step 11

12 Switch to Design View.

13 Click in any row in the first column in the design grid and then click the Property Sheet button in the Show/Hide group.

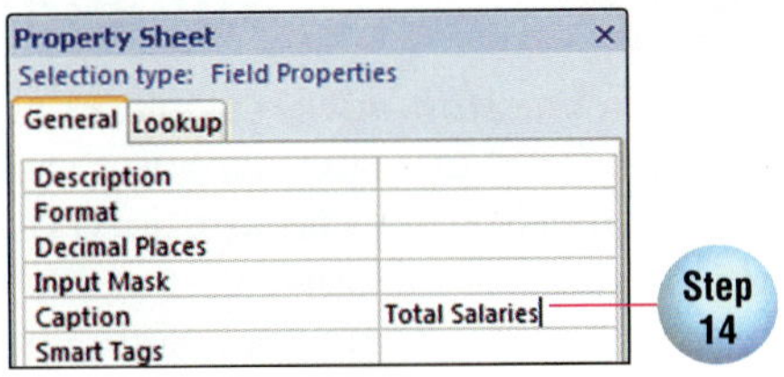

14 Click in the *Caption* property box and then type **Total Salaries**.

15 Click in any row in the second column in the design grid.

16 Click in the *Caption* property box and then type **Average Salary**.

17 Repeat Steps 15–16 to change the *Caption* field property for the third and fourth columns to **Maximum Salary** and **Minimum Salary**, respectively.

18 Close the Property Sheet task pane and then click the Run button.

19 Adjust all column widths to Best Fit in the query results datasheet and then print the datasheet.

Salary_Statistics

Total Salaries	Average Salary	Maximum Salary	Minimum Salary
$1,019,045.00	$46,320.23	$69,725.00	$38,175.00

Steps 18–19

20 Switch to Design View.

21 Click the Office button and then *Save As*. Change the name in the *Save 'Salary_Statistics' to* text box to **Salary_Statistics_byDept** and then press Enter or click OK.

22 Double-click *Department* in the field list box for the Employees table. ***Note: You may have to scroll down the field list box to find the* Department *field.***

The *Department* field is added to the design grid with *Total* automatically set to *Group By*. Adding this field produces a row in the query results datasheet for each department in which Access calculates the aggregate functions.

23 Run the query and then print the query results datasheet in landscape orientation.

Salary_Statistics_byDept

Total Salaries	Average Salary	Maximum Salary	Minimum Salary	Department
$325,004.00	$46,429.14	$69,725.00	$38,175.00	European Distribution
$368,046.00	$46,005.75	$69,725.00	$38,175.00	North American Distribution
$325,995.00	$46,570.71	$69,725.00	$38,175.00	Overseas Distribution

Steps 21–23

24 Close the Salary_Statistics_byDept query. Click Yes when prompted to save changes to the query design.

In Brief

Using Aggregate Functions

1. Create new query in Design view.
2. Add required table(s).
3. Close Show Table dialog box.
4. Add desired field once for each function.
5. Click Totals button.
6. Change *Total* option to desired function in each column.
7. Save query.
8. Run query.

Activity 4.2

Summarizing Data Using a Crosstab Query

A ***crosstab query*** calculates aggregate functions such as Sum and Avg in which field values are grouped by two fields. A wizard is included that guides you through the steps to create the query. The first field selected causes one row to display in the query results datasheet for each group. The second field selected displays one column in the query results datasheet for each group. A third field is specified that is the numeric field to be summarized. The intersection of each row and column holds a value that is the result of the specified aggregate function for the designated row and column group. For example, suppose you want to find out the total sales achieved by each salesperson by state. Each row in the query results could be used to display a salesperson's name with the state names in columns. Access summarizes the total sales for each person for each state and shows the results in a spreadsheet-type format.

Project

Worldwide Enterprises

Rhonda Trask wants to find out the salary cost that has been added to the payroll each year by department. You will use a crosstab query to calculate the total value of annual salaries for new hires in each year by each department.

1. With **WEEmployees4.accdb** open, click the Create tab and then click the Query Wizard button in the Other group.
2. Click *Crosstab Query Wizard* in the New Query dialog box and then click OK.

   The fields that you want to use for grouping must all exist in one table or query. In situations where the fields that you want to group by are in separate tables, you would first create a new query that contains the fields you need and then start the Crosstab Query Wizard. In your project, all three fields that you need are in one table.
3. At the first Crosstab Query Wizard dialog box with *Tables* selected in the *View* section, click *Table: Employees* and then click Next.

   In the second Crosstab Query Wizard dialog box you choose the field in which the field's values become the row headings in the query results datasheet.

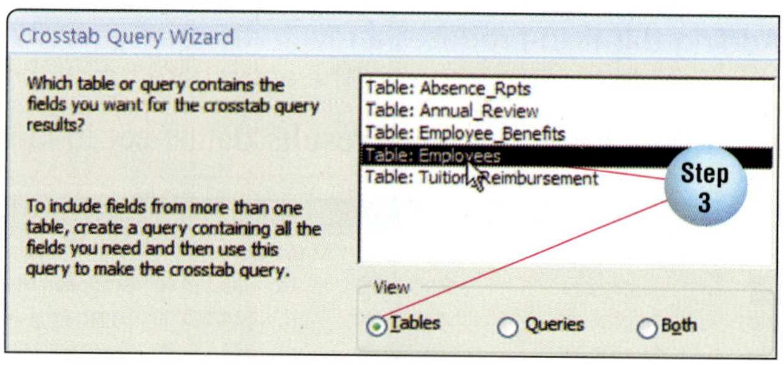

4. At the second Crosstab Query Wizard dialog box, double-click *Department* in the *Available Fields* list box to move the field to the *Selected Fields* list box and then click Next.

   At the next dialog box you choose the field in which the field's values become the column headings in the query results datasheet.

5. At the third Crosstab Query Wizard dialog box, click *Hire_Date* in the field list box and then click Next.

   Whenever a date/time field is chosen for the column headings, Access displays a dialog box asking you to choose the time interval to summarize by with the default option set to *Quarter*.

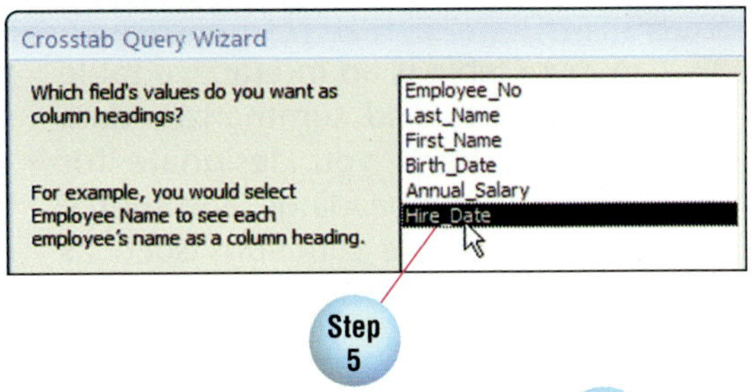

6. At the fourth Crosstab Query Wizard dialog box, click *Year* in the list box and then click Next.

   The final field to be selected is the numeric field to be summarized and the aggregate function to be used to calculate the values.

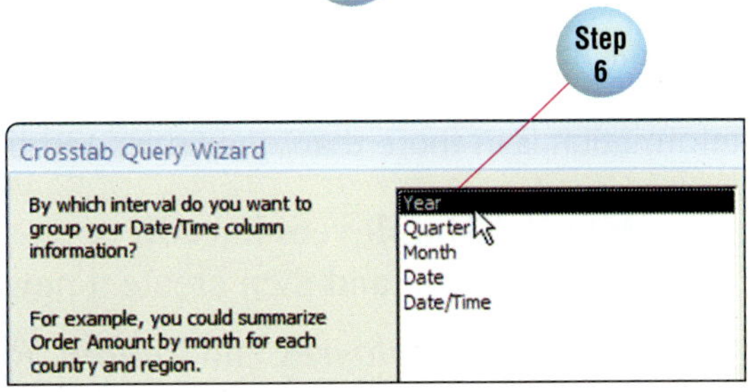

7. At the fifth Crosstab Query Wizard dialog box, click *Annual_Salary* in the *Fields* list box and then click *Sum* in the *Functions* list box.

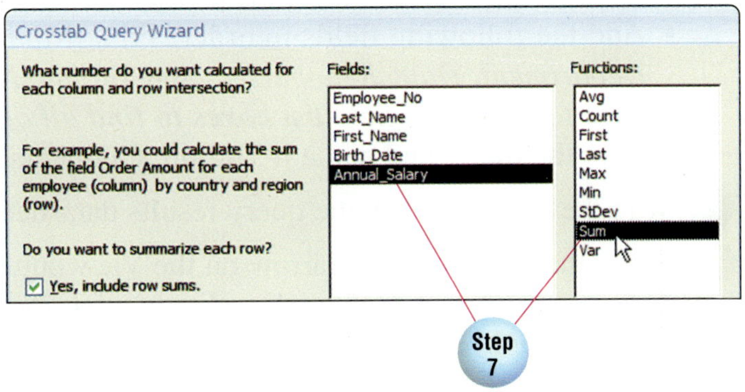

8. Look at the datasheet layout displayed in the *Sample* section and then click Next.

9. Select the existing text in the *What do you want to name your query?* text box, type **Payroll_byDept_byYear**, and then click Finish.

   The query results datasheet displays as shown below. Notice the total column next to each department name with the total broken down to show the amount for each year that makes up each department's payroll cost.

10. Minimize the Navigation pane and Best Fit each column's width.

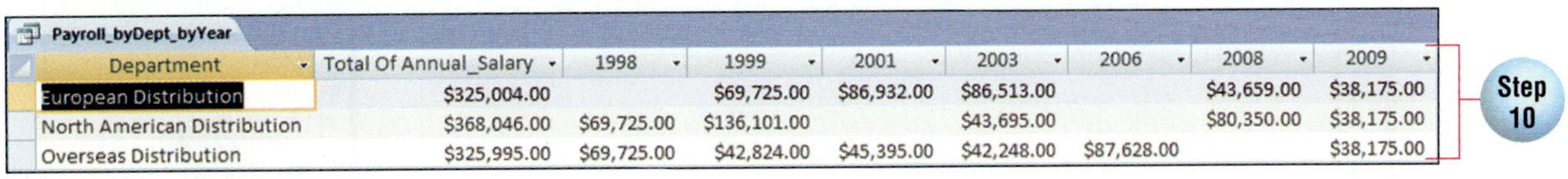

Department	Total Of Annual_Salary	1998	1999	2001	2003	2006	2008	2009
European Distribution	$325,004.00		$69,725.00	$86,932.00	$86,513.00		$43,659.00	$38,175.00
North American Distribution	$368,046.00	$69,725.00	$136,101.00		$43,695.00		$80,350.00	$38,175.00
Overseas Distribution	$325,995.00	$69,725.00	$42,824.00	$45,395.00	$42,248.00	$87,628.00		$38,175.00

11. Print the query results datasheet in landscape orientation and with a left and right margin of 0.5 inch.

12. Close the Payroll_byDept_byYear query. Click Yes to save changes to the layout.

13. Redisplay the Navigation pane.

In Brief

Create Crosstab Query

1. Click Create tab.
2. Click Query Wizard button.
3. Click Crosstab Query Wizard and click OK.
4. Choose table or query name and click Next.
5. Choose field for row headings and click Next.
6. Choose field for column headings and click Next.
7. Choose numeric field to summarize and function to calculate and click Next.
8. Type query name and click Finish.

Activity 4.3

Summarizing Data Using PivotTable View

A PivotTable is an interactive table that organizes and summarizes data based on the fields you designate for row headings, column headings, and source record filtering. Aggregate functions such as Sum, Avg, and Count are easily added to the table. A PivotTable provides more options for viewing data than a crosstab query because you can easily change the results by filtering data by an item in a row, a column, or for all source records. This interactivity allows you to analyze the data for numerous scenarios.

Project

Rhonda Trask has requested a report that summarizes the tuition reimbursement paid to employees by department and by month. You will begin by creating a query, since the required information is in more than one table, and then use a PivotTable to summarize the data.

Worldwide Enterprises

1. With **WEEmployees4.accdb** open and the Create tab active, click the Query Design button and then create a new query as follows.
   - Add the *Employees* and *Tuition_Reimbursement* tables to the design grid.
   - Drag the *Employee_No* field from the *Employees* field list box to the *Employee_ID* field in the *Tuition_Reimbursement* field list box.
   - Add the following fields in order: *First_Name, Last_Name, Department, Date_Reimbursed,* and *Tuition*. ***Note: You will have to scroll the field list boxes to find all of the fields.***
   - Save the query and name it Tuition_Payments.
2. Run the query to view the query results datasheet.
3. Click the down-pointing arrow on the View button in the Views group in the Home tab and then click *PivotTable View* at the drop-down list.

   The datasheet changes to PivotTable layout with four sections and a PivotTable Field List box.

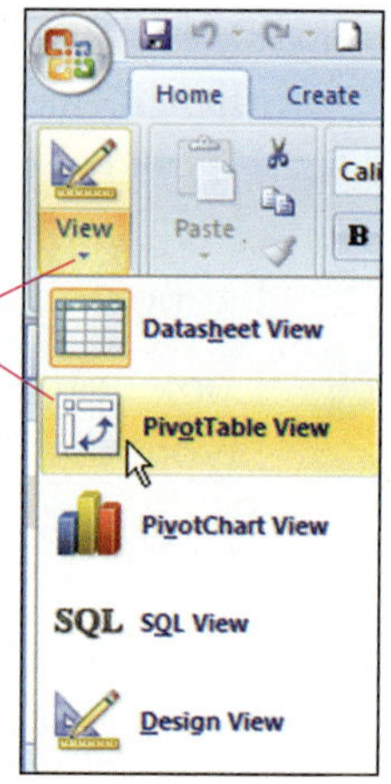

4. Click *Last_Name* in the PivotTable Field List box, drag the field to the section labeled *Drop Row Fields Here* until a blue border outlines the section, and then release the mouse.

   A row for each *Last_Name* field value appears with the heading *Last_Name* and a filter arrow at the top of the list.

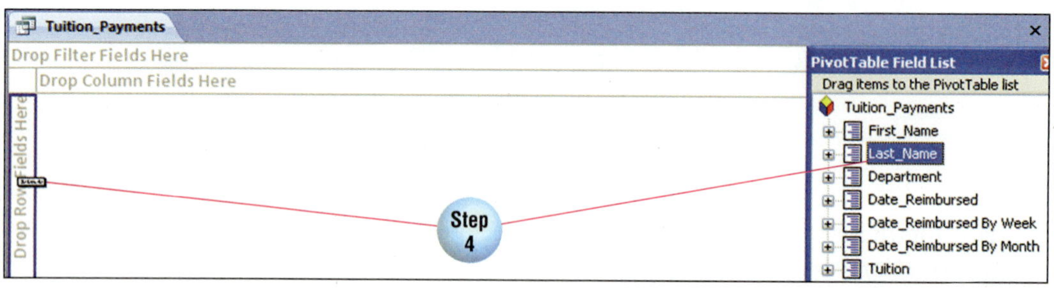

5. Click *Date_Reimbursed* in the PivotTable Field List box, drag the field to the section labeled *Drop Column Fields Here* until a blue border outlines the section, and then release the mouse.

   A column for each *Date_Reimbursed* field value appears with the heading *Date_Reimbursed* and a filter arrow above the list.

6. Click *Department* in the PivotTable Field List box and then drag the field to the section labeled *Drop Filter Fields Here*.

7 Click *Tuition* in the PivotTable Field List box and then drag the field to the section labeled *Drop Totals or Detail Fields Here.*

Access summarizes the values in the tuition field by name and by date paid.

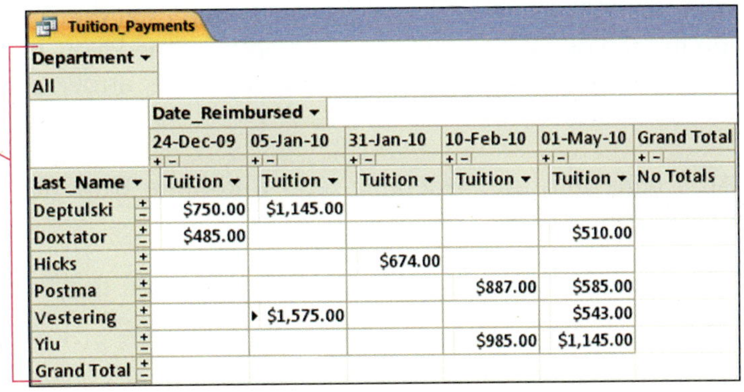

8 Click one of the *Tuition* column headings.

All cells in the table containing values from the *Tuition* field are selected as indicated by the light blue color.

9 Click the AutoCalc button Σ in the Tools group of the PivotTable Tools Design tab and then click *Sum* at the drop-down list.

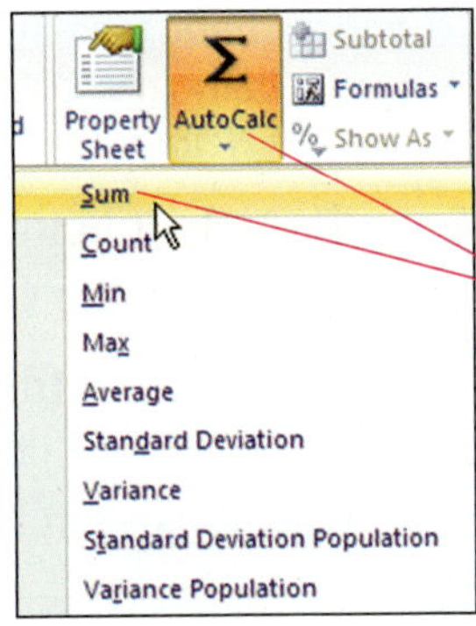

Each employee's tuition payments are subtotaled and the Grand Totals are now calculated. A *Totals* field showing the *Sum of Tuition* function is also added to the top of the PivotTable Field List box.

10 Click the filter arrow (black down-pointing arrow) to the right of *Department*.

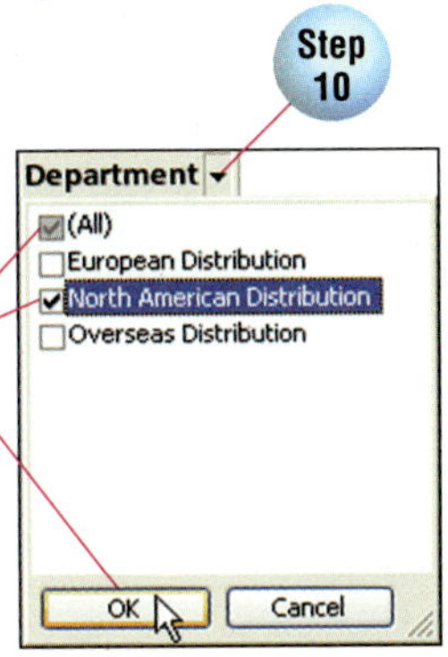

11 Click the *(All)* check box to clear the box for all department names, click the *North American Distribution* check box to insert a check mark, and then click OK.

The PivotTable hides all data except the tuition payments for employees in the North American Distribution department.

12 Right-click the *Sum of Tuition* column heading and then click *Properties* at the shortcut menu.

13 Click the Captions tab in the Properties sheet, click in the *Caption* text box, delete *Sum of Tuition*, and then type **Total Tuition**.

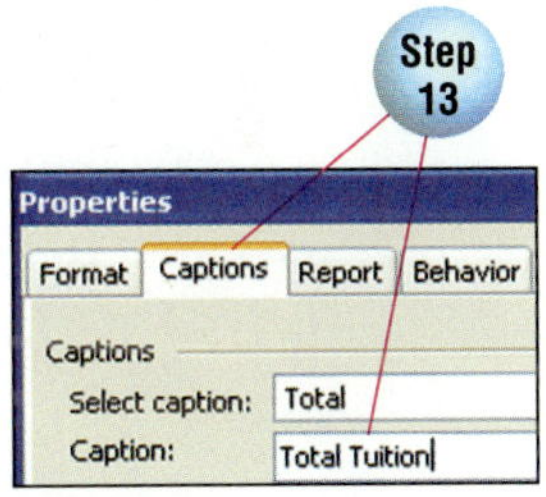

14 Click the Format tab, click the Bold button, click the *Fill Color* arrow next to *Background color,* click the *SkyBlue* color square (first from left in fourth row), and then close the Properties sheet.

15 Right-click the *Grand Total* row heading and click *Properties* at the shortcut menu. If necessary, click the Format tab. Click the red Font Color button in the *Text format* section and then close the Properties sheet.

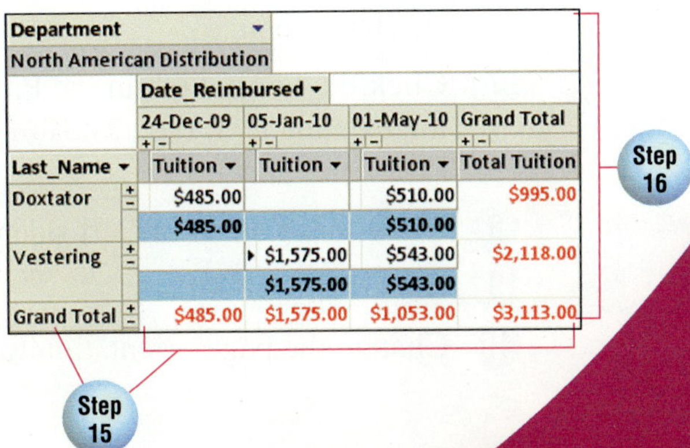

16 Change the font color of the values in the *Grand Total* column by completing steps similar to those in Step 15.

17 Save and then print the PivotTable.

18 Close the Tuition_Payments query. Click Yes if prompted to save layout changes.

In Brief

Create PivotTable

1. Open table or query.
2. Change view to PivotTable view.
3. Drag required field names from PivotTable Field List box to each section in PivotTable.
4. Save query.

Sum PivotTable Field

1. Open table or query.
2. Change view to PivotTable view.
3. Click desired column heading.
4. Click AutoCalc button.
5. Click *Sum*.
6. Save query.

Activity 4.4

Summarizing Data Using PivotChart View

A PivotChart performs the same function as a PivotTable with the exception that the source data is displayed in a graph instead of a table. A chart is created by dragging fields from the Chart Field List box to the Filter, Data, Category, and Series sections of the chart. By default, the Sum function is used to total the summarized data. As with a PivotTable, the PivotChart can be easily altered using the filter arrows.

Project

After reviewing the PivotTable report, Rhonda Trask has asked for two more reports in chart form.

Worldwide Enterprises

1. With **WEEmployees4.accdb** open, open the Tuition_Payments query.
2. Click the View button arrow in the Views group in the Home tab and then click *PivotChart View* at the drop-down list.

   The information created in the PivotTable in the previous activity is graphed automatically in a column chart with filter buttons for *Department*, *Last Name*, and *Date_Reimbursed*.
3. Click the Field List button in the Show/Hide group in the PivotChart Tools Design tab to close the Chart Field List box.
4. Click the *Department* filter arrow (blue down-pointing arrow), click the *(All)* check box to select all departments, and then click OK.

   The chart updates to reflect tuition payments for employees in all departments.

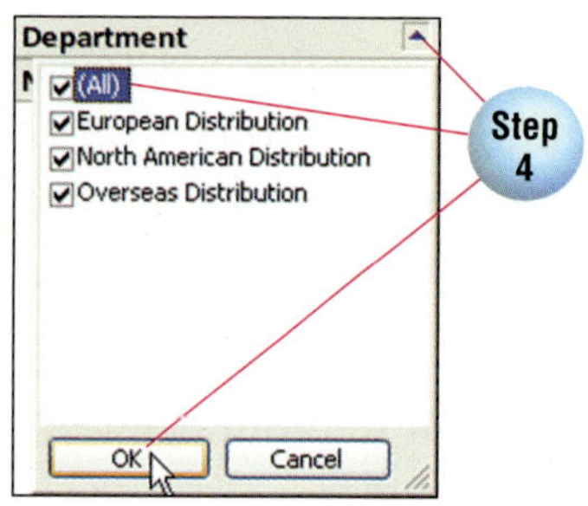

5. Click the *Date_Reimbursed* filter arrow, click the *(All)* check box to clear all dates, click the *01-May-10* check box, and then click OK.

   The chart is updated to reflect only tuition payments made on May 1, 2010 for employees in all departments.
6. Right-click *Axis Title* at the bottom of the chart and then click *Properties* at the shortcut menu.
7. Click the Format tab in the Properties sheet, click in the *Caption* text box, delete the existing text, type **Tuition Payments for May 1, 2010**, and then close the Properties sheet.
8. Click *Axis Title* at the left side of the chart to select the title and then press Delete.
9. Click the Save button.
10. Change the page orientation to landscape and then print the PivotChart.

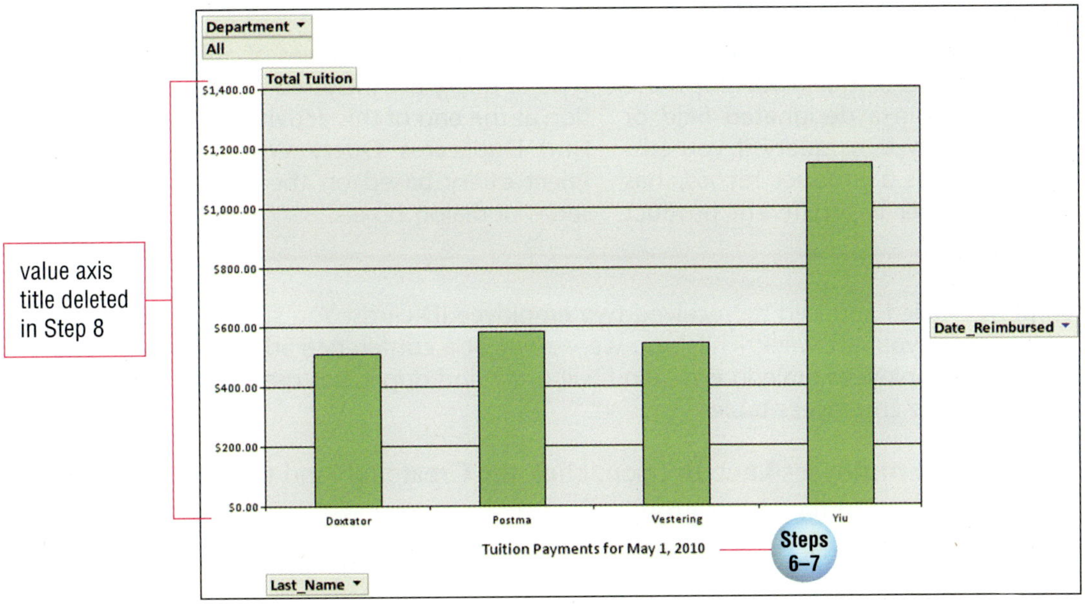

11 Change to PivotTable view.

Notice the PivotTable is linked dynamically to the PivotChart. Changes made to the filter settings in Chart view are also updated in Table view.

12 Click the *Department* filter arrow, click the *North American Distribution* check box to clear the check box, and then click OK.

The PivotTable updates to reflect tuition payments for employees in all departments except North American Distribution.

Step 11

Department ▾		
All		
	Date_Reimbursed ▾	
	01-May-10	Grand Total
Last_Name ▾	Tuition ▾	Total Tuition
Doxtator	$510.00	$510.00
	$510.00	
Postma	$585.00	$585.00
	$585.00	
Vestering	$543.00	$543.00
	$543.00	
Yiu	$1,145.00	$1,145.00
	$1,145.00	
Grand Total	$2,783.00	$2,783.00

13 Change to PivotChart view.

14 Print the revised PivotChart.

15 Save and then close the Tuition_Payments query.

In Brief

Create PivotChart

1. Open table or query.
2. Change view to PivotChart view.
3. Drag field for *x*-axis category from Chart Field List box to *Drop Category Fields Here*.
4. Drag field to use for filtering data from Chart Field List box to *Drop Filter Fields Here*.
5. Drag field(s) with data to be graphed to *Drop Data Fields Here*.
6. Change or delete axis titles as required.
7. Filter data as required.
8. Save query.

In Addition

Creating a PivotChart from Scratch

In this project, a PivotChart was created automatically when you selected PivotChart view because an existing PivotTable was saved with the query. When you open a table or query without an existing PivotTable and choose PivotChart view, the screen looks like the one shown at the right. Drag the fields from the PivotChart Field List box to the appropriate sections in the chart. You will create a PivotChart from scratch in a Skills Assessment project at the end of this section.

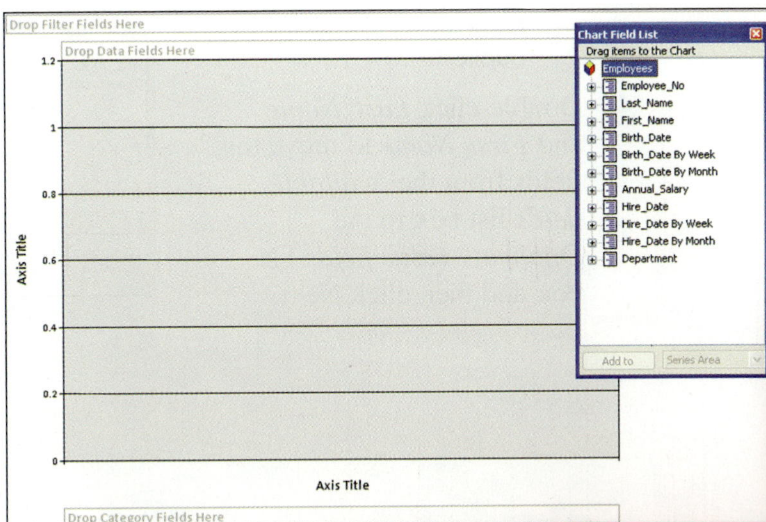

Activity 4.5

Using a Query to Find Duplicate Records

A ***find duplicates query*** searches a specified table or query for duplicate field values within a designated field or fields. Create this type of query if you suspect a record, such as a product record, has been entered twice under two different product numbers. Other examples of applications for this type of query are included in the In Addition section at the end of this activity. Access provides the Find Duplicates Query Wizard that builds the select query based on the selections made in a series of dialog boxes.

Project

Worldwide Enterprises

An employee called and said he received two employee ID cards. You suspect that someone who filled in for you last week while you were away at a conference added an employee record to the Employees table in error. You will use a find duplicates query to check for this occurrence in the Employees table.

1. With **WEEmployees4.accdb** open, click the Create tab and then click the Query Wizard button in the Other group.
2. Click *Find Duplicates Query Wizard* in the New Query dialog box and then click OK.

   At the first dialog box in the Find Duplicates Query Wizard, you choose the table or query in which you want Access to look for duplicate field values.

3. With *Tables* selected in the *View* section of the first Find Duplicates Query Wizard dialog box, click *Table: Employees* and then click Next.

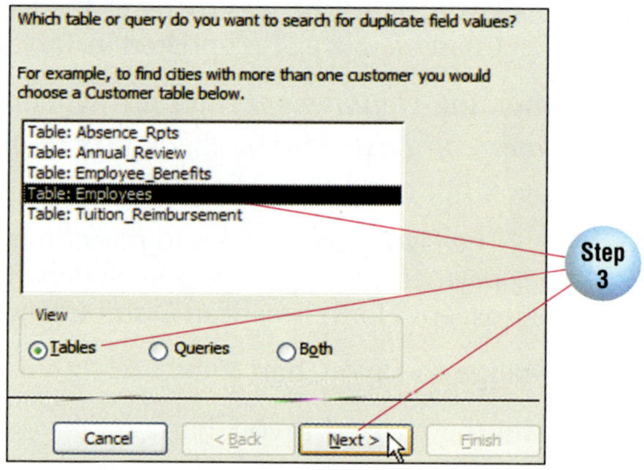

   At the second Find Duplicates Query Wizard dialog box you choose the fields that may contain duplicate field values. Since *Employee_No* is the primary key field in the Employees table you know that it is not possible for an employee record to be duplicated using the same employee number, therefore, you will use the name fields to check for duplicates.

4. Double-click *Last_Name* and *First_Name* to move the fields from the *Available fields* list box to the *Duplicate-value fields* list box and then click Next.

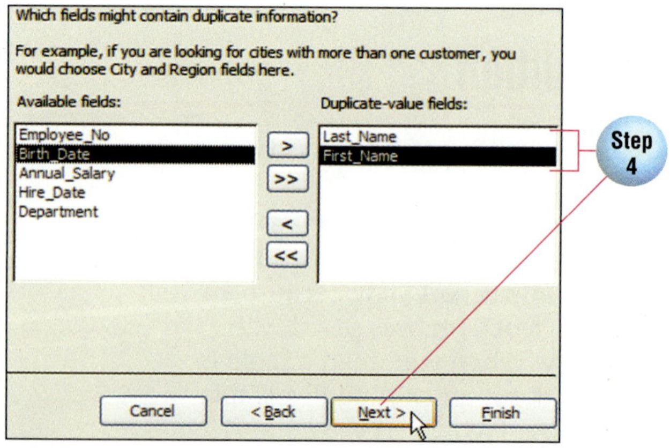

5 Move all of the fields from the *Available fields* list box to the *Additional query fields* list box and then click Next.

If an employee record has been duplicated, you want to see all of the fields to ensure that the information in both records is exactly the same. If not, you need to check which record contains the accurate information before deleting the duplicate.

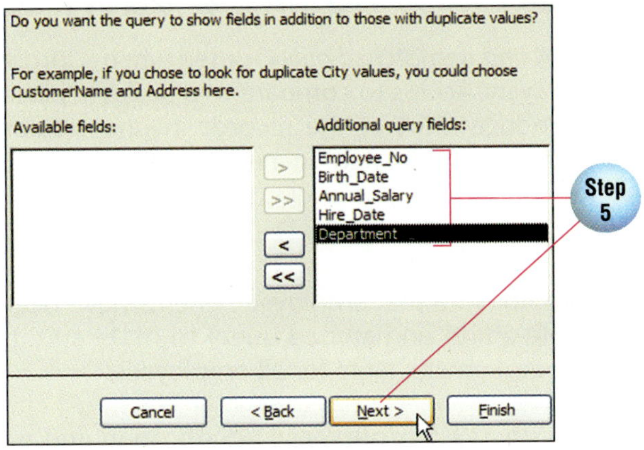

6 With the text already selected in the *What do you want to name your query?* text box, type **DuplicateRecordCheck_Employees** and then click Finish.

The query results datasheet displays showing that Pat Hildebrand has two records in the Employees table under two different employee numbers.

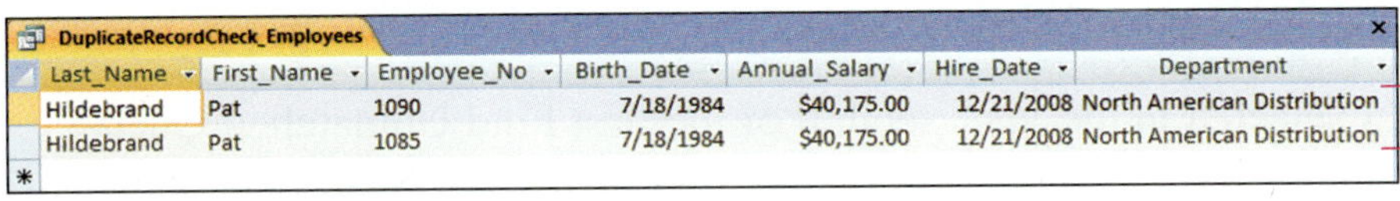

query results datasheet showing two records for *Pat Hildebrand* at Step 6

7 Print the query results datasheet in landscape orientation.

8 Move the mouse pointer in the record selector bar next to the first record (with *Employee_No 1090*) until the pointer changes to a right-pointing black arrow, right-click, and then click *Delete Record* at the shortcut menu.

9 Click Yes to confirm the record deletion.

10 Close the DuplicateRecordCheck_Employees query.

11 Double-click *DuplicateRecordCheck_Employees* in the Navigation pane to reopen the query. The query results is now a blank datasheet. Since you deleted the duplicate record for Pat Hildebrand in Step 8, duplicate records no longer exist in the Employees table.

12 Close the DuplicateRecordCheck_Employees query.

In Brief

Create Find Duplicates Query

1. Click Create tab.
2. Click Query Wizard button.
3. Click *Find Duplicates Query Wizard* and click OK.
4. Choose table or query to search for duplicates and click Next.
5. Choose field(s) that might contain duplicate field values and click Next.
6. Choose additional fields to display in query results and click Next.
7. Type query name and click Finish.

In Addition

More Examples for Using a Find Duplicates Query

In this project you used a find duplicates query to locate and then delete an employee record that was entered twice. A find duplicates query has several other applications. Consider the following examples:

- Find the records in an Orders table with the same customer number so that you can identify who your loyal customers are.
- Find the records in a Customer table with the same last name and mailing address so that you send only one mailing to a household to save on printing and postage costs.
- Find the records in an Expenses table with the same employee number so that you can see which employee is submitting the most claims.

Activity 4.6

Using a Query to Find Unmatched Records

A ***find unmatched query*** is used when you want Access to compare two tables and produce a list of the records in one table that have no matching record in the other related table. This type of query is useful to produce lists such as customers who have never placed an order or an invoice with no payment record. Access provides the Find Unmatched Query Wizard that builds the select query by guiding the user through a series of dialog boxes.

Project

You are not sure that employee benefits have been entered for all employees. You decide to create a find unmatched query to make sure that you have entered a record in the Employee_Benefits table for all employees.

1. With **WEEmployees4.accdb** open and with the Create tab active, click the Query Wizard button in the Other group.

2. Click *Find Unmatched Query Wizard* in the New Query dialog box and then click OK.

   At the first dialog box in the Find Unmatched Query Wizard, you choose the table or query in which you want to view records in the query results datasheet. If an employee is missing a record in the benefits table, you will need the employee's number and name, which are in the Employees table.

3. With *Tables* selected in the *View* section of the first Find Unmatched Query Wizard dialog box, click *Table: Employees* and then click Next.

   At the next dialog box, you choose the table or query that you want Access to compare with the first table selected.

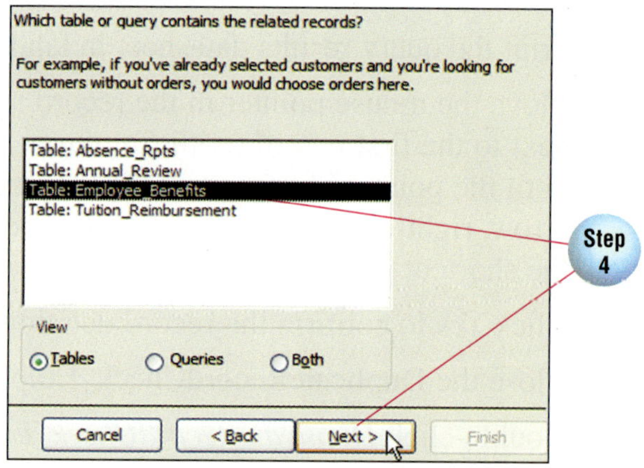

4. At the second Find Unmatched Query Wizard dialog box, click *Table: Employee_Benefits* in the table list box and then click Next.

   In order for Access to compare records you need to specify the field in each table that would have matching field values.

5. With *Employee_No* already selected in the *Fields in 'Employees'* and *Fields in 'Employee_Benefits'* list boxes at the third Find Unmatched Query Wizard dialog box, click Next.

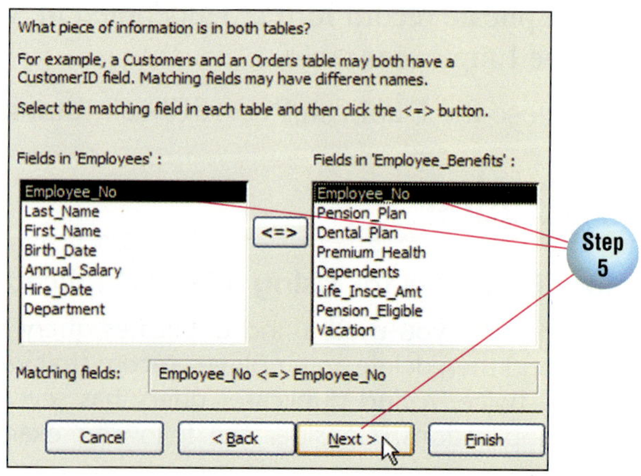

6. At the fourth Find Unmatched Query Wizard dialog box, double-click *Employee_No, Last_Name*, and *First_Name* to move the fields from the *Available fields* list box to the *Selected fields* list box and then click Next.

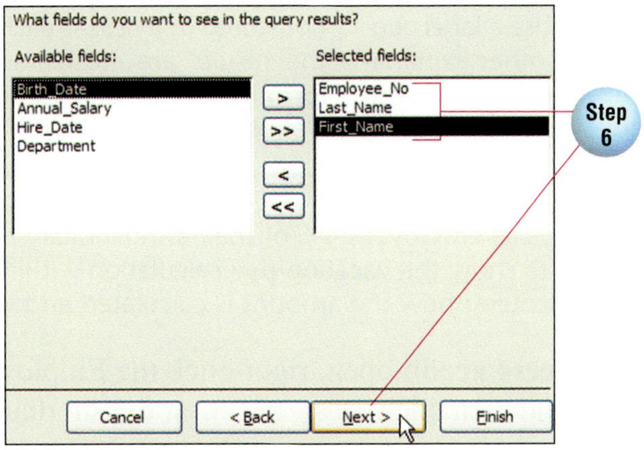

7. With the text already selected in the *What would you like to name your query?* text box, type **Unmatched_Employee_Benefits** and then click Finish.

8. Look at the three records displayed in the query results datasheet. These are the employee records for which no record with a matching employee number exists in the Employee_Benefits table.

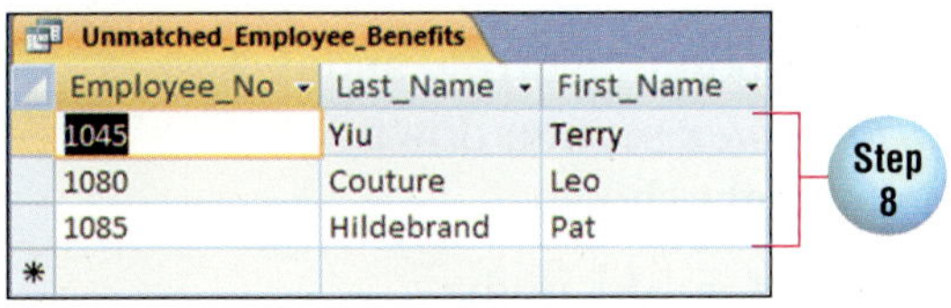

9. Print the query results datasheet and then close the Unmatched_Employee_Benefits query.

10. Open the Employee_Benefits table and then add the following records to the table.

Employee_ No	Pension_ Plan	Dental_ Plan	Premium_ Health	Dependents	Life_Insce_ Amt	Pension_ Eligible	Vacation
1045	Yes	No	Yes	**3**	**$150,000**	**01-May-04**	2 weeks
1080	Yes	No	No	**0**	**$100,000**	**01-Feb-11**	1 week
1085	Yes	Yes	Yes	**4**	**$185,000**	**01-Jan-12**	1 week

11. Close the Employee_Benefits table.

In Brief

Create Find Unmatched Query

1. Click Create tab.
2. Click Query Wizard button.
3. Click *Find Unmatched Query Wizard* and click OK.
4. Choose table or query to display in query results and click Next.
5. Choose related table or query and click Next.
6. Choose matching field in each table field list and click Next.
7. Choose fields you want to view in query results and click Next.
8. Type query name and click Finish.

Activity 4.7

Adding a Label and Calculation to a Form Using Design View; Sorting Data in a Form

A label control object containing text that is not bound to a field in a table or query can be added to a form. Use a label control object to add instructions or other explanatory text for the users of a form. A calculated control object containing a formula is created using a text box control object. As with a calculated field in a query, a calculated control object in a form is not stored as a field—each time the form is opened, the results are calculated dynamically. Display a form in Design view to add label or text box control objects.

Project

Worldwide Enterprises

Worldwide Enterprises pays its employees 4% of their annual salary each year on July 1 as vacation pay. You decide to show the vacation pay calculation within the Employees form with explanatory text describing how the amount is calculated and when it is paid.

1. With **WEEmployees4.accdb** open, right-click the Employees form in the Navigation pane and then click *Design View* at the shortcut menu.

   A form opens in Design view containing three sections as shown in Figure 4.1. The control objects for the fields in the table are displayed in the *Detail* section. Using buttons in the Controls group of the Form Design Tools Design tab, you will add the label and text box control objects.

2. Minimize the Navigation pane to display more space in the work area.

3. Position the mouse pointer at the top of the blue Form Footer section border until the pointer displays with a horizontal line with an up- and down-pointing arrow and then drag the *Form Footer* section down to the approximate height shown.

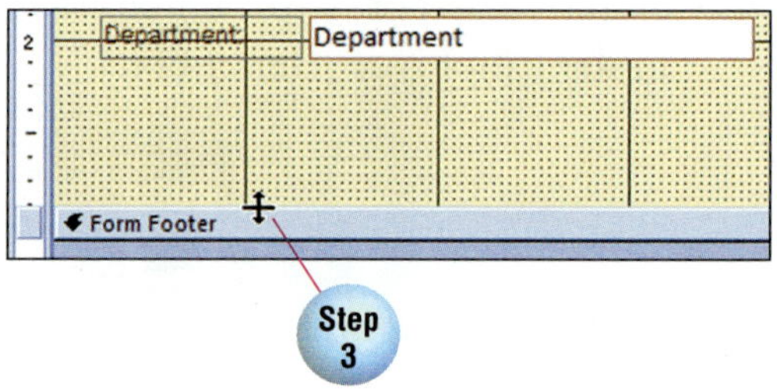

4. Click the Text Box button **ab|** in the Controls group in the Form Design Tools Design tab.

FIGURE 4.1 Employees Form in Design View

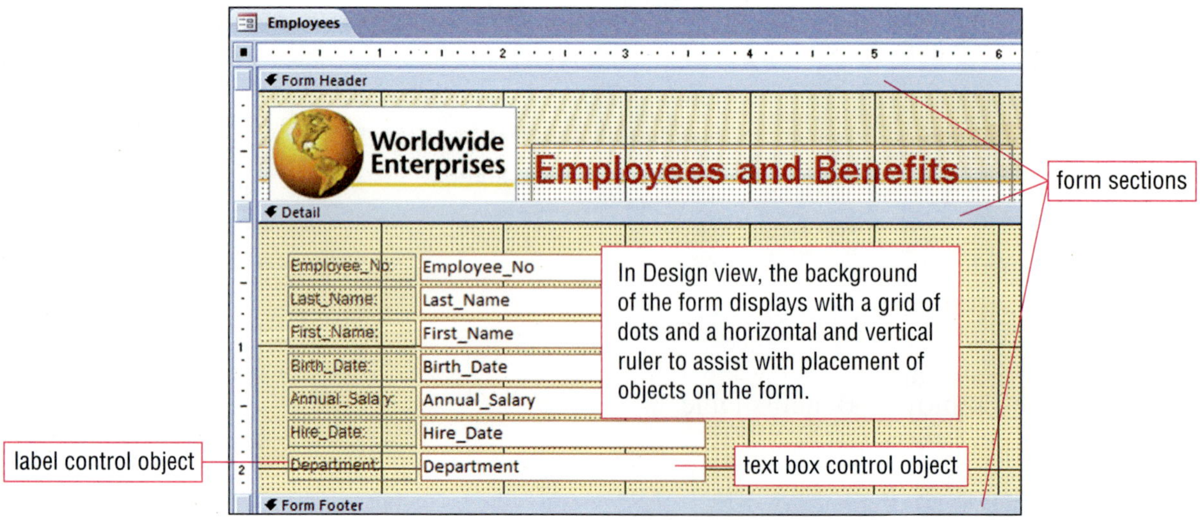

5 Position the crosshairs pointer with the text box icon attached below the *Department* text box control, drag to create the object the approximate height and width shown below, and then release the mouse button.

A text box label control object and an unbound control object box appear with selection handles. An ***unbound control*** contains data that is not stored anywhere. The other text box control objects in the Detail section of the Employees form are considered ***bound controls*** since the contents displayed in the objects are bound to the Employees table.

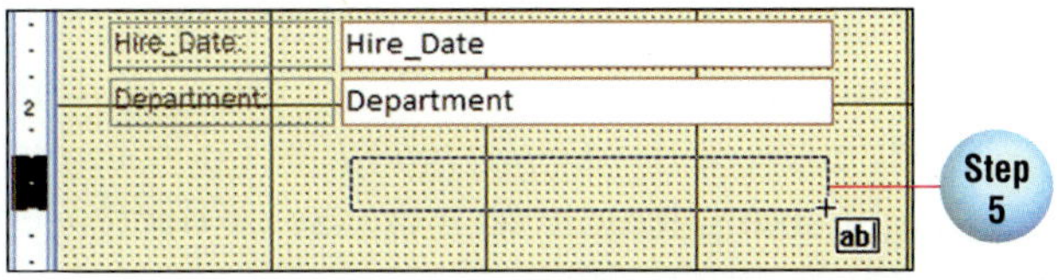

6 Click in the *Unbound* text box control.

An insertion point appears so that you can type a formula. A mathematical expression in a text box control begins with the equals sign (=) and field names are encased in square brackets.

7 Type **=[Annual_Salary]*0.04** and then press Enter.

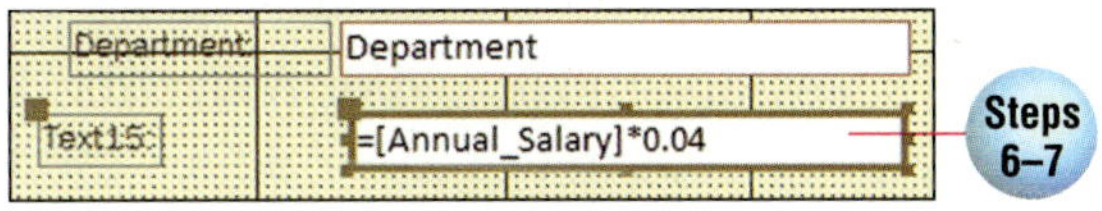

In Form view the object displays the calculated values in place of the formula.

8 With the calculated control object selected, click the Property Sheet button in the Tools group in the Form Design Tools Design tab.

9 With the All tab active in the Property Sheet task pane, click in the *Format* property box, click the down-pointing arrow that appears, and then click *Currency* at the drop-down list.

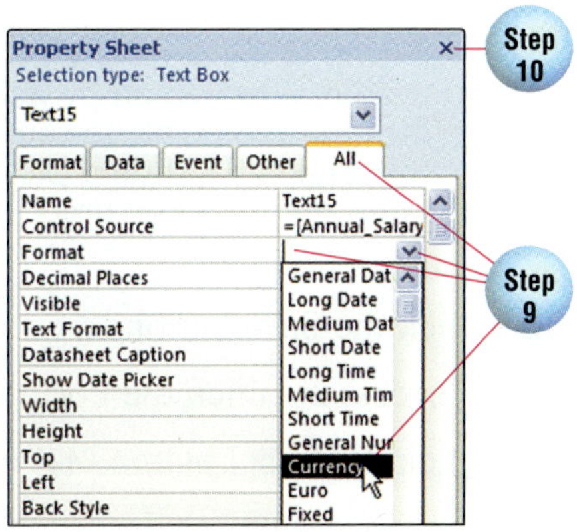

10 Close the Property Sheet task pane.

11 Click to select the label control object adjacent to the calculated text box control (currently displays *Text##* [where ## is the number of the label object]).

12 Click a second time inside the selected label control object to display the insertion point inside the object, delete the current text, type **Vacation_Pay:**, and then press Enter.

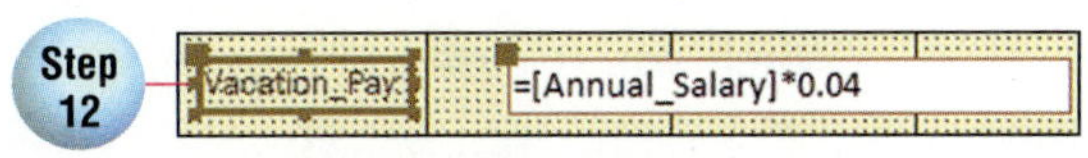

The width of the box increases automatically as you type the text.

13 With the *Vacation_Pay* label control still selected, point to the border of the object until the pointer displays with the four-headed move icon attached and then drag the control object until its left edge aligns with the left edge of the *Department* label control and the vertical space between *Department* and *Vacation_Pay* is consistent with the labels above.

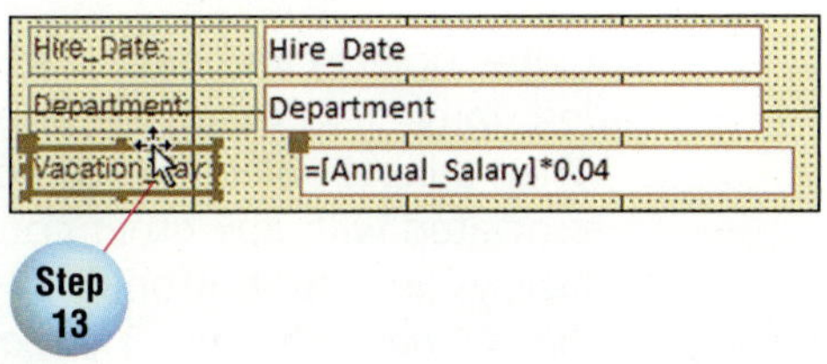

continues

14 With the *Vacation_Pay* label control still selected, drag the middle right sizing handle right until the right edge aligns with the right edge of the *Department* label control above.

15 Click to select the calculated text box control object and then drag the large sizing handle at the top left of the control until the left edge of the object aligns with the left edge of the *Department* text box control above. If necessary, use the middle right sizing handle to increase or decrease the width so that the right edges of both controls align.

Dragging the large handle at the top left of the text box control allows you to move the object independently of the label control associated with it.

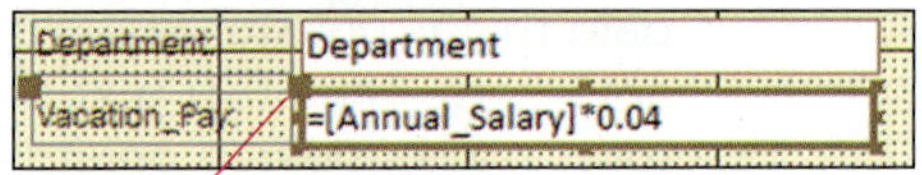

Drag large handle at top left to move calculated text box control object independently in Step 15.

16 Click in a blank area of the form to deselect the control objects.

17 If necessary, move and/or resize the *Vacation_Pay* label control or the calculated text box control to further adjust the width or position of the controls.

PROBLEM

Trying to move or resize by a very small increment? The Snap to Grid feature is turned on by default. This option pulls an object to the nearest grid point. To turn this feature off, click the Form Design Tools Arrange tab and then click the Snap to Grid button [Snap to Grid] in the Control Layout group.

18 Click the Save button.

19 If necessary, click the Form Design Tools Design tab.

20 Click the Label button [Aa] in the Controls group.

21 Position the crosshairs pointer with the label icon attached below the calculated text box control object and then drag to create the object the approximate height and width shown at the right.

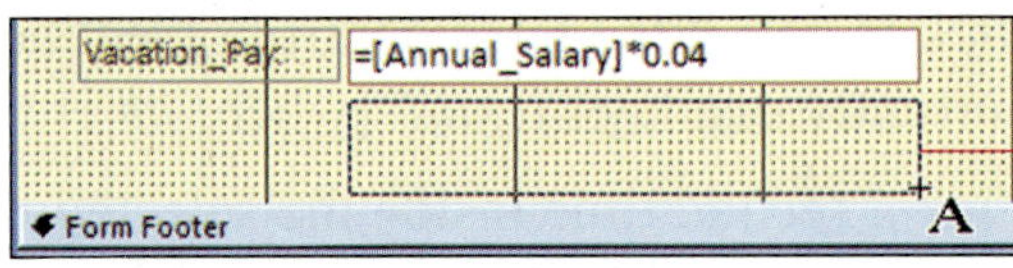

Step 21

When you release the mouse, an insertion point appears inside the object.

22 Type **Vacation Pay is calculated at 4 percent of salary and paid July 1 each year** and then press Enter.

A label object can be used to add any descriptive text to any section of a form. When a label object is created that is not associated with any other control, Access displays an error button with the ScreenTip *This is a new label and is not associated with a control.* You can ignore the error button since the label object is for descriptive text only.

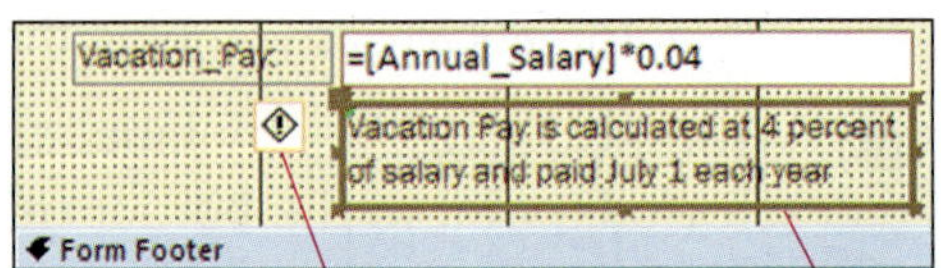

Error button displays when a new label object is added that is not associated with a control.

Step 22

23 Click the Save button and then switch to Form view.

24 Scroll through a few records in the form and notice the calculated text box control object update for each record.

25 Switch to Layout view.

26 Click to select the calculated text box control object and then click the Align Left button in the Font group in the Form Layout Tools Format tab.

27 Switch to Design view.

In the next step, you will decrease the width of the form so that printing a record in Form view does not exceed the page width.

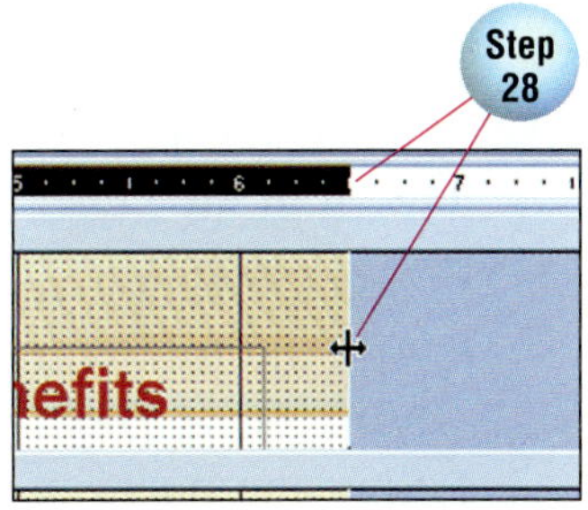

28 Position the mouse pointer on the right edge of the form's grid until the pointer changes to a vertical line with a left- and right-pointing arrow, drag the edge of the form left to position 6.5 on the horizontal ruler, and then release the mouse.

29 Switch to Form view.

30 Click in the *Last_Name* field in the first record.

31 Click the Ascending button in the Sort & Filter group of the Home tab to sort the records by the *Last_Name* field values.

The first record changes to display the data for Lyle Besterd.

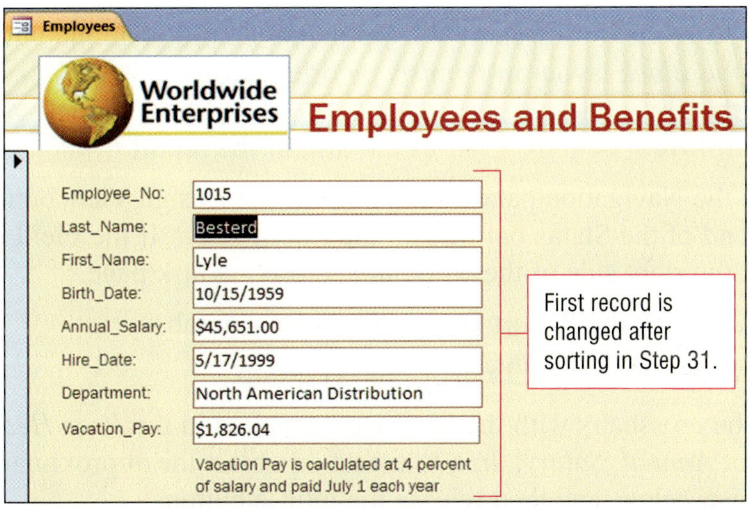

32 With the record for *Employee_No* 1015 displayed, click the Office button, click Print, click *Selected Record(s)* in the *Print Range* section, and then click OK.

33 Close the Employees form. Click Yes when prompted to save changes to the form design.

34 Redisplay the Navigation pane.

In Brief

Add Calculated Control Object to Form

1. Open form in Design view.
2. Click Text Box button.
3. Drag control in design grid to approximate height and width desired.
4. Click in Unbound control object and type formula.
5. Change format properties for unbound control as required.
6. Type desired label in text box label control.
7. Click Save button.

Add Label Control Object to Form

1. Open form in Design view.
2. Click Label button.
3. Drag control in design grid to approximate height and width desired.
4. Type label text and press Enter.
5. Click Save button.

Sort Data in Form

1. Open form in Form view.
2. Click in field by which to sort records.
3. Click Ascending or Descending button.

Activity 4.8

Adding a Label and Calculation to a Report Using Design View; Sorting Data in a Report

Labels and calculations are added to a report using Design view by applying the same techniques as those learned in the previous activity. When fine tuning a report design, switch often between Layout view and Design view since columns are easier to move and resize in Layout view.

Project

Worldwide Enterprises

Rhonda Trask estimates that Worldwide Enterprises incurs costs of an additional 22% of an employee's annual salary to pay for the benefit plans offered to employees. You will create a query and then a report to show the estimated benefit cost by employee.

1. With **WEEmployees4.accdb** open, click the Create tab, click the Query Design button in the Other group and then create a new query as follows.
   - Add the Employees table to the design grid.
   - Add the following fields in order: *Employee_No, First_Name, Last_Name, Hire_Date, Department,* and *Annual_Salary*.
   - Save the query and name it **Employee_List**.
2. Run the query, view the query results datasheet, and then close the query.
3. Click the Create tab, click the Report Wizard button, and then create a new report as follows.
   - Add all fields from the Employee_List query.
   - Double-click the *Department* field at the second Report Wizard dialog box to group the entries in the report by department.
   - Click Next at the third Report Wizard dialog box to continue without sorting.
   - Choose the *Block* layout in *Landscape* orientation.
   - Choose the *Trek* style.
   - Type **Employee_Benefit_Cost** as the title of the report.
4. Minimize the Navigation pane and then click the Design View button near the right end of the Status bar next to the Zoom slider. If the Field List task pane is open at the right side of the work area, close the task pane.
5. If necessary, click the Report Design Tools Design tab.
6. Click the Label button in the Controls group.
7. Position the crosshairs with the label icon attached in the *Page Header* section to the right of *Annual_Salary*, drag to create an object the approximate height and width shown below, and then release the mouse button.

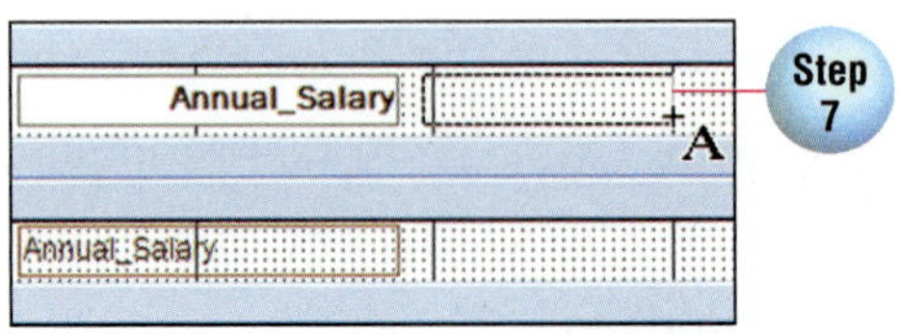

8. Type **Benefit_Cost** and then press Enter.
9. Click the Text Box button [ab|] in the Controls group.
10. Position the crosshairs with the text box icon attached in the *Detail* section below the *Benefit_Cost* label, drag to create an object approximately the same height and width as the label, and then release the mouse button.
11. Click in the text box control (displays *Unbound*), type **=[Annual_Salary]*0.22**, and then press Enter.

    Do not be concerned if the entire formula is not visible within the object box. If necessary, the formula can be seen in its entirety by displaying the Property Sheet.

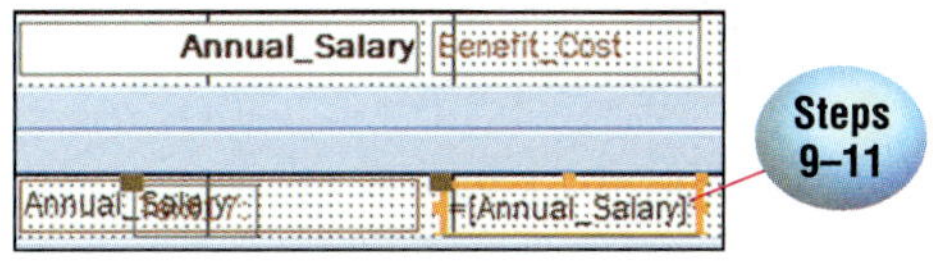

12. Click the label control to the left of the text box control (displays *Text##* [where ## is the text box label number]) and then press Delete.

PROBLEM

Not sure where the label control is located? The label control object is probably overlapping the *Annual_Salary* text box control adjacent to the calculated text box control. Look for the large sizing handle to locate the outline of the box.

13. Click the Print Preview button near the right end of the Status bar.
14. Notice the calculated values are aligned at the left edge of the column, do not display a consistent number of decimal places, and border lines are not surrounding the values as in the remainder of the report.

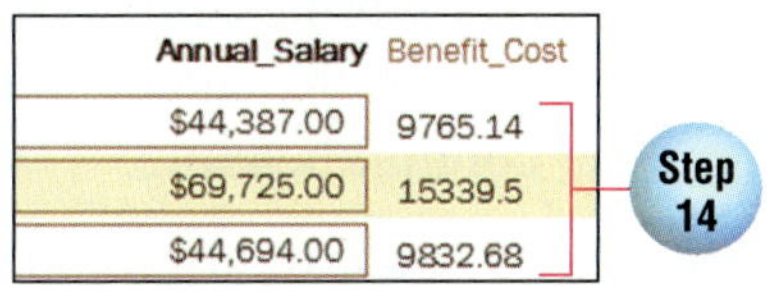

15. Click the Design view button near the right end of the Status bar.
16. Click the *Annual_Salary* control in the *Detail* section, click the Format Painter button in the Font group of the Report Design Tools Design tab, and then click the calculated text box control object containing the mathematical expression.

    The border attributes are copied to the calculated control object.

17. Click the *Annual_Salary* control in the Page Header section, click the Format Painter button, and then click the adjacent *Benefit_Cost* control to copy the formatting attributes to the new label object.
18. Right-click the calculated text box control object, click *Properties* at the shortcut menu, click the Format tab in the Property Sheet task pane, and then change the following properties.
    - *Format* property to *Currency*.
    - *Text Align* property to *Right*.
19. Close the Property Sheet task pane.
20. Click the *Annual_Salary* control in the Detail section, hold down the Shift key and click the adjacent calculated text box control object.

continues

21 With both objects selected, click the Report Design Tools Arrange tab and then click the Top button [Top] in the Control Alignment group.

Buttons in the Control Alignment group in the Report Design Tools Arrange tab align a group of selected objects at the topmost, leftmost, bottommost, or rightmost position.

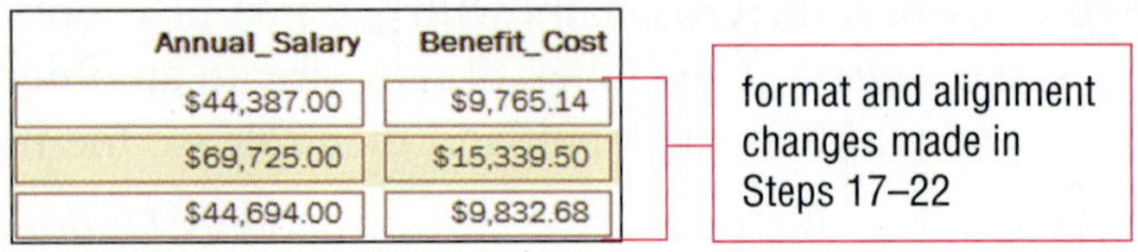

22 Repeat Steps 20–21 for the above two labels in the *Page Header* section.

23 Switch to Layout view.

You decide the employee numbers are not required in the report and want to delete the field to make more room on the page.

24 Right-click the *Employee_No* column heading and then click *Delete* at the shortcut menu.

25 Click to select the *Department* column heading and then drag the right border of the selected heading right until all of the text in the column is visible for all three departments.

26 Click the Save button.

27 Click the *Benefit_Cost* column heading.

28 Hold down the Shift key and click over any one of the calculated objects below the column heading.

29 Position the mouse pointer inside the selected column until the pointer changes to display the four-headed arrow move icon and then drag the column right approximately one-half inch.

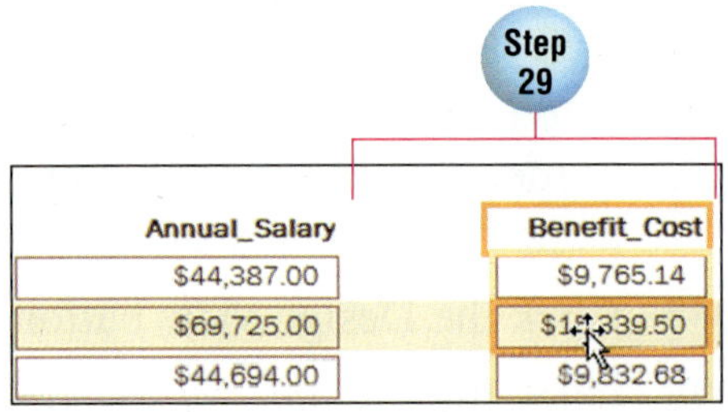

30 Click the *Hire_Date* column heading, position the pointer inside the dotted box of the selected column until the pointer displays with the four-headed arrow move icon, and then drag the column right to position it after *Annual_Salary*.

31 Drag the right border of the *Hire_Date* column heading to widen the column until all of the dates are visible within the column.

32 Move the *Benefit_Cost* column left until the space between the *Hire_Date* and *Benefit_Cost* columns is consistent with the spacing between the other columns in the report. Refer to Steps 27–29 if you need assistance.

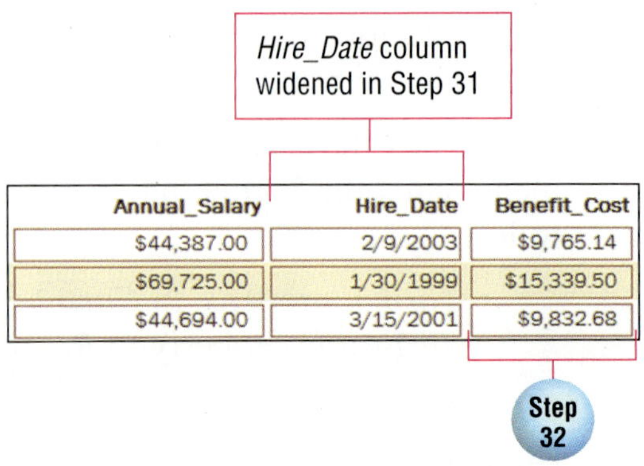

33 If necessary, move, resize, and/or make further height or width adjustments to the column headings.

34 If necessary, switch to Design view and make further height or width adjustments to the calculated text box control until the values in the *Benefit_Cost* column are aligned and sized the same as the values in the adjacent columns.

35 In Layout view, edit the report title to replace the underscore characters between the words with spaces.

As your final task before printing the report, you decide to sort the report by the last names.

36 With the report still in Layout view and the Report Layout Tools Format tab active, click the Group & Sort button in the Grouping & Totals group.

A Group, Sort, and Total pane opens at the bottom of the screen.

37 Click the Add a sort button (Add a sort) in the Group, Sort, and Total pane and then click *Last_Name* at the pop-up field list box.

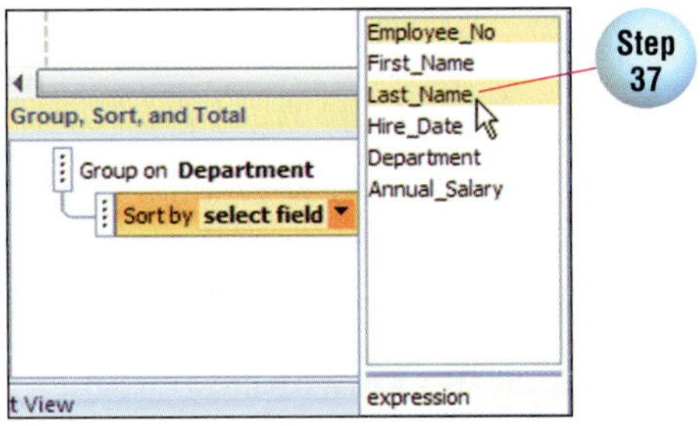

38 Click the Group & Sort button to remove the Group, Sort, and Total pane.

The report is now grouped by the Department names arranged alphabetically and within each department group the records are sorted by the last names.

39 Display the report in Print Preview and then print the report.

Employee Benefit Cost

Department	First_Name	Last_Name	Annual_Salary	Hire_Date	Benefit_Cost
European Distribution	Leo	Couture	$43,659.00	1/17/2008	$9,604.98
	George	Featherstone	$38,175.00	5/15/2009	$8,398.50
	Valerie	Fitsouris	$44,694.00	3/15/2001	$9,832.68
	Donald	McKnight	$42,126.00	6/22/2003	$9,267.72
	Hanh	Postma	$69,725.00	1/30/1999	$15,339.50
	Terry	Yiu	$42,238.00	4/12/2001	$9,292.36
	Carl	Zakowski	$44,387.00	2/9/2003	$9,765.14
North American Distributio	Lyle	Besterd	$45,651.00	5/17/1999	$10,043.22
	Jorge	Biliski	$44,892.00	12/1/1999	$9,876.24

Records are grouped first by *Department*.

Within each *Department* group, records are sorted by *Last_Name*.

40 Close Print Preview and then close the Employee_Benefit_Cost report. Click Yes when prompted to save changes to the report design.

41 Redisplay the Navigation pane.

42 Close **WEEmployees4.accdb**.

In Brief

Add Label Control Object to Report
1. Open report in Design view.
2. Click Label button.
3. Drag control in design grid to approximate height and width desired.
4. Type label text and press Enter.
5. Click Save button.

Add Calculated Control Object to Report
1. Open report in Design view.
2. Click Text Box button.
3. Drag control in Detail section of design grid to approximate height and width desired.
4. Click in Unbound control object and type formula.
5. Change format properties for unbound control as required.
6. Edit label text or delete label control object box.
7. Click Save button.

Sort Data in Report
1. Open report in Layout view.
2. Click Report Layout Tools Format tab.
3. Click Group & Sort button.
4. Click Add a sort button in Group, Sort, and Total pane.
5. Click field name by which to sort.
6. Click Group & Sort button to close Group, Sort, and Total pane.
7. Click Save button.

Activity 4.9

Creating a New Database Using a Template

Access provides database templates that can be used to create new database files. The templates are databases that have tables, queries, forms, and reports already created for you. In some cases, sample records are entered for you to illustrate how to use the objects. You can start a new database using a template and then customize the objects to suit your needs.

Project

You decide to experiment with a database template to create a new database to store contact information for Worldwide Enterprises.

1. At the *Getting Started with Microsoft Office Access* screen, double-click *Contacts* in the Featured Online Templates section in the center pane.
2. Click the Browse button (displays as a file folder icon) next to the *File Name* text box in the right pane.
3. At the File New Database dialog box, navigate to the AccessS4 folder on your storage medium, edit the name in the *File Name* text box to **WEContacts4.accdb**, and then click OK.
4. Click the Download button.

   Access downloads the database template from Microsoft Office Online and in a few seconds displays the Contact List form with the Access Help window in the foreground.

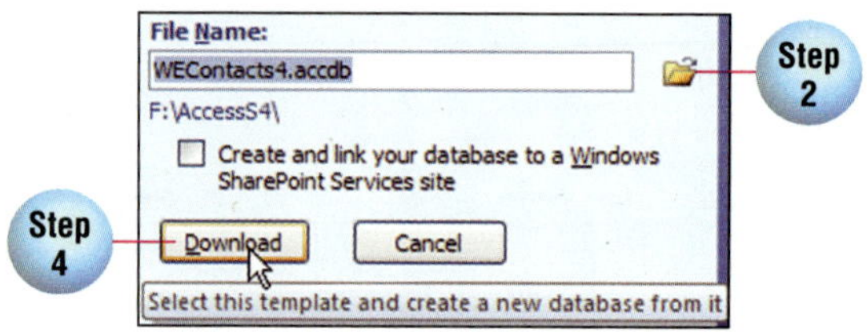

5. Close the Help window and redisplay the Navigation pane.
6. Click the down-pointing arrow to the right of Contacts Navigation at the top of the Navigation pane and then click *Object Type* at the drop-down list.

   Changing the Navigation pane to display objects grouped by type will allow you to quickly decipher how many tables, queries, forms, and reports are in the database template.

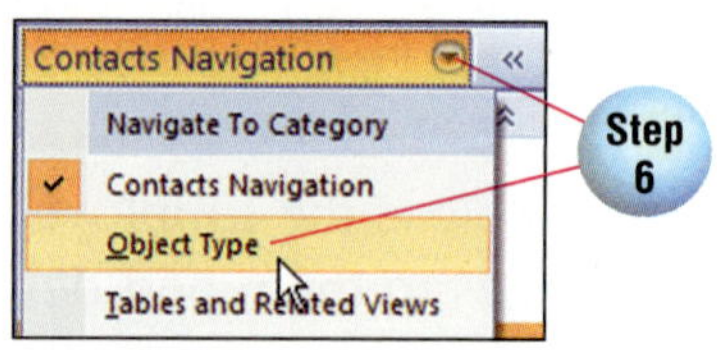

7. Notice the Contacts database template has one table, one query, two forms, and two reports created.
8. Close the Contact List form and then open the Contacts table datasheet.
9. Switch to Design view.

10 Review the field names, data types, and field properties for each field in the table and then close the table.

11 Open the Contact Details form and enter data into the new blank record as shown below.

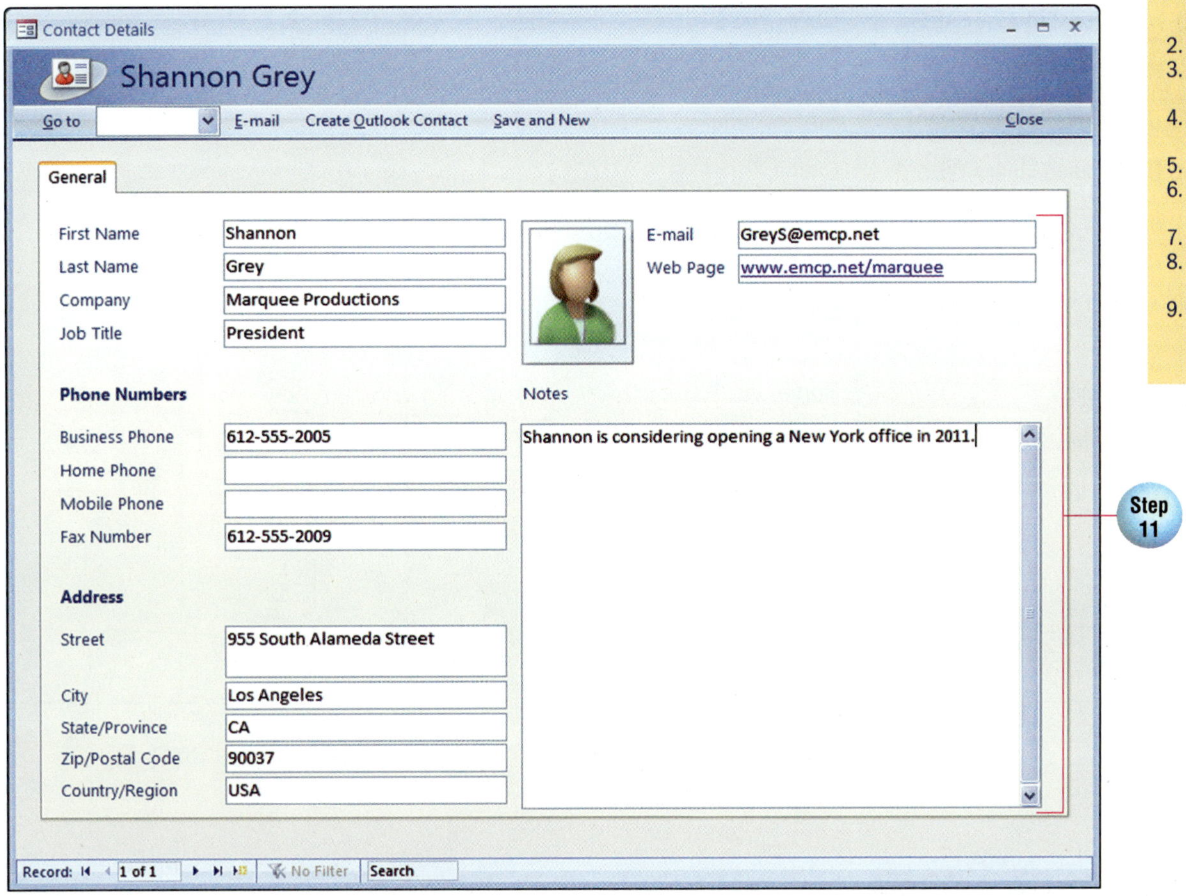

12 Close the Contact Details form.

13 Open each of the other objects and review the data for Shannon Grey.

14 Close **WEContacts4.accdb**.

In Brief

Create New Database Using Template

1. Double-click desired template at *Getting Started with Microsoft Office Access* screen.
2. Click Browse button.
3. Navigate to desired drive and/or folder.
4. Enter file name in *File Name* text box.
5. Click OK.
6. Click Download button.
7. Close Help window.
8. Display Navigation pane.
9. Explore objects created in database.

Features Summary

Feature	Ribbon Tab, Group	Button	Keyboard Shortcut
aggregate functions	Query Tools Design, Show/Hide	Σ	
Crosstab Query Wizard	Create, Other		
Find Duplicates Query Wizard	Create, Other		
Find Unmatched Query Wizard	Create, Other		
Group, Sort, and Total pane	Report Layout Tools Format, Grouping & Totals		
label control in form or report	Form Design Tools Design, Controls OR Report Design Tools Design, Controls	Aa	
PivotChart view	Home, Views		
PivotTable view	Home, Views		
Property sheet	Form Design Tools Design, Tools OR Report Design Tools Design, Tools		Alt + Enter
sort in ascending order in form	Home, Sort & Filter		
text box control in form or report	Form Design Tools Design, Controls OR Report Design Tools Design, Controls	ab|	

Knowledge Check

Completion: In the space provided at the right, indicate the correct term, command, or option.

1. Click this button in the Query Tools Design tab to add a row to the design grid from which you can choose an aggregate function such as Sum. ____________
2. This query wizard can be used to sum data that is grouped by two fields. ____________
3. This is the name of the view in which you can create an interactive table that organizes and summarizes data based on fields you drag and drop for row and column headings. ____________
4. Create this type of chart by dragging fields from a Field List box to Filter, Data, and Category sections. ____________
5. Start this query wizard if you suspect someone has added a record twice in the same table. ____________
6. Use this query wizard to produce a datasheet showing names and telephone numbers from a Customer table for those customers that have no record in a related Orders table. ____________
7. Open a form or report in this view to add a calculation. ____________

8. A calculation added to a form or report is started by clicking this button and dragging to create the outline of a control object. ________
9. Descriptive text can be added to a form or report using this button. ________
10. To format a calculated control object to display the values in Currency format, open this task pane. ________
11. To sort records in a form display the form in this view. ________
12. Hold down this key to select multiple objects in a form or report. ________
13. Buttons to align a group of selected objects in a report at the same top, left, bottom, or right position are found in the Control Alignment group of this tab. ________
14. To sort records in a report display this pane. ________
15. These are databases that have tables, queries, forms, and reports already created for you. ________

Skills Review

Review 1 Creating a Crosstab, Find Unmatched, and Find Duplicates Query

Worldwide Enterprises

1. Open **WEEmployees4.accdb** and enable all content.
2. Create a crosstab query that summarizes tuition payments by employee by quarter using the following information:
   a. Choose the Tuition_Payments query.
   b. Display the employee last names in rows.
   c. Display the reimbursement date by quarter intervals in columns.
   d. Sum the tuition amounts.
   e. Name the crosstab query **Tuition_byEmp_byQtr**.
3. Add a total row to the query results datasheet and sum each column.
4. Adjust column widths as necessary and then print the query results datasheet.
5. Close the Tuition_byEmp_byQtr query saving changes.
6. Use the Find Unmatched Query Wizard to compare the Employees table with the Absence_Rpts table and produce a list of employees who have not submitted an absence report. Display the fields *Employee_No, First_Name,* and *Last_Name* in order in the query results. Name the query **Unmatched_Employee_Absences**.
7. Print and then close the Unmatched_Employee_Absences query results datasheet.
8. Use the Find Duplicates Query Wizard to analyze the *Employee_No* field in the Absence_Rpts table and produce a list of employees who have submitted more than one absence report. Display the remaining fields in the query results. Name the query **DuplicateAbsenceRpts**.
9. Print the DuplicateAbsenceRpts query results datasheet in landscape orientation and then close the query.

Review 2 Creating a PivotTable

Worldwide Enterprises

1. With **WEEmployees4.accdb** open, open the Employee_List query.
2. Switch to PivotTable view.
3. Create a PivotTable that summarizes the annual salaries of employees by hire dates using the following information:
   a. Drag the *Department* field to *Drop Row Fields Here*.
   b. Click the expand button (displays as plus symbol) next to *Hire_Date by Month* in the PivotTable Field List box and then drag the *Years* field to *Drop Column Fields Here*.
   c. Drag the *Annual_Salary* field to *Drop Totals or Detail Fields Here*.
4. Close the PivotTable Field List box.
5. Filter the PivotTable on the *Department* field to display only the European Distribution and Overseas Distribution departments.
6. Filter the PivotTable on the *Years* field to display only those employees hired after the year 2000.
7. Calculate the row and column grand totals using the Sum function.
8. Select any of the *Annual_Salary* column headings and open the Properties dialog box. At the Format tab, change the font color to blue.
9. Format the grand total row and column values to bold dark green font color.
10. Save and print the PivotTable in landscape orientation.
11. Close the Employee_List query.

Review 3 Creating and Modifying a Report; Creating a Calculated Control

Worldwide Enterprises

1. With **WEEmployees4.accdb** open, create a new report using the Report Wizard based on the Employee_List query as follows:
   a. Add all of the fields from the query to the report.
   b. Do not include any grouping or sorting.
   c. Select the *Columnar* layout in *Portrait* orientation.
   d. Select the *Solstice* style.
   e. Title the report **Employee_MthlySalary**.
2. Modify the report as follows:
   a. Insert a label control object in the Report Header section that prints the text *Report design by: Student Name*. Substitute your first and last names for *Student Name*. Position the control near the right edge of the section and change the font size to 12-point. If necessary, resize the control after changing the font size. Select the report title and label control and then use the Bottom button in the Control Alignment group to position the bottom edges of both controls at the same position.
   b. Create a calculated control object to the right of the *Annual_Salary* text box control that calculates the monthly salary by dividing Annual_Salary by 12. Type the label **Monthly_Salary** for the calculated control object.
   c. Format the calculated control object to *Currency*.
   d. Use Format Painter to copy the border style from the *Annual_Salary* text box control object to the calculated control object.
   e. Select the *Annual_Salary* label and text box controls and the *Monthly_Salary* label and text box controls. Use the Top button in the Control Alignment group to adjust both sets of controls to the same position.
   f. Edit the report title to **Employee Salaries**.

3. Display the report in Print Preview. If necessary, switch to Layout view or Design view and make further adjustments to the calculated control objects size or position.
4. Save and then print the first page only of the report.
5. Close the Employee_MthlySalary report.
6. Close **WEEmployees4.accdb**.

Skills Assessment

Assessment 1 Adding a Calculated Control to a Form

Performance Threads

1. Staff have commented positively on a form created for the inventory table; however, they would like the form modified to include the daily rental fee amount with the tax included.
2. Open **PTCostumeInventory4.accdb** and enable content.
3. Open the Costume_Inventory form and review the current form layout and design.
4. Make the following changes to the form design.
   a. Create a calculated control object below the *DailyRentalFee* object that calculates the DailyRentalFee amount with 6% GST included. (GST is the goods and services tax levied on all purchases by the government of Canada.)
   b. Type **Fee with GST:** as the label for the calculated control.
   c. Format the calculated control object to *Currency*.
   d. Move and/or use buttons in the Control Alignment group to make sure the label and calculated control objects align at the same left positions as the *DailyRentalFee* object.
   e. If necessary, resize the label and text box control to the same width as the other controls on the form.
   f. Make sure the new object is the same text alignment as the other objects on the form.
5. Save the revised form.
6. Display the form in Form view and then print the first record only.
7. Close the Costume_Inventory form.
8. Close **PTCostumeInventory4.accdb**.

Assessment 2 Creating and Modifying a Report; Sorting a Report

Worldwide Enterprises

1. Heidi Pasqual, financial officer, requires a report that prints the names and addresses of the Canadian distributors. Since Heidi is not familiar with Access, she has asked you to create the report for her.
2. Open **WEDistributors4.accdb** and enable content.
3. Create a new report using the Report Wizard as follows:
   a. Select the *CompanyName, StreetAdd1, StreetAdd2, City, Province,* and *PostalCode* fields from the CDN_Distributors table.
   b. Do not include any grouping or sorting.
   c. Choose the *Tabular* layout in *Portrait* orientation.
   d. Choose the *Civic* style.
   e. Accept the default title of *CDN_Distributors*.
4. As you preview the report, notice that some of the data is truncated.

5. Modify the report as follows:
   a. In Layout view, resize columns as necessary so that all data is entirely visible in the report.
   b. In Design view, add a label object at the left side of the report in the Report Footer section that includes the text *Report design by: Student Name*. Substitute your first and last names for *Student Name*. ***Hint: Drag the bottom of the Report Footer section bar down to create space in the design grid to add objects.***
   c. Edit the report title to **Canadian Distributor Addresses**.
6. Save, print, and then close the CDN_Distributors report.
7. Close **WEDistributors4.accdb**.

Assessment 3 Creating a PivotChart

1. Dana Hirsch, manager, is reviewing the recent purchases made by the executive chef and has requested a chart showing the dollar value of inventory purchases by item.
2. Open **WBInventory4.accdb** and enable content.
3. Open the PurchaseItems query and review the query results datasheet.
4. Switch to Design view and add the *SupplierCode* field to the design grid.
5. Save the revised query.
6. Switch to PivotChart view.
7. Create a PivotChart as follows:
   a. Drag the *SupplierCode* field to *Drop Filter Fields Here.*
   b. Drag the *ItemDescription* field to *Drop Category Fields Here.*
   c. Drag the *Amount* field to *Drop Data Fields Here.*
8. Close the Chart Field List box.
9. Print the chart in landscape orientation.
10. Filter the chart to display only those items purchased from the supplier whose supplier code is 1.
11. Print the chart.
12. Redisplay all items in the chart.
13. Save and then close the PurchaseItems query.
14. Close **WBInventory4.accdb**.

Assessment 4 Calculating Statistics; Creating a Crosstab Query

1. Dana Hirsch, manager, has requested statistics from the inventory database. Dana would like to know the total purchases made, grouped by supplier code. Dana has also requested the total purchases made by inventory item by supplier code.
2. Open **WBInventory4.accdb** and enable content.
3. Create a new query in Design view using the Inventory_List and Purchases table that displays one row for each supplier code with the sum of the purchase amounts. Title the statistic column **TotalPurchases**. Name the query **Total_bySupplier**.
4. Run the TotalPurchases query and print the query results datasheet.
5. Close the TotalPurchases query.
6. Create a crosstab query to sum the purchases by supplier code and by inventory item as follows:
   a. Base the crosstab query on the PurchaseItems query.

b. Choose *ItemDescription* for the row headings.
c. Choose *SupplierCode* for the column headings.
d. You determine the remaining steps in the Crosstab Query Wizard.
e. Name the crosstab query **Purchases_byItem_bySC**.
f. Adjust column widths as necessary.

7. Add a totals row to the Purchases_byItem_bySC query results datasheet and sum each column.
8. Print the Purchases_byItem_bySC query results datasheet in landscape orientation.
9. Close the Purchases_byItem_bySC query. Click Yes when prompted to save changes.
10. Close **WBInventory4.accdb**.

Assessment 5 Finding Information on Adding an Image to a Report

1. Use the Help feature to find out how to add a picture or other image to a report.
2. Print the Help topic that you find.
3. Open **WEDistributors4.accdb** and enable content.
4. Open the CDN_Distributors report in Design view.
5. Increase the height of the Report Header section by dragging the top of the Page Header section bar down approximately 2 inches.
6. Add the image named **canada_flag.jpg** to the right side of the Report Header section and resize the image appropriately.
7. Decrease the height of the Report Header section to end the section just below the flag image.
8. Make sure the right edge of the report does not extend beyond 8 inches on the horizontal ruler. If necessary, drag the right edge of the design grid to position 8.
9. Save, print, and then close the CDN_Distributors report.
10. Close **WEDistributors4.accdb**.

Assessment 6 Researching Salary Statistics on the Internet

1. You decide to track salary statistics for your field of study.
2. Search the Internet for salary information by state or province for your field of study. Be sure to find consistent information for all states or provinces. For example, collect data that is based on the same unit such as annual salary, hourly wage, or other unit of pay.
3. Create a new database and name it **SalaryStatistics.accdb**. Design and create a table to store the location and salary statistics that you found. Include a field to store the date the statistic references and another to describe the source agency or Web site from which you obtained the data.
4. Design and create a form for the table and then enter records for the locations you researched.
5. Design and create a query to calculate the average salary, maximum salary, and minimum salary. Print the query results.
6. Design and create a report to print the records.
7. Save, print, and close the report.
8. Close **SalaryStatistics.accdb**.

Marquee Challenge

Challenge 1 Summarizing Catering Event Information

1. Dana Hirsch, manager, has requested a summary report and chart from the catering information database. Dana would like the summary report to group catering revenue by type of event and by date in quarter intervals. In the report, Dana wants the data sorted in descending order by total revenue so that the highest revenue events are listed first. Dana would like a chart showing the second and third quarter's catering revenue summarized by banquet room. Dana created a query that contains the fields and calculations needed but does not know how to group the data and has asked for your assistance.
2. Open **WBCateringContracts4.accdb** and enable content.
3. Look at the report in Figure 4.2. The data is grouped by type of event in rows and by date of event in quarter intervals in columns.
4. Create a crosstab query to generate the data for the report. Name the query **Revenue_byEvent_byQtr** and base it on the Revenue_and_Gratuity query.
5. Design and create a report similar to the one shown in Figure 4.2 based on the Revenue_byEvent_byQtr query. Use your best judgment to determine the style and report formatting elements. Make adjustments in both Layout view and Design view. ***Hint: The column labels are best edited in the report (not the query) in Layout view.***
6. Name the report the same name as the source query.
7. Print the report.
8. Open the Revenue_and_Gratuity query.
9. Display the query in PivotChart view and then create the chart shown in Figure 4.3. ***Hint: The chart is filtered to show only Qtr2 and Qtr3 data.***
10. Print the chart in landscape orientation.
11. Save and then close the Revenue_and_Gratuity query.
12. Close **WBCateringContracts4.accdb**.

FIGURE 4.2 Challenge 1 Report

Revenue by Type of Event by Quarter

Event	Quarter 1	Quarter 2	Quarter 3	Total Revenue
Wedding	$7,700.70	$8,937.75	$3,514.50	$20,152.95
Engagement Party	$5,124.15	$2,460.75	$2,096.25	$9,681.15
Birthday Party	$4,434.65	$2,186.10		$6,620.75
Business Meeting	$2,326.70	$2,044.85	$1,173.55	$5,545.10
25th Wedding Anniversary	$2,547.60	$1,725.30		$4,272.90
50th Wedding Anniversary		$2,042.90		$2,042.90
Baby Shower			$1,360.90	$1,360.90
	$22,133.80	**$19,397.65**	**$8,145.20**	**$49,676.65**

FIGURE 4.3 Challenge 1 PivotChart

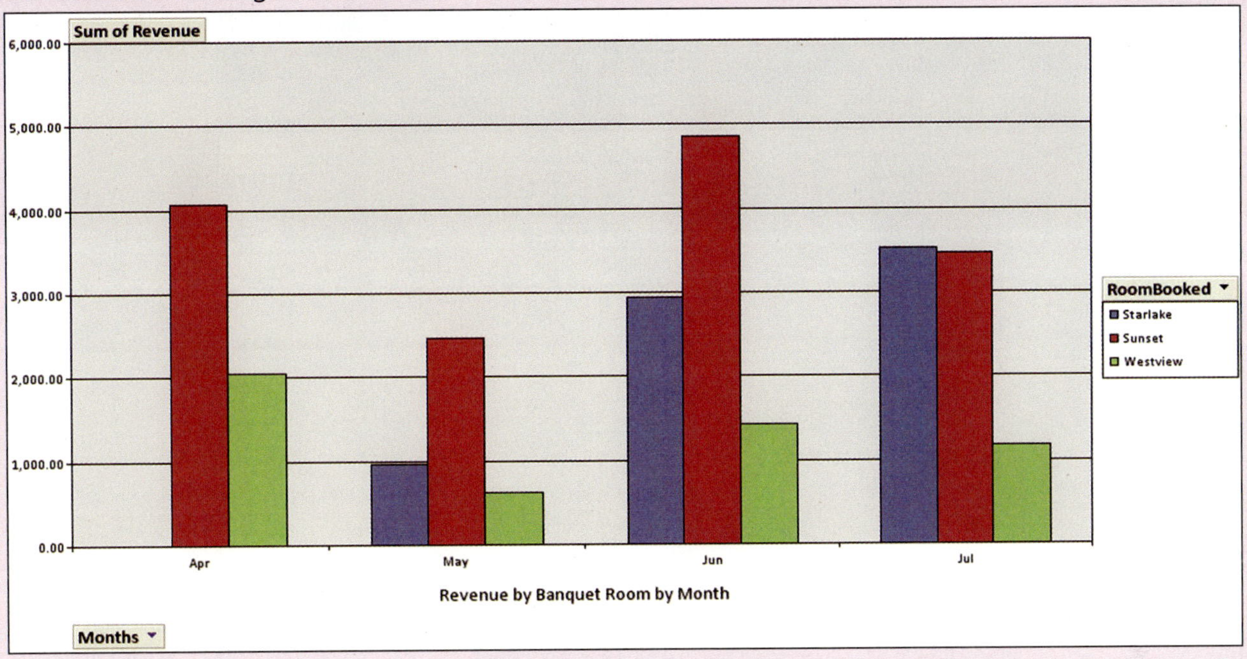

Challenge 2 Summarizing Costume Rental Revenue

1. Bobbie Sinclair, business manager, has created a query in the costume inventory database that calculates the rental revenue from costumes in 2009. Bobbie would like a report from the query that groups the records by month and includes a subtotal for each month and a grand total at the end of the report.
2. Look at the partial report in Figure 4.4. This figure shows the first three months of activity in the rental revenue report for 2009. Notice the subtotal at the end of each month.
3. Open **PTCostumeInventory4.accdb** and enable content.
4. Use the Report Wizard to create a report from the Rental_Revenue query. Add all fields to the report. At the second Report Wizard dialog box, double-click *DateOut* to group the report by date by month. Use the default options for the remainder of the dialog boxes except title the report **Rental_Revenue_GroupedbyMonth**.
5. Modify the report in Layout view. Use your best judgment to determine the style and report formatting elements.
6. Turn on the Group, Sort, and Total pane. Use Access Help or experiment with options in the pane to add a sum total to the *RentalFee* column for each group and a grand total at the end of the report. ***Hint: Modify the* Group on DateOut *options.***
7. Save, print, and close the report. (The report is two pages.)
8. Close **PTCostumeInventory4.accdb**.

FIGURE 4.4 Challenge 2 Partial Report

Costume Rental Revenue by Month

DateOut by Month	CostumeNo	CostumeTitle	DateOut	DateIn	DaysRented	RentalFee
May 2009						
	S-101	Macbeth	5/12/2009	6/30/2009	49	$9,115.47
	A-176	Pietro Gorski	5/2/2009	6/10/2009	39	$4,774.77
	S-102	Lady Macbeth	5/12/2009	6/30/2009	49	$10,128.30
	A-144	Kelly Williams	5/2/2009	6/11/2009	40	$4,218.80
						$28,237.34
June 2009						
	A-152	Hannah Sorenti	6/1/2009	7/12/2009	41	$5,019.63
						$5,019.63
July 2009						
	A-160	William Mercer	7/7/2009	7/10/2009	3	$387.96
	A-110	Tony Salvatore	7/15/2009	8/12/2009	28	$3,695.16
	D-105	Nala	7/1/2009	7/31/2009	30	$6,002.25
	A-102	Eunice Billings	7/7/2009	7/15/2009	8	$1,055.76
	D-107	Scar	7/1/2009	7/31/2009	30	$6,320.25
	A-198	Nanci Lasertol	7/22/2009	8/15/2009	24	$3,103.68
	D-101	Simba	7/1/2009	7/31/2009	30	$7,147.05
	D-102	Timon	7/1/2009	7/31/2009	30	$2,718.90
	A-101	Val Wingfield	7/7/2009	7/31/2009	24	$3,167.28
	D-104	Rafiki	7/1/2009	7/31/2009	30	$4,595.10
	D-106	Zazu	7/1/2009	7/31/2009	30	$2,718.90
	A-180	Robert Foullette	7/15/2009	7/31/2009	16	$1,738.40
	S-110	Othello	7/22/2009	8/31/2009	40	$5,300.00
	D-108	Mufasa	7/1/2009	7/31/2009	30	$6,852.90
	S-106	Hamlet	7/1/2009	7/31/2009	30	$3,975.00
	D-103	Pombah	7/1/2009	7/31/2009	30	$3,585.45
						$62,364.04

At the Group, Sort, and Total pane, add totals to each group and a grand total to the end of the report.

Integrating Programs
Word, Excel, and Access

Skills

- Export Access data in a table to Excel
- Export Access data in a table to Word
- Export Access data in a report to Word
- Import Excel data to a new Access table
- Link data between an Excel worksheet and an Access table
- Edit linked data

Student Resources

Before beginning this section:

1. Copy to your storage medium the Integrating2 subfolder from the Integrating folder on the Student Resources CD.
2. Make Integrating2 the active folder.

In addition to containing the data files needed to complete section work, the Student Resources CD contains model answers in PDF format for each of the projects in this section; model answers for end-of-section activities are not provided.

Projects Overview

Niagara Peninsula College

Export grades for AC215-03 from an Access table to an Excel worksheet. Import grades for a theater class from an Excel worksheet into an Access database table. Link grades for TRA220 between an Excel worksheet and an Access database table.

Worldwide Enterprises

Export data on U.S. distributors from an Access table to a Word document. Export data on Canadian distributors from an Access report to a Word document.

Performance Threads

Export data on costume inventory from an Access table to an Excel worksheet. Export data on costume inventory from an Access report to a Word document. Import data on costume design hours from an Excel worksheet into an Access table.

The Waterfront B·I·S·T·R·O

Export data on inventory from an Access table to a Word document.

First Choice TRAVEL

Link data on booking commissions between an Excel worksheet and an Access table and then update the data in the Excel worksheet.

Activity 2.1

Exporting Access Data to Excel

One of the advantages of a suite program like Microsoft Office is the ability to exchange data from one program to another. Access, like the other programs in the suite, offers a feature to export data from Access into Excel and/or Word. Export data using the Excel button in the Export group in the External Data tab. You can export an Access object such as a table, form, and query.

Project

You are Katherine Lamont, Theatre Arts Division instructor at Niagara Peninsula College. You want to work on your grades for your AC-215 class over the weekend and you do not have Access installed on your personal laptop. You decide to export your Access grading table to Excel.

Niagara Peninsula COLLEGE

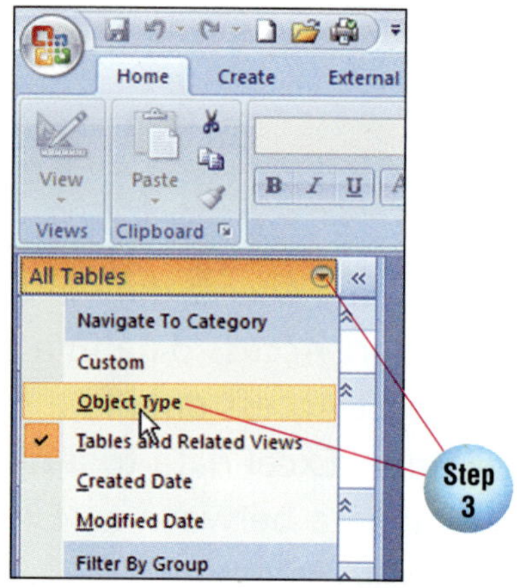

1. Open Access and then open the **NPCStudentGrades.accdb** database.
2. If necessary, click the Options button in the message bar. At the Microsoft Office Security Options dialog box, click the *Enable this content* option and then click OK.
3. Click the down-pointing arrow in the upper right corner of the Navigation pane and then click *Object Type* at the drop-down list.
4. Click once on the *StudentGradesAC215-03* query.
5. Click the External Data tab.
6. Click the Excel button in the Export group.
7. At the Export - Excel Spreadsheet dialog box, click the Browse button.
8. At the File Save dialog box, navigate to the Integrating2 folder on your storage medium and then click the Save button.

   Notice that the export wizard automatically inserts the name of the query in the *File name* text box.

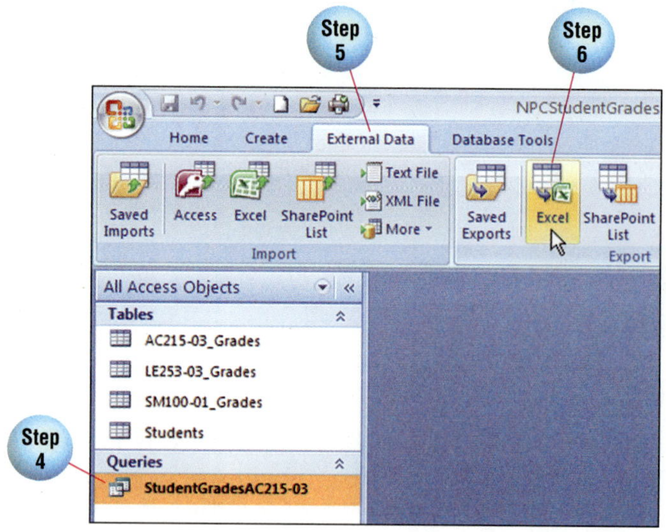

9. At the Export - Excel Spreadsheet dialog box, click the *Export data with formatting and layout* check box to insert a check mark.
10. Click the *Open the destination file after the export operation is complete* check box to insert a check mark and then click the OK button.

    Excel opens with the grades from the query in cells in the workbook.

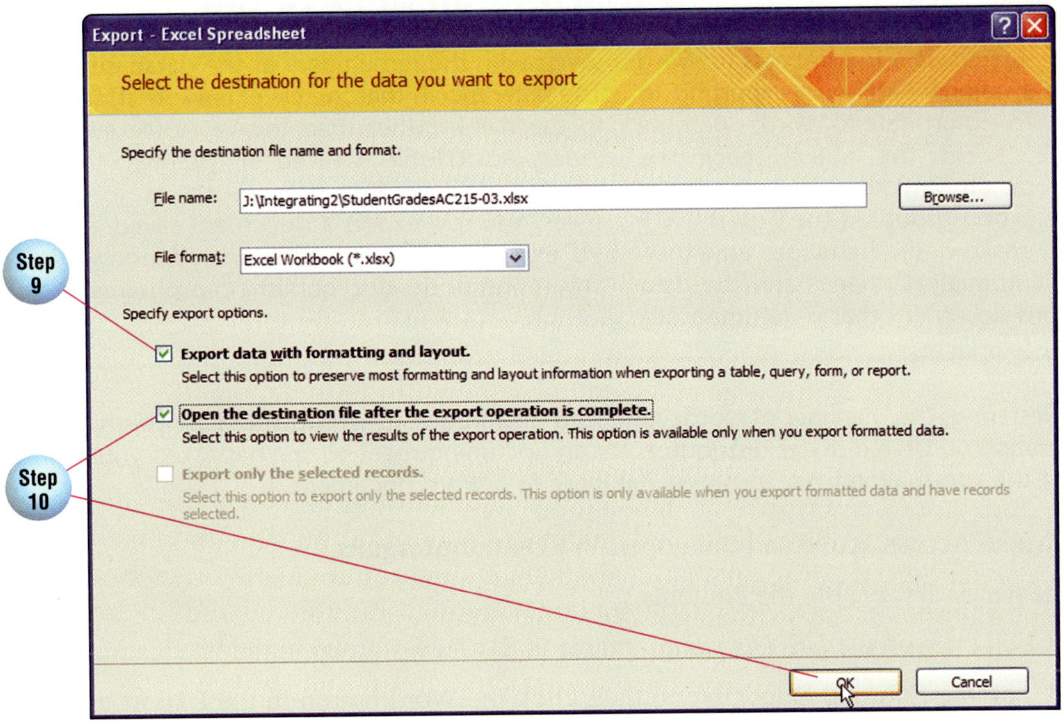

In Brief

Export Access Table, Form, or Query to Excel

1. Open database.
2. Click desired object in Navigation pane.
3. Click External Data tab.
4. Click Excel button in Export group.
5. At Export - Excel Spreadsheet dialog box, click Browse button.
6. At File Save dialog box, navigate to desired folder, then click Save button.
7. Click desired options at Export - Excel Spreadsheet dialog box.
8. Click OK.

11. Click the button on the Taskbar representing the **NPCStudentGrades.accdb** database.
12. Click the Close button at the Export - Excel Spreadsheet dialog box.
13. Close **NPCStudentGrades.accdb**.
14. Click the button on the Taskbar representing **StudentGradesAC215-03.xlsx**.
15. In the **StudentGradesAC215-03.xlsx** workbook, insert the following grades in the specified cells:

D4	C
D8	B
D10	F
D14	A
D16	C
D18	B

16. Save, print, and then close **StudentGradesAC215-03.xlsx**.

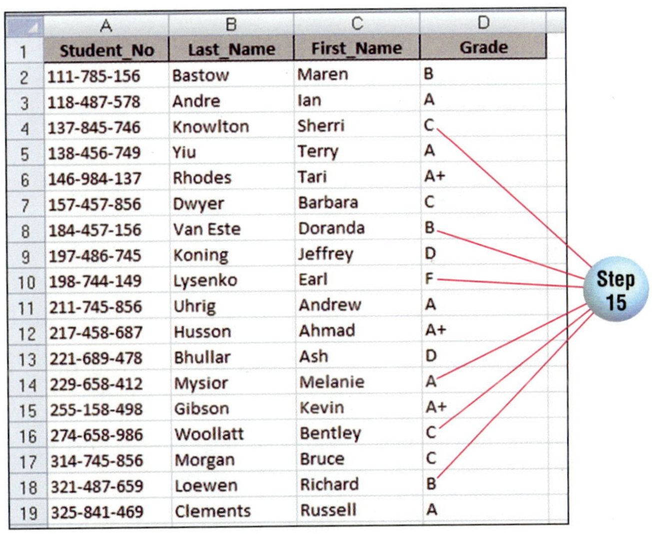

	A	B	C	D
1	Student_No	Last_Name	First_Name	Grade
2	111-785-156	Bastow	Maren	B
3	118-487-578	Andre	Ian	A
4	137-845-746	Knowlton	Sherri	C
5	138-456-749	Yiu	Terry	A
6	146-984-137	Rhodes	Tari	A+
7	157-457-856	Dwyer	Barbara	C
8	184-457-156	Van Este	Doranda	B
9	197-486-745	Koning	Jeffrey	D
10	198-744-149	Lysenko	Earl	F
11	211-745-856	Uhrig	Andrew	A
12	217-458-687	Husson	Ahmad	A+
13	221-689-478	Bhullar	Ash	D
14	229-658-412	Mysior	Melanie	A
15	255-158-498	Gibson	Kevin	A+
16	274-658-986	Woollatt	Bentley	C
17	314-745-856	Morgan	Bruce	C
18	321-487-659	Loewen	Richard	B
19	325-841-469	Clements	Russell	A

In Addition

Exporting Considerations

You can export to Excel a table, form, or query but you cannot export a macro, module, or report. If a table contains subdatasheets or a form contains subforms, you must export each subdatasheet or subform to view them in Excel.

Activity 2.2

Exporting an Access Table to Word

Export data from Access to Word in a manner similar to exporting to Excel. To export data to Word, open the database, select the object, click the External Data tab, and then click the Word button in the Export group. At the Export - RTF File dialog box, make desired changes and then click OK. Word automatically opens and the data displays in a Word document that is automatically saved with the same name as the database object. The difference is that the file extension .rtf is added to the name rather than the Word file extension .docx. An RTF file is saved in "rich-text format," which preserves formatting such as fonts and styles. You can export a document saved with the .rtf extension in Word and other Windows word processing or desktop publishing programs.

Project

Worldwide Enterprises

Sam Vestering, the manager of North American distribution for Worldwide Enterprises, needs information on United States distributors for an upcoming meeting. He has asked you to export the information from an Access database to a Word document.

1. Make Access active and then open **WEDistributors.accdb**.
2. If necessary, enable the contents.
3. Click once on the *US_Distributors* table in the *Tables* group in the Navigation pane.
4. Click the External Data tab and then click the Word button in the Export group.

Step 4

Step 3

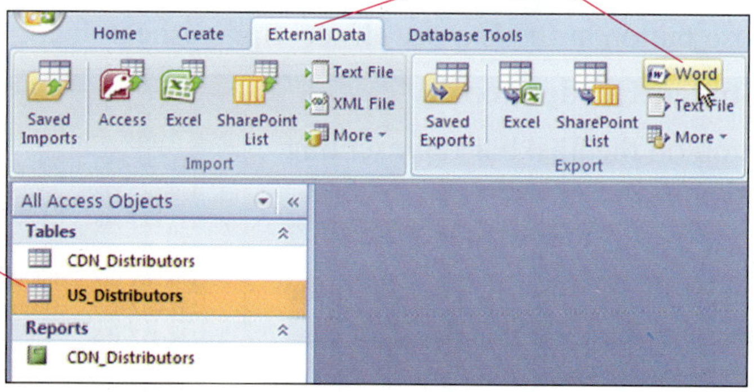

5. At the Export - RTF File dialog box, click the Browse button.
6. At the File Save dialog box, navigate to the Integrating2 folder on your storage medium and then click the Save button.

   Notice that the export wizard automatically inserts the name of the table in the *File name* text box.

7. At the Export - RTF File dialog box, click the *Open the destination file after the export operation is complete* check box and then click OK.

   Microsoft Word opens and the information for U.S. distributors displays in a Word document.

8. Click the button on the Taskbar representing the **WEDistributors.accdb** database.
9. Click the Close button at the Export - RTF File dialog box.
10. Close **WEDistributors.accdb**.
11. Click the button on the Taskbar representing **US_Distributors.rtf**.

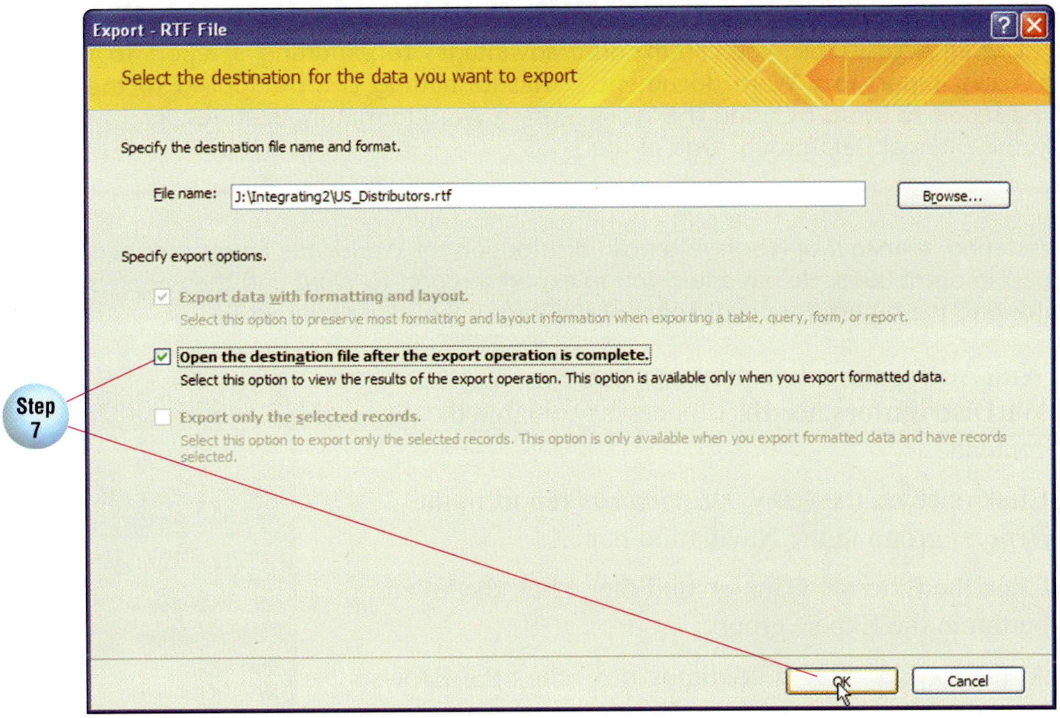

In Brief

Export Access Table to Word

1. Open database file.
2. Click table in Navigation pane.
3. Click External Data tab.
4. Click Word button in Export group.
5. At Export - RTF File dialog box, click Browse button.
6. At File Save dialog box, navigate to desired folder, then click Save button.
7. Click desired options at Export - RTF File dialog box.
8. Click OK.

12. Change the orientation to landscape by clicking the Page Layout tab, clicking the Orientation button in the Page Setup group, and then clicking *Landscape* at the drop-down list.

13. Click in any cell in the table.

14. Autofit the contents by clicking the Table Tools Layout tab, clicking the AutoFit button in the Cell Size group, and then clicking *AutoFit Window* at the drop-down list.

15. Save, print, and then close **US_Distributors.rtf**.

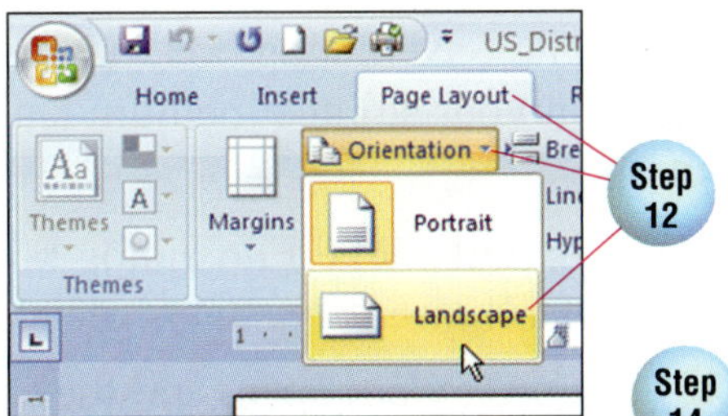

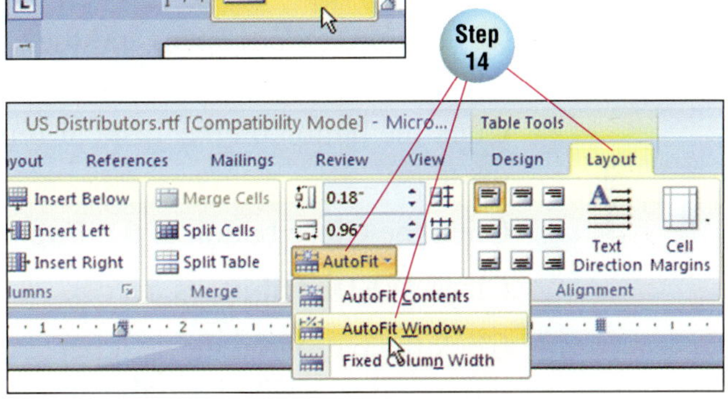

In Addition

Adjusting a Table

In this section, you adjusted the Word table to the cell contents. The Table AutoFit feature contains three options for adjusting table contents as described below.

Option	Action
AutoFit Contents	Adjusts table to accommodate the table text.
AutoFit Window	Resizes table to fit within the window or browser. If browser changes size, table size automatically adjusts to fit within window.
Fixed Column Width	Adjusts each column to a fixed width using the current widths of the columns.

Activity 2.3

Exporting an Access Report to Word

Like an Access table, you can export an Access report to a Word document. Export a report to Word by using the Word button in the External Data group. One of the advantages to exporting a report to Word is that formatting can be applied to the report using Word formatting features.

Project

Sam Vestering, manager of North American distribution for Worldwide Enterprises needs a list of Canadian distributors. He has asked you to export a report to Word and then apply specific formatting to the report. He needs some of the information for a contact list.

1. With Access the active program, open **WEDistributors.accdb**. If necessary, enable the contents.
2. Click once on the *CDN_Distributors* report in the *Reports* group in the Navigation pane.
3. Click the External Data tab and then click the Word button in the Export group.
4. At the Export - RTF File dialog box, click the Browse button.
5. At the File Save dialog box, navigate to the Integrating2 folder on your storage medium and then click the Save button.

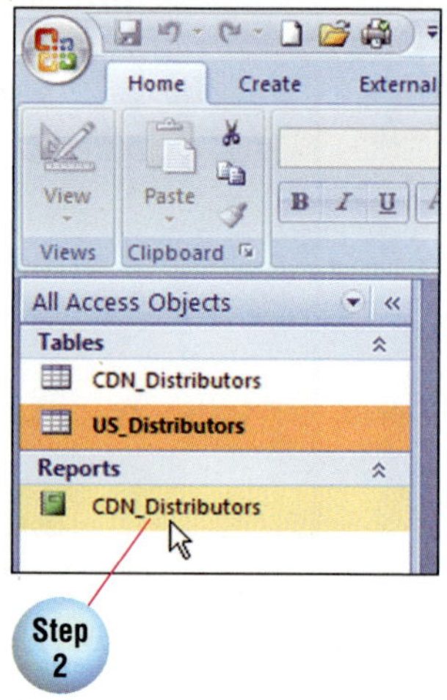

6. At the Export - RTF File dialog box, click the *Open the destination file after the export operation is complete* check box and then click OK.

   Microsoft Word opens and the Canadian Distributors report displays in a Word document.

7. Click the button on the Taskbar representing the **WEDistributors.accdb** database.
8. Click the Close button at the Export - RTF File dialog box.
9. Close **WEDistributors.accdb**.
10. Click the button on the Taskbar representing **CDN_Distributors.rtf**.
11. Convert the text to a table. To begin, move the insertion point to the left margin of the line that begins with *CompanyName*, press F8, and then press Ctrl + End.

    Make sure that you select the tab symbol that precedes the text *CompanyName*. (You might want to turn on the display of nonprinting characters.)

12. Click the Insert tab, click the Table button, and then click *Convert Text to Table* option at the drop-down list.

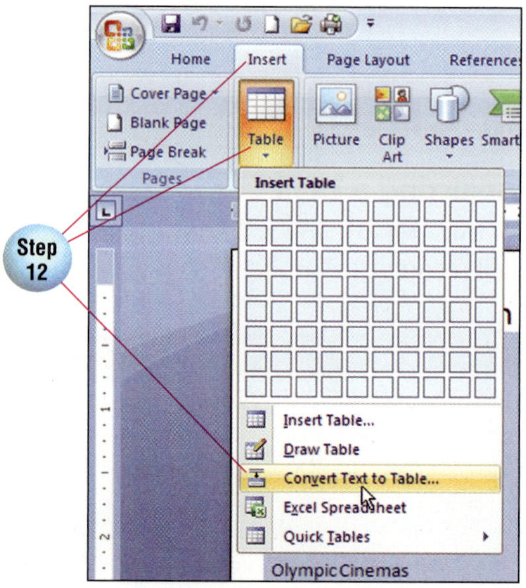

13 At the Convert Text to Table dialog box, make sure *7* displays in the *Number of columns* text box, make sure *Tabs* is selected in the *Separate text at* section, and then click OK.

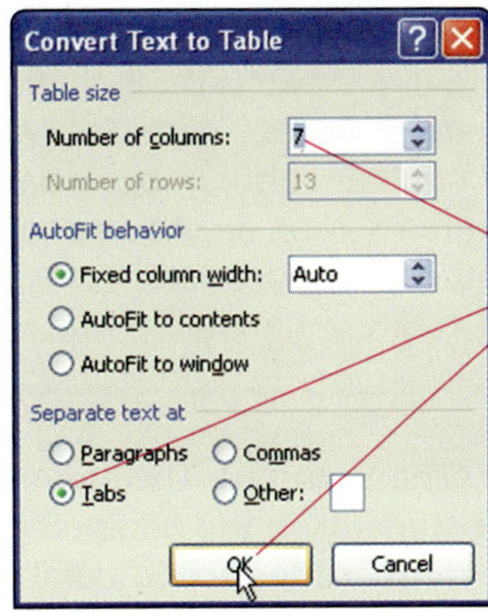

14 Click in any cell in the first column (this column does not contain data) and then click the Table Tools Layout tab. Click the Delete button in the Rows & Columns group and then click *Delete Columns* at the drop-down list.

15 Change the left and right margins by clicking the Page Layout tab, clicking the Margins button in the Page Setup group, and then clicking *Normal* at the drop-down list.

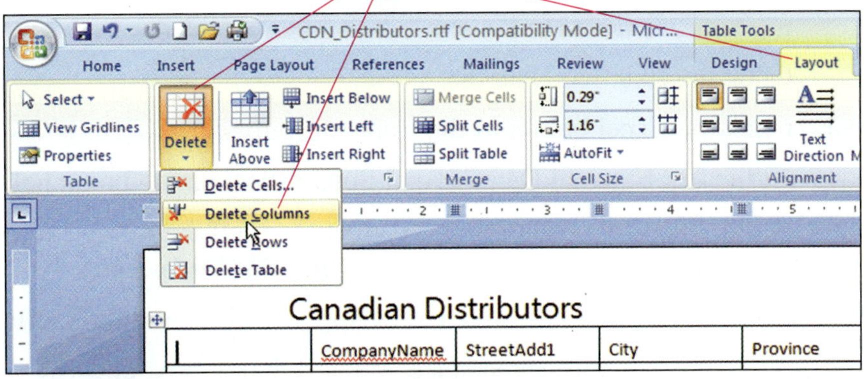

16 Click the Table Tools Layout tab, click the AutoFit button in the Cell Size group, and then click *AutoFit Contents* at the drop-down list.

17 Click the Table Tools Design tab, click the More button at the right side of the Table Styles group, and then click the fourth option from the left in the fourth row in the *Built-In* section (*Medium Shading 1 - Accent 3*).

18 Click in the title *Canadian Distributors* and then click the Center button in the Paragraph group in the Home tab.

19 Save, print, and then close **CDN_Distributors.rtf**.

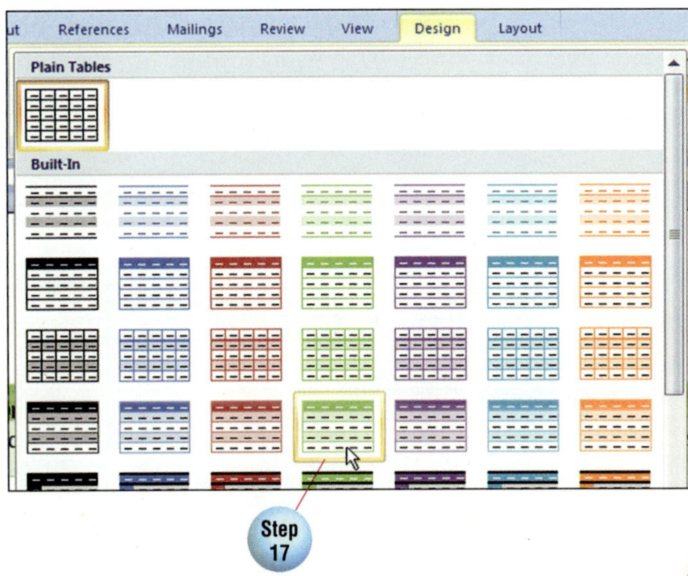

In Brief

Export Access Report to Word

1. Open database file.
2. Click report in Navigation pane.
3. Click External Data tab.
4. Click Word button in Export group.
5. At Export - RTF File dialog box, click Browse button.
6. At File Save dialog box, navigate to desired folder, then click Save button.
7. Click desired options at Export - RTF File dialog box.
8. Click OK.

In Addition

Merging Access Data with a Word Document

Word includes a mail merge feature you can use to create letters and envelopes and much more, with personalized information. Generally, a merge requires two documents—the ***data source*** and the ***main document***. The data source contains the variable information that will be inserted in the main document. Create a data source document in Word or create a data source using data from an Access table. When merging Access data, you can either type the text in the main document or merge Access data with an existing Word document. To merge data in an Access table, open the database and then click the table in the Navigation pane. Click the External Data tab, click the More button in the Export group, and then click *Merge it with Microsoft Office Word* at the drop-down list. Follow the steps presented by the mail merge wizard.

Activity 2.4

Importing Data to a New Table

In the previous three sections, you exported Access data to Excel and Word. You can also import data from other programs into an Access table. For example, you can import data from an Excel worksheet and create a new table in a database file. Data in the original program is not connected to the data imported into an Access table. If you make changes to the data in the original program, those changes are not reflected in the Access table.

Project

You are Gina Simmons, Theatre Arts instructor, and have recorded grades in an Excel worksheet for your students in the Beginning Theater class. You want to import those grades into the **NPCStudentGrades.accdb** database.

Niagara Peninsula College

1. Make Access active and then open the **NPCStudentGrades.accdb** database. If necessary, enable the contents.
2. Click the External Data tab.
3. Click the Excel button in the Import group.
4. At the Get External Data - Excel Spreadsheet dialog box, click the Browse button.
5. At the File Open dialog box, navigate to the Integrating2 folder on your storage medium and then double-click ***NPCBegThGrades.xlsx***.
6. At the Get External Data - Excel Spreadsheet dialog box, click the OK button.
7. At the first Import Spreadsheet Wizard dialog box, click the Next button.
8. At the second dialog box, insert a check mark in the *First Row Contains Column Headings* option and then click the Next button.

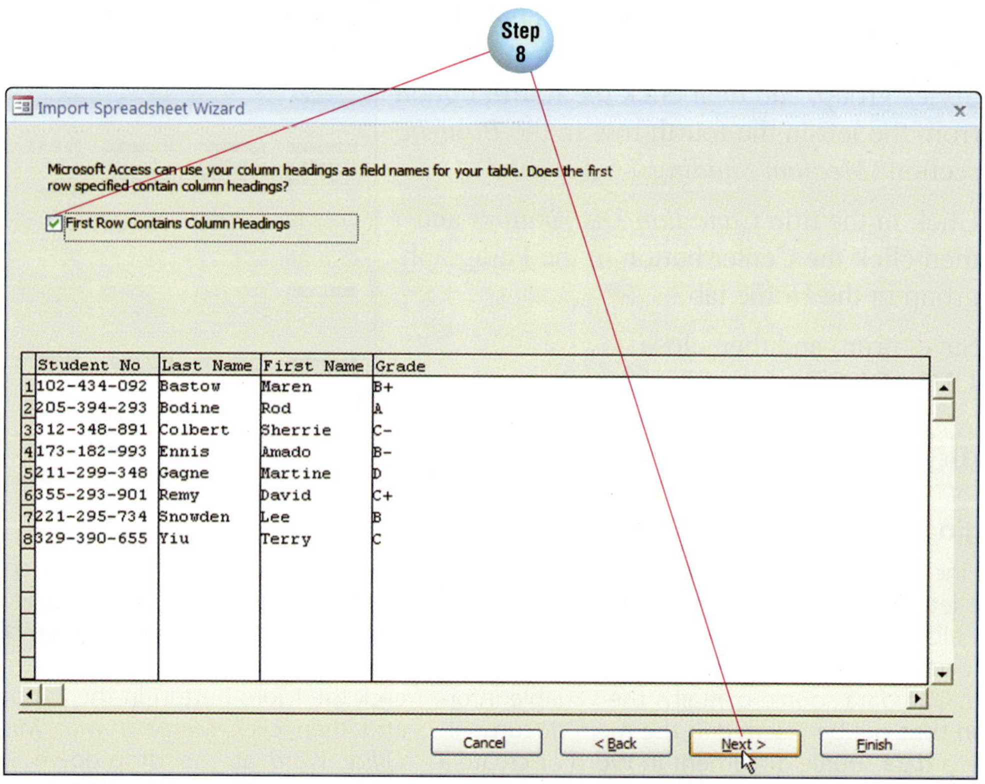

9. At the third dialog box, click the Next button.
10. At the fourth dialog box, click the *Choose my own primary key* option (this inserts *Student No* in the text box located to the right of the option) and then click the Next button.

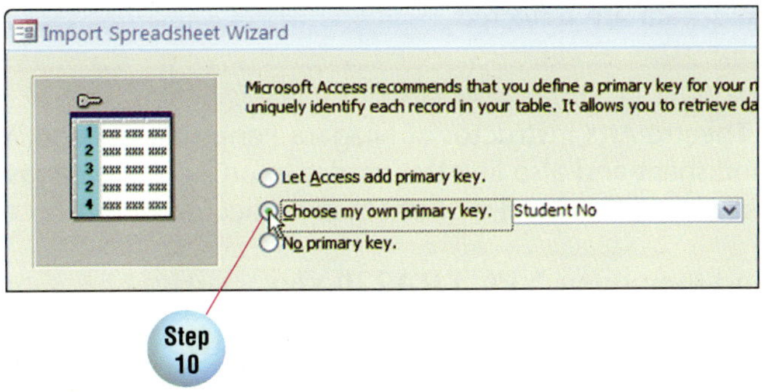

11. At the sixth dialog box, type **BegThGrades** in the *Import to Table* text box and then click the Finish button.

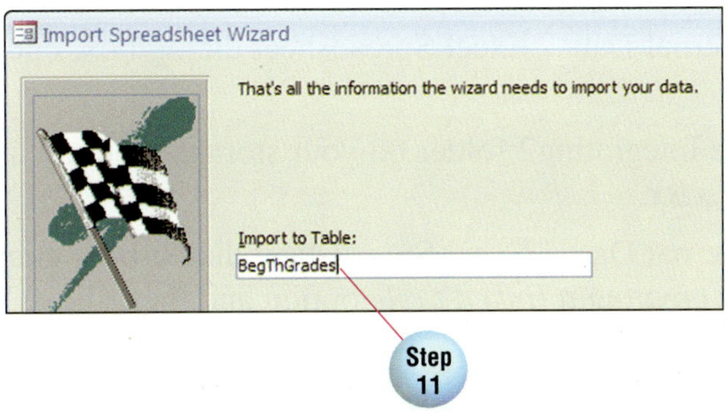

12. At the Get External Data - Excel Spreadsheet dialog box, click the Close button.
13. Open the new table by double-clicking *BegThGrades* in the list box.
14. Print and then close BegThGrades.
15. Close **NPCStudentGrades.accdb**.

In Brief

Import Data to New Table

1. Open database.
2. Click table in Navigation pane.
3. Click External Data tab.
4. Click Excel button in Import group.
5. Click OK at Get External Data - Excel Spreadsheet dialog box.
6. Follow Import Spreadsheet Wizard steps.

In Addition

Importing or Linking a Table

You can import data from another program into an Access table or you can link the data. Choose the method depending on how you are going to use the data. Consider linking an Excel file instead of importing if you want to keep data in an Excel worksheet but use Access to perform queries and create reports. In Access, you can only update linked data in one direction. Once an Excel table is linked to Access, you cannot edit data in the Access table. You can update the data in the Excel file and the Access table will reflect the changes but you cannot update data within Access.

Activity 2.5

Linking Data to a New Table

Imported data is not connected to the source program. If you know that you will use your data only in Access, import it. However, if you want to update data in a program other than Access, link the data. Changes made to linked data are reflected in both the source and destination programs. For example, you can link an Excel worksheet with an Access table and when you make changes in the Excel worksheet, the change is reflected in the Access table.

Project

You are Cal Rubine, Theatre Arts instructor at Niagara Peninsula College. You record students' grades in an Excel worksheet and also link the grades to an Access database file. With the data linked, changes you make to the Excel worksheet are reflected in the Access table.

1. Open Excel and then open **NPCTRA220.xlsx**.
2. Save the worksheet with Save As and name it **IntE2-01**.
3. Print and then close **IntE2-01.xlsx**.
4. Make Access the active program, open the **NPCStudentGrades.accdb** database.
5. Click the External Data tab and then click the Excel button in the Import group.
6. At the Get External Data - Excel Spreadsheet dialog box, click the Browse button.
7. Navigate to the Integrating2 folder on your storage medium and then double-click ***IntE2-01.xlsx***.
8. At the Get External Data - Excel Spreadsheet dialog box, click the *Link to the data source by creating a linked table* option and then click OK.

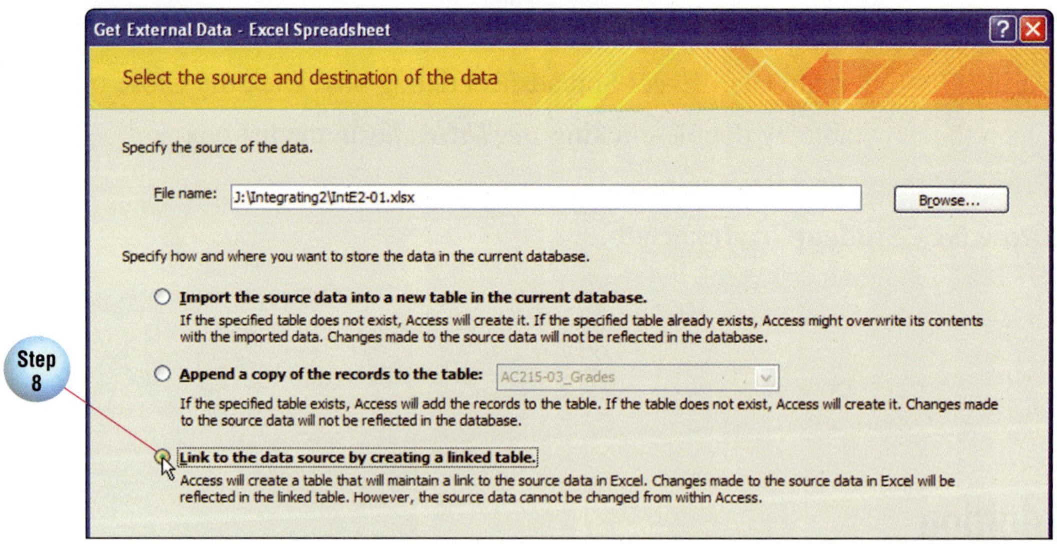

9. At the first Link Spreadsheet Wizard dialog box, click the Next button.
10. At the second dialog box, make sure the *First Row Contains Column Headings* option contains a check mark and then click the Next button.

11. At the third dialog box, type **LinkedGrades** in the *Linked Table Name* text box and then click the Finish button.

12. At the message stating the link is finished, click OK.

    Access uses different icons to represent linked tables and tables that are stored in the current database. Notice the icon that displays before the *LinkedGrades* table.

13. Open the new LinkedGrades table in Datasheet view.
14. Close the LinkedGrades table.
15. Make Excel the active program and then open **IntE2-01.xlsx**.
16. Make cell E2 active, click the Sum button arrow, click *Average* at the drop-down list, and then press Enter.

    This inserts *3.00* in cell E2.

17. Copy the formula in cell E2 down to cells E3 through E9.
18. Save, print, and then close **IntE2-01.xlsx**.
19. Close Excel.
20. With the **NPCStudentGrades.accdb** database open, open the LinkedGrades table and notice that the worksheet contains the average amounts.

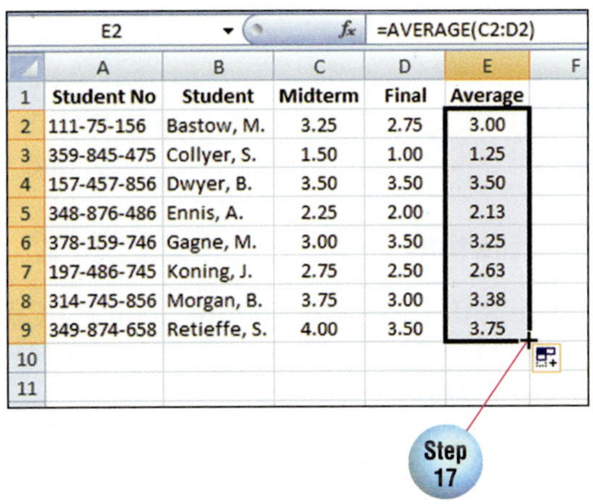

	A	B	C	D	E	F
1	Student No	Student	Midterm	Final	Average	
2	111-75-156	Bastow, M.	3.25	2.75	3.00	
3	359-845-475	Collyer, S.	1.50	1.00	1.25	
4	157-457-856	Dwyer, B.	3.50	3.50	3.50	
5	348-876-486	Ennis, A.	2.25	2.00	2.13	
6	378-159-746	Gagne, M.	3.00	3.50	3.25	
7	197-486-745	Koning, J.	2.75	2.50	2.63	
8	314-745-856	Morgan, B.	3.75	3.00	3.38	
9	349-874-658	Retieffe, S.	4.00	3.50	3.75	
10						
11						

21. Print and then close the table.
22. Close **NPCStudentGrades.accdb** and then close Access.

In Brief

Link Data to New Table

1. Open database file.
2. Click table in Navigation pane.
3. Click External Data tab.
4. Click Excel button in Import group.
5. Click *Link to the data source by creating a linked table* option at Get External Data - Excel Spreadsheet dialog box, then click OK.
6. Follow Import Spreadsheet Wizard steps.

In Addition

Deleting the Link to a Linked Table

If you want to delete the link to a table, open the database and then click the table in the Navigation pane. Click the Home tab and then click the Delete button in the Records group. At the question asking if you want to remove the link to the table, click Yes. Access deletes the link and removes the table's name from the Navigation pane. When you delete a linked table, you are deleting the information Access uses to open the table, not the table itself. You can link to the same table again, if necessary.

Skills Review

Review 1 Exporting Access Data to Excel

Performance Threads

1. Open Access and then open the **PTCostumes.accdb** database.
2. Click the *CostumeInventory* table in the Navigation pane and then export the data to Excel.
3. When the data displays in Excel, make the following changes in the specified cells:
   C4 Change *110.00* to *120.00*
   C5 Change *110.00* to *125.00*
   C7 Change *99.50* to *105.00*
4. Save, print, and then close **CostumeInventory.xlsx**.
5. Click the button on the Taskbar representing the Access database **PTCostumes.accdb**. Close the Export - Excel Spreadsheet dialog box and then close the database.

Review 2 Exporting Access Data to Word

The Waterfront B·I·S·T·R·O

1. With Access the active program, open **WBSupplies.accdb**.
2. Click the *InventoryList* table and then export the table to Word.
3. When the data displays on the screen in Word, apply a table style of your choosing to the table.
4. Move the insertion point to the beginning of the document, press the Enter key, and then type **The Waterfront Bistro - Inventory List**.
5. Select *The Waterfront Bistro - Inventory List* and then change the font size to 20 points.
6. Save, print, and then close **InventoryList.rtf**.
7. Click the button on the Taskbar representing the Access database **WBSupplies.accdb**. Close the Export - RTF File dialog box and then close the database.

Review 3 Exporting an Access Report to Word

Performance Threads

1. With Access the active program, open **PTCostumes.accdb**.
2. Click the *CostumeInventory* report in the Navigation pane and then export it to a Word document.
3. When the data displays in Word, change the page orientation to landscape.
4. Save, print, and then close **CostumeInventory.rtf**.
5. Exit Word.
6. With Access the active program, close the Export - RTF File dialog box and then close the database.

Review 4 Importing Data to a New Table

1. In Access, open the **PTCostumes.accdb** database.
2. Import the Excel workbook named **PTCostumeHours.xlsx**. (Do not make any changes to the first Import Spreadsheet Wizard dialog box. At the second dialog box, make sure the *First Row Contains Column Headings* option contains a check mark. Do not make any changes to the third dialog box. Click the *No primary key* option at the fourth dialog box. At the fifth dialog box, type **DesignHours** in the *Import to Table* text box and then click the Finish button.)
3. Open the new DesignHours table.
4. Print and then close the DesignHours table.
5. Close the **PTCostumes.accdb** database.

Review 5 Linking Data to a New Table and Editing Linked Data

1. Open Excel and then open **FCTBookings.xlsx**.
2. Save the workbook with Save As and name it **IntE2-R2.xlsx**.
3. Make Access the active program and then open the **FCTCommissions.accdb** database.
4. Link the Excel workbook **IntE2-R2.xlsx** with the **FCTCommissions.accdb** database. (At the Get External Data - Excel Spreadsheet dialog box, click the *Link to the data source by creating a linked table* option. At the third Link Spreadsheet Wizard dialog box, type **LinkedCommissions** in the *Linked Table Name* text box.)
5. Open, print, and then close the new LinkedCommissions table.
6. Click the button on the Taskbar representing the Excel worksheet **IntE2-R2.xlsx**.
7. Make cell C2 active and then type the formula **=B2*0.03** and then press Enter.
8. Make cell C2 active and then use the fill handle to copy the formula down to cell C13.
9. Save, print, and then close **IntE2-R2.xlsx**.
10. Click the button on the Taskbar representing the **FCTCommissions.accdb** Access database and then open the LinkedCommissions table.
11. Save, print, and then close the LinkedCommissions table.
12. Close the **FCTCommissions.accdb** database.
13. Exit Access and then exit Excel.

Microsoft® PowerPoint® 2007

Introducing

PowerPoint 2007

Create colorful and powerful presentations using PowerPoint, Microsoft's presentation program that is included in the Office 2007 suite. With PowerPoint, you can organize and present information and create visual aids for a presentation. PowerPoint is a full-featured presentation program that provides a wide variety of editing and formatting features as well as sophisticated visual elements such as clip art, pictures, SmartArt, WordArt, and drawn objects. While working in PowerPoint, you will produce presentations for the following six companies.

First Choice Travel is a travel center offering a full range of traveling services from booking flights, hotel reservations, and rental cars to offering travel seminars.

The Waterfront Bistro offers fine dining for lunch and dinner and also offers banquet facilities, a wine cellar, and catering services.

Worldwide Enterprises is a national and international distributor of products for a variety of companies and is the exclusive movie distribution agent for Marquee Productions.

Marquee Productions is involved in all aspects of creating movies from script writing and development to filming. The company produces documentaries, biographies, as well as historical and action movies.

Performance Threads maintains an inventory of rental costumes and also researches, designs, and sews special-order and custom-made costumes.

The mission of the Niagara Peninsula College Theatre Arts Division is to offer a curriculum designed to provide students with a thorough exposure to all aspects of the theater arts.

In Section 1 you will learn how to

Prepare a Presentation

Prepare a presentation using a template provided by PowerPoint or create your own presentation and apply formatting with a design theme. Preparing a presentation consists of general steps such as creating and editing slides; adding enhancements to slides; and saving, running, previewing, printing, and closing a presentation. When running a presentation, how one slide is removed from the screen and the next slide is displayed is referred to as the ***transition***. You can add interesting transitions to slides as well as sound to a presentation.

Create presentations using PowerPoint design themes and apply various slide layouts to change the appearance of slides.

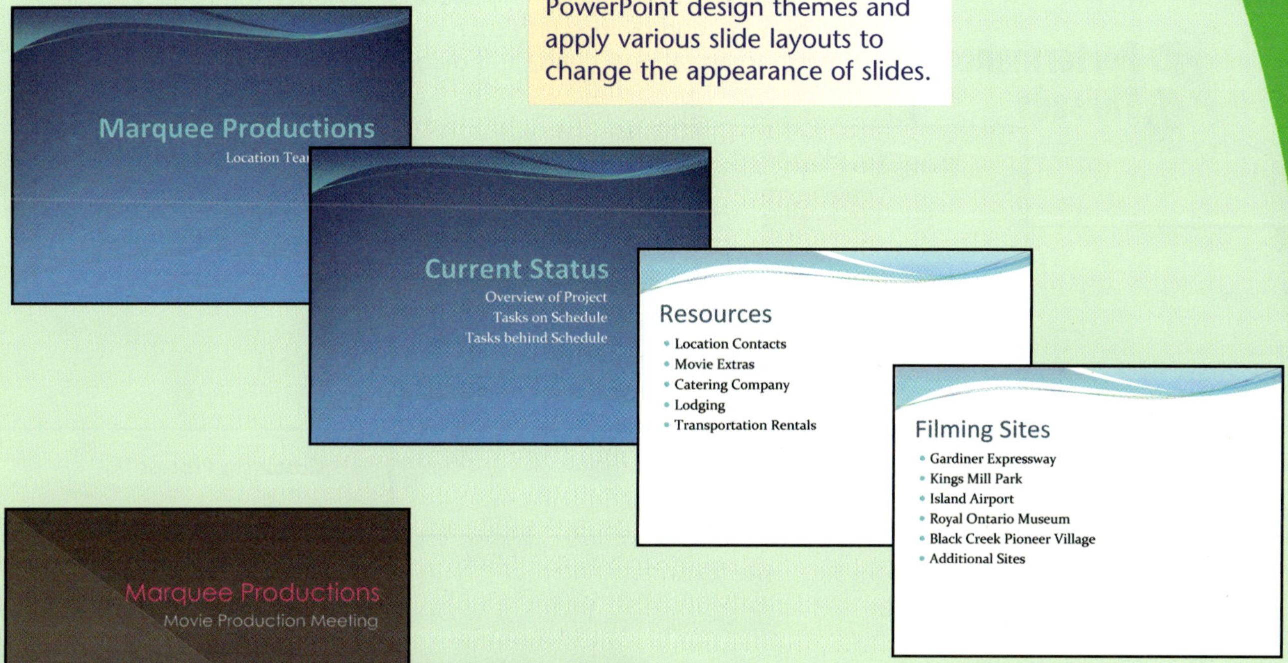

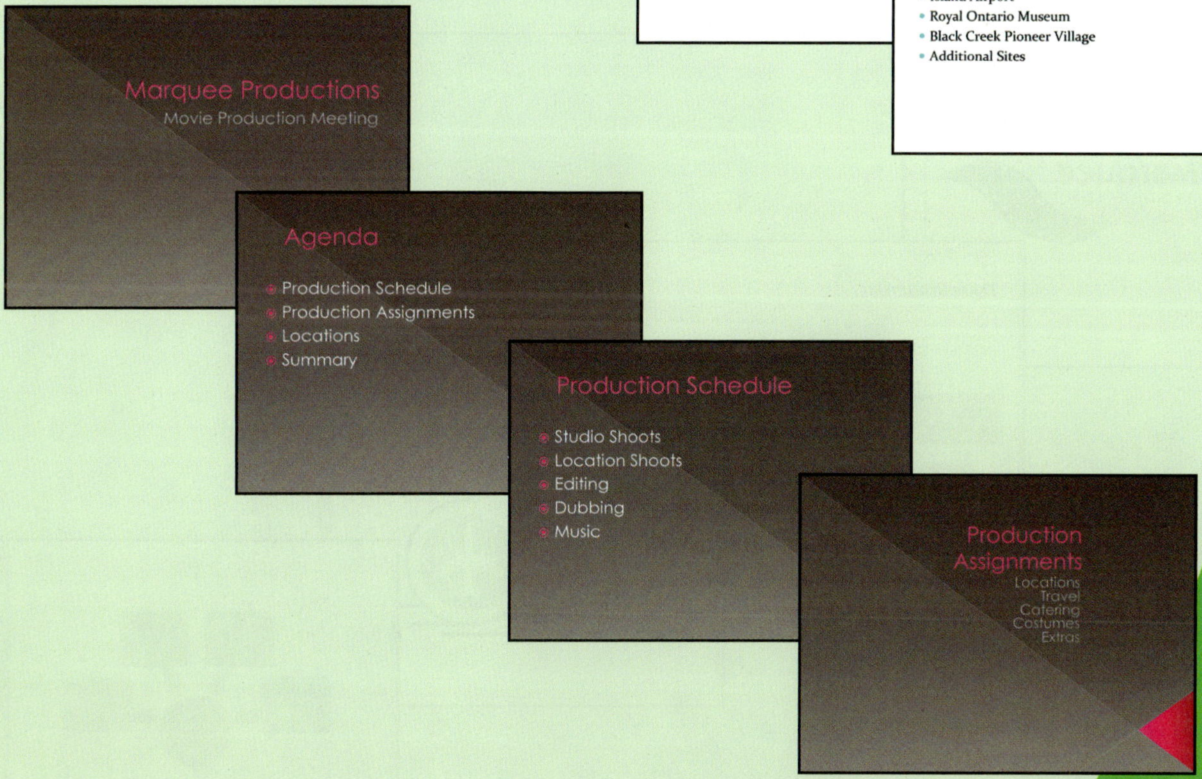

In Section 2 you will learn how to

Edit and Enhance Slides

Edit slides and slide elements in a presentation to customize and personalize the presentation. Editing can include such functions as rearranging and deleting slides; cutting, copying, and pasting text; changing the font, paragraph alignment, and paragraph spacing; and changing the design theme, theme color, and theme font. Add visual appeal to a presentation by inserting clip art images, pictures, and SmartArt organizational charts and diagrams.

Edit slides by performing such actions as rearranging and deleting slides. Perform editing tasks on text in slides such as changing the font, paragraph alignment, and spacing. Enhance the visual appeal of a presentation by inserting such elements as a company logo, clipart, organizational chart, and diagram.

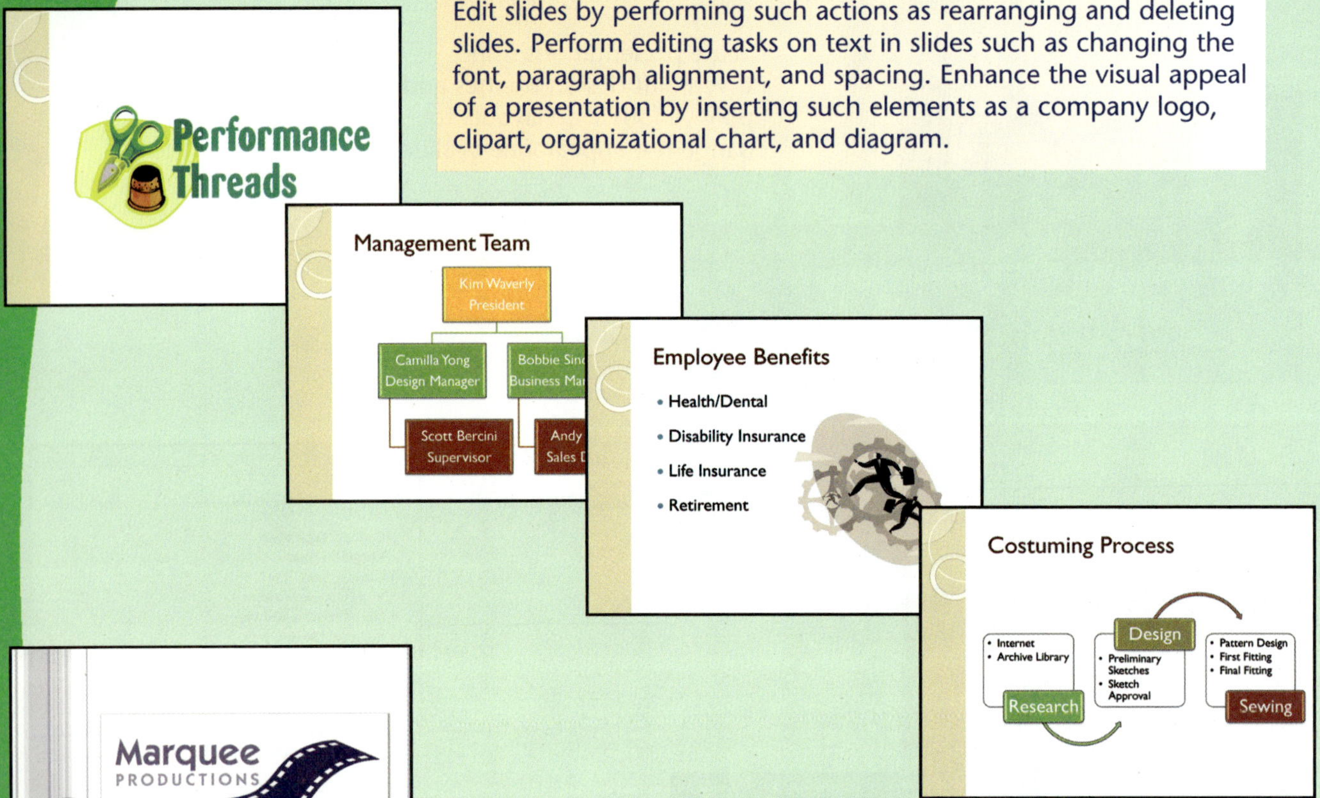

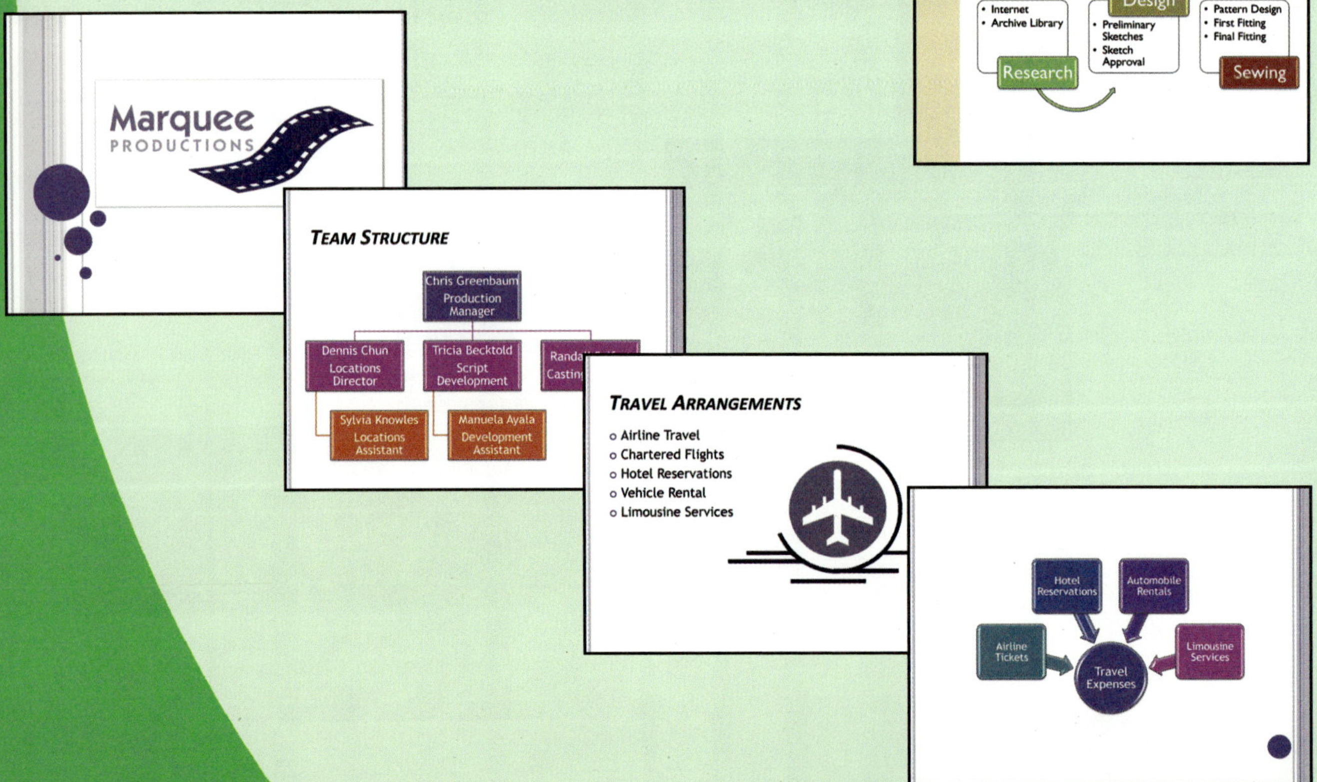

In Section 3 you will learn how to

Customize Presentations

Customize a presentation with the WordArt feature and by drawing and formatting objects and text boxes. Additional features for customizing a presentation include using the Clipboard; inserting and formatting a table; inserting actions buttons, hyperlinks, and headers and footers; and inserting sound and video.

Further customize presentations with features such as headers and footers, sound and video, WordArt, shapes, text boxes, and tables.

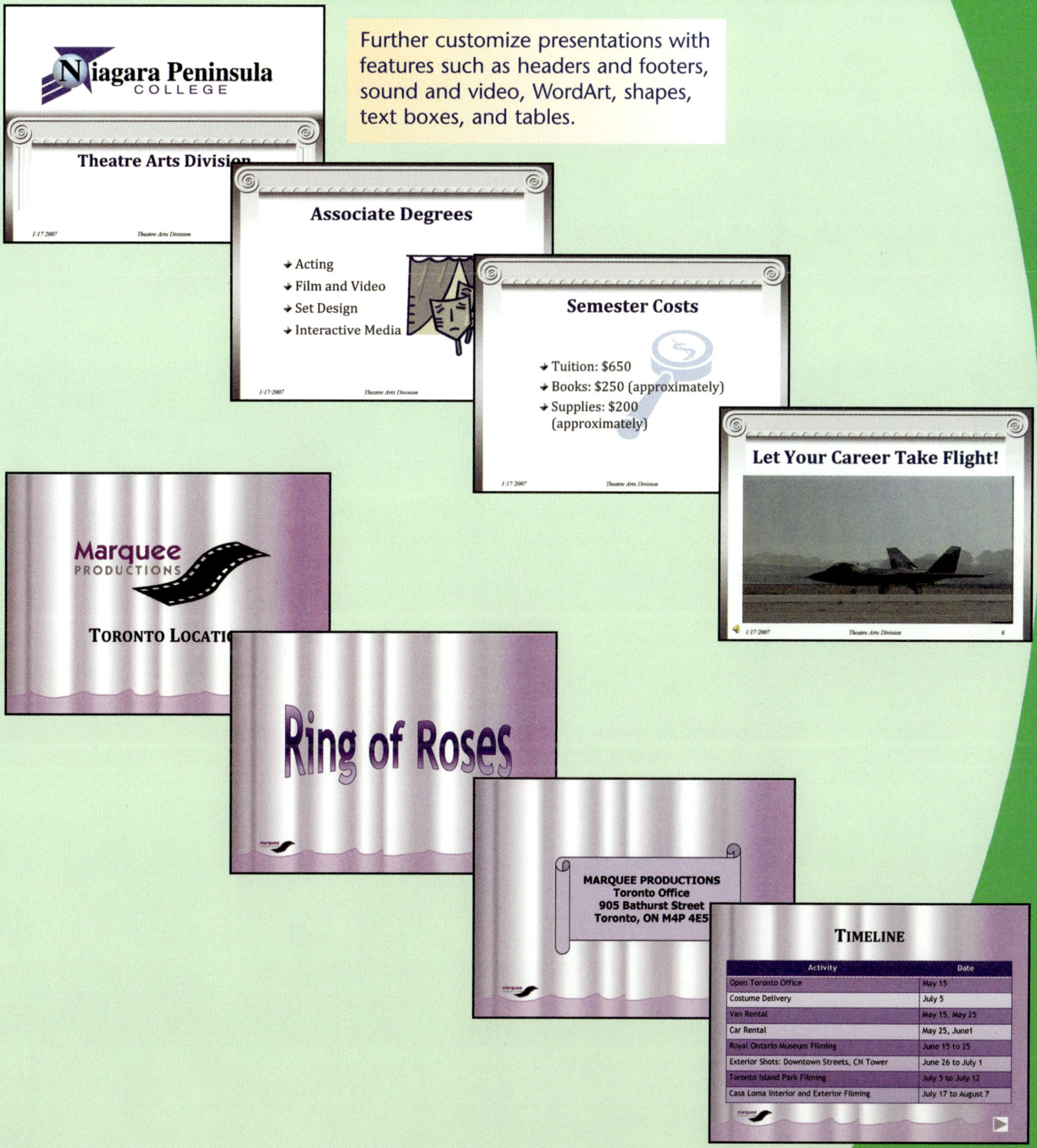

PowerPoint SECTION 1

Preparing a Presentation

Skills

- Complete the presentation cycle
- Choose a design theme
- Add a new slide to a presentation
- Navigate in a presentation
- Insert a slide in a presentation
- Change the presentation view
- Change the slide layout
- Use the Help feature
- Check spelling in a presentation
- Use Thesaurus to display synonyms for words
- Run a presentation and use the pen and highlighter during a presentation
- Add transition and sound to a presentation
- Print and preview a presentation

Student Resources

Before beginning this section:

1. Copy to your storage medium the PowerPointS1 subfolder from the PowerPoint folder on the Student Resources CD.
2. Make PowerPointS1 the active folder.

In addition to containing the data files needed to complete section work, the Student Resources CD contains model answers in PDF format for each of the projects in this section; model answers for end-of-section activities are not provided.

Projects Overview

Marquee Productions: Use an installed template to prepare a presentation about the new features in PowerPoint 2007; prepare a movie production meeting presentation and a location team meeting presentation.

Worldwide Enterprises: Prepare an executive meeting presentation for Worldwide Enterprises.

The Waterfront Bistro: Prepare a presentation containing information on the accommodations and services offered by The Waterfront Bistro.

First Choice Travel: Locate information on vacationing in Cancun using the Internet and then use that information to prepare a presentation for First Choice Travel; prepare a presentation on Toronto, Ontario, Canada.

Performance Threads: Prepare a presentation for a costume meeting.

Activity 1.1

Completing the Presentation Cycle

PowerPoint is a presentation graphics program you can use to organize and present information. With PowerPoint, you can create visual aids for a presentation and then print copies of the aids as well as run the presentation. Preparing a presentation in PowerPoint generally follows a presentation cycle. The steps in the cycle vary but generally include opening PowerPoint; creating and editing slides; saving, printing, running, and closing the presentation; and then closing PowerPoint.

Project

Marquee PRODUCTIONS

You are an employee of Marquee Productions and Office 2007 has just been installed on your computer. You need to prepare a presentation in the near future so you decide to open a presentation provided by PowerPoint and experiment with running the presentation.

1. Open PowerPoint by clicking the Start button (start) on the Windows Taskbar, pointing to *All Programs*, pointing to *Microsoft Office*, and then clicking *Microsoft Office PowerPoint 2007*.

   Depending on your system configuration, the steps you complete to open PowerPoint may vary.

2. At the PowerPoint window, click the Office button and then click *New* at the drop-down list.

3. At the New Presentation dialog box, click the *Installed Templates* option that displays in the *Templates* section in the left panel and then double-click the *Introducing PowerPoint 2007* template in the *Installed Templates* panel.

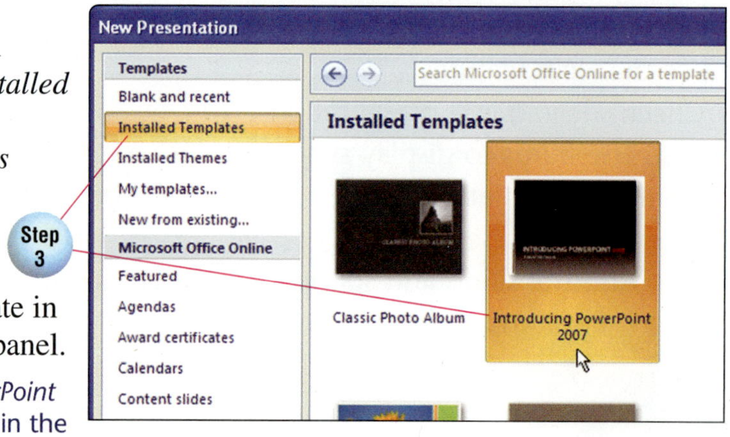

   The *Introducing PowerPoint 2007* template opens in the PowerPoint window. What displays in the PowerPoint window will vary depending on what type of presentation you are creating. However, the PowerPoint window contains some consistent elements as identified in Figure 1.1. Refer to Table 1.1 for a description of the window elements.

4. Run the presentation by clicking the Slide Show tab and then clicking the From Beginning button in the Start Slide Show group.

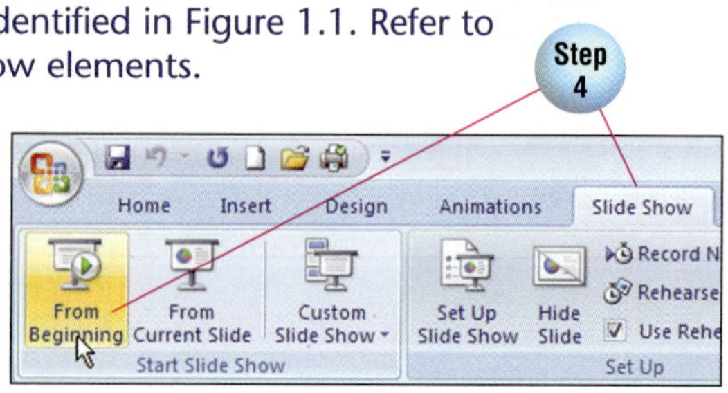

5. When the first slide fills the screen, read the information and then click the left mouse button. Continue reading the information in each slide and clicking the left mouse button to advance to the next slide. When a black screen displays, click the left mouse button to end the slide show.

6. Save the presentation by clicking the Save button on the Quick Access toolbar.

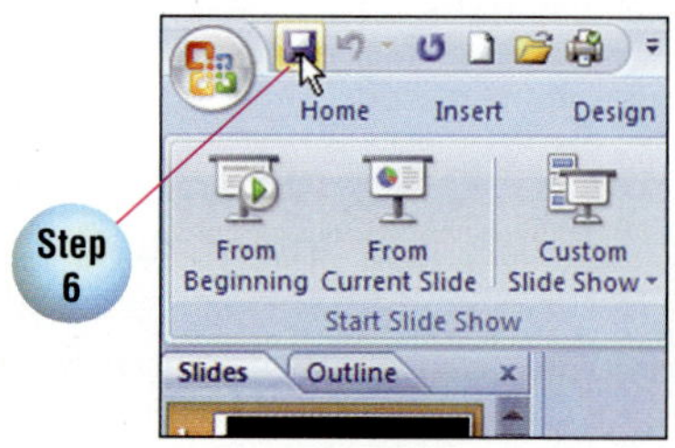

In Brief

Create Presentation with Installed Template

1. Click Office button.
2. Click New.
3. Click *Installed Templates* option.
4. Double-click desired template.

FIGURE 1.1 PowerPoint Window

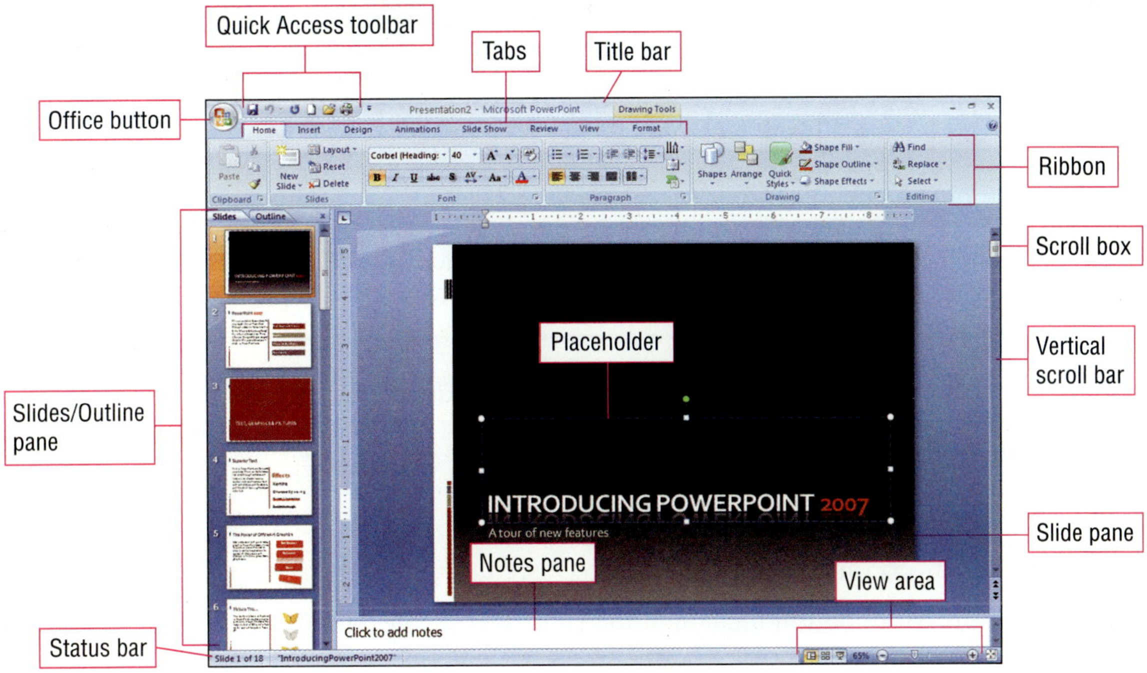

7. At the Save As dialog box, make sure the PowerPointS1 folder on your storage medium is the active folder, type **MPPowerPoint2007** in the *File name* text box, and then press Enter.

   The *Save in* option at the Save As dialog box displays the active folder. If you need to make the PowerPointS1 folder on your storage medium the active folder, click the down-pointing arrow at the right of the *Save in* option, click your storage medium, and then double-click *PowerPointS1* in the list box.

8. At the PowerPoint window, print the presentation information in outline view by clicking the Office button and then clicking *Print* at the drop-down list.
9. At the Print dialog box, click the down-pointing arrow at the right of the *Print what* option and then click *Outline View*.
10. Click OK to close the Print dialog box.
11. Close the presentation by clicking the Office button and then clicking *Close* at the drop-down list.

    If a message displays asking if you want to save the presentation, click *Yes*.

12. Close PowerPoint by clicking the Office button and then clicking the Exit PowerPoint button that displays in the lower right corner of the drop-down list.

TABLE 1.1 PowerPoint Window Elements

Feature	Description
Office button	Displays as a Microsoft Office logo and, when clicked, displays a list of options and most recently opened presentations.
Quick Access toolbar	Contains buttons for commonly used commands.
Title bar	Displays file name followed by program name.
tabs	Contain commands and features organized into groups.
ribbon	Area containing the tabs and commands divided into groups.
Slides/Outline pane	Displays at the left side of the window with two tabs—Slides and Outline. With the Slides tab selected, slide miniatures display in the pane; with the Outline tab selected, presentation contents display in the pane.
Slide pane	Displays the slide and slide contents.
Notes pane	Add notes to a presentation in this pane.
vertical scroll bar	Display specific slides using this scroll bar.
horizontal scroll bar	Shifts text left or right in the Slide pane.
I-beam pointer	Used to move the insertion point or to select text.
insertion point	Indicates location of next character entered at the keyboard.
View area	Located toward right side of Status bar and contains button for changing presentation view.
Status bar	Displays number of pages and words, View buttons, and Zoom slider bar.

Activity 1.2

Choosing a Design Theme; Creating Slides; Closing a Presentation

Create a PowerPoint presentation using an installed template as you did in the previous activity or begin with a blank presentation and apply your own formatting or apply formatting with a slide design theme. To display a blank PowerPoint presentation, click the New button on the Quick Access toolbar, press Ctrl + N, or click the Office button, click New, and then double-click the *Blank Presentation* option at the New Presentation dialog box. A PowerPoint presentation screen displays in Normal view with three panes available for entering text—the Slides/Outline pane, Slide pane, and Notes pane. Use either the Slide pane or the Slides/Outline pane with the Outline tab selected to enter text in a slide. Use the Notes page to insert a note in a slide.

Project

Chris Greenbaum, production manager for Marquee Productions, has asked you to prepare slides for a movie production meeting. You decide to prepare the presentation using a design template offered by PowerPoint.

1. Open PowerPoint.
2. At the PowerPoint window, click the Design tab.
3. Click the More button located at the right side of the Themes icons.

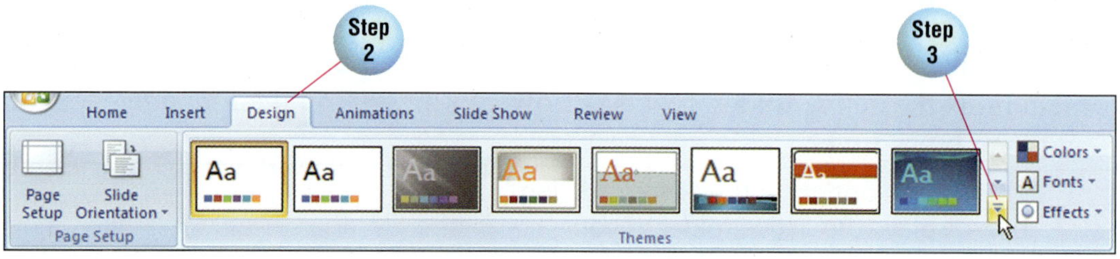

4. Click *Verve* at the drop-down gallery (last option in the *Built-In* section).

When you click the More button, a drop-down gallery displays. This gallery is an example of the ***live preview*** feature. When you hover your mouse pointer over one of the design themes, the slide in the Slide pane displays with the design theme formatting applied. With the live preview feature, you can view a design theme before actually applying it to the presentation.

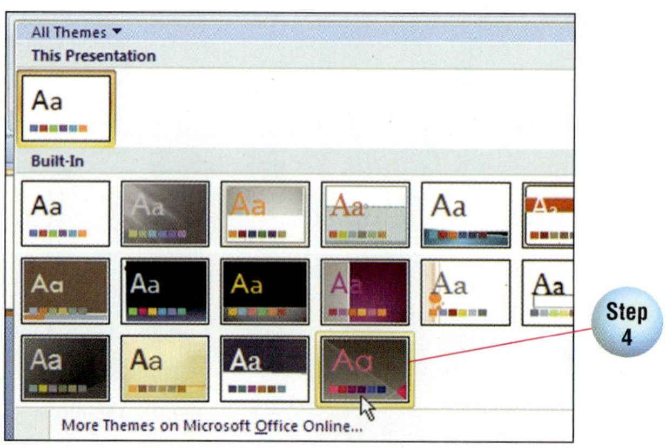

5 Click anywhere in the text *Click to add title* that displays in the slide in the Slide pane and then type **Marquee Productions**.

6 Click anywhere in the text *Click to add subtitle* that displays in the slide and then type **Movie Production Meeting**.

7 Click the Home tab and then click the New Slide button in the Slides group.

When you click this button, a new slide displays in the Slide pane with the Title and Content layout. You will learn more about layouts in Activity 1.4.

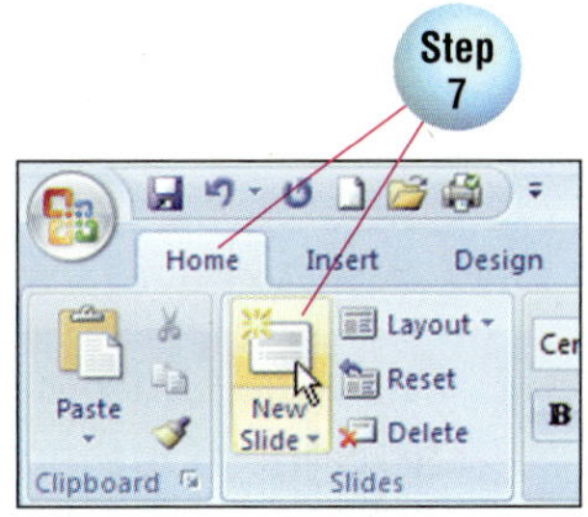

8 Click anywhere in the text *Click to add title* that displays in the slide and then type **Agenda**.

9 Click anywhere in the text *Click to add text* that displays in the slide and then type **Production Schedule**.

10 Press the Enter key and then type the following agenda items, pressing the Enter key after each item except the last: **Production Assignments**, **Locations**, and **Summary**.

You can use keys on the keyboard to move the insertion point to various locations within a placeholder in a slide. A placeholder is a location on a slide marked with a border that holds text or an object. Refer to Table 1.2 for a list of insertion point movement commands.

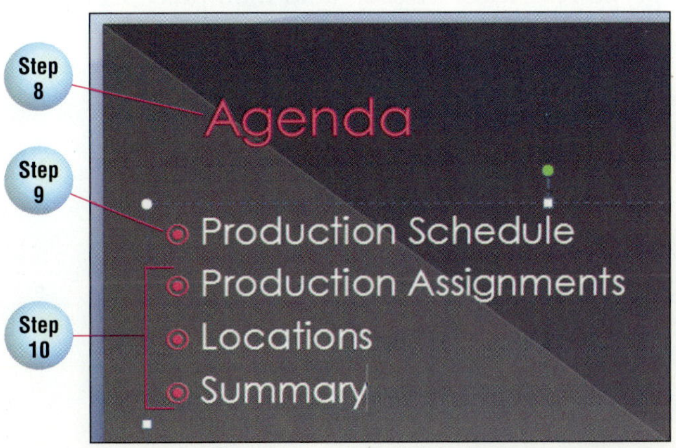

continues

TABLE 1.2 Insertion Point Movement Commands

To move insertion point	Press
One character left	Left Arrow
One character right	Right Arrow
One line up	Up Arrow
One line down	Down Arrow
One word to the left	Ctrl + Left Arrow
One word to the right	Ctrl + Right Arrow
To end of a line of text	End
To beginning of a line of text	Home
To beginning of current paragraph in placeholder	Ctrl + Up Arrow
To beginning of previous paragraph in placeholder	Ctrl + Up Arrow twice
To beginning of next paragraph in placeholder	Ctrl + Down Arrow
To beginning of text in placeholder	Ctrl + Home
To end of text in placeholder	Ctrl + End

Step 12

11. Click the New Slide button in the Slides group in the Home tab.
12. Click the Outline tab located toward the top of the Slides/Outline pane.
13. Click in the Slides/Outline pane immediately right of the slide icon after the number *3*, type **Locations**, and then press Enter.
14. Press the Tab key, type **Studio Shoots**, and then press the Enter key.

    Pressing the Tab key demotes the insertion point to the next level while pressing Shift + Tab promotes the insertion point to the previous level.

15. Press the Tab key, type **Vancouver Studio**, and then press Enter.
16. Type **Los Angeles Studio** and then press Enter.
17. Press Shift + Tab, type **Location Shoots**, and then press Enter.
18. Press the Tab key, type **Stanley Park**, and then press Enter.
19. Type **Downtown Streets**.

Steps 13–19

20 Click anywhere in the text *Click to add notes* in the Notes pane and then type **Camille Matsui will report on the park location.**

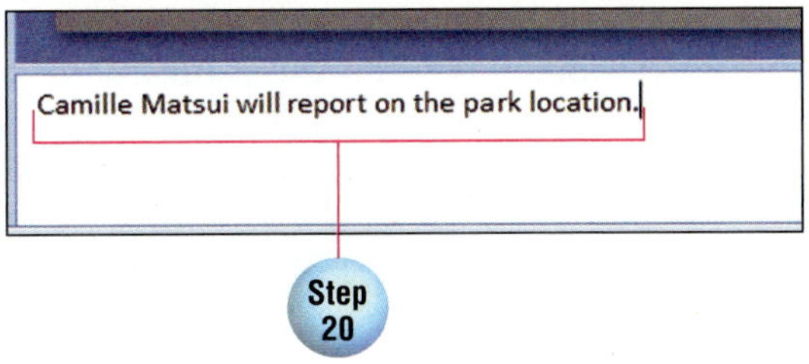

21 Click the Slides tab located toward the top of the Slides/Outline pane.

22 Click the Save button in the Quick Access toolbar.

23 At the Save As dialog box, make sure the PowerPointS1 folder on your storage medium is the active folder, type **PPS1-01** in the *File name* text box, and then press Enter.

24 Close the presentation by clicking the Office button and then clicking *Close*.

In Brief

Choose Slide Design
1. Click Design tab.
2. Click More button at right side of Themes icons.
3. Click desired theme at drop-down gallery.

Add Slide
1. Click Home tab.
2. Click New Slide button.

Save Presentation
1. Click Save button on Quick Access toolbar.
2. At Save As dialog box, type presentation file name.
3. Press Enter.

Close PowerPoint
1. Click Office button.
2. Click Close.

In Addition

Using Tabs

The ribbon area displays below the Quick Access toolbar. The buttons and options in the ribbon area vary depending on the tab selected. PowerPoint commands and features are organized into command tabs that display in the ribbon area. Commands and features are organized into groups within a tab. For example, the Home tab contains the Clipboard, Slides, Font, Paragraph, Drawing, and Editing groups. When you hover the mouse over a button, a ScreenTip displays with the name of the button, a keyboard shortcut (if any), and a description of the purpose of the button.

Activity 1.3

Opening, Navigating, and Inserting Slides in a Presentation

Open a saved presentation by displaying the Open dialog box and then double-clicking the desired presentation. Display the Open dialog box by clicking the Open button on the Quick Access toolbar or clicking the Office button and then clicking *Open* at the drop-down list. Navigate through slides in a presentation with buttons on the vertical scroll bar, by clicking text in the desired slide in the Slides/Outline pane, or using keys on the keyboard. Insert a new slide with a specific layout by clicking the New Slide button arrow and then clicking the desired layout at the drop-down list.

Project

Chris Greenbaum has asked you to add more information to the movie production meeting presentation. You will insert a new slide between the second and third slides in the presentation and then add a slide at the end of the presentation.

1. Click the Open button on the Quick Access toolbar.

   If the Open button does not display on the Quick Access toolbar, click the Customize Quick Access Toolbar button that displays at the right side of the toolbar and then click *Open* at the drop-down list.

2. At the Open dialog box, make sure the PowerPointS1 folder on your storage medium is the active folder and then double-click ***PPS1-01.pptx*** in the list box.

   PROBLEM

   If PPS1-01.pptx does not display in Open dialog box, you may need to change the folder. Check with your instructor.

3. With **PPS1-01.pptx** open, click the Next Slide button located at the bottom of the vertical scroll bar.

   Clicking this button displays the next slide, Slide 2, in the presentation. Notice that *Slide 2 of 3* displays at the left side of the Status bar.

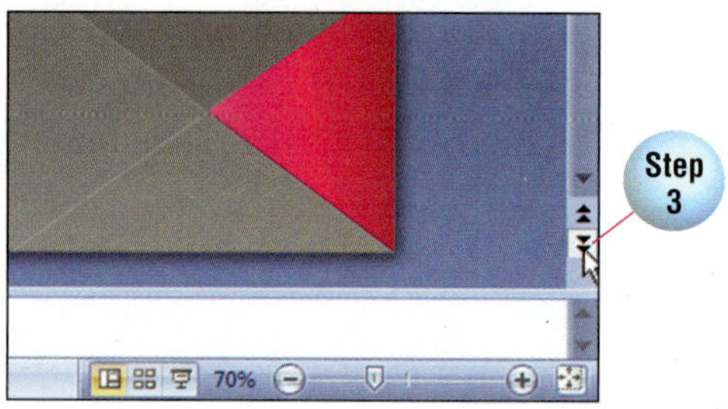

4. Click the Previous Slide button located toward the bottom of the vertical scroll bar to display Slide 1.

   When you click the Previous Slide button, *Slide 1 of 3* displays at the left side of the Status bar.

5. Display Slide 2 in the Slide pane by clicking the Next Slide button located at the bottom of the vertical scroll bar.

6. Insert a new slide between Slides 2 and 3 by clicking the New Slide button in the Slides group in the Home tab.

7 Click anywhere in the text *Click to add title* in the slide in the Slide pane and then type **Production Schedule**.

8 Click anywhere in the text *Click to add text* located in the slide and then type the bulleted text as shown in the slide at the right. Press the Enter key after each item *except* the last item.

9 Click the Outline tab located toward the top of the Slides/Outline pane.

10 Click immediately right of the text *Music* located toward the middle of the Slides/Outline pane, press the Enter key, and then press Shift + Tab.

This moves the insertion point back a level and inserts the number *4* followed by a slide icon.

11 Type **Production Assignments**, press the Enter key, and then press the Tab key. Type the remaining text for Slide 4 as shown at the right. Do not press the Enter key after typing *Extras*.

When you are finished typing the text, the presentation will contain five slides.

12 Click the Save button on the Quick Access toolbar to save **PPS1-01.pptx**.

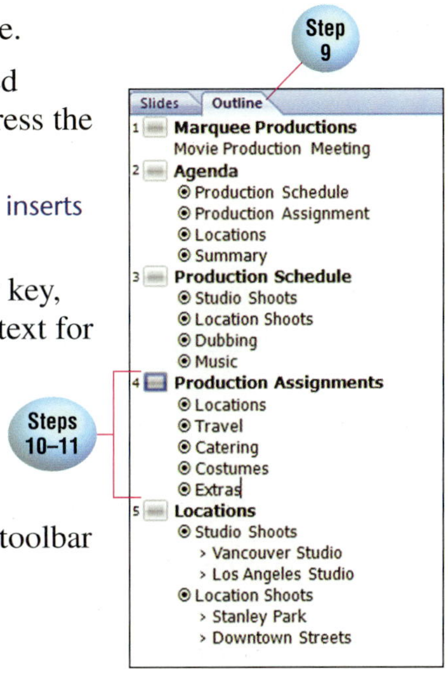

In Brief

Open Presentation
1. Click Open button on Quick Access toolbar.
2. At Open dialog box, double-click desired presentation.

In Addition

Planning a Presentation

Consider the following basic guidelines when preparing the content for a presentation:

- **Determine the main purpose of the presentation.** Do not try to cover too many topics. Identifying the main point of the presentation will help you stay focused and convey a clear message to the audience.
- **Determine the output.** To help decide the type of output needed, consider the availability of equipment, the size of the room where you will make the presentation, and the number of people who will be attending the presentation.
- **Show one idea per slide.** Each slide in a presentation should convey only one main idea. Too many ideas on a slide may confuse the audience and cause you to stray from the purpose of the slide.
- **Maintain a consistent design.** A consistent design and color scheme for slides in a presentation will create continuity and cohesiveness. Do not use too much color or too many pictures or other graphic elements.
- **Keep slides easy to read and uncluttered.** Keep slides simple and easy for the audience to read. Keep words and other items such as bullets to a minimum.
- **Determine printing needs.** Will you be providing audience members with handouts? If so, will these handouts consist of a printing of each slide? an outline of the presentation? a printing of each slide with space for taking notes?

Activity 1.4

Changing Views; Choosing a Slide Layout

PowerPoint provides viewing options for a presentation. Change the presentation view with buttons in the Presentation Views group in the View tab or with buttons in the View area on the Status bar. The Normal view is the default view and displays three panes—Slides/Outline, Slide, and Notes. You can change the view to Slide Sorter view or Notes Page view. Choose the view based on the type of activity you are performing in the presentation. You can also increase the size of the slide in the Slide pane by closing the Slides/Outline pane. Do this by clicking the Close button located in the upper right corner of the pane. Click the New Slide button arrow located in the Slides group in the Home tab and a drop-down list displays with layout choices. Choose the layout that matches the type of text or object you want to insert in the slide.

Project

After reviewing the movie production presentation, Chris Greenbaum has asked you to edit a slide and add a new slide.

Marquee PRODUCTIONS

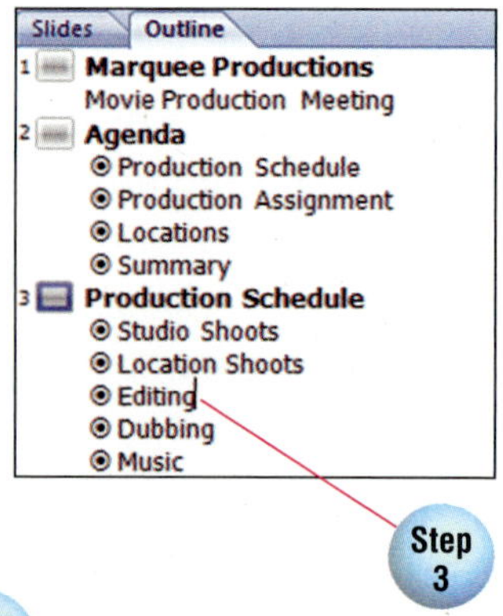

1. With **PPS1-01.pptx** open, check to make sure the Outline tab is selected in the Slides/Outline pane.
2. Click immediately right of *Location Shoots* in the third slide.
3. Press the Enter key and then type **Editing**.

   This inserts *Editing* between *Locations Shoots* and *Dubbing*.

4. Display the slides in Notes Page view by clicking the View tab and then clicking the Notes Page button in the Presentation Views group.

   In Notes Page view, an individual slide displays on a page with any added notes displayed below the slide.

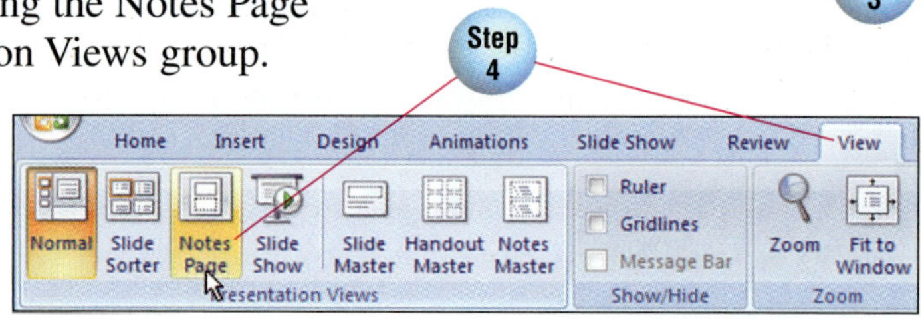

5. Click the Next Slide button on the vertical scroll bar until Slide 5 (the last slide) displays.

   Notice that the note you created about Camille Matsui displays below the slide in the page.

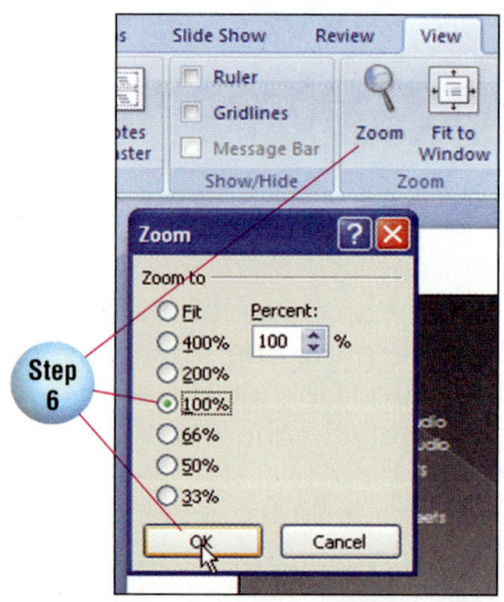

6. Increase the zoom by clicking the Zoom button in the Zoom group in the View tab, clicking *100%* at the Zoom dialog box, and then clicking OK.
7. You can also change the zoom using the Zoom slider bar. Change the zoom by positioning the mouse pointer on the Zoom slider bar button located at the right side of the Status bar. Hold down the left mouse button, drag to the right until the zoom percentage at the left side of the Zoom slider bar displays as approximately *136%*, and then release the mouse button.

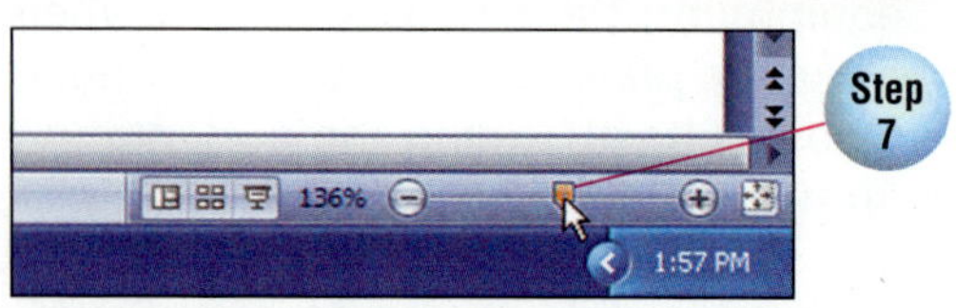

8. Click the minus symbol that displays inside a circle at the left side of the Zoom slider bar until *70%* displays at the left side of the slider bar.

   Click the minus symbol to decrease the zoom display and click the plus symbol to increase the display.

9. View all slides in the presentation in slide miniature by clicking the Slide Sorter button in the Presentation Views group.

10. Click the Normal button in the Presentation Views group.

11. Click the Slides tab in the Slides/Outline pane.

    With the Slides tab selected, slide miniatures display in the Slides/Outline pane.

12. Click below the Slide 5 miniature in the Slides/Outline pane.

    When you click below the slide miniature, a blinking horizontal line displays below Slide 5.

13. Click the Home tab, click the New Slide button arrow, and then click the Title Slide layout that displays in the drop-down list.

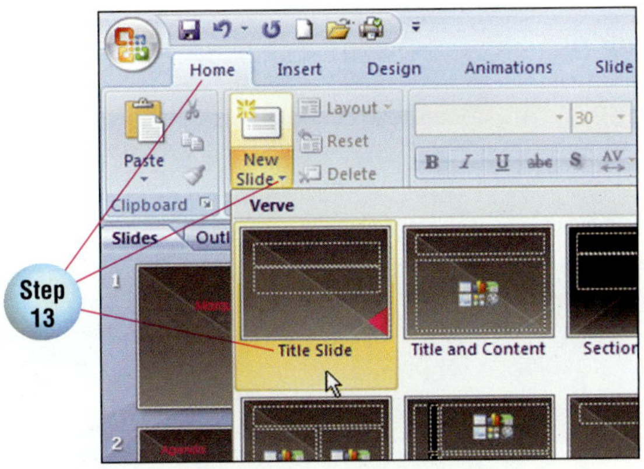

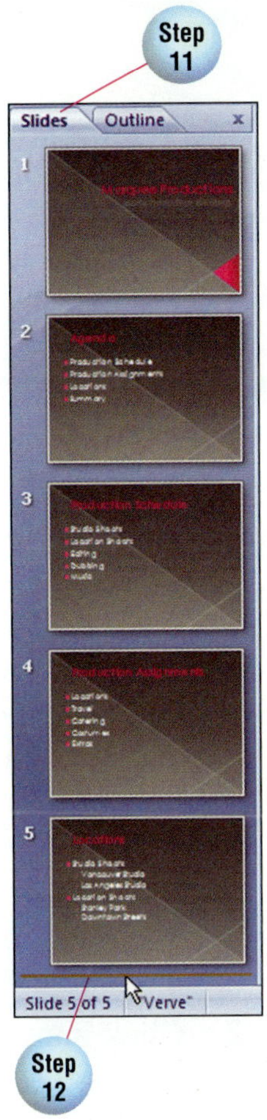

In Brief

Normal View
1. Click View tab.
2. Click Normal button.

OR
Click Normal button in View area on Status bar.

Slide Sorter View
1. Click View tab.
2. Click Slide Sorter button.

OR
Click Slide Sorter button in View area on Status bar.

Notes Page View
1. Click View tab.
2. Click Notes Page button.

14. Click the text *Click to add title* and then type **Production Leader**.

15. Click the text *Click to add subtitle* and then type **Chris Greenbaum**.

16. Save **PPS1-01.pptx**.

In Addition

Correcting Errors in PowerPoint

PowerPoint's AutoCorrect feature automatically corrects certain words as you type them. For example, type *teh* and press the spacebar, and AutoCorrect changes it to *the*. PowerPoint also contains a spelling feature that inserts a wavy red line below words that are not contained in the Spelling dictionary or not corrected by AutoCorrect. If the word containing a red wavy line is correct, you can leave it as written since the red wavy line does not print. If the word is incorrect, edit it.

Activity 1.5

Changing the Slide Layout; Selecting and Moving a Placeholder

The slides you have created have been based on a slide layout. You can change the slide layout by clicking the Layout button in the Slides group in the Home tab and then clicking the desired layout at the drop-down list. Objects in a slide such as text, a chart, a table, or other graphic element, are generally positioned in a placeholder. Click the text or object to select the placeholder and a dashed border surrounds the placeholder. You can move, size, and/or delete a selected placeholder.

Project

You have decided to make a few changes to the layout of slides in the movie production presentation.

1. With **PPS1-01.pptx** open, make sure Slide 6 displays in the Slide pane.

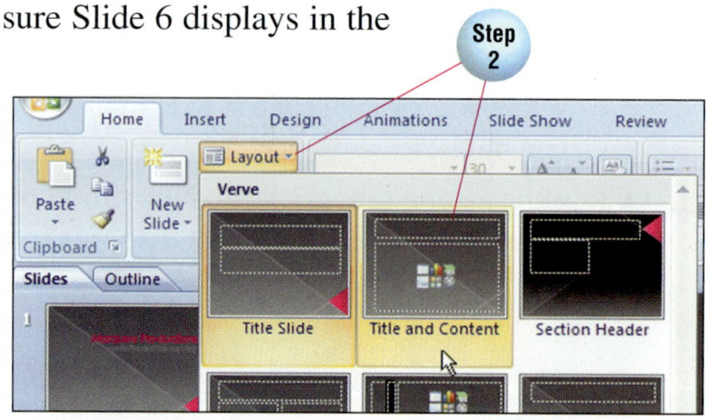

2. Click the Layout button [Layout] in the Slides group in the Home tab and then click the *Title and Content* layout at the drop-down list.

   Position the mouse pointer on a slide layout and the name of the layout displays in a box.

3. Click immediately right of the *r* in *Leader* (this selects the placeholder), press the Backspace key until *Leader* is deleted, and then type **Team**.

   Sizing handles display around the selected placeholder. Use these sizing handles to increase and/or decrease the size of the placeholder.

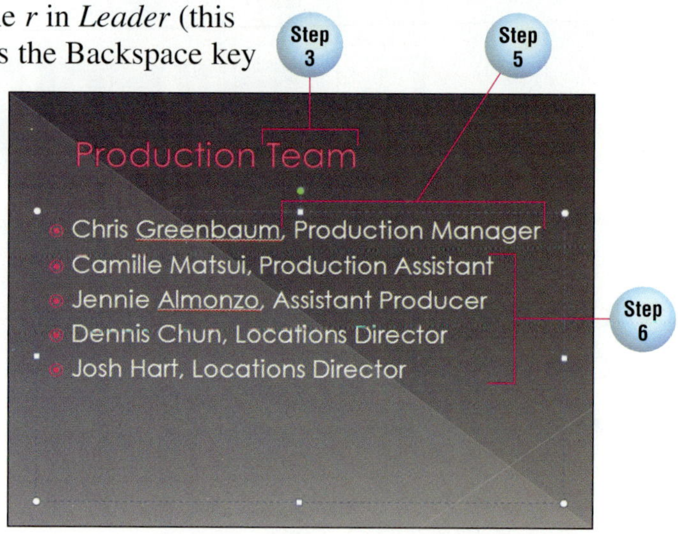

4. Click immediately right of the *m* in *Greenbaum*.
5. Type a comma (**,**), press the spacebar, and then type **Production Manager**.
6. Press the Enter key and then type the remaining names and titles shown in the slide above. (Do not press the Enter key after typing *Josh Hart, Locations Director*.)
7. Click the Previous Slide button [▲] on the vertical scroll bar until Slide 4 displays.
8. Change the slide layout by clicking the Layout button [Layout] and then clicking the *Title Slide* layout at the drop-down list.

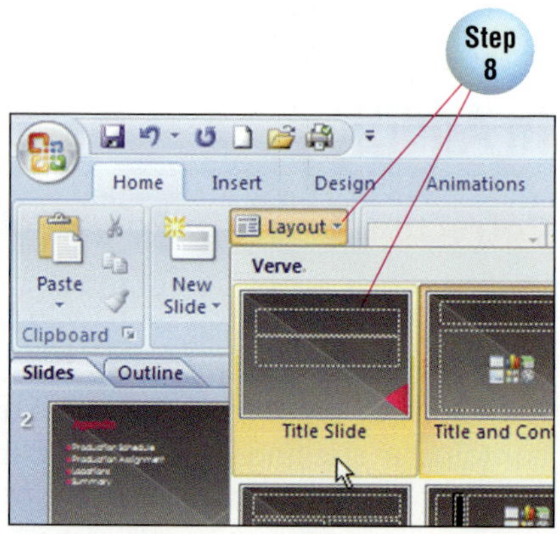

9 Click anywhere in the title *Production Assignments.*

This selects the placeholder.

10 Decrease the size of the placeholder by positioning the mouse pointer on the middle sizing handle at the left side until the pointer turns into a double-headed arrow pointing left and right. Hold down the left mouse button, drag to the right until the placeholder border is positioned at the left side of the *n* in *Production*, and then release the mouse button.

Decreasing the size of the placeholder causes the word *Assignments* to wrap to the next line.

11 Click anywhere in the text *Locations.*

This selects the placeholder containing the text.

12 Drag the left side of the placeholder border until it is positioned approximately one-half inch to the left of the beginning of the text.

13 Move the title placeholder so it positions the title as shown in Figure 1.2. To do this, click on any character in the title, position the mouse pointer on the border of the placeholder until the mouse pointer displays with a four-headed arrow attached, hold down the left mouse button, drag to the approximate location shown in the figure, and then release the mouse button.

14 Move the content placeholder so it positions the text as shown in Figure 1.2.

15 Click outside the placeholder to deselect it.

If you are not satisfied with the changes you make to a placeholder, click the Reset button Reset in the Slides group in the Home tab. This resets the position, size, and formatting to the default settings.

16 Save **PPS1-01.pptx**.

FIGURE 1.2 Slide 4

In Brief

Change Slide Layout
1. Make desired slide active.
2. Click Home tab.
3. Click Layout button.
4. Click desired layout at drop-down list.

Move Placeholder
1. Click inside placeholder.
2. Drag with mouse to desired position.

Size Placeholder
1. Click inside placeholder.
2. Drag sizing handles to increase/ decrease size.

In Addition

Using the AutoFit Options Button

When you selected the placeholder in Slide 4, an AutoFit Options button displayed at the left side of the placeholder. Click the AutoFit Options button and a list of choices displays as shown at the right for positioning objects in the placeholder. The *AutoFit Text to Placeholder* option is selected by default and tells PowerPoint to fit text within the boundaries of the placeholder. Click the middle choice, *Stop Fitting Text to This Placeholder*, and PowerPoint will not automatically fit the text or object within the placeholder. Choose the last option, *Control AutoCorrect Options* to display the AutoCorrect dialog box with the AutoFormat As You Type tab selected. Additional options may display depending upon the placeholder and the type of data inserted in the placeholder.

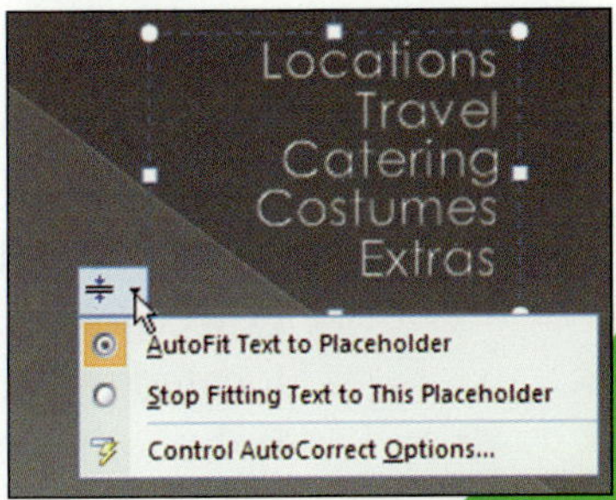

Activity 1.6

Using Help; Checking Spelling; Using the Thesaurus

Use the PowerPoint Help feature to display information on PowerPoint. To use the Help feature, click the Microsoft Office PowerPoint Help button (a circle with a question mark inside) located toward the upper right corner of the screen. At the PowerPoint Help window that displays, type the text for which you want information and then press Enter or click the Search button. A list of topics related to the search text displays in the results window. Click the desired topic and information displays in the PowerPoint Help window. Use PowerPoint's spelling checker to find and correct misspelled words and find duplicated words (such as *and and*). The spelling checker compares words in your slide with words in its dictionary. If a match is found, the word is passed over. If no match is found for the word, the spelling checker stops, selects the word, and offers replacements. Use the Thesaurus feature to find synonyms, antonyms, and related words for a particular word. To use the Thesaurus, click the word for which you want to display synonyms and antonyms, click the Review tab, and then click the Thesaurus button in the Proofing group. This displays the Research task pane with information about the word where the insertion point is positioned.

Project

Marquee PRODUCTIONS

You have decided to create a new slide in the movie production presentation. Because several changes have been made to the presentation, you know that checking the spelling of all the slide text is important, but you are not sure how to do it. You will use the Help feature to learn how to complete a spelling check and then use the Thesaurus feature to replace a couple of words with synonyms.

1. With **PPS1-01.pptx** open, position the mouse pointer on the scroll box located on the vertical scroll bar at the right side of the screen. Hold down the left mouse button, drag the scroll box to the bottom of the scroll bar, and then release the mouse button.

   This displays Slide 6 in the Slide pane. As you drag the scroll box on the vertical scroll bar, a box displays indicating the slide number.

2. Click the New Slide button in the Slides group in the Home tab.

   This inserts a new slide at the end of the presentation.

3. Click the text *Click to add title* and then type **Summary**.

4. Click the text *Click to add text* and then type the text shown in the slide at the right.

   Type the words exactly as shown. You will check the spelling in a later step.

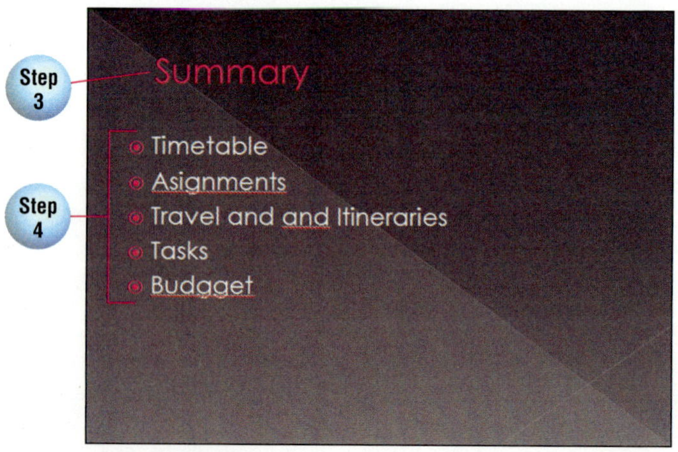

5. Learn how to complete a spelling check by clicking the Microsoft Office PowerPoint Help button located toward the upper right corner of the screen.

6 At the PowerPoint Help window, type **spell checking** and then press Enter.

7 Click *Check spelling and grammar* in the PowerPoint Help window.

8 Read the information that displays about spell checking and then click the Close button located in the upper right corner of the PowerPoint Help window.

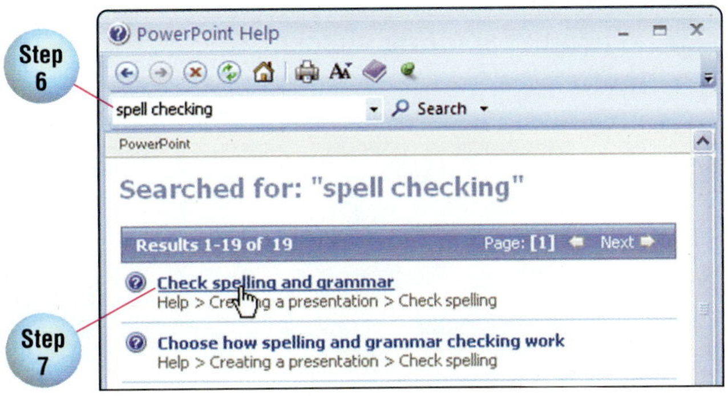

9 Complete a spelling check by moving the insertion point to the beginning of Timetable, clicking the Review tab, and then clicking the Spelling button in the Proofing group.

10 When the spelling checker selects *Asignments* in Slide 7 and displays *Assignments* in the *Change to* text box in the Spelling dialog box, click the Change button.

Refer to Table 1.3 for a description of the Spelling dialog box options.

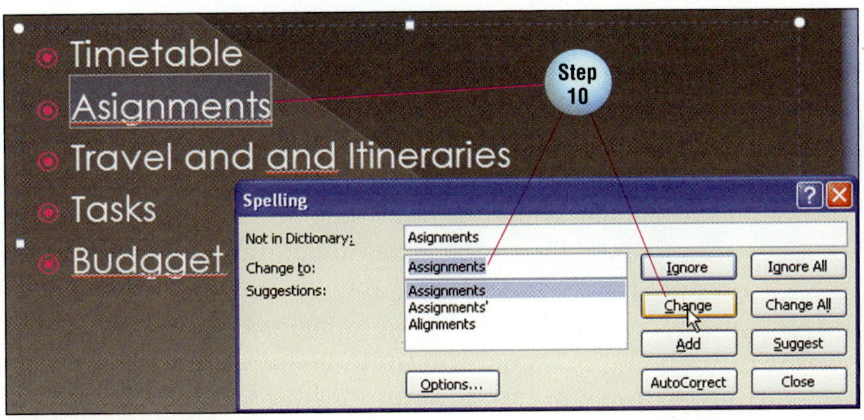

TABLE 1.3 Spelling Dialog Box Options

Button	Function
Ignore	skips that occurrence of the word and leaves currently selected text as written
Ignore All	skips that occurrence of the word and all other occurrences of the word in the presentation
Delete	deletes the currently selected word(s)
Change	replaces selected word in sentence with selected word in the *Suggestions* list box
Change All	replaces selected word with selected word in *Suggestions* list box and all other occurrences of the word in the presentation
Add	adds selected word to the main spelling check dictionary
Suggest	moves the insertion point to the *Suggestions* list box where you can scroll through the list of suggested spellings
AutoCorrect	inserts selected word and correct spelling of word in AutoCorrect dialog box
Options	displays a dialog box with options for customizing a spelling check

continues

11 When the spelling checker selects the second *and* in the slide, click the Delete button.

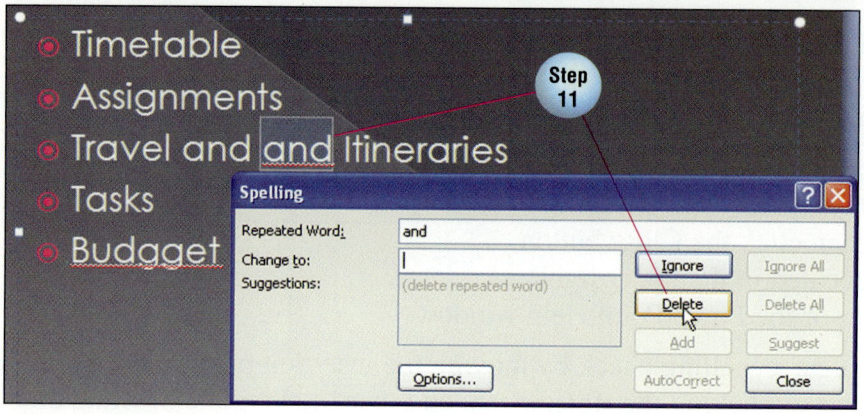

12 When the spelling checker selects *Budgget* in Slide 7 and displays *Budget* in the *Change to* text box in the Spelling dialog box, click the Change button.

13 When the spelling checker selects *Greenbaum* in Slide 6, click the Ignore button.

Greenbaum is a proper name and is spelled correctly. Clicking the Ignore button tells the spelling checker to leave the name as spelled.

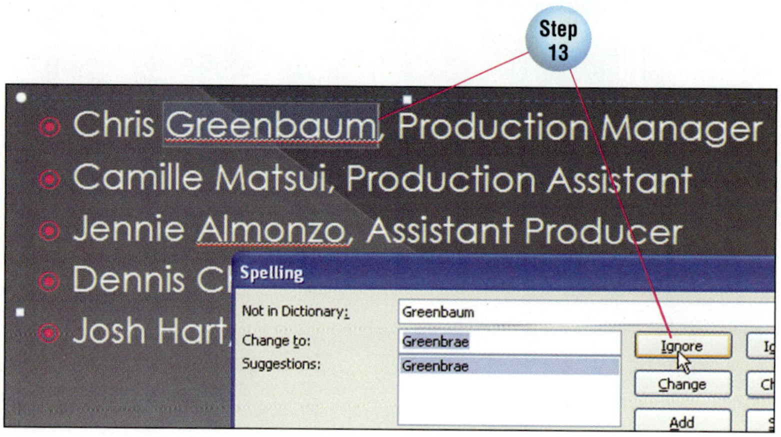

14 When the spelling checker selects *Almonzo* in Slide 6, click the Ignore button.

15 At the message telling you that the spelling check is complete, click the OK button.

16 Display Slide 7 in the Slide pane and then click the word *Timetable*.

17 Look up synonyms for *Timetable* by clicking the Thesaurus button in the Proofing group.

This displays the Research task pane containing lists of synonyms for *Timetable*. Depending on the word you are looking up, the words in the Research task pane list box may display followed by *(n.)* for *noun*, *(adj.)* for *adjective*, or *(adv.)* for *adverb*. Antonyms may display in the list of related synonyms, generally at the end of the list of related synonyms, and are followed by *(Antonym)*.

18 Position the mouse pointer on the word *schedule* in the Research task pane, click the down-pointing arrow at the right of the word, and then click *Insert* at the drop-down list.

This replaces *Timetable* with *Schedule*.

19 Close the Research task pane by clicking the Close button located in the upper right corner of the task pane.

20 Right-click on the word *Tasks*, point to *Synonyms*, and then click *responsibilities*.

The shortcut menu offers another method for displaying synonyms for words.

21 Capitalize the *r* in *responsibilities*.

22 Save **PPS1-01.pptx**.

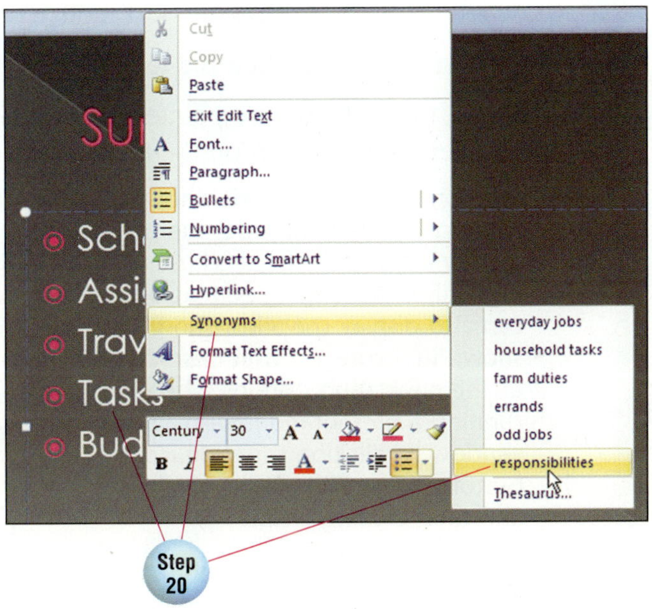

In Brief

Use Help
1. Click Microsoft Office PowerPoint Help button.
2. Type text for desired information.
3. Click Search button.

Complete Spelling Check
1. Click Review tab.
2. Click Spelling button.
3. Change or ignore highlighted words.
4. When spelling check is completed, click OK.

Use Thesaurus
1. Click desired word.
2. Click Review tab.
3. Click Thesaurus button.
4. Position mouse pointer on desired replacement word in Research task pane, click down-pointing arrow at right of word, and then click *Insert*.

In Addition

Changing Spelling Options

Control spelling options at the PowerPoint Options dialog box with the Proofing option selected. Display this dialog box by clicking the Office button and then clicking the PowerPoint Options button at the drop-down list. At the PowerPoint Options dialog box, click *Proofing* at the left side of the dialog box. With options in the dialog box, you can tell the spelling checker to ignore certain types of text, create custom dictionaries, and hide spelling errors in the presentation.

Editing While Checking Spelling

When checking a presentation, you can temporarily leave the Spelling dialog box by clicking in the slide. To resume the spelling check, click the Resume button, which was formerly the Ignore button.

Activity 1.7

Running a Presentation

You can run a presentation in PowerPoint manually, advance the slides automatically, or set up a slide show to run continuously for demonstration purposes. To run a slide show manually, click the Slide Show tab and then click the From Beginning button in the Start Slide Show group or click the Slide Show button in the View area on the Status bar. You can also run the presentation beginning with the currently active slide by clicking the From Current Slide button in the Start Slide Show group. Use the mouse or keyboard to advance through the slides. You can also use buttons on the Slide Show toolbar that display when you move the mouse pointer while running a presentation.

Project

You are now ready to run the movie production meeting presentation. You will use the mouse to perform various actions while running the presentation.

1. With **PPS1-01.pptx** open, click the Slide Show tab and then click the From Beginning button in the Start Slide Show group.

   Clicking this button begins the presentation, and Slide 1 fills the entire screen.

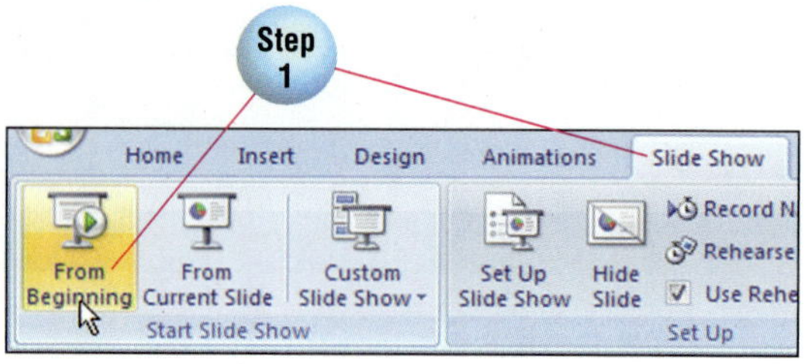

2. After viewing Slide 1, click the left mouse button to advance to the next slide.
3. After viewing Slide 2, click the left mouse button to advance to the next slide.
4. At Slide 3, move the mouse pointer until the Slide Show toolbar displays and then click the left arrow button on the toolbar to display the previous slide (Slide 2).

   With buttons on the Slide Show toolbar you can display the next slide, the previous slide, display a specific slide, and use the pen and highlighter to emphasize text on the slide. You can also display the Slide Show Help window shown in Figure 1.3 that describes all the navigating options when running a presentation. Display this window by clicking the slide icon button on the Slide Show toolbar and then clicking Help.

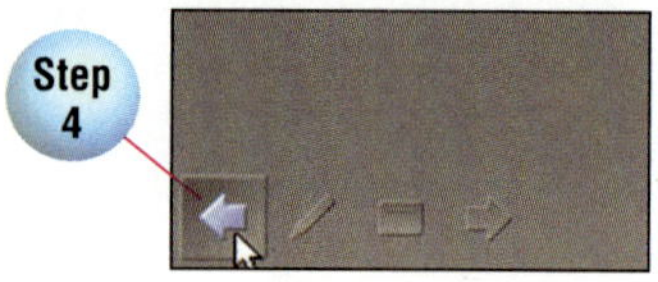

5. Click the right arrow button on the Slide Show toolbar to display the next slide (Slide 3).
6. Display the previous slide (Slide 2) by clicking the *right* mouse button and then clicking *Previous* at the shortcut menu.

   Clicking the *right* mouse button causes a shortcut menu to display with a variety of options including options to display the previous or next slide.

FIGURE 1.3 Slide Show Help Window

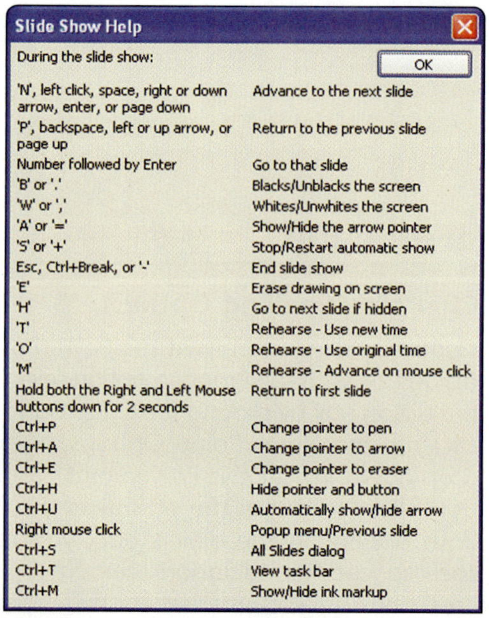

7. Display the next slide by clicking the slide icon button on the Slide Show toolbar and then clicking the *Next* option.

8. Display Slide 5 by typing the number *5* on the keyboard and then pressing Enter.

   Move to any slide in a presentation by typing the slide number and pressing Enter.

Step 7

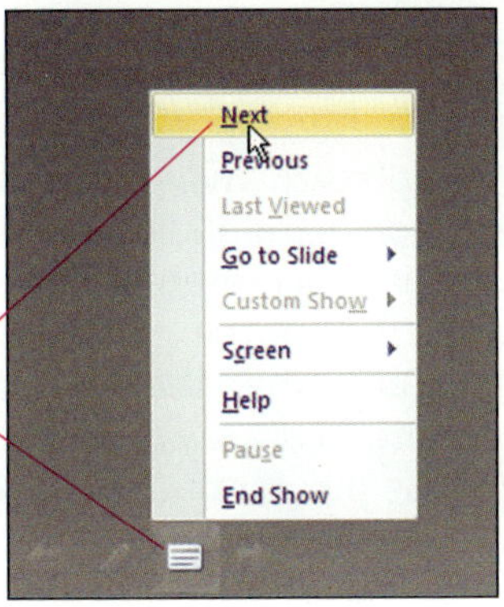

In Brief

Run Presentation

1. Click Slide Show tab.
2. Click From Beginning button or From Current Slide button.

OR

Click Slide Show button in View area on Status bar.

9. Change to a black screen by typing the letter *B* on the keyboard.

   When you type the letter B, the slide is removed from the screen and the screen displays black. This might be useful in a situation where you want to discuss something with your audience unrelated to the slide.

10. Return to Slide 5 by typing the letter *B* on the keyboard.

    Typing the letter *B* switches between the slide and a black screen. Type the letter *W* if you want to switch between the slide and a white screen.

11. Click the left mouse button to display Slide 6. Continue clicking the left mouse button until a black screen displays. At the black screen, click the left mouse button again.

    This returns the presentation to the Normal view.

12. Drag the scroll box up to the top of the vertical scroll bar and then release the mouse button.

    This displays Slide 1 in the Slide pane.

13. Display Slide 2 by clicking the Next Slide button located at the bottom of the vertical scroll bar.

14. Click the From Current Slide button in the Start Slide Show group in the Slide Show tab.

    Clicking this button begins the presentation with the active slide.

15. Run the presentation by clicking the left mouse button at each slide. At the black screen, click the left mouse button again.

In Addition

Showing Presenter View

If you want to view your speaker notes and any timings applied to slides while running a presentation, click the *Use Presenter View* check box in the Monitors group in the Slide Show tab. With this option active, you can run your presentation on one monitor while displaying speaker notes and timings on a second monitor. For this feature to work, you must have two monitors attached to your computer or be using a laptop computer that has dual-display capabilities.

Activity 1.8

Using the Pen and Highlighter during a Presentation

Emphasize major points or draw the attention of the audience to specific items in a slide during a presentation using the pen or highlighter. To use the pen on a slide, run the presentation, and when the desired slide displays, move the mouse to display the Slide Show toolbar. Click the mouse pointer button on the toolbar and then click either *Ballpoint Pen* or *Felt Tip Pen*. The felt tip pen draws a thicker line than the ballpoint pen. Use the mouse to draw in the slide to emphasize a point or specific text. If you want to erase the marks you made with the pen, click the mouse pointer button and then click *Eraser*. This causes the mouse pointer to display as an eraser. Drag through an ink mark to remove it. To remove all ink marks at the same time, click the *Erase All Ink on Slide* option. When you are finished with the pen, click the *Arrow* option to return the mouse pointer to an arrow.

Project

You will run the movie production meeting presentation again for another group of Marquee Production staff and use the pen and highlighter to emphasize points in slides.

1. With **PPS1-01.pptx** open, click the From Beginning button in the Start Slide Show group in the Slide Show tab.
2. With the first slide filling the screen, click the left mouse button to advance slides until Slide 3 displays. (This is the slide with the title *Production Schedule*.)
3. Move the mouse to display the Slide Show toolbar, click the pen button, and then click *Felt Tip Pen*.

   This turns the mouse pointer into a small circle.

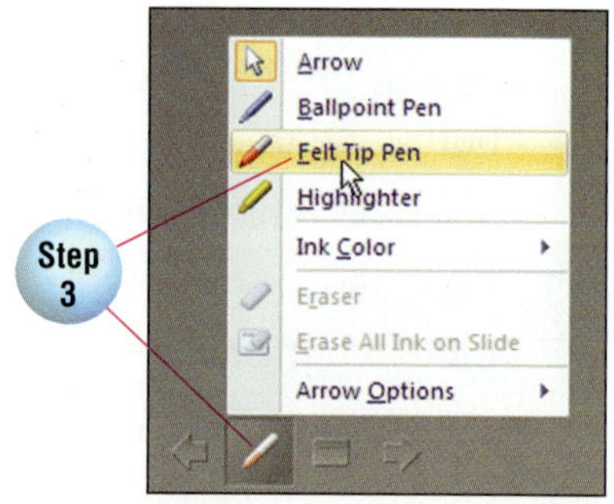

4. Using the mouse, draw a circle around the text *Location Shoots*.
5. Using the mouse, draw a line below *Dubbing*.
6. Erase the pen markings by clicking the pen button on the Slide Show toolbar and then clicking *Erase All Ink on Slide*.

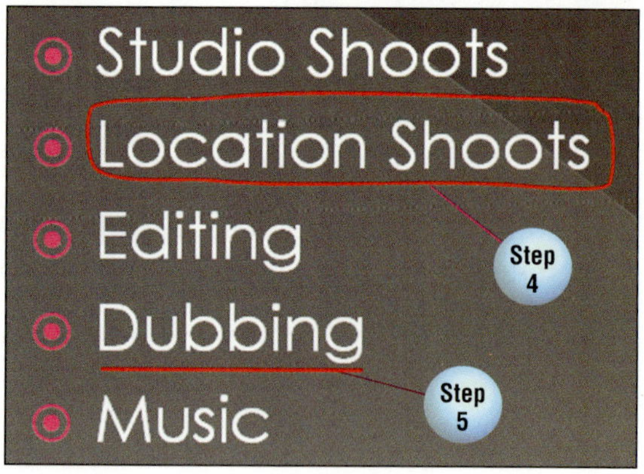

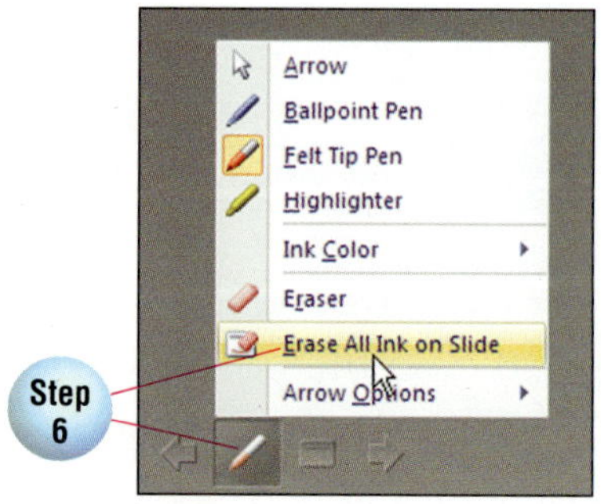

7 Change the color of the ink by clicking the pen button, pointing to *Ink Color*, and then clicking the bright yellow color.

8 Draw a yellow line below the word *Music*.

9 Return the mouse pointer back to an arrow by clicking the pen button and then clicking *Arrow* at the pop-up list.

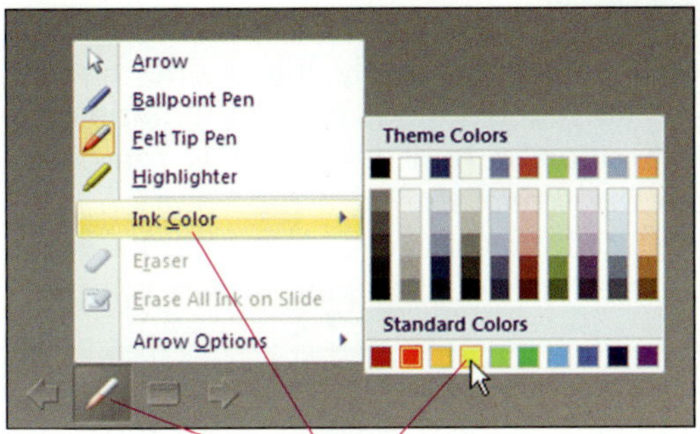

Step 7

10 Click the left mouse button to advance to Slide 4.

11 Click the pen button and then click *Highlighter* at the pop-up list.

This changes the mouse pointer to a light yellow rectangle.

12 Drag through the word *Locations* to highlight it.

13 Drag through the word *Costumes* to highlight it.

Step 12

Step 13

14 Return the mouse pointer back to an arrow by clicking the pen button and then clicking *Arrow*.

15 Press the Esc key on the keyboard to end the presentation without running the remaining slides. At the message asking if you want to keep your ink annotations, click the Discard button.

In Brief

Use Pen/Highlighter When Running Presentation

1. Run presentation.
2. At desired slide, move mouse.
3. Click pen button on Slide Show toolbar.
4. Click pen or highlighter option.
5. Draw in slide with pen/highlighter.

In Addition

Hiding/Displaying the Mouse Pointer

When running a presentation, the mouse pointer is set, by default, to be hidden automatically after three seconds of inactivity. The mouse pointer will appear again when you move the mouse. You can change this default setting by clicking the pen button on the Slide Show toolbar, pointing to *Arrow Options* and then clicking *Visible* if you want the mouse pointer always visible or *Hidden* if you do not want the mouse to display at all as you run the presentation. The *Automatic* option is the default setting.

Activity 1.9

Adding Transition and Sound

You can apply interesting transitions and sounds to a presentation. A transition is how one slide is removed from the screen during a presentation and the next slide is displayed. Interesting transitions can be added such as fades, dissolves, push, cover, wipes, stripes, and bar. Add a sound to a presentation and the sound is heard when a slide is displayed on the screen during a presentation. Add transitions and sounds with options in the Animations tab.

Project

You have decided to enhance the movie production meeting presentation by adding transitions and sound to the slides.

Marquee PRODUCTIONS

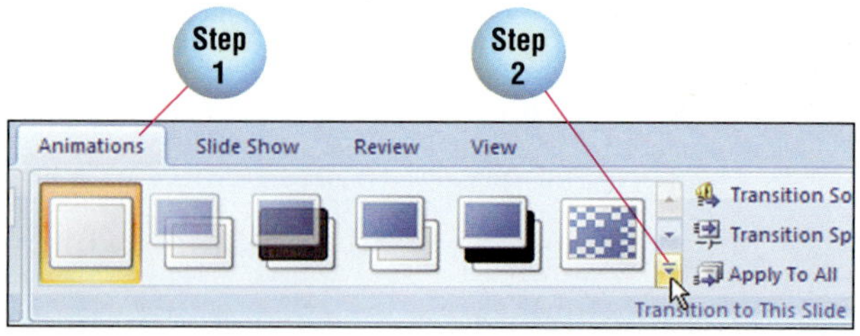

1. With **PPS1-01.pptx** open, click the Animations tab.
2. Click the More button located at the right side of the transition icons that display in the Transition to This Slide group.
3. At the drop-down gallery, click the *Newsflash* option (last option in the *Wipes* section).

   A gallery contains the live preview feature that shows the animation in the slide in the Slide pane as you hover the mouse over an animation option in the drop-down gallery.

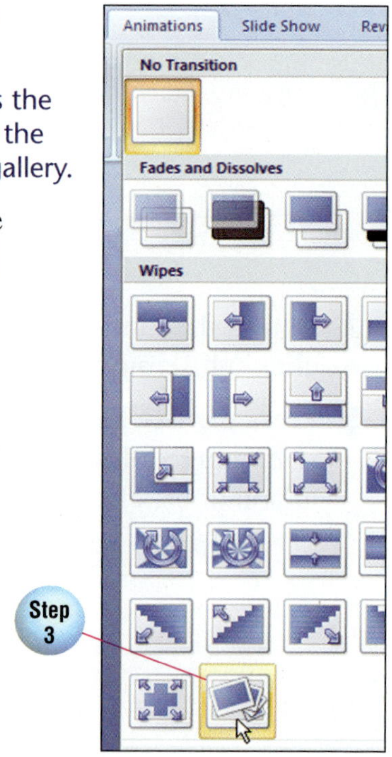

4. Click the down-pointing arrow at the right side of the Transition Sound button Transition Sound [No Sound] in the Transition to This Slide group.
5. At the drop-down gallery that displays, click the *Click* option.

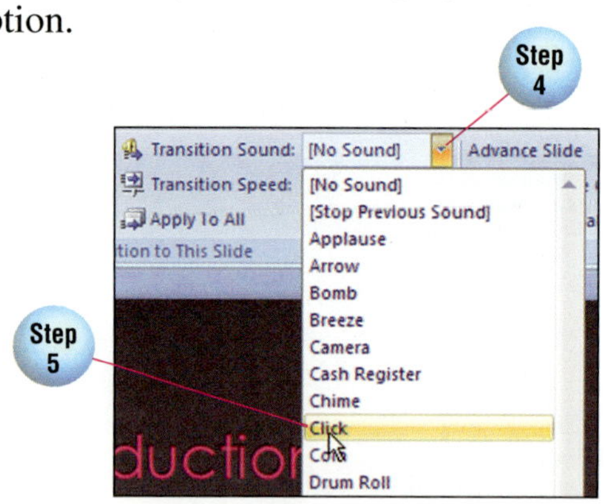

6. Click the down-pointing arrow at the right of the Transition Speed button Transition Speed Fast in the Transition to This Slide group and then click *Medium* at the drop-down list.
7. Click the Apply To All button Apply To All in the Transition to This Slide group.

   Notice that a transition icon displays below the slide miniatures in the Slides/Outline pane.

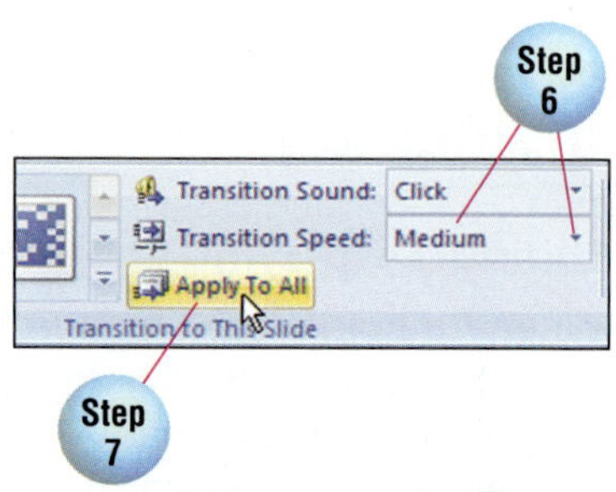

8. Click the Slide 1 miniature in the Slides/Outline pane.
9. Run the presentation by clicking the Slide Show button in the View area on the Status bar.

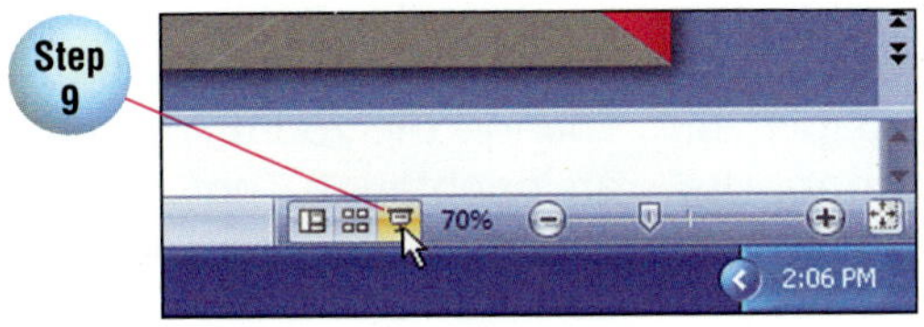

10. Click the left mouse button to advance each slide.
11. At the black screen that displays after the last slide, click the left mouse button again to return the presentation to the Normal view.
12. Click the More button located at the right side of the transition icons that display in the Transition to This Slide group.
13. Scroll down the drop-down gallery and then click the *Random Transition* option (last option in the *Random* section).
14. Click the down-pointing arrow at the right of the Transition Speed button [Transition Speed Fast] and then click *Fast* at the drop-down list.
15. Click the Apply To All button [Apply To All] in the Transition to This Slide group.
16. Run the presentation.
17. Save **PPS1-01.pptx**.

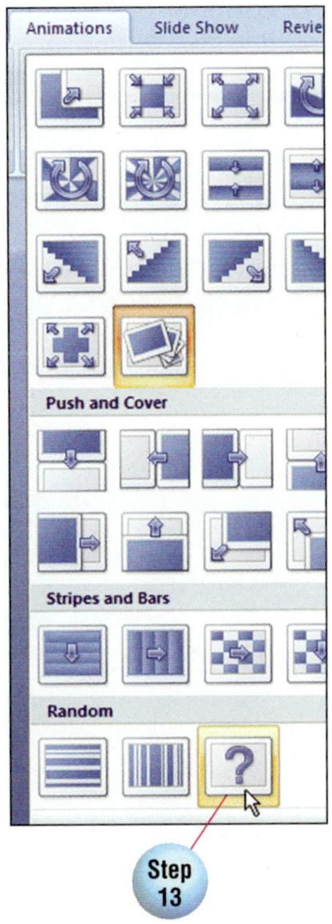

In Brief

Add Transition to All Slides in Presentation

1. Click Animations tab.
2. Click More button at right side of transition icons.
3. Click desired transition at drop-down gallery.
4. Click Apply To All button.

Add Transition Sound to All Slides in Presentation

1. Click Animations tab.
2. Click Transition Sound button arrow.
3. Click desired option at drop-down gallery.
4. Click Apply To All button.

In Addition

Running a Slide Show Automatically

Slides in a slide show can be advanced automatically after a specific number of seconds by inserting a check mark in the *Automatically After* check box in the Transition To This Slide group. Change the time in the text box by clicking the up- or down-pointing arrow at the right side of the text box or by selecting any text in the text box and then typing the desired time. If you want the transition time to affect all slides in the presentation, click the Apply To All button. In Slide Sorter view, the transition time displays below each affected slide. Click the Slide Show button to run the presentation. The first slide displays for the specified amount of time and then the next slide automatically displays.

Activity 1.10

Printing and Previewing a Presentation; Changing Page Setup

You can print each slide on a separate piece of paper; print each slide at the top of the page, leaving the bottom of the page for notes; print up to nine slides or a specific number of slides on a single piece of paper; or print the slide titles and topics in outline form. Use the *Print what* option at the Print dialog box to specify what you want printed. Before printing a presentation, consider previewing the presentation. To do this, click the Office button, point to the Print option and then click *Print Preview.* Use options in the Print Preview tab to display the next or previous slide, display the Print dialog box, specify how you want the presentation printed, change the zoom (percentage of display), choose an orientation (portrait or landscape), and close Print Preview. You can also change page orientation with the Slide Orientation button in the Page Setup group in the Design tab or with options at the Page Setup dialog box.

Project

Staff members need the movie production meeting slides printed as handouts and as an outline. You will preview and then print the presentation in various formats.

1. With **PPS1-01.pptx** open, display Slide 1 in the Slide pane. Click the Office button, point to *Print*, and then click *Print Preview*.

   This displays Slide 1 in the Print Preview window as it will appear when printed.

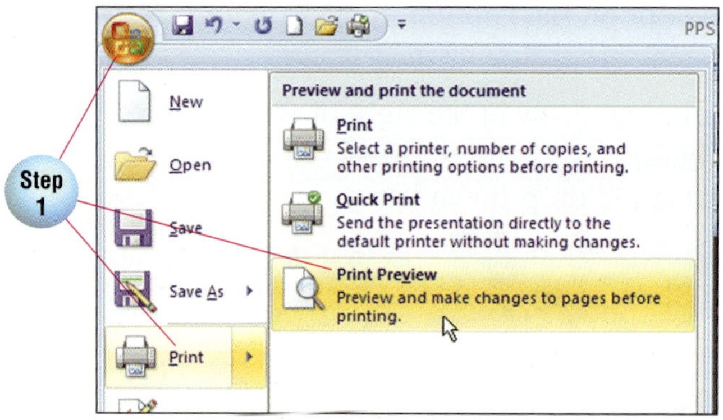

2. Click the Next Page button in the Preview group in the Print Preview tab.

   This displays Slide 2 in the Print Preview window.

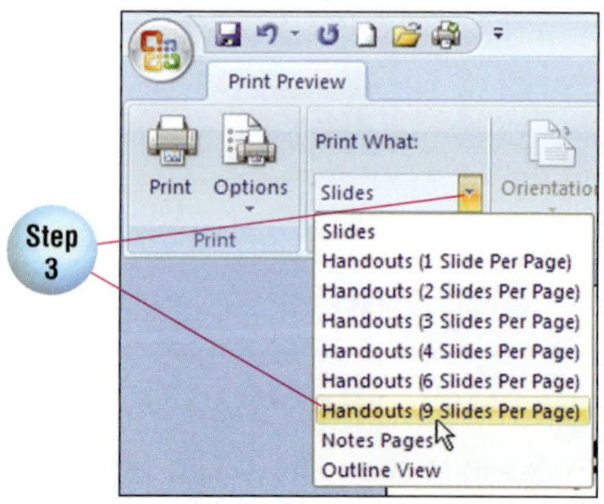

3. You decide to print all slides on one page and you want to preview how the slides will appear on the page. To do this, click the down-pointing arrow below the *Print What* option box, and then click *Handouts (9 Slides Per Page)* at the drop-down list.
4. Click the Print button in the Print group in the Print Preview tab.
5. At the Print dialog box, click OK.
6. Click the Close Print Preview button.
7. You want to print all slide text on one page and use the printing as a reference. To do this, click the Office button and then click *Print* at the drop-down list.

8. At the Print dialog box, click the down-pointing arrow at the right side of the *Print what* option and then click *Outline View* at the drop-down list.

9. Click OK.

   With the Outline View option selected, the presentation prints on one page with slide numbers, slide icons, and slide text in outline form.

10. Change the slide orientation from landscape to portrait by clicking the Design tab, clicking the Slide Orientation button in the Page Setup group, and then clicking *Portrait* at the drop-down list.

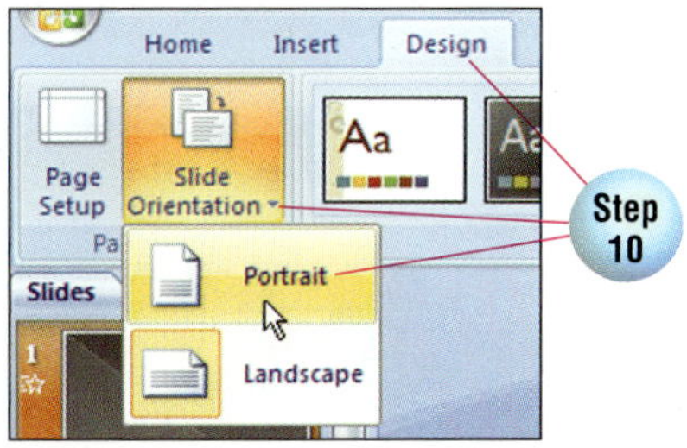

11. You need a printing of Slide 6. To do this, click the Office button and then click *Print* at the drop-down list.

12. At the Print dialog box, click the down-pointing arrow at the right side of the *Print what* option and then click *Slides* at the drop-down list.

13. Click the *Slides* option in the *Print range* section, type **6** in the text box, and then click OK.

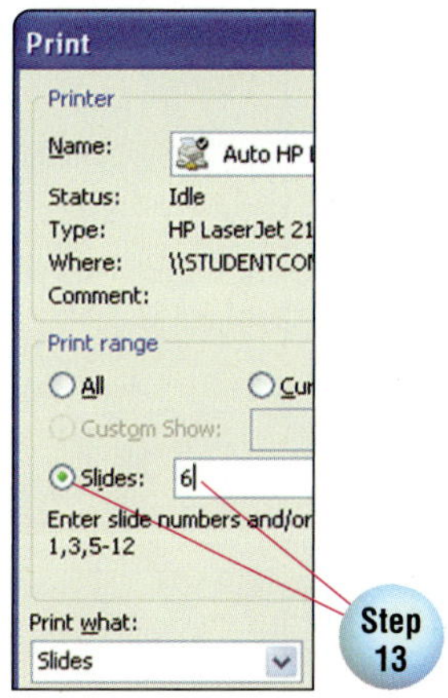

14. Return the orientation for slides back to landscape by clicking the Slide Orientation button in the Page Setup group in the Design tab and then clicking *Landscape* at the drop-down list.

15. Save **PPS1-01.pptx**.

16. Close the presentation by clicking the Office button and then clicking *Close* at the drop-down list.

In Brief

Print Presentation
1. Click Office button.
2. Click *Print.*
3. At Print dialog box, specify how you want presentation printed.
4. Click OK.

Preview Presentation
1. Click Office button.
2. Point to *Print.*
3. Click *Print Preview.*

Change Slide Orientation
1. Click Design tab.
2. Click Slide Orientation button.
3. Click desired orientation at drop-down list.

In Addition

Using Options at the Page Setup Dialog Box

You can change orientation with the Slide Orientation button or with options at the Page Setup dialog box shown at the right. Display this dialog box by clicking the Design tab and then clicking the Page Setup button. With options at this dialog box you can specify how you want slides sized; page width and height; orientation for slides; and orientation for notes, handouts, and outline.

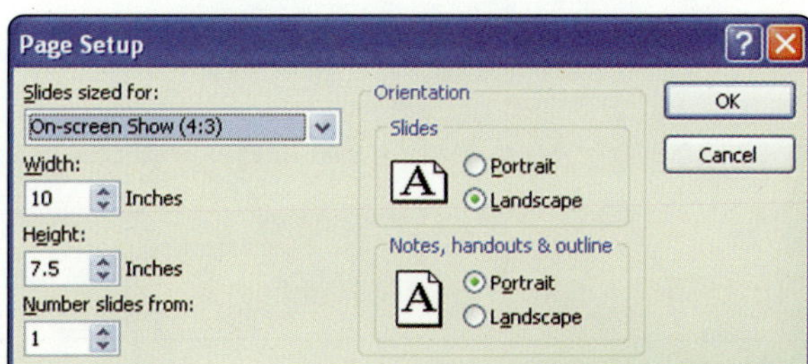

Features Summary

Feature	Ribbon Tab, Group	Button	Quick Access Toolbar	Office Button Drop-down List	Keyboard Shortcut
apply transitions and sounds to all slides	Animations, Transition to This Slide	Apply To All			
close				Close	
exit PowerPoint		Exit PowerPoint		Exit PowerPoint	
Help					F1
layout	Home, Slides	Layout			
New Presentation dialog box				New	
new slide	Home, Slides				
Normal view	View, Presentation Views				
Notes Page view	View, Presentation Views				
open blank presentation					Ctrl + N
Open dialog box				Open	Ctrl + O
Print dialog box				Print	Ctrl + P
print presentation					
Print Preview				Print, Print Preview	
run presentation from current slide	Slide Show, Start Slide Show				Shift + F5
run presentation from Slide 1	Slide Show, Start Slide Show				F5
save					Ctrl + S
save with a new name				Save As	F12
slide orientation	Design, Page Setup				
Slide Sorter view	View, Presentation Views				
Spelling	Review, Proofing				F7
themes	Design, Themes				
Thesaurus	Review, Proofing				Shift + F7

continues

Feature	Ribbon Tab, Group	Button	Quick Access Toolbar	Office Button Drop-down List	Keyboard Shortcut
transitions	Animations, Transition to This Slide				
transition sound	Animations, Transition to This Slide	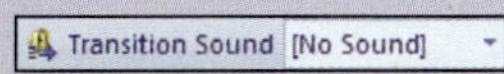			
transition speed	Animations, Transition to This Slide	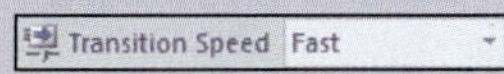			
Zoom dialog box	View, Zoom				

Knowledge Check

Completion: In the space provided at the right, indicate the correct term, command, or option.

1. Display the New Presentation dialog box by clicking this button and then clicking *New* at the drop-down list. ________________
2. To run a presentation beginning with Slide 1, click the Slide Show tab and then click this button. ________________
3. The Save button is located on this toolbar. ________________
4. The Normal view contains the Slides/Outline pane, the Slide pane, and this pane. ________________
5. The New Slide button is located in this tab. ________________
6. The Zoom slider bar is located at the right side of this bar. ________________
7. Click the Microsoft Office PowerPoint Help button and this displays. ________________
8. Use this feature to find synonyms, antonyms, and related words for a particular word. ________________
9. The Spelling button is located in the Proofing group in this tab. ________________
10. Move the mouse while running a presentation and this toolbar displays. ________________
11. Press this key on the keyboard to change to a black screen while running a presentation. ________________
12. Press this key on the keyboard to end a presentation without running all of the slides. ________________
13. Add transitions and sounds to a presentation with options in this tab. ________________
14. The Slide Orientation button is located in the Page Setup group in this tab. ________________

Skills Review

Review 1 Creating a Presentation for Marquee Productions

1. With a blank presentation in PowerPoint open, click the Design tab, click the More button at the right side of the Themes group, and then click *Flow* in the drop-down gallery.
2. Type the title and subtitle for Slide 1 as shown in Figure 1.4.
3. Click the Home tab and then click the New Slide button in the Slides group.
4. Type the text shown for Slide 2 in Figure 1.4.
5. Continue creating the slides for the presentation as shown in Figure 1.4.
6. Insert a new Slide 3 between the current Slides 2 and 3 with the text shown in Figure 1.5.
7. Display Slide 2 in the Slide pane and then change the slide layout to Title Slide.
8. Click the text *Current Status* to select the placeholder and then move the placeholder to the left approximately one inch.
9. Click in the text *Overview of Project* to select the placeholder and then move the placeholder to the left approximately one inch. Make sure the right side of the title and text below align at the right side.
10. Click the Animations tab, click the More button located at the right side of the transition icons that display in the Transition to This Slide group, and then click a transition of your choosing.
11. Click the down-pointing arrow at the right of the Transition Sound button and then click a transition sound of your choosing.
12. Apply the transition and sound to all slides in the presentation.
13. Save the presentation and name it **PPS1-R1**.
14. Run the presentation beginning with Slide 1.
15. Print the presentation in outline view.
16. Print the presentation with all five slides on one page.
17. Save and then close **PPS1-R1.pptx**.

FIGURE 1.4 Review 1

Slide 1	Title	Marquee Productions
	Subtitle	Location Team Meeting
Slide 2	Title	Current Status
	Bullets	• Overview of Project • Tasks on Schedule • Tasks behind Schedule
Slide 3	Title	Filming Sites
	Bullets	• Gardiner Expressway • Kings Mill Park • Island Airport • Royal Ontario Museum • Black Creek Pioneer Village • Additional Sites
Slide 4	Title	Key Issues
	Bullets	• Equipment Rental • Budget Overruns • Transportation Concerns • Location Agreements

FIGURE 1.5 Review 1

Slide 3	Title	Resources
	Bullets	• Location Contacts • Movie Extras • Catering Company • Lodging • Transportation Rentals

Skills Assessment

Assessment 1 Preparing a Presentation for Worldwide Enterprises

1. Prepare a presentation for Worldwide Enterprises with the information shown in Figure 1.6. (You determine the design template.)
2. Add a transition and sound of your choosing to all slides in the presentation.
3. Run the presentation.
4. Print the presentation with all five slides on one page.
5. Save the presentation and name it **PPS1-A1**.
6. Close **PPS1-A1.pptx**.

Assessment 2 Preparing a Presentation for The Waterfront Bistro

1. Prepare a presentation for The Waterfront Bistro with the information shown in Figure 1.7. (You determine the design template.)
2. Add a transition and sound of your choosing to all slides in the presentation.
3. Run the presentation.
4. Print the presentation with all five slides on one page.
5. Save the presentation and name it **PPS1-A2**.
6. Close **PPS1-A2.pptx**.

FIGURE 1.6 Assessment 1

Slide 1	Title	Worldwide Enterprises
	Subtitle	Executive Meeting
Slide 2	Title	Accounting Policies
	Bullets	• Cash Equivalents • Short-term Investments • Inventory Valuation • Property and Equipment • Foreign Currency Translation
Slide 3	Title	Financial Instruments
	Bullets	• Investments • Derivative Instruments • Credit Risks • Fair Value of Instruments
Slide 4	Title	Inventories
	Bullets	• Products • Raw Material • Equipment • Buildings
Slide 5	Title	Employee Plans
	Bullets	• Stock Options • Bonus Plan • Savings and Retirement Plan • Defined Benefits Plan • Foreign Subsidiaries

FIGURE 1.7 Assessment 2

Slide 1	Title	The Waterfront Bistro
	Subtitle	3104 Rivermist Drive Buffalo, NY 14280 (716) 555-3166
Slide 2	Title	Accommodations
	Bullets	• Dining Area • Salon • Two Banquet Rooms • Wine Cellar
Slide 3	Title	Menus
	Bullets	• Lunch • Dinner • Wines • Desserts
Slide 4	Title	Catering Services
	Bullets	• Lunch – Continental – Deli – Hot • Dinner – Vegetarian – Meat – Seafood
Slide 5	Title	Resource
	Subtitle	Dana Hirsch, Manager

Assessment 3 Finding Information on Setting Slide Show Timings

1. Open **MPProject.pptx** and use the Help feature to learn how to save a presentation with Save As.
2. Save the presentation with Save As and name it **PPS1-A3**.
3. Use the Help feature or experiment with the options in the Animations tab and learn how to set slide show timings manually.
4. Set up the presentation so that, when running the presentation, each slide advances after three seconds.
5. Run the presentation.
6. Save and then close **PPS1-A3.pptx**.

Assessment 4 Locating Information and Preparing a Presentation for First Choice Travel

1. You are Melissa Gehring, president of the Los Angeles branch of First Choice Travel. You are interested in arranging a vacation travel package to Cancun, Mexico. Connect to the Internet and search for information on Cancun. (One possible site for information is www.cancun.com.) Locate information on lodging (hotels), restaurants, activities, and transportation.
2. Using PowerPoint, create a presentation about Cancun that contains the following:
   - Title slide containing the company name, *First Choice Travel*, and the subtitle *Vacationing in Cancun*.
   - Slide containing the names of at least three major airlines that travel to Cancun
   - Slide containing the names of at least four hotels or resorts in Cancun
   - Slide containing the names of at least four restaurants in Cancun
   - Slide containing at least four activities in Cancun
3. Run the presentation.
4. Print all of the slides on one page.
5. Save the presentation and name it **PPS1-A4**.
6. Close **PPS1-A4.pptx**.

Marquee Challenge

Challenge 1 Preparing a Presentation on Toronto, Ontario, Canada

1. Create the presentation shown in Figure 1.8. Apply the appropriate design theme and slide layouts, and size and move placeholders so your slides display as shown in the figure.
2. Save the completed presentation and name it **PPS1-C1**.
3. Print the presentation as a handout with all six slides on the same page.

FIGURE 1.8 Challenge 1

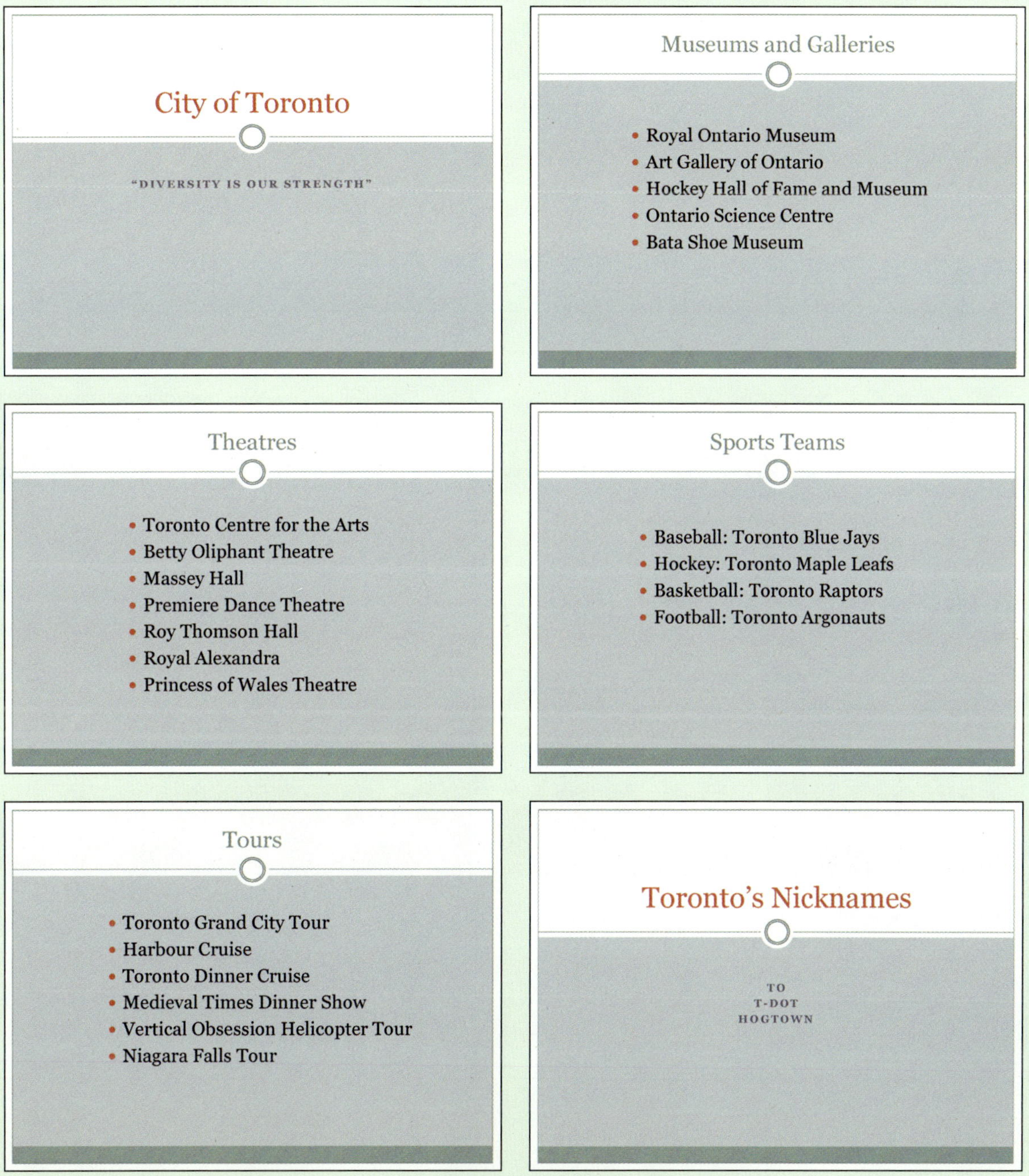

Challenge 2 Preparing a Presentation for Performance Threads

1. Create the presentation shown in Figure 1.9. Apply the appropriate design theme and slide layouts and size and move placeholders so your slides display as shown in the figure.
2. Save the completed presentation and name it **PPS1-C2**.
3. Print the presentation as a handout with all six slides on the same page.

FIGURE 1.9 Challenge 2

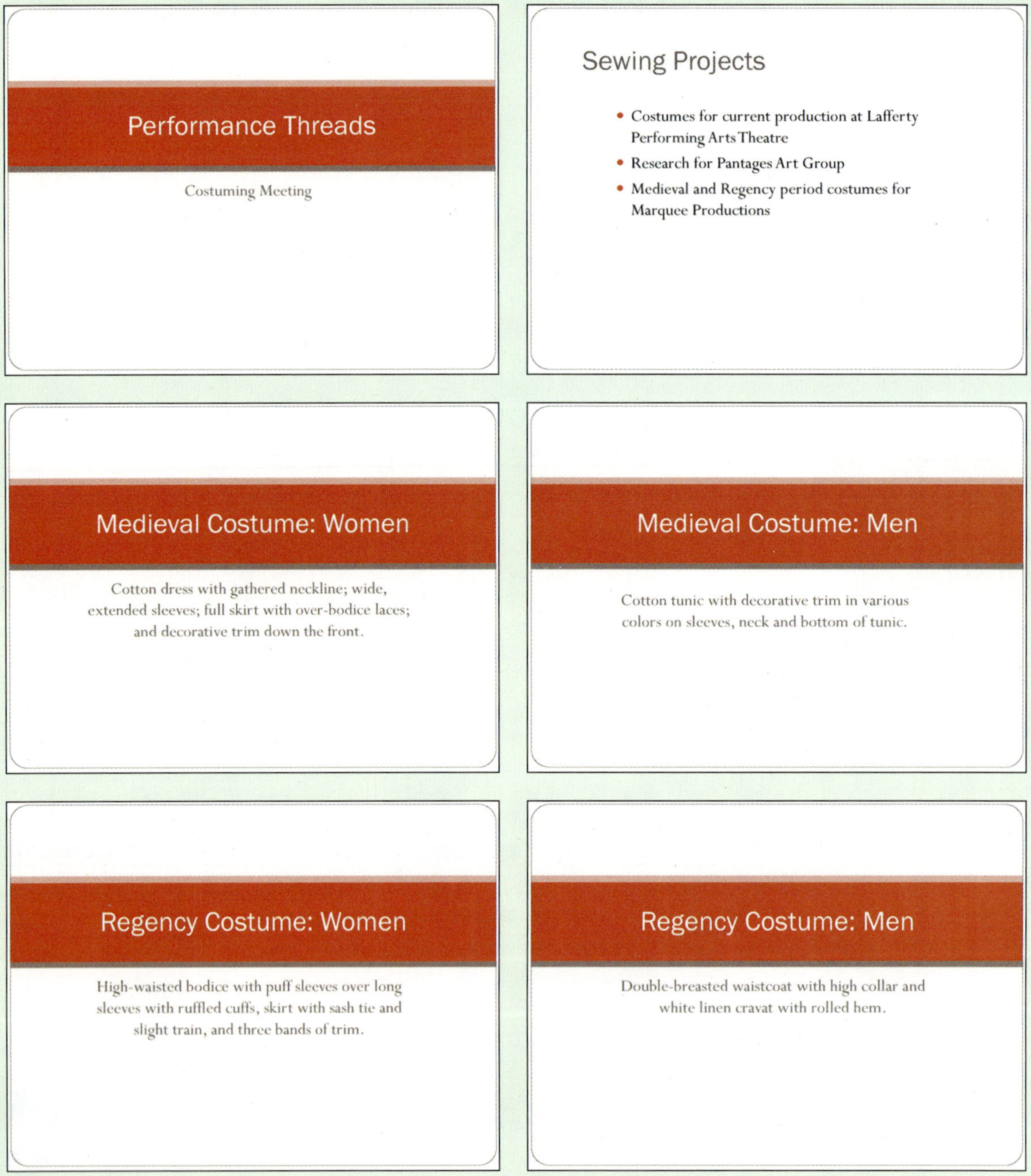

PowerPoint SECTION 2

Editing and Enhancing Slides

Skills

- Open a presentation and save it with a new name
- Rearrange, delete, and hide slides
- Increase and decrease the indent of text
- Select, cut, copy, and paste text
- Apply font and font effects
- Find and replace fonts
- Apply formatting with Format Painter
- Change alignment and line and paragraph spacing
- Change the design theme, theme color, and theme font
- Insert, size, and move images
- Insert and format clip art images
- Insert and format a SmartArt organizational chart
- Insert and format a SmartArt diagram
- Apply animation to an object in a slide

Student Resources

Before beginning this section:

1. Copy to your storage medium the PowerPointS2 subfolder from the PowerPoint folder on the Student Resources CD.
2. Make PowerPointS2 the active folder.

In addition to containing the data files needed to complete section work, the Student Resources CD contains model answers in PDF format for each of the projects in this section; model answers for end-of-section activities are not provided.

Projects Overview

Marquee Productions

Open an existing project presentation for Marquee Productions, save the presentation with a new name, and then edit and format the presentation. Open an existing annual meeting presentation for Marquee Productions and then save, edit, and format the presentation.

Niagara Peninsula College

Open an existing presentation for the Theatre Arts Division of Niagara Peninsula College and then save, edit, and format the presentation.

First Choice Travel

Open an existing presentation containing information on vacation specials offered by First Choice Travel and then save, edit, and format the presentation.

The Waterfront B·I·S·T·R·O

Locate information on the Internet on competing bistros in and around the Toronto area and then prepare a presentation to the owners of the bistro containing the information located. Prepare and format a presentation on the services offered by the bistro.

Performance Threads

Prepare and format a presentation on the company structure, policies, and benefits.

Worldwide Enterprises

Prepare and format a presentation for a planning meeting of the distribution department.

Activity 2.1

Rearranging, Deleting, and Hiding Slides

If you open an existing presentation and make changes to it, you can then save it with the same name or a different name. Save an existing presentation with a new name at the Save As dialog box. PowerPoint provides various views for creating and managing a presentation. Use the view that most easily accomplishes the task. For example, consider using the Slide Sorter view to delete, rearrange, and hide slides in a presentation.

Project

You want to create another version of an existing project presentation for Marquee Productions. The changes for the second version include deleting, rearranging, and hiding slides in the presentation.

1. With PowerPoint open, click the Open button on the Quick Access toolbar.
2. At the Open dialog box, make sure PowerPointS2 is the active folder and then double-click ***MPProject.pptx*** in the list box.
3. Click the Office button and then click *Save As*.
4. At the Save As dialog box, type **PPS2-01** in the *File name* text box and then press Enter.
5. Click the Slide Sorter button in the View area on the Status bar.
6. Click Slide 2 to select it and then click the Delete button [Delete] in the Slides group in the Home tab.

   A slide selected in Slide Sorter view displays surrounded by an orange border. You can also delete a selected slide by pressing the Delete key on the keyboard.

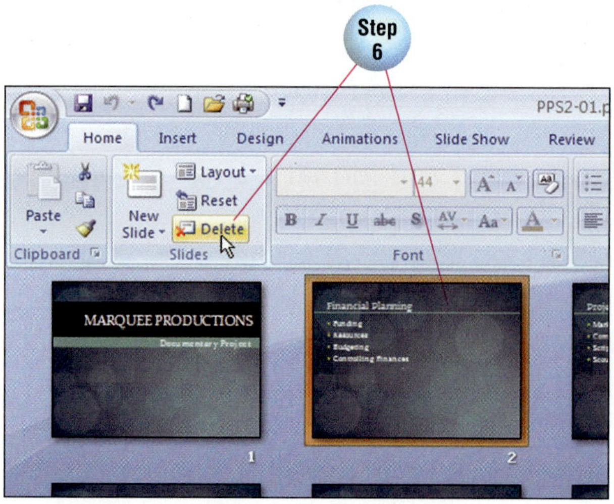

7. Click Slide 6 to make it active.
8. Position the mouse pointer on Slide 6, hold down the left mouse button, drag the arrow pointer (with a square attached) to the left of Slide 3, and then release the mouse button.

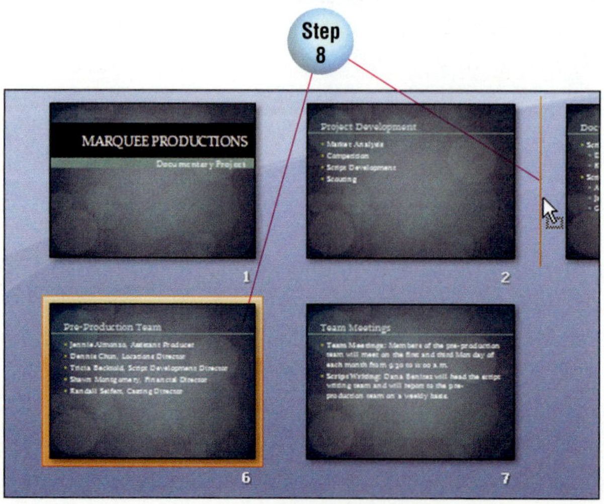

9. Click the Normal button located in the View area on the Status bar.
10. Click the Slides tab in the Slides/Outline pane. (Skip this step if the Slides tab is already selected.)
11. Scroll down the Slides/Outline pane until Slide 7 displays. Position the mouse pointer on the Slide 7 miniature, hold down the left mouse button, drag up until a thin, horizontal line displays immediately below the Slide 2 miniature, and then release the mouse button.
12. With the Slide 3 miniature selected in the Slides/Outline pane (miniature displays with an orange background), hide the slide by clicking the Slide Show tab and then clicking the Hide Slide button in the Set Up group.

When a slide is hidden, the slide miniature displays dimmed.

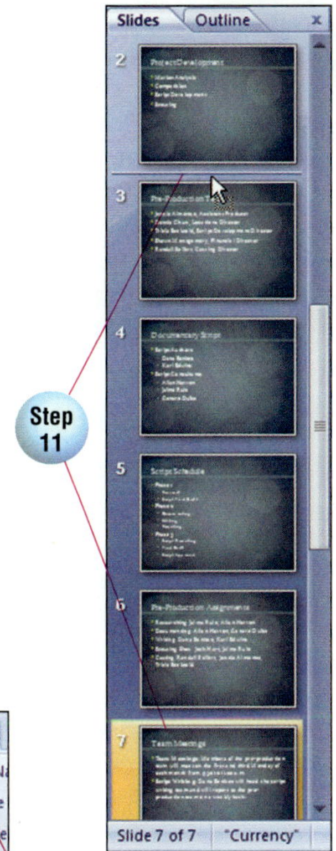

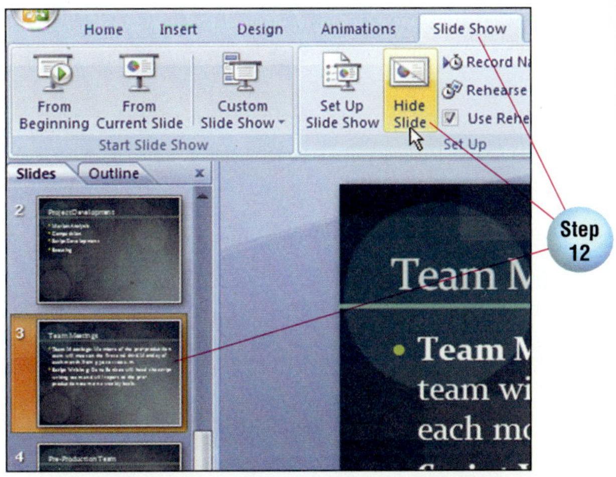

In Brief

Save Presentation with New Name
1. Click Office button, click *Save As*.
2. Type presentation name.
3. Click Save or press Enter.

Delete Slide
1. Click Slide Sorter button in View area on Status bar.
2. Click desired slide.
3. Press Delete key.

Move Slide
1. Click Slide Sorter button in View area on Status bar.
2. Click desired slide.
3. Drag slide to desired position.

13. Run the presentation by clicking the From Beginning button in the Start Slide Show group. Click the left mouse button to advance each slide.
14. After running the presentation, you decide to redisplay the hidden slide. To do this, make sure the Slide 3 miniature is selected in the Slides/Outline pane and then click the Hide Slide button in the Set Up group.
15. Save **PPS2-01.pptx** by clicking the Save button on the Quick Access toolbar.

In Addition

Copying Slides within a Presentation

Copying a slide within a presentation is similar to moving a slide. To copy a slide, first change to the Slide Sorter view. Position the arrow pointer on the desired slide, hold down the Ctrl key and the left mouse button. Drag to the location where you want the slide copied, release the left mouse button, and then release the Ctrl key. When you drag with the mouse, the mouse pointer displays with a square and a plus symbol next to the pointer.

Activity 2.2

Increasing and Decreasing Text Level Indent; Cutting, Copying, and Pasting Text

In the Slides/Outline pane with the Outline tab selected, you can organize and develop the content of the presentation by rearranging points within a slide, moving slides, or increasing and decreasing text level indent. Click the Decrease List Level button in the Paragraph group in the Home tab or press Shift + Tab to decrease text to the previous level. Click the Increase List Level button or press Tab to increase text to the next level. You can also increase and/or decrease the indent of text in the slide in the Slide pane. You can select text in a slide and then delete the text from the slide, cut text from one location and paste into another, or copy and paste the text. Use buttons in the Clipboard group in the Home tab to cut, copy, and paste text.

Project

As you edit the documentary project presentation, you will increase and decrease text level and select, delete, move, copy, and paste text in slides.

1. With **PPS2-01.pptx** open, click the Home tab and then display Slide 5 in the Slide pane.
2. You decide to promote the names below *Script Authors*. To do this, position the mouse pointer immediately left of the *D* in *Dana*, click the left mouse button, and then click the Decrease List Level button in the Paragraph group in the Home tab.

3. Position the insertion point immediately left of the *K* in *Karl* in Slide 5 and then promote the text to the previous level by pressing Shift + Tab.
4. Demote two of the names below *Script Consultants* by clicking immediately left of the *J* in *Jaime* and then clicking the Increase List Level button in the Paragraph group in the Home tab.
5. Position the insertion point immediately left of the *G* in *Genaro* and then press the Tab key.
6. Display Slide 6 in the Slide pane.

7 Position the mouse pointer on the bullet that displays before *Script Rewriting* until it turns into a four-headed arrow and then click the left mouse button.

This selects the text *Script Rewriting*. Refer to Table 2.1 for additional information on selecting text.

8 Press the Delete key.

This deletes the selected text.

9 Display Slide 5 in the Slide pane, position the mouse pointer on the bullet that displays before *Genaro Dufoe* until it turns into a four-headed arrow, and then click the left mouse button.

In Brief

Decrease Text Level Indent
Click Decrease List Level button or press Shift + Tab.

Increase Text Level Indent
Click Increase List Level button or press Tab.

Cut and Paste Text
1. Select text.
2. Click Cut button.
3. Position insertion point.
4. Click Paste button.

Copy and Paste Text
1. Select text.
2. Click Copy button.
3. Position insertion point.
4. Click Paste button.

10 Click the Cut button in the Clipboard group in the Home tab.

The keyboard shortcut to Cut text is Ctrl + X.

11 Position the mouse pointer immediately left of the *A* in *Allan Herron*, click the left mouse button, and then click the Paste button in the Clipboard group.

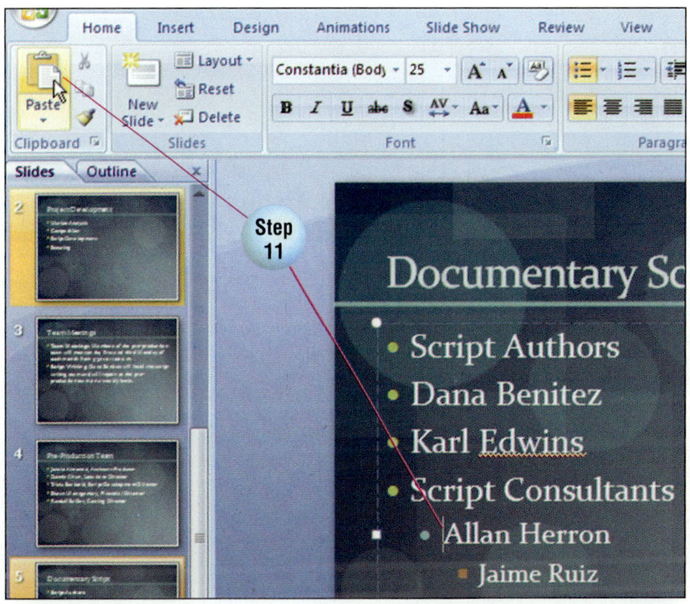

12 Select the text *Script Authors* and then click the Copy button in the Clipboard group.

The keyboard shortcut to copy text is Ctrl + C.

13 Make Slide 2 active, position the insertion point immediately left of the *S* in *Scouting*, and then click the Paste button in the Clipboard group.

If *Script Authors* and *Scouting* display on the same line, press the Enter key. The keyboard shortcut to paste text is Ctrl + V.

14 Save **PPS2-01.pptx**.

TABLE 2.1 Selecting Text

To select	Perform this action
entire word	Double-click word.
entire paragraph	Triple-click anywhere in paragraph.
entire sentence	Ctrl + click anywhere in sentence.
text mouse pointer passes through	Click and drag with mouse.
all text in selected object box	Click Select button in Editing group and then click *Select All*; or press Ctrl + A.

Activity 2.3

Applying Fonts and Font Effects

The Font group in the Home tab contains two rows of buttons. The top row contains buttons for changing the font and font size and a button for clearing formatting. The bottom row contains buttons for applying font effects such as bold, italic, underline, strikethrough, subscript, and superscript as well as a button for changing the case of selected text and font color.

Project

Certain text elements on slides in the documentary project presentation need to be highlighted to make them stand out. You will apply font effects to specific text and change the font size of selected text.

1. With **PPS2-01.pptx** open, display Slide 1 in the Slide pane.
2. Select the title *MARQUEE PRODUCTIONS* and then click the Italic button **I** in the Font group in the Home tab.

3. Select the subtitle *Documentary Project*, click the Increase Font Size button **A**, the Bold button **B** and then the Italic button **I** in the Font group.

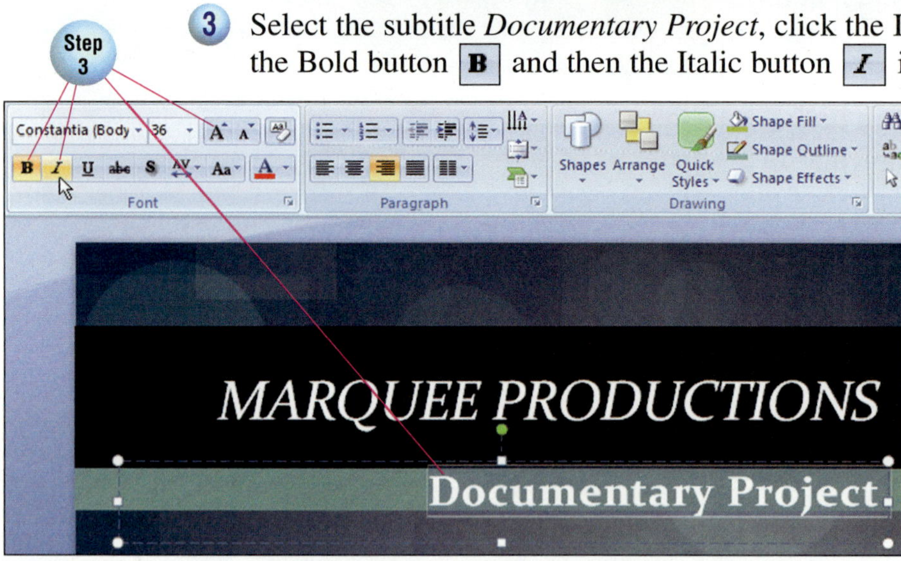

4. Make Slide 6 active in the Slide pane, select the text *Phase 1*, and then click the Underline button **U** in the Font group.
5. Select and then underline the text *Phase 2*.
6. Select and then underline the text *Phase 3*.
7. Make Slide 1 active.

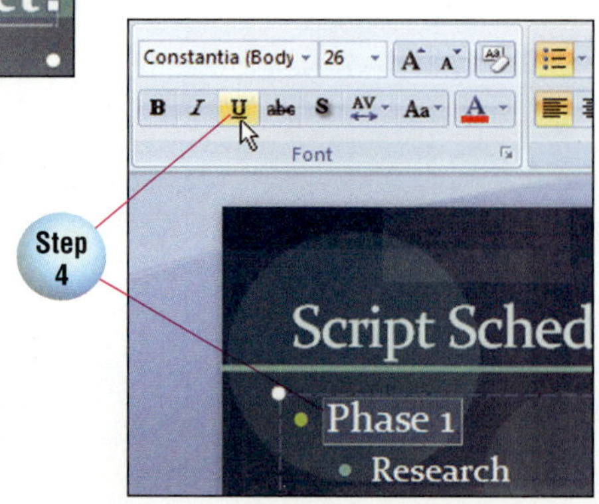

In Brief

Apply Font Effects with Font Group
1. Select text.
2. Click button in Font group.

8. Select the title *MARQUEE PRODUCTIONS*, click the Font button arrow in the Font group, scroll down the drop-down gallery (fonts display in alphabetical order), and then click *Calibri*.

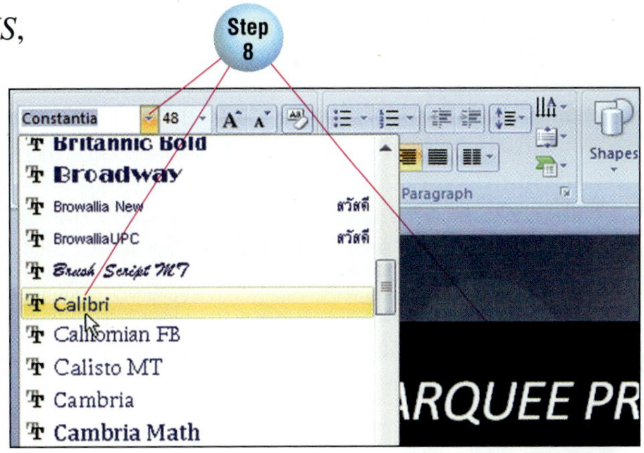

9. Select the subtitle *Documentary Project*, click the Font button arrow, and then click *Calibri* at the drop-down gallery.

   The drop-down gallery displays the most recently used fonts toward the beginning of the gallery.

10. Make Slide 6 active, select the text *Phase 1*, click the Underline button **U** to remove underlining, and then click the Bold button **B** to apply bold formatting.

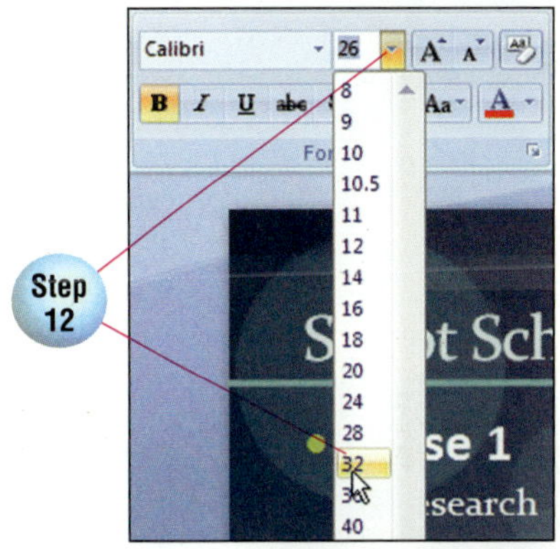

11. With *Phase 1* still selected, click the Font button arrow and then click *Calibri* at the drop-down gallery.
12. Click the Font Size button arrow, scroll down the drop-down gallery, and then click *32*.
13. Select the text *Phase 2*, remove the underlining, turn on bold, change the font to Calibri, and change the font size to 32.
14. Select the text *Phase 3*, remove the underlining, turn on bold, change the font to Calibri, and change the font size to 32.
15. Print slides 1 and 6. Begin by pressing Ctrl + P to display the Print dialog box.

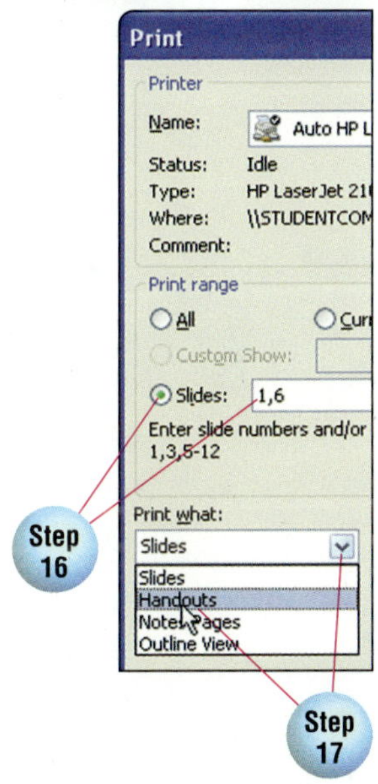

16. At the Print dialog box, click the *Slides* option in the *Print range* section and then type **1,6**.
17. Click the down-pointing arrow at the right side of the *Print what* text box and then click *Handouts* at the drop-down list.
18. Click OK to close the Print dialog box.

    The two slides print in miniature on the same page.

19. Save **PPS2-01.pptx**.

In Addition

Choosing Typefaces

A typeface is a set of characters with a common design and shape. PowerPoint refers to a typeface as a ***font***. Typefaces can be decorative or plain and are either monospaced or proportional. A monospaced typeface allots the same amount of horizontal space for each character while a proportional typeface allots a varying amount of space for each character. Proportional typefaces are divided into two main categories: serif and sans serif. A serif is a small line at the end of a character stroke. Consider using a serif typeface for text-intensive slides because the serifs help move the reader's eyes across the text. Use a sans serif typeface for titles, subtitles, headings, and short text lines.

Activity 2.4

Changing the Font at the Font Dialog Box; Replacing Fonts

In addition to buttons in the Font group in the Home tab, you can apply font formatting with options at the Font dialog box. With options at this dialog box, you can change the font, font style, and size; change the font color; and apply formatting effects such as underline, shadow, emboss, superscript, and subscript. If you decide to change the font for all slides in a presentation, use the Replace Font dialog box to replace all occurrences of a specific font in the presentation.

Project

Still not satisfied with the font choices in the documentary project presentation, you decide to change the font for the title and subtitle and replace the Tahoma font on the remaining slides.

1. With **PPS2-01.pptx** open, make Slide 1 active.
2. Select the title *MARQUEE PRODUCTIONS*.
3. Display the Font dialog box by clicking the Font group dialog box launcher in the Home tab.

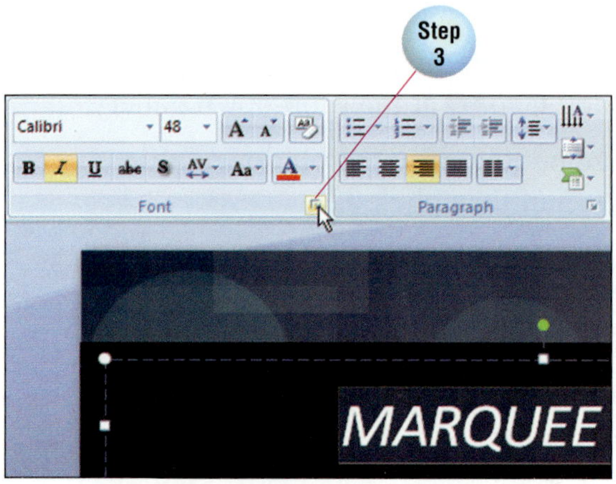

4. At the Font dialog box, click the down-pointing arrow at the right side of the *Font style* option box and then click *Bold Italic* at the drop-down list.
5. Select the current measurement in the *Size* text box and then type **50**.
6. Click the Font color button in the *All text* section and then click the *Teal, Accent 1, Lighter 60%* option.

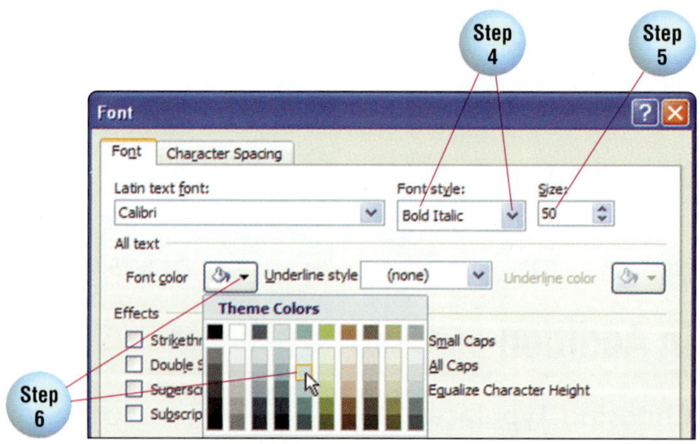

7. Click OK to close the Font dialog box.
8. Select the subtitle *Documentary Project*.
9. Click the Font group dialog box launcher.

10 At the Font dialog box, select the current measurement in the *Size* text box and then type **40**.

11 Click the Font color button in the *All text* section and then click the black color (*Black/Background 1*) that displays in the upper left corner of the color palette.

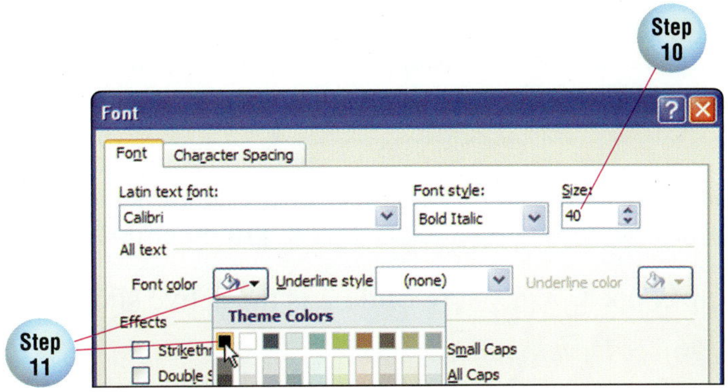

12 Click OK to close the Font dialog box.

13 Make Slide 2 active.

14 You decide to replace all occurrences of the Constantia font with the Cambria font. To begin, click the Replace button arrow in the Editing group in the Home tab and then click *Replace Fonts* at the drop-down list.

15 At the Replace Font dialog box, click the down-pointing arrow at the right side of the Replace option box and then click *Constantia* at the drop-down list.

16 Click the down-pointing arrow at the right side of the *With* option box and then click *Cambria* at the drop-down list. (You will need to scroll down the list box to display *Cambria*.)

17 Click the Replace button and then click the Close button.

18 Save **PPS2-01.pptx**.

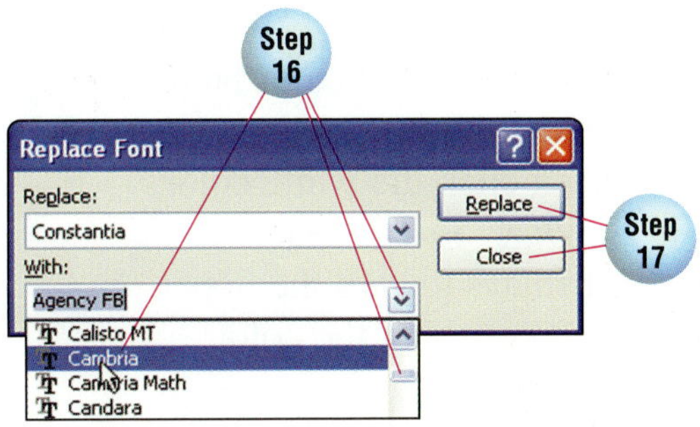

In Brief

Change Font at Font Dialog Box

1. Select text.
2. Click Font group dialog box launcher.
3. Click desired options at Font dialog box.
4. Click OK.

Change All Occurrences of Font

1. Click Replace button arrow, then click *Replace Fonts*.
2. At Replace Font dialog box, make sure desired font displays in *Replace* text box.
3. Press Tab.
4. Click down-pointing arrow at right of *With*, click desired font.
5. Click Replace button.
6. Click Close button.

In Addition

Choosing Presentation Typefaces

Choose a typeface for a presentation based on the tone and message you want the presentation to portray. For example, choose a more serious typeface such as Constantia or Times New Roman for a conservative audience and choose a less formal font such as Comic Sans MS, Lucida Handwriting, or Mistral for a more informal or lighthearted audience. For text-intensive slides, choose a serif typeface such as Constantia, Times New Roman, Georgia, or Bookman Old Style. For titles, subtitles, headings, and short text items, consider a sans serif typeface such as Calibri, Arial, Tahoma, or Univers. Use no more than two or three different fonts in each presentation. To ensure text readability in a slide, choose a font color that contrasts with the slide background.

Activity 2.5

Formatting with Format Painter

Use the Format Painter feature to apply the same formatting in more than one location in a slide or slides. To use the Format Painter, apply the desired formatting to text, position the insertion point anywhere in the formatted text, and then double-click the Format Painter button in the Clipboard group in the Home tab. Using the mouse, select the additional text to which you want the formatting applied. After applying the formatting in the desired locations, click the Format Painter button to deactivate it. If you need to apply formatting in only one other location, click the Format Painter button once. The first time you select text, the formatting is applied and the Format Painter is deactivated.

Project

Improve the appearance of slides in the documentary project presentation by applying a font and then using the Format Painter to apply the formatting to other text.

1. With **PPS2-01.pptx** open, make sure Slide 2 is the active slide.
2. Select the title *Project Development*.
3. Click the Font group dialog box launcher.
4. At the Font dialog box, click the down-pointing arrow in the *Latin text font* option box and then click *Calibri* at the drop-down list.

   You will need to scroll down the list to display *Calibri*.
5. Click the down-pointing arrow at the right side of the *Font style* option box and then click *Bold Italic* at the drop-down list.
6. Select the current measurement in the *Size* text box and then type **40**.
7. Click the Font color button in the *All text* section and then click the white color (*White, Text 1*) that displays toward the upper left corner of the color palette.
8. Click OK to close the Font dialog box.
9. At the slide, deselect the text by clicking in the slide outside the selected text.
10. Click anywhere in the title *Project Development*.
11. Double-click the Format Painter button in the Clipboard group in the Home tab.

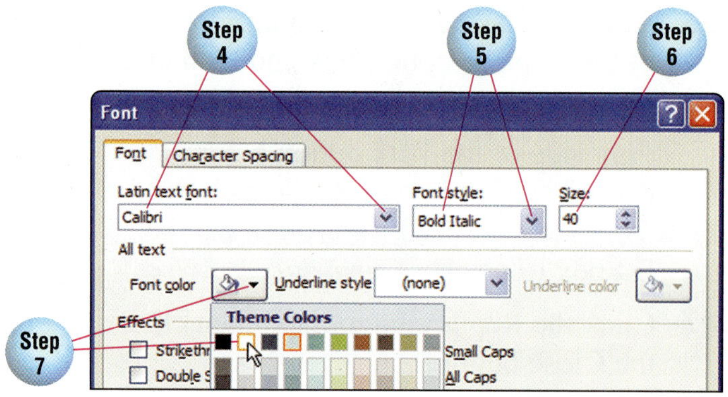

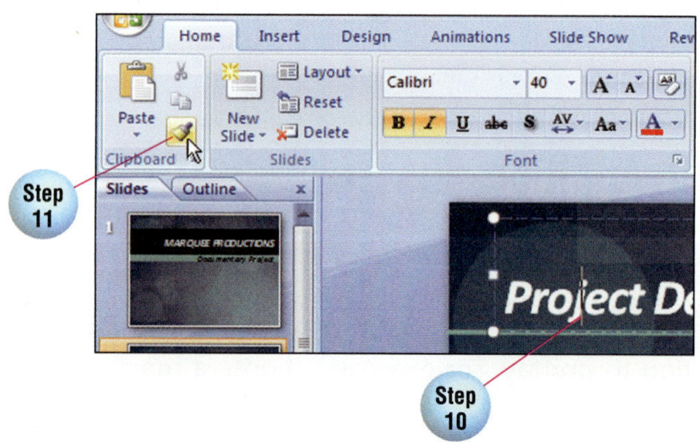

12 Click the Next Slide button to display Slide 3.

13 Using the mouse, click the word *Team* and then click the word *Meetings* in the title placeholder.

The mouse pointer displays with a paintbrush attached. This indicates that the Format Painter feature is active. You can also apply the formatting by selecting the title.

14 Click the Next Slide button to display Slide 4.

15 Using the mouse, click each word in the title *Pre-Production Team*.

PROBLEM

If the paintbrush is no longer attached to the mouse pointer, Format Painter has been turned off. Turn it back on by clicking in a slide title with the desired formatting and then double-clicking the Format Painter button.

16 Apply formatting to the titles in the remaining three slides.

17 When formatting has been applied to all slide titles, click the Format Painter button in the Clipboard group in the Home tab.

Clicking the Format Painter button turns off the feature.

18 Save **PPS2-01.pptx**.

In Brief

Format with Format Painter

1. Position insertion point on text containing desired formatting.
2. Double-click Format Painter button.
3. Select text to which you want to apply formatting.
4. Click Format Painter button.

In Addition

Choosing a Custom Color

Click the Font Color button at the Font dialog box, and a palette of color choices displays. Click the *More Colors* option and the Colors dialog box displays with a honeycomb of color options. Click the Custom tab and the dialog box displays as shown at the right. With options at this dialog box you can mix your own color. Click the desired color in the *Colors* palette or enter the values for the color in the *Red*, *Green*, and *Blue* text boxes. Adjust the luminosity of current color by dragging the slider located at the right side of the color palette.

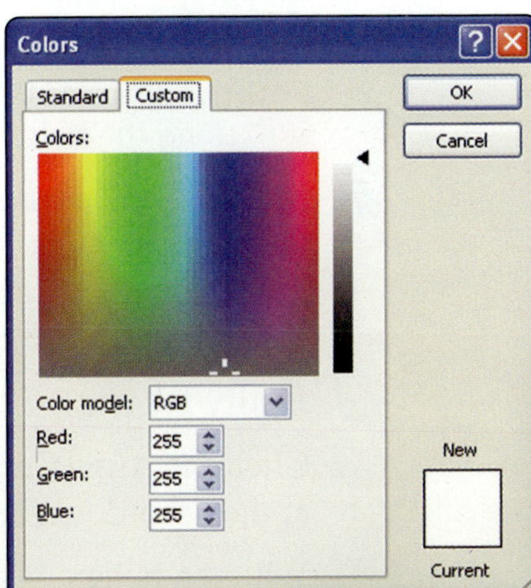

Activity 2.6

Changing Alignment and Line and Paragraph Spacing

The slide design template generally determines the horizontal and vertical alignment of text in placeholders. Text may be left-aligned, center-aligned, or right-aligned in a placeholder as well as aligned at the top, middle, or bottom of the placeholder. You can change alignment for specific text with buttons in the Paragraph group in the Home tab or with options from the Align Text drop-down list. Use options at the Line Spacing button drop-down list or the *Line Spacing* option at the Paragraph dialog box to change line spacing. The Paragraph dialog box also contains options for changing text alignment and indentation and spacing before and after text.

Project

Change the alignment for specific text in slides and improve the appearance of text in slides by adjusting the vertical alignment and paragraph spacing of text.

1. With **PPS2-01.pptx** open, make Slide 1 active.
2. Click anywhere in the text *Documentary Project* and then click the Center button in the Paragraph group in the Home tab.

   You can also change text alignment with the keyboard shortcuts shown in Table 2.2.

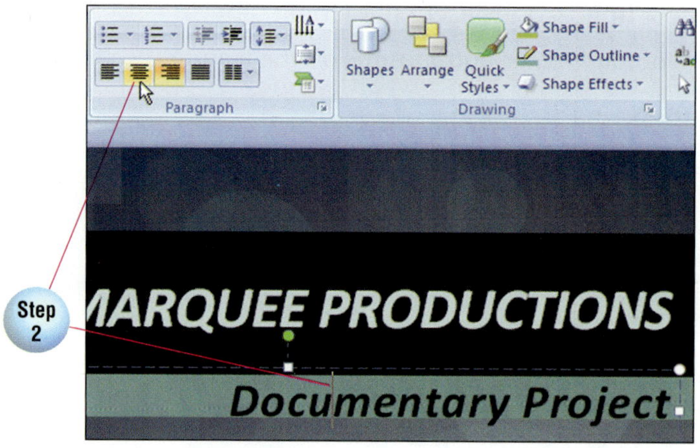

3. Click anywhere in the text *Marquee Productions* and then click the Center button.
4. Click the Align Text button in the Paragraph group and then click *Bottom* at the drop-down list.

   This aligns *MARQUEE PRODUCTIONS* along the bottom of the placeholder.

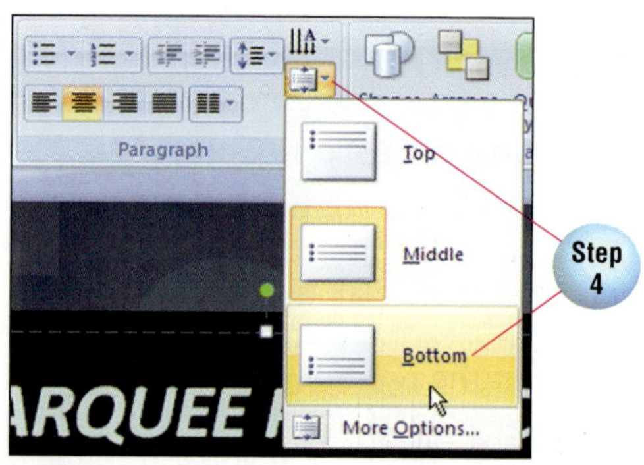

5. Make Slide 3 active (this slide contains the heading *Team Meetings*), click once in the bulleted text, and then press Ctrl + A to select all of the bulleted text.
6. Justify the text by clicking the Justify button in the Paragraph group.
7. Click the Align Text button in the Paragraph group and then click *Middle* at the drop-down list.
8. With the bulleted text still selected, click the Line Spacing button and then click *Line Spacing Options* at the drop-down list.

9 At the Paragraph dialog box, click once on the up-pointing arrow at the right side of the *After* option in the *Spacing* section.

This inserts *6 pt* in the *After* option box.

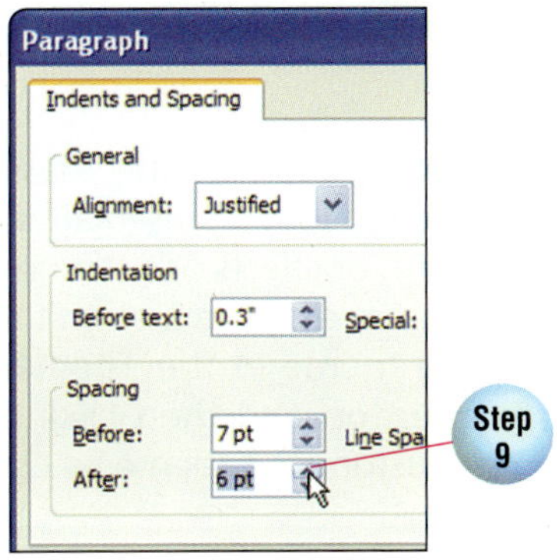

10 Click OK to close the dialog box.

11 Make Slide 4 active (contains the title *Pre-Production Team*).

12 Click once in the bulleted text and then select all the bulleted text by clicking the Select button Select in the Editing group in the Home tab and then clicking *Select All* at the drop-down list.

13 Click the Line Spacing button and then click *1.5* at the drop-down list.

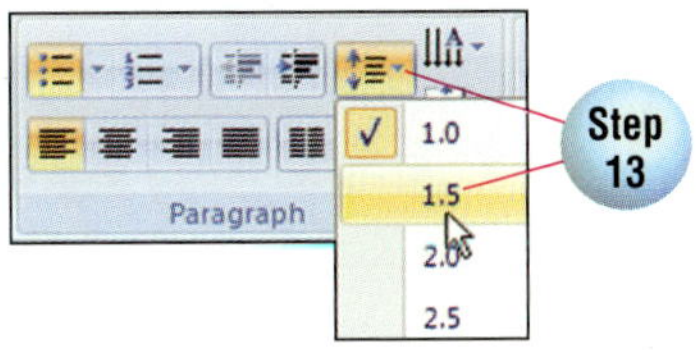

14 Make Slide 7 active (contains the title *Pre-Production Assignments*).

15 Click once in the bulleted text and then press Ctrl + A.

16 Click the Line Spacing button in the Paragraph group and then click *Line Spacing Options* at the drop-down list.

17 At the Paragraph dialog box, click once on the up-pointing arrow at the right side of the *After* option in the *Spacing* section.

This inserts *6 pt* in the *After* option box.

18 Click OK to close the dialog box.

19 Save **PPS2-01.pptx**.

In Brief

Change Horizontal Text Alignment

1. Select text or click in text paragraph.
2. Click desired alignment button in bottom row of Paragraph group.

Change Vertical Text Alignment

1. Click Align Text button.
2. Click desired alignment at drop-down list.

Change Line Spacing

1. Click Line Spacing button.
2. Click desired spacing at drop-down list.

OR

1. Click Line Spacing button.
2. Click *Line Spacing Options* at drop-down list.
3. At Paragraph dialog box, specify desired spacing.
4. Click OK.

TABLE 2.2 Alignment Shortcut Keys

Alignment	Keyboard Shortcut
left-align	Ctrl + L
center-align	Ctrl + E
right-align	Ctrl + R
justify-align	Ctrl + J

In Addition

Inserting a New Line

When creating bulleted text in a slide, pressing the Enter key causes the insertion point to move to the next line, inserting another bullet. Situations may occur where you want to create a blank line between bulleted items without creating another bullet. One method for doing this is to use the New Line command, Shift + Enter. Pressing Shift + Enter inserts a new line that is considered part of the previous paragraph.

Activity 2.7

Changing the Design Theme, Theme Color, and Theme Font

You can change the design theme applied to slides in a presentation or change the color, font, or effects of a theme. To change the design theme, click the Design tab and then click the desired theme in the Themes group or click the More button and then click the desired theme. You can customize a theme by changing the colors, fonts, and effects. Click the Colors button in the Themes group and then click the desired color scheme at the drop-down gallery. Click the Fonts button and then click the desired font at the drop-down gallery. Theme effects are sets of lines and fill effects. You can change theme effects with options from the Effects button drop-down gallery.

Project

You are not pleased with the design theme for the documentary project presentation and decide to apply a different theme and then change the color and font for the theme.

Marquee PRODUCTIONS

1. With **PPS2-01.pptx** open, click the Design tab.
2. Click the More button that displays at the right side of the Themes icons.

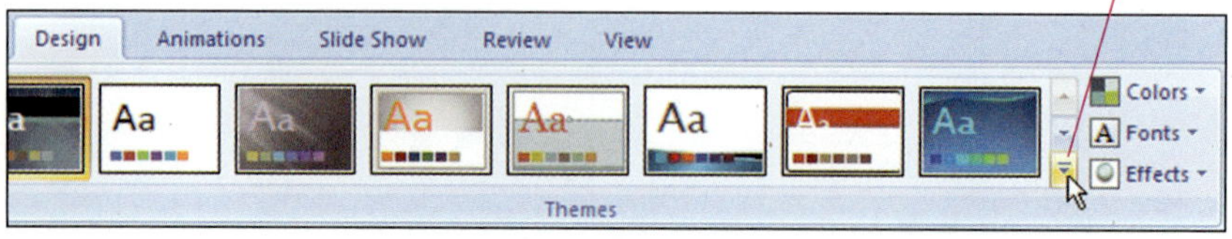

3. At the Themes drop-down gallery, click the *Oriel* theme.

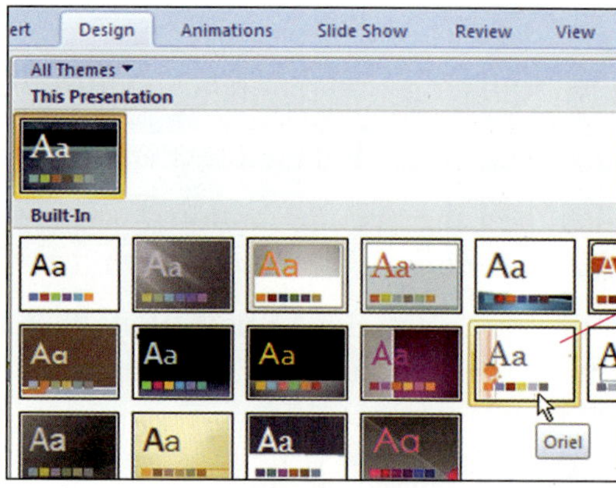

4. Run the presentation beginning with Slide 1 and notice how the theme change affected the slides.
5. Display the presentation in Normal view, make Slide 2 active, and then click the Design tab.
6. Click the Colors button Colors in the Themes group and then click *Foundry* at the drop-down gallery.

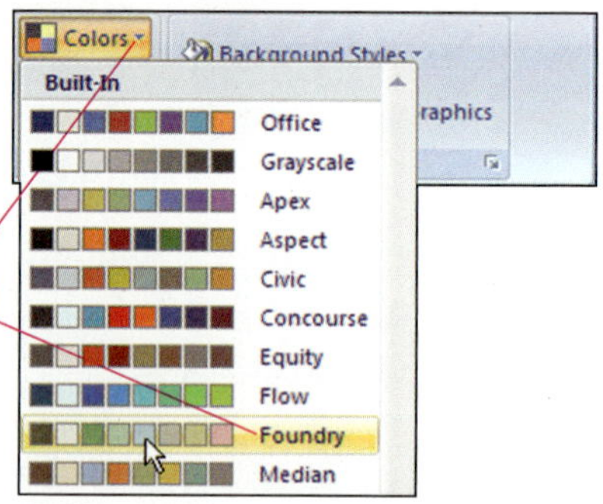

7. Run the presentation beginning with Slide 1 and notice how the color change affected the slides.
8. Click the Design tab, click the Colors button Colors, and then click *Urban* at the drop-down gallery.

   You may need to scroll down the drop-down gallery to display *Urban*.

9. Make Slide 2 active.
10. Click the Fonts button Fonts in the Themes group and then click *Opulent* at the drop-down gallery.

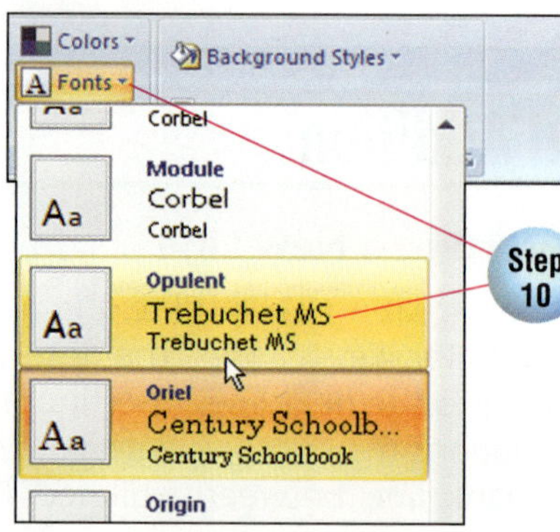

11 Apply a background style by clicking the Background Styles button [Background Styles] in the Background group and then clicking the *Style 10* option (second option from the left in the third row) at the drop-down gallery.

Background styles display in slides in a presentation but do not print.

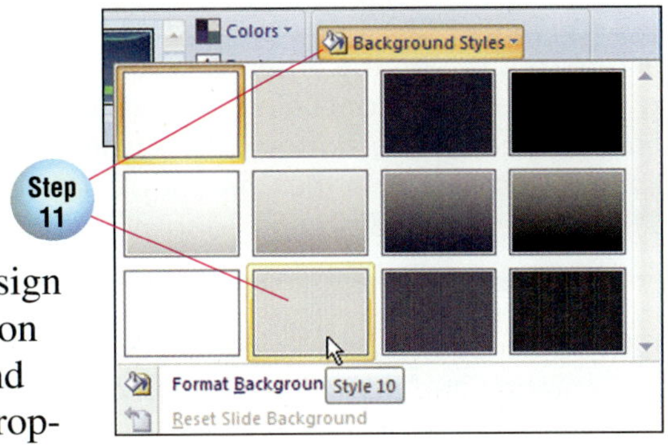

12 Run the presentation beginning with Slide 1.

13 After running the presentation, remove the background style by clicking the Design tab, clicking the Background Styles button [Background Styles] in the Background group, and then clicking *Style 1* at the drop-down gallery (first option from the left in the top row).

14 Make Slide 1 active.

15 Delete the title and placeholder. To do this, click in the title text, position the mouse pointer on the placeholder border until the pointer displays with a four-headed arrow attached, and then click the left mouse button. With the placeholder selected (displays with a solid border line), press the Delete key.

This deletes the title text and placeholder and then displays the title placeholder.

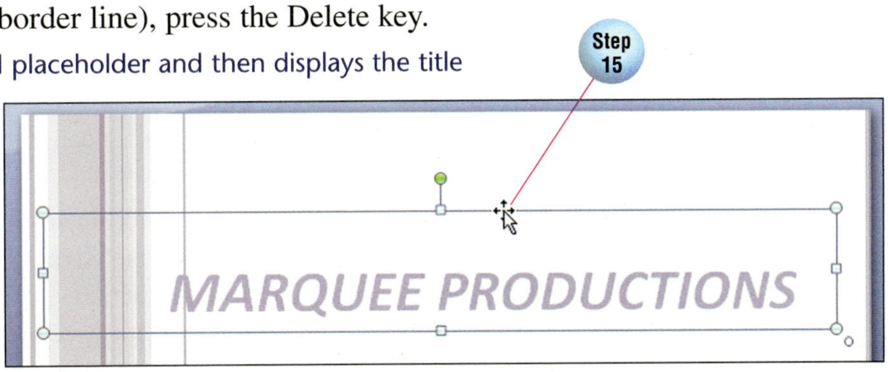

16 Position the mouse pointer on the CLICK TO ADD TITLE placeholder border until the pointer displays with a four-headed arrow attached, click the left mouse button, and then press the Delete key.

Slide 1 is now blank except for the formatting applied by the Oriel theme.

17 Save **PPS2-01.pptx**.

In Brief

Change Design Theme
1. Click Design tab.
2. Click More button at right side of Themes icons.
3. Click desired theme at drop-down gallery.

Change Theme Colors
1. Click Design tab.
2. Click Colors button.
3. Click desired option at drop-down gallery.

Change Theme Fonts
1. Click Design tab.
2. Click Fonts button.
3. Click desired option at drop-down gallery.

In Addition

Customizing Theme Colors

Design theme colors consist of four text colors, six accent colors, and two hyperlink colors. You can customize these theme colors with options at the Create New Theme Colors dialog box shown at the right. Display this dialog box by clicking the Colors button in the Themes group in the Design tab and then clicking *Create New Theme Colors* at the drop-down list. Change a color by clicking the desired color option in the *Theme colors* section and then clicking the desired color at the color palette. Changes made to colors display in the *Sample* section of the dialog box. You can name a custom color theme with the *Name* option in the dialog box. Click the Reset button to return the colors to the default theme colors.

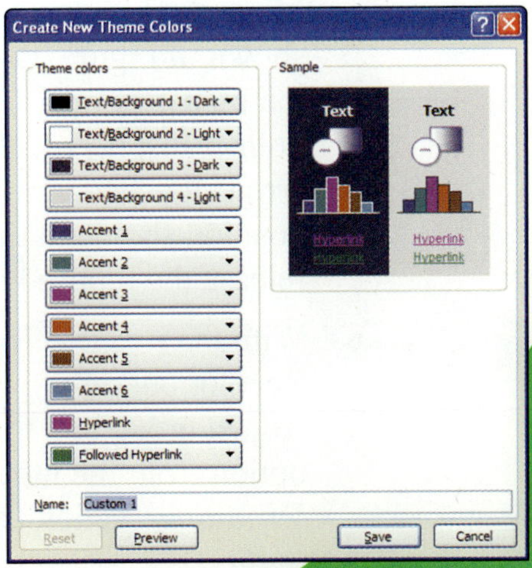

Activity 2.8

Inserting, Sizing, and Moving an Image

Add visual appeal to a presentation by inserting a graphic image such as a logo, picture, or clip art in a slide. Insert an image from a drive or folder with the Picture button in the Insert tab or by choosing a slide layout containing a Content placeholder. Click the Picture button in the Insert tab or click the picture image in the Content placeholder and the Insert Picture dialog box displays. At this dialog box, navigate to the desired drive or folder and then double-click the image. Use buttons on the Picture Tools Format tab to recolor the picture, apply a picture style, arrange the picture in the slide, and size the image. You can also size an image using the sizing handles that display around the selected image and move the image using the mouse.

Project

Chris Greenbaum has asked you to insert a slide at the beginning of the documentary project presentation and insert the company logo on the new slide.

Marquee PRODUCTIONS

1. With **PPS2-01.pptx** open, make sure Slide 1 is active.
2. Insert the company logo in the new slide as shown in Figure 2.1. To begin, click the Insert tab and then click the Picture button in the Illustrations group.

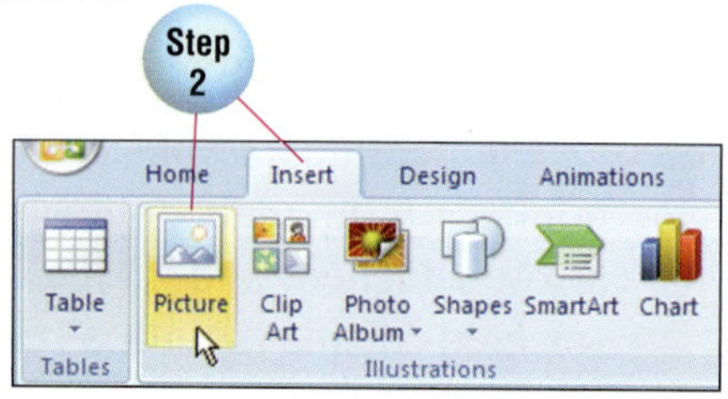

3. At the Insert Picture dialog box, navigate to the PowerPointS2 folder on your storage medium and then double-click the file named ***MPLogo.jpg***.

   The image is inserted in the slide, selection handles display around the image, and the Picture Tools Format tab is selected.

4. Increase the size of the logo by clicking in the *Shape Width* measurement box in the Size group, typing 7, and then pressing Enter.

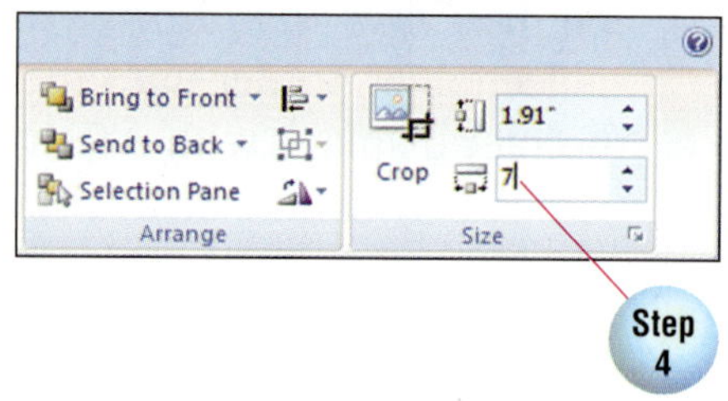

   When you change the width of the logo, the height automatically changes to maintain the proportions of the logo. You can also size an image using the sizing handles that display around the selected image. Use the middle sizing handles to increase or decrease the width of an image. Use the top and bottom handles to increase or decrease the height and use the corner sizing handles to increase or decrease both the width and height of the image at the same time.

5. Move the logo so it is positioned as shown in Figure 2.1. To do this, position the mouse pointer on the image until the pointer displays with a four-headed arrow attached, drag the image to the position shown in the figure, and then release the mouse button.
6. With the image selected, click the Recolor button in the Adjust group and then click the second option from the left in the *Light Variations* section (*Accent color 1 Light*).

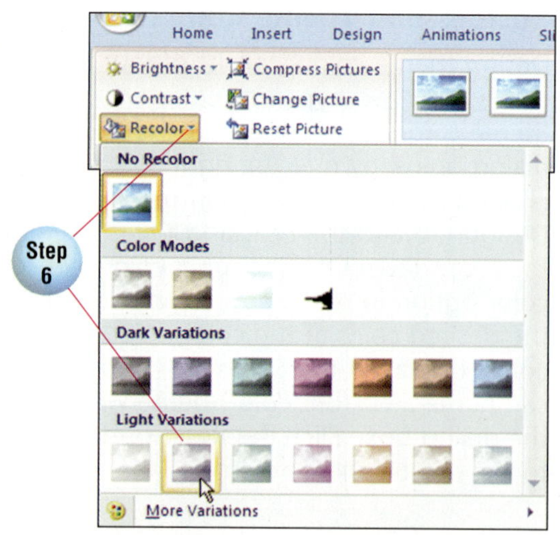

7 Click the *Beveled Matte, White* option in the Picture Styles group.

8 Click the Picture Effects button Picture Effects in the Picture Styles group, point to *Shadow*, and then click *Offset Right* at the drop-down gallery.

9 Click outside the logo to deselect it.

10 Save **PPS2-01.pptx**.

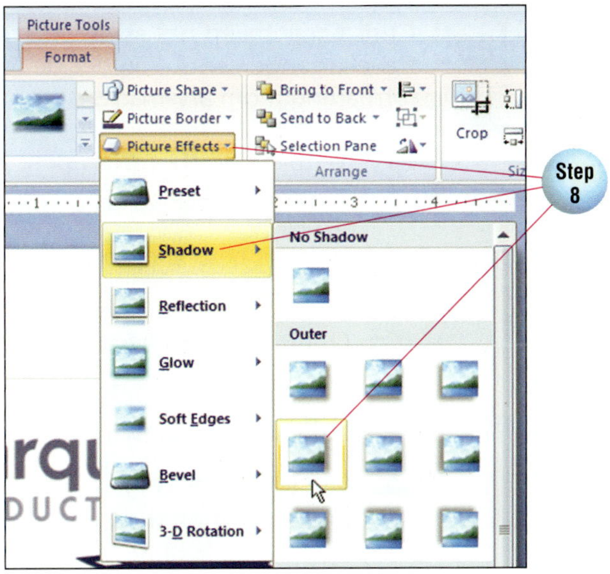

FIGURE 2.1 Slide 1

> **In Brief**
>
> **Insert Image**
> 1. Click Insert tab.
> 2. Click Picture button.
> 3. At Insert Picture dialog box, navigate to desired folder.
> 4. Double-click desired picture file.

In Addition

Formatting with Buttons in the Picture Tools Format Tab

You can format images in a slide with buttons and options in the Picture Tools Format tab shown below. Use buttons in the Adjust group to control the brightness and contrast of the image; recolor the image; change to a different image; reset the image to its original size, position, and color; and compress the image. Compress a picture to reduce resolution or discard extra information to save room on the hard drive or to reduce download time. Use buttons in the Picture Styles group to apply a predesigned style, insert a picture border, or apply a picture effect. The Arrange group contains buttons for positioning the image, wrapping text around the image, and aligning and rotating the image. Use options in the Size group to crop the image and specify the height and width of the image.

Activity 2.9

Inserting and Formatting Clip Art Images

Microsoft Office includes a gallery of clip art images you can insert in an Office program such as PowerPoint. Insert a clip art image at the Clip Art task pane. Display this task pane by clicking the Clip Art button in the Illustrations group in the Insert tab or clicking the Insert Clip Art button in a Content placeholder. At the Clip Art task pane, type a category in the *Search for* text box and then press Enter. In the list of clip art images that displays, click the desired image. The image is inserted in the slide and the Picture Tools Format tab is selected. Use buttons and options in this tab to format and customize the clip art image.

Project

Chris Greenbaum has asked you to include an additional slide containing information on travel arrangements. You decide to enhance the visual appeal of the slide by inserting and formatting a clip art image.

1. With **PPS2-01.pptx** open, make Slide 7 active.

   This is the last slide in the presentation.

2. Insert a new slide by clicking the New Slide button in the Slides group in the Home tab.
3. Click the text *CLICK TO ADD TITLE* and then type **Travel Arrangements**.
4. Click the text *Click to add text* and then type the bulleted text shown in the slide in Figure 2.2.
5. Click the Insert tab and then click the Clip Art button in the Illustrations group.

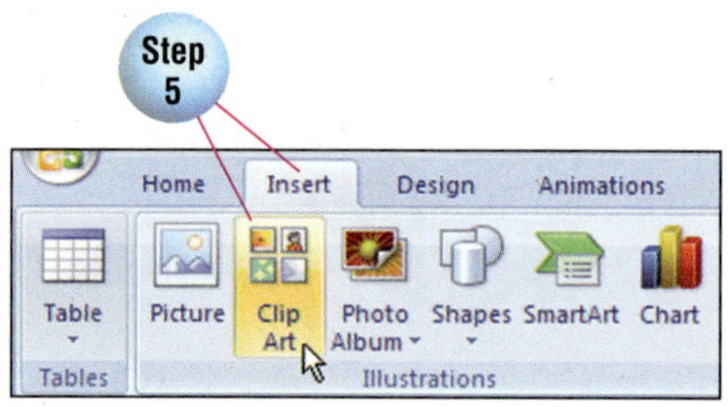

6. At the Clip Art task pane, type **transportation** in the *Search for* text box and then press Enter.

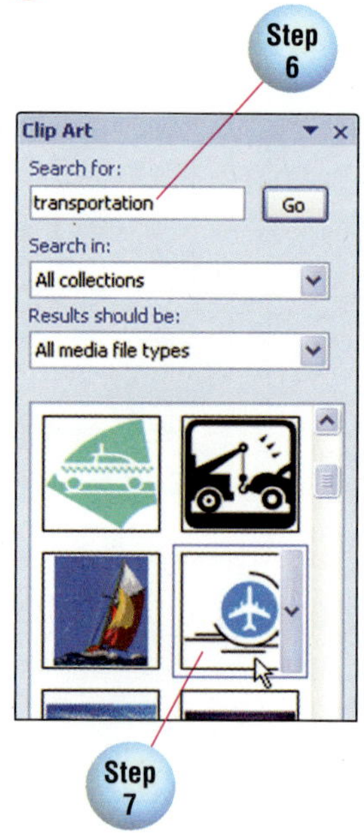

7. Scroll down the list of clip art images and then click the image shown in Figure 2.2.

? PROBLEM

If the jet image is not available, check with your instructor to determine which clip art image you should substitute.

FIGURE 2.2 Slide 1

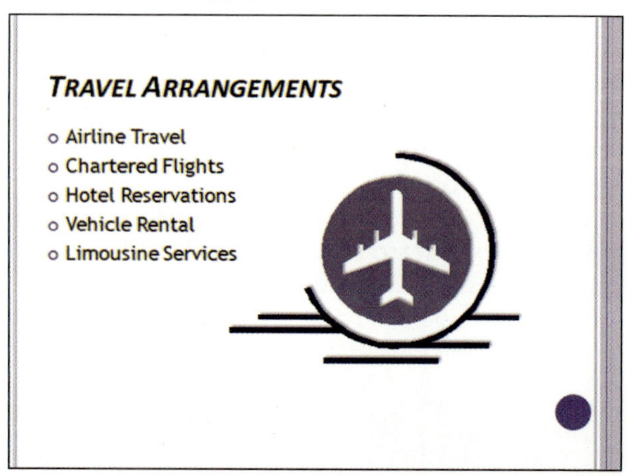

8. Close the Clip Art task pane by clicking the Close button (contains an X) that displays in the upper right corner of the task pane.
9. Recolor the image so it complements the slide design color scheme. To do this, click the Recolor button in the Adjust group in the Picture Tools Format tab and then click the *Accent color 1 Light* option in the *Light Variations* section.
10. Click the Brightness button in the Adjust group and then click *-20 %* at the drop-down gallery.
11. Click the Picture Effects button in the Picture Styles group, point to *Shadow*, and then click the *Offset Diagonal Top Right* option (first option from the left in the bottom row of the *Outer* section).
12. Click in the *Shape Height* measurement box, type **3.5**, and then press Enter.

    When you change the height measurement, the width measurement changes automatically to maintain the proportion of the image.
13. Using the mouse, drag the image so it is positioned as shown in Figure 2.2.
14. Make Slide 7 active and then click the Home tab.
15. Click on any character in the title *PRE-PRODUCTION ASSIGNMENTS* and then double-click on the Format Painter button in the Clipboard group.
16. Make Slide 8 active and then click each word in the title *TRAVEL ARRANGEMENTS*.

    This applies 40-point Calibri bold and italic formatting.
17. Click the Format Painter button to turn the feature off.
18. Save **PPS2-01.pptx**.

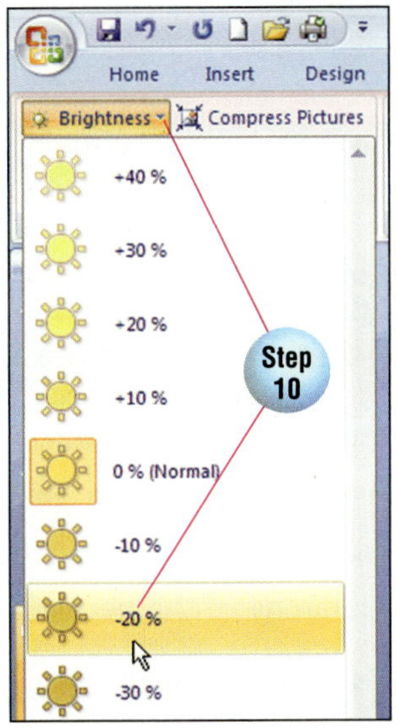

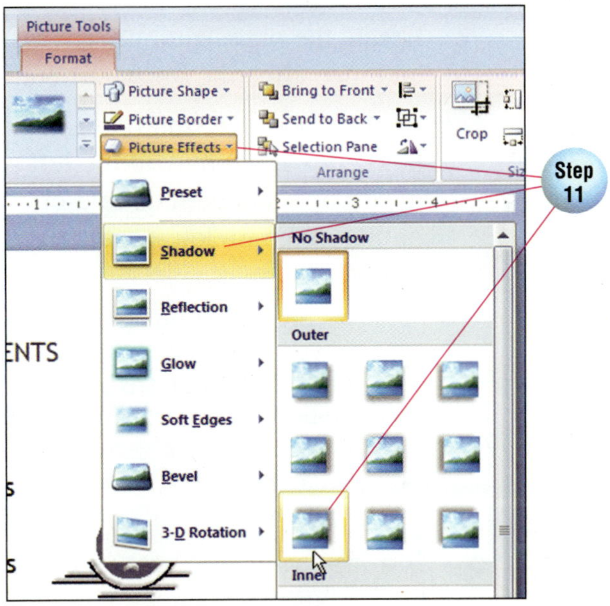

In Brief

Insert Clip Art Image
1. Click Insert tab.
2. Click Clip Art button.
3. At Clip Art task pane, type desired category, press Enter.
4. Double-click desired clip art image.

In Addition

Downloading Clip Art Images

If you are connected to the Internet, click the Clip art on Office Online that displays toward the bottom of the task pane. This takes you to the Office Online Clip Art window where you can search for and download a wide variety of images. Type the desired category in the search text box and then press Enter. At the list of clip art images, click the check box below the desired image. This inserts the image in the selection basket. When you have finished making all clip art selections, click the *Download* option in the *Selection Basket* section located at the left side of the window.

Activity 2.10

Inserting and Formatting a SmartArt Organizational Chart

If you need to visually illustrate hierarchical data, consider creating an organizational chart with SmartArt. To display a menu of SmartArt choices, click the Insert tab and then click the SmartArt button in the Illustrations group. This displays the Choose a SmartArt Graphic dialog box. At this dialog box, click *Hierarchy* in the left panel and then double-click the desired organizational chart in the middle panel. This inserts the organizational chart in the document. Some diagrams are designed to include text. You can type text in a diagram by selecting the shape and then typing text in the shape or you can type text in the *Type your text here* window that displays at the left side of the diagram.

Project

Chris Greenbaum has asked you to create a slide of an organizational chart illustrating the hierarchy of the people involved in production.

1. With **PPS2-01.pptx** open, make Slide 2 active and then click the New Slide button in the Slides group in the Home tab.
2. Create the organizational chart shown in Figure 2.3. To begin, click the Insert tab and then click the SmartArt button in the Illustrations group.
3. At the Choose a SmartArt Graphic dialog box, click *Hierarchy* in the left panel of the dialog box and then double-click the first option in the middle panel, *Organization Chart*.

   This displays the organizational chart in the slide with the SmartArt Tools Design tab selected. Use buttons in this tab to add additional boxes, change the order of the boxes, choose a different layout, apply formatting with a SmartArt style, and reset the formatting of the organizational chart.

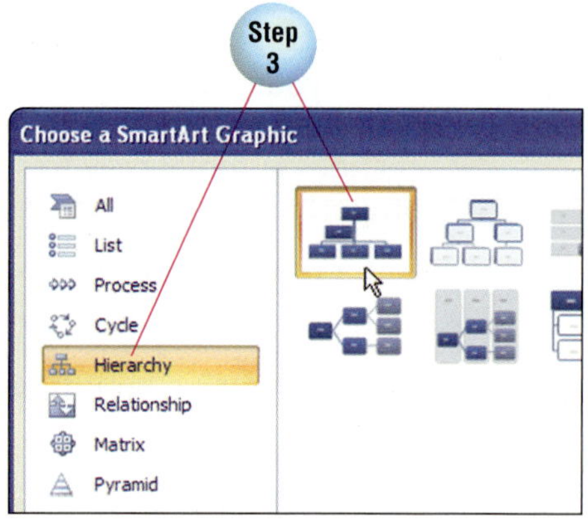

4. If a *Type your text here* window displays at the left side of the organizational chart, close it by clicking the Text Pane button in the Create Graphic group.

   You can also close the window by clicking the Close button that displays in the upper right corner of the window.
5. Delete one of the boxes in the organizational chart by clicking the border of the second box from the top at the left side to select the border and then pressing the Delete key.

   Make sure that the selection border that surrounds the box is a solid line and not a dashed line. If a dashed line displays, click the box border again. This should change it to a solid line.
6. With the bottom left box selected, click the Add Shape button in the Create Graphic group.

   This inserts a box below the selected box.
7. Click the middle bottom box and then click the Add Shape button.

   Your organizational chart should contain the same boxes as shown in Figure 2.3.

8. Click *[Text]* in the top box, type **Chris Greenbaum**, press the Enter key, and then type **Production Manager**. Click in each of the remaining boxes and type the text as shown in Figure 2.3.

9. Click the Change Colors button in the SmartArt Styles group in the SmartArt Tools Design tab and then click the second color option from the left in the *Colorful* section (*Colorful Range - Accent Colors 2 to 3*).

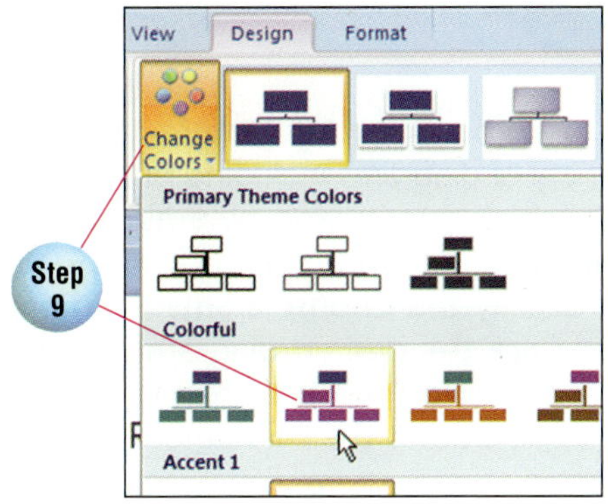

In Brief

Create Organizational Chart

1. Click Insert tab.
2. Click SmartArt button.
3. Click *Hierarchy* at Choose a SmartArt Graphic dialog box.
4. Double-click desired organizational chart.

10. Click the More button located at the right side of the SmartArt Styles group.

11. Click the *Cartoon* option located in the *3-D* section.

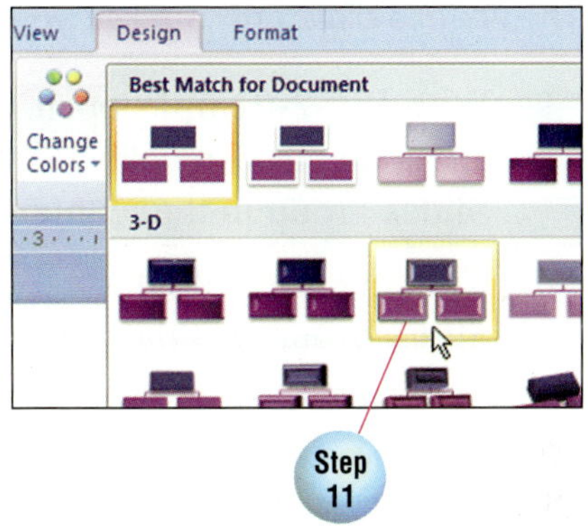

12. Click the SmartArt Tools Format tab.

13. Click the Size button located at the right side of the tab, click in the Width measurement box, type **8.4**, and then press Enter.

14. Click the text *Click to add title* and then type **Team Structure**.

15. Make Slide 2 active and then click the Home tab.

16. Click on any character in the title *Project Development* and then double-click the Format Painter button in the Clipboard group.

17. Make Slide 3 active and then click each word in the title *Team Structure*.

    This applies 40-point Calibri bold and italic formatting.

18. Click the Format Painter button to turn off the feature.

19. Save **PPS2-01.pptx**.

FIGURE 2.3 Organizational Chart

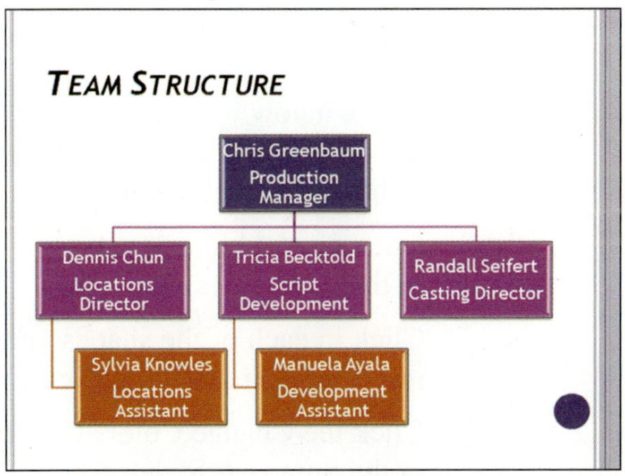

In Addition

Moving a SmartArt Organizational Chart or Diagram

Move an organizational chart by positioning the arrow pointer on the chart border until the pointer displays with a four-headed arrow attached, holding down the left mouse button, and then dragging the diagram to the desired location. You can increase the size of the diagram with the *Height* and *Width* options or by dragging a corner of the diagram border. If you want to maintain the proportions of the diagram, hold down the Shift key while dragging the border to increase or decrease the size.

Activity 2.11

Inserting and Formatting a SmartArt Diagram; Applying Animation to an Object

Use the SmartArt feature to create a variety of diagrams including process, cycle, relationship, matrix, and pyramid diagrams. Click the Insert tab and then click the SmartArt button to display the Choose a SmartArt Graphic dialog box. Click the desired diagram type in the left panel of the dialog box and then use the scroll bar at the right side of the middle panel to scroll down the list of diagram choices. Double-click a diagram in the middle panel of the dialog box and the diagram is inserted in the document. Use buttons in the SmartArt Tools Design tab and the SmartArt Tools Format tab to customize a diagram. You can animate an individual object in a slide with options from the Animate button located in the Animations group in the Animations tab.

Project

The finance director has asked you to include a slide containing a diagram of travel expenses.

1. With **PPS2-01.pptx** open, make Slide 9 active and then click the New Slide button in the Slides group in the Home tab.
2. Click the Layout button in the Slides group and then click the *Blank* layout at the drop-down list.
3. Create the diagram shown in Figure 2.4. To begin, click the Insert tab and then click the SmartArt button in the Illustrations group.
4. At the Choose a SmartArt Graphic dialog box, click *Relationship* in the left panel of the dialog box and then double-click the third option from the left in the fifth row (*Converging Radial*).
5. If necessary, close the *Type your text here* window by clicking the Close button that displays in the upper right corner of the window.
6. Click the Add Shape button in the Create Graphic group.
7. Click in each of the shapes and insert the text shown in Figure 2.4.
8. Click the Change Colors button in the SmartArt Styles group and then click the second color option from the left in the *Colorful* section (*Colorful Range - Accent Colors 2 to 3*).
9. Click the More button located at the right side of the SmartArt Styles group.

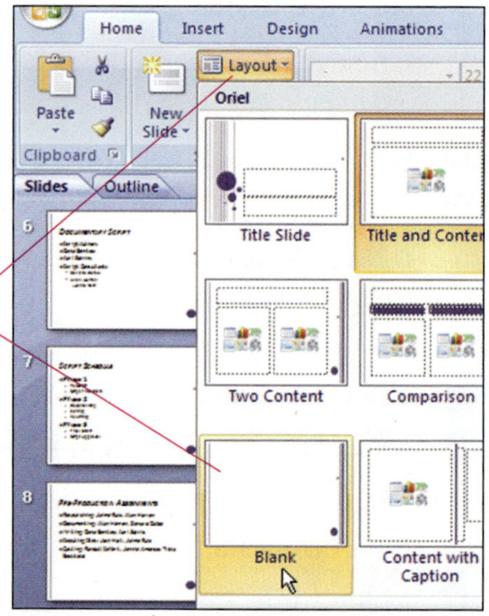

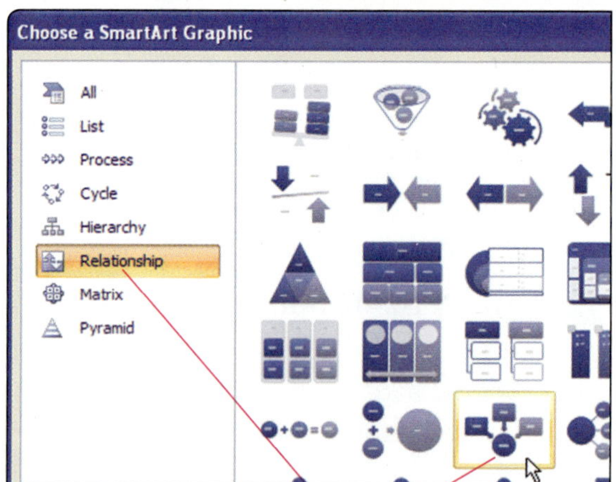

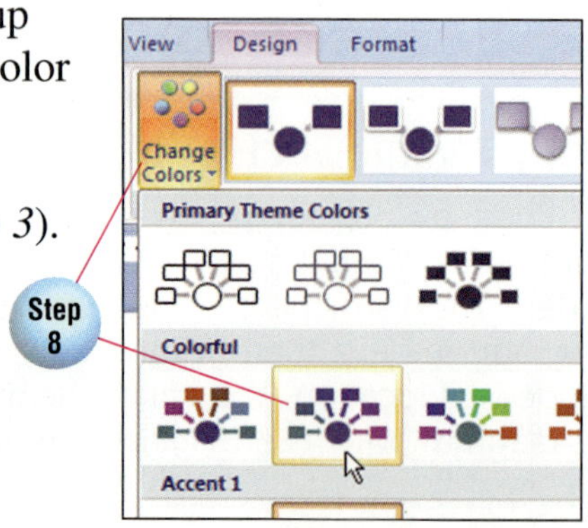

10. Click the *Cartoon* option located in the *3-D* section.
11. With the diagram selected, apply an animation. Begin by clicking the Animations tab.
12. Click the down-pointing arrow at the right side of the *Animate* option box in the Animations group and then click *From center one by one* in the *Fly In* section of the drop-down gallery.

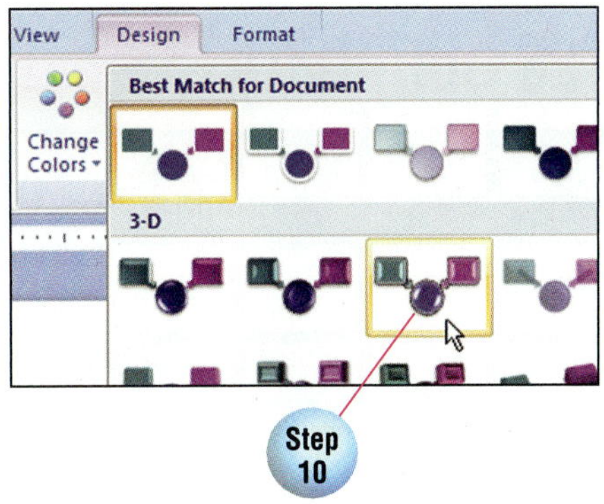

> **In Brief**
>
> **Create Diagram**
> 1. Click Insert tab.
> 2. Click SmartArt button.
> 3. Click desired category in left panel of Choose a SmartArt Graphic dialog box.
> 4. Double-click desired chart.

13. Make Slide 3 active and then click the organizational chart to select it.
14. Click the down-pointing arrow at the right side of the *Animate* option box and then click *By branch one by one* in the *Wipe* section.
15. Click Slide 5 to make it active and then click in the bulleted text to select the placeholder.
16. Click the down-pointing arrow at the right side of the *Animate* option box and then click *By 1st Level Paragraphs* in the *Fly In* section.

    Applying this animation creates a ***build*** for the bulleted items. A build displays important points in a slide one point at a time and is useful for keeping the audience's attention focused on the point being presented rather than reading ahead.

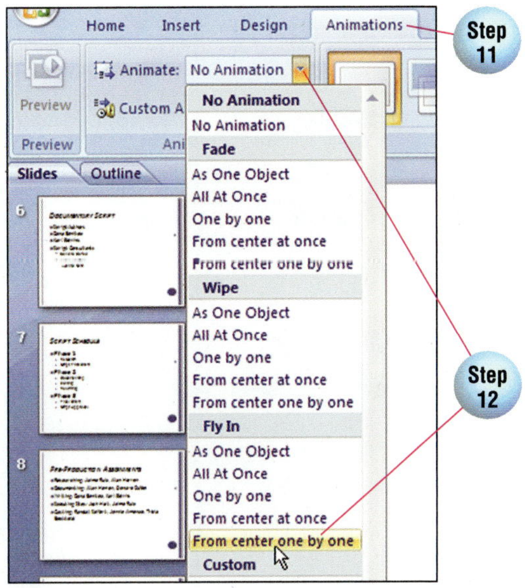

17. Make Slide 1 active and then run the presentation. Click the mouse button to advance slides and to display the individual organizational chart boxes, bulleted items, and diagram boxes.
18. Print the presentation as handouts with six slides per page. To do this, press Ctrl + P to display the Print dialog box.
19. At the Print dialog box, click the down-pointing arrow at the right side of the *Print what* option box and then click *Handouts* at the drop-down list. Make sure the *Slides per page* option displays as *6* and then click OK.
20. Save and then close **PPS2-01.pptx**.

FIGURE 2.4 Diagram

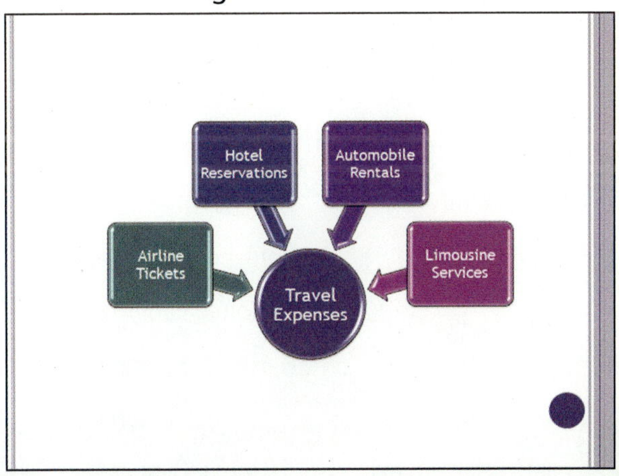

In Addition

Applying a Custom Animation

Apply custom animation to selected objects in a slide by clicking the Custom Animation button in the Animations group in the Animations tab. This displays the Custom Animation task pane at the right side of the screen. Use options in this task pane to control the order in which objects appear on a slide, specify entrance and exit effects, choose animation direction and speed, and specify how objects will appear in the slide.

Features Summary

Feature	Ribbon Tab, Group	Button	Keyboard Shortcut
align text left	Home, Paragraph		Ctrl + L
align text right	Home, Paragraph		Ctrl + R
align text vertically	Home, Paragraph		
animate object	Animations, Animations	Animate No Animation	
bold	Home, Font	B	Ctrl + B
center	Home, Paragraph		Ctrl + E
copy selected text	Home, Clipboard		Ctrl + C
cut selected text	Home, Clipboard		Ctrl + X
decrease font size	Home, Font		Ctrl + Shift + <
decrease text level	Home, Paragraph		Shift + Tab
delete slide	Home, Slides	Delete	Delete
design theme	Design, Themes		
font	Home, Font	Calibri	
font color	Home, Font		
Font dialog box	Font group dialog box launcher		Ctrl + Shift + F
font size	Home, Font	11	
Format Painter	Home, Clipboard		
hide slide	Slide Show, Set Up		
increase font size	Home, Font		Ctrl + Shift + >
increase list level	Home, Paragraph		Tab
insert clip art image	Insert, Illustrations		
insert picture	Insert, Illustrations		
insert SmartArt	Insert, Illustrations		
italic	Home, Font	I	Ctrl + I
justify	Home, Paragraph		Ctrl + J
line spacing	Home, Paragraph		
paste selected text	Home, Clipboard		Ctrl + V
theme colors	Design, Themes	Colors	
theme effects	Design, Themes	Effects	
theme fonts	Design, Themes	Fonts	
underline	Home, Font	U	Ctrl + U

Knowledge Check

Completion: In the space provided at the right, indicate the correct term, command, or option.

1. Delete a slide by selecting the slide and then clicking the Delete button in this group in the Home tab. ________________
2. The Hide Slide button is located in this tab. ________________
3. Increase the text level by clicking the Increase List Level button or by pressing this key on the keyboard. ________________
4. Decrease the text level by clicking the Decrease List Level button or by pressing these keys on the keyboard. ________________
5. The Cut button is located in this group in the Home tab. ________________
6. This is the keyboard shortcut to copy selected text. ________________
7. Use this feature to apply the same formatting in more than one location in a slide or slides. ________________
8. Press these keys on the keyboard to select all text in a placeholder. ________________
9. Click this button in the Paragraph group in the Home tab to change the text alignment to right. ________________
10. Change the vertical alignment of text in a placeholder with options from this button drop-down list. ________________
11. This dialog box contains options for changing line spacing and text alignment, indentation, and spacing. ________________
12. Click this tab to display the Themes group. ________________
13. Use buttons in this tab to recolor the selected picture, apply a picture style, arrange the picture, and size the picture. ________________
14. Display the Clip Art task pane by clicking the Insert tab and then clicking the Clip Art button in this group. ________________
15. Use this feature to create an organizational chart or a variety of diagrams. ________________
16. The Animate button is located in this tab. ________________

Skills Review

Review 1 Editing and Formatting a Presentation for Marquee Productions

1. Open the presentation named **MPAnnualMeeting.pptx** located in the PowerPointS2 folder.
2. Save the presentation with Save As and name it **PPS2-R1**.
3. Apply the Urban design theme to the slides in the presentation and change the theme colors to Civic.
4. Change to the Slide Sorter view and then select and delete Slide 5 (contains the title *Financial*).

5. Move Slide 7 (*Expenses*) immediately after Slide 3 (*Review of Goals*).
6. Move Slide 6 (*Future Goals*) immediately after Slide 7 (*Technology*).
7. Change to the Normal view and then make Slide 4 (*Expenses*) the active slide.
8. Decrease the indent of *Payroll* so it displays aligned at the left with *Administration*.
9. Decrease the indent of *Benefits* so it displays aligned at the left with *Payroll* and *Administration*.
10. Make Slide 6 (*Technology*) active and then increase the indent of *Hardware* to the next level, the indent of *Software* to the next level, and the indent of *Technical Support* to the next level.
11. Make Slide 7 (*Future Goals*) active, select the name *Chris Greenbaum*, and then click the Copy button. (Make sure you select only the name and not the space following the name.)
12. Make Slide 3 (*Review of Goals*) active.
13. Move the insertion point immediately to the right of *Overview of Goals*, press the Enter key, press the Tab key, and then click the Paste button. (Clicking the Paste button inserts the name *Chris Greenbaum*.)
14. Move the insertion point immediately to the right of *Completed Goals*, press the Enter key, press the Tab key, and then click the Paste button.
15. Make Slide 7 (*Future Goals*) active, select the name *Shannon Grey* (do not include the space after the name), and then click the Copy button.
16. Make Slide 3 (*Review of Goals*) active and then paste the name *Shannon Grey* below *Goals Remaining* at the same tab location as *Chris Greenbaum*.
17. Paste the name *Shannon Grey* below *Analysis/Discussion* at the same tab location as *Chris Greenbaum*.
18. Make Slide 1 active, select the text *Marquee Productions*, change the font to Candara, the font size to 54, and turn on bold.
19. Select the text *Annual Meeting*, change the font to Candara, the font size to 44, and turn on bold.
20. Make Slide 2 (*Agenda*) active, select the title *Agenda*, change the font to Candara, the font size to 48, and turn on bold.
21. Using Format Painter, apply the same formatting to the title in each of the remaining slides.
22. Make Slide 6 active, select all of the bulleted text, and then change the line spacing to 1.5.
23. Make Slide 8 active, select all of the bulleted text, and then change the spacing before paragraphs to 6.
24. Apply a transition and sound of your choosing to each slide in the presentation.
25. Run the presentation.
26. Print the presentation as handouts with all eight slides on one page.
27. Save and then close **PPS2-R1.pptx**.

Review 2 Formatting a Presentation for Performance Threads

1. Open **PTPresentation.pptx** and then save the presentation and name it **PPS2-R2**.
2. Make Slide 1 active and then insert the **PTLogo.jpg** file from the PowerPointS2 folder. (Use the Picture button in the Illustrations group in the Insert tab.) Change the height of the logo to 4″ and then position the logo in the middle of the slide.
3. Make Slide 3 active, select the bulleted text, and then change the line spacing to 1.5.
4. Make Slide 4 active, select the bulleted text, and then change the line spacing to 1.5.
5. Make Slide 2 active and then insert the organizational chart shown in Figure 2.5 with the following specifications:
   - Click the *Hierarchy* option in the left panel at the Choose a SmartArt Graphic dialog box and then double-click *Organization Chart*.
   - Change the color of the organizational chart to *Colorful Range - Accent Colors 3 to 4*.
   - Apply the *Cartoon* SmartArt style to the organizational chart.
   - Customize the boxes as shown and then type the text in each box as shown in Figure 2.5.
6. Make Slide 3 active and then insert the clip art image shown in Figure 2.6 with the following specifications:
   - At the Clip Art task pane, type **people** in the *Search for* text box, press Enter, and then click the image shown in Figure 2.6.
   - Change the height of the clip art image to 4″.
   - Recolor the clip art image to Sepia (located in the *Color Modes* section of the Recolor button drop-down gallery).
   - Position the clip art as shown in Figure 2.6.
7. Make Slide 5 active and then insert the diagram shown in Figure 2.7 with the following specifications:
   - Click the *Process* option in the left panel at the Choose a SmartArt Graphic dialog box and then double-click *Alternating Flow*.
   - Change the color of the diagram to *Colorful Range - Accent Colors 4 to 5*.
   - Apply the *Cartoon* SmartArt style to the diagram.
   - Type the text in the boxes as shown in Figure 2.7.
8. Make Slide 2 active, click the organizational chart, and then animate the organizational chart using the *Animate* option box in the Animations group in the Animations tab. (You determine the type of animation.)
9. Make Slide 5 active, click the diagram, and then animate the diagram using the *Animate* option box in the Animations group in the Animations tab. (You determine the type of animation.)
10. Run the presentation.
11. Print the presentation as handouts with all five slides on one page.
12. Save and then close **PPS2-R2.pptx**.

FIGURE 2.5 Slide 2

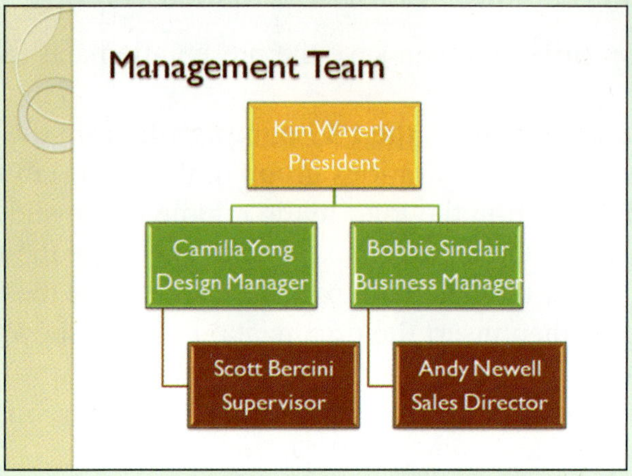

FIGURE 2.6 Slide 3

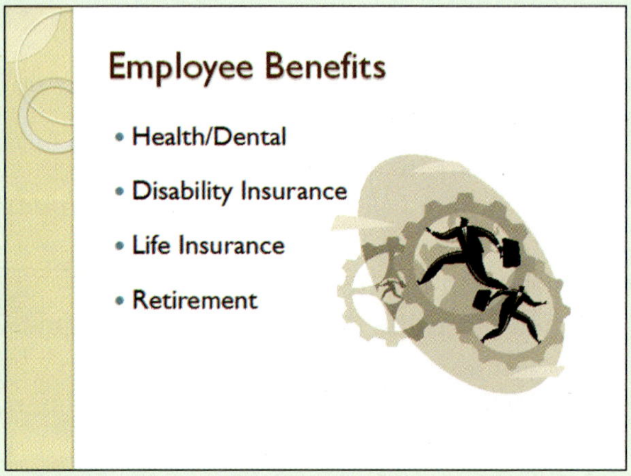

FIGURE 2.7 Slide 5

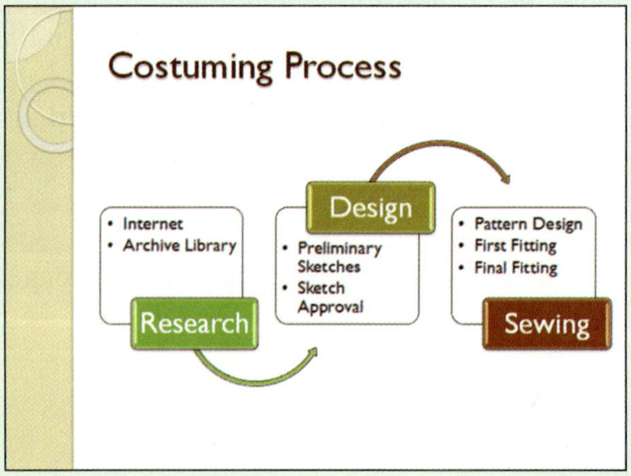

Skills Assessment

Assessment 1 Formatting a Presentation for Niagara Peninsula College, Theatre Arts Division

1. Open **NPCTheatreArts.pptx** and then save the presentation and name it **PPS2-A1**.
2. Change the theme colors to *Office* and change the theme font to *Paper*.
3. Move Slide 7 (*Associate Degrees*) immediately after Slide 2 (*Mission Statement*).
4. Move Slide 6 (*Semester Costs*) immediately after Slide 7 (*Fall Semester Classes*).
5. Make Slide 2 (*Mission Statement*) active, click in the paragraph below the title *Mission Statement*, and then change the alignment to justify.
6. Change the line spacing to 1.5 for the bulleted text in Slides 5 and 7.
7. Make Slide 5 active, select the bulleted text, and then apply italics formatting.
8. Make Slide 1 active and then insert the logo file named **NPCLogo.jpg** into the slide. Increase the size of the logo and then position it above the column ledge.
9. Make Slide 3 active and then insert a *Radial Cycle* diagram (located in the *Cycle* category in the Choose a SmartArt Graphic dialog box) in the slide. Insert the text *Theatre Arts Division* in the middle circle and then insert the following text in the remaining four circles: *Production*, *Acting*, *Set Design*, and *Interactive Media*. Apply a color and SmartArt style of your choosing to the diagram. Apply any other formatting you desire to enhance the visual display of the diagram. Position the diagram on the slide as necessary.
10. Make Slide 4 active and then insert an *Organization Chart* organizational chart (located in the *Hierarchy* category in the Choose a SmartArt Graphic dialog box) in the slide with the boxes and text shown in Figure 2.8. Apply a color and SmartArt style of your choosing to the organizational chart. Apply any other formatting you desire to enhance the visual display of the organizational chart. Position the chart on the slide as necessary.
11. Make Slide 7 active and then insert a clip art image related to "money." Size, position, and recolor the image so it enhances the slide.
12. Apply an animation of your choosing to the money clip art image.
13. Make Slide 3 active and then apply an animation of your choosing to the diagram.
14. Make Slide 4 active and then apply an animation of your choosing to the organizational chart.
15. Run the presentation.
16. Print the presentation as handouts with all eight slides on one page.
17. Save and then close **PPS2-A1.pptx**.

FIGURE 2.8 Slide 2 Organizational Chart

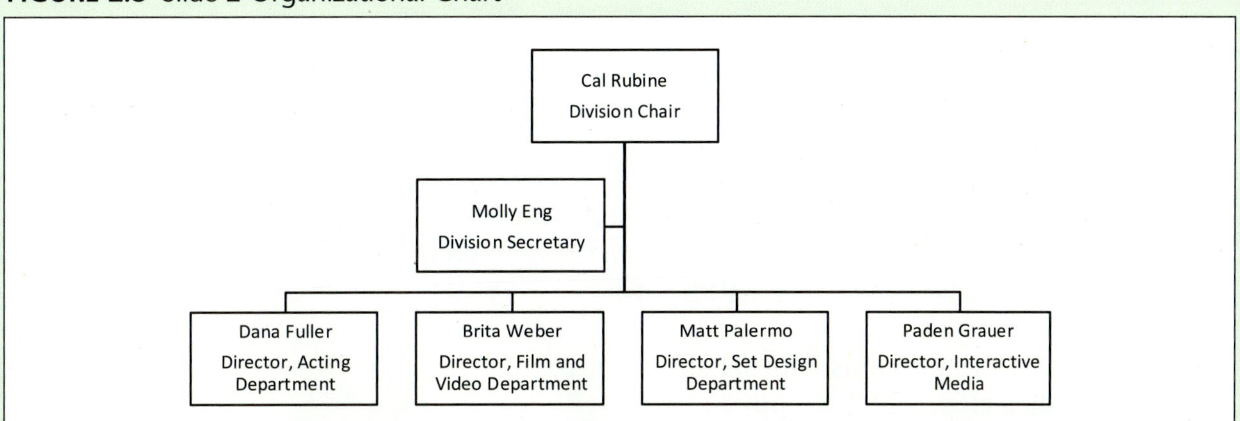

Assessment 2 Formatting a Presentation for First Choice Travel

1. Open **FCTVacations.pptx** and then save the presentation and name it **PPS2-A2**.
2. Change the theme colors to *Flow*.
3. Change the theme font to *Foundry*.
4. Increase the font size of the subtitle *Vacation Specials* located in Slide 1 (you determine the size).
5. Apply bold formatting and change to left alignment for each heading in Slides 2 through 6.
6. Make Slide 1 active and then insert the **FCTLogo.jpg** file into the slide. You determine the size and position of the logo.
7. Apply any formatting you feel is necessary to improve the appearance of each slide.
8. Apply a transition and sound to each slide in the presentation.
9. Run the presentation.
10. Print the presentation as handouts with all six slides on one page.
11. Save and then close **PPS2-A2.pptx**.

Assessment 3 Finding Information on Converting Text to a SmartArt Graphic

HELP

1. Open **PPS2-A2.pptx** and then save the presentation and name it **PPS2-A3**.
2. Use the Help feature to learn how to convert text in a slide to a SmartArt graphic.
3. After learning how to convert text, make Slide 4 active and then convert the bulleted text to a SmartArt diagram of your choosing.
4. Apply formatting to enhance the visual display of the diagram.
5. Save and then close **PPS2-A3.pptx**.

Assessment 4 Locating Information and Preparing a Presentation for The Waterfront Bistro

1. You are Dana Hirsch, manager of The Waterfront Bistro. The owners of the bistro are interested in opening a bistro in Toronto and you need to prepare a presentation on currently open bistros in and around the Toronto area. Connect to the Internet and search for information on bistros in Toronto. (One possible site for information is the *Toronto Life Restaurant Guide* site.)
2. Using PowerPoint, create a presentation on competing bistros that contains a title slide with the **TWBLogo.jpg** file inserted and include an appropriate subtitle. Create additional slides that include information on at least four bistros in and around Toronto. Create a slide for each bistro. You determine what information to put on the slide. (Consider information such as name, address, telephone number, Web site, type of food, hours, and so on.)
3. Insert an appropriate clip art image in any slide where it seems appropriate.
4. Apply a transition and sound to each slide in the presentation.
5. Save the presentation and name it **PPS2-A4**.
6. Run the presentation.
7. Print the slides as handouts with six slides per page.
8. Save and then close **PPS2-A4.pptx**.

Marquee Challenge

Challenge 1 Preparing a Presentation for Worldwide Enterprises

1. Create the presentation shown in Figure 2.9. Apply the *Median* design theme, the *Trek* theme colors, and the *Foundry* theme font. Insert the logo file named **WELogo.jpg** in Slide 1. Insert the clip art images in Slides 3 and 6 using *business* as the search category. Format, size, and position the clip art images as shown. Create and format the diagram shown in Slide 5.
2. Save the completed presentation and name it **PPS2-C1**.
3. Print the presentation as a handout with all six slides on the same page.

FIGURE 2.9 Challenge 1

Challenge 2 Preparing a Presentation for The Waterfront Bistro

1. Create the presentation shown in Figure 2.10. Apply the *Concourse* design theme, the *Office* theme colors, and then *Opulent* font. Insert the logo file named **TWBLogo.jpg** in Slides 1 and 2. Create and format the organizational chart in Slide 3. When creating the organizational chart, insert the appropriate boxes and then change the layout to *Hierarchy*. This will position the boxes as shown in the slide. Create and format the diagram shown in Slide 4. Insert the clip art image as shown in Slide 6 using *food* as the search category.
2. Save the completed presentation and name it **PPS2-C2**.
3. Print the presentation as a handout with all six slides on the same page.

FIGURE 2.10 Challenge 2

PowerPoint SECTION 3

Customizing a Presentation

Skills

- Copy and paste items using the Clipboard task pane
- Find and replace text
- Insert and format WordArt
- Draw and customize objects
- Display gridlines
- Insert a text box
- Copy and rotate shapes
- Create and format a table
- Insert action buttons
- Insert a hyperlink
- Format with a Slide Master
- Insert headers and footers
- Add sound and video
- Set and rehearse timings for a presentation

Student Resources

Before beginning this section:

1. Copy to your storage medium the PowerPointS3 subfolder from the PowerPoint folder on the Student Resources CD.
2. Make PowerPointS3 the active folder.

In addition to containing the data files needed to complete section work, the Student Resources CD contains model answers in PDF format for each of the projects in this section; model answers for end-of-section activities are not provided.

Projects Overview

Marquee PRODUCTIONS

Open a presentation on filming in Toronto, save the presentation with a new name, and then format the presentation and add visual appeal by inserting WordArt, shapes, text boxes, and a table. Open an existing presentation on a biography project, save the presentation with a new name, and then format and add visual appeal by inserting WordArt, shapes, text boxes, clip art, a logo, and a footer. Open an existing presentation on the annual meeting, apply a design theme, theme colors, and theme fonts and format using a slide master. Prepare and format a project schedule presentation.

Niagara Peninsula COLLEGE

Open a presentation on the Theatre Arts Division, save the presentation with a new name, and then format the presentation with headers and footers and enhance the presentation by inserting a sound clip and movie clip.

Performance Threads

Open a presentation on costume designs for Marquee Productions, save the presentation with a new name, and then format the presentation and add visual appeal by inserting a logo, WordArt, shapes, text boxes, a table, and a footer. Locate sites on the Internet where employees can do costume research and then prepare a presentation containing the information and a hyperlink to a site on the Internet.

First Choice TRAVEL

Open a presentation on a vacation cruise, save the presentation with a new name, and then format the presentation and add visual appeal by inserting a logo and sound clip, setting and rehearsing timings, and setting up the presentation to run continuously. Open a presentation on tours in Australia and New Zealand and then enhance the presentation by inserting WordArt, a footer, a sound clip, setting and rehearsing timings, and setting up the presentation to run continuously. Prepare a presentation on a Moroccan tour.

Activity 3.1

Using the Clipboard Task Pane

Display the Clipboard task pane and you can collect up to 24 different items and then paste them in various locations. To display the Clipboard task pane, click the Clipboard group dialog box launcher. The Clipboard displays at the left side of the screen. Select data or an object you want to copy and then click the Copy button in the Clipboard group. Continue selecting text or items and clicking the Copy button. To insert an item, position the insertion point in the desired location and then click the item in the Clipboard task pane. If the copied item is text, the first 50 characters display. After inserting all desired items, click the Clear All button to remove any remaining items.

Project

In preparation for a meeting on the Toronto location shoot, you will open the **MPToronto.pptx** presentation and then copy and paste multiple items in the appropriate slides.

1. Open **MPToronto.pptx** in the PowerPointS3 folder in your storage medium and then save the presentation and name it **PPS3-01**.
2. Display the Clipboard task pane by clicking the Home tab and then clicking the Clipboard group dialog box launcher. If items display in the Clipboard task pane, click the Clear All button located in the upper right corner of the task pane.
3. Make Slide 2 active and then select the name *Chris Greenbaum.*

   Make sure you do not select the space after the name.
4. With *Chris Greenbaum* selected, click the Copy button in the Clipboard group.

   When you click the Copy button, the name *Chris Greenbaum* is inserted as an item in the Clipboard task pane.

Step 4

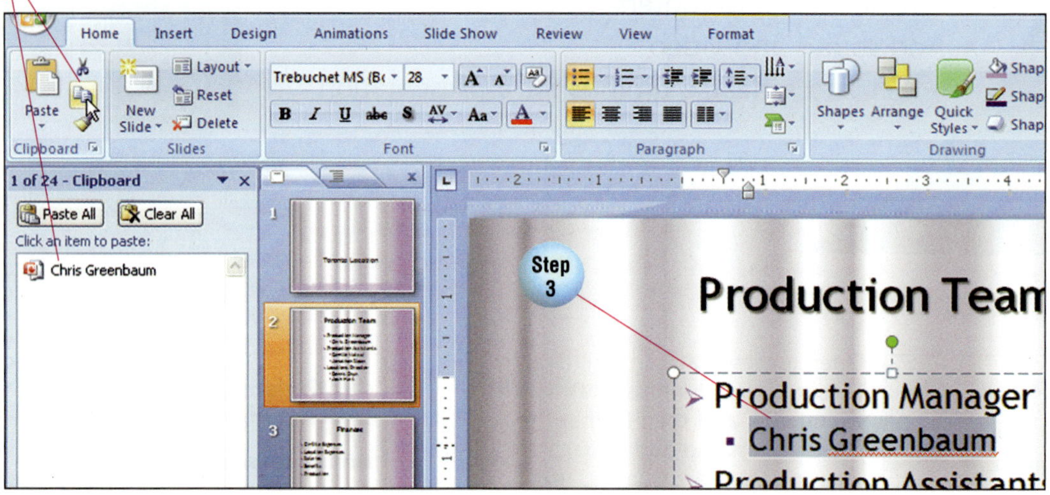

5. Select the name *Camille Matsui* (do not include the space after the name) and then click the Copy button. Select the name *Dennis Chun* (without the space after) and then click the Copy button. Select the name *Josh Hart* (without the space after) and then click the Copy button.
6. Make Slide 3 active, position the insertion point immediately to the right of *Location Expenses*, press the Enter key, and then press the Tab key.
7. Click the item in the Clipboard task pane representing *Chris Greenbaum.*

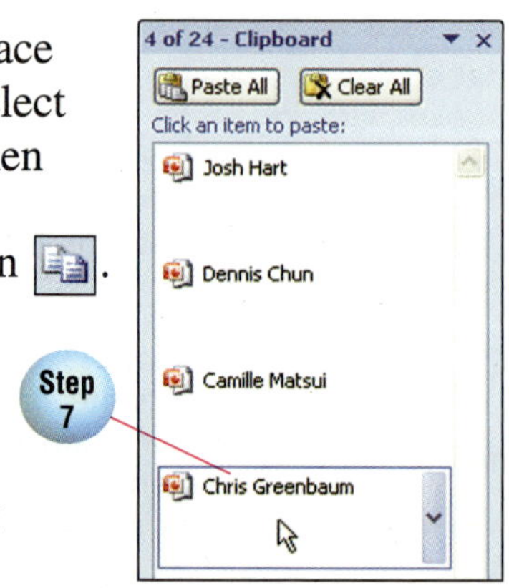

8. Position the insertion point immediately right of *Production*, press the Enter key, press the Tab key, and then click the item in the Clipboard task pane representing *Camille Matsui*.

9. Make Slide 4 active, position the insertion point immediately right of *Royal Ontario Museum*, press the Enter key, press the Tab key, and then click the item in the Clipboard task pane representing *Dennis Chun*.

10. Position the insertion point immediately to the right of *Island Airport*, press the Enter key, press the Tab key, and then click the item in the Clipboard task pane representing *Dennis Chun*.

11. Position the insertion point immediately to the right of *King Street*, press the Enter key, press the Tab key, and then click the item in the Clipboard task pane representing *Josh Hart*.

12. Click the Clear All button in the Clipboard task pane and then click the Close button located in the upper right corner of the task pane.

13. Make Slide 1 active and then insert the **MPLogo.jpg** file. To begin, click the Insert tab and then click the Picture button in the Illustrations group. Make PowerPointS3 the active folder and then double-click ***MPLogo.jpg***.

14. With the logo inserted in the slide, set the background color of the logo to transparent (so the slide design theme shows through) by clicking the Recolor button in the Adjust group in the Picture Tools Format tab and then clicking *Set Transparent Color* at the drop-down list.

    The mouse pointer displays with a tool attached.

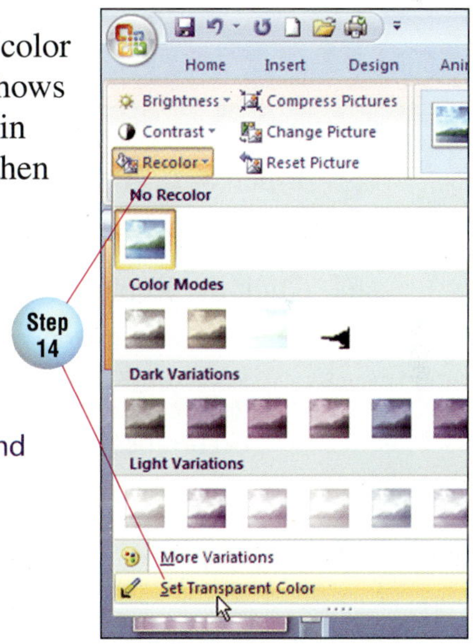

15. Position the mouse pointer in the white background color of the logo and then click the left mouse button.

    This makes the white background color transparent and displays the design theme behind the logo.

16. Size and move the logo so it better fills the slide.

17. Save **PPS3-01.pptx**.

In Brief

Use Clipboard Task Pane

1. Click Clipboard group dialog box launcher.
2. Select text, click Copy button.
3. Continue selecting text and clicking Copy button.
4. Position insertion point.
5. Click desired item in Clipboard task pane.
6. Insert additional items.
7. Click Clear All button.
8. Close Clipboard task pane.

In Addition

Clipboard Task Pane Options

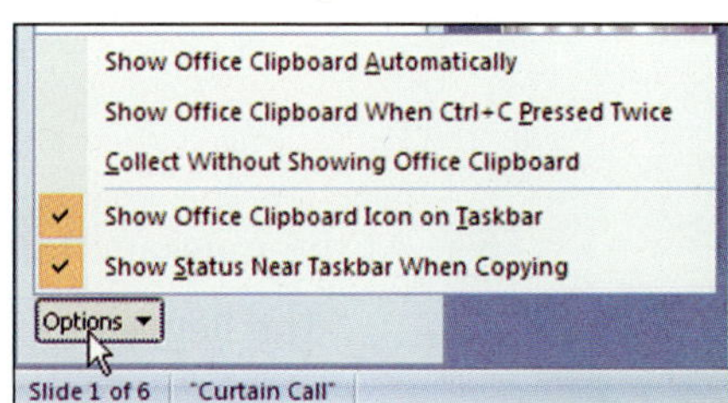

Click the Options button located toward the bottom of the Clipboard task pane and a drop-down menu displays with five options as shown at the right. Insert a check mark before those options that you want active. For example, you can choose to display the Clipboard task pane automatically when you cut or copy text, cut and copy text without displaying the Clipboard task pane, display the Clipboard task pane by pressing Ctrl + C twice, display the Office Clipboard icon near the Taskbar when the clipboard is active, and display the item message when copying items to the Clipboard.

Activity 3.2

Finding and Replacing Text

Use the Find and Replace feature to look for specific text or formatting in slides in a presentation and replace it with other text or formatting. Display the Find dialog box if you want to find something specific in a presentation. Display the Replace dialog box if you want to find something in a presentation and replace it with another element.

Project

A couple of people have been replaced on the Toronto location. Use the Replace feature to find names and replace them with new names in the Toronto location presentation.

1. With **PPS3-01.pptx** open, make Slide 1 active.
2. Camille Matsui has been replaced on the project by Jennie Almonzo. Begin the find and replace by clicking the Replace button Replace in the Editing group in the Home tab.

   This displays the Replace dialog box with the insertion point positioned in the *Find what* text box.

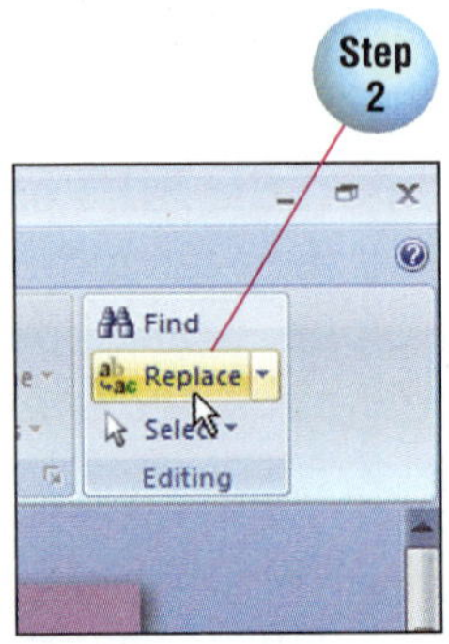

3. Type **Camille Matsui** in the *Find what* text box.
4. Press the Tab key and then type **Jennie Almonzo** in the *Replace with* text box.
5. Click the Replace All button.

   Clicking the Replace All button replaces all occurrences of the text in the presentation. If you want control over what is replaced in a presentation, click the Replace button to replace text or click the Find Next button to move to the next occurrence of the text.

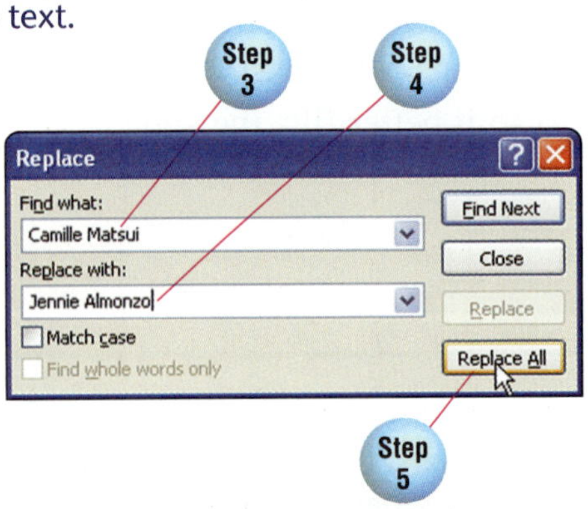

6. At the message telling you that two replacements were made, click OK.

   The Replace dialog box remains on the screen.

7 Josh Hart had to leave the project and is being replaced by Jaime Ruiz. At the Replace dialog box, type **Josh Hart** in the *Find what* text box.

When you begin typing the name *Josh Hart*, the previous name, *Camille Matsui*, is deleted.

8 Press the Tab key, type **Jaime Ruiz** in the *Replace with* text box, and then click the Replace All button.

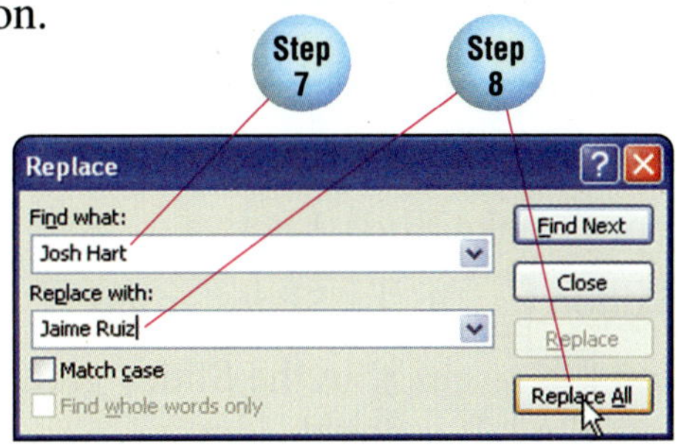

9 At the message telling you that two replacements were made, click OK.

The Replace dialog box remains on the screen.

10 The title *Manager* has been changed to *Director*. At the Replace dialog box, type **Manager** in the *Find what* text box.

11 Press the Tab key, type **Director** in the *Replace with* text box, and then click the Replace All button.

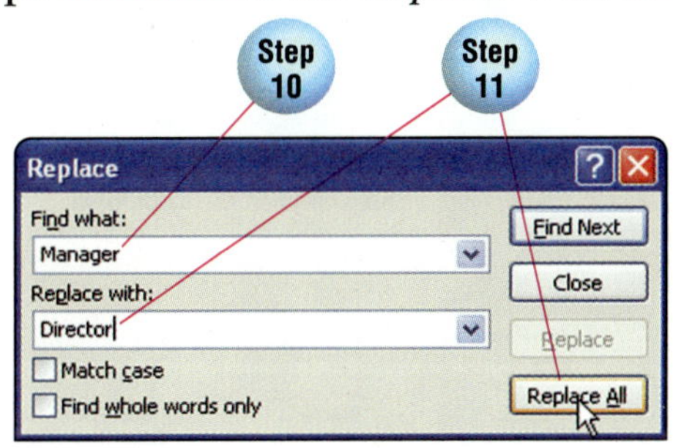

12 At the message telling you that one replacement was made, click OK.

13 Close the Replace dialog box by clicking the Close button located at the right side of the dialog box.

14 Save **PPS3-01.pptx**.

In Brief

Find and Replace Text

1. Click Replace button.
2. At Replace dialog box, type find text.
3. Press Tab, type replace text.
4. Click Replace All button.
5. Click Close button.

In Addition

Using Replace Dialog Box Options

The Replace dialog box shown at the right contains two options for completing a find and replace. Choose the *Match case* option if you want to exactly match the case of the find text. For example, if you look for *Company*, PowerPoint will stop at *Company* but not *company* or *COMPANY*. Choose the *Find whole words only* option if you want to find a whole word, not a part of a word. For example, if you search for *his* and did *not* select *Find whole words only*, PowerPoint will stop at t*his*, *his*tory, c*his*el, etc.

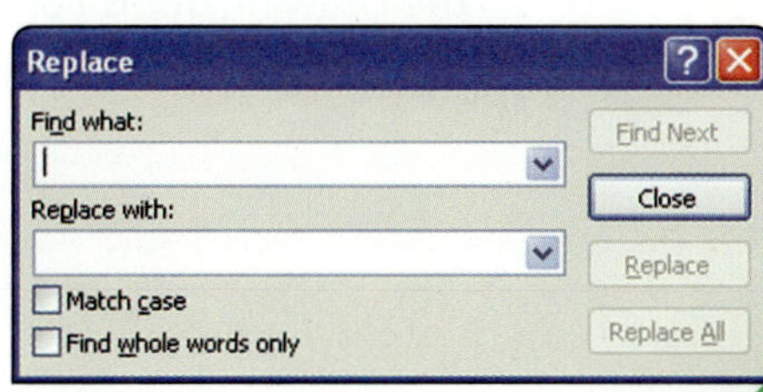

Activity 3.3

Inserting and Formatting WordArt

Use the WordArt application to distort or modify text and to conform to a variety of shapes. To insert WordArt, click the Insert tab, click the WordArt button in the Text group, and then click the desired WordArt style at the drop-down gallery. When WordArt is selected, the Drawing Tools Format tab displays. Use options and buttons in this tab to modify and customize WordArt.

Project

You want to improve the visual appeal of the slide on exterior shots by changing text to WordArt and also insert a new slide containing the title of the film using WordArt.

Marquee PRODUCTIONS

1. With **PPS3-01.pptx** open, make Slide 1 active.
2. Click the New Slide button in the Slides group.
3. Click the Layout button [Layout] in the Slides group and then click the *Blank* layout (first option from the left in the third row).

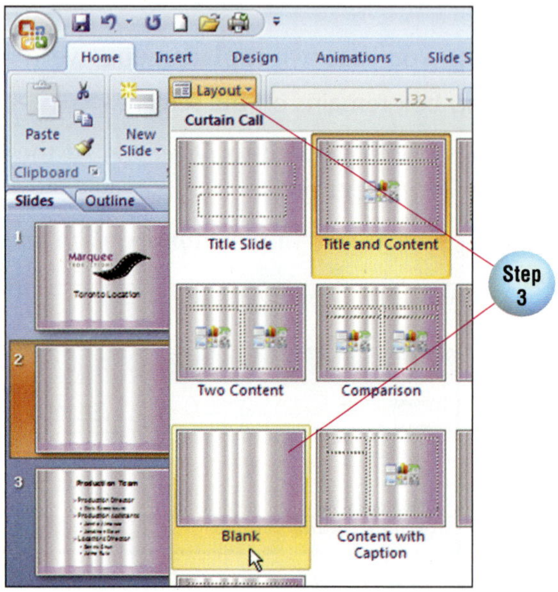

4. Insert WordArt by clicking the Insert tab, clicking the WordArt button in the Text group, and then clicking *Gradient Fill - Accent 1* (fourth option from the left in the third row).

   This inserts a text box with *Your Text Here* inside and also selects the Drawing Tools Format tab.

5. Type **Ring of Roses**.

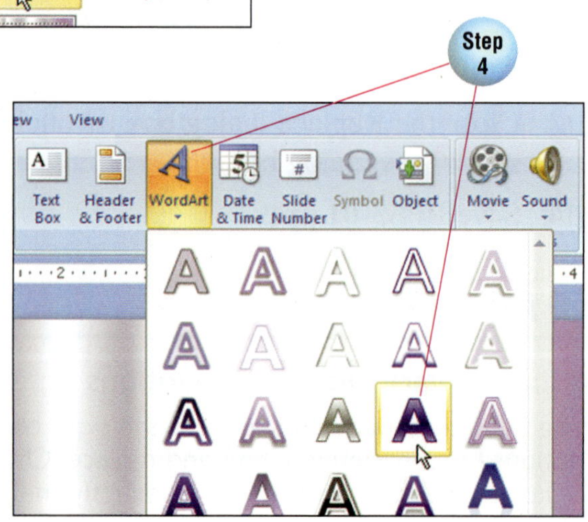

6. Select the text *Ring of Roses*, click the Text Effects button in the WordArt Styles group, point to *Transform* at the drop-down list, and then click *Deflate* at the drop-down gallery (second option from the left in the sixth row in the *Warp* section).
7. Click in the Shape Height measurement box in the Size group, type **3**, and then press Enter.
8. Click in the Shape Width measurement box in the Size group, type **7**, and then press Enter.

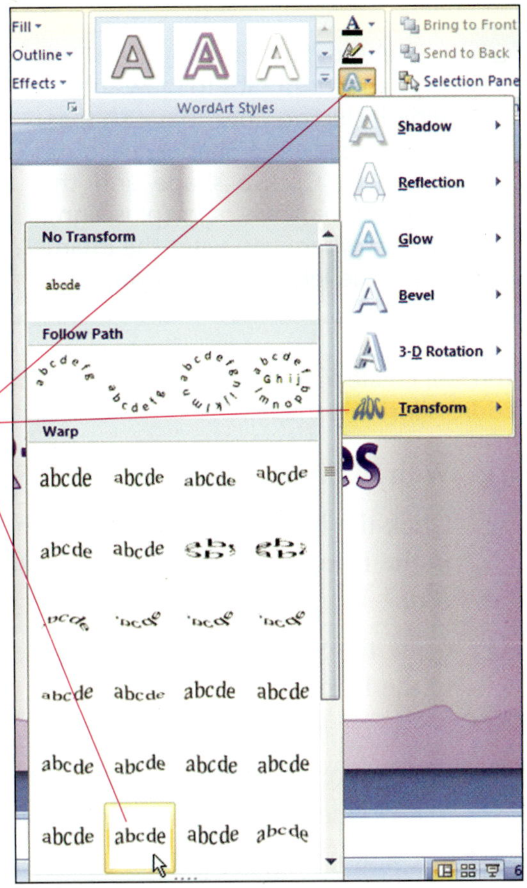

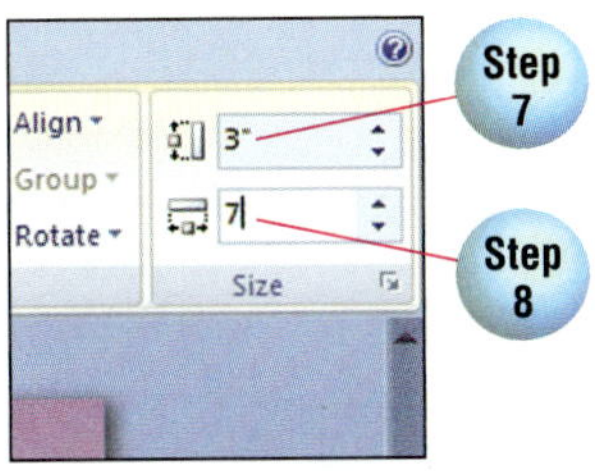

FIGURE 3.1 Slide 2

9. Drag the WordArt text so it is centered on the slide as shown in Figure 3.1.
10. Make Slide 4 active and then insert a clip art image related to money. You determine the size, position, and coloring of the clip art image.
11. Save **PPS3-01.pptx**.

In Brief

Insert WordArt

1. Click Insert tab.
2. Click WordArt button.
3. Click desired WordArt option.
4. Type WordArt text.
5. Apply desired formatting.

In Addition

Using Buttons and Options in the Drawing Tools Format Tab

When WordArt is selected in a slide, the Drawing Tools Format tab displays as shown below. You can draw a shape or text box with buttons in the Insert Shapes group. Apply a style, fill, outline, and effects to the WordArt text box with options in the Shape Styles group. Change the style of the WordArt text with options in the WordArt Styles group, specify the layering of the WordArt text with options in the Arrange section, and identify the height and width of the WordArt text box with options in the Size section.

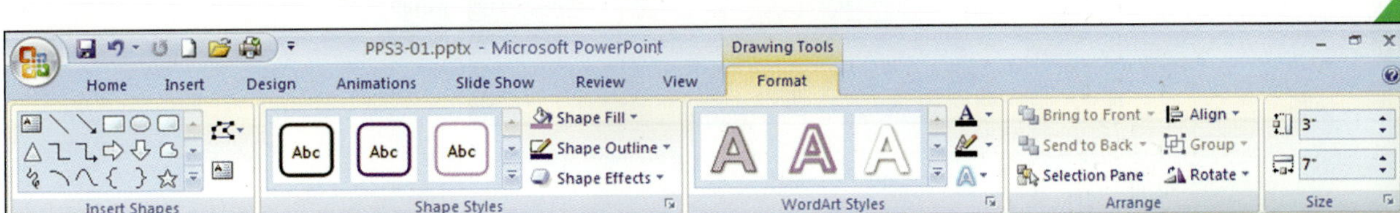

Activity 3.4

Drawing and Customizing Shapes

Use the Shapes button in the Home and Insert tabs to draw shapes in a slide including lines, basic shapes, block arrows, flow chart shapes, callouts, stars, and banners. Click a shape and the mouse pointer displays as crosshairs (plus sign). Position the crosshairs where you want the image to begin, hold down the left mouse button, drag to create the shape, and then release the mouse button. This inserts the shape in the slide and also displays the Drawing Tools Format tab. Use buttons in this tab to change the shape, apply a style to the shape, arrange the shape, and change the size of the shape. Use the Text Box button in the Text group in the Insert tab to type text in a shape.

Project

You will create a new slide for the Toronto site presentation that includes the Toronto office address inside a shape.

1. With **PPS3-01.pptx** open, make Slide 2 active.
2. Click the New Slide button in the Slides group in the Home tab. (Make sure the slide layout is *Blank*.)
3. Click the Shapes button in the Drawing group in the Home tab.
4. Click *Horizontal Scroll* at the drop-down list (sixth option from the left in the bottom row of the *Stars and Banners* section).
5. Position the mouse pointer in the slide, hold down the left mouse button, drag to create the shape as shown below, and then release the mouse button.

   If you are not satisfied with the size and shape of the image, press the Delete key to remove the image and then draw the image again.

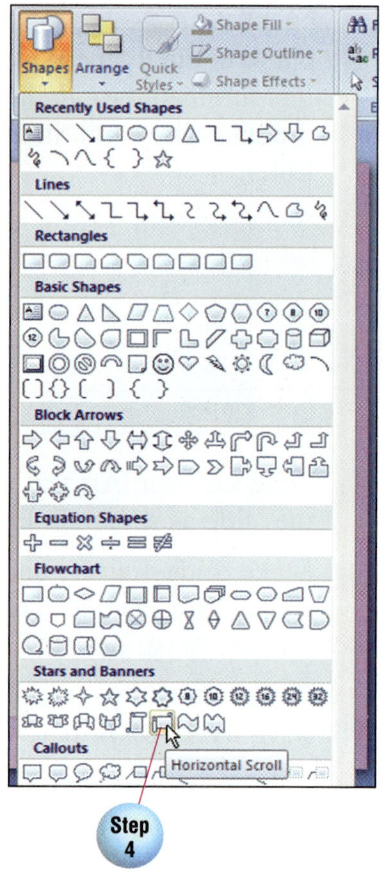

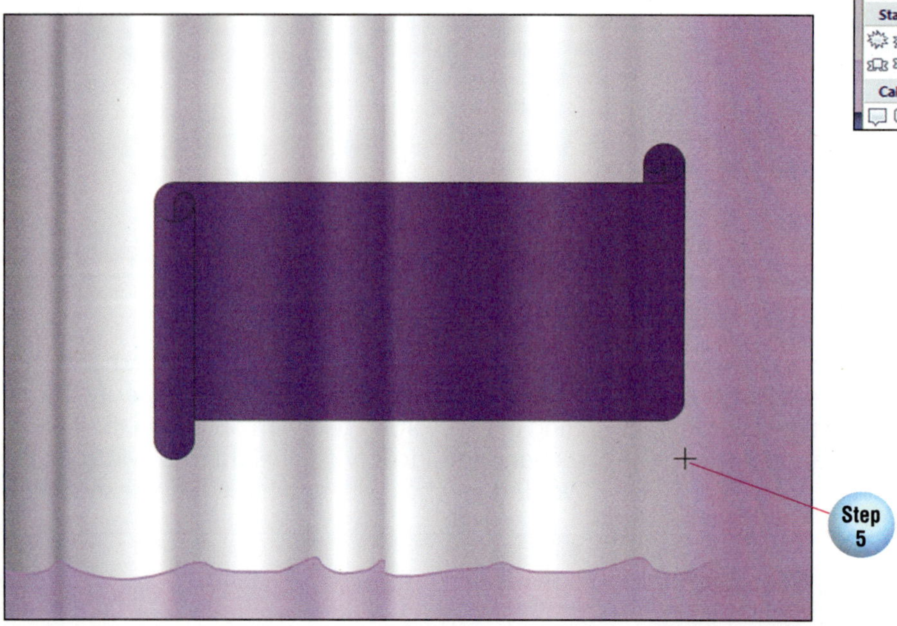

6. With the image selected, change the fill by clicking the Shape Fill button arrow in the Drawing group and then clicking the *Lavender, Accent 5, Lighter 60%* option.

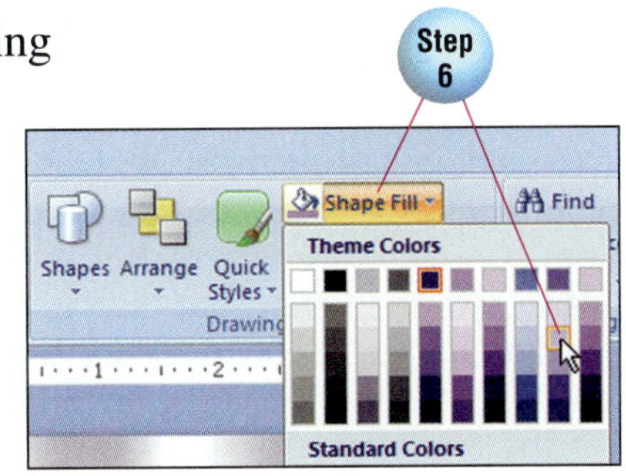

7. Click the Drawing Tools Format tab.
8. Click the Text Box button in the Insert Shapes group and then click inside the shape.

   When you click the Text Box button, the mouse pointer displays as a vertical line with a short horizontal line at the bottom.

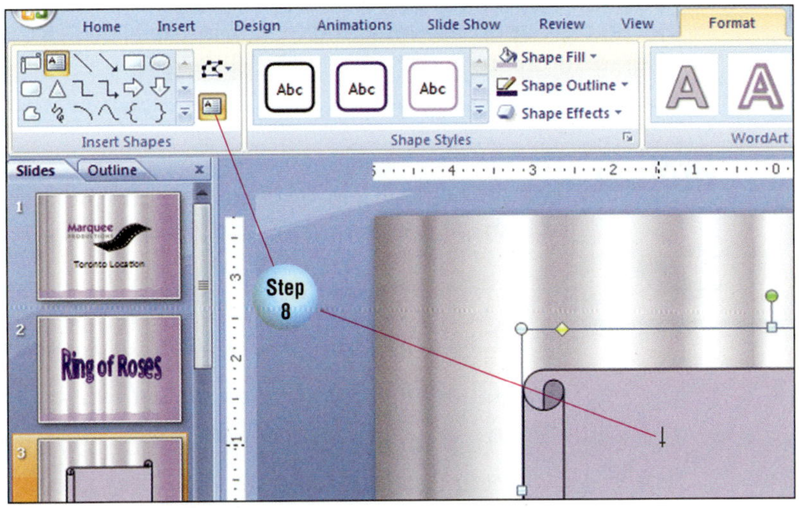

9. With the insertion point inside the text box, click the Home tab, click the Font Size button arrow, and then click *24* at the drop-down gallery.
10. Click the Bold button in the Font group and then click the Center button in the Paragraph group.
11. Type the following text in the text box:

MARQUEE PRODUCTIONS
Toronto Office
905 Bathurst Street
Toronto, ON M4P 4E5

12. Click the Align Text button in the Paragraph group and then click *Middle* at the drop-down list.
13. Save **PPS3-01.pptx**.

In Brief

Draw Shape

1. Click Home tab or Insert tab.
2. Click Shapes button.
3. Click desired shape at drop-down list.
4. Drag in slide to draw shape.

In Addition

Displaying the Selection and Visibility Pane

If you want to select an object or multiple objects in a slide, consider turning on the display of the Selection and Visibility pane. Turn on the display of this pane by clicking the Selection Pane button in the Arrange section in the Drawing Tools Format tab (see example at right). Select an object by clicking the object name in the Selection and Visibility pane list box. Select multiple objects by holding down the Ctrl key as you click objects. Click the button that displays at the right side of the object name to turn on/off the display of the object.

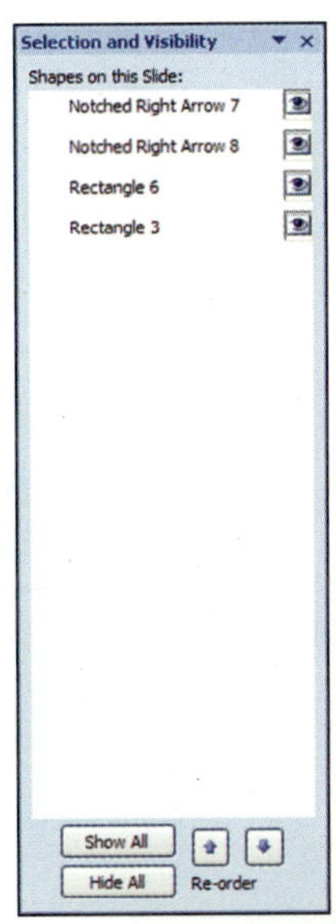

Activity 3.5

Displaying Gridlines; Inserting a Text Box; Copying and Rotating Shapes

To help position elements such as shapes and images on a slide, consider displaying gridlines. Gridlines are intersecting horizontal and vertical dashed lines that display on the slide in the Slide pane. Display gridlines by clicking the View tab and then clicking the *Gridlines* check box in the Show/Hide group. Create a text box in a slide by clicking the Text Box button in the Text group in the Insert tab. Click in the slide or drag to create a text box in the slide. Draw a shape in a slide and the selected shape displays with a yellow adjustment handle and a green rotation handle. Rotate a shape with the rotation handle or with the Rotate button in the Arrange group in the Drawing Tools Format tab. If you draw more than one object in a slide, you can select the objects as a unit so you can work with them as if they were a single object. You can format, size, move, flip, and/or rotate selected objects as a single unit.

Project

You need to create a new slide for the Toronto site presentation that displays the date for the last day of filming in Toronto. To highlight this important information, you will insert an arrow autoshape and then copy and rotate the shape.

1. With **PPS3-01.pptx** open, make Slide 8 active and then click the Home tab.
2. Click the New Slide button arrow and then click *Title Only* at the drop-down list.
3. Click in the text *Click to add title* and then type **Last Day of Filming**.
4. Turn on the display of gridlines by clicking the View tab and then clicking the *Gridlines* check box in the Show/Hide group.

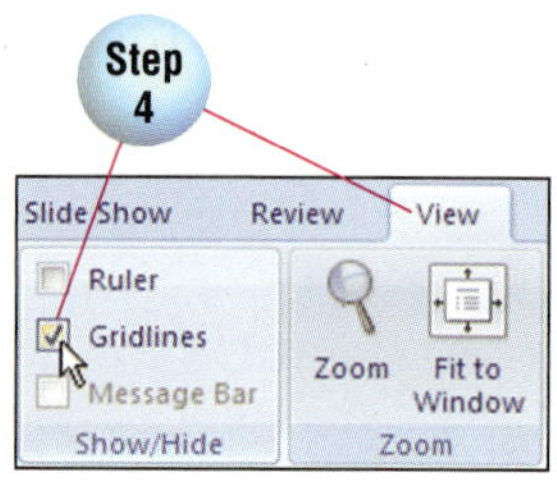

5. Click the Insert tab and then click the Text Box button in the Text group.
6. Position the mouse pointer in the slide and then draw a text box similar to what you see below. Use the gridlines to help you position the mouse before drawing the text box.

7. Change the font size to 24, turn on bold, change the alignment to center, and then type **August 27**. Click outside the text box to deselect it.
8. Click the Insert tab, click the Shapes button, and then click the *Notched Right Arrow* shape (sixth shape from the left in the second row of the *Block Arrows* section).

9 Position the mouse pointer at the left side of the slide, hold down the left mouse button, drag to create the arrow shape as shown at the right, and then release the mouse button.

Use the gridlines to help position the arrow.

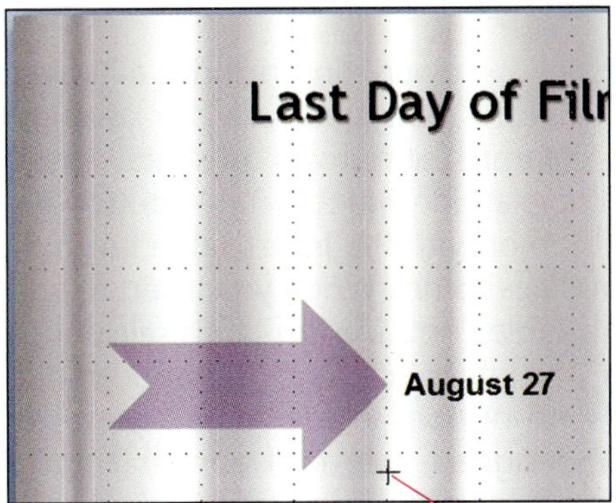

Step 9

10 With the arrow image selected, copy the arrow by positioning the mouse pointer inside the image until it displays with a four-headed arrow attached. Hold down the Ctrl key and then the left mouse button. Drag the arrow to the right side of the date, release the left mouse button, and then release the Ctrl key.

11 Click the Drawing Tools Format tab and then flip the copied arrow by clicking the Rotate button [Rotate] in the Arrange group and then clicking *Flip Horizontal* at the drop-down list.

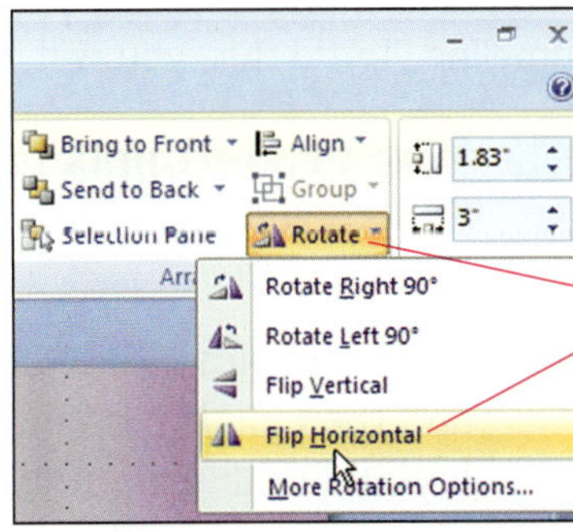

Step 11

12 Using the mouse pointer, draw a border around the three objects.

When you release the mouse button, the three objects are selected.

13 Click the Drawing Tools Format tab and then center-align the three grouped objects by clicking the Align button [Align] in the Arrange group and then clicking *Align Middle* at the drop-down list.

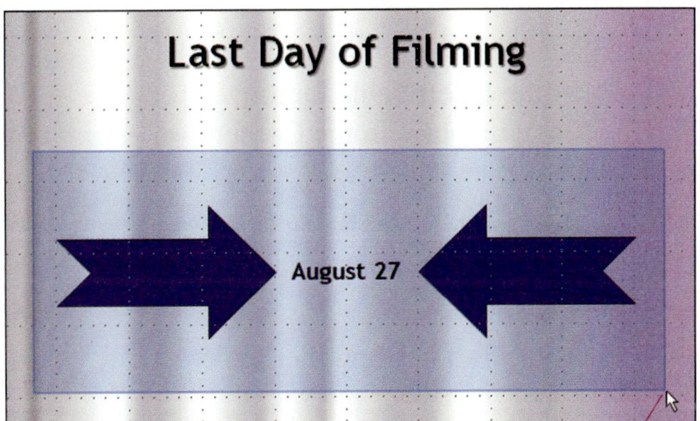

Step 12

14 Turn off the display of the gridlines by clicking the Align button [Align] and then clicking the *View Gridlines* option at the drop-down list.

15 Click outside the objects to deselect them.

16 Save **PPS3-01.pptx**.

In Brief

Display Gridlines
1. Click View tab.
2. Click *Gridlines* check box.

Insert Text Box
1. Click Insert tab.
2. Click Text Box button.
3. Click in slide or drag to create text box.

In Addition

Rotating Objects

Use the rotation handle that displays near a selected object to rotate the object. Position the mouse pointer on the rotation handle until the pointer displays as a circular arrow as shown at the right. Hold down the left mouse button, drag in the desired direction, and then release the mouse button.

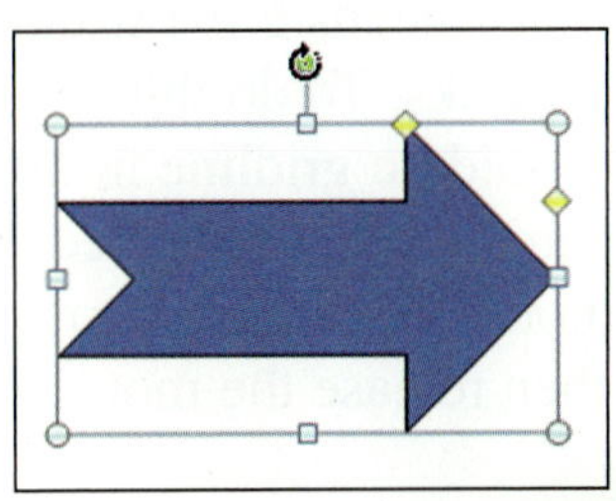

Activity 3.6

Creating a Table in a Slide

PowerPoint includes a Table feature you can use for displaying columns and rows of data. Insert a table in a slide with the Table button in the Insert tab or with the Insert Table button in a Content placeholder. When you insert a table in a slide, the Table Tools Design tab is selected. Use buttons in this tab to enhance the appearance of the table. With options in the Table Styles group, apply a predesigned style that applies color and border lines to a table. Maintain further control over the predesigned style formatting applied to columns and rows with options in the Table Style Options group. Apply additional design formatting to cells in a table with the Shading and Borders buttons in the Table Styles group. Draw a table or draw additional rows and/or columns in a table with options in the Draw Borders group. Click the Table Tools Format tab and display options and buttons for inserting and deleting columns and rows; changing cell size, alignment, direction, and margins; changing the table size; and arranging the table in the slide.

Project

After reviewing the slides, you decide to include additional information on the location timeline. To do this, you will insert a new slide and then create a table with specific dates.

1. With **PPS3-01.pptx** open, make Slide 8 active and then click the Home tab.
2. Click the New Slide button arrow and then click the *Title and Content* layout at the drop-down list.

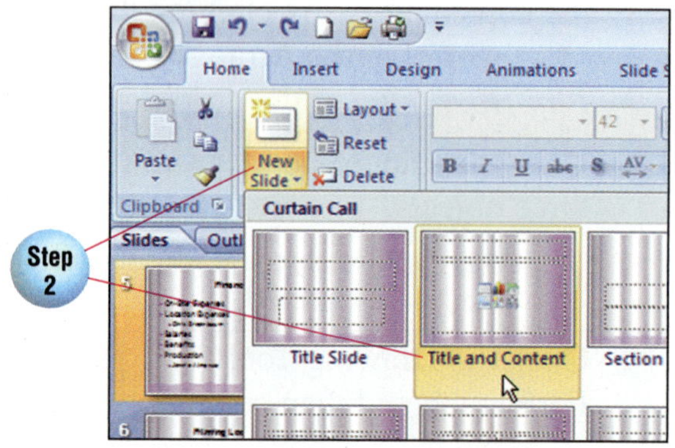

3. Click the text *Click to add title* in the new slide and then type **Timeline**.
4. Click the Insert Table button that displays in the Content placeholder.

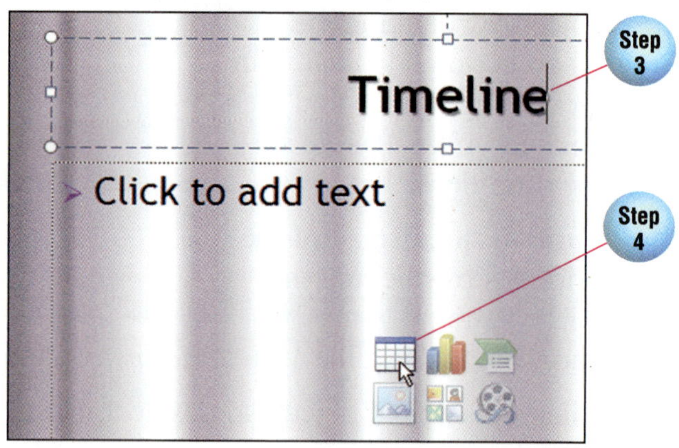

5. At the Insert Table dialog box, type **2** in the *Number of columns* text box.
6. Press the Tab key and then type **9** in the *Number of rows* text box.
7. Click OK to close the Insert Table dialog box.
8. Make sure the horizontal and vertical rulers display. If they do not, turn on the display of rulers by clicking the View tab and then clicking the *Ruler* check box in the Show/Hide group.

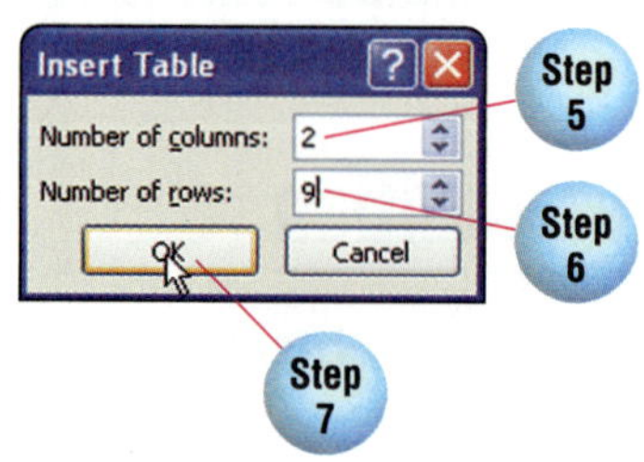

9. Column 1 needs to be widened to accommodate the project tasks. To do this, position the mouse pointer on the middle gridline in the table until the pointer turns into a double-headed arrow with two short lines between. Hold down the left mouse button, drag to approximately the 6-inch mark on the horizontal ruler, and then release the mouse button.

10 With the insertion point positioned in the first cell, type the text shown in Figure 3.2. Press the Tab key to move the insertion point to the next cell. Press Shift + Tab to move the insertion point to the previous cell.

11 Click the More button at the right side of the Table Styles group in the Table Tools Design tab.

12 Click *Themed Style 1 - Accent 1* in the drop-down gallery (second option from the left in the top row in the *Best Match for Document* group).

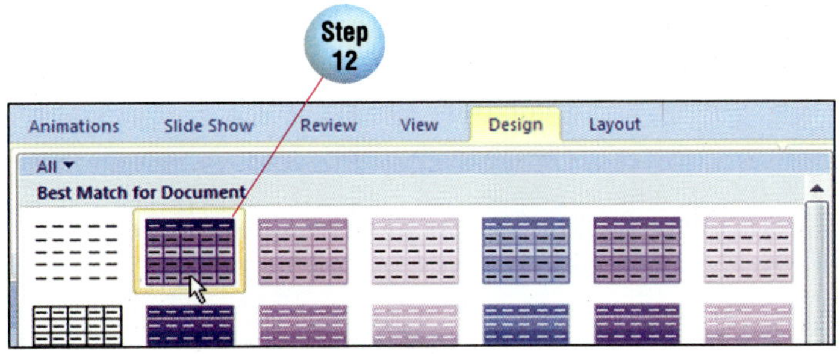

13 Click the Table Tools Layout tab.

14 Select the first row in the table by positioning the mouse pointer at the left side of the first row in the table until the pointer turns into a black, right-pointing arrow and then clicking the left mouse button.

15 Click the Center button in the Alignment group.

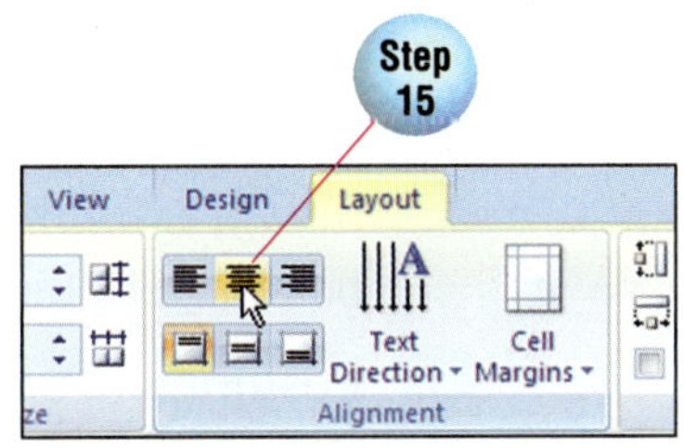

16 Click in the *Height* measurement box in the Table Size group, type **4.5**, and then press Enter.

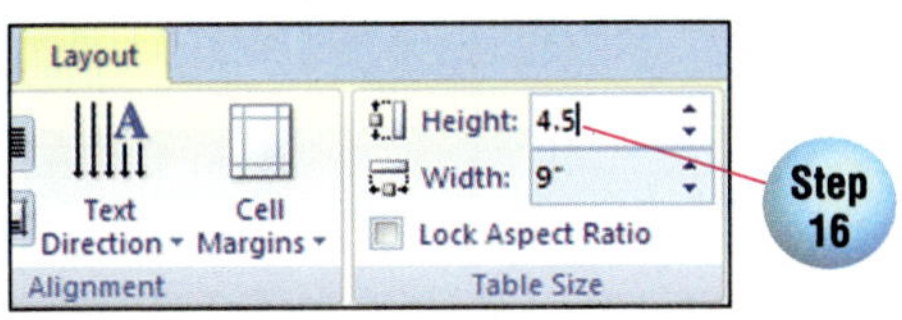

17 Save **PPS3-01.pptx**.

FIGURE 3.2 Slide Table

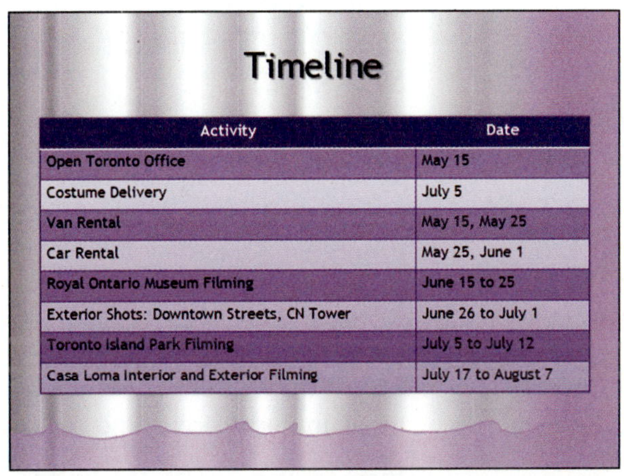

In Brief

Create Table
1. Click Insert Table button in Content placeholder.
2. At Insert Table dialog box, type desired number of columns and rows.
3. Click OK.

In Addition

Moving and Sizing a Table

Increase or decrease the size of a table by typing the desired measurements in the *Height* and *Width* measurement boxes in the Table Size group in the Table Tools Layout tab. You can also drag a table border to increase or decrease the size. When the insertion point is positioned in a table, a light turquoise border surrounds the table. This border contains sizing handles that display as a series of dots in the middle of the top, bottom, left, and right borders as well as each corner. Position the mouse pointer on one of the sizing handles until the pointer displays as a two-headed arrow, hold down the left mouse button, and then drag to increase or decrease the size. Drag a corner sizing handle to change the size of the table proportionally. To move the table, position the mouse pointer on the table border until the pointer displays with a four-headed arrow attached and then drag to the desired position.

Activity 3.7

Inserting Action Buttons and Hyperlinks

Action buttons are drawn objects on a slide that have a routine attached to them that is activated when the presenter clicks the button. For example, you can insert an action button that displays a specific Web page, a file in another program, or the next slide in the presentation. Creating an action button is a two-step process. The first step is to draw the button in the slide and the second step is to define the action that will take place using options in the Action Settings dialog box. You can customize an action button using the same techniques as customizing drawn shapes. You can insert a hyperlink in a slide that, when clicked, will display a site on the Internet or open another presentation or document. Insert a hyperlink with the Hyperlink button in the Insert tab.

Project

Marquee PRODUCTIONS

To automate the running of the presentation, you decide to insert an action button at the bottom of each slide that will link to the next slide or the first slide and insert a hyperlink to a Web site.

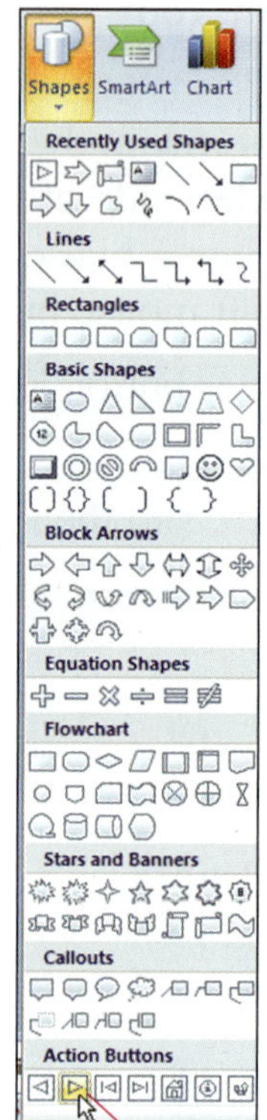

Step 2

Step 3

1. With **PPS3-01.pptx** open, make Slide 1 active.
2. Insert an action button that, when clicked, will display the next slide. To begin, click the Insert tab, click the Shapes button, and then click the *Action Button: Forward or Next* option (second button from the left in the *Action Buttons* section).
3. Position the crosshair pointer in the lower right corner of Slide 1 and then drag to create a button that is approximately one-half inch tall and wide.
4. At the Action Settings dialog box that displays, click OK. (The default setting is *Hyperlink to Next Slide*.)
5. With the button selected, click the Drawing Tools Format tab and then click the *Colored Outline - Accent 2* option in the Shapes Styles group.
6. Select the current measurement in the height measurement box, type 0.5, and then press Enter. Select the current measurement in the width measurement box, type 0.5, and then press Enter.
7. Instead of drawing the button on each slide, you decide to copy and then paste it in other slides. To do this, make sure the button is selected, click the Home tab, and then click the Copy button in the Clipboard group.
8. Make Slide 2 active and then click the Paste button in the Clipboard group. Continue pasting the button in Slides 3 through 9. (Do not paste the button on the last slide, Slide 10.)
9. Make Slide 10 active and then insert an action button that displays the first slide. To begin, click the Insert tab, click the Shapes button, and then click *Action Button: Home* (fifth option from the left in the *Action Buttons* section).
10. Position the crosshair pointer in the lower right corner of Slide 10 and then drag to create a button that is approximately one-half inch tall and wide.

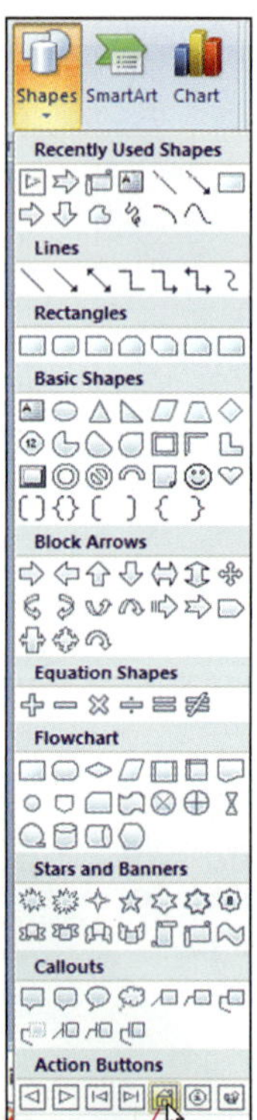

Step 9

11 At the Action Settings dialog box that displays, click OK. (The default setting is *Hyperlink to First Slide*.)

12 With the button selected, click the Drawing Tools Format tab and then click the *Colored Outline - Accent 2* option in the Shapes Styles group.

13 Click in the Shape Height measurement box, type **0.5**, and then press Enter. Click in the Shape Width measurement box, type **0.5**, and then press Enter.

14 Make Slide 6 active and then create a hyperlink to the museum Web site. To begin, select *Royal Ontario Museum*, click the Insert tab, and then click the Hyperlink button in the Links group.

Step 14

15 At the Insert Hyperlink dialog box, type **www.rom.on.ca** in the *Address* text box and then press Enter.

PowerPoint automatically inserts *http://* at the beginning of the Web address. The hyperlink text displays underlined and in a different color in the slide.

16 Run the presentation beginning with Slide 1. Navigate through the slide show by clicking the action buttons. When Slide 6 displays (*Filming Locations*), click the Royal Ontario Museum hyperlink.

Step 16

17 After viewing the museum Web site, close the browser by clicking the Close button in the upper right corner of the browser window. Continue running the presentation. After viewing the presentation at least twice, press the Esc key to end the presentation.

18 Save **PPS3-01.pptx**.

In Brief

Insert Action Button

1. Click Insert tab.
2. Click Shapes button.
3. Click desired action button at drop-down list.
4. Drag in slide to create button.
5. At Action Settings dialog box, click OK.

In Addition

Linking with Action Buttons

You can specify that an action button links to a Web site during a presentation. To do this, draw an Action button. At the Action Settings dialog box, click the *Hyperlink to* option, click the down-pointing arrow at the right side of the *Hyperlink to* option box, and then click *URL* at the drop-down list. At the Hyperlink To URL dialog box, type the Web address in the *URL* text box and then click OK. Click OK to close the Action Settings dialog box. Other actions you can link to using the *Hyperlink to* drop-down list include: *Next Slide*, *Previous Slide*, *First Slide*, *Last Slide*, *Last Slide Viewed*, *End Show*, *Custom Show*, *Slide*, *URL*, *Other PowerPoint Presentation*, and *Other File*. The Action Settings dialog box can also be used to run another program when the action button is selected, to run a macro, or to activate an embedded object.

Activity 3.8

Formatting with a Slide Master

If you use a PowerPoint design theme, you may choose to use the formatting provided by the theme or you may want to customize the formatting. If you customize formatting in a presentation, PowerPoint's slide master can be very helpful in reducing the steps needed to format slides. A slide master is added to a presentation when a design theme is applied. A slide design theme generally contains a slide master for each of the various slide layouts. To display slide masters, click the View tab and then click the Slide Master button in the Presentation Views group. The available slide masters display in the slide thumbnail pane at the left side of the screen. Apply formatting to the desired slide masters and then click the Close Master View button in the Close group to return to the Normal view.

Project

As you finalize the presentation, you decide to make one last formatting change and then insert the company logo so it appears on each slide. Since the logo already displays on Slide 1, you decide to insert the logo in the lower left corner of the remaining slides.

1. With **PPS3-01.pptx** open, make Slide 1 active.
2. Click the View tab and then click the Slide Master button in the Presentation Views group.

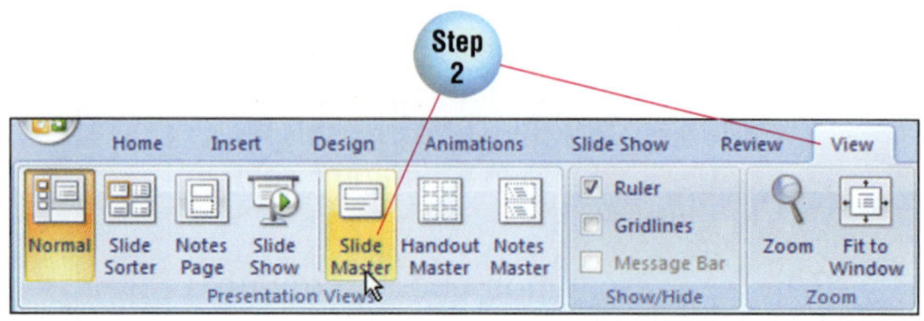

3. Select the text *Click to edit Master subtitle style*, click the Home tab, and then click the Font group dialog box launcher.
4. At the Font dialog box, change the font to Cambria, the font style to Bold, turn on small caps, and then close the Font dialog box.

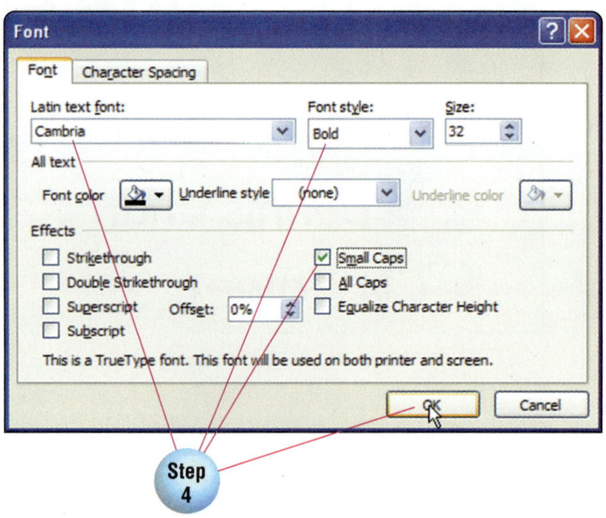

5. Click the top slide master located in the slide thumbnail pane at the left side of the screen.
6. Select the text *Click to edit Master title style* and then click the Font group dialog box launcher.

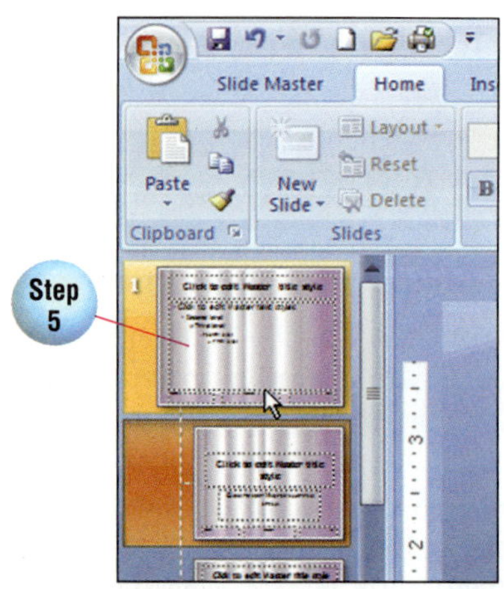

7. At the Font dialog box, change the font to Cambria, the font style to Bold, turn on small caps, and then close the Font dialog box.
8. Insert the Marquee Productions logo in the slide master (so it prints on all slides *except* the first one). Begin by clicking the Insert tab and then clicking the Picture button in the Illustrations group.
9. Navigate to the PowerPointS3 folder on your storage medium and then double-click ***MPLogo.jpg***.
10. Make sure the logo is selected.
11. Click the Recolor button in the Adjust group in the Picture Tools Format tab and then click *Set Transparent Color* at the drop-down list.

    The mouse pointer displays with a tool attached.

12. Position the mouse pointer in the white background color of the logo and then click the left mouse button.

    This makes the white background color transparent and displays the design theme behind the logo.

13. Click in the Shape Height measurement box, type **0.5**, and then press Enter.
14. Drag the logo to the lower left corner of the slide master as shown at the right.
15. Click the Slide Master tab.
16. Click the Close Master View button in the Close group located at the right side of the Slide Master tab.
17. Print the presentation as handouts with six slides per page.
18. Save and then close **PPS3-01.pptx**.

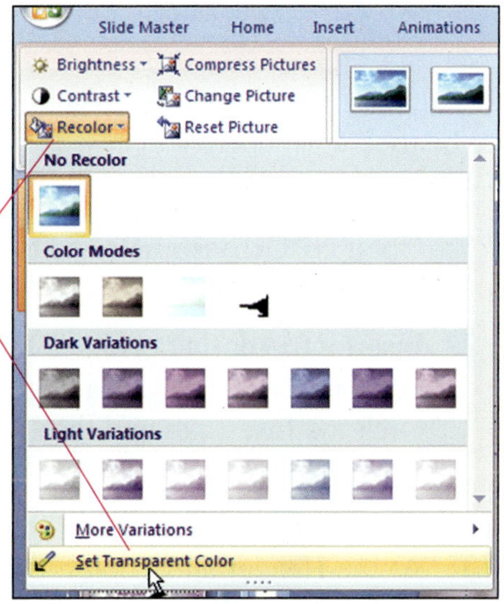

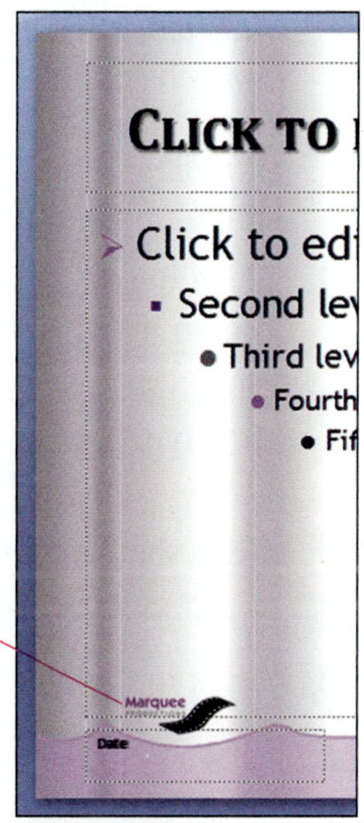

In Brief

Format in Slide Master View

1. Click View tab.
2. Click Slide Master button.
3. Make desired editing changes.
4. Click Close Master View button.

In Addition

Applying More Than One Slide Design Theme to a Presentation

Each design theme applies specific formatting to slides. You can apply more than one design template to slides in a presentation. To do this, select the specific slides and then choose the desired design theme. The design theme is applied only to the selected slides. If you apply more than one design theme to a presentation, multiple slide masters will display in Slide Master view.

Activity 3.9

Inserting Headers and Footers

Insert information you want to appear at the top or bottom of each slide or on note and handout pages with options at the Header and Footer dialog box. If you want the information to appear on all slides, display the Header and Footer dialog box with the Slide tab selected. With options at this dialog box, you can insert the date and time, insert the slide number, and create a footer. To insert header or footer elements in notes or handouts, choose options at the Header and Footer dialog box with the Notes and Handouts tab selected.

Project

Niagara Peninsula College

Cal Rubine, the chair of the Theatre Arts Division, has asked you to complete a presentation to be used at an upcoming college fair. The first task you need to complete is to insert the current date and slide number in the presentation and create a header for notes pages.

1. Open **NPCDivisionPresentation.pptx** and then save the presentation and name it **PPS3-02**.
2. Insert a footer that prints at the bottom of each slide. To begin, click the Insert tab and then click the Header & Footer button in the Text group.

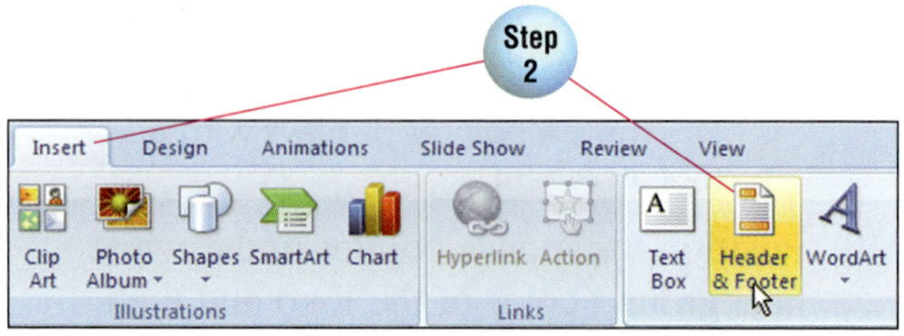

3. At the Header and Footer dialog box with the Slide tab selected, click the *Date and time* check box to insert a check mark. Click the *Update automatically* option to insert a circle in the option button.
4. Click the *Slide number* check box to insert a check mark.
5. Click the *Footer* check box and then type **Theatre Arts Division** in the *Footer* text box.
6. Click the Apply to All button.

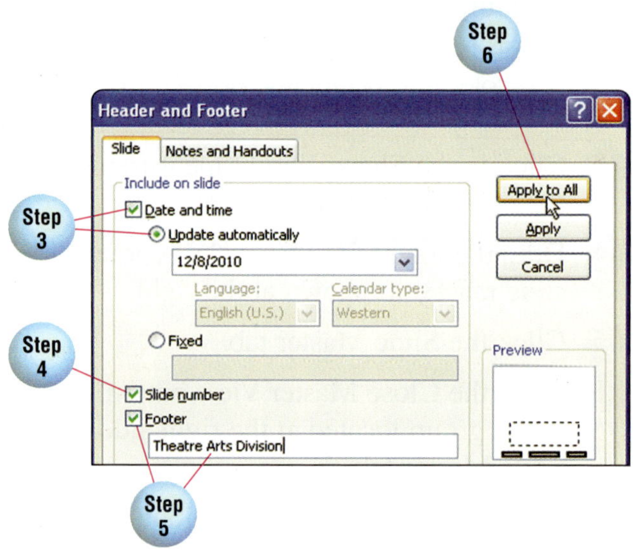

7. Make Slide 4 active.
8. Click in the Notes pane and then type **Include additional costs for equipment, costuming, set design, and other required expenses.**

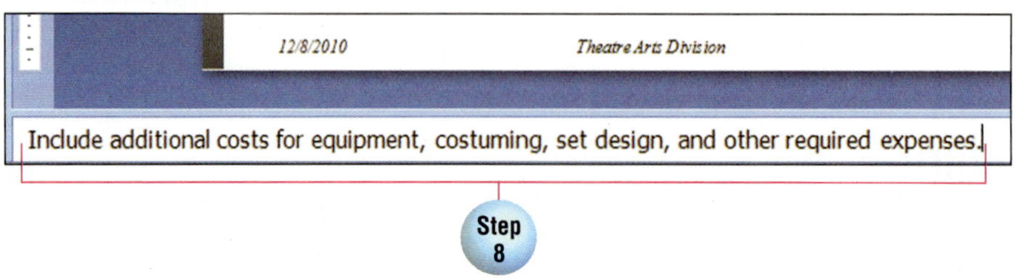

9. Insert a header in notes and handouts by clicking the Header & Footer button in the Insert tab.
10. At the Header and Footer dialog box, click the Notes and Handouts tab.
11. Click the *Date and time* check box to insert a check mark and then, if necessary, click the *Update automatically* option to insert a circle in the option button.
12. Click the *Header* check box and then type **Niagara Peninsula College**.
13. Click the *Footer* check box and then type **Theatre Arts Division**.
14. Click the Apply to All button.

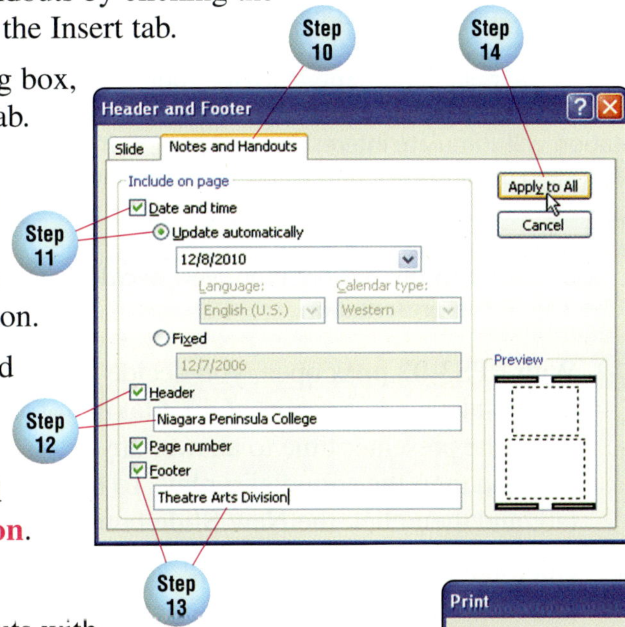

15. Print the presentation as handouts with nine slides per page.
16. Print Slide 4 as a notes page. To do this, press Ctrl + P. At the Print dialog box, click the down-pointing arrow at the right side of the *Print what* option and then click *Notes Pages*.
17. Click in the *Slides* option button and then type **4**.
18. Click OK to close the Print dialog box.
19. Save **PPS3-02.pptx**.

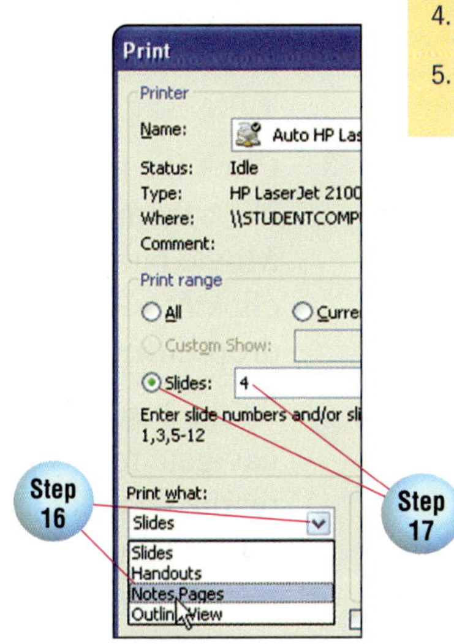

In Brief

Insert Header/Footer on Slide

1. Click Insert tab.
2. Click Header & Footer button.
3. At Header and Footer dialog box with Slide tab selected, choose desired options.
4. Click Apply to All button.

Insert Header/Footer in Notes and Handouts

1. Click Insert tab.
2. Click Header & Footer button.
3. At Header and Footer dialog box, click Notes and Handouts tab.
4. Choose desired options.
5. Click Apply to All button.

In Addition

Using the Package for CD Feature

The safest way to transport a PowerPoint presentation to another computer is to use the Package for CD feature. With this feature you can copy a presentation onto a CD or to a folder or network location and include all of the linked files, fonts, and PowerPoint Viewer program in case the destination computer does not have PowerPoint installed on it. To use the Package for CD feature, click the Office button, point to *Publish*, and then click *Package for CD*. At the Package for CD dialog box, type a name for the CD and then click the Copy to CD button.

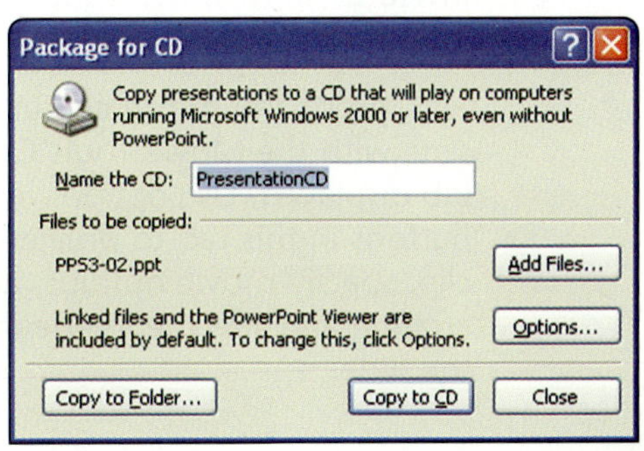

Activity 3.10

Adding Sound and Video

Adding sound and/or video effects to a presentation will turn a slide show into a true multimedia experience for your audience. Including a variety of elements in a presentation will stimulate interest in your presentation and keep the audience motivated. Use the Sound button in the Media Clips group in the Insert tab to insert a sound file into a presentation and use the Movie button to insert a video clip. You can insert a sound or video clip from a folder or from the Microsoft Clip Organizer. You will need access to the Internet to access the Clip Organizer.

Project

To add interest to the presentation, you decide to experiment with adding a sound file and a video clip in the presentation.

Niagara Peninsula COLLEGE

1. With **PPS3-02.pptx** open, you decide to insert a slide at the end of the presentation that displays a video clip of a jet taking off and then plays a sound clip. This will allow the presenter time to answer any questions from the audience while the video clip and then the sound clip play. To begin, make Slide 7 active, click the Home tab, and then click the New Slide button.

2. Click the text *Click to add title* and then type **Let Your Career Take Flight!**

3. Click the text *Click to add text*, click the Insert tab, click the Movie button arrow, and then click *Movie from File* at the drop-down list.

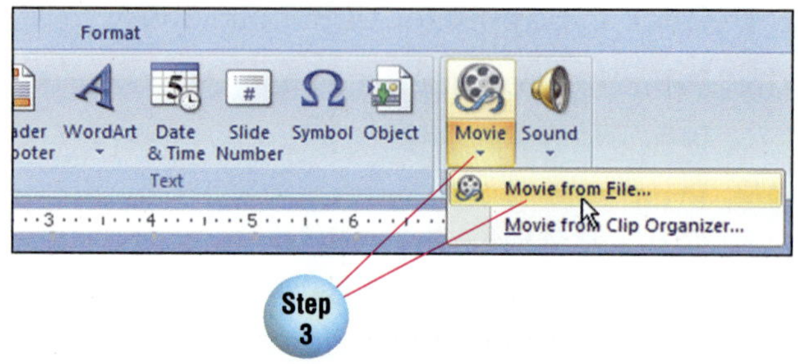

4. At the Insert Movie dialog box, navigate to the SoundandVideo folder on the CD that accompanies this textbook and then double-click the file named ***TakeOff.mpeg***.

PROBLEM

If the **TakeOff.mpeg** file does not display, make sure you navigated to the correct file folder on the CD.

5. At the message asking how you want the movie to start in the slide show, click the Automatically button.

   This inserts the movie clip in the slide with the Movie Tools Options tab displayed. Use options and buttons in this tab to preview the clip, specify movie options, and arrange and size the image in the slide.

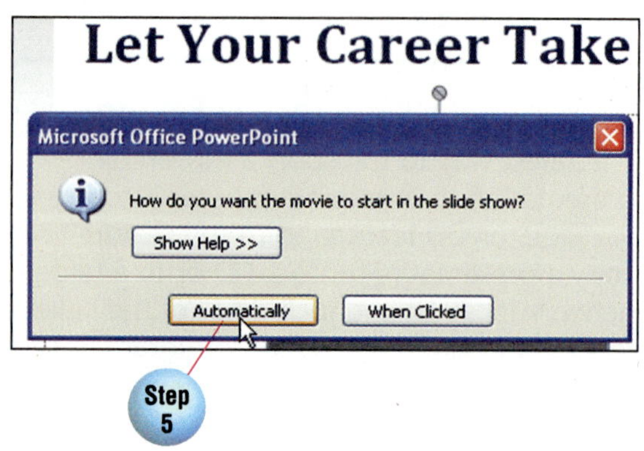

6 Click the Slide Show Volume button in the Movie Options group in the Movie Tools Options tab and then click *Low* at the drop-down list.

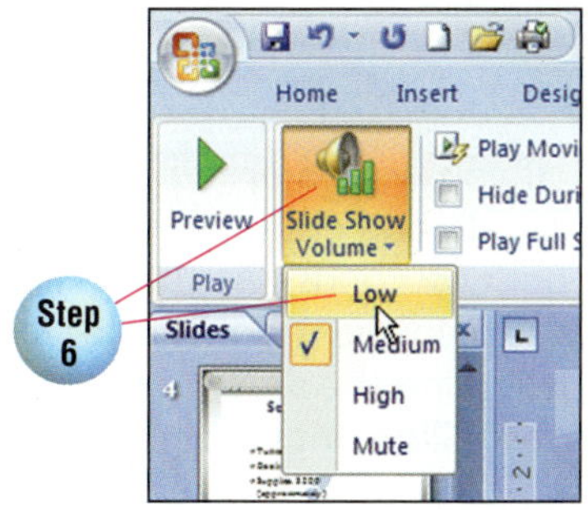

7 Click the *Rewind Movie After Playing* check box in the Movie Options group to insert a check mark.

8 Resize and position the movie on the slide so it fills the text placeholder.

9 Add a sound clip by clicking the Insert tab, clicking the Sound button arrow, and then clicking *Sound from File* at the drop-down list.

10 At the Insert Sound dialog box, navigate to the SoundandVideo folder on the CD that accompanies this textbook and then double-click the file named ***SoundClip.mid***.

11 At the message asking how you want the sound to start in the slide show, click the Automatically button.

This inserts the sound clip in the slide with the Sound Tools Options tab displayed. Use options and buttons in this tab to preview the sound, specify sound options, and arrange and size the sound icon in the slide.

12 Click the *Hide During Show* check box in the Sound Options group to insert a check mark.

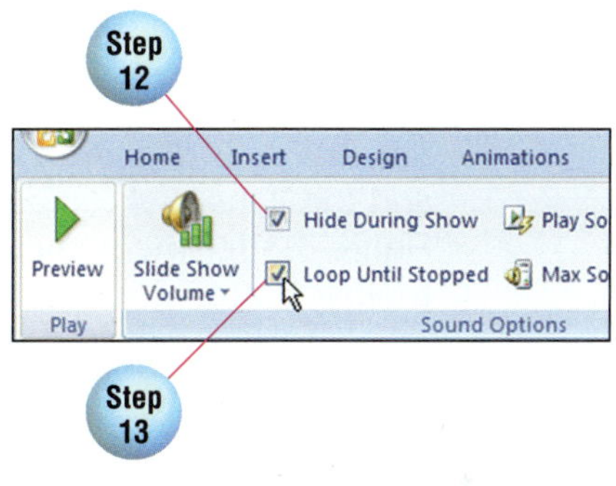

13 Click the *Loop Until Stopped* check box to insert a check mark.

14 Drag the sound icon so it is positioned in the lower left corner of the slide.

15 Run the presentation beginning with the first slide and navigate through the presentation. When Slide 8 displays, the movie clip will begin automatically and, after the video clip is finished, the sound clip will begin.

16 After listening to the sound clip for a short period of time, press the Esc key to end the presentation.

17 Print only Slide 8.

18 Delete Slide 8. (This slide requires quite a bit of additional storage space.)

19 Save **PPS3-02.pptx**.

In Brief

Insert Video Clip

1. Click Insert tab.
2. Click Movie button arrow.
3. Click *Movie from File*.
4. Navigate to desired folder.
5. Double-click desired video clip file.

Insert Sound Clip

1. Click Insert tab.
2. Click Sound button arrow.
3. Click *Sound from File*.
4. Navigate to desired folder.
5. Double-click desired sound clip file.

In Addition

Formatting Video and Sound Clip Display

When you insert a video clip in a slide, the Movie Tools Options tab is active. You can also format the movie clip with options at the Picture Tools Format tab. Click this tab and options display for changing the brightness, contrast, and color of the movie clip; applying a picture style; and arranging and sizing the clip. The Picture Tools Format tab is also available when you insert a sound clip.

Activity 3.11

Setting and Rehearsing Timings for a Presentation

If you want a presentation to run automatically and each slide to display a specific number of seconds, use the Rehearse Timings feature to help set the times for slides as you practice delivering the slide show. To set times for slides, click the Slide Show tab and then click the Rehearse Timings button in the Set Up group. The first slide displays in Slide Show view and the Rehearsal toolbar displays. Use buttons on this toolbar to specify times for each slide. Use options at the Set Up Show dialog box to control the slide show. Display this dialog box by clicking the Set Up Slide Show button in the Set Up group. Use options in the *Show type* section to specify the type of slide show you want to display. If you want the presentation to be totally automatic and run continuously until you end the show, click the *Loop continuously until 'Esc'* check box to insert a check mark. In the *Advance slides* section, the *Using timings, if present* option should be selected by default. Select *Manually* if you want to advance the slides using the mouse during the slide show instead of the slides advancing using your preset times.

Project

Cal Rubine has asked you to make the presentation self-running so it can be run continuously at the college fair.

Niagara Peninsula COLLEGE

1. With **PPS3-02.pptx** open, make Slide 1 active.

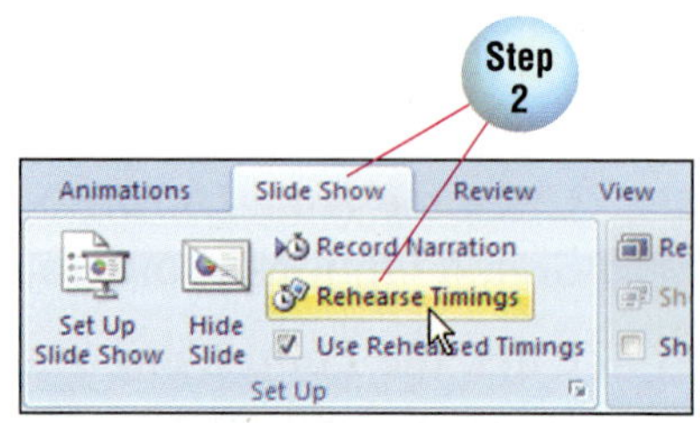

2. Click the Slide Show tab and then click the Rehearse Timings button [Rehearse Timings] in the Set Up group.

   The first slide displays in Slide Show view and the Rehearsal toolbar displays. Refer to Figure 3.3 for the names of the Rehearsal toolbar buttons.

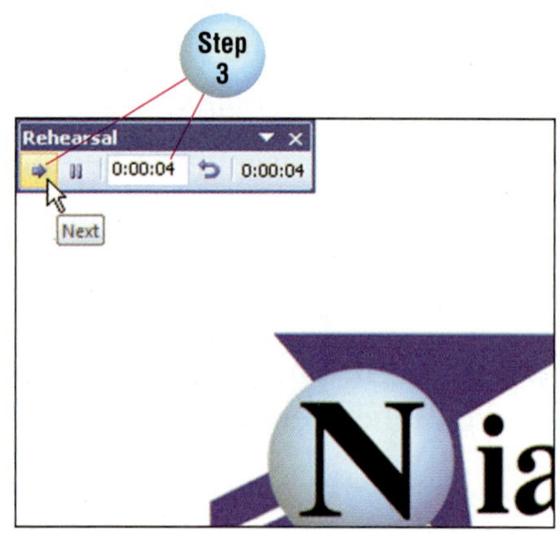

3. Wait until the time displayed for the current slide reaches four seconds and then click the Next button.

   If you miss the time, click the Repeat button to reset the clock back to zero for the current slide.

4. Set the following times for the remaining slides:

Slide 2	5 seconds	Slide 5	6 seconds
Slide 3	4 seconds	Slide 6	7 seconds
Slide 4	4 seconds	Slide 7	8 seconds

5. After the last slide has displayed, click Yes at the message asking if you want to keep the new slide timings.

   This displays the slides in Slide Sorter view.

6. Double-click Slide 1 to change to Slide view.

FIGURE 3.3 Rehearsal Toolbar Buttons

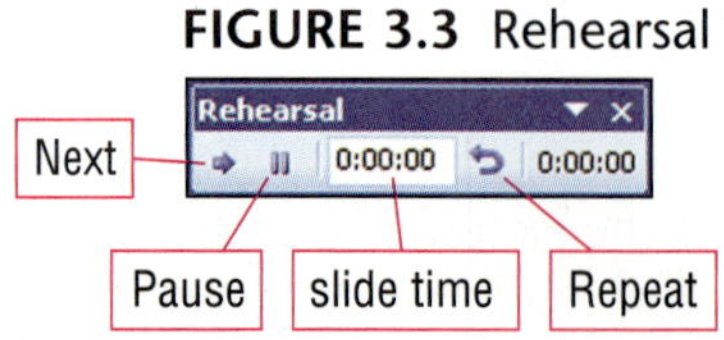

7. Set up the slide show to run continuously by clicking the Set Up Slide Show button in the Slide Show tab.
8. At the Set Up Show dialog box, click the *Loop continuously until 'Esc'* check box.

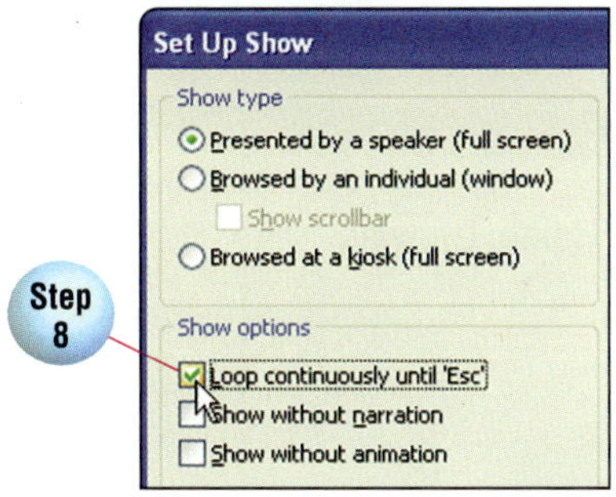

9. Click OK to close the dialog box.
10. Insert a sound clip that will play continuously throughout the presentation. To begin, click the Insert tab, click the Sound button arrow, and then click *Sound from File* at the drop-down list.
11. At the Insert Sound dialog box, navigate to the SoundandVideo folder on the CD that accompanies this textbook and then double-click the file named ***SoundClip.mid***.
12. At the message asking how you want the sound to start in the slide show, click the Automatically button.
13. Click the *Hide During Show* check box in the Sound Options group in the Sound Tools Options tab to insert a check mark.
14. Click the down-pointing arrow at the right side of the Play Sound option box and then click *Play across slides* at the drop-down list.
15. Drag the sound icon to the lower left corner of the slide.
16. Run the presentation beginning with Slide 1. The slide show will start and run continuously. Watch the presentation until it has started for the second time and then end the show by pressing the Esc key.
17. Print the presentation as handouts with nine slides per page.
18. Save and then close **PPS3-02.pptx**.

In Brief

Set and Rehearse Timings

1. Click Slide Show tab.
2. Click Rehearse Timings button.
3. When desired time displays, click Next button.
4. Continue until times are set for each slide.
5. Click Yes at message.

Set Up Show to Run Continuously

1. Click Slide Show tab.
2. Click Set Up Slide Show button.
3. Click *Loop continuously until 'Esc'* check box.
4. Click OK.

In Addition

Setting Times Manually

The time a slide remains on the screen during a slide show can be manually set using the *Automatically After* option in the Transition to This Slide group in the Animations tab. To use this feature, click the Animations tab and then click the *On Mouse Click* check box to remove the check mark. Click the *Automatically After* check box to insert a check mark and then insert the desired time in the time box. Click the Apply To All button to apply the time to each slide in the presentation.

Features Summary

Feature	Ribbon Tab, Group	Button	Keyboard Shortcut
action button	Insert, Links		
Clipboard task pane	Home, Clipboard		
draw shape	Insert, Illustrations OR Home, Drawing		
Find	Home, Editing		Ctrl + F
gridlines	View, Show/Hide	Gridlines	Shift + F9
header and footer	Insert, Text		
hyperlink	Insert, Links		Ctrl + K
movie clip	Insert, Media Clips		
rehearse timings	Slide Show, Set Up	Rehearse Timings	
replace	Home, Editing	Replace	Ctrl + H
sound clip	Insert, Media Clips		
table	Insert, Tables		
text box	Insert, Text		
WordArt	Insert, Text		

Knowledge Check

Completion: In the space provided at the right, indicate the correct term, command, or option.

1. Display this task pane to collect and paste multiple items. ____________
2. The Replace button is located in this group in the Home tab. ____________
3. Use this feature to distort or modify text and to conform to a variety of shapes. ____________
4. When you insert a shape in a slide, this tab is available for formatting the shape. ____________
5. These are horizontal and vertical dashed lines that you can display on a slide. ____________
6. To copy a shape, hold down this key while dragging the shape. ____________
7. Use this feature for displaying columns and rows of data. ____________
8. These are drawn objects that have a routine attached to them. ____________
9. Create a hyperlink by clicking the Hyperlink button in this group in the Insert tab. ____________
10. When you click the Hyperlink button in the Insert tab, this dialog box displays. ____________
11. Create footer text that displays at the bottom of all slides with options at this dialog box. ____________
12. Click this button in the Insert tab to insert a video clip. ____________

13. When the desired time displays on the Rehearsal toolbar, click this button on the Rehearsal toolbar to display the next slide. ______________
14. The Sound button is located in this group in the Insert tab. ______________
15. Click this button on the Rehearsal toolbar to reset the clock back to zero for the current slide. ______________

Skills Review

Review 1 Formatting and Customizing a Biography Project Presentation

Marquee PRODUCTIONS

1. Open **MPBiography.pptx** and then save the presentation and name it **PPS3-R1**.
2. Make Slide 4 active, turn on the display of the Clipboard task pane, and clear any contents in the task pane.
3. Select and then copy *Chris Greenbaum.*
4. Select and then copy *Camille Matsui.*
5. Select and then copy *Amy Eisman.*
6. Select and then copy *Tricia Becktold.*
7. Make Slide 5 active.
8. Position the insertion point immediately to the right of *On-Site Expenses*, press the Enter key, press the Tab key, and then click *Camille Matsui* in the task pane.
9. Position the insertion point immediately to the right of *Benefits*, press the Enter key, press the Tab key, and then click *Chris Greenbaum* in the task pane.
10. Position the insertion point immediately to the right of *Production*, press the Enter key, press the Tab key, and then click *Amy Eisman.*
11. Press the Enter key and then click *Tricia Becktold.*
12. Clear the contents of the Clipboard task pane and then close the task pane.
13. Make Slide 1 active and then find all occurrences of *Camille Matsui* and replace with *Jennie Almonzo.*
14. Find all occurrences of *Tricia Becktold* and replace with *Nick Jaffe.*
15. Make Slide 1 active and then insert the file named **MPLogo.jpg**. Size and position the logo on the slide. Recolor the background of the logo to transparent color.
16. Make Slide 2 active and then insert the name of the biography, *Silent Streets*, as WordArt. You determine the formatting and shape of the WordArt. Increase the size of the WordArt so it fills most of the slide and position the WordArt so it is centered in the slide.
17. Make Slide 6 active and then create the table shown in Figure 3.4. Apply the *Themed Style 1 - Accent 2* table style, select all cells in the table, and then change the font size to 24. Size and position the table and table columns as shown.
18. Make Slide 7 active, create the arrows shown in Figure 3.5, and insert the text in text boxes in the shapes as shown. Apply the *Light 1 Outline, Colored Fill - Accent 5* shape style to the shapes and change the text font size to 40.
19. Make Slide 1 the active slide and then draw an action button named Action Button: Forward or Next in the lower right corner of the slide. Fill the button with a color that complements the slide design. Copy the button and paste it in Slides 2, 3, 4, 5, and 6.
20. Insert a footer that prints *Silent Streets* at the bottom center of each slide.

21. Make Slide 4 active and then insert a clip art image related to “people” or “team.” You determine the size, positioning, and coloring of the clip art.
22. Make Slide 5 active and then insert a clip art image related to “money” or “finance.” You determine the size, positioning, and coloring of the clip art.
23. Run the presentation beginning with Slide 1.
24. Print the presentation as handouts with nine slides per page.
25. Save and then close **PPS3-R1.pptx**.

FIGURE 3.4 Slide 6

Activity	Date
Completed Script	October 31
Final Budget	November 15
Location Confirmation	November 15
Casting Decisions	January 1
Begin Filming	January 15

FIGURE 3.5 Slide 7

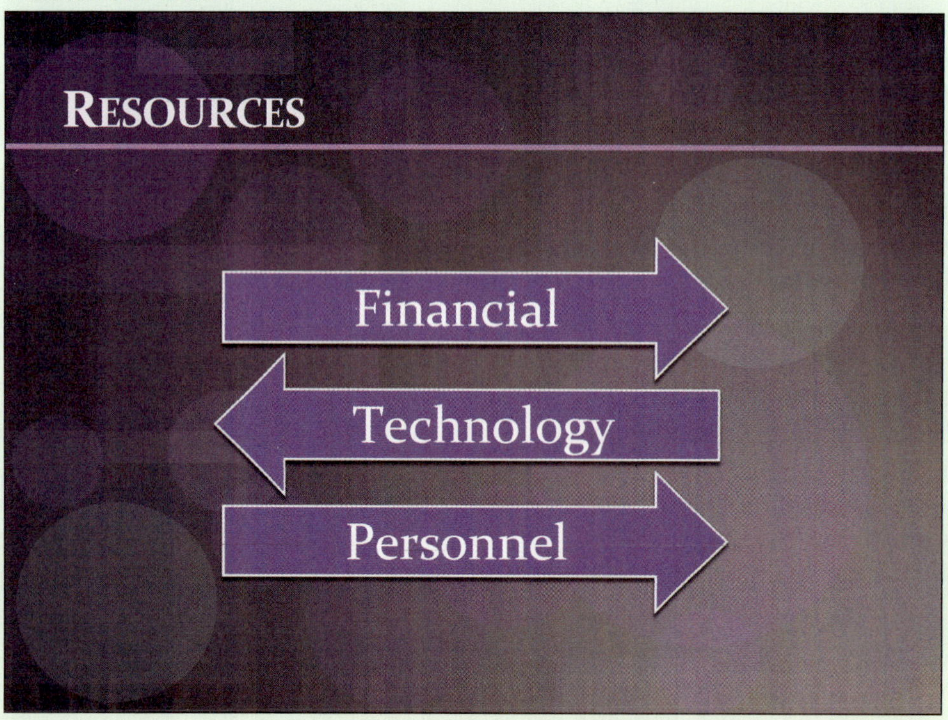

Review 2 Formatting with Slide Masters

1. Open **MPAnnualMeeting.pptx** and then save the presentation and name it **PPS3-R2**.
2. Apply the Oriel design theme, change the theme colors to Office, and change the theme font to Opulent.
3. Display the presentation in Slide Master view, click the top slide miniature in the slide thumbnail pane, and then make the following changes:
   - Select the text *CLICK TO EDIT MASTER TITLE STYLE* and then change the font size from 30 to 40.
   - Select the text *Click to edit Master text styles* and then change the font size from 24 to 32.
   - Select the text *Second level* and then change the font size from 21 to 24.
   - Insert the **FCTLogo.jpg** file in the slide. Recolor the logo to follow the color scheme of the theme. Decrease the size of the logo so the height is approximately 0.5″. Drag the logo to the lower left corner of the master slide.
4. Close the Slide Master view.
5. Apply a slide transition and sound to each slide.
6. Run the presentation.
7. Print the presentation as handouts with nine slides per page.
8. Save and then close **PPS3-R2.pptx**.

Review 3 Formatting a Vacation Cruise Presentation to Run Automatically

1. Open **FCTCruise.pptx** and then save the presentation and name it **PPS3-R3**.
2. Make Slide 1 active and then insert the **FCTLogo.jpg** file. Size and position the logo on the slide.
3. Rehearse the timings and set the following times for the slides:

   Slide 1 4 seconds
   Slide 2 8 seconds
   Slide 3 8 seconds
   Slide 4 4 seconds
   Slide 5 7 seconds
4. With Slide 1 active, insert the sound clip named **SoundClip.mid** (from the SoundandVideo folder on the CD that accompanies this textbook). At the message asking how you want the sound to start in the slide show, click the Automatically button. Click the *Hide During Show* check box (to insert a check mark), click the down-pointing arrow at the right side of the *Play Sound* button, and then click *Play across slides*.
5. Set up the slide show to run continuously.
6. Run the presentation and view it at least twice.
7. Print the presentation as handouts with six slides per page.
8. Save and then close **PPS3-R3.pptx**.

Skills Assessment

Assessment 1 Formatting a Presentation for Performance Threads

1. Open **PTCostumes.pptx** and then save the presentation and name it **PPS3-A1**.
2. Make Slide 1 the active slide and then insert the file named **PTLogo.jpg**. Size and position the company logo on the slide.
3. Make Slide 3 active and then insert the movie name *Ring of Roses* as WordArt. You determine the formatting, shape, size, and position of the WordArt in the slide.
4. Make Slide 5 the active slide, create a shape (you determine the shape), and then copy the shape two times (so the slide contains a total of three shapes). Insert *Research* in the first shape, *Design* in the second shape, and *Production* in the third shape. Format, size, and position the shapes in the slide.
5. Make Slide 6 the active slide and then insert the following information in a table:

Designer	**Date**
Scott Bercini	June 21
Terri Cantrell	June 13
Paul Gottlieb	June 28
Tae Jeong	June 13
Rosa Levens	June 28

6. Insert the footer *Performance Threads* on each slide.
7. Run the presentation.
8. Print the presentation as handouts with nine slides per page.
9. Save and then close **PPS3-A1.pptx**.

Assessment 2 Formatting a Presentation for First Choice Travel

1. Open **FCTSouthernTours.pptx** and then save the presentation and name it **PPS3-A2**.
2. Make Slide 2 active and then insert *Australia* as WordArt. You determine the formatting, size, and position of the WordArt in the slide.
3. Make Slide 6 active and then insert *New Zealand* as WordArt. You determine the formatting, size, and position of the WordArt in the slide.
4. Insert a footer that prints *Southern Tours* at the bottom center of each slide.
5. Rehearse the timings and determine the seconds for each slide.
6. Insert the sound clip **SoundClip.mid** (from the SoundandVideo folder on the CD) that will play automatically and loop until stopped.
7. Set up the slide show to run continuously.
8. Run the presentation and view it at least twice.
9. Print the presentation as handouts with nine slides per page.
10. Save and then close **PPS3-A2.pptx**.

Assessment 3 Learning about Custom Shows

1. Open **FCTSouthernTours.pptx** and then save the presentation and name it **PPS3-A3**.
2. Use the Help feature to learn about custom shows.
3. Create a custom show containing Slides 1, 7, 8, and 9. (You determine the name of the show.)
4. Run the custom show.
5. Save and then close **PPS3-A3.pptx**.

Assessment 4 Locating Information and Preparing a Presentation for Performance Threads

1. You are Sophie Yong, design manager for Performance Threads. You are responsible for preparing a presentation on resources for Performance Threads employees. You need to find Internet sites where employees can do costume research (such as museum sites), sites on costume design, and sites on costume supplies. Locate at least two sites in each category (research, design, supplies).
2. Using PowerPoint, create a presentation on the costume resources you have located on the Internet. You determine how to arrange the information and what information to include in the presentation. Create a hyperlink to the Internet sites you mention in the slides.
3. Apply an animation scheme to all slides in the presentation.
4. Save the presentation and name it **PPS3-A4**.
5. Run the presentation.
6. Print the presentation as handouts with six slides per page.
7. Save and then close **PPS3-A4.pptx**.

Marquee Challenge

Challenge 1 Preparing a Project Schedule Presentation for Marquee Productions

1. Create the presentation shown in Figure 3.6. Apply the Opulent design theme and the Office theme colors. Insert the WordArt text and clip art images as shown in the figure. Use the category *finances* to find the clip art image in Slide 4 and use the category *teamwork* to find the clip art image in Slide 5. If you do not have access to the clip art images shown, choose your own. Create and format the table shown in Slide 3.
2. Save the completed presentation and name it **PPS3-C1**.
3. Print the presentation as a handout with all six slides on the same page.

Challenge 2 Preparing a Moroccan Tour Presentation for First Choice Travel

1. Create the presentation shown in Figure 3.7. Apply the Trek design theme. Create the WordArt text and insert the **FCTLogo.jpg** file in Slide 1. Insert the clip art images in Slides 3 and 5 and create and format the table in Slide 6. Use the category *mountains* to find the clip art image in Slide 3 and use the category *cities* to find the clip art image in Slide 5. If you do not have access to the clip art images shown in the figure, choose your own.
2. Save the completed presentation and name it **PPS3-C2**.
3. Print the presentation as a handout with all six slides on the same page.

FIGURE 3.6 Challenge 1

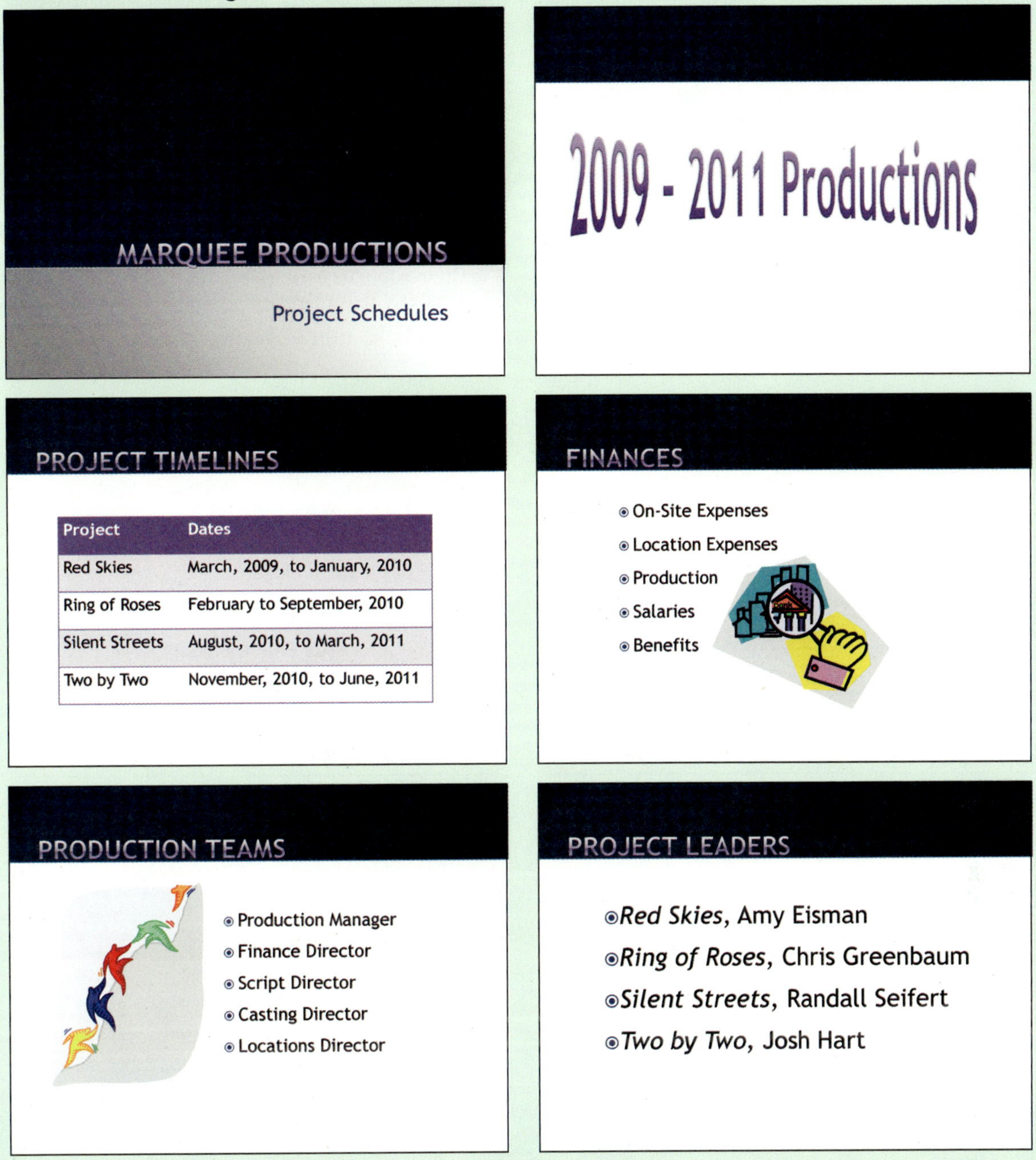

FIGURE 3.7 Challenge 2

Morocco Tour

First Choice TRAVEL

MOROCCO FACTS

- Location: Northern Africa between Algeria and Western Sahara
- Government: Constitutional monarchy
- Capital: Rabat
- Population: Approximately 35 million
- Official language: Arabic

SCENIC HIGHLIGHTS

- Barbary Coast
- Route de Fez
- Middle Atlas Range
- High Atlas Range
- Ziz and Todra Gorges
- Dades Valley
- Tizi-n-Tichka Pass

ACCOMMODATIONS

- Casablanca: Royal Meridien
- Fez: Zalagh Plaza
- Erfoud: Le Berbere Resort
- Ouarzazate: Belere Palace
- Marrakesh: Saadi Hotel

ITINERARY

- Casablanca: Three days, two nights
- Fez: Three days, two nights
- Erfourd: Two days, one night
- Marrakesh: Two days, one night

DATES AND PRICES

Dates	Land and Air	Land Only
January 17 through 27	$2,359	$1,599
March 8 through 18	$2,359	$1,599
June 6 through 16	$2,119	$1,399
September 20 through 30	$2,119	$1,399

Integrating Programs

Word, Excel, and PowerPoint

Skills

- Export a PowerPoint presentation to a Word document
- Export a Word outline document to a PowerPoint presentation
- Link an Excel chart with a Word document and a PowerPoint presentation
- Edit a linked object
- Embed a Word table in a PowerPoint presentation
- Edit an embedded object

Student Resources

Before beginning this section:

1. Copy to your storage medium the Integrating3 subfolder from the Integrating folder on the Student Resources CD.
2. Make Integrating3 the active folder.

In addition to containing the data files needed to complete section work, the Student Resources CD contains model answers in PDF format for each of the projects in this section; model answers for end-of-section activities are not provided.

Projects Overview

Marquee Productions: Create presentation handouts in Word for an annual meeting PowerPoint presentation.

Worldwide Enterprises: Prepare a presentation for the Distribution Department of Worldwide Enterprises using a Word outline. Copy an Excel chart and link it to the Distribution Department meeting presentation and to a Word document and then edit the linked chart. Copy a Word table containing data on preview distribution dates, embed it in a PowerPoint slide, and then update the table.

First Choice Travel: Export a PowerPoint presentation containing information on vacation specials offered by First Choice Travel to a Word document.

Niagara Peninsula College: Link an Excel chart containing information on department enrollments to a PowerPoint slide and then update the chart in Excel. Embed a Word table in a PowerPoint slide and then edit the table in the slide.

Activity 3.1

Exporting a PowerPoint Presentation to Word

You can send data in one program to another program. For example, you can send Word data to a PowerPoint presentation and data in a PowerPoint presentation to a Word document. To send presentation data to Word, click the Office button, point to *Publish*, and then click *Create Handouts in Microsoft Office Word*. At the Send To Microsoft Office Word dialog box that displays, specify the layout of the data in the Word document, whether you want to paste or paste link the data, and then click OK. One of the advantages to sending presentation data to a Word document is that you can have greater control over the formatting of the data in Word.

Project

Create a handout as a Word document that contains slides from a PowerPoint presentation on the Theatre Arts Division at Niagara Peninsula College.

1. Make sure both Word and PowerPoint are open.
2. With PowerPoint the active program, open the presentation named **NPCDivisionPresentation.pptx**.
3. Save the presentation and name it **IntP3-01**.
4. Click the Office button, point to *Publish*, and then click *Create Handouts in Microsoft Office Word.*

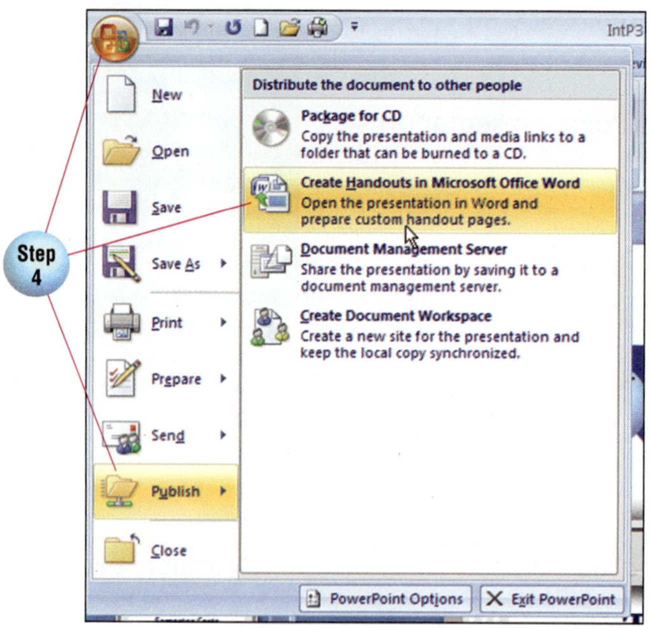

5. At the Send To Microsoft Office Word dialog box, click the *Blank lines next to slides* option.
6. Click the *Paste link* option located toward the bottom of the dialog box and then click OK.

   In a few moments, the slides will display in a Word document.

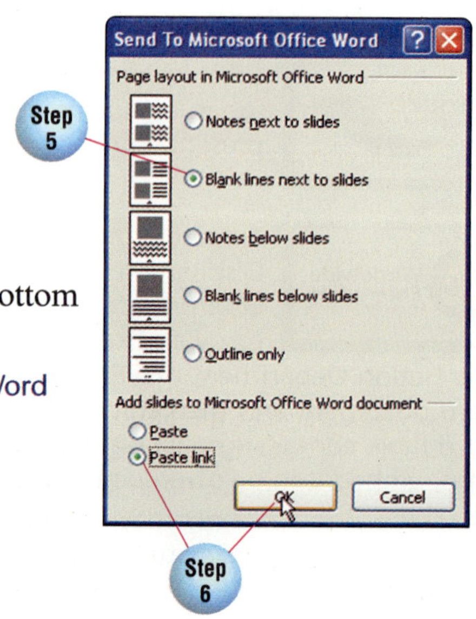

7. Save the Word document and name it **IntW3-01**.
8. Print and then close **IntW3-01.docx**.
9. Click the button on the Taskbar representing the PowerPoint presentation **IntP3-01.pptx**.
10. Make Slide 4 active and then change *$650* to *$750*, change *$250* to *$350*, and change *$200* to *$250*.

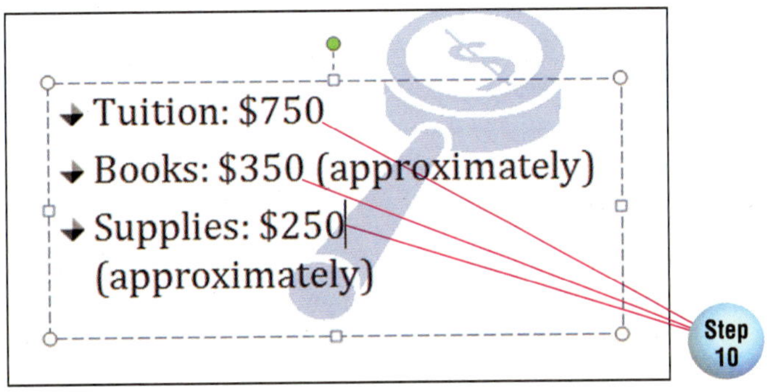

11. Save and then close **IntP3-01.pptx**.
12. Make Word the active program and then open **IntW3-01.docx**. At the message asking if you want to update the document with the data from the linked files, click the Yes button.
13. Scroll through the document and notice that the amounts in Slide 4 reflect the changes you made to Slide 4 in the PowerPoint presentation.
14. Save, print, and then close **IntW3-01.docx**.

In Brief

Export PowerPoint Presentation to Word

1. Open presentation.
2. Click Office button, *Publish, Create Handouts in Microsoft Office Word.*
3. Choose desired options at Send To Microsoft Office Word dialog box.
4. Click OK.

In Addition

Pasting and Linking Data

The *Paste* option at the Send To Microsoft Office Word dialog box is selected by default and is available for all of the page layout options. With this option selected, the data inserted in Word is not connected or linked to the original data in the PowerPoint presentation. If you plan to update the data in the presentation and want the data updated in the Word document, select the *Paste link* option at the Send To Microsoft Office Word dialog box. This option is available for all of the page layout options except the *Outline only* option.

Activity 3.2

Exporting a Word Outline to a PowerPoint Presentation

As you learned in the previous section, you can send data in one program to another program. For example, you can send Word data to a PowerPoint presentation and data in a PowerPoint presentation to a Word document. You can create text for slides in a Word outline and then export that outline to PowerPoint. PowerPoint creates new slides based on the heading styles used in the Word outline. Paragraphs formatted with a Heading 1 style become slide titles. Heading 2 text becomes first-level bulleted text, Heading 3 text becomes second-level bulleted text, and so on. If styles are not applied to outline text in Word, PowerPoint uses tabs or indents to place text on slides. To export a Word document to a PowerPoint presentation, you need to insert the Send to Microsoft Office PowerPoint button on the Quick Access toolbar.

Project

Prepare a presentation for the Distribution Department of Worldwide Enterprises using a Word outline.

Worldwide Enterprises

1. Make sure both Word and PowerPoint are open.

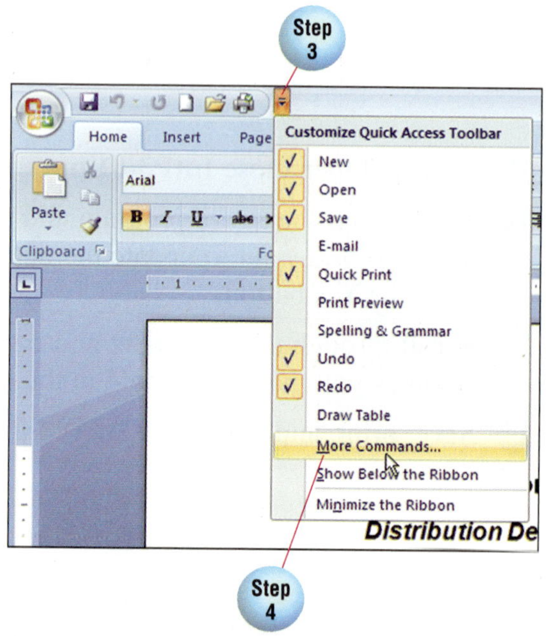

2. With Word the active program, open the document named **WEOutline.docx**.

   Text in this document has been formatted with the *Heading 1* and *Heading 2* styles.

3. Insert a Send to Microsoft Office PowerPoint button on the Quick Access toolbar. Begin by clicking the Customize Quick Access Toolbar button that displays at the right side of the Quick Access toolbar.
4. Click *More Commands* at the drop-down list.
5. Click the down-pointing arrow at the right side of the *Choose commands from* list box and then click *All Commands* at the drop-down list.

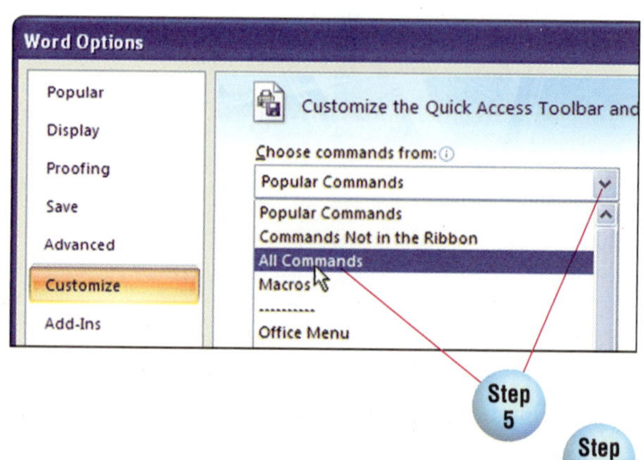

6. Scroll down the list box that displays below the *Choose commands from* list box and then double-click *Send to Microsoft Office PowerPoint*.

   Items in the list box display in alphabetical order.

7. Click OK to close the Word Options dialog box.
8. Send the outline to PowerPoint by clicking the Send to Microsoft Office PowerPoint button on the Quick Access toolbar.

9 When the presentation displays on the screen, make sure Slide 1 is the active slide.

The presentation is created with a blank design template.

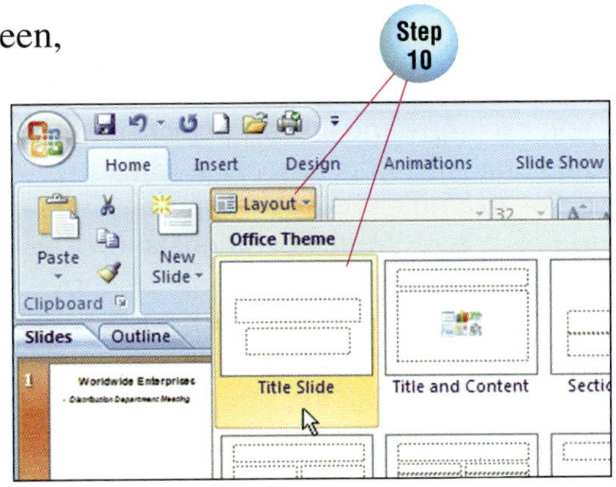

10 With Slide 1 active, change the layout by clicking the Layout button in the Slides group in the Home tab and then clicking *Title Slide* at the drop-down list.

11 Make Slide 4 active and then change the layout to *Title Only*. Make Slide 5 active and then change the layout to *Title Only*. Make Slide 6 active and then change the layout to *Title Only*.

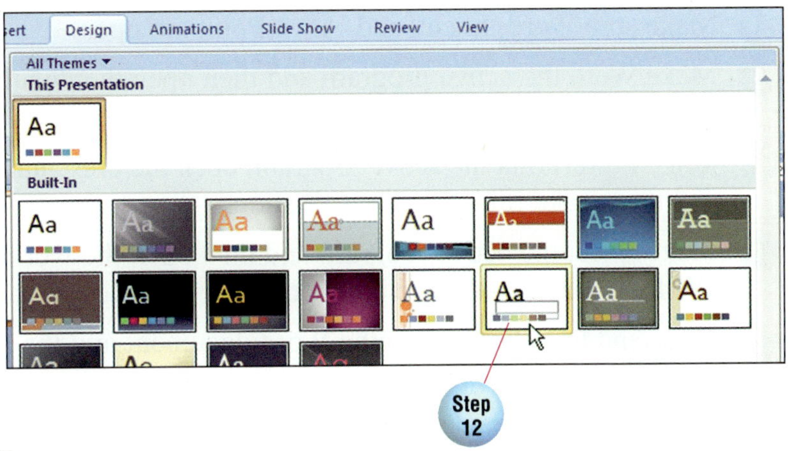

12 Apply a design theme by clicking the Design tab, clicking the More button at the right side of the Themes icons, and then clicking *Origin*.

13 Save the presentation and name it **IntP3-02**.

14 Close **IntP3-02.pptx**.

15 Click the button on the Taskbar representing the Word document **WEOutline.docx**.

16 Right-click the Send to Microsoft Office PowerPoint button on the Quick Access toolbar and then click the *Remove from Quick Access Toolbar* option at the shortcut menu.

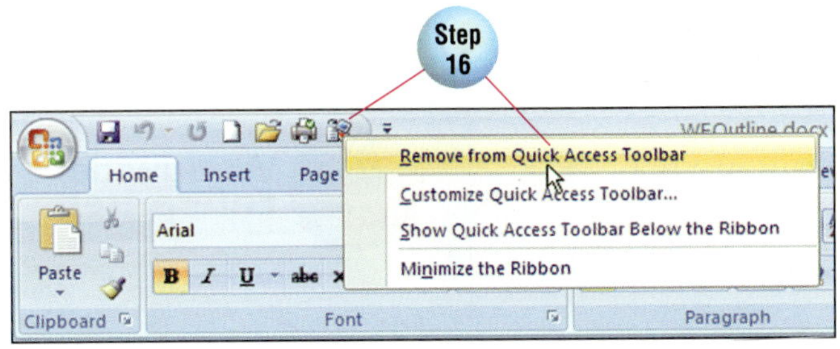

17 Close **WEOutline.docx**.

In Brief

Insert Send to Microsoft Office PowerPoint Button on Quick Access Toolbar

1. Click Customize Quick Access Toolbar button at the right side of Quick Access toolbar.
2. Click *More Commands*.
3. Click the down-pointing arrow at right side of *Choose commands from* list box.
4. Click *All Commands*.
5. Scroll down *Choose commands from* list box, double-click *Send to Microsoft Office PowerPoint*.
6. Click OK.

Send Word Outline to PowerPoint Presentation

1. Open Word document.
2. Click Send to Microsoft Office PowerPoint button on Quick Access toolbar.

In Addition

Applying a Style in Word

Heading styles were already applied to the text in the **WEOutline.docx** Word document. If you create an outline in Word that you want to export to PowerPoint, apply styles using options in the Styles group in the Home tab. A Word document contains a number of predesigned formats grouped into style sets called Quick Styles. Display the available Quick Styles sets by clicking the Change Styles button in the Styles group in the Home tab and then pointing to Style Set. Choose a Quick Styles set and the four styles visible in the Styles group change to reflect the set. To display additional available styles, click the More button (contains a horizontal line and a down-pointing triangle) that displays at the right side of the styles. To apply a heading style, position the insertion point in the desired text, click the More button at the right side of the styles in the Styles group, and then click the desired style at the drop-down gallery.

Activity 3.3

Linking an Excel Chart with a Word Document and a PowerPoint Presentation

You can copy and link an object such as a table or chart to documents in other programs. For example, you can copy an Excel chart and link it to a Word document and/or a PowerPoint presentation. The advantage to copying and linking over just copying and pasting is that you can edit the object in the originating program, called the ***source*** program, and the object is updated in the linked documents in the ***destination*** programs. When an object is linked, the object exists in the source program but not as a separate object in the destination program. Since the object is located only in the source program, changes made to the object in the source program are reflected in the destination program.

Project

In preparation for a company meeting, you will copy an Excel chart and link it to the Worldwide Enterprises Distribution Department meeting presentation and to a Word document.

Worldwide Enterprises

1. Make sure Word, Excel, and PowerPoint are open.
2. Make Word the active program and then open the document named **WERevDocument.docx**. Save the document with Save As and name it **IntW3-02**.
3. Make PowerPoint the active program, open the presentation named **IntP3-02.pptx**, and then make Slide 6 the active slide.
4. Make Excel the active program and then open the workbook named **WERevChart.xlsx**. Save the workbook with Save As and name it **IntE3-01**.
5. Copy and link the chart to the Word document and the PowerPoint presentation by clicking once in the chart to select it.

   Make sure you select the chart and not a specific chart element. Try selecting the chart by clicking just inside the chart border.

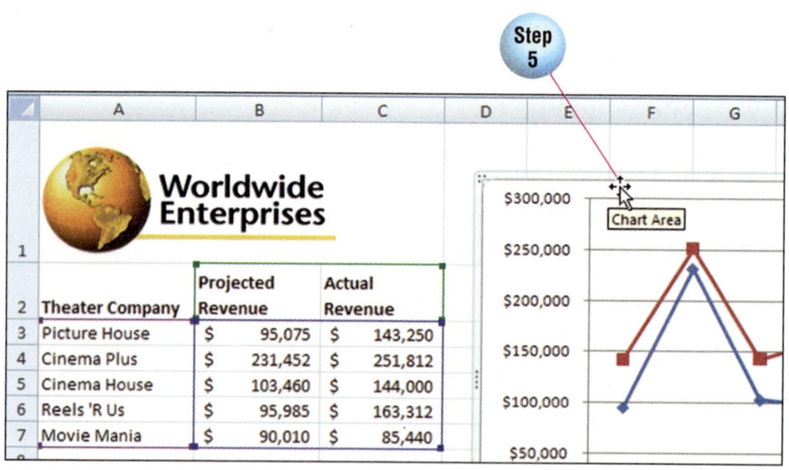

6. With the chart selected, click the Copy button in the Clipboard group in the Home tab.
7. Click the button on the Taskbar representing the Word document **IntW3-02.docx**.
8. Press Ctrl + End to move the insertion point to the end of the document.
9. Click the Paste button arrow and then click *Paste Special* at the drop-down list.

10. At the Paste Special dialog box, click the *Paste link* option, click the *Microsoft Office Excel Chart Object* option in the *As* list box, and then click OK.
11. Save, print, and then close **IntW3-02.docx**.
12. Click the button on the Taskbar representing the PowerPoint presentation **IntP3-02.pptx**.
13. With Slide 6 the active slide, make sure the Home tab is selected, click the Paste button arrow, and then click *Paste Special*.
14. At the Paste Special dialog box, click the *Paste link* option, make sure *Microsoft Office Excel Chart Object* is selected in the *As* list box, and then click OK.
15. Increase the size of the chart so it better fills the slide and then move the chart so it is centered on the slide.
16. Click outside the chart to deselect it.
17. Save the presentation with the same name (**IntP3-02.pptx**), print only Slide 6, and then close **IntP3-02.pptx**.
18. Click the button on the Taskbar representing the Excel worksheet **IntE3-01.xlsx**. Click outside the chart to deselect it.
19. Save, print, and then close **IntE3-01.xlsx**.

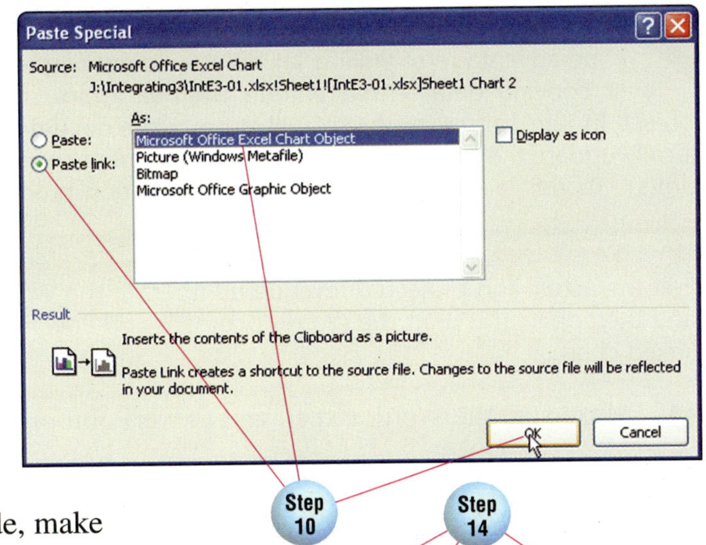

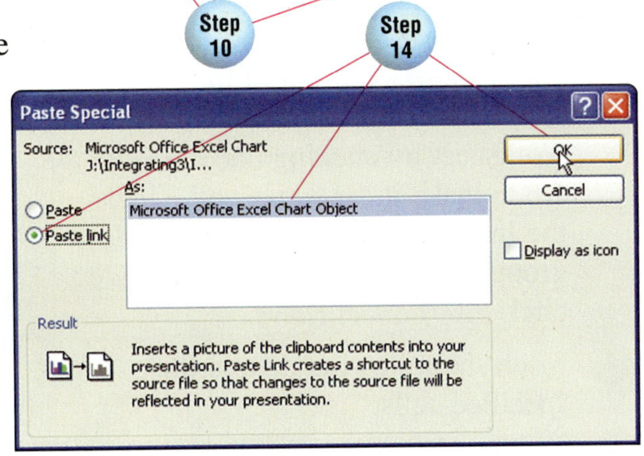

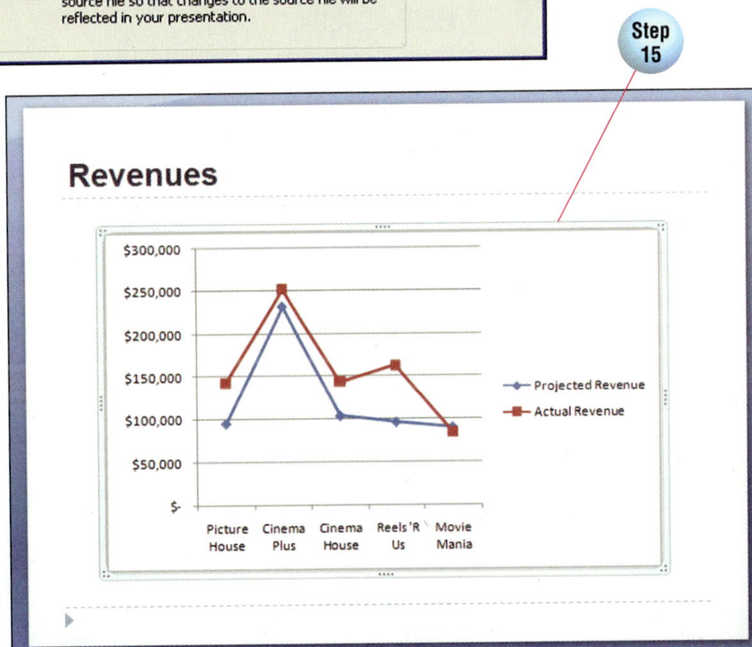

In Brief

Link Object between Programs

1. Open source program, open file containing object.
2. Select object, click Copy button.
3. Open destination program, open file into which object will be linked.
4. Click Paste button arrow, *Paste Special*.
5. At Paste Special dialog box, click *Paste link*, click OK.

In Addition

Linking Data or an Object within a Program

In this section, you learned to link an object between programs using the Paste Special dialog box. You can also link an object in Word using options at the Object dialog box. To do this, click the Insert tab and then click the Object button. At the Object dialog box, click the *Create from File* tab. At the dialog box, type the desired file name in the *File name* text box or click the Browse button and then select the desired file from the appropriate folder. Click the *Link to file* check box to insert a check mark and then click OK.

Activity 3.4

Editing a Linked Object

The advantage of linking an object over copying data is that editing the object in the source program will automatically update the object in the destination program(s). To edit a linked object, open the document containing the object in the source program, make the desired edits, and then save the document. The next time you open the document, worksheet, or presentation in the destination program, the object is updated.

Project

Worldwide Enterprises

Edit the actual and projected revenue numbers in the Worldwide Enterprises Excel worksheet and then open and print the Word document and PowerPoint presentation containing the linked chart.

1. Make sure the Word, Excel, and PowerPoint programs are open.
2. Make Excel the active program and then open the workbook named **IntE3-01.xlsx**.
3. You discover that one theater company was left out of the revenues chart. Add a row to the worksheet by clicking once in cell A6 to make it the active cell. Click the Insert button arrow in the Cells group in the Home tab and then click *Insert Sheet Rows*.

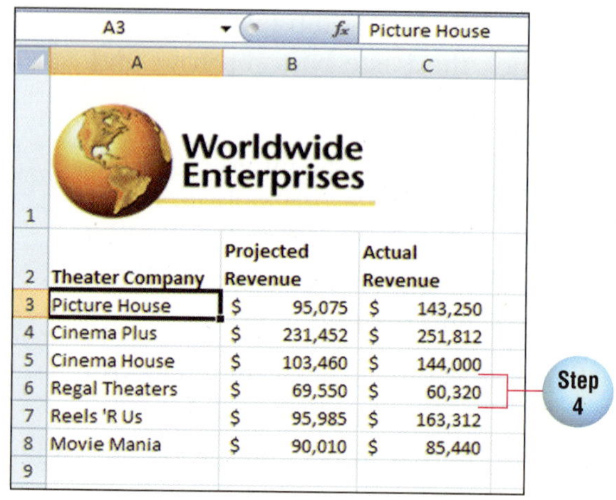

4. Insert the following data in the specified cells:

   A6 **Regal Theaters**
   B6 **69,550**
   C6 **60,320**

5. Click in cell A3.
6. Save, print, and then close **IntE3-01.xlsx**.
7. Make Word the active program and then open **IntW3-02.docx**. At the message asking if you want to update the linked file, click the Yes button.
8. Notice how the linked chart is automatically updated to reflect the changes you made to the chart in Excel.

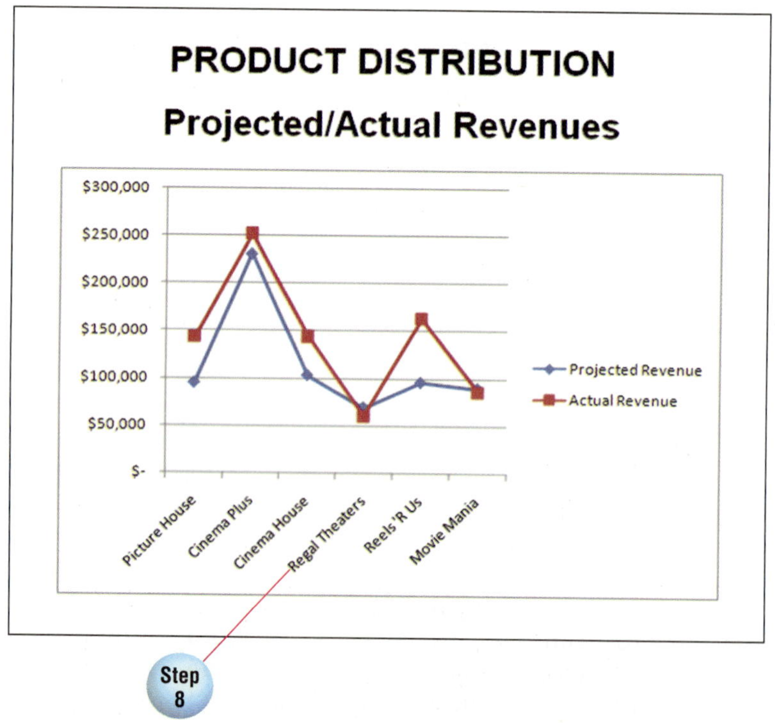

9. Save, print, and then close **IntW3-02.docx**.
10. Make PowerPoint the active program and then open **IntP3-02.pptx**.
11. At the message telling you that the presentation contains links, click the Update Links button.
12. Make Slide 6 the active slide and then notice how the linked chart is automatically updated to reflect the changes you made to the chart in Excel.

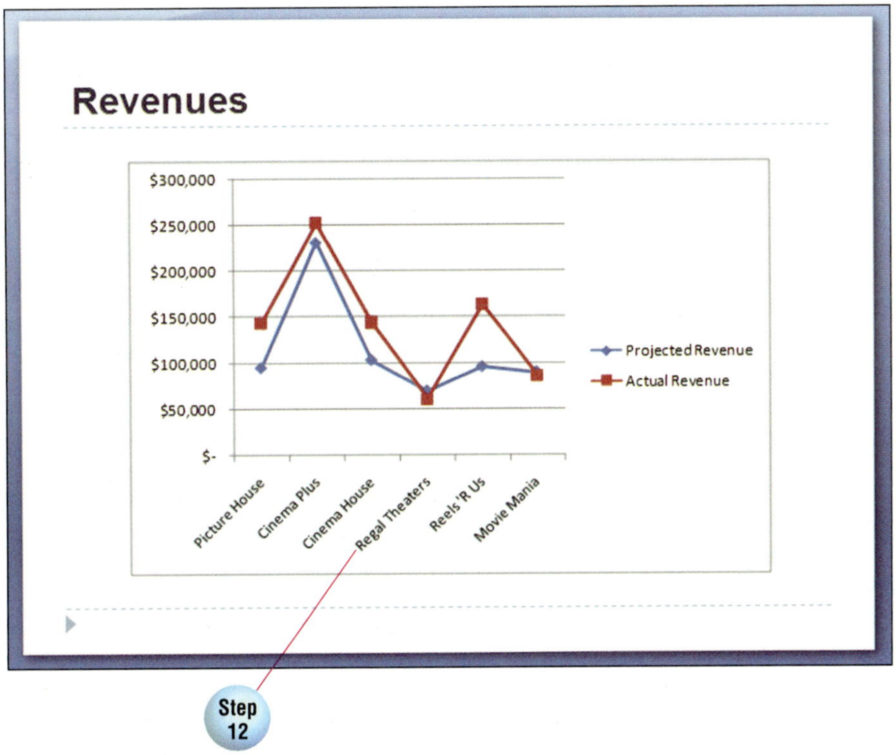

13. Save **IntP3-02.pptx**.
14. Print only Slide 6.
15. Close **IntP3-02.pptx**.

In Addition

Updating a Link Manually

You can choose to update a link manually in the destination program. To do this, open a Word document containing a linked object. Right-click the object, point to *Linked (type of object) Object*, and then click *Links*. At the Links dialog box, click the *Manual update* option and then click OK. With *Manual update* selected, a link is only updated when you right-click a linked object and then click *Update Link*; or display the Links dialog box, click the link in the list box, and then click the Update Now button.

Activity 3.5

Embedding and Editing a Word Table in a PowerPoint Presentation

You can copy an object from one file and paste it into a file in another application or you can copy and link an object or copy and embed an object. A linked object resides in the source program but not as a separate object in the destination program. An embedded object resides in the document in the source program as well as the destination program. If you make a change to an embedded object at the source program, the change is not made to the object in the destination program. Since an embedded object is not automatically updated as is a linked object, the only advantage to embedding rather than simply copying and pasting is that you can edit an embedded object in the destination program using the tools of the source program.

Project

Worldwide Enterprises

Copy a Word table containing data on preview distribution dates for Worldwide Enterprises and then embed the table in a slide in a PowerPoint presentation. Update the distribution dates for the two embedded tables.

1. Make sure the Word and PowerPoint programs are open.
2. Make PowerPoint the active program and then open **IntP3-02.pptx**.
3. At the message telling you the presentation contains links, click the Update Links button.
4. Make Slide 4 the active slide.
5. Make Word the active program and then open the document named **WETable01.docx**.
6. Click in a cell in the table and then select the table. To do this, click the Table Tools Layout tab, click the Select button in the Table group, and then click *Select Table* at the drop-down list.
7. With the table selected, click the Home tab and then click the Copy button in the Clipboard group.
8. Click the button on the Taskbar representing the PowerPoint presentation **IntP3-02.pptx**.
9. With Slide 4 the active slide, click the Paste button arrow and then click *Paste Special* at the drop-down list.
10. At the Paste Special dialog box, click *Microsoft Office Word Document Object* in the *As* list box and then click OK.

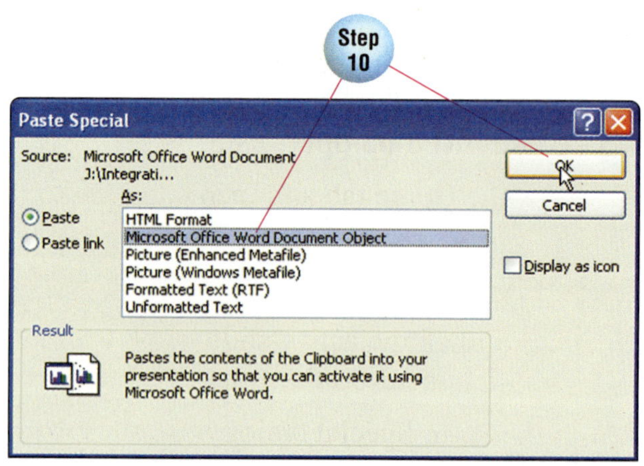

11 With the table selected in the slide, use the sizing handles to increase the size and change the position of the table as shown below.

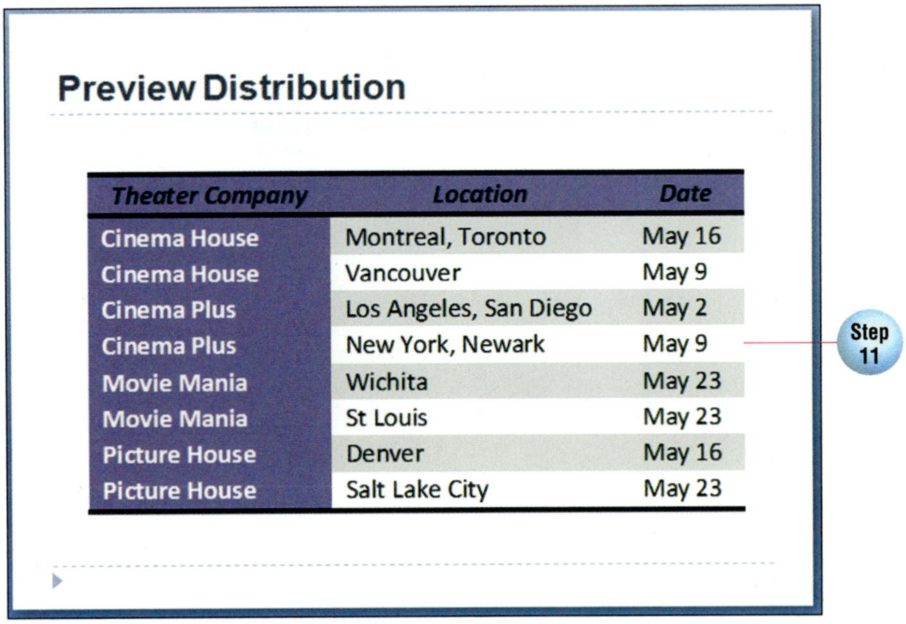

12 Click outside the table to deselect it.

13 Save **IntP3-02.pptx** and then print Slide 4 of the presentation.

14 Click the button on the Taskbar representing the Word document **WETable01.docx** and then close the document.

15 With **IntP3-02.pptx** open, make Slide 5 the active slide.

16 Make Word the active program and then open the document named **WETable02.docx**.

17 Click in a cell in the table and then select the table. To do this, click the Table Tools Layout tab, click the Select button in the Table group, and then click *Select Table* at the drop-down list.

18 Click the Home tab and then click the Copy button in the Clipboard group.

19 Click the button on the Taskbar representing the PowerPoint presentation **IntP3-02.pptx**.

20 With Slide 5 the active slide, click the Paste button arrow and then click *Paste Special* at the drop-down list.

21 At the Paste Special dialog box, click *Microsoft Office Word Document Object* in the *As* list box and then click OK.

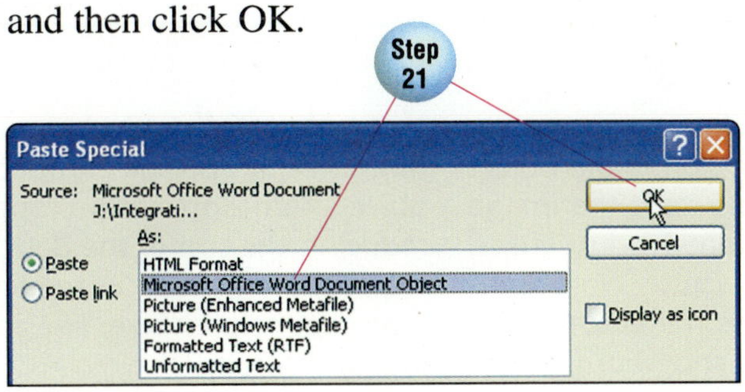

continues

In Brief

Embed Object

1. Open source program, open file containing object.
2. Select object, click Copy button.
3. Open destination program, open file into which object will be embedded.
4. Click Paste button arrow, *Paste Special*.
5. At Paste Special dialog box, click object in *As* list box.
6. Click OK.

Edit Embedded Object

1. Open file containing embedded object.
2. Double-click object.
3. Make edits, click outside object.

22 Increase the size and position of the table in the slide so it displays as shown at the right.

23 The distribution date to Cinema Plus in Sacramento and Oakland has been delayed until May 30. Edit the date by double-clicking the table in the slide.

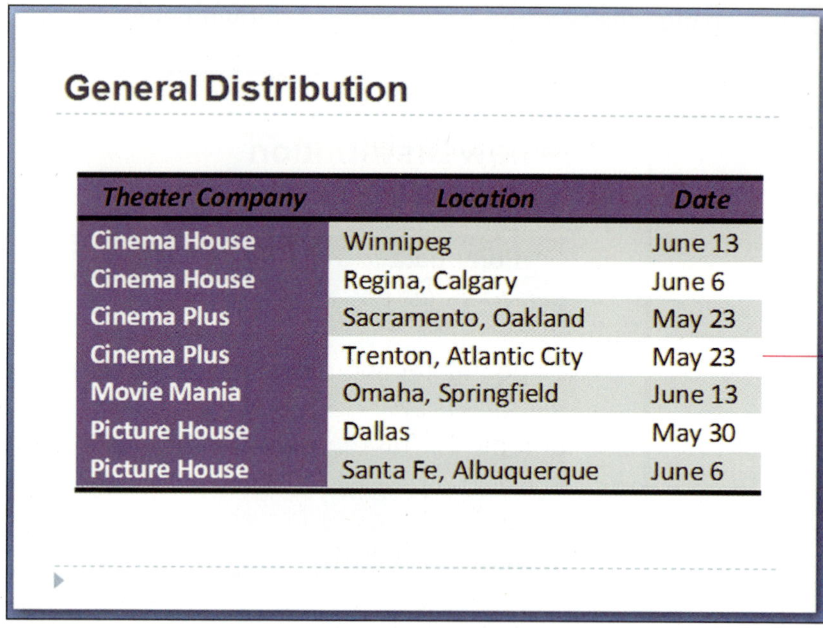

Step 22

Double-clicking the table displays the Word tabs and ribbon at the top of the screen. A horizontal and vertical ruler also display around the table.

24 Using the mouse, select *23* after *May* and then type **30**.

25 Click outside the table to deselect it.

Clicking outside the table deselects it and also removes the Word tabs.

26 Print Slide 5 of the presentation.

27 Apply a transition and sound of your choosing to all slides in the presentation and then run the presentation.

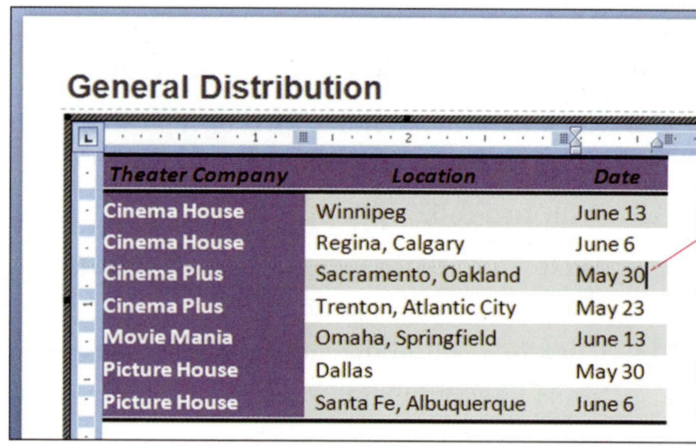

Step 24

28 Save and then close **IntP3-02.pptx**.

29 Click the button on the Taskbar representing the Word document **WETable02.docx** and then close **WETable02.docx**.

In Addition

Working with a Cropped Object

Some embedded or linked objects may appear cropped on the right or bottom side of the object even if enough room is available to fit the image on the page or slide. A large embedded or linked object may appear cropped because Word converts the object into a Windows metafile (.wmf), which has a maximum height and width. If the embedded or linked object exceeds this maximum size, it appears cropped. To prevent an object from appearing cropped, consider reducing the size of the data by changing formatting such as reducing the font size, column size, line spacing, and so on.

Skills Review

Review 1 Exporting a PowerPoint Presentation to Word

1. Open Word and PowerPoint.
2. With PowerPoint the active program, open the presentation named **FCTVacations.pptx** and then save it with Save As and name it **IntP3-R1**.
3. Send the PowerPoint data to Word as slides with blank lines next to the slides. Click the *Blank lines next to slides* option and the *Paste link* option at the Send To Microsoft Office Word dialog box.
4. Save the Word document and name it **IntW3-R1**.
5. Print and then close **IntW3-R1.docx**.
6. Click the button on the Taskbar representing the PowerPoint presentation **IntP3-R1.pptx**.
7. Make Slide 4 active and then change *$950* to *$1,050*, change *$1,175* to *$1,275*, and change *$1,215* to *$1,315*.
8. Save the presentation, print Slide 4, and then close the presentation.
9. Make Word the active program, open **IntW3-R1.docx**, and then click Yes at the question asking if you want to update the link.
10. Print only page 2 of **IntW3-R1.docx**.
11. Save and then close the document.

Review 2 Linking and Editing an Excel Chart in a PowerPoint Slide

1. Open Excel and PowerPoint.
2. With PowerPoint the active program, open **NPCEnrollment.pptx**.
3. Save the presentation with Save As and name it **IntP3-R2**.
4. Make Slide 4 active.
5. Make Excel the active program and then open the workbook named **NPCChart01.xlsx**. Save the workbook with Save As and name it **IntE3-R1**.
6. Click the chart once to select it (make sure you select the entire chart and not a chart element) and then copy and link the chart to Slide 4 in the **IntP3-R2.pptx** PowerPoint presentation. (Be sure to use the Paste Special dialog box to link the chart.)
7. Increase the size of the chart to better fill the slide and then center the chart on the slide.
8. Click outside the chart to deselect it.
9. Save the presentation with the same name (**IntP3-R2.pptx**).
10. Print only Slide 4 of the presentation and then close **IntP3-R2.pptx**.
11. Click the button on the Taskbar representing the Excel workbook **IntE3-R1.xlsx**.
12. Click outside the chart to deselect it.
13. Save and then print **IntE3-R1.xlsx**.
14. Insert another department in the worksheet (and chart) by making cell A7 active, clicking the Insert button arrow in the Cells group in the Home tab, and then clicking *Insert Sheet Rows* at the drop-down list. (This creates a new row 7.) Type the following text in the specified cells:

    A7 **Directing**
    B7 **18**
    C7 **32**
    D7 **25**

15. Click in cell A4.
16. Save, print, and then close **IntE3-R1.xlsx**.
17. Click the button on the Taskbar representing PowerPoint and then open **IntP3-R2.pptx**. At the message telling you that the presentation contains links, click the Update Links button. Display Slide 4 and then notice the change to the chart.
18. Save **IntP3-R2.pptx** and then print only Slide 4.

Review 3 Embedding and Editing a Word Table in a PowerPoint Slide

Niagara Peninsula COLLEGE

1. Open Word and PowerPoint.
2. Make PowerPoint the active program, open **IntP3-R2.pptx**, and then make Slide 5 the active slide.
3. Make Word the active program and then open the document named **NPCContacts.docx**.
4. Select the table and then copy and embed it in Slide 5 in the **IntP3-R2.pptx** presentation. (Make sure you use the Paste Special dialog box.)
5. With the table selected in the slide, use the sizing handles to increase the size and change the position of the table so it better fills the slide.
6. Click outside the table to deselect it and then save **IntP3-R2.pptx**.
7. Double-click the table, select *Editing* in the name *Emerson Editing*, and then type **Edits**.
8. Click outside the table to deselect it.
9. Print Slide 5 of the presentation.
10. Apply a transition and sound of your choosing to all slides in the presentation.
11. Run the presentation.
12. Save and then close **IntP3-R2.pptx** and then exit PowerPoint.
13. Close the Word document **NPCContacts.docx** and then exit Word.

INDEX

A

B

E

F

G

H

I

P

Q

R

S

U

V

W

X

Z

Using Student Resources

Completing Section Activities and End-of-Section Exercises

Most of the projects in this textbook require you to open an existing file. The student data files needed for each section are organized in subfolders on the Student Resources CD. On the front page of each section, instructions will direct you to copy the necessary folder from the CD to your storage medium.

Copying a Folder from the Student Resources CD

Copy a folder from the CD to your storage medium (such as a USB flash drive) using the My Computer window by completing the following steps:

1. Insert the CD that accompanies this textbook in the CD drive.
2. Insert your USB flash drive in an available USB port. ***Note: When you plug in a USB flash device that contains content, Windows XP opens a window displaying "What do you want Windows to do?" Click the Cancel button to remove the window. You may receive startup messages in Windows XP. Check with your instructor if you need assistance using the storage device.***
3. At the Windows XP desktop, open the My Computer window by clicking the Start button and then clicking My Computer at the Start menu.
4. Double-click the CD drive in the contents pane (displays as *MarqueeStudentCD* followed by the drive letter).
5. Double-click the desired program folder name in the contents pane.
6. Click once on the desired section subfolder name to select it.
7. Click the Copy this folder hyperlink in the *File and Folder Tasks* section of the task pane.
8. At the Copy Items dialog box, click the drive letter for the storage medium (drive containing your USB flash drive) and then click the Copy button. For example: Removable Disk (F:).
9. After the folder is copied, close the My Computer window by clicking the Close button (white X on red background) that displays in the upper right corner of the window.

Deleting a Folder from Your Storage Medium

Note: Check with your instructor before deleting a folder. If storage capacity is an issue, delete previous section folders before copying a section folder onto your storage medium. Delete a folder by completing the following steps:

1. Insert your storage medium (such as a USB flash drive) in the USB port.
2. At the Windows XP desktop, open the My Computer window by clicking the Start button and then clicking My Computer at the Start menu.
3. Double-click the drive letter for the storage medium (drive containing your USB flash drive). For example: Removable disk (F:).
4. Click the section folder in the list box.
5. Click the Delete this folder hyperlink in the *File and Folder Tasks* section of the task pane.
6. At the message asking if you want to remove the folder and all its contents, click the Yes button.
7. If a message display asks if you want to delete a read-only file, click the Yes to All button.
8. Close the My Computer window by clicking the Close button (white X on red background) that displays in the upper right corner of the window.

Viewing or Printing Section Activities Model Answers

The Student Resources CD also contains model answers in PDF format for the activities within each section so you can check your work. These PDF files are locked and watermarked. (Model answers are not provided for the end-of-section exercises.)

To access the PDF files you will need to use Adobe Reader. You can download the free program by clicking the Get Adobe Reader button at www.adobe.com. Once Adobe Reader is installed, double-click the *MarqueeStudentCD* icon in the My Computer window, double-click the *ActivitiesModelAnswers* folder, double-click the desired program subfolder name, double-click the desired section subfolder name, and then double-click the appropriate file name to open a file. You can view and/or print a file to compare it with your own completed work.